ENGLISH CONSTITUTIONAL HISTORY

AUSTRALIA
The Law Book Co. of Australasia Pty Ltd.
Sydney : Melbourne : Brisbane

CANADA
The Carswell Company Ltd.
Toronto

INDIA
N. M. Tripathi Private Ltd.
Bombay

NEW ZEALAND
Sweet & Maxwell (N.Z.) Ltd.
Wellington

PAKISTAN
Pakistan Law House
Karachi

U.S.A.
Houghton Mifflin Company
Boston

TASWELL-LANGMEAD'S
English Constitutional History

From the Teutonic Conquest
to the Present Time

ELEVENTH EDITION

BY

THEODORE F. T. PLUCKNETT

M.A.London, LL.B., M.A., Litt.D.Cambridge, LL.D.Glasgow, F.B.A.,
Fellow of University College, London,
Honorary Fellow of Emmanuel College, Cambridge,
Literary Director of the Selden Society,
Professor of Legal History in the University of London

HOUGHTON MIFFLIN COMPANY
BOSTON
1960

First Edition	(1875)	By Thomas Pitt Taswell-Langmead
Second Edition	(1879)	,, ,, ,, ,,
Third Edition	(1886)	By C. E. H. Carmichael
Fourth Edition	(1890)	,, ,,
Fifth Edition	(1896)	By P. A. Ashworth
Sixth Edition	(1905)	,, ,,
Seventh Edition	(1911)	,, ,,
Eighth Edition	(1919)	By C. Phillipson
Ninth Edition	(1929)	By A. L. Poole
Tenth Edition	(1946)	By T. F. T. Plucknett
Eleventh Edition	(1960)	,, ,,

PRINTED IN GREAT BRITAIN
BY
THE EASTERN PRESS LTD.
OF LONDON AND READING

PREFACE

THE principles upon which the last edition of this work was prepared were shortly explained in the preface to the tenth edition. The rearrangement in this, the eleventh, edition has not been at all extensive and has been confined to a very few pages.

On another group of matters rather more serious treatment seemed necessary. First, there has been some excision from Chapter 21, where a large mass of detail, particularly financial, seemed unsuitable in a book which is primarily concerned with *constitutional* history. Secondly, the whole of Chapter 22 has been excised, since its subject-matter (although much of it is indeed " constitutional ") is not necessarily *English*. The removal of these portions of the work is the more justifiable now that the practice is growing for their treatment separately in their proper environment of " Social Services " or " Constitutional Laws of the Commonwealth."

For the rest, there still remains a formidable mass of primarily English constitutional history covering more than a thousand years, and the main duty of an editor was to see that this was presented in as attractive and informative a manner as possible, with guides to recent literature on subjects which could be pursued further with profit.

June 14, 1960.   T. F. T. P.
THE LONDON SCHOOL OF ECONOMICS.

v

TABLE OF CONTENTS

TABLE OF LAWS, STATUTES, AND CONSTITUTIONAL DOCUMENTS

CHAPTER 1

ANGLO-SAXON PERIOD

THE first step in a history of the institutions of the English people is to determine the elements of the English nationality. It is not unusual to speak of the English as a mixed race formed out of the fusion of the Britons, the Anglo-Saxons, the Danes, and the Normans; but this form of expression is apt to convey an erroneous idea of the facts. No modern European nation is, indeed, of pure unmingled race; yet in all some one element has maintained a clear and decided predominance. In the English people this predominant element is the Germanic or Teutonic.

THE EARLY CONQUESTS

The Teutonic conquest of Britain was something more than a mere conquest of the country; it was in all senses a national occupation, a sustained immigration of a new race, whose numbers, during a hundred and fifty years, were continually being augmented by fresh arrivals from the fatherland.

Before the end of the sixth century, the Teutonic invaders had established a dominion in Britain, extending from the German Ocean to the Severn and from the English Channel to the Firth of Forth. The Britons were soon driven into the western parts of the island, where they maintained themselves for a time in several small states. The remnant of the country which they retained was indeed at first of considerable extent, including not only modern Wales but the great kingdom of Strathclyde, stretching from Dumbarton to Chester, together with Cornwall, Devon, and part of Somerset. But the eastern boundary of this territory yielded more and more to the influence of the invaders; and it was only in the mountains of Wales and Cumbria that the Britons preserved for any length of time their ever-decreasing independence. During the long-continued and peculiarly ferocious series of contests between the natives and invaders, vast numbers of the flower of the British race perished. Many Britons sought refuge in emigration to the Continent. Not a few of the less warlike doubtless remained as slaves to the conquerors, and a still greater infusion of the Celtic element may have been effected by the intermarriages of the victors with the women of the vanquished.[1] But

---

[1] This hypothesis is strengthened by the fact that the few words in our language which have been retained from the original Celtic (about thirty-two in number, excluding proper names) have all relation to inferior employments, and for the most part apply exclusively to articles of feminine use or to the domestic occupations of women. (See a list of these words, made by Garnett, in *Transactions of the Philological Society*, i, 171.) On the other hand, the tribal or family organisation of the Germans points to the strong improbability of any general amalgamation through intermarriage. The Britons also were long averse to such an admixture. See Stubbs, *Constitutional History*, i, 62.

1

the Germanic element has always constituted the main stream of our race, absorbing in its course and assimilating each of the other elements. It is " the paternal element in our system natural and political."[2] Since the first immigration, each infusion of new blood has but served to add intensity to the national Teutonic element. The Danes were very closely allied in race, language and institutions to the people whom they invaded; and the Normans, though speaking a different language, and possessing different political and social institutions, were yet descended from a branch of the same ethnic stock.

Celtic and Roman Influences. But whatever be the proportion in which the various national elements have coalesced, it is certain that the principles of our constitution are in no wise derived from either Celt or Roman. The civilisation of the Romans, for the most part, departed with them.[3] The Roman law disappeared from the judicial system of our country. After the conversion of the English to Christianity, however, it must indirectly have exercised some degree of influence on Anglo-Saxon jurisprudence, through the medium of the dignified ecclesiastics who in Witenagemot and Shiremoot took a prominent part in the making of laws and the administration of justice.[4] Roman legal learning was re-introduced more directly from the Continent in the twelfth century, as a consequence of the revived study of jurisprudence, which had there taken place. The so-called *Leges Henrici Primi*, written probably shortly before 1118, contains but one citation from the Theodosian Code, and that at third-hand.[5] In the year 1149, however, or perhaps a little earlier, Vacarius, a Lombard jurist, who had studied at Bologna, was invited to England by Archbishop Theobald, and taught the civil law at Oxford to a band of students, for whose use he wrote his *Liber Pauperum*, consisting of annotated extracts from the Digest and the Code.[6] Although Vacarius was soon silenced by King Stephen, the impulse which he had given to the study of Roman law was not arrested.[7] The legal treatises of

---

[2] Stubbs, *Select Charters* (ed. H. W. C. Davis, 1913), Introductory Sketch, p. 3. See also for the character of the Anglo-Saxon settlement, Chadwick, *Origin of the English Nation* (1907); Vinogradoff, *The Growth of the Manor* (2nd ed., 1911), pp. 117 *et seq.*

[3] See Haverfield, *The Roman Occupation of Britain*, revised by Macdonald (1924), Lecture vi. His general conclusion is that " racially, topographically, culturally, ancient Rome has nothing to do with modern Britain " (p. 286); *cf.* R. G. Collingwood and J. N. L. Myres, *Roman Britain and the English Settlements* (1937).

[4] *Cf.* Maitland, *The Constitutional History of England*, ed. H. A. L. Fisher, p. 5: "Roman jurisprudence did not survive, but the traditions of Roman civilisation were of great importance. The main force which made for the improvement of law was the Church, and the Church, if it was Catholic, was also Roman. Thus, for example, at quite an early time we find the Anglo-Saxons making wills. This practice, we may safely say, is due to the Church; the Church is the great recipient of testamentary gifts." See generally, T. F. T. Plucknett, " The relations between Roman Law and English Common Law down to the sixteenth century," *University of Toronto Law Journal*, III, 24–50, for a review of the controversy, and R. C. van Caenegem, *Royal Writs* (Selden Society), pp. 360 *et seq.*

[5] Liebermann, *Über das Englische Rechtsbuch " Leges Henrici,"* p. 22. *Cf.* also Pollock & Maitland, *History of English Law*, 2nd ed., i, 99 *et seq.*

[6] For the life of Vacarius see Professor de Zulueta's introduction to his edition of the *Liber Pauperum* (Selden Society, vol. 44, 1927), pp. xiii *et seq.*

[7] John of Salisbury, *Polycraticus*, lib. viii, c. 22.

both Glanvill and Bracton, the latter especially, are strongly marked in some places by a large infusion of Roman principles and terminology.[8] As a system, however, the Roman law was soon rejected in England; but from time to time some of its forms and principles were absorbed into and amalgamated with the system which our own courts of justice had been gradually developing for themselves out of the primitive national usages.[9]

Germanic Influences. The germs of our present constitution and laws must, therefore, be sought in the primeval institutions of the first Teutonic immigrants. Of these institutions we have little positive knowledge. According to Bede,[10] the original immigrants consisted of the three kindred tribes of Angles, Saxons, and Jutes.[11] Of these Tacitus does not even mention the Saxons or Jutes, and only names the Angles as one of a number of North German tribes, without fixing their locality. In the second century Ptolemy identifies the seats of the Saxons and Angles as the district between the Elbe, the Eyder, and the Warnow, now constituting the modern duchies of Holstein, Lauenburg, and Mecklenburg. Before the age of Bede the name of Saxon had been extended from the designation of a single insignificant tribe to that of a wide confederacy of North German tribes. Retaining their independence of Rome, tenacious of their heathen worship and their primitive barbarism, they habitually plundered the richer nations who had succumbed to the Roman sway.

Scarcely, if at all, affected by contact with Roman influences, the Teutonic tribes who invaded Britain had probably a less distinctly marked political organisation than that of their kindred on the banks of the Rhine and the Danube, a picture of whose institutions has been handed down to us in the pages of Caesar and Tacitus. But after making due allowance for this difference, for the indistinctness of the picture itself, and for the contradictory ways in which it has been interpreted, we may yet gather

---

[8] Bracton was largely indebted to Azo's *Summae* on the Code and Institutes of Justinian (Savigny, *Geschichte des Römischen Rechts*, iv, 538 *et seq.*). Bracton's knowledge of, and indebtedness to, Roman law is disputed: see Maine, *Ancient Law* (ed. Pollock), 87; Maitland, *Bracton and Azo* (Selden Society); Woodbine in *Yale Law Journal*, xxxi; Vinogradoff, *Collected Papers*, i, 237; Plucknett in *Toronto Law Journal*, iii, 24, and *Concise History of the Common Law* (1956), 261–262; H. Kantorowicz, *Bractonian Problems* (Glasgow, 1941); Woodbine in *Yale Law Journal*, lii, 428; Schulz in *Law Quarterly Review*, lix, 179, lxi, 286, *Seminar*, ii, 41, *English Historical Review*, lx, 136; McIlwain in *Harvard Law Review*, lvii, 220; Richardson in *English Historical Review*, lix, 22, 376; Post in *Traditio*, iv, 197; Richardson in *Traditio*, vi, 61; R. C. van Caenegem, *Royal Writs in England*, 360 *et seq.*

[9] See generally, the brief but masterly survey of Sir Paul Vinogradoff, *Roman Law in Mediaeval Europe* (ed. F. de Zulueta), and *cf.* Hazeltine in *Cambridge Mediaeval History*, v; Meynial in Crump and Jacob, *Legacy of the Middle Ages*.

[10] Bede (*b.* 672, *d.* 735) records very few circumstances relative to the English conquest of Britain from his own sources, but for the most part uses the *De Excidio Britanniae*, composed about 540, of Gildas.

[11] Chadwick, in *Origin of the English Nation*, Chap. 4, contends that the Angles and Saxons were essentially the same race. See his conclusion, p. 88, " the people of the ' Saxon ' kingdoms as a whole were not of a distinct nationality from those of the ' Anglian kingdoms,' " and again, " the invaders of Britain belonged not to three but to two distinct nationalities, which we may call Jutish and Anglo-Saxon. The former occupied Kent and southern Hampshire, the latter the rest of the conquered territory."

from this source some general knowledge of the primitive institutions of our Teutonic forefathers.

Teutonic Society. In the time of Tacitus, Germany appears to have been divided among a number of independent tribes, who had ceased to be nomadic and occupied fixed seats in settled communities. The whole land of the settlement according to one view belonged to the community (*vicus*), who annually allotted the arable land among the freemen, while the pasture-land was both held and used in common.[12] An aggregate of communities (*vici*) of the same tribe constituted the *pagus* (the *gau*); and an aggregate of *pagi* made up the *civitas*, or *populus*.

In their political life the monarchic, aristocratic, and democratic elements were clearly marked; but the ultimate sovereignty seems to have resided in a free and armed people.[13] Some of the tribes had kings selected from particular families; others had not. But the king had only a limited power,[14] and was rather the representative of the unity of the tribe than its ruler. In the *vici* and *pagi* justice was administered by *principes* elected by the nation in the popular assembly, and assisted in each district by a hundred companions or assessors.[15] They had also *duces*, their leaders in war, elected probably from among the *principes*, but whose authority was based, not like that of the kings, on noble birth, but on personal valour.[16] Each district contributed its hundred fighting men to the host. The *principes* were attended by bands of retainers (*comites*), who protected the person of their lord in war and upheld his state in peace,[17] receiving in return such presents as their leader could confer. The power of all the chiefs, whether *reges*, *duces*, or *principes*, was greatly limited. All important state affairs were discussed and determined in the national assemblies, held at stated times, and attended by all the freemen of the tribe. Questions of minor importance were settled by the *principes*, meeting as a separate body, and this body also appears to have taken the initiative in bringing matters before the large assembly.

Below the freemen was a class of men intermediate between the slaves and the freemen. They were not slaves, but they had no political rights. They were the cultivators of the soil which they held under the freemen, to whom they rendered a part of its produce as rent. Last of all came the mere slaves, chiefly made up of prisoners of war and of freemen who had been degraded for some crime.

---

12 Tacitus, *Germania*, c. xxvi; extracts in W. Stubbs, *Select Charters*. On the peculiar difficulties of this passage, and the various interpretations of it, see Stubbs, *Constitutional History*, i, 19, n. 3; Seebohm, *English Village Community*, 342 *et seq.*; Maitland, *Domesday Book and Beyond*, 346 *et seq.* and 347, n. 1; *Cambridge Economic History* (1941), i, 13, and Dopsch, *Economic and Social Foundations of European Civilization* (1937), 30–45. Current opinion rejects the older view that the Teutons practised agrarian communism.

13 *Ibid.*, c. xi.

14 *Ibid.*, c. vii.

15 *Ibid.*, c. xii.

16 *Ibid.*, c. vii.

17 *Ibid.*, c. xiii.

Among the freemen there were differences of rank and social status; some were of noble blood and some were not; but this distinction carried with it no inequality of political rights. Military valour was shared by the Germans with all the northern nations; but one of their national traits was remarkable from the earliest times—the respect paid by them to the women of their race,[18] who on their side were celebrated for an exceptional chastity. The tie of kindred was strong and all-pervading; it formed the basis of social organisation, and entered into the military, the legal and the territorial arrangements. Side by side with it may be discerned the germ of feudalism in the relation existing between the *princeps* and his *comites*, though it was as yet unconnected with the tenure of land.[19]

Such were the general features of the political and social system which our Teutonic forefathers brought with them to their new island home. But the process of migration and conquest necessarily produced certain modifications and developments of the primitive institutions. One of the earliest of these developments was the institution of royalty.

According to the Saxon Chronicle, the chieftains of the first settlers were only distinguished by the title of *ealdorman*, or *heretoga*, the former word expressing the civil, the latter the military, aspect of the same office.[20] But the successful leader soon won for himself a position much stronger than that of any chief in the old land, and, in most cases, assumed the regal title, as more accurately denoting his altered relation to his followers. The word "cyning," or "king," connected with *cynn*, or kin, marked out the bearer of the title as the representative of the race, the head and leader of the people, not the lord of the soil. His reputed descent from Woden, the god from whom all the English kings professed to descend, invested with a semi-sacred character the authority which his own prowess and the will of the people had conferred upon him.

Christianity. The conversion of the English to Christianity exercised an important influence upon the national development. The church not only introduced a higher civilisation, mitigated the original fierceness of the heathen conquerors, softened their pride of birth and race, and exalted the power of the intellect above that of brute force, but also supplied a new and powerful bond of union to a divided people. Once within the pale of the universal Christian church, the English, moreover, were necessarily brought into relations with the general political society of Europe; and in the highly organised system of ecclesiastical synods they

[18] On the position of women in early Teutonic settlements see G. Waitz, *Deutsche Verfassungsgeschichte* (Kiel, 1880), i, 48, 67–69. *Cf.* F. M. Stenton, " The historical bearing of place-name studies: the place of women in Anglo-Saxon society," *Transactions of the Royal Historical Society*, 4th ser., xxv, 1.

[19] See Tacitus, *op. cit.*, for the importance of the family tie; its bearings on the host, c. 7; feuds, c. 21; inheritance, c. 20; the kin of the unfaithful wife, c. 19; exogamy unusual, c. 4. Dopsch, *op. cit.*, 44, emphasises the extent of Teutonic feudalism and suggests that they already had an incipient manorialism.

[20] Freeman, *Norman Conquest*, i, 77. But see for different meanings of the words Liebermann's Glossary in *Die Gesetze der Angelsachsen*, ii, 359, under *Ealdorman*, 5.

found a pattern by which to regulate the procedure of their own political assemblies. From the first the church entered into the closest alliance with the state, and while paying respectful deference to the Roman See, grew up with a distinctly marked national character. Theodore of Tarsus, enthroned Archbishop of Canterbury in 668, reduced the whole ecclesiastical organisation of the various kingdoms into one national church.[21] Henceforward the church existed as a united, central and national institution, in spite of the separation and frequent hostility of the states to which the clergy individually belonged. Thus the ecclesiastical unity preceded and pointed the way to the civil unity of the nation. After the first missionary prelates had passed away, the highest spiritual dignities were filled by Englishmen, members, for the most part, of noble and powerful families. The tie thus created between the clergy and the state was strengthened by the union of secular and spiritual functions. The bishops were prominent members of the Witenagemot, and frequently acted as the chief ministers of the king. They also shared with the ealdormen in the local judicial administration. The church thus entered into close combination with the civil organisation, gradually intertwining itself with all the feelings and customs of the people, and acquiring in the process its exceptionally national character.

The Bretwaldas. During the whole period commonly called the Heptarchy,[22] the land was full of petty kings or princes, some one of whom, from time to time, obtained a forcible predominance over his neighbours. Bede enumerates seven who are said to have enjoyed such a predominance or leadership over nearly the whole island; and the Saxon Chronicle speaks of Egbert as "the eighth king who was Bretwalda."[23] What were the exact nature and extent of the dominion of these Bretwaldas is very doubtful; but we may accept as a fact that each of the seven had acquired and exercised some kind of supremacy over all his neighbours. The existence of the Bretwaldas would seem to indicate certain earlier attempts at a union of the whole English race, which was ultimately carried out by the West Saxon kings in the ninth and tenth centuries.[24]

The three kingdoms of Wessex, Mercia, and Northumbria at length became predominant. Egbert, king of the West Saxons (802–839), not only added to his dominions the dependent kingdoms of Kent and Essex, but compelled the extensive states of Mercia and Northumbria to acknowledge his supremacy. Still the Mercians, East Anglians, and Northumbrians

---

21 Bede, *Historia Ecclesiastica*, iv, 2: Isque primus erat in archiepiscopis cui omnis Anglorum ecclesia manus dare consentiret.

22 There were at least nine, if not ten, independent states founded by the invaders; and there was never a confederate government composed of the different states as members. The word Heptarchy, therefore, is not accurate, but it is convenient if taken to denote the greater prominence of seven states out of the number.

23 Bede, *Historia Ecclesiastica*, ii, 5; *Chronicle Anglo-Saxon*, ann. 827; Kemble, *Saxons in England*, i, 20; Sir John Rhys, *Celtic Britain*, p. 136; Sir Frank Stenton, *Anglo-Saxon England*, 34–35.

24 Freeman, *Norman Conquest*, i, 28. *Cf.* Chadwick, *Origin of the English Nation*, pp. 12 et seq.

retained each their ancient line of kings, and neither Egbert nor his five immediate successors assumed any other title than that of king of the West Saxons. This is the only style used by Alfred (871–899) in his will.

The Danish Invasion (787–1070). The consolidation of the various kingdoms into one was hastened by the invasions of the Danes, by which the three kingdoms of Mercia, Northumbria, and East Anglia were over-whelmed, and even that of the West Saxons was brought to the brink of destruction. Led by their famous sea-kings, these " slayers of the north " ravaged almost every European coast during the ninth and tenth centuries. They were closely akin to the English, and spoke another dialect of the same common Teutonic speech. Their institutions exhibited a striking similarity to those of the English, and, even where differing in detail, were generally governed by identical principles. The first recorded descent of the Danes upon the shores of England occurred toward the end of the eighth century. They reappeared again and again, and at length, instead of making mere predatory excursions, began to form permanent settle-ments in the island. The genius and heroism of Alfred alone rescued the English from their imminent peril. Yet he was never able to expel the Danes from England, or to become its sole master. By the treaty of Alfred and Guthrum (885 ?), the limits of the Danish occupation southward were defined " up on the Thames, and then up on the Lea, along the Lea unto its source, then right to Bedford, then up on the Ouse unto Watling Street." [25] To the north it extended as far as the Tyne, and on the west to· the mountain districts of Yorkshire, Westmorland and Cumberland. Throughout this district—the *Denalagu*, or region where the Danish law was in force—the *armies*, as the Saxon Chronicle terms them, of the Danes continued to occupy the land, governing, as a military aristocracy, the subject Anglian population. The victorious arms of Alfred's three able and energetic successors, Edward the Elder (899–925), Athelstan (925–939), and Edmund (939–946), succeeded in reducing the Danes to something like real submission; and at length, in 959, Edgar (957–975), having outlived the last Danish king of Northumbria, received the crown as king of all England, uniting in his person, as the elect of all three provinces of England, the threefold sovereignty of the West Saxons, Mercians, and Northumbrians. The English and the Anglo-Danes gradually coalesced, the English language and institutions maintaining the ascendancy, though appreciably influenced by contact with the foreign element in their midst.

After the death of Edgar the Peaceable in 975 the minority and feeble character of Ethelred the Unready (979–1013) provoked fresh attacks from Denmark. These now assumed the form of a regular war of conquest, conducted by the kings of a country which had at length been admitted within the civilising pale of Christendom, and whose people were no longer

[25] In F. L. Attenborough, *Laws of the Earliest English Kings*, 98; and in Stubbs, *Select Charters*, 9th ed., p. 72.

ferocious pirates like their ancestors in the former invasions. The English
royal house was for a time supplanted by its Danish rival, but the polity
of the kingdom was not changed. The English still outnumbered their
conquerors; and on the death of Harthaknut, in 1042, the ancient line of
the West Saxon kings regained the throne with the accession of Edward
the Confessor (1042–1066).

ENGLISH SOCIETY AND INSTITUTIONS

Before the Norman conquest, the various Teutonic tribes had coalesced
with one another and with the descendants of the Danish settlers, and had
become fused into one nation. We have now to inquire what was the
constitution of the English nation from the seventh to the eleventh century,
a constitution which survived the Norman conquest, and which in all its
essential principles—developed and adapted from time to time to meet
the requirements of successive generations—has continued down to our
own day.

Of the exact process by which the territory conquered by each of the
invading tribes was divided amongst the settlers, we have no positive
knowledge. Any statement on this point must therefore necessarily be
hypothetical. But there can be little doubt that, as to a large portion of
the land of each settlement, a principle of allotment was generally adopted
based upon the existing divisions of the host into companies, each consisting of a hundred warriors united by the tie of kinship. The allotment of
land made to each hundred warriors would be subdivided, according to
the minor divisions of the kindred, into *maegths*, *i.e.*, a greater or less
number of settlers closely connected by the family tie.[26]

Besides the land thus divided among the simple freemen, a further
portion of the territory was retained by the chief of the tribe as his private
estate; and it is probable that the nobles also and leaders of subordinate
rank either themselves appropriated, or received, grants of estates in
severalty.[27]

During the pre-Norman period, moreover, the whole land of England
may be broadly divided under the two great heads of (1) *folcland*; and
(2) *bocland*.[28]

Folcland was land held by folkright or popular custom,[29] and in
principle it was inalienable.

[26] See Vinogradoff, *Growth of the Manor*, pp. 144 *et seq.* (There is no connection between
this conjecture and the later territory and jurisdiction called the " Hundred.")

[27] See Chadwick, *Origin of English Nation*, pp. 158, 185; Stevenson, *English Historical
Review*, iv, p. 356; Beck, *Cambridge Mediaeval History*, ii, pp. 387–388; Corbett, *ibid.*,
iii, pp. 566 *et seq.*, esp. p. 573.

[28] The law of Edward the Elder, I Edward 2 (Attenborough, *Laws*, 117) implies that these
two forms of land tenure cover all landed property, " we have declared what he is liable
to, who withholds from another his rights either in *bocland* or *folcland*."

[29] The error of regarding *folcland* as the land of the people, *ager publicus*, originated with
John Allen, *Inquiry into the Rise and Progress of the Royal Prerogative in England*, 1830,
and was followed by all historians till the true meaning, as Spelman knew it in the seventeenth century, was restored by Vinogradoff, *English Historical Review*, viii, 1893. *Cf.*
also Maitland, *Domesday Book and Beyond*, pp. 244 *et seq.* On the recent revival of

Bocland, on the other hand, was land held under a charter, a book, or, to use a modern term, under a title deed. Unlike *folcland*, it was easily alienable and devisable by will. It might be entailed or limited in descent, in which case the owner was deprived of his power of alienation.[30] It was a privileged form of ownership, often carrying with it freedom from the customary burdens which fell upon land except the *trimoda necessitas* or liability to military service and to a contribution for the repair of fortresses and bridges (*fyrd-fare, burh-bot,* and *brycg-bot*); *bocland*, it appears, was held only by churches and by very great men.[31]

Both folkland and bookland might be leased out to free cultivators in such quantities and on such terms as the holders pleased. When so leased out, it was termed *laenland* (land lent or loaned).

Units of Government. The smallest unit of the territorial division was the *tun*, township,[32] or vill, occupied by a body of owners associated by the tie of local contiguity, and also as representing either the original *maegth* community of allottees, or the dependent settlers on the estate of the immigrant chief. At times, the township had its *gemot*,[33] or assembly of freemen, and a reeve as its head man or chief executive officer. The townships were grouped together into *hundreds*, or as they were called in the Danish districts, *wapentakes*. An aggregation of hundreds constituted the *shire*, and the union of shires made up the later kingdom.

The origin of the hundred, or wapentake, has most frequently been sought in the primitive settlements, varying in geographical extent, of each hundred warriors of the invading host, a group of a hundred households or hides.[34] In England the names " hundred " and " wapentake "

the controversy, see Plucknett, " Bookland and Folkland," *Economic History Review*, vi, 64–72.

[30] Alfred, 41 (Attenborough, *Laws*, 83, and Stubbs, *Select Charters*, p. 71): "The man who has boc-land, which his kindred left him, then ordain we that he must not give it from his maeg-burg, if there be writing or witness that it was forbidden by those men who at first acquired it, and by those who gave it to him."

[31] Maitland, *Domesday Book and Beyond*, p. 257.

[32] " The *tun* is originally the enclosure or hedge, whether of the single farm or of the enclosed village, as the *burh* is the fortified house of the powerful man. The corresponding word in the Norse is *gardr*, our *garth* or *yard*. The equivalent German termination is *heim*, our *ham*; the Danish form is *by* (Norse *bú* = German *bau*)."—Stubbs, *Constitutional History*, i, 88, n. 5 (*Cf.* also the Flemish and Frisic *hem* and *um*.)

[33] Maitland doubted whether a village had a court in early times (*Domesday Book and Beyond*, p. 185); it is now clear that at least some townships had moots (Maitland, *Collected Papers*, ii, 363–364; Vinogradoff, *Growth of the Manor*, 194, 273).

[34] Vinogradoff, *Growth of the Manor*, p. 144; *English Society in the Eleventh Century*, p. 100. The difficulty in determining the principle upon which the hundreds were established is increased by the fact that they are most numerous in some of the smaller shires. Kent contains 61, Sussex 65, Dorsetshire 34 hundreds; while Lancashire has only six. The latest discussion by Sir Frank Stenton, *Anglo-Saxon England*, 295–298 regards the hundred as having been necessarily an old institution; the view by J. E. A. Jolliffe, *Constitutional History*, 116–120, that the hundred only appears late in Anglo-Saxon history, may be compatible with the strengthening of an institution which was already old. There are also some divisions which are confined to certain localities; thus the county of Kent is divided into six *lathes*, of nearly equal size, having the jurisdiction of the hundreds in other shires. The lathe may be derived from the Jutish " *lething* " (in modern Danish " *leding* "—a military levy). Sussex is divided into six " rapes," each of which is subdivided into hundreds. The old Norse " *hreppr* " denoted a nearly similar territorial division. (See Lappenberg, *England under the Anglo-Saxons*, ed. Thorpe, i, 96, 107.) Two counties,

first appear, however, in the laws of Edgar (A.D. 959–975) in connection with the police organisation of the kingdom[35]; by that time (it was believed) the term hundred, originally denoting certain personal relations of the inhabitants of a district, had probably acquired its territorial signification as a subdivision of the shire or kingdom to which it belonged. A recent suggestion is that the hundred was originally a voluntary association of neighbours for the detection of thieves, and that subsequently (by steps which can be traced) it received powers of trial as well as of arrest.[36] It had its *hundred-gemot*, held every four weeks, which was attended by the thegns of the hundred and by the representative reeve and four men from each township. The chief executive officer was the *hundred-man* or *hundreds-ealdor*, who convened the *hundred-gemot*. He was perhaps at first elective; but as the personal gradually gave way to the territorial influence, he was in many places nominated by the thegn or other great man to whom the hundred belonged.

The division into *shires* (a word originally signifying merely a subdivision or share of any larger whole) is very ancient, but the period at which it arose is uncertain. We have evidence that in Wessex the division into shires existed as early as the end of the seventh century, long anterior to the time of Alfred, to whom their institution has been popularly attributed. In the laws of Ine [Ine 36, sec. 8], king of the West Saxons (*cir.* A.D. 690), provision is made for the case of a plaintiff failing to obtain justice from his *scirman*, or other judge; if an ealdorman compound a felony it is declared that he shall forfeit his *scir*: and the defendant is forbidden secretly to withdraw from his lord into another *scir*. As Wessex gradually annexed the other kingdoms, these were organised into shires, sometimes on the basis of old divisions, sometimes on that of districts created by the Danes centring round a fortified town.[37]

The *boroughs* of England had many different origins. Some no doubt grew out of already existing villages or *tuns*, and the rural aspect is a marked feature of the early medieval town.[38] Some developed from the

---

Yorkshire and Lincolnshire, were divided into Trithings or Thirds (which still subsist in Yorkshire under the corrupted name of Ridings), and these were subdivided generally into wapentakes which came to be regarded as equivalent to hundreds (*Cf.* Gneist, *History of the English Constitution*, p. 41, and footnote.)

[35] There is in fact an earlier reference to the hundred in the Laws of Edmund (III 2), c. 940–946; A. J. Robertson, *Laws*, 13.

[36] J. E. A. Jolliffe, *Constitutional History of Mediaeval England*, 116–123. The *Judicia Civitatis Londoniae* (VI Athelstan, Attenborough, *Laws*, 157–169) mentioned below, p. 11, note 42, is the best known. For the later history see H. M. Cam, *The Hundred and the Hundred Rolls*, and *Studies in the Hundred Rolls*. See the comments in note 34 above.

[37] On the various origins of the different historical shires or counties, see Stubbs, *Constitutional History*, i, § 48, who says: " The constitutional machinery of the shire represents either the national organisation of the several divisions created by West Saxon Conquest, or that of the early settlements which united in the Mercian Kingdom, as it advanced westward; or the rearrangement by the West Saxon dynasty of the whole of England on the principles already at work in its own shires." For the origin of the Midland shires, see Chadwick, *Anglo-Saxon Institutions*, pp. 202 *et seq.*, 269 *et seq.* *Cf.* below, p. 22, n. 84.

[38] The transition from the village to the borough in the case of Cambridge is described by Maitland, *Township and Borough*. See generally, James Tait, *The Medieval English Borough* (1936). *Cf.* also Petit-Dutaillis, *Studies Supplementary to Stubbs' Constitutional History*, i, pp. 75 *et seq.*

burh, which in its origin may be described as " a more strictly organised form of the township. It was probably in a more defensible position; had a ditch or mound instead of the quickset hedge or " tun " from which the township took its name; and as the " tun " was originally the fenced homestead of the cultivator, the " burh " was the fortified house and courtyard of the mighty man—the king, the magistrate, or the noble." [39]

The necessity of defence during the Danish invasions led to the fortification of many centres, and from this time the term *burh* came to denote a group of fortified houses, a borough. Other towns again arose round great monasteries, or in places where merchants and traders would congregate such as the fords of rivers, or the crossing of important highways, or harbours. But whether the origin of a town can be traced to a pre-existing village, to a military defensive work, to a monastery, or to a meeting place of merchants, it was always the commercial and industrial needs of the country which provided the stimulus for its development. [40]

Within the walls of the town the traders enjoyed a greater security than they could find in the open country, for it was protected by the special peace of the king, and heavy fines were exacted from those who violated it. The towns (or some of them) soon had their own *moot* or court, parallel to that of the hundred; sometimes also they had gilds, but these were voluntary associations for religious, charitable or social purposes analogous to our modern clubs. [41] Of the Merchant Gild, which took a prominent place in later municipal history, there is no trace before the Norman Conquest.

Some *gilds* had for their principal object the mutual defence of their members and the preservation of peace; and by the laws of Ine and Alfred, in case of homicide of or by one of the members, the gild-brethren were to share in the receipt or payment of the *wergild*. [42]

The *City of London* has always occupied an exceptional position above other towns of the kingdom. The citizens took part in the election of Edmund Ironside, of Harold Harefoot, and of William the Conqueror [43]; witena-gemots were held there more frequently than at other places. [44]

---

[39] Stubbs, *Constitutional History*, i, 99.

[40] In this connection the prevalence of the word *port* as a term for town is significant. It is derived from the Latin word *portus*, harbour or wharf, and was applied to inland as well as sea-coast towns. *Cf.* the law of Edward the Elder (I Edward 1; Attenborough, *Laws*, 115) that no one shall buy except in a *port*, and he shall have the witness of the *portreeve*; and II Athelstan 14 (Attenborough, *Laws*, 135) that no one shall mint money except in a *port*. *Poort* is the old name for a town in Flanders. *Cf.* Petit-Dutaillis, *op. cit.*, p. 83.

[41] See Gross, *The Gild Merchant*, vol. i, App. B.

[42] In the *Judicia Civitatis Lundoniae*, drawn up under King Athelstan (*cir.* 930) by the bishops and reeves belonging to London, and confirmed by the pledges of the " frith-gegildas," is preserved a complete code of a " frith-gild " of the city of London, with minute directions for the pursuit and convictions of thieves, the exacting of compensation, and the carrying out of the dooms which Athelstan and the Witan had enacted at Greatley, Exeter, and Thundersfield.—VI Athelstan; Attenborough, *Laws*, 157–169; *Select Charters*, 75 *et seq.*

[43] See Liebermann, *The National Assembly in the Anglo-Saxon Period*, p. 37. " At the paramount function of the National Assembly, therefore, the city played a considerable part, which was continued under Stephen, Richard and John. This role forms an important link between the Anglo-Saxon and Norman assemblies."

[44] *Ibid.*, p. 45.

It had its folkmoot, the open-air gathering of the people, and its small weekly husting court of Danish origin, but there is as yet no evidence of a more developed constitution. It was and continued to be through the Norman period " a collection of small communities, manors, parishes, church-sokens and gilds, held and governed in the usual way." [45]

Towards the close of the pre-Norman period the two chief officers of the City of London were the port-reeve [46] and the bishop. It is to these two that the charter of William the Conqueror confirming to London the laws which it had enjoyed under King Edward is addressed : " William the King greets William the Bishop and Gosfrith the port-reeve, and all the burghers within London, French and English, friendly: and I do you to wit that I will that ye twain be worthy of all the law that ye were worthy of in King Edward's day. And I will that every child be his father's heir after his father's day ; and I will not endure that any man offer any wrong to you. God keep you." [47]

The original *Bishoprics* were conterminous with the limits of the various kingdoms at the time of the conversion to Christianity ; but under Archbishop Theodore the dioceses were subdivided on the lines of the still earlier territorial divisions. As churches were gradually erected throughout the country, the township, or, in thinly populated districts, a cluster of small townships, naturally became in its ecclesiastical aspect the parish of a single priest. [48]

The Officers of Government. The government of the shire was administered by an ealdorman, rendered in Latin as *princeps* or *dux*, and later by *comes*. [49] The ealdorman ranked very high in the social scale; the compensation due to him for *burgbryce* (*i.e.*, breaking into his fortified house) was equal to that of the bishop and twice that of the ordinary noble. [50] His functions were both military and civil; he commanded the fyrd, he administered justice, and he was responsible for the carrying out of the laws of his province. [51] In early times it appears that each shire had its own ealdorman, but from the reign of Edward the Elder it became usual for a group of shires to be governed by a single ealdorman. Under the Danish kings in the eleventh century, the title of ealdorman was generally

---

[45] Stubbs, *Constitutional History*, i, p. 442.

[46] The *port-reeve* is the sheriff, *vice-comes*, of Henry I's charter to London (see *infra*, p. 51). He was sheriff of London and Middlesex, but as in the case of London the town was more important than the shire, the officer took his title (until the twelfth century) from the former: he was called *port-reeve*, not *shire-reeve*. See Round, *Geoffrey de Mandeville*, pp. 352 *et seq*. On early London history generally, see Round, *op. cit.* and his *Commune of London*; Petit-Dutaillis, *Studies Supplementary to Stubbs*, I, 91–106; *Victoria County History of London* (in progress); M. Weinbaum, *Verfassungsgeschichte Londons* 1066–1268, and *London unter Eduard I und II* (2 vols.).

[47] Stubbs, *Select Charters*, 97.

[48] Stubbs, *Constitutional History*, i, 244–247.

[49] He is the *scirman* of Ine's law, c. 8 (Attenborough, *Laws*, 39; Stubbs, *Select Charters*, p. 67.)

[50] Laws of Alfred, c. 40 (Attenborough, *Laws*, 83).

[51] Chadwick, *Anglo-Saxon Institutions*, pp. 168 *et seq.*, 171 *et seq.*

supplanted by that of eorl or earl, as the official title of the governor of a shire or province.[52]

When in the tenth century an ealdorman had charge of several shires, he was unable to give personal attention to the administrative business of each separate one; he required a deputy, and the natural deputy was the *gerefa*, the king's reeve.[53] From about the time of Edgar the king's reeve becomes the shire reeve, the *sheriff*, or as he was termed after the Norman conquest, *vice-comes*. He became the special representative of the regal or central authority, and as such was usually nominated by the king. In the absence of the ealdorman he presided over the shire court; he was responsible for the maintenance of the peace and the police regulations; he was the fiscal agent of the king; he was the executor of the law and steward of the royal demesne. Gradually the civil administration became almost entirely concentrated in the sheriff, leaving to the earl, as his principal function, the command of the military force of the shire.[54] Unlike the office of ealdorman, the sheriffdom, as a rule, did not become hereditary. This circumstance was productive of important constitutional effects after the Norman conquest, as the kings found ready to hand a machinery which enabled them effectually to assert the central authority in every shire, and thus to check the growth of local feudal jurisdictions.

RANKS OF THE PEOPLE

Slaves. Turning from the divisions of the land to those of the people, we find at the bottom of the social scale the mere *slaves* (*theowas, esnas*), of whom, under the name of *servi*, 25,000 are numbered in Domesday Book, or nearly one-eleventh of the registered population. These were of two kinds—(1) hereditary, consisting partly of the descendants of the conquered Britons, partly of persons of the common German stock either descended from the slaves of the first colonists, or from freemen who had lost their liberty; (2) penal slaves (*wite-theowas*), freemen who had been reduced to slavery on account of crime, or through failure to pay a *wergild*, or by voluntary sale—the father having power to sell his child of seven, and a child of thirteen having power to sell himself.

As among the Germans of Tacitus we find the distinction between the noble and common freemen, so among the English the freemen were broadly divided into eorls and ceorls, the modern meaning of which may be rendered by gentle and simple, or esquire and yeoman.

---

[52] The title of *eorl* occurs early in the laws of the Kentish king Ethelbert, 13, 14 (Attenborough, 7), and was probably of Jutish origin, but its use as a substitute for *ealdorman* was borrowed from the Danish *jarl*.

[53] The " sheriff " seems to appear in some charters, but not in the Anglo-Saxon Laws; see F. E. Harmer, *Anglo-Saxon Writs*, pp. 48 *et seq.*; F. Liebermann, *Gesetze*, ii, 649; W. A. Morris, *The Medieval Sheriff*; Sir Frank Stenton, *Anglo-Saxon England*, 540; for the king's reeve see also Larson, *The King's Household in England before the Norman Conquest* (Madison, Wis. 1904), Chap. 4; and Chadwick *Anglo-Saxon Institutions*, Chap. 7.

[54] After the Conquest the earl had no connection with the administration of the county except the right to receive a third of its pleas, " the third penny." As Maitland observes, in spite of this Latin title, the sheriff was never the deputy or assistant of the earl (*comes*): Pollock and Maitland, *History of English Law*, i, 533.

Eorls; Gesiths; Thegns. The rank of the *eorl* rested upon noble birth but in England, as in other Germanic countries, a new kind of nobility speedily grew up—nobility by service. This arose in part out of the development of the *comitatus*, described by Tacitus, the band of personal followers of the king or other leader. These followers were the *gesiths* (= companions), and we find them endowed with substantial grants of land, part of which they used for the maintenance of their own dependants.[55] Then, by a different line of development, the relations existing between the lord and his followers appear to have gradually assumed a somewhat different type; this produced the rise of the *thegn* (= servant[56]), and the service of the king, or other great lord, was eagerly sought by freemen as well for the social dignity as for the material rewards which it ensured. We read of the king's dish-thegn (*disc-thegn*), bower-thegn (*bur-thegn*), and horse-thegn,[57] as personages of high rank and great influence; a feature in our early institutions which has survived to the present day in such offices as those of lord chamberlain (bower-thegn) and master of the horse. Service to the king, or some great lord, gradually became the only avenue to distinguished rank. The dignity of thegn was also closely connected with the possession of landed property; so much so that the possession of a certain quantity of land came to be regarded as a foundation of nobility.[58] The simple freeman who acquired five hides of land, and was attached by special services to the court, entered into the ranks of the thegnhood.[59] For the position of ealdorman the possession of at least forty hides was necessary. This intimate connection between social status and the ownership of large landed estates, which has continued with but slight modification down to our own times, may be traced even in the early institutions of our Teutonic ancestors. Among this nobility by service the highest rank comprised the king's thegns, whilst in a lower class were the thegns of the ealdorman or bishop.[60]

[55] See the valuable discussion in Jolliffe, *Constitutional History*, 17–20.

[56] For thegns, and especially king's thegns, see Jolliffe, 88. Bede uses *comes* as the Latin for *gesith*, and *minister* as the Latin for *thegn*: his A.-S. translator sometimes renders Bede's *miles* as *thegn*.

[57] He was not the same as the *staller* as till recently it was supposed; the office of *staller* is of Norse origin and was introduced into England by the Danish kings. See Larson, *The King's Household in England*, p. 147.

[58] See Larson, *op. cit.*, p. 103. " Before the Danish invasion the *ministri* were something more than great landed proprietors with certain military obligations; they composed an aristocracy bound to the King by peculiar personal ties and forming an extension of his court into the various parts of his kingdom. From the humbler realms of household service, the order had risen, first to the plane of honor as a royal *comitatus*, and next to the plane of influence as a landed nobility. In the days of its prosperity it formed the great outer circle of the royal service."

[59] *Cf.* People's Ranks and Law, c. 2 (*Select Charters*, p. 88), " If a ceorl throve, so that he had fully five hides of his own land, church and kitchin, bell house, and burh-gate, seat and special duty in the king's hall, then was he thenceforth of thegn-right worthy." Another clause of the same tract states that a merchant who " fared thrice over the wide sea by his own means " became worthy of thegn-right (c. 6).

[60] See Maitland, *Constitutional History*, ed. Fisher, p. 147: " But it is not only the King who has thegns—great men may have them; indeed, it seems that a thegn may have lesser thegns dependent on him—just as in after-days the King's tenant *in capite* might have tenants holding of him by knights' service." See the important Chapter IV (" Thegns and Knights ") in F. M. Stenton, *First Century of English Feudalism* (1932).

Ceorls. Below the thegns were the free peasants, the *ceorls*, who appear in the Domesday survey under the names of *liberi homines, soc-manni, villani, bordarii, cotarii,* and *cotseti,* indicating doubtless some peculiarity of service or tenure. Their position on the whole was depressed by the growth of thegnhood; those who did not rise by the acquisition of five hides of land to the rank of thegn sank into a state of dependence. In this way the rise of a landed aristocracy effected great changes in the organisation of society. The churches and thegns who acquired from the king large estates or the royal rights over portions of the land developed a seignorial power, and often a seignorial jurisdiction (*sac* and *soc*). The free *ceorl* requiring protection for his person and his land placed himself under some powerful neighbour; he *commended* himself to a lord (*hlaford*). For the sake of security he lost his independence. Purely voluntary in its origin, commendation rapidly grew to be universally compulsory. It soon came to be regarded as a principle that every free-man, not being a *hlaford*, must be attached to some superior, to whom he was bound by fealty, and who, in return, was his legal protector and the guarantee for his good behaviour. The freeman had indeed the right of choosing the lord to whom he should commend himself; but if he failed to do so, his kindred were bound to present him to the folk-moot and name a lord for him.[61] In some cases the freeman might change his lord at will, could " go with his land where he pleases "; but more usually he could not—he had to remain attached to his patron. " Patronage had a tendency to strike roots and to develop into a lasting lordship over freemen and their land." [62]

Clergy. As the result alike of their almost entire monopoly of learning and of the veneration, not unmixed with superstition, which the sacerdotal character inspired in the laity, the *clergy,* as a class, held a very high political and social status.[63] The poorest priest ranked as a mass-thegn; the bishop was on a par with the ealdorman and presided with him in the shire-moot, and the archbishop was never valued, in the eye of the law, at less than an atheling, or member of the king's family. Whilst all laymen, even of the highest rank, were bound to find a number of com-purgators in addition to their own oath, in order to clear themselves from a charge, the simple oath of a priest was accepted as sufficient. In every great council the prelates appear to have taken a prominent part, church and state working together in the closest alliance; while for purely church matters the clergy, from an early period, had their own synods.

---

[61] II Athelstan 2 (Attenborough, *Laws,* 129; *Select Charters,* p. 74).

[62] Vinogradoff, *Growth of the Manor,* p. 213. *Cf.* also Maitland, *Domesday Book and Beyond,* pp. 69–75.

[63] Lappenberg (*England under the Anglo-Saxons,* ed. Thorpe, ii, p. 322) suggests, as a further explanation of the high position of the Christian priesthood, the account given by Tacitus of the vast influence in secular affairs possessed by the Pagan German priesthood, in whom exclusively resided the power of life and death. " Such a primitive influence tended, no doubt, greatly to facilitate the domination of the Roman papal church, and a part of their jurisdiction, the ordeals or so-called judgments of God, may have had their origin in the legal usages of the heathen priests."

The King. At the head of the nation was its elected chief and representative, the *cyning* or *king*. The royal power was, however, limited in practice rather than in theory by that of the witan or national council; but with the extension of the national territory and the growth of the thegnhood, the personal dignity and power of royalty gradually but steadily increased. The king became the personal lord as well as the chief and representative of his people. From the time of Athelstan the kings began to assume imperial titles, with which the extensive European connections of that sovereign had doubtless rendered them familiar.[64] These titles were probably not mere grandiloquent sounds, but were intended to proclaim the imperial character of the sway which the king of the English asserted over the inhabitants of the whole island, and his independence of any external potentate. In his imperial character, as overlord, the king called himself *rex, imperator, casere, basileus, totius Britanniae* or *totius Albionis*; but in his regal character he is still king of the people, not lord of the soil— *rex Anglorum*, not *rex Angliae*.[65] The prerogatives and immunities of the king were extensive. Like every other individual, he had originally a *wer-gild*, or fixed price for his life; but Alfred made plotting against the king's life " death-worthy." He was entitled to maintenance for himself and his retinue in public progresses; to wrecks, tolls, the profits of markets, mines, and salt works, and to the forfeited possessions of outlaws.[66] A *wite*, or fine, was also payable to him, on every breach of the law, in addition to the compensation (*bot*) due to the person injured. The breach of the king's *frith* or peace, and the violation of his *mund*,[67] or special security granted to anyone, were severely punished. He alone had *soken*, or jurisdiction, over persons of the highest rank, and was charged with the duty of executing justice in the last resort. Lastly, he was commander-in-chief of the national host (*fyrd*).

The Queen. The consort of the king, in accordance with the high respect in which women were held by the Germans, seems to have occupied a very exalted position. She was styled " the wife," the " queen " (*cwen*) and " lady " (*hlaefdige*). As late as the Statute of Treason (1352) she was described as the king's " companion " (*ma dame sa compaigne*). The crimes of Edburga, who poisoned her husband King Beorhtric (in 802), caused the West Saxons, for a considerable period, to withhold from the king's wife the name and authority of queen. In 856 Ethelwulf gave deep offence to his people by causing his second wife, Judith, to be crowned;

[64] Four of Athelstan's sisters were married to foreigners.

[65] On the imperial character of the early English kings, see Palgrave, *English Commonwealth*, pp. 627, cccxlii–cccxliv; Freeman, *Norman Conquest*, i, 148, and Jolliffe, *Constitutional History*, 101–102.

[66] Treasure trove is not traceable before the Conquest (Sir George Hill, *Treasure Trove*, 186); the royal right of wreck may be as old as the Confessor (Marsden, *Select Pleas in Admiralty* (Selden Soc.), ii, xxxix). On the position of the Anglo-Saxon crown generally, see Jolliffe, *Constitutional History*, 41–55, 106–114.

[67] The original signification of " *mund* " is *hand*. It specially denoted the power of the head of the family over his wife, children, and slaves, in which sense it may be compared with the similar use of *manus* in the ancient legal phraseology of the Romans.

but from the date of Edgar's second marriage with Elfthrytha, in 965, the rank of queen appears to have been restored. Emma, wife and queen of Ethelred II (and after his death, of King Cnut), seems to have held the city of Exeter as her peculiar property, and to have governed it by her own officers. In Mercia and East Anglia the queen-consort was entitled to the payment of an extra tenth, called *aurum reginae* (*gersuma*), or queen-gold, on every fine or oblation of more than ten marks paid to the king. This ancient due was claimed so late as the time of Charles I, by Queen Henrietta Maria.[68]

The Athelings. The sons and brothers of the king were distinguished by the title of athelings. The word *atheling*, like eorl, originally denoted noble birth simply; but, as the royal house of Wessex rose to pre-eminence, and the other royal houses and the nobles generally were thereby reduced to a relatively lower grade, it became restricted to the near kindred of the national king. The more remote members of the royal house fell into the ranks of the ordinary nobility without any distinctive appellation, on the same principle as that by which the descendant of an English nobleman at the present day, if not heir to the ancestral title, bears, in the third generation, no external sign of his noble relationship.

THE WITENAGEMOT

The supreme council of the nation, which performed the functions of the Teutonic national assembly described by Tacitus, was the *Witenagemot*, or meeting of the wise.[69] Concerning the constitution of this assembly there exists considerable difference of opinion. It has been supposed that in the local moots every freeman had a right to attend, so that every freeman, whether eorl or ceorl, had a voice in the folkmoot of the shire, the shire-moot or county court of later times. But here the divergence makes itself manifest. It was once held that every freeman had also the right to attend the national assembly (although this right had practically gone out of use at an early period) and that the witenagemot was " democratic in ancient theory, aristocratic in ordinary practice," a view which to a certain extent was supported by the high authority of Kemble.[70]

The Nature of the Witan. But it is now generally believed that the central assembly was never in historic times formed on the model of the lower courts as the folkmoot of the whole nation, the ordinary freemen

[68] Lappenberg, A.-S. ii, 310, 311. On " Queen " and " Lady," see Freeman, *Norman Conquest*, iv, 765 *et seq.*, Appendix Q, and P. E. Schramm, *History of the English Coronation*. *Cf.* Alistair Campbell, " The status of Queen Emma," in his edition (p. 62) of *Encomium Emmae Reginae* (1949). For queen-gold, see W. Prynne, *Aurum Reginae* (1668) and Coke, 12 Rep. 21.

[69] *Witan* is the nominative plural and *Witena* is genitive plural of *wita*, a wise man. On the whole subject see Liebermann, *The National Assembly in the Anglo-Saxon Period* (Halle, 1913), and Jolliffe, *Constitutional History*, 25–29, 103.

[70] Freeman, *Norman Conquest*, i, 107; Kemble, *Saxons*, ii. 239 *et seq.*

never rising higher than their respective shire-moots. The witenagemot was an aristocratic body. Its members were the king, the ealdormen or governors of shires, the king's thegns, the bishops, abbots, and generally the *principes* and *sapientes* of the kingdom. *Sapientes* = witan = wise men, was the common description of those who attended it. The lesser thegns, if entitled to be present, did not, probably, attend in any numbers, so that the assembly can never have been very large. " The largest amount of signatures," says Kemble, " which I have yet observed is 106, but numbers varying from 90 to 100 are not uncommon, especially after the consolidation of the monarchy. In earlier times, and smaller kingdoms, the numbers must have been much less. . . . Other meetings, which were rather in the nature of conventions, and were held in the presence of armies, may have been much more numerous and tumultuary—much more like the ancient armed folkmoot on the famous day which put an end to the Merwingian dynasty among the Franks. Such, perhaps, was the gemot which, after Eàdmund Irensída's death, elected Cnut sole king of England, or that in which Earl Godwine and his family were out-lawed." [71] Although the witenagemot was not a representative body in the modern sense, it was unquestionably looked upon as representing in some sort the whole people, and consequently the national will.[72] It is especially necessary to avoid the view of the witan, and other institutions, as having a constitution, with members who exercise rights of being present, of discussing, of voting, and the like. They were assuredly not like share-holders at a company meeting.

The power of the witenagemot was extensive although ill-defined:

(1) **The Deposition of Kings.** We find it deposing the king for mis-government. So great a step would generally be taken only at rare intervals. In Northumbria, indeed, the deposition of kings, with more or less of violence and bloodshed, is extraordinarily frequent; but two only, Ethel-wald (probably) in 765 and Alcred (certainly) in 774, can be said to have been regularly deposed by the witenagemot.[73] In the royal line of the West Saxons, which grew into the royal line of the English, there were two instances of deposition by the witan. In 755, Sigebert of Wessex was deposed by the witan, and Cynewulf, his kinsman, elected in his stead.[74] Ethelred II was in like manner practically deposed in 1013, and again

---

[71] Kemble, *Saxons in England*, ii, 200, 201, n. *Cf.* Liebermann, *National Assembly*, 40, 42.

[72] In a charter of Athelstan, in 931, the act is said to have been confirmed " toto plebis generalitate ovante "; and the act of a similar meeting at Winchester in 934, which was attended by the king, four Welsh princes, two archbishops, seventeen bishops, four abbots, twelve dukes, and fifty-two thegns, making a total of ninety-two persons, is described as being executed " tota populi generalitate."—Kemble, *Saxons*, ii, 199.

[73] As to Alcred, see Simeon of Durham, *s.a.*, 774. Of fifteen kings of Northumbria in the eighth century, thirteen ended their reigns by extraordinary means. See the list in Stubbs, *Constitutional History*, i, 153.

[74] *Chronicle Anglo-Saxon, ann.* 755; Florence of Worcester, *ann.* 755; *cf.* Kemble, *Saxons*, ii, 219.

restored in 1014.[75] Since the Norman conquest, the deposing power has
been three times exercised by the national parliament, in the cases of
Edward II in 1327, Richard II in 1399, and James II in 1688.

(2) **The Election of Kings.** The witenagemot elected the king. All
the old Teutonic kingdoms were elective; but in every kingdom there was
a royal family, out of which the witan had to elect the most competent
member to discharge the functions of king. The eldest son of the last
king, if of full age and not manifestly incompetent, was usually chosen to
succeed his father. But at a period when the personal character and
military prowess of the king were of the utmost importance, minorities
were too dangerous to be endured. Thus when Ethelred I died in 871,
leaving only young children, he was succeeded by his younger brother
Alfred. King Athelstan, again, though reputed illegitimate, was preferred
in 925 to the younger but legitimate sons of Edward the Elder.[76] In 946
Edwy, son of Edmund, was passed by in favour of his uncle Edred;
and in 1042 Edward the Confessor was chosen in preference to the absent
son of his elder brother Edmund Ironside. Finally, in 1066, the whole
royal house was passed by, and Earl Harold, the most able general and
statesman of his time, was elected king. The race of Cerdic had once
before been passed by, when, in 1017, Cnut was chosen king; but this
election, though good in form, was made under duress. A certain preference seems to have been given to the issue born after the accession of the
father to the throne—the *porphyrogeniti*, sons born in the purple; and a
certain preference was also acquired by the recommendation of the last
king; thus Edgar recommended his son Edward to the witan, and Edward
the Confessor recommended Earl Harold.[77] " The technical expression
for ascending the throne is being *gecoren and âhafen to cyninge*, elected
and raised to be king "; where the *âhafen* refers to the old Teutonic custom
of what we still at election times call chairing the successful candidate,
and the *gecoren* denotes the positive and foregone conclusion of a real
election." [78]

(3) **The Witan and Government.** The witenagemot could take a direct
share in any act of government. In conjunction with the king, the witan
might enact laws and levy taxes for the public service; make alliances
and treaties of peace; raise land and sea forces when occasion demanded;
sanction royal grants of bookland; appoint and depose the bishops,
ealdormen of shires, and other great officers of church and state; adjudge

---

[75] Florence of Worcester, *ann.* 1013, 1014; *Chronicle Anglo-Saxon*, 1014. The ealdormen of
    Wessex and all the thegns of the West came to Swend at Bath and submitted to him, giving
    hostages. " Putting the language of the different accounts together," says Freeman
    (*Norman Conquest*, i, 396), " there can be little doubt that this was, or professed to be, a
    formal act of the Witan of Wessex, deposing Ethelred and raising Swend to the throne."
    But see Stubbs, *Constitutional History*, i, 156.
[76] Illegitimacy, however, says Kemble, " was not considered a valid ground of objection
    among the Anglo-Saxons, if the personal qualities of the prince were such as to recommend
    him."—*Saxons in England*, ii, 37, n.
[77] See Freeman, *Norman Conquest*, i, 118.
[78] Kemble, *Saxons in England*, ii, 215. *Cf. infra*, p. 474.

the lands of offenders and intestates dying without heirs to be forfeit to the king; and authorise the enforcement of ecclesiastical decrees. Lastly, the witan acted from time to time as a supreme court of justice, both in civil and criminal causes.[79]

But although the powers of the witan were so extensive, the active exercise of them varied greatly with the personal character and influence of each occupant of the throne. Strong kings, like Alfred and Athelstan, were able, by the legitimate exercise of personal influence, to lead the witan in whatever direction they pleased, and thus to attain the practical enjoyment of supreme power. Towards the close of the pre-Norman period, many of the powers which had been originally shared by the king and the witan were in fact exercised by the king alone; but in the two cardinal matters of legislation and the imposition of extraordinary taxation, the participation of the witan in giving counsel and consent was at all times recognised.

THE JUDICIAL SYSTEM

The great original principle of the English judicial system was that of trial in local courts popularly constituted, or as it was termed in later times, trial *per pais*, in the presence of the county as opposed to a distant and unknown tribunal. This was at once an evidence of freedom and the surest guarantee for its permanence. But before describing the different local courts it is necessary to notice, shortly, the principle of pledges, by which provision was made that every man should be either personally forthcoming, or have some representative bound to answer for him, in every case of litigation.

Frankpledge. A collective responsibility for producing an offender appears originally to have lain upon the *maegth* or community of the kindred [80]; it then devolved upon the voluntary associations called *gilds*; and later on the gild was superseded by the local responsibility of the *tithing*, the exact nature of which is doubtful, but which seems to have been a personal and territorial subdivision of the hundred practically identical with the township. Eventually, though probably not much earlier than the Norman conquest, for the local tithing was substituted the personal collective *friborh*, or frankpledge. Every freeman over twelve years of age, not being a *hlaford*, was bound to be enrolled in a *friborh*, or *tenmannetale* as it was called in the north: that is, an association of ten men who formed a perpetual collective bail for the appearance of any one of their number when required to answer in a court of law. Each association had its head-man, the *borhs-ealdor*, who was also called the *tithing-man*, as the body of ten was also called the *tithing*. If an accused member appeared and was condemned, he had to make reparation by his

---

[79] See Kemble, *Saxons in England*, ii, 204–240; Liebermann, *National Assembly*, 59–75.
[80] For all that follows, see generally W. A. Morris, *The Frankpledge System* (1910).

own property or by personal punishment; but if he fled from justice, the other members of the tithing, in default of exculpating themselves from all share in his crime or escape, were pecuniarily liable for the penalty.

Lord and Man. Side by side with the collective responsibility of the local community or of the personal association, was the individual responsibility of the *hlaford* for his men. By a law of Athelstan (*c.* 928), every landless man was to have a lord to answer for his appearance; and by an ordinance of King Edgar (*c.* 962) it was enacted: " Let every man so order that he have a ' *borh* ' [surety]; and let the ' *borh* ' then bring and hold him to every justice; and if any one then do wrong and run away, let the ' *borh* ' bear that which he ought to bear. But if it be a thief, and if he can get hold of him within twelve months, let him deliver him up to justice, and let be rendered unto him what he before had paid." [81]

The Hundred Court. The two principal local courts were those of the hundred and the shire. The hundred court was held once a month, under the presidency of the sheriff or his deputy. The judges of the court were originally the whole body of freeholders within the hundred; but, as often happened, the duty became eventually attached to the ownership of particular plots of land; especially in the Danelaw it became the custom to delegate the judicial powers of the whole body of suitors to a representative committee, generally twelve or some multiple of twelve in number, and either chosen for the occasion or permanently appointed.[82] The court of the hundred exercised jurisdiction both civil and criminal, voluntary and contentious; and litigants were bound to seek justice in this court before applying to a higher tribunal. On the institution of the *friborh* or frankpledge, the hundred court twice a year undertook the duty of seeing that every man was regularly enrolled in his tithing, a practice which continued long after many of the hundred courts had fallen into private hands, as the sheriff's tourn, or the two occasions in the year when the sheriff held the courts to take the view of frankpledge.

In numerous cases the owner of the hundred also enjoyed the right of view of frankpledge to the exclusion of the sheriff; instead of the sheriff holding a tourn, therefore, the lord held his " court leet."

Private Jurisdictions. From an early period certain districts within the hundred were detached from its jurisdiction and subjected to the *socn* of the church or of the secular lords to whom they belonged. Such districts formed private *franchises* or liberties. The *hlaford* possessing a

---

[81] II Athelstan 2; Edgar's Secular Ordinance, III Edgar 6; Robertson, *Laws*, 27; *Select Charters*, 83. *Fri-borg* (free pledge = Frankpledge) is historically more correct; the form *frith-borg* (peace pledge) was due to an erroneous conjecture by post-conquest writers as to the origin of the institution; Morris, *op. cit.*, 2.

[82] This seems to be a post-conquest development; *cf.* Tait, *The Medieval English Borough* (1936), 287 n. 3.

private soken over his lordship, or manor as it was subsequently termed, was wont to dispense justice in the hall of his mansion, whence his court was called a hall-mote, the precursor of the feudal court-baron. Sometimes the jurisdiction of a whole hundred, or of several hundreds, was granted to churches or private individuals. The process began by royal grants to a subject of the monetary profits of justice; much later, the grantees began to exercise jurisdiction in private courts of their own in virtue of explicit royal grants: " the passing of the men of the folk-moots into the view of private courts can be proved to have been in progress in the eleventh century, and may fairly be conjectured of the tenth century, but of earlier centuries it cannot be proved, nor is it, indeed, probable." [83]

The Shire-moot. The *scir-gemot*, or, as it was called after the Norman conquest, the *comitatus*, was not only the court of the shire, but also the *folc-gemot*, the general assembly of the folk of the shire.[84] The shire-moot was convened by the sheriff twice in a year. It was attended by the ealdorman, the bishop, and all other public officers, by all lords of lands, and by the reeve and four men and the parish priest from each township. The jurisdiction of the shire-moot extended to every kind of suit, except such as concerned a high officer of state, or a king's thegn, which were reserved for the king's immediate cognisance. But the shire-moot could not be resorted to until justice had first been sought and denied in the court of the hundred; and on the same principle no appeals could be carried to the king, unless the shire-moot had previously failed to do justice. The court of the shire, though it gradually lost much of its importance after the Norman conquest, especially after the institution of the justices itinerant, long continued to exercise an extensive original civil jurisdiction in small causes, and remained the general assembly of all the freeholders of the shire for county purposes.[85]

---

[83] Jolliffe, *Constitutional History*, 64. The argument of Maitland, *Domesday Book and Beyond*, 258–290 predicating private courts in the early ninth century has been subjected to keen criticism by Jolliffe, *loc. cit.*, and (in greater detail) by Julius Goebel, *Felony and Misdemeanor* (1937), i, 342–378.

[84] " If the shire be the ancient under-kingdom, or the district whose administrative system is created in imitation of that of the under-kingdom, the shire-moot is the folk-moot in a double sense, not merely the popular court of the district, but the chief council of the ancient nation who possessed that district in independence, the witenagemot of the pre-heptarchic kingdom. Such a theory would imply the much greater preponderance of popular liberties in the earlier system, for the shire-moot is a representative assembly, which the historical witenagemot is not; and this is indeed natural, for the smaller the size of the districts and the more nearly equal the condition of the landowners or sharers in the common land, the more easy it would be to assemble the nation, and so much the less danger of the supreme authority falling into the hands of the king and the magistrates without reference to the national voice. But this can only be matter of conjecture."— Stubbs, *Constitutional History*, i, 130.

[85] There is a growing literature, B. H. Putnam, *Statute of Laborers* (1908), 162, *391; W. A. Morris, *The County Court* (1926); R. Stewart-Brown, *County Rolls of Chester* (1925); G. H. Fowler, *Rolls from the Office of Sheriff* (1929); articles by Sir Hilary Jenkinson (*English Historical Review*, xliii, 21, *Cambridge Historical Journal*, i, 103), Plucknett (*Harvard Law Review*, xlii, 639, xliii, 1,111), Woodbine (*ibid.*, xliii, 1,083), and Lapsley (*Law Quarterly Review*, li, 299). Still further material is in G. O. Sayles, *King's Bench* (Selden Society), iii, p. xcv.

PROCEDURE

Nearly all the work of judicature consisted in the declaration of the law applicable to each case, as distinguished from the finding of the facts. The *law* was declared by the presiding magistrates—the ealdorman, or sheriff, and the bishop. The *facts* (except in a certain class of civil causes to be presently noticed) were decided either by compurgation or by ordeal.

Compurgation. The accused might clear himself by his own oath strengthened by the oaths of certain compurgators, usually twelve in number, and either his relatives or immediate neighbours, who testified to the trustworthiness of the person on whose behalf they came forward. The compurgators were in reality " witnesses to character."[86] But the oaths of different men varied in legal value and credit according to the rank and property of the swearer. The oath of one thegn counterbalanced that of six ceorls. If the accused were subject to a lord, the lord or his reeve might offer to swear on behalf of the accused. But if the testimony of the lord were not in his favour, the accused was bound either to produce a triple number of compurgators or to undergo an ordeal of threefold rigour. Not only the accused, but the accuser also, was bound to take an oath (*fore-oath*) that he was not actuated by interested or vindictive motives.

Ordeal. But compurgation was not always allowed. In certain cases, as when a man was taken red-handed, or bearing other proofs of guilt, he was obliged to submit to the ordeal. The ordeal was also compulsory—(1) where the accused was unable to produce a sufficient number of compurgators; (2) where he had been notoriously guilty of perjury on a previous occasion; (3) where he was not a freeman—unless his lord swore to his belief in the innocence of the accused, or bought him off by paying the wergild.

The ordeal, or judgment of God, was of three kinds—hot iron, hot or cold water, and the *corsnaed*, or accursed morsel. It was to be undergone (except as to the cold water ordeal) in a church, and under the superintendence of the priests. It is very difficult for us to understand how even the most innocent could have escaped condemnation under this process, except by the collusion of the officials; but there is no doubt that in its origin the ordeal was intended as a reverent appeal to God, in the firm belief that He would make the truth manifest.

Transaction witnesses. Besides the compurgators or witnesses to character, there was also in civil causes a special class of witnesses appointed by law for the attestation of facts in bargains and sales. In some respects they are analogous to the public notaries of the present day. They are

---

[86] On the importance of the oath, both for status and procedure, and on the choice of compurgators, see Jolliffe, *Constitutional History*, 58.

first mentioned in a law of King Athelstan (924–940), which enacted that there should " be named in every reeve's ' manung ' (district) as many men as are known to be unlying, that they may be for witnesses in every suit." [87] But the most explicit information about these legal witnesses is contained in the Laws of Edgar (959–975): " This, then, is what I will: that every man be under *borh* both within the *burhs* and without the *burhs*; and let witness be appointed to every *burh* and to every hundred. To every *burh* let there be chosen 36 as witnesses. To small *burhs* and in every hundred 12, unless ye desire more. And let every man, with their witness, buy and sell every of the chattels that he may buy, or sell, either in a *burh* or in a wapentake; and let every of them, when he is first chosen as witness, give the oath that he never, neither for money, nor for love, nor for fear, will deny any of those things of which he was witness, nor declare any other thing in witness save that alone which he saw or heard; and of such sworn men let there be at every bargain two or three as witness." [88] The sworn testimony of these official pre-ordained witnesses was decisive of any dispute which might subsequently arise.

Punishments. The principle that every injury either to person or property might be compensated by a money payment was common to all the northern nations. It was introduced into Gaul by the conquering Franks, and into Britain by the English invaders. Every man's life had a fixed money value, called the *wergild*. In the case of a freeman, this compensation for murder was payable to his kindred; in that of a slave, to his master. The amount of the wergild varied, according to a graduated scale, with the rank of the person slain. For a ceorl it was fixed at 200 shillings; for a lesser thegn, 600 shillings; for a king's thegn, 1,200 shillings.[89] For bodily injuries a *bot* was payable, being highest in amount where any disfigurement ensued. In every case the king was entitled to a *wite*, or fine, for the breach of his peace. In the course of time capital punishments were introduced for offences against the state, or the king as its representative. Alfred declared that treason against a lord he dared not pardon; and fighting in the king's hall and several other state offences were made " death-worthy." At a later period the severity of the laws increased, especially as to theft, which was sometimes capitally punished. But neither severity nor lenity seems to have availed to restrain the general turbulence of the people. The laws are filled with complaints of the open violations of the public peace. The relatives of a murdered man freely maintained the right to vengeance; and the private feud frequently went

[87] Concilium Exoniensis, V Athelstan, 1, 5; Attenborough, *Laws*, 155; *Select Charters*, 75.
[88] Secular Ordinance, IV Edgar, cap. 3, 4, 5, 6. Robertson, *Laws*, 33–35; Stubbs, *Select Charters*, 84 [" *borh* " = surety, " *burh* " = a borough or fortified place].
[89] From the amount of his *wer* a thegn was sometimes called a *twelf-hynde man* (hynde, hund, here = a hundred), a lesser thegn a *six-hynde man*, and a ceorl a *twy-hynde man*. The *six-hynde man* disappears after the time of Alfred, except perhaps in the west midlands where he may be identified with the *radcniht*. It seems to have comprised the landless gesith and also Welsh landed proprietors. See Chadwick, *Anglo-Saxon Institutions*, 90–98.

on for a long period between the two families. The law of money compensation must be regarded therefore as showing rather what society was intended to be, than what in very many instances it actually was. For certain offences, the punishment of exile was inflicted; and the man who fled from trial became an outlaw, whom any one might slay as he would a wild beast.[90]

THE ANGLO-SAXON LAWS

The laws of the English extend in an unbroken series from the laws of Ethelbert, the first Christian king of Kent (600), down to the present time. The earliest written collections are simply digests of local unwritten customs which had been handed down by oral tradition, and put into writing to meet the requirements of a more developed and centralised state organisation. Many of these early laws consist of amendments of older unwritten customs, and from our lack of knowledge of the customs intended to be amended, are necessarily somewhat obscure. Even when the laws are clear, the great bulk of them " concern chiefly such questions as the practice of compurgation, ordeal, wergild, sanctity of holy places, persons or things; the immunity of estates belonging to churches, and the tables of penalties for crimes, in their several aspects as offences against the law, the family, and the individual "; but scattered through the collection there occur from time to time many enactments of the highest interest and importance as elucidations of the early history of the constitution.[91]

Some of these laws, e.g., those of Alfred (circa 890), of Ethelred (978–1016), and of Cnut (1016–1035), exhibit traces of early attempts at codification. But the name " code " cannot with propriety be applied to them. They are unsystematic and fragmentary, and such general principles as they enunciate are not legal definitions, but maxims drawn from religion or morality.

Of all our early kings, Alfred the Great has enjoyed the widest fame as a legislator. Popular legend has represented him as the personal author of nearly all our institutions, of many of which the germs existed ages before, while the existing form cannot be discerned till ages after him. There is no doubt that, like many others of our early kings, Alfred collected and arranged the laws of his predecessors; but his real position, as a compiler of old rather than an originator of new legislation, is accurately set forth by himself in the preamble to his " dooms ": " I then, Aelfred, King, these together gathered, and had many of them written which our fore-gangers held, those that me-liked. And many of them that me-not-liked, I threw aside, with my Wise Men's thought, and

---

[90] The gradual development of capital and corporal punishments, forfeitures of chattels or land, and money fines—truly punitive measures taken by the state—was the result of a long struggle with this older system, whose principal objects were vindictive or remedial, rather than penal. For all this, see Julius Goebel, *Felony and Misdemeanor* (1937).

[91] These passages are collected by Stubbs, *Select Charters*, pp. 66–92.

no other wise bade to hold them. For why, I durst not risk of my own much in writ to set, for why, it to me unknown was what of them would like those that after us were. But that which I met, either in Ine's days my kinsman, or in Offa's the King of the Mercians,[92] or in *Aethelberht's* that erst of English kin baptism underwent, those that to me rightest seemed, those have I herein gathered, and the others passed by. I then, Aelfred, King of the West Saxons, to all my Wise Men these showed, and they then quoth that to them it seemed good all to hold." [93]

CONCLUSION

The general features of the institutions and laws of the English people during the five hundred years preceding the Norman conquest have now been briefly surveyed. In different districts and at different periods a great diversity of local customs prevailed; but amidst many varieties of detail the essential principles and general machinery of government possessed throughout the characteristics which have been described. It must not, however, be supposed that during this lengthened period the institutions of the English were at any time stationary. They were subject to a marked though gradual process of development, the general tendency of which may be described as a movement from the personal organisation characteristic of all ancient systems of government towards the territorial organisation which forms the basis of the modern state. At the beginning of the period, the Anglo-Saxon kings were the leaders of the people, not the lords of the soil, their jurisdiction was primarily over the persons of their subjects, not over the territories included within the geographical boundaries of their kingdom.[94]

Towards the close of the pre-Norman period, the king, though still " King of the English," had become, in addition, lord of the English land. Nearly two centuries were indeed to lapse before King John should declare himself, on his great seal, *Rex Angliae* instead of *Rex Anglorum*, but the transition from the tribal to the territorial system, from the kingship of the people to the conception of the king as feudal lord of both kingdom and people, was already far advanced towards completion.[95]

---

[92] These laws of Offa, which King Alfred evidently had seen, are no longer extant.

[93] Alfred's Dooms. Thorpe, *Ancient Laws and Institutes*, i, 58, 59; Attenborough, *Laws*, 63; Stubbs, *Select Charters*, 70. See Maitland, *Constitutional History*, pp. 2, 3: " Beginning with Alfred's we have now a continuous series of laws covering the whole of the tenth century and extending into the eleventh, laws from Edward the Elder, Aethelstan, Edmund, Edgar and Ethelred. . . . These Anglo-Saxon laws or dooms—as they call themselves—after having lain hid in MS. for several centuries, were dug up in the sixteenth century as antiquarian curiosities. Lambard published some of them in 1568 under the title *Archaionomia*. In 1840 they were published for the Record Commissioners with a modern English translation under the title *Ancient Laws and Institutes of England*: they were again published in 1865 with a German translation by Dr. Reinhold Schmid." The best edition is now that of F. Liebermann, *Die Gesetze der Angelsachsen*, 3 vols. Halle, 1898–1916. A convenient edition with an English translation is in *The Laws of the Earliest English Kings*, edited by F. L. Attenborough, 1922, and *The Laws of the Kings of England from Edmund to Henry I*, edited by A. J. Robertson, 1925.

[94] Palgrave, *English Commonwealth*, Pt. i, Chap. 3. That is also one of the principal themes in the treatment of this period in Mr. Jolliffe's *Constitutional History*.

[95] Stubbs, *Constitutional History*, i, 183–185.

But whilst, in theory, the power of the king was rising higher and higher, it was practically limited by the simultaneous advance in the power of the great nobles, who were constantly tending towards a position not far removed from that of the great feudatories of the continent. Under Edward the Martyr the condition of England was not unlike that of France under Charles the Bald. The great earls, or ealdormen of provinces, were forming a separate order in the state inimical alike to the supremacy of the king and the liberty of their fellow subjects. Cnut divided the kingdom into four great earldoms or duchies; and the same policy was continued by Edward the Confessor, in whose reign the whole land seems to have been divided among five earls, three of them being Earl Godwin and his sons Harold and Tostig. The power and statesmanship of William the Norman prevented the threatened disintegration of the kingdom.

CHAPTER 2

THE NORMAN CONQUEST

The Succession. On the death of Edward the Confessor (January 5, 1066), the succession to the crown was disputed. The heir of the house of Cerdic, Edgar the Atheling, grand-nephew of the late king, was not only of tender age, but, as his after-life showed, of feeble character and mediocre intellect. The political exigencies of the kingdom imperatively demanded an able and resolute man at its head. King Edward on his death-bed had recommended as his successor his brother-in-law, Earl Harold. The earl was the most able general and statesman of the time, already exercising a quasi-royal authority through his own personal influence and the vast possessions of the Godwin family. He was allied to the English royal house by affinity, and by blood to the Danish house, which had so lately occupied the throne.[1] The witan, who were at this time assembled in their ordinary mid-winter session, approving of Edward's recommendation, elected Earl Harold king of the English, and he was forthwith anointed and crowned by Aldred, Archbishop of York.[2]

But there was another competitor for the crown in the person of William, Duke of Normandy, who was cousin to Edward the Confessor through that king's mother, Emma of Normandy, and now claimed the throne under an alleged earlier appointment of his late kinsman. If such appointment or promise had indeed been made, which seems probable,[3] it was superseded by the last expression of King Edward's wishes. Under any circumstance it could merely amount to a recommendation to the witan. A king of the English had never possessed the right to bequeath his kingdom like a private estate. The right of electing a king resided in the witan alone, acting on behalf of the whole nation. Their choice, it is true, had hitherto, when freely exercised, been restricted to the members of the royal house; but failing an eligible descendant of Cerdic, the choice of the nation was unlimited.

The Conquest. William, however, professed to be asserting his legal right, and further alleged that Harold himself had once sworn to recognise his claim to the throne.[4] Having secured the moral and religious support of the papal benediction, which the Roman see, in its anxiety to reduce the independence of the national English church, was most ready to bestow, and leading a large army of Normans and other foreigners, all

---

[1] Harold's sister Edith was the wife of Edward the Confessor, and his mother, Gytha, was a sister of Ulf Jarl and first cousin once removed of King Cnut.
[2] Florence of Worcester, *an.* 1066.
[3] See Freeman, *Norman Conquest* (3rd ed.), ii, 302–309.
[4] The story is obscure. See Ramsay, *Foundations of England*, i, 496, ii, 21.

inured to warfare and eager for booty, William landed in England to decide by the fate of arms between himself and the " usurper " Harold. At the decisive battle of Hastings the Normans were victorious, Harold, his brothers, and the flower of English thegnhood being left dead on the field. Although on the news of Harold's death, the Londoners at once chose Edgar Atheling king, disunion and the lack of effective organisation prevented any successful resistance to the onward march of the invaders. William had as yet conquered but a very small portion of the kingdom, but such was the panic of the nation that he was elected king by the witan, and crowned at Westminster on Christmas Day, 1066, by the same Archbishop Aldred of York who had crowned the unfortunate Harold.[5] In conformity with his original pretensions, he assumed the title of " king of the English," and entered into the usual compact with the nation in the ancient coronation oath.

The Conqueror's Rule. William evidently began with the intention of reigning as the appointed heir of Edward and the lawful successor of the English kings. In that character he was obliged to respect the laws and customs of the kingdom, though in practice he acted in defiance of everything but his own wishes. The continuity of the English constitution was not broken by the Norman conquest. That event ought to be regarded, not as a fresh starting-point, but as " the great turning-point " in the history of the English nation.[6]

The infusion of Norman blood has been considered extensive enough to count as one of the four chief elements of the present English nation; but it was still only an infusion. In the course of little more than a century it became absorbed, as the smaller Celtic and larger Danish elements had been absorbed previously, in the predominant English nationality. The fusion was doubtless facilitated by the common Teutonic descent of the two peoples.[7] The Normans were in fact Northmen, who, instead of coming direct from Scandinavia, had sojourned for a century and a half in a French home. While retaining much of the Norse character, they had acquired, during the interval, the language and civilisation of the romanised Gauls and Franks, developing in the process a brilliant nationality distinct alike from the nationality of their origin and of their new home. The conquerors, moreover, were by no means utter strangers to the people whom they subdued. The vicinity of so remarkable a nation as the Normans had early begun to produce an influence upon the public mind of England, and had to some extent prepared the way for their ultimate supremacy. " Before the Conquest, English princes received their education in Normandy, English sees and English estates were bestowed on Normans. The French of Normandy was familiarly spoken in the palace of Westminster. The court of Rouen seems to have been to the court of

---

[5] William of Poitier, *Gesta Willelmi* (ed. Maseres), p. 145; Florence of Worcester, *an.* 1066.
[6] See Freeman, *Norman Conquest*, i, 1.
[7] *Supra*, p. 2.

Edward the Confessor what the court of Versailles long afterwards was to the court of Charles the Second."[8]

The immediate changes which the conquest introduced were undoubtedly great, but they were practical rather than formal. The power of the crown was vastly increased. As the government became more centralised, local self-government, the essential characteristic of our Teutonic constitution, was for a time depressed; but only to arise again later on, when the nobles and people became united against the tyranny of the crown. The social aspect of England was enormously changed. The old dynasty had been supplanted by an alien family. The old aristocracy was superseded by a new nobility. The old offices received new names—the ealdorman, or earl, became the *comes*, the sheriff the *vice-comes*; and with the new names and alien officials, the old laws, though retained and even promulgated anew, must have been considerably modified in practical administration.

FEUDALISM

The most important result of the conquest, in its constitutional aspect, was the assimilation of all the institutions of the country, from the highest to the lowest, to the feudal type.[9] This was a consequence of the immense confiscations of landed estates which, occurring not all at once, but from time to time, ultimately placed King William in the position of supreme landowner, and established the feudal system in England.

The steps by which this great change was brought about, and the nature of the system of tenure thus established, demand some consideration.

At first the Conqueror,[10] with an appearance of strict legality, appropriated merely the extensive royal domains now finally changed into *terra regis*—and the large forfeited estates of the Godwin family and all of those who had, or were suspected of having, taken up arms against him. Reserving to himself as the demesne of the crown more than a thousand manors scattered over various counties, he divided the rest among his companions in arms. Although William affected to regard all Englishmen as more or less tainted with treason and liable to forfeiture of their estates, inasmuch as they had either fought against him or failed to range themselves on his side, yet the bulk of the landowners were at first suffered to retain their possessions. But there is reason to believe that this was subject to the condition of accepting a regrant from the Conqueror; the more

---

[8] Macaulay, *History of England*, i, 10.

[9] For feudalism generally, see the basic introduction by F. L. Ganshof, *Qu'est-ce que la Féodalité?* (translated by P. Grierson as *Feudalism*), and the brilliant survey by Marc Bloch, *Le Régime Féodal* (2 vols., 1939). On the subject of feudalism in England see Pollock and Maitland, *History of English Law*, i, Book ii, Chap. 1; Maitland, *Constitutional History*, pp. 23–24, and 141–164; Round, *Feudal England*, pp. 225 *et seq.*, and especially F. M. Stenton, *The First Century of English Feudalism* (1932).

[10] It is perhaps scarcely necessary to remark that the term " Conqueror " did not in the language of the time of which we are treating imply subjugation, but signified merely one who " had sought and obtained his right." In reality, however, the modern meaning of the term more accurately describes William's practical position, which was, as he himself once expressed it, " king by the edge of the sword."

important personages, in return for their adhesion, receiving back their estates as a free gift, the smaller owners on payment of a money consideration.[11] By this means William procured a peaceable acknowledgment of his title over extensive districts into which his arms had not yet penetrated.

Insurrections. During the Conqueror's first absence from England a reaction set in after the panic; and the oppression and insolence of the Normans, Odo of Bayeux and William FitzOsbern, who had been left in charge of the kingdom, excited the natives to rebel. One rising was no sooner suppressed than others broke out in different parts of the kingdom, and the first four years of his reign were occupied by William in acquiring the actual sovereignty of his new dominions. Each insurrection, as it occurred, was followed by a confiscation of the estates of those who in the eye of the law were rebels, however patriotic and morally justifiable may have been the motives by which they were actuated. Thus, by a gradual process and with an outward show of legality, nearly all the lands of the kingdom came into the hands of the king, and were by him granted out to his Norman nobles, to be held by the feudal tenure, to which they were alone accustomed in their own country. The maxim of later times, "Tout fuit in luy et vient de luy al commencement"[12] seems to have been something more than a fiction. At the time of the domesday survey there still remained some few exceptions to the general feudal tenure, but before the accession of Henry I all tenures seem to have become uniformly feudal.[13]

French Feudalism. At the period of the Norman conquest, feudalism in both tenure and government was well established in France, the country of its historic development, and in most of the continental countries of Europe.[14] It had grown up gradually, deriving its elements partly from a Roman, partly from a Teutonic source. Indirectly and in part, it may be traced to Roman practices; but its direct and principal sources were (1) the system of beneficiary grants which grew up under the Frank kings and emperors, working in combination with (2) the practice of personal commendation or vassalage, which seems to have superseded and absorbed the primitive and, in many respects, analogous German *comitatus*.

On the Continent, feudalism had become much more than a mere system of tenure. It was inseparably bound up with the system of government and the legal and social relations of the people. To the possession

---

[11] The contemporary Peterborough chronicler speaks of all who did homage to William at or soon after his coronation as " buying " their land. *Select Charters*, 94–95.

[12] Year Book 24 Edward III, f. 65, no. 70 (1350).

[13] Stubbs, *Select Charters*, Introductory Sketch, 14–15.

[14] For recent views on the origins of feudalism see the chapter by Sir Paul Vinogradoff in *Cambridge Mediaeval History*, ii, Chap. xx, and Marc Bloch, *Le Régime Féodal* (1939). For a survey of recent controversies, see H. A. Cronne, " Origins of Feudalism," *History*, xxiv, 251–259 (1939), and F. L. Ganshof, " Benefice and Vassalage," *Cambridge Historical Journal*, vi, 145–175 (1939); C. E. Odegaard, *Vassi and Fideles* (1945).

of a fief was united the right of local judicature. Originally tenable for
life only, fiefs soon came to be hereditary.[15] The practice of " sub-infeudation " naturally followed. The great feudatory who had received large
grants of land from his sovereign retained a certain portion for his own
demesne and then parcelled out the remainder amongst his own dependants, to be held by services similar to those which he himself owed. The
provincial governors, who held the largest beneficiary estates, found
themselves strong enough to establish a number of provincial principali-
ties—*imperia in imperio*—in which, while admitting a nominal dependence
on the sovereign, they claimed and exercised a practically independent
military and civil jurisdiction. It was of the essence of a fief that its tenant
owed fealty to his immediate lord rather than to the state or the sovereign.
The king might be the immediate lord; but in this case obedience was
due to him, not so much in his political capacity as sovereign, as in his
feudal capacity as lord. Thus during the height of the feudal system in
France, the tenants of the immediate vassals of the crown never hesitated
to follow their lord's standard against the king.[16]

The general conversion of allodial into feudal tenure was also due,
in a great degree, to the voluntary action of the smaller free proprietors,
who, in an age of lawlessness and rapine, were glad to submit their persons
and estates, by way of *commendation*, to some powerful neighbouring
lord.[17] Not only the possessions of laymen, but those of the church,
became subject to the all-pervading feudal influence—the bishops and
abbots, equally with the feudal nobles amidst whom they lived, swearing
fealty for their lands to the king or other superior, and exercising feudal
jurisdiction and authority over their own vassals.

English Feudalism. In England an indigenous growth of feudalism
had been going on, but its development had been slower and more purely
Teutonic than on the Continent, where the legal principles and practices
of Imperial Rome exercised an accelerating influence. As a system,
feudalism cannot be said to have been established in England prior to the
conquest, but all its elements had long existed, both separately and sometimes in combination.[18] The two chief elements of feudalism are: (1)
The personal relation of lord and vassal founded on contract, and binding
the parties to mutual fidelity, the one owing protection, the other service.
(2) The holding (*dominium utile*) of land on the condition of rendering
military service, the ultimate property (*dominium directum*) remaining in

---

[15] Conrad II seems to have been the first to declare the fiefs of sub-tenants hereditary by his
edict of 1037. See *Monumenta Germaniae Historica, Constitutiones*, i, 89 *et seq.*, and
Cambridge Mediaeval History, iii, 266.

[16] Such no doubt was their natural tendency. Whether " ideal " feudalism enjoined or
reproved such conduct is open to argument; *v*. Adams, *Origin of the English Constitution*,
187, 190.

[17] The practice of commendation had originally no connection with land, but created a
merely personal tie of mutual protection and fidelity, similar to the Roman *clientela*.

[18] For a summary of recent work on this difficult and contentious subject, see Douglas
" The Norman Conquest and English Feudalism," *Economic History Review*, ix, 128.

the lord, the grantor.[19] Combined, these two elements constitute feudalism; apart, neither is sufficient. In the personal relation which existed between the Teutonic *princeps* and his *comites*, between the English lord and thegn, we have the first element of feudalism in its integrity. We have seen how universal the practice of commendation became, in so much that the lordless man was soon looked upon as an anomaly in the state and treated as an outlaw.[20] One of the most natural modes in which the lord would reward his followers would be by a grant of land, subject to the condition of service, even military service of a sort. By the beginning of the eleventh century the king seems to have assumed the right of disposing of land to his followers as a reward for past, a retainer for future, services. Moreover, by means of sub-infeudation and commendation, a very large part of the land of England had come to be held by dependent tenure, in contradistinction from allodial ownership, which remained the privilege of the few.[21] But up to this stage feudality had affected only the tenure of land. The policy initiated by Cnut, and continued under Edward the Confessor, of dividing the country among a few great earls, who in some cases succeeded in transmitting their jurisdictions to their children, carried the feudal tendency a step farther; and but for the Norman conquest would probably have resulted in the development of a feudalism very similar to that which existed on the Continent.

Both in the kingdom of France and in his duchy of Normandy, William had been familiar with the evils of feudalism, in the form in which it was there established. His recollection of contests with his own barons was too keen and too recent not to induce him to prevent, if possible, a recurrence of the struggle in his newly acquired kingdom. From the very first he took measures to check the natural development of feudalism in England; and although by gradually substituting the Frankish system of land tenure for the complicated system which had grown up in England, he may be said to have established the feudal system, it was as a system of tenure only, not of government organisation. He was determined to reign as the king of the nation, not merely as feudal lord. While, therefore, availing himself of all the advantages of the feudal system, he broke into its most dangerous tendency, the exclusive dependence of a vassal upon his lord, by requiring, in accordance with the old English practice, that all landowners, mesne tenants as well as tenants-in-chief, should take the oath of fealty to the king.

[19] These two phrases were used when Continental lawyers tried to express in terms of Roman law the situation which feudalism had finally brought about. Our own common law did not use the expressions, because there was no need to reconcile feudalism with the Roman idea of *dominium*; Pollock and Maitland, *History of English Law*, ii, 6; Declareuil, *Histoire du droit français*, 272 *et seq.*

[20] *Supra*, p. 15.

[21] The " dependent," remarks Stubbs, " might be connected with the king (1) by service, (2) by comitatus, (3) by commendation, (4) by reception of land as a benefice. Frank feudalism grew out of the two latter, the English nobility of service from the first two. . . . The feudalism that followed the Conquest was Frank and territorial, that which preceded it grew from personal and legal, not from territorial influences." *Constitutional History*, i, 170 n.

The Salisbury Oath. This was formally decreed at the celebrated gemot held on Salisbury Plain, on August 1, 1086, at which the witan and all the landowners of substance in England, whose vassals soever they were, " became his men and swore oaths of fealty to him that they would be faithful to him against all other men."[22]

Domesday Book. This national act of homage and allegiance to the king followed immediately upon the compilation of the domesday survey, which had been decreed in the memorable mid-winter gemot of Gloucester, 1085–1086. The recently attempted invasion from Denmark seems to have impressed the king with the desirability of an accurate knowledge of his fiscal resources. The survey was completed in the remarkably short space of a single year. In each shire the commissioners made their inquiries by the oaths of the sheriffs, the barons and their Norman retainers, the parish priests, the reeves and six ceorls of each township. The result of their labours was a minute description of all the lands of the kingdom, with the exception of the four northern counties of Northumberland, Cumberland, Westmorland, and Durham and part of what is now Lancashire. It enumerates the tenants-in-chief, under-tenants, freeholders, villeins, and serfs, describes the nature and obligations of the tenures, the value in the time of King Edward, at the conquest, and at the date of the survey, and, which gives the key to the whole inquiry, informs the king whether any advance in the valuation could be made.[23]

---

[22] For the earlier oath in III Edmund 1 (*circ.* A.D. 943) see A. J. Robertson, *The Laws from Edmund to Henry I*, 13, 298, and Stubbs, *Select Charters*, 77; for the oath to William, see Wl. art., 2 and Wl. art. retr. 2 in Robertson, 239, 245, and Stubbs, *Select Charters*, 98; *Anglo-Saxon Chronicle*, *s. a.* 1086 *ibid.* p. 96. Davis, *England under the Normans and Angevins*, p. 37, and Adams, *Origin of the English Constitution*, 186–187, consider that the importance of the oath of Salisbury has been exaggerated. Recent work suggests that the oath of Salisbury had real significance. It was not " anti-feudal "; but " the point that needs to be insisted upon is that feudal organisation in England did in practice from the start display different characteristics from those prevailing elsewhere."—D. C. Douglas, *Feudal Documents* (1932), c. note 1; *cf.* F. M. Stenton, *First Century of English Feudalism*, 111–113, and H. A. Cronne in *History*, xix, 248. For an extreme feudal interpretation of this assembly, see J. H. Round, *Peerage and Pedigree*, i, 335. Henry I also exacted an oath at Salisbury; *infra*, p. 127.

[23] The returns were transmitted to Winchester, digested, and recorded in two volumes which have descended to posterity under the name of Domesday Book. The author of the *Dialogus de Scaccario* gives the more probable explanation, " Hic liber ab indigenis *Domesdei* nuncupatur, id est, *Dies Judicii*, per metaphoram," I xvi, 3. It was " the book by which all men would be judged " (*New English Dictionary*) and " is the Register from which judgment was to be given upon the value, tenure, and services of lands therein described " (*cf.* Ellis, *General Introduction*). It is certain that the name was applied to several similar records, as we have notices of the Domesday of St. Paul's, the Domesday of Chester, the Domesday of York, &c. From this authentic record our most certain information is obtained as to old English law, as it appears in the local customs referred to; the character of the municipal government and " consuetudines " of the towns; the financial system of the shires whilst still under the administration of the earls; and the general political and social condition of England towards the end of William's reign. George III caused this complete national register to be printed in two folio vols. in 1783; to these came four supplementary registers and indices in two additional vols. of the Record Commission in 1816. Sir Henry Ellis, the editor of the last two volumes, wrote a brilliant introduction which was published separately in 1833. Later still, Domesday Book was reproduced in facsimile. A very valuable account of the surviving two volumes and of their physical structure, was published for the Record Office by the Stationery Office in *Domesday Rebound*, 1954, on the occasion of their being rebound. The best

The Great Feudatories. In addition to his exactions of homage from his sub-tenants, William took other effective measures to keep the great feudatories in check. The lordships which he bestowed upon his principal barons were scattered over the kingdom, so that in no one district should the territories of one man be great enough to tempt him to rebellion.[24] William abolished the great earldoms which had threatened the integrity of the kingdom under Edward, and, reverting to the earlier English practice, restricted the jurisdiction of the earl to a single shire. The government of the shire—judicial, military, and financial—was, moreover, practically executed by the sheriff, who was directly responsible to the king. An apparent exception to the general policy pursued by the Conqueror occurs in the creation of the three Palatine counties of Chester, Durham, and Kent. The extraordinary powers thus conferred were, however, requisite for the defence of the kingdom against attacks from Wales, Scotland, and the Continent respectively, and two of the persons entrusted with them were ecclesiastics, who could not become the founders of families. A further check to the power of the baronage resulted from the maintenance in full vigour of the popular courts of the shire and the hundred, by which the private manorial jurisdictions of the nobles were restrained, as far as possible, within narrow limits.

Tenures: Knight's Service. Prior to the conquest all lands had been subject to the *trimoda necessitas*.[25] This obligation still continued. But after the feudal system of tenure had been fully established, all lands were held subject to certain additional obligations, which were due either to the king (not as sovereign, but as feudal lord) from the original grantees called tenants-in-chief (*tenentes in capite*), or to the tenants-in-chief themselves from their under-tenants,[26] or to mesne tenants from their

analyses of the contents of Domesday Book are Maitland's *Domesday Book and Beyond* and J. H. Round, *Feudal England*. An excellent short introduction, with a summary of recent research and select bibliography, is given by D. C. Douglas, " The Domesday Survey," *History*, xxi, 249 (1936). The study of Domesday Book is inevitably a matter of great technicality.

[24] From Domesday we learn that the vast possession of the king's brothers, Odo, Bishop of Bayeux, and Robert, Count of Mortain, were scattered over seventeen and twenty counties respectively. Eustace, Count of Boulogne, held fiefs in twelve counties. Hugh (Lupus) of Avranches held lands in twenty-one counties, exclusive of those in his palatine earldom of Chester. *Cf.* the Index of Tenants in Ellis' *Introduction*. The granting of scattered estates was perhaps as much due to the piecemeal character of the Conquest as to William's political design, see Davis, *England under the Normans and Angevins*, p. 31. Note the suggestion in Stenton, *English Feudalism*, 29, that the scattering of estates prevented the formation of local racial groups, and promoted the assimilation of the invaders.

[25] The erroneous form " *trinoda* " was due to Selden; the true form was established by G. J. Turner in the *Encyclopaedia Britannica* (1911) xxvii, 287, and by W. H. Stevenson in *English Historical Review*, xxix, 689. The triple burden was service in the fyrd, repair of bridges, and repair of fortresses, and the crown insisted that no one was exempt (in fact, only one genuine exemption is known). The services are usually named expressly; the words *trimoda necessitas* occur but once, and that in a suspicious charter.

[26] The tenants-in-chief, including the ecclesiastical corporations, enumerated in Domesday, amounted to about fifteen hundred. The under-tenants were about eight thousand in number, and largely consisted of the ousted English owners, who had been reduced from the degree of thegn to the condition of simple freeholders or franklins, holding under a Norman lord.

own under-tenants. Of these obligations the most important was that of knight's service. This was the tenure by which the king granted out fiefs to his followers, who in turn provided him with a certain number of knights properly armed and accoutred to serve in the army for forty days in the year at their own expense (*servitium debitum*).[27] The lands of the bishops and dignified ecclesiastics, and of religious foundations, were also generally held by this tenure. Sometimes, however, religious bodies and ecclesiastics in right of their churches held land by a tenure known as frankalmoign, or free alms; they rendered no earthly service to the lord, but an indefinite spiritual service, prayers for the soul of the donor.

On the grant of a fief, the tenant was publicly invested with the land by a symbolical or actual delivery, termed *livery of seisin*.[28] He then did *homage*, so called from the words used in the ceremony: " Je deveigne votre *homme*." Humbly kneeling before his lord, with sword ungirt and head uncovered, he placed his hands between those of his lord, and pronounced the words: " I become your man from this day forward, of life and limb, and of earthly worship; and unto you shall be true and faithful, and bear to you faith for the tenements I claim to hold of you."[29] The lord then kissed his vassal on the cheek and received the oath of *fealty*.[30] In the case of a sub-tenant (vavasor), his oath of fealty was guarded by a reservation of the faith due to his sovereign lord the king.

In addition to service in war-time, the tenants-in-chief were also bound to attend the king's court at the three great festivals of the year; and on the same principle every mesne lord having two or more freehold tenants had a right to compel their attendance (termed *suit of court*, from *suivre*, to follow) at the court-baron of the manor.[31]

Incidents of Knight's Service. Tenure by knight's service was also subject to several other incidents of a burdensome character, the unfair and oppressive exactions of which by the Norman and earlier Angevin kings supplied one of the chief incentives to the barons who wrested the Great Charter from King John.[32] These incidental burdens were:

27 See Round, *Feudal England*, " The Introduction of Knight's Service into England," pp. 225 *et seq*. William I arbitrarily fixed the obligation of each tenant-in-chief (*cf*. H. M. Chew, *Ecclesiastical Tenants in Chief*, and M. D. Knowles, *Monastic Order*, 610). The *servitium debitum* was not determined in exact proportion to the value or extent of the land granted. A summary of Round's theory will be found in Petit-Dutaillis, *Studies and Notes Supplementary to Stubbs' Constitutional History*, " English Society during the Feudal Period," i, pp. 52 *et seq*. For his theory of *constabularia* see A. L. Poole, *Obligations of Society*, 48–51.

28 Pollock and Maitland, *History of English Law*, ii, 83–89.

29 Littleton (*temp*. Edw. IV), lib. ii, c. i, s. 85. *Cf*. Glanvill (*temp*. Henry II), lib. ix, c. 1; Pollock and Maitland, i, 296–307.

30 The taking of homage had considerable effects in the private law of land, but that lies outside the field of constitutional law.

31 For manorial jurisdiction, see Maitland, *Select Pleas in Manorial and other Seignorial Courts*, and *The Court Baron* (both published by the Selden Society). *Cf*. also Holdsworth, *History of English Law*, i, 181–187.

32 This, and subsequent enactments upon feudal matters, are described in Plucknett, *Legislation of Edward I*.

(1) The tenant was at first expected, and afterwards obliged to render to his immediate lord certain contributions termed *aids* when the lord found himself in an emergency—thus a lord might demand aid in paying his debts, paying his relief to his own lord, stocking his land, etc. These, which were to be reasonable in amount, were finally limited to three special occasions—to ransom the lord's person from captivity; to make his eldest son a knight; and to meet the expense of marrying his eldest daughter.[33] The Statute of Westminster I (1275) fixed the reasonable aid of under-tenants to their lords at 20s. for every knight's fee, and for every £20 value of land in socage.[34]

(2) On the death of the tenant, his fief descended to his heir, sons being preferred to daughters, and the elder to the younger son. But before taking up his ancestor's estate, the heir, if of age, had to pay a fine called a *relief*, which closely resembled and was apparently a feudalised form of the ancient English heriot.[35] By demanding arbitrary and exorbitant reliefs the Norman kings, William Rufus especially, often obliged the heir in effect to purchase or redeem his lands. This abuse was specially provided against in the charter of Henry I, in which the king promised to exact, and required his tenants to exact from their under-tenants, only just and legal reliefs.[36] Glanvill, in the reign of Henry II, tells us that the reasonable relief for a knight's fee was 100s., and for socage, one year's rent, but that the sum due for a barony varied *juxta voluntatem et misericordiam domini regis*. The amount was not finally fixed till Magna Carta defined the *antiquum relevium* as £100 for a barony, 100s. for a knight's fee.[37]

Tenants-in-chief were subject to a kind of additional relief, termed *primer seisin*, which consisted in the right of the king, on the death of one of his tenants leaving an heir of full age, to receive one year's profits of the inherited land.[38]

(3) If the heir were under age, the lord was entitled, under the name of *wardship*, to the custody of his body and lands without any account of the profits. At the age of twenty-one in males, and fourteen in females, the wards were entitled to *ousterlemain* or " sue out their livery "—that is, to require delivery of their lands out of their guardians' hands, on payment of half a year's profits in lieu of all reliefs and primer seisins.[39]

---

[33] Glanvill, lib. ix, c. 8; Magna Carta, c. 12 (*infra*, chap. 4).

[34] 3 Edw. I, c. 36; *Select Charters*, 442. The aids of tenants-in-chief to the king were fixed at the same figures in 1352 (25 Edw. III, stat. 5, c. 11).

[35] Stubbs, *Constitutional History*, ii, 284; Pollock and Maitland, i, 312, *et seq.*

[36] *Select Charters*, 118.

[37] *Infra*, Chap. 4. Glanvill, lib. ix, c. 4; *ibid.* 193.

[38] *Coke upon Littleton*, sect. 103, p. 77A. It was by analogy to the feudal incident of primer seisin, that the popes—who, in carrying out Hildebrand's ideas, claimed to be feudal lords of the lands of the church—subsequently exacted from every beneficed clergyman in England the *first-fruits* of his benefice.

[39] The rights of wardship and marriage, the most oppressive of feudal exactions, were greatly abused by William Rufus. Though Henry I, in his coronation charter promised redress, he did not keep his promises. The feudal lawyers justified the right of wardship on the ground: as to land, that the infant heir being incapable of rendering the military service, ought not to hold the fief; as to the person of the heir, that it was the interest of

(4) The lord also possessed the right of disposing of his female wards in marriage. The rejection by the ward of a suitable match incurred the forfeiture of a sum of money equal to the value of the marriage—that is, as much as the suitor was willing to pay down to the lord as the price of the alliance. If the ward presumed to marry without the lord's consent, she forfeited double the market value of the marriage. This right, which applied not only to female wards, but to daughters who were the presumptive heirs of living vassals, was originally intended as a security against the lord being obliged to receive the homage of a hostile or otherwise objectionable tenant [40]; but it was afterwards, without any feudal justification, extended to male wards, and used as a lucrative source of extortion both by the crown and mesne lords.[41]

(5) The right of devising land by will ceased (with a few local exceptions) at the conquest, and for some time afterwards the freedom of alienation *inter vivos*, as in Anglo-Saxon times, seems to have been limited by certain restrictions in favour of the heir. Indirectly, however, alienation of portions of fiefs was effected through the medium of sub-infeudation, a process which by the time of Henry II had been most extensively applied throughout the country. By this time also the ancestor appears to have acquired a limited right to defeat the expectation of his heir.[42] Subsequently, by the statute of *Quia Emptores* (18 Edw. I, c. 1), 1290,[43] subinfeudation was forbidden, and every freeman was allowed to alienate his land at pleasure (except by will), to be held not of the alienator, but of the lord of whom the alienator had immediately held. All tenants-in-chief, however, still required a licence from the king before they could alienate, for which a fine was of course demanded. By a statute of Edward III [44] the necessity for a licence was done away with, and tenants-in-chief were allowed to alienate at will, on payment of a reasonable fine to the king.

(6) Lastly, there was the valuable right of *escheat*, by which, on the determination of the tenant's estate—either on failure of legal heirs (*propter defectum sanguinis*), or on conviction of the actual tenant of felony (*propter delictum tenentis*)—the fief reverted to the lord by whom or by whose ancestors it had been originally granted. Independently of escheat, the lands of a convicted traitor were liable to *forfeiture* to the crown (which defeated the escheat to the mesne lord). The lands of a convicted felon, however, *escheated* to the lord, the crown having previously exercised its " year, day and waste."

the lord to educate him properly for military service. *Cf.* Fortescue, *De Laudibus Legum Angliae*, c. xliv. A Norman contemporary of Glanvill argued seriously that an infant heir is less likely to be murdered by his lord than by his relatives; Pollock and Maitland, i, 326. *Cf.* R. Génestal, *La Tutelle* (1930) for the conflict of feudalism and the family.

40 Glanvill, lib. vii, c. 12.

41 Statute of Merton, 20 Henry III, c. 6. Glanvill (*temp.* Henry II) expressly limits the lord's right of marriage to female wards. Bracton (*temp.* Henry III) extends it to both, " sive sit masculus, sive foemina." By the Statute of Merton the lord's right of selling the ward in marriage, or else receiving the value of it, is expressly declared.

42 Glanvill, lib. vii, c. i; Pollock and Maitland, i, 329 *et seq; infra.* p. 89.

43 *Select Charters*, 437 *et seq.*; Pollock and Maitland, i, 337 (for a different view, see Plucknett, *Concise History of the Common Law* (5th edn.), 540).   44 1 Edw. III, stat. 2, c. 12.

Tenure by Serjeanty. Besides the tenure by knight's service properly so-called, there was a species of tenancy by *serjeanty*, whereby the tenant was bound, instead of serving the king generally in his wars, to do some special service in his own proper person, as to carry the king's banner or lance, or to be his champion, butler, or other officer at his coronation.[45] The great officers of the household, the steward, marshal, constable and chamberlain, held their lands by serjeanty. Grants of land were also made by the king to his inferior followers and personal attendants, to be held by meaner services. Among the tenants-in-chief mentioned in Domesday occur the names of the king's foresters, huntsmen, falconers, farriers, cooks, and similar officers. In later times a distinction was made between what was called " grand " and what was called " petty " serjeanty. The latter came to be restricted to tenure by the service of rendering yearly some implement of war to the king.[46] It was, in fact, merely a dignified species of the tenure in socage, which has next to be noticed.

Tenure in Free Socage. Tenure in *free socage*[47] (which still subsists under the modern denomination of freehold) denotes, in its most general and extensive signification, a tenure by any certain and determinate but non-military service, as to pay a fixed money rent, or to plough the lord's land for a fixed number of days in the year. In this sense it is constantly opposed, by our ancient legal writers, to tenure by knight's service, where the service, though esteemed more honourable, was more onerous.[48] Not being held by military service, socage tenure lacked one of the elements of a fief, but the spirit of feudalism was all-embracing and affected every tenure and every institution. Thus we find that tenure in socage, like that by knight-service, was created by words of pure donation accompanied by livery of seisin, and was liable to the obligation of fealty invariably, sometimes of homage; and was in like manner subject, but in a modified form, to many of the incidents of tenure by knight's service. Though considered less honourable than the latter, socage was practically much more beneficial, especially in its freedom from the grievous burdens of scutage, feudal wardship and marriage.[49]

Socage tenure comprised also two other particular species, burgage and gavelkind.

---

[45] *Coke upon Littleton*, i, sect. 153. A man might also hold by serjeanty of a mesne tenant, see Pollock and Maitland, i, 285. On the whole subject see Round, *The King's Serjeants and Officers of State with their Coronation Services* (1911), and A. L. Poole, *Obligations of Society*, 57 et seq.

[46] *Coke upon Littleton*, ss. 159, 160. " Per servitium reddendi nobis cultellos vel sagittas, vel hujusmodi." Magna Carta, c. 37, *infra*, Chap. 4.

[47] For the derivation of the word, see Pollock and Maitland, i, 294.

[48] Bracton, lib. 2, c. 16, s. 9; Fleta, lib. 3, c. 14, s. 9. See Pollock and Maitland, i, 294.

[49] The wardship and marriage of an infant tenant of a socage estate (up to the age of fourteen, when wardship ceased) devolved upon his nearest relation not being one to whom the inheritance could descend. Conversely to the rule in knight-service, the guardian in socage was strictly accountable to the infant for the rents and profits; and if he allowed his ward to marry under the age of fourteen, he was bound to account to the ward for the value of the marriage, even though nothing had been received for it, unless he had married him to advantage: Statute of Marlborough, c. 17 (1267).

Tenure in *burgage* was a kind of town socage.[50] It applied to tenements in any ancient borough, held by the burgesses, of the king or other lord, by fixed rents or services.[51] At the conquest the cities and boroughs were retained by the king as part of the demesne of the crown, but a large number were subsequently granted out to his barons. This tenure was subject to a variety of local customs, the most remarkable of which was that of *borough-English*, by which the burgage tenement descended to the youngest instead of the eldest son.[52]

Gavelkind[53] was almost confined to the county of Kent, whose inhabitants are said to have secured this and other privileges by special favour of the Conqueror.[54] The lands are held by suit of court and fealty, a service in its nature certain.[55] The tenant in gavelkind retained many rights and customs which in other parts of the country were submerged by the common law; his lands were devisable by will; in case of intestacy, they descended to all his sons equally; they were not liable to escheat for felony, the maxim being " the father to the bough, the son to the plough "; and they could be alienated by the tenant at the age of fifteen.

Tenure in Villeinage. Below free socage was the tenure in *villeinage*, by which many agricultural labourers held the land which was to them in lieu of money wages. The terms of the tenancy varied with the local customs of different manors, but it was always more or less precarious. Bracton, writing under Henry III, describes two kinds of tenure in villeinage, pure and privileged. Pure villeinage, he tells us, was the tenure by which the demesne of mesne lords was held by tenants who, whether free or unfree, were bound to do whatever work was set them, and who " knew not in the evening what was to be done in the morning." They were occupiers of the land at the lord's will. Privileged villeinage, or villein socage, was the tenure by which tenants of the king's demesnes held their land on condition of performing base services, but certain, and who could not be removed from the land as long as they were willing and able to perform the service due. It was this kind of " privileged villeins," or " villein socmen," who were properly termed " *glebae ascriptitii.*"[56]

---

[50] Stubbs, i, 445 and note. See Pollock and Maitland, i, 295, for the peculiarities of burgage tenure.

[51] *Coke upon Littleton*, ss. 162, 163; M. de W. Hemmeon, *Burgage Tenure in Medieval England* (1914).

[52] Littleton, s. 165; *Third Real Property Report*, p. 8; Mary Bateson, *Borough Customs* (2 vols., Selden Society) is a valuable *corpus* of material, and James Tait, *The Medieval English Borough*, especially c. iv, is indispensable.

[53] Gavelkind, A.-S. *gafolcund* = " rent-yielding " land, *gafol* = " rent " or " customarie paiment of woorkes." Lambarde, *Perambulation of Kent* [ed. 1826], p. 477; *Account Book of a Kentish Estate*, ed. E. C. Lodge (British Academy, 1927), pp. xvi, xvii; N. Neilson, " Custom and the Common Law in Kent ", *Harvard Law Review*, xxxviii, 482.

[54] But see Pollock and Maitland, i, p. 187, " a legend grew up telling how the men of Kent had made special terms with the Conqueror—but probably we shall do well in looking for the explanation of what has to be explained to the time which lies on this side of the Conquest " (*cf. ibid.*, ii, 271–272). Holdsworth, *History of English Law*, iii, 260–263, gives the most plausible of the modern conjectures on this important but difficult problem.

[55] Wright, *Tenures*, 210.

[56] Bracton, f. 208 b-209, *Select Charters*, p. 415. On the personal status of the villeins and the nature of the tenure by which they held their lands, see *infra*, pp. 178 *et seq.*

Law under William I

Whilst availing himself of every advantage which his position as feudal lord paramount gave him over his baronage, William was careful to maintain his rights, and, as a rule, endeavoured to perform his duties as king of the English, preferring " the forms of ancient royalty to the more ostentatious position of a feudal conqueror."[57]

The Curia Regis. He held his court on the three great festivals of the year at Winchester, Westminster and Gloucester at which the archbishops and bishops, abbots and earls, thegns and knights attended.[58] Although these meetings bore a close resemblance to those of the national assembly of the Anglo-Saxon period,[59] they were in fact essentially different. William's court, as we see it in retrospect, was a new court, a feudal court. The Anglo-Saxon chronicler continues to use the name *Witan* with which he is familar,[60] but the qualification for attendance tends to be no longer wisdom, but tenure, and the personnel are felt to be not *sapientes* but *barones*. The feudal principle acquired the predominating influence in every department of the state, and the national council almost insensibly changed from the assembly of the Wise Men into the *Curia Regis*, the court of the king's tenants-in-chief.[61]

William's legislation. William made but few changes in the national laws. It was their administration by foreign officials which constituted the grievance most heavily felt. Early in his reign, when the work of conquest had been completed, he ordained that peace and security should be observed between his English and Norman subjects, and renewed the law of Edward the Confessor, with certain additions made by himself " ad utilitatem populi Anglorum." [62] In like manner Cnut, fifty-two years before, had reconciled the English and Danes at a gemot at Oxford, and renewed the law of Edgar the Peaceful.[63] This renewal by William is the first mention of the famous laws of King Edward, which Normans as well as English soon learnt to demand in every reign, until Magna Carta supplied them with a more substantial foundation for their liberties. By the " laws of Edward " they probably meant not the laws which he had promulgated, but those which he had observed.[64] The phase imported a demand for a mild and good government as opposed to harsh and unjust innovations. As for the text known as *Leges Edwardi Confessoris*, " it

---

[57] Stubbs, *Constitutional History*, i, 314.

[58] *Anglo-Saxon Chronicle*, s. a. 1087. This was a Norman innovation; see Liebermann, *National Assembly in the Anglo-Saxon Period*, p. 82.

[59] Liebermann, *op. cit.*, 75–88.

[60] *Anglo-Saxon Chronicle*, s. a. 1086.

[61] See Round, " Origin of the House of Lords," in *Pedigree and Peerage*, i, 324 *et seq.*

[62] Wl. art. 7 (Robertson, *Laws of the English Kings*, 240); *Select Charters*, 98–99.

[63] Florence of Worcester, s. a. 1018; Cn. 1020, 13 (Robertson, *Laws*, 142).

[64] The remark is William of Malmesbury's: Hallam, *Middle Ages*, ii, 325. The story in Hoveden, *Chronicle*, ii, 218, s. a. 1070 that the Conqueror summoned juries to declare Edward's law " is not very probable ": Pollock and Maitland, i, 104 n. 3.

should only be used with extreme caution, for its statements, when not supported by other evidence, will hardly tell us more than that some man of the twelfth century, probably some man of Henry I's day, would have liked those statements to be true."[65]

Normans and English were, in theory, equal before the law; but the distinction of personal law was, for some purposes, allowed. The Normans were accustomed to the *wager of battle*,[66] the English to the ordeal and compurgation. King William allowed the man of each race to be tried by the customs of his own country.[67] But *Francigenae* (who would be mostly Normans), settled in England previously to the conquest, were to be treated as Englishmen.[68]

The English frequently revenged themselves on their local tyrants by assassination. To check this, William ordained that the whole hundred, within whose limits a Norman should be secretly slain, should be liable to a heavy amercement.[69] In connection with this enactment there grew up the famous law of " *Englishry*," by which every murdered man was presumed to be a Norman, unless proofs of " Englishry " were made by the four nearest relatives of the deceased.[70] Although so early as the reign of Henry II we are told that the two races (with the exception of the villeins) had become so blended, through inter-marriages, that the distinction between Norman and Englishman had almost entirely disappeared,[71] liability to the murder fine continued till 1340, when it was abolished by statute.[72]

The public peace which William established and maintained was the greatest benefit of his reign. He permitted no rapine but his own. Meting out stern justice to Norman and Englishman alike, he yet abolished the punishment of death, and substituted what was possibly regarded as the milder punishment of mutilation.[73] He also, like his predecessors Ethelred and Cnut, prohibited the infamous practice of selling men into foreign slavery.[74]

[65] Pollock and Maitland, i, 104; the text of the *Leges Edwardi Confessoris* is in Liebermann's *Gesetze*, i, 627–670. Even Bracton used it, and so did Coke.

[66] " The trial by battle, which on clearer evidence seems to have been brought in by the Normans, is a relic of old Teutonic jurisprudence, the absence of which from the Anglo-Saxon courts is far more curious than its introduction from abroad."—Stubbs, *Constitutional History*, i, 299 (and *cf.* particularly Brunner, *Die Entstehung der Schwurgerichte*). As late as 1818, in the case of *Ashford* v. *Thornton* (Barn. & Ald. i, 405 *et seq.*), the judges held that trial by battle in appeals of murder was still a part of English criminal procedure; the next year battle in civil and criminal procedure was abolished by 59 Geo. 3, c. 46. The last case in which trial by compurgation was claimed was that of *King* v. *Williams*, 2 B. & C. 538 (1824). Wager of law was abolished in 1833 by 3 & 4 Will. 4, c. 42, s. 13. *Cf.* Stephen, *History of Criminal Law*, vol. i, p. 244, note 2. See G. Neilson, *Trial by Combat* (Glasgow, 1890). *Cf.* also *infra*, chap. 4, text note to Magna Carta, sec. 54.

[67] Wl. lad. 2 = Wl. art. 6 (Robertson, 232, 241).

[68] Wl. art. 4; *Select Charters*, 98.

[69] Wl. art. 3, sec. 1, Leis Wl. 22 (Robertson, 238, 264); *Dialogus de Scaccario*, lib. i, c. 10; *Select Charters*, 98, 218; Pollock and Maitland, i. 89.

[70] Bracton, f. 134 *b*. The crime of murder (*murdrum*) was anciently restricted to *secret* killing. *Dialogus de Scaccario*, lib. i, c. 10. On *Murdrum*, *cf.* Maitland, *Pleas of the Crown of Glouc.* (Introd. xxix) and Yntema, " Lex Murdrorum," *Harvard Law Review*, xxxvi, 146.

[71] *Cf. Dialogus de Scaccario*, lib. i, c. 10; *Select Charters*, 218.

[72] 14 Edw. 3, st. 1, c. 4.

[73] Wl. art. 10; *Select Charters*, 99.   [74] *Ibid., c.* 9.

The Forests. The love of field sports amounted in the Conqueror to an ungovernable passion. " He loved the tall deer," says the Anglo-Saxon chronicler, " as if he were their father "; and the laying waste of 17,000 acres for the formation of the New Forest in Hampshire, made a deep impression on the popular mind. The forest laws which William introduced, though not so cruel as they subsequently became under Henry I, were yet marked by extraordinary harshness.

The penalty for killing a hart or hind was loss of sight. The killing of even wild boars and hares was forbidden. The beginning of forest laws is traceable to the legislation of Cnut; but by him the right of every man to hunt on his own ground was expressly recognised.[75] Up to the period of the conquest, hunting was still regarded not merely as a pastime but as a means of exterminating noxious animals and of procuring food. Under William it became a mere sport for pleasure, and the exclusive privilege of the king and those whom he allowed to share it.[76] Though mitigated under Henry III and in succeeding reigns, yet " from this root," says Blackstone, " afterwards sprung a bastard slip known by the name of the game law "—a system which, down to the reign of William IV, made it illegal for any man to take or sell game, even on his own land, unless possessed of a real property qualification of at least £100 a year.

The Church. Previous to the conquest the English church had enjoyed what has been termed " an insular and barbaric independence." The conquest brought it into much closer connection with Rome. Foreign ecclesiastics were substituted in high places for the native clergy. But while the church lost some of its national independence, it gained in power. As secular government gained in force through the strong centralisation system of the Conqueror, so the power of the church increased through its more complete subordination to the papacy. The Conqueror, however, had no intention of admitting the interference of the Pope in the English church or state to a greater extent than he himself might judge to be expedient. He was, indeed, under great obligations to the papacy, and was at all times regarded as a favoured son of the church. But he resolutely refused to admit the haughty pretensions of Hildebrand (Pope Gregory VII), who in the prosecution of his scheme of ecclesiastical feudalism, in which all kings of the earth were to hold their kingdoms as fiefs of the Holy See, called upon William to do fealty for the crown of England.[77]

Under the pre-Norman kings the church and the state had been practically identical, earls and bishops were alike elected and deposed, and laws

[75] II Cnut, 80; *Select Charters*, p. 88. The laws ascribed to Cnut, known as the *Constitutiones de Foresta*, have been shown by Liebermann to be a forgery. *Cf. Select Charters*, p. 185.
[76] See Freeman, *Norman Conquest*, iv, 607 *et seq.*, and especially G. J. Turner, *Select Pleas of the Forest* (Selden Society), and N. Neilson in the *English Government at Work*, 1327–1336 (ed. J. Willard and W. A. Morris).
[77] See Z. N. Brooke, " Pope Gregory VII's Demand for Fealty from William the Conqueror," *English Historical Review*, xxxi, 225 *et seq.* (1911), and his *English Church and the Papacy* (1931), 140 *et seq.*

spiritual and temporal were enacted by the king in co-operation with the witan.[78] The bishop and the ealdorman sat side by side at the gemot of the shire or hundred, deciding all causes, ecclesiastical as well as civil. One of the most important acts of William's reign was the separation of the ecclesiastical from the civil jurisdiction of the courts of law. He directed that from henceforth no bishop or archdeacon should hold pleas of ecclesiastical matters in the shire or hundred court; but that all such pleas should be determined according to the canon and ecclesiastical laws before the bishop, at the place which he should appoint for the purpose. All sheriffs and other lay persons were prohibited from interfering in spiritual causes.[79] But in making this change William took care to preserve the ancient supremacy of the state, by laying down his three famous canons of the royal supremacy, *viz.*:

(1) That no pope should be acknowledged, or papal letters received, in England, without the king's consent.

(2) That the decrees of national synods should not be binding without the king's confirmation.

(3) That the king's barons and officers should not be excommunicated, or constrained by any penalty of ecclesiastical rigour, without his permission.[80]

JUDICIAL ORGANISATION

The judicial organisation of the kingdom at the end of William's reign was but slightly altered from what it had been under Edward the Confessor. The spiritual courts had now, as we have seen, exclusive jurisdiction in spiritual matters; but for civil matters the ordinary courts were still those of the shire, the hundred, or the borough, together with the manorial courts baron of the king or other lord. In the court of the shire all the freeholders of the shire,[81] in the court baron all the free tenants of the manor,[82] acted as judges, and doubtless gave judgment in accordance with the ancient local customs; but in the shire and hundred courts the Norman sheriff, or *vice-comes*, now presided with a power and authority far less limited than the power and authority of any of his English predecessors.

[78] See Liebermann, *National Assembly*, pp. 62–65.

[79] See the Ordinance of William in *Select Charters*, 99–100.

[80] Eadmer, *Historia Novorum*, i, p. 6; *Select Charters*, 96; *cf.* Stubbs, *Constitutional History*, i, 310: " A further usage, which was claimed by Henry I as a precedent, was the prohibition of the exercise of legatine power in England, or even of the legates landing on the soil of the kingdom without royal licence." See generally, Z. N. Brooke, *The English Church and the Papacy* (1931), 132.

[81] See the accounts of the suits between the Bishop of Rochester and Pichot, the sheriff on behalf of the king, *Textus Roffensis*, ed. Hearne, 150; between Bishop Wulstan and Abbot Walter of Evesham, " judicante et testificante omni vice-comitatu." Heming, *Chartulary*, ed. Hearne, p. 77; and between Archbishop Lanfranc and Odo, Bishop of Bayeux, 'Textus Roffensis,' in Wharton, *Anglia Sacra*, i, 334. Great meetings of the shire held before royal commissioners could be described by the word *witenagemot* as late as 1124; below, p. 52, note 19.

[82] Coke, *Fourth Institutes*, 46, 268; *Coke on Littleton*, 58A. In Domesday mention is made of one lord lending another some free tenants to make up his court, *propter placita sua tenenda*. Spence, *Equitable Jurisdiction*, i, 100, n. (a).

The supreme court of the kingdom was the *Curia Regis*, at once the council of the king and the witenagemot of the nation, with whose counsel and consent the king discharged both legislative and judicial functions. The immense amount of business to be transacted and the frequent absence of the king in Normandy caused the appointment of a new officer of the highest dignity, the *justiciar*, who represented the king in all matters, acted as regent in his absence, and at all times administered the legal and financial business of the country. The office of *chancellor*, who, as official keeper of the royal seal, first appears under Edward the Confessor (the first of our kings who had a seal), was continued; but he was subordinate to the justiciar, heading the king's clerks or chaplains, who performed the duties of secretaries.

RETROSPECT

William was reputed to be the most opulent prince in Christendom. As king of the English, feudal superior of his tenants-in-chief, and personal lord of all his subjects, William exercised a power far greater than that which any of his predecessors had ever wielded. Though the formal changes which he had made in our constitution and laws were few in number, his government was practically despotic and his administration harsh. His tyranny, says Hallam, " displayed less of passion or insolence than of that indifference about human suffering which distinguishes a cold and far-sighted statesman." [83] It was in this spirit that to resist a threatened invasion from Denmark he caused the whole country between the Tyne and the Humber to be laid waste, so that for some years afterwards there was not an inhabited village and hardly an inhabitant left.[84]

The reign of the Conqueror was on the whole beneficial to the nation, which required welding together and organising by means of a strong central government; and he himself was both a wise and, from his own standpoint, a just king.[85] But his stern nature and the hardness of his rule made him an object of fear to all ranks of his subjects. In the picturesque language of the Anglo-Saxon chronicler: " He was a very stark man and very savage; so that no man durst do anything against his will. He had earls in his bonds who had done against his will; bishops he set off their bishoprics, abbots off their abbotries, and thegns in prison, and at last he did not spare his own brother Odo." " Truly in his time men had mickle suffering and very many hardships. Castles he caused to be wrought and poor men to be oppressed. He was so very stark. He took from his subjects many marks of gold and many hundred pounds

[83] *Middle Ages*, ii, 305.
[84] William of Malmesbury, *Gesta Regum*, lib. iii, s. 249. On this " harrying of the North," see some recent work by T. A. M. Bishop, " The Norman Settlement of Yorkshire," in *Studies presented to F. M. Powicke* (1948), 1–14.
[85] Gregory VII extols his love of justice: " Quoniam, licet in vobis per misericordiam Dei multae et egregiae sint virtutes, haec tamen est praeclara et famosissima et quae gloriam vestram Deo praecipue commendat et hominibus, quod justiciam, quam vos facere prompti estis, aliis etiam facientibus diligitis atque probatis," *Reg.* iv, 17.

of silver; and that he took, some by right and some by mickle might, for every little need." " He let his lands to fine as dear as he could: then came some other and bade more than the first had given, and the king let it to him who had bade more. Then came a third and bid yet more, and the king let it into the hands of the man who bade the most. Nor did he reck how sinfully his reeves got money of poor men, or how many unlawful things they did. As man spake more of right law, so man did more unlaw. His rich men moaned and his poor men murmured; but he was so hard that he recked not the hatred of them all." [86]

[86] *Anglo-Saxon Chronicle, s. a.* 1086, 1087.

CHAPTER 3

THE NORMAN AND FIRST ANGEVIN KINGS

William Rufus, A.D.	1087–1100.	*Henry II*, A.D.	1154–1189.
Henry I	1100–1135.	*Richard I*	1189–1199.
Stephen	1135–1154.		

WILLIAM II, RUFUS

THE constitutional importance of the reign of William Rufus consists mainly: (1) in the systematic elaboration by Ranulf Flambard of the theory of the incidents of feudal tenure, and its rigid application in practice, as a fiscal expedient, to ecclesiastical and lay tenants alike; and (2) in the continued struggle between the royal and feudal powers, which caused the king to throw himself upon the support of the native English, and led to the ultimate breaking up of the baronage of the Conquest. A despot of the worst sort, William devoted himself almost entirely to his pleasures, and after the death of Archbishop Lanfranc, his ablest adviser, left nearly all the work of government to his justiciar.

Ranulf Flambard. This great official was not, as in the Conqueror's days, a powerful baron, but a humble and clever court chaplain, of congenial and compliant tastes, Ranulf Flambard,[1] by whom the church, the feudal vassals, and the people, were all subjected to systematic oppression and extortion. As justiciar, he controlled and directed the whole fiscal and judicial business of the kingdom; and in order to supply the prodigality of the master who had raised him to this exalted position, he directed his ingenuity, like Empson and Dudley four centuries later, to turning the feudal rights of the king and the procedure of the courts of justice into instruments of pecuniary extortion. The feudal incidents of relief, wardship, and marriage, which under the Conqueror had been based on true feudal principles, and, for the most part, reasonably exacted, were now systematically organised as a method of arbitrarily taxing the tenants-in-chief, under colour of exacting a legal due. The system of extortion thus fixed upon the tenants of the king was naturally, indeed

---

[1] Ranulf was the son of a priest of the diocese of Bayeux; he took orders and came to England with the Conqueror; he appears in Domesday, i, 51, as a small landowner in Hampshire. He was at one time in the service of Maurice, Bishop of London; and then chaplain to William Rufus, who made him chief justiciar. *Ordericus Vitalis*, ed. Le Prevost, iii, 310; iv, 107. William of Malmesbury, iv, 314. See R. W. Southern, "Ranulf Flambard and Early Anglo-Norman Administration," *Transactions of the Royal Historical Society* (1933), 95–128. *Cf.* Davis, *England under the Normans and Angevins*, p. 78. For the office of justiciar, see *infra*, p. 94. There seems no contemporary warrant for regarding either Lanfranc, Flambard or Roger of Salisbury as the holders of a single definite office; there might be several " chief justiciars " (Jolliffe, *Constitutional History*, 192, n. 1, 196).

necessarily, extended by them to their sub-tenants, and in this way all holders of land by military tenure became subject to the new imposts.[2] The fiefs of the church were assimilated by Ranulf as far as possible to lay fiefs. Bishoprics and abbeys were purposely kept vacant for years together, during which time the king claimed, on the analogy of the wardship of a lay fief, to receive all the profits for his own use; and when at length a successor was nominated to the vacant benefice, a fine was demanded equivalent at least to the relief which would have been payable by a lay heir.[3]

Insurrections. The great struggle between the royal and feudal powers, which began under the Conqueror himself in the conspiracy of Ralph de Guader, Earl of Norfolk, and Roger, Earl of Hereford (1075), was actively carried on under Rufus. Taking advantage of the claim of Duke Robert to the throne of England, the larger part of the barons eagerly seized the opportunity of siding with him against the king (1088). Seven years later (1095) an attempt was made to set aside the line of the Conqueror altogether in favour of Stephen of Aumale, grandson of Duke Robert I of Normandy. On both occasions the insurrections were unsuccessful; and being followed by considerable forfeitures, served only to bring about the decay, ultimately the almost utter extinction, of the baronage of the Conquest.[4] In order to maintain his ground, the king was compelled to court the support of his English subjects, who eagerly and successfully fought for him against their feudal oppressors. On three separate occasions—at his coronation, at the outbreak of the rebellion of his Norman barons almost immediately afterwards, and again in 1093, when ill and in fear of death—he sought to engage the affections of the people by issuing constitutional manifestos in which he promised good laws, lighter taxation, and free hunting.[5] But his promises were never fully kept. Instead of the free hunting promised, he made the capture of a stag a capital offence.[6] Like the others of his race, however, even Rufus left his mark upon the growing fabric of judicial organisation.[7]

---

[2] Two lines of development contributed to this result. (1) The practice of the crown fixed the law of feudal incidents, which the tenants in chief proceeded to apply to their own tenants; and (2) the mesne tenant had for a time legal right to the assistance of his sub-tenants to meet the feudal claims of the lord paramount, Glanville, lib. ix, c. 8; even villeins might be called upon to contribute, F. M. Stenton, *The First Century of English Feudalism*, 183.

[3] *Ordericus Vitalis*, viii, 8: " He desired to be the heir of every one, churchman or layman." *Anglo-Saxon Chronicle, s. a.* 1100; Stubbs, *Constitutional History*, i, 325. For an example of Ranulf's methods see the Writ of 1095 (Round, *Feudal England*, p. 310, *Select Charters* p. 109), in which, on the death of the Bishop of Worcester, he demands the payment of a relief from all the tenants of the See.

[4] Stubbs, *Constitutional History*, i, 321. For the rather different view that William I and Rufus had co-operated closely with the feudatories, see Jolliffe, *Constitutional History*, 200.

[5] William of Malmesbury, *Gesta Regum*, lib. iv, § 306; Eadmer, *Historia Novorum*, p. 30; *Select Charters*, 109.

[6] William of Malmesbury, *Gesta Regum*, iv, § 319.

[7] Below, p. 51 at notes 15 and 16.

Henry I

Henry I, on his accession, issued a Charter of Liberties which is in form an amplification of the covenant made by the king with his people in the coronation oath. Copies were despatched to the several counties and deposited in the principal monasteries.

Charter of Henry I (1100). In this charter Henry endeavoured to propitiate all classes of his subjects by abolishing the *malae consuetudines*, the illegal exactions with which the clergy, the baronage, and the people generally had been oppressed during the reign of the late king. (1) To the church he promised that on the death of an archbishop, bishop, or abbot, he would neither sell [8] nor let to farm the possessions of the church or its tenants, nor receive anything, during the vacancy of the benefice. (2) To his barons and other tenants-in-chief he promised a remission of various illegal exactions, to which they had been subjected under cover of the incidents of feudal tenure. The heir should not be compelled to *redeem* his land, as in the time of the late king, William Rufus, but should pay only a lawful and just relief. The king's licence for the marriage of his vassal's daughter or other female relative must still be obtained, but it should be given without payment, and should not be refused unless the intended husband were the king's enemy. In the case of an heiress the king would take the advice of his baronage before giving her in marriage. Widows should not be given in marriage against their will. Widows without children should possess their dowers unconditionally; if with children, so long as they continued chaste.

The wardship of the persons and lands of children should belong to the mother or other relation.

Knights, holding by military service, should have their demesne lands free from all geld and work, in order that they might the more efficiently equip themselves for the defence of the king and kingdom.

The right of the king's vassals to bequeath their personal property by will was recognised; and in case of intestacy, the deceased person's wife, children, relations, or vassals legally authorised, were to dispose of it for the good of his soul, as to them should seem good.

Fines for offences should not be assessed at the king's mercy, as in the time of his father and brother, but according to the nature of the offence, as in the time of the king's " other ancestors." Thus early had the Norman barons begun to claim for themselves the benefit of the old English laws.

(3) To the nation at large the king granted the law (*lagam*) of Edward the Confessor with the emendations made by the Conqueror with the consent of his barons. The claims of the people were also recognised in the proclamation of the king's peace, and especially in the express extension

---

[8] This might refer to simoniacal sale of the office, not alienation of church property. *Cf.* the Second Charter of Stephen, *infra*, p. 53, and Stubbs, *Lectures on Early English History*, p. 110. But see also McKechnie, *Magna Carta*, p. 97, who takes it as referring to alienation.

to all under-tenants of the benefits granted to the king's immediate vassals. The king further promised to exact no moneyage which had not been levied in the time of King Edward, and to punish all coiners or utterers of base money. He forgave the debts due to his late brother; and all murder-fines (*murdra*) up to the day of his coronation. Such fines should in future be regulated by the law of King Edward.[9]

The only unpopular clause in the charter was that in which Henry declared his intention to retain the forests in his own hand as his father had held them, a personal indulgence for which he pleads the " common consent " of his barons.[10]

Historically, the charter records the nature and recent introduction of the illegal exactions which it specifically abolishes; constitutionally, it is important as a formal and deliberate recognition, by a practically despotic king, of the ancient and lawful freedom of the nation, and of the limitation of the royal power. It seems to have been re-issued by Henry at various times; but as soon as he found himself firmly seated on the throne, he never hesitated to disregard its provisions. It was renewed by Stephen and by Henry II; and under John it served, in the hands of the archbishop, Stephen Langton, as a text upon which the barons founded their claim for a restoration of the ancient liberties of the nation.

This charter of liberties is the sole legislative enactment of Henry's reign; for the so-called " Laws of Henry I " were not legislative enactments, but an unofficial treatise on English law written by a private jurist.[11]

Domestic policy. His somewhat questionable title to the throne, at a time when canons of hereditary descent (whether to land or to the crown) were as yet hardly established, the contest with his elder brother Robert, and the difficulty of keeping in check a turbulent and powerful baronage, caused Henry to court the alliance and support of the native population. The people were already predisposed in his favour as being the first of the new dynasty who had been born and educated in England. His politic marriage with the " good Queen Maud," daughter of Malcolm Canmore, king of Scots, by Margaret, sister of Edgar Atheling, gave him still stronger claim to national support. Moreover, the feudal barons, ever seeking to achieve their independence, were the common enemies of both king and people. Impelled alike by national sentiment and unity of interest, and encouraged by the king's promises of good government, the

---

[9] By the consensus of modern opinion, there was no law regulating murder fines in the time of King Edward, for the fine was a Norman innovation to protect the lives of Normans (see *supra*, p. 42). However, this chapter can be used (with other material) to make a case for the pre-conquest and perhaps Danish origin of the fine; see the discussion in Yntema, " Lex Murdrorum," *Harvard Law Review*, xxxvi, 146.

[10] See the Charter in full, Robertson, *Laws*, 276, and *Select Charters*, pp. 117–119.

[11] See Liebermann, *Ueber das englische Rechtsbuch Leges Henrici* (Halle, 1901) and Pollock and Maitland, *History of English Law*, i, 99. The text is in B. Thorpe, *Ancient Laws and Institutes* (1840), and in Liebermann, *Gesetze* (1903). Extracts are printed in *Select Charters*, 123–126. There is no translation into English.

people steadily supported the crown against all assailants. Henry was thus enabled to obtain a complete triumph over his rebellious vassals, many of the most powerful of whom, including Robert de Belesme, Earl of Shrewsbury, the most dangerous of them all, were expelled the kingdom with the forfeiture of their English estates.[12] In the end Henry acquired a plenitude of royal power equal, if not superior, to that which the Conqueror had enjoyed. In the redistribution of the forfeited lands and jurisdictions he carried out his father's policy of keeping within moderate limits the possessions of any one vassal. As a further check to the still formidable nobility of the conquest he raised to the baronage a number of new men, whom he placed on an equality with the proudest of their fellow barons.[13]

THE LOCAL COURTS

During the late reign the feudal nobles appear to have extended their hereditary franchises to the detriment of the national courts of the shire and the hundred. Henry restored the jurisdiction of these courts to its ancient vigour by ordering that they should be held at the same places and during the same terms as in the time of King Edward. All suits respecting lands between tenants-in-chief of the crown were to be determined in the king's court, but, like suits between vassals of different mesne lords, were to be heard in the county court.[14] Another measure of great importance was the erection (in the last years of the eleventh century) of royal justiciars in the counties, whose powers prevented the sheriffs from becoming independent hereditary despots.[15] The proper jurisdiction of the baronial court over the disputes of two or more tenants of the same lord was not interfered with.

The king also granted charters to several boroughs confirming and augmenting their ancient privileges. His charter to the citizens of London is remarkable for the amount of municipal independence and self-government which it accorded. But London had always held an exceptional position; and its privileges were far in advance of those as yet granted to the other towns of the kingdom.[16]

[12] *Cf.* Ordericus Vitalis, *Ecclesiastica Historia*, xi, 3.
[13] Ordericus Vitalis, *Ecclesiastica Historia*, xi, c. 2; *Select Charters*, 114.
[14] See the order in Robertson, *Laws*, 286, *Select Charters*, 122, and G. B. Adams, in *American Historical Review*, viii, 487. The address, " Henricus Rex Anglorum Samsoni episcopo et Ursoni de Abetot et omnibus baronibus suis Francis et Anglis de Wirecestrescira salutem," is remarkable for two reasons: (1) the bishop of the diocese is joined with the sheriff, in the ancient form, notwithstanding the separation of the spiritual and temporal jurisdictions decreed by the Conqueror; (2) English barons are mentioned.
[15] G. B. Adams, *Council and Courts in Anglo-Norman England* (1926). 142, 148 *et seq.*
[16] *Cf.* the charter to London with that granted to Beverley and with the customs of Newcastle-on-Tyne.—*Select Charters*, 129–134. London was deprived by Stephen of many of the privileges granted by the charter of Henry I, such as the right to appoint a sheriff and justiciar. For the constitutional development of London see Petit-Dutaillis, *Studies Supplementary to Stubbs' Constitutional History*, i, chap. ix, " London in the Twelfth Century."

Centralisation

At the same time that Henry strengthened the local courts of the shire, the hundred, and the borough, as a check to the feudal nobility from below, he endeavoured to curb them from above by centralising and systematising the royal administration. Roger le Poer, Bishop of Salisbury, having served as chancellor from 1101 to 1103, was appointed in 1107 chief justiciar—or so the later chronicles describe him.[17] Under his direction, during his thirty-two years' tenure of this high office, the administration of the Curia Regis was organised for judicial and financial purposes. A regular routine of business was established. The annual courts were still held as before during the great festivals at Gloucester, Winchester, and Westminster; but they were found inadequate for the increasing business of the nation.

Judicial circuits. The chief justiciar, therefore, accompanied by some of the other justices of the king's court, began towards the end of Henry's reign to make occasional circuits round the kingdom principally for fiscal but partly also for judicial purposes.[18] The local courts were thus brought into closer connection with the supreme national tribunal. By introducing order and system into the administration of law and government, Henry prepared the way for the important reforms which the reign of his grandson will present to our notice.

The severity with which Henry punished offences against the laws caused him to be popularly regarded as the " Lion of Justice " described in the prophecies of Merlin. William Rufus had reintroduced the punishment of death for offences against the forest laws; by Henry it was extended to ordinary crimes. In the year 1124 no less than forty-four thieves were hanged in Leicestershire at one time.[19] " No man," says the Anglo-Saxon Chronicle, " durst misdo against another in his time. He made peace for man and beast. Whoso bare his burden of gold or silver, no man durst say to him aught but good." [20] By severe punishments he effectually checked the malpractices of the moneyers, which had caused a general depreciation of the coinage. He also checked the abuse of the royal right of purveyance by the officers of his court. But the expenses of his foreign wars and home administration necessitated the imposition of heavy and

---

[17] See above, p. 47, n. 1.

[18] Towards the close of the reign of William Rufus, in 1096, we find two itinerant commissioners, Bishops Walkelin and Flambard, despatched to Exeter and to Cornwall to hold royal pleas (cf. Bigelow, *Placita Anglo-Normanica*, p. 69). It is probable that no practice of the kind had as yet been established, and that this journey was on some special business. Gneist, *Constitutional History of England*, i, 273, remarks: " The administration of the counties by the *vice-comites* had from the first suffered from grave abuses. For this reason, even under Henry I the *vice-comites* had begun to be relieved of certain judicial business by commissioners sent from the royal court," and refers to the Pipe Roll, 31 Hen. I (1130), as showing that at that date the commission of itinerant justices had become an institution. It is probable that their duties were originally financial, but sitting as they did in the shire courts, they gradually came to discharge judicial business also. Cf. Stubbs, *Constitutional History*, i, 423; Jolliffe, *Constitutional History*, 193–194.

[19] *Anglo-Saxon Chronicle*, 1124 E (where the session is described as a " gewitenemot ").

[20] *Anglo-Saxon Chronicle, sub ann.* 1135; *Select Charters*, 115.

regular taxation, of which the contemporary chroniclers complain in bitter terms.[21]

The investiture contest. After the triumph of Henry over the baronage, the only class in the state strong enough to offer any resistance to the royal power consisted of the clergy. The contest between the king and Archbishop Anselm on the question of investitures ended in a compromise. The ring and crosier, as denoting spiritual jurisdiction, were in future to be conferred by the pope; fealty and homage, being civil duties, were still to be rendered to the king, in return for the temporalities of the see. Thus the national church regained her spiritual freedom, which the rapid growth of the feudal principle had injuriously affected, and the king retained all that he could justly claim—the supremacy in things temporal.[22] The chief constitutional importance of the struggle consists in the successful imposition of a limit to the royal power.

STEPHEN

On his coronation, Stephen issued a *charter* briefly confirming, in general terms, to the barons and men of England all the liberties and good laws which his uncle Henry, King of the English, had granted them, as well as all the good laws and good customs which they possessed in the time of King Edward.[23] After a short interval the king held his first Great Council at Oxford,[24] at which most of the English, together with several Norman, prelates and barons attended. In this assembly a *second charter* was drawn up and promulgated by the king. It is more definite in form than the earlier one, and was attested by no less than thirty-seven witnesses, of whom fourteen were bishops (eleven of English and three of Norman sees), and the rest lay vassals, for the most part of high rank and official position.

As Stephen owed his election chiefly to the favour of the clergy, who were greatly influenced by his brother Henry, Bishop of Winchester, it is not surprising to find the greater part of the second charter devoted to concessions to the church.

Concessions. (1) *The Clergy.* The king promised to repress all simony, and to maintain the jurisdiction of the bishops over all clerical persons and their possessions. Ecclesiastical dignities, with their privileges and ancient customs, should remain inviolate. The church should retain possession of all estates which it had enjoyed by an uncontested title at

---

[21] Florence of Worcester, *sub ann.* 1104; *Select Charters*, 113. See also *Anglo-Saxon Chronicle, sub ann.* 1104, 1105, 1110, 1118, 1124.

[22] Stubbs, *Constitutional History*, i, 266–267. *Cf.* Adams, *Political History of England*, ed. Hunt and Poole, p. 148. On the problem of Church and State in the Anglo-Saxon period, in Normandy, and in England after the Conquest, see M. D. Knowles, *The Monastic Order in England*, and Z. N. Brooke, *The English Church and the Papacy*.

[23] *Select Charters*, 142.

[24] This Council met first at London at Easter and was adjourned to Oxford, where it met in April. Round, *Geoffrey de Mandeville*, pp. 21–22.

the death of the Conqueror, or which the liberality of the faithful had since then conferred. But if it should demand anything which it held or possessed prior to the death of the Conqueror, but had since lost, the king reserved to his indulgence and dispensation either to refuse or restore it. He renounced all claim to the property of deceased clergymen, whether dying testate or intestate; and ordered that every vacant see with its possessions should be committed to the custody of the clergy, or other upright men of the see, until a pastor be appointed. (2) To the *people* generally Stephen promised to maintain peace and justice in all things. All exactions and extortions, wickedly introduced by sheriffs or any other persons, he totally abolished; and promised to observe and cause to be observed good laws and the ancient and just customs in cases of *murdrum* and other pleas and suits.

He reserved to himself the *forests* made and held by William his grandfather and William his uncle; but those added by King Henry he restored to the church and realm. All these things the king granted and confirmed, " saving his royal and just dignity "—a somewhat vague and elastic reservation.[25]

The anarchy. During the tumult and anarchy of what can scarcely be termed the " reign " of Stephen, in which all central authority collapsed, the provisions of these charters fell into abeyance, together with the whole legal and administrative machinery. But they are important as forming another link in the chain by which the ancient liberties of the nation, symbolised in the popular mind by the laws of Edward the Confessor, were handed down in unbroken series to the framers of the Great Charter.

Brave, energetic, and personally popular, Stephen lacked administrative ability and the art of governing men. The barons, taking advantage of his weakness, fortified their castles, and, under colour of supporting either the king or the Empress Matilda, made themselves practically independent of both. They claimed and exercised all the most obnoxious privileges of continental feudalism. " Quot domini castellorum," says the chronicler, " tot reges vel potius tyranni." [26] The king endeavoured to strengthen his position by creating new earldoms, supported by extravagant grants from the crown-lands and the exchequer. The only result was to impoverish himself and arouse the jealousy of the old nobility. His justifiable but impolitic violence towards the three bishops, Roger of Salisbury and his nephews, Nigel of Ely and Alexander of Lincoln, secured, indeed, the surrender of their castles, but alienated the entire body of the clergy, who had been the king's chief supporters, and threw into confusion the whole administration of the government, over which

[25] *Select Charters*, 143–144.
[26] William of Newburgh, *Historia Anglica*, i, 22: *ibid.*, 139.

Bishop Roger, as justiciar, had hitherto continued to preside.[27] Even the king's brother, Henry of Winchester, went over to the side of the empress. During the long period of civil war the condition of the people was most lamentable. Both sides employed mercenary troops, principally from Flanders, who behaved with the greatest insolence and barbarity. " In this king's time," says the Anglo-Saxon chronicler, " was all dissension and evil and rapine . . . . Never yet was there more wretchedness in the land." [28]

Treaty of Winchester. At length, in 1153, after the death of Stephen's eldest son Eustace, a pacification was brought about at Winchester, through the mediation of the bishops.[29] It was agreed between the king and young Henry, Matilda's son, now in his twenty-first year, and ratified by the assent and homage of the bishops and barons on both sides, that Henry should give up his claim to the present possession of the throne, and should be acknowledged as the rightful successor on the death of Stephen, that war should cease, the mercenaries be dismissed, and the " adulterine " castles be demolished.[30]

In less than a year from the date of the treaty, the death of Stephen, on October 25, 1154, handed over the imperfectly accomplished work of restoring order and good government to Henry of Anjou.

HENRY II

Henry II succeeded to the throne, pursuant to the treaty of Winchester, without the faintest appearance of opposition. The regularity of his succession was doubtless facilitated by the great strength which his extensive continental possessions gave him.[31] To the English people, moreover, he was welcome as a descendant of their ancient royal house; and throughout his reign they faithfully supported him in every emergency. But though claiming, through his mother, to be at once Norman and

---

[27] " The arrest of Bishop Roger was perhaps the most important constitutional event that had taken place since the Conquest; the whole administration of the country ceased to work, and the whole power of the clergy was arrayed in opposition to the king. It was also the signal for the civil war, which lasted, with more or less activity, for fourteen years."—Stubbs, *Constitutional History*, i, 352 *et seq.*

[28] *Anglo-Saxon Chronicle* (ed. Ingram), pp. 364, 367.

[29] The terms arranged at Winchester were ratified at Westminster, *Select Charters*, 141.

[30] Later chronicles allege that a comprehensive scheme of reform was drawn up, to be carried out by both Stephen and Henry, for the restoration of good government and national prosperity. It included the resumption by the king of the royal rights which had been usurped by the barons; the restoration to the lawful owners of the estates of which they had been deprived by intruders; the restoration of agriculture by means of a system of state subventions to the impoverished farmers; the maintenance of the rights of the clergy; the revival of the sheriffs' jurisdiction, and the appointment of impartial men to that office; the strict administration of justice; the encouragement of commerce; and a reform of the coinage. *Cf.* Stubbs, *Constitutional History*, i, 360.

[31] From his father Henry had inherited Anjou and Touraine; in right of his mother he possessed Normandy and Maine, and with his wife Eleanor, who had been divorced from Louis VII of France, he had received the seven provinces of Poitou, Saintonge, Auvergne, Périgord, Limousin, Angoumois, and Guienne. *Cf.* also Stubbs, preface to Benedict of Peterborough [Rolls Series], vol. ii.

English, Henry was by birth and character neither Norman nor English.[32]
He introduced a new and foreign dynasty, the Angevin, or Plantagenet,
as it was subsequently called,[33] which was destined to rule over England
for a period of more than three centuries (*viz.*, 1154–1485). Henry himself
endeavoured to rule England as an English king, and he was far too able
and energetic ever to succumb to a favourite, foreign or native. But under
his sons Richard and John, and his grandson Henry III the evils of a
foreign dynasty made themselves felt, and the descendants of both English
and Norman alike experienced the bitterness of being governed by a set
of foreign favourites, supported by the swords of foreign mercenaries.

Coronation charter. Henry II had the advantage of coming to the
throne after a long civil war, during which the nation had become
thoroughly weary of anarchy. At his coronation, or shortly afterwards, he
issued a charter, briefly and in general terms granting and confirming to
the church, and all earls and barons, and all his men, all the liberties and
free customs granted by the charter of his grandfather, King Henry, and
abolishing and remitting all the evil exactions which that king had abolished
and remitted.[34] Without any delay the young king set himself energetically
to the task, which he persistently worked at throughout his reign, of
establishing law and order upon a permanent basis. Taking as his
immediate model the government of his grandfather, Henry I, he reconstructed the disorganised administrative and judicial machinery of the
kingdom, but with developments and innovations which were the outcome
of his own individual policy.[35]

Inquest of Sheriffs, 1170. His determination to prevent peculation
and other abuses in the administration of the royal officials is shown by
his remarkable action in 1170, when in a Great Council at London he
dismissed nearly all the sheriffs of the kingdom, with their bailiffs, for
alleged misconduct in their office. The dismissed functionaries were
compelled to give pledges to answer, and make compensation for, all
wrongful exactions proved against them, and a special commission was
issued by the king with instructions to make in every county an exhaustive

---

[32] See Freeman, *Growth of the English Constitution*, 72. " The peculiar position of Henry II
was something like that of the Emperor Charles V—that of a prince ruling over a great
number of distinct states without being nationally identified with any of them. Henry
ruled over England, Normandy, and Aquitaine, but he was neither English, Norman,
nor Gascon."—*Ibid.*, 177.

[33] "The Angevin family are commonly known as the Plantagenets; but the name was never
used as a surname till the fifteenth century."—*Ibid.*, 176.

[34] *Statutes of the Realm*—Charter of Liberties, p. 4; *Select Charters*, 158.

[35] " Henry II is the first of the three great kings who have left on the constitution indelible
marks of their own individuality. What he reorganised Edward I defined and completed.
The Tudor policy, which is impersonated in Henry VIII, tested to the utmost the soundness
of the fabric. . . . Each of the three sovereigns had a strong idiosyncrasy, and in each
case the state of things on which he acted was such as to make the impression of personal
character distinct and permanent."—Stubbs, *Constitutional History*, i, 483. See further,
Pollock and Maitland, *History of English Law*, i, 136 *et seq.*; and for a retrospect of the
legal activity of this reign, Maitland, *Constitutional History*, pp. 10–14.

inquisition by the oaths of all the barons, knights, freeholders, and even the villeins of the county, into the receipts of the sheriff and of all persons in any way accountable to the exchequer.[36]

The aim of his policy through life appears to have been the consolidation and centralisation of the kingly power in his own hands, and the rounding off, as it were, of his great empire, extending from the Cheviots to the Pyrénées. He attempted, though with only partial success, to reduce the Welsh to obedience; Ireland, unfortunately for herself only imperfectly conquered, was annexed to the English crown; and Scotland acknowledged his superiority.

The two great constitutional results of Henry's reign were: (1) the reorganisation and full development of the kingship as a monarchy at once feudal and national; and (2) the maintenance of the legal supremacy of the state over the national church. In working out his policy, the king had to contend with two powerful opponents—(1) the feudal baronage, whose power and privileges it was necessary largely to curtail, and (2) the clergy, who, under the system of separate spiritual and temporal jurisdictions initiated by the Conqueror, had succeeded in obtaining a mischievous and even dangerous immunity from all the ordinary processes of law.

Administrative reforms. Over the barons Henry was completely successful. The programme of administrative reform, which had been included in the terms of the pacification of Winchester, was strictly carried out. The " adulterine " castles were destroyed; the alienated demesnes of the crown resumed; the foreign mercenaries banished; the coinage reformed,[37] and returns exacted from tenants-in-chief declaring the number and names of their knightly sub-tenants, so that the king could impose heavier services upon them.[38] With the aid of counsellors whose ability he had the discernment to detect,[39] he reorganised and extended

[36] Benedict Abbas, i, 5. The comprehensive instructions to the Commissioners comprised in fifteen articles, are given in *Select Charters*, 175, from Bodleian MS., Rawlinson, C. 641. For some textual additions and a facsimile from this manuscript, see *Pleas before the King* (Selden Society, ed. Lady Stenton), i, 151–154. " The sheriffs removed on this occasion from their offices were most of them local magnates, whose chances of oppression and whose inclination towards a feudal administration of justice were too great. In their place Henry instituted officers of the Exchequer, less closely connected with the counties by property, and more amenable to royal influence as well as more skilled administrators " —*ibid.*

[37] William of Newburgh, ii, c. 1; *Select Charters*, 151; Robert de Monte, *s. a.* 1155, ed. Howlett, *Chronicles of the reigns of Stephen, Henry II and Richard I* (Rolls Series), iv, 183. For the new coinage, *cf.* Benedict Abbas, i, 263, *s. a.* 1180. But Henry did not, as often stated, extinguish the earldoms created by Stephen; see Round, *Geoffrey de Mandeville*, 274 *et seq.*

[38] These are the *cartae baronum* of 1166 discussed by J. H. Round, *Feudal England*, 236 *et seq.* and F. M. Stenton, *First Century of English Feudalism*, 136 *et seq.*

[39] Henry's first ministers were " Archbishop Theobald, who had been firmly attached to the interests of the empress throughout the later years of the struggle, Bishop Henry [of Blois] of Winchester, and Nigel of Ely, who represented the family, and the official training of Roger of Salisbury, the justiciar of Henry I; the Earl of Leicester, Robert de Beaumont, and Richard de Lucy, who had charge of the castle of Windsor and the Tower of London, at the peace, who had possibly acted as justiciar during the last year of Stephen, and who filled the office for the first twenty-five years of Henry's reign. In a subordinate capacity was Thomas Becket of London, the pupil of Theobald and future

the judicial and financial administration of the Curia Regis and exchequer. He renewed the provincial visitations of itinerant justices, increased their number and assigned them regular circuits. Another legal improvement in this reign was the institution of the Grand Assize and several " petty " assizes, whereby litigants could have questions decided by the recognition of a jury, instead of the old method of trial by battle. The principle of recognition by a jury was extended to all descriptions of business, fiscal and legal. In conjunction with the visits of the itinerant justices, it exercised a very important influence in training the people for self-government.[40]

By means of Henry's administrative reforms, not only did the mass of the people obtain the enjoyment of an orderly and legal security, but the feudal baronage, a source of danger to crown and people alike, were kept in strict subordination, and the executive power taken out of their hands. After the inquest of 1170, instead of bestowing the office of sheriff on the great barons, who had evinced a tendency to make it hereditary in their families, Henry gave it to men trained in the Exchequer. For the office of chief justiciar he selected the ablest laymen instead of ecclesiastics, thus curbing the power of both bishops and barons. The power of the latter was still further, and permanently, diminished by the development, on the occasion of the Toulouse war, of a commutation of military service for the money payment termed scutage.[41] The money thus raised was employed for hiring mercenaries who proved more reliable than the feudal levies. Henry also rendered himself more independent of the feudatories by reviving in the Assize of Arms (an ordinance issued in 1181) the ancient *fyrd*, or national militia.[42]

The effect of Henry's policy was greatly to augment the power of the crown. But while maintaining a strong central government he never aimed at despotic power. He appears to have been imbued with a sincere regard for constitutional government of the feudal type. He was continually calling his Great Council together. No public matter of importance was transacted, no law issued, without their consent and advice.

archbishop and martyr."—Stubbs, *Constitutional History*, i, 486. De Lucy was succeeded as justiciar in 1180 by Ranulf de Glanvill in whose time was written the famous (but anonymous) treatise.

[40] For a more detailed consideration of Henry's legal and administrative reforms, see *infra*, Chap. 5.

[41] Robert de Monte, *s. a.* 1159; Gervase of Canterbury, i, 167; *Select Charters*, 152. Scutage was not an innovation of Henry II; the payment of a sum of money in lieu of military service was permitted in certain cases at least as early as the reign of Henry I. Henry II required personal service from lay tenants-in-chief, but churches and mesne tenants were allowed to commute their service at the rate of two marks on the knight's fee. See Pollock and Maitland, *History of English Law*, vol. i, pp. 266 *et seq.*, and Round, *Feudal England*, pp. 262 *et seq.*; J. F. Baldwin, *The Scutage and Knight-Service in England* [Chicago, 1897]. " The king's power was now re-established over the feudal world and the way was clear for the development of scutage into the constitutional imposition which bore that name in the thirteenth century."—Stenton, *English Feudalism*, 185.

[42] Benedict Abbas, i, 278; Hoveden, ii, 261; *Select Charters*, 183–184.

Henry II and Becket

In his contest with Becket and the clergy, Henry was only partially successful, for he was obliged to surrender two important claims of the church—the right of appeals to Rome and the jurisdiction over criminous clerks (1164).

The celebrated **Constitutions of Clarendon** (1164), sixteen in number, are in form a record and acknowledgment by the archbishops and bishops, in presence of the earls, barons, and other *proceres* of the kingdom, clerical and lay, of the customs ascertained by recognition to have regulated the relations of church and state in the time of Henry I.[43] The record is expressed as being made on account of the dissensions and discord which had arisen between the clergy and the king's justices and barons concerning the nature of these customs, and contains the distinct promise of the archbishops and bishops faithfully to observe them as therein defined.

The most important articles may be conveniently arranged in five groups.[44]

(1) All clerks accused of any crime were to be summoned in the first instance before the king's justices, who should determine whether the cause ought to be tried in the secular or spiritual court. In the event of the cause being remitted to the spiritual court, a royal officer should be sent by the king's justices to watch the proceedings; and the accused, if found guilty, should not be protected thereafter by the church (cap. iii). All matters pertaining to the king's court should be terminated there; but causes which appeared to fall within the jurisdiction of the ecclesiastical courts should be sent thither to be dealt with (cap. vii). The distinction between the civil and ecclesiastical jurisdictions introduced by William the Conqueror was thus maintained. But the king's court was first to decide the fact whether or not the accused was entitled to be tried in the spiritual court; the latter court then decided the fact of the guilt or innocence of such accused persons as were remitted to it; and the king's court sentenced and punished the guilty.

All disputes concerning advowsons and presentations to livings, whether between laymen or clerks, or laymen and clerks, were to be dealt with and terminated in the king's court (cap. i).[45]

The king's court should have jurisdiction over all pleas of debt,

---

[43] "They are no mere engine of tyranny, or secular spite against a churchman; they are really a part of a great scheme of administrative reform, by which the debatable ground between the spiritual and temporal powers can be brought within the reach of common justice, and the lawlessness arising from professional jealousies abolished."—Stubbs, *Constitutional History*, i, 503.

[44] For the text of the Constitutions see Stubbs, *Select Charters*, 163–167. For discussions see Pollock and Maitland, i, 447 *et seq.*; Maitland, " Henry II and the Criminous Clerks " *English Historical Review*, vii, 224 *et seq.*, reprinted in *Canon Law in the Church of England*, 132 *et seq.*; Z. N. Brooke, *The English Church and the Papacy*, chap. xiii; A. L. Poole, " Outlawry as a punishment of criminous clerks " (*Essays in honour of James Tait*, 239); C. R. Cheney, " Punishment of Felonious Clerks," *English Historical Review*, li. 215.

[45] This completes the process by which the patronage of churches was assimilated to real property; *cf.* H. Böhmer, " Eigenkirchentum in England " (*Festgabe für Liebermann*), and M. D. Knowles, *Monastic Order in England*, c. xxxiv.

whether accompanied by a pledge of faith (of which the church claimed exclusive cognisance) or not (cap. xv).

In disputes between laymen and clerks as to land which the clerk asserts to be held in frankalmoign, the chief justice should decide, by the recognition of twelve lawful men, whether it was held by lay or by eleemosynary tenure (frankalmoign), and should refer the suit accordingly to the lay or ecclesiastical tribunal (cap. ix).

Laymen should be tried in the bishop's court only if accused by lawful and specific accusers and witnesses. If no one should be willing, or dare, to appear as accuser against a powerful delinquent, the sheriff, at the request of the bishop, should empanel and swear twelve lawful men of the vicinage to tell the truth (cap. vi).

(2) No tenant-in-chief of the king or officer of his household should be excommunicated, nor his lands put under interdict, without the previous consent of the king, or, in his absence from the kingdom, of his justiciar (cap. vii).

On the same principle, tenants of any of the king's cities, castles, boroughs, or demesne manors, refusing to appear when cited by the archdeacon or bishop to answer for any wrong falling within his lawful jurisdiction, might be placed under interdict, but not excommunicated until application had first been made for the intervention of the king's chief local officer (cap. x).

(3) The custody of vacant archbishoprics, bishoprics, abbeys, and priories of the royal demesne should be in the king's hand, and their revenues paid to him.[46]

Election of a new incumbent should take place, in obedience to the king's writ, by the chief clergy of the church, assembled in the king's chapel, with the assent of the king, and with the advice of such persons of the kingdom as the king might summon for the purpose.

Before consecration, the incumbent elect should do homage and fealty to the king as his liege lord, of life, limb, and earthly honour, saving the rights of his order (cap. xii).

Archbishops, bishops, and all the beneficed clergy of the kingdom, holding of the king *in capite*, should answer for their baronies to the king's justices and officers, and follow and observe all royal rights and customs; and, like the rest of the barons, ought to take part in the judgments of the king's court, except in cases involving loss of life or limb (cap. xi).

No archbishop, bishop, or beneficed clergyman should quit the realm without licence from the king. Those who were permitted to leave should give pledge, if required, not to contrive any hurt to the king or kingdom during their absence (cap. iv).

(4) Appeals ought to proceed from the archdeacon to the bishop, and from the bishop to the archbishop. If the archbishop failed to do justice, resort should be had, in the last instance, to the king, so that by his order

---

[46] On the rise and abuse of this right, see M. D. Knowles, *The Monastic Order*, 612.

the controversy might be terminated in the archbishop's court and not proceed farther (*i.e.*, to the pope), without the king's assent (cap. viii).

(5) Lastly, the sons of villeins (*rusticorum*) were not to be admitted to orders without the assent of the lord on whose land they were born (cap. xvi).

The intention of the king and barons, in this article of the Constitutions of Clarendon, probably went no farther than to protect the legal property which every feudal lord had in the service of his villeins. But its practical effect was undoubtedly still further to depress the lowest class of the population. The prohibition is extended in the Assize of Clarendon, issued by Henry in 1166, to entry into monasteries; and more than two hundred years afterwards, in 1391, we find the Commons' House of Parliament petitioning that villeins might not be allowed to put their children to school in order to advance them by the church, " and this for the honour of the freemen of the kingdom."[47] Under Richard II it is not so much the feudal and proprietary as the anti-democratic and caste feeling which is manifested.

RICHARD I

The reign of Richard I belongs not so much to the history of England as to the history of Christendom. He was the " creation and impersonation of his own age,"[48] and occupied a central place in the history of his times.

With the exception of about four months immediately following his coronation, and the two months which he spent in England in 1194 after his release from captivity, Richard was absent from his kingdom during the whole ten years of his reign.[49] By birth, education, and sympathies essentially a foreigner, he seems to have regarded England merely as an appanage to his continental possessions, and a profitable source of revenue. It was the strong administrative system, established under his father, by which the power of the crown was so largely augmented, that rendered it possible for Richard thus to govern as an absentee king.

Taxation. To support his expedition to Palestine, to pay his ransom from captivity, and to carry on his wars in France, every known source of taxation was exhausted. Public offices and dignities were openly sold to the highest bidder; the demesne lands of the crown were first sold, and then, after a time, forcibly resumed; all the feudal dues were rigorously exacted; the old danegeld, under the thin disguise of a " carucage," was revived in a more stringent form; not only land, but personal property,

---

[47] *Rotuli Parliamentorum*, iii, 294 (the royal assent was refused); Hallam, *Middle Ages*, iii, 181.

[48] Stubbs, *Itinerarium Ricardi Primi* (Rolls Series), xi.

[49] Gneist, *Constitutional History*, i, 294, says: " The absence of this knight-errant from English soil, which was, with the exception of a few months, continuous, proved extremely beneficial, in so far as it rendered the continuance of an organised internal government possible."

which had already been subjected to taxation in the Saladin tithe granted to Henry II in 1188,[50] was laid under a heavy impost; the gold and silver of the churches were seized; and the Cistercian monks compelled to compound for all their wool.[51] These systematic and oppressive exactions appear to have been borne by the nation with remarkable patience. The rising of the populace of London, under William with the Beard, " quidam legis peritus," was not so much a resistance to taxation as to its unjust assessment, because the rich citizens " sparing their own purses, willed that the poor should pay the whole." [52] The only real opposition proceeded from the clergy. In 1198 the regular clergy refused to pay the carucage, or tax of five shillings imposed on each carucate (or hundred acres) of land. The king immediately issued a proclamation directing that on the one hand no layman should be liable to make satisfaction for an injury committed against a clerk, and, on the other, that every clerk injuring a layman should be forthwith compelled to give redress.[53] This amounted to virtual outlawry, and the monastic clergy were forced to submit. A more important and successful stand was made in the same year by the bishops Hugh of Lincoln and Herbert of Salisbury. In a council of the barons, summoned at Oxford by the justiciar, Archbishop Hubert Walter, to consider the king's demand for an aid of three hundred knights, each to receive three shillings a day, and to serve with him for a year against Philip of France, the two bishops alone had the courage to refuse; alleging that the lands of their sees were liable for military service within the kingdom only and not abroad.[54] The opposition was successful; the king's demand was withdrawn; and shortly afterwards the justiciar resigned.[55]

Rule by justiciar. During the all but continuous absence of Richard, the administration of the kingdom was carried on by four successive justiciars who acted as viceroys. (1) William Longchamp, Bishop of Ely, a Norman of servile birth, was both a justiciar and chancellor. As a *parvenu* he excited the jealousy of the barons, and by his vigorous assertion

---

[50] The Saladin Tithe (*Select Charters*, 189) was not the first occasion on which moveable property was subjected to taxation. In 1166 every man was required to contribute a penny in the pound on moveable property towards a fund for the relief of the Holy Land. See Davis, *England under the Normans and Angevins*, p. 271.

[51] Benedict Abbas, ii, 90. For the various modes of taxation, see Roger Hoveden, iii, 210, 240, *s. a.* 1193–1194; *Select Charters*, 244–246.

[52] Roger Hoveden, iv, 5, *s. a.* 1196. The tallage was assessed as a poll-tax equally on all the citizens rich and poor. Fitz-Osbert wished it to be assessed in proportion to the property of each citizen.

[53] Roger Hoveden, iv, 66; *Select Charters*, 251.

[54] *Vita Magna St. Hugonis*, p. 248; *Select Charters*, 248.

[55] " This event is a landmark of constitutional history; for the second time a constitutional opposition to a royal demand for money is made, and made successfully. It would perhaps be too great an anticipation of modern usages to suppose that the resignation of the minister was caused by his defeat."—Stubbs, *Constitutional History*, i, 548. The first case of opposition to the king in the matter of taxation to which Stubbs refers (p. 500) was Becket's refusal to accede to Henry II's proposal to appropriate to his revenues the sheriff's aid, *auxilium vicecomitis*. Stubbs mistook this for danegeld. See *Select Charters*, 152, and Round, *Feudal England*, 497–502.

of the royal rights raised up a strong opposition headed by Earl John, who was ever plotting against his brother's government. The struggle ended in 1191 with the deposition of Longchamp from the justiciarship by a great council of the bishops, earls and barons of England, and the citizens of London, assembled at St. Paul's by Earl John, and apparently acting in concert with Walter of Coutances, Archbishop of Rouen, whom the king had sent over from Messina some months previously with a secret appointment to the officer of justiciar, to be produced only if circumstances should require it.[56] This proceeding has been characterised as " the earliest authority for a leading principle of our constitution, the responsibility of ministers to parliament."[57] But this view seems to invest the action of the Council of St. Paul's with too great importance. It can at most be regarded as a rude anticipation, by an irregularly constituted assembly acting as if it represented the nation, of that constitutional control over ministers of the crown which the regular national council was later on to claim and obtain. (2) The assembly which deposed Long-champ recognised the Archbishop of Rouen as his successor. At the close of the year 1193, the Archbishop of Rouen gave place to (3) Hubert Walter, Archbishop of Canterbury, who had been brought up in the household of his celebrated uncle, Ranulf de Glanvill; and on the resignation of Hubert Walter in 1198, (4) Geoffrey FitzPeter, Earl of Essex, the fourth and last of Richard's justiciars, entered into office.

Coroners: administrative developments. Under the rule of each of the justiciars, but more especially of Hubert Walter and his successor, Geoffrey FitzPeter, the administrative system established by Henry II was maintained and considerably developed. By the extensive application of the principle of representation to the assessment of the taxes on both real and personal property, the people were gradually educated for self-government. In the year 1194, the principle of election in the appointment of county officers was introduced. " Keepers of the pleas of the crown," three knights and a clergyman, were ordered to be elected in every county.[58] The advance made by the boroughs towards independence through the charters which, as a means of raising money, were extensively sold to them, is also an important feature of this reign. In some instances the privileges granted were assimilated to those of the citizens of London, which served as a model for the provincial towns, and included the right of electing the town-reeve.[59] On the occasion of Longchamp's deposition, in which, as we have seen, the citizens of London concurred, they secured a formal recognition, by the justiciar and barons, of their existence as a " *communa*,"

---

[56] Benedict Abbas, ii, 213, *s. a.* 1191; *Select Charters*, 245.

[57] Hallam, *Middle Ages*, ii, 325. For a valuable account of this episode embodying the results of modern studies in administrative history, see Jolliffe, *Constitutional History*, 229–235.

[58] *Capitula placitorum Coronae Regis*, cap. 20; *Select Charters*, 254. For the question whether this is the origin of the coroner, or whether that office existed before 1194, see Gross, *Coroners' Rolls* (Selden Society), and I. L. Langbein, " The Jury of Presentment and the Coroner," *Columbia Law Review*, xxxiii, 1329.

[59] *Cf.* Charter of Richard I to Lincoln, 1194, in Rymer, i, 52, and *Select Charters*, 261.

the exact meaning of which is not quite clear, but which was certainly a near approach to what is understood by a " corporation." [60] In connection, doubtless, with this establishment of the *communa*, the mayor now appears for the first time.

On the whole, the reign of Richard, through no merit, however, of his own, was beneficial to the liberties of the people. They became accustomed to the rule of law as opposed to the rule of force. Even the unexampled taxation was levied with the appearance of legal formality. The immense sums raised are a proof that the kingdom had rapidly advanced in wealth during the preceding reign. The baronage, which had been severely repressed under Henry II, became at once more orderly and less inclined than formerly to submit to the caprice of the sovereign, to whose personal interference they had become unaccustomed.[61] The fusion of the two races, nearly accomplished under Henry II, was silently worked out under Richard; and in the following reign we shall find the barons and people claiming for themselves against the crown the common liberties of Englishmen.

---

[60] Benedict Abbas, ii, 214, *s. a.* 1191; *Select Charters*, 245. No boroughs were expressly incorporated as municipal corporations, in the modern sense of the term, till the reign of Henry VI—Merewether and Stephens on *Boroughs*, vol. i, Introd. Round, *Commune of London*, p. 245, has suggested that the constitution of London was modelled upon that of Rouen. But see Miss Bateson, " A London Municipal Collection of the reign of John," in *English Historical Review*, xvii, 480 *et seq.* For a summary of the question, see Petit-Dutaillis, *Studies Supplementary to Stubbs' Constitutional History*, i, 96 *et seq.* The commune, a French institution, has been defined as a *seigneurie collective populaire*; it is compared with English institutions in J. Tait, *Medieval English Borough*, 159 *et seq.*

[61] As a recent writer has expressed it: " The crisis of 1191 marks the entry of the baronage into the political field, not as individual parties to tenurial contracts, but as critics of and participators in government, and is in a sense a prelude to the greater effort of 1215."—Jolliffe, *Constitutional History*, 237.

Chapter 4

MAGNA CARTA

THREE great political documents, traditionally regarded as being in the nature of fundamental compacts between the crown and the nation, stand out as prominent landmarks in English constitutional history. Magna Carta, the Petition of Right, and the Bill of Rights constitute, in the words of Lord Chatham, " the Bible of the English Constitution." In each of these documents, whether it be of the thirteenth or of the seventeenth century, is observable the common characteristic of professing to introduce nothing new. Each professed to assert rights and liberties which were already old, and sought to redress grievances which were for the most part themselves innovations upon the ancient liberties of the people.[1] In the practical combination of conservative instincts with liberal aspirations, in the power of progressive development and adaptation to the changing political and social wants of each successive generation, have always lain the peculiar excellence, and at the same time the surest safeguard, of our constitution.[2]

The eminently moderate, practical, and conservative character of the barons' demands is especially noticeable. Magna Carta was in fact a treaty of peace between the king and his people in arms; yet their ancient rights and liberties, the acknowledgment of which had been extorted from the king, were expressed to flow from his charter, which was not only a " grant," but also a " confirmation "—which were becoming words of power in the nascent science of conveyancing. " On the whole, the charter contains little that is absolutely new. It is restorative. John in these last years has been breaking the law, therefore the law must be defined and set in writing." [3]

Its political ideas. We shall come nearest to the contemporary view of this momentous document if we regard it as a solemn statement of sound policy which commended itself to the most influential men of the day, and as an attempt to reduce to writing the principles which in their view should govern the relationship of king and people. From the days of antiquity onwards there have been numerous examples of such an endeavour to take stock of public affairs. Some of them were philosophical,

---

[1] *Cf.* the paper by C. H. McIlwain, " Magna Carta and Common Law," in *Magna Carta Commemoration Essays* (1917), pp. 122–179.
[2] *Cf.* Palgrave, *English Commonwealth*, i, 6.
[3] Pollock and Maitland, i, 172.

abstract and *doctrinaire*—and they laid the foundations of modern political science. Others took little heed of theory, and confined themselves to examining practical difficulties in the art of government, and finding practical solutions for them. It is in this latter class that we must place the Charter. In it there is nothing theoretical or revolutionary, no declaration of abstract principles of government; but merely a practical assertion of rights as between the crown and the subject, and, as a natural corollary under a system of feudal tenures, between mesne lords and their sub-vassals.

The coronation oath. Taken in this sense, the Charter is the product of a long line of earlier precedents. The earliest attempts to define the position of the monarch took the form of a solemn oath tendered to the new king upon his coronation. The continuous history of the coronation rite[4] dates from the days of St. Dunstan, Archbishop of Canterbury, and about the year 960 the king was already expected to make three "precepts" of government[5]; in 973 these precepts become "promises" made prior to the unction and crowning. In the following century the oath was sometimes enlarged to cover the special circumstances of each accession, and the Conqueror himself took a number of oaths as well as the traditional simple coronation oath.

Earlier charters. The high importance attached to such undertakings can be seen in the fact that they came to be supplemented by fuller engagements entered into by some kings on the occasion of their corona-tions (although not as part of the ceremony), or even independently of a coronation. Thus Canute's charter[6] covers much the same ground (although merely a letter in form) as the traditional oath.

William the Conqueror soon after his accession issued his famous charter to London,[7] and although Rufus issued no charter his successor, Henry I, renewed his father's example and issued the first strictly corona-tion charter in the year 1100.[8] This is a document of high importance, for it was the immediate and direct model for the Great Charter. Stephen issued two coronation charters and Henry II one; Richard I and John, none at all.

EVENTS LEADING TO THE CHARTER

Several causes worked together to bring about the state of affairs which compelled John to grant the Great Charter. Foremost among these

---

[4] On all this, see P. E. Schramm, *History of the English Coronation* (Oxford, 1937) which throws valuable light upon the medieval conception of monarchy. *Infra*, p. 532.

[5] They were: " that God's church and all Christian people keep a true peace for ever; that he forbid all rapine and iniquity to all ranks; that he enjoin equity and mercy in all judgements . . ."—Stubbs, *Select Charters*, 69 (but for the date see Schramm, 19).

[6] Text in A. J. Robertson, *Laws of the Kings of England*, 141, and Stubbs, *Select Charters*, 90. The date is 1020.

[7] Stubbs, *Select Charters*, 97; Robertson, *Laws*, 231.

[8] Stubbs, *Select Charters*, 117–119; Robertson, *Laws*, 277.

was the fortunate loss of Normandy. The barons, confined within the limits of England, concentrated their attention upon its affairs. They became thoroughly English in interests and sympathies, and united with the people against the tyranny of the king.[9] Moreover, a great part of the baronage now consisted of the new ministerial families raised up by the policy of Henry I and Henry II. These were far less closely connected with Normandy than the baronage of the conquest, and their sympathies were national rather than feudal.

The loss of Normandy[10] was itself in a great measure due to the decay of feudalism, the result of Henry II's policy. John, who was not altogether destitute of energy and courage, made some efforts to recover Normandy, but the barons, especially in the north of England, where the possessions of the new families chiefly lay, refused to follow the king, alleging that they were not bound to military service abroad.

The king. Intimately connected with this refusal, and with the exaction of the Charter, was the personal character of the king, which inspired utter distrust and aversion in all classes of his subjects. In disposition and character John was an oriental despot, a tyrant of the worst sort. Under Henry II and the ministers of Richard I, the nation had become accustomed to the rule of law; John set at defiance all laws, human and divine.[11] Supported in his tyranny by bands of foreign mercenaries, he not only taxed and fined his subjects of every degree, with an open disregard of all legal restraints, but was guilty of acts of cruelty rivalling those of Nero.[12] The church, the baronage and the people, united by common

---

[9] " The talents and even the virtues of England's first six French kings were a curse to her. The follies and vices of the seventh were her salvation. . . . John was driven from Normandy. The Norman nobles were compelled to make their election between the island and the continent. Shut up by the sea with the people whom they had hitherto oppressed and despised, they gradually came to regard England as their country, and the English as their countrymen. The two races, so long hostile, soon found that they had common interests and common enemies. Both were alike aggrieved by the tyranny of a bad king. Both were alike indignant at the favour shown by the court to the natives of Poitou and Aquitaine. The great-grandsons of those who had fought under William and the great-grandsons of those who had fought under Harold began to draw near to each other in friendship; and the first pledge of reconciliation was the Great Charter, won by their united exertions and framed for their common benefit."—Macaulay, *History of England*, i, 12.

[10] The Channel Islands—the only Norman territory not lost—still continue attached, as a separate dependency, to the English Crown. " The Isle of Man and the Channel Islands are not parts of the United Kingdom, though king and Parliament can make laws for them. The statutes made by Parliament do not affect them, unless they are specially mentioned, or it is evident from the context that they were within the purview of the legislature. The appeal from their courts is not to the House of Lords, but to the king in council. The interest of these small dependencies lies in this, that the relation between them and England formed a precedent for the treatment of the vaster dependencies which have gradually collected round the United Kingdom."—Maitland, *Constitutional History*, p. 337. J. H. Le Patourel, *The Medieval Administration of the Channel Islands* (Oxford, 1937) is a valuable study of this very interesting jurisdiction. See also Anson, *Law and Custom of the Constitution*, (1935), ii, pt. 2, 54–61.

[11] *Annals of Waverley* (ed. Luard), p. 282.

[12] *Annals of Waverley*, pp. 264–265; Roger of Wendover, *Flores*, ii, 77. For valuable recent estimates of John's tyranny, see Jolliffe, *Constitutional History*, 247 *et seq.* For the interplay of papal and baronial politics, see F. M. Powicke in *Cambridge Medieval History*, vi, 232 *et seq.* Still more recently it has been suggested that John was deeply interested in

oppression in a common hatred of the tyrant, were compelled to make a stand not so much for constitutional government as for personal liberty.

The pope. In his struggle with Pope Innocent III, arising out of the disputed election of a successor to Hubert Walter in the archiepiscopal see of Canterbury, John had to deal with a man of consummate ability, who had carried to the highest point, both in theory and practice, the doctrine of the paramount suzerainty of the pope. As a matter of fact, freedom of election to the higher ecclesiastical benefices, however it might accord with canonical requirements, had never been practically recognised by the English kings. Prior to the Norman conquest, the appointments had been made in the Witenagemot, and afterwards by the king in the *Curia Regis,* or great council of the realm. The political power of the bishops, of the Archbishops of Canterbury especially, was so great in medieval times that it would seem to have been a state necessity that their nomination should rest with the supreme civil authority. Although the form of election was conceded by Henry I the process, which subsequently became a *congé d'élire,* was free only in name. At this time the monastic chapter of Christ Church, Canterbury, attempted to assert their right of election without consulting the bishops of the province, and hastily chose their sub-prior. In the meantime the king directed the suffragan bishops to elect John de Grey, Bishop of Norwich. The case was carried before Innocent, who set both elections aside (the one as clandestine, the other as *ultra vires*), and procured the election in his own presence of Stephen Langton, an Englishman of the highest character and great reputation for learning.[13]

John determined not to submit, and refused to receive Langton as archbishop. The pope then (1208) placed the kingdom under interdict (which suspended the whole religious life of the nation). The people were made to suffer in order that pressure might be put on the king. John's reply was the wholesale confiscation of ecclesiastical property; that was followed by his excommunication (1209) and the declaration (1212) that his kingdom was forfeit.

Threatened by Philip Augustus, king of France, whom the pope had encouraged to take possession of the forfeited kingdom of England, and placing no reliance on the support of his alienated people, John at length gave in. From the extreme of arrogance and violence he now passed to the extreme of abject submission. He not only accepted Langton as archbishop, and promised restitution of the money extorted from the church, but surrendered his kingdom to Pandulf, the pope's envoy,

law reform, as well as passably pious: Lady Stenton, introduction to *Pipe Roll*, 6 *John* (1940) xxxiii. King John was much maligned by the chroniclers Roger of Wendover and Matthew Paris; for a more favourable view of his character see A. L. Poole, *Domesday Book to Magna Carta,* 425.

[13] The claim of the bishops to take part in the election of the archbishop, which was occasionally advanced during the twelfth century, was rejected by Innocent III and was never raised afterwards—Stubbs, *Constitutional History,* iii, 313. No such claim was made in the province of York.

receiving it back as a fief of the Holy See, subject to the annual tribute of one thousand marks.[14] A few months afterwards, the act of submission was renewed to Nicholas, Bishop of Tusculum, with the actual performance of liege homage on the part of the king.[15] This submission was undoubtedly a disgrace, although not quite to the same extent as it would be now. It was, however, a startling falling off from the position which Henry II had occupied, that one of his sons should do homage to the emperor and another to the pope.

The barons. The surrender of the temporal and spiritual independence of the kingdom completed the alienation of the people from the king, whose misgovernment had brought on this national humiliation. On the other hand, the pope now, having secured submission, changed his tactics, and supported the tyranny of his vassal. The barons determined upon resistance, and the national church,[16] headed by Archbishop Langton, gave the weight of its influence to the patriotic side.

It may be convenient briefly to notice the most important events which immediately led up to the grant of the Charter.[17] The open quarrel with the barons began in July 1213, with the refusal of the northern nobility to follow John to France. While the king was vowing vengeance against his recalcitrant vassals, two important councils of the bishops and barons were held, the first at St. Albans, on August 4,[18] the second at St. Paul's, London, on August 25. They were summoned ostensibly for the purpose of assessing the compensation promised to the church; but the justiciar, Geoffrey FitzPeter, and Archbishop Langton seized the opportunity of introducing a discussion on the king's general misgovernment. The half-forgotten charter of Henry I, having been referred to generally at St. Albans as the standard of the people's liberties, was at St. Paul's produced by the archbishop, and adopted as the basis of the barons' demands.

During the greater part of the year 1214, John was absent on the Continent, whence he returned in October. In the meantime, the barons met at Bury St. Edmunds, and entered into a confederacy binding them, if the king would not acknowledge the rights which they claimed, to withdraw their fealty and make war upon him until by a sealed charter he should confirm the laws and liberties of the people.[19]

---

[14] See the concession of the kingdom to the pope and the form of oath of fealty in Rymer, i, 111, and *Select Charters*, 279. The 1,000 marks were apportioned 700 for England and 300 for Ireland. It will be remembered that Richard I had already surrendered England as a fief to be held of the Emperor; Pope Innocent III and the Emperor Henry VI were competing for universal sovereignty. *Cf.* A. L. Poole, *op. cit.*, 366.

[15] *Annals of Waverley*, 277, 278; *Select Charters*, 272.

[16] On the danger of using this and like expressions with modern implications, see Z. N. Brooke, *English Church and the Papacy* (Cambridge, 1931), Chap. 1.

[17] For a more detailed statement, see Stubbs, *Constitutional History*, i, 565–571; J. H. Ramsay, *Angevin Empire*, 466 *et seq.*; McKechnie, *Magna Carta* (2nd ed., 1914), 27–36; A. L. Poole, *Domesday Book to Magna Carta*, 459 *et seq.*

[18] For the Council at St. Albans, see *infra*, p. 129.

[19] Matthew Paris, *Chronica Majora*, ed. Luard, ii, 583. *Select Charters*, 273.

On January 6, 1215, the barons in arms presented their demands to the king at the Temple, and, at his urgent request, conceded a respite until after Easter, in order that he might have time for consideration.[20]

In this interval John did all he could to break up the combination against him. He granted a separate charter to the church, giving freedom of election of bishops and abbots[21]; he ordered the sheriffs to administer the oath of allegiance and fealty to the freemen of every shire; he assumed the cross, in order to gain the special protection of the church as a crusader; and he attempted to detach the barons by offering them special terms. But the national party continued firm and united. The barons, strengthened by numerous adhesions since the Councils of St. Albans and St. Paul's, assembled in arms at Stamford; and when the stipulated time had expired without an answer from the king, marched to Brackley, in Northamptonshire, where they appointed Robert Fitzwalter " Marshal of the army of God and of the Holy Church," having formally " defied " the king by denouncing the homage they had done—a necessary preliminary to a feudal rising. Here the king sent to ask their demands, but when these were submitted to him, peremptorily refused to grant them.

The Londoners. The barons now continued their march to London, which they entered on May 17, amidst the acclamations of the citizens.[22] The support of the Londoners seems to have decided the contest. The small, but by no means unimportant, section of the baronage, which had hitherto remained faithful to the king, now went over to the confederacy, and with them most of the officials of the *Curia Regis* and Exchequer and even of the king's household.[23]

Deserted by all but a few personal adherents, chiefly of foreign extraction, and utterly incapable of further resistance, John accepted the Articles of the Barons, which were embodied in the Great Charter at Runnymede, on June 15, 1215.[24]

---

[20] *Ibid.*

[21] *Select Charters*, 283. First granted November 21, 1214; re-issued January 15 following.

[22] A few days before, on May 9, John had attempted to win the support of London by the grant of a charter giving " the barons " of the city the right to elect their mayor annually: *Select Charters*, 311. For the attitude of the Londoners, see Matthew Paris: " Favebant enim baronibus divites civitatis, et ideo pauperes obloqui metuebant ": *Select Charters*, 274. The towns and sea ports were in general loyal to the king and the poorer classes in the country at large were either indifferent or mildly favourable: Jolliffe, *Constitutional History*, 248.

[23] Blackstone, *Introduction to the Charters* (1759) reprinted in his *Law Tracts* (1762) and his *Tracts* (1771). The still older views of the Charter will be found in Sir Edw. Coke's *Second Institute* (1642 and later eds.).

[24] The Articles of the Barons and the Great Charter are printed in *Select Charters*, 285–302, and in McKechnie, where a translation and a commentary on each clause are appended. " The Documents of the Great Charter of 1215," by A. J. Collins, *Proceedings of the British Academy* (1948), 233–279, is an important study. On the whole subject, see W. S. McKechnie, *Magna Carta* (2nd ed., Glasgow, 1914); Holdsworth, *History of English Law*, ii, 207–216; *Magna Carta Commemoration Essays*, ed. H. E. Malden (Royal Historical Society, London, 1917); G. B. Adams, *The Origin of the English Constitution* (Yale University Press, 1920), Chap. vi; Charles Bémont, *Chartes des Libertés Anglaises* (Paris, 1892). " It is dated June 15; but in several writs the king speaks of June 19 as the day on which peace was concluded. Probably the Articles were accepted as the basis of peace on June 15, and the final copy of Magna Carta was only sealed on June 19 ": *Select Charters*, 285.

ANALYSIS AND SUMMARY OF THE CHARTER

Magna Carta contains, in addition to the preamble, sixty-three clauses inserted without much regard to orderly arrangement. Its chief provisions (preceded by the conventional numbering of the chapters or clauses) may be conveniently grouped and summarised as follows, square brackets enclosing the more important of those portions which were omitted or seriously modified in later issues:

1. Commencing with the declaration that the church shall be free with all her rights and liberties inviolate [and expressly confirming the freedom of election which he had already granted by separate charter], John grants to all the freemen of the kingdom[25] the following liberties:

I.—Feudal Obligations

2, 3. (*Reliefs*.) The heir (if of age) shall pay only " the ancient relief "— *viz*., in the case of an earl or baron, £100; of a knight, 100s.; of one holding less than a knight's fee, less in proportion.[26] A minor, who is in ward, shall have his inheritance, on coming of age, without relief or fine.

> By the charter of Henry I, c. 2, reliefs were to be " justa et legitima." The sum is now defined.[27]

4, 5. (*Wardships*.) Guardians shall take only reasonable fruits and profits, without destruction or waste; and shall keep up the estate in proper condition during the wardship.

> By Henry I's charter, c. 4, the widow or next of kin was to be the guardian. The Assize of Northampton (1176), c. 4, directed that the lord of the fee should have the wardship and thus recognised the victory of feudal over family ties. Magna Carta remedies the *abuses* of wardship.[28]

6. (*Marriage*.) Heirs shall be married without disparagement [their near blood relations having notice beforehand].

> Henry I's charter, c. 3, bound the king to consult his baronage as to the marriage of heiresses. In the Articles of the Barons, c. 3, " haeredes " were to be married " *per consilium* propinquorum de consanguinitate sua." In the Charter itself this is softened down to barely giving *notice* to the relations; and even this requirement was omitted in Henry III's re-issues.[29]

---

[25] Coke thought that the term *liber homo* included the villein, but it seems clear that in the charter the phrase is equivalent to freeholder; see McKechnie, 114 *et seq.*; Vinogradoff in *Magna Carta Commemoration Essays*, 80–83; Powicke, *ibid.*, 103–109; Holdsworth, *History of English Law*, ii, 211–212.

[26] On " barons " and " knights " in the Great Charter, see the paper by J. H. Round, in *Magna Carta Commemoration Essays* (1917), pp. 46–77.

[27] *Supra*, pp. 37, 49. The relief of a barony was reduced in the time of Edward I to 100 marks.

[28] *Supra*, pp. 37, 49.

[29] *Supra*, pp. 38, 49. It has been commonly said that by a strained construction the word " haeredes " in this clause was held to include male as well as female heirs. But see Pollock and Maitland, i, 324: " We can trace the sale of the marriages of boys back to a very few years after Glanvill's death."

7, 8. (*Widows.*) A widow shall receive freely, within forty days of her husband's death, her dower and inheritance; and shall have her quarantine (forty days' residence) in the family mansion. She shall not be forced to remarry; but if she wish to do so, must obtain the lord's consent.

> The king and other feudal lords sometimes forced the widows of their tenants to remarry in order to gain the fine payable for consenting to the marriage. This abuse is here forbidden.

15. (*Aids.*) [The king shall not empower mesne lords to exact other than the three ordinary aids—to ransom the lord's person, to knight his eldest son, and once to marry his eldest daughter—and these of reasonable amount.]

16. (*Services.*) No one shall be compelled to render more than the due service for a knight's fee or other free tenement.

29. (*Castle-guard.*) No knight shall be compelled to pay for castle-guard, if he be willing to perform the service in person, or (on reasonable excuse) by a proper deputy; and whilst on service in the army, he shall be free from the duty of castle-guard.

32. (*Lands of felons.*) The king shall not hold the lands of convicted felons except for a year and a day, at the expiration of which time the lands shall be given up to the lords of the fees.

> By the common law, the lands of a person found guilty of treason were forfeited to the crown; but on conviction of petit-treason or felony, they escheated to the immediate lord, subject, however, in this case, to the king's right to hold them for a year and a day.[30] By 54 George 3, c. 145 (1814), the forfeiture was limited (except in the cases of treason, petit-treason, or murder) to the life interest of the offender; but the personal property of all felons continued liable to be forfeited to the crown down to 1870. In former times attainder also worked " corruption of blood," the effect of which was to prevent any inheritance being claimed from or through the attainted person. This harsh law was considerably mitigated by 54 George 3, c. 145, and other statutes, and finally by 33 & 34 Vict. c. 23, passed in 1870, it was enacted that (with the single exception of forfeiture consequent upon outlawry) " no confession, verdict, inquest, conviction, or judgment of or for treason, or felony, or *felo de se*, shall cause any attainder, or corruption of blood, or any forfeiture or escheat." There is much valuable material on the early history of forfeiture, amercement and corruption of blood in Julius Goebel, *Felony and Misdemeanor* (New York, 1937), vol. i.

37. (*Mesne wardships.*) The king shall not have the wardship of land held in chivalry of a mesne lord, by reason of the sub-tenant also holding other land of the king, either in fee-farm, socage, burgage, or petit-serjeanty; nor the wardship of such fee-farm unless it owe military service.[31]

---

[30] Hawkins, *Pleas of the Crown*, ii, c. 49, ss. 1–3. During that interval the crown was entitled to waste the tenement—" year, day and waste " is the usual expression. It is curious that the Charter omits mention of waste.

[31] For an explanation of these feudal tenures, see *supra*, pp. 43 *et seq.*

If the sub-tenant holds a tenement of the .crown by knight service, however, the king's " prerogative wardship " will attach to all his land, of whomsoever held.

43. (*Escheated baronies.*) The tenants of baronies escheated to the crown shall only pay the same relief and perform the same services as if the land were still held of a mesne lord.

It will be observed that forfeiture, or escheat for failure of heirs, continually reduced the number of tenants in chief *ut de corona*, and that the sub-tenants who thereby came to hold of the crown were only tenants in chief *ut de escaeta* and so were not subject to the heavy burdens of their predecessors. The crown's rights are thus continually diminishing.

46. (*Custody of abbeys.*) Barons who have founded abbeys shall have the custody of them when vacant.

The constitutional importance of these remedial provisions, grouped under the above head of " Feudal Obligations," consists in the evidence which they afford of the vexatious and increasingly onerous character of the exactions of the feudal monarchy of the Norman and early Angevin kings.

II.—*Administration of Law and Justice*

17. *Common Pleas* shall not follow the king's court, but be held in some certain place.

The intent of this clause was that suitors might always have a fixed and settled court to resort to, instead of being subjected, as formerly, to the great expense and inconvenience of following the king in his progresses through the kingdom.

18, 19. (*Assizes.*) The recognitions of *novel disseisin, mort d'ancestor,* and *darrein presentment* shall only be held in the county where the lands in question lie. The king; or in his absence the chief justice, shall send two justices into each county [four times] a year, who, with [four] knights [to be chosen by the county court], shall hold such assizes. [If all the matters cannot be determined on the day appointed for each county, a sufficient number of knights and freeholders present at the assizes shall stay to decide them.]

The charters of 1217 and 1225 have " once " instead of " four times " and omit the passages in brackets.

20. (*Amercements.*) A freeman shall only be amerced, for a small offence after the manner of the offence, for a great crime according to the heinousness of it, saving to him his contenement; and, after the same manner, a merchant saving his merchandise, and a villein saving his wainage; the amercements in all cases to be assessed by the oath of honest men of the neighbourhood.

21. Earls and barons shall not be amerced but by their peers, and according to the degree of the offence.

22. No clerk shall ·be amerced for his lay tenement except according to the proportions aforesaid, and not according to the value of his ecclesiastical benefice.

These clauses (20, 21, 22) were primarily intended as a safeguard against the tyrannical extortions, under the name of amercements, with which John had oppressed his people. At the same time they inculcate the general principle that amercements ought to be proportioned to the offence, and that the amount must be fixed not arbitrarily by the king but by a local group of neighbours in the case of the ordinary freeman, the merchant and the villein, and by judgment of peers in the case of earls and barons.[32] The term " amercement " is derived through the old French *amercier*, from the Low Latin *amerciare*, both meaning " to fine," and signified the pecuniary mulct laid upon an individual who had done wrong. It was usually the penalty for procedural or administrative faults, or for petty offences in manorial courts, where certain of the suitors " affeered " (fixed) the sum. Latin plea rolls would say that the party was " in mercy," but properly, the amercement was a moderate fixed payment. On the other hand a court might order serious offenders to " make fine " with the king; that meant making the best bargain they could with the exchequer. Fines fixed by the court or by statute are rare in the Middle Ages. " Contenement " signifies that which is indispensable for a man's support and maintenance, according to his rank or social condition.[33] Thus in Glanvill,[34] the mesne lord is to demand reliefs from his sub-tenants " secundum facultates, ne nimis gravari inde videantur vel suum *contenementum* amittere." " Wainage " was the crops or tillage of the villein or husbandman.[35]

24. (*Pleas of the crown.*) No sheriff, constable, coroner, or bailiff of the king shall hold pleas of the crown.

This clause is important as marking an era in the history of our criminal judicature. It secured the trial of all serious crimes before the king's justices, men of learning and experience in the law and to some degree, at least, free from local connections. Its practical effect was to take away from the county court and the other inferior local tribunals the jurisdiction of nearly all criminal matters. This important judicial reform was not a sudden act, but the result of a gradual process. By the Assize of Clarendon, 1166, sheriffs were to send those accused of robbery, murder or theft to the royal justice for trial[36]; and in 1194 it was ordered that no sheriff should be a justice in his own county.[37] Magna Carta

---

[32] On what the barons meant by *per pares suos* in this chapter, see McKechnie, 295–297. On amercement, see Sir John Fox, *Contempt of Court*, 119 *et seq.* and Goebel, *Felony and Misdemeanor*, 1.

[33] The word derived from the French *contenir* and was not a compound from *tenementum*. See Tait, *English Historical Review*, xxxvii, 720 *et seq.* (1912); Pollard, *English Historical Review*, xxviii, 117; so in 1327 Crown process against its debtors was to be " saving their countenance." *Rotuli Parliamentorum*, ii, 8, No. 8. *Cf.* the discussion in *Dialogus de Scaccario*, II, xiv.

[34] In lib. ix, c. 8. *Cf. ibid.*, c. 11 " ne aliquid de suo honorabili contenemento amittat."

[35] Tait, *loc. cit.* Wainage was not the wagon or wain and other implements of husbandry, but is a latinised form of the French *gagnage*. The object of saving the villein's " tillage " was to prevent him being completely impoverished, for his tillage was his means of sustenance, the basis of his *contenementum*.

[36] Assize of Clarendon, c. 1. (*Select Charters*, 170.)

[37] Forma procedendi in placitis Coronae Regis (1194), c. 21. Hoveden, ii, 262–267. *Select Charters*, 254.

now deprived sheriffs and other local officers of all jurisdiction over pleas of the crown.[38] Henceforth, he could take indictments and keep prisoners accused or suspected, but only royal justices could try them. " Pleas of the crown " are criminal prosecutions carried on in the name of the sovereign, " who is supposed by the law," remarks Blackstone, " to be the person injured by every infraction of the public rights of the community." The word " constables " meant castellans, or constables of castles, of which in the time of Henry II there were upwards of eleven hundred in England. These constables possessed considerable power, and within the precincts of the manors upon which their castles were built, held trials of criminal charges, as the sheriffs did within their respective counties. In manors not having a castle, the criminal and civil jurisdiction of the lords was exercised by the stewards or bailiffs. The convenience of secure prisons afforded by these private castles caused prisoners charged with crimes in the counties to be frequently committed to the custody of the constables, who too often abused their trust. Nearly two hundred years after the Great Charter, a statute (5 Henry 4, c. 10) directed justices of the peace to imprison in the common gaol, " because that divers constables of castles within the realm of England be assigned to be justices of the peace by commission from our lord the king, and by colour of the said commission they take people to whom they bear ill-will and imprison them within the said castles till they have made fine and ransom with the said constables for their deliverance." To deprive such men of the power to try prisoners was a great boon to the people.

34. (*Writ of praecipe.*) The writ called *praecipe* shall not in future be issued to anyone regarding any tenement so as to cause a freeman to lose his court.

> This clause attempts to maintain the strict feudal rule that the solemn writ of right for land should be addressed to the lord of the fee from whom the land is held. The case thus began in the lord's court (but could be evoked thence into the king's court). The abuse here attacked was the issue of the writ in the form *praecipe quod reddat* which was addressed to the sheriff, and thus deprived the lord of the profits of his jurisdiction, and might imperil the tenure.[39]

36. (*Writ De odio et atia.*) The writ of inquest of life or limb shall be given *gratis*, and not denied.

> The writ referred to was that " *De odio et atia*," of " malice and hate." A man appealed, *i.e.*, accused by a private individual of homicide or felony (see *infra*, p. 78), claimed that the charge was not a bona fide

---

[38] Certain powers were however still retained by the sheriff. See McKechnie, 309: " Along with the coroners, he conducted preliminary inquiries even into pleas of the Crown; while in his tourn (which was specially authorised to be held twice a year by chapter 42 of the second reissue of the Charter in 1217) he was made responsible for every stage in the trial of trivial offences."

[39] See the writ in Glanvill, lib. i, c. 5, *Select Charters*, 190. Magna Carta left to the king the right to use the writ for the purpose of settling disputes between tenants-in-chief or where the tenure was disputed, and Glanvill, i, 5, had stated a generation earlier that the crown could use its discretion in the matter. By the end of the century, Hengham (ed. W. H. Dunham), *Summa Magna*, 7, could say that lords of courts got little or no profit out of holding such pleas. The clause was soon evaded by writs of entry and became inoperative. See Plucknett, *Statutes and their Interpretation*, 82–83; McKechnie, 346–355; Pollock and Maitland, ii, 63–70.

one, but brought through spite, and the decision on this point, which came to be regarded as a final verdict of guilt or innocence, was made by the local jury. It afforded to the accused, therefore, the opportunity of escaping the *duellum*, and was also a means by which a person imprisoned on such a charge could procure the privilege, in certain circumstances, of being released on bail to await the *iter* of the king's justices. The writ was not, however, issuable as of right, but only as a matter of royal favour *ex regiae potestatis beneficio*.[40] Advantage was taken of this circumstance during John's reign to extort large sums of money for the privilege. Magna Carta made it grantable as a matter of right, and without payment.[41]

38. (*Wager of law.*) No bailiff for the future shall put anyone to his law (*ad legem*) upon his own bare saying, without credible witnesses to prove it.

The meaning of this clause has been disputed from the early fourteenth century onwards.[42] To put a man to his law was to put him upon his defence,[43] and thus in jeopardy, and strenuous efforts were made during the Middle Ages and long after to prevent the oppressive use of criminal and civil procedure. It was often insisted that legal proceedings in the king's courts could only be begun by original writ, appeal or indictment. Hence the early opposition to equity on the ground that subpoena was not an original writ, and to the council and Star Chamber on the ground that they proceeded without indictment. Both ecclesiastical and royal procedure had to deal with the problem caused by the facts that many honest persons were loth to prosecute, and that many unscrupulous persons were eager to do so. In both cases justice failed. The church had long ago developed the synodal jury[44] and in 1164 Henry II gave the church the co-operation of the sheriffs in summoning synodal juries, but insisted that laymen should not be tried by the church unless accused by substantial witnesses or by a synodal.[45] A few years earlier he had ordained in Normandy[46] that a rural dean's bare word was insufficient as an accusation. In 1166 these experiments with church procedure were transferred to royal procedure with the regularisation of the indictment.[47] The present clause (with its mention of " bailiffs ") seems to carry the matter a stage further and into the seignorial courts where bailiffs had ample opportunities for petty oppressions and vindictiveness. The bailiff commonly prosecuted in manorial courts, and the accused seems generally to have defended himself " against the bailiff and his

---

[40] Glanvill, lib. xiv, c. 3.

[41] This chapter has no bearing, as often supposed, on the history of habeas corpus. The writ is fully discussed in Elsa de Haas, *Antiquities of Bail* (New York and Oxford, 1940), Chap. iv.

[42] On the various interpretations see McKechnie, 370–375. That suggested above is substantially new, though based on a hint in Pollock and Maitland, i, 151, n. 1, and somewhat differently put, *ibid.*, ii, 606.

[43] But in the second re-issue of 1217 the wording was slightly altered to ad legem manifestam nec ad juramentum.

[44] *Cf.* Fournier " l'Oeuvre canonique de Réginon de Prüm " (1920) *Bibliothèque de l'Ecole des Chartes*, LXXXI, 5, 23.

[45] Constitutions of Clarendon, c. 6 (Stubbs, *Select Charters*, 165); Pollock and Maitland, i, 151–152; Haskins, *Norman Institutions*, 219, 329.

[46] " Ordinance of Falaise " (1159), in C. H. Haskins, *loc. cit.*

[47] Assize of Clarendon, c. 4 (Stubbs, *Select Charters*, 170).

suit "[48]—we may well suspect that this suit was often little more than a fiction.

42. (*Ne exeat regno*.) [In future anyone may leave the kingdom and return at will, unless in time of war, when he may be restrained " for some short space for the common good of the kingdom." Prisoners, outlaws, and alien enemies are excepted, and foreign merchants shall be dealt with as provided in the 41st clause.] [49]

This clause has some ecclesiastical interest, as it removed a practical impediment in the way of appeals to Rome. It was among the clauses reserved for further consideration in Henry III's first re-issue of the Charter, and was never afterwards restored. The sovereign still retains the prerogative of preventing any subject from quitting the realm, by the writ *ne exeat regno*. Coke points out [50] that although by the common law everyone had liberty to go abroad when he would, unless specially enjoined to remain at home, there were formerly certain orders of men under a continual prohibition from quitting the realm, without the king's previous licence. Peers were thus prohibited, because they were the counsellors of the crown; knights, because they were to defend the kingdom from invasion; all ecclesiastics, because they were confined by a special law (Constitutions of Clarendon, 1164), on account of their attachment to the see of Rome; and all archers and artificers, lest they should instruct foreigners how to rival the manufactures of England. In 1381 a statute (5 Ric. 2, st. 1, c. 2) prohibited all persons whatever from going abroad without licence, except only the lords and other great men of the realm, true and notable merchants, and the king's soldiers. This was not repealed till 4 James 1, c. 1, s. 22. In his reign, however, various Acts were passed restraining, as a particular guard against the papacy, the sending, without licence, any children out of the realm, to seminaries beyond sea, or for any cause whatever (3 Jac. 1, c. 5). The writ *ne exeat* is now, in practice, only used to prevent a party to an action in respect of equitable debts and claims from withdrawing his person and property from the jurisdiction of the court.

44. (*The Forests*.) [Persons dwelling without the limits of a forest shall not in future be compelled to attend the king's forest courts upon common summons, unless they be impleaded or be pledges for others attached for forest offences.]

Henry II in the Assize of Woodstock (1184), had established an exact analogy between the courts of the shire and those of the forest, all men being required to attend the king's forest court, which exercised supreme jurisdiction over all woods and forests, whether a part of the royal demesne or not. He appointed justices to visit the forests at the same time and on the same system as the justices itinerant. The forest clauses were omitted from the Charter in 1217, and were embodied with other remedial provisions in the separate Carta de Foresta of Henry III (1217).[51]

---

[48] *Cf.* Maitland, *The Court Baron* (Selden Society), 20–39 *passim*; T. F. T. Plucknett, *The Mediaeval Bailiff* (1954), 11–13.
[49] See *infra*, p. 83, commenting on clause 41.   [50] 3 *Inst.* c. 84.
[51] *Infra*, p. 89. The principal authorities on forest law are Manwood, *Lawes of the Forrest* (1598, 1615), G. J. Turner, *Select Pleas of the Forest* (Selden Society, 1899), C. Petit-Dutaillis, *Studies Supplementary to Stubbs*, i, 148–251, N. Neilson in *The English Government at Work* (ed. J. F. Willard and W. A. Morris, 1940) 394–467 and A. L. Cross,

45. (*Judges and ministers.*) [We will appoint as justices, constables, sheriffs, and bailiffs only " such as know the law and mean duly to observe it."]

54. (*Women's appeals.*) No one shall be taken or imprisoned on the appeal of a woman except for the death of her husband.

> In cases of death by murder or manslaughter, an " appeal " of felony was allowed to be brought only by certain relations or by the feudal lord of the deceased; by the widow for the death of her husband, or by the heir male for the death of his ancestor. The word " appeal " is not used here in the ordinary sense of a complaint to a higher court for injustice done by an inferior one; but signifies an accusation or challenge, an original suit by one subject against another, rather because of his own peculiar damage than for an offence against the public. The defendant in an appeal had the right of trial by battle (a rule of Norman origin). The parties were obliged to fight in their own persons, unless the appellant were a woman, a priest, an infant, lame, blind, or sixty years old, any of whom were permitted to hire a champion. The appeal by a woman was therefore disliked and limited to the death of a husband. The appellee in these cases could clear himself by the ordeal, or, after the virtual abolition of this procedure, by trial by a jury " per patriam." [52] If the appellee were worsted in the combat, or found guilty, he suffered the same judgment as if convicted on an indictment; but the crown had no power to pardon him, because an " appeal " was a private suit. [53] An appeal might be brought even after the appellee had been tried and acquitted on an indictment. The period within which this right could be exercised was limited by the Statute of Gloucester (6 Edw. 1, c. 9) to a year and a day. The " battel " took place in the presence of the judges of the Court of King's Bench or Common Pleas, attired in their scarlet robes, who sat looking on while the combatants each armed with a staff an ell long, and a leathern shield, cudgelled each other from sunrise to star-rising, or until one of them cried " craven." Though long obsolete, neither appeals nor trials by battle were legally abolished till the early part of the nineteenth century. [54] In 1817 a writ of appeal was tried in the court of King's Bench against Abraham Thornton, for the alleged rape and murder of Mary Ashford. The appellee, who had already been tried and acquitted at Warwick Assizes on the same charge, cast down his glove in open court and formally demanded trial by battle against the appellant, the brother of the deceased. The court having allowed the demand, time was given for due consideration of the novel circumstances of the case; ultimately the appellant declined to accept the challenge, and the defendant was discharged without bail on Oct. 20, 1818. [55] This led to the passing (June 22, 1819) of the statute 59 George 3, c. 46, intituled " An Act to abolish appeals of murder, treason, felony, or other offences, and wager of battel, or joining issue and trial by battel in writs of right." [56]

Eighteenth Century Documents relating to the Forest (Ann Arbor, 1928). Compare S. Deck, *Etude sur la Forêt d'Eu* (Caen, 1929).

[52] *Cf.* McKechnie, pp. 451–452; Neilson, *Trial by Combat,* Chap. xvi; Sayles, *Select Cases in King's Bench* (Selden Soc.), iii, p. lxxii; Stephen, *History of Criminal Law,* i, 244; Holdsworth, iii, 608.

[53] See Glanvill, lib. xiv; Bracton, lib. iii; Britton, lib. i; Hawkins, *Pleas of Crown,* ii, 392.

[54] See *supra,* pp. 42 *et seq.*   [55] See *Ashford* v. *Thornton* (1818) 1 Barn. & Ald. 405.

[56] Note that trial by battle in real actions was fought by champions, and not by parties. The case of *Ashford* v. *Thornton* is fully dealt with in the *Famous Trials* series.

III.—*Fundamental Principles of the Constitution*

12. (*Scutage.*) [No scutage or aid shall be imposed unless *per commune consilium regni*, except in the three cases of ransoming the king's person, making his eldest son a knight, and once for marrying his eldest daughter; and for these the aids shall be reasonable. In like manner it shall be concerning the aids of the city of London.]

14. (*Common counsel.*) [In order to take the common counsel of the kingdom in the imposition of aids (other than the three regular feudal aids) and of scutage, the king shall cause to be summoned the archbishops, bishops, abbots, earls, and greater barons, by writ directed to each severally, and all other tenants *in capite* by a general writ addressed to the sheriff of each shire; a certain day and place shall be named for their meeting, of which forty days' notice shall be given; in all letters of summons the cause of summons shall be specified; and the consent of those present on the appointed day shall bind those who, though summoned, shall not have attended.]

These two clauses (12, 14) were often said to amount to the surrender of the royal claim to arbitrary taxation, and to lay down the principle that the nation ought not to be taxed except by consent of the national council. But they deal not with taxation in general but with specific dues, scutages and extraordinary aids from the feudal tenants, and aids from the city of London. Tallages upon towns are not included.[57] The towns were still to a great extent in the position of demesne lands of the king or other lord, and their inhabitants in a state of quasi-villeinage. It is noticeable that in the Articles of the Barons c. 32 (the rough draft of the barons' demands, subsequently embodied in the Charter), after the provisions against levying scutage or aids except by consent of the national council, occur the words: " Simili modo fiat de *tallagiis* et auxiliis de civitate Londonarium *et de aliis civitatibus* quae inde habent libertates." It may be that the barons in excluding tallages (the crown's right to which was only abolished in 1340) and omitting the other chartered towns were making a concession to John in matters where their own interests were not concerned. Nevertheless, sub-tenants did benefit by this chapter, because lords subjected to exactions from the crown had the right of calling upon their tenants for help in meeting them.[58] The word " baron " was of wide signification, and had not yet become a title in its modern acceptation. The citizens of London and of the Cinque Ports were sometimes designated " barons." While the " greater barons " developed into the House of Lords, the lesser barons lost their separate and political identity in the mass of the commonalty, and were represented, together with the towns, in the House of Commons. The significance of the 14th clause, as defining the method of summoning the national council, will be discussed later on in the chapter on the " Origin of Parliament." Although the 12th and 14th clauses were omitted in Henry III's renewals of the Charter, the form of a grant of scutages and aids appears to have been generally observed throughout

[57] *Cf.* McKechnie, pp. 238–239.
[58] F. M. Stenton, *English Feudalism*, 183. *Cf. infra*, p. 139.

his reign.[59] Moreover, although this chapter only deals with royal dues, we find lords applying the principle in their relations with their own tenants. Thus Henry de Tracy in 1235 summoned his knights, and they, in court assembled, granted him an aid.[60]

39. (*False imprisonment.*) No free man shall be taken or imprisoned or disseised, or outlawed, or exiled, or anyways destroyed; nor will we go upon him, nor will we send upon him, unless by the lawful judgment of his peers, or by the law of the land.

40. (*Sale of justice.*) To none will we sell, to none will we deny or delay, right or justice.

Earlier exponents of the Charter have read into these clauses legal conceptions of a later age and tended to exaggerate the importance of the principles embodied in them. Sir James Mackintosh remarks,[61] for example, that here " are clearly contained the habeas corpus and the trial by jury, the most effectual securities against oppression which the wisdom of man has hitherto been able to devise "; and Hallam has termed them " the essential clauses," as being those which " protect the personal liberty and property of all freemen, by giving security from arbitrary imprisonment and arbitrary spoliation."[62] These views require some modification. Neither the petty criminal jury nor the writ of habeas corpus was yet in existence, and from time to time kings continued to claim and to exercise the prerogative of arbitrarily committing to prison persons suspected of designs against the crown until the right was abolished by the Petition of Right on the alleged ground that it was contrary to the tenor of Magna Carta.[63] These clauses were intended, not to enunciate new principles, but to protect the freeman against the arbitrary acts in which King John had indulged.[64] That in no wise diminishes their importance. A fundamental advance took place when the life, liberty and property of the freeman were subjected to law alone, and no longer lay at the whim of the monarch: the case in *Bracton's Note Book*, no. 857, which confirmed this principle in 1234 in respect of Hubert de Burgh, is one of the most important (and little known) cases in our constitutional history.

(1) *Nullus liber homo capiatur vel imprisonetur*, meaning that no freeman could be arrested or detained in prison without a trial.

[59] *Cf.* writ for collection of scutage, 1235; *Select Charters*, 357. In clause 44 of the second re-issue of the Charter (1217) scutage was to be taken in future according to the custom of Henry II. There is no reference to aids. For a suggestion that recent changes in the nature of scutage made the clauses unnecessary, thus accounting for their omission, see Lapsley's note in Pasquet, *Origins of the House of Commons*, App. III, c.

[60] *Bracton's Note Book* (ed. Maitland), 1146.

[61] *History of England*, i, 219–220.

[62] Hallam, *Middle Ages*, ii, 327.

[63] McKechnie, 392–395. Vinogradoff, in *Magna Carta Commemoration Essays*, 94. Such action generally aroused protests, and sometimes Magna Carta was expressly invoked. Arrest was followed by trial, although sometimes of an archaic sort. *Cf.* Plucknett, " Origins of Impeachment," *Transactions of the Royal Historical Society* (1942), 47. Even later, somewhat similar powers were claimed by Privy Councillors and Secretaries of State (below, p. 308–310).

[64] *Cf.* Powicke, *Magna Carta Commemoration Essays*, 103: " The thirty-ninth clause was intended to lay stress not so much on any form of trial as on the necessity for protection against the arbitrary acts of imprisonment, disseisin, and outlawry in which King John had indulged." On Hubert de Burgh's case see *Bracton's Note Book*, no. 857; Pollock and Maitland, ii, 581.

(2) *Aut dissaisietur de libero tenemento suo, vel libertatibus, vel liberis consuetudinibus suis* [65]; meaning thereby that no man shall be dispossessed of his freehold or of his liberties or free customs—that is, of such feudal franchises, immunities and privileges as had been granted to him.

(3) *Aut utlagetur, aut exuletur, aut aliquo modo destruatur.* By " outlawry " is signified the ejecting of a person, by public proclamations, from the benefit of the law, a process which, from the time of Alfred until long after the reign of William the Conqueror, was available in the case of felony only, for which the penalty was death; and therefore an outlaw, having, as it was said, a wolf's head, might be slain by any man. Early in Edward III's reign it was decided that none but the sheriff should put an outlaw to death, under pain of being considered guilty of felony; the only exception was when an outlaw was slain during an attempt to capture him. Outlawry was regularly used where trial was impossible because the accused had fled, and was roughly equivalent to a conviction. By " exile " is signified not so much formal banishment, as that degree of oppression which compels a tenant great or small to abandon his holding.[66] " Destroyed " is most probably a colloquial expression with the sense of " ruined."

(4) *Nec super eum ibimus nec super eum mittemus*; Coke erroneously explained these words in connection with the forms of legal procedure, but their significance is brought out correctly by Lingard, who remarks that John had hitherto been in the habit of *going* with an armed force, or *sending* an armed force on the lands and against the castles of all whom he knew or suspected to be his secret enemies, without observing any form of law.[67] The king's letters patent,[68] dated at Windsor the 10th day of May, in the 16th year of his reign, about a month before the meeting at Runnymede, attempted to detach the barons from the confederacy against him, by promising to them and their retainers specially what was afterwards granted to all the freemen of the realm: " Sciatis nos concessisse baronibus nostris qui contra nos sunt quod nec eos nec homines suos capiemus, nec dissaisiemus, nec super eos *per vim vel per arma* ibimus nisi per legem regni nostri, vel per judicium parium suorum *in curia nostra*."

(5) *Nisi per legale judicium parium suorum, vel per legem terrae.* These words have been variously interpreted. Whether *vel* is conjunctive or disjunctive has been much argued; the best suggestion is still Maitland's, namely that it is " subdisjunctive," with the meaning " and/or." [69] It is probable, as Professor Adams concludes,[70] " that what the barons had in mind in this clause was not chiefly the form of trial, but was the general body of the law and the rights which it secured them." The

---

[65] The words *de libero tenemento suo, vel libertatibus, vel liberis consuetudinibus suis* were added in the second re-issue of the Charter in 1217. The words *de libertatibus* cannot be understood, as Coke interpreted them, so as to include a general prohibition of monopolies.

[66] Statute of Marlborough (1267), c. 23, uses " exile " to mean the sort of waste which compels villeins to flee from their holdings, thus impoverishing the manor.

[67] Lingard, *History of England*, iii, c. 1. Glanvill, ix, 1, uses the expression *ire contra* of private feudal warfare; *cf.* Stenton, *Feudalism*, 250, n. 2.

[68] *Rotuli Patentium* 16 Joh. part 1, m. 3, d, ed. Hardy, p. 141; Blackstone, *Introduction to the Charters*, xiii.

[69] See Adams, *Origin of the English Constitution*, 262 *et seq.*; McKechnie, 381; Vinogradoff, in *Magna Carta Essays*, 80. But *cf.* Powicke, *ibid.*, 90 *et seq.* Pollock and Maitland, i, 173, n. 3 is of capital importance.

[70] Adams, *op. cit.*, 242. So also Vinogradoff, 85: " The struggle was waged to secure trial in properly constituted courts of justice and in accordance with established justice "; and Powicke, 120: " In 1215 neither baron nor freeman was concerned primarily with a judgment of peers so much as with justice."

" judicium parium " of Magna Carta is a phrase of wide signification referring to a long familiar legal principle rather than the technical definition of a mode of trial. " It lay at the foundation of all German law; and the very formula here used is probably adopted from the laws of the Franconian and Saxon Caesars." [71] The peers were the fellow suitors: in the case of the baron, the other tenants-in-chief in the *Curia Regis*; in the case of the tenants of a mesne lord, the other suitors in the Court Baron.[72]

(6) *Nulli vendemus, nulli negabimus, aut differemus, rectum aut justiciam.* The proviso was probably mainly directed against the bribes or fines which were anciently paid to delay or expedite judicial proceedings.[73] The words " to none will we sell " were intended to abolish the fines paid for procuring right or judgment; " to none will we deny " referred to the stopping of suits and the denial of writs; " to none will we delay " meant the delays caused either by the counter-fines of defendants (who sometimes outbid the plaintiffs), or by the will of the king. This clause of the Charter, says Madox, was so far effectual that fines for law proceedings became more moderate, and the evils alluded to gradually fell into disuse.[74]

IV.—*Cities, Boroughs, Commerce*

13. (*London.*) The city of London shall have all its ancient liberties and free customs, and so of all other cities, boroughs, towns, and ports.

33. All weirs (" kydelli ") in the Thames and Medway and throughout England shall be put down, except on the sea-coast.

Kydelli were fish-weirs. The object of their removal was not, as often stated, in order to prevent private appropriations of the right of fishing in public rivers, but to remove from rivers all obstacles likely to interfere with navigation.[75] The removal of weirs from the Thames and Medway is directed in several ancient charters besides the present, and by many statutes.

35. (*Weights and Measures.*) There shall be one standard . . . of measures and one standard of weights throughout the kingdom.

Uniformity of weights and measures had been enjoined in an assize of Richard I; and in the Articles of Visitation, issued by that king in 1194, the itinerant justices were directed to inquire " de vinis venditis contra assisam, et de falsis mensuris tam vini quam aliarum rerum." [76]

---

[71] Stubbs, *Constitutional History*, i, 577. *Cf.* the Constitution " De Beneficiis" of Conrad the Salic, 1037 (*Monumenta Germaniae Historica, Constitutiones.* i, 89). Similarly, Lothair II declares: Sancimus ut nemo miles adimatur de possessione sui beneficii nisi convicta culpa quae sit laudanda *per judicium parium suorum* sicut supra dictum est. In the *Leges Henrici Primi* (xxxi, 7) we find the same principle expressed in nearly the same words: Unusquisque *per pares suos judicandus est.*

[72] *Cf.* B. C. Keeney, *Judgment by Peers.* It should be noted that it is not " trial " but " judgment " which was the concern of the peers; " trial " was generally by ordeal or by battle.

[73] Instances are given in Madox, *History of the Exchequer*, Chap. xii.

[74] But see Pollock and Maitland, i, 195, and McKechnie, 395–398. On the subject of payments for writs, Turner has pointed out that the crown could, and did, charge when a plaintiff wanted to bring his case in some particular court, or at some particular time: *Brevia Placitata* (Selden Society), xlix *et seq.*

[75] See McKechnie, 343–344.

[76] Hoveden, iii, 263; iv, 33; *Select Charters*, 254.

41. (*Foreign merchants.*) All merchants shall have liberty safely to enter, to dwell and travel in, and to depart from England, for the purposes of commerce, without being subjected to any evil tolls, but only according to the ancient and allowed customs, except in time of war. On the breaking out of war, merchants of the hostile state who may be in England shall be attached, without damage to their bodies or goods, until it be known how our merchants are treated in such hostile state; and if ours be safe, the others shall be safe also.

> This provision in favour of merchants has been eulogised, as showing something like free-trade sentiments in days when the feudal barons throughout Europe were accustomed to oppress and pillage commerce; there has also been the contrary suggestion that it was in the interest of the barons to encourage foreign trade for they were the chief consumers of wines and luxuries imported from the Continent, and that this clause was opposed to the interests of the English traders. The first view is clearly untenable. The second contains more truth. " On the whole the king, the prelates and barons support the merchants: they are useful, they lend money, they lower prices, they will pay for favours." [77] Several authors have remarked upon the conflict between this and c. 13.[78] The present chapter maintains the old customs (which restrained the merchant's stay to forty days, and his trade to wholesale transactions, etc.) and merely relieves him of " evil tolls." The decent treatment of foreign merchants in England was in the interests of merchants generally, for reprisals were a common feature of international commerce. The merchant towns, in fact, secured the ratification of their old customs, which contributed greatly to the disabilities of the foreign merchant; this chapter only fetters the king. In Henry III's first re-issue of the Charter, the words " nisi publice antea prohibiti fuerint " were inserted immediately after " Omnes mercatores." The effect of this was to restore to the king full discretionary authority over foreign trade.[79]

V.—*Purveyance and other Royal Exactions*

28. (*Purveyance.*) No constable or other royal bailiff shall take any man's corn or other chattels without immediate payment, unless the seller voluntarily give credit.

30, 31. (*Purveyance*: *Impressment.*) Nor shall the king, his sheriffs, or bailiffs, take any horses or carriages of freemen for carriage, or any man's timber for castles or other uses, unless by consent of the owner.

> Purveyance (from *pourvoir*, to provide) was a prerogative enjoyed by the crown of " buying up provisions and other necessaries, by the intervention of the king's purveyors, for the use of his royal household, at an appraised valuation, in preference to all others, and even without the consent of the owner, and also of forcibly impressing the carriages and horses of the subject to do the king's business on the public road . . . upon paying a settled price; a prerogative which prevailed pretty generally

---

[77] Pollock and Maitland, i, 464. For the importance of the foreign merchants in England at this time, *cf.* Cunningham, *Growth of English Industry and Commerce*, i, 194.

[78] *e.g.*, Pollock and Maitland, i, 465; McKechnie, 404; Lipson, *Economic History*, i, 449.

[79] McKechnie, 404.

throughout Europe." [80] In Henry III's charters the restrictions on purveyance were modified and a scale of prices added. The abuses to which this system gave rise were manifold and grievous. The evil was never completely suppressed until the prerogative itself was resigned by Charles II.[81] The right was even extended to men's labour as well as to their goods. Thus, Edward III granted a commission to William of Walsingham, to impress painters for the works at St. Stephen's Chapel, Westminster, " to be at our wages as long as shall be necessary," and directed all sheriffs to arrest and imprison such as should refuse. Masons were frequently impressed,[82] and Edward IV granted a similar commission for the impressment of workers in gold for the royal household.[83]

23. (*Bridges*.) Neither a town nor any man shall be distrained to make bridges at river banks, unless anciently and of right bound to do so.[84]

25. (*Ferm of counties, etc.*) [Counties, hundreds, wapentakes, and trithings [85] shall stand at the ancient ferms, without any increase, except the manors of the royal demesne.]

It was customary for the king to farm out by the year, to the highest bidder, the sheriffdoms of counties and other offices. The officials recouped themselves by the exaction of excessive fines and fees, so that the people were the real sufferers by the exaction of an increased rental. This chapter was omitted from all re-issues.

9. (*Debts due to the crown.*) Land or rent shall not be seized for any debt due to the crown, so long as the chattels of the debtor will suffice; sureties shall not be distrained while the principal debtor is capable of payment, and if they have to pay, they shall, if they wish, hold of the lands and rents of their principal until they are satisfied.

The grant of the right of indemnity to the sureties of crown debtors—a right not enjoyed (apart from covenant) by sureties of other debtors [86] is noteworthy. The procedure is an anticipation of *elegit*.[87]

10, 11. (*Jews*.) [Debts due to the Jews are to bear no interest during the minority of the heir of a deceased debtor; the widow shall have her dower, and pay nothing of the debt; and the children shall be provided with necessaries before payment of the debt out of the residue.]

In all debts due to the Jews, the crown had an ulterior interest. They were the king's bondmen, and are so described in " Les Estatutz de la Jeuerie " of Edward I's reign, which direct that every Jew of the age of twelve years and upwards shall pay threepence annually " de taillage au rey ky serf il est," and that they shall not pay scot or lot, or be taxed with the men of the cities or boroughs, " cum il sunt taillables

---

[80] Blackstone, *Commentaries*, i, 287.
[81] 12 Car. 2, c. 24 (1660).
[82] D. Knoop and G. P. Jones, in *Economic History Review*, VIII, 57.
[83] Rymer, vi, 417; xi, 852; Hallam, *Middle Ages*, iii, 149.
[84] The king's interest in the repair of bridges was partly connected with falconry. For this aspect see McKechnie, 300–302. For the normal common law duty of communities or specific landowners to repair bridges—one of the most ancient heads of local government law—see Sir Cyril Flower, *Public Works in Mediaeval Law* (2 vols., Selden Society).
[85] Third parts of counties or ridings. Yorkshire and Lincolnshire were so divided.
[86] *Cf.* R. M. Jackson, *History of Quasi-Contract*, 4.
[87] Plucknett, *Concise History of the Common Law* (5th ed.), 390–391.

al rey comes ses serfs e a nul autres for a rey." [88] Under the Norman and early Angevin kings the Jews were employed " as a sponge " to suck up the wealth of their subjects, and be periodically squeezed to supply the wants of the Crown. Madox thus sums up their position as disclosed by the Exchequer records: " The king seemed to be an absolute lord of their estates and effects, and of the persons of them, their wives, and children. 'Tis true he let them enjoy their trade and acquests, but they seemed to trade and acquire for his profit as well as their own; for at one time or other their fortunes, or great part of them, came into his coffers." [89]

26. (*Decedents' chattels.*) On the death of a tenant *in capite* of a lay fee, indebted to the crown, the sheriff or other bailiff may attach the chattels of the deceased found upon his lay fee, to the value of the debt, by the view of lawful men; and nothing shall be removed until the whole debt be paid, the surplus being left to the executors to fulfil the testament of the deceased. If nothing be found due to the king, all the chattels shall go to the use of the deceased, saving to his wife and children their reasonable shares.[90]

27. (*Intestacy.*) [If any freeman shall die intestate, his chattels shall be distributed by the hands of his nearest kinsfolk and friends, under supervision of the church, saving to everyone the debts which the deceased owed to him.] [91]

By clause 60, to which reference has already been made, all the foregoing rights and liberties granted to the king's vassals are expressly extended to the tenants of mesne lords. The Charter concludes: " 63. Wherefore we will and firmly enjoin that the Church of England be free, and that all men in our kingdom have and hold the aforesaid liberties, rights, and concessions, well and in peace, freely and quietly, fully and wholly, to them and their heirs, of us and our heirs, in all things and places for ever as aforesaid." This is followed by the oath to be taken by the king and the barons, mutually to observe all the articles of the Charter, in good faith and without evasion.

Clauses 47, 48, 49, 50, 51, 52, 53, 55, 56, 57, 58, 59 and 62 have been omitted from this summary, as being mainly of a special and temporary character. They relate principally to the reform of the forests, the surrender of charters and hostages placed in the king's hands as securities, the dismissal of his foreign servants and mercenary troops, the rights of

---

[88] *Statutes of the Realm*, i, 221, 222. The date is 1275; G. J. Turner, in *Law Magazine and Review* (4th ser.), xxi, 310.

[89] Madox, *History of the Exchequer* (2nd ed.), i, 221 *et seq.* All contracts of debt due to Jews were to be in writing, drawn out in several copies and examined by two Jews, two Christians, and two public officers, and then filed. Hoveden, iii, 266. For the Exchequer of Jews, see J. M. Rigg, *Select Pleas from the Exchequer of the Jews* (Selden Society).

[90] For the light thrown by this chapter on the right of making wills, see McKechnie, pp. 323–326.

[91] This clause was omitted from subsequent re-issues, but it settled the law of intestacy. The church supervised the administration of the personal estate of an intestate. See Pollock and Maitland, ii, 357.

the Welsh and of the King of Scots, and the grant of a general political amnesty.

VI.—*Enforcement by the Twenty-five*

61. (*Enforcement.*) There remains only the 61st clause, by which means were provided for enforcing the due observance of the Charter. The question, how should the compact between the king and his people be enforced, was at once difficult and pressing. The king was left in possession of the regal power and dignity; experience had shown the ease with which former sovereigns had broken their most solemn written engagements; and the insincerity of John was notorious. At this period there were no effective constitutional checks against the king; and so a rude device was hit upon, in its nature really impracticable, by which John granted, according to a widespread opinion, to all his subjects a qualified liberty of rebellion. The whole baronage were to elect a Council of twenty-five barons charged to take care with all their might that the provisions of the Charter were carried into effect. If the king or any of his officers should violate the Charter in the smallest particular, these barons, or four of their number, were to complain to the king, or in his absence to the justiciar, and demand instant redress. If no redress be given within forty days, " the said five-and-twenty barons, together with the commonalty of the whole land (*communa totius terrae*), shall distrain and distress us in all possible ways, by seizing our castles, lands, possessions, and in any other manner they can, till the grievance is redressed according to their pleasure, saving harmless our own person and the persons of our queen and children; and when it is redressed they shall obey us as before. And any person whatsoever in the land may swear that he will obey the orders of the five-and-twenty barons aforesaid in the execution of the premises, and will distress us, jointly with them, to the utmost of his power; and we publicly and freely give liberty to any one that shall please to swear this, and never will hinder any person from taking the same oath. As to all those in the land who will not of their own accord swear to join the five-and-twenty barons in distraining and distressing us, we will issue orders to make them take the same oath as aforesaid."

> Much has been written about this remarkable clause. Stubbs thought that the twenty-five were empowered to make war against the king himself,[92] and the most recent commentator has used similar words.[93] It is difficult to find evidence for this view either in the Articles of the Barons or in the Charter. There is no mention of war, or of the " defiance," *diffidatio*, which preceded hostilities between a tenant and his lord. All the barons demanded, and all that the king conceded, was that the royal castles, lands and possessions should lie open to distress. In doing that, he was following what was a common form among conveyancers who daily inserted powers of distress in deeds creating rent

[92] Stubbs, *Constitutional History*, i, 605.
[93] J. E. A. Jolliffe, *Constitutional History* (1937), 258.

charges and similar obligations. In this case, however, the power is given not to the party grieved but to a standing body of barons whose position has been compared to the *fidejussores* or guarantors who frequently supervise the application of twelfth century treaties.[94] This is a fruitful and novel suggestion. It would certainly be wrong to regard them as in any way constituting a court.

The men of 1215 were well aware that the constitution was not a self-winding and self-regulating clock. With our additional centuries of experience, we are aware that no mechanism is likely to reach that impossible perfection. Outside intervention will occasionally be necessary to effect repairs and adjustments, and those occasions—rare in a well-ordered polity—call for skill and sense. The barons of 1215 showed those qualities in the charter as a whole, and especially in this clause. They did not resort to that *doctrinaire* anarchy which is often attributed to them, but employed a well-tried lawyerly device, a covenant for distress.[95]

(*The majority rule.*) There is one other provision of this charter which has received very little attention, although it is the one provision in the whole document with a truly modern ring. This is a clause saying that the opinion of the majority of those present of the twenty-five shall prevail. It is an early statement of the majority rule. Without such a rule modern government would be impossible and it is lamentable that so little is known of its history in England.[96]

John, the Pope and the Charter. John soon gave evidence of his intention to break from the Charter if he could. He applied for aid to the pope, now his suzerain, who declared the Charter void,[97] excommunicated the barons, and suspended Archbishop Langton. The city of London also,

---

[94] *Op. cit.*, 258–259.

[95] Medieval thought steadily contemplated the possibility of rebellion being the only practicable means of redress, however; see the chapter on the " right of resistance " in Fritz Kern, *Kingship and Law in the Middle Ages* (tr. S. B. Chrimes, 1939), 81–133, and Marc Bloch, *Régime Féodale*, ii, 259, but Gneist already noticed that the chapter was concerned rather with distress: " A contractual right of distress was so bound up with the legal customs of the Middle Ages that the Committee of Resistance almost lost thereby its apparently revolutionary character."—Gneist, *The English Parliament*, p. 85. The view in the text is a little elaborated in T. F. T. Plucknett, *Legislation of Edward I*, 75–76; see the reservations in A. L. Poole, *Domesday Book to Magna Carta*, 476, n. 3.

[96] See *Encyclopaedia of the Social Sciences*, x, 54. To the bibliography there, add J. Redlich, *Procedure of the House of Commons*, ii, 261–264, and O. Prausnitz, " Representation and the Majority Principle," *Politica*, i, 215–223.

[97] The text is in Rymer, *Foedera*, i, pp. 203–205 and Bémont, *Chartes*, 41. See the paper by G. B. Adams, " Innocent III and the Great Charter," in *Magna Carta Commemoration Essays* (1917), pp. 26–45 (and in his *Council and Courts*, 353); T. F. Tout, *Collected Papers*, ii, 285. The pope's action was based on a number of grounds and on a review of the whole course of recent events. The feudal overlordship was mentioned, but the principal justification was the church's frequently exercised jurisdiction to absolve from oaths extorted by " such threats as might move the most constant man." This formula is as old as Gaius (in Dig., 4, 2, 6) and exercised the minds of medieval Romanists (*cf.* H. Kantorowicz, *Studies in the Glossators*, 189–190) and common lawyers (*cf.* F. W. Maitland, *Bracton and Azo*, 184, and the curious example of a forced marriage in Jolliffe, *Constitutional History*, 283, n. 2) as well as canonists. The church's view seems to have been that the moral obligation of a " dictated peace " rested on its intrinsic justice, and not upon the fact that it had been successfully imposed by force. For this and other events following the Charter, see H. G. Richardson in *Bulletin of John Rylands Library*, xxviii and xxix.

which had ardently supported the barons in their demands, and whose
mayor was one of the council of twenty-five executors, was laid under
interdict. In addition to these spiritual arms, John sent for a body of
mercenaries and renewed the civil war. The mercenaries, as professional
soldiers, proved themselves an overmatch for the barons with their
half-trained retainers. In this extremity, the barons determined to renounce
their allegiance to John and to dethrone him by the aid of Louis, eldest
son of Philip Augustus of France, to whom they made a formal offer of
the English crown.[98] Louis at once sent aid to the barons, and himself
landed in England on May 21, 1216. But for John's unexpected death,
on October 19 following, it is highly probable that a change of dynasty
would have been carried out.

THE GREAT CHARTERS OF HENRY III

At the death of John things looked bad for the succession of his son
Henry, then only nine years old. Louis was in the south, the Scots in the
north, as enemies, and the Welsh march was for a time the only place of
refuge for the Angevin dynasty. Without delay, on October 28, 1216,
the boy Henry was crowned at Gloucester under the authority of the
papal legate Gualo [99]; and William Marshal, Earl of Pembroke, assumed,
with the assent of the friendly barons, the title of *Rector Regis et Regni*.
The regent, by his politic conduct, contrived, within the space of a twelve-
month, to bring over the disaffected baronage to the king's side, and to
induce Louis, after the " Fair of Lincoln " (May 19, 1217), and the loss
of his reinforcements in the naval engagement off Dover (August 24),
to abandon his pretensions to the English crown.

The Charter of 1216. One of the first acts of the Earl of Pembroke
had been to renew the Great Charter at a meeting of the royalist prelates
and barons held at Bristol on November 12, 1216, a few weeks after John's
death. The alterations in the re-issue are numerous. The merely temporary
provisions of John's Charter were omitted as a matter of course. But
there were also omitted the 12th and 14th clauses, forbidding the levying
of extraordinary aids without the common counsel of the realm, and
regulating the mode in which that counsel was to be had, as well as all
other clauses which in any way restricted the king's power to increase his
revenue. In clause 42 of the re-issue the king's ministers assign as their
reason for the omission that these articles being " gravia et dubitabilia,"
the prelates and barons had thought it best that the consideration of them
should be respited until such time as, together with such other things as
pertained to the welfare of all, they could be fully considered and established. The 42nd clause of John's Charter, in restraint of the king's

---

[98] *Annals of Waverley* 283; *Select Charters*, 275; Rymer, i, 140; Matt. Paris, *Chronica Majora* (ed. Luard), ii, 647.
[99] As regards this vexed question of the part played by the papal legate at the coronation, see Stubbs, *Constitutional History*, ii, p. 18, note; Norgate, Minority of Henry III, p. 4; P. E. Schramm, *History of the English Coronation*, 45.

prerogative to prevent any of his subjects from quitting the kingdom, and the 45th, as to the qualifications of the king's justices, were also left out. The alterations in the feudal clauses are characterised by the greater authority conceded to the mesne lords over their sub-vassals, a retrograde policy which was probably dictated by a desire to conciliate the baronage.[1]

The Charter of 1217. In the following year (1217), after Louis had finally quitted the kingdom, the Great Charter was again re-issued (it was thus Henry III's second Charter), with many further important omissions, alterations and additions. The forest clauses, which had been retained in the preceding Charter, were now omitted, being embodied in the Charter of the Forest, which was issued about the same time.[2] The respiting clause (1216), c. 42, was also left out, provision being made in this and the Forest Charter for several of the matters previously respited, and as to the other matters, their absence was to some extent supplied by a new clause in this re-issue (1217), c. 46, saving all existing liberties and free customs. The chief alterations are: In the " essential clauses " of John's Charter (39, 40), the words already referred to[3] were added, apparently for the sake of greater accuracy; and, probably, as a concession to the old feudal party, who regarded with dislike all extension of the central royal jurisdiction, the assizes of the itinerant justices were reduced from four to one annually; and the direction for the election by each county of four knights to take the recognitions is omitted, the knights of the county generally being substituted.

In addition to the 46th, the other new clauses in Henry's second Charter are the 39th, 42nd, 43rd, 44th and 47th. By clause 39 land was forbidden to be alienated by gift or sale, unless sufficient were retained to answer for the services due to the superior lord of the fee.[4] The 42nd directs that the county court shall be holden but from month to month,

---

[1] A duplicate of Henry III's first charter was transmitted to Ireland, under the seals of the legate and the protector, for the benefit of the king's faithful subjects there, with some few alterations which the local necessities of that island required. The adaptation to local conditions seems to have been done later in Ireland, although possibly authorised (at least in the compiler's view) by the covering letter which accompanied the text of the Charter of Nov. 12, 1216. *Cf.* H. G. Richardson, " Magna Carta Hiberniae," *Irish Historical Studies*, iii, 31–33.

[2] No Forest Charter was issued by John separately from the Forest clauses (44, 47, 48) of Magna Carta. The Forest Charter issued by the Earl Marshal in Henry III's name, on November 6, 1217, contains seventeen articles, by which the most grievous burdens of the Forest laws, as formulated by Henry II in the Assize at Woodstock, 1184, were either repealed or mitigated. The forests were still suffered to remain " an oasis of despotism in the midst of the old common law "; but the restriction on the jurisdiction of the Forest Courts imposed by the 44th clause of John's Charter was maintained, and all lands afforested by Richard and John were to be at once disafforested, as well as such lands afforested by Henry II as were not within the bounds of the Royal demesne. The penalty of death or mutilation was forbidden for the future, fine, imprisonment, or banishment from the realm being substituted (art. 10); but the cruel mutilation of dogs, in order to prevent them from being used in hunting, was expressly retained and regulated (three claws of the forefoot were to be cut off). See the Charter of the Forest, and the Assize of Woodstock, with which it should be compared in *Select Charters*, 186–188, 344–348.

[3] See *supra*, p. 81, n. 65.

[4] *Supra*, p. 38.

the sheriff's Tourn but twice in the year, and the view of frankpledge at Michaelmas; regulations relieving the public from compulsory attendance at courts whose excessive frequency was due to the cupidity of those who drew fees and fines from them.

The 43rd restrains fraudulent gifts in mortmain to religious corporations: " It shall not be lawful from henceforth to anyone to give his lands to any religious house, and to take the same land again to hold of the same house; nor shall it be lawful for any religious house to take the lands of anyone and to hand them back to be held by him of whom it received them. If anyone from henceforth give his lands to any religious house, and thereupon be convict, the gift shall be utterly void, and the land shall accrue to the lord of the fee." [5]

The 44th clause asserts the king's right to scutage " sicut capi consuevit tempore Henrici regis avi nostri " ; and the 47th directs the immediate destruction of the " castra adulterina " (a phrase forcibly recalling the disorders of Stephen's reign), either erected or rebuilt since the commencement of the barons' war.

The Charter of 1225. In the ninth year of his reign, Henry, who was now declared of age, re-issued Magna Carta and the Charter of the Forest, in consideration of the grant of an aid of a " fifteenth." They are Henry III's third issue of the Charter, 1225, and contain only two alterations of importance: (1) In the preamble, the words " spontanea et bona voluntate nostra " were substituted for the " consilio "; a change which, though capable of being interpreted as an assertion on the king's part of his independence of the counsel of his baronage, was, with greater probability, intended to obviate any subsequent evasion by him on the ground that his former charters, having been granted by others in his name during his minority, were no longer binding on himself.[6] (2) A final clause was added specifying the grant of the " fifteenth " as the price of the king's concession: " And for this our gift and grant of these liberties and of other liberties contained in our charter of liberties of the forest, the archbishops, bishops, abbots, priors, earls, barons, knights, freeholders, and all our subjects have given unto us the fifteenth part of all their movables." [7]

Confirmatio Cartarum, 1297. It is in the form in which the Great Charter, and the Charter of the Forest, were promulgated in 1225,

---

[5] The earlier measures seem to have been specially directed against the fraud so frequently committed upon the feudal lords by pretended and colourable donations to religious houses with the intention of receiving the lands back again freed from the feudal obligations, and the present clause of the Great Charter seems to refer to fraudulent as opposed to innocent alienations. But in the following reign the statute *de Religiosis* (7 Edw. 1), prohibited gifts of land to religious houses generally—*i.e.*, even in cases where the religious house did not give the land back to hold of the house, but kept it in its own hands. The clerical evasions of this statute were successively and at length effectually met by 15 Ric. 2, c. 5.

[6] *Annals of Dunstable*, p. 93, *s. a.* 1225; *Select Charters*, 322.

[7] *Statutes of the Realm, Charters of Liberties*, 22–25; *Select Charters*, 350.

9 Henry III, that the charters were confirmed by Edward I, in 1297, the twenty-fifth year of his reign. Regarding the Charter as the palladium of the nation's liberties, the people for centuries were ever ready to purchase its confirmation from successive kings by the grant of a liberal subsidy. In this way it was solemnly confirmed no less than thirty-seven times down to the second year of Henry VI.[8]

THE SIGNIFICANCE OF THE CHARTER

The place of Magna Carta in the history of its own time must be considered first. It has already been remarked that it was a link in a long chain of documents which stated the best contemporary opinions on the problems of government. Its merit is to have been more specific and detailed than any of its predecessors. Nor must it be dismissed as " merely feudal." Those words can only mean that it was in fact intensely practical in handling the contemporary problems of a feudal state. Still less is it " class-legislation " in the modern sense. The hierarchy of tenures in England never constituted class distinctions[9]; the definition of feudal duties benefited every free feudal tenant, high or low. The political unit was the *liber homo* and it was for him, and not merely for the barons alone, that the Charter secured the greatest of its liberties. It was, moreover, the barons themselves who inserted this demand in their original list of Articles.

But the Great Charter was not a unique document, nor a private revelation of political wisdom to Englishmen exclusively. Many towns were also securing charters defining and enlarging their rights[10]; the Earl of Chester granted a great charter to his tenants[11]; the kingdom of Hungary gained a remarkable charter[12] a few years later, and over a century earlier the Emperor Conrad II issued a charter which has an important parallel to chapter 39.[13] In 1188 the Cortes of Leon had anticipated in some measure the same chapter.[14] In other words, many countries whose structure was feudal were feeling the same difficulties and resorting to the same remedies, allowance being duly made for the

---

[8] The Charter was confirmed:—

	6 times by Henry III			6 times by Henry IV	
3	,, ,, Edward I			Once by Henry V	
14	,, ,, Edward III			,, ,, Henry VI	
6	,, ,, Richard II				

On these confirmations, see F. Thompson, *The First Century of Magna Carta*.

[9] See the example in Pollock and Maitland, i, 296. The view that the Charter was merely class-legislation without broad significance was propounded in a brilliantly provocative article by Professor Jenks, " The Myth of Magna Carta " (*Independent Review*, 1904); Robert Brady had had the same idea in 1685. *Cf.* the survey of opinions on the Charter by L. Leclère, in *Revue de l'Université de Bruxelles* (1913), xviii, 481.

[10] John had been lavish in granting charters.

[11] Text in J. Tait, *Chartulary of Chester Abbey* (Chetham Society, N.S. 79).

[12] For the Golden Bull of Andrew II (1222) see E. Sayous, *Histoire générale des hongrois* (2nd ed., 1900), 116–121; Fest, " Bulle d'Or et Magna Carta: les premières influences anglaises en Hongrie " (*Nouvelle Revue de la Hongrie*, LIII, 33).

[13] In 1037; text in *Monumenta Germaniae Historica, Legum Sectio* IV, i, 90; and *cf.* Stubbs, *Germany in the Middle Ages*, 146.

[14] Discussed by R. Altamira in *Magna Carta Commemoration Essays*, 227.

countless differences of detail which are as great a characteristic of feudalism as the uniformity of its general outline. The insistence of this type of document upon seeming details of real property law is an inevitable result of feudal conditions; it was also a source of strength. In an age of fierce antagonisms, the land and its law was one of the most settled and developed of secular institutions. Peaceful inheritance was the most conspicuous sign of good government—witness the Conqueror's charter to London, and contrast the reckless disseisins of John which united the nation against him.[15] The fixed and orderly relations of king and subject are thus the natural product of two most potent factors: first, the feudal fact that those relationships are really relationships of lord and tenant; and second, the conviction that land law is law *par excellence*. For centuries to come private law was the principal ingredient of our constitution and often private litigation provided constitutional precedents. It is true, no doubt, that kings and lawyers, even in the Middle Ages, felt that a king was something more than a feudal lord. There was speculation enough about the problem, and a few notorious tags from Roman law were only too well known. The attempts to draw practical conclusions from them, however, were doomed to fail as long as the Middle Ages lasted in England; sooner or later they came to grief on the solid rock of the common law.

The Charter was constantly invoked as long as its detailed provisions continued to apply to the current law and feudal structure. With the decline of feudalism, moreover, the Charter took a strange new life, and a legendary charter rivalled in potency the original.

From the time of Coke till the nineteenth century it was thought that almost every fundamental principle of the English Constitution could be traced to Magna Carta. " It was declaratory," wrote Coke, " of the principal grounds of the fundamental laws of England," and Hallam has characterised it as the " keystone of English liberty," to which all that has since been added is " little more than confirmation or commentary." This is extravagance and hyperbole, no doubt; but we may not condemn a cause because its advocates are eloquent. If the Charter, century after century, aroused the generous emotions of public-spirited men, then we need only be the more grateful that the practical expedient of one age became the consecrated legend of the next, fit to do even greater deeds in the days of Coke than in the days of Stephen Langton.

---

[15] *Cf.* also the significant language of Orderic quoted *supra*, p. 48, n. 3.

CHAPTER 5

INSTITUTIONS UNDER THE NORMAN AND PLANTAGENET KINGS

AT the head of the whole administrative system was the king himself, personally taking part not only in legislation but in fiscal, judicial, and every other kind of executive business.[1]

THE KING AND HIS GREAT OFFICERS

It was not till long after the Conquest that the kings of the English ceased, occasionally at least, to attend and take part in the proceedings of their courts of law.

The king as judge. Henry II was accustomed to assist in dispensing justice both in the *Curia Regis* and in its financial committee the Exchequer.[2] Some of his sayings on the judgment-seat have been preserved. In a case tried before him, shortly after his accession to the throne in 1154, the defendant alleged that a charter of Henry I produced in evidence had been improperly obtained. " Per oculos Dei," exclaimed the king, taking the charter in his own hands, " si cartam hanc falsam comprobare posses, lucrum mille librarum mihi in Anglia conferres."[3] In another case, a dispute between Baldwin, Archbishop of Canterbury, and the Abbot of St. Edmunds as to a territorial franchise, we are told that the king, puzzled by the production of conflicting charters, declared " Nescio quid dicam: nisi ut cartae ad invicem pugnent." And when the archbishop subsequently refused to accept the abbot's offer to submit the dispute to the verdict of the counties of Norfolk and Suffolk, the king angrily arose and left the court, saying, " Qui potest capere capiat."[4] King John personally decided a case in the Exchequer in the sixth year of his reign. Henry III frequently sat in Westminster Hall with his judges; and several instances are recorded of criminal jurisdiction exercised in person by John, Henry III, Edward I and Edward II.[5]

[1] *Cf.* Stubbs, *Constitutional History*, i, 366; Gneist, *English Constitution*, Chap. 16, i, 246.
[2] *Dialogus de Scaccario*, i, c. 4. (The text entire is in the first eight editions of Stubbs, *Select Charters*; extracts only in the 9th ed. The critical edition by A. Hughes, C. G. Crump and C. Johnson (Oxford, 1902) has valuable notes, and has now been re-issued with a translation by C. Johnson. R. L. Poole, *Exchequer in the Twelfth Century* (Oxford, 1912), is a valuable commentary.)
[3] *Abbot of Battle* v. *Balliol* (*Chronicon Monasterii de Bello*, 106; Bigelow, *Placita Anglo-Normannica*, 175). This case is interesting for the light which it throws alike on the working of the feudal tenures, the system of judicature, and the social aspects of the twelfth century.
[4] *Archbishop of Canterbury* v. *Abbot of St. Edmunds. Circa* 1186. *Chronicon Jocelin de Brakelonda*, p. 37 (Camden Soc.); Bigelow, *Placita Anglo-Normannica*, 238.
[5] Madox, *History of the Exchequer*, i, 191; *Dialogus de Scaccario*, i, c. 4; Palgrave, *English Commonwealth*, i, 292; *cf.* a good story about Edward I in Y.B. 3 Edw. II (Selden Society), 196–197. In early times even queens-consort sometimes sat in court. Matilda, in the

Still the exercise of ordinary jurisdiction by the king was an exception to the general rule. Edward IV, we are told, sat in the King's Bench for three consecutive days, in order to see how his laws were executed, but it is not said that he interfered in the proceedings.[6] By the usage of many centuries it has now been long an undisputed principle that, although the king may be present in a court of justice, he is not entitled to " determine any cause but by the mouth of his judges, to whom he has committed the whole of his judicial authority."[7] When James I sat personally in court, and wished to interfere, he was told by the judges that he could not deliver an opinion.[8]

The justiciar. Next to the king in power and authority was his chief minister, the justiciar, the supreme administrator of law and finance. He was " the greatest subject in England," the representative of the king in all matters, and, by virtue of his office, lieutenant, viceroy, or regent of the kingdom during the king's absence. The justiciar was, as we have seen, a new officer appointed by the Conqueror, not only to carry on the government during his frequent absence from England, but at all times to relieve him from the pressure of the vast amount of business which the government of that newly-acquired dominion involved. The justiciar, in short, stood to the king in the whole kingdom in the same relation as the sheriff did in each shire.[9] The dignity of the justiciar's office remained unimpaired until the death of King John, when Hubert de Burgh, the justiciar, being besieged in Dover Castle, the barons who proclaimed Henry III constituted the Earl of Pembroke " *Rector regis et regni*," de Burgh still retaining his office.[10] In 1241 the Archbishop of York was appointed regent during Henry's absence in Poitou, without the title of justiciar. But the office was still considered of such importance that in 1258, in the Provisions of Oxford, the barons demanded that the justiciar should be annually chosen with their approbation. At length Edward I dispensed with the office altogether; and the chancellor, who now entered into many of the rights and dignities formerly enjoyed by the justiciar, became the principal minister.

---

absence of William the Conqueror, held pleas in person in the County Court (Domesday; Heming, *Cartulary*, p. 512 " coram Regina Matilda in praesentia iv vice-comitum "). The " good Queen Maud," wife of Henry I, was present at a trial in the Exchequer between the men of Periton and the Abbot of Abingdon (*Chronicon Monasterii de Abingdon*, ii, 116 [Rolls Ser.]; Bigelow's *Placita Anglo-Normannica*, 99). Henry III's queen also held pleas in person (Spence, *Equitable Jurisdiction*, 101, n.).

[6] Stow, *Chronicon*, 41 (1631). Foss, *Judges*, iv, 215.

[7] Coke, 4th *Inst.*, 73.

[8] Blackstone, iii, 41.

[9] *Supra*, pp. 51, 71. The fullest discussion is in Sayles, *Cases in King's Bench* (Selden Society), I, xxvi *et seq. Cf.* Stubbs, *Select Charters*, Introduction, 17–18, and *Constitutional History*, i, 374, where the Norman seneschalship is suggested as a likely model. For the increasingly judicial character of the office, see Treharne, *Baronial Plan of Reform*, 10–14.

[10] The fall of Hubert de Burgh in 1232 marks the end of the office of great justiciar. *Cf.* Stubbs, *Constitutional History*, ii, 280, " the office of great justiciar, after the fall of Hubert de Burgh, lost its importance, and may be said to have become practically extinct."

The chancellor. The title of chancellor was introduced into England under Edward the Confessor,[11] as the designation of the official keeper of the royal seal and chief of the king's chaplains. With the chancellor at their head, the king's chaplains, like the "clerks of the palace" of the Frankish monarchs, formed a select body of scribes or secretaries, who, under the justiciar, drew up and sealed the royal writs, conducted the king's correspondence, and assisted the treasurer in keeping the royal accounts.[12] Under the Norman kings the office of chancellor, though dignified and important, was thrown into the shade by the justiciarship. From the time of Becket, however, the chancellorship appears to have steadily advanced in dignity until, on the abolition of the office of justiciar, it attained, as we have seen, the foremost rank.

The Curia Regis. The term *Curia Regis*, in its widest signification, seems to have denoted the national or great council of the realm—the witenagemot in its feudalised form—at the threefold sessions of which the bishops and earls and all tenants-in-chief had the duty of attending. There was however from the first a small *curia* composed of a select body of officials who met at more frequent intervals to deal with the regular business of government. It was the same institution differing from the larger body only in size and manner of meeting.[13] In addition to its political function of giving "counsel and consent" to legislative changes and other acts of national importance, the Curia, in its judicial aspect, was invested with the old appellate jurisdiction of the witenagemot, and with a direct jurisdiction, as the feudal court of the king's vassals, in all disputes between the tenants *in capite*. It possessed originally all those different powers which were subsequently distributed among the three courts of the King's Bench, the Common Pleas, and the Exchequer. In the *Curia Regis* were discussed and tried all pleas immediately concerning the king and the realm; it superintended the assessment and collection of the royal revenue; decided all appeals; and to it suitors were allowed, on payment of a fine, to remove their plaints from the older but inferior courts of the shire and hundred.[14]

THE EXCHEQUER AND FINANCE

The administration of the justiciar was first systematically organised under Henry I, by Roger, Bishop of Salisbury, the founder of a family

---

[11] T. F. Tout, *Administrative History*, i, 127 *et seq.*; new doubts have been raised by F. E. Harmer, *Bulletin of John Rylands Library*, xxii, 339. On the nature of the problem whether there existed an Anglo-Saxon chancery, see R. C. van Caenegem, *Royal Writs in England* (Selden Soc.), 135 *et seq.*

[12] Palgrave, *English Commonwealth*, i, 177. The name is derived probably from the *cancelli* or screen behind which the secretarial work of the royal household was carried on: Stubbs, *Constitutional History*, i, 380–381.

[13] See Adams, *Origin of the English Constitution*, p. 375. Tout, *Administrative History*, i, 10, gives a warning that the household element is as prominent as the feudal element in the history of the *Curia Regis*.

[14] See Adams, *op. cit.*, 57 *et seq.*, 373 *et seq.*; Holdsworth, *History of English Law*, i, 32 *et seq.*

of officials.   From the reign of that king, at the latest, a committee or branch of the *Curia Regis* was specially devoted to fiscal matters, and when so employed, sat in the chamber and was known by the name of the Exchequer (*Curia Regis ad Scaccarium*).[15]   Twice in each year, at Easter and Michaelmas, every sheriff was bound to appear at the Exchequer in the Palace of Westminster and account for the sums due from his shire.

Sources of revenue.   These were mainly of two kinds: (1) The ancient national payments (which required no new authorisation), consisting of (a) the *ferm of the shire*, that is the royal rents and dues of the county formerly paid in kind, now commuted for fixed sums; (b) *danegeld*, a tax of two shillings on every hide of land, originally imposed under Ethelred II, to raise a tribute exacted by the Danes, and by the Norman kings turned into a permanent contribution for the public defence[16]; (c) the *fines* of local courts—the old English *wite* payable to the king. (2) The new *feudal aids*, *reliefs*, and other payments, for which also no authorisation was required except when some extraordinary gift was demanded.   In addition to these sources of revenue the demesne lands of the king and the towns were liable to tallage, which was arbitrarily exacted without the consent of parliament, until the right was surrendered by Edward III.[17]   No inconsiderable income was also received by the Exchequer from the fines and other proceeds of the " *pleas of the crown*," from the amercements payable in respect of a large class of small offences of commission or omission, and from the fines paid to the king by the parties to suits at law, either by the plaintiff to obtain speedy judgment, or by the defendant in order to delay or put an end to further proceedings.

Taxation.   Henry II introduced important changes in taxation.   All classes of the people and all kinds of property were brought under contribution.   Scutage, a tax imposed upon the tenants in chivalry, clerical as well as lay, and rated, not upon the ancient basis of the hide, but upon the knight's fee, although traceable to the reign of Henry I, was largely extended by Henry II.[18]   Danegeld after 1162 was allowed to drop out of the fiscal system, but only to be almost immediately revived under the name of *donum* or hidage.   Under Richard I it became the " carucage," a tax levied upon all holders of land of whatever tenure.   But Henry's

---

[15] The members of the Curia were all termed justices, their head being the *capitalis justiciarus*; but in the Exchequer they were called barons, *barones scaccarii*.   The Exchequer derived its name from the " chequered cloth which covered the table at which the accounts were taken, a name which suggested to the spectator the idea of a game of chess between the receiver and the payer, the treasurer and the sheriff "—Stubbs, *Constitutional History*, i, 407. *Dialogus de Scaccario*, i, 1.   On the whole subject see Poole, *The Exchequer in the Twelfth Century*.

[16] The latest instance of its payment is in the 8th of Henry II; but Richard I practically revived it under the disguise of a " carucage," or land-tax.

[17] 14 Edw. 3, st. 2, c. 1 (1340).   Stubbs, *Constitutional History*, ii, 402.

[18] *Supra*, p. 58.   The quantity or value of land constituting a knight's fee was not uniform. The usual value requisite for a knight's fee was £20, *temp.* Edw. 1 (*Parliamentary Writs*, i, 214).

most important innovation was the taxation of income and personal property, which, as we have seen,[19] were made contributory by his ordinance of the Saladin Tithe in 1188. The practice, when once introduced, was speedily extended and permanently retained. For the ransom of Richard I in 1193, every person in the realm was called upon to pay one-fourth of revenue or goods. King John exacted, in 1203, a seventh of the movables of his barons, and in 1207 a thirteenth from the whole people.[20]

Respite of knighthood. Edward I employed an expedient for raising money analogous to the institution of scutage by Henry II. It was one of the liabilities of a tenant by knight's service to be obliged, on attaining full age, to receive the order of knighthood and to provide himself with the arms and equipment appropriate to that dignity. Henry III, in 1224, had directed the sheriffs to enforce this obligation against all lay holders of a knight's fee[21]; an order which was repeated in 1234 as to tenants *in capite* only.[22] In 1278, Edward I, being pressed for funds, issued stringent orders to the sheriffs to compel all persons, as well tenants of mesne lords as tenants-in-chief, who held land to the value of £20 a year, or one whole knight's fee of the same annual value, and who ought to be knights, to take up their knighthood.[23] Those who preferred to pay a fine *pro respectu militiae* were excused. The distraint of knighthood was not merely a method of raising money; it was also intended to effect the military object of augmenting the knightly body from competent freeholders, and to replenish the class of knights whose presence was necessary for a number of legal purposes, especially on juries and assizes and in numerous administrative duties.[24] But the early abuse of this prerogative is shown by the institution in 1274 of an inquiry into the misconduct of the sheriffs and others in reference to the compulsory knighthood,[25] and by the remedial measure (sometimes called a " statute ") *De militibus* ascribed to the first year of Edward II. It prescribed that tenants whose lands did not exceed the value of £20 a year, or who were under age, or in holy orders, or whose lands were held by socage or burgage tenure, should not be compelled to receive knighthood; and that

[19] *Supra,* p. 62.
[20] In subsequent times the usual grant became a fifteenth from the county and a tenth from the borough. From 8 Edward III a " fifteenth and tenth " signified a fixed sum according to an assessment of the value made in that year, 1334. The sum amounted to between £38,000 and £39,000. See Dowell, *History of Taxation,* i, 96–97. Ramsay, *Revenues of the Kings of England,* ii, 285, reckons the amount of a tenth and fifteenth at a slightly lower figure—between £36,000 and £38,000. The working of the system is fully described in J. F. Willard, *Parliamentary Taxes on Personal Property, 1290–1334.* Like the " fifteenth," the " subsidy " of the sixteenth century, a property tax of 4s. in the pound for land and 2s. in the pound for goods, also became a fixed amount; one " subsidy " = £80,000.
[21] *Rotuli Litterarum Clausarum,* ii, 69.
[22] *Royal Letters* [Hen. III], ed. Shirley (Rolls Series), i, 456.
[23] *Parliamentary Writs,* i, 214. *Select Charters,* 448.
[24] A. L. Poole, *Obligations of Society,* 53 *et seq. Cf.* the requirement that a jury in replevin should contain six knights girt with swords: *De Banco* roll 40/189, m. 335d (at foot); 1311.
[25] Rymer (Record Commission), i, 517.

other persons, if of great age, afflicted with bodily injury or incurable disease, or burdened by the charge of children or by suits, should be excused on payment of a " reasonable " fine.[26] This mode of raising money without the consent of parliament was vexatiously employed in later times by Edward VI, Elizabeth and Charles I. It was abolished, with the other incidents of feudal tenure, by the Act of Charles II.[27]

Indirect taxation. Besides the various forms of direct taxation under the Norman and early Angevin kings, the prisage of imported wines and the customs duties on certain other imports and exports (based upon the ancient right of levying toll, which in some places was exercised even by the lords of manors), formed the nucleus of a system of indirect taxation which gradually grew up with the expansion of commerce and the increasing pecuniary necessities of the crown. The early abuse of the king's claim to customs is shown by the provision in Magna Carta (c. 41), that merchants may buy and sell *sine omnibus malis toltis, per antiquas et rectas consuetudines*. The constitutional aspect of the later struggles between the king and the parliament on the subject of indirect taxation will be discussed hereafter.

Judicial System

Down to the reign of Henry II the *Curia Regis* still continued as the one supreme court, of which some of the judges, selected from time to time out of the whole body, and varying in number and combination, held a practically continuous session at the Exchequer for all financial business. Under Henry II—more especially during the decade beginning with the Assize of Clarendon in 1166 and ending with the Assize of Northampton in 1176—the great increase in the business of the Curia, both in its central sessions and on its fiscal and judicial circuits, caused the staff of judges to be gradually augmented to eighteen. But in the year 1178, the king, finding this number too great, reduced the judges in the Curia from eighteen to five (two clerics and three laymen); and at the same time deprived the court of its character of a court of final appeal, by reserving to his own hearing in council causes in which the Curia should fail to do justice.[28] It was not the king's intention to create a new court; but clearly his frequent resort to " temporary " expedients of this kind (and several such are known) had the final result that there sprang up the court of Common Pleas (*i.e.*, principally for civil suits between private individuals).[29] This court continued to follow the king's person; but the

---

[26] *Statutes of the Realm*, i, 229. The date is *circa* 1278: H. G. Richardson in *Law Quarterly Review*, l, 221, n. 17 (and his *Early Statutes*, 51, n. 17). On the financial limits of distraint of knighthood, see N. Denholm-Young, *Collected Papers*, 64.

[27] 12 Car. 2, c. 24 (1660).

[28] Benedictus Abbas, i, 207. *Select Charters*, 155.

[29] Pike, *History of the House of Lords*, 31 *et seq.*; Adams, *Origin of the English Constitution*, 136 *et seq.* Some reservations on points of detail have been suggested by Sayles, *Select Cases in King's Bench* (Selden Soc.), i, pp. xx *et seq.*; iv, pp. xxvii *et seq.*

practice being found productive of great inconvenience to both suitors and witnesses, it was provided by Magna Carta that common pleas should be held in some certain place, and the court became fixed at Westminster.[30]

Division of the Curia. By the end of the reign of Henry III the *Curia Regis* in its judicial aspect was permanently divided into three institutions or courts, each taking a certain portion of the business: (1) Fiscal matters were confined to the Exchequer; (2) civil disputes, where no matter savouring of a criminal nature or the suit of the crown was involved, were decided in the Common Pleas; and (3) the court of King's Bench, at first actually and later theoretically a court held before the king himself, *coram rege*, retained all the remaining business together with the very important jurisdiction of correcting the errors of the court of Common Pleas.[31] Some trace of their ancient unity of organisation always survived, however, in the assembly of all the judges in the Exchequer Chamber[32]; until at length after six centuries of independent existence they were again united by the Judicature Act.[33]

Together with the Court of Chancery and the Probate, Divorce, and Admiralty courts, they now form divisions of a consolidated High Court of Justice, itself a branch of the Supreme Court of Judicature.[34]

---

[30] Magna Carta, c. 17, *supra*, p. 73.

[31] The process of separation was slow and indistinct. The court *coram rege* long remained almost undistinguishable from the council during the minority of Henry III. See Baldwin, *King's Council*, Chap. iii; Holdsworth, *History of English Law*, i, 194–212; Maitland, *Constitutional History*, 133–135. For the jurisdiction of the King's Bench, see Holdsworth, *op cit.*, 212. The later history of these courts belongs to legal rather than constitutional history.

[32] Four distinct bodies were all called courts of Exchequer Chamber down to the passing of the Judicature Act, 1873:

(1) A court of mere debate, into which causes of great weight and difficulty might be adjourned, before judgment was given upon them in the court below (as was done in *Calvin's Case*, 2 St.Tr. 559). The court was then composed of all the judges of the three superior courts, and sometimes the Lord Chancellor also. This assembly did not become prominent until the fifteenth century. See Hemmant, *Exchequer Chamber* (Selden Society).

(2) A Court of Error created by statute 31 Edw. 3, st. 1, c. 12 (1357) to determine errors from the common law side of the Court of Exchequer. Composed of the Lord Chancellor, and Lord Treasurer, with the Justices of the King's Bench and Common Pleas as assistants.

(3) A further Court of Exchequer Chamber erected by statute 27 Eliz. 1, c. 8 (1585), to determine writs of error from the King's Bench. Composed of the Justices of the Common Pleas and the Barons of the Exchequer.

Both (2) and (3) were abolished, and

(4) the court was reconstituted by 11 Geo. 4 & 1 Will. 4, c. 70 (1830), s. 8. Judgments of each of the superior courts of Common Law (upon proceedings in error in law being instituted) were subject to revision by the judges of the other two courts sitting collectively as a Court of Error in the Exchequer Chamber.

By the Supreme Court of Judicature Act, 1873, the jurisdiction of the Court of Exchequer Chamber was merged in that of the new Court of Appeal. *Cf.* Holdsworth, *History of English Law*, i, 242–246.

[33] 36 & 37 Vict. c. 66.

[34] The Queen's Bench Division, the Common Pleas Division and the Exchequer Division, were by Order in Council of December 16, 1880, amalgamated into the Queen's Bench Division of the High Court of Justice. The President is the Lord Chief Justice of England, and the powers of the former Chief Justice of the Common Pleas and of the Chief Baron

Itinerant justices. The system of itinerant justices, or justices in eyre (*in itinere*), was not invented by Henry II, but its establishment as an organised and permanent institution in this country is due to him. As early as the reign of Henry I, some of the justices of the *Curia Regis* were occasionally appointed by the king to go from county to county to collect the revenue and hold pleas, civil and criminal.[35] Their chief duty, originally, was to collect the revenue, determine disputes as to the amounts payable, and detect and punish frauds on the part of the sheriffs and other fiscal officers. But they also supplied the place both of the old English royal progresses during which the kings had been wont to hear and determine complaints of failure of justice in the lower tribunals, and also of the courts which the Conqueror and his two sons held by custom at Gloucester, Winchester and Westminster, on the three great festivals of the year. Even during the anarchy of Stephen's reign the provincial visitation never quite ceased[36]; Henry II restored the practice. The instructions contained in the Assize of Clarendon in 1166 are evidently intended for the guidance of a body of itinerant justices who were about to visit each county, and in conjunction with the sheriffs, try all offenders accused by the jury of presentment.[37]

Regular circuits formed. In 1176, at the great council of Northampton, Henry divided the kingdom for fiscal and judicial purposes into six circuits, to each of which three itinerant judges were assigned.[38] The justices in eyre came to act as the king's agents for squeezing money out of the people and they were therefore intensely unpopular. In the reign of Henry III it became the practice for the justices to make the eyre only once in seven years, and it was finally given up at the end of the fourteenth century.[39]

From their first institution the itinerant justices were accustomed on circuit to sit in the full county court, which was summoned to meet them. Their provincial visitations thus form " the link between the *Curia Regis* and the shiremoot, between royal and popular justice, between the old system and the new."[40] This direct connection between the court of the king and the court of the shire had most important constitutional effects, hereafter to be noticed, on the growth of the national representative

of the Exchequer (these two offices being abolished by the Order) are vested in him. The High Court of Justice now comprises three divisions:

    (1) The Queen's Bench Division (with which is incorporated the former Court of Bankruptcy) consisting of the Lord Chief Justice of England as president, and seventeen other judges;

    (2) The Chancery Division consisting of the Lord Chancellor as president and six other judges;

    (3) The Probate, Divorce and Admiralty Division consisting of the president and one other judge.

[35] Hardy, *Introduction to Close Rolls*, p. xxiv, n. 3.
[36] Madox, *Exchequer*, i, 146, quoted by Holdsworth, *History of English Law*, i, 49.
[37] *Select Charters*, 167–173.
[38] Benedict Abbas, i, 107; *Dialogus de Scaccario*, ii, c. 2; *Select Charters*, 154 and 228.
[39] Holdsworth, i, 272.
[40] Stubbs, *Constitutional History*, i, 648.

assembly; and to the same cause is mainly due both the uniformity of our common law, and the repression within due limits of the local feudal jurisdictions.[41]

Assize and Nisi Prius. From the time of Henry II justices were sent into the counties to take assizes of mort d'ancestor, novel disseisin, and darrein presentment. By Magna Carta (c. 18) two justices were to be sent four times a year, but in the second re-issue of the Charter by Henry III, in 1217, this was altered (c. 13) to one annual visitation.

By the Statute of Westminster II, 13 Edw. 1, c. 30 (1285), judges of assize and *nisi prius* were ordered to be assigned out of the king's sworn justices, associating to themselves two discreet knights of each county, to try matters of fact at the courts of assize and *nisi prius*.[42] These justices of assize superseded the old justices in eyre, and have continued to the present day.[43]

EARLY HISTORY OF THE JURY

To Henry II must also be ascribed, in addition to his other legal reforms, the wide expansion and regular establishment of the system of recognition by sworn inquest, that is, the finding of facts by the oath of a body of impartial witnesses, who represent the testimony of the local community, and are summoned and examined by an official acting under the king's writ. From this institution our modern trial by jury is lineally descended.

The origin of this " most democratical of juridical institutions," the cherished bulwark of constitutional liberty, has been the subject of much learned discussion, and of numerous conflicting theories. Some eminent writers, including the learned author of the *History of Trial by Jury*,[44] have stoutly maintained that the English jury is of indigenous growth, and was not derived, directly or indirectly, from any of the tribunals that existed on the Continent. By others the Anglo-Saxon compurgators (or

---

[41] The shire court summoned to meet the itinerant judges was a much more complete representation of the county than the ordinary county court. A writ of Henry III, issued in 1231, directs the summons to the county court to be addressed to " archbishops, bishops, abbots, priors, earls, barons, knights, and freeholders; four men of each township, and twelve burghers of each borough, to meet the justices "—Stubbs, *Constitutional History*, i, p. 651, and n. 2, *ibid.*; *Select Charters*, 354. *The Eyre of Kent in 1313–1314* (3 vols., Selden Soc.), gives a vivid picture of the later eyre. Earlier ones will be found in the Society's vols. 53, 56 and 59. Two errors which must be avoided are (1) the view that the eyre was equal or superior to the King's Bench, and (2) the view that the eyre exercised equitable jurisdiction.

[42] The sheriff was instructed to summon jurors to Westminster unless before that day (*nisi prius*) justices should come into the county. This gave the justices of assize jurisdiction over civil cases begun in the courts of Common Pleas or King's Bench. See Holdsworth, i, 278; Maitland, *Constitutional History*, 139. The fullest discussion of *nisi prius* origins is in the introductions by G. J. Turner to the Selden Society's *Year Book Series*, vols. iv and ix.

[43] Provincial justice has always been administered under a variety of distinct authorisations, corresponding to the several commissions of the judges. Blackstone (iii, 60) describes the judges of assize as sitting under five commissions : (1) of the peace ; (2) of oyer and terminer ; (3) of gaol delivery ; (4) of assize ; (5) of *nisi prius*.

[44] Forsyth, *History of Trial by Jury* (1852), p. 13.

sworn witnesses to credibility), the sworn witnesses to facts, the *friborh*, the twelve senior thegns of Ethelred's law who were sworn to accuse none falsely, the system of trial in local courts by the whole body of the shire or hundred, have all been regarded as containing, severally or in combination, the germ of the modern jury.[45] Yet, with the exception of what may be termed Ethelred's jury of presentment (which will be considered in connection with the grand jury of later times), not one of these supposed origins will be found, on careful examination, to possess much more than a superficial analogy to the inquest by sworn recognitors, the historic progenitor of the existing jury.

Brunner's theory of Norman origins. The theory which presents the fewest *a priori* difficulties, and which is supported by arguments and evidence only falling short of actual demonstration, regards the English system of sworn inquests as an importation from Normandy. There, both before and after the cession of the Neustrian province to Rollo, by Charles the Simple in 911, it had existed, as in the rest of France, from its establishment under the Carolingian kings, whose capitularies contain minute instructions for inquisitions by sworn witnesses in the local courts.[46] But whatever may be the remote source of this institution out of which trial by jury grew, and whether we regard it as a modification of the old English judicial system, or as an inheritance derived through the Normans from the Carolingian kings, two points would necessarily follow: (1) That the system of inquest by sworn recognitors, even in its rudest and simplest form, should appear for the first time in England subsequently to and shortly after the Norman Conquest, and (2) That this system was in England, from the first, worked in close combination with the previously existing procedure of the shiremoot.[47]

Some recent criticisms. Of those two propositions there has been some further and more detailed study, especially since 1952 when the surviving Anglo-Saxon writs were collected and elaborately edited,[48] and since

---

[45] For a revival of this point of view, see Ernst Mayer, *Geschworenengericht* (1916).

[46] See Palgrave, *English Commonwealth* (1832), i, Chap. 8; Brunner, *Entstehung der Schwurgerichte* (1872), who traces the inquest by jury, both Norman and English, from the Carolingian *Inquisitiones*; and Stubbs, who, adopting in the main the theory of Palgrave corrected and adjusted by the later work of Brunner, says: " The truth seems to be that the inquest by sworn recognitors is directly derived from the Frank Capitularies, into which it may have been adopted from the fiscal regulations of the Theodosian Code, and thus own some distant relationship with the Roman jurisprudence. . . . The continuance of the system in France from the Karolingian times and through the Norman period is proved by Dr. Brunner. . . . The most curious phenomenon in connexion with it is the fact that it was only on English soil that it gained much development, the Norman lawyers seeing themselves rapidly outstripped by those of England, and the institution withering away in the rest of France until it became extinct." *Constitutional History*, i, 656, 657, n. 2. *Cf.* also Pollock and Maitland, i, 140 *et seq.*; Haskins, *Norman Institutions*, Chap. 6.

[47] See the celebrated trials in the reign of William the Conqueror between Lanfranc, Archbishop of Canterbury, and Odo, Bishop of Bayeux, on Pennenden Heath (Bigelow, *Placita Anglo-Normannica*, 5); and between Gundulf, Bishop of Rochester, and Picot, Sheriff of Cambridgeshire (*ibid.*, 34).

[48] F. E. Harmer, *Anglo-Saxon Writs*.

1958, when the writs from the conquest to Glanvill were also collected and studied afresh with special reference to the problem of the origins of the jury.[49] In consequence, it would now appear that the pre-Conquest inquisition certainly is to be found in England before the Conquest, although its use was not compulsory and the selection of the recognitors was for the parties to agree between themselves, and the crown did not choose them or summon them. As Dr. van Caenegem remarks: " We have here [in a case under Edward the Confessor] the free popular recognition as we shall find it in later generations; a procedure distinct altogether from the royal inquest, without any order from above and without any administrative or fiscal intention or any impannelling by an official." There are numerous examples of similar procedure being used after the Conquest and before the crucial assizes of Henry II. We are thus confronted with an impressive and well-documented case for the use of the recognition before the great assizes of the twelfth century.

Nevertheless, we need not abandon completely the remarkable researches of Brunner, and their valuable continuation by Haskins. The crown, with its Norman heritage, rich with Carolingian memories, had much to contribute to practices which seem to have come principally, and ultimately, from popular Anglo-Saxon, rather than from royal (indeed, imperial) and Norman sources. The one thing needful, here as in other departments of the law, was royal initiative, and firm enforcement. The abundant good will which had alone made this part of Anglo-Saxon law workable may well excite our wonder, but it was the assizes of Henry II which made recognitions compulsory in certain cases, and (except for the grand assize), made the sheriff, and not the parties, the choosers of the jury[50]; and it was the centralised royal judicial machinery which he created which undertook to enforce the recognitions which the assizes made, and the judges pronounced.

Growth of the civil jury. It was only gradually, however, that the advantages of the principle of recognition by jury in its application to judicial procedure became impressed upon the minds of both rulers and ruled. At first the sworn inquest seems to have been chiefly applied to matters not judicial, such as the domesday survey,[51] the assessment of feudal taxation under William Rufus and Henry I, and the customs of the church of York, which the latter monarch, in 1106, directed five commissioners to verify by the oath of twelve of the citizens.[52] There are, however, equally early instances of strictly legal matters being decided by the recognition on oath of a certain number of *probi et legales homines,* selected from the men of the county to represent the neighbourhood and testify to facts of which they had special knowledge. In a suit

[49] R. C. van Caenegem, *Royal Writs in England from the Conquest to Glanvill* (Selden Soc.).
[50] The rule was that four knights should be chosen in the county court, and that those four should choose the members of the grand assize.
[51] *Supra,* p. 34.
[52] Thoroton, *Nottinghamshire,* iii, 77.

as to certain lands of the church of Ely, the Conqueror directed his justiciars to assemble the shiremoots of the shires in which the possessions of the abbey of Ely lay, and ascertain the truth by the oath of a number of English to be chosen for their knowledge of the state of lands in the time of King Edward.[53] A like proceeding is directed with reference to the rights of the monks of Ramsey in an extant writ of William Rufus directed to the sheriff of Northamptonshire.[54] One of the most marked of these early instances of the *probi vicini* being summoned as a jury for judicial purposes occurs in the reign of Henry I. A writ was addressed in the name of William the Atheling to the sheriff of Kent, requiring him to summon " Hamo the son of Vital, and the *probi vicini* of Sandwich whom Hamo has named, to say the truth " respecting the freedom from toll of a vessel belonging to the abbot of St. Augustine's, which seems to have been seized for non-payment of dues. By a subsequent writ the sheriff was directed to restore the vessel to the abbot, according to the verdict or recognition of the good men of the county (*sicut recognitum fuit per probos homines comitatus*).[55] Henry II applied recognition by jury to every description of business, fiscal and legal, and henceforth down to the reign of Edward I it was, in particular, the most usual machinery employed for the assessment of taxation.[56]

Henry II's assizes. The use of a jury, whether for criminal presentment or civil inquest, is mentioned for the first time in our statute law in the Constitutions of Clarendon (1164). The way in which the jury is therein referred to seems to imply that it had already grown into general use and favour. When no one could be found to accuse a powerful layman amenable to the bishop's jurisdiction, the sheriffs, at the bishop's request, were directed (by cap. 6) to " swear twelve lawful men of the neighbourhood to tell the truth, according to their conscience," and the same Constitutions, cap. 9, declared that " by the recognition of twelve lawful men," the chief justice should decide all disputes as to the lay or clerical tenure of land.[57]

It was in the *Grand Assize*,[58] probably enacted at a council held at

[53] *Liber Eliensis*, ed. D. J. Stewart (Anglia Christiana Society, 1848), 256. Bigelow, *Placita Anglo-Normannica*, 24.

[54] Palgrave, *English Commonwealth* (Proofs), clxxix.

[55] Elmham, *Historia Monasterii S. Augustini*, ed. Hardwick (Rolls Series), pp. 353–354; Palgrave, *loc. cit.*; Forsyth, *Trial by Jury*, 104.

[56] The variations in the mode of assessing taxation during this period and the increasing use of the jury for that purpose, are traced by Stubbs, *Select Charters*, pp. 184, 189, 249, 254, 348, 351, 356, 358. By the Great Charter of John, c. 20, amercements were only to be imposed " per sacramentum proborum hominum de visneto."

[57] Cap. 6 raises obscure questions of the use of " synodal " juries by the Church; see p. 76 at note 44, *supra*. Cap. 9 establishes the assize *Utrum*, as to which see Thorne in *Columbia Law Review*, xxxiii, 428.

[58] Assisa seems to mean in the first instance a sitting, a session for example of the king and his barons; then the name is transferred to an ordinance made at such a session (we have the Assize of Clarendon, the Assize of Northampton, etc.); then again it is transferred to any institution which is created by such an ordinance (*e.g.*, certain forms of action, and, finally, the juries which tried the issues in them). Maitland, *Constitutional History*, 12.

Windsor in 1179,[59] that the principle of recognition by jury, having gradually grown into familiar use in various civil matters, was applied by Henry II, as a regular part of normal procedure, to the decision of actions to try the right to land. It is described by Glanvill as a royal boon conferred on the people, with the counsel and consent of the *proceres*, to relieve freeholders from the hardship of defending the title of their lands by the doubtful issue of trial by battle.[60] By the Grand Assize the defendant was allowed his choice between wager of battle and the recognition of a jury of twelve sworn knights of the vicinage chosen by four other knights who had been summoned for that purpose by the sheriff.

In actions not seeking to determine the absolute right to land, but dealing with recent changes of seisin only (of which the *assize of novel disseisin* was the most important), the sheriff himself chose twelve knights or freeholders (*legales homines*) of the vicinage, who were sworn to try the question. In both cases the recognitors were sworn to found their verdict upon their own knowledge, gained either by eye-witness or by the words of their fathers, or by such words as they are bound to have as much confidence in as if they were their own.[61] If all were ignorant of the facts, a fresh jury had to be summoned; if some of them only were ignorant, or if they could not agree, others were to be added—a process subsequently called " afforcing " the jury—until a unanimous verdict could be obtained from the jury, or assize, of twelve lawful men.[62]

The remedy by assize was subsequently improved by several Acts of Parliament, particularly 13 Edw. 1, c. 25; and as all actions on the assize were tried in the King's Court or in that of the justices itinerant, the jurisdiction of the feudal, county and hundred courts began, from this period, rapidly to decline.

THE JURY AND CRIME

The twelve senior thegns. As regards criminal trials, we do indeed meet in the ordinance of King Ethelred II (978–1016) with a species of jury of accusation clearly analogous to our grand jury, and possibly its direct progenitor. In the gemot of every wapentake the twelve senior thegns, with the reeve, were directed to go apart and accuse, or, as we should say, present, on oath, all whom they should believe to have committed any crime.[63] The twelve thegns seem to have performed the

---

[59] Round, *Athenaeum*, Jan. 28, 1899, *English Historical Review*, xxxi, 268; Davis, *England under Normans and Angevins*, 280.

[60] Lib. ii, c. 7; *Select Charters*, 190–191.

[61] *Ibid.*, c. 17.

[62] Lib. ii, c. 17; Bracton, f. 185 b. An example of the whole jury being ignorant of the facts, and of the summons of a fresh one in consequence, occurs in *Placitorum Abbreviatio*, 11. For the various " petty assizes " see Maitland, *Forms of Action*.

[63] " And that a gemot be held in every wapentake; and the xii senior thegns go out, and the reeve with them, and swear on the relic which is given them in hand, that they will accuse no innocent man, nor conceal any guilty one." III Aethelred 3 (1), Robertson, *Laws*, 65; *Select Charters*, 84–85.

part of public prosecutors; but the fact of the guilt or innocence of the accused person had still to be determined by compurgation, or the ordeal. This primitive grand jury, it has been conjectured, probably continued in use after the conquest, until its reconstitution by Henry II, and thus the criminal jury, although, doubtless, largely influenced in its later development by the co-existence of the inquest by jury in civil matters, possesses strong claims to a purely indigenous origin.[64]

The grand jury. By the Assize of Clarendon (1166) the principle of recognition by jury was extended to criminal cases. It was ordained that in every county twelve lawful men of each hundred, with four lawful men from each township, should be sworn to present all reputed criminals of their district in each county court. The persons so presented were to be at once seized and sent to the water ordeal.[65] This was perhaps a reconstitution or revival, in an expanded form, of the old English institution analogous to a grand jury, which, as we have seen, had existed in the time of King Ethelred II

By the Chapters of the Eyre issued under Richard I in 1194, as instructions to the itinerant justices, the election and constitution of the jury of presentment established by Henry II was further regulated and assimilated to the system already in use for nominating the recognitors of the Grand Assize.[66] From this developed jury of presentment the later grand jury has historically descended.[67]

---

[64] Vinogradoff considered that the admitted Frankish-Norman origin of the jury inquisition " does not preclude that in preconquestual England itself there had existed legal customs which prepared the way for the indictment jury of the twelfth century. The leading men of the wapentake, to judge by the Wantage enactment, were called up to point out persons who had to be accused of crimes. . . . Nor is the remarkable coincidence with the twelve lawful men of the Clarendon Assize, on the one hand, with the twelve *lagmen* of the Danish boroughs, likely to be fortuitous ": *English Society in the Eleventh Century*, p. 7. For a recent attempt to give proofs for the propositions which Mr. Taswell-Langmead put forward as conjectures in the above paragraph, see N. D. Hurnard in *English Historical Review*, lvi, 374–410 (1941). For the twelve *lagmen* of the Danish boroughs in Domesday, see the *Customs of Lincoln, Select Charters*, 105. The Pipe Roll of 31 Hen. I contains references to the *judices* and *juratores* of the shire and hundred courts.

[65] Assize of Clarendon, c. 1, *Select Charters*, 170. Even those who successfully passed through the ordeal, if they were shown to be of evil character by the testimony of the neighbourhood, were to abjure the kingdom within eight days : c. 14.

[66] Hoveden, iii, 262; *Select Charters*, 252.

[67] Under the modern grand jury system twenty-four freeholders of the county were summoned by the sheriff. Of these, a certain number, varying from twelve to twenty-three, were sworn, and having been previously instructed in the articles of enquiry by a " charge " from the judge, withdrew to examine indictments and hear privately the evidence for the prosecution only. If twelve of them were satisfied of the truth of the accusation, the grand jury found " a true bill," and the prisoner was then put on his trial in open court before a judge and twelve petty jurymen. If not satisfied, the grand jury found " no true bill." This is termed " ignoring " the bill, from the word " ignoramus," which was formerly indorsed on it. A famous historic case of " ignoramus " occurred on the trial of Lord Shaftesbury for high treason in 1681, when the grand jury of London ignored the bill.— *State Trials*, viii, 759. A more recent case, arising out of the Jamaica rebellion, was the ignoring the indictment for murder against Governor Eyre. Any person could present a bill to a grand jury accusing any other person of any crime whatever. This is the general rule to which, as yet, hardly any exception has been made. Thus anyone may prefer a bill against any one of the king's ministers.—Maitland, *Constitutional History*, p. 475. Grand juries were abolished, for most purposes, by the Administration of Justice Act, 1933.

The establishment of this system of presentment and ordeal had the effect of supplanting, in all criminal cases, the ancient practice of compurgation by the oath of friends, " the manifest fountain of unblushing perjury." [68]

The petty or trial jury. In the year 1215, the ordeal was in effect abolished throughout Christendom by the fourth Lateran Council, since the church forbade clergy to take part, and there remained only, for criminal trials the combat, in which the participation of the clergy was not required. But the combat (or " trial by battle ") was not applicable unless an injured prosecutor or " appellant " came forward to demand it; and the practice (which had been introduced even before the abolition of ordeal) gradually grew up of allowing a second, or petty, jury to affirm or traverse the testimony of the first set of inquest-men. This became the general usage in the reign of Henry III. Still for a long time no prisoner was compelled to plead, that is, he might refuse to be tried by the jury; but in this case he was remanded to prison, and from the date of the Statute of Westminster I, c. 12 (3 Edward I, 1275) was liable to strict imprisonment, which later practice transformed into the barbarous punishment called *peine forte et dure*, which was only abolished so late as the reign of George III.[69]

It is important to bear in mind that in trial by jury as permanently established, both in civil and criminal cases, by Henry II and his successors, the function of the jury long continued very different from that of the modern tribunal. The jurymen were still mere recognitors, deciding simply on their own knowledge or from the belief of the countryside, and not upon evidence produced before them, and their position is best understood as being substitutes for the old ordeals. It was for this reason that they were always selected from the hundred or vicinage in which the question arose.[70]

The jury as judge of facts. The later development, common to the civil and criminal jury alike, by which the jurors gradually changed from recognitors into judges of fact, the proof of which rested exclusively on the evidence of others, has now to be considered. The number of the recognitors was at first undefined, but when Glanvill wrote, under Henry II, twelve appears to have been the usual, though not the invariable, number

[68] In boroughs, compurgation was retained some time longer. Wager of law was abolished in 1833, by 3 & 4 Will. 4, c. 42, s. 13.

[69] 12 Geo. 3, c. 20. For an account of the *peine forte et dure*, see Palgrave, *English Commonwealth* (Proofs and Illustrations), clxxxix. For a fuller discussion of the jury in its various forms and of the ordeals which it replaced, see T. F. T. Plucknett, *Concise History* (5th ed.), 106–136; R. C. van Caenegem, *Royal Writs* (Selden Society), 51–81.

[70] On the development of the jury, see the works cited in the previous footnote, and J. B. Thayer, *Preliminary Treatise on Evidence*; Wells, in *Law Quarterly Review*, xxvii, 347, and xxx, 97; Stephen, *History of Criminal Law*, and Holdsworth, *History of English Law*, i, 312. On ordeals and battle see also H. C. Lea, *Superstition and Force*, and G. Neilson, *Trial by Battle*.

mentioned in the king's writs. We have seen that it was necessary that twelve jurymen should concur in their verdict, and this result, in civil cases at least, was procured by " afforcing " the jury, that is, adding other recognitors from the vicinage who were acquainted with the matter. But the difficulty of procuring a verdict of twelve caused for a time the verdict of a majority to be received. In the reign of Edward III, however, the necessity for a unanimous verdict of twelve was re-established.[71]

Under Henry III special witnesses (such as the witnesses to a deed) were sometimes summoned together with, and formed part of, the jury.

In the Year Books of 23 Edward III mention is made of witnesses being adjoined to the jury to give them their testimony, but without having any voice in the verdict. This is the first indication of the jury deciding on evidence formally produced in addition to their own knowledge, and forms the connecting link between the ancient and the modern jury.[72]

Late in the reign of Henry IV a further advance was made. All evidence was required to be given at the bar of the court, so that the judges might be enabled to exclude improper testimony.[73]

From this change flowed two important consequences: (1) From the exercise of control on the part of the judges sprang up the whole system of rules as to evidence. (2) The practice of receiving evidence openly at the bar of the court produced a great extension of the duty of an advocate. Henceforward " witnesses were examined and cross-examined in open court: the flood-gates of forensic eloquence were opened, and full scope given to the advocate to exercise his ingenuity and powers of persuasion on the jurors, to whose discretion the power of judging on matters of fact were now entrusted." [74]

In the treatise of Chief Justice Fortescue, *De Laudibus Legum Angliae*, written in or about the year 1470, we have clear evidence that the mode of procedure before juries by *viva voce* evidence was the same as at present.[75]

But juries were still for a long time entitled to rely on their own knowledge in addition to the evidence. In the first year of Queen Anne, the Court of Queen's Bench decided that if a jury gave a verdict of their own knowledge, they ought so to inform the court, that they might be sworn as witnesses. This, and a subsequent case in the reign of George I,

---

[71] Holdsworth, i, 318.

[72] 23 Ass. 11 (1349); Spence *Equitable Jurisdiction*, i, 129.

[73] Y.B. 11 Hen. IV, Mich. No. 41 (1409), a verdict was set aside because the jury, on retiring to consider their verdict, had taken with them an escrow which had *not been proved in evidence at the bar by the party, nor delivered to them by the court*. Starkie, " Trial by Jury " (*Law Review and Quarterly Journal of British and Foreign Jurisprudence*, No. iv, Aug. 1845, p. 397).

[74] Y.B. 11 Hen. IV, Mich. No. 41 (1409). For the suggestion that these developments began as early as the reign of Edward II, see the introduction by G. J. Turner to Selden Society, *Year Book Series*, ix, lxiii.

[75] Fortescue, *De Laudibus Legum Angliae* (ed. S. B. Chrimes), c. 26. Trial procedure in the days of Elizabeth is minutely described by Sir Thomas Smith, *De Republica Anglorum* (ed. Alston), 94–103.

at length put an end to all remains of the ancient functions of juries as recognitors.[76]

In the same way the ancient rule requiring jurors to be returned from the vicinage or hundred, which arose when jurymen relied upon their own knowledge, was, after various modifications, abolished in all civil actions in the reign of George II,[77] and it was directed that juries should be summoned from the body of the county.

The control of juries. While the jurymen were mere recognitors they would usually be guilty of perjury if they gave a wrong verdict. Hence, at common law, they became liable to the writ of attaint, which, in the time of Henry II, was restricted to pleas of assize only (novel disseisen, etc.), but was afterwards, by various statutes, extended to " every plea, real as well as personal." [78]

In attaint the cause was tried again by a jury of twenty-four. If the verdict of the second jury was opposed to that of the first, the original twelve jurors were arrested and imprisoned, their lands and chattels were forfeited to the king, and they became for the future infamous. At a later period other severities were added to the sentence.[79]

After the jury ceased to be recognitors, attaint gradually fell into disuse. Sir Thomas Smith, in 1583, says " attaints be very seldom put in use." [80] In 1757, Lord Mansfield said " the writ of attaint is now a mere sound in every case " [81]; but it was not legally abolished till the reign of George IV.[82]

Long before the legislative abolition of attaint, the important object which that proceeding indirectly gained—a review of the first verdict— had been otherwise secured, in practice, by the motion for a new trial.[83]

Besides the legal method of attaint, there was also another and illegal method of punishing a jury for a false verdict, frequently employed by the Tudor and Stuart sovereigns for political purposes. This was by fine and imprisonment by the court of the Star Chamber. In the first year of Queen Mary's reign, in 1554, Sir Nicholas Throckmorton was tried and acquitted by a jury on a charge of high treason in connection with Sir Thomas Wyatt's rebellion. Thereupon " the court, being dissatisfied with the verdict, committed the jury to prison." Some of the jury apologised and were liberated, the rest were fined by the court of Star Chamber and kept in prison till the fines were paid.[84]

---

[76] (1702) 1 Salk. 405; (1726) *Kitchen* v. *Manwaring*, cited in *Smith* v. *Parkhurst*, Andrew, 315; see " On the Trial by Jury," *Law Review and Quarterly Journal* (1845), ii, 370, 400 (the author, according to Spence, *Equity Jurisdiction*, i, 130, was Thomas Starkie).

[77] 4 & 5 Anne, c. 3 (1706), and 24 Geo. 2, c. 18 (1751).

[78] 34 Edw. 3, c. 7 (1360). An attaint lay in civil cases only. *Bushell's Case* (1670) 6 St.Tr. 999; Hawkins, *Pleas of the Crown*, bk. i, Chap. 72, s. 5.

[79] Broom, *Constitutional Law*, 154 [2nd ed. by G. Denman, 1885].

[80] Smith, *De Republica Anglorum* (ed. Alston, 1906), iii, Chap. 2, p. 111.

[81] *Bright* v. *Eynon* (1757) 1 Burr. 393.

[82] 6 Geo. 4, c. 50 (1825), s. 60.

[83] Holdsworth, i, 225. The practice became common in the seventeenth century.

[84] 1 St.Tr., 869.

Bushell's Case, 1670. After the abolition of the Star Chamber the crown made use of the judges to intimidate juries. At length the immunity of juries was finally established in 1670, by the celebrated decision of Chief Justice Vaughan in *Bushell's Case*.[85] Edmund Bushell was foreman of the jury who acquitted the famous William Penn and William Mead, the Quakers, on a prosecution for having preached to a large assemblage of people in Gracechurch Street, contrary to the Conventicle Act.[86] The recorder of London fined each of the jury 40 marks (£26 13s. 4d.); and Bushell, having been committed to prison for refusing to pay, sued out his writ of habeas corpus in the Court of Common Pleas. On the return being made that he had been committed for finding a verdict " against full and manifest evidence and against the direction of the court," Chief Justice Vaughan held the ground to be insufficient, and discharged the prisoner.

In his judgment in this case, Chief Justice Vaughan was led to affirm the legal right of the jury, without the direction of the judge, to find a general verdict in criminal cases, that is, to determine not only the truth of the facts, but their quality of guilt or innocence.[87] This question came up again with reference to the law of libel. In the trial of the Seven Bishops, in 1688, the jury asserted their right to decide upon the purport of the libel, but subsequently in the trial of the printers of the *North Briton* in 1764, Lord Mansfield ruled that it was the province of the court alone to judge of the criminality of a libel, a doctrine wholly subversive of the rights of juries. This doctrine, after being both assailed and maintained for a long time, was at length reversed, in opposition to all the judges and chief legal authorities of the time, by the passing, in 1792, of Fox's Libel Act,[88] which, in the form of a declaratory law, enacted that the jury may give a general verdict of guilty or not guilty upon the whole matter put in issue.[89]

THE COUNCIL AND ITS OFFSHOOTS

After the old *Curia Regis* had been permanently split up into the three separate courts of King's Bench, Common Pleas, and Exchequer, each under its own chief, the ancient personal jurisdiction of the king still continued to be exercised by him in his Council (the source of the later Privy Council),[90] not only as an upper court of appeal, but as a direct

---

[85] Vaughan, 135; 6 St.Tr., 999; Broom, *Constitutional Law*, 120–138; Robertson, *Documents*, 362. Cf. *Floyd* v. *Barker* (1607) 12 Rep. 23; *Earl of Macclesfield* v. *Starkey* (1684) 10 St.Tr. 1330.

[86] 16 Car. 2, c. 4.

[87] 6 St.Tr. 1013–1014.

[88] 32 Geo. 3, c. 60.

[89] See the full discussion in Holdsworth, *History of English Law*, x, 673–696; May, *Constitutional History*, ii, 253–263; *infra*, p. 667.

[90] " During the reign of Edward II *secretum consilium* and *privatum consilium* appear upon the regular rolls. French equivalents also gain currency, such as *le prive conseil*. . . . But never during the Middle Ages did ' the privy council ' become a term of general acceptance, as it is in modern times. It was seldom used, in fact, unless a certain distinction was necessary, and then it meant not especially a small council, nor yet a more highly

court of royal justice in all cases which had not been specially delegated to the recently constituted courts of common law. It was, however, during the minority of Henry III that the king's continual or permanent Council, as distinct alike from the *Curia Regis* of Henry II's time and from the large and solemn assemblies which were soon to become known as parliaments, acquired special prominence and strength. It comprised not only the officers of state and of the royal household, with the whole body of the judges, but a varying number of bishops and barons, as well as others, both clerical and lay, whose sole official status appears to have been that of counsellors.[91] Maintained by Henry III throughout his long reign, and further developed by Edward I, the royal council became henceforth the special representative and instrument of the kingly power acting side by side with, often in opposition to, the power of the national council. The royal council, as its designation " continual " denotes, was always sitting for the despatch of business,[92] and for that purpose it occupied different chambers about the palace, among which the Star Chamber, *la Chambre des Etoiles*, is specially mentioned in the records of Edward III's reign.[93] Its powers were most extensive, and indeed indefinite. It was the king's standing council of advice in all matters of administration ; it received, discussed, and remitted to the proper courts a vast number of petitions, which were constantly being presented, praying for relief in various matters of judicial cognisance [94]; it exercised by itself, in conjunction with the lords' house in parliament, a very great jurisdiction in causes both civil and criminal; and in matters of a temporary, partial, or comparatively unimportant nature, it assumed, by issuing ordinances claiming the force of statutes, the exercise of legislative powers.

organised or more select council than usual, but simply a *secret* council " : Baldwin, *King's Council*, 105. The term " ordinary council," *consilium ordinarium*, " nowhere occurs in the Middle Ages, and not till the reign of Henry VIII is there mention of ' the king's ordinary counsellors ' " : *ibid.*, 112. The term *le conseil continuel* " appears for the first time prominently in 1376, and it arose from the desire which had been stated many times before of having councillors ' continually present ' " : *ibid.*, 106. Baldwin concludes his discussion on this subject by stating : " The main fact, which takes away all reason for subdivision, is that the *consilium regis* unqualified by any adjective was inclusive and flexible enough to answer all the purposes required of the great council, the secret council, and the ordinary council. The only vital distinction of this kind which the Middle Ages really demanded was that between the Parliament and the Council. Here were two institutions of a common origin, which came to be positively differentiated both in organization and functions " : *ibid.*, 114. It may be added that the words *commune consilium regni* in Magna Carta (1215), c. 12 (*supra*, p. 79) mean the general approval of the kingdom, and that there was no institution called " the Common Council of the Realm." A. B. White, " Was there a ' Common Council ' before Parliament? " *American Historical Review*, xxv, 1–17 (1919).

[91] See Stubbs, *Constitutional History*, ii, 41, 269 *et seq*. For the composition of the council, see particularly Baldwin, Chap. iv.

[92] Sir N. H. Nicolas, Preface to *Proceedings of Privy Council*, i, p. iii.

[93] See *infra*, pp. 118 *et seq*. *Chambre des estoiles*, a translation of the mediaeval Latin term *camera stellata* soon became the popular name for what was called in 1343 " the new chamber upon the water " " next to the exchequer " " ordained for the council " : Baldwin, 356.

[94] The general nature of these petitions appears from the answers of the Council which have been preserved : " Sue at Common Law " ; " sue in the Exchequer " ; " sue in Chancery " ; " a writ on the subject shall be dispatched out of Chancery " ; " the King will consider " ; " a remedy shall be provided," etc.—Hardy, *Introduction to Close Rolls*, i, p. xxvi.

The Council's judicial work. As regards the particular description of judicial business, civil and criminal, disposed of by the Council itself, we have seen that Henry II, in 1178, had employed it as a court of appeal for all such causes as the ordinary judges should be incapable of determining.[95] The Council also exercised a convenient and salutary jurisdiction in cases of injury and oppression where, from the heinousness of the offence, the rank or power of the defendant, popular riots, or other causes, it was likely that a fair trial in the inferior courts could not be obtained, or that the process of the courts would be resisted by force. The rapine and oppression committed by the powerful nobility during the Middle Ages, more especially under the weak administration of the Lancastrian kings, frequently called for the interposition of this paramount authority.[96] Further, where a person was suffering imprisonment by the process of an inferior court, the double remedy of a subpoena against the pursuing party and a writ of *habeas corpus cum causa* (by which the cause itself and the body of the defendant were brought to be dealt with by the Council) was sometimes given. The Council had also the power of issuing writs into all special jurisdictions or franchises, such as Wales and Ireland[97]; and the poor, in theory at least, were the objects of its special care.[98]

The chancellor's jurisdiction. In the exercise of its judicial functions, the Council appears to have been generally presided over by the chancellor, who, until the reign of Edward III, was always an ecclesiastic of high dignity, and was peculiarly entrusted with the duty of redressing the grievances of the king's subjects. This great officer, independently of his connection with the Council, exercised an ordinary legal jurisdiction of much importance.[99] But in the reign of Edward I (according to some

---

[95] *Supra*, p. 98.

[96] In " Provisions for the good of the gouvernance of this land, that the Lordes, which ben of the K. Counsaill desireth," of the second year of Henry VI, subsequently embodied, with additions, in the Articles for the Regulation of the Council agreed to in Parliament, the eighth year of his reign, we read : " Item, that all the Billes that comprehende materes terminable atte the Commune Lawe . . . be remitted there to be determined ; but if so be that the discretion of the Counsaill feele to greet myght on that oo syde and unmyght oo that othir, [or elles other cause reasonable yai shall meve hem.]"—*Rotuli Parliamentorum*, iv, 201, 343.

[97] Palgrave, *Essay on the Jurisdiction of the King's Council*, 19, 90, 134. For the whole subject, see Baldwin, *King's Council*, Chap. xi.

[98] *Rotuli Parliamentorum*, iv, 201. 2 Hen. VI, 1423. On the council generally, see Baldwin, *The King's Council*; *Select Cases in Council* (Selden Society); Palgrave, *Jurisdiction of the King's Council*; A. V. Dicey, *Privy Council*; Lord Eustace Percy, *Privy Council under the Tudors*; and Plucknett, " Place of the Council in the Fifteenth Century," in *Transactions of the Royal Historical Society*, 4th series, i, 157 ; C. G. Bayne, *Select Cases in the Council of Henry VII* (Selden Society).

[99] On the chancellor's ordinary jurisdiction, see Spence, *Equitable Jurisdiction*, i, 336. The proceedings were by common law process ; but as the chancellor had no authority to summon a jury, issues of fact were remitted for trial to the Court of King's Bench. Blackstone (3 Comm. 47) and Lord Campbell (*Lives of the Chancellors*, Intro.) suggest that from the earliest times the chancellor was keeper of the king's conscience and explain thereby his equitable jurisdiction. The expression seems no older than Hatton's oration of 1587 (Spence, *Equitable Jurisdiction*, i, 406, 414). The common notion that the chancellor was the king's confessor is a legend without any foundation in fact. (There are lists of royal confessors in *The Antiquary*, xxii, 114, 159, 262, xxiii, 24, and in *Home Counties Magazine*, 1910.)

historians) we begin to perceive signs of the rise of the extraordinary or equitable jurisdiction of the chancellor. In their view, the numerous petitions addressed to the king and his Council, seeking the interposition of the royal grace and favour either to mitigate the harshness of the common law or supply its deficiencies, had been in the special care of the chancellor, who examined and reported upon them to the king. The inconvenience arising from the " multitude " of petitions in the year 1280 caused a special order to be issued by Edward I, directing that all petitions be examined, and according as they concerned the seal, the exchequer, the law of the land, or Jewry, they should go primarily to the chancellor, the exchequer, the justices, or the justices of the Jewry. But if the wants of the petitioners were of a nature so great, or so much of grace, that the chancellor and the justices could not act without the king, then they should be brought before the king to learn his will; but so that no petition come before the king and his Council except by the hands of the chancellor and the other chief ministers.[1] This monarch was wont to assign by writ under the privy seal certain of the petitions addressed to him, praying extraordinary remedies, to the chancellor and master of the rolls, or to either separately, with directions to give such remedy as should appear to be consonant with honesty (or equity, *honestati*).[2] During the reign of Edward II the jurisdiction of the court of chancery was considerably extended, and there occurs frequent and familiar mention of the *consuetudo cancellariae*.[3] At length, in 1349, by a writ or ordinance of the twenty-second year of Edward III, all such matters as were " of grace " were directed to be dispatched by the chancellor or by the keeper of the privy seal.[4] This was a great step in the recognition of the equitable jurisdiction of the court of chancery as distinct from the legal jurisdiction of the chancellor and of the courts of common law, although it was not until the following reign that it can be said to have been permanently established.[5]

---

[1] *Calendar of Close Rolls* (1279–1288), 56–57; Ryley's *Placita Parliamentaria*, 442. Spence's view given in the text, that equity was administered in the chancery as early as Edward I, has been revived by recent constitutional historians (Baldwin, *King's Council*, 241; B. Wilkinson, *Chancery under Edward III*, 48, and *Studies in Constitutional History*, 205). Legal historians have failed to find any trace of it until slightly before the accession of Richard II (Baildon, *Select Cases in Chancery*; Maitland, *Constitutional History*, 222–225; Holdsworth, *History of English Law*, i, 451 *et seq.*, citing fifteenth century cases). The latter view is clearly preferable. For the suggestion that chancery jurisdiction grew out of the " Latin side " of Chancery, see A. D. Hargreaves, " Equity and the Latin side of Chancery," *Law Quarterly Review*, lxviii, 481.

[2] Spence, *Equitable Jurisdiction*, i, 335. " Quale de jure et gratia cancellariae " occurs in a writ of 12 Edw. I; *ibid.*

[3] Lord Campbell, *Lives of the Chancellors*, i, 207.

[4] Baildon, *Select Cases in Chancery* (Selden Society), xvii; Sir T. Duffus Hardy, *Introduction to Close Rolls*, xxviii. While it is possible that " matters of grace " may mean equitable intervention, it must also be remembered that there were numerous petitions asking for money, church livings and similar favours, and that the ordinance may be concerned only with these latter.

[5] " By ' equitable jurisdiction ' must be understood," says Lord Campbell (*op. cit.*, i, 8, 9), " the extraordinary interference of the Chancellor, without common-law process or regard to the common law rules of proceeding, upon the petition of a party grieved who was without adequate remedy in a court of common law; whereupon the opposite party was

The Council, not content with its admitted sphere of action, assumed original jurisdiction in cases cognisable at common law. In direct violation of the liberties guaranteed by the Great Charter, men were arbitrarily imprisoned without the legal process of indictment or presentment, and their lands seized into the king's hands.

Restraining statutes. During the reign of Edward III a series of statutes were passed, in answer to the repeated complaints of the commons, restraining these illegal invasions by the Council upon the rights of property and personal liberty. In the 5th Edward III (1331), it was enacted that " no man from henceforth shall be attached by any accusation, nor forejudged of life or limb, nor his lands, tenements, goods, nor chattels seized into the king's hands, against the form of the Great Charter and the law of the land."[6] Twenty years later, the commons again petitioned against the illegal proceedings of the Council. Receiving a somewhat unsatisfactory reply from the king, they repeated their petition to parliament in the following year (1352), and obtained the enactment of a statute which, expounding the words of Magna Carta, explicitly declares: " Whereas it is contained in the Great Charter of the franchises of England, that none shall be imprisoned nor put out of his freehold, nor of his franchises nor free customs, unless it be by the law of the land; it is accorded, assented, and established, That from henceforth none shall be taken by petition or suggestion, made to our lord the king or to his Council, unless it be by indictment, or presentment of good and lawful people, of the same neighbourhood where such deeds be done, in due manner, or by process made by writ original at the common law, nor that none be ousted of his franchises nor of his freeholds, unless he be duly brought into answer and forejudged of the same by the course of the law; and if anything be done against the same it shall be redressed and holden for naught."[7]

Similar provisions were contained in a short enactment of 1354[8]; yet in 1362 we find the commons again complaining, and it was " ordained and established by the assent of the prelates, dukes, earls, barons, and the commons, that the charters and statutes be held and put in execution according to the said petition."[9] In the following year another statute was passed in these terms: " Though it be contained in the Great Charter

---

compelled to appear and to be examined, either personally or upon written interrogatories; and evidence being heard on both sides, without the interposition of a jury, an order was made *secundum aequum et bonum*, which was enforced by imprisonment."

[6] 5 Edw. 3, c. 9.

[7] 25 Edw. 3, st. 5, c. 4; *Rotuli Parliamentorum*, ii, 239, no. 19.

[8] 28 Edw. 3, c. 3.

[9] *Rotuli Parliamentorum*, ii, 269. The mention here of dukes as a separate rank is noteworthy, The title had been bestowed for the first time in England only twenty-five years previously (in 1337), when the Black Prince was created Duke of Cornwall. Henry, Earl of Lancaster (great-grandson of Henry III), was, in 1351, the next recipient; he died March 24, 1360, and his title was revived this very year, 1362, in his son-in-law, John of Gaunt. The only other English duke then in existence, besides the Black Prince and John of Gaunt, was their brother Lionel, created Duke of Clarence, September 15, 1362.

that no man be taken nor imprisoned nor put out of his freehold without process of the law; nevertheless divers people make false suggestions to the king himself as well for malice as otherwise, whereat the king is often grieved and divers of the realm put in great danger and loss against the form of the said Charter; wherefore it is ordained that all they which make such suggestions shall be sent with the same suggestions to the Chancellor, Treasurer, and his Grand Council, and that they there find surety to pursue their suggestions, and incur the same pain that the other should have had, if he were attainted, in case that the suggestion be found evil; and that then process of law be made against them without being taken or imprisoned against the form of the said Charter and other statutes."[10]

In 1368 the commons again petitioned: "Because many of your Commons are hurt and destroyed by false accusers, who make their accusations more for their revenge and particular gain than for the profit of the king or of his people; and of those that are accused by them some have been taken, and others are made to come before the King's Council by writ, or other commandment of the king, upon grievous pain contrary to the law: That it would please our lord the king, and his good Council, for the just government of his people, to ordain that, if hereafter any accuser propose any matter for the profit of the king, the same matter be sent to his justices of the one bench or of the other, or of the Assizes to be inquired of and determined according to the law; and if it concern the accuser or party, that he have his suit at the common law; and that no man be put to answer without presentment before the justices, or matter of record, or by due process and original writ, according to the ancient law of the land. And if anything henceforth be done to the contrary, that it be void in law and held for error." The answer to this petition, whereon a statute to the same effect was grounded, runs: "Because this article is an article of the Great Charter, the king willeth that this be done, as the petition doth demand."[11]

Acts of Parliament, however, were of little avail against the stubborn perseverance of king and Council in retaining the power which they had been so long accustomed to use. The civil jurisdiction of the Council was at this time principally exercised in conjunction with the chancery, now growing in importance, and the two are henceforth generally named together in the remonstrances which the commons still from time to time continued to present. To a petition in the 13th of Richard II (1389), that neither the chancellor nor the king's council should make any ordinance against the common or statute law, or the ancient customs of the land, "but that the common law have its course for all the whole people, and that no judgment rendered be annulled without due process of law," the king returned the unsatisfactory answer: "Let it be done as

[10] 37 Edw. 3, c. 18. (Hallam, *Middle Ages*, iii, 253 appears to have misapprehended the purport of this obscurely worded statute.)
[11] *Rotuli Parliamentorum*, ii, 295, and 42 Edw. 3, c. 3.

has been usual heretofore, provided the royal prerogative be saved (issint que la Regalie du Roi soit sauve); and if any one feel aggrieved, let him show it specially and right shall be done him." [12]

Parliament in the fourteenth century regarded the Council's jurisdiction with suspicion chiefly on the ground of its association with the crown and the prerogative—and expressed the general feeling against the exercise of arbitrary power. The lawyers, too, of the ordinary courts were a numerous and influential group among the commons, and manifested much professional jealousy of the growing jurisdiction of chancery, the procedure of which was less cumbrous than that of the common law courts.

The writ subpoena. Suits in chancery were commenced by petition or bill, without any preliminary writ, followed by a subpoena,[13] summoning the party complained against to appear before the court and make answer. Disputed facts might be established by the personal examination of the parties on oath, a proceeding unknown to the common law, but employed by this tribunal and by the Council from which it branched off. During the reigns of Henry IV and Henry V, and in the minority of Henry VI, the commons continued to remonstrate against the encroachments of the chancery. But from the time of Edward IV, although the judges still disputed the chancellor's authority to interfere with the proceedings of the common law courts, we do not trace any further opposition on the part of the commons; and down to the reign of Charles II the court continued to be substantially the same as it was in the reign of Edward IV.[14]

The great council. The continual council has been considered with reference to its independent jurisdiction; but it was also equally conspicuous in its relation to the High Court of Parliament. The growth of parliament has yet to be considered; but we may anticipate so far as to note that even after the permanent establishment of a parliament of the three estates under Edward I, the baronage, spiritual as well as temporal, still retained, independently of parliament, certain powers which had been theirs when they alone constituted the national assembly, and which they ultimately transmitted to the House of Lords. Under the title of *Magnum Consilium* they continued to meet at intervals during the thirteenth, fourteenth and fifteenth centuries, sometimes in conjunction with the king's continual council, and occasionally also in an assembly

---

[12] *Rotuli Parliamentorum*, iii, 266. For another view upon this series of statutes, see Plucknett, *Concise History of the Common Law* (1956), 187 *et seq.*

[13] Holdsworth, i, 485–487. The subpoena appears as early as 1363; the tradition that John de Waltham invented it in Richard II's reign is without foundation. He probably initiated the practice of issuing it under the privy seal and it was this which was particularly resented in the fifteenth century. See Baldwin, *Select Cases before the King's Council* (Selden Society), p. xxxix. A frequent objection was that the subpoena (unlike common-law writs) gave no indication of the nature of the matter involved.

[14] Spence, *Equitable Jurisdiction*, i, 349.

containing all the elements of parliament.[15] As the commons took no part in the judicial power of parliament,[16] its function as the king's great and extraordinary court of justice was performed by the king's great council—the lords' house in parliament blended with the ordinary council.

House of Lords: Judicial Committee. It is from the mixed powers of this assembly, and the double capacity of the peerage as members both of the parliament or legislative council and of the deliberative and judicial council, that the House of Lords derived its judicial character as a court of appeal, and the king's council its legislative character, which it attempted to carry out in the shape of ordinances.[17] The judges and other official members of the king's continual council originally attended as constituent members of the great council, and in that capacity, although not peers, seem to have had the right of suffrage[18]; but under Edward III the lords successfully asserted their ascendancy over the judges and the rest of the council, and took the decisive jurisdiction into their own hands. Their ancient colleagues of the council, not being lords, were thus reduced to the position of assistants and advisers, a position which they have ever since held in the judicial proceedings of the upper house, the heir and representative of the medieval great councils.[19]

The original tribunal, the king's continual council, retained throughout its extraordinary jurisdiction. After throwing off as branches or offsets the court of Requests,[20] and the more famous court of Star Chamber, it transmitted its judicial powers to the Privy Council, by whom, through the medium of a Judicial Committee,[21] they are still exercised.

[15] Stubbs, *Constitutional History*, ii, 273; Committee on House of Commons Personnel, *Interim Report*, 1932 (Cmd. 4130), 108; Plucknett, " The Council in the Fifteenth Century," *Royal Historical Society, Transactions* (4th series), i, 165 *et seq.*

[16] The commons acknowledged in 1 Henry IV (1399) that they had no right to interfere in judicial matters (*Rotuli Parliamentorum*, iii, 427; *cf. Report on the Dignity of a Peer*, i, 360); but in the next reign they began to concern themselves with the petitions of private individuals to the lords or Council which in many instances were answered in the form of statutes with the express assent of all parts of the legislature. Hence originated private Acts of Parliament.—See Hallam, *Middle Ages*, iii, 92; Clifford, *History of Private Bill Legislation*.

[17] Stubbs, *Select Charters*, Introductory Sketch, 26. On the judicature of the House of Lords, *cf.* Pike, *Constitutional History of House of Lords*, pp. 279 *et seq.* For the whole subject see Baldwin, *King's Council*, Chap. xii, and Holdsworth, i, 351 *et seq.*

[18] Hale, *Jurisdiction of the Lords' House* (ed. by Hargrave), pp. 6, 8.

[19] Palgrave, *King's Council*, 54; Hallam, *Middle Ages*, iii, 145; Baldwin, 318; Holdsworth, i, 356.

[20] The conjectures that the origin of this court is as old as 1349 (Spence, *Equitable Jurisdiction*, i, 337) cannot be confirmed. The court certainly was in existence in the reign of Henry VII; see Tanner, *Tudor Constitutional Documents*, 299; Pollard traced its origin at least as early as the reign of Richard III, *English Historical Review*, xxxvii, 345 (1922). This court continued to be resorted to down to 1598, when (according to Coke, 4 Inst. 97) it was virtually abolished by a decision of the Court of Common Pleas (*Stepney* v. *Flood*). In spite of this decision, however, the court continued to thrive till 1642. See Tanner, 299–302; Holdsworth, i, 413–416. *Infra*, p. 253.

[21] The Judicial Committee of the Privy Council was established in 1833 by 3 & 4 Will. 4, c. 41. After hearing the allegations and proofs the Committee make their report to the Queen in Council, by whom the judgment is finally given. This Act was the work of Lord Brougham (see Greville's *Memoirs*, 1st series, vol. ii, p. 364). It has been amended in some respects by the Appellate Jurisdiction Acts of 1876 (39 & 40 Vict. c. 59) and 1887 (50 & 51 Vict. c. 70). By the Judicial Committee Amendment Act, 1895 (58 & 59 Vict.

Court of Star Chamber. As regards the origin of the court of Star Chamber, it has already been mentioned that in the reign of Edward III the king's continual council was in the habit of sitting in what was called the Star Chamber (*Chambre d'Estoiles*, or *Chambre des Estoylles*).[22] After the establishment of the court of Chancery as a separate and independent jurisdiction taking cognisance of the greater portion of the civil business of the Council, the latter body appears to have usually sat in the Star Chamber while exercising jurisdiction over such cases as were not sent to the chancery. " The continual complaints of the Commons," says Lord Hale,[23] " against the proceedings before the Council in causes civil and criminal, although they did not always attain their concession, yet brought a disreputation upon the proceedings of the Council, as contrary to Magna Carta and the known laws," and the jurisdiction appears to have gradually declined in the later years of Henry VI, and for a short period was all but in abeyance [24]; a revival set in towards the end of the reign of Edward IV and under Henry VIII " there is ample evidence of a policy not merely of rehabilitating the council, but of employing it with greater vigour than ever." [25] In the third year of his reign (1487) he established what may be termed a " statutory committee of the council," [26] sometimes inaccurately identified with the Star Chamber. This new committee consisted of the chancellor, treasurer, and lord privy seal, or two of them, together with a bishop, a temporal lord of the council, and the two chief justices, or in their absence two other justices.[27] By a later statute, 21 Henry 8, c. 20 (1529), the president of the council was added to the number of the judges. Neither in this statute, nor in that of the 3rd Henry VII, is the name of Star Chamber applied to this committee,[28] which seems to have been set up for the purpose of dealing with the general disorders prevalent at the accession of Henry VII arising from livery and maintenance, the corruption of juries and " great riots and unlawful assemblies "; it was a temporary expedient and when the need for it had passed it fell into abeyance. But it did not affect either the composition or the jurisdiction of the Council. In the Council Ordinances of 1526 a distinction was drawn between the two branches of the Council's activities, the executive and the jurisdictional: the former was to be in continual attendance on the king and became the Privy Council, while the latter remained at Westminster to deal with the judicial work and became the court of Star Chamber.[29]

c. 44), Privy Councillors, who have been colonial chief justices or justices or judges of colonial superior courts, are, to the number of five, but no more, enabled to sit on the Judicial Committee. For the privy council of the Tudors, see *infra*, p. 255.

[22] *Supra*, pp. 111 *et seq.*
[23] *Jurisdiction of the Lords' House* (ed. Hargrave), p. 39.
[24] Baldwin, *King's Council*, 205, 428.   [25] *Ibid.*, 435; *infra*, pp. 216, 226.
[26] Tanner, *Tudor Constitutional Documents*, 250.
[27] 3 Hen. 7, c. 1; Tanner, 258.
[28] The title " Pro Camera Stellata " was prefixed to the statute of 1487 at a later date: Tanner, p. 249. *Infra*, p. 226.
[29] See Tanner, pp. 216 *et seq.*, 249 *et seq.*; Holdsworth, *History of English Law*, i, 493 *et seq.*; Leadam, *Select Cases in the Star Chamber* (Selden Society), 2 vols., 1902, 1910; Plucknett, *Concise History of the Common Law* (1956), 182.

The Star Chamber exercised a jurisdiction analogous, in principle and procedure, to that of the court of Chancery, and founded on the inefficiency of the ordinary tribunals to do complete justice in criminal and other offences of an extraordinary or dangerous character.[30] Its civil jurisdiction comprised disputes between alien merchants and Englishmen, questions of prize or unlawful detention of ships, and other matters of maritime law; certain testamentary causes, and suits between corporations. These were gradually absorbed by the admiralty, chancery, and common law courts, leaving to the Star Chamber its criminal jurisdiction. As a court of " criminal equity," it took cognisance of forgery, perjury, riot, maintenance, fraud, libel and conspiracy; and generally of all misdemeanours, especially those of a public nature, among which were included all breaches of proclamations, without regard to the illegality of the proclamations themselves. Fine and imprisonment were the usual punishments inflicted; but the court was held competent to pronounce any sentence short of death. The fines were frequently of enormous amount, and though, as a rule, they were reduced or remitted, they in many cases proved ruinous to the sufferers. The pillory, whipping, branding and cruel mutilations were inflicted upon political offenders by the sentence of this court [31]; and at length the tyrannical exercise and illegal extension of its powers became so odious to the people that it was abolished by the Long Parliament in 1641.[32]

Admiralty. In 1691 by 2 William and Mary, sess. 2, c. 2 (amended in 1820 by 1 Geo. 4, c. 90, and in 1827 by 7 & 8 Geo. 4, c. 65), the Lords Commissioners [33] of the Admiralty are vested with all the jurisdictions and powers formerly vested in the Lord High Admiral of England. Much of that jurisdiction had been won by the Admiral by the close of the Middle Ages from the many seaports which enjoyed maritime courts of their own, administering a traditional sea-law, especially the " laws of Oléron " (Rôles, Jugements et Lois d'Oléron), a collection of ancient rules and usages observed by the Maritime Court of that island, lying off the west coast of France. They had been introduced into England perhaps as early as the reign of Richard I, and were adopted as a standard whereby maritime causes should be determined.[34] The office of Lord High Admiral is

---

[30] The Act of 1487 recognised the practice of examining defendants on oath; it also gave statutory sanction to the issue of writs of subpoena and privy seal for summoning persons accused of the offences specified in the statute.

[31] These punishments were not, as is often said, introduced into the practice of the court by the Stuart kings. *Cf.* J. R. Tanner, *Tudor Constitutional Documents*, pp. 256–257; " nothing was done under the Stuarts by way of fine and corporal punishment that had not been already done under the Tudors. The later unpopularity of the court was due to a change in the popular point of view, and not in the action of the court."

[32] 16 Car. 1, c. 10.

[33] James II had been the last Lord High Admiral, save for short intervals: 1702–1709 and 1827–1828.

[34] *Cf.* F. R. Sanborn, *Early English Maritime and Commercial Law* (1930); Art. " Sea Laws " in *Encyclopaedia Britannica*, 11th ed., vol. xxiv, pp. 535–537; Reeves, *History of English Law*, iii, 369; *Documents relating to Law and Custom of the Sea*, 2 vols., ed. R. G. Marsden (Navy Records Society, 1915–1916). The customs of Oléron were inserted in the *Black Book of the Admiralty* (ed. Twiss, Rolls Series).

first heard of in the reign of Edward I, and the first admiral to be known as " Admiral de la Mer du Roy d'Angleterre," was William de Leyburne in 1297. From the beginning of the fourteenth century the office became permanent. At first the admiral possessed only a disciplinary jurisdiction over the fleet under his command (with the particular care of seeing that hostilities were not carried on against friendly ships, or during truces), but from about the middle of the fourteenth century his jurisdiction was extended so as " to enable him to hold an independent court and administer complete justice in piracy and other maritime cases." [35]

The jurisdiction of this court of Admiralty became so far-reaching, and encroached so much upon the rights of the sea-coast towns which possessed admiralty jurisdiction,[36] that in the reign of Richard II and Henry IV statutes were passed for restricting the scope of its powers.[37] However, the High Court of Admiralty continued throughout the Middle Ages as a court taking cognisance of all causes, criminal and civil, relating to maritime matters, which were without the pale of the common law courts of the country, and thus its jurisdiction extended over all the high seas. It was, however, virtually deprived of its criminal jurisdiction by the Act of 1536 (28 Hen. VIII, c. 15), which provided that treasons, felonies, robberies, murders and confederacies committed within the admiral's jurisdiction should be tried by commissioners appointed by the crown. As these commissioners " came to be invariably the judges of the common law courts, the indirect result of the Act was to transfer the criminal jurisdiction of the Admiralty to the judges of the courts of common law." [38] In the sixteenth and seventeenth centuries admiralty and common law were in frequent conflict, and in the eighteenth century the use of admiralty jurisdictions in the American colonies was the cause of much friction. In 1834 the jurisdiction of these commissioners was transferred to the Central Criminal Court. By the Judicature Act of 1873 the civil juris-diction and the prize jurisdiction hitherto exercised by the court of Admiralty became merged in that of the High Court of Justice.

Military and Police Organisation

One of the special characteristics of the English constitution—the permanence combined with progressive development of its primitive institutions—is illustrated by the system which we find in use under the Norman and Plantagenet kings, for the preservation of the internal peace of the country, and its defence against hostile invasion. There were two principal methods by which these ends were attained in ancient times, the one civil, the other military: (1) The police organisation of the mutual

[35] *Select Pleas of the Admiralty* (Selden Society), i, Introduction xxxv, quoted by Holdsworth, i, 545.
[36] The jurisdiction of the court of Admiralty " comprised the ordinary criminal and civil jurisdiction of later days, the prize jurisdiction, and the jurisdiction over wreck and other droits of the Crown or the admiral."—*Ibid.*, 548.
[37] 13 Ric. 2, st. i, c. 5 (1389); 15 Ric. 2, c. 3 (1391); 2 Hen. 4, c. 11 (1401).
[38] Holdsworth, i, 551.

frithborh, or frankpledge, supplemented by the " hue and cry " in pursuit of offenders, in which all the inhabitants of the hundred or tithing were bound to join; (2) the *fyrd*, or national militia, available not only for the defence of the country, but for the maintenance of peace at home. Service in this national force was one of the three duties—the *trimoda necessitas*—to which all freemen were subject. These primitive institutions, which may be traced to the laws of Edgar and Cnut, and had probably been customary for some centuries, are all met with in full vigour long after the Norman Conquest, "working their way through the superstratum of feudalism and gaining strength in the process." [39]

The old military system. The *fyrd* was originally the only military system known to our ancestors. The Danish conqueror, Cnut, introduced the germ of a standing army in the bodyguard with which he surrounded himself, composed of mercenaries drawn from various nations. But these *hus-carls* were not very numerous, being variously estimated at from three to six thousand. The limited period of service to which the feudal vassals were bound by tenure, and their general unmanageableness, caused both William the Conqueror and the succeeding Norman and early Angevin kings to employ mercenary forces, who, however, soon became odious in the eyes of the nation, and had eventually to be given up. Throughout this period the ancient national militia, though thrown into the shade for a time by the feudal and mercenary troops, still subsisted, and occasionally did good service in defence of their country, as in the battle of the Standard, in 1138, which was won by their exertions, and again in 1174, at the battle of Alnwick. The use of scutage, on the occasion of the Toulouse war in 1159, as a commutation of personal service, had the effect of diminishing the feudal levies; and although Henry II was enabled with the money thus obtained to hire mercenaries for his foreign wars, the hatred of the English towards these forces prevented him from employing them for the purposes of home defence, while the feudal army, besides being insufficient, was too much under the influence of the barons, whose power he was bent upon curtailing.

Assize of Arms. Under these circumstances, the king determined to resuscitate the ancient national force. By the Assize of Arms, issued in the year 1181, in addition to requiring every military tenant to keep in readiness a coat of mail, with helmet, shield and lance, for as many knights as were charged on demesne,[40] it was ordained that every free layman having chattels or rent to the value of sixteen marks should be armed in like manner; that he who was worth only ten marks should

[39] Stubbs, *Select Charters*, 463.
[40] See Round, *Feudal England*, 241: " When the number of knights' fees created was not sufficient to discharge the baron's service, the balance of that service remained charged on the uninfeudated portion of his fief, that is on the ' demesne.' " This clause requires him " to keep in readiness harness sufficient for those knights whom he would have to provide himself to discharge that balance."

possess a hauberk, an iron skull cap, and a lance; and that all burgesses and the whole community of freemen (" tota communa liberorum hominum ") should furnish themselves with quilted doublets, iron skull caps and lances. To enforce this, the itinerant justices were charged to ascertain, by the recognition of a jury of lawful knights, or other free and lawful men of the hundred or borough, the value of the rents and chattels of all freemen, and to enrol their names in separate classes, with the nature of the arms appertaining to each; and then, after causing the schedule to be read in open court, to oblige all to swear that they would provide themselves with these arms within a stated time, and be true and faithful to the king.[41]

Thirteenth-century developments. The two military systems, the ancient traditional, and the more modern feudal, continued for some time side by side without coalescing, but tending more and more to amalgamate into the general national armament which we meet with under Henry III and Edward I.

In 1205, a writ of King John,[42] directs that every nine knights throughout England shall provide a tenth well equipped with horses and arms for the defence of the kingdom, and shall contribute two shillings per diem for his keep. This tithe of knights is to repair to London three weeks after Easter, ready to go wherever ordered, and to remain in the king's service, for the defence of the kingdom as long as need shall require. So far, the military tenants only are affected; but a connection with the national militia is traceable in the provision which follows, that in case of foreign invasion, " all men shall unanimously hurry to meet the enemy with force and arms, without any excuse or delay, at the first rumour of their coming "; and also in the penalties for neglect, which were, in the case of a knightly or other landholder (unless his absence had arisen from infirmity), the absolute forfeiture by him and his heirs of the land which he held; in the case of knights or others having no land, perpetual serfdom for them and their heirs (" ipsi et haeredes sui servi fient in perpetuum "), with the obligation to pay an annual poll tax of fourpence each.

In the following reign we find the two military forces amalgamated for the purposes of national defence. In 1217, a writ, issued during the minority of Henry III, shortly after the battle of Lincoln, and while Louis of France was still in the country, directs the sheriff of Berkshire to bring up the whole force of his county, both the feudal levy and also the *jurati ad arma*, the ancient local militia as reorganised under the Assize of Arms.[43] In 1231 the plan already adopted in the case of the military tenants, of dispensing with the personal service of a part on the condition

---

[41] Benedictus Abbas, i, 278; Hoveden, ii, 261; *Select Charters*, 183–184.

[42] Issued " cum assensu archiepiscoporum, episcoporum, comitum, baronum, et omnium fidelium nostrorum Angliae." *Select Charters*, 276.

[43] *Report on Dignity of a Peer*, App., p. 2; *Select Charters*, 340.

of contributing to the equipment of the remainder, was applied to the *jurati ad arma.*[44]

Hue and cry. Concurrently with the development of the ancient *fyrd,* the primitive police organisation had also been undergoing a process of expansion. The system of frankpledge was maintained with even increased stringency. It was enforced by an injunction of William the Conqueror, and by the Assize of Clarendon under Henry II.[45] By a royal decree issued in 1195 by Archbishop Hubert Walter, Richard I's chief justiciar, the " hue and cry " was enforced, and knights were assigned to receive the oaths for the preservation of the peace. All men above the age of fifteen years were required to swear to keep the peace of the lord the king; to be neither themselves outlaws, robbers, or thieves, nor to aid such persons as receivers or consenting parties; to follow up the hue and cry in pursuit of offenders, and seize as malefactors all who failed to join or withdrew from the pursuit, and to deliver them to the knights assigned for this purpose who should deliver them to the sheriff, from whose custody they should not be liberated except by order of the king or of his chief justice.[46]

Watch and ward. In 1233, the old police organisation, proving inadequate, was supplemented by a system of watch and ward in every township throughout the country.[47] In 1252 and 1253 further regulations were issued extending and enforcing the watch and ward, and combining it, for the preservation of internal peace, with the Assize of Arms. (1) Watch was to be kept from sunset to sunrise between Ascension Day and Michaelmas; in the cities by companies of six armed men stationed at every gate, in the boroughs by a company of twelve, and in the townships by six, or four at least, according to the number of the inhabitants. Any stranger attempting to pass through was to be arrested till the morning, and then, if suspected of any crime, delivered to the sheriff and kept in custody and liberated " per legem terrae." Even a stranger who arrived by daylight was not to remain in any village for more than a day, or two at most, except during harvest-time, unless his host would become surety for his conduct. A merchant on his road was entitled, after counting his money in the presence of the mayor and bailiffs of any city or borough, to demand of them a guard " per malos passus et loca ambigua," and if

---

[44] Rymer, i, 200; *Select Charters,* 355. *Cf.* also Assize of Arms of 1252. *Ibid.,* 362.

[45] Wl. art. 8 (Robertson, *Laws,* 239); Assize of Clarendon, cc. 9, 10, 15, 16 (*Select Charters,* 99, 171–172).

[46] R. Hoveden, iii, 299; *Select Charters,* 257–258. In 1 Edgar 2 (Ordinance of the Hundred, 959–975) it was ordered: " That a thief will be pursued. . . . If there be present need, let it be made known to the hundredmen, and let him make it known to the tithingmen, and let all go forth to where God may direct them to go. Let them do justice on the thief, as it was formerly the enactment of Edmund." And in 2 Cnut 21 (Secular Dooms): " And we will that every man above xii years make oath that he will neither be a thief nor cognizant of theft."—*Select Charters,* 81, 87; Robertson, *Laws,* 17, 185.

[47] Writ of Henry III to the Sheriff of Kent: De forma pacis conservanda, Rymer, i, 209; Stubbs, *Select Charters* (8th ed.; omitted in 9th), 362.

subsequently robbed, could claim restitution from the inhabitants.[48]
(2) The Assize of Arms was renewed and the classification remodelled,
all men, " citizens, burgesses, free tenants, villeins, and others," between
the ages of fifteen and sixty, being ranked according to the value of their
land or movables, from fifteen pounds annual rent in land down to forty
shillings in chattels.[49] (3) All these were sworn to provide themselves with
the arms proper to their class, and ordered to join the hue and cry whenever
required. For this purpose they were placed under the command of the
local civil authorities, the mayor and bailiffs in cities and boroughs, and
the constable in each township, the supreme authority over all being vested
in the chief constable of each hundred.[50]

Statute of Winchester. Under our " English Justinian," Edward I,
whose " legislation is so full that the laws of the next three centuries are
little more than a necessary expansion of it," [51] the celebrated Statute of
Winchester,[52] which though now to a great extent obsolete has been the
foundation of modern laws, elaborated and completed the various
regulations for watch and ward, reception of strangers, hue and cry, and
the Assize of Arms. It was also specially provided that the whole hundred
where any robbery should be committed should be answerable for the
damage, unless the felons be brought to justice ; and that highways leading
from one market town to another should be widened, " so that there be
neither dyke, tree nor bush, whereby a man may lurk to do hurt," within
200 feet of each side of the road.

The provisions of the Statute of Winchester with respect to the arming
of the men of each county were more immediately directed to the preservation of internal peace, by rendering more effective the power of summoning
the *posse comitatus*, which the sheriff, as chief conservator of the peace
of the county, had always possessed. But these local forces still continued
available for the purposes of national defence ; and from the thirteenth
down to the middle of the sixteenth century, it was customary, whenever
invasion was apprehended from Scotland or France, to empower special
" Commissioners of Array " to muster and train all or a portion of the
men of each county capable of bearing arms, and to hold them in readiness
to defend the kingdom.

The ancient obligation to keep sufficient arms according to each man's
estate was enforced by statutes of Philip and Mary, and the kind of

---

[48] Henry III's father-in-law had enacted a similar rule in Provence ; Matthew Paris castigates
it as a " Savoyard " innovation and says it was withdrawn as the barons protested.
Pollock and Maitland, i, 181.
[49] The owner of land worth £15 a year, and the owner of chattels of the value of 60 marks
(£40), were classed together with respect to their armour, and served in what may be
termed the " Yeomanry Cavalry " of that period. Each had to provide himself with a
coat of mail, an iron headpiece, sword, small knife and a horse. The other classes served
on foot.
[50] Writs of 36 & 37 Hen. 3 (1252–1253) ; Rymer, i, 281, 292 ; *Select Charters*, 362 ; Pollock
and Maitland, i, 565.
[51] Stubbs, *Select Charters*, Introduction 38.
[52] 13 Edw. 1, c. 6, 1285 ; *Select Charters*, 463–469.

weapons changed for those of more modern fashion[53]; but under James I these provisions were abrogated.[54] In 1638 Charles I issued an unconstitutional Order in Council obliging every freeholder whose land was of the clear yearly value of £200 to furnish a horse-soldier when called upon to do so by the lord lieutenant of his county.

The Militia. The command of the Militia, as the local forces were usually denominated, formed the final ground of rupture between Charles and his parliament, the latter having passed ordinances (February 16 and March 5, 1642) superseding the king's commissions of lieutenancy by the appointment of fifty-five Commissioners of Array, with power to suppress " all rebellions, insurrections, and invasions." [55] This proceeding, however necessary it may have been at the time for the peace and safety of the kingdom, was clearly illegal. After the Restoration, an Act of Parliament declared that " the sole supreme government, command, and disposition of the militia, and of all forces by sea and land, and of all forts and places of strength is, and by the laws of England ever was, the undoubted right of the kings and queens of England," and that neither House of Parliament could pretend to the same, nor lawfully levy war, offensive or defensive, against the king.[56] By another Act, provision was made for calling together, arming, and arraying the militia, by the king's lieutenants of counties, and for charging the cost upon the landholders in proportion to the value of their estates.[57] But concurrently with the growth of a standing army,[58] the local forces languished for a lengthened period, until revived and remodelled in 1757, in consequence of a panic caused by rumours of a French armament, as the national militia.[59]

Militiamen were to be chosen by ballot to serve for a limited number of years, but were not to be compelled to leave their own county except in case of invasion or rebellion. In 1829, the practice was commenced, and was subsequently continued, of passing an annual Act suspending the militia ballot, the supply being furnished by voluntary enlistment.[60]

---

[53] 4 & 5 Phil. and Mary, c. 2 and c. 3. Penalties were imposed on persons absenting themselves when commanded to muster by the sovereign, or any *lieutenant* authorised for the same. This was a new officer, the lord lieutenant, introduced under the Tudors as the chief military officer of the crown in every county. For the early history of the office see Scott Thomson, *Lords Lieutenants in the Sixteenth Century* (London, 1923). Thenceforward the sheriff became practically a purely civil officer. By the Army Regulation Act, 1871 (34 & 35 Vict. c. 86, s. 6), the jurisdiction and command of the lords lieutenant of counties over the militia and other auxiliary forces have been revested in the crown, to be exercised through the Secretary of State for War, and officers appointed with his advice.

[54] 1 Jac. 1, c. 25, s. 46.

[55] Gardiner, *Documents*, 245.

[56] 13 Car. 2, st. 1, c. 6; Robertson, *Documents*, 29.

[57] 14 Car. 2, c. 3.

[58] A standing army under the direct command of the crown was, as a result of suppression of the great rebellion, regarded as a menace to free rights of the people. (*Cf.* the Bill of Rights, 1688.) Hence extraordinary powers annually renewable under strict conditions were granted to the crown by the Mutiny Act (1 Will. and Mary, c. 5). See *infra*, Chap. 15.

[59] Pitt's Militia Act, 30 Geo. 2, c. 25; Robertson, *Documents*, 230; *cf.* Hallam, *Constitutional History*, ii, 133; iii, 259 *et seq.*

[60] The old militia came to an end in 1908, but the name has since been applied to a newer statutory force (Territorial Army and Militia Act, 1921, s. 2).

Conservators of the peace. In the appointment of knights to receive the oaths [61] may probably be discerned the germ of the office of conservator, later justice, of the peace. *Custodes pacis* were assigned in 1252, 1253 and 1264 [62] and from 1285 were closely associated with the enforcement of the Statute of Winchester. They afterwards appear to have been occasionally chosen by the landholders of the county, but were finally appointed to their office by the royal writ or commission. Their constant function was to take indictments of felonies and misdemeanours, and to hold the accused until trial by royal judges. In 1329, 1332, 1338, and from 1350 to 1364 they were given powers to try their prisoners, and this became permanent in 1368. Their early functions of supervising the militia were soon transferred to separate commissions of array, but after the Black Death they frequently dealt with the new labour and price-control legislation. The local courts paled before them, the sheriff became their servant, and parliament (where many J.P.s sat in the House of Commons) constantly confided new and important tasks to them. [63]

County coroner. The office of county coroner had already been instituted under Richard I, in 1194. [64] It is regulated partly by common law, partly by a long series of statutes. Although their name would imply that they were appointed by the crown, the coroners have always been elective officers. Till 1888 they were always elected by the freeholders, " commons of the counties," in full county court. They are now appointed by the county council. [65]

---

[61] In 1195; *supra*, p. 123.

[62] See the writs in Rymer, i, 281, 292, 442; *Select Charters*, 364, 399.

[63] For the whole subject see B. H. Putnam, *Proceedings before Justices of the Peace* (Ames Foundation) which supersedes all previous work.

[64] Forma procedendi in placitis Coronae Regis, c. 20 in Hoveden, iii, 262 and *Select Charters*, 254.

[65] Coroners held inquests in cases of suspicious death, on treasure trove, etc. They received the abjuration of fugitives who had taken sanctuary, and conducted outlawry proceedings in the county court. If a sheriff had an interest in litigation in his county, the writs were directed to the coroners instead of to the sheriff. See Gross, *Coroners' Rolls* (Selden Society); W. Blake Odgers, *Local Government*; Maitland, *Constitutional History*, pp. 43, 44; R. H. Wellington, *The King's Coroner*, 2 vols. (1905–1906). Recent controversies on the origin of the office are discussed by I. L. Langbein in *Columbia Law Review*, xxxiii, 1329–1365.

CHAPTER 6

ORIGIN OF PARLIAMENT

ENGLAND has never been without a national assembly,[1] by whose " counsel and consent " the work of government has been carried on. But, whilst retaining its historical continuity, the name, powers, and constitution of this assembly have varied from time to time.

EARLY FORMS OF NATIONAL ASSEMBLY

The nature and functions of the old English witenagemot have been already sufficiently described.[2] After the Norman Conquest, with the introduction of the feudal principle, the meeting of the wise was replaced by the *Curia Regis*, the court of the king's feudal vassals. All immediate tenants of the crown by military service, however small might be their holdings, had originally a duty to appear when summoned to the national council of the realm. The bishops and principal abbots continued to be summoned without any intermission, though their ancient character of witan appears to have become gradually merged in that of feudal barons. The earls also never lost their right to attend. But as regards all other military tenants *in capite*, although they may have owed suit of court to the *Curia Regis*, it is highly probable that the king early assumed the power of selecting the persons to whom writs of summons should be addressed.[3] Thus the same indefiniteness and uncertainty which had characterised the constitution of the witenagemots continued as a feature of the feudal great councils.

Lay and spiritual lords. With the exception of the famous meeting of Salisbury in 1086, which was attended not only by the tenants-in-chief but also by the under-tenants,[4] and the similar general muster of land-owners held by Henry I at Salisbury in 1116,[5] the complete assembly of all the tenants-in-chief can hardly ever have taken place. Still, when councils were summoned for the purpose of granting extraordinary aids,

---

[1] This expression is used merely as a modern description, to avoid any implication that contemporaries had a technical name for such meetings. The editor has likewise avoided the words *Commune Concilium Regni*, which were used by Stubbs, Maitland and Taswell-Langmead, since they are not the contemporary name for an institution but are based on a misunderstanding of Magna Carta (1215), cc. 12, 14; *cf.* A. B. White, *American Historical Review*, xxv, 1–17 (1919).
[2] *Supra*, pp. 17 *et seq.*
[3] The Constitutions of Clarendon (1164), c. 11, imply that attendance on the *curia regis* was an obligation of tenants by barony only. The issue between G. B. Adams (*Origins of the English Constitution*, 193) and Maitland (*Constitutional History*, 163) as to whether the *curia regis* was purely feudal or not, is largely a matter of words.
[4] See *supra*, p. 34.
[5] Florence of Worcester, *s. a.* 1116.

the king promised on such occasions to summon all tenants *in capite*, the archbishops, bishops, abbots, earls, and *majores barones* individually, and the rest generally through the sheriff.[6] This difference in the mode of summons—a difference which had been observed for at least half a century[7] and probably from a still earlier period—is evidence of the inequality then existing among the tenants-in-chief. Though formally recognised by Magna Carta, the right of the inferior tenants-in-chief to attend the national council must soon have become impracticable through the increase in their numbers (arising from the subdivision of tenures), their comparative poverty, and the personal inconvenience of attending at long distances from home. Thus the ancient national assembly gradually ceased to be anything more than an assembly of the " greater barons," and ultimately developed into a hereditary House of Lords, the upper house of the national parliament.[8]

Hereditary lords. The hereditary character of the House of Lords— now long regarded as fixed and fundamental—accrued slowly, as a consequence of the hereditary descent of the baronial fiefs in right of which summonses to the national council were issued. But, in addition to the barons by tenure, the king asserted the right at least as early as the reign of Edward I of summoning other persons who held nothing of the crown by barony. It is certain that a summons was not at first regarded as conferring even a lasting personal right, much less one that was hereditary; but by the time that the custom arose of creating baronies by letters patent (the first instance of which was the creation in 1387 of Sir John Beauchamp of Holt as Lord Beauchamp of Kidderminster, in the 11th of Richard II), the hereditary nature of the baronage, irrespective of tenure, may be regarded as the established rule.[9] Still, the rule has never been without exception.

Spiritual lords. The presence of the bishops in the House of Lords is at once an exception to the principle of hereditary right, and a continuing witness of the times when such right had no existence. Down to the suppression of the monasteries by Henry VIII, in 1539, while the abbots and priors sat with the bishops, the spiritual lords sometimes actually outnumbered the lords temporal; and even after the abbots and priors had been removed the bishops alone formed about one-third of the House of Lords.[10]

---

[6] Magna Carta (1215), c. 14.

[7] In 1164, Archbishop Becket felt himself insulted by receiving a summons to the Great Council in Northampton, not by special writ, but through a common summons directed to the Sheriff of Kent. William Fitz-Stephen in *Materials for the History of Becket*, ed. Robertson (Rolls Series), iii, 51. Stubbs, *Constitutional History*, i, 504.

[8] Round, " The Origin of the House of Lords," in *Peerage and Pedigree*, i, 324 *et seq.*

[9] Pike, *Constitutional History of the House of Lords*, pp. 99 *et seq.*

[10] May, *Constitutional History*, i, 201.

ELECTION AND REPRESENTATION

As the ordinary tenant-in-chief became gradually merged in the general mass of freeholders, his theoretical right of attending the national assembly in person was exchanged for the practical right of electing representatives, who in his name consented to the imposition of taxes. The ideas of election and representation, both separately and in combination, had been familiar to the nation, in its legal and fiscal system, long before they were applied to the constitution of the national parliament. The English kingship was always in theory, and to a great extent in practice, elective. The bishops were supposed to be elected by the clergy, and the abbots generally were elected by their fellow monks. The Dominican friars since 1221 even had a system of assemblies attended by elected priors and elected representatives and the canonists soon developed a body of practice,[11] out of which the philosophers were to evolve a theory of representation.[12] In the local courts of the hundred and the shire the reeve and four men attended as representatives from each township and twelve burgesses from each borough. Subsequently, in the system of recognition by jury, as developed by Henry II, the principles of election and representation were successively applied to almost every description of business—fiscal, judicial, and administrative. In the four sworn knights summoned by the sheriff to nominate the recognitors of the Grand Assize we have, probably, the first germ of a county representation.[13]

St. Albans, 1213. The first suggested instance of the extension to a national assembly of the representative machinery which had long existed in the folkmoot of the shire is afforded by the council held at St. Albans on August 4, 1213, after John's submission to the pope, and during his dispute with the northern barons on the question of foreign service. To this assembly were summoned, according to Roger of Wendover, not only the bishops and barons, but also the reeve and four men from each township on the royal demesne; the chronicler however does not state that these representatives actually attended the council. The immediate business to be transacted was the assessment of the amount due by way of restitution to the church; but several other matters of national importance appear to have been discussed by the assembly. Their representative capacity may be doubted, and the suggestion has been made that they were more probably the " four legal men " who in 1208 supervised locally

---

[11] *Cf.* Powicke, *Henry III*, i, 269.

[12] M. V. Clarke, *Medieval Representation and Consent.*

[13] Stubbs, *Select Charters*, Introductory Sketch, 27. For the influence of ecclesiastical assemblies on the development of the representative system, see E. Barker, *The Dominican Order and Convocation, a study of the growth of representation in the Church during the XIIIth century*, and the criticisms of Pasquet in *An Essay on the Origins of the House of Commons*, pp. 19–23. *Cf.* G. de Lagarde in *Revue Historique de Droit* [1937], 756. Throughout this chapter, it should be remembered that to elect is merely to choose, and that the process of election was not expressly prescribed; it would be misleading to think of it as a count of votes. Compare the commission of 1282 to " elect " 1,000 men for the army—which can only mean to pick or impress; Palgrave, *Parliamentary Writs*, i, 228.

the king's confiscatory measures. The chroniclers' brief narratives leave so much room for conjecture that it is hardly possible to determine the proper place of this incident in our constitutional history, although its general significance is undeniable.[14]

Four instances of summoning representatives of the shires to the national council are met with prior to de Montfort's celebrated parliament of 1265, which is sometimes erroneously spoken of as the " origin of popular representation." [15]

Oxford, 1213. (1) The first occurred during the contest between John and the barons, when both sides found it necessary to seek the support of the free tenants of the counties. In 1213 the king, by his writ to the sheriffs, directed four discreet knights of each shire to be sent to him on November 15, at Oxford " ad loquendum nobiscum de negotiis regni nostri." [16] There is no indication on the face of this writ whether the four knights were to be elected by the county or returned at the discretion of the sheriff; but as there already existed a recognised machinery for the election, in the county court, of four knights to nominate the recognitors in civil suits and the grand jury for the presentment of criminals, it may reasonably be concluded that the accustomed machinery was now used for the novel purpose of county representation in the general assembly. It is probable also that the 14th clause of John's Charter, which promised that the minor barons should be summoned generally by the sheriff, though it undoubtedly recognised their personal right to attend, was practically interpreted by the light of the county representation system already introduced less than two years previously.

A long interval of forty years elapsed before the presence of representatives of the counties at national assemblies is again recorded. But the period is marked by the increasing use of representatives elected in the

---

[14] Wendover, ed. Hewlett (Rolls Series), ii, 82; *cf.* Matthew Paris, ii, 550–551 (in Stubbs, *Select Charters,* 271). The passage has been variously interpreted. H. W. C. Davis, *English Historical Review,* xx, 289 (1905), suggests that the reeve and four men were not to appear at St. Albans, but were merely to make recognition of the facts before the sheriff in the county court. G. J. Turner, *ibid.,* xxi, 297 (1906), thinks that the representatives were summoned not from the vills of the king's demesne but of the bishops' demesne. A. B. White, *American Historical Review,* xvii, 12 *et seq.* (1911), on a comparison with a passage in the *Annals of Waverley* (*sub anno* 1208), concludes that the representatives summoned to St. Albans were the persons to whom the administration of Church property was entrusted in 1208. *Cf.* C. R. Cheney, " King John's Reaction to the Interdict," [1949] *Transactions of the Royal Historical Society,* 130. Concurring in G. J. Turner's view, E. Barker, *Dominican Order,* 52 (1913), observes that in substance it was a matter of juries assessing damages. Pasquet, *op. cit.* 42 (1914), suggests that the chronicler had before him the writ summoning the reeve and four men of the vills in demesne in Hertfordshire to St. Albans, and concluded that representatives from all the vills had been similarly summoned to St. Albans, whereas in the writs addressed to the sheriffs of other counties, other places of meeting may have been indicated. The whole controversy is conveniently summarised in Pasquet's *Essay,* 38–43.

[15] Hallam, *Middle Ages,* iii, 27.

[16] *Report on Dignity of a Peer,* App. i, 2. *Select Charters,* 282. (Earlier editions of Stubbs' *Charters* contained the erroneous reading *homines* instead of *milites,* and thus occasioned some confusion in the discussion of this assembly); *cf. English Historical Review,* xxxi, 85; A. L. Poole, *Domesday Book to Magna Carta,* 463, n. 2.

county court for fiscal and other purposes. Thus, in 1220 and 1225, two writs of Henry III direct the election of knights for the assessment and collection of subsidies,[17] and in 1226 writs were directed to the sheriffs of eight counties to send to the king, at Lincoln, four knights elected in each county, to make complaints against the sheriffs, concerning an alleged infringement of the Great Charter.[18] To a general assembly of the prelates, earls and barons of London in 1246 the name of parliament, which had previously been indiscriminately ascribed to assemblies of various kinds, is for the first time given by a contemporary chronicler, Matthew Paris.[19] Henceforth it became specially, though not for many years exclusively, the appellation of the national council.[20]

Westminster, 1254. (2) The second instance of county representation in parliament is met with in 1254, when Henry III was in Gascony, and in want of men and money. By his direction Queen Eleanor and the Earl of Cornwall, the regents, issued writs to the sheriffs to cause to come before the King's Council at Westminster two lawful and discreet knights from each county, whom the men of the county shall have chosen for this purpose in the place of all and each of them, to consider, together with the knights of the other counties, what aid they will grant the king in such an emergency. These writs possess both a positive and a negative importance. On the one hand we have it clearly directed that the two knights are to be chosen by the county—that is, in the county court; that they are to represent the whole county, and are to have a deliberate voice in the assembly; on the other, the absence of any restriction of the elective franchise to tenants *in capite*, or to knights, is sufficient evidence that no such restriction then existed.[21]

The utter falseness of Henry III—who persistently disregarded the Great Charter, notwithstanding his repeated solemn confirmations of it— his devotion to successive sets of foreign favourites, his foolish and expensive attempt to secure the crown of Sicily for his son Edmund, his illegal exactions, prodigality and support of the papacy, excited in all

[17] *Close Rolls*, i, 437; Rymer, i, 177. *Select Charters*, 349, 351.

[18] *Report on Dignity of a Peer*, App. i, 4. *Select Charters*, 353.

[19] " Parliamentum generalissimum "; *Chronica Majora*, ed. Luard, iv, 518. *Select Charters*, 328.

[20] In a writ of 1248 the expression " coram rege et toto parliamento " is used; *Close Rolls*, vi, 107. Even after the national council had permanently in 1295 assumed the form of a perfect representation of the three estates of the realm, the name of parliament continued to be applied both to the terminal sessions of the king's council, and to the occasional assemblies of the *Magnum Concilium*. A not infrequent term in early use for the sessions of the national council was the Latin *colloquium* (often with *et tractatus* added); and " it is by no means unlikely," remarks Stubbs, " that the name of Parliament, which is used as early as 1175 by Jordan Fantosme, may have been in common use. . . . When the term comes into use it is applied retrospectively; and in a record of the 28th year of Henry III the assembly in which the Great Charter was granted is mentioned as the ' Parliamentum Runimedae.' "—*Constitutional History*, i, 611. Much illuminating material on the history and early use of the word and a comparison with French institutions is collected by Richardson in *Transactions of the Royal Historical Society*, 4th series, xi. 137.

[21] *Report on Dignity of a Peer*, i, 95, and App. i, p. 13. *Select Charters*, 365. *Cf.* Pasquet, 33 *et seq.*

classes of his subjects feelings of animosity and resistance equal to, if not exceeding in intensity, those which had inspired the combination against John.

Provisions of Oxford, 1258. Matters came to a crisis in the great council or parliament, which met at London on April 2, 1258; and after stormy debates, lasting till May 5, the king found himself obliged to submit wholly to the guidance of the barons.[22] At their desire he consented to the appointment of a committee of twenty-four persons, to be elected, twelve by the barons and twelve by the king, in a parliament summoned to meet at Oxford on June 11. To these twenty-four unlimited power was confided to carry out all necessary reforms. They began by drawing up the set of articles known as the Provisions of Oxford, under which all the powers of government were placed in the hands of a kind of representative oligarchy.[23] By a rather complicated process, bearing some resemblance to the Venetian constitution, each twelve of the twenty-four selected two from the other twelve, and the four thus chosen elected fifteen as a continual council of state. Another committee of twenty-four was appointed for the special business of treating of the aid required by the king for the war; and in order, as was alleged, to spare the other members the expense of frequent attendance in parliament (which was to meet three times a year), a third body of " twelve honest men " was elected by the barons, as representatives of the community, to treat with the king's council of the common need.[24]

Although representatives of the shires were not summoned to the Oxford Parliament, the machinery of county representation was made use of for the other purposes under the Provisions, each county being directed to elect " four discreet and lawful knights " to inquire into abuses. The application, moreover, of the principles of election and representation to the constitution of the governing body of the kingdom under the Provisions, was probably not without effect in securing popular representation in parliament. In these Provisions the barons are designated as " the party of the commonalty "; and in the proclamation in English of the king's adhesion to the Provisions, he speaks of his councillors as " chosen by us and by the *landsfolk* of our kingdom," [25] an expression which calls to mind the " landsittende men " who attended King William's gemot at

---

[22] The events of these years are the subject of a considerable literature; E. F. Jacob, *Baronial Rebellion and Reform* (Oxford, 1925), R. F. Treharne, *Baronial Plan of Reform* (Manchester, 1932) and F. M. Powicke, *Henry III and the Lord Edward* (Oxford, 1947), i, 302 *et seq.*, are the major works.

[23] Text in Stubbs, *Select Charters*, 378–387. The government in England has on four occasions been placed for a time in the hands of an oligarchy. In John's reign, the 25 barons of Magna Carta; under Henry III, the Oxford Committee of 24; under Edward II, the 21 Lords Ordainers; and under Richard II, the 5 Lords Appellant. For the name " Mad Parliament " inaptly applied to this body, see *Bulletin of the Institute of Historical Research* iii, 110, plate I (1925), and C. Bémont, *Simon de Montfort* (ed. E. F. Jacob), 155, n. 1.

[24] See the series of documents relating to the Provisions of Oxford in Stubbs, *Select Charters*, 369–397.

[25] Rymer, i, 378. *Select Charters*, 387.

Salisbury in 1086. It would seem that at least all the landed proprietors of the realm, and not merely the barons, or even the tenants-in-chief, were regarded as directly or indirectly represented in the governing council.

St. Albans, 1261. (3) In 1261 the king openly refused to abide by the Provisions of Oxford, and civil war broke out. During the contest, the confederate barons summoned to St. Albans three knights from each county, " secum tractaturi super communibus negotiis regni "; where-upon the king, in opposition, issued other writs directing the sheriffs to enjoin the same knights to repair instead, on the day originally fixed, to the king at Windsor, " nobiscum super praemissis colloquium habituros." [26]

De Montfort's first Parliament, 1264. (4) The decisive victory at the battle of Lewes, on May 14, 1264, followed by the surrender of the king and his son Edward, placed the supreme power in the hands of Simon de Montfort. Although the arbitration of St. Louis of France and his award in Henry's favour (January 23, 1264) had served only to rekindle the flame of civil war, a proviso was inserted in the Mise of Lewes, referring all controversies between the king and the barons to the decision of a second arbitration. In the meantime, de Montfort, having placed friendly garrisons in all the royal castles, issued writs in the king's name, appointing certain extraordinary magistrates, called guardians of the peace, in every county and summoning four lawful and discreet knights, " per assensum ejusdem comitatus ad hoc electos pro toto comitatu illo," to attend the king in parliament at London " nobiscum tractaturi de negotiis praedictis." [27]

De Montfort's second Parliament, 1265. If not " the founder of representative government in England," as Guizot has termed him,[28] Simon de Montfort may justly be regarded as the " founder of the House of Commons." [29] An assembly of knights of the shire, exclusively represent-ing the landowners of the kingdom, and closely united by descent, interest, and sympathies with the great barons, could never have formed a really popular chamber, entitled to speak in the name and on behalf of the whole commonalty of the realm. To Simon, Earl of Leicester, belongs the lasting glory of having been the first to admit within the pale of our political constitution the really popular and progressive burgher class.[30]

---

[26] *Report on Dignity of a Peer*, App. i, p. 23; Shirley, *Royal Letters of Henry III*, ii, 179; *Select Charters*, 394. The king's writs went only to Norfolk, Suffolk, and the counties south of the Trent. There is no evidence that the meeting at Windsor actually took place.

[27] Rymer, i, 442. *Select Charters*, 400.

[28] *Histoire des Origines du Gouvernement Représentatif*, ii, 173.

[29] " Der Schöpfer des Hauses der Gemeinen " (" the founder of the House of Commons "). —Pauli, *Simon von Montfort*. On his career, see particularly his life by Bémont.

[30] The claim of Simon de Montfort to be the creator of the House of Commons is much disputed. The assembly of 1265 was a meeting of the Earl's partisans, a large body of ecclesiastics, a small body of barons (5 earls and 18 barons), and the representatives of the shires and boroughs; and they were called together in order to sanction the newly

This " bold and happy innovation " was effected on December 14, 1264 (49th Henry III), when de Montfort, in the name of the captive king, summoned his famous parliament to meet at London on the 20th of the following January. Writs were issued to all the sheriffs directing them to return not only two knights from each shire, but also two citizens from each city, and two burgesses from each borough.[31]

Borough representation. The towns of England, from a position of dependence, were slowly attaining to the possession of liberty, wealth, and the political franchise. Originally the demesne of the king or other lord, spiritual or temporal, they long continued subject to arbitrary tallage and other exactions. Before the Norman Conquest the towns had acquired an individuality distinct from the hundred in which they were locally comprised. Instead of attending at the court of the hundred, the townsmen had their own gemot, presided over by the elective or nominated reeve, assisted by a body of councillors.[32] As the boroughs increased in wealth and population, the burghers began to purchase from their lords the *firma burgi*, thus commuting their individual payments for a fixed sum, to be rendered by them in respect of the whole borough, and re-apportioned amongst themselves at their own discretion. The burgesses acquired the freehold of their houses and tenements in burgage tenure, which was analogous to that in free socage, being subject only to a fixed annual rent payable to the lord. During the lapse of two hundred years after the conquest, the citizens and burgesses were enabled to extort, from the pecuniary necessities of the kings, charters of liberties varying greatly in extent, but all conceding more or less self-government through the medium of elected and representative magistrates.[33]

established form of government. It was an extraordinary assembly summoned for an extraordinary purpose, and there is no reason to suppose that the experiment was intended to be repeated. Simon, like Edward I later, called the Commons to strengthen his power against the attacks of the baronage. " The novelty," says Stubbs, " was simply the assembling the representatives of the towns in conjunction with those of the counties " (*Select Charters*, 398). The importance of the novelty must not however be underrated. Pasquet (p. 60) concludes : " The parliament of January, 1265, was the *first* in which representatives of the counties and of the towns took part, if not side by side, at least simultaneously. In this sense Simon de Montfort was the creator of the House of Commons," and with certain reservations he maintains that " it must be admitted that the precedent set by Simon de Montfort was of extreme importance for the future." Its chief significance lies in the fact that the precedent was copied by Edward I, who held a fully representative assembly, not as was once thought for the first time in 1295 after thirty years of constitutional experiments, but in 1275, in the first parliament of his reign, just ten years after the parliament of Simon.

[31] See the writ in Rymer, i, 449; and *Select Charters*, 403.

[32] *Supra*, pp. 10 *et seq.*

[33] The progressive liberties granted to the towns should be studied in the charters of Henry I, Henry II, Richard I, and John, collected in Stubbs, *Select Charters*, 128–134, 195–199, 258–262, 304–314; and on the difficult and obscure subject of the various constitutions of the cities and boroughs, see his *Constitutional History*, ii, 216, 232; F. W. Maitland, *Township and Borough* (1898); A. Ballard, *Domesday Boroughs* (1904); and especially Tait, *The Medieval English Borough* (Manchester, 1936); the charters have been collected in *British Borough Charters* (1042–1216) ed. Ballard, continued (1216–1307), ed. Ballard and Tait, and (1307–1660), ed. Weinbaum. The custumals are collected in *Borough Customs* (ed. Bateson, 2 vols., Selden Society).

As in the case of the counties, so in that of the boroughs, the representative machinery was first employed for judicial and financial purposes before its extension to the domain of politics. In the court of the shire—the ancient folk-moot, or assembly of the people—all the national elements had from time immemorial been wont to meet together, the bishops and other dignified clergy, earls, barons, knights, and freeholders in person[34]; the townships each by their representative reeve and four men. As the boroughs gradually grew into incorporate municipalities, they also sent their representatives to the assembly of the shire. This is apparent from a very important writ, issued by Henry III in 1231 to the sheriff of Yorkshire, for assembling the county court before the justices itinerant, in which he is directed to summon for that purpose not only the persons already enumerated, but also twelve lawful burgesses as representatives from every borough.[35]

It is probable that from an early period some of the wealthy burghers of important towns occasionally attended the general assembly.[36] The letter addressed to the pope by the parliament of 1246 is written in the name, not only of " totius regni Angliae barones, proceres, et magnates," but also of " nobiles portuum maris habitatores, necnon et clerus et populus universus."[37] We are not, however, justified in attributing any representative character to these barons of the Cinque Ports, or to the other burghers whose presence in parliament is sometimes recorded or implied prior to the year 1265. The only object for summoning representatives of the towns was to secure their consent to taxation, and hitherto the kings had found it more convenient to treat separately, through the officers of the Exchequer, with each town in the royal demesne.

Parliament takes shape, 1265–1295. The innovation of Simon de Montfort in calling to the central assembly elected representatives of the boroughs, completed the formation of the national parliament on substantially the basis which it has ever since retained. But its existence during the next thirty years was still precarious. From 1265 to 1295 was

[34] As to the personal attendance of the freeholders generally in the county court, after the conquest, Maitland, *Constitutional History*, p. 42, wrote: " The freeholder was entitled and bound to be present. In such an assembly the tenants-in-chief of the Crown have to meet their own vassals on a footing of legal equality; a tenant may find himself sitting as peer of his own lord." On second thoughts he withdrew this opinion: Pollock and Maitland, *History of English Law*, i, 538 *et seq.* Great lords did not necessarily attend in person; they might send their stewards, or a tenant who had been enfeoffed on condition of doing the suit.

[35] The words of the writ are: " omnes archiepiscopos, episcopos, abbates, priores, comites, barones, milites, et omnes libere tenentes, de tota ballia tua, et de qualibet villa, quatuor legales homines et praepositum, et de quolibet burgo duodecim legales burgenses."— Shirley, *Royal Letters*, i, 325. *Select Charters*, 354. Stubbs, commenting on this writ, points out that the county court contained all the elements that were united in the national assembly at the time, and in addition the representatives of the townships and boroughs. *Ibid.*

[36] See White, *American Historical Review*, xix, 742 *et seq.* (1914). There is no warrant for regarding the representation of vills (if such it was) in August, 1213 (*supra*, p. 129) as being in any way connected with borough representation; Pasquet, 43.

[37] Matt. Paris, *Chronica Majora*, iv, 533.

a transitionary period; and it is only from the latter year that we can date the regular and complete establishment of a perfect representation of the three estates in parliament. There is no proof that representatives of either counties or boroughs attended the parliaments of the later years of Henry III's reign. The statement, however, in the preamble to the Statute of Marlborough (52 Henry III) that the king had called together the more discreet men of the realm " tam ex majoribus quam minoribus " affords a strong presumption that the knights of the shire attended the parliament of 1267.[38] A contemporary chronicler, moreover, records the summoning in 1269 of representatives from the cities and boroughs, to assist at the translation of the body of Edward the Confessor to Westminster Abbey, and that on the conclusion of the ceremony a parliament was held, at which a subsidy on the movables of all laymen was granted to the king. But it is not certain that the representatives of boroughs remained for the parliament; indeed, the language of the chronicler would rather seem to imply that they did not.[39] The fact, however, that they were summoned on this occasion, together with the prelates and magnates of the kingdom, is evidence of the greatly increased importance with which the civic element in the nation was now regarded.

PARLIAMENTS OF EDWARD I

Under Edward I instances of representation are few, while great councils, attended only by the prelates and magnates, are very frequent. At this period there appears to have been no legal or definite distinction between complete parliaments and great councils of the realm, and neither expression had yet become a technical term; nor did the word " parliament " imply the summons of the commons. Several of the most important statutes of Edward's reign were passed in assemblies at which no representatives of the commons attended. During the first twenty years of his reign there were about thirty parliaments, but only occasionally did they contain representatives from either counties or boroughs, or from both.

At the national assembly, summoned after the death of Henry III to meet at Westminster on January 14, 1273, to swear allegiance to Edward I, who was still in Palestine, there attended not only the prelates and barons, but four knights from each county, and four citizens from every city.[40]

On his return to England, Edward summoned " his first general

---

[38] *Statutes of the Realm,* i, 19; Stubbs, *Select Charters,* 333, and *Constitutional History,* ii, 233. The same expression is used in French in the preamble of the Statute of Gloucester (1278): "appelez les plus descrez de sun reaume, ausi bien des greindres, cum des meindres." *Select Charters,* 449.

[39] Chronicle of T. Wykes in *Annales Monastici,* iv, 226, 227. Stubbs, *Constitutional History,* ii, 234.

[40] *Annales Monastici* (Winchester), ii, 113; *Select Charters,* 421. The absence of the word " parliament " from the chronicler's brief note seems without significance.

parliament" [41] at Westminster in April, 1275. In the preambles of the important statutes therein enacted (the Statute of Westminster I and the statute granting to the king the custom on wool, woolfells, and leather), they are said to be made " by his council and by the assent of the archbishops, bishops, abbots, priors, earls, barons, and the commonalty of the land [42] thither summoned," and the custom is specially said to be granted by the " communitates regni ad instantiam et rogatum mercatorum," as well as by the prelates and barons. [43] The probability implied in these expressions, that representatives of the commons attended this meeting, became a certainty when in 1910 were discovered writs addressed to the sheriffs of certain counties directing them to send " four knights who were more discreet in the law and also six or four citizens, burgesses or other honest men from each of the cities, boroughs and market towns . . . to discuss together with the magnates of our kingdom the affairs of the kingdom." This parliament, therefore, except in one respect, in the summons of the lower clergy, foreshadows the famous assembly of 1295. [44]

Knights of the shire were summoned to the parliament which met in October, 1275, and possibly again to the parliament of Gloucester in 1278. [45]

Extraordinary assemblies. In 1282, while the king, the barons, and the military force of the kingdom were at Rhuddlan, intent upon the conquest of Wales, two extraordinary assemblies were summoned, the one at Northampton, the other at York, to raise additional forces and grant subsidies. Writs were issued on November 24 to the sheriffs, ordering them to send to Northampton or York, as the case might be, on January 20, 1283 : (1) all freeholders, not already with the army capable of bearing arms, and holding lands of more than £20 annual value; (2) four knights from each county having full power for the community of the same county; and (3) two men from each city, borough, and market town, having like power for the community of the same, " ad audiendum et

---

[41] So described in the preamble to the statute, meaning possibly the first at which the king presided in person. A meeting to which some, but not all, the magnates were convoked in 1284 was described by the annalist of Osney as " singulare, non generale, parliamentum "; *Select Charters*, 425.

[42] On the changing implications of the *communitas regni* see W. A. Morris, " Magnates and Community of the Realm in Parliament, 1264–1327 " in *Medievalia et Humanistica* (1943), i, 58–94 (a criticism of J. R. Strayer, " Statute of York and the Community of the Realm," in *American Historical Review* (1941), xlvii, 1–17).

[43] Statute of Westminster I, *Statutes of the Realm* i, 26; Palgrave, *Parliamentary Writs*, i, 2. *Select Charters*, 442–443.

[44] The writs are printed by Jenkinson in *English Historical Review*, xxv, 231 *et seq.* (1910); *Select Charters*, 441–442; *English Historical Review*, lviii, 462, see also Pasquet, 75–80. Representatives of the market towns (villae mercatoriae) appear in parliament only on one other occasion, in 1283. The requirement that the knights be conversant with legal matters is peculiar, and suggests that the king desired their help in framing his great statute.

[45] Above, p. 136, note 38. See Pasquet, p. 82.

faciendum ea quae sibi ex parte nostra faciemus ostendi."[46] The parliamentary proceedings of this year are important, as " marking the point of final transition from the system of local to that of central assent to taxation."[47] The king had already, in order to raise funds for the Welsh war, successfully negotiated for a subsidy with the counties and boroughs separately.[48] But the sums raised not proving sufficient, the necessity for a general grant became apparent and led to the general assemblies of representatives of the counties and boroughs above described. Convocations of the bishops, abbots, priors, and other heads of religious houses, with the proctors of the cathedral clergy of the provinces of Canterbury and York, were also summoned, through their respective archbishops, to meet at Northampton and York on the same day as the estate of the commons, for the purpose of making a grant to the king.[49] On the ground that the parochial clergy were unrepresented, the convocation of Canterbury refused to contribute anything; and it was not until after a long delay, during which the diocesan synods were separately consulted, that a " twentieth " (half the sum originally demanded by the king) was at length granted in another convocation, held in November, and attended by two proctors from the parochial clergy of each diocese.[50]

Acton Burnell, 1283. In June of the same year, Edward, being at Rhuddlan, summoned a national council to meet at Shrewsbury on September 30, for the purpose of passing judgment of treason on David, brother and successor of Llewelyn, Prince of Wales, who had surrendered as prisoner after the conquest of that country.

Besides the earls and barons who were individually summoned, writs were issued (1) to the sheriffs throughout England, directing the attendance at Shrewsbury of two elected knights from each county, and (2) to the magistrates of London and twenty other towns, directing the return from each of two elected representatives " nobiscum super hoc [sc. quid de David fieri debeat] et aliis locuturi."[51] This assembly is called by contemporaries the parliament of Shrewsbury or Acton Burnell. It will be noticed that there is no proof that any of the clergy were present,[52] and that the representatives of the twenty-one towns were summoned by separate writs, instead of through the sheriffs in the usual way. But however imperfect the composition of this parliament may have been, we have here an unequivocal instance of the representation of both sections of the commons in the central assembly of the nation. The

---

[46] Palgrave, *Parliamentary Writs*, i, 10. *Select Charters*, 458. The bishops and clergy of either province were similarly convoked ; there are no writs to the barons, no doubt because they were already with the king in his army.

[47] Stubbs, *Select Charters*, 452.

[48] *Parliamentary Writs*, i, 384, 387.

[49] *Parliamentary Writs*, i, 10. *Select Charters*, 459.

[50] *Ibid.* The convocation of York seem to have been more compliant, but their promised contribution was still unpaid three years afterwards. *Constitutional History*, ii, 120.

[51] *Parliamentary Writs*, i, 16; *Select Charters*, 460–461.

[52] The fact that the principal object of the assembly was a trial for a capital offence sufficiently accounts for their non-summons.

commons would appear to have left David of Wales to be tried by his peers at Shrewsbury, while they themselves adjourned to Acton Burnell to discuss the " other matters " referred to in the writ. The Statute of Acton Burnell or *De Mercatoribus*,[53] though published in the name of the king and his council only, was the outcome of the deliberations of this assembly of the commons. It is noteworthy that the parliaments at Westminster and Winchester, which produced statutes of the highest importance in 1285, seem not to have been attended by the commons.

Parliaments of 1290. The state of parliament is peculiarly illustrated by the proceedings of the year 1290. The king had already held a parliament on the octave of St. Hilary (Jan. 20), to which the magnates and *proceres* only were summoned.[54] In a second parliament, begun at Easter, consisting only of prelates, earls, barons, and *proceres*, the assembled magnates granted on the morrow of Holy Trinity (May 29), for the marriage of the king's eldest daughter—(1) that he should take an aid of the same kind and amount as his father King Henry had taken from the kingdom for the marriage of his daughter to the King of Scots, and (2) after reciting that King Henry had only received from each knight's fee two marks (one mark = 13s. 4d.) they further granted that the king, for this turn, should take forty shillings on every knight's fee ; but on condition that the present grant should not form a precedent to their prejudice, and that the aid should be levied in the same manner as that granted to King Henry.[55] It is remarkable that the aid was further declared by the magnates to be granted " pro se et communitate totius regni quantum in ipsis est," words which seem to express a doubt of their competency to make a grant, even on the knight's fee, for the whole community, without the presence of the commons, or at least of the minor tenants-in-chief. The aid *pur fille marier* was one of the three ancient feudal imposts excepted from the twelfth section of King John's Magna Carta, and, even if that section had not been omitted from every subsequent re-issue of the Charter, would not appear, in strict law, to have required a parliamentary authorisation. But the *amount* of the aid in the case of tenants *in capite* was not yet fixed by law,[56] and hence the necessity, as a matter of politics if not of law, for an agreement with them on this point. A further reason is carefully concealed by the official documents, which

---

[53] 11 Edw. 1, confirmed and much enlarged in its scope by the more famous statute of 1285, 13 Edw. 1, Statute of Merchants. Both are discussed in T. F. T. Plucknett, *Legislation of Edward I*, Chap. VI.

[54] At this parliament new judges were appointed to replace those removed for misconduct in the great purge of 1289. *Cf.* Tout, *State Trials of Edward I.*

[55] *Rotuli Parliamentorum*, i, 25 ; *Select Charters*, 472. For the obscure chronology of this period, see Richardson and Sayles in *Bulletin of the Institute of Historical Research*, v. 143 *et seq.*

[56] The aids payable by the tenants of mesne lords, for making the eldest son a knight or marrying the eldest daughter, had been fixed in 1275 by the Statute of Westminster I, c. 36, at 20s. on the knight's fee. It was not until 1352, by 25 Edw. 3, st. 5, c. 11, that the same was done for the tenants *in capite*.

speak of the king's " eldest " daughter; in fact it was his second daughter whose marriage was in view.[57]

This parliament continued to sit, apparently, and some matter arose (we are not informed of its nature—it may have been the expulsion of the Jews) which made a wider assembly desirable; and so, on June 14, 1290 (18th Edward I), writs were issued to the sheriffs to send from each shire, to a parliament at Westminster on July 15, two or three elected knights, of the most discreet and capable of hard work, " ad consulendum et consentiendum pro se et communitate comitatus, hiis quae comites, barones, et proceres tunc duxerint concordanda." [58] No townsmen were asked for. Meanwhile, on July 8, before the commons had arrived in accordance with the summons for the 15th of the month, the king, at the instance of the magnates alone ("ad instantiam magnatum regni sui "), enacted the celebrated Statute of Westminster the Third or *Quia Emptores*, by which a stop was put to the practice of subinfeudation[59]; that the right to share in general legislation of even that section of the commons which was closely allied to the baronage was not at this time established is evident from the publication by the king of a statute affecting all land-owners with the counsel and consent of the baronage alone, and without the assent of the representatives of the shires. The aid granted by the baronage was laid aside for a time (it was not levied till twelve years later, in 1302)[60] and in lieu thereof the king appears to have accepted a " fifteenth " from the laity and a " tenth " from the clergy who were assembled at Ely.[61]

Parliament of 1294. Four years later, on October 8, 1294, the king being in want of money, both for the suppression of the Welsh rebellion and for his projected expedition against Philip the Fair for the recovery of Gascony, again summoned to a parliament, which was to meet at Westminster on November 12, two elected knights from each shire " ad consulendum et consentiendum pro se et communitate illa hiis quae comites barones et proceres praedicti concorditer ordinaverint in prae-missis." On the following day fresh writs were issued summoning two other knights from each county to attend in addition to those previously called " ad audiendum et faciendum quod eis tunc ibidem plenius in-jungemus." [62] The barons and knights granted a " tenth "; and a " sixth," probably by way of tallage, was exacted from the towns.[63]

---

[57] J. H. Ramsay, *Dawn of the Constitution*, 367.

[58] *Report on the Dignity of a Peer*, App. i, 54; Palgrave, *Parliamentary Writs*, i, 24; *Select Charters*, 472–473.

[59] *Supra*, pp. 38, 89; T. F. T. Plucknett, *Legislation of Edward I*, 102–108.

[60] *Rotuli Parliamentorum*, i, 266.

[61] *Annals of Dunstable*, p. 362.

[62] *Report on the Dignity of a Peer*, App. i, 60; *Select Charters*, 476–477. The writs use the words *colloquium* and *tractatus*, but not *parliamentum*; the form using all three words did not become invariable until Edward III's early years. See Plucknett, " Parliament," in *English Government at Work*, 1327–1336 (ed. J. F. Willard and W. A. Morris), 84 *et seq.*

[63] *Flores Historiarum*, iii, 275; Stubbs, *Constitutional History*, ii, 132.

Lords and Commons in Parliament, 1295. The following year, 1295 (23rd Edward I), foreshadows the regular establishment of a representation of the estates of the realm in parliament, although it should be remembered that the discovery of the writs of summons for the parliament of 1275 has considerably lessened the importance of the parliament of 1295 as " an epoch in parliamentary history "; and that for the next thirty years, during which nearly fifty parliaments were called, there were about fifteen to which apparently no commons were summoned. Edward's difficulties had become serious. The expedition to France was still delayed by the rebellion of the Welsh, and before their obstinate resistance could be subdued, war with Scotland supervened. The French had not only overrun Gascony, but had sent a fleet to the English coast, which effected a landing at Dover and burnt a convent and several houses on August 1— the very day on which a parliament had been summoned to meet at Westminster [64] to consider, among other things, the proposals of two legates sent by the pope to endeavour to bring about peace between France and England.[65] The legates were ultimately empowered to conclude a truce [66]; but the position of the kingdom was still critical, and Edward seems to have felt that he required to be backed up by the whole nation, supporting him as well by their common counsel and approval as by a general and adequate grant of an aid. He accordingly, on September 30, summoned a parliament to meet at Westminster in the November following, so constituted as to represent, and have the power to tax, the whole nation. The summons to the bishops enters with unusual detail into the causes which had rendered it necessary to call parliament together, and is prefaced by a citation from Justinian's Code—" quod omnes tangit ab omnibus approbetur " [67]—which happily expresses both the theory and the practice of the English constitution of later times. In its beneficent influence upon the development of constitutionalism this maxim of Roman law may be regarded as an antidote to its more famous fellow maxim, " quod principi placuit legis habet vigorem," which, in the mouths of the medieval jurists, did so much to build up the despotic power of

[64] Rymer, i, 822. The writs call it a " parleamentum "; all the usual prelates and magnates were summoned, but no commons.
[65] Florence of Worcester (*Contin.*), ii, 276.
[66] Rymer, i, 825.
[67] *Cod.* V, 59, 5 §3. It occurs also in the canon law, c. 7, X 1. 23 (and *cf. De Regulis Juris*, in VI°, 29). But it seems to have been familiarly known in England; *cf. Chapters of the English Black Monks* (ed. W. A. Pantin), i, 19, "ut quod omnes tangit, per omnes vel per eorum partem saniorem agatur " (1225); Matt. Paris (*anno* 1251), *Chronica Majora*, v. 225, " quod enim omnes angit et tangit ab omnibus habet trutinari "; and the *Vita Edwardi II* in *Chronicles of Edward I and II*, ed. Stubbs (Rolls Series), ii, 170. *Cf.* Stubbs, *Constitutional History*, ii, 133, n. 4; Lapsley's note in Pasquet, 243–244; Vinogradoff, *Collected Papers*, ii, 245–246; Gaines Post, " A Romano-Canonical maxim ' *Quod omnes tangit*' in Bracton," *Traditio*, iv, 197; the phrase does not occur in the writs to the laity, whether lords or commons. Ernst H. Kantorowicz, *The King's Two Bodies* (see p. 556 for refs.). It had long played a part in English ecclesiastical politics: M. V. Clarke, *Representation and Consent*, 264 *et seq.* The whole preamble of the writs to the archbishops and bishops is remarkable; contrast the writs to the lay baronage, sheriffs, elected knights, citizens, and burgesses where the phrase is not used: *Reports on Dignity of a Peer*, App. i, 66, 67; *Select Charters*, 480–482. Surtees Society, clv, 212.

the kingly office.[68] Besides the ordinary summons to the lay and spiritual baronage, writs were issued to the sheriffs ordering the election and return of two knights from each county, two citizens from each city, and two burgesses from each borough, "ad faciendum quod tunc de communi consilio ordinabitur in praemissis."

Inferior clergy in parliament. But together with the knights and burgesses, the whole inferior clergy, by their representatives under the *praemunientes* clause, were now for the first time united with the assembled baronage in the national parliament. In the writs addressed to the Archbishops of Canterbury and York, each was directed not only to be present at the parliament, but also to *premonish* the prior (or the dean) of his cathedral and the archdeacons of his diocese to attend in person, and the chapter of the cathedral and the parochial clergy by their representative proctors.[69] This great assembly did not form a single body. The aid was discussed and voted by each of the three bodies separately. Each made a different proportional grant. The barons and knights gave the king one-eleventh of their movables, the burgesses one-seventh, the clergy only one-tenth.

Convocation. The summons to parliament of representatives of the inferior clergy was partly due, like that of the citizens and burgesses, to the pecuniary necessities of the king. It was doubtless the intention of Edward's legal and systematic mind to make the representatives of the clergy an effective branch of a comprehensive national parliament. But this design was defeated by the action of the clergy themselves. Averse, by the nature of their calling, from interfering in the ordinary subjects of secular legislation, despising as barbarous the system of common law, and desirous of keeping themselves as a privileged class and maintaining their independence of the crown, they unwillingly obeyed a summons the primary object of which they well knew was to get from them as much money as possible. The clergy, moreover, had long possessed their own peculiar assemblies or convocations which, earlier in the reign of Edward I, had already been remodelled upon the representative basis.[70] In these assemblies, one for each province, sitting at London (as being more convenient than Canterbury) and York, they preferred to grant their aids; and, although regularly summoned to parliament under the

---

[68] *Dig.* I, 4, 1; *Inst.* I, 2, 6. Glanvill, prologue, and Bracton, f. 1, try to escape the implications of the maxim (*cf.* C. H. McIlwain, *Political Thought in the West*, 195, and Selden, *Dissertatio ad Fletam* (ed. David Ogg), *passim*).

[69] There were summoned to this parliament, eight earls, forty-one barons, the two archbishops and the bishops, sixty-seven abbots, the masters of the Temple and of Sempringham and the prior of the Hospital of St. John of Jerusalem, the prior (or dean) and one proctor from the chapter of each cathedral, the archdeacons, and two proctors from the parochial clergy of each diocese, two knights from each county, and two citizens or burgesses from each city or borough in every shire.

[70] See the series of summonses to convocation, 1225-1277, in Stubbs, *Select Charters*, 444–447, and the Introductory Sketch, p. 41.

praemunientes clause, their attendance was always reluctant and intermittent, and in the fourteenth century ceased altogether.[71]   For two hundred years after they had ceased to attend parliament, the clergy retained the function of taxing themselves in convocation.   But from the reign of Henry VIII, when the reformed church, which in its national aspect was itself the creation of parliament, was placed in strict subordination to the state,[72] the subsidies granted in convocation were (since 1540) always confirmed by Act of Parliament.   At length, in 1664, the practice of ecclesiastical taxation was discontinued, without the enactment of any special law, and the clergy, being henceforth taxed at the same rate and in the same manner with the laity, assumed and have ever since enjoyed the right of voting in the election of members of the House of Commons.[73]

Model parliaments.   The great assemblies of 1275 and 1295 may well be called " Model " since in the fullness of time the long succession of English parliaments finally conformed to that pattern ; but many national assemblies, for half a century after 1275, were less comprehensive.   Often there were no commons at all; sometimes there were knights but no burgesses ; nor did the dispersal of the commons prevent the parliament from continuing to transact business.   The representation of the capitular and parochial clergy was a problem met by constantly changing expedients, and was finally settled only by subterfuge.   The use or avoidance of the word " parliament " in contemporary documents and narratives does not correspond with either the composition or the functions of these assemblies, nor can we draw distinctions of a legal and constitutional nature between them.   Political expediency was a sufficient guide in determining whether a larger or smaller representation was desirable, or none at all.   To say that some of these meetings were " parliaments " while others were not is to introduce a distinction which contemporaries did not feel necessary, and to exclude evidence which is clearly relevant to the study of parliamentary origins.   Many meetings of very different sorts must have formed part of the political experience and personal recollection of a bishop, a baron or a local magnate in the last years of Edward I, and so have contributed to the broad foundation which determined the shape of the future structure.

Clericis laicos.   The years immediately following 1295 are occupied by a succession of grave crises, political, military, financial and

---

[71] For convocations see M. V. Clarke, *Representation and Consent* (1936); E. Barker, *Dominican Order and Convocation* (1913); D. B. Weske, *Convocation of the Clergy* (1937); and F. Makower, *Constitutional History of the Church of England* (1895).

[72] By 25 Hen. 8, c. 19, convocation was forbidden to enact constitutions or canons without the king's licence.

[73] The taxation of the clergy out of convocation was termed by Bp. Gibson " the greatest alteration in the constitution ever made without an express law." It was settled by a mere verbal agreement between Archbishop Sheldon and the Lord Chancellor Clarendon. (Hallam, iii, 243 n. cites as his authority a note by Speaker Onslow to Burnet's *History*, iv, 508.)

ecclesiastical. In order to carry on his extensive wars, Edward I was in constant need of large sums of money, which he raised by arbitrary exactions from all classes of his subjects, lay and clerical. In vain did the clergy endeavour to shelter themselves under the bull of Boniface VIII, *Clericis laicos* (February 24, 1296), which absolutely forbade, under pain of excommunication, the payment to laymen of any tax whatever on the revenues of the church. The practical outlawry of the whole clerical body (January 30, 1297), and the temporary confiscation of the estates of the see of Canterbury (February 12, 1297), compelled the clergy to abandon their untenable position and to yield *per se*, or *per mediatores*.[74]

The merchants. Whilst the clergy were exasperated by these violent proceedings, the merchants were equally aggrieved by the heavy impositions placed on the export of their wool by the actual seizure of the greater part of it, for which payment was nominally given by tallies upon the Exchequer. Large quantities of provisions were, in the same manner, exacted from the men of each county for the king's expedition to Flanders, and, in the words of the chronicler, " multae fiebant oppressiones in populo terrae." [75]

The baronage. The baronage also were irritated by the king's open disregard of many of the provisions of the Great Charter, and the Charter of the Forest, both of which he persistently refused to confirm. They had, moreover, a personal grievance in the king's demand of foreign service which, they alleged, neither they nor their ancestors had ever been liable to perform.[76] On February 24 Edward held a " parliament " at Salisbury, to which only the lay baronage, without any bishops or representatives of the commons, was summoned. He here proposed that the barons should go to Gascony, while he himself proceeded to Flanders. On their refusal,[77] he threatened to take away their lands and give them to those who would go. This led to a personal altercation with Roger Bigod, Earl of Norfolk, the Marshal of England,[78] which ended in the breaking up of the assembly, and the withdrawal of the marshal, and of Humphrey Bohun, Earl of Hereford, the constable, who, supported by a large number of the magnates and a force of 1,500 cavalry, stopped the king's officials from seizing the wool, hides, and other commodities on their estates, and resolutely prepared for armed resistance.

[74] *Annales Triveti*, p. 353, *s. a.* 1297; *Select Charters*, 431.
[75] Walter of Hemingburgh, ii, 120, *s. a.* 1297 (now re-edited by H. Rothwell as *Chronicle of Walter of Guisborough*, p. 289); *Select Charters*, 431.
[76] W. Rishanger, *Chronica*, 175, *s. a.* 1297; *Select Charters*, 434.
[77] *Cf.* the refusal of foreign service by St. Hugh of Lincoln in 1198 (*supra*, p. 62), and by the barons of King John (*supra*, p. 67).
[78] The altercation is graphically described by Walter de Hemingburgh, ii, 121; *Select Charters*, 431–432.

CONFIRMATIO CARTARUM, 1297

On May 15, Edward issued writs to the bishops, barons, and sheriffs for a general military levy of all the landholders of the kingdom whose lands were of £20 annual value and upwards, whether tenants in chief or holding of mesne lords. They were to assemble in London on July 7, with horses and arms, ready to cross the sea under the king's personal command.[79] On the 7th the force met; the constable and marshal, when called upon by the king, refused to perform the duties of their offices, in taking the lists of the army, and at their own request were superseded. The summons of the whole force of the kingdom for the purpose of an aggressive foreign war was such a violent straining of the military obligations, alike of feudal tenants and national militia, that the two earls might well have based their refusal on the broad ground of the unconstitutionality, if not of the illegality, of the king's proceedings. They chose, however, to base their refusal on what looks very like a bit of special pleading as to the wording of the summons. Edward, distrustful apparently of the legality of his position, had employed the words " affectuose requirimus et rogamus," instead of the usual imperative formula, in his summons to the earls and barons, and the constable and marshal professed to have regarded this as a mere informal invitation, and not a legal summons.[80] Their answer had probably been deliberately determined upon as most appropriate in the circumstances; for we know from the *Flores Historiarum*[81] that the earls and barons had been concerting their measures in what is termed a parliament of their own (" parliamentum suum ") in the forest of Wye in the Welsh march. In dealing with a man of Edward's well-known legal proclivities, they might have thought it prudent in the coming contest to cover themselves with the shield of technical legality, while at the same time accentuating the fact, which might otherwise have been overlooked, that the king had not ventured to command what they alleged, and he himself ultimately admitted, to be an illegal requisition.[82] Hallam's eulogium upon these two leaders of the political party, which forced from the king the Confirmatio Cartarum, may require some qualification. They were probably actuated quite as much by personal claims as by motives of true patriotism. But whatever were their motives, it is mainly to their combined courage and prudence, and to the patriotic exertions of Archbishop Winchelsey, that we owe the addition of " another pillar to our constitution not less important than the Great Charter itself." [83]

[79] Palgrave's *Parliamentary Writs*, i, 281. A preliminary writ to the sheriffs to summon the landholders, but without specifying the intended voyage beyond the sea, was issued on May 5.

[80] Stubbs, *Constitutional History*, ii, 140-141; H. M. Chew " Scutage under Edward I," *English Historical Review*, xxxvii, 321.

[81] *Flores Historiarum*, iii, 294.

[82] From Bartholomew de Cotton (*Historia Anglicana*, p. 327) we learn that in the same year " concessit dominus rex omnibus qui debebant sibi servitium, et omnibus viginti libratas terrae habentibus, non teneri ire secum in Flandriam, nisi ad vadia, et pro stipendiis dicti regis." *Select Charters*, 435.

[83] Hallam, *Middle Ages*, iii, 3. The documents are collected and discussed by C. Bémont, *Chartes des Libertés Anglaises* (1892); compare the accounts in Pasquet, *Origins of the*

Edward's speech to the people. In his extremity, Edward determined to appeal to the people. Having made friends with the archbishop and restored the confiscated lands of the see of Canterbury, he proceeded, on July 14, to make a public harangue, standing upon a wooden stage erected in front of the great hall at Westminster, and accompanied by his young son Edward (afterwards Prince of Wales), together with the archbishop and the Earl of Warwick. With visible emotion (" erumpentibus lacrymis " are the words of the chronicler) he humbly asked forgiveness for his past acts, admitting that he had not governed them so well and peaceably as became a king; but reminding them that such small portions of their property as they had given him, or as his servants without his knowledge had extorted, had been accepted by him in order that by the expenditure of a part the bulk might be possessed in greater quietude, and that he might be enabled to overcome the injurious attempts of enemies who were thirsting for English blood. " Behold," he added, " I am going to expose myself to danger for your sakes; I pray you, if I return, receive me as you have me now, and I will restore to you all that has been taken. But if I return not, crown my son as your king."[84]

The Crisis. The hearts of the people were touched by this politic and affecting address; and with uplifted hands they promised fealty to the king. But Edward was still in want of money: and the barons, when appealed to, insisted on the various grievances of the nation, and demanded the confirmation of the Charters. By promising to comply with this demand the king ultimately, after many of the barons had departed, induced an irregular assembly of some of the barons and others who had attended the military summons, to make a grant of an " eighth " from the barons and knights and a " fifth " from the towns.[85] After a vain effort to negotiate with the absent constable and marshal, Edward gave orders (July 30) for the collection of the eighth and fifth, and again directed the seizure of all the wool of the kingdom, promising to pay for it as soon as he was able.[86] The clergy, who were still hampered by the prohibitions of the bull *Clericis Laicos*, expressed (Aug. 10) their willingness to make a grant as soon as they could obtain the pope's permission, which they had good hopes of getting.[87] But the king, impatient at the delay, directed the seizure of a third of their temporal goods.[88] A few

House of Commons, and Hubert Hall, " Negotiations preceding the *Confirmatio Cartarum*," *Transactions of the Royal Historical Society*, N.S., iii, 281. See now the discussion in J. G. Edwards, " *Confirmatio Cartarum* and Baronial Grievances in 1297," *English Historical Review*, lviii, 147, 273, and Harry Rothwell, " Confirmation of the Charters, 1297," *ibid.*, lx, 16, 177, 300; see also Harry Rothwell, " Edward I and the Struggle for the Charters, 1297–1305," *Studies presented to Powicke*, 319–332.

[84] *Flores Historiarum*, iii, 295.   [85] *Ibid.*
[86] *Rotuli Parliamentorum*, i, 239; Bartholomew Cotton, *Historia Anglicana*, 338.
[87] Bartholomew Cotton, *Historia Anglicana*, 327, 335.
[88] Palgrave, *Parliamentary Writs*, i, 396. All articles dedicated to spiritual purposes were excepted, and clerks whose benefices were under 5 marks in value were exempt. Lay fees of the clergy, not appurtenant to their churches, were to be taxed with those of the laity, but they might be quit of the whole by payment of a fifth of their goods temporal and spiritual.

days previously he had issued a manifesto to the people justifying his action in the dispute with the two earls, excusing his exactions as being necessary for the defence of the nation, and promising to set things right on his return.[89] Shortly afterwards, while the king was at Winchelsea preparing to embark, messengers arrived from the earls and presented to him what, to anticipate the language of a later age, may be termed a Grand Remonstrance in the name of the " archbishops, bishops, abbots and priors, earls and barons, and the whole community of the land," setting forth the evils of which they complained and demanding redress.

The schedule of grievances. (1) In the first place, they said, it seems to the whole community of the land that the summons made to them by the king's writ was not sufficient, because it did not mention any certain place to which they were to go; yet it was on the place that the nature of the outfit and requisite amount of money depended. But whether they were bound to serve or not, it was commonly said that their lord wishes to cross the sea to Flanders, and it seems to them that they are not bound to perform any service whatever there; for neither they nor their predecessors or ancestors ever served in that land. Even if they were bound to serve there or elsewhere, yet they have not the necessary means; so afflicted are they by divers tallages, aids, and prises (to wit, of corn, oats, malt, wool, hides, oxen, kine, salt meat), exacted without payment of a single penny by which they might sustain themselves.

(2) Further, they say they are unable to grant an aid, because of their poverty arising from the aforesaid tallages and prises; for they have hardly wherewithal to support themselves " et multi sunt qui nullam sustentationem habent, nec terras suas colere possunt."

(3) They are not dealt with (" tractantur ") according to the laws and customs of the land as their ancestors were wont to be dealt with, nor have they the liberties which they were wont to have, but are arbitrarily refused them; for they were wont to be dealt with in accordance with Magna Carta, but now all its provisions are disregarded to the exceeding damage of the whole people. Wherefore they beseech their lord the king to correct these things, both for his own honour and the salvation of his people.

(4) Moreover, the community of the land feels itself sorely aggrieved concerning the Assize of the Forest, which is not kept as formerly; neither is the Charter of the Forest observed, but attachments are made at will, beyond the jurisdiction, contrary to custom.

(5) The tax on wool is too heavy, namely 40s. on each sack and of broken wool 7 marks [= £4 13s. 4d.] per sack; for the wool of England amounts to the value of half the whole land, and the tax paid on it to a fifth part of the whole land.

(6) Lastly, the community wishing, as it ought to wish, honour and safety to the king, considers it not for the king's good that he should go

89 Rymer, i, 872; Stubbs, *Constitutional History*, ii, 143.

into Flanders unless he have further assurance as regards the Flemings, both for himself and his people; and further, on account of Scotland, which is already beginning to rebel now that he is going, and will assuredly do worse when they know that he has crossed the sea. Nor is it Scotland only that has to be considered: there are other lands also which are not yet duly secured.[90]

To this remonstrance the king declined to return any specific answer without the advice of his Council, part of which had already sailed for Flanders while the other part was in London.[91] A few days afterwards (Aug. 22), he himself proceeded to Ghent, leaving his son, Edward, Prince of Wales, as regent. As soon as the king had departed, the earls seized the opportunity to press their demands. Entering the Exchequer they peremptorily forbade the barons there to levy the aid, the grant of which they asserted had been illegally obtained, until the charters had been confirmed.

Confirmation of the Charters, 1297. Supported by a large military following, and backed up by the citizens of London, they were masters of the situation, and the young prince and his Council found it necessary to yield. The *Confirmatio Cartarum*[92] which, although reckoned later as a statute, is drawn up in the form of a charter, was published on October 10, 1297, in a parliament to which knights of the shire were summoned in order to receive copies of the confirmation, as well as an unusually small number of the lay and clerical baronage. It was immediately sent over to King Edward at Ghent, and there confirmed by him on November 5 following.[93] The former grant of an eighth and a fifth was treated as invalid, and a fresh grant of a ninth was substituted.[94] The constitutional opposition had now been completely successful. The *Confirmatio Cartarum* was not merely a re-issue of Magna Carta and the Charter of the Forest, with special provisions for their distribution throughout the realm and annual publication, but the enactment of a series of new provisions intended to deprive the crown in the future of its assumed right of arbitrary taxation.

[90] Rishanger, *Chronica*, 175–176 [*s. a.* 1297]; *Select Charters*, 434–435. For a full discussion, see J. G. Edwards, " *Confirmatio Cartarum* and Baronial Grievances in 1297," *English Historical Review*, lviii, 147, 273 (1943).

[91] *Ibid.*

[92] 25 Edw. 1, st. 1; *Select Charters*, 490–493.

[93] In 1298, the Earls of Hereford and Norfolk, doubting the king's sincerity or the binding force of his confirmation at Ghent of his son's acts, demanded a second formal confirmation. This the king reluctantly granted on March 8, 1299, but with a comprehensive proviso, as to the forests, saving the rights of the crown (" salvis semper juramento nostro, jure coronae nostrae, et rationibus nostris atque calumpniis ac omnium aliorum "). The openly expressed discontent of the people at the unlooked-for reservation induced Edward to repeat the process shortly afterwards without the obnoxious " salvo." The charters were twice again confirmed by Edward, in the *Articuli Super Cartas*, on March 6, 1300, and finally on February 14, 1301, in return for a grant of a " fifteenth." Notwithstanding this, Edward secretly sought and obtained, in 1305, from Pope Clement V an absolution from the observance of the Confirmation of the Charters; but to his credit, be it said, the absolution, except as to the Forest Articles, was never acted upon.

[94] Palgrave, *Parliamentary Writs*, i, 63.

By the fifth section of this statute the king expressly renounced as precedents the " aids, tasks, and prises " before taken. The next section proceeds:

" vi. Moreover, we have granted for us and our heirs, as well to archbishops, bishops, abbots, priors, and other folk of the holy Church, as also to earls, barons, and to all the commonalty of the land, that for no business from henceforth will we take such manner of aids, tasks, nor prises from our realm, but by the common consent of all the realm, and for the common profit thereof, saving the ancient aids and prises due and accustomed."

By section vii the " maltolt of wools, that is, to wit, a toll of forty shillings for every sack of wool," is released, and the king grants " that we shall not take such thing nor any other " without the common consent and good will of the commonalty of the realm, "saving to us and our heirs the custom of wools, skins, and leather granted before by the commonalty aforesaid."

De Tallagio non Concedendo. The saving words in this statute would appear to have preserved to the king the ancient custom on wool (as distinguished from the " evil toll "), and even the legal right of tallaging the towns and royal demesne, a right which he exercised in 1304.[95] It appears that Edward was not prepared to make such wide concessions as the barons desired. The latter's demands are probably represented by the so-called *Statutum de Tallagio non Concedendo*, by the first clause of which no tallage or aid was to be levied without the consent, not only of the magnates, but " also of the knights, burgesses, and other free men." That the king gave his sanction to a document drafted in vague rather than precise terms implies that he did not intend to go so far.[96]

---

[95] See the king's writ in *Rotuli Parliamentorum*, i, 266. There was also an " ancient prise " of wines imported—a duty of two tuns from every vessel. The expression " maltolt " is at least as old as 1215: Magna Carta, c. 41 *supra*, p. 98; *cf. infra*, pp. 159–160.

[96] See Pasquet, p. 109, and note by Lapsley in App. iii, pp. 237–238. See also Bémont, *Chartes des Libertés Anglaises*, pp. xliii, and 87.

The " Statutum de Tallagio non Concedendo " is quoted as a statute in the preamble of the Petition of Right, and *thenceforth* acquired the authority of a statute. In 1637 it was decided to be a statute by the judges. See Stubbs, *Select Charters*, 493. To the two articles mentioned *supra*, p. 148, note 90, must now be added those by H. Rothwell who prints a new text of De Tallagio non Concedendo in *English Historical Review*, lx. 300–315.

CHAPTER 7

GROWTH OF PARLIAMENT

THE preceding chapter has given a brief summary of the more conspicuous facts in the early history of parliament. The nature of parliament, as contemporaries understood it, and the motives which led kings to convoke these assemblies, can now only be guessed at, and so it is not surprising to find a bewildering mass of conjecture on the subject.

LORDS AND COMMONS

In the first place we must beware of assuming that Edward I foresaw the future greatness of parliament and that he deliberately created it with that end in view. It is equally unlikely that he ever thought of sharing his power with any class or group of persons.[1] Moreover, the great variety of the assemblies which have been described is in itself a sufficient indication that no single motive could have prompted all of them. The forty years or more of intense political activity recounted in the last chapter seem rather to show us politicains turning feverishly from one expedient to another as crisis succeeded crisis. If Edward called parliaments, it was because he saw some immediate advantage in doing so, not because he intended to found an institution to illustrate a novel political ideology.

The purpose of parliament. Secondly, we must remember that counsel was a practical necessity to kings as well as to the rest of mankind, and that kings might take counsel upon every sort of matter. Thus assemblies of prelates and magnates might be consulted upon foreign or domestic politics, finance, administration, law reform or adjudication. If for any reason it seemed desirable to have further information or closer contact with local institutions, then representatives could be summoned. If on the other hand, the government felt sufficiently sure of itself to proceed without these precautions, then it did so. In neither case was any principle of constitutional law involved. Under such conditions it is impossible to regard any one factor as being of the essence of parliament. Thus, it is true to say that parliament was a " court " and that adjudication was often conspicuous among its activities [2]; it is equally true that the assembly of representatives enabled the government to keep a close watch upon the abuses of sheriffs and local officials, and that it facilitated the

---

[1] The writings of Hallam and Stubbs may have created this impression on some readers who have neglected their cautious qualifications.
[2] Maitland, *Memoranda de Parliamento* (1893); C. H. McIlwain, *High Court of Parliament* (1910); A. F. Pollard, *Evolution of Parliament* (1920, 1926).

grant and collection of taxes [3]; from time to time contemporaries also regarded parliament as containing all the social elements or " estates " which mattered politically.[4] No one of these factors was enough by itself to account for the rise of parliament, but taken together they formed a long series of incidents and expedients whose frequent recurrence gradually resulted in a permanent institution.

The structure of parliament. Moreover, it is natural to find that the structure of parliament should reflect the different origins of its parts. At its centre was the king and his council, surrounded by the lords spiritual and temporal who had been summoned " to consult " together upon his arduous affairs. To such a " parliament " as this the local communities were sometimes ordered to send representatives. Most frequently the commons were asked not to " consult " but to " consent to whatever should be decided," or to " do what would be told them "; the writs often require them to come furnished with full powers from their constituents so that their consent should bind the electors effectively.[5] Nor were the knights and townsfolk regarded as part of the parliament [6]— they were in fact merely deputations which waited upon the council, spoke if they were invited to do so, and were sent away when they had given their consent to what the king and magnates had decided. These deputations represented various local communities, *comunaultés, communes*, and taken together they come to be described as the " commons." [7]

The Commons. It had long been customary for the king, his council, the magnates and the prelates to meet in solemn plenary sessions (although subordinate discussions may well have taken place in smaller groups). If commons attended on such occasions, they seem to have stood or knelt at the lower end of the hall.[8] Their own private confabulations followed various methods, but by the middle of the fourteenth century the knights of the shire and the citizens and burgesses habitually met together.[9] It

[3] L. Riess, *English Electoral Law* (1885, tr. K. L. Wood-Legh, 1940).

[4] *Cf.* M. V. Clarke, *Representation and Consent* (1936).

[5] Examples in Pasquet, *Origin of the House of Commons*, 135; J. G. Edwards, " *Plena Potestas* of English Parliamentary Representatives," in *Oxford Essays presented to H. E. Salter*. There are 14th century examples in *Rough's Register* (Kent Archaeological Society, Records Branch xvi), and Tudor examples in *York Civic Records*, v. 7, 31, 87, 93, *et seq.* (Yorkshire Archaeological Society, Record Series, cx). *Cf. infra*, p. 618.

[6] Indeed, such an expression would be impossible during most of the Middle Ages, for a parliament then was not an institution, but an event—a discussion.

[7] *Cf. supra*, p. 137, note 42; J. E. A. Jolliffe, *Constitutional History*, 328–330.

[8] There is much interesting material on this in A. F. Pollard, *Evolution of Parliament* (2nd. ed.).

[9] The first mention in the rolls of parliament of a separate session occurs in 1332; *Rotuli Parliamentorum*, ii, 66, No. 3 (E. C. Lodge and G. A. Thornton, *English Constitutional Documents, 1307-1485*, 132). From 1339 the division may be regarded as permanent. In 1352 the Chapter House of Westminster Abbey was the chamber of the Commons (*Rotuli Parliamentorum*, ii, 237, No. 8; Stubbs, *Constitutional History*, iii, 444, 445). It should be noted that it was only the accidental circumstance of the withdrawal of the clergy from all participation in secular legislation that prevented us from having, as was generally the case in continental constitutions, *three* houses of nobles, clergy, and commons (*supra*, pp. 142 *et seq.*). Stubbs (*Constitutional History*, ii, 198) points out that there was

must be borne in mind that the knights belonged socially to the same class as the barons, but the representatives of boroughs, belonging to a lower grade, formed a distinct social group whose separate interests are evident from the grants of subsidies which, for many years after the introduction of the commons, were voted in different proportions by (1) the earls, barons, and knights, (2) the clergy, and (3) the citizens and burgesses.[10]

There is reason to believe that the knights, even while still voting taxes separately, occasionally joined with the burgesses in petitions. This development was slow, for normally most of the petitions in early parliaments came from individuals, and were not presented by the elected representatives. It is also obscure, for a petitioner with a grievance is tempted to describe himself somewhat unwarrantably as " the people of England," or " the commons of the realm." In the early years of Edward III, however, the commons in parliament began to segregate the petitions which they were ready to support by putting them together on a separate roll, sometimes indented, with the heading *communes petitions*, " common petitions," and it becomes clear that they received particular attention by the king and his council.[11]

The complete fusion of the two elements of the lower house into one assembly—the result of one of those unions of happy accident and practical wisdom to which the English constitution owes so much—was fraught with the most important consequences. The knights, who represented the landed property of the country, gave to the house of commons, from the first, stability, weight, and permanence, and obtained for it a respect which the citizens and burgesses alone could not have commanded, in a country so permeated with feudal ideas as England then was. Without the knights of the shire the burgesses would have been mere deputies to consent to taxation and advise on matters of trade; united with them on equal terms, they were enabled at once to claim a voice in the government of the nation, and to defend the liberties of the people against both king and nobles. Moreover, the smooth working of parliament was frequently secured by the device of small bodies of commons " intercommuning "

even at one time a possibility that the lawyers and the merchants might have been grouped in separate sub-estates. On the question of the division of parliament into estates, see Pollard, *Evolution of Parliament*, Chap. iv, " The Myth of the Three Estates "; Pasquet, pp. 136–139; S. B. Chrimes, *Constitutional Ideas of the Fifteenth Century*, 81 *et seq.*; *Selden's Table Talk* (ed. Pollock, Selden Society), 150.

[10] In 1296, the barons and knights and the clergy gave each a twelfth, and the burgesses an eighth; in 1306 the barons and knights and the clergy gave a thirtieth, the burgesses a twentieth; in 1307 the barons and knights gave a twentieth, the clergy and the burgesses each a fifteenth. In the 6th of Edward 3 (1332) the rates were for the barons and knights and the clergy a fifteenth, for the burgesses a tenth; but on this occasion the knights and burgesses deliberated, although they did not vote, in common. In 1344 the knights granted two-fifteenths, the burgesses two-tenths, while the lords promised to follow the king in person and granted nothing.

[11] For the controversy on this matter see H. L. Gray, *Influence of the Commons in Early Legislation* (1932); S. B. Chrimes, *English Constitutional Ideas* (1936); G. L. Haskins, " Petitions of Representatives in the Parliament of Edward I," *English Historical Review*, liii, 1 (1938); T. F. T. Plucknett, " Parliament," in *English Government at Work* (ed. J. F. Willard, 1940).

with equally small bodies of lords, so that even the principal division of
" lords " and " commons " ceased to be a serious impediment to the
essential unity of the fourteenth century parliament.[12]

The Lords. The commingling of the knights and burgesses in a single
house was rendered possible by the existence in the English constitution
of a peculiarity which most prominently and honourably distinguished
it from nearly every kindred constitution in Europe—the absence of an
exclusive noble caste. In most of the continental states the nobles formed
a distinct class, distinguished by privileges inherent in their blood, from
ordinary freemen, and transmitting their privileges, and in some countries
their titles also, to all their descendants in perpetuity. The words " nobleman " and " gentleman " were strictly synonymous; the estate of the
nobles (wherever the system of estates obtained) represented in the
national assembly not only the high nobility, but the class who in England
formed the " landed gentry," while the commons, the " tiers état,"
consisted almost exclusively of the citizens and burgesses. In England,
on the contrary, the privileges of nobility have always, except perhaps in
the days of the ancient eorls, been confined to one only of the family at
a time, the actual possessor of the peerage. The sons of peers are commoners, and on a perfect equality, as regards legal and political privileges,
with the humblest citizen. Even the eldest son, the heir to the peerage,
though he may bear a title by courtesy, is still, so long as his father lives,
a commoner like his younger brothers. No restraint seems ever to have
lain upon the free inter-marriage of all ranks.[13] Their lands were governed
by the same rules as those of all other freemen.[14] The highest offices of

[12] This practice is described, and its implications examined, in J. G. Edwards, *The Commons
in Medieval Parliaments* (1958).

[13] " It was regarded as no disparagement for the daughter of a duke, nay, of a royal duke,
to espouse a distinguished commoner. Thus Sir John Howard married the daughter of
Thomas Mowbray, Duke of Norfolk, Sir Richard Pole married the Countess of Salisbury,
daughter of George, Duke of Clarence. Good blood was indeed held in high respect;
but between good blood and the privileges of peerages, there was, most fortunately for
our country, no necessary connection. There was therefore here no line like that which in
some other countries divided the patrician from the plebeian. Our democracy was, from
an early period, the most aristocratic, and our aristocracy the most democratic in the
world."—Macaulay, *History of England*, i, 30, 31. The present doctrine of ennobled blood
is a foreign importation made under Henry VIII which, having no roots in English history,
has wrought much confusion. Thus bishops (who in the 14th century were regarded as
peers: *infra*, p. 163) are now held to be " lords of parliament " only and not " peers ";
not being ennobled in blood, they are " not of trial by nobility," and would be tried for a
capital offence by a jury of commoners. *Lords' Standing Orders*, No. 79, 1692; trials of
Bishop Fisher and Archbishop Cranmer, 1 Howell, *State Trials*, pp. 399, 771. " It seems,"
writes Pike (*Constitutional History of the House of Lords*, p. 221), " to have been settled
law that bishops do not enjoy the right of being tried by peers of the realm, either in
parliament, or in the Court of the Lord High Steward," and cites especially Staunford,
Les Plees del Coron, p. 153 and 3 Inst. 30, in support of this statement. For pungent
criticisms of peerage law by a historian, see J. H. Round, *Peerage and Pedigree*, and the
bibliography in his *Family Origins*. As regards the barons or peers for life, whose status
as lords of parliament was especially determined by the Appellate Jurisdiction Act,
1887, sec. 2, it would appear certain that they, not being *ennobled in blood*, would be only
triable before a common jury.

[14] The appearance of the idea of " ennobled blood " was accompanied by (unsuccessful)
attempts to create a special property law for peers: T. F. T. Plucknett, " Some Proposed
Legislation of Henry VIII," *Transactions of the Royal Historical Society* (1936), 122 *et seq.*;

the state were always legally open to all freemen. All ranks, moreover, have at all times borne a share of the public burthens without claiming any of those unjust exemptions from taxation which the continental *noblesse* habitually enjoyed.

Few things are more important in our early constitution, or have exercised a more potent and beneficial influence upon the political and social conditions of the people, than this civil equality of all ranks below the peerage. Had it been otherwise, the house of commons could scarcely have become what it is at the present day. " The knight of the shire was the connecting link between the baron and the shopkeeper. On the same benches on which sat the goldsmiths, drapers, and grocers, who had been returned to parliament by the commercial towns, sat also members who, in any other country, would have been called noblemen, hereditary lords of manors, entitled to hold courts and to bear coat armour, and able to trace back an honourable descent through many generations. Some of them were younger sons and brothers of lords. Others could boast of even royal blood. At length the eldest son of an Earl of Bedford, called in courtesy by the second title of his father, offered himself as candidate for a seat in the house of commons,[15] and his example was followed by others." [16] In this way the house of commons has at length come to represent not any single order in the state, but, with the exception of the actual members of the house of lords, the whole nation; and, as a natural consequence, has drawn to itself " the predominant authority in the state." [17]

But the growth of the powers of the commons has been very gradual. At first the burgesses deferred to their aristocratic associates, the knights of the shire, and these naturally followed the lead of the barons.[18]

Holdsworth, *History of English Law*, iv, 572 *et seq.* For the political implications of the later peerage notions and of the hereditary offices, *cf.* T. F. T. Plucknett, " Rise of the English State Trial," *Politica* (1937), ii, 557, and the references of G. Barraclough in *Law Quarterly Review*, lvi, 82 n.

[15] In 1550 and in 1575 a member of the commons after his election became heir apparent of the Earl of Bedford ; the House resolved in both cases that his seat was not thereby vacated. E. and A. G. Porritt, *Unreformed House of Commons*, i, 123.

[16] Macaulay, *History of England*, i, 32.

[17] May, *Constitutional History*, ii, 83. The difference between the House of Commons as representing " the whole community of England " and the House of Lords as representing only themselves, is strongly insisted upon by the writer of the " Modus Tenendi Parliamentum." The date of this treatise is uncertain, but it " is found in manuscripts of the 14th century and although, on reference to contemporary writs and documents, it is found to be frequently misleading, it may be accepted as a theoretical view for which the writer was anxious to find a warrant in immemorial antiquity."—Stubbs, *Select Charters*, 500–506. The *Modus*, re-edited, is the principal theme of M. V. Clarke, *Representation and Consent*; *cf.* Galbraith in *Journal of the Warburg Institute*, xvi, 81–89.

[18] " Their co-operation has been commonly regarded as the outcome of a deliberate determination of the knights to throw in their lot with the burgesses rather than with the lords; but this view presupposes too great an influence of the burgesses in parliament. There is hardly a definite trace of parliamentary action on their part before 1340, while there are many occasions on which the knights were consulted without any reference to burgesses at all. It would appear that the knights had already established the habit of independent deliberation, and that the fusion of the county and civic representatives was rather due to the burgesses attaching themselves to the knights. No doubt there must have been a reciprocal willingness on the side of the knights, and it is a peculiar and remarkable feature of the English constitution that the knights, in spite of their social and

EDWARD II: 1307–1327

Under Edward II, jealousy of the successive favourites, Gaveston and the Despensers, threw the baronage into chronic opposition to the king; and on two occasions, in 1312 and again in 1321, drove them into open revolt. The ultimate deposition of the king was also mainly the work of the barons acting in concert with the queen.

So early in this reign as 1309, the commons manifested a knowledge of their power and rights by granting a subsidy " upon this condition that the king should take advice and grant redress upon certain Articles, in which their grievances were set forth." These Articles of Stamford, eleven in number, present a concise summary of the grievances—arising in many cases from distinct violations of the existing law—by which the nation had been more or less oppressed under all the successors of Henry of Anjou, which the Lords Ordainers endeavoured to redress in 1311, but which continued for at least another century to form the burden of the complaints of the commons in parliament.[19]

Articles of Stamford, 1309. They are to the following effect: " Les bones gentz du roialme qi sont cy venuz au Parlement," after a general prayer for the observance of the Great Charter, and that the oppressions of " those who call themselves the king's servants " may be restrained, specifically complain: 1. That the king's purveyors seize great quantities of corn, malt, meat, and other provisions, without any payment, not even by tallies. 2. That new customs are exacted on wine, cloth, and other imports, whereby the price to the people is enhanced. 3. That the current coin is accepted by traders at only half its nominal value, notwithstanding the king's proclamation to the contrary. 4, 5. That the steward and marshal illegally enlarge their jurisdiction beyond measure, to the oppression and impoverishment of the people. 6. That the commons find no one to receive petitions in parliament, as in the time of the king's father. 7. That the collectors of the king's dues (" pernours de prises ") at fairs and in cities take prises of commodities in excess of the king's needs, and barter away the surplus for their own advantage. 8. That men are delayed in their actions at law by writs of protection. 9. That felons escape punishment by too easily procuring charters of pardon, so that those who have indicted them are afraid to stay in their own districts, and many forbore, on this account, from prosecuting. 10. That the constables of the king's

---

political bonds with the barons—such as common military tenure-in-chief and common ideas of chivalry—should have found it easier to work with burgesses than with barons; indeed it would not have been possible but for the shrinking of the baronage into the peerage. The fusion of knights and burgesses was, however, a slow process, the steps of which might be traced in some detail in the ' Rolls of Parliament '; possibly the Good Parliament of 1376 exemplifies the first-fruits of amalgamation. In any case, separate consultation of knights and burgesses grew rarer, while their joint deliberation in the ' *domus communis* ' grew more regular and well defined."—Pollard, *Evolution of Parliament* (2nd ed.), 124–125; and see also the Creighton Lecture mentioned above at note 12.

[19] *Rotuli Parliamentorum*, i, 443–445. (Sometimes called the " Statute " of Stamford, 3 Edw. 2.)

castles take cognisance of common pleas. 11. That the king's escheators oust men of lands held *in capite* by them and their ancestors from time immemorial, under pretence of an inquest of office, without summoning them before the king's court. Edward accepted all the articles unreservedly, except the second, which had reference to the new customs of 2s. on the tun of wine, 2s. on the piece of foreign cloth, and 3d. on the pound avoirdupois of other merchandise, originally conceded to Edward I by the foreign merchants in 1303. As to this the king, at the request of the people, granted that the "little custom" should be taken off until it should appear whether any advantage would accrue to him and his people thereby, and afterwards he would take counsel thereon. The "ancient prises and customs anciently due and approved" were not to be affected. In 1310 the "little custom" was again imposed, on the ground that no reduction in prices had followed the remission.[20] In the following year the Ordainers declared it illegal.

The Lords Ordainers. The appointment in 1310 of the twenty-one " Lords Ordainers " who were to draw up a scheme of reform, like the previous appointment of similar committees in the reign of Henry III, and of the subsequent commissions of reform under Richard II, was an extraordinary and revolutionary remedy to meet exceptional circumstances. At the time when kings governed as well as reigned, their personal character was of the utmost importance. The practical effect to the nation was much the same whether the king was wicked or only weak. When, from either cause, mis-government reached a certain pitch of intensity, an attempt appears to have been made to reconcile the continuance of the king upon his throne with the enjoyment of good government, by temporarily putting into commission, as it were, the powers of the kingship. In Edward II's case, it was doubtless the personal jealousy of the barons against Gaveston and the king's other favourites, quite as much as a desire for the public weal, which actuated the Ordainers.

The Ordinances, 1311. Yet most of their comprehensive " Ordinances," [21] by which remedies were provided for the old and undoubted grievances of the nation, were highly beneficial; and others, which trenched on the prerogative of the crown, were in many cases but anticipations of that direct parliamentary control over the appointment of the king's ministers, and the action of the executive, which was subsequently attained for a time, and which is now exercised by parliament indirectly. Among

---

[20] *Parliamentary Writs*, II, ii, App. 30.

[21] Printed in *Rotuli Parliamentorum*, i, 281–286, and *Statutes of the Realm*, i, 157 *et seq*; extracts in E. C. Lodge and G. A. Thornton, *English Constitutional Documents, 1307–1485* (Cambridge, 1935), 12–17. There are detailed studies by James Conway Davies, *Baronial Opposition to Edward II* (1918), and T. F. Tout, *The Place of Edward II* (1914; 1936, ed. H. Johnstone), both emphasising the development of central administration during the reign. *Cf.* S. B. Chrimes, *Introduction to the Administrative History of Mediaeval England* (1952), 173 *et seq*. Brief introductions to this important aspect are in Tout, *Collected Papers*, iii, 191, 223. On the Ordainers and the Council, see *infra*, p. 215.

the Articles of this nature may be noted: (ix) That the king should not leave the kingdom,[22] or levy war, without the consent of the baronage in parliament; and in the case of his absence with such consent, a guardian of the realm should be chosen by the common assent of the baronage in parliament; (xiv) That the chancellor, two chief justices, treasurer, and other great officers of the crown, should be chosen by the counsel and assent of the barons in parliament; and (xxix) That to prevent delay in the administration of justice, parliaments should be holden once in every year, or twice if need be, and in convenient places.

The Statute of York, 1322. The right of the commons to concur in legislation of national importance was affirmed in 1322, by the Statute of York which repealed the Ordinances when the baronial opposition had been defeated in the battle of Boroughbridge. It was declared (1) that the Ordinances be repealed; (2) that statutes duly made by the king remained in force; (3) that no ordinance destroying the essential nature of the crown can be made by subjects, whatever power or commission they may claim to have; and (4) that " the matters which are to be established for the estate of our lord the king and his heirs, and for the estate of the realm and of the people, shall be treated, accorded, and established in parliaments by our lord the king, and by the assent of prelates, earls, and barons, and the commonalty of the realm, according as it hath been heretofore accustomed." [23]   Edward II had already applied this principle, over a year earlier, when he forbad a group of magnates from gathering together to discuss matters affecting the crown.[24]

The situation was too complicated for so simple a solution. In 1327 Edward II was deposed with solemnities which were a still more desperate attempt to state in words the fundamental assumptions of orderly government.[25]

EDWARD III: 1327–1377

Under Edward III the barons, instead of opposing the king, rallied round the throne, and the commons, ceasing to be mere auxiliaries of the lords, became the chief asserters of constitutional rights against the arbitrary power of the crown. They did not, however, so much curb the

---

[22] The Act of Settlement was trying to enforce this rule as late as 1701; below, p. 463 (c. 3).

[23] 15 Edw. 2, *Statutes of the Realm*, i, 189; Lodge and Thornton, 128–129. The following references contain an important debate on the significance of the statute: G. Lapsley, *English Historical Review*, xxviii, 118 (1913); T. F. Tout, *Edward II*, 136 (1914); J. C. Davies, *Baronial Opposition*, 513 (1918); H. G. Richardson, *Bulletin of the Institute of Historical Research*, vi, 76 (1928); G. L. Haskins, *The Statute of York* (1935); G. Lapsley in *Law Quarterly Review*, liii, 125–127 (1937); M. V. Clarke, *Representation and Consent*, 138, 172, 196 (1936); B. Wilkinson, *Studies in Constitutional History*, 236 (1937); J. E. A. Jolliffe, *Constitutional History*, 370–371 (1937); G. L. Haskins, *English Historical Review*, lii, 74 (1937); G. Lapsley, *ibid.*, lvi, 22, 411 (1941); J. R. Strayer, *American Historical Review*, xlvii, 1 (1941); W. A. Morris, *Medievalia et Humanistica*, i, 59 at 83–84 (1943); B. Wilkinson, *Speculum*, xix, 445 (1944); W. Ullmann, *Medieval Papalism*, 24 (1949).

[24] *Parliamentary Writs*, II, ii, 155.

[25] *Infra*, pp. 487 *et seq*.

royal power as consolidate their own. No reign, perhaps, is so replete with illegalities as that of Edward III; but they were admitted to be exceptions, and disowned as precedents, while the legal rule was firmly established.

More regular parliaments. The regularity with which parliament was assembled by Edward III confirmed the power of the commons, by affording them an opportunity for its frequent exercise. To defray the enormous expenses of his wars, the king was perpetually compelled to solicit the aid of his people, and during the fifty years of his reign, forty-eight sessions of parliament are recorded.

It was, moreover, twice declared by statute (as it had been previously directed by the Lords Ordainers in 1311), that parliament should be held annually—by which appears to have been meant, not that there should be annual sessions of the same parliament, but a newly elected parliament every year.[26] Thus, in 1330, it was enacted: " A parliament shall be holden every year once, and more often if need be "; and again in 1362: " For redress of divers mischiefs and grievances which daily happen a parliament shall be holden every year, as another time was ordained by statute." [27]

The growth of the Commons. During the long reign of Edward III, the commons asserted three great claims:

I. That all taxation without the consent of parliament is illegal.

II. The necessity for the concurrence of both Houses in legislation.

III. The right of the commons to inquire into and amend the abuses of the administration.

Growing out of these, two derivative claims were also made by the commons for the first time: (a) The right to examine public accounts and appropriate the supplies, which was involved in Nos. I and III; and (b) The right to impeach the king's ministers for misconduct, which was a corollary to No. III.

I. Taxation without consent illegal. In spite of the *Confirmatio Cartarum*, both Edward I and his son occasionally, and Edward III constantly, continued to levy arbitrary imposts of every kind. The commons, however, by their continual remonstrances, their conditional grants and their liberal subsidies, whenever the king applied to them for aid, succeeded at length in establishing a control over direct taxation.

In 1332 (6 Edward III) a rebellion having broken out in Ireland, the king assigned certain commissioners to tallage the cities, towns and royal demesnes throughout England; but revoked these commissions at the request of the prelates, earls, barons and knights of the shire, who granted

---

[26] See Stubbs, *Constitutional History*, iii, 393. The Provisions of Oxford of 1258 proposed three parliaments a year. A single short session was normal. The deliberate prolongation of a parliament by holding several sessions first becomes common under Edward IV.

[27] 4 Edw. 3, c. 14; 36 Edw. 3, st. 1, c. 10. In the year 1328, no less than four parliaments were held, and three in 1340. Stubbs, *Constitutional History*, ii, 645.

instead a tenth from the cities, boroughs, and royal demesnes, and a fifteenth from " the commonalty," the king promising that in time to come he would not set such tallage, except as it had been done in the time of his ancestors, and as he might reasonably do.[28]

In 1339 (13 Edward III), the prelates, earls and barons made a grant of one-tenth of their corn, fleece and lambs, but only with a stipulation that the " maltolt," or illegal custom on wool, should be abolished, and their present grant not drawn into precedent.[29] The commons professed themselves most willing to grant a subsidy, but unable to do so without first consulting their constituents, for which purpose they desired that another parliament might be summoned, and that the sheriffs be directed that no knight of the shire be returned to the next parliament who is himself a sheriff or other official.[30] They complained of the increased imposition on wool and lead, and boldly asserted that " inasmuch as it is enhanced without assent of the commons, or of the lords, as we understand," " any one of the commons may refuse it (le puisse arester) without being troubled on that account (saunz estre chalangee)." [31] The new parliament duly met in 1340, the terms of the bargain were embodied in an indenture, and a statute declared that no charge or aid should be raised without the common assent of the prelates, lords and commons given in parliament.[32]

Two years later, in 1342, the king being much pressed for money, assembled, with the concurrence of the lords, a council of merchants, and procured from them, without the assent of the commons, a grant of forty shillings " in addition to the lawful maltolt " on every sack of wool that should be exported. It seems to have been contended that this duty did not fall upon the people, but upon the foreign purchaser; but the commons in the following year in their remonstrance showed that they possessed some rudimentary knowledge of the principles of political economy, alleging that the tax actually fell on the seller, the foreign merchants refusing to give the accustomed price on account of the additional duty.[33] In 1346 (20 Edward III) parliament again prayed the king that this forty shillings on the sack of wool might be taken off, but it was answered that the prelates and other magnates [grantz], seeing the necessity of the king, had assented, with the accord of the merchants, that he should have the said subsidy of wool for the prosecution of the war; and that as it had been pledged to his creditors, it must continue; whereupon the commons gave way.[34] In 1363, however, upon the petition

---

[28] Rotuli Parliamentorum, ii, 66 no. 3. The grant thus charged the country generally, instead of merely the special classes affected by a tallage.

[29] Rotuli Parliamentorum, ii, 104, no. 5. On the " maltolt " cf. p. 149, n. 95, supra.

[30] Ibid., ii, 104, no. 8.

[31] Ibid., ii, 105, no. 13.

[32] Ibid., ii, 107, no. 7; Lodge and Thornton, 133–134; 14 Edw. 3, st. 2, c. 1.

[33] Ibid., ii, 140, no. 5; for a list of such assemblies of merchants, see Interim Report of Committee on House of Commons Personnel, 109 (1932, Cmd. 4130).

[34] Rotuli Parliamentorum, ii, 161, no. 18.

of the commons it was finally declared that no grants of subsidies upon wool were to be made by merchants without the consent of parliament.[35]

In 1348 (22 Edward III), the commons made a conditional grant, and required the conditions—the most important being that the king should henceforth levy no " imposition, tallage, or charge by way of loan or in any other manner, without the grant and assent of the commons in parliament "—to be entered on the roll " as a matter of record, whereby they may have remedy if anything should be attempted to the contrary in time to come." [36] In these conditional grants originated the doctrine and practice that " supply should depend upon redress of grievances."

But while conceding the technical illegality of the proceeding, Edward seems always to have claimed a kind of moral right to impose charges upon his subjects in cases of great necessity, and for the defence of the kingdom. This was asserted even in his last parliament, in 1377 [37]; and long previously, in 1339, with reference to the heavy impositions laid on the people on the occasion of the war with Scotland, the king had urged the same plea in a letter to the Archbishop of Canterbury: " That whereas the people were burdened with divers charges, tallages, and impositions, which he could not mention but with much grief, yet being enforced by inevitable necessity, could not as yet ease the people of them, he required the archbishop to exhort the people patiently and humbly to bear the burden for a while, and to excuse him towards the people, hoping he should ere long recompense his said people and give them comfort in due time." [38]

Appropriation of supplies. The first unequivocal instance of appropriation of supplies occurred in 1353, when a subsidy on wool was granted, to be applied solely for the purposes of the war.[39]

Audit of tax accounts. In 1340 a parliamentary committee was appointed to examine into the accounts of the collectors of the last subsidy; and in the following year the king granted, at the request of the commons, that commissioners should be assigned for a similar purpose.[40] Inquiry into the accounts of the collectors was the first step towards examining into the application of the money by the king's ministers; but that some investigation of fiscal matters was absolutely necessary at this time, if only for the purpose of obtaining statistics, is evidenced by the ludicrous miscalculation made by the parliament in 1371 (45 Edward III) as to the number of parishes in England. A subsidy

---

[35] *Ibid.*, ii, 271, no. 26.
[36] *Ibid.*, ii, 200–201. This was an improvement on the indenture of 1340 which was not enrolled.
[37] *Ibid.*, ii, 366, no. ix.
[38] See Broom, *Constitutional Law*, (ed. Denman), 269.
[39] *Rotuli Parliamentorum*, ii, 252, no. 35. The enrolment (extracts in Lodge and Thornton, 142–143) describes this gathering as a great council; elected commons were present.
[40] *Ibid.*, ii, 114 no. 22, 128 no. 12, 130 no. 38 (and in Lodge and Thornton, 138–139). Earlier attempts of this sort occur in 1237 and 1244; Stubbs, *Constitutional History*, ii, 596–597.

was granted of £50,000, to be collected by an assessment of 22s. 3d. upon every parish, the number of parishes being assumed to be nearly 45,000. After the parliament had been dismissed, it was discovered that the number of parishes was not much more than 8,600, and that the sum raised would not exceed £10,000. To repair the error the king summoned a Great Council, at Winchester, consisting of one selected member out of the two who had sat in the last parliament for each county, city, and borough. He excused himself for not summoning a full parliament on the ground of relieving his people from the additional expense [41]; and the facts of the case having been laid before the assembly, they increased the parochial assessment, of their own authority, to 116s.[42] No complaint appears to have been made of this irregularity, by which the main intention of parliament was carried into effect. In the following year (1372) there occurred a more serious disregard of constitutional formalities, tending to destroy the unity of the House of Commons by reviving the former separation of the borough from the county members. After the petitions of the commons had been answered, the knights were dismissed; but the burgesses were convened before the Prince of Wales and the prelates and barons " in a chamber near the White Chamber," and induced, as a return for the continual safe convoy of merchant shipping, to renew for a year a subsidy formerly granted upon imports.[43]

II. Legislation. Legislation raises a different problem: " the nation granted the tax, the king enacted the law." [44] The Statute of York in 1322 solemnly affirmed this principle with the important requirement of the parliamentary assent of the prelates, lords and commonalty of the realm.[45]

From the year 1318 down to the accession of Edward III the form of enacting words in statutes invariably runs: " by the assent of the prelates,

---

[41] Knights of the shire and townsmen were entitled to their expenses, which became burdensome to their constituents; see *infra*, p. 646. Those contemporary officials who called the Winchester gathering a " parliament " seem to have been mistaken: T. F. Tout, *Chapters in Administrative History*, iii, 268, n. 4.

[42] *Rotuli Parliamentorum*, ii, 304 no. 10.

[43] *Ibid.*, p. 310 no. 15 (Lodge and Thornton, 145); and see Hallam, *Middle Ages*, iii, 47.

[44] Stubbs, *Constitutional History*, ii, 267. On the development of legislation, *cf.* C. H. McIlwain, *High Court of Parliament* (1910); T. F. T. Plucknett, *Statutes and their Interpretation* (1922) and *Legislation of Edward I* (1948); P. H. Winfield, *Sources of English Legal History* (1925); W. S. Holdsworth, *Sources of English Law* (1925); C. K. Allen, *Law in the Making* (1927, 6th ed. 1958); H. L. Gray, *Influence of the Commons on early Legislation* (1932); H. G. Richardson and G. O. Sayles, *The Early Statutes* (1934, reprinted from *Law Quarterly Review*, l, 201, 540); G. O. Sayles, *Cases in King's Bench*, iii, Intro. xi-xlii (Selden Society, 1939); T. F. T. Plucknett, *Concise History of the Common Law* (1956); S. E. Thorne, intro. to *A Discourse upon the Statutes* (1942); Plucknett, *Law Quarterly Review*, lx, 242.

[45] *Supra*, p. 157. The importance to be attached to the assent of the commons should not be exaggerated. *Cf.* Pasquet, p. 174, who, referring to parliament under Edward I, writes: " Legislation was a royal prerogative, in which subjects took no part, except to give counsel, when the king demanded it of them. . . . So little importance was attached to the presence and the opinion of the commons that in 1290 the statute *Quia Emptores*, although it affected the knights, was promulgated a week before the delegates of the counties arrived at the parliament." For many examples under Edward I of statutes dated after the dismissal of the commons, see Stubbs, *Constitutional History*, ii, 247, n. 2.

earls, barons, and the commonalty of the realm." Under Edward III
this form alternates with another, in which the share of the commons is
expressed as that of petitioners—" at the request of the commons and
by the assent of the prelates, earls, and barons." This was owing to the
fact that at this time statutes were almost always founded upon the
petitions of the commons, which expounded grievances and prayed for
specific remedies.[46] In 1340 a committee, consisting of the Archbishop
of Canterbury and a certain number of bishops and barons (with whom
were associated several of the justices), and twelve knights and six
burgesses (chosen by the commons), was appointed to convert such
petitions and answers as were fit to be perpetual into statutes.[47] Matters
of a temporary nature might be regulated by ordinances, which differed
little from statutes, except in their less solemn and less permanent character,
and in the fact that they were sometimes made, not in parliament, but in
a great council. The great councils, however, sometimes contained all
the elements of a parliament, the only difference being that the summonses
were not in parliamentary form; but in ordinary cases the lords and the
king's council were the only members. In 1363, when it was proposed to
enact the first sumptuary laws, the lords and commons were asked,
" inasmuch as the matter agreed upon in parliament was novel and un-
heard of before," whether they would prefer an ordinance or a statute.
They decided to proceed " by way of ordinance and not by statute, in
order that, if anything should need amendment, it might be amended
at the next parliament."[48] The important " Ordinances of the Staple,"
which, among other things, prohibited English merchants from exporting
wool under pain of death, were promulgated in a great council held in
1353, at which one knight from each shire and certain citizens and
burgesses attended. The introduction of a new capital offence was clearly
a matter of such grave consequence that the commons present at the great
council prayed " that the said articles might be recited at the next parliament and entered upon the parliament roll, for this cause that ordinances
and agreements made in council are not of record, as if they had been
made in a general parliament." In the next parliament the ordinances
were expressly confirmed " to be holden for a statute to endure always,"
and it was enacted at the same time that no alteration or addition should
be made in future without the assent of parliament.[49]

---

[46] Sometimes the commons merely prayed for a declaration of the existing law, in which
case their assent to the declaration in answer was usually assumed without being positively
given. This was the case with the great Statute of Treasons, 1352 (25 Edw. 3, st. 5, c. 2;
Lodge and Thornton, 21–22). The petition upon which this Act is founded simply prayed
that " whereas the king's justices in different counties adjudge persons indicated before
them to be traitors for sundry matters not known by the commons to be treason, it would
please the king by his council, and by the great and wise men of the land, to declare what
are treasons in this present parliament." The king's answer to this petition, entitled
" A Declaration which Offences shall be adjudged Treason," constitutes the existing
statute.

[47] Rotuli Parliamentorum, ii, 113 no. 7.

[48] Ibid., ii, 280 no. 39.

[49] Ibid., ii, 253, 257 no. 16 (Lodge and Thornton, 143). The latest investigators
of the distinction between statute and ordinance conclude that " it would almost

Edward III's announcement in 1341 that the statute 15 Edward III, st. 1, was abrogated because his royal assent was feigned, and because his ministers regarded it as prejudicial to the prerogative, is based upon grounds which, however plausible,[50] failed to become a permanent part of English constitutional thought.

III. Parliament and government. On two occasions during the reign of Edward III the commons interfered with great boldness in matters of governmental administration.

Ministerial responsibility. (1) In the parliament which met in April 1341 (15 Edward III), they made, in conjunction with the lords, a praiseworthy but premature attempt to establish the responsibility of the king's ministers to parliament. Edward's quarrel with the archbishop, John Stratford, whom he accused of mismanagement, and the ex-minister's vigorous defence, had raised the question of the right of peers to be tried by their peers in parliament, and a committee of the lords reported in the affirmative. When the question of supply came up, each of the three estates made a series of conditional demands, three of which are of special interest. (1) The lords required a statute enacting, in conformity with the recent report of their committee: That when the king was prosecutor (" ou le roi se fait partie "), no peer of the land, whether minister or not, and whether on account of his office or for any other cause, should be brought to trial, lose his lands, tenements, goods or chattels, be arrested, imprisoned, outlawed or forfeited, or be bound to answer or be judged, except in full parliament and before the peers; saving unto the king the laws rightfully used by due process, and saving also suits between party and party.[51] It was a peculiar situation; an ex-minister sought the protection of parliament on losing the confidence of his sovereign, and parliament was eager to protect him.[52] The lords and commons together petitioned: (2) That commissioners should be appointed to inquire into the accounts of such as had received the aids

---

seem as though there were in the background a draftsman of methodical mind who failed to win assent to his categories and terminology ": H. G. Richardson and G. O. Sayles, *The Early Statutes*, 37 (and in *Law Quarterly Review*, l, 560).

[50] See the discussion, *op. cit.*, 27 *et seq.*; P. Birdsall, in *Essays in honour of C. H. McIlwain*, 41. A regular parliamentary repeal took place in 1343: *Rotuli Parliamentorum*, ii, 139 no. 23. *Cf. infra*, p. 164.

[51] *Rotuli Parliamentorum*, ii, 127 no. 7 (Lodge and Thornton, 137–138). Anciently the bishops would appear to have been regarded as peers; *cf. supra*, p. 153, n. 13. On the meaning of " peers " in 1340, see T. F. Tout, *Chapters in Administrative History*, iii, 136–139.

[52] The whole crisis is of great constitutional interest; see G. Lapsley in *English Historical Review* (1915), xxx, 6, 193; Dorothy Hughes, *Early Years of Edward III* (1915); and for a different view, B. Wilkinson, *Chancery under Edward III* (1929), 111 *et seq.*; for the administrative side, see T. F. Tout, *Chapters in Administrative History*, iii, 121 *et seq.*, and for some legal aspects, see T. F. T. Plucknett, in *Transactions of the Royal Historical Society* (1942), 65 *et seq.* A significant feature of the conflict was the appeal to public opinion by the archbishop in his sermons and by the king in a manifesto (printed in Rymer, ii, 1147), which got the name of the *libellus famosus*; *cf.* T. F. Tout, " Parliament and Public Opinion," in his *Collected Papers*, ii, 174.

and other public moneys [53]; and (3) That the ministers and judges should be appointed in parliament, and sworn to observe Magna Carta and the other statutes.[54]

The most important of these demands, and at the same time the most obnoxious to the king, were the parliamentary appointment of the ministers and judges, and the auditing of accounts, which, combined, would at once have involved ministerial responsibility. Finding, however, that a subsidy could only be obtained on condition that the petitions were granted, the king reluctantly allowed them to be embodied in a statute; but with a slight modification by which he was still to appoint, " with the advice of his council," the ministers and judges, who, however, should be bound to surrender their offices at the next parliament, and be there responsible to all having cause of complaint against them.[55] The passing of this statute gave rise to the first protest on the rolls of parliament, the chancellor, treasurer and judges recording their dissent.[56] On the dissolution of parliament Edward had recourse to the violent measure of declaring this statute null and void, in a proclamation addressed to all the sheriffs.[57]

Impeachment. (2) In 1376 (50 Edward III) the commons initiated proceedings which later legal theory regards as the origin of impeachment.[58] During the declining age of the king and the lingering illness of the Black Prince, John of Gaunt, Duke of Lancaster, had acquired the chief direction of affairs. His administration was exceedingly unpopular, and was subjected to a prolonged and determined attack in the " Good Parliament," as that which met in the 50th of Edward III was long called among the people.[59] Fifty years before, a combination of the barons against the Lancastrian party would doubtless have been the form which the opposition would have assumed. Now, the Prince of Wales and the Earl of March (the husband of Philippa, daughter and heiress of Lionel, Duke of Clarence) found that the best means of effecting their object was by combining with the Lower House in a political attack upon the government. The commons voted a subsidy, but under the intrepid leadership of their spokesman, Sir Peter de la Mare (who, significantly, was

[53] *Rotuli Parliamentorum*, ii, 128 no. 12, 130 no. 38 (Lodge and Thornton, 138, 139).
[54] *Ibid.*, ii, 128 nos. 10, 15 (Lodge and Thornton, 56), 131 no. 41; and see Stubbs, *Constitutional History*, ii, 409.
[55] 15 Edw. 3, st. 1. [56] *Rotuli Parliamentorum*, ii, 131 no. 42.
[57] *Supra*, p. 163, n. 50.
[58] See T. F. T. Plucknett, " Origin of Impeachment," in *Transactions of the Royal Historical Society* (1942); the story is continued in " The impeachments of 1376" (*ibid.*, 1951), " State trials under Richard II " (*ibid.*, 1952), and " Impeachment and Attainder " (*ibid.*, 1953). For a different view, see M. V. Clarke, in *Fourteenth Century Studies* (reprinted from *Oxford Essays presented to H. E. Salter*, 1933), criticised by B. Wilkinson, *Studies in Constitutional History* (1937); see also Anson, *Law and Custom of the Constitution*, vol. i, pp. 362 *et seq.*; Maitland, *Constitutional History*, pp. 317, 318.
[59] A great deal of new and vivid detail on the discussions among the commons in this parliament is now to be found in the *Anonimalle Chronicle of St. Mary's, York* (ed. V. H. Galbraith, 1927); *cf.* A. F. Pollard, in *English Historical Review*, liii, 577 (1938). On this parliament see the articles mentioned in the last footnote, and also T. F. Tout, *Collected Papers*, ii, 173 (1934), and A. Steel, *Richard II*, 23 *et seq.* (1941).

steward of the Earl of March), they insisted that the council should be strengthened by the addition of ten or twelve lords, prelates, and others, " to be constantly at hand so that no business of weight should be despatched without the assent and advice of all." After complaining, in general terms, that the king and kingdom had been greatly impoverished " for the private advantage of some near the king, and of others by their collusion," the commons proceeded to impeach, at the bar of the House of Lords, two peers, Latimer and Nevill, who held office under the king, and four commoners, Lyons, Ellys, Peachey and Bury, farmers of the customs and of certain monopolies. The grounds of impeachment were various, but the three principal allegations against the accused were: (1) That they had procured and advised the removal of the Staple from Calais, where it had been fixed by parliament; (2) that they had lent money to the king at exorbitant usury; and (3) that they had purchased, at a low price, old debts due from the crown, and afterwards paid themselves in full out of the treasury. The House of Lords tried and convicted all the accused, with the exception of Bury, who did not appear to take his trial. Lord Latimer was expelled from the council and placed under arrest; Lord Nevill was deprived of all his offices; while Lyons, Ellys and Peachey were imprisoned and placed at the king's mercy.[60] But the commons were not strong enough to stand alone. By the death of the Prince of Wales (June 8, 1376), they lost their chief supporter. On the dissolution of the " Good Parliament," the Duke of Lancaster resumed the chief place in the administration; the new council of twelve was removed; the former partisans of the duke returned to court; and Sir Peter de la Mare was arrested under unstated charges, and imprisoned in Nottingham Castle. In the following year a parliament, believed by a chronicler to have been packed with the duke's supporters,[61] undid the work of its predecessors, and reversed the judgments given against the impeached ministers. Most of the work of the Good Parliament was thus undone by its successor. There remained the new and dangerous weapon of impeachment, and, still more important, a great impression upon public opinion, which now became deeply interested in parliament. Nor need we assume that the commons were unduly subservient to their speakers, successively stewards of March and Lancaster; in 1377 the commons under Hungerford did in fact protest effectively against some aspects of Gaunt's policy.[62]

The commons and national politics. The intervention of the commons was not confined to questions of internal administration. Under Edward III we find them constantly consulted and giving advice on questions of war

---

[60] *Rotuli Parliamentorum*, ii, 323–329; extracts in Lodge and Thornton, 146–149. For the financial operations involved, see T. F. Tout, *Chapters in Administrative History*, iii, 289.
[61] *Chronica Angliae*, p. 112. The charge is now known to be baseless: Lord Wedgwood, in *English Historical Review*, xlv, 623; H. G. Richardson, in *Bulletin of the John Rylands Library*, xxii; A. Steel, *Richard II*, 32–33. It is noteworthy, however, that such a suspicion was current. In any case, the new Speaker, Sir Thomas Hungerford, was Gaunt's steward.
[62] A. Steel, *Richard II*, 29–33.

and peace. In 1328, while he was still a minor, and Mortimer held the reins of power, the treaty of peace with Scotland, by which that kingdom was liberated from all feudal subordination to England, was concluded with the consent of parliament, the commons being expressly mentioned. In 1331 the king consulted only the lords in parliament on the question of peace or war with France, and was advised in favour of peace [63]; but in 1333 the knights of the shire were asked to advise on Scottish relations, because half of the magnates and nearly all the prelates had not put in an appearance. [64]

In 1343 parliament was asked to advise the king as to making peace with France. The lord chamberlain, Sir Bartholomew de Burghersh, announced on the part of the king that " as the war was begun by the common advice of the prelates, great men, and commons, the king could not treat of, or make, peace without the like assent." The lords and commons, after separate deliberation, gave their opinion that the king ought to make peace if he could obtain a truce that would be honourable and advantageous to himself and his friends, but if not, the commons declared that they would aid and maintain his quarrel with all their power. [65]

In 1344 parliament, on being consulted, again urged that the war should be prosecuted energetically; but in 1348, when asked for advice (the expenses of the war having in the meantime proved exceedingly burdensome), the commons returned a very discreet and guarded answer. " Most dread lord," they said, " as to your war and the array thereof, we are so ignorant and simple that we cannot give you advice. We therefore pray your gracious lordship to excuse us, and that it please you, with the advice of the great men and of the sages of your council, to ordain what shall in this matter seem best to you for the honour and profit of yourself and your kingdom; and whatever shall be thus ordained by the consent and agreement of you and of the great men aforesaid, we readily assent to, and will hold it firm and established." [66]

In 1354, the king informed the parliament, through the lord chamberlain, that there was great hope of bringing about a peace with France, but that as he would not conclude anything without the assent of the lords and commons, he wished to know whether they would agree to peace if it might be had by treaty. To this the commons at first replied " that whatever should be agreeable to the king and the lords in making of this treaty, would be so to them "; but on being asked again, " whether they consented to a treaty of perpetual peace if it might be had? " they all with one voice cried out, " Aye ! Aye ! ". [67]

When at length peace was concluded in 1360 by the Treaty of Brétigni,

---

[63] *Rotuli Parliamentorum*, ii, 60 no. 2.

[64] *Ibid.*, ii, 69 no. 6.

[65] *Ibid.*, ii, 136 no. 8.

[66] *Ibid.*, ii, 165 no. 5; Lodge and Thornton, 140–141.

[67] *Ibid.*, ii, 262 no. 58.

parliament was summoned, and the treaty submitted to its inspection and formally approved.

In 1368, when David Bruce offered peace with Scotland on condition of being relieved from all homage for his crown to the king of England, the lords in parliament, who alone were consulted upon this occasion, answered that " they could not assent to any such peace, upon any account, without a disherison of the king, his heirs, and crown, which they themselves were sworn to preserve." [68]

These examples show the practice during the reign of Edward III, and from that time questions of war and peace have been admitted, both by the sovereigns who have requested, and by the parliaments which have freely offered, counsel and advice, to be proper subjects of parliamentary cognisance. The commons were by no means always included in these consultations, but as wars became steadily more costly, so the financial co-operation of the commons became more necessary—not as a requirement of constitutional law, but as a dictate of political.prudence.[69]

In many other affairs of state, beside those already enumerated, the commons, under Edward III, took an active part. The statute of Provisors (25 Edw. 3)—which checked the power assumed by the pope of nominating foreign clerks to fill the ecclesiastical benefices and dignities of England— was passed in consequence of " the grievous complaints of all the commons of the realm." [70]

Eligibility of the commons. In this reign also we meet with the first efforts to repress electoral abuses. In addition to several petitions that none but knights or reputable esquires might be allowed to serve as county members, it was enacted in 1372 (46 Edw. 3) that no lawyer practising in the king's court, nor sheriff during his shrievalty, should be returned or accepted as knight of the shire. The reason alleged was that many lawyers had procured seats in parliament for the purpose of putting forward, in the name of the commons, petitions which only concerned their private clients; and that sheriffs, being common ministers for the people, ought to reside in their official districts to administer right to all.[71]

RICHARD II: 1377–1399

The reign of Richard II is one of the most interesting periods in the constitutional history of medieval England. The recent discovery of new sources, and the re-examination of old ones, moreover, has shown that the situation was more complex than the older historians had suspected.

---

[68] *Ibid.*, ii, 295 no. 7.

[69] For instances of parliament being consulted as to peace or war in the fifteenth century, see p. 193, *infra*; under Henry VII, James I, and Queen Anne, see *Parliamentary History*, i, 452; i, 1293; vi 609.

[70] The equally important statute of Premunire (27 Edw. 3) was made at a great council, on the petition of the commons there present.

[71] *Rotuli Parliamentorum*, ii, 310 no. 13 (where it is called " an ordinance "), Lodge and Thornton, 144–145; see Stubbs, *Constitutional History*, ii, 445 and *infra*, p. 363. Though long obsolete, this statute was not formally repealed till 1871.

The history of the reign is therefore more difficult to recount shortly, but even richer in constitutional significance.[72]

Under Richard II not only did the commons confirm by frequent exercise the three main rights established under Edward III, that (1) no money could be levied or (2) laws enacted without their assent, and that (3) the administration of government was subject to their inspection and control; but they also secured on an equally firm basis the two derivative rights which had been asserted for the first time in the late king's reign—namely, (1) the right to examine the public accounts and appropriate the supplies, and (2) the right to impeach the king's ministers for misconduct.

In taking a rapid survey of the principal constitutional events of the twenty-two years of Richard's reign, it will be convenient to divide it into three periods: I. From 1377 to the *coup d'état* of 1389, when the king suddenly declared himself of age and took the reins of government into his own hands. II. From 1389 to the second *coup d'état* of 1397, when the king seized the Duke of Gloucester and the Earls of Warwick and Arundel (three of the five " lords appellant "). III. From 1397, when the king began to exercise despotic power, until his deposition in 1399. IV. The Peasants' Revolt of 1381, raising somewhat different questions, will be mentioned by way of conclusion.

First period, 1377–1389. During this period of minority, parliament assumed an aggressive character, and for some years " the whole executive government was transferred to the two Houses." [73]

Councils and the minority. As soon as the coronation of the boy-king was over, the prelates and barons held a great council, and chose, " in aid of the chancellor and treasurer," twelve councillors to act as a quasi-regency.[74] About three months afterwards a parliament was summoned (October, 1377), and the House of Commons, to which had been returned a large proportion of the knights who sat in the " Good Parliament " which impeached the Lancastrian ministry, elected as their speaker their old leader Sir Peter de la Mare, now released from prison. The commons at once proceeded to assert their right to a voice in the government; and at their request, the lords, in the king's name, appointed a permanent council of nine, without whose unanimous consent no business of importance was to be transacted. They also petitioned that, during the king's minority, the chancellor, treasurer, judges, and other high officers, should be made in parliament; and procured the appointment of two London

---

[72] New sources are the " Dieulacres Chronicle " (ed. M. V. Clarke and V. H. Galbraith, *Bulletin of the John Rylands Library*, xiv, 1930), and the " Kirkstall Chronicle " (ed. M. V. Clarke and H. Denholm-Young, *ibid.*, xv, 1931). The introductions, with other essays, are reprinted in M. V. Clarke, *Fourteenth Century Studies*. A new survey of the reign is made by A. Steel, *Richard II* (1941); *cf.* V. H. Galbraith, in *History*, xxvi, 223.

[73] Hallam, *Middle Ages*, iii, 59.

[74] Rymer, vii, 161–162 (Lodge and Thornton, 61–62).

merchants, William Walworth and John Philypot (the latter of whom is celebrated as the first Englishman who has left behind him the reputation of a financier), as sworn parliamentary treasurers to receive and disburse the liberal subsidy granted for the French war.[75] When the next parliament (at Gloucester, 1378) asked for Walworth's full accounts, the government produced them, but only as an act of grace and without creating a precedent.[76]

Appropriation : Accounts. The heavy expenses attending the prosecution of this war—a legacy which Richard had inherited from his grandfather— and the usual want of economy incident to a minority, necessitated frequent and urgent appeals to parliament, and the commons were always careful to tack conditions to their grants. In the second year of Richard's reign, the kingdom was in imminent danger of invasion. The council, not wishing to call a parliament so soon after the dissolution of the last, had convoked a great council of peers and other great men in January, 1379, who, finding the absolute necessity of preparation for defence, and that the king wanted money for that purpose, declared that they could not provide a remedy without charging the commons of the realm, which could not be done without parliament; but as the necessity was very urgent, all the lords there present voluntarily lent divers large sums of their own money, as did also " the good men of London and many other towns, and several persons in the kingdom to whom the king applied with the assent of the said great council." The lords then strongly advised that a parliament should be presently summoned, as well for the repayment of their loan as for further supply.[77] This advice was acted upon, and it is significant of the real progress made that as soon as parliament met, the king voluntarily, without reservation and without waiting for a petition, informed the commons that the treasurers were ready to exhibit the accounts before them; and a committee was appointed to inquire generally into the state of the revenue.[78] A similar committee, but with more extended powers, was appointed in the following year [79]; and the right of the commons to investigate the accounts and appropriate the supplies was clearly established.[80]

In the parliament which met after the insurrection of the villeins in 1381, the language of the commons was characterised by a remarkable

---

[75] *Rotuli Parliamentorum*, iii, 5–7; extracts in Lodge and Thornton, 62–64, 151–154.

[76] *Ibid.*, iii, 35 no. 20, 36 no. 21.

[77] *Ibid.*, iii, 55 no. 5. For the frequent great councils of this period, see Tout, *Chapters in Administrative History*, iii, 336.

[78] *Rotuli Parliamentorum*, iii, 56, no. 7 (Lodge and Thornton, 154), 57 no. 12 (*ibid.*, 155). It will be remembered that this was a concession by the council rather than the king, who was still a minor.

[79] *Rotuli Parliamentorum*, iii, 71 no. 3 (1380).

[80] Henry IV in 1406 made an attempt to silence the demand of the commons for the audit of accounts, telling them " kings do not render accounts." But he had to give way. Under the Yorkists and Tudors the right fell into disuse. It was revived in 1624 and 1641, and again firmly established as an undisputed principle under Charles II in 1666.—Hallam, *Constitutional History*, ii, 356.

boldness. After expressing their conviction that, " unless the government of the realm were speedily amended, the realm itself would be utterly lost and ruined for ever," they made many bitter complaints against the administration, whereupon a commission of reform was appointed " to survey and examine in private council both the state and government of the king's person and of his household, and to suggest proper remedies." [81]

John of Gaunt, Duke of 'Lancaster, had quickly recovered from the attacks of the Good Parliament of 1376 and until 1386 was the dominant influence in English politics, domestic, foreign, commercial and ecclesiastical.[82] From 1386 to 1389, however, he took his considerable private army to Spain in an endeavour to secure the crowns of Castile and Leon.

Suffolk's Impeachment, 1386. His absence provided the opportunity for the anti-Lancastrian factions. As a result the commons were induced to impeach the chancellor, Michael de la Pole, Earl of Suffolk. This prosecution confirmed to the commons their newly acquired right of impeaching the ministers of the crown. In the parliament which met on October 1, 1386, both Houses jointly requested the removal of the chancellor. The king, who, after the opening of parliament, had withdrawn to Eltham, with characteristic impetuosity and arrogance replied " that he would not for them, or at their instance, remove the meanest scullion from his kitchen." The lords and commons returned a joint answer, refusing to proceed with any business until the king should come back to his parliament and remove the obnoxious minister from office.[83] At length Richard was rash enough to threaten to call in the advice of the king of France; a threat which produced the memorable address in answer, in which the parliament referred to the deposition of Edward II, and plainly intimated to the king that his continued contumacy would produce a similar result.[84] After this Richard yielded; the chancellor was removed, and his enemy Arundel, bishop of Ely, appointed in his

---

[81] *Rotuli Parliamentorum*, iii, 100, 101, no. 18; Lodge and Thornton, 65–66. For details, see Tout, *Chapters in Administrative History*, iii, 381. For the next fifty years, the lords took great enjoyment from their interference with the king's domestics. There was the additional incentive that the household was now a considerable factor in politics. For this complicated though vital aspect in the situation see T. F. Tout, *Chapters in Administrative History*, iii, 194 *et seq.*, 329 *et seq.*, and A. Steel, *Richard II*, 111.

[82] The complicated story will be found in A. Steel, *Richard II*, 94 *et seq.* and M. V. Clarke, *Fourteenth Century Studies*, 36–52.

[83] Knighton, ii, 215–216; extracts in Lodge and Thornton, 23–25. For the name " Wonderful," traditionally given to this parliament, see A. Steel, *Richard II*, 119, n. 3.

[84] Their words were : " We have an ancient statute, and it was not many years ago experimented (it grieves us that we must mention it) that if the king through any evil design or foolish obstinacy, or contempt, or out of a perverse or froward wilfulness, or by any other irregular courses, shall alienate himself from his people, and refuse to govern by the laws, statutes, and laudable ordinances of the realm, with the salutary counsel of the lords and great men of the realm, but will throw himself headlong into wild designs, and wantonly exercise his own singular arbitrary will,—from that time it shall be lawful for his people, by their full and free assent and consent, to depose the king himself from his royal throne, and in his stead to raise up some other of the royal race upon the same."—Knighton, ii, 219. There was, of course, no such " statute " authorising the deposition of kings. The reference was to the measures taken for the deposition of King Edward II. On Richard's alleged appeal to France, see A. Steel, *Richard II*, 122.

stead. In a bill of impeachment, divided into seven heads, Suffolk was charged with divers crimes and misdemeanours, and especially with having obtained from the king grants beyond his deserts and contrary to his oath of office, and with having enriched himself by defrauding the crown. He made a very able defence and was acquitted on some of the charges; but being found guilty on the rest was condemned to forfeit all his grants, and to be committed to prison until he should pay a fine or ransom.[85]

Commission of Reform. Acting on the precedents of the reigns of John, Henry III, and Edward II, and of the third and fifth years of the king's own reign, the commons now petitioned for the appointment of a commission of reform. The king at first resolutely refused to give his assent, and threatened to dissolve parliament, but at length he was forced to yield, and a commission, consisting of fourteen persons of the highest eminence, was appointed by statute, with almost unlimited powers, for the space of one year only.[86]

Richard, who now was in his twentieth year, had no intention of submitting to this drastic attempt to continue the conditions of his minority. Before the dissolution of parliament he had made a verbal protestation that nothing done therein should be in prejudice of his prerogatives [87]; and a few months afterwards, having in the meantime released Suffolk and restored him to favour, he summoned the judges to Nottingham, and propounded to them the famous set of ten questions.

Questions to the Judges, 1387. The judges gave their answers in writing under seal: (1) That the late statute, ordinance, and commission were derogatory to the king's prerogatives, particularly as they were made without his will; (2) that all who procured the said statute, ordinance, and commission to be passed, or (3) persuaded or (4) compelled the king to consent to it, or (5) impeded the king in the exercise of his prerogative, were deserving of the punishment of death; (6) that the king, and not the lords and commons, had the power to determine the order in which business should be proceeded upon in parliament; (7) that the king could dissolve parliament at pleasure and that any proceedings thereafter were treasonable; (8) that his ministers could not be impeached without his consent; (9) that he who had moved that the statute deposing Edward II should be sent for, and he who had carried it in, were punishable as traitors; and (10) that the judgment against the Earl of Suffolk was altogether erroneous, and might be revoked.[88] All the judges, except one,

---

[85] *Rotuli Parliamentorum*, iii, 216–220. There is reason to believe that Suffolk was as much " sinned against as sinning." As a *parvenu* he was regarded with enmity and jealousy by the old nobility, headed by the king's uncle, the Duke of Gloucester; *cf.* Steel, *op. cit.*, 123, and N. B. Lewis, *English Historical Review*, xlii, 402–407.

[86] *Rotuli Parliamentorum*, ii, 221 no. 18 (Lodge and Thornton, 67); the commission is in *Calendar of Patent Rolls* (1385–1389), 244; *cf.* T. F. Tout, Chapters, iii, 416; A. Steel, *Richard II*, 125. Its term was from November 20, 1386–November 19, 1387.

[87] *Rotuli Parliamentorum*, iii, 224 no. 35; Lodge and Thornton, 25.

[88] *Rotuli Parliamentorum*, iii, 233; partly in Lodge and Thornton, 25–26.

subsequently protested that these answers had been extorted by threats. Whatever may have been the motive which dictated them, they were undoubtedly both servile and sanguinary, unconstitutional for the most part, even as the constitution was then understood, and utterly inconsistent with the continued existence and future development of parliamentary liberty.

The preceding sentence, written in 1875, represents a view of this incident which has been widely held down to recent times.[89] Considerable revision is necessary if a truthful account is to be made from the standpoint of 1387. Mr. Steel has observed that there is no evidence that Richard coerced the judges, nor did the judges suggest it until a year later when they were on trial—and then in very real peril of their lives. He further suggests that it is dangerous to speak of a " constitution " at this date.[90] That also is true, save in the untechnical sense of a complex of institutions, procedures and conventional conduct in public affairs. From that point of view, the judges' opinions seem to be a defensible statement of fourteenth-century practice. Points 1, 2, 3, 4 and 5 reaffirm the principle of the statute of York of 1322 [91]; points 6 and 7 state the undoubted fact that parliament was effectively the king's parliament, concerned with the king's affairs; points 8 and 10 rest on the principle that ministers are the king's ministers, responsible primarily to him. They also show the unsettled problems involved in the process of impeachment.[92] Most ominous is the use of the word " treason." [93] In short, the answers are a case for the crown, arguable if not conclusively convincing, when tested by contemporary practice; like any purely legal statement on constitutional matters, they emphasise old-established rules, and miss those changes in thought and political development which so often carry the working constitution in advance of the strictly legal constitution.[94]

The Lords Appellant, 1388. The king had hoped to use this opinion to rid himself of the obnoxious commission, but the baronial leaders forestalled him. Although the commission had expired, its members continued notwithstanding to exercise their extraordinary powers. Then five lords (the Duke of Gloucester and the Earls of Warwick and Arundel, joined later by the Earls of Derby and Nottingham) solemnly accused (or " appealed ") several of the king's ministers and supporters of treason.[95]

[89] T. F. Tout, *Chapters in Administrative History* (1928), iii, 423–424, for example.

[90] A. Steel, *Richard II*, 130. *Cf.* B. Wilkinson, *Studies in Constitutional History*, 254, 259.

[91] *Supra*, pp. 157.

[92] Point 8 negatives the claim of the commons to impeach without the concurrence of the king. Could the king impeach without the concurrence of the commons? Charles I thought he could. Both propositions are obscure.

[93] For one view, see M. V. Clarke, *Fourteenth Century Studies*, 123 *et seq.* The subject is too difficult to treat here.

[94] The latest examination of the incident is by Professor S. B. Chrimes, in *Law Quarterly Review*, lxxii, 365 (1956).

[95] For details, see A. Steel, *Richard II*, 136 *et seq.* Appeals of treason were not unknown at common law (Maitland, *Select Pleas of the Crown*, no. 115; L. W. Vernon Harcourt, *His Grace the Steward* (1907), 349n.; Pollock and Maitland, *History of English Law*, ii, 507), but were a novelty in parliament. The issue might be tried by battle.

The reasons for using the appeal are evident—it was the only criminal procedure which the crown could not initiate, nor prevent, nor nullify after the event by a pardon. The king transferred the appeals to be tried in parliament. The judges and the council reported that the appeals were defective both in common law and in civil law.[96] The lords rejected this politic advice and made the dangerous declaration that momentous matters of this sort concerning peers were determinable in parliament alone, and that neither civil nor common law governed them, but only the " law of parliament."[97] To Richard's claim in the ten questions that parliament is the king's parliament, the barons now reply that parliament is theirs, to be used in their absolute discretion against the ministers of the crown—just as in 1341 they had claimed to use parliament to protect ministers against the king. The appeals being disposed of,[98] the judges who had given the opinions on Richard's ten questions were impeached and banished. The baronial triumph was thus complete,[99] and parliament voted the huge sum of £20,000 to the appellants for their services.

Deprived, by death or exile, of all his favourites, Richard remained for nearly a year subservient to the Duke of Gloucester's party; until, taking advantage of the growing disunion in their ranks, and of a reaction in public opinion, he suddenly announced (in 1389) that he was now in his twenty-second year, that he repudiated the tutelage of the past twelve years, and that, like every other heir, he was now going to manage his own affairs.

Second period, 1389–1397. During this period of nearly eight years, comparative harmony subsisted between Richard and his parliament, and the return of John of Gaunt, who had been absent during the late revolutionary proceedings, prosecuting his claim to the throne of Castile, served to keep his brother of Gloucester in check, and exercised a mitigating influence over the excited passions of all parties. The leaders among the nobles were moreover divided by personal jealousies. The series of truces with France obviated the necessity for oppressive taxation. Parliament refrained from interfering with the king's household expenses, but they continued the practice of making conditional grants, to be levied only in case of an expedition against the enemy, and on account of the non-fulfilment of this condition, several subsidies were remitted by proclamation. The king on his side behaved with unusual courtesy. In 1389, he ordered the chancellor, treasurer, and other members of his Council,

---

[96] The appeals had previously been laid in the court of the constable, which professed to follow Roman procedure. These judges were men recently appointed by the appellants themselves.

[97] *Rotuli Parliamentorum*, iii, 236, 244 no. 7 (Lodge and Thornton, 156, 158). Parliament thus claimed to be a special court for state trials, and to be subject to no law but its own (*cf.* T. F. T. Plucknett, in *Politica*, ii, 558).

[98] Tresillian (ex-Chief Justice) and Brembre (ex-Mayor of London) were executed. De la Pole and De Vere fled abroad and died in exile.

[99] Among the appellants' reforms are the first extant orders of chancery: Tout, *Chapters in Administrative History*, iii, 443–449; text in B. Wilkinson, *Chancery under Edward III*, 217 *et seq.*

to resign their offices in parliament, and submit themselves to its judgment in case any charge should be brought against them. After a day's deliberation the commons declared, in full parliament, that nothing amiss had been found in the conduct of the ministers, who were consequently restored to their former positions; the king protesting that his complaisance on this occasion was not to be drawn into a precedent.[1]

Haxey's Case, 1397. As soon, however, as Richard, having secured an alliance with the royal family of France, and perceiving the disunion which existed among his principal nobility, fancied himself secure upon his throne, he ventured once more to indulge his natural arbitrary and tyrannical disposition. The first incident was provoked by a " bill," *i.e.*, a petition or remonstrance, in the commons' house during the parliament of 1397. The grievances for which it prayed remedy were : (1) That the statute requiring sheriffs and escheators to be persons of sufficient lands and rent, and that they should not retain office for more than a year, was not kept. (2) In the Scottish march, great oppressions and outrages were inflicted by the Scots, contrary to the truces between the two kingdoms. (3) That retainers (" vadletz appellez yomen ") of the lords, although they were not household servants, wore liveries contrary to the statute passed with the object of preventing maintenance and duress, by colour of such liveries. (4) That the excessive charge of the king's household should be diminished: to wit, of the multitude of bishops, who have lordships, and with their retinue are supported by the king; and also of many ladies and their attendants who dwell in the palace of the king and at his cost.[2] Richard sent for the lords, who were considering the bill, declared it to be an invasion of his prerogative, and ordered the Duke of Lancaster to demand from the commons the name of the person who had introduced it. This request the commons, with many humble apologies, complied with by delating the name of Sir Thomas Haxey, an ecclesiastic; and being intimidated by the king, and unsupported in this instance by the nobility, they remained passive while the lords and the king determined the point of law by declaring that it was treason for any person to move the commons of parliament or anyone else to remedy anything appertaining to the king's person, rule, or royalty. Two days after (February 7), under this law, Haxey was condemned, on his own confession, to suffer the punishment of a traitor.[3] This violent proceeding was undoubtedly (to quote the words used

---

[1] *Rotuli Parliamentorum*, iii, 258 no. 6. For the independent attitude of the council towards the king, and their sense of their responsibility to parliament at this moment, see Tout, *Chapters in Administrative History*, iii, 469 *et seq.*

[2] *Rotuli Parliamentorum*, iii, 339 no. 13. In the recital of Haxey's bill contained in the pardon ultimately granted to him (*ibid.*, iii, 407–408), he is also made to complain of the imposition by the pope of a tax of 4d. in the pound on the clergy of the province of Canterbury.

[3] *Ibid.*, iii, 339 nos. 14–17, 341 no. 23, 407, 408. His life was spared at the intercession of the bishops as a matter of grace (treason was not within the benefit of clergy); and a full pardon was granted him on the 27th of May.

in Henry IV's first parliament, when the judgment was reversed in both Houses), " encontre droit et la course quel avoit este use devant en Parlement en anientisement des custumes de lez communes." [4]

There has been so much misunderstanding of this case in the past, that the following points must be made clear.[5] (1) Haxey was not an elected member of the commons, nor did he attend under the *premunientes* clause; he was in fact keeper of the rolls in the court of common pleas. (2) Richard's rage is explicable by the fact that this impertinent personal attack came from a senior civil servant of fifteen years' standing who had received much valuable preferment through the royal bounty (resources which he augmented by a profitable business in money-lending). (3) Even so, the judgment against him was merely *in terrorem*, and within a fortnight he began to regain his many pluralities. (4) Haxey's " treason " was not newly created by the lords for the purposes of this case, but was a corollary to the judges' opinion of 1387, which Richard always treated as sound law. (5) Somewhat later it would have been regarded as a breach of privilege for the king to take notice of matters pending in the commons and to draw the attention of the lords to them, but no such privilege existed in 1397; it would be hazardous to conclude from the extremely vague language used in reversing the case, that the commons were now setting up such a privilege. (6) Since Haxey was not a member of either house, no other question of privilege could arise.

Third period, 1397–1399. The prosecution of Haxey was quickly followed up by the execution of the king's project of revenge, the first step towards which was the arrest of the Duke of Gloucester and the Earls of Warwick and Arundel (three out of the five " lords appellant ") who were possibly involved in an obscure conspiracy. The conduct of the new parliament of September, 1397, was so servile as to prompt the statement of the anonymous monk of Evesham in his *Life of Richard II*,[6] that it was surrounded by the king's troops, and thus coerced into compliance with his wishes. Notwithstanding the general and special pardons formerly granted, appeals of treason were brought by the king's friends against the accused lords; the Duke of Gloucester, who had been sent to Calais and there murdered, was attainted after his death; the Earl of Arundel was beheaded; his brother, the Archbishop of Canterbury, impeached and banished, and the Lords Warwick and Cobham sent beyond sea. In its second session, during which this parliament re-assembled at Shrewsbury on January 28, 1398, and sat only to the end of the month, the proceedings of the Merciless Parliament (1388) and the commission

---

[4] *Ibid.*, iii, 434 no. 104; Lodge and Thornton, 159; *infra*, p. 195.
[5] See J. E. Neale, " Commons' Privilege of Free Speech " (in *Tudor Studies presented to A. F. Pollard*, 1924); T. F. Tout, *Chapters in Administrative History*, iv, 17–19; A. Steel, *Richard II*, 224–227. For Haxey's career, see *Chichele's Register* (ed. E. F. Jacob), ii, 657.
[6] *Vita Ricardi* (ed. Hearne), 133. Otterbourne, (p. 191) says that the knights returned were elected " non per communitatem, ut mos exigit, sed per regiam voluntatem." Of this there is no evidence; H. G. Richardson, in *Bulletin of the John Rylands Library* xxii, 35–42.

of reform of 1386 were annulled. The answers of the judges to the questions put by the king at Nottingham, which had been punished by death and exile, were declared to be just and legal. An attempt was also made to bind future parliaments by enacting that every judgment, statute, or ordinance, made in the present parliament, should in all time to come have the full force of statutes, and that any man who should attempt to repeal or overturn them should be adjudged, and have execution as, a traitor to the king and realm.[7] The commons then set the dangerous precedent of granting the king a tax (upon wool and hides) for the term of his life.[8]

Appointment of eighteen commissioners. The concluding act of the session proved the most disastrous of all to constitutional liberty. It had been the custom to dismiss the members as soon as ever public business would permit, and to appoint a committee to hear and determine such petitions as had not been answered during the sitting of parliament. Accordingly, a committee of twelve peers and six commoners was appointed to sit after the dissolution and to deal with this business " by authority of parliament." [9] It is evident that no further power was intended by parliament to be delegated to these eighteen commissioners than such as had been conferred upon previous occasions. But the words of their appointment were of somewhat indefinite scope, and there is reason to believe that Richard had the rolls of parliament falsified in order to enlarge the committee's terms of reference; indeed, this accusation was specifically made at his deposition.[10]

The obscure quarrel between the Dukes of Hereford and Norfolk (the two remaining " lords appellant ") gave Richard an excuse for banishing them both—just as they were about to enter the lists to try their appeal by battle. The king was now triumphant over all his enemies. The grant of a revenue for life relieved him from the immediate necessity of summoning a parliament; and a former declaration of the two Houses, that the king's prerogative was as free and unimpaired as that of any of his predecessors,[11] was now construed as giving him the power to dispense with such statutes as controlled it.

His deposition. The career of tyranny and extortion upon which Richard had entered alienated all classes of the nation, and speedily led to his deposition. The time had now come of which the parliament had warned the king in 1386, when it became " lawful with the common

---

[7] *Rotuli Parliamentorum*, iii, 350–352.
[8] *Ibid.*, 368 no. 75 (Lodge and Thornton, 158–159).
[9] *Ibid.*, iii, 368 no. 74 (Lodge and Thornton, 158). See J. G. Edwards, " The Parliamentary Committee of 1398," *English Historical Review*, xl, 321; T. F. Tout, *Chapters in Administrative History*, iv, 31, 35–41; A. Steel, *Richard II*, 246–251.
[10] There is interesting matter for contrast as well as comparison in the Lords of the Articles to whom Scottish parliaments delegated their powers. See generally, R. S. Rait, *Parliaments of Scotland* (1924).
[11] *Rotuli Parliamentorum*, iii, 279 no. 15.

assent and consent of the people of the kingdom to depose the king from his royal throne, and in his stead to raise up some other of the royal race upon the same." In the solemn exercise of the greatest of its powers, parliament was careful to observe every formality and precaution which the constitutional lawyers of that day could suggest. But although Richard was induced to resign the crown, and Henry of Lancaster laid claim to it, the deposition, the vacancy of the throne, and the subsequent election of Henry, are each recorded in the most distinct terms in the official entry on the rolls of parliament.[12]

THE PEASANTS' REVOLT, 1381

The formidable insurrection of the villeins in 1381 had forcibly called the attention of the knights and burgesses, who had hitherto been intent upon the maintenance of their own political liberties, to the growing feeling of discontent among the agricultural labourers. Forming probably a majority of the whole nation, they were not destitute of political privileges, but harassed by vexatious restrictions on the freedom of their labour, and in many cases were in a state of personal bondage.

For a long time prior to the Conquest, the condition of a large number of the ceorls had been gradually becoming more and more depressed.[13] Although they were all freemen, an increasing number had lost the privilege of commending themselves to whatever hlaford they pleased, and were unable to quit the soil which they cultivated for their own and their lord's benefit. Although the so-called laws of William the Conqueror declare that " Coloni et terrarum exercitores non vexentur ultra debitum et statutum, nec licet dominis removere colonos a terris dummodo debita servitia persolvant," [14] the general status of all agricultural tenants was lowered under the harsh rule of their new military masters. The multitude of smaller or larger " manors " with which the whole of England appears covered in the first century after the conquest, were not indeed of Norman origin, though called by a Norman name; but the strict application of the feudal system to all kinds of land, which was a result of the Conquest, must have tended very much to throw the small landed proprietors under manorial lordships.[15] The ceorl, who had previously been at liberty to go where he willed, would now tend to the position of one bound to the soil; and the service which was formerly certain in amount would now in many cases be exacted at the will of the lord. Some of the ceorls retained their free status, as *libere tenentes* or *socmanni*, rendering, by way of rent, fixed agricultural services, exclusive of, or in conjunction with, a

[12] *Ibid.*, iii, 416–424. On the deposition procedure see *infra*, pp. 487–492.

[13] For general surveys of the very difficult problem of villeinage and the manor, see E. Lipson, *Economic History*, i (7th ed., 1937), and the *Cambridge Economic History* (1941) i, 224. See the material collected in A. E. Bland, P. A. Brown and R. H. Tawney, *English Economic History: Select Documents*, 56–110.

[14] *Lois de Guillaume le Conquérant* (ed. Matzke), c. 29, and *Leis Willelme*, 29 (in A. J. Robertson, *Laws of the English Kings*, 269).

[15] Bracton, lib. i, c. 11 (f. 7; ed. Woodbine, ii, 37).

money payment; but the rest, under the generic term *villani*, were the agricultural labourers upon land which they cultivated for the lord. Amongst the villeins there were various grades, of which the higher, possessing larger holdings, probably approached very near to the *socmanni*; while the lower, such as the *bordarii*, *cottarii*, and *cotseti*, with but scanty allotments, would be liable in many cases to become gradually confounded with the *servi*, who, soon after the date of Domesday, disappear as a class distinct from the *villani*.

Status of the villeins. Glanvill, writing in the reign of Henry II, speaks of the *nativi* as being absolutely dependent upon their lords' will, and so destitute of any kind of property that they were legally incapable of purchasing their own redemption from villeinage.[16] Here we may probably trace the influence of the Roman law as to slavery,[17] in exaggerating the servile aspect of villeinage in the eyes of the medieval lawyers. This view, however accurately it states the strictly legal position, is inconsistent with what we learn from other historic sources. That villeins had property, notwithstanding the general statements of Bracton and other legal writers to the contrary, seems to be clearly proved. Thus, in the chronicle of Simeon of Durham, we read (*s. a.* 1096): " Comites, barones, vice-comites suos milites et villanos spoliaverunt, et regi non modicam summam auri et argenti detulerunt." [18] So in the *Dialogus de Scaccario*, among possible debtors to the king are enumerated *miles, vel liber alius, aut ascriptitius*.[19] In *Magna Carta* (1215, c. 20), the " wainage " (the tillage) of a villein is specially excepted from liability to seizure for a fine due to the king. Henry III, in a writ issued in 1225 for the collection of a " fifteenth," excepts from assessment the arms which a villein was sworn to keep for service in the local militia, as well as his household utensils, and such of his provisions, hay, and provender as were not for sale.[20] In 1232 a " fortieth " is declared to have been granted by the " archbishops, bishops, abbots, priors, clergy holding lay fees, earls, barons, knights, freeholders, and *villeins*." [21]   Five years later a " thirtieth " is declared to be granted by the freeholders, *pro se et suis villanis*, and a distinction is drawn between the villeins, and the poor having less than forty pence, *in bonis*, who are to pay nothing.[22] All through the fourteenth century the common law courts continued to maintain a theory completely at variance with social practice. Bondmen were able and willing to pay

[16] Glanvill, lib. v, c. 5 (ed. Woodbine, 86); see also *Dialogus de Scaccario* (ed. Hughes, Crump and Johnson), lib. i, c. 11; lib. ii, c. 14; *Select Charters*, 192, 221, 240.
[17] *Cf.* Vinogradoff, *Villainage in England*, p. 47; Holdsworth, *History of English Law*, iii, 491 *et seq.*; and for a later period, Maitland, *English Law and the Renaissance* (1901), 23, 83 n. 54 (but note *contra* H. Nabholz in *Cambridge Economic History*, i, 553).
[18] *Ibid.*, ii, 227.
[19] Lib. ii, c. 13.
[20] Rymer, i, 177. *Select Charters*, 352–353.
[21] Matt. Paris, iii, 230; *Select Charters*, 356.
[22] Rymer, i, 232; *Select Charters*, 358.

huge sums for their liberty, and sometimes rose to high civic office—although all their land and chattels were technically their lords'.[23]

Change in meaning of the word " villein." It seems clear that the word *villanus* had undergone a change of meaning between the times when Domesday was compiled and when Bracton wrote under Henry III. In Domesday the men who, though performing base services, were still free, are carefully distinguished from the *servi*. But both the *villani* and *servi* received their means of subsistence in land, which, however it might differ in quantity, was still held by the same villein tenure, and for which they rendered services the same in kind though differing in extent. From the status of the *servi*—the lowest species of tenants-in-villeinage—the generic term " villein " seems gradually to have acquired a lower sense and meaning, and came at length to denote the condition of personal servitude.[24] The word *servus* disappeared as the name of a class, but villeins, in the lower sense of the term, are generally specifically described as *nativi*—villeins by birth, not merely by tenure—or by the addition of the word *servus* after *villanus*. The double signification of the word is evident from the returns in the Hundred Rolls (*temp.* Edw. I), where, in certain cases, it is specially stated, *villani sunt servi*, or *nativi*,[25] while, on the other hand, in the decisions of the Curia Regis of the same period, the word *villanus* is used to designate the state of personal serfdom.[26] We are expressly told by Bracton (*temp.* Hen. III) that a freeman might hold a tenement in villeinage, in which case his personal liberty existed along with the burdens of territorial servitude.[27] He distinguishes two kinds of villeinage, socage and pure. The *villani socmanni*, who were chiefly to be found on the king's demesne, were bound to fixed services, but while they could not, so long as they performed the service due, be removed from their land against their will, they could at any time voluntarily leave it. They had no power, however, any more than the tenant in pure villeinage, to confer on another any right or interest in the land occupied; they could only by a bargain with the lord surrender it to him

[23] G. G. Coulton, *Medieval Village*, 502; *cf.* Y.B. 1 & 2 Edw. 2, 11–13 (ex-Sheriff of London claimed as a villein); Y.B. 11 Rich. 2, 168–174 (arbitrators in 1387 fix the price of freedom at £1,000); Y.B. 13 Rich. 2, 122–128 (a mayor of London holding land said to be villeinage); and other examples in Holdsworth, iii, 503 *et seq.*, and Bland, Brown and Tawney, *Documents*, 98–102, 231.

[24] " It may be doubted whether the word *villani* had during the twelfth century fully acquired the meaning of servitude which was attached to it by the later lawyers."—Stubbs, *Constitutional History*, i, 467. " For some purposes, indeed—chiefly in connection with the law as to wrongs—the distinction between free and slave was clearly drawn in the law books. But for many purposes the distinction was not very apparent. In Domesday-Book, ' the *servus* who has land and oxen may be casually called a *villanus*, and we cannot be sure that no one whom our record calls a *servus* has the wergild of a free man ' ": W. S. Holdsworth, *History of English Law*, ii, 42, citing Maitland, *Domesday Book and Beyond*, pp. 30–33; *cf.* also Vinogradoff, *English Society*, pp. 217, 218.

[25] *Rotuli Hundredorum*, ii, 324, 327, 329, 822. *Cf.* E. A. Kosminsky, in *Economic History Review* (1931), iii, 16–44.

[26] *Placitorum Abbreviatio*, pp. 25, 161.

[27] Bracton, l, ii, c. 8; iv, c. 28; *Select Charters*, 415; see also *Placitorum Abbreviatio*, 29 Edw. 1, p. 243.

or his steward, so that it might be let out afresh to the person in whose favour it had been relinquished. The " pure " villein, on the contrary, according to Bracton, might be subject to unlimited services and burdens, " nec scire debeat sero quid facere debeat in crastino, . . . talliari . . . potest . . . ad plus vel minus." He had not the smallest right in the land which he cultivated, and was in the strongest sense of the word a predial serf.[28]

The manor. It is important to bear in mind that manorial property differed in many respects from the modern landed estate. " It was not a breadth of land, which the lord might cultivate or not as he pleased, suffer it to be inhabited, or reduce it to solitude and waste; but it was a dominion or empire, within which the lord was superior over subjects of different ranks, his power over them not being absolute, but limited by law and custom. . . . The demesne, the assised,[29] and the waste lands were his; but the usufruct of the assised land belonged, on conditions, to the tenants, and the waste lands were not so entirely his that he could exclude the tenants from the use of them." [30]

The natural tendency of the customary law by which each manor was regulated was towards certainty: certainty of services, certainty of tenure. Accordingly we find in the Hundred Rolls and in the land registers of the thirteenth century exact specifications of the services due from the various denominations of tenants; and even those villeins who are entered as liable to be tallaged at the will of the lord have their agricultural services accurately determined both in kind and extent. There was another circumstance which favourably affected the condition of the agricultural population. A money economy, as opposed to barter in kind, was established in England at a much earlier period, and far more extensively than in the great inland countries of the European continent.[31]

Rise of free labourers. The lords of manors found it more profitable and convenient to receive money payments in lieu of the ancient predial services, and the tenants were very willing by such payments to relieve themselves from the burden of personal performance of the services. This change was gradually carried out between the middle of the twelfth

[28] But " the slave is free against everybody but his lord "—" and even against his lord had some standing ground for a civil action." Vinogradoff, *Villainage in England*, pp. 69, 70. The whole subject of villeinage is exhaustively and admirably treated in this work, which brings out many new points, and firmly establishes them. See also Maitland, *Constitutional History*, pp. 33 *et seq.*; and Pollock and Maitland, *History of English Law*, i, 412–432, where the status of the villein is fully considered. *Cf.* also Holdsworth, *History of English Law*, iii, 491–509; Lipson, *Economic History of England*, i, 32–45; *Cambridge Economic History*, i, 438–446; E. A. Kosminsky, *Studies in Agrarian History* (1956).

[29] *Assised* lands = parts of the demesne granted out to tenants subsequently to the original formation of the manor. See Vinogradoff, pp. 333–334.

[30] Hale, *Domesday of St. Paul's*, Introduction, xxxii–xxxiii.

[31] Nasse, *Agricultural Community of the Middle Ages* (translated by Ouvry, 1872), p. 67. *Cf.* N. Neilson in *Cambridge Economic History*, i, 465.

and the middle of the fifteenth centuries.[32] In this way a numerous class of free labourers arose, and the lords of manors passed into the condition of the landlord of modern times, who must hire, but cannot command, labour. The process was slow and varied; sometimes the commutation was complete and permanent, sometimes partial, sometimes revocable. The villein might be released from some of his obligations in return for a money payment, while others—often the most burdensome—he was still compelled to perform. Commutation was also adopted as a temporary expedient which could be abandoned when it suited the lord's convenience. There was no uniformity in the process, and in its later stages there was on some estates a tendency to revert to labour services and to increase such labour services as were still due. It was long before all the villeins had ceased to be mere tenants-at-will and had become copyholders with inheritable estates in their lands subject to fixed services.[33]

Statutes of Labourers. The dreadful pestilence of 1348, by greatly reducing the number of the new class of hired labourers, nearly doubled the value of their labour—to the great loss of those landed proprietors who had commuted the predial services of their tenants. The government, without any intention of oppressing the labourers but hoping to avert a serious economic catastrophe, had recourse to the ordinance of 1349, and to a series of statutes of greater severity between 1351 and 1368, by which every able-bodied man, not living of his own nor by any trade, was compelled to hire himself to any master who should demand his services, at such wages as were paid three years previously, or for some time preceding. Simultaneously, the prices of food and articles of necessity were likewise fixed. These statutes, while failing in the object which they had in view, as appears by the frequent complaints of the commons that they were not kept, greatly increased the general discontent of the . peasantry.[34] In a great many manors at this period the ancient services still remained due, but the villeins, lured by the prospect of high wages, impatient of the burdens of predial service, and animated by the general spirit of unrest which resulted from the Black Death, often left their holdings to offer themselves as hired labourers, and began to confederate for the purpose of resisting their lords. A statute of 1377, passed " at the

---

[32] The remarkable transmutation of villein-tenure into copyhold reached a decisive stage in the reign of Edward IV, when the judges permitted the copyholder to bring an action of trespass against his lord for dispossession. *Cf.* Lipson, *Economic History*, 136 *et seq.*; Holdsworth, ii, 379 *et seq.*, iii, 201–213, vii, 296–312.

[33] For the whole subject of commutation see the important study by M. Postan in the *Transactions of the Royal Historical Society*, 4th series, xx, 169–193 (1937); *cf.* Lipson, Chap. III; Page, *The End of Villeinage in England*, and the review of this book by Vinogradoff in *English Historical Review*, vol. xv, 1900 (reprinted in his *Collected Papers*, Oxford (1928), i, 129 *et seq*); and Plucknett, *Legislation of Edward I*, 65; for comparative studies, see F. Joüon des Longrais, " *La vilainage anglais*," in *Recueil de la Societé Jean Bodin* (1937), and his *L'Est et L'Ouest* (1958), Chap. III (ii).

[34] See 25 Edw. 3, st. II (1351), Putnam, *Enforcement of the Statutes of Labourers*, and Petit-Dutaillis, *Studies Supplementary to Stubbs' Constitutional History*, ii, 264 *et seq.* The ordinance of 1349 and cases illustrating the enforcement of the legislation will be found in Bland, Brown and Tawney, *Documents*, 164–178.

grievous complaint of the lords and commons of the realm, as well men of holy church, as other," for the punishment of recalcitrant villeins, recites that " villeins and tenants of land in villeinage who owe services and customs to their lords, had of late withdrawn their customs and services from them, by comfort and procurement of others their counsellors, maintainers, and abettors, who had taken hire and profit of the said villeins and land tenants; and under colour of exemplifications out of Domesday Book of the manors and vills in which they dwelt, and by wrong interpretation of those exemplifications, claimed to be quit and discharged of all manner of service either of their body or of their lands, and would suffer no distress or other course of justice to be taken against them; and did menace the servants of their lords with peril to life and limb, and what is more, did gather together in great routs, and bind themselves mutually by such confederacy that each one should aid the other to resist their lords with the strong hand." [35]

The Peasants' Revolt, 1381. The discontent of the peasants, the grievances of the lower clergy, who as a class had, perhaps, suffered more severely from the pestilence than any other, the French war bringing with it heavy taxation, especially the irritating poll-tax of twelvepence a head exacted from rich and poor alike,[36] were among the chief causes which gave rise to the formidable insurrection of 1381.[37]   The actual demands of the insurgents as declared by Wat Tyler at Smithfield comprised " that there should be no law within the realm save the law of Winchester, and that from henceforth there should be no outlawry in any process of law . . . and that the goods of Holy Church should not remain in the hands of the religious, nor of parsons and vicars, and other churchmen, but the clergy already in possession should have a sufficient sustenance from the endowments, and the rest of the goods should be divided among the people of the parish . . . and that there should be no more villeins in

[35] 1 Ric. 2, c. 6. (If it could be shown that a manor was ancient demesne—by inspecting Domesday Book—the tenants had a remedy in the common law courts if the lord increased their services; Pollock and Maitland, i, 378.)

[36] It was ordered, however, that the richer should aid the poorer, and that individual contributions might range from 20s. down to 4d. *Rotuli Parliamentorum*, iii, 90. But this left much scope for oppression on the part of the collectors of the tax.

[37] On the variety of causes which led to the revolt of 1381 see the essay already quoted by Petit-Dutaillis. " Whether one considers its principal or its secondary causes," he says, p. 274, " it is true to say that the revolt of 1381 was, so to speak, a settlement of old scores of every kind. It was above all an eruption of long-cherished envy, hatred, and malice—feelings which had every excuse—towards the selfishness of the rich . . . it altogether lacked unity, and it was directed by demagogues of only mediocre ability. It had some of the characteristics of a political movement, of a religious movement, and especially of a social movement; but none of these terms defines it sufficiently, and even if one uses all three to describe it, there is still a danger of giving a false impression." Recent research is embodied in A. Steel, *Richard II* (1941), 58–91, and in H. Nabholz in *Cambridge Economic History* (1941), i, 508–524. In addition to the works already cited, see Reville and Petit-Dutaillis, *Le Soulevement des Travailleurs d'Angleterre en 1381*; Oman, *The Great Revolt of 1381*; Trevelyan, *England in the Age of Wycliffe* and *The Peasants' Revolt and the Lollards*; Powell, *The East Anglia Rising in 1381*.

England, and no serfdom or villeinage, but that all men should be free and of one condition." [38]

The immediate effect of the violence of the democratic party was to create a reaction of stern repression. The general charter of manumission extorted from Richard by the rioters was annulled by royal proclamation and by statute,[39] both Houses of Parliament unanimously refusing to accept the king's offer to agree to the entire abolition of the state of bondage, and affirming, in the exaggerated language of panic, that they would never consent to such a measure even to " save themselves from perishing altogether in one day." [40] No immediate improvement in the condition of the peasants seems to have resulted from the rising. The peasants continued to struggle for higher wages and for commutation of services. The revolt unsettled society, and gave rise to revolutionary ideas among the workers, and among the lords a constant fear of another general rising. It was only when the panic had passed away that the process of the break-up of the old manorial system, which had begun in the previous century, proceeded once more and was consummated by the Wars of the Roses, which weakened the authority of the lords over all classes of their tenants, and enabled the latter, in the midst of the political confusion, to make good their independence. In a few exceptional instances the state of servitude lingered on till the commencement of the seventeenth century, when it became extinct without any legislative abolition.[41]

---

[38] *The Anonimalle Chronicle of St. Mary's Abbey, York*, ed. Galbraith (1927), p. 147. The Law of Winchester " substituted the mutilation and blinding of felons for common hanging, and was a coveted privilege in early borough charters," *ibid.*, 196.

[39] Rymer, iv, 126; 5 Ric. 2, st. 1, c. 7.

[40] *Rotuli Parliamentorum*, iii, 100.

[41] *Cf.* Holdsworth, *History of English Law*, iii, 505 *et seq.* The last case in which villeinage was pleaded was that of *Pigg* v. *Caley* (1618), Noy, 27. The plaintiff, Pigg, sued the defendant in trespass for taking his horse. The defendant pleaded that he was seised of the manor of D., to which Pigg was a villein regardant, and that defendant and those seised of the said manor had been seised of the plaintiff and his ancestors. The plaintiff replied that he was free, and this issue was found in his favour. Since the extinction of villeinage no form of slavery in England has been recognised by law. But in the colonies it was legalised, and the status of a colonial slave when in England long continued doubtful. As early as Queen Anne's reign, Lord Chief Justice Holt expressed an opinion that " as soon as a negro comes into England he becomes free," and Mr. Justice Powell also declared that " the law took no notice of a negro " (*Smith* v. *Brown and Cooper* (1707) 2 Salk. 666); but the first express adjudication on the subject was not given till 1771, when Lord Mansfield, in the celebrated case of the negro Sommersett, pronounced the decision of the Court of King's Bench that slavery in England is illegal, and that the negro must be set free. (20 St.Tr. 1; Broom, *Constitutional Law*, 65 *et seq.*; see the full discussion by E. Fiddes in *Law Quarterly Review* (1934), 1, 499.) Four years later, in the case of the negro Knight, the Court of Session in Scotland declared the unlawfulness of negro-slavery in that country (Morrison, *Dictionary of Decisions*, iii, 14545). It was not, however, till 1799 that the colliers and salters of Scotland, who, by force of a comparatively modern custom which had grown into recognition since the extinction of the ancient feudal villeinage, had been reduced to a state of serfdom, were declared absolutely free by Statute 39 Geo. 3, c. 56. Seven years later the slave trade was prohibited: 47 Geo. 3, sess. 1, c. 36; and from August 1, 1834, colonial slavery itself was abolished: 3 & 4 Will. 4, c. 73 (1833).

CHAPTER 8

PARLIAMENT UNDER THE LANCASTRIAN AND YORKIST KINGS

General characteristics. Under the Lancastrian kings, parliament was occupied rather in the consolidation and regulation of the results of former contests with the crown, than in the acquisition of any new fundamental rights. The commons continued to exercise, with but slight opposition, the main rights which they had established during the fourteenth century—voting taxes, appropriating the supplies, which they made dependent upon the redress of grievances, examining public accounts, controlling the internal administration, sharing in legislation, and intervening in questions of war and peace, and in all important business, foreign and domestic. But the chief characteristic of the period was the settlement of the internal constitution of parliament, and the establishment of its principal forms of procedure and most essential privileges. During the latter half of the fifteenth century, the House of Commons became somewhat less dependent than it had been under Edward III, Richard II, or Henry IV. The Wars of the Roses in the first place enhanced the power of the nobles at the expense of the commons, who proved invariably ready to give a parliamentary sanction to the claims of a victorious military leader; and, finally, by almost annihilating the ancient nobility, left the lower House to face unaided the augmented power of the crown. But the growing importance of the popular assembly is proved by the attempts, which were now systematically made by the crown and the nobility, to influence the elections in boroughs as well as in counties. A seat in the House of Commons, even as the representative of a borough constituency, became an object of ambition to the members of what would now be termed county families, and the higher social status to which the burgesses had attained is marked by the fact to which Hallam calls attention, that in the reign of Edward IV, and not before, a few of them received the addition of " esquire " in the returns made by the sheriffs.[1]

Parliament in Eclipse. Under Edward IV and Richard III parliamentary history is obscure. The steadily diminishing frequency of parliaments,

---

[1] *Middle Ages*, iii, 119. The importance attached to a seat in parliament at this time, and the attempts made to influence the electors, are shown in the contemporary Paston correspondence. In vol. i, p. 337 (ed. Gardner) we find the Duchess of Norfolk soliciting the influence of John Paston, Esq., at a county election. " It is thought right necessarie," she tells him, " for divers causes that my lord have at this tyme in the Parlement suche persones as longe unto him, and be of his menyall servaunts, wherein we conceyve your good will and diligence shall be right expedient." The " menyall servaunts " were " our right welbelovid cosin and servaunts, John Howard and Syr Roger Chambirlayn." In vol. iii, p. 51, is a letter to the bailiff of Maldon recommending the election of Sir John Paston. On the use and significance of the terms " valet," " yeoman," " esquire," " gentleman," etc., see below, pp. 203–204, note 80.

184

which is characteristic of the century, is still more marked under Edward IV, who met only seven parliaments in a reign of twenty-two years. One of them sat intermittently from 1472 to 1475, but generally one or two short sessions of a few weeks sufficed. There were several intervals of two years without a parliament, the longest interval being from February 1478 to January 1483—nearly five years. The nobility, thinned by civil war and the hands of the executioner, and split up into contending factions, were unable to offer any political resistance to the power of the crown. The commons, by themselves, were as yet unequal to the contest. Under Edward IV both lords and commons, instead of contending, like their predecessors, for the establishment of rights and the redress of grievances, were subservient to the royal will. His legislation is scanty and concerned almost exclusively with minute trade and tariff matters; parliament's whole attention seems to have been devoted to the patient reconstruction of commerce after the ravages of international and internecine wars. His was the first reign in which no public remedial statute was passed, nor even a petition presented similar to those with which we have seen the commons, in former reigns, approaching the throne.[2] In money matters Edward appears to have made himself, as far as possible, independent of parliamentary grants. He derived a very large income from the numerous forfeited estates of his enemies; and all the feudal dues and the customs duties on merchandise were exacted with the greatest rigour. At least once in his reign the lords in parliament taxed themselves by a ten per cent. income tax without charging the commons.[3]

Benevolences. He also extorted frequent tenths from the clergy, and, discarding the specious appellation of " loans," by which former kings had endeavoured to disguise the forced contributions of their subjects, he compelled the richer classes to make apparently voluntary gifts, under the new and less plausible name of " benevolences." As already mentioned, no complaint of any kind appears in the parliamentary records of his reign; but it is evident from a passage in the remarkable address presented to Richard Duke of Gloucester, when invited, in 1483, to assume the crown, that the nation, though hitherto silent, had not been insensible to the illegality. " For certainly wee be determined," say the authors of the address, " rather to aventure and committe us to the perill of oure lyfs and jopardye of deth, than to lyve in suche thraldome and bondage as we have lyved long tyme heretofore, oppressed and injured by Extorcions and newe Imposicions, ayenst the Lawes of God and Man, and the Libertee, old Police and Lawes of this Realme, wheryn every Englishman

---

[2] In Edward IV's last parliament, in 1483, the commons ventured to make some complaints with respect to the wearing of liveries, the maintenance of the public peace, and one or two other topics: *Rotuli Parliamentorum*, vi, 198.

[3] *Rotuli Parliamentorum*, vi, 6 no. 9 (Lodge and Thornton, 177); the full text is lengthy and contains stringent provisions for making it effective and equitable. (The suggestion, *ibid.* 178, that there was a demand for redress of grievances before supply in 1484 is erroneous.)

is enherited." [4]   Accordingly, in Richard III's only parliament, benevolences were declared by statute to be for ever illegal.[5]

TAXATION

Instances of direct taxation without parliament's assent are very rare under the Lancastrian kings. Under Richard II the system of forced loans, of which we find the commons complaining for the first time in 1379,[6] had been very extensively made use of, but the Lancastrian kings seldom had recourse to this means of filling their coffers. In 1400, Henry IV appears to have obtained an aid in men and ships from a great council, but its members did not pretend to charge any beside themselves.[7] There is also an instance, during the minority of Henry VI, of the Duke of Bedford and other lords declaring in parliament, with the advice of the judges and others learned in the law, that a subsidy granted upon certain conditions by the commons in the previous parliament was to be at all events collected and levied for the king's use, notwithstanding any condition in the grant.[8]   But these were merely occasional exceptions to the admitted legal rule. In the same parliament the commons, in making a fresh grant, not only renewed the former conditions, but appropriated the supply, declaring that " it ne no part thereof be beset ne dispendid to no othir use, but oonly in and for the defense of the seid roialme." [9]   Similar precautions had been taken in the grants made to Henry IV. In the sixth year of his reign (1404) the commons granted a large subsidy on condition that it should be expended for the defence of the kingdom according to the form and extent of the grant, and not otherwise, and two treasurers of war, Thomas, Lord Furnivall, and Sir John Pelham, were appointed and sworn in parliament to receive it, and account to the commons at the next parliament.[10]   Thus, conditional grants, appropriation of supplies, and examination of accounts became the established usage.

Supply and redress.   The dependence of supplies on the redress of grievances had been successfully asserted on a few occasions in the fourteenth century when the political situation had been favourable;

---

[4] *Rotuli Parliamentorum*, vi, 241.

[5] 1 Ric. 3, c. 2; Lodge and Thornton, 179.

[6] *Rotuli Parliamentorum*, iii, 62 no. 30 (1379).

[7] Nicolas, *Proceedings of the Privy Council*, i, 107–111 (where the documents are inaccurately printed); the great council recommended that subscriptions be invited from the monasteries. This was done, and many promised support.

[8] *Rotuli Parliamentorum*, iv, 301 no. 22 (1426). This seems another example of the feeling that constitutional concessions accepted by an adult monarch ought not to be used to the detriment of an infant king. *Cf. supra*, pp. 89-90, 169–170, note 78. The conditions were (*Ibid.*, iv, 276 no. 17) that the grant should be void unless certain rebates were allowed— the aim being to compel the crown to accept the grant *in toto*.

[9] *Ibid.*, iv, 302, no. 24.

[10] *Ibid.*, iii, 546 no. 9; *cf. ibid.*, 529 no. 33 (in Lodge and Thornton, 160). These concern only the accounting of extraordinary war taxes. This is our earliest income tax: Gray, *English Historical Review*, xlix, 607.

it became an issue of principle under Richard II.[11] It had previously been usual for the king not to answer petitions until the last day of the session, when the supplies had of course been granted. The attempt to invert this order of proceeding had been declared by Richard II's judges to be high treason.[12] But in 1401 (2 Henry 4) the commons again endeavoured to secure this important lever for the application of parliamentary power. The king resisted firmly, and the commons gave way for the time,[13] but the practice gradually gained ground.

Collision between the Houses. In 1407 (9 Henry 4) a proceeding took place which is interesting both as the first instance of a collision between the two Houses, and as the earliest authority for what are now two well-known axioms of parliamentary law, *viz.*: (1) That all money bills must originate in the House of Commons, and (2) that the king ought not to take notice of matters debated in parliament, until a decision be come to by both Houses, and such decision be regularly brought before him. It appears that the lords, in the king's presence, had held a debate on the state of the kingdom, and, in answer to his demands, had specified certain subsidies as being requisite for the national defence. The king then requested the commons to send a deputation to the House of Lords to hear and report to their fellows what they should have in command from the king, " to the end that they might take the shortest course to comply with the intention of the said lords." Twelve of the commons accordingly attended and made their report to the rest of the lower House, who were thereupon " greatly disturbed at it, saying and affirming it to be much to the prejudice and derogation of their liberties." " And after that our lord the king had heard this," the entry on the roll proceeds, " not willing that anything should be done at present, or in time to come, that might anywise turn against the liberty of the Estate for which they are come to Parliament,[14] nor against the liberties of the Lords—wills and grants, and declares, by the advice and assent of the Lords, in manner following: that it shall be lawful for the Lords to commune amongst themselves in this present Parliament, and in every other in time to come, in the absence of the king, of the state of the realm, and of the remedy necessary for the

---

[11] As early as 1309 (2 Edw. 2), a twenty-fifth was granted the king by the commons on the condition of his redressing eleven grievances, that were laid before him; which he promised to do: *Rotuli Parliamentorum*, i, 443–445. So too in 1348 (*Ibid.*, ii, 201 *et seq.*) in 1344 the commons stipulated not for the redress of grievances but that the king should either win the war or make peace (*Ibid.*, ii, 148 nos. 8 and 9).

[12] *Supra*, p. 171. Stubbs, *Constitutional History*, ii, 601.

[13] *Rotuli Parliamentorum*, iii, 458 no. 23 (Lodge and Thornton, 159–160) cf. Stubbs, *Constitutional History*, ii, 601.

[14] The true position of the House of Commons as not being in itself an estate of the realm but the representative of the estate of the commons of England, is here expressed. In the same way, the knights, citizens, and burgesses assembled in the parliament of 1406 (7 Hen. 4), which settled the succession to the crown, are described as the " procurators and attorneys of all the counties, cities, and boroughs, and of the whole people of the kingdom." Although only elected by a portion of the population they were regarded as in effect procurators and attorneys for the whole; M. V. Clarke, *Representation and Consent*, 171; S. B. Chrimes, *Constitutional Ideas*, 131.

same. And that in like manner, it shall be lawful for the Commons, on their part, to commune together of the state and remedy aforesaid. Provided always that the Lords on their part, and the Commons on their part, shall not make any report to our said lord the king of any grant by the Commons granted, and by the Lords assented to, nor of the communications of the said grant, before the Lords and Commons shall be of one assent and one accord in such matters, and then in manner and form accustomed, that is to say, by the mouth of the Speaker of the Commons, in order that the Lords and Commons may have their will (lour gree) of our said lord the king."[15]

LEGISLATION

The practice of drawing up the statutes from the petitions and answers after the session of parliament had closed, afforded opportunities of fraud on the part of the king's officers, who might enter acts of parliament on the rolls, differing materially from what the commons had petitioned for. In 1414 (2 Henry 5) they presented a petition to the king, which is not only important on account of its subject-matter, but interesting as the earliest instance in which the House of Commons adopted the English language in their petitions.[16] After asserting that it had ever been their liberty and freedom that there should be no statute or law made unless with their assent, the commons proceed: " Consideringe that the Comune of youre lond, the whiche that is, and ever hath be, a membre of youre Parlement, ben as well Assentirs as Peticioners, that fro this tyme foreward, by compleynte of the Comune of eny myschief axkynge remedie by mouthe of their Speker for the Comune, other ellys by Petition writen, that ther never be no Lawe made theruppon, and engrosed as Statut and Lawe, nother by addicions, nother by diminucions, by no maner of terme ne termes, the whiche that sholde chaunge the sentence, and the entente axked by the Speker mouthe, or the Petitions biforesaid yeven up yn writyng by the manere forsaid, withoute assent of the forsaid Comune. Consideringe oure soverain lord, that it is not in no wyse the entente of youre Comunes, zif hit be so that they axke you by spekying or by writyng, two thynges or three, or as manye as theym lust. But that ever it stande in the fredom of your hie Regalie, to graunte whiche of thoo that you luste, and to werune the remanent." In reply the king, " of his grace especial graunteth that fro hensforth no thyng be enacted to the Peticions of his Comune, that be contrarie of hir askyng, wharby they shuld be bounde withoute their assent. Savyng alwey to our liege Lord his real Prerogatif, to graunte and denye what him lust of their Petitions and askynges aforesaide." The crown, in fact, had always

---

[15] *Rotuli Parliamentorum*, iii, 611 no. 21 (Lodge and Thornton, 163–164); Stubbs, *Constitutional History*, iii, 62; Anson, *Law and Custom of the Constitution*, i, 269. The sense of the last line is that the Houses should not compete for royal favour by making separate offers, but that both should share equally in the king's good will. *Cf. infra*, p. 195.

[16] Hallam, *Middle Ages*, iii, 90. As early as 1363, the chancellor addressed the parliament in English in his opening address. *Rotuli Parliamentorum*, ii, 283. See also Stubbs, iii, 496.

exercised discretion by basing legislation only in a very general way upon petitions, especially as the drafting of statutes became more technical. The present protest was provoked by the drastic use of this latitude in respect of the proceedings of the previous parliament, and the commons committed themselves to a stricter thesis than the crown could accept. The royal reply merely undertook to stop short of totally misrepresenting their wishes, and the crown continued for some years to exercise a wide discretion in the matter.[17]

Formam actus in se continens. Under Henry VI, we find the apparently formal but essentially important innovation of introducing complete statutes under the name of bills—" petitiones formam actuum in se continentes." The classical doctrine of Stubbs regarded this as a device by the commons to force the crown to accept or reject a bill *in toto*, thereby considerably improving their position. This is no longer sustained by recent research. We suggest the following alternative. In the first place, there were several occasions when it was necessary that the authentic text of a parliamentary document should be preserved; thus in 1327 the commons suspected that supposititious documents were going forward, and declared that none had their support save those in a certain indenture[18]; grants of taxes were technical documents whose " form " was carefully drawn and adopted—in the fifteenth century invariably drawn as indentures.[19] The same development went on in the council, where petitioners seeking grants, franchises and the like would submit a draft of the document they desired.[20] In 1423 a petitioner introduced into parliament the exact text of the letters patent she wanted,[21] and in 1439 the crown presented to the commons a " schedule or bill " containing technical changes in the settlement of certain crown lands to the uses of Henry V's will. The commons agreed, and then the king and lords agreed that the document should be " enacted of record."[22] The first known document containing the actual words " formam actus in se continens " was the attainder of Henry VI in 1461, which was followed by other attainders and by acts of resumption. These were all highly technical documents prepared in government offices, beyond a doubt.

---

[17] *Rotuli Parliamentorum*, iv, 22 no. 22 (Lodge and Thornton, 165–166). On the whole matter see the discussions between H. L. Gray, *Influence of the Commons on Early Legislation* (1932), 261–287, and S. B. Chrimes, *English Constitutional Ideas in the Fifteenth Century* (1936), 159 *et seq.*, 245 *et seq.*; W. H. Dunham, *The Fane Fragment* (1935), 63–84.

[18] *Rotuli Parliamentorum*, ii, 11 no. 38; Stubbs, ii, 608–609 following Ruffhead's *Statutes at Large*, i, xvi. The view in the text is based partly upon the works of Gray, 177–183, and Chrimes (*supra*, note 17). Gray has shown that there is no foundation for Stubbs' distinction between bills and petitions.

[19] A few indentures of taxes (*e.g.*, those of 1346, 1373) are found even in the fourteenth century; see the discussion in J. G. Edwards, *The Commons in Medieval Parliaments* (1958), 23 *et seq.*

[20] Maxwell Lyte, *The Great Seal*, 196, contains an example of 1402.

[21] *Rotuli Parliamentorum*, iv, 242 no. 32 (contrast no. 31). For an example of 1455, see N. H. Nicolas, *Proceedings and Ordinances of the Privy Council*, vi, 254–255.

[22] *Rotuli Parliamentorum*, v. 8 no. 19. Compare the not dissimilar practice of the papacy: A. de Boüard, *Manuel de Diplomatique*, i, 69, n. 1.

It thus appears that the device was not invented by the commons as a constitutional weapon, but by the crown as an improvement in business method.

" But a good deal might turn upon whether the king or the commonalty should originate legislation . . . and there is no question that in form at least, the initiative is passing in the fourteenth century, from the king to his subjects."[23]   This was especially true under the first three Edwards; the adoption of this procedure served to obscure what was happening, however, and under Henry VIII ordinary legislation came to be introduced by this method, thus making it clear that the crown no longer waited for suggestions from the commons, but undertook the initiation of a regular programme of statute-making. Bills might also originate in the House of Lords and be sent thence to the commons; and it gradually became the established rule of parliament, that with the exception of money bills, which must come from the commons, and of bills affecting the peerage (e.g., for the restitution of forfeited honours), which must come from the lords, all other bills might be originated in either House.

Dispensing and suspending powers. The legislative authority of parliament was subject to the exercise of the dispensing and suspending powers of the crown.[24]   These two terms must be carefully distinguished, for there is a very appreciable difference in their strict signification.   (1) The dispensing power was frequently used in the Middle Ages, and consisted in the exemption of particular persons, under special circumstances, from the operation of penal laws; being, in fact, an anticipatory exercise of the undoubted right of the king to pardon individual offenders. (2) The suspending power was employed during the later part of the seventeenth century only, and consisted in temporarily suspending the entire operation of any statute or any number of statutes ; and was in its nature incompatible with the existence of constitutional government.[25]

The dispensing power was expressed in a form of words derived from the practice of the papacy, whose example in issuing bulls " *non obstante* any law to the contrary," was soon followed by our kings in their proclamations, grants, and writs.   Henry III was perhaps the first to make use of the *non obstante* clause, and his successors throughout the Plantagenet period frequently used it.   Thousands of licences authorised the gift of land to the church *non obstante* the statute of mortmain, and still others permitted international trading operations in spite of statutory regulations.

The commons disliked its exercise, but when they felt it desirable, would expressly grant it (or at least something rather like it); thus, in

---

[23] Richardson, " The Coronation Oath," *Transactions of the Royal Historical Society* (1941), 147.

[24] *Cf.* E. F. Churchill, in *Law Quarterly Review*, xxxvii, 412, xxxviii, 297, 420; P. Birdsall in *Essays in honour of C. H. McIlwain*, 37–76.

[25] *Infra*, pp. 426, 442.

1391 they " assented, in full parliament, that the king, by the advice and assent of the said lords, might make such sufferance respecting the Statute of Provisors as should seem reasonable and profitable to him until the next parliament, but so that the said statute be not repealed in any article of the same . . . and, moreover, that the commons may disagree to such sufferance at the said next parliament and resort to the statute "; protesting, at the same time, that this assent " which was a novelty and had never been given before " should not be drawn into precedent. The same power of dispensation was renewed a few years later, and enlarged to include " full power and authority to modify the said statute " —an interesting and early example of delegated legislation.[26] But in the first year of Henry V, when the commons prayed for a statute driving aliens out of the kingdom, the king granted their request with a proviso that he might dispense (*souffrer ou dispencer*) with the statute when he pleased.[27] In 1446, however, it was specially enacted by a statute which declared void all patents to hold the office of sheriff for more than a year, not only that the king should not dispense by the words *non obstante* with this provision, but that all pardons and remissions of penalties granted by him to persons acting contrary to it, should be of no effect.[28] It appears, therefore, that parliament sometimes expressly granted the power, and sometimes excluded it; meantime, the crown continued to exercise it as a prerogative. This obscure legal situation was partially explored in a case in Henry VII's reign in which it was decided that the king could not dispense with penalties for an act which was *malum in se*; but that he could do so with respect to an act which was *malum prohibitum* merely (that is, an offence created solely by statute).[29] Subject to this restriction, and some others, the dispensing power was repeatedly exercised during the fourteenth and fifteenth centuries and acknowledged as a legal prerogative of the crown.

CRITICISM OF THE GOVERNMENT

The right of enquiring into public abuses, and controlling the royal administration of both home and foreign affairs, was frequently exercised by the commons during the Lancastrian period. In the fifth year of Henry IV the commons requested the king to remove several of his ministers, together with his confessor, and although the king protested that he knew

---

[26] *Rotuli Parliamentorum*, iii, 285 no. 8 (1391), no. 8 (1393).

[27] *Ibid.*, iv, 13 no. 37 (1413). Apparently *souffrer* is merely to refrain from prosecuting; while *dispencer* is to grant a formal licence. The commons disclaimed any denial of the power: *ibid.*, 5, no. 15.

[28] 23 Hen. 6, c. 7. Alluding to this statute, Lord Bacon (*Maxims*, regula xix) argued that the dispensing power could not be restrained by statute, as it was an " inseparable prerogative." It came to be believed that the Sheriff's Case, Y. B. Mich. 2 Hen. 7, no. 20 (1486) was an authority for this, but there is in fact no such decision; see Plucknett, " Bonham's Case and Judicial Review," *Harvard Law Review*, xl, 46. Coke agreed with Bacon in this view: 12 Rep. 18.

[29] Y. B. Mich. 11 Hen. 7, no. 35 (1495) and in S. B. Chrimes, *Constitutional Ideas*, 388. (The text is corrupt.) See Holdsworth, *History of English Law*, vi, 217 *et seq.* and *infra* p. 440.

of no cause or occasion for their removal, yet being assured that whatever
the lords and commons did or ordained was for the benefit of himself
and the kingdom, he removed them, adding that he would do as much
by any other about his person whom he should find to have excited the
hatred or indignation of his people.[30] The " Unlearned Parliament,"
as that of 1404 (6 Henry 4) was termed, because lawyers were excluded
from it, rescinded the grants already made by the crown, and prohibited
the king from alienating the ancient royal inheritance without consent
of parliament.[31]

The Thirty-one Articles. In 1406 (8 Henry 4) the commons presented
their famous petition of Thirty-one Articles, which Hallam idealised as
" a noble fabric of constitutional liberty, and hardly perhaps inferior
to the Petition of Right under Charles I." The political scene in fact
was sombre. Scots ravaged the north; pirates controlled the English
Channel; Wales was in revolt aided by French and Spanish arms and an
English Earl; religious dissidents attacked the church and alleged that
Richard II was still alive and in Scotland; the king was ill and listless. The
Articles were in fact the fruit of the bewilderment and frustration which
oppressed the commons, who found their traditional scapegoats in the
royal household and the " foreigners." The articles were explicitly stated
to be temporary, and are illuminating because they express in detail the
canons of good government to which experienced politicians repeatedly
appealed in the fifteenth century when things went ill. Henry accepted
all the articles without reserve. The most important provisions were:
(i) The king " should elect and name sixteen counsellors and officers
pleasing to God and agreeable to his people, on whom he could rely, to
advise him and be of his continual council until the next parliament, and
a reasonable number of whom should be continually about his person ";
they were to be salaried according to their degree. (ii) The chancellor and
privy seal [32] should pass no grant or other matter of the seals contrary to
law, or delay any which ought to be passed. (iii) Persons about the court
stirring up the king's or queen's minds against any of their lieges, and
duly convicted thereof, to lose their offices and be fined. (vi) The king's
ordinary revenue should be wholly appropriated to his household and
the payment of his debts; no grant of wardship or other profit to be made
therefrom, nor any forfeiture to be pardoned. (viii) The king " considering the wise governance of other well governed Christian princes, and
conforming himself thereto," was to assign two days in the week for the
reception of petitions, " it being a most honourable and necessary thing,
that such of his lieges as desired to petition him should be heard." No

[30] *Rotuli Parliamentorum*, iii, 525, no. 16 (1404).

[31] *Ibid.*, iii, 547, no. 14. The writs of summons excluded lawyers in virtue of an Act of 1372
(*Ibid.*, ii, 310 no. 13) which was not put on the statute roll.

[32] On the great constitutional significance of the struggle for the control of the seals, see
Plucknett, " Place of the Council in the Fifteenth Century," *Transactions of the Royal
Historical Society*, 4th ser., i, 157.

officer of the treasury, chancery, or the household was to enjoy his place for life or term of years; he should personally perform his duties, without appointing a substitute, or letting his office to farm. (x) The council should determine nothing cognisable at common law, unless for a reasonable cause and by the advice of the judges. (xi) The statutes and ordinances regulating purveyance, both those of the household and those made in parliament, were affirmed. (xii–xxii) Abuses of various kinds in the council and the courts of justice, including bribery and the exaction of excessive fees, were enumerated and forbidden. (xxiii) The election of knights of the shire was regulated.[33] (xxiv) The council and chief officers of state were to be sworn in parliament to observe the common law of the land, and the statutes and ordinances before made and ordained, as well for the king's household as for the good government of the realm of England. (xxvi–xxx) The administration of the courts of law and of the household was to be regulated, and full enquiry made by the chancellor and treasurer of England, the seneschal and treasurer of the household, the justices of either bench and the barons of the Exchequer, each in his place and office, into all torts, oppressions and defaults done to the people who had had business therein, and a report sent in to the great council in order that full and due correction might be made. (xxxi) Finally these articles should be in force only from the beginning of the then present parliament until the close of the next.[34]

Questions of war and peace. The right to be consulted in questions of war and peace, which the commons had established under Edward III, and maintained under Richard II, was extended under the Lancastrians so as to include all questions of national interest. In the fourth of Henry V the parliament confirmed the league between the king and the Emperor Sigismund; and the important Treaty of Troyes was similarly submitted to and ratified by both Houses.[35] By one of the articles of this treaty it was stipulated that no negotiations with the Dauphin should be undertaken without the consent of the three estates of both kingdoms; accordingly, under Henry VI both Houses of Parliament granted leave to commissioners on the king's behalf to treat of peace with France. In the same reign, parliament also concurred in the appointment of commissioners to treat of the deliverance of the King of Scots; in the grant of denization to the Duchesses of Gloucester and Bedford; and in the appointment of mediators to reconcile the Dukes of Gloucester and Burgundy.[36]

Impeachment. The judicial power, which had occasionally been exercised by the whole parliament, had been declared in 1399, at the

---

[33] This petition gave rise to the statute 7 Hen. 4, c. 15, discussed *infra*, pp. 200, 202.

[34] *Rotuli Parliamentorum*, iii, 585–589 (extracts in Lodge and Thornton, 73–75).

[35] *Ibid.*, iv, 99 no. 14 (1416), 135 no. 18 (1421).

[36] *Ibid.*, iv, 371 no. 18 (French negotiations, 1431); 211 no. 27 (King of Scots, 1424); 242 nos. 31, 32 (Denization, 1423); 277 no. 19 (Gloucester, 1425).

suggestion of the commons themselves, to reside in the lords only.[37] The right of impeaching ministers lay dormant from the reign of Richard II until 1450; unless we may regard as an informal exercise of it the proceeding of the commons in the first year of Henry IV, when, without preferring specific articles of accusation, they petitioned the king that Justice Rickhill, who had been employed to take the late Duke of Gloucester's confession at Calais, and the lords who had formerly impeached the duke and his associates of treason, should be put on their defence before the peers.[38] In 1450 (28 Henry 6) the commons determined to prosecute the Duke of Suffolk, William de la Pole (grandson of Michael), on charges of high treason, chiefly relating to his conduct in France while negotiating the unpopular marriage of the king with Margaret of Anjou. They drew up a bill of impeachment containing eight charges of high treason, and subsequently produced eighteen additional articles, but the king, in order to screen his favourite minister and save the life of a probably innocent man, banished him for five years. Suffolk had abstained from putting himself upon his peerage, and while protesting his innocence, placed himself entirely in the king's hands; the king moreover declared that he acted by his own advice and not that of the lords, and not by way of judgment, but on the ground of the duke's submission. But the lords immediately protested against the proceedings and declared that it should form no precedent to bar them or their heirs of the privileges of peerage. The whole tragic story shows that the nature of impeachment was still unsettled; Richard II's question whether the crown's consent was necessary was still undecided, although in effect, Henry VI frustrated the proceedings; and as Sir James Ramsay remarked, the extravagance of the commons' charges shows how little real knowledge they possessed of the state of public affairs.[39]

PRIVILEGES OF PARLIAMENT

It was under the Lancastrian kings that the privileges of parliament first began to attract attention.

As enjoyed by either House, in its collective capacity or in the persons of its individual members, these privileges are various and important. They all rest either upon the ancient law and custom of parliament solely, or upon that law and custom as defined by statute. Three of them claim special attention: (1) freedom of speech; (2) freedom from arrest and special protection against assault; (3) the right of the commons to determine contested elections.[40]

---

[37] *Rotuli Parliamentorum*, iii, 427 no. 79.

[38] *Ibid.*, iii, 439 no. 92; 449–452.

[39] *Ibid.*, v, 176–182 (extracts in Lodge and Thornton, 172–173). See the discussions in Stubbs, *Constitutional History*, iii, 149–152, and J. H. Ramsay, *Lancaster and York*, ii, 113–121. For a vindication of Suffolk, see C. L. Kingsford, *Prejudice and Promise*, 146–176. Suffolk was intercepted by a ship of the royal navy, manned by pirates, and beheaded.

[40] For a historical and legal account of the various branches of parliamentary privilege, see May, *Parliamentary Practice* (13th ed., 1924), pp. 70 *et seq.* and with respect to the House of Lords Pike, *Constitutional History of the House of Lords*, pp. 258 *et seq.*; his account

I. Freedom of speech is an essential attribute of every free legislature under modern conditions. " The Commons did oftentimes, under Edward III," says Elsynge,[41] " discuss and debate amongst themselves many things concerning the king's prerogative, and agreed upon petitions for laws to be made directly against his prerogative, as may appear by divers of the said petitions, yet they were never interrupted in their consultations, nor received check for the same, as may appear also by the answers to the said petitions." Things tolerated by Edward III under political pressure, however, might seem inexpedient to his successors, and when later kings acted upon that view, there was no formal and recognised principle of free speech which the commons could invoke. The establishment of the " privilege " was the slow and arduous work of the fifteenth and sixteenth centuries, and cannot be regarded as successfully accomplished until it had passed through the ordeal of the Stuart conflict.

The peculiar circumstances of *Haxey's Case* under Richard II have already been noticed.[42] In the first year of Henry IV (1399) the judgment against Haxey was twice reversed and annulled; in the first instance, on his own petition, by the king and the lords spiritual and temporal sitting as a court of error, it would seem; and again on the petition of the commons. In neither case was any reason given. The commons said nothing of free speech nor of privilege; the " custom " and " use " which they vaguely invoked refers probably to the procedural peculiarities of the trial and the extreme view of the law of treason involved. The real importance of the case lies not in the year 1399 but in the seventeenth century when parliamentarians used it unhistorically but with telling effect in the controversies of that age.[43]

The king and speeches in parliament. In the next parliament (1401) the commons, by their Speaker,[44] showed the king " how that when certain matters were moved among them, some of their body, to please the king, and to advance themselves, would inform the king of such matters, before the same had been determined and discussed or agreed upon among the said commons, by which the king might be incensed against them or some of them "; wherefore they prayed him not to take notice of any reports that might be made to him of their proceedings. To this he replied that " it was his wish that the commons should deliberate and treat of all matters amongst themselves, in order to bring them to the best conclusion, . . . that he would hear no person, nor give him any credit, before

should be read as supplementary to May's treatment of the subject. *Cf.* C. Wittke, *History of English Parliamentary Privilege* (Columbus, Ohio, 1921). J. E. Neale, " The Commons' Privilege of Free Speech " (*Tudor Studies presented to A. F. Pollard*, 257-286) is of fundamental importance; *cf.* Anson, *Law and Custom of the Constitution*, i, 157 *et seq.*; Maitland, *Constitutional History*, pp. 375 *et seq.*
[41] Elsynge, *Ancient Method of holding Parliaments* (ed. 1675), p. 177.
[42] *Supra*, pp. 174-5.
[43] *Rotuli Parliamentorum*, iii, 430 no. 90, 434 no. 104 (and Lodge and Thornton, 159); May, *Parliamentary Practice* (13th ed. 1924), p. 104.
[44] *Infra*, pp. 207 *et seq.*

such matters were brought before the king by the advice and consent of all the commons, according to the purport of their petition."[45]

The declaration of the king, in the ninth year of his reign (1407), acknowledging the right of the commons to initiate money bills, and also undertaking to have no communications on the subject until the houses are agreed, has been already referred to.[46]

In 1455 (33 Henry 6) *Thomas Yonge*, one of the " knights for the shire and town of Bristol," complained to the commons that he had been arrested and imprisoned in the Tower, five years previously, " for matters by him showed in the House "—namely, a motion made by him that, the king then having no issue, the Duke of York might be declared heir-apparent to the crown. The Duke was now protector, and the occasion, therefore, favourable for the presentation of Yonge's complaint and claim for compensation. His petition is notable for its claim, " unique in the middle ages," that the commons by their ancient liberty ought to speak in the House of their assembly unrestrainedly, without being accountable elsewhere. It seems clear that opinion was moving in that direction, but we have no more of this proposition, although Yonge did get redress. The commons transmitted his petition to the lords, and the king " willed that the lords of his council do and provide for the said suppliant, as by their discretion shall be thought convenient and reasonable." [47]

II. The privilege of freedom from arrest can be compared with the much older legal principle attaching specially heavy penalties to the molestation of those engaged in public functions, which is probably coeval with the first existence of national councils in England. A law of Ethelbert, the first Christian King of Kent, at the end of the sixth century, provides that " If the king call his ' leod ' (people) to him [*i.e.*, in the witenagemot] and any one there do them evil, let him compensate with a twofold ' bot ' and fifty shillings to the king." So Cnut, in the early part of the eleventh century, declares " that every man be entitled to ' grith ' [immunity from molestation] to the gemôt and from the gemôt, except he be a notorious thief." [48] Immunity from arrest (except for treason, felony, or breach of the peace) is useful and indeed necessary; but formerly not only the members of both Houses, but their servants and their property also, were included in it, during the time over which the privilege was supposed to extend, *i.e.*, forty days before and after the meeting of parliament.

In 1290 (18 Edward 1) the Master of the Temple petitioned the king for leave to distrain for the rent of a house held of him by the *Bishop of*

---

[45] *Rotuli Parliamentorum*, iii, 456 no. 11.
[46] *Supra*, pp. 187–188.
[47] *Rotuli Parliamentorum*, v, 337 no. 15 (and Lodge and Thornton, 176). *Cf.* Neale, *loc. cit.*, 265.
[48] Ethelbert, c. 2; Cnut, Secular Dooms, c. 83; *Select Charters*, pp. 66, 88. Cnut's law was evidently intended to apply to persons coming to the witenagemot on private business as well as those summoned to give counsel and consent. So the pseudo-Leges Edwardi Confessoris art. 2, cl. 8 provide " ad synodos ad capitula venientibus, sive submoniti sint, sive per se quid agendum habuerint, sit summa pax."—Liebermann, *Gesetze*, i, 629.

St. David's, and was answered: " It does not seem fit that the king should grant that they who are of his council should be distrained in time of Parliament "; but at another time let him distrain " per hostia et fenestras prout moris est." [49] Both petition and answer therefore recognised the privilege. The privilege was also distinctly acknowledged by the crown in 1315 (9 Edward 2) in the case of the *Prior of Malton* who had been arrested by his goods on his way from parliament " in contempt of the king, in prejudice of the crown . . . and against the king's peace "—words which indicate that the privilege was the king's, rather than parliament's.[50] In 1429 *William Larke*, a member's servant, was imprisoned by the court of common pleas in an action of trespass, having been condemned in damages to the plaintiff and a fine to the king. The commons protested that although the judgment was given before parliament met, the arrest was made during parliament time. The king and lords refused to admit the privilege of freedom from arrest, and only released Larke as a matter of grace, with the consent of the plaintiff, and after many precautions. The affair was hardly a triumph for the House.[51] Immunity from a landlord's distress was undoubted; immunity from the process of the court of common pleas was clearly a more serious matter. The fact that Larke was merely a member's servant, and the ambiguous nature of the action of trespass (which contained criminal as well as civil elements), may have weakened the case still further.

Indeed, a very eminent member was unsuccessful in claiming the privilege for his own person. This was the celebrated case of *Thomas Thorpe*, Speaker of the Commons, and a baron of the Exchequer in 1454 (31 Henry 6) who, during a prorogation of parliament, was imprisoned in the Fleet on an execution, issuing out of his own court of the Exchequer, for non-payment of a fine due to the king for a trespass committed in seizing certain goods of the Duke of York. The commons sent some of their members to complain to the king and lords, and demand the release of the Speaker, and of Walter Rayle, another imprisoned member. As in Larke's case, counsel for the plaintiff in the previous action was heard, who opposed Thorpe's release since the Duke would be deprived of his legal remedy. The judges, on being consulted by the lords, declared by the mouth of the chief justice, speaking in the name of them all, " after sadde communication and mature deliberation hadde amonge theim," that " they ought not to aunswere to that question, for it hath not be used aforetyme that the Justicez shuld in eny wyse determine the Privelegge of this high Court of Parlement; for it is so high and so mighty in his nature that may make lawe, and that that is lawe it may make noo lawe; and the determination and knowlegge of that Privilegge belongeth to the Lordes of the Parlement, and not to the Justices." But they went on to

---

[49] *Rotuli Parliamentorum*, i, 61 no. 192; the Master alleged, it seems, that there was nothing distrainable there except during parliament time.

[50] Hatsell, *Precedents*, i, 12; Prynne, *Animadversions*, 20.

[51] *Rotuli Parliamentorum*, iv, 357 no. 57.

admit the privilege, asserting that " if any persone that is a membre of this high Court of Parlement be arrested in suche cases as be not for treason or felony, or suerte of the peas, or for a condempnation hadde before the Parlement, it is used that all such persones shuld be relessed of such arrestes, and make an Attourney, so that they may have theire fredom and libertee frely to entende upon the Parlement." " As for declaration of procedyng in the lawer Courtes," they observed, " ther be many and diverse Supersedeas of Privelegge of Parlement brought in to the Courtes, but there ys no generall Supersedeas brought to surcesse of all processes; for if ther shuld be, it shuld seeme that this high Court of Parlement, that ministreth all Justice and equitee, shuld lette the processe of the commune lawe, and so it shuld put the partie compleynaunt withoute remedie, for so muche as actions atte commune lawe be not determined in this high Court of Parlement." Although, according to this opinion of the judges (notwithstanding their evident disinclination to " lette the processe of the commune lawe "), Thorpe was clearly entitled to his release, the lords determined " that the seid Thomas, accordyng to the lawe, shuld remayne stille in prison for the causes abovesaid, the Privelegge of the Parlement, or that the same Thomas was Speker of the Parlement, not-withstondyng "; and the commons were directed in the king's name to proceed " with all goodly hast and spede " to the election of a new Speaker, which they did the next day.[52] This extraordinary decision was possibly not unconnected with the fact that Thorpe was a staunch Lancastrian, and an old enemy of the Duke of York. The whole case was subsequently characterised in parliament as " begotten by the iniquity of that time,"[53] but it must be remembered that the judges' difficulty was real, and that for centuries to come there was sharp conflict between the rights of the subject and the claims of privilege.

In spite of Thorpe's case, the recognition and enforcement of the privilege soon became regular; thus William Hyde, a judgment debtor, was released from prison in 1475,[54] and in 1478 writs were authorised superseding processes of the Exchequer which were out against John Atwyll, although he had not yet been apprehended[55]; both were members of the commons.

The existence of this privilege, recognised as it had been by statute, by declarations of both Houses, by the frequent assent of the king, and by the opinion of the judges, to which reference has been made, was un-doubted; but it was not until the year 1543 that the commons proceeded to deliver a member out of custody, or to commit any one to prison, by their own sole authority. Down to that year members had been released either by virtue of a special Act of Parliament; or by a writ of privilege

[52] *Ibid.*, v, 239 nos. 26–28.
[53] *Commons' Journals*, i, 546.
[54] *Rotuli Parliamentorum*, vi, 160 no. 55 (and Lodge and Thornton, 177–178).
[55] *Ibid.*, vi, 191, no. 35.

issued by the chancellor.[56] In both cases the commons had to petition the king, and the concurrence of the lords was recorded.

Assaults upon Members. The foregoing cases are all concerned with the relief of members from certain lawful constraints to which the generality of the public were subject, *i.e.*, extra-judicial distress, and arrest of the person or goods by court process in civil litigation. Somewhat similar to that privilege was the provision of special sanctions to protect members from assault and battery by evil-doers on their way to and from parliament, and during its continuance. We have already seen that the principle was recognised in Anglo-Saxon times; in the fifteenth century the commons secured legislation to that effect. In 1404 Richard Chedder, a member's servant, was " emblemished and maimed " by one Savage; the commons prayed for a declaration that murdering a member should be treason, maiming him should entail the loss of a hand, and assaulting him should be punished with imprisonment. This the crown refused, granting only a civil, not a criminal, remedy, namely, that Savage should be attainted by fine and double damages unless he appeared for trial.[57] In 1433 the rule of double damages was again enacted by statute.[58]

III. Parliamentary elections. The growing power of the House of Commons is specially marked, during the Lancastrian period, by the earnest attention bestowed by parliament upon the subject of elections.

The misconduct of sheriffs. Owing to the ill-defined power of the sheriffs, gross abuses in the return of members very early crept in. It was to the sheriff of each county that the king's writ was addressed, requiring him to return two knights for the county and two citizens or burgesses for each borough in his bailiwick. But as no particular cities or boroughs were specified in the writ, this functionary assumed the power of determining what cities and boroughs should exercise the franchise; and it became a frequent practice to omit boroughs which had been in the recent habit of electing members, and to return upon the writ, " There are no more cities or boroughs within my bailiwick." There is some excuse for the sheriffs in the fact that the boroughs for the most part were anxious to be omitted, so as to escape the burden of paying the wages of their members, and frequently set at naught the writ ordering an election, by

---

[56] Hatsell, i, 53; May, *Parliamentary Practice* (13th ed. 1924), p. 112. Special Acts were passed to enable the Chancellor to issue writs for the release of Larke, a member's servant, in 8 Hen. 6, of Clerke, 39 Hen. 6, of Hyde, and of Atwyll, 14 & 17 Edw. 4.—*Rotuli Parliamentorum*, iv, 357; v, 374; vi, 160, 191; Hatsell, i, 17–22, 35–37. For the later history, see pp. 249 *et seq.*, 332 *et seq, infra.*

[57] *Rotuli Parliamentorum*, iii, 542 no. 78 (Lodge and Thornton, 161–162), re-drafted as statute 5 Hen. 4, c. 6, since the principle was to be general for the future. The attainder clause is remarkable. At the same time a petition by the commons that treble damages be exacted from plaintiffs issuing process to arrest members or their servants was rejected: *Rotuli Parliamentorum*, iii, 541 no. 71.

[58] 11 Hen. 6, c. 11. The clergy had already secured similar protection for themselves and their servants going to convocation, by 8 Hen. 6, c. 1.

sending no return.[59]   A further element of confusion was due to the fact
that the three lists of (1) boroughs by charter or prescription, (2) boroughs
paying a tenth when the counties were taxed at a fifteenth, and (3) boroughs
which customarily returned representatives to parliament, did not entirely
correspond.[60]   But the discretionary power of the sheriffs was often
abused by them for the purpose of influencing the elections and falsifying
the returns either at the instigation of the crown or of great local
magnates.[61]   Several statutes were from time to time passed to prevent
these malpractices.   So early as the reign of Edward I, the Statute of
Westminster I, c. 5 (1275) declared that elections ought to be free, and
forbade any disturbance of their freedom.[62]   In 1382 an Act was passed
imposing a fine on sheriffs who should neglect to make a return to parliamentary writs, or omit from such return any city or borough which was
bound and formerly accustomed to send members to parliament.[63]
A statute of 1406, made " on the grievous complaints of the commons of
the undue election of the knights of shires for parliament," regulated the
time and manner of electing knights and provided for a true return into
chancery by the sheriff of the result of the election, by requiring the names
of the members to be written in an indenture, authenticated by the seals
of the persons who had elected them.[64]   An Act, passed four years later-
(1410), gave the justices of assize power to inquire into the legality of
returns, and inflicted the penalty of one hundred pounds on any sheriff
who should return a member not duly elected.[65]   In 1445, a further attempt
was made to check abuses by an Act which gave an additional penalty,
upon a false return, to the party aggrieved, and required every sheriff
duly to deliver a proper precept to the mayor and bailiff of each city or
borough in his shire, to elect representatives for parliament, and every
mayor and bailiff to make a true return of the members chosen.[66]

Jurisdiction in election disputes.   Election disputes were originally
dealt with by the king and his council, and where it was alleged that the

---

[59] Torrington, in Devonshire, and Maldon, Essex, even obtained charters of exemption from
sending burgesses to parliament—A. F. Pollard, *Evolution of Parliament*, 394; so also
Woodstock, M. Weinbaum, *British Borough Charters*, 95. M. McKisack, *Parliamentary
Representation of the English Boroughs* (1932) contains much material of interest.

[60] J. F. Willard in *Essays in Honour of James Tait* (1932), 417 *et seq.*

[61] In 1319 Matthew Crauthorne complained that the sheriff of Devon, instead of returning
him, a duly elected member, had returned members not chosen by the commons of the
county (Prynne, *Animadversions*, 31; Palgrave, *Parliamentary Writs*, II, ii, App., p. 138).
Crauthorne seems to imply that he was " elected " by the Bishop of Exeter, and his
fellow knight " by the other good folk of the county." In 1386, the bailiffs of Barnstaple
in reply to writs ordering them to pay £6 8s. as the expenses of John Henrys, one of their
representatives in the parliament of Oct. 1385 (9 Ric. 2), excused themselves on the double
ground that he was not an inhabitant of the county of Devon nor having any property
therein, and that James de Chuddelegh, the sheriff of Devon, had returned the said John
without their assent or knowledge, at the motion of the said John and his friends, for the
sake of gain. *Return of Members of Parliament*, 1213–1702 (printed by authority of
Parliament, 1878), p. 225.

[62] The statute does not specify what elections it means; it seems unlikely that it means
parliamentary elections.   [63] 5 Ric. 2, st. ii, c. 4.

[64] 7 Hen. 4, c. 15 (Lodge and Thornton, 162); *cf.* p. 193 *supra.*

[65] 11 Hen. 4, c. 1 (Lodge and Thornton, 164).

[66] 23 Hen. 6, c. 14 (Lodge and Thornton, 171–172); *infra*, p. 201.

sheriff was at fault, the matter might be remitted to the Exchequer, which had special jurisdiction over sheriffs.[67] The first instance of the intervention of the commons in such matters occurred under Richard II, whose reign was so fruitful in constitutional precedents.

In 1384 (7 Richard 2) the borough of Shaftesbury presented a petition to the king, lords, and commons, complaining of a false return by the sheriff of Dorset, and praying them to order remedy.[68] In the 5th Henry 4 (1404) the commons prayed the king and lords in parliament that an improper return by the sheriff of Rutland might be examined in parliament, and exemplary punishment inflicted in case of default found. The lords thereupon sent for the sheriff and for William Ondeby, the knight returned, as well as for Thomas de Thorp, who had been duly elected, and having examined into the facts of the case, directed the return to be amended by the insertion of Thorp's name in lieu of Ondeby's, and committed the sheriff to the Fleet till he should pay a fine at the king's pleasure.[69]

In a subsequent case, in the 18th Henry 6 (1439), where the sheriff of Cambridgeshire had failed to make any return, the commons are not even named, but the matter was determined by the king and the lords.[70]

Under Edward IV, Henry VII and Henry VIII there is no record of any interference on the part of the commons; we may venture the conjecture that this was a result of the statute of 1445 which gave the defrauded candidate a penalty payable by the sheriff. His remedy is therefore an action of debt in the court of common pleas, and at least one case there has long been in print.[71]

THE PARLIAMENTARY FRANCHISE

It was under the Lancastrian dynasty that the first statutes were passed regulating the qualifications of parliamentary electors and of persons to be elected.

County franchise. It is probable that from the first introduction of county representation, but certainly as early as the year 1254,[72] the knights of the shire were elected, not merely by the knights or tenants *in capite*, but by all the freeholders of the county assembled in the county court. In the " Good Parliament " of 1376 the commons, in their anxiety to prevent the malpractices of the sheriffs, appear to have attempted to restrict the electoral body in counties. They petitioned that knights of the shire might be chosen by common election of the better folk of the shires,

---

[67] As in 1319; Prynne, *Animadversions on Coke's Fourth Institute*, 31; Palgrave, *Parliamentary Writs*, II, ii, App. 138.
[68] Stubbs, *Constitutional History*, iii, 436, discusses this and other like cases.
[69] *Rotuli Parliamentorum*, iii, 530 no. 38 (Lodge and Thornton, 160–161); Hallam, *Middle Ages*, iii, 110.
[70] *Ibid.*; *Rotuli Parliamentorum*, v, 7 no. 18.
[71] *Buckley* v. *Rice Thomas* (1555) Plowd. 118, which contains some interesting details about elections.
[72] *Supra*, p. 131.

and not nominated by the sheriff alone without due election. Edward III replied that the knights should be elected by common assent of the whole county.[73] The earliest statute regulating their election, 7 Henry 4, c. 15 (1406) [74]—which, having been enacted in answer to a complaint of the commons of " undue " election, may be taken to be declaratory and confirmatory only of the existing custom—places the franchise upon a very popular basis, so as to include not only all freeholders, but all freemen present at the county court on the day of election. It was enacted " that at the next county court to be holden after the delivery of the writ of the parliament, proclamation shall be made, in full county court, of the day and place of the parliament, and that all they that be there present, as well suitors duly summoned for the same cause as others, shall attend to the election of the knights for the parliament; and then, in full county, they shall proceed to the election, freely and indifferently, notwithstanding any request or command to the contrary." [75]

Property qualification of voters. But in 1430 was passed a very remarkable measure—the first disfranchising statute on record—by which the qualification of county electors was restricted to freeholders, and of them to such only as " have free land or tenement to the value of forty shillings by the year at least, above all charges "; with power to the sheriff to examine each elector on oath as to the annual value of his property (8 Henry 6, c. 7). This must have disfranchised not merely all landless freemen and leaseholders, but a very large number of the smaller freeholders. The county franchise, which had reached its maximum by the time of Henry IV, was now reduced to its minimum. The recital in the Act of the reasons which were thought to render it necessary complained that elections of knights of shires had of late been made " by very great, outrageous, and excessive number of people dwelling within the same counties, of the which most part was people of small substance and of no value, whereof every of them pretended a voice equivalent, as to such elections to be made, with the most worthy knights and esquires dwelling within the same counties—whereby manslaughters, riots, batteries, and divisions among the gentlemen and other people of the same counties shall very likely rise and be unless convenient and due remedy be provided." [76]

---

[73] *Rotuli Parliamentorum*, ii, 355 no. 186 (Lodge and Thornton, 150); Stubbs, *Constitutional History*, ii, 453.

[74] *Supra*, pp. 193, 200.

[75] The language of the Act is not free from ambiguity; and some have regarded it as conferring an extension of the suffrage. See Homersham Cox, *Antient Parliamentary Elections* (1868), 105; Stubbs, however (*Constitutional History*, iii, 419, n. 3) maintains, and his contention is supported by the natural inference from the petition of the commons in 1376, together with the king's answer, that " before the close of the reign of Edward III the whole body of persons assembled made the election whether they were legal suitors or not " and that the Act of 1406 introduced no alteration.

[76] 8 Hen. 6, c. 7 (Lodge and Thornton, 167).

Residence. Besides fixing a property qualification for voters, this statute also required that both the electors and the elected should be actually resident in the county. This had already been insisted on in 1413, as to both counties and boroughs, by a statute of Henry V [77]; and another statute in 1432 (10 Henry 6, c. 2) required that the land which qualified the holder for the county vote should be situate within the county. The restrictions as to residence seem to have been generally evaded as early as the reign of Edward IV; and the statute of Henry V, having proved " almost a solitary instance in the law of England wherein the principle of desuetude has been avowedly set up against an unrepealed enactment," was at length repealed in 1774 by 14 George 3, c. 58.[78]

Qualification by birth. The Act of 1445 (23 Hen. 6, c. 14) has been already referred to in reference to the restraints put upon the malpractices of the sheriffs; but it is more important on account of one of its provisions, which attempted to establish not only a property qualification for members (as distinct from voters), but also a qualification of gentle birth, contrary to that important constitutional principle—the legal equality of all free-men below the peerage—which has exercised so beneficial an influence over the English nation.[79] It would seem that the knights of the shire, who had long ceased to be in all cases knights in the strict sense of the term, were sometimes not even gentlemen by birth, and it was now enacted that henceforth the county representatives should be " notable knights of the same counties for which they shall be chosen, or otherwise such notable esquires, gentlemen born, of the same counties as shall be able to be knights; and no man to be such knight which standeth in the degree of a yeoman (*vadlet*) or under." [80]

---

[77] 1 Hen. 5, c. 1 (Lodge and Thornton, 165).

[78] Hallam, *Middle Ages*, iii, 119. See also Peckwell, *Reports of Contested Elections*, i, 53, note D.

[79] *Cf. supra*, p. 153.

[80] *Cf.* K. L. Wood-Legh, " Sheriffs, Lawyers and Belted Knights in the Parliaments of Edward III," *English Historical Review*, xlvi, 372–388. In 1322 eight knights of the shire returned to the parliament which met in November have the word *valettus* against their names in the enrolment of the writs *de expensis*. They are: for Devon, Richard Chissebych; Worcestershire, John de Stone; Herefordshire, John de Brugge and Philip de Canvouwe; Leicester, Robert de Gaddesby and William Jaunvill; Middlesex, Richard Duraunt and William le Rous. The exact meaning of the term " valettus " at this date is doubtful. In 1445 it was clearly synonymous with " yeoman," and so it would appear to have been in 1397, when " vadletz appellez yomen," are complained of in Haxey's Bill (*supra*, p. 174), and are, by a statute of the same year (20 Ric. 2, c. 2), apparently founded on Haxey's complaint, restrained, as well as all others, " de meindre estat," from wearing the " livery of company " pertaining to any lord. " Valet " or " vadelect " seems to have originally denoted honourable service. Selden (*Titles of Honour*, 3rd ed., 688) speaks of it as being anciently a name specially denoting young gentlemen, even though of great descent or quality, but as subsequently given to persons of the rank of yeoman. A " yeoman " is defined by Sir Tho. Smith (*De Republica Anglorum*, lib. i, c. 23) as he whom our law calls *legalis homo*, a free-born man that may dispend of his own free land in yearly revenue to the sum of forty shillings. But it had also a more general application, denoting, like " valet," a higher kind of service, which still survives in the current phrase to do " yeo-man's service." In the household of the medieval knight or baron, the younger sons of yeomen would form a large proportion of the servitors, and share with the younger sons of knight or esquire the common name of *valetti*. The yeomen, too, who lived on their own land, but wore the " livery of company " of some baron or lesser territorial

Property qualification of members.   The property qualification thus established was considerable, the amount of land which made its owner eligible for knighthood being estimated at £20 annual value. The celebrated statute of Queen Anne—passed in 1710 to correct the evils of bribery caused by the candidature of rich commercial men without local connections—excluded all but landowners from the House of Commons, the qualification being fixed at £600 a year for county, and £300 a year for borough, members, which was to be exclusively derived from freehold

magnate, would also be his " valets." See now, Mildred Campbell, *The English Yeoman under Elizabeth and James I* (Yale Press, 1942).

The medieval " yeoman " was the tenant of land in free socage. The extent of his holding might be large or small. Fortescue, *De Laudibus*, c. 29 (ed. Chrimes), 68, emphasises his wealth. From the year 1278, if it amounted to £20 annual value, he was liable, like the tenant in chivalry, to be compelled to take up knighthood; a burden from which he was nominally relieved by the Statute *De Militibus* c. 1278 (*supra*, p. 97.).   Gentle birth constituted then as now a social distinction, but had as yet received no legal recognition. If a freeholder below the rank of a peer were not a knight, or an esquire, he would, we apprehend, have been classified as a yeoman, " gentleman " not having yet become a designation of legal status.

It was not till 1353 that the words " *gentilis homo* " were adjudged a good addition (Cowell's *Interpreter*, under " gentleman ") : and both " esquire " and " gentleman " are rarely found before the statute 1 Hen. 5, c. 5 (1413), which required the addition, in original writs and other legal processes, of the " estate, degree or mystery " of the defendant. In 1447, the members returned for Surrey were : " John Stanley, squyer," and " William Weston, gentylman." (*Parliamentary Return*, 1878, Part i, p. 337.) A hundred and twenty years previously Weston would probably have been described as *valettus* or " yeoman." Some of the *valetti* returned in 1322 may, however, have been early instances of county representation by members who were socially as well as legally of yeoman status. Down to 1324 the writs required the election of actual knights, but these were not always obtainable; and as early as 1311, two *homines*, Ralph de Bellafago and Nicholas de Burton, were returned for Rutlandshire. (Palgrave, *Parliamentary Writs*, ii, Div. ii, 51.) But they were probably not of a lower social grade than that of the ordinary county member. N. de Burton sat again in 1315 and 1318; and William de Burton, *miles*, was member in 1353 and 1357. A John de Bellafago was returned in 1327 and 1328, and Roger de B. in 1338 and 1341. (*Return of Members of Parliament.*) In 1324 the parliamentary writs directed the return of two knights " or others." (*Parliamentary Writs*, ii, Div. ii, 317.)

An examination of the *Parliamentary Return of Members*, already cited, gives evidence that most of the eight *valetti* of Nov. 1322 were of the class from which county members were usually drawn. The name of " Richardus de Chissebech, *miles*," occurs as one of the members for Devon in the parliament which met in May of the same year, 1322. The *valettus* of this name in the November parliament could scarcely have been the same person, but was clearly of the same family, probably a son or other relative, who being neither a knight nor an esquire was properly designated *valettus* or yeoman. Richard de Chissebech was also member in 1316, 1319, 1323, and 1324; and R. de C., *miles*, in 1318, Jan. and Oct. John de Stone, the Worcestershire *valettus* of 1322, appears also as member for that county in 1320, and subsequently in 1323, and in six other years down to 1339. Of the Herefordshire *valetti*, John de Brugge does not appear as a member either before or after 1322, but he is stated in Burke's *Extinct Peerage* to have been a grandson (Collins, *Peerage*, ed. 1756, says " the eldest son ") of Sir Simon de Brugge (Bruges or Brydges) of that county, an ancestor of the Duke of Chandos. Philip de Canvouwe occurs again in 1337 as " Claynvou." Robert de Gaddesby was member for Leicestershire in 1319, and again in 1327. The name of " Jaunvill " does not again occur, but it has not a plebeian sound. It was probably a various spelling of " Genevill," a baronial family of the *fourteenth* century. Of the two remaining *valetti*, William le Rous was again member for Middlesex in 1324, and was evidently related to the Richard le Rous who, sometimes with the addition of *miles* and sometimes without, sat for that county in nine parliaments from 1297 to 1313. The name of Richard Durant does not appear again, and he may not improbably have been of the yeoman class. The names of William " Tornegold " and Richard " Tulusan " which appear as members for Middlesex, " *loco militum* " in 1319 (*Parliamentary Return*, p. 58), seem indicative of a mercantile element in the county representatives.

or copyhold estate.[81] This invidious and unjust law was maintained until 1838, when the monopoly of the landowners was surrendered, and personal property was admitted as a qualification.[82] At length, in 1858, the law of property qualification, having been systematically evaded from its first establishment, even at the risk of perjury, was abolished altogether.[83] There is only one recorded instance in which the oligarchic provision of Henry VI's statute, that knights of the shire should be of gentle birth, was alleged as a disqualification against a parliamentary candidate, and this occurred six years after the law was passed.[84] But it would be very rare during the reactionary period upon which England had now entered that men who were not of aristocratic birth should be returned as county members.

The statutes and cases dealing with elections, of which only a select number has been cited here, taken into consideration with other evidence such as we find in the *Paston Letters*, or even in the chronicles (some of which assert from time to time that a parliament was packed),[85] justify the conclusion that there was now a lively interest in the representative system. Magnates and ambitious candidates spared no efforts to influence election results. The knights of the shire were themselves men of weight and experience whose leadership in the commons was unchallenged. It was inevitable, however, that they in turn should normally find themselves under the ultimate leadership of the lords. There was no deep gulf, legal or social, to compel a divergence of the two groups. On the other hand, the numerous ties of family and the community of interest between substantial landowners produced the natural result of lords and commons working together as a matter of course. The relationship is further illustrated by the way in which the House of Commons, and the landowning class outside the peerage, reflected the vicissitudes of the Wars of the Roses.[86]

---

[81] 9 Anne, c. 5. A Bill to the same effect passed both Houses in 1696, but William III withheld the royal assent. The members for the universities were excepted.

[82] 1 & 2 Vict. c. 48.

[83] 21 & 22 Vict. c. 26. For the unhappy case which led to the repeal, see Porritt, *Unreformed House of Commons*, i, 177.

[84] In 1450 (29 Hen. 6) there was a contested election for Huntingdonshire. Robert Stonham and John Styuecley (or " Stucle "), " notabiles armigeri," who had sat for the county in several preceding parliaments, were opposed by a certain Henry Gymber, who was probably the candidate of the yeomen or smaller freeholders, and stood in much the same position as a tenant-farmer candidate at the present day. He secured 70 votes, but the old members polled 424, and in the end were duly returned by the sheriff. The under-sheriff, however, had endeavoured to put in force the provisions of the Act of 1430 as to the examination of electors on oath, and Gymber's supporters threatened a riot; whereupon 124 of the principal freeholders who had voted for Stonham and Styuecley, fearing lest the sheriff should be induced to make a false return, forwarded a statement of the facts to the king, setting forth the number of the votes on each side, and objecting, further, to the return of Gymber, on the ground that he was not " of gentell berthe "—Prynne's *3rd Register*, p. 157; *Return of Members of Parliament*, Part i (1878), pp. 336, 338, 342, 344; and see Stubbs, *Constitutional History*, iii, 423, 437.

[85] *Supra*, pp. 165, 175 n. 6

[86] So, too, the various sudden changes of fortune in the York and Lancaster feud from 1376 to the fall of Richard II. The high estimate of the commons' independence formed by Stubbs has been variously qualified by recent scholars: K. B. McFarlane in *Transactions of the Royal Historical Society* (1944), 53; J. G. Edwards, *The Commons in Medieval English Parliaments* (1958).

Borough elections. In boroughs, prior to the passing of the Act of Queen Anne above referred to, no other qualification was required in the members except that imposed by 1 Henry 5, c. 1, that they should be " citizens and burgesses resiant, dwelling and free, in the same cities and boroughs." The question, Who were the original electors in boroughs ? has been the subject of much controversy, and scarcely admits of a general answer, owing to the infinite variety of local electoral customs which municipal records, so far as they have yet been explored, disclose. Perhaps originally the elective franchise was enjoyed by all burgesses, that is, by all the free inhabitant householders paying scot and bearing lot, and sworn and enrolled at the court leet of the borough. The court leet, or burgh-moot, was the folkmoot of the borough, just as the shiremoot was the folkmoot of the shire. Those householders only who bore their share of the burdens of the place, who paid scot and bore lot, were entitled to the privilege ; those who, from poverty or other cause, did not pay the charges, nor serve the public offices of the borough, were not " burgesses," and therefore excluded. But whoever may have been the original electors— whether the scot and lot householders, the tenants in burgage, the free-holders generally, or the freemen—very few boroughs retained their electoral system unaltered for any length of time ; all were subject to the changes arising from the development of local custom, and the tendency of such development was generally towards a restriction of the franchise.[87] On receipt of the writ for the election of county and borough representa-tives, it was the sheriff's duty to issue his precept to the cities and towns in his county ; and it was customary for delegates, appointed by their fellow burgesses for the purpose, to attend in the county court and there either to report the choice of the borough, or themselves to elect the members to serve in parliament. Gradually various select bodies of burgesses, by whatever names distinguished, acquired the power, and by long usage a kind of prescriptive right, of election. By the end of the fifteenth century these select bodies had in many places substituted self-election for the suffrages of the whole body of the burgesses. In some boroughs a lengthy series of indirect elections led up to the final choice of the parliamentary representatives. Hitherto these encroachments on the rights of the town populations had gone on in each borough independently and spontan-eously, deriving their sanction solely from the binding force of particular local custom.

Franchise by charter. But from the accession of the House of Tudor, the rights of the inhabitants of boroughs were subjected to renewed and more rigid restrictions, through the charters of municipal incorporation

---

[87] On the very difficult subject of the medieval borough electorate, see the valuable study of May McKisack, *The Parliamentary Representation of the English Boroughs during the Middle Ages* (Oxford, 1932) ; and *cf.* Stubbs, *Constitutional History*, iii, 427–435 ; Anson, *Law and Custom of the Constitution*, i, p. 107 ; Maitland, *Constitutional History*, pp. 88–90, 355–357 ; Porritt, *History of the Unreformed House of Commons*, i, Chap. iii. One of the members for the city of Rochester in 1383 appears to have been employed as a labourer at 3d. a day at the castle : F. F. Smith, *Rochester in Parliament* (1933).

which now began to be granted in increasing numbers by the crown.[88] With the privilege of incorporation was usually combined the gift, or renewal, of the right of sending representatives to parliament. This right was in many cases exclusively vested in the municipal governing body (the mayor and town council) which as a rule was nominated in the first instance by the crown, and afterwards maintained by self-election. These close corporations tended more and more to fall under the influence of the local territorial magnate. Thus, " for national, as well as local government," it has been well observed, " the burgesses were put beyond the pale of the constitution. The power of the crown and aristocracy was increased at the expense of the liberties of the people. The same policy was pursued by the Stuarts; and the two last of that race violated the liberties of the few corporations which still retained a popular constitution after the encroachments of centuries." [89]

Although these developments were in some places reversed after the Revolution, yet in others they were continued and sanctioned by legal authority. By these various means the right of voting in many (but by no means all) cities and boroughs became generally restricted either to the mayor and town council, or to that body and its own nominees, the freemen; and by the growth of an infinite variety of local usages, which, though in many cases not really ancient, were judicially recognised as such, the electoral, as well as the municipal, system of boroughs became greatly changed from its primitive popular character. The mass of abuses and anomalies was at length swept away by the Reform Act of 1832,[90] and the Municipal Corporations Act of 1835.[91] Finally, the Reform Act of 1867 admitted to the borough franchise all male occupiers of dwelling-houses of full age who had resided for twelve months on July 31 in any year, and had been rated to the poor rates as ordinary occupiers, and had, on or before July 20, paid such rates up to the preceding January 5. It also admitted lodgers who had occupied for the same period lodgings of the annual value, unfurnished, of £10.[92]

THE OFFICE OF SPEAKER

The development of the office of Speaker [93] was one of the most important contributions of this period to our constitutional history. Here, as in many other instances, the first impression derived from a casual examination is one of remarkable continuity; closer study, however, will

---

[88] The first charter of municipal incorporation in the classical form had been granted in 1440 to Hull.

[89] May, *Constitutional History*, iii, 279–280; *Case of Quo Warranto* (1683) 8 St.Tr. 1039; Hallam, *Constitutional History*, iii, 74.

[90] 2 & 3 Will. 4, c. 45.

[91] 5 & 6 Will. 4, c. 76, amended by 22 Vict. c. 35.

[92] 30 & 31 Vict. c. 102. See Anson, *Law and Custom*, i, 113–114. *Cf. infra*, pp. 574 *et seq.*

[93] A. I. Dasent, *The Speakers of the House of Commons* (1911), has a very useful chronological list, but is hardly a history of the office; E. Porritt, *The Unreformed House of Commons* (1903), i, 432–488 is valuable for the eighteenth century; W. Stubbs, *Constitutional History*, iii, Chap. xx, is slight on the beginnings of the office.

show that beneath the familiar appearances there are fundamental differences which make it dangerous to regard the medieval Speaker as though his office resembled that of his modern successors.

Early spokesmen. In the Middle Ages it was always hoped that an assembly would speak " with one voice " and " with one accord." [94] Ordinarily this was possible, no doubt, and a murmur of assent was probably sufficient in many cases to assure the king of the concurrence of his parliament. When more difficult matters were involved, the lords might each in turn announce his opinion. It might be necessary to transmit to the king the results of a lengthy consultation, and then a spokesman was needed—sometimes several, when the consultations took place in separate groups. [95]   An early example occurs in 1301 when the lords, having prepared an " outrageous " Bill, unheroically left it to a knight of the shire (*Sir Henry Keighley*) to convey the dangerous document to the king. The knight's temerity landed him in the Tower. [96] More usually the lords deputed one of their own number to communicate to the king the result of their deliberations, as for example in 1332 when Lord Beaumont spoke on their behalf. [97]

Sometimes dimly felt legal difficulties produced curious results. At the deposition of Edward II there was much concern to make it clear that the proceedings were the work of all the estates, and for this purpose *Sir William Trussel* acted as spokesman of the whole parliament, [98] being himself neither one of the lords nor of the commons. By a curious coincidence another *Sir William Trussel* in 1343 spoke on behalf of the commons in parliament, although he too was not a member. [99]

The above are clearly examples of temporary expedients for dealing with casual emergencies. A great step in the direction of a more permanent office was taken by the Good Parliament of 1376. The *Anonimalle Chronicle* shows that there was another problem in organising the work of a large assembly in the middle ages. Business men, like the teachers and students of those days, made very little use of temporary written notes, compared with modern practice; they relied to a much greater

---

[94] " *Les Prelatz & Sieurs très-touz se leveront & excuseront a une voice* "—*Rotuli Parliamentorum*, iii, 5 no. 14 is typical.

[95] Examples in Plucknett, " Parliament " (*English Government at Work*, ed. J. F. Willard and W. A. Morris), 107–108.

[96] Stubbs, *Constitutional History*, ii, 158 ; for Keighley see J. E. A. Jolliffe, *Constitutional History*, 361–362.

[97] *Rotuli Parliamentorum*, ii, 64 no. 5.

[98] *Rotuli Parliamentorum Inediti* (ed. H. G. Richardson and G. O. Sayles), 101 ; M. V. Clarke, *Representation and Consent*, 184–185, 191, 347. He was a familiar of the Duke of Lancaster (Clarke, *op. cit.*, J. C. Davies, *Edward II*, 462, 590 no. 109) and on various occasions had been knight of the shire and sheriff, T. F. Tout, *Edward II* (ed. Hilda Johnstone, 91 note 4 ; J. H. Ramsay, *Genesis of Lancaster*, i, 158 ; R. Somerville, *History of the Duchy of Lancaster* (1953), 347.

[99] *Rotuli Parliamentorum*, ii, 136 no. 9 ; Trussel was employed by the king as a confidential messenger, *ibid.*, ii, 121 no. 28, 122 no. 29.

extent than we do upon memory. Now it is clear that in the Good Parliament [1] there was a man exceptionally gifted in this respect, *Sir Peter
de la Mare*. After a long debate, he would sum up in an orderly fashion
the various points made, to the admiration and complete satisfaction of
his fellow members. We need not be surprised, for de la Mare was
steward to the Earl of March, who like other great lords doubtless had
his council in which the steward was the outstanding figure, and it is
safe to assume that the management of the vast economic and political
interests of the March estate would only be entrusted to a man of considerable ability. The commons without any hesitation chose de la Mare
as their spokesman [2] and before the assembled lords and commons he
presented their views with accuracy and assurance. The significance of
de la Mare's position is not so much his acting as spokesman—others
had done so long before—as the fact that he enjoyed a vague but powerful
supremacy inside the House, and exerted a directing influence over its
debates. And finally, he acted continuously ever since his first emergence
until the end of the parliament. Already, then, several of the Speaker's
characteristics are to be found in the work of Sir Peter de la Mare; but
the title is not accorded him in any official document.

Sir Thomas Hungerford, 1377. The rolls of parliament for the very
next year contain the first mention of a Speaker by title: "*Monsieur Thomas
de Hungerford, chivaler, qi avoit les paroles pur les Communes d'Engleterre
en cest Parlement.*" [3] These words seem to imply a function extending
throughout the parliament, but in fact, Hungerford is only mentioned
in the proceedings of the last day of the parliament.[4]

Sir Peter de la Mare. We are on surer ground when we read in the
next parliament of " *Monsieur Peres de la Mare, chivaler, q'avoit les
paroles de par la Comune, faisant sa protestation.*" It is indeed poetic
justice that the doughty de la Mare, who had suffered imprisonment for
his intrepid leadership of the Good Parliament of 1376, should be destined
to complete in 1377 the edifice he had begun in 1376. Unlike Hungerford,
de la Mare appears as Speaker at the very beginning of the parliament,
and he is the first Speaker to make his formal " protestation " [5]—that
what he is about to say is not his own invention, but the considered
opinion of all the commons, and that if he forgets anything, or misreports

---

[1] *Supra*, p. 165.

[2] They " prierent a luy qil vodroit prendre la charge pur eux davoir la sovereinte de pronun-
cier lour voluntes en le graunt parlement avaunt les ditz seignours " : *Anonimalle Chronicle*
(ed. Galbraith), 83. De la Mare spoke several times for the commons before the lords,
but generally claimed that he was only their spokesman " for this time " or " for today."

[3] *Rotuli Parliamentorum*, ii, 374 no. 87 (Lodge and Thornton, 151–152).

[4] Earlier communications from the commons (as *Rotuli Parliamentorum*, ii, 363 no. 18)
are not stated to have been made by Hungerford.

[5] *Rotuli Parliamentorum*, iii, 5 no. 15 (part only in Lodge and Thornton, 152). Sir Peter
de la Mare in 1376 had used words which amounted to much the same thing: *Anonimalle
Chronicle*, 85.

anything, his companions should correct him then and there (but Sir Peter of the faultless memory had nothing to fear on that score). Successive Speakers made " protestations " in varying terms, and in the next century the important claim to freedom of speech was inserted.[6]

It is instructive to observe the type of man chosen for the office, especially in the early formative years. De la Mare's successor, Hungerford, was his opposite in politics but his fellow in everything else. Hungerford, in fact, was steward to the Duke of Lancaster, as de la Mare was steward to the Earl of March. The first two Speakers were thus managers of two great fortunes,[7] and both succeeded in wielding the whole weight of the commons in the interests of a political party. The government quickly learnt the lesson, and thenceforward speakers were almost always drawn from the higher ranks of the royal service. During the minority of Richard II they seem to have been non-political administrators; with the assertion of Richard's personal rule the type changes and one of his most intimate friends and devoted followers, Sir John Bussy (executed 1399), was Speaker of the later parliaments of the reign.[8]

Perils of the Speakership. The Lancastrian kings likewise secured the election of their most trusted councillors to the chair of the commons' house. John Durward, for example, was much employed by the king in carrying confidential verbal messages—duties requiring great discretion and a memory like de la Mare's.[9] The Speakers under Henry IV and Henry V were almost all constantly attending in the king's council, and the same is true of several of the Speakers under Henry VI and Edward IV. Although much still remains obscure, it seems clear that the crown fully realised the importance of the office and was willing, perhaps eager, to see it filled by men who were familiar with the small inner circle of administrators who conducted the daily work of government. What steps were taken to secure this important liaison between the government and the commons we can hardly guess. The commons seem always to have been regarded as electing their Speaker and it may well be that they felt the House would benefit from having such an intimate link with the king. We hear only once during this period of a contest, and that was in 1420 when Roger Hunt gained the nomination over Richard Russell by a majority of four votes.[10] The general impression made by all this seems

---

[6] Cf. Pickering's protestation in 1378 in *Rotuli Parliamentorum*, iii, 34 no. 16 (Lodge and Thornton, 154); the variations are discussed by J. E. Neale, " Free Speech in Parliament," *Tudor Studies presented to A. F. Pollard*; *infra*, p. 246.

[7] The race of great business managers is at least as old as the days of Adam Statton (for whose colourful career see N. Denholm-Young, *Seignorial Administration*, 77–85—he had been steward to Isabella de Force); and *cf.* William Cade, whose career, a century earlier, is studied by Sir Hilary Jenkinson in *English Historical Review*, xxviii, 209, 731.

[8] For Sir John Bussy, or Bushy, see Tout, *Administrative History*, iv, 12 *et seq.*, and A. Steel, *Richard II*.

[9] J. F. Baldwin, *The King's Council*, 150; there is a note upon him by J. H. Round, *English Historical Review*, xxix, 717–719.

[10] This interesting discovery was made in the borough archives of King's Lynn by Miss M. McKisack, *Representation of Boroughs*, 142.

to be that the Speaker's position in the commons must have been something like the Lord Chancellor's in the lords at the present day; in both
cases the presiding officer was not only a spokesman on behalf of the
House to the king, but also a representative of the government in the
House.

We have already seen that the office was perilous. Sir Peter de la
Mare was imprisoned, but worse befell some of his successors, for whom
the speakership was a stage in the hazardous career of politics. Bussy,
William Tresham, Thomas Tresham, Thorpe, Wenlock, Catesby, Empson,
Dudley, Sir Thomas More—all came to violent ends on the scaffold, in
civil war or by assassination. The list illustrates most strikingly the type
of man, adventurous, and deeply committed in partisan politics, who often
filled the office.

The history of parliament is of absorbing interest; but it was not the
only factor in the constitution. Indeed, during the fifteenth century there
were but fifty-six parliaments. The session was very generally about six
weeks, and one session a year the normal practice, although there were
years without a session, and such periods became longer and more
numerous as the century drew to its close. So intermittent an organ
could only exert occasional influence upon the course of events. The fact
that it still continued to be summoned in spite of its waning activity is a
remarkable testimony to the soundness of the foundations laid in the
preceding century. If we can judge it fairly by its works, then it would
appear that from about 1461 onwards it was the mercantile classes with
their constant demands for tariffs and regulations who kept parliament
alive.[11]

ADMINISTRATIVE TENDENCIES

Meanwhile, the work of government went on with the appearance,
at least, of growing efficiency. The surviving archives show us machinery
of ever-increasing elaboration operated by a large professional civil
service.

Institutions, new and old. The oldest institutions—the exchequer,
chancery, common law courts—were now solemn and formal bodies
employed in ancient procedures which were slow, highly technical, inflex-
ible and at times ineffective. Their official heads were officers of great
dignity and occasionally became conspicuous ministers. For the most
part, however, they were content to devote themselves to the formalities
rather than to the substance of government. Newer institutions, less
dignified, less encumbered with elaborate procedure, but much more
adaptable and active, began to supplement the ancient bodies. The

---

[11] Borough members were active in keeping their constituents informed about parliamentary
proceedings and were doubtless busy in promoting the interests of the towns; several of
the cases of parliamentary privilege during the fifteenth century involved burgesses—M.
McKisack, *Representation of the English Boroughs*, Chap. vii.

wardrobe and the chamber became great financial institutions; the signet and privy seal offices [12] drafted documents which the chancery merely copied: the council and the star chamber undertook tasks which the common law courts were incapable of dealing with.

These two sets of institutions, the new and the old, could hardly avoid conflict, and they have bequeathed to later ages two views of government, both of them valuable, yet so mutually inconsistent, that for centuries the most that could be hoped for was a tolerable balance between them, rather than a genuine reconciliation. Thus, the rigidity of the common law courts gave us the principles of the rule of law and of due process of law.[13] The conciliar courts on the other hand worked out the idea of equity and insisted that formal rules ought to yield before substantial justice. Each of these ideas is of fundamental value; their fierce conflict in the Stuart period was inevitable; but the eighteenth century patiently achieved a balance, and the nineteenth century a reconciliation of law and equity. Much the same antinomy existed in administration, and the war between parliament and prerogative was, partly at least, concerned with the issue between strict and discretionary administration which is a current problem today; so far, a balance rather than a reconciliation seems to be the immediate aim.

The king's clerks. These new organs of administration were staffed with active and well-trained men who in general were bent on making a career; the great offices of state, on the other hand, were becoming more and more confined to the great baronial families.[14] Moreover, these newer institutions were intimately connected with the king and his household. Constantly attendant upon him, they were always available for consultation, always ready to receive the royal commands, and consequently became the prompt and effective instruments of the royal will.

They were instruments only; the *primum mobile* of the entire system was the king, and upon his character and political judgment everything depended. Equally for good and for ill, the civil service was a powerful tool in his hands. It is not surprising that the baronage, and large numbers of others who shared their sentiments, should have viewed these developments with considerable misgiving. Some feeling of resentment among an agricultural aristocracy against the professional administrators of a centralised government is generally to be found in the Middle Ages in England and on the Continent. The motives varied in quality. Some felt it an affront to be taxed, examined and ordered about by obscure clerks of doubtful origin; others looked enviously at the rapid increase

[12] These institutions are discussed at large by T. F. Tout, *Chapters in Administrative History* (6 vols., Manchester, 1920–33); brief introductions to this newly discovered aspect of constitutional history will be found in his *Collected Papers*, ii, 191, 223; iii, 143; S. B. Chrimes, *Administrative History* (1952); G. R. Elton, *Tudor Revolution in Government* (1953).

[13] W. S. Holdsworth, *Some Lessons from our Legal History*, Chap. ii.

[14] *Handbook of British Chronology* (ed. F. M. Powicke) has very useful lists of office holders down to 1939.

in wealth of royal clerks; many were unable to understand the process of administration and felt sure that they were often corrupt; still others saw a menace to their liberties in the growth of royal administration. Clearly there were some grounds for this attitude. Royal clerks were zealous rather than scrupulous, and certainly became prosperous; and their activities were by no means easy to explain or justify in some cases. It is undeniable that the continental absolutisms were established by the efforts of such men.

The barons in politics. Coupled with this, were the political demands of the baronage. From the early thirteenth century onwards it is clear that there was a group of men who were interested in politics, considered themselves competent in public affairs, thought that they ought to be consulted upon momentous matters, and were prepared in the last resort to impose their views upon the king, and on several occasions did so. The composition of this class, whom we may call " the politically effective public," varied from time to time. In its early stages, historians can describe it with rough accuracy as " the earls "; it soon becomes enlarged to " the magnates " or " the baronage." In the fifteenth century it is still the baronage which provides the opposition when there is one, and for the most part the knights followed in their train.

The barons and the council. The struggle is therefore between the baronage and the knights, usually their sympathisers, on one side, and the king, his council and the administrators (especially the household officers) on the other. It will be noted that the bishops were territorial magnates like the barons, although they often attained their sees after long service as administrators. They often had the choice, therefore, of throwing their influence on one side or the other, or of acting as mediators between the two. A few bishops of character and ability could thus play a very important role upon occasion. For over two centuries the council was the strategical key to the situation. Many times the baronage insisted that the council should consist of a precise list of persons whose names should be publicly known; sometimes they would force the king to accept a council of persons nominated by them. In 1234 the bishops joined the barons in forcing the king to remove Poitevins from his council [15]; in 1237 a council of twelve was named and sworn [16]; in 1244 there was talk of confiding all business to four of the greatest magnates [17]; in 1258 the barons imposed an elaborate paper constitution embodying their ideas and went to war in defence of it [18]; in 1264 they produced a scheme which went to the opposite extreme of

[15] J. F. Baldwin, *The King's Council in the Middle Ages* (Oxford, 1913), 26; Matthew Paris, *Chronica Majora*, iii, 269.
[16] Baldwin, 27; Matthew Paris, *Chronica Majora*, iii, 382.
[17] Baldwin, 28–29; Matthew Paris, *Chronica Majora*, iv, 366 *et seq*.
[18] *Supra*, p. 132.

simplicity.[19] The long reign of Henry III was thus a continuous struggle. The king was too weak, financially and politically, to maintain his council in which foreigners were so unpopular an element—although they were sometimes able administrators. The barons, on the other hand, sought a council of magnates and claimed the great offices of state for members of their own order.

Under Edward I things were very different. The council became a more definite body and its members took an oath of office—which in the Middle Ages was a potent factor in imposing a sense of responsibility, and to some extent served to define the scope of an office. The official and household element was dominant in the council, which, moreover, kept a firm hold upon administration. The barons, on the other hand, now had parliament as their constant organ for participating in the government, or for criticising it, and in the sharp conflicts which arose the king personally was the object of attack rather than the council.

The reign of Edward II saw the council once again the storm centre, and the lords ordainers produced yet another experiment in remodelling the system of government; it is significant that one of their great concerns was that the king should not make grants without the consent of six magnates [20]—this matter of the disposal of the royal patronage in offices, lands, wardships, livings, pensions and money gifts is one that constantly recurs. The ordainers insisted that the great offices should be filled to the satisfaction of the baronage,[21] and for this and several other purposes they took their stand upon the dogma of annual parliaments, which they wished to make supreme over king, council and ministers alike.[22] The policy was carried further in 1341 when the baronage, now describing themselves as " peers," undertook to defend magnates who had held high office from the wrath of the king.[23] Under Richard II, the magnates started with the initial advantage of a minority, which gave them ample opportunity of setting up councils to their liking, and were very reluctant to surrender this position when the king came of age.[24]

The council under the Lancastrians. The accession of the house of Lancaster was only made possible by a combination of great baronial families, and Henry IV was never allowed to forget it. Before his accession he doubtless had shared the general views upon government held by the magnates, and now that he was king he seemed hardly able to

---

[19] Baldwin, 32–33; Rymer, *Foedera* (Rec.Comm.), i, 443 (Stubbs, *Charters*, 401).

[20] Ordinances (1311), c. 3; *cf. supra*, p. 156. The barons had made a similar attempt in 1258 by the Provisions of Oxford, *Ceo jura le Chanceler* (Stubbs, *Charters*, 380). The policy was based on a fear of favouritism, and the belief that these casual revenues should serve to relieve the taxes. In fact, they were used to reward men who would nowadays be salaried civil servants—although the undeserving often outran the meritorious in the race for favours.

[21] Ordinances (1311), c. 14 (Lodge and Thornton, 14).

[22] Ordinances (1311), c. 29 (Lodge and Thornton, 16).

[23] *Supra*, pp. 163–164.

[24] *Supra*, pp. 168, 171; note that typically baronial demands are made ostensibly by the commons.

dispute them. Archbishop Arundel pointedly commended the new king as a " knowing and discreet man, who is willing to be governed and counselled by the Sages and Ancients of the Realm." [25] Parliaments met fairly regularly, and extra-parliamentary meetings of the magnates in great councils were also often called. Major issues of policy seem to have been decided in parliament or great council, thus leaving the small council for the day-to-day work of administration.[26] Such a development should have left the council outside of politics, but this was not to be. In the first place, the burden of work, much of it quasi-judicial, was overwhelming, and in spite of heroic efforts the councillors could not keep up with it. There was also the dangerous question of the royal patronage, and the barons (or some of them) desired to capture it and use it to build up their own " influence "—in very much the same way as the Whig magnates were to exploit royal patronage in the eighteenth century. To effect this object, the barons embarked upon a struggle for the control of the small seals, which by this time automatically authorised the application of the great seal to the documents by which royal grants were made.[27] Several times the barons successfully demanded that the names of the councillors should be publicly disclosed, and magnates appear in the list with increasing frequency; there is record, moreover, of their dogged application to masses of administrative detail.

Henry V had to treat the magnates with great caution in order to manoeuvre the declaration of war upon France which neither the lords nor commons wished [28]; but once the war began, the attention of the magnates was diverted from the council board to the campaign. The minority of Henry VI gave the magnates another chance which they eagerly accepted. A council was named and it only consented to serve on condition of disposing of the whole royal patronage, to the exclusion of the Lord Protector.[29] A long series of ordinances which aim at regulating the procedure of the council makes it clear that its business was extremely heavy [30]; it is equally clear that the magnates had little taste for it unless their personal interests happened to be involved. Attendance became irregular as magnates discovered that their zeal for public affairs did not extend to several hours' office work daily. Heavy charges were incurred by paying substantial salaries, which some of the bishops patriotically gave back to the Exchequer. The lords of the council, from the dukes downwards, were certainly drawing large sums; " the patent rolls are filled with grants to lords Cromwell, Hungerford, Tiptoft " [31] (all three

[25] *Rotuli Parliamentorum*, iii, 415 no. 2.
[26] Baldwin, *King's Council*, 152.
[27] *Rotuli Parliamentorum*, iii, 572–573; Plucknett, " Place of the Council in the Fifteenth Century," in *Transactions of the Royal Historical Society* (1918), 177 *et seq. Cf. Rotuli Parliamentorum*, iii, 586 no. 68.
[28] Plucknett, *loc. cit.*, 167–168.
[29] Baldwin, *King's Council*, 172; *Rotuli Parliamentorum*, iv, 176 no. 29 (partly in Lodge and Thornton, 75–77).
[30] There are extracts from some of them in Lodge and Thornton, 73–79.
[31] Baldwin, *King's Council*, 179.

were prominent councillors). There can be no doubt that there was much corruption and that poor suitors received no relief unless they could buy the interest of some councillor.

The young king began to intervene in business in 1437, when he reserved to himself the more important patronage [32]; in 1444 he secured control of the seals [33] and at last reduced the council to its normal position. It was too late. Irreparable harm had come from the previous twenty years. The demoralisation of those who should have been the nation's leaders, the immense increase in maintenance, livery, embracery and public disorder, the development of fierce feuds among the magnates, and finally the revival of the ancient hatreds to which York and Lancaster were heirs, all combined to involve the baronage and the king himself in the ruin of the Wars of the Roses.

Edward IV. The new dynasty has left us little material for the history of the council. [34] The general impression is of a strong personal government, little troubled with parliaments, conducting the work of government through a council which seems to have been numerous, but for the most part consisting of industrious officials. When magnates did assemble in council, they were especially engaged in judicial business in the star chamber. That court, in fact, was the true heir of the medieval council; but when the Tudors needed advice they turned to a body which came, as it were, only by a collateral and junior line from the Middle Ages; this came to be known as the privy council. [35]

Fortescue on the council. A valuable contemporary commentary upon council government has been left us by Sir John Fortescue, who was Chief Justice of the King's Bench from 1442 to the close of the year 1460, becoming thenceforward the titular chancellor to Henry VI's fugitive court in Scotland and France. His remarks [36] were written after the final fall of the Lancastrian house in 1471, and when he was eventually reconciled to Edward IV and admitted to his council. He is emphatic that the crown was being impoverished by the distribution of royal patronage among the dependants of the magnates. To point the moral, " he sketches a model council of twelve laymen and twelve spiritual men—the wisest and best that can be found—who are to counsel continually. These, it should be noted, contained not a single lord, but to them the king might add four nobles and four prelates. At their head was to be a *Capitalis Consiliarius*, but this dignity was reserved not for a Bedford or a Gloucester, but for one of the simple twenty-four. Further,

---

[32] *Rotuli Parliamentorum*, v, 439.

[33] Nicolas, *Proceedings and Ordinances*, vi, 316–320 (*c.* 1440–1443); Rymer, *Foedera*, xi, 75.

[34] Baldwin, *King's Council*, 419.

[35] *Ibid.*, 450; *infra*, pp. 252 *et seq.*; but see C. G. Bayne in *Select Cases in the Council of Henry VII* (Selden Society, 1958), xxiv.

[36] Fortescue, *The Governance of England* (ed. Plummer), 145–149 (and in Lodge and Thornton, 88–90).

the simple men were to be paid a salary, but the noble men none. . . . The chancellor, treasurer, keeper of the privy seal and the chamberlains had long been the most assiduous members of the council, but Fortescue holds them all suspect; they may come to his ideal council if they like. he says, but he does not welcome them. . . . Fortescue is Lancastrian enough to call the lords at large *consiliarii nati*, but he will only have their presence when it is invited, and even the eight lords and prelates nominated by the king were to receive no salaries, and so they too could be trusted to stay away." [37] As a practical statesman Fortescue thus expresses the utmost distrust of the magnates; he was a keen observer, and his verdict that Lancastrian government was essentially government by the magnates, and that it failed by the fault of the magnates, is amply confirmed by the history of the fifteenth century. His ideal council was indeed a feeble suggestion; its great vice was that it merely ignored the social problem which had wrecked the scheme of Lancastrian government. That problem, which is not inaptly described as " bastard feudalism," [38] has left its mark on the statute book and parliament rolls in a long series of acts against the giving of liveries and the maintenance of huge retinues of dependants which were a constant temptation to private war, the intimidating of juries and similar excesses. Underlying these conspicuous symptoms was a deeper and less obvious economic movement which contemporaries found puzzling, and which still furnishes a difficult chapter in our economic history.[39]

Lawyers and parliament. Fortescue's political experience led him, and rightly, to regard the council as the crux of the situation. He tells us little about parliament.[40] The material briefly reviewed in this chapter can easily give the impression that parliament in the fifteenth century was not unlike that of the nineteenth. This resemblance is undeniable, but it is superficial. The Lancastrian parliaments had indeed developed forms and even procedures which were to persist for centuries to come. They were, moreover, of a sort which later centuries, searching for precedents, found particularly useful. The greatest contribution which this century made was possibly that very fact that its rolls contained precedents which later ages could appeal to, and which seemed especially weighty in the Stuart Age when a historical argument had a great advantage over an analytical one. There is reason to believe that there had been as yet little systematic thought about parliament. Much was written in the Middle Ages about monarchy in all its aspects, theological, political and practical; Fortescue (who had studied some of that literature to

---

[37] Plucknett, " Place of the Council in the Fifteenth Century," in *Transactions of the Royal Historical Society* (1918), 159–160.

[38] Good descriptions of the state of affairs are given in the introductions to the *Paston Letters* (ed. J. Gairdner) and Fortescue's *Governance of England* (ed. C. Plummer); cf. K. B. McFarlane in *Transactions of the Royal Historical Society* (1944), 53–79.

[39] The problem has been recently surveyed by M. Postan in the *Economic History Review*, ix, 160, xii, 7.

[40] As has been noticed by S. B. Chrimes, *Constitutional Ideas*, 67.

good purpose) could also add something on the practical aspects of counsel, but much less progress had been made in thinking about parliament. The lawyers had been compelled to consider the problem in occasional cases which raised points of constitutional law.[41] They regarded parliament as a feudal court, and surmised that taxation was possibly a feudal profit arising from it. The idea of representation was familiar, at least in the form of the powers of attorney in private law. They realised, too, that parliament was a group, and that there was also a " community " of the realm. The relations between those groups and their individual members aroused some discussion. The characteristic of all these debates is their reliance upon concepts of private law, and their failure to reach any solid conclusions in terms of constitutional theory. Nor is this surprising, for in the Middle Ages the only part of the law to be developed in considerable depth was the law of property.

Fortescue on monarchy. Parliament might be baffling, but monarchy was familiar, and Fortescue wrote upon it in several books. These were based partly on the academic political science of his day which drew its thought from Aristotle through the scholastic theologians, and from the Roman lawyers; but it also owed something to experience and the observation of English and French institutions at work. We may conclude this chapter with a quotation from his *De Laudibus Legum Anglie:* " A king of England cannot at his pleasure make any alterations in the laws of the land, for the nature of his government is not only regal, but political. Had it been merely regal, he would have a power to make what innovations and alterations he pleased in the laws of the kingdom, impose tallages and other hardships upon the people whether they would or no, without their consent, which sort of government the civil laws point out, when they declare ' Quod principi placuit legis habet vigorem.' [42] But it is much otherwise with a king whose government is political, because he can neither make any alteration or change in the laws of the realm without the consent of the subjects, nor burden them against their wills with strange impositions, so that a people governed by such laws as are made by their own consent and approbation enjoy their properties securely, and without the hazard of being deprived of them, either by the king or any other." [43]

---

[41] Some cases are discussed in Plucknett, " The Lancastrian Constitution," in *Tudor Studies presented to A. F. Pollard*; cf. S. B. Chrimes, *English Constitutional Ideas in the Fifteenth Century*, and M. V. Clarke, *Medieval Representation and Consent*. Cf. *infra*, p. 492.

[42] Inst. 1, 2, 6; Dig. 1, 4, 1.

[43] *De Laudibus*, c. 9. There is an excellent edition by Chrimes (Cambridge, 1942), who has also treated his political ideas at length in *English Constitutional Ideas* (Cambridge, 1936). Cf. M. A. Shepard in *Essays in Honour of C. H. McIlwain* (1936), 289–319.

CHAPTER 9

THE EARLIER TUDORS (1485–1558)

General characteristics. The Tudor period is almost synchronous with the sixteenth century, an age remarkable for its material prosperity, and for its intellectual and religious activity. The mighty impulse given to commerce by the discovery of America and of the passage to the East Indies by the Cape of Good Hope, coupled with the certainty imparted to the science of navigation by the use of the compass, caused an enormous increase of the wealth of the middle classes. Intent upon the acquisition of private gain, the merchants and traders were for the most part satisfied to leave questions of government to others, so long as they themselves were permitted to pursue their avocations in peace. Simultaneously with the extraordinary expansion of commerce there were other causes at work which tended to withdraw men's minds from the consideration of purely political topics.

The revival of learning, and its rapid dissemination among all classes through the medium of the printing press, the profound religious agitation of the Reformation, and the spirit of bold enquiry which it excited concerning matters of the deepest interest hitherto generally accepted as beyond dispute—all contributed to concentrate popular attention upon intellectual and religious progress, to the neglect of politics. On the continent of Europe, the introduction of standing armies, and the revolution in the art of war which made it " a distinct science and a distinct trade," had emancipated rulers from the chief restraint on their power— the fear of an armed people—and enabled them either utterly to sweep away, or reduce to empty formalities, the national assemblies which had once been as free and as potent as our own early parliaments. The free constitutions of Castile and Aragon were successfully overthrown by Charles V and Philip II; and the States-General of France, after languishing for a time, ceased altogether in 1614, until resuscitated in 1789, for their final meeting on the eve of the Great Revolution. In England, too, parliamentary institutions passed through a season of trial. That they did not perish here as on the Continent was partly due to the Lancastrian tradition which the Tudors to some extent inherited and partly to the personal character of Henry VIII, who " sought to make Parliament not the rival, still less the master, but the foundation of the royal authority." [1]

---

[1] Pollard, *Factors of Modern History*, 108–111. " We shall find that Henry VIII was anything but hostile to his Parliaments; that under him the Parliamentary system is extended and developed; that Parliamentary privileges are asserted and maintained; and that Parliament is educated up to a national sense of duty. Parliament in fact owes much more to the Tudor monarchy than a democratic age is willing to admit," p. 109. *Cf.* also Fisher, *Political History of England* (ed. Hunt and Poole) vol. v, pp. 6–7.

The rule of Henry VIII. Despot as he was, he was yet animated by a scrupulous regard for the letter of the law. "While his fellow tyrants abroad were everywhere overthrowing free institutions, Henry was in all things showing them the deepest outward respect. Through his reign he took care to do nothing except in outward and regular legal form, nothing for which he could not shelter himself under the sanction either of precedent or of written law." If he "could get the letter of the law on his side, he was satisfied; otherwise his conscience was uneasy." [2] This peculiar character of Henry's despotism, his anxiety to do everything in proper parliamentary and judicial form, "while it degraded parliamentary and judicial institutions at the time, really did a great deal to strengthen and preserve them for better days." [3] The parliament often served to cover his most outrageous proceedings with a convenient and plausible appearance of popular approbation. When Henry had Anne Boleyn's head cut off on one day and married Jane Seymour the next morning, the parliament gravely listened to a speech from the lord chancellor, assuring the world that the king did not do it "in any carnal concupiscence," and immediately proceeded to pass an Act declaring that it was all done "of the king's most excellent goodness." [4] Nevertheless Henry's proposals were sometimes opposed, and bills were rejected and amended by the House of Commons [5]; and with some show of truth he could write to the pope in 1529: "The discussions in the English parliament are free and unrestricted; the crown has no power to limit their debates, or to control the votes of their members. They determine everything for themselves, as the interests of the commonwealth require." [6]

The Renaissance, like the Reformation, is one of those broad movements of intellectual history which must certainly be mentioned here, but cannot be treated in any detail; its effects are all-pervasive in art, literature, science, law, politics, theology. It exerted influence upon Roman and canon law, as well as upon English common law, and the relations between English and Roman law have for centuries claimed the attention of English scholars. Those relations were partly in the nature of conflict, or opposition; but the opposition of two legal systems may sometimes be a stimulus to a better understanding—a notable example is the discussion by Stephen Gardiner of the place of king and parliament in English practice, portions of which have long been in print in Foxe's *Book of Martyrs*.[7]

---

[2] Freeman, *Growth of the English Constitution*, 101.

[3] *Ibid.*

[4] Speech of Lord Chancellor Audley in 1536, *Lord's Journals*, p. 84; 28 Hen. 8, c. 7; Froude, *History of England*, ii, 535, 539.

[5] Pollard, *Factors of Modern History*, 123–125. "The idea that Parliament did nothing but register royal edicts cannot stand for a moment after an examination of the Parliamentary proceedings of the reign" (p. 125); *infra*, p. 245. See also Tanner, *Tudor Documents*, 518 *et seq.*

[6] Froude, *History of England*, i, 209.

[7] For the twelfth century, see R. C. van Caenegem, *Royal Writs in England from the Conquest to Glanvil* (Selden Society, vol. 77), pp. 360–390; for the thirteenth, Plucknett, *Earl/*

Independently of the general political apathy to which allusion has been made, the attitude of parliament during the Tudor Age, so unlike its demeanour at an earlier and at a later period, is to be accounted for by the fact that the old nobility, the leaders in former struggles for liberty, had been cut off in the Wars of the Roses, and the commons had not yet acquired sufficient importance and self-reliance to act alone. The temporal lords summoned by Henry VII to the parliament of 1485 were only twenty-eight in number, and of these several were new creations. The new nobility which grew up under Henry VII and his son owed everything to the royal favour, and were restrained from independent action alike by gratitude, by interest, and by fear of the resolute vengeance which those monarchs unsparingly dealt out to all who opposed them. A watchful jealousy of all individuals likely to disturb their power was a characteristic of all the Tudor sovereigns. The nobles found safety and advancement by acting the part of courtiers, rather than of medieval parliamentary barons. Henry VII, says Lord Bacon, " kept a strait hand on his nobility; and chose rather to advance clergymen and lawyers, which were more obsequious to him, but had less interest in the people." [8] The same policy was pursued by Henry VIII and Elizabeth. The remnant of the old nobility, the Percies, Nevilles, and Howards, were disgusted at the advancement in the course of a generation of men like Wolsey, Cromwell, Cecil, Bacon and Walsingham. The rising of 1536 which called itself the " Pilgrimage of Grace," and the later rebellion of the Earls of Northumberland and Westmorland in 1569, were as much a protest against the " newe set-upp nobles," as against the " newfound religion " and the incarceration of Mary Queen of Scots, the representative of the ancient faith.[9] At the same time under Henry VIII there is little evidence of government interference with election to parliament. In the reigns of Edward VI, Mary, and Elizabeth, a large number of small boroughs were created; but if the object of their creation was to increase the royal influence in the House of Commons, it singularly failed.[10] Moreover the anxiety which the Tudor monarchs generally displayed to secure the sanction of parliament for all their proceedings, affords the strongest testimony to the real power and importance of the national assembly. Under Elizabeth, the commons began to resume their firm tone and bearing, and thenceforth never desisted

English Legal Literature; for the sixteenth century, Maitland, *English Law and the Renaissance* (Cambridge, 1901), reprinted in his *Collected Papers*, his *Selected Historical Essays* (ed. H. M. Cam); *Letters of Stephen Gardiner* (ed. J. A. Muller), no. 130, especially pp. 398–399—the whole letter is very illuminating.

[8] *History of the Reign of Henry VII*, ed. Lumby, p. 217.

[9] The pilgrims of 1536 swore to " expulse all villain blood from the king's grace and his privy council "—*Letters and Papers of Henry VIII*, xi, no. 892. In their proclamation the rebels of 1569 justified their proceedings on the ground that the queen was surrounded " by divers newe set-upp nobles, who not onlie go aboute to overthrow and put downe the ancient nobilitie of the realme, but also have misused the queen's majestie's owne personne, and also have by the space of twelve yeares nowe past set upp and mayntayned a new-found religion and heresie contrary to God's word "—Lingard, viii, 45.

[10] See Pollard, *Factors in Modern History*, pp. 120–123, and *infra*, p. 243 note 77.

until they had won back their ancient liberties and established them on a sure foundation.

During the 120 years spanned by the Tudor dynasty, the power of the crown was strongly exerted; but it was usually exercised with discretion; and the want of a standing army acted as a perpetual restraint which did not indeed prevent the crown " from sometimes treating an individual in an arbitrary and even in a barbarous manner, but which effectually secured the nation against general and long-continued oppression." [11] In the meantime, amidst the political lethargy of the great mass of the people, a silent transfer of power was taking place. The commercial wealth of the middle classes enabled them to buy up the estates of the old landed proprietors, and feudalism gradually died out. [12] The persecution of the Puritans roused up a spirit of opposition to the crown, and the struggle for religious freedom led on to the vindication of political freedom also. Under Elizabeth, opposition was restrained by her personal popularity, and by the feeling that a strong government was necessary amidst the perils to which both she and the nation were exposed from the pope, from Spain, and from France; but this forbearance ended with the advent of the House of Stuart.

HENRY VII: 1485–1509

The results of the protracted contest between the crown and the people during the Middle Ages are thus concisely summed up by Hallam, in enumerating the essential checks upon the royal authority existing at the accession of Henry VII.

Hallam's checks. (1) " The king could levy no sort of new tax upon his people, except by the grant of his parliament, consisting as well of bishops and mitred abbots, or lords spiritual, and of hereditary peers or temporal lords, who sat and voted promiscuously in the same chamber, as of representatives from the freeholders of each county, and from the burgesses of many towns and less considerable places, forming the lower or Commons' House. (2) The previous assent and authority of the same assembly were necessary for every new law, whether of a general or temporary nature. (3) No man could be committed to prison but by a legal warrant specifying his offence; and by an usage nearly tantamount to constitutional right, he must be speedily brought to trial by means of regular sessions of gaol-delivery. (4) The fact of guilt or innocence on

---

[11] Macaulay, *History of England*, i, 34. *Cf.* also Maitland, *Constitutional History*, p. 237: "The Tudor monarchy is indeed something very different from the Lancastrian—the latter was a very limited monarchy; the former, if we regard its practical operation, seems almost unlimited. Still the difference, when we look into it, is found not so much in the nature of institutions which exist as in the spirit in which they work; the same machinery of king, lords, commons, council, law courts, seems to bring out very different results."

[12] H. M. Cam, " The decline and fall of English Feudalism," *History*, xxv, 216–233; K. B. McFarlane, " Parliament and ' Bastard Feudalism,' " *Transactions of the Royal Historical Society* (1944), 53–73; R. H. Tawney, " The Rise of the Gentry," *Economic History Review* xi, 1–38; below, p. 226, n. 21.

a criminal charge was determined in a public court, and in the county where the offence was alleged to have occurred, by a jury of twelve men, from whose unanimous verdict no appeal could be made. Civil rights, so far as they depended on questions of fact, were subject to the same decision. (5) The officers and servants of the crown, violating the personal liberty or other right of the subject, might be sued in an action for damages to be assessed by a jury, or, in some cases, were liable to criminal process; nor could they plead any warrant or command in their justification, nor even the direct order of the king." [13] To these may be added, (6) The liability of the king's ministers to be impeached by the commons for misgovernment. This constitutional right had not indeed been exercised since the reign of Henry VI, [14] and lay dormant throughout the Tudor period, but it was dormant only, and with the revival of the spirit of liberty under James I the right of impeachment was reasserted. Hallam added a general warning that all these securities, though undoubtedly established by law, were more or less evaded in actual practice by the Tudor sovereigns: " the general privileges of the nation were far more secure than those of private men "; and on the whole " there was, perhaps, little effective restraint upon the government, except in the two articles of levying money and enacting laws."

Effectiveness of Hallam's checks. A careful examination of Hallam's famous " checks " is therefore necessary if correct estimates are to be formed of the achievements of medieval constitutional lawyers, and the nature of Tudor government. (1) Direct taxation was certainly limited in the manner which Hallam described; but the incidents to be related in the course of the present chapter will show how frequently the crown levied direct contributions which were sometimes, but not always, condoned *ex post facto* by parliament. The whole question of indirect taxation in the form of customs dues was still open, and only in Stuart times was it seriously examined from a constitutional point of view. Both Henry VIII and Edward VI, moreover, made drastic use of their prerogative in debasing the coinage. (2) There was indeed by this time an ascertained list of documents called statutes, and additions to the collection could only be made by parliamentary means. The Tudors, however, were active in developing other types of legislation which were powerful instruments of government in spite of the fact that they were not equated with statutes by the lawyers. These were proclamations principally, but some matters, notably the printing and publishing of books, were regulated by decrees of the council published in the star chamber. (3) The idea of due process of law, especially in criminal matters, was familiar and cherished, but the hardest part of the struggle for its recognition still lay in the future, when the pretensions of the privy council and of the secretaries of state seriously threatened the principle,

[13] Hallam, *Constitutional History*, i, 2.
[14] *Supra*, pp. 193-194.

and the technical deficiencies of the writ of habeas corpus jeopardised its enforcement. (4) Jury trial, likewise, was to meet grave dangers in the sixteenth century. Chancery and star chamber had already gone far in eliminating the jury from their trial procedure in civil and criminal matters respectively; from the first days of the Tudor Age, moreover, parliament itself began the practice of confiding powers of summary trial without jury to the justices of the peace.[15] (5) The principle of liability here stated was old and well understood, but it was too often frustrated by the equally ancient grievance that crown officers, even without invoking the prerogative, had ample opportunity of evading the law and of intimidating their adversaries. (6) The point about impeachment, which Mr. Taswell-Langmead added to the five others, he has himself very properly and sufficiently qualified. As we shall see, Tudor ministers were in peril, not of the commons, but of the king, who had no difficulty in adapting common law trials or parliamentary attainders to suit his purposes.

Henry VII's legislation. Henry VII has been eulogised by Lord Bacon as " the best lawgiver to this nation after Edward I." His laws are characterised by the same author as " deep and not vulgar, not made upon the spur of a particular occasion for the present, but out of providence for the future, to make the estate of his people still more and more happy, after the manner of the legislators in ancient and heroical times." [16] Besides a considerable number of valuable trade and commercial enactments which reflect the great economic development of the period, and some important conveyancing statutes (including four statutes of uses), the laws of Henry VII contain two, which for their political and constitutional importance require special notice—the statute for the security of the subject under a king *de facto*, and the statute " giving the Court of Star Chamber Authority to punish divers Misdemeanours." It is a curious feature of both these acts that in the course of succeeding centuries they acquired a completely new, and much wider, significance.

Statute upon a *de facto* king. By the first of these it was declared that " no person nor persons, whatsoever he or they be, that attend upon the King and Sovereign Lord of this land for the time being in his person, and do him true and faithful service of allegiance in the same, or be in other places by his commandment, in his wars within this land or without, that for the same deed and true service of allegiance he or they be in no wise convict or attaint of high treason nor of other offences for that cause by Act of Parliament or otherwise by any process of law, whereby he or any of them may forfeit life, lands, etc." Further, any " Act made contrary to this statute shall be void and of no effect." [17] The attempt

---

[15] The material is collected and discussed by F. Frankfurter and T. G. Corcoran in the *Harvard Law Review*, xxxix, 917.
[16] Bacon, *History of Henry VII* (ed. J. R. Lumby), 69.
[17] 11 Hen. 7, c. 1 (1495); J. R. Tanner, *Tudor Constitutional Documents*, 5–6.

to bind future parliaments was of course nugatory; " for a supreme and absolute power cannot exclude itself; neither can that which is in its nature revocable be made fixed." [18]

If this Act had been passed in 1485 it could easily have been construed as a magnanimous gesture to the adherents of Richard III. Its date is ten years later, however, and Richard's partisans had long before paid the penalty for supporting a king in possession, whom his successor regarded as a usurper. Now 1495 was a year when Perkin Warbeck's operations were most ominous, and it seems that the Act was meant to rally wavering Lancastrians rather than to conciliate defeated Yorkists. The only conduct which the Act mentions is being with the king (or under the king's command) in his wars, at home or abroad, and it enacts that those who stood by the " king for the time being " should be protected against criminal proceedings in respect of their service; on the other hand, the Act further provides that those who "decline from their allegiance" (presumably, by refusing to serve Henry, or by joining the Yorkists) are excluded from the benefits of the Act (in the event, no doubt, of a temporary Yorkist ascendancy being followed by Henry's restoration).

The Act is a good example of the typical Tudor technique of mingling promises with threats, and it would therefore seem to be a political move directed to a particularly critical situation, and not an attempt to deal in general terms with the tragically difficult legal and moral problem (which faces several countries at the present day) of how much obedience is due to a *de facto* government. The liberal and humane policy which later ages found in the Act certainly did not govern Henry VII's own conduct.[19] As late as 1553 it would seem that no general significance had yet been attached to it, for in that year the Duke of Northumberland was tried by Queen Mary for having adhered to Lady Jane Grey (who had been queen for nine days); he did not appeal to the Act—as he assuredly would, if it had then been regarded as laying down the humane principle now associated with it. In the course of the seventeenth century it came to be an accepted constitutional maxim that " possession of the throne gives a sufficient title to the subject's allegiance, and justifies his resistance of those who may pretend to a better right "; and in support of that proposition, this statute was regularly cited. It was one of the reasons advanced by timid souls who urged Cromwell to assume the crown, and thus bring his supporters within the terms of the statute; and at the trial of the regicides after the Restoration, some of them endeavoured to justify themselves under this Act by pleading that they had obeyed

---

[18] Bacon, *Henry VII*, 133.

[19] Hatred of the House of York was with Henry VII a passion which even political considerations of expediency could hardly control. " He never seemed to be weary," says Mr. Campbell (*Materials for History of Henry VII*, Roll Series, i, Introduction xiii), " of branding the name of the Yorkists and their supporters with the gravest charges of rebelliousness and want of patriotism; and we shall see that the name of the late king is never mentioned by him without the favourite iteration of ' king in dede but not in right.'" This was Yorkist dogma originally applied to the Lancastrians: *infra*, p. 497.

the government which was in possession, and were therefore not traitors. The judges, however, held that although this would have been a good defence for acts done by authority of a usurping king, it would not avail to cover the proceedings of a non-regal government against one who was indicted and executed being king. At the Revolution of 1688, the provisions of the Act were much relied upon in argument as a reason for accepting William III as king, instead of establishing a regency, as suggested by Archbishop Sancroft and certain of the Tory party.[20]

Act of 1487, Pro Camera Stellata. Henry's attention was early directed to the prevention of conspiracies among the adherents of the House of York, by which his throne was perpetually threatened during the earlier portion of his reign. The practice of "maintenance" by which a number of individuals associated together under some powerful nobleman, whose livery they wore and to whom they were bound by oaths and promises, for the purpose of forcibly maintaining his and their own private quarrels, afforded a ready means of raising forces at short notice to assist the claims of any pretender.[21] Although prohibited by many statutes, this practice of giving liveries to numerous retainers had become general throughout the kingdom. With a view of effectually suppressing it, Henry procured the passing of the statute in the third year of his reign, by which a group of councillors was established to deal with the particular offences which were the cause of the disturbed state of the kingdom at the end of the fifteenth century.[22] The offences dealt with by the Act were maintenance, livery, the endenture of retainers, embracery, packing or bribing juries, riot and unlawful assembly. The Act was construed as making the chancellor, treasurer and privy seal the sole judges; the presence of the others mentioned in the Act was held to be essential (two councillors and two justices) but their position was

---

[20] The view in the text is based in part on A. F. Pollard, " Tudor Gleanings," *Bulletin of the Institute of Historical Research*, vii, 1–12, where the views of Coke, Bacon, Hobbes, Hawkins, Blackstone, Hallam and Stubbs are examined. For a different view, see K. Pickthorn, *Early Tudor Government*, i, 151 *et seq.*

[21] For a detailed study and bibliographical references, see William Huse Dunham, " Lord Hastings' indentured Retainers, 1461–1483," *Transactions of the Connecticut Academy of Arts and Sciences*, xxxix, 1–175 (1955).

[22] 3 Hen. 7, c. 1 (Tanner, *Tudor Constitutional Documents*, 258); *supra*, p. 118. The growth of the legend associating the Act with the Star Chamber is discussed by A. F. Pollard in *English Historical Review*, xxxvii, 520–529. It seems to appear first in Plowden's argument for the plaintiff in *Earl of Leicester* v. *Heydon* (1571) Plowd. 384 at 393. Compare the tradition mentioned by Hudson in F. Hargrave, *Collectanea Juridica*, ii, 50–51. The title *Pro Camera Stellata* is added to the statute roll in a later hand, *Bulletin of the Institute of Historical Research*, iii, 115 and Plate II. The Star Chamber differed from the committee set up by the Act of 1487 inasmuch as all members of the Council were members of it, and its jurisdiction was not confined to the particular offences enumerated in the Act. So Maitland, *Constitutional History*, p. 262, referring to the court of Star Chamber, remarks: " Now, was this the court created by the Statute of Henry VII? Under Charles I the opinion had gained ground that it *was*, that consequently whatever it did beyond the sphere marked out by that statute was an unlawful usurpation of jurisdiction. When the time for abolishing it had come, it was abolished on this score. But the general opinion now seems to be that the jurisdiction of this court of Star Chamber was in truth the jurisdiction which the King's Council had exercised from a remote time, despite all protests and all statutes made against it."

that of assessors only. Procedure was upon information and summons by privy seal; the trial by examination without jury. Punishments were to be in accord with the existing Acts which created the offences. This Act is best regarded as one of the many examples of the tendency to set up special courts for the trial of statutory offences.[23]

Financial exactions. Henry VII has been reproached with his insatiable avarice, but it is improbable that he amassed money merely for its own sake. As a clever and unscrupulous political adventurer, who had taken advantage of the disturbed state of the kingdom, after an exhausting and protracted civil war, to seize the throne by the aid of the Lancastrian faction, he had learnt the value and power of money as a means of buying future, and rewarding past, support. Taxation, moreover, was the one point which the mass of the people seemed to have considered worth fighting about. Twice during his reign, when several subsidies were granted, formidable insurrections broke out: in 1489 in the north, under John à Chambre and Sir John Egremont; in 1497 in Cornwall, under Thomas Flamank, an attorney, and Michael Joseph, a farrier, who, with 16,000 followers, marched as far as Blackheath in Kent, and, having been joined by Lord Audley, engaged the king's troops, surrendering only after 2,000 of their number had been killed. Henry therefore deemed it politic to squeeze money out of the rich, and to avoid general impositions affecting the poorer classes. He first had recourse to benevolences, which, as we have seen, had been abolished in Richard III's only parliament as an intolerable grievance.[24] A benevolence extorted by the king in the seventh year of his reign, received, four years later (1495), a kind of parliamentary sanction by " a shoring or under-propping Act," making legally payable, under pain of imprisonment, the arrears which private individuals had promised but not brought in.[25] The inquisitorial and arbitrary nature of the exaction appears from the statement of Lord Bacon that " there is a tradition of a *dilemma* that Bishop Morton the Chancellor used, to raise up the benevolence to higher rates; and some called it his fork, and some his crotch. For he had couched an article in the instructions to the commissioners who were to levy the benevolence, that if they met with any that were sparing, they should tell them that they must needs have, because they laid up; and if they were spenders, they must needs have, because it was seen in their port and manner of

---

[23] On such special courts, see T. F. T. Plucknett, *Concise History of the Common Law* (5th ed.), 183 and " Some proposed legislation of Henry VIII," *Transactions of the Royal Historical Society* (1937), 119–144; *infra*, p. 234 n. 45. For this present Act, and the judicial construction of it in Y.B. 8 Hen. 7, Pasch. no. 70, f. 13 (1493) see C. H. Williams, " The so-called Star Chamber Act," *History*, xv, 129. The jurisdiction of council and chancery (by writs of great and privy seals) had been temporarily, and very cautiously, reinforced by statute 31 Hen. 6, c. 2 in 1453.

[24] *Supra*, p. 185–186.

[25] 11 Hen. 7, c. 10; Bacon, *Henry VII*, 134. Promises to pay a benevolence were unenforceable for lack of consideration; the statute supplied the defect, by applying to them the exchequer procedure for recovering crown debts of record, thus imposing imprisonment. It also hinted that there had been some embezzlement by the collectors.

living; so neither kind came amiss."[26]   In addition to benevolences
Henry extorted large sums by suing for penalties under obsolete statutes,
by rigorously exacting the extreme feudal rights of the crown, and by
employing the various processes of the courts of law, not for the dispensation of justice, but for the accumulátion of fines and penalties.
During the latter part of his reign he made use, for this purpose, of the
notorious Richard Empson and Edmund Dudley, " lawyers in science
and privy councillors in authority," who " turned law and justice into
wormwood and rapine."[27]   At the accession of Henry VIII they were
both committed to prison, tried, and executed, on a frivolous charge of
treason.   But, while sacrificing to popular resentment the agents of his
father's extortions, the new king was careful to retain the fruits of their
iniquity in his treasury.

Parliament.   Throughout his reign of twenty-four years Henry VII
summoned parliament only seven times, and during the last thirteen
years only once, in 1504.   To obtain money was the object on each occasion; but, like his predecessors, he submitted the expediency of his wars
to the consideration and advice of the national council.   His first parliament had granted him the duties on tonnage and poundage for life,[28]
and the wealth which he amassed by the various means already referred
to, by the attainder of the most opulent of the Yorkists, and by revocation,
on parliamentary authority, of all crown grants made since the 34 Henry
6 (1454–55), rendered him the richest prince in Christendom, and thus
practically independent of parliamentary control.[29]

HENRY VIII: 1509–1547

Henry's first parliament granted him tonnage and poundage for life;
but with a proviso " that these grants be not taken in example to the
kings of England in time to come."[30]

Wolsey and the commons.   Liberal subsidies were granted by the four
following parliaments for the prosecution of the war with France; but,
in 1523, Wolsey took the indiscreet step of going to the House of Commons, and personally urging the grant of £800,000, an unprecedented

[26] Bacon, *Henry VII*, 93. The story has also been told of Foxe: A. F. Pollard, *Reign of Henry VII*, ii, 47 n. 1.

[27] Bacon, *Henry VII*, 190. The employment of uses made it increasingly difficult to trace the old feudal relationships and to ascertain the crown's rights—hence Henry VIII's great statute of 1536, the last of a long line (Plucknett, *Concise History of the Common Law* (1956), 578–587. There is a valuable account of Dudley by Miss D. M. Brodie in *Transactions of the Royal Historical Society* (1932), 133. Henry VIII made some slight restitution of these extortions, as his father's will commanded: Holdsworth, *History of English Law*, iv, 27, n. 1.

[28] *Rotuli Parliamentorum*, vi, 268.

[29] *Ibid.*, vi, 336 *et seq.* (1485); to the sweeping measure proposed by the commons, the king attached a number of exceptions in the interests of " equity."   On the subject of finance under the Tudors, see Tanner, *Tudor Documents*, 598 *et seq.*

[30] 1 Hen. 8, c. 20 (Tanner, *Tudor Documents*, 601).

sum, to be raised by a property tax of 20 per cent. on lands and goods. Many members were inclined to resist his admission into the House, his presence there being evidently calculated to intimidate the members, and thus silence all opposition. It was resolved, however, to admit him, and on the suggestion of Sir Thomas More, the Speaker, not with a few followers only, but " with all his pomp, with his maces, his pillars, his poleaxes, his crosses, his hat, and great seal too." The cardinal made a long and eloquent oration in favour of joining the Emperor Charles V in a war against France, and urged the grant of the sum demanded as the estimated cost of the expedition. But all the independent members offered a vigorous resistance. Wolsey came down to the House a second time, but the commons received his harangue with silence; and when the cardinal demanded of particular members some reasonable answer, every member held his peace. At last the Speaker, " reverently upon his knees, excusing the silence of the house, abashed at the presence of so noble a personage, able to amaze the wisest and best learned in the realm," endeavoured to show the cardinal that " for them to make answer was it neither expedient, nor agreeable with the ancient liberty of the house,"[31] it being the usage of the commons to debate only amongst themselves. After fifteen days' debate, a subsidy much inferior in amount to that which the cardinal had demanded, was at length granted, mainly through the influence of the court party in the House. " I beseke almightie God," wrote a member of the commons to the Earl of Surrey, " it maye bee well and peasibly levied, and surely payed unto the Kings Grace, with oute grudge, and specially with oute losyng the good wills and true herts of his subjects which I rekene a ferre grettir treasure for a King then gold or silver. And the gentilmen which muste take payne to levie this money amongs the Kings subjects, I think shalhave no litle besynes about the same."[32] This manifestation of an independent spirit among some of the commons' House was agreeable neither to the king nor the cardinal; and for nearly seven years parliament was not again summoned.

Forced loans and benevolences. In the meantime recourse was had to forced loans and benevolences. A forced loan had been already exacted in 1522, every man being required to swear to the value of his possessions, and to contribute a rateable portion according to such declaration, on the king's promise of repayment out of the next subsidy granted by parliament. In 1525, soon after the news of the battle of Pavia had been received, fresh commissioners were appointed with instructions to demand the sixth part of the goods of the laity and the

[31] Roper, *Life of Sir T. More* (ed. E. V. Hitchcock), pp. 17–19; *cf.* R. W. Chambers, *Thomas More* (1935) 203–205. Wolsey was not the first chancellor who attempted to use his personal weight with the commons; Warham had done the same in 1514—apparently without protest from the House: *Parliamentary History*, i, 482. Henry VIII himself once visited the burgesses to promote a bill which he was interested in : *Letters and Papers*, x, no. 462 (p. 190); K. Pickthorn, *Early Tudor Government*, ii, 275, n. 2.

[32] Ellis, *Letters Illustrative of English History*, i, 221.

third part of the goods of the clergy, on the pretext that the king was about to lead an army into France. This demand was unanimously resisted. The mayor and citizens of London on attemping to remonstrate were warned to beware, lest " it may fortune to cost some their heads." The clergy boldly stood upon their privilege to grant money only in convocation; asserting that the commission was contrary to the liberties of the realm, inasmuch as the king could take no man's goods without the authority of parliament. By preaching and example they animated the people to resistance. " When this matter was opened through Englande," says the old chronicler Hall, " howe the great men toke it was marvel, the poore cursded, the riche repugned, the light wittes railed, but, in conclusion, all people cursded the Cardinal, and his coadherentes as subversor of the Lawes and libertye of Englande. For thei saied, yf men should geve their goodes by a Commission, then wer it worse than the taxes of Fraunce, and so England should be bond and not free." The royal commissioners being forcibly resisted in several counties, and a serious insurrection having broken out in Suffolk, Henry was at length obliged to annul the obnoxious commission, and " the demande of money seased in all the realme for well it was perceived that the commons should none paie." [33]

The forced loan having failed, recourse was now had to the more specious demand for a voluntary benevolence. This, however, being objected to by the citizens of London, as illegal, under the statute of Richard III, had also to be withdrawn.

In 1544 another forced loan was exacted from all persons rated at £50 per annum; and in the following year a general benevolence from all persons having land to the annual value of 40s., or chattels worth £15. The commissioners were instructed that if any one should withstand their gentle solicitations, alleging either poverty or some other pretence which the commissioners should deem unfit to be allowed, then, after failure of persuasions and reproaches for ingratitude, they were to command his attendance before the Privy Council, at such time as they should appoint, to whom they were to certify his behaviour, enjoining him silence in the meantime, that his evil example might not corrupt the better disposed. [34] The consequence of refusing to contribute may be learnt from the oppressive treatment of an alderman of London, Richard Reed, who was sent down to serve as a common soldier on the Scottish border, where the English army was then in the field, with special instructions to the general to employ him on the hardest and most perilous duty, and to " use him in all things after the sharp military discipline of the northern wars, whereby he might somewhat be instructed of the difference between the sitting quietly in his house, and the travail and danger which others

---

[33] Hall, *Union of . . . York and Lancaster* (ed. Whibley), ii, 36, 43. *Cf.* Tanner, *Tudor Documents*, 620–624.
[34] Lodge, *Illustrations of British History*, i, 91, Hallam, *Constitutional History*, i, 24.

daily do sustain." [35] Having been taken prisoner in the first engagement, the unhappy alderman was compelled to pay much more for his ransom than the benevolence required of him.

Default on royal loans. The forced loans were nominally secured, as we have seen, by the king's promises of repayment; but even this shadowy hope of reimbursement was taken away by Act of Parliament. On two occasions the king was formally released from his debts. In 1529 a statute was passed by which the parliament, " for themselves and all the whole body of the realm whom they do represent, freely, liberally, and absolutely, give and grant unto the king's highness, by authority of this present parliament, all and every sum and sums of money which to them and every of them is, ought, or might be due, by reason of any money, or any other thing to his grace at any time heretofore advanced or paid by way of prest or loan, either upon any letter or letters under the king's privy seal, general or particular, letter missive, promise, bond, or obligation of repayment, or by any taxation of other assessing by virtue of any commission or commissions, or by any other mean or means, whatsoever it be, heretofore passed for that purpose." [36] When this release of the loan, Hall tells us, " was knowen to the commons of the Realme, Lorde so they grudged, and spake ill of the hole Parliament; for almoste euery man counted it his dette, and reconed suerly of the payment of the same, and therefore some made their wylles of the same, and some other dyd set it ouer to other for debt, and so many men had losse by it, whiche caused them sore to murmur, but ther was no remedy." [37] Again, in 1544, just after the exaction of a fresh loan, an Act was passed granting to the king all sums borrowed from any of his subjects since 1542, with a further provision that any money which his Majesty should have already paid in discharge of these debts, should be refunded by the creditor or his heirs. [38]

New treasons created by statute. Under Henry VIII, the offence of high treason was vexatiously and wantonly extended far beyond the limits marked out by the ancient statute of Edward III. It was made treason to dispute, and afterwards to maintain, the validity of the king's marriage with Anne Boleyn, or the legitimacy of her daughter Elizabeth. It was declared treason to marry without the royal licence, or have a criminal intercourse with any of the king's children " lawfully born, or otherwise commonly reputed or taken for his children," or his sister, aunt, or niece; or for any woman to marry the king himself, unless she were chaste, or had previously revealed to him her former incontinence. It was treason to wish by words to deprive the king of his title, name, or

[35] Lodge, *Illustrations*, i, 100.
[36] 21 Hen. 8, c. 24.
[37] Hall (ed. Whibley), ii, 169.
[38] 35 Hen. 8, c. 12.

dignity (including the title of supreme head on earth of the Church of England); to call the king a heretic, or schismatic, openly to wish him harm, or to slander him, his wife, or his issue.[39] The guilt of treason was even extended from deeds and assertions to the very thoughts of men. It was incurred by any person who should " by words, writing, imprinting, or any other exterior act, directly or indirectly accept or take, judge, or believe " that either of the royal marriages, that with Catherine or that with Anne Boleyn, was valid, or who should protest that he was not bound to declare his opinion, or should refuse to swear that he would answer truly such questions as should be asked him on these subjects.[40] " It would be difficult," says Lingard, " to discover, under the most despotic governments, a law more cruel and absurd. The validity or invalidity of the two marriages was certainly matter of opinion, supported and opposed on each side by so many contradictory arguments, that men of the soundest judgment might reasonably be expected to differ from each other. Yet Henry by this statute was authorised to dive into the breast of every individual, to extort from him his secret sentiments upon oath, and to subject him to the penalties of treason, if those sentiments did not accord with the royal pleasure." [41]

The Earl of Suffolk, nephew of Edward IV; the Duke of Buckingham, also of royal descent and the first in rank and consequence among the nobility; the aged Countess of Salisbury, daughter of Edward IV and mother of Cardinal Pole; Queen Anne Boleyn; Bishop Fisher; Sir Thomas More; Thomas Cromwell; the Earl of Surrey; and the Duke of Norfolk, ordered for execution but saved by the opportune death of the king, were among the most conspicuous victims to Henry's ferocious vengeance, policy or caprice. The forms of law became the engines for the perpetration of judicial murders; the most trivial evidence was regarded as sufficient to support a conviction for treason; and during the latter part of Henry's reign even the few advantages which the accused possessed in the ordinary courts were taken away by the habitual employment of bills of attainder.

Bills of attainder. A bill of attainder differs from an impeachment thus: Impeachment is a judicial proceeding in which the commons are prosecutors, supporting their accusations by evidence, and the lords are the sole judges. Attainder is a legislative act, which must pass through the same stages as any other Act of Parliament. It may be introduced

---

[39] 25 Hen. 8, c. 22; 26 Hen. 8, c. 13; 28 Hen. 8, c. 24; 32 Hen. 8, c. 25; 33 Hen. 8, c. 21. See Tanner, *Tudor Documents*, 375 *et seq.*, where most of these statutes are given. On this legislation see I. D. Thornley, " Treason Legislation of Henry VIII," *Transactions of the Royal Historical Society* (1917), 87-123; I. D. Thornley, " Treason by words in the fifteenth century," *English Historical Review*, xxxii, 556 (but note the dissent of Sir William Holdsworth, *History of English Law*, iii, 293 n. 5); S. Rezneck, " Constructive treason by words in the fifteenth century," *American Historical Review*, xxxiii, 544; S. Rezneck, " Trial of Treason in Tudor England," *Essays in Honour of C. H. McIlwain*, 258-288; S. Rezneck, " History of the parliamentary declaration of Treason," *English Historical Review*, xlii, 497 (continued in *Law Quarterly Review*, xlvi, 80).

[40] 28 Hen. 8, c. 7.   [41] *History of England*, vi, 484.

in either the lords or commons, and after passing through both Houses receives the royal assent. No evidence is necessarily adduced to support it. It is analogous to a bill of pains and penalties, and was originally intended for the punishment of those who fled from justice. In its earliest form, therefore, an act of attainder did no more than a common law outlawry, which was the regular proceeding against those who fled from a charge of felony (for an accused person cannot be tried in his absence). Attainder became thoroughly indefensible when it was used against persons who were actually in custody and so could be regularly tried by common law. This procedure was employed by the Lancastrians against the leaders of the Yorkist party in 1459, and two years later the victorious Yorkists used the same weapon against Henry VI, his queen and a number of his prominent supporters.[42]

To obviate all danger of refutation or of unpleasant disclosures, Cromwell, by the king's express command, inquired of the judges whether, if parliament should condemn a man " who was forthcoming " (and who could therefore have been given a common law trial) to die for treason without hearing him in his defence, the attainder could ever be disputed. They replied that it would form a dangerous precedent; that parliament should rather set an example to inferior courts by proceeding according to justice; but that the court of parliament being supreme, an attainder in parliament could never, under any circumstances, be subsequently questioned in a court of law. The final step in the degradation of this procedure was therefore the work of Cromwell and the timid judges of Henry VIII. By the irony of fate, Cromwell was himself the first to perish by an Act of attainder hurried through parliament without hearing him in his defence.[43]

Enforcement of proclamations, 1539. A remarkable example of the way in which Henry VIII contrived to unite the exercise of practically absolute power with respect for constitutional forms—to play the despot by the co-operation of his parliament—is afforded by the Act giving the king's proclamations the force of law. The king having issued certain royal proclamations, the judges held that those who disobeyed them

---

[42] " The proceedings of Parliament in passing bills of attainder, and of pains and penalties, do not vary from those adopted in regard to other bills. They may be introduced into either House, but ordinarily commence in the House of Lords: they pass through the same stages; and, when agreed to by both Houses, they receive the royal assent in the usual form. But the parties who are subjected to these proceedings are admitted to defend themselves by counsel and witnesses before both Houses; and the solemnity of the proceedings would cause measures to be taken to enforce the attendance of members upon their service in Parliament. In evil times this summary power of Parliament to punish criminals by statute has been perverted and abused; and in the best of times it should be regarded with jealousy; but, whenever a fitting occasion arises for its exercise, it is undoubtedly the highest form of parliamentary judicature."—May, *Parliamentary Practice* (1883), p. 744; *cf.* 13th ed. 1924, pp. 379, 655.

[43] Coke, *Institutes*, iv, 37. *Cf.* Tanner, *Tudor Documents*, p. 423. An Act of attainder might follow a conviction (or even execution) at common law; here the object was to enact the forfeiture of equitable and entailed estates which often escaped at common law: *cf.* Plucknett, " Impeachment and Attainder," *Transactions of the Royal Historical Society* (1953), 145 at 155.

could not be punished by the Council. The king then appealed to parliament to give to his proclamations the force of statutes. This request was complied with, but not without "many large words." The Act recites the contempt and disobedience of the king's proclamations by some who did not consider "what a king by his royal power may do," and then, in order that the king might "not be driven to extend the liberty and supremacy of his regal power," enacts that proclamations made by him, with the advice of a majority of his Council, should, under the penalty of fine and imprisonment, have the force of statutes, but so that they should not be prejudicial to any person's inheritance, offices, liberties, goods and chattels, or infringe the established laws. It was, moreover, specially declared that such proclamations should derive all their force from the "authority of this Act," and that no persons should "by virtue of this Act suffer any pains of death"; but from this provision against capital punishment there was a formidable exception of such persons as "shall offend any proclamation to be made by the king's highness, his heirs or successors, for and concerning any kind of heresies against Christian religion."[44] As Hallam remarks, the fact that the king was obliged to obtain this statute, the difficulty he experienced in getting it through the commons, and the considerable limitations with which it was granted, afford "a striking testimony to the free constitution it infringed, and demonstrate that the prerogative could not soar to the heights it aimed at, till thus impelled by the perfidious hand of parliament."[45] It would be a mistake, however, to regard the statute of proclamations as being a sort of English *Lex Regia*. The matters excepted from the operation of the statute include the whole of the common and statute law; the proclamations actually issued contain nothing after the statute which is not also to be found before. Its principal object was doubtless the special tribunal and procedure which it set up. At the same time, Sir William Holdsworth observes, the problem of delegated legislation had become urgent, and he regards the Act as "an extremely able attempt by king and parliament to deal finally with the problem in a manner which should commend itself to the public opinion of the day." Sir Cecil Carr has made the interesting suggestion that ultimately the Act weakened the crown, because it created the impression that the proclaiming power was statutory, whereas historically the crown already possessed it by prerogative.[46]

[44] 31 Hen. 8, c. 8 (1539); Tanner, *Tudor Documents*, p. 532.

[45] Hallam, *Constitutional History*, i, 35. By the Act of 31 Hen. 8, c. 8, transgressors against the king's proclamations were to be tried and punished by certain persons enumerated therein, consisting of the usual officers of the Privy Council, together with some bishops and judges, "in the star-chamber or elsewhere." The tribunal thus constituted is substantially the same as that set up in the Act of 1487 (*supra*, p. 226). The prescribed number proving inconveniently large, another Act was passed in 1543 (34 & 35 Hen. 8, c. 23) by which the jurisdiction was given to a tribunal of nine privy councillors. Both were repealed by 1 Edw. 6, c. 12 (1547).

[46] Holdsworth, *History of English Law*, iv, 102, 296; E. R. Adair, "The Statute of Proclamations," *English Historical Review*, xxxii, 34–46; C. T. Carr, *Delegated Legislation*, 52; K. Pickthorn, *Tudor Government*, ii, 414 *et seq.*

Ecclesiastical supremacy. The royal authority was still further augmented by the assumption of the ecclesiastical supremacy, and the practical transfer to the crown of the immense power which the church had
hitherto wielded. The dissolution of the monasteries not only supplied
Henry with vast wealth with which to bribe the temporal peerage into
implicit conformity with his will, but at the same time, by depriving
thirty-one mitred abbots of their seats in the House of Lords, reduced,
from a majority to a minority, the spiritual peerage, who alone were likely
to be sufficiently independent to offer a serious opposition.[47]

Popularity of Henry VIII. Notwithstanding his many vices, Henry
VIII was on the whole popular with the mass of his subjects. The times
were peculiarly favourable for the exercise of a strong paternal government. Henry secured to the people that domestic peace for which they
so ardently longed. During the earlier portion of his reign at least he
displayed a frank, affable and generous temper; he was no mean scholar;
expert in all manly exercises; of noble presence and elegant bearing;
and he at all times devoted a large portion of time to the arduous duties
of personal government. Amidst the perils and dangers, foreign and
domestic, to which the nation was on several occasions exposed during
Henry's reign, men felt that in him they possessed an able, vigorous and
thoroughly national administrator.

Wales. The consolidation of the kingdom with respect to both Wales
and Ireland was considerably advanced under Henry VIII. By the
Statute of Wales (12 Edw. 1, 1284) the land of Wales had been wholly
annexed and united to the English crown. But, although many material
alterations were at the same time made in the Welsh laws, the conquered
people still retained several provincial immunities and disabilities. They
preserved their ancient rule of inheritance, similar to the English gavelkind,
by which lands were divided equally among all the issue male, instead
of descending to the eldest son alone [48]; but on the other hand, with the
exception of two parliaments of Edward II in 1322 and 1327, to which
twenty-four representatives were summoned from South and twenty-
four from North Wales,[49] the Welsh people had continued without any
representation in the House of Commons. From the beginnings of parliament, however, the four Welsh bishops had sat among the lords. By

---

[47] See Tanner, *Tudor Documents*, p. 514: " Whereas Henry VII's House of Lords contained
49 spiritual peers to 29 temporal peers, after the Dissolution Henry VIII's House only
contained 26 spiritual peers, while his temporal peerage was never less than 36 and often
nearer 50." To the 21 old bishoprics, Henry VIII subsequently added 6 new ones in
succession to the great abbeys previously existing there—Westminster (suppressed in 1550),
Bristol, Chester, Gloucester, Oxford and Peterborough, which still exist.

[48] On this, see Plucknett, " The Legal Position of Wales," in *Year Book Series* (Selden
Society), xxiv, pp. lxvii *et seq.* (1953), and A. J. Otway-Ruthven, " The Constitutional
position of the great lordships of South Wales," *Transactions of the Royal Historical
Society* (1958), 1 *et seq.*

[49] Rymer, ii, 484, 649.

the statute 27 Hen. 8, c. 26 (1536), Wales was thoroughly incorporated into and united with England; all persons born in the principality were admitted to enjoy and inherit all the freedoms, liberties, rights, privileges and laws of England; and lands in Wales were declared to be inheritable after the English tenures and rules of descent. By a subsequent statute in 1543 (34 & 35 Hen. 8, c. 26) Wales was divided into twelve counties,[50] each empowered to send one knight to parliament; and every borough, being a shire town, was to send one burgess. In the same year the County Palatine of Chester was admitted to parliamentary representation, two knights for the county and two burgesses for the city of Chester.[51]

Ireland. During the Wars of the Roses the authority of the English crown over Ireland had sunk to a very low ebb. At the accession of Henry VIII it was practically limited, with the exception of the principal seaports, to the English pale, consisting of the eastern half of the four counties of Louth, Meath, Dublin and Kildare. The western half of these counties was a march land, more disorderly, if possible, than the rest of the island, which was divided among a large number of petty chieftains, mainly of Irish but partly of English origin, who governed the inhabitants of their respective territories and made war upon each other with the freedom of independent princes. Under the strong government of the Tudor kings the English ascendancy in Ireland was reasserted and placed upon a firmer basis than it had occupied since the days of Henry II. Richard, Duke of York, father of Edward IV, laid the foundations of Yorkist influence there while he was Lieutenant of Ireland, from 1449 to his death in 1460; in the contest between the rival houses of York and Lancaster, the Anglo-Irish for the most part espoused the cause of the White Rose, and readily gave their support to the two pretenders who successively put in jeopardy the throne of Henry VII.[52]

---

[50] This was exclusive of Monmouthshire, which, though formerly part of Wales, had been made, by the 27 Hen. 8, c. 26, before mentioned, one of the counties of the realm of England, and as such entitled to return two knights of the shire to parliament. Under the statute 34 & 35 Hen. 8, c. 26 (1543), superior courts of justice called courts of Great Session were established, with a jurisdiction independent of the process of Westminster Hall. These continued to administer both law and equity in civil cases, and also criminal matters arising within the principality, down to the year 1830, when the courts were abolished by statute (1 Will. 4, c. 70), and it was enacted that assizes should be held in the principality for the trial of all matters criminal and civil in like manner and form as had been usual for the counties in England. The peculiarity of common law judges assuming equity jurisdiction is discussed by W. H. D. Winder, " Equity in the Courts of Great Sessions," *Law Quarterly Review*, lv, 106. The Act of 1543 also defined the jurisdiction of the Council of Wales, which had been in existence since the reign of Edward IV. " It exercised a criminal jurisdiction similar to that exercised by the Court of Star Chamber, and a civil and an equitable jurisdiction co-ordinate with that of the Courts of Great Session ": Holdsworth, *History of English Law*, i, 126. The Council fell into abeyance in the seventeenth century, and was finally abolished in 1689 (1 Will. & Mar. c. 27). For the whole subject, see Holdsworth, *op. cit.*, pp. 117-132; C. A. J. Skeel, *The Council in the Marches of Wales* (1904); Tanner, *Tudor Documents*, pp. 331-334.

[51] 34 & 35 Hen. 8, c. 13.

[52] Lambert Simnel was undoubtedly an impostor. It was long a question of much uncertainty who the young man really was who called himself Richard, Duke of York, son of Edward IV, and who is generally styled Perkin Warbeck. Gairdner, however, has furnished evidence

Poynings' Law, 1495. It was with the view of reducing to subjection the settlers within the pale that the Irish parliament in 1495 passed the celebrated Poynings' Law, as the Statute of Drogheda was styled from Sir Edward Poynings, the deputy of young Henry, Duke of York (afterwards Henry VIII), who at the age of three years had been appointed lord lieutenant of Ireland. This statute contained a variety of provisions for restraining the power of the great lords within the pale, and strengthening the royal authority. Its two most important enactments were: (1) All statutes " late made within the realm of England and belonging to the public weal of the same " should have the force of law in Ireland; (2) No parliament should in future be holden in Ireland till the king and his Council had been informed by the lieutenant of the necessity of the same, and of the Acts proposed to be passed in it, and the royal licence and approbation had been previously obtained. By securing the initiative power to the king and his English Council, a check was placed upon the action of every Irish parliament, and upon the lord-deputies, sometimes powerful Irish nobles "whom it was dangerous not to employ, but still more dangerous to trust." The immediate objects of the Act are clear. Experience had shown that the Irish parliament was merely a tool in the hands of the governors, who had frequently used it in the Yorkist interest; the restriction on the powers of Irish parliaments was thus an attempt to curb the governors, in the first place. "Whatever might be its motives," says Hallam, "it proved, in the course of time, the great means of preserving the subordination of an island, which, from the similarity of constitution, and the high spirit of its inhabitants, was constantly panting for an independence which her more powerful neighbour neither desired nor dared to concede."

The whole situation, in which Poynings' Act was a conspicuous detail, later acquired a significance far more extensive than purely Irish affairs. As England acquired more and more overseas possessions and the problem of their constitutional position became more urgent, lawyers found their earliest precedents in Ireland's relations to England. In particular, the power of the English parliament to legislate for Ireland was constantly invoked in discussing the relations of the English parliament to the local legislatures of the American and other colonies—indeed, an attempt was made in 1678 to extend the principle of Poynings' Act to Jamaica.[53]

which almost conclusively proves that he also was an impostor (" The Story of Perkin Warbeck from Original Documents," printed at the end of Gairdner's *Life of Richard III*). For Irish history generally, see Edmund Curtis, *History of Mediaeval Ireland, 1110-1513* (2nd ed., 1938); R. Bagwell, *Ireland under the Tudors* (3 vols., 1885-1890), and *Ireland under the Stuarts* (3 vols., 1909-1916); W. E. H. Lecky, *Ireland in the Eighteenth Century* (5 vols., 1892); some documents are collected in A. F. Pollard, *Reign of Henry VII*, iii, 259-313.

[53] Hallam, *Constitutional History*, iii, 362. *Cf.* also Fisher, *Political History*, pp. 60-61. For the text of Poynings' Act see A. F. Pollard, *Henry VII*, iii, 298, where other acts and Year Book cases on the position of Ireland are printed. For its interpretation, see D. B. Quinn in *Irish Historical Studies*, ii, 241, and R. D. Edwards and T. W. Moody, " The history of Poynings' Law," *ibid.*, ii, 415. The Jamaican episode is told in A. B. Keith,

The stern and systematic despotism of Henry VIII, coupled with the intimidation produced by his relentless vengeance against the powerful family of Fitzgerald, had still greater effect in reviving the royal authority. From a lordship—the title which it had hitherto borne under the successors of Henry II—Ireland was raised to the higher rank of a kingdom [54]; the native chiefs came in and submitted; peerages were sought and obtained, not only by the Anglo-Irish, but by some of the most powerful of the old Irish families [55]: and although still far from secure, the English government in Ireland assumed during the last years of Henry VIII a much more settled aspect than it had borne for very many years previously.

EDWARD VI: 1547–1553

The ecclesiastical changes under Edward VI and Mary, as well as those effected by Henry VIII, will be treated in the succeeding chapter on the " Reformation in England." In their civil aspect the reigns of Edward VI and Mary were scarcely, if at all, less despotic than that of their father, although we shall see some signs that the House of Commons as beginning to reassert more of its ancient independence. The youth of Edward VI precluded him from exercising any but a very slight influence upon affairs, the royal power being practically vested first in the protector, Edward Seymour, Duke of Somerset (brother of Jane Seymour, and thus uncle to Edward VI), and afterwards in John Dudley, Duke of Northumberland (son of Henry VII's minister).

Treason legislation. One of the first acts of the young king's advisers was to endeavour to propitiate the nation by abrogating some of the sanguinary and oppressive laws of Henry VIII. By a statute of Edward's first parliament all new treasons and felonies created during the last reign were abolished; and the Act of Edward III again became the standard of high treason, except that to affirm in saying or writings that the king was not, or that the pope was head of the church, still remained a treasonable offence.[56]

In 1552, however, after the fall of Somerset, many of the treasons created under Henry VIII, and abolished by this statute, were re-enacted, together with some new ones.[57] But in this parliament the commons

Constitutional History of the first British Empire, 12 (*cf. ibid.*, 82, for Virginia). For the Irish legal position see A. B. Keith, *op. cit.*, C. H. McIlwain, *The American Revolution*, R. L. Schuyler, *Parliament and the British Empire*, Holdsworth, *History of English Law*, xi, 21 *et seq.*

[54] Henry assumed the style of King of Ireland, January 23, 1542, ûnder an Irish statute, 33 Hen. 8, c. 1. The change was confirmed in 1543 by an English Act of Parliament, 35 Hen. 8, c. 3. *Cf.* Alice Stopford Green, " Henry VIII, ' King of Ireland,' " *Miscellany presented to Kuno Meyer* (Berlin, 1912), 278–285.

[55] William Birmingham was created Lord Carbery in 1514; Con O'Neill and his son Matthew, respectively Earl of Tyrone and Lord Dungannon, in 1542; Morogh O'Brien was made Earl of Thomond, Ulick de Burgh, Earl of Clanricarde, and Donough O'Brien, Lord Ibracken, in 1543.

[56] 1 Edw. 6, c. 12. Tanner, *Tudor Documents*, pp. 401–404. *Cf. supra*, p. 231.

[57] 5 & 6 Edw. 6, c. 11; Tanner, p. 405.

exhibited an unwonted independence, and zeal for liberty and justice. They threw out the bill as originally framed by the ministers, and substituted one of a much more moderate nature, in which was embodied what has been justly described as " one of the most important constitutional provisions which the annals of the Tudor family afford."[58] The constant complaint of persons accused of treason, that they could not establish their innocence because never confronted with their accusers, had brought home to the public mind the iniquity of the usual method of procedure. It was now enacted that no person should in future be indicted or attainted for any manner of treason except on the testimony of two lawful witnesses, who should be brought face to face with the accused at the time of his trial, unless he should willingly confess the charges. Although shamelessly evaded, or utterly disregarded in the state trials under Elizabeth and James I, this salutary statute was ultimately recognised, when all ranks and parties had learnt moderation in the school of adversity, as the foundation of a rule of procedure which has afforded to the subject " a mighty safeguard against oppressive prosecutions."[59]

Proclamations. The same Act of Edward's first parliament which repealed the new-made treasons of Henry VIII repealed also the statute which had given to that monarch's proclamations the force of law. But this made little practical change with regard to royal proclamations. Several were issued during Edward's reign, enforced by penalty of fine and imprisonment; and by one issued in 1549, all justices of the peace were commanded to arrest " sowers and tellers abroad of forged tales and lies," and to commit them to the galleys, there to row in chains as slaves during the king's pleasure.[60] The same practice was continued under Mary, who in the last year of her reign went so far as to issue a proclamation which, after denouncing the importation of books filled with heresy and treason from beyond sea, declared that whosoever should be found to have such books in his possession should be reputed and taken for a rebel, and executed according to martial law.[61]

Ket's Rebellion. The year 1549 was remarkable for the tumults and insurrections of the common people which arose in many counties.

[58] Hallam, *Constitutional History*, i, 40. *Cf. infra*, p. 518.
[59] Foster, *Crown Law*, 238; 5 & 6 Edw. 6, c. 11, s. 9; a similar clause appeared in the Act of 1547 (s. 23) but in a less satisfactory form.
[60] Strype, ii, 149; Hallam, *Constitutional History*, i, 38. The proclamation could be justified under the Act of 12 Ric. 2, c. 11, which gave the council power to punish spreaders of false news at its discretion; *cf.* Plucknett, *History of the Common Law*, 429–430. Richard II's Act was re-enacted in 1554 and 1559.
[61] Strype, iii, 459; Hallam, *Constitutional History*, i, 43. There was some excuse for this arbitrary proceeding in the fact that a violent libel had recently been written at Geneva by Goodman, a refugee, inciting the people to dethrone the queen; and that, in 1557, Sir Thomas Stafford, a grandson of the Duke of Buckingham beheaded by Henry VIII, had sailed from Dieppe with the connivance of the French king, and landing at Scarborough with a small force had vainly endeavoured to raise the people in rebellion against " the most devilish devices of Mary, unrightful and unworthy queen." (Strype, iii, App. No. 71, 259–262).

In Cornwall and Devonshire under Humphrey Arundel, and in Norfolk under Ket, the risings assumed formidable dimensions, and were suppressed with some difficulty. They arose partly from opposition to the reformed doctrines, but mainly from discontent at the proceedings of the landowners, who, regardless of the ancient commonable rights of their tenants, made large enclosures of the waste or common lands of manors; and, experience having shown that the growth of wool was more profitable than that of corn, converted the arable land into pasture. This strictly commercial mode of dealing with their estates was especially adopted by the newly made nobles and gentry who had acquired a large share of the confiscated abbey lands, and both they and the reformed religion which they professed became objects of hatred to the thousands of agricultural labourers whom the restriction of tillage had thrown out of employment, and the cultivation of commons had deprived of one great source of support.[62] For the suppression of these risings in future, a very severe Act was passed by parliament against unlawful and rebellious assemblies, by which it was declared to be treason for any twelve persons to meet together on any matter of state, and felony if the object of the assembly was to destroy enclosures.[63]

MARY: 1553–1558

Independently of the sanguinary religious persecutions of Mary's reign, her civil government was characterised by much violence and arbitrariness. Reference has already been made to her proclamation ordering the possessors of heretical and seditious books to be executed by martial law. She followed the example of her predecessors in extorting loans from her subjects.[64] She imposed a duty upon foreign cloth without

---

[62] " Parallel to the religious Reformation, social changes of vast importance were silently keeping pace with it. In the break-up of feudal ideas the relations of landowners to their property and their tenants were passing through a revolution; and between the gentlemen and the small farmers and yeomen and labourers were large differences of opinion as to their respective rights. The high price of wool and the comparative cheapness of sheep farming continued to tempt the landlords to throw their plough lands into grass, to amalgamate farms, and turn the people who were thrown out of employment adrift to shift for themselves. The commons at the same time were being largely enclosed, forests turned into parks, and public pastures hedged round and appropriated. Under the late reign these tendencies had with great difficulty been held partially in check; but on the death of Henry they acquired new force and activity. The enclosing, especially, was carried forward with a disregard of all rights and interests, except those of the proprietors." Froude, *History of England*, v, 107. " It is the common custom with covetous landlords to let their housing so decay that the farmers should be fain for small regard or coin to give up their leases, that they, taking the ground into their own hands, may turn all into pasture. So now old fathers, poor widows, and young children lie begging in the streets." Sermon of Lever quoted by Froude, v, 112, note from Strype's *Memorials*. See especially, R. H. Tawney, *Agricultural Problem of the Sixteenth Century*.

[63] 3 & 4 Edw. 6, c. 5.

[64] In the directions to the commissioners for a forced loan in 1557 they are informed that should any persons be " froward " they were to be compelled to find sureties to appear before the Privy Council when called on, or else to be arrested on the spot and sent to London. £110,000 was collected under this commission, in spite of outcry and resistance. Commission for the Loan, State Papers, Mary, Domestic, vols. xi, xii, cited in Froude, *History of England*, vi, 486. Compare the entries relating to the loan of 1556 in Tanner, *Tudor Documents*, 624.

the assent of parliament; and illegal modes of punishment, the torture especially, are " perhaps more frequently mentioned in her short reign than in all former ages of our history put together." [65]

In 1557, a commission was issued to Bishop Bonner and others authorising them to inquire rigorously concerning " devilish and clamorous persons " who spread seditious reports or brought in heretical and seditious books, or neglected or contemned the ceremonies of the church, and in some instances to fine, imprison, or " otherwise punish " the guilty; in others of a graver nature, to remit them to the spiritual courts. It was feared at the time that this proceeding was a preliminary to the establishment of the inquisition; it proved, in fact, to be one more precursor of the High Commission Court of the next reign.[66]

The violence of Mary's reign is in curious contrast with the humane and enlightened sentiments enunciated in the preamble of the first Act upon her statute book.[67] Like her immediate predecessor, Mary began her reign by a statute repealing all new treasons and felonies, although, as in this case, new treasons were very soon again introduced. In the preamble of the abolishing statute it is recited that the state of a king " standeth more assured by the love and favour of the subject towards their sovereign ruler and governor than in the dread and fear of laws made with rigorous pains and extreme punishment "; and that laws made without extreme punishment are more often obeyed than laws made with extreme punishment.

Powers of a queen regnant. Mary was the first queen regnant of England (for it is unnecessary to take into account the few days' reign of the unfortunate Lady Jane Grey),[68] and some doubts were at one time raised as to her constitutional powers. Some of the reformed preachers even went so far as to contend that the government of a woman was both prohibited by the word of God, and unrecognised by the laws of the land, which conferred no authority upon queens. On the other hand a silly book was written to exalt Mary's prerogative, on the pretence that as queen she was not bound by the laws of former kings. Mary showed her contempt for this sophism by herself throwing the book into the fire. But to set all questions at rest an Act was passed in 1554 to declare that the royal power and dignities are invested in a queen the same as in a

---

[65] Hallam, *Constitutional History*, i, 42. C. H. Williams, *Tudor Despotism*, contains an important new estimate of her reign and character.

[66] Burnet, *History of the Reformation*, ii, 347, and Collection of Records, No. 32, ii, p. 311. The first such commission was issued to Thomas Cromwell in 1535, Tanner, *Tudor Constitutional Documents*, 360, *infra*, p. 303.

[67] 1 Mary, c. 1, an Act to " repeal and take away treasons, felonies, and cases of praemunire."

[68] Jane was nominally queen from July 6 to 19, 1553, but Mary dated her second regnal year from July 6, 1554, thus ignoring the short reign of Jane. After the capture of King Stephen at the battle of Lincoln, in February, 1141, the Empress Matilda was elected " *Domina Angliae* " on April 8 following; but although she held courts and issued charters in royal form, she never succeeded in making good her claim to the crown.

king, and that all statutes in which a king was named applied equally
to a queen.[69]

PARLIAMENT UNDER THE EARLIER TUDORS

The momentous events related in the present and succeeding chapters
were accompanied by equally important developments in the history of
institutions.

Parliament was necessarily associated with the religious revolutions
which swayed to and fro as Tudor succeeded Tudor. This was partly
because parliament's position as the supreme legislative organ of the
crown was so well established in history and public sentiment as to be
beyond challenge; partly also because Henry VIII liked to regard parliament as adding lustre to his already glittering majesty,[70] and thus
employ it for the purpose of impressing his brother monarchs. The
progress of research makes it increasingly evident that parliament was
no cypher, but an active partner in the Tudor adventure—unwilling,
perhaps, critical and sometimes recalcitrant, but still an essential partner
which had to be hectored or humoured into collaboration. The Tudors
were skilled in the use of both these devices, and needed all their skill
to keep the partnership together. On matters of regular taxation, the
commons were at their strongest. We have already seen that the appari-
tion of the cardinal in all his glory reduced the commons to silence but
not to compliance with the king's demands, and that he withdrew with
no answer save an ironic compliment from Mr. Speaker More.[71] In the
end, the statute book is witness to the fact that by fair means or foul
the Tudors contrived to maintain the association of parliament with their
projects, and to following ages, when there was inquiry into what parliament could do, and had done, there were prodigious precedents to be
cited from this period.[72]

Infrequent sessions. The infrequency of Henry VII's parliaments has
already been noted[73]; his son pursued the same policy. In a reign of
nearly thirty-eight years Henry VIII summoned nine parliaments. The
first sat for only a month and the sixth for nearly six weeks; the others
held two or three sessions lasting about a month or six weeks each. The
Reformation Parliament was exceptional in having eight sessions (according to modern reckoning) between its assembly on November 4, 1529,
and its dissolution on April 14, 1536 (although there was no session in
the years 1530 and 1535). Its nearest rival in longevity so far was the long
parliament of Edward IV whose seven sessions extended from October

---

[69] 1 Mary, sess. 3, c. 1 (Tanner, *Tudor Constitutional Documents*, 123). It was thus in large
part a sort of Interpretation Act. The main object, according to Dr. Tanner, was to make
it clear that the royal power was wholly in Mary notwithstanding her approaching marriage
with Philip of Spain, the treaty for which was confirmed in this parliament.

[70] *Cf.* his letter to the pope (*supra*, p. 220) and his speech in *Ferrers' Case, infra*, p. 250.

[71] *Supra*, p. 229.

[72] As in Blackstone, *Commentaries*, i, 161.

[73] *Supra*, p. 228.

1472 to November 1475. There were numerous instances of a whole year passing without a parliamentary session; still more remarkable is the fact that the seven years from 1515 to 1523 and the six years from 1523 to 1529 saw no parliament. Edward VI had annual sessions of his first parliament (save for one interval of nearly two years), and Mary's reign looks almost medieval with its five parliaments holding seven sessions in a reign of five years. Elizabeth reverted to the practice of Henry VIII. The growing rarity of parliaments did nothing, however, to diminish public interest in the institution. At the parliament of 1523 " Cardinal Wolsey found himself much grieved with the burgesses thereof for that nothing was so soon done or spoken therein but that it was immediately blown abroad in every ale house." [74]

Composition of the lords. Over the composition of parliament, the crown exerted increasing influence. With the disappearance of the abbots, the bishops became still more important for they had long been in substance royal nominees. Henry VIII created new sees for Oxford, Peterborough, Gloucester, Bristol and Chester (Westminster was soon suppressed), but the lay peerage he kept small, with very few new creations. One of the projects preceding the Statute of Uses shows that he was willing to give extraordinary privileges to the peers, making their lands inalienable, and giving to them exclusively the right of entail; but the commons defeated the proposal and when the Statute of Uses finally passed it conformed to the settled tradition of the country by making no distinction between noble and commoner. [75]

Composition of the commons. Notable additions were made to the commons by the statutory grant of representation to Wales and Chester. [76] Henry VIII created only five new borough constituencies by prerogative, but Edward VI created or restored twenty-two boroughs, of which at least half, including seven in Cornwall, were places of no kind of importance. Mary added fourteen to the number, and Elizabeth, in a similar manner, increased the representation in parliament by no less than sixty-two members. [77] The interference of the crown in elections was exerted

[74] William Roper, *Life of Thomas More* (ed. Hitchcock), 16.
[75] *Cf. supra*, p. 153 Holdsworth, *History of English Law*, iv, 540 *et seq.*; Maitland, *English Law and the Renaissance* (1901), 45, note 11. The tendency to formalise the social distinctions, although their medieval significance had largely disappeared, is seen in the statute of 1539 fixing the order of precedence (31 Hen. 8, c. 10), in the creation of the Heralds' College under Richard III, the numerous heraldic visitations *temp.* Henry VIII and later, the numerous acts graduating the dress of all ranks of the peerage and society, and the rise of the doctrine of ennobled blood (*supra*, p. 153, note 14; *cf.* 21 Hen. 8, c. 13, ss. 14 *et seq.*).
[76] *Supra*, pp. 235–236.
[77] But *cf.* Pollard, *Factors in Modern History*, p. 122, who points out the significant fact that Peter Wentworth, " one of the most courageous and assertive champions of Parliamentary liberty who ever opposed the Crown," and his brother Paul, " who was scarcely less distinguished as a Parliamentary critic of the Crown," sat for the two Cornish boroughs of Tregony and Liskeard respectively. " If," says Professor Pollard, " these Cornish boroughs were really created in order to make the House of Commons subservient, the Crown was indeed hoist with its own petard."

in the most open manner. In 1553 Edward VI directed a circular letter to all sheriffs, commanding them to apprise the freeholders, citizens, and burgesses of their respective counties, " that our pleasure and command-ment is, that they shall choose and appoint, as nigh as they possibly may, men of knowledge and experience within their counties, cities, and boroughs "; and especially that whenever the Privy Council, or any of them, having instructions on the king's behalf, should " recommend men of learning and wisdom, in such case their directions be regarded and followed." Accordingly several persons—all of them belonging to the court, or in places of trust about the king—were recommended by letters to the sheriffs, and elected as knights for different shires.[78] The writs for the parliament summoned by Mary in 1554, to sanction the return of the country to obedience to the apostolic see, were accompanied in like manner by royal circulars requiring the mayors, sheriffs, and other influential persons to admonish the electors to " choose of their inhabi-tants, as being eligible by order of our laws, may be of the wise, grave, and catholic sort." [79]

The king's servants in the commons. Contemporaries are all agreed that " the king's servants " exerted a powerful influence in the commons. They might be household officers, courtiers, lawyers or aspiring politicians; the most eminent of them were members of the king's council, however, and their position in both bodies gave them the opportunity of serving as the link between the king and the commons. They took charge of royal business in the House, and kept the king informed of the sentiments of the commons.[80] Promising young members who showed ability in opposition attracted the king's attention, and he took pains to attach to his court those who seemed able to impress the House—Sir Thomas More and Thomas Cromwell are examples under Henry VIII. The government had its " bills " ready drafted by the council,[81] and it was for the king's servants to pilot them through the House.

---

[78] Hallam, *Constitutional History*, i, 46, citing Strype, ii, 394. What appear to be first drafts of circular letters are preserved in Lansd. MS. 3, cited by Froude, v, 464, n. 1. In some instances the orders of the crown were sent direct to the candidate himself. The Council, in a letter to Sir P. Hoby, inform him " that his Majesty hath willed us to signify unto you this his pleasure to have you one of the Commons House, which thing we also require you to foresee, that either for the county where ye abide ye be chosen knight, or else otherwise to have some place in the House, like as all others of your degree be appointed. And herein, if either his Majesty or we knew where to recommend you, according to your own desires, we would not fail but provide the same." Harl. MS. 523, in Froude, v, 465. *Cf.* further instances in Pickthorn, *Tudor Government*, ii, 404.

[79] Letter of the Queen to the Earl of Sussex in Burnet, *Collection*, iii, 210. *Cf.* Froude, vi, 260. These general directions were copied from a form which had been in use under Henry VII.

[80] On all this see W. Notestein, *The Winning of the Initiative by the House of Commons* (British Academy, 1924).

[81] *Cf. supra*, pp. 188–190. Before, or during, parliament the judges could be consulted upon legislative policy, and traces of their debates may be found in the Year Books, *e.g.*, 1 Hen. 7, Mich., No. 5 (1485), a case whose genuineness seems established by Dr. M. Hemmant in the Selden Society publications, vol. 51, p. 185; and 1 Hen. 7, Hil. no. 25 (1486). Both cases are reprinted in A. F. Pollard, *Henry VII*, ii, 10–11.

Parliament and legislation. It is hardly possible to determine how far the legislation of Henry VIII, Edward VI and Mary (and especially their ecclesiastical measures) enjoyed the unfeigned assent of the commons, or how far the commons themselves represented the opinion of the country. As we have seen, the crown had considerable opportunities of securing the election of a number of its nominees, and they in turn formed a compact group of government supporters within the House. Notwithstanding these very real advantages, the crown had to face serious opposition in the commons. Parliament was far from being merely the registrar of royal ordinances. In some cases surviving documents show how stubborn was the resistance of the commons and how successful they were in materially modifying the crown's legislative projects. Thus a very long and elaborate series of negotiations, beginning in 1529, led up to the great Statute of Uses of 1536.[82] Neither the king nor the peers secured the measures they desired, both having to accept the compromise which for nearly four centuries stood upon the statute book. The Statute of Wills of 1540 was reluctantly accorded by the crown after the Pilgrimage of Grace had made it clear that landowners would have to be placated if the crown wished to retain their support. There, possibly, lay the key to the situation. The routine work of local government, and the application of any special policies which the crown or parliament might adopt, depended upon the principal gentry of the counties for their effective conduct and enforcement. These men were indispensable in quarter sessions and upon countless commissions, and their political influence in the countryside could be a decisive factor. In the House of Commons their attitude was no less vital. Nor was this independent temper of the commons confined to questions of fiscality and private law. It is now known that the treason legislation of Henry VIII was hotly debated; some treason bills were rejected, or had to be withdrawn; others were much amended; the Act of Six Articles and the Statute of Proclamations are other examples.[83] The lords were also willing to make a stand: the king was given to understand that they would reject the bill of attainder against More and Fisher unless More's name was omitted. At first the king proposed to go to the House and bluster it through; he soon thought better of it and More's name was omitted.[84]

THE SPEAKERS

The Speaker of the commons during this period continued to rise in importance. The tendency seems to have shifted towards selecting lawyers rather than business men and civil servants. Both Sir Edmund Dudley and Sir Thomas More were Under-Sheriffs of London when

[82] The whole story, which is an excellent illustration of Tudor technique, must be read in Holdsworth, *History of English Law*, iv, 450–466.
[83] I. D. Thornley, " Treason Legislation of Henry VIII," in *Transactions of the Royal Historical Society* (1917), 87–123; K. Pickthorn, *Tudor Government*, ii, 407, 414.
[84] R. W. Chambers, *Thomas More*, 299–300.

elected Speaker—a judicial office with an important commercial jurisdiction which was a good training for subsequent trade missions. Three
of Henry VII's Speakers (Mordaunt, Empson and Bray) soon became
chancellors of the duchy of Lancaster; three of Henry VIII's became
chancellors of England (More, Audley, Rich). Under Edward VI and
Mary the judiciary seems the commonest destination of the Speaker:
Dyer and Brooke became famous as chief justices of the common pleas,
and others became either master of the rolls, chief baron, or chancellor
of the exchequer, and similar careers are thenceforward frequent until
the early eighteenth century, when politics rather than law lay before
the retiring Speaker. Not until the nineteenth century did the Speakership cease to be merely an incident in the professional life of a lawyer
or politician, and attain its present position.

The Speaker and the commons. The development of the office under
Henry VIII was not spectacular, although subsequent events show that
it was in a significant direction. Short as sessions were, there was difficulty
in keeping members in attendance until the end, and so by an Act of
1515 (6 Hen. 8, c. 16) members were forbidden to depart " except
they have licence of the Speaker and commons in the said parliament
assembled, and the same licence be entered of record in the book of the
clerk of the parliament appointed . . . for the Commons' House." It
is notable that this delegation of royal power is made not only to the
Speaker (who was in any case very much of a royal officer) but to the
Speaker and the commons, thus beginning that characteristic relationship
whereby the commons controlled their own members through the
Speaker. It could hardly have been foreseen in 1515 that in the end the
Speaker would cease to be a royal supervisor and become in effect the
impersonation of the House's independence.[85]

The Speaker's claim for free speech. The newly elected Speaker,
on being presented to the king in the House of Lords, made his " protestation." As we have seen [86] this was in varying terms. Quite early
we find Speaker Pickering demanding " for himself " the usual permission
to correct mistakes, and demanding further " for the commons " that if
he should say anything on their behalf which angered the king, he would
overlook it—a claim, in fact, for the Speaker to have liberty of speech
when he speaks for the commons in parliament.[87] After 1413 this formula seems to disappear,[88] and in any case it did not refer to speech

---

[85] *Cf.* J. E. Neale in *Tudor Studies presented to A. F. Pollard*, 265–266. The act implies the
existence of a " book " of the commons; the earliest journal of the commons now extant,
however, is from 1547. There are Lords' Journals from 1509 onwards. See A. F. Pollard,
" Authenticity of the Lords' Journals," *Transactions of the Royal Historical Society*
(1914), 17 and J. E. Neale, " The Commons' Journals," *ibid.* (1920), 136.

[86] *Supra,* p. 209.

[87] *Rotuli Parliamentorum,* iii, 34 no. 16 (1378; Lodge and Thornton, 154, and *cf.* in 1411
ibid., iii, 648 no. 9). Taken together, these two passages suggest that the claim was to
free speech for the Speaker in parliament rather than for the commons among themselves.

[88] Neale, *loc. cit.*, 264.

among the commons in their separate consultations. Nor did *Haxey's Case* or *Yonge's Case* add anything at all definite to the problem, although the latter case unmistakably shows that the commons desired the recognition of the principle. Even so, Yonge had to wait for a political revolution before he could raise the matter, five years afterwards.[89] All the same, there are indications that a practice, if not yet a privilege, was growing up; thus in 1515 Convocation claimed to be as free in this matter as parliament—at least to the extent of one body not being punishable by the other for transgressing the boundaries of church and state as they were then understood.[90]

The next step was taken by Sir Thomas More when he was Speaker in 1523. To the traditional protestation he added a request that every man should discharge his conscience and declare his advice boldly " among us," without fear of the king's displeasure.[91] Here, then, is a clear claim for freedom of speech within the commons' House, covering the members and not merely the Speaker. The persuasive preamble suggests that More was making a new departure and not merely relying upon a time-honoured privilege. There was undoubtedly much free speaking in the commons and, indeed, in the lords, during the reign of Henry VIII,[92] but there was also a solid phalanx of privy councillors and minor ministers who marked well what was said, and kept the king informed. Often he discussed matters personally with his opponents and " forgave " them, but ultimately there were ways and means of applying stern sanctions.[93] Whether succeeding speakers continued More's claim is difficult to ascertain, for the entries in the Lords' Journal are quite unreliable. We can be sure that free speech was claimed in 1542, in 1554 and throughout Elizabeth's reign.[94] The commons, therefore, had achieved something: they had framed a form of words which embodied a principle, and time after time their claim was solemnly repeated. But it still remained for them to translate that claim into the peaceful enjoyment of a privilege.

PRIVILEGE

Strode's Case (1512). It was believed by Stuart lawyers that an important contribution was made to the subject of freedom of debate in

---

[89] *Supra*, p. 196.

[90] *Letters and Papers of Henry VIII*, II (ii), 1105, 1312, 1313. This was part of Dr. Standish's case, for which see K. Pickthorn, *Tudor Government*, ii, 115 *et seq.* for Keilway's *Reports* (used by Brewer in the *Letters and Papers*) see now A. W. B. Simpson in *Law Quarterly Review* (1957), lxxiii, 89 *et seq.*

[91] W. Roper, *Life of More* (ed. E. V. Hitchcock), 16 (and in J. R. Tanner, *Constitutional Documents of James I*, 382–383); Neale, *loc. cit.*, 267.

[92] In 1547 Gardiner could refer to debates in Henry VIII's House of Lords " where was free speech without danger ": *Letters of Stephen Gardiner* (ed. J. A. Muller), 392; *cf. ibid.*, 398–399: " Doctor Crome, a mean man, preached against our late sovereign lord's determinations, and how daintily was he handled to relieve his conscience!"

[93] Neale, *loc. cit.*, 269–270.

[94] Supplicavit Regie Majestati: " Ut in dicendis sententiis quivis libere et impune eloqui posset quid animi haberet et quid consilii "—*Lords' Journals*, i, 167; Tanner, *Tudor Constitutional Documents*, 551; Prothero, *Constitutional Documents*, 117; Neale, *loc. cit.*, 271.

1512 (4 Henry 8), when, in consequence of the proceedings in *Strode's Case*, an important Act was passed, which it was thought not only admitted, by implication, the existence of the privilege, but was also designed to protect, in future, all members of either House from any question on account of their speeches or votes in parliament. As there has been much misapprehension over the case for some centuries, it is particularly necessary to examine the Act with care. The facts seem to be as follows. Richard Strode, member for the borough of Plympton in Devonshire, had proposed certain bills in parliament to regulate the tinners in that county. Those who thought their interests were being prejudiced took the view that Strode's activities were an offence against an act of their local stannary " parliament " which imposed a penalty on all who obstruct tin mining. They therefore procured (without his knowledge) his conviction in the Stannary Courts [95] on four indictments alleging that he had, " at the Parliament holden at Westminster the fourth day of February last past, letted, vexed and troubled one William Read . . . and all other tinners in the same parliament for digging of tin . . . contrary to this our Act made." He was in consequence fined and imprisoned,[96] as the statute recites, " in a doungen and a depe pytt under grounde in the Castell of Lidford, and there and elsewhere remayned by the space of thre wekys and more, unto such tyme he was delyvered by a wrete of Privilege out of the Kyngges Eschequer Westminster, for that he was one of the collectours in the said countie for the first of the twoo quyndezims graunted at and in this present Parliament." The statute proceeds to declare these proceedings of the Stannary Court void, and further: " That sutes, accusementes, condempnacions, execucions, fynes, ameriamentes, punysshmentes, etc., putte or had, or hereafter to be put or hadde unto or uppon the said Richard, and to every other of the person or persons afore specified

---

[95] The court for the Stannaries of Cornwall and Devon is a court of special jurisdiction, similar in character to the court of the Lord Warden of the Cinque Ports, the courts of the Counties Palatine of Lancaster and Durham, and other special courts instituted in derogation from the general jurisdiction of the courts of common law, for the local redress of private wrongs. It is founded on an ancient privilege granted to the workers in the tin mines to sue and be sued (in all matters arising within the Stannaries, excepting pleas of life, land, or members) in their own court before a judge called the vice-warden of the Stannaries. This privilege was confirmed by charter of 23 Edw. 1, and by statutes 50 Edw. 3, and 16 Car. 1, c. 15, and the court has been regulated by several later statutes. Formerly an appeal lay from the Stannary Court to the lord warden, from thence to the privy council of the Prince of Wales as Duke of Cornwall, from thence to the sovereign; but by statute 18 & 19 Vict. c. 32, s. 26, an appeal from all decrees and orders of the vice-warden was given to the lord warden assisted by two legal assessors, and from the lord warden a final appeal to the Judicial Committee of the Privy Council. By the Supreme Court of Judicature Act, 1873 (36 & 37 Vict. c. 36), all the jurisdiction and powers of the lord warden of the Stannaries assisted by his assessors were transferred to the new Court of Appeal established by that Act. By the Stannaries Court Abolition Act, 1896 (59 & 60 Vict. c. 45), this court, which still lingered in that of the vice-warden, was finally abolished, and its powers transferred to such of the new county courts as the lord chancellor should direct. *Cf.* Holdsworth, *History of English Law*, i, 151–165; G. R. Lewis, *The Stannaries*.

[96] At the suit (in an action of debt) of one to whom the crown had assigned a part of the (as yet unpaid) penalty.

that nowe be of this present Parliament, or that of any Parliament hereafter shalbe, for any bill, spekyng, reasonyng, or declaryng of any mater
or maters concernyng the Parliament, to be communed and treated of,
be utterly voyd and of non effecte."

Such is the story told in the lengthy Act which finally gave Strode
his remedy.[97] It is immediately clear that the root of the matter is the
schedule to the Act which contains the text of the preposterous indictments against Strode. The point raised was simple: could Strode be
indicted under a local by-law against hindering miners because he had
promoted bills in parliament on the subject of mining? The Act gave the
only possible answer, but in a flood of indignant verbiage which acquired
a new meaning, as we shall see, in the next century.[98] In 1512 (some
years before Sir Thomas More made his tentative claim to liberty) the
question of free speech in parliament was still very obscure but this at
least was sure—members were not indictable in petty tribunals for their
actions in parliament.[99]

Ferrers' Case (1543): writ of privilege. The cases of privilege so far
considered were dealt with either by the king, lords and commons concurring (as in *Strode's Case*) in an " Act," or by writ of privilege issued
on application to the chancellor.[1] The first occasion on which the commons acted independently of any other power in the vindication of their
privilege was in the important case of George Ferrers, a member who, in
1543, was arrested, as surety for the debt of another, by process out of
the King's Bench. On hearing of the arrest, the House sent their serjeant
to demand the release of the imprisoned member. The serjeant, being
resisted by the gaolers and sheriffs of London, was obliged to return
empty-handed; whereupon the House rose as a body and laid their case
before the lords " who, judging the contempt to be very great, referred
the punishment thereof to the order of the Commons' House." The
lord chancellor offered them a writ of privilege, but they refused it, " being
in a clear opinion that all commandments and other acts proceeding from
the Nether House were to be done and executed by their serjeant without
writ, only by show of his mace, which was his warrant." Accordingly,
the serjeant was again ordered by the commons to go to the sheriffs and
demand the delivery of Ferrers; but in the meantime the sheriffs, becoming
alarmed, had surrendered the prisoner. They were, however, ordered
by the House to attend at the bar, together with the gaolers and even
the plaintiff in the suit, and on appearing were all committed to prison
for contempt. These proceedings were reported to King Henry VIII,
who thereupon summoned the chancellor, judges, the Speaker, and some

[97] 4 Hen. 8, c. 8; Tanner, *Tudor Documents*, 558, which omits large portions, and the schedule.
[98] *Infra*, p. 378 note 55.
[99] Under any other view most borough members would be in peril from town corporations
and guilds whose interests (usually fortified by by-laws) might be affected by proposed
legislation.
[1] *Supra*, pp. 198–199.

of the gravest persons of the commons, and delivered a very remarkable address. After commending the wisdom of the commons in maintaining the privileges of their House, and stating that even their cooks and horse-keepers were free from arrest, he is reported to have said: " And further we be informed by our judges that we at no time stand so highly in our estate royal, as in the time of Parliament; wherein we as head, and you as members, are conjoined and knit together into one body politick, so as whatsoever offence or injury, during that time, is offered to the meanest member of the House is to be judged as done against our person and the whole court of Parliament; which prerogative of the court is so great (as our learned counsel informeth us), as all acts and processes coming out of any other inferior courts must, for the time, cease, and give place to the highest." Following the king, " Sir Edward Montagu, lord chief justice, very gravely told his opinion, confirming by divers reasons all that the king had said, which was assented unto by all the residue, none speaking to the contrary." [2] Ferrers was a servant of the king, who, probably on that account, was the more inclined to regard the energetic proceedings of the commons with favour.

Henceforward, although a writ of privilege was still occasionally employed to effect the release of members, it was not permitted to be obtained without a previous warrant from the Speaker.

Membership of the commons. This assumption by the commons, with the acquiescence of the king, of jurisdiction to maintain their privilege without recourse to any outside authority placed the commons on the same footing, procedurally, as the courts of law, which had long exercised the right of protecting their members, staff and litigants from molestation, and this newly won position was to become in future centuries the basis of their most sweeping claims. For the moment, however, it was merely one of several features which contributed to the enhancement of the commons' dignity and, to some extent, of their effective management of their own affairs. We have already seen that the Speaker and the House were given some statutory power over members [3]; in the middle of the century they assumed the jurisdiction of passing upon the qualification of members. Thus in 1550 they determined that Sir Francis Russell should continue a member although he had subsequently become heir-apparent to the Earl of Bedford [4]; and in 1553, the first year of Queen Mary, the journals of the commons record the appointment of a committee to inquire if Alexander Nowell, prebendary of Westminster, may be of the House. On the following day they reported that " Alexander Nowell, being prebendary in Westminster, and thereby having voice in the Convocation House, cannot be a member

[2] Holinshed, *Chronicle*, iii, 824; Tanner, *Tudor Documents*, 580–583.
[3] *Supra*, p. 246.
[4] *Commons' Journals*, i, 15; Tanner, *op. cit.*, 596; *supra*, p. 154 n. 15. Sir Edwin Sandys sat in parliament, 1586–1593, while holding a prebend at York, but he was a layman.

of this House, and the queen's writ to be directed for another burgess in that place." [5]

King and ministers. The Tudor age is the age of over-great ministers, and it is instructive to observe their careers and the fate awaiting them. Henry VII's Empson and Dudley, both of them ex-Speakers, rose to no great office, although their political influence was very considerable. Their " fall " was certainly not the result of attacks by the public, or by political opponents, but was deliberately contrived by the crown, since it would provide good publicity for the new reign. In short, it was an example of the new politics of prestige, such as Machiavelli had described. Wolsey's career was a novel combination of age-old elements. To the position of favourite and confidential adviser he added the office of lord chancellor, which by itself conferred the outward symbols of the king's principal minister in the medieval tradition. To this formidable combination of power Wolsey added the jurisdiction of *legatus a latere* which made him for many purposes equivalent to the pope for English affairs. It needed the Act of Supremacy to make Henry himself the successor of Wolsey. Wolsey's fall, again, was not primarily the work of his enemies, but of the king who had no further use for him since he had failed to secure the divorce. Sir Thomas More's short tenure of the great seal shows that the office alone did not guarantee that its holder would be the principal minister—that role was already being played by Thomas Cromwell. Cromwell's official position was that of king's secretary (the first holder of the office to become prominent). Later, as vicar-general, he exercised Henry's ecclesiastical supremacy, much as Wolsey had exercised the pope's as legate *a latere*. Like Wolsey, he fell from office for the sole reason that the king withdrew his confidence. Henry VIII's ministers were heartily hated by the nobility and by the public generally, but their rise and fall was the work of the crown, and not the result of public or parliamentary pressure.

MINISTERS AND COUNCILS

King and baronage. The theme, so familiar in the later Middle Ages, of the baronial opposition, finally disappears from English history under the Tudors. This was primarily a social and economic phenomenon, but its constitutional results were momentous. The peers, in spite of their temporary alliance with the crown, had been signally defeated in the negotiations for the Statute of Uses; many of them were tied to the government by the monastic lands granted to them; their most prominent leaders often derived their influence, not from their own territorial resources or their personal qualities, but from their bonds of kindred or affinity with the monarch.[6]

[5] *Commons' Journals*, i, 27; Tanner, *op. cit.*, 596; *cf. supra*, p. 143 n. 73.
[6] Notably the Seymours and the Howards through their marriages with Henry VIII.

The Council under the Tudors. The decline of the peerage is particularly evident in the history of the council. Their pretensions in the fourteenth, and their disastrous achievements in the fifteenth centuries have already been mentioned.[7] The failure of the Lancastrian experiment—which was essentially an experiment in baronial, rather than in parliamentary government—prompted the Yorkists to pursue a different policy, which seems to have been continued by Henry VII and in the earlier years of Henry VIII.[8] This consisted in having a large number of people who are described individually as " councillors " although " the council " as an assembly seems to have been rather less numerous. One has the impression of a large panel of technicians, ecclesiastical, financial, legal, diplomatic, etc., who could be consulted as occasion demanded, but who did not habitually meet all together as members of a " council." In both cases the lords are fewer in number and clearly less influential.

The Star Chamber. Nevertheless, the medieval council continued to exist uninterrupted, and to conduct its business in the sixteenth as in the fifteenth century in its traditional quarters, the star chamber. That business was becoming steadily more legal and less political; indeed, it was too large and miscellaneous a body to be entrusted with the confidential discussion of high policy. The plausible suggestion has been made that it was too large even for the task of maintaining public order, and that the select body set up by the " Star Chamber " Act of 1487 was made necessary by the fact that the council as a whole might include some notable offenders.[9] Moreover, its judicial functions meant also that the star chamber sat in public. In the sixteenth and seventeenth centuries its opening and closing sessions of the term, when attendance was particularly large, were renowned as magnificent and impressive spectacles, often marked by an important speech from the throne on the general political situation.

The king himself sometimes presided at these public sessions; in his absence, the chancellor took his place, and, as in the Middle Ages, remained the most constant and most influential member of the court. Already, therefore, the office of chancellor was becoming exceptionally laborious, for its holder had not only his department to administer, but also the court of chancery where he was the sole judge, and the star chamber where he was the presiding officer for most practical purposes. In composition the court was certainly large. If the most intimate councillors of the king, and the highest officials, formed the core, there was also assembled round them a varying number of common law judges

---

[7] *Supra*, pp. 213 *et seq.*

[8] On all that follows, see the important contributions of A. F. Pollard, " The Council under the Tudors," *English Historical Review*, xxxvii, 337–360, 516–539, xxxviii, 42–60, and C. G. Bayne, *Select Cases in The Council of Henry VII* (Selden Society, vol. 75). There is a good selection of material from the contemporary legal writers, and the records, in Tanner, *Tudor Documents*, 249–298.

[9] Pollard, *English Historical Review*, xxxvii, 526. The work of the Star Chamber in its general aspects has already been noticed: *supra*, pp. 118–119, 216, 226.

and other specialists, together with an array of distinguished persons, whose principal function was to lend dignity to the proceedings. It was occasionally urged that all peers were entitled to attend, but they were never recognised as members of the court merely in virtue of their peerage.[10]

The history of the clerkship of the council is an interesting testimony to the continuity of the institution.[11] In the fifteenth century the principal clerk was generally also the secondary of the privy seal, and to ease his burden he was often provided with a deputy or associate who devoted his time principally to the council's business, and so it was this latter who came to be described as clerk of the council. At the close of the century one or both of these officers was frequently a civilian, several of them becoming admiralty judges. It is clear that the practice grew up of describing the clerk of the council as " clerk of the council in the Star Chamber " (for other councils elsewhere now had clerks of their own) and finally as " clerk of the Star Chamber."

Court of requests. In 1483 an additional (but less lucrative) clerkship appears, whose holder is to keep order in the already voluminous archives of " requests " (or poor persons' petitions, which had long been regarded by the council as entitled to especially sympathetic and expeditious handling); he is styled " clerk of the council of the said requests " [12] and his appointment is a clear indication that " requests " are now being administered separately—a differentiation which results in a definitely separate institution when the council thrusts away the burden upon a group of specially appointed " masters of requests." By Wolsey's time the court of requests was insufficient, and so the cardinal organised poor persons' courts before the king's almoner, in the lord treasurer's chamber, and at the Rolls, as well as in the older court of requests whose sittings were now fixed in the white hall.[13] The " court of conscience in the Guild Hall " of London, founded it seems in 1518, may also be due to Wolsey's solicitude for the poor.[14] Meantime, yet another junior clerkship had appeared from 1509 onwards, and this developed slowly into the clerkship of the privy council.[15]

The council attendant upon the king. Space, as well as time, played a part in moulding our institutions. The king during the Middle Ages and for long afterwards was constantly perambulating the country;

[10] Pollard, *English Historical Review*, xxxvii, 536.
[11] The details, though complicated, are tolerably clear : J. F. Baldwin, *The King's Council*, 362 *et seq.*; A. F. Pollard, *English Historical Review*, xxxvii, 343–351.
[12] Pollard, *loc. cit.*, 344.
[13] Pollard, *loc. cit.*, 532.
[14] I. S. Leadham, *Select Cases in the Court of Requests* (Selden Society), liii.
[15] It would be well to mention here the " Council learned in the Law," of which Mr. R. Somerville has written in *English Historical Review*, vol. liv; " there can be little doubt that the Council learned was part of the machinery by which the well-known exactions of Empson and Dudley were carried out " : C. G. Bayne in Selden Society, vol. lxxv, p. xxviii. *Cf.* H. E. Bell, *Court of Wards*, 4–5, 10–12.

moreover, from time to time he was on the Continent, campaigning. Wherever he was, he needed counsel. On the other hand, the routine work of government was concerned with the direction of several departments of state, each with a large permanent staff, and dependent upon an elaborate equipment of files and records; in other words, the system required a fixed seat of government. As early as the twelfth century these conditions were already in existence and as we have seen [16] they compelled the *Curia Regis* to assume two forms, one fixed, and the other following the king. The same causes were to produce the same result with the council. In the Middle Ages the council frequently broke into two groups, one remaining at the seat of government (usually Westminster or London) and the other following the king; as soon as circumstances permitted, the council once again became a single body. Indeed, it never really ceased to be one, for there was never any question of creating two separate institutions.[17]

The same situation prevailed during the first half-century of the Tudor era. As early as 1504 a statute made certain offenders answerable " before the chancellor . . . in the star chamber, or before the king in his Bench, or before the king and his council attending upon his most royal person wheresoever he be." [18] If the council, fixed in the star chamber, and the council attendant upon the king became distinct institutions, it is because there was more than the merely geographical factor involved. The council in the star chamber, in fact, was becoming so immersed in judicial affairs that it was unsuitable for advisory and executive action, and so a small group of confidential advisers, attendant upon the king wherever he happened to be, came into existence as the normal body for consultation upon political matters. One obvious difference between the two bodies was the fact that in the star chamber the proceedings were public; the inner group however was concerned only with the king, and to describe it as " privy " was merely a statement of fact. Under Henry VII and also under Henry VIII there was experiment and variation, but the general direction of development is clear. A stage is marked by the " Eltham Ordinance " for the regulation of the royal household which Wolsey drew up in 1526.[19] That scheme was not strictly carried out, but it did state the significant policy that the king ought to have about twenty councillors attendant upon his person; from the twenty names it mentions it is clear that about half of the persons suggested would also be normally with the council in the star chamber—and thus unable to attend the king if he were more than a few miles from Westminster.

[16] *Supra*, p. 111.
[17] J. F. Baldwin, *The King's Council*, 397.
[18] 19 Hen. 7, c. 14.
[19] Printed in *Ordinances for the Household* (Society of Antiquaries, 1790), 159; Tanner, *Tudor Documents*, 220–221. For the textual problem, see Pollard, *English Historical Review*, xxxvii, 358, n. 7.

The privy council. After a long period of experiment, the " privy council " attained a fairly stable position by 1540.[20]   Already in 1538 the appointment of a separate clerk with the title " clerk of the privy council," to distinguish him from the clerk of the star chamber, had marked the essential separateness of the newer body from the council. At the same time, the indefinite mass of " ordinary " councillors or " councillors at large " was left in the outer darkness while a small circle of " privy " councillors tightened their grip upon the conduct of the most important affairs.   In 1540 the appearance of the first of a series of privy council registers is the visible sign of the reorganised and stabilised privy council.

Its numbers were kept very close to nineteen, which some years of experience had shown to be more effective than the large bodies which there was always a tendency to create.   Its membership contained few nobles (and they of recent creation), and even fewer bishops—so complete was the break with the tradition of the medieval council.   From 1540 onwards, Henry VIII likewise excluded judges from the privy council (although they were, of course, prominent in the judicial work of the star chamber).   The interesting suggestion has been made by Professor Pollard that so strong a government could afford to separate the judicial from the executive function, and thus to leave the privy council as a purely executive body.   The two chief justices reappear however in the privy councils of Edward VI and Mary; under Elizabeth no judge sat in the privy council for forty years until in 1599 Chief Justice Popham joined it—thus foreshadowing the dangerous Stuart policy of assimilating the composition of the privy council and star chamber.

Council government. Having become a distinct institution, the privy council rapidly acquired a position of supremacy among the organs of government.   Its own administrative machinery was enlarged to meet the immense demands upon its activity, and through its control of subordinate councils of the West, of Calais, of Boulogne, of New Haven, of Limerick, of the Scottish Border, of the North, it held the central position in a coherent system of conciliar government.[21]

---

[20] Pollard, *English Historical Review*, xxxviii, 42–60.
[21] The creation, or re-creation, of several of these bodies seems to owe much to Wolsey, who had in mind a plan of conciliar government.   For a brief account see Tanner, *Tudor Documents*, 314 *et seq.*   Important monographs are C. A. J. Skeel, *The Council in the Marches of Wales* (1904); R. R. Reid, *The Council of the North* (1921); and C. A. J. Skeel, " The Council of the West," *Transactions of the Royal Historical Society* (1921), 62—this last, founded in 1539, did not survive Henry VIII.

CHAPTER 10

THE REFORMATION IN ENGLAND

THE separation of the Church of England from that of Rome, formally accomplished under Henry VIII, was a political and legal rather than a religious reformation. The doctrinal changes which followed under Edward VI and Elizabeth were an unintentional consequence, to which Henry and his parliament more than once declared themselves utterly repugnant. But in reality the reformation, in both its political and religious aspects, was the effect of causes which had been in operation for centuries, not only in England, but throughout Europe. " No revolution," says Hallam, " has ever been more gradually prepared than that which separated almost one half of Europe from the communion of the Roman see; nor were Luther and Zwingli any more than occasional instruments of that change which, had they never existed, would at no great distance of time have been effected under the names of some other reformers. At the beginning of the sixteenth century, the learned doubtfully and with caution, the ignorant with zeal and eagerness, were tending to depart from the faith and rites which authority prescribed." [1]

THE ENGLISH CHURCH AND THE PAPACY

In England, the spiritual primacy of the pope and his authority in matters of faith were reverently admitted, but the exorbitant claims of jurisdiction and territorial power asserted by Hildebrand and his successors, together with the pecuniary exactions founded on those claims, were persistently, though with varying degrees of firmness, resisted by the English kings and people. Impatience at discipline, and discontent at taxation, however, need not imply a denial of the fundamental right of government; clergy and nobles grumbled loudly at the new vigour of a succession of powerful reforming and centralising popes, but they had no answer to the logic of the theologians and the canonists. That canon law, moreover, was accepted by English ecclesiastical courts as the undoubted law of the church, and it is erroneous to suppose that the English church ever asserted its independence by denying it.[2]

Until Henry III. Prior to the Norman Conquest, church and state in England were so intimately united that they were practically identical.

---

[1] Hallam, *Constitutional History*, i, 57.
[2] For the whole subject, see Maitland, *Roman Canon Law in the Church of England* (1898); A. L. Smith, *Church and State in the Middle Ages* (1913); Z. N. Brooke, *The English Church and the Papacy* (1931). All these authors reject the view of Stubbs in the *Report of the Ecclesiastical Courts Commission* of 1883, and in his *Seventeen Lectures* (1886) reprinted in *Select Essays in Anglo-American Legal History*, i, 248, who had maintained that canon law was of persuasive but not of binding authority in England.

William of Normandy, to further his designs on England, entered into an alliance with the papacy; and when the Conquest—which it had been his object to present to the eyes of Europe somewhat in the light of a crusade—had been effected, the ecclesiastical power was to a great extent separated from the civil power and placed in much closer communion with and subordination to the papal see. But anxious as he was to propitiate the see of Rome, William was careful not to surrender the ancient supremacy of the state over the national church.[3] Still, the impetus given by the Conquest to the papal power in England caused it to go on rising, until—notwithstanding the partial checks which it received under Henry I and Henry II, on the questions of investitures and clerical immunity from civil jurisdiction—it reached its acme under John and Henry III. For one hundred and fifty years succeeding the Conquest the right of influencing and assenting to the election of the archbishops, bishops, and mitred abbots had been claimed and exercised by the king. This right had been specially asserted by the Constitutions of Clarendon, which also provided that the revenues of vacant sees should belong to the crown.[4] But John admitted all the papal claims, surrendering even his kingdom to the pope, and receiving it back as a fief of the holy see. By the charter granted to the church in 1214, which was confirmed by the Great Charter in the following year, the church recovered its liberties, the right of free election was conceded to the cathedral chapters and the religious houses, and the right of custody of vacant churches was alone reserved to the crown.[5] Every election was, however, subject to the approval of the pope, which was signified, in the case of archbishops, by the gift of the pallium. Under Henry III the popes by means of provision and reservation interfered extensively with the rights of private patrons, lay and ecclesiastical; and Gregory IX even went to the length of ordering the bishops of Lincoln and Salisbury to provide for not less than three hundred foreign ecclesiastics. The system of papal provision was so greatly abused that it soon degenerated into a mere channel for draining money into the Roman exchequer.

Edward I and the Pope. Under Edward I the barons, if not the king himself, firmly withstood the exactions of the pope, and re-asserted the independence of both church and crown. To the letter of Boniface VIII claiming to be feudal lord of Scotland, and commanding Edward I to withdraw his troops from that kingdom and submit his pretensions to the decision of the papal see, the parliament of England drew up in 1301 a very emphatic repudiation of the pope's temporal jurisdiction in a letter to which seven earls and ninety-seven barons affixed their seals. " The kings of England," they said, " have never pleaded, or been bound to plead, respecting their rights in the kingdom of Scotland, or any othe'

[3] *Supra*, pp. 43 *et seq.*
[4] Cap. xii; Stubbs, *Select Charters*, p. 166; *supra*, pp. 60.
[5] *Select Charters*, pp. 283 *et seq.*, and Magna Carta, c. 1.

their temporal rights, before any judge, ecclesiastical or secular. It is, therefore, and by the grace of God shall always be, our common and unanimous resolve that with respect to the rights of his kingdom of Scotland, or other his temporal rights, our aforesaid lord the king shall not plead before you, nor submit in any manner to your judgment, nor suffer his right to be brought in question by any inquiry, nor send agents or procurators for that purpose to your Court. . . . Neither do we, nor will we, permit, as we neither can nor ought, our aforesaid lord the king to do, or attempt to do, even if he wished it, any of the things aforesaid." [6] The letter was never sent. Edward I, like many other monarchs, discovered that public protests could be combined with private compromises according to the requirements of the diplomacy of the moment.

Statute of Carlisle. In the last year of Edward I's reign began a series of statutes passed to check the aggressions of the pope, and restore the independence of the national church and kingdom. They dealt with a number of different, although related, problems, *viz.*, remittances by the English branches of certain orders to the mother house on the continent; the claim of the papacy to exercise, by its prerogative and often in favour of aliens, the patronage belonging to English ecclesiastical persons and bodies; and the papal claim to be not only the ultimate court of appeal, but also a universal court of first instance, thus attracting much important litigation to Rome.

The first of the series was passed in the parliament of Carlisle, 1307. It recites that " the abbots, priors, and governors of religious houses, and certain aliens their superiors, as the abbots and priors of the Cluniac, Cistercian, and Premonstratensian orders, the orders of Saint Augustine and of Saint Benedict, and many more of other religions and orders, have at their own pleasure set divers unwonted, heavy, and unportable tallages, payments and impositions upon every of the said monasteries and houses subject unto them in England, Ireland, Scotland and Wales, without the privity of the king and his nobility, contrary to the laws and customs of the said realm "; and that in consequence of such impositions, " the service of God is diminished; alms are not given to the poor, the sick, and the feeble; the health of the living and the souls of the dead be miserably defrauded; hospitality, almsgiving and other godly deeds do cease; and so that which in times past was charitably given to godly uses and to the increase of the service of God, is now converted to an evil end, by permission whereof there groweth great scandal to the people." It was therefore enacted—" the king considering it would be very prejudicial to him and his people, if he should any longer suffer so great losses and injuries to be winked at "—that for the future no abbot or other religious person should, directly or indirectly, secretly or openly, carry or send any tax, rent or tallage, imposed by the superiors, or assessed

[6] Rymer, ii, 873–875.

amongst themselves, out of the kingdom; and that "priors aliens" should not presume to impose any such payment whatever upon religious houses subject to them. Here again, the barons had taken the initiative, having proposed such a measure in 1305; it was published as a statute in 1307 at Carlisle, reciting the assents of the king, lords and commons (but not of the bishops); but the king had diplomatic reasons for not enforcing the statute.[7] This statute was confirmed under Edward III in the 4th, and again in the 5th year of his reign.

Statute of Provisors, 1351. In the 25th of his reign, roused "by the grievous complaints of all the commons of his realm," the king and parliament passed the famous Statute of Provisors of 1351, aimed directly at the pope, and emphatically forbidding his nominations to English benefices.[8] The preamble recites that "the holy church of England was founded in the estate of prelacy within the realm of England," by the king's progenitors and the ancestors of "the earls, barons, and other nobles of his realm, to inform them and the people of the law of God, and to make hospitalities, alms, and other works of charity, in the places where the churches were founded, for the souls of the founders, their heirs, and all Christians; and certain possessions as well in fees, lands, rents, as in advowsons, which do extend to a great value, were assigned by the said founders to the prelates and other people of the Holy Church of the said realm to sustain the same charge . . . the same kings, earls, barons, and other nobles, as lords and advowees, have had, and ought to have, the custody of such voidances, and the presentments and the collations of the benefices being of such prelacies: And the said kings in times past were wont to have the greatest part of their council, for the safeguard of the realm when they had need, of such prelates and clerks so advanced; but the pope of Rome accroching to him the seignories of such possessions and benefices, doth give and grant the same benefices to aliens, which did never well in England, and to cardinals which might not dwell here, and to others as well aliens as denizens, as if he had been patron or advowee of the said dignities and benefices, as he was not of right by the law of England. . . . And . . . now of late, our holy father the pope . . . taketh of all such benefices the first fruits and many other profits, and a great part of the treasure of the said realm is carried away and dispended out of the realm by the purchasers of such graces aforesaid: and also by such privy reservations, many clerks advanced in this realm by their true patrons which have peaceably holden their advancements by long time, be suddenly put out." It was therefore declared that the elections of bishops and other dignitaries should be free as in time past; that the rights of all patrons should be

---

[7] 35 Edw. 1, st. i, cc. 1–4; *cf.* the documents printed by H. G. Richardson and G. O. Sayles in *English Historical Review*, liii, 425 *et seq.* For Anglo-papal diplomacy, see G. Mollat, *Les papes d'Avignon* (Paris, 1920), 273 *et seq.*

[8] *Cf.* A. Deeley, "Papal provision and royal rights of patronage in the early fourteenth century," *English Historical Review*, xliii, 497; Maitland, *Canon Law*, 63 *et seq.*

preserved; and penalties of imprisonment, forfeiture, or outlawry, according to the degree of the offence, were enacted against all " provisors," who should obtain benefices from Rome by purchase or otherwise.[9] Like the Statute of Carlisle, this statute was enacted by the king, lords and commons, without the bishops. The crown made little effort to exercise its rights under the Act, and lawyers believed that it never had been enforced.[10] Edward III like his grandfather preferred to drop the issue of principle, and share (by diplomatic means) in the fruits of the papal victory which it had helped to secure.

Citations to Rome. Two years afterwards it was found necessary to pass a statute, forbidding citations to the court of Rome. It was based upon " the grievous and clamorous complaints of the great men and commons, how that divers of the people be and have been drawn out of the realm to answer of things whereof the cognisance pertaineth to the king's court; and also that the judgments given in the same court be impeached in the court of another in prejudice and disherison of our lord the king, and of his crown, and of all the people of his said realm, and to the undoing and destruction of the common law of the same realm at all times used." The cumulative penalties of outlawry, forfeiture of lands and goods, and imprisonment at the king's pleasure, were therefore enacted against all people of the king's legiance who should " draw any out of the realm in plea, whereof the cognisance pertaineth to the king's court, or of things whereof judgment be given in the king's court, or who do sue in the court of another, to defeat or impeach the judgments given in the king's court," and who should fail to appear, within two months after summons before the king and his council, or in his chancery, or before the king's justices, to answer in their proper persons for the contempt so committed.[11] For over a century it had been a common law offence to sue in the papal or the local ecclesiastical courts, upon matters within the royal jurisdiction. The old procedure had been slow; this statute imposed outlawry after a very short period of contumacy, but if the party appeared within the two months, the common law applied unchanged.[12] As early as 1304 the penalty by the common law on conviction was already total forfeiture.[13] As in the two preceding statutes, there is a formal peculiarity to be noted:

---

[9] 25 Edw. 3, st. 4; Lodge and Thornton, 300–302. The statute only deals with dignities and benefices in the gift of spiritual persons. The popes did not attempt to provide to parish churches in the gift of lay patrons (Maitland, *Canon Law*, 67, n. 2). Had they done so, the patrons would certainly have used their effective common law remedies. Spiritual patrons were afraid to pursue their common law remedies, hence the need for the statute.

[10] See the cases in Plucknett, *Concise History of the Common Law* (5th ed.), 338 n. 4.

[11] 27 Edw. 3, st. 1, c. 1; Lodge and Thornton, 303–304.

[12] There are numerous examples of the old " attachment on prohibition " in *Bracton's Note Book* and in the earlier Year Books. On these, see Norman Adams, " The writ of prohibition to Court Christian," *Minnesota Law Review*, xx, 272 (1936), and a series of articles on the same subject by Father G. B. Flahiff in *Medieval Studies* (Pontifical Institute of Toronto). For the new statutory procedure, see E. B. Graves, " Legal significance of the statute of praemunire," in *Haskins Anniversary Essays*, 57–80.

[13] Sayles, *Cases in King's Bench* (Selden Society), iii, pp. xix, 137.

the concurrence of the bishops is lacking, and the statute's authority is derived from the king, magnates and commons in great council—not parliament. From this statute originated several senses of the word *praemunire* (from the words of the writ *praemunire facias*, requiring the sheriff to warn the accused to appear and answer the contempt on a day fixed). Later legislation used it to mean (1) the offence of suing in contempt of the king at Rome or elsewhere, and (2) the procedure and penalties contained in this Act, which were sometimes transferred by statute to other offences.

These statutes evaded. Statutes, however, were of little avail. The law still continued to be defied, or evaded, very frequently by the king himself, or with his connivance—indeed, Edward III and Gregory XI concluded a formal concordat on the matter in 1376—although several fresh Acts of Parliament to the same effect as the former were promulgated from time to time.[14]

The general ecclesiastical situation was grave. In the words of an eminent authority, " neither king nor pope realised that the constant complaints of the commons in parliament would finally spread to the masses of the people, and give rise to a most dangerous opposition to the papacy. The discontent of a whole people cannot be stifled indefinitely. It is perhaps an exaggeration to say that there was already a tendency towards the formation of a national church, but at least it is certain that minds were disposed to listen to the violent attacks of Wycliffe against the organisation of the Roman church, and that England was gradually ripening for the schism." [15]

More stringent legislation. In 1390, there was an expectation that the pope was about to attempt to enforce his claims by excommunicating those who rejected them. The parliament at once passed a highly penal statute, which, besides re-enacting in the most emphatic terms the former prohibitions of papal provisors, declared that " if any man bring or send within the realm or the king's power any summonses, sentences, or excommunications against any person of what condition that he be," because of his assent to or execution of the Statute of Provisors, he should incur pain of life and member, with forfeiture of lands and goods; and if any prelate should execute such sentences or excommunications, " let his temporalities be taken, and abide in the king's hands, till due redress and correction be thereof made." [16] The two archbishops protested against the statute, but the king and lords sent a copy of it to Rome for the information of Boniface IX.

Matters were shortly afterwards brought to a crisis (1391) by Boniface IX, who, after declaring the statutes enacted by the English parliament

---

[14] 38 Edw. 3, st. 2; 3 Ric. 2, c. 3; 7 Ric. 2, c. 12; 12 Ric. 2, c. 15.

[15] G. Mollat, *Les papes d'Avignon* (3rd ed., 1920), 287.

[16] 13 Ric. 2, st. 2, c. 3; Lodge and Thornton, 310–311; " inciting " royal letters to the pope are heavily penalised by this statute.

null and void, granted to an Italian cardinal a prebendal stall at Wells, to which the king had already presented. Cross suits were at once instituted by the two claimants in the papal and English courts. A decision was given by the latter in favour of the king's nominee, and certain bishops, having agreed to support the crown, were excommunicated by the pope.

The commons were now roused to the highest pitch of indignation. They drew up, in the form of a petition to the king, a declaration of the circumstances which had occurred, and affirmed that " the said things so attempted be clearly against the king's crown and his regality, used and approved of the time of all his progenitors; wherefore they and all the liege commons of the same realm will stand with our said lord the king, and his said crown, and his regality, in the cases aforesaid, and in all other cases attempted against him, his crown, and his regality, in all points to live and to die." After this emphatic assertion of their own opinion, they prayed the king, " and him require by way of justice," to examine severally all the lords spiritual and temporal in the parliament how they thought and how they would stand. The lay lords answered directly, and the spiritual lords indirectly, to the same effect as the commons.[17] Whereupon the petition and the separate declarations of the three estates of parliament were incorporated in the great Statute of Praemunire, 16 Ric. 2, c. 5, 1393.[18]

Statute of Praemunire. It begins with a lengthy and argumentative preamble setting out the proceedings in parliament, in the course of which it is asserted that the jurisdiction over the right of patronage is a lay plea belonging to the king's court, and that bishops and others are bound to give effect to the judgments of the royal courts in these matters; nevertheless, the pope has excommunicated bishops who carry out judgments of the royal courts, and threatens to translate others to remote places without their consent or the king's. All this is to the prejudice of the crown, and would subject the laws and statutes of the realm to the pope's will. It is therefore enacted, that " if any purchase or pursue . . . in the court of Rome, or elsewhere, such translations, processes, and sentences of excommunications, bulls, instruments, or any other things whatsoever, which touch the king, against him, his crown, and his regality, or his realm, as is aforesaid, and they which bring them within the realm, or them receive, or make thereof notification or any other execution whatsoever within the same realm or without, that they, their notaries, procurators, maintainers, abettors, fautors, and counsellors, shall be put out of the king's protection, and their lands and tenements, goods and chattels, forfeit to our lord the king; and that they be attached by their bodies, if they may be found, and brought before the king and his

---

[17] *Rotuli Parliamentorum*, iii, 304.
[18] See the ample commentary by W. T. Waugh, " The Great Statute of Praemunire," *English Historical Review*, xxxvii, 173–205.

council, there to answer to the cases aforesaid, or that process be made against them by *praemunire facias* in manner as it is ordained in other statutes of provisors, and others which do sue in the court of another in derogation of the regality of our lord the king."[19]

In the minds of those who enacted it, it is clear that the statute is directed against the papal policies which the preamble so indignantly denounces, and that the penalties of the act apply to those who procure the excommunication or translation of bishops who have executed royal judgments in cases of advowsons. As years went by, however, the Act came to be read without the preamble, with the result that its words acquired a very sweeping construction. The penalties which the Act prescribed for the very particular offences named in it, were held to apply to any conduct which might prejudice the crown's claims to jurisdiction in matters of an ecclesiastical nature. This process was carried to the extreme of absurdity and injustice when Wolsey, all the clergy, and the whole of the laity were " put in praemunire " by Henry VIII—under the assumption that any conduct which could be construed as a recognition of papal authority, even in matters undoubtedly spiritual, was an offence under the Act. The legend of the statute became even more monstrous when Coke held that praemunire lay against those who obtained injunctions in chancery against common law proceedings.[20]

THE SPREAD OF LOLLARDY

Strange doctrine. It was at this moment that the spread of heretical doctrine became, for the first time in English history, a matter of serious concern. The movement centred round John Wycliffe, and was in part an academic dispute on abstruse matters of philosophy, theology and political science. There was also a popular side to the movement, and for a time (especially through the influence of John of Gaunt) Lollardy became a factor in national domestic politics.[21] Wycliffe collected together a band of " poor priests " or " itinerant preachers," whom he sent about the country to preach the gospel and denounce abuses, " clad in long russet gowns of one pattern, going on foot," ventilating his opinions among the people.[22] They carried with them copies or pages of the Bible which had been translated under Wycliffe's direction.

But the " poor priests " had other doctrines besides those which they found in the Bible. The tenets of Wycliffe himself were not free from revolutionary tendencies, though probably intended by him, so far as regarded temporal matters, as mere idealistic theories; his followers

---

[19] 16 Ric. 2, c. 5.

[20] Holdsworth, *History of English Law*, v. 440; S. E. Thorne, " Praemunire and Sir Edward Coke," *Huntingdon Library Quarterly*, ii, 85 (but the date is 1616, not 1615). For Wolsey, see *infra*, p. 271 ; *supra*, p. 251.

[21] For an account of Wycliffe's work, see H. B. Workman, *John Wyclif* (1926); G. M. Trevelyan, *England in the Age of Wycliffe* (1904). For his political thought, see R. L. Poole, *Illustrations of Medieval Thought*, and C. H. McIlwain, *Growth of Political Thought*, 315 *et seq.*

[22] *Chronicon Angliae* (ed. E. Maunde Thompson) (Rolls Series), p. 395.

superadded, and propagated among their ignorant proselytes, wild socialistic views which did much harm, not only to their cause but to the reputation of their master. Although there is no evidence that Wycliffe himself had any hand in exciting the insurrection of the villeins in 1381, the complicity of some of his followers, the Lollards, is not beyond suspicion. John Ball, the fanatical leader of the insurgents, is said to have confessed before his execution that he had been for two years a pupil of Wycliffe, and had imbibed his views on the Eucharist.[23] The insurrection was in fact a great blow to Wycliffe and the Lollards. A reaction set in. In the parliament which met in May 1382, Archbishop Courtenay procured a statute to be irregularly passed, without the assent of the commons, ordering that commissions should issue out of the chancery directing the sheriffs to arrest all persons certified by the bishops to be preachers of heresy, and their abettors, and to keep them in prison " until they will justify themselves according to law and the reason of Holy Church." [24] Prosecutions followed; but Wycliffe petitioned against the measure, and in the succeeding parliament the commons demanded and obtained its repeal, on the ground that their assent had never been given.[25]

During the remainder of Richard's reign there was no further legislation, but the crown issued a new set of commissions in 1388, by prerogative, to search and seize heretical books, and the people who dealt in them. In the proceedings that followed, the king's council took an active part even to the extent of holding preliminary examinations of the accused —without, however, directly challenging the church's undoubted exclusive jurisdiction to try for heresy. The king and council, in fact, had quietly obtained control of heresy cases, and the clergy were well aware of the fact. At last, a particularly audacious Lollard manifesto stung them

---

[23] Fasciculi Zizaniorum Magistri Johannis Wyclif, edited by Canon Shirley (Rolls Series), p. 273. But cf. the continuator of Knighton's Chronicle (ed. Lumby) (Rolls Series), ii, 151, who regards Ball as Wycliffe's precursor; speaking of the latter he says: " hic habuit praecursorem Johannem Balle, veluti Christus Johannem Baptistam, qui vias suas in talibus opinionibus praeparavit." On the whole question, see E. Powell and G. M. Trevelyan, The Peasants' Rising and the Lollards.

[24] 5 Ric. 2, st. 2, c. 5. The terms of the commissions as issued differed materially from the provisions of this statute: H. G. Richardson, " Heresy and the lay power under Richard II," English Historical Review, li, 1–28 at 8.

[25] In this statute the assent of lords and commons is not expressed (" it is ordained and assented in the present Parliament "); the government probably regarded it as an administrative measure of some importance and desired it to be proclaimed in the counties, and so sent it out with the statutes. Consequently it came to be enrolled among the statutes. In the next parliament, which met in October of the same year, 1382, the commons, reciting this statute, declared it was never assented to or granted by them, but that what had been proposed in this matter was without their assent, and prayed " that the statute might be annulled "; for it was never their intent, they said, to be judged by, or to bind themselves or their descendants to, the bishops more than their ancestors had been bound in times past. The king returned an answer agreeing to their petition (Rotuli Parliamentorum iii, 141, no. 53). This was clearly meant to be a repeal; but the repeal was not put on the statute roll and so was forgotten. The principal Act was assumed to be still in force, and was expressly confirmed, by 25 Hen. 8, c. 14. The latter was repealed by 1 Edw. 6, c. 12, but re-enacted by 1 & 2 Phil. & Mar. c. 6. The last was repealed by 1 Eliz. 1, c. 1. The original Act of Richard II (as distinguished from its re-enactments) was thought to be still in force until it was expressly repealed by the Statute Law Revision Act, 1863.

into petitioning Richard II in 1397 to impose the death penalty by statute.[26] That final step was not taken until the accession of the new dynasty.

De Haeretico Comburendo, 1401. It was the policy of Henry IV to gain the support of the prelates by sustaining them against their new adversaries, who, moreover, as disturbers of order, were equally obnoxious to the secular power.[27] With this object was passed, in the second year of his reign, at the instigation of Archbishop Arundel, the celebrated statute *De Haeretico Comburendo.* The preamble recites that " divers false and perverse people of a certain new sect, of the faith, of the sacraments of the church, and the authority of the same damnably thinking, and against the law of God and of the church usurping the office of preaching, do perversely and maliciously in divers places within the said realm, under colour of pretended holiness, preach and teach in these days, openly and privily, divers new doctrines, and wicked, heretical and erroneous opinions, contrary to the same faith and blessed determinations of holy church. And of such sect and wicked doctrine and opinions they make unlawful conventicles and confederacies; they hold and exercise schools; they make and write books; they do wickedly instruct and inform people; and, as much as they may, excite and stir them to sedition and insurrection; . . . the diocesans and their jurisdictions spiritual, and the keys of the church with the censures of the same, they do utterly contemn and despise; and so their wicked preachings and doctrines doth from day to day continue, to the hatred of right and reason, and utter destruction of order and good rule." To remedy these evils it was enacted, that the bishops should have power to arrest and imprison persons defamed or vehemently suspected of such offences, until they should make canonical purgation; and, if convicted, to punish them with fine and imprisonment. And if any person so convicted should refuse to abjure such preachings, doctrines, opinions, schools, and misinformations, or, after abjuration, should be proved to have relapsed, then the sheriff of the county, or the mayor and bailiffs of the nearest borough, should, on requisition, be present at the pronunciation of the sentence, should receive the persons so condemned into custody, " and them before the people, in an high place, do to be burnt, that such punishment may strike in fear to the minds of others." [28]

The statute was made by the king, with the assent of the magnates at the petition of the clergy, and the commons were not mentioned as assenting parties to it, although in fact they had petitioned for strong

[26] Richardson, *ut supra,* 21.

[27] At the same time that Henry IV was supporting the church against domestic adversaries of its doctrine, he was careful to maintain the policy of resistance to the aggressions of the pope. See statutes 2 Hen. 4, c. 3; 2 Hen. 4, c. 4; 5 Hen. 4, c. 11; and 9 Hen. 4, c. 9.

[28] 2 Hen. 4, c. 15 (1401); Lodge and Thornton, 314–317. The writ *De Haeretico Comburendo,* " all processes and proceedings thereupon, and all punishment by death in pursuance of any ecclesiastical censures," were finally abolished by statute, 29 & 30 Car. 2, c. 9.

measures against the Lollards.[29]   Their agreement was therefore genuine, although not embodied in the text.   Throughout the whole of Henry IV's reign, they manifested nevertheless a very hostile spirit to the clergy; and on two occasions, in 1404 and again in 1410, they proposed that the temporalities of the church should be confiscated to the use of the state; but the king refused to countenance the scheme.[30]

Sawtrey's Case, 1401.   In connection with this Act, a very important constitutional issue was deliberately raised, with important consequences for the future.   A writ *De Haeretico Comburendo* actually issued from parliament, and execution of it made, about a week before the statute was passed.   This was the famous case of William Sawtrey.   The question therefore arises as to the legal authority for Sawtrey's execution.   The answer seems to be that it was the joint effect of a constitution of the Emperor Frederick II enacting that heretics should be burnt, and a decretal of Boniface VIII ordering that Frederick's constitution be observed everywhere.   In short, Sawtrey was burnt by authority of the canon law, and the haste in his execution seems to be designed to make it clear that a statute was not strictly necessary (at least by canonical theory).   Later ages drew a similar conclusion, but with this difference: to them it seemed that heresy was a crime at common law, apart from the statute.   Hence, although the statute was repealed, it was still possible for the writ to issue, on the assumption that it was at common law.   This actually happened under Edward VI.[31]

Insurrection under Sir John Oldcastle, 1413.   The abortive insurrection of the Lollards at the commencement of Henry V's reign, under the leadership of Sir John Oldcastle, had the effect of adding to the penal laws already in existence against the sect.   In a proclamation, the king asserted that the insurgents intended to destroy him, his brothers, and several of the spiritual and temporal lords, to confiscate the possessions of the church, to secularise the religious orders, and to appoint Sir John Oldcastle president of the commonwealth.[32]   In 1414 a statute was passed which, after reciting that "great rumours, congregations and insurrections of people here in the realm of England, by divers of the king's liege people, as well by them which were of the sect of heresy commonly called Lollardy, as by other of their confederacy, excitation, and abetment, now of late were made to the intent to annul and subvert the Christian faith, and the law of God, and holy church,

---

[29] *Rotuli Parliamentorum*, iii, 473, no. 91.

[30] Walsingham, *Historia Anglicana* (ed. Riley) (Rolls Series), ii, 283.   From the superfluous revenues of the church, the commons asserted that the king might maintain 15 earls, 1,500 knights, and 6,200 esquires; and also support 100 hospitals for the relief of the poor.

[31] The facts of Sawtrey's case are discussed in J. F. Stephen, *History of Criminal Law*, ii, 445 *et seq.*; the view of the law given above is that of Maitland, *Roman Canon Law*, 176 *et seq.*; *cf.* Pollock and Maitland, *History of English Law*, ii, 546; J. R. Tanner, *Tudor Constitutional Documents*, 95; Holdsworth, *History of English Law*, i, 617–618.

[32] Rymer, ix, 170 *et seq*.   *Cf*. H. G. Richardson, "John Oldcastle in Hiding," *English Historical Review*, lv, 432–438.

and also to destroy the sovereign lord the king and all other manner of
estates of the realm as well spiritual as temporal, and also all manner of
policy, and finally the laws of the land," enacted that the lord chancellor,
the judges, and all magistrates should be sworn to use their best power
and diligence to detect and arrest persons suspected of Lollardy, and
deliver them over to the ecclesiastical courts (since cognisance of heresy
belongs to the spiritual and not to the secular judges), and that the prisoners on conviction should forfeit lands, goods and chattels, as in cases
of felony.[33]

Although repressed and discredited, Lollardy was by no means
extinguished. Henry VI, in 1431, writes of the Lollards: "As God
knoweth, never would they be subject to His laws nor to man's, but would
be loose and free to rob, reve, and despoil, slay and destroy all men of
estate thrift and worship, as they proposed to have done in our father's
days; and of lads and lurdains would make lords."[34] The revolutionary
tendencies of the Lollards were indeed effectually crushed out; but
"the fire of heresy continued to smoulder," and copies of Wycliffe's
Bible were still read in secret with fear and trembling.[35] During the
troubled period of the Wars of the Roses we hear little of heretical doctrines, but from the last years of the fifteenth century the chronicles
and records of the bishops' courts are filled with accounts of prosecutions
for heresy.[36] Under Henry VII and in the first years of Henry VIII
several persons were burnt for this crime, while others only escaped by
abjuring their errors.

Dr. Standish's Case, 1515. One of the most mischievous of clerical
privileges was the immunity of all tonsured persons from secular punishment for crimes.[37] This had been partially restrained under Henry VI,
by the practice of requiring that clerks arrested on any criminal charge,
instead of being instantly claimed by the bishop, should plead their
privilege at the time of arraignment, or after conviction. Under a statute
of 1490 (4 & 5 Henry 7, c. 13), all clerks not actually in orders, who had
once had benefit of clergy and were a second time convicted of felony,
were ordered to be burned in the hand; and by a temporary Act in 1512,
the "benefit of clergy" was taken away from persons committing murder
or felony in any church, hallowed place or highway, those within holy
orders only excepted.[38] The Act only remained in force till the opening
of the next parliament in 1515; but in that year a friar, Dr. Standish,
defended the principle of the Act, which was before parliament with a

[33] 2 Hen. 5, st. 1, c. 7 (1415); partly in Lodge and Thornton, 317.
[34] *Archaeologia*, xxiii, 342.
[35] *Cf.* M. Deanesly, *The Significance of the Lollard Bible* (1951).
[36] For late fifteenth-century cases, see Pollard, *Henry VII*, iii, 235–246.
[37] *Supra*, p. 59. See L. C. Gabel, *Benefit of Clergy in the Later Middle Ages* (1929); R.
Génestal, *Privilegium Fori* (1921–24); W. S. Holdsworth, *History of English Law*, iii,
293–302.
[38] 4 Hen. 8, c. 2.

view to its renewal, and denied the right of clerks to be exempt from the jurisdiction of the king's courts. He was attacked by convocation, which put him on trial in respect of a number of fundamental points of political theory, and parliament petitioned the king to support him against his enemies. The king, after hearing both sides, decided in favour of Standish. In giving his decision the king is reported to have asserted his supremacy: " By the permission and ordinance of God, we are king of England; and the kings of England in times past never had any superior but God only. Therefore, know ye well, that we will maintain the right of our crown, and of our temporal jurisdiction as well in this as in all other points, in as ample a manner as any of our progenitors have done before our time." [39] The king succeeded in rescuing Standish from convocation, and frustrated the proposal to remove the case to Rome; but the Act was not renewed—in spite of the popular indignation aroused by the mysterious death of a Londoner, Hunne, in an episcopal prison.

The abuse was again attacked in the Reformation Parliament, and by an Act of 1532 no person below the order of sub-deacon committing petty treason, murder or felony was permitted to claim benefit of clergy.[40] The immunity was, however, still enjoyed by priests, deacons, and sub-deacons, but by the Act of 1532 safeguards against the worst abuses were imposed, and a clerk could be degraded by the ordinary and handed over to the justices of the King's Bench for punishment. The privilege was still further modified by subsequent legislation of Henry VIII, but it was not finally abolished until 1827.[41]

Richard Hunne's Case, 1514. In 1514 popular indignation was greatly excited against the clergy by the case of Richard Hunne, a citizen of London, who having been cited in the spiritual court for declining to pay a mortuary fee, himself brought an action of *praemunire* against the plaintiff on the ground that the spiritual court sat by the authority of the legate. He was then, by way of retaliation, prosecuted in the bishop's court for heresy, and having been committed to the bishop's prison, was found hanged in his chamber. The bishop's chancellor and sumner were indicted for the murder on such vehement presumption that, a conviction being almost certain, the bishop appealed to Wolsey to defer the trial, declaring that the London juries were so " maliciously set *in favorem haereticae pravitatis* that they would condemn any clerk though he were as innocent as Abel." [42]

---

[39] For the important questions raised in this case, see H. A. L. Fisher, *Political History of England*, v, 211–215, and K. Pickthorn, *Tudor Government*, ii, 115–117; see further below, p. 350.

[40] 23 Hen. 8, c. 1.

[41] See Plucknett, *Concise History of the Common Law* (5th ed.), 439–441; Tanner, *Tudor Constitutional Documents*, p. 15.

[42] On this, see Fisher, *op. cit.*, 208; Pickthorn, *op. cit.*, 112–114, 117; E. Jeffries Davis, " The authorities for the Case of Richard Hunne," *English Historical Review*, xxx, 477; and A. Ogle, *The Tragedy of Richard Hunne* (1947).

Luther; Henry VIII; the Divorce. Such was the state of popular feeling in England when Martin Luther nailed his theses to the church door of Wittenberg, and set in motion that mighty religious revolution which, while it has to some extent affected the destinies of all western nations, has in an especial manner influenced the religious and political development of the English people.

Inclined as a man of Henry's intelligence and force of character must have been to reform the abuses of the ecclesiastical system and curb the excesses of clerical power, he was altogether opposed to doctrinal innovations. In defence of orthodoxy, he even condescended to a polemic contest with Luther, and for the treatise, *Assertio Septem Sacramentorum adversus Martinum Lutherum*, received from Pope Leo X the title of " Defender of the Faith." But among the people the writings of the " arch-heretic," and of other foreign reformers, were sedulously circulated until at length, under Edward VI and Elizabeth, English Lollardism, stimulated and developed by the influence of Germanic protestantism, brought about the doctrinal, as Henry VIII had brought about the political and legal, reformation of the national church. Some reform of the ecclesiastical system, and even of the doctrines of the church, must certainly have been carried out at no great distance of time even had no quarrel arisen between Henry VIII and the papacy. The crisis was precipitated by the famous divorce suit against Queen Catherine. It is unnecessary here to discuss the merits of the case, or to dwell upon the " vacillation and duplicity " of Pope Clement VII, " the assurances he gave the king and the arts with which he receded from them, the unfinished trial in England before his delegates, Campeggio and Wolsey, the opinions obtained from foreign universities in the king's favour, not always without a little bribery, and those of the same import at home, not given without a little intimidation, or the tedious continuance of the process after its adjournment to Rome." [43]

More than five years elapsed between Henry's first application to the pope, in 1527, for a bull annulling his marriage with Catherine as being originally contrary to the laws of God, and the celebration of his marriage with Anne Boleyn in January 1533. On May 23, Archbishop Cranmer pronounced sentence of divorce from Catherine; and on September 7 following Anne became the mother of Elizabeth. On March 23, 1534, the pope, urged by the cardinals to extreme measures, pronounced a definite sentence in favour of Catherine, and required the king under pain of excommunication to take her back as his wife. Henceforth, the breach between the king and the pope was irreparable; but long before the final rupture Henry had entered upon the course of ecclesiastical reform, which was retarded or accelerated as the progress of the great suit seemed to call for a conciliatory or threatening attitude on the part of the king.

---

[43] Hallam, *Constitutional History*, i, 61.

THE REFORMATION PARLIAMENT

It is remarkable that the seven years' legislation which abolished the papal supremacy in England, reformed the constitution and administrative system of the Anglican Church, and established the royal supremacy, was the work of one and the same parliament. The " Reformation Parliament " met in London on November 4, 1529, and it was continued by prorogations—unusual in those days—from year to year, until it was finally dissolved on April 14, 1536, having completed the task for which it had been specially summoned. We shall consider the ecclesiastical reforms of the Reformation Parliament in the chronological order of its seven sessions.[44]

Fees and pluralities. Three statutes were passed in the first session (November 4–December 17, 1529, 21 Hen. 8), in restraint of the personal privileges and emoluments of the clergy.

(1) The fees, hitherto assessed at discretion, upon the granting of probates and administration by the ecclesiastical courts were reduced to fixed and moderate proportions.

This was a mode of ecclesiastical extortion which had been long and bitterly resented. A statute of 1357 (31 Edward 3, st. 1, c. 4) had been passed to repress the " outrageous and grievous fines and sums of money taken by the ministers of bishops and other ordinaries [45] of holy church for the probate of testaments "; and another statute of 1416 (3 Hen. 5, st. 2, c. 8) had been made temporary only by reason that " the ordinaries did then promise to reform and amend the oppressions and exactions complained of "; but as the abuse still continued, " nothing reformed nor amended but greatly augmented and increased against right and justice," it was now effectually restrained by this statute of Henry's reign which established a scale of fees and made useful reforms in probate and administration procedure.[46]

(2) The mortuary fees, or " corse presents," of the parochial clergy were regulated. After reciting that these fees had been " over excessive to the poor people and other persons of this realm, and also had been demanded and levied for such as at the time of their death have had no property in any goods or chattels, and many time, for wayfaring travelling men in the places where they have fortuned to die," the statute fixed the fees on a graduated scale, from three shillings and fourpence up to ten shillings, according to the value of the deceased person's property, but with an entire exemption when the goods of the deceased were less than

---

[44] According to modern reckoning there were eight sessions, but it seemed unnecessary to change the settled tradition which has treated the prorogation from March 28 to April 10, 1532, as merely an Easter adjournment. The more important documents of the Reformation Parliament are printed, with historical prefaces, in Tanner, *Tudor Constitutional Documents*, pp. 13 *et seq.*

[45] The term *ordinary* is generally synonymous with bishop; but it includes every ecclesiastical judge who has the regular *ordinary* jurisdiction independent of another: Co.Litt., 344.

[46] 21 Hen. 8, c. 5.

ten marks in value, and in the case of married women, children, persons not keeping house, and wayfaring men.[47]

(3) Pluralities, non-residence, farming and trading by the clergy were forbidden. It was enacted [48] that no clergyman should thenceforth take any land to farm beyond what was absolutely necessary for the support of his own household; or should buy merchandise to sell again; or keep tanneries or brewhouses,[49] or otherwise directly or indirectly trade for gain. Pluralities were not to be permitted with respect to benefices above the yearly value of £8; and residence was made obligatory. Papal and episcopal dispensations for pluralities and non-residence were declared illegal, and persons procuring them rendered liable to heavy penalties; but power was reserved to the king to grant such dispensations to a numerous list of chaplains (of the king, the nobility, the judges, and other officials), to the brothers and sons of temporal peers and of knights, and to persons holding the degree of doctor or bachelor of divinity or law. The crown thus acquired a powerful means —hitherto enjoyed by the pope—of influencing the lower house of convocation.

Proctors and pardoners. In the second session (January 16–March 31, 1531, 22 Hen. 8), no statute directly aimed at either pope or clergy was passed. But in an Act for the punishment (by whipping, pillory and loss of ears) of beggars and vagabonds, were significantly included " all proctors and pardoners going about the country without sufficient authority." [50] Proctors were properly officers of the ecclesiastical courts analogous to attorneys of the civil courts, but the word was also used (as here) of persons who collected alms for the benefit of hospitals and the like; pardoners were the itinerant vendors of indulgences and relics from the court of Rome. The Act also included " scholars of the Universities of Oxford and Cambridge that go about begging " (unless licensed by the Vice-Chancellor). No doubt many rascals throve by fraudulently pretending to be in one or another of these categories, and it was against them that the Act was directed.

Wolsey in a praemunire. This was followed by the Act for the pardon of the clergy in the matter of the praemunire to which they were very harshly and unfairly held to have rendered themselves liable, in consequence of admitting the legatine authority of Cardinal Wolsey. The cardinal had been indicted in October 1529, upon the statute of praemunire of the 16th Richard II, for having obtained bulls from Rome, which he caused to be publicly read, and by which he exercised jurisdiction and legatine

---

[47] 21 Hen. 8, c. 6. *Cf.* M. R. James, " Medieval Ghost Stories," *English Historical Review*, xxxvii, 413.

[48] 21 Hen. 8, c. 13.

[49] The commons, in a petition to the king concerning clerical abuses, had made a particular complaint of reverend tanners and brewers. A. Amos, *Statutes of the Reformation Parliament* (1859), p. 237.

[50] 22 Hen. 8, c. 12; Tanner, *Tudor Documents*, 478.

authority, to the deprivation of the king's power established in his courts of justice. Wolsey had been careful to obtain the king's licence under the great seal authorising him to exercise the legatine authority; and although the king may be considered to have exceeded his legal right in granting such a licence, still, as the dispensing power had been continuously claimed and frequently exercised by the crown, both with respect to the statute of praemunire and others, there was equally an equitable and moral if not a legal defence to the charge.[51]   Wolsey, however, thinking it prudent not to plead his royal licence, was found guilty on his own confession; and after being plundered, received the king's pardon.   The whole episode was disgraceful, but a vital constitutional principle lay behind it, as Stephen Gardiner realised when, in a letter of 1547 he put the question " whether the king may command against an Act of Parliament, and what danger they fall in that break a law with the King's consent."   The Cardinal's case gave the answer; " which conclusion I bare away, and take it for a law of the realm because the lawyers so said; but my reason digested it not."   The doctrine which had dismayed him in 1529, he himself now invoked in 1547.[52]

The clergy in a praemunire.   It was now contended, on the ground of his conviction, that all the clergy of the realm had been guilty of praemunire, because by admitting the jurisdiction they had become, in the language of the statute, his " fautors and abettors "; and the attorney-general was instructed to file an information against the whole clerical body in the Court of King's Bench.   The Convocation of Canterbury hastily assembled and offered the king £100,000 in return for a full pardon. This offer the king refused to accept, unless in the preamble of their petition he was acknowledged to be " sole protector and supreme head of the church and clergy in England."   After much discussion, the king finally consented to accept the acknowledgment of his supremacy with the qualifying words " as far as the law of Christ allows."[53]   The Convocation of York adopted the same language, and voted, for a like pardon, the sum of £18,840.[54]

It is remarkable in a reign when the power of the crown was at its highest, and when parliament even delegated to the king its legislative

---

[51] It had been decided in Henry VII's reign, that although the king could not dispense with penalties for an act against the common law, he could do so with respect to an act prohibited by statute only. See *supra*, p. 191. For this construction of praemunire, see *supra*, p. 263.

[52] *Letters of Stephen Gardiner* (ed. Muller), 390. The letter is a defence of Gardiner's refusal to obey orders in the name of Edward VI which were contrary to statute. The whole letter deserves careful study as an exposition of constitutional principle by an eminent canonist and civilian.

[53] 22 Hen. 8, c. 15; Tanner, *Tudor Documents*, 17–20. (Note that the words " supreme head " are an anticipation of the Act of Supremacy.)   The notion that all the clergy could be charged with praemunire was a development of a suggestion, made in 1515 in the course of the Standish affair by the common law judges, to the effect that all convocation had incurred praemunire by denying the king's temporal jurisdiction.

[54] The pardon to York was delayed until the next session: 23 Hen. 8, c. 19 (1532).

functions, that the king should have admitted his parliament to participate in the undoubted royal prerogative of pardoning offences. The unusual character of a pardon granted to a whole estate of the realm may have been a reason for a special parliamentary sanction, but a difficulty arose in the passage of the Bill of Pardon through the Lower House. The comprehensive words of the statute of praemunire applied not only to the clergy but to the Privy Council, the lords and commons, and indirectly to the whole nation, as having recognised Wolsey in his capacity as legate.

The laity also in a praemunire. The commons, therefore, fearing that the king might make the alleged praemunire an excuse for fleecing the laity as well as the clergy, boldly refused to pass the bill for the pardon of the latter, " except all men were pardoned, saying that all men which had anything to do with the cardinal were in the same case." The Speaker and a number of members subsequently waited upon the king, and in more submissive language declared " how the commons sore lamented and bewailed their chance to think or imagine themselves to be out of his gracious favour, because that he had graciously given his pardon of the praemunire to his spiritual subjects and not to them, wherefore they most humbly besought his grace of his accustomed goodness and clemency to include them in the same pardon." The king replied that he was their prince and sovereign lord, and that they ought not to restrain him of his liberty, nor to compel him to show his mercy, for it was at his pleasure to use the extremity of his laws, or mitigate and pardon the same, wherefore since they denied to assent to the pardon of the spiritual persons, which pardon he said he might give without their assent by his great seal, he would be well advised or [ere] he pardoned them, because he would not be noted to be compelled to do it." [55] However, a pardon to the laity was signed by the king, and embodied in an Act of Parliament, by which his Majesty " of his mere motion, and of his benignity, special grace, pity, and liberality, hath given and granted, and by authority of this present parliament giveth and granteth to all and singular his temporal and lay subjects and temporal bodies politic and corporate, and to every of them, his gracious, general and free pardon " for offences committed by them against the statutes of provisors and praemunire. This pardon of a whole nation is not only one of the most extraordinary events of this extraordinary reign, but it is probably unparalleled in history. It was all the more preposterous from the circumstance that, in effect, the lords and commons pardoned themselves.[56]

These proceedings had taken place in the early part of the year 1531,

---

[55] Hall (ed. Whibley), ii, 184.

[56] The pardon to the clergy of the province of Canterbury was by Stat. 22 Hen. 8, c. 15, the pardon of the laity by 22 Hen. 8, c. 16; the pardon of the clergy of York province by 23 Hen. 8, c. 19, passed in the following session. For more recent views of the praemunire thus presumed to have been incurred, and of the submission of the clergy to the king's supremacy, see Dixon, *History of the Church of England*, i, 53 *et seq.*, and " The Submission of the Clergy," *Quarterly Review*, Oct. 1879.

while the king's representatives at Rome were still pressing, though with diminished hopes, for a favourable termination of the king's suit. In the next (third, or third and fourth) session of parliament (January 15–March 28, April 10–May 14, 1532, 23 Hen. 8) while the clergy were still under the terror of their recent narrow escape from the penalties of a praemunire, the attack upon the papal and ecclesiastical privileges was renewed.

Citations. An Act was passed to restrain the citation of persons out of the dioceses in which they were resident. The preamble recites that a great number of the king's subjects as well men, wives, servants, as others, dwelling in divers dioceses of England and Wales, have been at many times called by citation and other processes compulsorily to appear in the Arches, audience and other high courts of the archbishops of this realm, far from their dwellings, and many times to answer to surmised and feigned causes, and suits of defamation, withholding of tithes, and such other like causes and matters, which have been sued more for malice and for vexation than for any just cause of suit; and not appearing they are excommunicated, or at least suspended from all divine services, and can only be absolved on payment of the fees of court, and also to the " summoner, apparitor, or other light literate person " by whom they were certified to be summoned, a further sum of 2d. for every mile distant from the court to the residence of the party. It was therefore enacted that, with certain exceptions, no person should be summoned out of the diocese in which he resided, and the fee for a citation was reduced from two shillings to threepence.[57]

Annates. Shortly afterwards an Act was passed depriving the pope of the annates, or first-fruits of benefices.[58] It recites that " The pope's holiness, his predecessors, and the court of Rome, by long time have heretofore taken of all and singular those spiritual persons which have been named, elected, presented, or postulated to be archbishops or bishops within this realm of England under the title of annates otherwise called first fruits " which they were compelled to pay before they could receive the pope's bulls for their elections to be confirmed; but " because the said annates have arisen, grown, and increased by an uncharitable custom

---

[57] 23 Hen. 8, c. 9.

[58] 23 Hen. 8, c. 20. As early as the 6th century it was customary for the ordaining authorities to demand a fee of those advanced to any ecclesiastical preferment, which amounted sometimes even to the whole of one year's income from the benefice. The " annates " in England, which had been usually paid to the Archbishop of Canterbury, were first claimed by Clement V in 1306, and later by Pope John XXII (1316–1334) for the space of three years, and by his successors until 1531 (Henry VIII). See W. E. Lunt, " The first levy of papal annates," *American Historical Review*, xviii, 48–64; G. Mollat and C. Samaran, *La fiscalité pontificale* (1905); W. E. Lunt, *Papal Revenues* (1934). At the close of the reformation the annates, as also the first-fruits or tenths, which were the tenth part of the annual profits of a church benefice, and also formerly paid to the pope, were made over to the crown (*infra*, p. 281); but were, in 1704, by Queen Anne, appropriated to the poorer clergy, and thus formed the " Queen Anne's Bounty." *Cf.* Anson, *Law and Custom of the Constitution*, vol. ii, pt. ii (4th ed.), pp. 269–270.

grounded upon no just or good title, and the payments thereof obtained by restraint of bulls . . . against all equity, and justice: the noblemen therefore of this realm and the wise, sage, politic commons of the same, considering that the court of Rome ceaseth not to tax, take and exact the said great sums of money under the title of annates " which were first taken " for the only defence of Christian people against the infidels, but now they be claimed and demanded as mere duty, only for lucre, against all right and conscience. . . . And albeit that our sovereign lord the king and all his natural subjects, as well spiritual as temporal, be as obedient, devout, catholic and humble children of God and holy church as any people be within any realm christened; yet the said exactions of annates be so intolerable and importable to this realm that it is considered and declared by the whole body of this realm now represented by all the estates of the same assembled in this present parliament, that the king's Highness before Almighty God is bound as by the duty of a good Christian prince, for the conservation and preservation of the good estate and commonwealth of this his realm, to do all that in him is, to obviate, repress and redress the said abusions and exactions of annates or first fruits." It was thereupon enacted " by the authority of this present parliament " (no mention being made of the assent of the lords spiritual) that the payment of annates should cease; that any bishop making such payments should forfeit all his lands and goods to the king; that if any bishop presented by the king to the pope should be letted or delayed through withholding of bulls, he should be consecrated in England by the archbishop; that every archbishop presented by the king, and from whom the pope should withhold the necessary bulls, should be consecrated by two bishops to be nominated by the king; that bishops so consecrated should be installed, accepted, and obeyed, and should enjoy their spiritualities and temporalities as completely as if they had obtained their bulls from Rome; and that any censures, excommunications, or interdicts issued in consequence by the pope should be utterly disregarded. A remarkable proviso was added, evidently with the object of influencing the pope in the negotiations for the divorce still pending at Rome. "Forasmuch as the king's Highness and this his high court of parliament neither have nor do intend to use in this or any other like cause, any manner of extremity of violence, before gentle courtesy and friendly ways and means first attempted," it was further enacted that, in order to come to an amicable composition with the pope, the king should have power to declare by his letters patent, before the beginning of the next session of parliament, " whether the premises or any part, clause or matter thereof," should be observed and take effect as a statute or not.

The fourth (or fifth) session of parliament lasted from February 4–April 7, 1533, 24 Hen. VIII. The king had been secretly married to Anne Boleyn in the January preceding; and arrangements were in contemplation for the sentence of divorce from Catherine which Archbishop Cranmer pronounced in the ensuing May.

Appeals to Rome. It was probably with the view of quashing Queen Catherine's pending appeal to Rome, and also, prospectively, any appeal which she might make against the archbishop's sentence, that an Act was now passed forbidding, under the penalty of praemunire, all appeals from the spiritual judges in England to the court of the pontiff. In a curious and lengthy preamble it is recited that " By divers sundry old authentic histories and chronicles it is manifestly declared and expressed that this realm of England is an empire, and so hath been accepted in the world, governed by one supreme head and king having the dignity and royal estate of the imperial crown of the same; unto whom a body politic, compact of spirituality and temporality, be bounden and owe to bear next to God a natural and humbled obedience." After referring to the statutes of Edward I, Edward III, Richard II and Henry IV made to keep " the imperial crown of this realm from the annoyance as well of the see of Rome as from the authority of other foreign potentates " [59] and reciting that since those good statutes and ordinances inconveniences and dangers not provided for plainly therein had arisen and sprung up by reason of appeals to Rome in causes testamentary, of matrimony and divorces, tithes, oblations and obventions, not only to the great vexation, trouble, costs and charges of the king's Highness and many of his subjects, but also to the great delay and let to the true and speedy determination of the said causes, for so much as the said parties appealing to the said court of Rome, most commonly do the same for the delay of justice, it was therefore enacted: That all causes testamentary, of matrimony and divorce, tithes, oblations, and obventions, already commenced or hereafter coming in contention, whether they concerned the king, his heirs or successors, or any subjects or resiants of what degree soever they be, should be heard and determined within the king's jurisdiction, and not elsewhere, in such courts, spiritual and temporal, as the case should require, any inhibitions or excommunications, or processes from the see of Rome notwithstanding; that any person procuring from Rome any foreign process should incur the penalties of praemunire; that the course of appeal should be from the archdeacon to the bishop, and from the bishop to the archbishop in his province; and that in any case touching the king or his successors, the appeal should be to the upper house of convocation.[60] To this Act the lords spiritual gave their assent.

Before the meeting of parliament for its fifth (or sixth) session (January 15–March 30, 1534, 25 Hen. 8), Archbishop Cranmer had pronounced the divorce of Henry from Queen Catherine, the king's marriage with Anne Boleyn had been publicly acknowledged, and a final breach with the pope appeared imminent.

The Supplication. Two years previously, in March, 1532, the commons had presented a petition to the king, containing what was in fact a formal

---

[59] *Supra*, pp. 257 *et seq.*
[60] 24 Hen. 8, c. 12.

acte d'accusation, with a detailed summary of grievances, against the clergy generally, and the bishops in particular. This " Supplication against the Ordinaries " had in fact been carefully drafted by Thomas Cromwell. It was referred by the king to the bishops, with a request that they would immediately answer its charges. The bishops replied in a lengthy document,[61] which was handed by the king to the commons with the remark, " We think their answer will smally please you, for it seemeth to us very slender." A few days later, "the king sent for the Speaker again, and twelve of the Commons House, having with him eight lords, and said to them, ' Well-beloved subjects ! we thought that the clergy of our realm had been our subjects wholly, but now, we have well perceived that they be but half our subjects ; yea, and scarce our subjects, for all the prelates, at their consecration, take an oath to the Pope clean contrary to the oath they make to us, so that they seem to be his subjects and not ours. Copies of both the oaths I deliver here to you, requiring you to invent some order that we be not thus deluded of our spiritual subjects'."[62] The ever-present difficulty of reconciling the papal pretensions with national independence is also clearly brought out. It was the divided allegiance of the bishops which especially struck Henry's mind, and which for national as well as personal reasons he was so anxious to determine. He doubtless saw that, in the impending struggle, the oaths sworn by the prelates to the pope would afford them too ready an excuse for taking part against him. Accordingly in May, 1532, the clergy in convocation were induced by the king to promise that they would never from thenceforth enact, promulge or execute, any new canons, constitutions, or ordinances, without the king's licence to make them and his approval of the same when made.

Submission of the Clergy, 1534. By an Act of 1534 this submission of the clergy was confirmed and recorded in statutory form, and the penalty of fine and imprisonment at the king's pleasure imposed upon all who should act contrary to its provisions. Appeals to Rome, which had been already prohibited in certain cases, were now, under penalty of a praemunire, forbidden in any case whatsoever ; and in lieu of the right thus abolished it was declared that appeals from the archbishops' courts should be made to the king in chancery, and that the king should appoint commissioners to hear and determine finally in the cause.[63]

---

[61] The " supplication " and the " answer " are both voluminous. They are printed in H. Gee and W. J. Hardy, *Documents Illustrative of English Church History*, 145–176.

[62] Hall (ed. Whibley), ii, pp. 209 *et seq.*

[63] 25 Hen. 8, c. 19, " An Act for the submission of the clergy to the King's Majesty." The Delegates of Appeals, as the commissioners were termed, continued to form the final court of ecclesiastical appeals, until superseded by the Judicial Committee of the Privy Council under the provisions of 2 & 3 Will. 4, c. 92 (1832) and 3 & 4 Will. 4, c. 41 (1833). By the Judicature Act, 1873, the queen was empowered, by Order in Council, to direct that all appeals and petitions, which according to the laws now in force ought to be heard by the Judicial Committee of the Privy Council, shall be referred to and heard by her Majesty's new Court of Appeal constituted by this Act, which, when hearing appeals in ecclesiastical causes, shall be " assisted by such assessors, being archbishops and bishops of the Church

Act of Annates, 1534; congé d'élire. The statute of 1532, by which the payment of annates to the pope had been contingently forbidden, and which had since been ratified by the king's letters patent, was re-enacted, with additional clauses providing a mode of nominating archbishops and bishops by *congé d'élire*, which is that now in force. For the future no archbishop or bishop was to be presented to " the bishop of Rome, otherwise called the pope," (the expression in the previous Act was " our holy father the pope,") for confirmation, or was to sue out any bulls in his court. But at every vacancy of any cathedral church the king should grant to the dean and chapter a licence under the great seal to elect the person named in the accompanying letters missive, and him they should choose and none other. Should they defer the election for more than twelve days, the king should elect by his letters patent. The prelate so elected or nominated should first swear fealty; after which the king should signify the election to the archbishop, or if there be no archbishop, to four bishops, requiring them to confirm the election and to invest and consecrate the bishop elect, who might then sue his temporalities out of the king's hands, making a corporal oath to the king and none other, and should receive the profits spiritual and temporal belonging to his bishopric.[64] The novelties in this Act were not the *congé d'élire* (which had been in use for over three centuries), nor the letters missive, but the statutory compulsion to obey the letters, the elimination of the pope from the procedure, and the possibility of appointment by patent.

Peter's Pence, etc. This statute was immediately succeeded by another lopping off a multitude of petty payments which the pope had been wont to exact both from the clergy and the laity. It is declared to be founded on the petition of the commons complaining to the king that his subjects were greatly decayed and impoverished by the intolerable exactions of the bishop and see of Rome, " the specialities whereof be over long, large in number, and tedious here particularly to be inserted; wherein the bishop of Rome hath not been only to be blamed for his usurpation " of the revenues, " but also for his abusing and beguiling your subjects, pretending and persuading to them that he hath full power to dispense with all human laws, uses and customs of all realms in all causes which be called spiritual . . . in great derogation of your imperial crown and authority royal . . . where this your grace's realm, recognising no superior under God but only your grace, hath been and is free from subjection to any man's laws but only to such as have been devised, . . . made, and ordained within

of England," as shall be directed by any general rules to be made by Order in Council: 36 & 37 Vict. c. 66, s. 21. Before this Act came into force, the Appellate Jurisdiction Act, 1876, abandoned the idea of a single court of appeal, and restored the position of the Judicial Committee. See also the Public Worship Regulation Act, 1874, 37 & 38 Vict. c. 85, which created a procedure for offences against the ceremonial law of the church; Anson, *Law and Custom of the Constitution*, vol. ii, pt. ii (4th ed.), p. 313; F. Makower, *Constitutional History of the Church of England*, 451.

[64] 25 Hen. 8, c. 20, " An Act restraining the payment of annates," etc.

this realm for the wealth of the same, or to such other as by sufferance of your grace and your progenitors the people of this your realm have taken at their free liberty by their own consent to be used amongst them, and have bound themselves by long use and custom to the observance of the same not as to the observance of the laws of any foreign prince, potentate, or prelate, but as to the accustomed and ancient laws of this realm originally established as laws of the same by the said sufferance, consents, and custom, and none otherwise." It was therefore enacted that Peter's pence and every other kind of payment made to the bishop of Rome, and " to his use and his chambers which he calleth apostolic," and every species of licence, dispensation and grant, accustomed to be obtained at Rome, should cease; that thereafter all such licences, faculties and other writings might be granted by the Archbishop of Canterbury; that children born of marriages solemnised by virtue of an archbishop's licence should be legitimate; and that the penalties of praemunire should be incurred by any one suing to Rome for any licences, bulls or instruments forbidden by the Act. It was, however, declared that the king, his nobles and subjects, did not intend by this Act " to decline or vary from the congregation of Christ's church in any things concerning the very articles of the catholic faith of Christendom, or in any other things declared by Holy Scripture and the Word of God necessary for salvation." In order, doubtless, to leave open a possibility of arrangement with the pope, it was provided that this Act should not take effect till the next feast of St. John the Baptist (June 24, 1534), unless the king before that feast should declare his will that it should take effect earlier, and at all times before the said feast he was empowered to annul the whole or any part of the Act at his pleasure.[65]

Royal Succession Act, 1534. The first of Henry's statutes for the settlement of the royal succession was also passed in this session. Its principal enactments were: an adjudication by authority of parliament of the nullity of the king's marriage with Queen Catherine and of the validity of that with Anne Boleyn; a declaration of fourteen prohibited degrees of marriage, the tenth on the list being the marriage of a brother with a brother's widow; an entail of the crown upon the children by Anne[66]; certain new treasons and misprisions of treason[67]; and an oath to observe and maintain the Act, to be taken by all subjects of full age under the penalty, on refusal, of being adjudged guilty of misprision of treason. The terms of the oath prescribed in the Act, were, that the deponents would " truly, firmly and constantly, without fraud or guile, observe, fulfil, maintain, defend and keep, to their cunning, wit, and uttermost of their powers, the whole effects and contents of this present Act." [68]

[65] 25 Hen. 8, c. 21, " An Act for the exoneration from exactions paid to the see of Rome."
[66] *Infra*, p. 501.
[67] It is declared high treason " by writing, print, deed, or act " to " procure or do or cause to be procured or done anything to the prejudice, slander, disturbance, or derogation " of the king's marriage or the succession.　　　　　　[68] 25 Hen. 8, c. 22.

But the oath actually tendered to be taken differed very materially from that required by the statute. Professedly drawn up in the sense of the statute, this oath was devised so as to include a virtual acknowledgment of the king's ecclesiastical supremacy, before that supremacy had been established by the legislature. In its amplified form, it included an abjuration of all faith, truth and obedience to any " foreign authority, prince or potentate " ; a declaration that the deponent reputed " as vain and annihilate " any oath already made or to be made to any person or persons other than the king and the heirs of his body ; and a promise not only to observe the late Act, but also " all other Acts and statutes made since the beginning of this present Parliament in confirmation or for due execution of the same." Sir Thomas More and Bishop Fisher, when called upon to take this amplified oath, which had no legislative authority, refused, and were in consequence illegally committed to prison, where they remained a long time without trial.[69]

In the sixth (or seventh) session of parliament (November 3–December 18, 1534, 26 Hen. 8) the legal difficulty was surmounted by a special Act, by which, after reciting the oath prescribed in the Succession Act for the maintenance and defence of the said Act, and then setting forth the tenor of the oath which was in fact used, it was enacted that the said last-mentioned oath should " be interpreted, expounded, reputed, accepted and adjudged the very oath that the king's Highness, the lords spiritual and temporal, and the commons of this present parliament meant and intended that every subject of this realm should be obliged and bounden to take and accept." [70] For refusing to take this substituted oath, More and Fisher—who were willing to swear to maintain the succession as settled by parliament, but had scruples as to the preamble of the oath denying the pope's right of dispensation—were shortly after, while close prisoners in the Tower, and without being heard in their defence, attainted by Acts of Parliament of misprision of treason. The penalty was prison and forfeiture.

Act of Supremacy, 1534. Shortly after the close of the preceding session, the news arrived in England of the pope's adjudication annulling Cranmer's sentence of divorce. This was followed by a royal proclamation ordering " all manner of prayers, oracions, rubrics, canons, or mass-books, and all other books in churches, wherein the bishop of Rome is named, or his presumptious and proud pomp and authority preferred, utterly to be abolished, eradicated and rased out, and his name and memory to be never more (except in his contumely and reproach) remembered, but perpetually suppressed and obscured." Parliament met after the prorogation (for its sixth, or seventh, session), on November 3, 1534, and sat till the 18th of the following month. Its first Act was the famous Act of Supremacy. The king had already been recognised by convocation

---

[69] R. W. Chambers, *Thomas More*, 301 *et seq.*
[70] 26 Hen. 8, c. 2.

—under the terror of the praemunire—"quantum per Christi legem licet Supremum Caput." It was now enacted (without the saving clause) that the king should be taken and reputed "the only supreme head in earth of the Church of England called *Anglicana Ecclesia*, and shall have and enjoy, annexed, and united to the imperial crown of this realm, as well the title and style thereof, as all honours, dignities, pre-eminences, jurisdictions, privileges, authorities, immunities, profits, and commodities, to the said dignity of supreme head of the same church belonging and appertaining"; with full power to visit, reform, and correct all heresies, errors, abuses, offences, contempts and enormities which, by any manner of spiritual authority or jurisdiction, ought to be reformed or corrected.[71] The royal supremacy was exercised through a new type of royal instrument, called Injunctions, which replaced the old canons of convocation in giving minute directions to the clergy as to their duties. In 1536 and 1538 Thomas Cromwell (as the king's vicegerent for ecclesiastical matters) issued injunctions which already began to attack time-honoured practices connected with images, relics and pilgrimages.[72]

The second Act of this session was that to which reference has already been made, as having been passed to justify retrospectively the imprisonment of Sir Thomas More and Bishop Fisher, for not taking an oath, which it was now declared [73] had been meant by the legislature to be taken although it had in fact prescribed a different oath.

First-fruits annexed to the crown. By another Act the first-fruits and tenths of the annual income of all ecclesiastical benefices—the payment of which to the pope had been stigmatised, in the third session of this parliament, as having arisen by an uncharitable custom against all equity and justice, and as being exacted only for lucre against all rights and conscience—were "united and knit to the king's imperial crown for ever." [74]

Treason Act, 1534. Another Act created a number of new treasons,[75] among them being by words or writing maliciously to wish, will or desire to deprive the king, the queen or their heirs apparent, of the dignity, title or name of their royal estates. As we have already seen, More and Fisher had been attainted for misprision. This new Act made it possible to indict them of treason, since they refused to acknowledge that the king

---

[71] 26 Hen. 8, c. 1.

[72] Printed in H. Gee and W. J. Hardy, *Documents Illustrative of Church History*, 269 *et seq.*, 275 *et seq.* Among the injunctions of 1536 is one requiring parish registers of baptisms, burials and marriages. A similar requirement was made in France in 1539: Esmein, *Histoire du droit Français* (ed. Génestal), 739.

[73] 26 Hen. 8, c. 2.

[74] 26 Hen. 8, c. 3. *Cf. supra*, 274 n. 58. In the following session of parliament "for the entire and hearty love that his grace beareth to the prelates and other incumbents," they were excused from the tenths in the same year that they paid their first-fruits. 27 Hen. 8, c. 8.

[75] 26 Hen. 8, c. 13; Tanner, *Tudor Documents*, 388.

was supreme head. For thus depriving the king of one of his titles, they were tried, convicted and executed (1535).

The destruction of the papal power, emoluments and influence in England, and the reduction of the national English Church under due subordination to the state, had now been accomplished. In its seventh (or eighth) and last session the Reformation Parliament commenced the " second grand innovation in the ecclesiastical polity of England " —the dissolution of the monasteries.

THE DISSOLUTION OF THE MONASTERIES

At various times in the past individual monasteries had been suppressed, by papal authority, so that their endowments could be transferred to other charitable or pious objects—Magdalen College, Oxford (1459) and Fisher's St. John's College, Cambridge (1511) are examples. Indeed, whole orders might be suppressed, such as the Templars in 1312 and the Friars of the Sack in 1274. The fate of the suppressed houses might be the result of their decay in numbers or their financial difficulties. Archbishop Morton, under Henry VII, had obtained a bull from the pope for the reform of the English monasteries, in which many of them were charged with dissoluteness of life; and the abbot of St. Albans was severely reprimanded by the same archbishop for the alleged scandalous vices of himself and his monks.[76] In 1523, Cardinal Wolsey, as papal legate, commenced a visitation of the professed as well as the secular clergy, in consequence of the general complaint against their manners. He also set the example of diverting the revenues of these institutions to more useful purposes, by procuring from Rome the suppression of many convents in order to endow a new college at Oxford, which, after his fall, was more completely established under the name of Christ Church. A decisive change of policy took place in 1532 when the priory of Christchurch, Aldgate, was suppressed. " Papal sanction was no longer possible, and it soon became evident that the property was not to be devoted to any pious or charitable use. The complete secularisation of a monastery, with all its possessions, was contemplated for the first time : the revolution had definitely begun."[77] The canons were induced, possibly by trickery, into executing a deed of surrender in favour of " the king," but the legal doubts raised by the deed compelled the crown to resort to an Act of Parliament to secure its title.[78]

[76] Whether the charges were true or not, does not appear: A. F. Pollard, *Henry VII*, iii, 223; J. Gairdner, " Archbishop Morton and St. Albans," *English Historical Review*, xxiv, 91, 319. For Gasquet's *Henry VIII and the English Monasteries* (1888) see M. D. Knowles, *Cardinal Gasquet as an Historian* (1957).

[77] E. Jeffries Davis, " The beginning of the Dissolution," *Transactions of the Royal Historical Society* (1925), 129.

[78] The capacity of the members of a corporation to dissolve it, and by their deed alienate its lands, was in doubt; the omission of words of inheritance would only give the king a life estate; and the crown cannot take by deed, but only by matter of record. That would normally be by the " office " of an escheator's jury; but the king would not trust himself to a London jury—hence an act of parliament was the only course : 25 Hen. 8, c. 33 (1534).

Smaller houses dissolved, 1536. That Act was the precedent for the first general Act of suppression of the smaller houses in 1536.[79] All religious houses under the yearly value of £200 were, to the number of 376, suppressed by Act of Parliament, and all their property, real and personal, given to the king, his heirs and assigns, " to do and use therewith his or their own wills to the pleasure of Almighty God and the honour and profit of this realm." To prepare the way for this measure, Thomas Cromwell, the king's chief minister and adviser since the death of Wolsey, had been appointed lord vicegerent of the king in all matters ecclesiastical and, at his suggestion, commissioners were nominated to make a general visitation of the monasteries. The nature of their report, which formed the basis of the subsequent legislation, is accurately described in the preamble of the Act. " Manifest sin," it is recited, " vicious, carnal, and abominable living, is daily used and committed amongst the little and small abbeys, priories and other religious houses of monks, canons, and nuns." Amendment has been long tried, " but their vicious living shamelessly increaseth and augmenteth." It scarcely admits of doubt that the commissioners conducted their investigations with unwarrantable harshness, and that their report is in particular cases exaggerated. It is a suspicious circumstance that all the smaller monasteries —whose suppression was alone immediately contemplated—are described as vicious, while those whose incomes rose above the hard-and-fast lines of £200 a year are not only not blamed but even praised. It looks very much as if the small and remote houses, having no one to speak in their favour, were condemned, while the larger, whose abbots could refute unfounded accusations by personal testimony from their seats in parliament, were conveniently spared till a more favourable opportunity. Yet there is no reason to doubt the substantial and general truth of the allegations of the commissioners.[80] Henry VIII may have been chiefly actuated by greed of gain and by hatred to the monastic orders, who, as the special protégés of the papacy, were the most obstinate opponents of his ecclesiastical policy. Their widespread influence over the mass of the people rendered them dangerous enemies to a ruler whose conduct they disapproved.

The Pilgrimage of Grace, 1536–37. This is evidenced by the insurrection in Lincolnshire and the great northern rebellion, styled by the insurgents the " Pilgrimage of Grace," which broke out on the suppression of the smaller monasteries, and was imputed to the " solicitation and traitorous conspiracy of the monks and canons." The movement is of great interest and significance.[81] Some of the insurgents were profoundly shocked at

---

[79] 27 Hen. 8, c. 28; Tanner, *Tudor Documents*, 58.

[80] Since Mr. Taswell-Langmead wrote, there has been a great deal of study upon this question; a more recent estimate is that " the commissioners were men upon whose word it is impossible to depend ": H. A. L. Fisher, *Political History of England*, v, 374.

[81] M. H. Dodds and R. Dodds, *The Pilgrimage of Grace* (2 vols., 1915) is the standard work; there is an extended account also in K. Pickthorn, *Tudor Government*, ii, 304–371.

the religious implications of the government's policy. Others rose in defence of the old feudal order which survived longest in the north, and denounced the thrusting plebeians, such as Cromwell, on the council [82]; the gentry protested against the statute of uses which frustrated their evasions of feudal dues, and put an end to their practice of devising the use of their land; the peasantry lamented the progress of enclosures; townsfolk had special grievances of their own. In spite of the incompatible aims of different sections, the revolt was formidable. Eventually, the insurgents submitted; the government's promises of pardon were thereupon repudiated, and repressive measures applied in the disaffected areas.[83]

The larger houses dissolved, 1539. The rebellion having been ruthlessly stamped out, Henry ventured to dissolve the larger monasteries also, without encountering any open resistance from a terrified people. A few had already been held, contrary to every principle of the common law, to be forfeited to the crown by the attainder of their abbots for high treason. The rest were all surrendered, practically under duress. It only remained for parliament to ratify the king's title under the surrenders and forfeitures, in order to obviate any objection on the score that as all the members of a foundation possessed only life-interests in the property, they could not, either singly or collectively, confer anything more on the sovereign. An Act was accordingly passed, which, after hypocritically reciting that the abbots, priors, abbesses and prioresses had made surrender, " of their own free and voluntary minds, goodwills, and assents, without constraint, coaction, or compulsion," vested in the king and his heirs for ever all the property, real or movable, of the religious houses which had been already or might be hereafter dissolved, suppressed, surrendered, or had or might by any other means come into the hands of the king.[84]

Constitutional implications. The momentous events which fill this chapter had results of the greatest consequence for English history. The exclusion of papal jurisdiction prepared the way for the dissolution, and that, in turn, facilitated the doctrinal revolution of the next reign. It is no part of the constitutional historian's task to inquire whether the

---

[82] *Cf. supra*, p. 221.

[83] On February 22, 1537, after the rebels in the north had dispersed, the king wrote to the Duke of Norfolk: " Forasmuch as our banner is outspread and displayed, by reason whereof, till the same shall be closed again, the course of our laws must give place to the ordinances and statutes martial, our pleasure is that before you close up our said banner again, you shall in any wise, cause such dreadful execution to be done upon a good number of the inhabitants of every town, village, and hamlet, that have offended in this rebellion, as well by the hanging of them up in trees, as by the quartering of them, and the setting of their heads and quarters in every town, great and small, and all such other places, as they may be a fearful spectacle to all other hereafter that would practise any like matter: which we require you to do without pity or respect, according to our former letters." The duke was also to " cause all the monks and canons that be in anywise faulty, to be tied up, without further delay or ceremony, to the terrible example of others; wherein we think you shall do unto us high service."

[84] 31 Hen. 8, c. 13.

marriage of Catherine and Henry was valid or invalid, nor whether the papal jurisdiction as exercised by Clement VII was defensible or not, nor can he discuss the question whether the monasteries deserved their fate. These matters must be studied in the broader setting of ecclesiastical history. Here, we are only concerned to note that Henry VIII did not unravel these knots, but cut them, and that the weapon he used was the omnipotence of the crown in parliament. The inescapable corollary from his action was the inherent right of the supreme authority of parliament to confiscate any property, private or corporate, lay or ecclesiastical, for reasons of which it is itself the sole judge.

The Act of attainder asserted the same irresponsible despotism over the individual as the Acts of suppression had done over ecclesiastical corporations, and both of them denied the profoundest conviction of the Middle Ages, namely, that the liberty of the subject rested upon the inviolability of his person and his property within the limits of due process of law.

The transference of papal jurisdiction to the crown was destined in time to effect a confusion between ecclesiastical and secular politics which incommoded both church and state. Each of them became involved in the difficulties of its partner. Under the early Stuarts religious dissent became political opposition—eventually, political revolution, and for a time puritanism laid low the crown itself. In revenge, the Hanoverians reduced the church to impotence, and almost to silence.

The vast wealth which accrued to the crown by the dissolution of the monasteries might have rendered the king, had he been able to retain it, independent of the commons. But he was obliged to bribe all around him to acquiesce in, and maintain, a measure the accomplishment of which had been attained not without great hazard and difficulty. Some portion was expended on public works and on the foundation of six new bishoprics, but the greater part was distributed among the nobles and gentry, either as gifts or by sale at low prices. The results of this policy were: (1) the new owners of monastic lands were engaged by the strongest ties of private interest to oppose the re-establishment of the papal dominion in England; (2) the territorial aristocracy were strengthened by the large infusion of wealth amongst the newly elevated and the more ancient but decayed families; and (3) land was rendered to a much greater extent than formerly an article of commerce. In connection with this latter result, it is remarkable that the very next year after the passing of the Act for the dissolution of the larger monasteries witnessed the enactment of a goodly array of laws to facilitate the transfer and enjoyment of real property, a circumstance which can scarcely be regarded as fortuitous.[85]

---

[85] A. Amos, *Reformation Parliament*, p. 313. The economic and agrarian results of the dissolution are the subject of a growing literature; see especially the works of S. B. Liljegren, A. Savine, and R. H. Tawney.

ANGLICAN DOCTRINE DEFINED

Henry had now been completely victorious in his contest with the pope; and the English clergy were so humbled and intimidated that they dared not offer any open resistance to the royal will. So far as he had advanced on the road of ecclesiastical reform, with the single exception of the confiscation of the monasteries, the king had probably been heartily supported by a majority of the nation. But there was a growing minority who were eagerly desirous of essential changes in religious faith. With these Henry had no sympathy. Concurrently with the series of political and legal changes which had been effected in the ecclesiastical system, severe measures of repression had been taken against the holders of heretical doctrines, and many had from time to time suffered for their opinions.

Statute of Six Articles, 1539. In his new character of supreme head of the church, Henry now determined to vindicate its doctrinal orthodoxy by imposing on his people a compulsory belief in all the leading doctrines of the Roman Church. By the " Statute of the Six Articles," as it is commonly called, it was affirmed: (1) That in the Sacrament of the Altar there is really present the natural body of Christ, under the forms, but without the substance, of bread and wine. (2) That communion in both kinds is not necessary to salvation. (3) That priests may not marry by the laws of God. (4) That vows of chastity ought to be observed. (5) That private masses ought to be retained " in this the King's English Church and Congregation." (6) That auricular confession is expedient and necessary, and ought to be retained. The penalties for writing, preaching, or disputing against these articles were: Against the first article, death as a heretic, without the option of abjuring; against the other five, the usual penalties of felony. The Act also declared the marriages of priests or nuns utterly void, ordered any such who were married to be immediately separated, and pronounced their future cohabitation to be felony. Lastly, persons contemptuously refusing to confess at the usual times, or to receive the sacrament, were, for the first offence, to be fined and imprisoned ; and for the second, to suffer the punishment of felony.[86]

The Bible in English. In some other respects Henry was induced by Cromwell and Cranmer to favour protestant doctrines. An English translation of the Bible was directed, by the Injunctions of 1538, to be set up in each parish church for the use of the people [87] ; and in the *Institution of a Christian man* (1537, commonly called " The Bishops' Book ") and *Necessary doctrine and erudition of a Christian man* (1543, " The King's Book ")—the latter published by royal authority—explanations

---

[86] 31 Hen. 8, c. 14, " An Act abolishing diversity in opinions "; Tanner, *Tudor Documents*, 95–98.

[87] In 1543, by an Act " for the advancement of true religion " (34 Hen. 8, c. 1), the liberty formerly granted of reading the Bible was restricted.

were given which, " if they did not absolutely proscribe most of the ancient opinions, threw at best much doubt upon them, and gave intimations which the people, now become attentive to these questions, were acute enough to interpret." [88]

EDWARD VI: 1547–1553

The actual reformation in religion was established in the early part of the reign of Edward VI, mainly through the instrumentality of Cranmer and the protector Somerset. A new set of injunctions, containing doctrine at variance with that laid down in Henry VIII's statutes (as yet unrepealed), was issued in August, 1547, and Stephen Gardiner was imprisoned for not subscribing to them. The first Act of Edward's first parliament (which met on November 4, 1547) directed (in response to a petition of convocation) that the sacrament of the altar be administered in both kinds, as being agreeable to primitive usage.[89] Another Act repealed the whole of Henry VIII's treason legislation together with his heresy laws and the Act of Six Articles, thus abandoning his attempt to stabilise religious doctrine, and almost inviting the expression of heterodox opinions—as well as relieving the injunctions from the constitutional objections raised by Gardiner.[90] The absence of parliamentary penalties for the heresies enumerated by Henry VIII, however, still left it possible to burn heretics under the subsisting general law, and two persons, each professing a different, but heinous Christological heresy, were thus executed.[91] Another Act dissolved large numbers of chantries, guilds and religious (but non-monastic) corporations.[92]

The first Book of Common Prayer, 1549. In 1549 was passed the " Act of Uniformity of Service and Administration of the Sacraments," ordaining that the " order of divine worship," contained in the Book of Common Prayer which had been drawn up by a committee of bishops and other divines appointed for that purpose, should in future be the only one to be used by all ministers in any cathedral, parish, or other church.[93] In the same session, the marriage of priests was declared lawful—again, in

[88] Hallam, *Constitutional History*, i, 82 ; E. G. Rupp, *English Protestant Tradition* (Cambridge, 1947).

[89] 1 Edw. 6, c. 1.

[90] 1 Edw. 6, c. 12 (1547); Tanner, *Tudor Documents*, 401 ; *supra*, p. 272.

[91] *Supra*, p. 266.

[92] 1 Edw. 6, c. 14 (1547); Tanner, *Tudor Documents*, 103. The Chantry Act of 1545 (37 Hen. 8, c. 4) had produced little result. For the effect on education, see A. F. Pollard, *Political History of England*, vi, 20.

[93] 2 & 3 Edw. 6, c. 1; Tanner, *Tudor Documents*, 108. The penalties for refusing to use, or speaking or writing in derogation of, the *Book of Common Prayer*, were, for the first or second offence, a fine ; for the third, forfeiture of goods and imprisonment for life. In 1552, a second Act of Uniformity (5 & 6 Edw. 6, c. 1) was passed, reciting that the *Book of Common Prayer* had been " perused, explained, and made fully perfect," and ordering the new (and very much modified) version alone to be used. Both books are easily accessible in the Everyman Library. On their liturgical aspects, see F. Procter and W. H. Frere, *New History of the Book of Common Prayer* (1901), and F. A. Gasquet and E. Bishop, *Edward VI and the Book of Common Prayer* (London, 1890).

response to a petition of the lower house of convocation [94]; and shortly afterwards images and pictures of saints in churches were ordered to be destroyed.[95] But these changes were not carried out without considerable opposition from a part of the nation. Insurrections of a serious nature broke out in Devonshire, Norfolk and several other counties; and religious persecution, " the deadly original sin of the reformed churches," was employed as vigorously, if not so extensively, as in the succeeding reigns of Mary and Elizabeth.

MARY: 1553–1558

During the short reign of Mary the papal religion was completely re-established, probably with the entire approval of a large portion, if not of a majority, of the nation, for whom the progress of the reformation doctrines had been too precipitate. All the laws made against the supremacy of the see of Rome, since the 20th year of Henry VIII, were formally repealed [96]; but it was found impossible to restore the ecclesiastical property in the hands of subjects; and even the bill for restoring to the church the first-fruits and impropriations in the queen's hands was passed not without difficulty. The cruel and widespread persecution of the protestants under Mary, far from eradicating the reformed faith, was instrumental in promoting it. The abhorrence and disgust excited in the people against Mary and the Roman hierarchy were extended to the doctrines which they professed. " Many," remarks Hallam, " are said to have become protestants under Mary, who, at her coming to the throne, had retained the contrary persuasion. And the strongest proof of this may be drawn from the acquiescence of the great body of the kingdom in the re-establishment of protestantism by Elizabeth, when compared with the seditions and discontent on that account under Edward." [97]

---

[94] 2 & 3 Edw. 6, c. 21.

[95] 3 & 4 Edw. 6, c. 10.

[96] 1 & 2 Phil. and Mar., c. 8, repealing " all statutes, articles, and provisions made against the See Apostolic of Rome, since the 20th year of King Henry VIII, and for the establishment of all spiritual and ecclesiastical possessions and hereditaments conveyed to the laity." The preamble recites that " much false and erroneous doctrine hath been taught, preached and written, partly by divers the natural-born subjects of this realm and partly being brought in hither from sundry other foreign countries, had been sown and spread abroad within the same."

[97] *Constitutional History*, i, 107.

CHAPTER 11

THE REIGN OF ELIZABETH I

THE reign of Elizabeth spans a period of very great political and religious ferment throughout Europe. It is the glory of this great queen that by her courage and wisdom, aided by the able policy of her statesmen, Cecil, Nicholas Bacon and Walsingham, she safely guided the nation through a sea of troubles, foreign and domestic, and achieved for England a position in the foremost rank of European monarchies. In commercial and naval enterprise, in every branch of material prosperity, the country advanced with sure and rapid strides, while literature was adorned by the writings of Shakespeare, Spenser, Sidney, Hooker and Jewel. But of constitutional progress during the greater part of Elizabeth's reign there is little to be recorded. From her father she had inherited the arbitrary Tudor notions of the royal prerogative. Her government was eminently despotic in both church and state; and it was only at intervals that the gradually developing spirit of liberty manifested itself in the House of Commons.[1]

ECCLESIASTICAL POLICY OF ELIZABETH

A brief consideration of the principal features of Elizabeth's ecclesiastical policy—so important in its influence on later English constitutional history—will appropriately precede a discussion of the civil government during her reign.

Act of Supremacy, 1559. The first care of Elizabeth's first parliament [2] —which met on January 23, 1559, about two months after her accession to the throne—was to restore the constitution and liturgy of the national church to nearly the same state in which Edward VI had left them at his death. This was effected by the statutes commonly known as the Acts of Supremacy and Uniformity.[3] By the Act of Supremacy, the statute of Philip and Mary (1 & 2 Phil. and Mary, c. 8), which had generally repealed all the previous statutes affecting religion, was abrogated, and

---

[1] For this and the following reign see G. W. Prothero, *Select Statutes and other Constitutional Documents, illustrative of the reigns of Elizabeth and James I* (Clarendon Press, 1906): J. R. Tanner, *Tudor Constitutional Documents* (Cambridge, 1930): and J. R. Tanner, *Constitutional Documents of James I* (Cambridge, 1930). For the political tactics behind the Elizabethan settlement, see Sir John Neale's *Elizabeth I and her Parliaments* (1559–1581): and see generally, the same author's *Elizabeth I* and *The Elizabethan House of Commons*.

[2] There is no evidence that the crown exerted undue influence over the elections: C. G. Bayne, "The first House of Commons of Elizabeth," *English Historical Review*, xxiii, 455 *et seq.*, 643 *et seq.*

[3] For their parliamentary history see F. W. Maitland, *Collected Papers*, iii, 185–209 (*Historical Essays* (ed. Cam) 229 *et seq.*) where useful light is thrown upon the procedure of amendment.

most (but not all) of the laws of King Henry VIII which established the ecclesiastical supremacy of the crown were expressly revived.

It was also particularly enacted: (1) That no foreign prince, person, prelate, state or potentate, spiritual or temporal, shall use, enjoy, or exercise any manner of power, jurisdiction, superiority, authority, pre-eminence, or privilege, spiritual or ecclesiastical, within this realm, or the dominions thereof. (2) That such jurisdictions, privileges, superiorities, pre-eminences, spiritual and ecclesiastical, as by any spiritual or ecclesiastical power or authority hath heretofore been, or may lawfully be, exercised or used for the visitation of the ecclesiastical state and persons, and for reformation, order, and correction of the same, and of all manner of errors, heresies, schisms, abuses, offences, contempts and enormities shall for ever be united and annexed to the imperial crown of this realm. (3) All beneficed ecclesiastics, and all judges, justices, mayors, and other laymen holding office under the crown, were required to take the oath of supremacy and allegiance, on pain of forfeiting their benefices or offices.[4] (4) Any person maintaining the spiritual or temporal jurisdiction of any foreign prince or prelate should, for the first offence, forfeit all his property real and personal; for the second, incur the penalties of prae-munire; and for the third offence, suffer death as a traitor. (5) The queen was also empowered to execute the ecclesiastical jurisdiction of every kind vested in her by the Act by means of commissioners appointed under the great seal for such time as she should direct.[5]

Court of High Commission. It was this last provision which gave statutory authority to the famous High Commission Court,[6] which became a powerful instrument of oppression in the hands of the crown until abolished by the Long Parliament under Charles I. There is one notable omission. Henry VIII's Act of Supremacy had conferred upon the sovereign and his successors the title of " Supreme Head." The commons certainly wished Elizabeth to assume this attribute, but the queen declined to take a step which might prejudice foreign relations. Henry VIII's Act of Supremacy was not expressly revived by Elizabeth's Act, and so Mary's repeal was still effective. Ecclesiastical jurisdiction in

---

[4] This oath, which remained unaltered till the Revolution, was thus worded: " I, *A.B.*, do utterly testify and declare in my conscience that the queen's highness is the only supreme governor of this realm, and of all other her highness's dominions and countries, as well in all spiritual and ecclesiastical things or causes, as temporal; and that no foreign prince, person, prelate, state or potentate hath or ought to have any jurisdiction, power, superiority, pre-eminence, or authority, ecclesiastical or spiritual, within this realm; and therefore I do utterly renounce and forsake all foreign jurisdictions, powers, superiorities and authorities, and do promise that from henceforth I shall bear faith and true allegiance to the queen's highness, her heirs and lawful successors, and to my power shall assist and defend all jurisdictions, pre-eminences, privileges, and authorities granted or belonging to the queen's highness, her heirs and successors, or united or annexed to the imperial crown of this realm "—Act of Supremacy, 1559, s. ix.

[5] 1 Eliz. 1, c. 1, " An Act restoring to the Crown the ancient jurisdiction over the state, ecclesiastical and spiritual, and abolishing all foreign power repugnant to the same." Prothero, *Documents*, 1 *et seq.*; extracts in Tanner, *Documents*, 130 *et seq.*

[6] *Cf. infra*, p. 303.

the widest possible terms was expressly vested in the queen by the new Act, but the oath prescribed in it only calls the queen " supreme governor of the realm. . . ." [7] In fact, Elizabeth had forestalled parliament by replacing the provocative title by the famous " &c." [8]

The Act of Supremacy raised, for the last time, a problem which had been in existence for two centuries and a half, viz., if all the bishops vote against a Bill, can it become a valid statute, and can the statute properly be said to have the consent of "the lords and commons," or of "the lords spiritual and temporal and commons"? An affirmative answer had already been given by the courts of Henry VIII, and although Bishop Bonner (advised by the great lawyer Plowden) was ready to dispute it, that answer, confirmed by the authority of Coke, became a definitive statement of the law. There are two estates in the lords, but the lords vote as one house and the vote binds both estates.[9]

Act of Uniformity, 1559. By the Act of Uniformity, the revised Book of Common Prayer as established by Edward VI in 1552 was, with a few alterations and additions, revived and confirmed. Any parson, vicar, or other minister, whether beneficed or not, wilfully using any but the established liturgy was to suffer, for the first offence, six months' imprisonment, and, if beneficed, forfeit the profits of his benefice for a year; for the second offence, a year's imprisonment; for the third, imprisonment for life. All persons absenting themselves, without lawful or reasonable excuse, from the service at their parish church on Sundays and holy days, were to be punished by ecclesiastical censures and a fine of one shilling for the use of the poor.[10]

By another Act of the same session, first-fruits and tenths, which the preamble states the late queen had given up, " upon certain zealous and inconvenient respects," were again vested in the crown, in order to lessen " the huge, immeasurable and inestimable charges of the royal estate." [11] Such religious houses as Queen Mary had refounded were suppressed, and their property also given to the crown.[12]

Thirty-Nine Articles. In 1563 the Articles of the English Church, forty-two in number, originally drawn up in 1551 under Edward VI,

---

[7] *Supra*, p. 289 n. 4.

[8] The curious story is told in Maitland, *Collected Papers*, iii, 185–209; for the " &c.," *ibid.* 157–165: reprinted in his *Historical Essays* (ed. Cam), 229–246, 211–216. (Some of Henry's Acts which referred to him as " Supreme Head " were among those expressly revived.) See generally, A. F. Pollard, *Political History of England*, vi, 201 et seq. There is a neat comment in Selden, *Table Talk* (ed. Pollock), 63, and in Prothero, 412.

[9] The problem dates from 1307 (*supra*, pp. 259 et seq., 275). The principal authorities are Keilwey's *Reports*, 184b and Coke, 2 Inst. 587; Maitland, *Collected Papers*, iii, 125–126; *cf.* the next footnote, and *infra*, p. 295.

[10] 1 Eliz. 1, c. 2, " An Act for the Uniformity of Common Prayer and Divine Service in the Church, and Administration of the Sacraments." Prothero, 13; extracts in Tanner, 136. The general heading to all the statutes of the session recites the consent of lords spiritual and temporal and commons, but the enacting clause omits to mention the bishops; as to this, *cf.* Maitland, *op. cit.*, iii, 207.

[11] 1 Eliz. 1, c. 4; Prothero, 22.

[12] 1 Eliz. 1, c. 24; Prothero, 27.

were revised in Convocation, and reduced to their present number, thirty-nine; but it was not until 1571 that they were made binding upon the clergy by Act of Parliament.[13]

These changes in religion were not effected without considerable opposition in the House of Lords. Nine temporal peers and all the bishops protested against the Bill of Uniformity establishing the Anglican liturgy and it passed the lords with a majority of only three votes. The first Supremacy Bill disappeared in committee in the commons; the second bill was heavily amended in the lords, refashioned by the commons, accepted by the lords and rejected by the queen; it was a third draft which finally became law. The commons, on the contrary, far from offering any opposition, were throughout Elizabeth's reign anxious for further reforms.

The formularies of the national church thus finally established, appear to have been designedly framed in a comprehensive spirit, so as to avoid giving offence to the moderate men of both the religious parties in the state. With reference to this peculiar character of the reformed national church as a compromise between the extreme parties of the old and new theology, Lord Macaulay has remarked: " She occupies a middle position between the churches of Rome and Geneva. Her doctrinal confessions and discourses, composed by protestants, set forth principles of theology in which Calvin or Knox would have found scarcely a word to disapprove. Her prayers and thanksgivings, derived from the ancient breviaries, are very generally such that Cardinal Fisher or Cardinal Pole might have heartily joined in them. . . . Nothing, however, so strongly distinguished the Church of England from other churches as the relation in which she stood to the monarchy. The king was her head. The limits of the authority which he possessed, as such, were not traced, and indeed have never yet been traced, with precision. . . . What Henry and his favourite counsellors meant, at one time, by the supremacy, was certainly nothing less than the whole power of the keys. The king was to be the pope of his kingdom, the vicar of God, the expositor of catholic verity, the channel of sacramental graces. He arrogated to himself the right of deciding dogmatically what was orthodox doctrine and what was heresy, of drawing up and imposing confessions of faith, and of giving religious instruction to his people. He proclaimed that all jurisdiction, spiritual as well as temporal, was derived from him alone, and that it was in his power to confer episcopal authority, and to take it away. . . . According to this system, as expounded by Cranmer, the king was the spiritual as well as the temporal chief of the nation. In both capacities his highness must have lieutenants. As he appointed civil officers to keep his seal, to collect his revenues, to dispense justice in his name, so he appointed divines of various ranks to preach the gospel, and to administer the

[13] 13 Eliz. 1, c. 12; Prothero, 64.

sacraments. . . . These opinions the archbishop, in spite of the opposition of less courtly divines, followed out to every legitimate consequence. He held that his own spiritual functions, like the secular functions of the chancellor and treasurer, were at once determined by a demise of the crown. When Henry died, therefore, the primate and his suffragans took out fresh commissions, empowering them to ordain and to govern the church till the new sovereign should think fit to order otherwise. . . . These high pretensions gave scandal to protestants as well as to catholics " ; and Elizabeth " found it necessary expressly to disclaim that sacerdotal character which her father had assumed, and which, according to Cranmer, had been inseparably joined, by divine ordinance, to the regal function . . .[14] The queen, however, still had over the church a visitatorial power of vast and undefined extent. . . . By the royal authority alone, her prelates were appointed. By the royal authority alone her convocations were summoned, regulated, prorogued and dissolved. Without the royal sanction her canons had no force. One of the articles of her faith was that without the royal consent no ecclesiastical council could lawfully assemble. From all her judicatures an appeal lay, in the last resort, to the sovereign, even when the question was whether an opinion ought to be accounted heretical, or whether the administration of a sacrament had been valid. Nor did the church grudge this extensive power to our princes. . . . All her traditions, all her tastes, were monarchical. Loyalty became a point of professional honour among her clergy, the peculiar badge which distinguished them at once from calvinists and from papists. Both the calvinists and the papists, widely as they differed in other respects, regarded with extreme jealousy all encroachments of the temporal power on the domain of the spiritual power. Both calvinists and papists maintained that subjects might justifiably draw the sword against ungodly rulers. In France, calvinists resisted Charles IX; papists resisted Henry IV; both papists and calvinists resisted Henry III. In Scotland calvinists led Mary captive. On the north of the Trent papists took arms against the English throne. The Church of England meantime condemned both calvinists and papists, and loudly boasted that no duty was more constantly or earnestly inculcated by her than that of submission to princes." [15]

The royal supremacy. When the oath of supremacy was tendered to the bishops, one only, Kitchin of Llandaff, was prevailed upon to take it; the rest, on refusal, were deprived of their sees.[16] But the general

[14] The 37th article of religion, framed under Elizabeth, declares in emphatic terms that the ministering of God's Word does not belong to princes.

[15] Macaulay, *History of England*, i, 44–49.

[16] It happened that ten sees were vacant at Elizabeth's accession, and fifteen more were vacated by the bishops who refused the oath of supremacy. Matthew Parker, who had been chaplain to Queen Anne Boleyn, was consecrated Archbishop of Canterbury, December 17, 1559, and before the end of 1562 all the sees, except Oxford, were filled by men eminent for their zeal in the protestant cause, many of whom had been exiles during the Marian persecution. Elizabeth kept the see of Oxford vacant for twenty-one years, appropriating its revenues, 1568–1589.

body of the beneficed clergy, with the exception of a very small number, acquiesced in the new order of things and retained their livings.[17]

Throughout her reign it was the constant policy of Elizabeth to maintain her ecclesiastical supremacy, and to enforce outward conformity with the religion established by law. This policy, which is expressed in a series of persecuting and disabling Acts against Roman Catholics and protestant sectaries, continued as a marked feature of our system of government for more than two centuries. The church and the throne mutually supported each other against the advocates of civil and religious freedom, and to the heat of political contests was added the bitterness of theological hatred.

The first attack upon the Romanists was made in Elizabeth's second parliament by a statute passed in 1563, " for the assurance of the queen's majesty's royal power over all estates and subjects within her highness' dominions." The preamble recites the " perils, dishonours and inconveniences " that have resulted from the usurped power of the see of Rome, and " the danger by the fautors of the said usurped power, at this time grown to marvellous outrage and licentious boldness, and now requiring more sharp restraint and correction of laws than hitherto in the time of the queen's majesty's most mild and merciful reign, have been had, used, and established." It was therefore enacted: (1) That the penalties of praemunire should be incurred by all who maintained the authority of the pope within the realm. (2) That the bishops and commissioners to be appointed under the great seal should have power to tender the oath of supremacy to, and that the same should be taken by, all persons who had ever been admitted into holy orders or to any degree in the universities; all schoolmasters and public and private teachers of children; and all barristers, attorneys, officers of the Inns of Court, and other persons engaged in the execution of the law. The penalty for the first refusal of this oath was that of praemunire, but if, after three months, there was a second tender and refusal, the offence was made high treason. (3) Every member of the House of Commons was to take the oath before entering upon his parliamentary functions; but it was not to be tendered to the temporal peers, in whom, although many of them were still Roman Catholics, the queen declared her full confidence.[18]

Opposition in both Houses. This severe statute excited some opposition in both Houses of Parliament. In the Upper House, Lord Montagu delivered a speech against it which is characterised by great liberality and tolerance, virtues which in that age were rarely advocated by any party except when itself the object of persecution. " This law," said

---

[17] Out of a body of nearly 9,000 only about 180 resigned their benefices or were deprived. See Tanner, *Documents*, 136, n. 2. *Cf.* also Pollard, *Political History*, p. 218, who estimates the number of beneficed clergy who lost their preferments considerably higher; but " the question cannot be settled by the data available at present."—J. B. Black, *Reign of Elizabeth* (1936) 17 n. 1.

[18] 5 Eliz. 1, c. 1; Prothero, *Documents,* 39–41.

Lord Montagu, " is not necessary; forasmuch as the catholics of this realm disturb not, nor hinder the public affairs of the realm, neither spiritual nor temporal. They dispute not, they preach not, they disobey not the queen, they cause no trouble nor tumults among the people. So that no man can say, that thereby the realm doth receive any hurt or damage by them. They have brought into the realm no novelties in doctrine and religion. This being true and evident, as it is indeed, there is no necessity why any new law should be made against them. . . . I do entreat," he continued, " whether it be just to make this penal statute to force the subjects of this realm to receive and believe the religion of the protestants upon pain of death. This I say, is a thing more unjust. . . . For this repugneth to the natural liberty of man's understanding. For understanding may be persuaded, but not forced." He concluded by pointing out the danger of driving the catholics to forcible resistance: " It is an easy thing to understand that a thing so unjustly, and so contrary to all reason and liberty of man, cannot be put in execution but with great incommodity and difficulty. . . . To be still and dissemble may be borne and suffered for a time; to keep his reckoning with God alone; but to be compelled to lie and to swear, or else to die therefor, are things that no man ought to suffer and endure. And it is to be feared, rather than to die, they will seek how to defend themselves; whereby should ensue the contrary of that every good prince and well-advised commonwealth ought to seek and pretend, that is, to keep their kingdom and government in peace." [19] This reasoning seems to have produced some effect on the government, although it did not prevent the passing of the statute. Archbishop Parker privately instructed the bishops to use great caution in tendering the oath of supremacy under the Act, and never to do so the second time, on which the penalty of treason might attach, without his previous authorisation. Some time afterwards, however, Horne, Bishop of Winchester, indiscreetly giving vent to his indignation against Bonner, the deprived Bishop of London, who was specially obnoxious on account of the prominent part taken by him in the Marian persecution, indicted him for refusing to take the oath of supremacy. Bonner, advised by Edmund Plowden, a catholic and the most eminent lawyer of the day, drew up an argument in the course of which he offered to maintain that the Act of Supremacy, which purported to impose the oath, was no lawful Act, since it had not the assent of the lords spiritual [20]; and furthermore that Horne was not a lawful bishop, and therefore had no authority to tender the oath. As we have seen,[21] authority was going against the first point; but the second point was difficult to meet in view of the special circumstances of Horne's appointment. The prosecution was therefore dropped; no trial took place, and Bonner was suffered to

[19] Strype, *Annals of the Reformation*, i, 296–297. *Cf.* for the general question, W. K. Jordan, *Development of Religious Toleration in England* (1932).
[20] Strype, *Annals of the Reformation*, I, ii, p. 4.
[21] *Supra*, p. 291.

remain in his prison in the Marshalsea, where he had been confined since the accession of the queen. As soon as Parliament was reassembled, an Act was passed declaring the consecration of the archbishops and bishops, as practised since the queen's accession, " good, lawful, and perfect." [22]

Eight years elapsed before further legislation was directed against the Roman Catholics; but in the meantime several circumstances had occurred, which rendered them specially obnoxious to the government not merely as being opponents of the established religion, but as tainted with disloyalty to the queen. At first the catholics generally had attended church, and yielded an apparent conformity to the English service; but in 1563, the Council of Trent, in its last session, pronounced a condemnation of such outward conformity. This censure was industriously circulated throughout England by William Allen [23] and other priests, who now ventured to return from the voluntary banishment into which they had gone on the death of Queen Mary. The Romanists, in consequence, began to decline attendance at church; and many withdrew abroad, where they formed centres of disaffection, in which plots were constantly being hatched against Queen Elizabeth.

Elizabeth's title to the throne. The relations of Elizabeth towards her Roman Catholic subjects were also materially affected by the special character of her title to the throne, and the uncertainty in which the succession was involved—an uncertainty which was increased by her repeated refusals to marry, or to agree to a parliamentary appointment of a successor. The queen's title to the throne depended absolutely on an Act of Parliament (35 Hen. 8, c. 1) by which the crown had been settled upon her. She had also been nominated in the succession, after her sister Mary, by her father's will, and her title had been ratified by the Act passed immediately after her accession (1 Eliz. 1, c. 3). Her right to the crown was therefore based upon the best of all titles, the will of the people expressed by their representatives in parliament. But the natural prejudice of most of the Roman Catholics in favour of a monarch of their own religion, and the impossibility of a catholic admitting that Elizabeth was legitimate, coupled with the preference felt by many for a strictly hereditary over a purely parliamentary title,

[22] 8 Eliz. 1, c. 1. The only irregularity in the consecration of the bishops had consisted in the use of the ordinal of Edward VI before it had been legally re-established. As the pre-reformation [Sarum] ordinal had been abolished, and that of Edward VI was not yet re-established, there existed at the time no form of consecration prescribed by the English law.

[23] Allen had been principal of St. Mary Hall, Oxford, in Mary's reign, and had gone into exile at Louvain in 1561. He founded a seminary at Douai, whither catholics of the best English families were sent to be educated, and whence a constant succession of priests passed into England, not only to look after the spiritual welfare of the Romanists, but to intrigue against the government. Allen was made a cardinal in 1587, put his signature to an admonition in favour of the projected Spanish Armada, and was rewarded by Philip II with the Archbishopric of Mechlin. He died in 1594. Lingard, *History of England*, vi, 331, 499, 706.

led them to regard the Queen of Scots, granddaughter of Henry VIII's elder sister Margaret, as having a prior right to the throne during Elizabeth's life, and in any case as its presumptive heir after her decease. Under the provisions of Henry's will—executed under parliamentary authority—the succession in remainder was vested in the junior line of the House of Suffolk to the postponement, if not exclusion, of the senior Scottish line. But the harsh and unjust condemnation of Lady Catherine Grey's private marriage with the Earl of Hertford (son of the Protector Somerset), which Elizabeth's jealous humour procured to be pronounced early in her reign,[24] cast a doubt upon the legitimacy of the protestant line of Suffolk, and thus strengthened the hope of the catholic adherents of Mary of Scotland. So early as 1563, Edmund and Arthur Pole, nephews of the late cardinal, were tried and convicted of high treason on a charge of designing to set the Queen of Scots on the throne and to re-establish Romanism in England. In 1568, Mary, having been driven from her throne, in a great measure owing to the intrigues of Elizabeth's ministers with the Scottish malcontents, escaped into England, only to endure a long imprisonment ending in a violent death. Her presence on English soil revived the hopes of the Romanists. Plots were formed for her liberation, for the invasion of England by Spain, and for the re-establishment of the Roman rite. In 1569 the Duke of Norfolk, the greatest and richest subject in England, was concerned in an extensive conspiracy, involving the deposition of the queen, his own marriage with Mary of Scotland, and the invasion of the kingdom by the Duke of Alva.[25]

The Pope deposes the Queen, 1570. Later in the same year the Earls of Northumberland and Westmorland took up arms in the north, with the design of restoring the old religion; and at the beginning of 1570, Pope Pius V, who had secretly instigated this insurrection, published his celebrated bull *Regnans in Excelsis*, excommunicating and deposing Elizabeth, and absolving all her subjects from their oaths of fidelity and allegiance.[26]

As soon as parliament met, in April 1571, two statutes were passed in reply to the pope's bull, and as a precaution against fresh attempts

---

[24] See the circumstances narrated in Pollard, *Political History of England*, vi, 243–244.

[25] He was convicted of treason and executed in 1572. *Infra*, p. 514.

[26] "The bull of Pius V," observes Hallam (*Constitutional History*, i, 137), "far more injurious in its consequences to those it was designed to serve than to Elizabeth, forms a leading epoch in the history of our English catholics. It rested upon a principle never universally acknowledged, and regarded with much jealousy by temporal governments, yet maintained in all countries by many whose zeal and ability rendered them formidable —the right vested in the supreme pontiff to depose kings for heinous crimes against the Church. One Felton affixed this bull to the gates of the Bishop of London's palace, and suffered death for the offence. So audacious a manifestation of disloyalty was imputed with little justice to the catholics at large, but might more reasonably lie at the door of those active instruments of Rome, the English refugee priests and Jesuits dispersed over Flanders, and lately established at Douai, who were continually passing into the kingdom, not only to keep alive the precarious faith of the laity, but, as was generally surmised, to excite them against their sovereign." Text in Prothero, 195; translation in Tanner, 144; *cf.* the comments of J. B. Black, *Reign of Elizabeth*, 134 *et seq.*

on the part of Mary's partisans. By the first of these: (1) It was made high treason to affirm that the queen was a heretic, schismatic, tyrant, infidel, or usurper of the crown; or that the common law, until altered by parliament, ought not to bind the right of the crown, or that the queen, with the authority of parliament, was not able to make laws limiting and binding the crown and the descent, inheritance, and government thereof. (2) And it was further declared to be an offence, punishable by imprisonment and forfeiture of goods, and on repetition by a praemunire, for anyone during the queen's life, and before the same had been established by parliament, to affirm, print, or write that any one particular person was or ought to be heir or successor of the queen, except the natural issue of her body.[27] The second Act refers specially to the pope's recent bull, and recites that " by colour of the said bulls and writings wicked persons very secretly and most seditiously in such parts of the realm where the people, for want of good instruction, are most weak, simple and ignorant, . . . have by their lewd and subtle practices and persuasions so far wrought, that sundry simple and ignorant persons have been contented to be reconciled to the usurped authority of the see of Rome, and to take absolution at the hands of the said naughty and subtle practicers whereby hath grown great disobedience and boldness in many, not only to withdraw and absent themselves from all divine service, but also have thought themselves discharged of all obedience to her majesty whereby most wicked and unnatural rebellion hath ensued." It was therefore enacted: (1) That any person publishing any bull from Rome, or absolving and reconciling any one of the Roman church, or being so reconciled, should incur the penalties of high treason. (2) Aiders and comforters after the fact were to incur praemunire; and any person to whom absolution should be offered, and who should not disclose such offer within six weeks to some member of the Privy Council, was to be held guilty of misprision of treason. (3) Praemunire was also imposed upon such as brought into the realm " things called Agnus Dei, or any crosses, pictures, beads, or such like vain and superstitious things, . . . hallowed and consecrated, as it is termed, by the bishop of Rome." [28]

The Jesuit mission, 1580. During an interval of ten years no further statute was passed against the Roman Catholics, but the existing laws were enforced by the government in all their severity. Persecution, however, served only to excite fresh manifestations of zeal. Missionary priests poured into the kingdom from Douai and Rome; and in 1580 a mission of the recently founded order of Jesuits, under the leadership of Robert Parsons and Edmund Campion, was dispatched by Pope Gregory XIII to bring about the re-conversion of England. The government was seriously alarmed. A proclamation was issued denouncing as aiders and abettors of treason all who should harbour or conceal any

[27] 13 Eliz. 1, c. 1, Prothero, *Documents*, 56–60; Tanner, 413. *Infra*, p. 503.
[28] 13 Eliz. 1, c. 2. Prothero, 60–63; Tanner, 146.

Jesuit or seminarist in the kingdom, and as soon as parliament met a severe Act was passed " to retain the queen's majesty's subjects in their due obedience." By this statute: (1) The former provisions making it high treason to reconcile any of her Majesty's subjects, or to be reconciled to the church of Rome, were re-enacted. (2) The celebration of the mass was made punishable with a fine of 200 marks and a year's imprisonment; hearing mass, with a fine of 100 marks and imprisonment for a like period. (3) All persons above sixteeen absenting themselves from church, unless they should hear the established service at home, were to forfeit £20 a month, or, in default of payment within three months after judgment, to be imprisoned until they should conform. (4) All schoolmasters were to be licensed by the ordinary, or suffer a year's imprisonment; and persons employing them unlicensed were to forfeit £10 a month.[29]

Shortly afterwards, the Jesuit Campion and several seminary priests from Flanders, after having eluded the vigilance of the government for some time, were seized and imprisoned in the Tower. It was alleged that under the pain of the rack [30] Campion revealed the names of several catholics who had sheltered him, but it is probable that these so-called " confessions " were forgeries.[31] Failing to give satisfactory answers as to the pope's deposing power, he was tried and condemned for high treason, and executed with two other priests.

Driven to desperation by the severity of the persecution, some of the more reckless spirits among the Roman Catholics now began to form plots for the assassination of the queen, as a step towards the elevation of Mary of Scotland to the throne. In September 1584, one Creighton, a Scottish Jesuit, was captured at sea, bearing about him the

[29] 23 Eliz. 1, c. 1; Prothero, 74; Tanner, 150. By a subsequent Act (28 & 29 Eliz. 1, c. 6; Prothero, 88) the queen was empowered, for default of payments of the fine, to seize two-thirds of the land and all the goods of the delinquents.

[30] " The common law of England . . . neither admits of torture to extort confession, nor of any penal infliction not warranted by a judicial sentence. But this law, though still sacred in the courts of justice, was set aside by the Privy Council under the Tudor line." Hallam, *Constitutional History*, i, 148. For a description of the different kinds of torture, see Lingard, viii. 521, note (G). Coke (3 Inst., p. 35) says the rack in the Tower was introduced by the Duke of Exeter under Henry VI, whence it obtained the name of " the Duke of Exeter's daughter." He adds, " there is no law to warrant tortures in this land, nor can they be justified by any prescription being so lately brought in." Under James I, the torture was employed in the case of the Gunpowder Plot conspirators, and on other occasions; but on the trial of Felton (1628) for the assassination of the Duke of Buckingham, when it was proposed in the Privy Council to put the accused on the rack in order to discover his accomplices, the judges (being consulted) declared unanimously that no such proceeding was allowable by the law. They equally refused, as being *ultra vires*, to add some additional punishment, at the king's request, to that which the law had ordained for murder. 3 St.Tr. 371–372. D. Jardine, in his " Reading on the use of Torture " (1837) says: " The last case of torture in England, of which I can find any trace, occurred in the year 1640." Maitland, *Constitutional History*, p. 221, remarks: " In Edw. IV's reign torture begins to make its appearance, we hear of it in 1468. It never becomes part of the procedure of the ordinary courts, but a free use is made of it by Council, and the rack becomes one of our political institutions."

[31] R. Simpson, *Life of Campion*, 224 *et seq.* The government endeavoured to underline the political rather than the religious side of the case by trying Campion under the Treason Act of 1352 instead of under the recent acts against Jesuits; *cf*. Pollard, *Political History of England*, vi, 376–377.

heads of a plan for a Spanish invasion and the deposition or death of the queen. When Elizabeth's fifth parliament met in November 1584, its first Act was one " for the security of the queen's majesty's most royal person and the continuance of the realm in peace." This statute legalised a voluntary association which had been formed shortly before, the members of which had sworn to protect the queen from assassination or to revenge her death. It also enacted that if any invasion or rebellion should be made by or for any person pretending title to the crown after the queen's decease, or if anything be compassed or imagined tending to the hurt of her person, with the privity of any such person, a number of peers, privy councillors, and judges, to be commissioned by the queen, should examine and give judgment on such offences and all circumstances relating thereto. All persons who should authorise such an attempt, or on whose behalf the same should be made, were declared to be incapable of ever inheriting the throne.[32]

Mary Queen of Scots. It was under the provisions of this statute that Mary Queen of Scots was tried and found guilty, in 1586, of having been privy to Babington's conspiracy to kill the queen, and of having herself " compassed and imagined within this realm of England divers matters tending to the hurt, death, and destruction of the royal person of our sovereign lady the queen."

The second Act of the parliament of 1584 was directed against " Jesuits, seminary priests, and such other like disobedient persons." All Jesuits, seminary and other Roman Catholic priests, whether ordained within or without the kingdom, were commanded to quit the realm within forty days, under the penalty of high treason; to aid or receive them was made felony; and any person knowing a priest to be within the kingdom and not disclosing the fact to a magistrate, was to be fined and imprisoned at the queen's pleasure. All students in the Romanist seminaries who should not return within six months after proclamation to that effect, and within two days afterwards take the oath of supremacy, should be punished as traitors; persons sending children abroad without licence were to forfeit £100 for each offence, and to incur a praemunire if they sent money to any already at a seminary; the children so sent were disabled from inheriting any property from the sender.[33]

So drastic a law as this would seem to have rendered any further penal legislation against the Roman Catholics unnecessary. The execution of Mary of Scotland on February 8, 1587, relieved the queen from the only dangerous pretender to the throne, and deprived the catholics of their last hope. The patriotism and loyalty displayed by them during the agonising crisis of the Armada would have been fitly acknowledged

[32] 27 Eliz. 1, c. 1. Prothero, 80; Tanner, 417.
[33] 27 Eliz. 1, c. 2. Prothero, 83.

by some remission of penalties. But far from being relaxed, the persecution became more rigorous,[34] and yet one more statute was passed against " popish recusants," as persons convicted for non-attendance at church were now denominated, restraining them to particular places of residence, from which they were not to travel more than five miles.[35]

The perils with which the throne of Elizabeth was constantly menaced by the perpetual conspiracy of Rome and Spain against her during the greater part of her reign, and the imputation of disloyalty necessarily attaching to all strict catholics after the promulgation of the pope's deposing bull, afforded some justification for the harsh persecution to which they were subjected.

Persecution of the protestant sectaries. For the simultaneous persecution of the protestant non-conformists no such extenuation can be pleaded. " The puritans," as Macaulay has justly remarked, " even in the depths of the prisons to which Elizabeth had sent them, prayed, and with no simulated fervour, that she might be kept from the dagger of the assassin, that rebellion might be put down under her feet, that her arms might be victorious by sea and land. One of the most stubborn of the stubborn sect, immediately after his hand had been lopped off for an offence into which he had been hurried by his intemperate zeal, waved his hat with the hand which was still left him, and shouted, ' God save the queen ! ' " [36]

The reformed Anglican church, as professedly " keeping the mean between the two extremes," had from the first been distasteful to a large body of the more zealous protestants, who were eager to discard all rites and ceremonies savouring in any degree of the Roman system of worship. During the Marian persecution many of these men sought refuge in Germany and Switzerland, where they imbibed calvinistic doctrines, and grew accustomed to a simple form of divine service and a democratic system of church government. Returning to England on the accession of Elizabeth, these exiles were dissatisfied at finding that far from proceeding in the path of reform, the queen and her ministers were inclined somewhat to recede even from the point which had been attained under Edward VI.[37] Though separated from the Roman communion,

---

[34] The Roman Catholic martyrs under Elizabeth have been reckoned at 187. Pollard, *Political History*, 376. Of these 110 suffered death between 1588 and 1603.

[35] 35 Eliz. 1, c. 2. Prothero, 92.

[36] *History of England*, i, 53. The person referred to was John Stubbe, a lawyer, and brother-in-law of Cartwright, the leader of the puritans. In 1579, the queen, much to the alarm of her protestant subjects, entered into negotiations for a marriage with the Duke of Alençon (afterwards Duke of Anjou). Stubbe ventured to remonstrate in a pamphlet entitled the " Discovery of a Gaping Gulph whereinto England is like be swallowed up by another French Marriage if the Lord forbid not the Banns, by letting her Majestie see the Sin and Punishment thereof." For this pamphlet, which, very far from being a virulent libel, is written in a sensible manner and with unfeigned loyalty and affection towards the queen, he suffered the mutilation mentioned in the text.

[37] The retention of vestments, instrumental music, and other features of the ancient church ceremonial, though thoroughly defensible on the grounds of decency and order, and as tending to conciliate the very large Roman party existing in the kingdom, was due in a

the Anglican reformers had by no means intended to abolish the binding nature of the authority in matters of religion, but merely to substitute one kind of authority for another. But the very fact of the separation was in its essence an assertion, however unintentional, of the right of private judgment. Having emancipated themselves by a great mental effort from the despotism of a church " strong in immemorial antiquity and catholic consent," the more ardent reformers were indignant at the attempt made to bind them anew by the authority of a church which they considered to be sprung from the exercise of that right of private judgment which it now sought to suppress.

Archbishop Parker's " Advertisements," 1566. For several years the deviations of many of the clergy from the uniformity prescribed by statute were connived at by the bishops, several of whom sympathised with the puritan party. But in 1565 the queen determined to put a stop to these irregularities, which in fact were practised in defiance of her prerogative in ecclesiastical affairs. At her instigation Archbishop Parker published a book of " Advertisements " to the clergy, containing strict regulations for their discipline.[38] Shortly before, Sampson, Dean of Christ Church, and Humphrey, Regius Professor of Divinity and President of Magdalen College, Oxford, two of the most eminent puritans, were cited to appear before Archbishop Parker and the commissioners for refusing to wear vestments, and the former was deprived of his deanery, and thirty-seven of the London clergy refusing to comply with the legal ceremonies were suspended from their ministry and threatened with the punishment of deprivation. Abandoning the churches, the lay puritans in London now began to form separate conventicles. In June 1567, a congregation of more than one hundred were seized at Plumbers' Hall, and about twenty of them subjected to a year's imprisonment for their contumacy. This was the first instance of actual punishment inflicted on protestant dissenters.

The puritans attack episcopacy. Hitherto the puritans had restricted their opposition to the retention of what they deemed superstitious ceremonies in the church services; but about the year 1570 attacks began to be made on the episcopal system of church government. The principal leader in this new movement was Thomas Cartwright, Lady Margaret Professor of Divinity at Cambridge, and the author of the " Second Admonition to the Parliament," published in 1572, which demanded,

---

large measure to the strong personal predilection of the queen. She manifested a very decided leaning towards the forms of worship and even to some of the doctrines of the Roman church, and resolutely opposed the marriage of the clergy. Although the marriage of bishops and priests was connived at, the queen would never consent to repeal the statute of Mary against it. Until the first year of James I, when this statute was explicitly abrogated, the offspring of clerical marriages were, in the eye of the law, illegitimate (1 Jac. 1, c. 25). Hallam, *Constitutional History*, i, 173.

[38] These were issued without specific royal sanction. See Pollard, *Political History*, 358; J. B. Black, *Reign of Elizabeth*, 157.

in bold and contemptuous language, a reform of the various abuses alleged to exist in the established church.[39] The puritans had many friends in the House of Commons, in the Queen's Council, and among the bishops. From time to time bills were introduced for abolishing various ecclesiastical rites and ceremonies, and even for abrogating some of the thirty-nine articles, but, mainly through the determined opposition of the queen, they were invariably withdrawn.

Prophesyings. Archbishop Grindal, who succeeded Parker in January 1576, was inclined to the views of the puritans, and for refusing to comply with the command to suppress certain meetings of the more precise clergy for prayer and exposition of Scripture, termed " Prophesyings," was sequestered from his see for five years, and only escaped deprivation by his death in 1583. Although primarily designed as meetings of clergy for devotion and instruction, these " exercises " or " prophesyings " tended to develop features which disquieted the queen, in spite of the fact that several bishops countenanced them. Thus, the laity were admitted as spectators; the members framed a confession of faith which they were ready to maintain even against the church; and they devised a system of discipline which simply ignored the church's existing organisa-tion. In all this Elizabeth discerned a movement to effect radical changes in church government by erecting a voluntary but rival system within the church.[40] Grindal was succeeded in the primacy by Whitgift, a strenuous opponent of the puritans.

High Commission Court. The Act of Supremacy of 1559 expressly sanctioned the issue of commissions for ecclesiastical causes, a practice which had already grown up from the necessity of exercising the authority vested in the crown by Henry VIII's assumption of the supreme headship of the church. It had been used by Henry, by Edward VI, and by Mary; under Elizabeth it took its final form. The strictly judicial side of the royal supremacy was entrusted to the statutory High Court of Delegates,[41] leaving to the commissioners a varied mass of disciplinary and administra-tive duties. Its wide supervisory powers in ecclesiastical matters gave it a position not unlike that of the Star Chamber and Privy Council in secular affairs.[42] During Elizabeth's reign the commission gradually

[39] See A. F. S. Pearson, *Thomas Cartwright and Elizabethan Puritanism* (1925) and *Church and State: Political Aspects of Sixteenth-Century Puritanism* (1928); H. C. Porter, *Reformation and Reaction in Tudor Cambridge* (1959). The first admonition was the work of John Field and Thomas Wilcox, who were, on account of it, committed to prison. Several of Elizabeth's bishops were vulnerable, having dealt simoniacally or irregularly with the endowments of their sees, and the queen herself was implicated in some of these trans-actions—J. B. Black, *Reign of Elizabeth*, 153–154.

[40] See the documents in Prothero, 202–208.

[41] 25 Hen. 8, c. 19 (Act for the Submission of the Clergy, 1534, *supra*, p. 290); expressly revived by 1 Eliz. 1, c. 1. This jurisdiction was transferred to the crown in council in 1832, and to the Judicial Committee of the Privy Council in 1833.

[42] The statement commonly made that the High Commission has its origin in the Act of Supremacy of 1559 is erroneous: see Usher, *The Rise and Fall of the High Commission* (Oxford, 1913); see also, for an excellent summary of the history and work of the High

developed the aspect of a court; by 1583 this development is clearly marked. The old inquisitorial functions came to be accompanied by newer judicial functions in suits between parties. It competed very successfully with the ancient church courts and especially with the High Court of Delegates.[43] Of the fourty-four members of the commission of 1584, twelve were prelates; and three, of whom one must be a bishop, formed a quorum. They were directed to inquire generally, as well by the oaths of twelve good and lawful men, as by witnesses, and all other means they could devise, into all matters affecting religion, such as heretical and schismatic opinions, absence from church, seditious books, slanderous words and sayings, incests, adulteries, and other immoralities; to examine all suspected persons on their oaths; to tender the oath of supremacy according to the Act of Parliament, and to punish all who should refuse to appear or to obey their orders by excommunication, fine and imprisonment.

The oath " ex officio." Under these extensive powers, such of the clergy as were suspected of puritanical tendencies were summoned before the court and required to take the famous oath *ex officio*, to answer truly a series of ecclesiastical interrogatories. This oath[44] was founded on the canon law, and Lord Burleigh, who strongly disapproved of the proceeding, described it as " so curiously penned, so full of branches, and circumstances," that he thought " the inquisitors of Spain use not so many questions to comprehend and to trap their preys."[45] The oppressive use made of this oath aroused great indignation, and played a part in introducing into our law the principle that no one can be compelled to accuse himself.[46]

The Mar-Prelate Tracts. Instead of producing conformity, the rigorous proceedings of the High Commission Court only served to exasperate the sectaries still more against the hierarchy. Declamatory and scurrilous pamphlets directed against the bishops, of which the most notable was a series published under the pseudonym of " Martin Mar-Prelate," rapidly issued from the press and obtained a wide popularity.

Commission, the same author's article in *Dictionary of English Church History* (ed. by Ollard and Crosse, 1912). *Cf.* also Tanner, 360 *et seq.* Several of the commissions are printed in Prothero, 227 *et seq.*

[43] Although by statute there was no appeal from the Delegates, Elizabeth exercised the prerogative of issuing commissions of review, and thus a case could always be reopened; but the decisions of the High Commission, like those of the Star Chamber, were absolutely final (save only between 1611 and 1625; Holdsworth, i, 608).

[44] See M. M. Maguire, "The oath *ex officio*," in *Essays in Honour of C. H. McIlwain* (1936), 199–229.

[45] Strype's *Whitgift* (ed. 1718), 157; Prothero, 213; Tanner, 373. An example of *ex officio* interrogatories dated 1584, together with the letter of Burleigh and Whitgift's defence of the procedure, are all printed in Tanner, *Documents of James I*, 164–172.

[46] *Nemo tenetur prodere seipsum* was a Canonist maxim to which there were some exceptions, but the High Commission treated the maxim itself as non-existent. On this, and the privilege against self-incrimination, see Holdsworth, ix, 199.

An Act had been passed in 1581, levelled at the writings of the seminary priests, by which it was made a capital felony " to write, print, or set forth any manner of book, rhyme, ballad, letter or writing, containing any false, seditious or slanderous matter to the defamation of the queen's majesty, or to the encouraging, stirring or moving of insurrection or rebellion within this realm." [47] By a strained construction of the judges it was held that the puritanical " libels," as they were termed, tending to subvert the constitution of the church and the ecclesiastical supremacy of the queen, were seditious, and punishable under the Act. One of the most conspicuous victims, John Udal, a puritan minister, was convicted for an alleged libel on the bishops in 1591, and sentenced to death. The extreme penalty was remitted, on the intercession of Whitgift, but the prisoner soon died from the severity of his confinement. [48] In 1593, Henry Barrow, a lawyer, and John Greenwood, a clergyman, were convicted and executed for writing " sundry seditious books, tending to the slander of the queen and state "; and the same year, John Penry, a young Welsh clergyman, who was strongly suspected of being one of the authors of the Martin Mar-Prelate tracts, was tried for " seditious words and rumours against the queen." Although the only evidence against him consisted of certain unconnected sentences discovered among his private papers and which had never been communicated to any other person, he was found guilty, and executed with great haste and cruelty. [49]

The Scottish Reformation. The position of ecclesiastical affairs in Scotland was at once an encouragement to the English puritans to persevere in their efforts and an incentive to Elizabeth and her councillors to enforce strict uniformity. The Scottish Reformed Church, as established in 1560, though retaining a nominal form of episcopacy, approached very early to the system of church polity advocated by the puritans, and in 1592 episcopacy was abolished altogether. About the same time a serious attempt was made, under the leadership of Cartwright, to set up the presbyterian system in England. Cartwright and nine of his associates were summoned before the High Commission Court, and, refusing to answer interrogatories under the oath *ex officio*, were committed to prison. In the Star Chamber—a tribunal possessing more extended powers of punishment—they still persisted in their refusal to incriminate themselves. They were ultimately liberated on bail, after satisfying the court on the question of the queen's supremacy.

The persecution of puritans. The favour with which the puritans were regarded in the Queen's Council, and especially in the House of Commons, had hitherto prevented any special legislation against them.

---

[47] 23 Eliz. 1, c. 2; for seditious words this statute imposed the loss of the offender's ears. The Act was to endure for Elizabeth's lifetime only.

[48] Extracts from the report of his trial are in Prothero, 442.

[49] See *The Notebook of John Penry, 1593* and Dr. Albert Peel's introduction (Royal Historical Society, 1944).

But in 1593, parliament was induced to pass an Act subjecting protestant nonconformists to penalties similar to those already imposed upon popish recusants. All persons above the age of sixteen denying or impugning the queen's supremacy, or obstinately refusing to come to the church established by law, or attending any assemblies, conventicles, or meetings, under colour or pretence of the exercise of religion, were to be imprisoned until they should openly conform. Failing to conform within three months, they were to abjure the realm, and for refusal to do so, or for returning after abjuration without licence, the punishment was to suffer death as a felon.[50]

The persecuting policy adopted by Elizabeth against the puritans had most important political results. " It found them a sect; it made them a faction. To their hatred of the church was now added hatred of the crown. The two sentiments were intermingled; and each embittered the other." [51] During the closing years of Elizabeth's reign, and throughout the Stuart period, the firmest champions of constitutional liberty against the arbitrary exercise of royal power were drawn from the puritan ranks.[52]

CIVIL GOVERNMENT OF ELIZABETH

The ecclesiastical despotism of Elizabeth was, at least, a legal despotism, based on the extraordinary powers which parliament in its wisdom had seen fit to confer upon the crown. Religious liberty indeed was as yet totally unrecognised by the constitution, either in theory or in practice [53] : for the crown was still regarded as the whole nation in its religious aspect, though in fact the church and the nation were ceasing to be co-extensive. For the despotic acts of Elizabeth's civil government, there was some excuse in the perils and dangers by which she was surrounded,

[50] 35 Eliz. 1, c. 1, " An Act to retain the queen's subjects in obedience."

[51] Macaulay, *History of England*, i, 52.

[52] " The slavish parliament of Henry VIII grew into the murmuring parliament of Queen Elizabeth, the mutinous parliament of James I, and the rebellious parliament of Charles I. The steps were many, but the energy was one—the growth of the English middle class, using that word in its most inclusive sense, and its animation under the influence of protestantism. No one, I think, can doubt that Lord Macaulay is right in saying that political causes would not alone have then provoked such a resistance to the sovereign, unless propelled by religious theory. . . . Gradually, a strong evangelic spirit (as we should now speak), and a still stronger anti-papal spirit, entered into the middle sort of Englishmen and added to that force, fibre, and substance which they have never wanted, an ideal warmth and fervour which they have almost always wanted." Bagehot, *English Constitution*, 282.

[53] " At the end of the sixteenth century, the simple proposition, that men for holding or declaring heterodox opinions in religion ought not to be burned alive, or otherwise put to death, was itself little else than a sort of heterodoxy; and, though many privately must have been persuaded of its truth, the Protestant churches were as far from acknowledging it as that of Rome. No one had yet pretended to assert the general right of religious worship, which, in fact, was rarely or never conceded to the Romanists in a Protestant country, though the Huguenots shed oceans of blood to secure the same privilege for themselves." Hallam, *Literature of Europe*, i, 559. " Even at the close of the seventeenth century, Bossuet was able to maintain that the right of the civil magistrate to punish religious error was one of the points on which both churches agreed; and he added that he only knew two bodies of Christians who denied it. They were the Socinians and the Anabaptists." Lecky, *Rationalism in Europe*, ii, 59.

and in the example of her immediate predecessors of the Tudor dynasty. Nevertheless protests against them were from time to time uttered in parliament, at first feebly and ineffectually, but later more vigorously, until by the end of her reign the opposition in the House of Commons was sufficiently strong and organised to compel the queen and her ministers to defer to its wishes.

The conduct of political trials. The administration of justice in all trials partaking in any degree of a political nature was characterised by that iniquitous straining of law and evidence in favour of the crown which was the common feature of all the Tudor reigns, and attained a still more disgraceful notoriety under the Stuarts. Hallam has denounced in eloquent language " those glaring transgressions of natural as well as positive law, that rendered our courts of justice in cases of treason little better than the caverns of murderers. Whoever was arraigned at their bar was almost certain to meet a virulent prosecutor, a judge hardly distinguishable from the prosecutor except by his ermine, and a passive pusillanimous jury." [54] The trials of Stubbe, of Penry and of Udal, already referred to, are samples of the kind of justice meted out by the legal tribunals to all who were obnoxious to the court.[55] But besides the ordinary judicial tribunals there existed the two courts of High Commission and Star Chamber, respectively taking cognisance of all offences against the ecclesiastical supremacy and the royal prerogative of the sovereign; special courts of commissioners occasionally appointed for the trial of offences; and the courts-martial by which the queen frequently superseded the operation of the common law.

Courts-martial. During a period of actual rebellion all governments have been wont to exercise the right of suspending the ordinary course of justice in favour of the more summary and awe-inspiring military tribunal. The medieval view was that common law alone applied as long as the courts were actually open; thus an earl captured at the head of a rebel army in battle was still entitled to a trial at common law.[56] In the fifteenth century John Tiptoft, Earl of Worcester, won ill-fame by his attempt to use the Court of the Constable and Marshal for political trials,[57] but nothing so drastic had yet been seen as the conduct of Sir George Bowes, who (as provost-marshal to the Earl of Sussex) executed 600 persons after the rebellion of the earls in 1569.[58] A royal proclamation, issued on July 1, 1588,[59] in the crisis of the Spanish invasion, directing that all persons importing or dispersing papal bulls,

[54] *Constitutional History*, i, 231.
[55] *Supra*, pp. 338 n., 342; but *cf*. Holdsworth, v, 347 *et seq*.
[56] *Thomas of Lancaster's Case, Rotuli Parliamentorum*, ii, 3 (1327); Plucknett, " Origin of Impeachment," *Transactions of the Royal Historical Society* (1942), 58, n. 2.
[57] Stubbs, iii, 281–283.
[58] The documents are in Sir Cuthbert Sharp, *Memorials of the Rebellion of 1569* (London, 1840).
[59] Strype, *Annals*, iii, 568 *et seq*.

or disloyal or traitorous books, should be instantly proceeded against and punished by martial law, was fairly justified, however unconstitutional in character, by the extraordinary perils of the time. But the hasty and arbitrary temper of Elizabeth led her to have recourse to this summary process when there existed no justification in the circumstances of the time. In 1573, one Peter Burchett, a puritan, who was probably insane, attempted to murder the famous sea-captain John Hawkins, in mistake for Sir Christopher Hatton, the captain of the queen's guard. Elizabeth wished to have him immediately executed by martial law, and was with great difficulty persuaded by her council to allow the civil jurisdiction to take its ordinary course.[60] A much more violent and illegal proceeding took place in July 1595. A street brawl, devoid of all political character, having taken place one Sunday evening between some riotous apprentices and the warders of the Tower, the queen issued a commission to Sir Thomas Wyllford, appointing him provost-marshal, with power to punish by martial law. Upon notification by a justice of the peace that a person was " rebellious and incorrigible," the provost-marshal was to take him and hang him forthwith. He was further empowered " to repair with a convenient company into all common highways near to our said city, where you shall understand that any vagrant persons do haunt, and calling to your assistance some convenient number of our justices and constables abiding about the said places, to apprehend all such vagrant and suspected persons, and them to deliver to the said justices, by them to be committed and examined of the causes of their wandering, and finding them notoriously culpable in their unlawful manner of life, as incorrigible, and so certified to you by the said justices, you shall by our Law Martial cause to be executed upon the gallows or gibbet some of them that are so found most notorious and incorrigible offenders." [61]

Commitments by the Council: the " Resolutions in Anderson." Another intolerable grievance by which the people were oppressed under Elizabeth was the discretionary power which the queen, and each member of her Privy Council, arrogated to themselves of committing to prison all persons who were on any account obnoxious to the court. Every obstacle was thrown in the way of a prisoner suing out a writ of habeas corpus; and even when liberty had been obtained by order of a court of law, the person so discharged was frequently recommitted by order of the council, while the officers of the court were imprisoned for having executed their duty. So flagrant were these abuses that, in 1591, the judges ventured to present a joint remonstrance to Sir Christopher Hatton, Lord Chancellor, and Sir William Cecil, Lord Burleigh, Treasurer. They desired that " order may be taken that her highness's subjects may

---

[60] Strype, *Annals*, ii, 288; Camden, *Annals*; Prothero, 176. While imprisoned in the Tower, Burchett murdered one of his keepers, for which offence he was hanged in due course of law.

[61] Rymer, xvi, 279; Prothero, 443. Five of the apprentices were executed as traitors on Tower Hill, July 24, 1595.

not be committed or detained in prison, by commandment of any noble-man or councillor, against the laws of the realm, to the grievous charges and oppression of her Majesty's said subjects." " For divers," the remonstrance continues, " have been imprisoned for suing ordinary actions and suits at the common law, until they will leave the same, or against their wills put their matter to order, although some time it be after judgment and accusation. *Item:* Others have been committed and detained in prison upon such commandment against the law; and upon the queen's writ in that behalf, no cause sufficient hath been certified or returned. *Item:* Some of the parties so committed and detained in prison after they have, by the queen's writ, been lawfully discharged in court, have been eftsoones recommitted to prison in secret places, and not in common and ordinary known prisons, as the Marshalsea, Fleet, King's Bench, Gatehouse, nor the custody of any sheriff, so as, upon complaint made for their delivery, the queen's court cannot learn to whom to award her Majesty's writ, without which justice cannot be done. *Item:* Divers serjeants of London and officers have been many times committed to prison for lawful execution of her Majesty's writs out of the King's Bench, Common Pleas, and other courts, to their great charges and oppression, whereby they are put in such fear as they dare not execute the queen's process. *Item:* Divers have been sent for by pursuivants for private causes, some of them dwelling far distant from London, and compelled to pay to the pursuivants great sums of money against the law, and have been committed to prison till they would release the lawful benefit of their suits, judgments or executions, for remedie in which behalf we are almost daily called upon to minister justice according to law, whereunto we are bound by our office and oath." Thus far the remonstrance of the judges, having regard to the fact that they were removable from office at the queen's pleasure, is a remarkably outspoken vindication of the right of personal freedom.[62] But it concludes rather tamely, by leaving to the executive government a great and dangerous latitude. " Whereas," the judges continue, " it pleased your lordships to will divers of us to set down when a prisoner sent to custody by her Majesty, her council, or some one or two of them, is to be detained in prison and not to be delivered by her Majesty's courts or judges : We think that, if any person shall be committed by her Majesty's special commandment or by order from the council-board, or [if any one or two of her council commit one] for treason touching her Majesty's person, which causes being generally returned into any court, is good cause for the same court to leave the person committed in custody." [63] The above text is from the original with the judges' signatures, printed for the first time by Hallam. Until 1827 it was only known through the garbled version in the posthumously published *Reports* of Anderson

[62] The instance is not isolated; *cf.* Holdsworth, v, 348.
[63] British Museum, Lansdowne MS., lxviii, 87; Hallam, *Constitutional History*, i, 235; Prothero, 446–447.

(1664) which contains the additional words in square brackets. It was in the less accurate version that the rules became an important document in the controversy over the powers claimed in the eighteenth century by secretaries of state, especially in the *Wilkes* cases.[64]

Proclamations. The royal proclamations put forth under Elizabeth seem to show that the crown then claimed not merely a kind of supplemental right of legislation, to perfect and carry out what the spirit of existing laws might require, but also " a paramount supremacy, called sometimes the king's absolute or sovereign power which sanctioned commands beyond the legal prerogative, for the sake of public safety, whenever the council might judge that to be in hazard." [65] Elizabeth exercised discretion in the use of proclamations, and it was not until the Stuart period that their abuse compelled a strict delimitation of their scope. New offences, unknown to the common law, and affecting the persons and property of whole classes of the queen's subjects, were from time to time constituted by royal proclamation alone, and made punishable with fine and imprisonment. The Press was placed under a strict censorship, and in 1586, at the instigation of Archbishop Whitgift, the trades of printing and bookselling were subjected to most stringent regulations by an ordinance, published in the Star Chamber, to restrain the " enormities and abuses as of late have been commonly used and practised by divers contentious and disorderly persons professing the art or mystery of printing or selling of books." [66]

Revenue of Elizabeth. The frugality of Elizabeth, and the sums which she received from the fines of recusants and from the grant of monopolies for the exclusive sale of commodities, enabled her to avoid frequent applications to parliament for money.[67] This greatly increased her popularity, and caused subsidies to be granted, when applied for, with both liberality and readiness. She indeed occasionally had recourse to the ancient practice of forced loans from the wealthy, notwithstanding the statute of Richard III against them. But she is honourably distinguished from her predecessors by the moderation and tact with which these loans were exacted and by her punctuality and speed in repayment.[68]

---

[64] Both texts are printed in Holdsworth, v, 495–497. For discussions see F. M. G. Evans, *Secretaries of State*, 258 *et seq*; Holdsworth, x, 661 *et seq.*

[65] Hallam, *Constitutional History*, i, 237. For the varied matters dealt with by proclamation, see Holdsworth, iv, 295–307.

[66] Strype, *Whitgift*, 222, Appendix, 94; a better text is in Prothero, 169–172. *Cf.* the full treatment in Holdsworth, vi, 360–379, and *infra*, p. 661.

[67] There are a few documents on finance in Prothero, 133–138, but the best collection, with commentary, is in Tanner, *Tudor Documents*, 598–626. The standard work is F. C. Dietz, *English Government Finance (1558–1641)*, New York, 1932.

[68] " In the time of Queen Elizabeth," said Mr. Justice Hutton, in his judgment in the *Case of Ship Money*, " in the end of her reign, whether through covetousness or by reason of the wars that came upon her, I know not by what counsel, she desired benevolence; the statute of 2nd Richard III was pressed, yet it went so far that by commission and direction money was gathered in every Inn of Court; and I myself, for my part, paid twenty shillings. But when the queen was informed by her judges that this kind of proceeding was against

Burleigh's administration. Very much of the credit, and a fair share of the odium, attaching to the government of Elizabeth, are of right due, not to her personally, but to the policy of her ministers, among whom Sir William Cecil, created Lord Burleigh in 1571, stands pre-eminent.[69] Under his administration England, it has been said, " was managed as if it had been the household and estate of a nobleman under a strict and prying steward. . . . It was a main part of his system to keep alive in the English gentry a persuasion that his eye was upon them. No minister was ever more exempt from that false security which is the usual weakness of a court. His failing was rather a bias towards suspicion and timidity; there were times, at least, in which his strength of mind seems to have almost deserted him through a sense of the perils of his sovereign and country. But those perils appear less to us, who know how the vessel outrode them, than they could do to one harassed by continual informations of those numerous spies whom he employed both at home and abroad. The one word of Burleigh's policy was prevention: and this was dictated by a consciousness of wanting an armed force or money to support it, as well as by some uncertainty as to the public spirit in respect at least of religion. But a government that directs its chief attention to prevent offences against itself is in its very nature incompatible with that absence of restraint, that immunity from suspicion, in which civil liberty, as a tangible possession, may be said to consist. It appears probable that Elizabeth's administration carried too far, even as a matter of policy, this precautionary system upon which they founded the penal code against popery; and we may surely point to a contrast very advantageous to our modern constitution in the lenient treatment which the Jacobite faction experienced from the princes of the House of Hanover. She reigned, however, in a period of real difficulty and danger. At such seasons few ministers will abstain from arbitrary actions, except those who are not strong enough to practise them." [70]

ELIZABETH AND HER PARLIAMENTS

Throughout the reign of Elizabeth the predominant party in the House of Commons was composed of members more or less imbued with the puritan doctrines. Amongst them were many bold and active spirits, well read in constitutional lore, who gradually organised an opposition to the despotism of the crown, and on several occasions successfully resisted all the efforts of the court party.

law, she gave directions to pay all such sums, as were collected, back; and so I (as all the rest of our house, and as I think of other houses too) had my twenty shillings repaid me again; and privy councillors were sent down to all parts, to tell them that it was for the defence of the realm, and it should be repaid them again." *State Trials*, iii, 1199.

[69] William Cecil contrived to serve Henry VIII, Somerset, Northumberland, Mary and Elizabeth—a remarkable feat of suppleness. He became Secretary of State in 1550, held the office until 1572 when he became Lord Treasurer, and died in 1598. His second son, Robert, became a Secretary of State in 1596 and held office until his death in 1612. He was created Earl of Salisbury in 1605.

[70] Hallam, *Constitutional History*, i, 247. Compare Lord Macaulay's famous essay on "Burleigh".

The two principal subjects upon which conflicts arose between the crown and parliament were the settlement of the succession to the throne, and a further reformation in the established church. Elizabeth took the view that high matters of state policy, such as her marriage and the problem of the succession, matters of her prerogative generally, and especially the ecclesiastical settlement and the exercise of the royal supremacy, ought not to be debated in parliament unless she had given leave to do so. This seems equivalent to the proposition that the most important political issues would be raised in the House by the ministers and councillors there, if the crown thought it proper to do so; until then, the House ought not to take the initiative. In opposition to that view, the House set up an enlarged conception of its freedom of speech, which it construed as meaning a freedom to initiate debates and to propose legislation on any matter whatever. These conflicts between queen and parliament therefore tended to raise discussions of the privilege of freedom of speech, although the underlying issue really belonged to a different category of ideas.

The succession question. At first the efforts of the commons were directed towards urging the queen to marry, a request to which she always returned evasive answers. As the hope of her marriage grew fainter, and the fears of the popular party increased lest the claim of Mary Queen of Scots should be preferred to the title of the house of Suffolk, parliament became more urgent for some " proclamation of certainty already provided," alluding to the settlement of the succession under Henry VIII's will, " or else by limitations of certainty if none be," by means of a fresh parliamentary settlement.[71] The queen resolutely declined to pronounce between the conflicting claimants to the throne; a policy in which she appears to have been supported by Cecil, who thought that no limitation of the crown could at that time be effected without great peril to the state. In 1566 this question gave rise to one of the most serious conflicts between the crown and the commons which had arisen since the days of Henry IV. Both Houses of parliament united to importune the queen to give way. In both very bold language was employed, and some peers, members of the queen's council, are even said to have insisted in their places that her Majesty ought to be compelled to take a husband, or else that a successor should be declared by parliament against her will. Elizabeth met the attack with boldness and tact. The recalcitrant peers were excluded from her presence until they had made submission, and the commons were induced, by the ministers in their House, to modify their request that the queen name her successor, by coupling with it an alternative request that she would take to herself a husband. To this she returned a vague but courteous answer. The

---

[71] D'Ewes, *Journal*, 82.

commons, however, were not satisfied, and continued to discuss the question of the succession. The queen at length positively enjoined them, through the Speaker, to proceed no further in the business. Hereupon a member, Paul Wentworth, moved to know whether the queen's command and inhibition were not against their liberties and privileges. Lengthened debates ensued, and at the expiration of several days the queen, finding it advisable to give way, informed the Speaker, that she revoked her former commandment and inhibition; " which revocation," says the *Journal*, " was taken by the House most joyfully with hearty prayer and thanks for the same." [72]

Five years elapsed before the queen summoned another parliament. At its meeting in April 1571, the lord keeper Bacon, in replying to the Speaker's customary demand of freedom of speech, said that " her Majesty having experience of late of some disorder and certain offences, which though they were not punished, yet were they offences still, and so must be accounted, therefore they should do well to meddle with no matters of state but such as should be propounded unto them, and to occupy themselves in other matters concerning the commonwealth." [73]

Ecclesiastical reforms. Silenced for a time on the question of the succession, the commons now turned their attention to another topic equally obnoxious to the queen. In this session no fewer than seven bills were introduced in the lower house for a further reformation of ecclesiastical affairs.

Strickland's Case, 1571. The commons resolved to petition the queen for leave to proceed, but Elizabeth was indignant at this interference with her supremacy, and Strickland, the mover of the bills, was sent for to the council and ordered not to appear again in his place in parliament. This proceeding was noticed in the House as being a violation of parliamentary privilege, and an injury not merely to himself but to his constituents whom he represented. The ministers endeavoured to excuse his detention on the ground that it was occasioned not by anything spoken in the House, but by his having introduced bills against the prerogative of the queen. Yelverton, however, maintained that although the queen's prerogative was to be upheld, it ought to be confined within reasonable limits; that as the queen could not make the law so she had no right to break it; and that as that House, where all things came to be considered, could determine the right to the crown—which it would be high treason to deny—it could certainly entertain motions respecting religious ceremonies. Seeing the resolute attitude of the House, the queen prudently permitted Strickland to return to his place. This was an important

[72] *Journals of the House of Commons*, i, 78; Prothero, 118. *Cf.* D'Ewes, *Journal*, 124–130, in Tanner, 560–562. Hallam, *Constitutional History*, i, 251.
[73] D'Ewes, *Journal*, p. 141; Prothero, 119; Tanner, 563.

victory for the commons, who thenceforth displayed increased confidence in asserting their privileges against the arbitrary pretensions of the crown.[74]

Peter Wentworth's Case, 1576. In February 1576, a speech of remarkable boldness in defence of the liberties and privileges of the commons was delivered by Peter Wentworth, member for Tregony, in Cornwall —a brother of the Paul Wentworth who had earlier distinguished himself in the same cause. " Sweet is the name," he said, " of liberty; but the thing itself a value beyond all inestimable treasure. So much the more it behoveth us to take care lest we, contenting ourselves with the sweetness of the name, lose and forgo the thing." " In the last and preceding session," he continued, " I saw the liberty of free speech . . . so much and so many ways infringed, and so many abuses offered to this honourable council, as hath much grieved me; . . . wherefore to avoid the like I do think it expedient to open the commodities that grow to the prince and whole state by free speech. . . . Without this it is a scorn and mockery to call it a parliament house; for in truth it is none but a very school of flattery and dissimulation. Two things do great hurt in this place: the one is a rumour which runneth about the House, and this it is, ' Take heed what you do; the queen's Majesty liketh not such a matter; whosoever preferreth it, she will be offended with him.' On the contrary, ' Her Majesty liketh of such a matter; whosoever speaketh against it, she will be much offended with him.' The other: sometimes a message is brought into the House, either of commanding or inhibiting very injurious to the freedom of speech and consultation. I would to God, Mr. Speaker, that these two were buried in hell. . . . Hereunto agreeth the most excellent words of *Bracton* who saith *the king hath no peer nor equal in his kingdom*; he hath no equal, for otherwise he might lose his authority for commanding, sithence that an equal hath no rule of commandment over his equal. *The king ought not to be under man but under God and the law, because the law maketh him a king*. . . . A message was brought last session into the House, that we should not deal in any matters of religion, but first to receive from the bishops. Surely this was a doleful message, for it was as much as to say, Sirs, you shall not deal in God's causes." He proceeded to express great indignation at the queen's refusal to assent to the attainder of Mary of Scotland; boldly exclaimed, " None is without fault, no, not our noble queen, since her Majesty hath committed great fault, yea dangerous faults to herself "; rudely, but withal loyally, accused her Majesty of ingratitude and unkindness towards her subjects; and declared that his only object was " the advancement of God's glory, our honourable sovereign's safety and the sure defence of this noble isle of England, and all by maintaining of the liberties of this honourable council, the fountain

---

[74] D'Ewes, 156, 175, 176; Tanner, 565–567; Prothero, 119–120. Although Strickland resumed his seat, the Queen had not surrendered her principle, and the next year she demanded to see two ecclesiastical bills then before the House—and " seemed utterly to mislike them." D'Ewes, 213–214; Tanner, 568.

from whence all these do spring." [75] This direct attack upon the queen alarmed the House of Commons. They deemed it prudent to anticipate any action from without by themselves sequestering Wentworth, and appointing a committee of all the privy councillors in the House to examine him. On being assured that the committee sat not as councillors but as members of the commons only, he submitted to their authority, and, on their report to the House, was committed to the Tower. After a month's confinement, the queen informed the commons that she had remitted her displeasure against him, and the House, having first exacted an acknowledgment of his fault upon his knees, released him with a reprimand from the Speaker.

Mr. Cope's Bill and Book, 1587. Twelve years later Peter Wentworth again suffered imprisonment for his bold resistance to the queen's interference with the liberty of parliament. In February 1587, Anthony Cope submitted to the House of Commons a very sweeping measure of ecclesiastical reform, consisting of a bill and a book. By the bill it was proposed to annul all laws affecting ecclesiastical government then in force, and to establish a new form of Common Prayer, which was contained in the book annexed. The Speaker ineffectually endeavoured to stop the reading of the bill by alleging the queen's commands not to meddle in the matter. A day was passed in discussing the question; but before the next meeting of the House, her Majesty sent for the Speaker and obtained from him both bill and book. As soon as the House reassembled, Peter Wentworth submitted to the Speaker, for the purpose of being read to the House, a series of questions of which the principal points were: " Whether this House be not a place for any member freely and without controlment of any person, or danger of laws, by bill or speech, to alter any of the griefs of the commonwealth whatsoever touching the service of God, the safety of the prince and this noble realm ? Whether that great honour may be done unto God, and benefit and service unto the prince and state, without free speech in this council, which may be done with it ? Whether there be any council which can make, add to, or diminish from the laws of the realm but only this council of parliament ? Whether it be not against the orders of this council to make any secret or matter of weight, which is here in hand, known to the prince or any other concerning the high service of God, prince or state, without the consent of the House ? Whether the Speaker, or any other, may interrupt any member of this council in his speech used in this House tending to any of the forenamed high services ? Whether the Speaker may raise when he will any matter being propounded without consent of the House or not ? Whether the Speaker may overrule the House in any matter or cause there in question; or whether he is to be ruled or over-ruled in any matter or not ? Whether the prince and state can continue, stand, and be maintained, without this council of parliament, not altering

[75] D'Ewes, 236–241; Tanner, 537 *et seq*; Prothero, 120 *et seq*.

the government of the state ? " For these queries (which the Speaker declined to read to the House), Wentworth was again committed to the Tower; a fate which Cope and those members who had supported his motion also shared. At the dissolution of parliament, three weeks afterwards, they were released.[76]

Elizabeth and liberty of speech, 1593. At the opening of the parliament which met in February, 1593, the Speaker having made the usual request of liberty of speech, received for answer: " Privilege of speech is granted, but you must know what privilege you have; not to speak every one what he listeth, or what cometh in his brain to utter that; but your privilege is *Ay* or *No*." [77]

On the fifth day of the session the undaunted Peter Wentworth, together with Sir Henry Bromley, another member, delivered a petition to the lord keeper desiring the lords to be suppliants with the lower house to her Majesty to entail the succession of the crown, for which they had already prepared a bill. For this boldness they were summoned before the council and committed to prison.[78]

A few days later, Morice, the attorney of the Court of Wards, introduced a bill to reform the practice of the ecclesiastical courts, especially in the matter of the oath *ex officio*. The queen immediately sent for the Speaker, who on his return informed the House that " she wondered that any could be of so high commandment to attempt a thing so expressly contrary to that which she had forbidden. . . . Her Majesty's present charge and express commandment is, that no bill touching matters of state, or reformation in causes ecclesiastical, be exhibited. And upon my allegiance I am commanded, if any such bill be exhibited, not to read it." Not content with this general reprimand, Morice himself was arrested in his place, committed to prison, deprived of his office in the Court of Wards, and disabled from practising as a barrister.[79]

The conflict involved a still broader question of constitutional principle which neither the queen nor the commons could be expected to appreciate at so early a date, although the queen came nearer to the root of the matter than the commons. The controversy between them was consistently argued in terms of prerogative on one side and of freedom of speech on the other. Freedom of speech, however, was acquiring a new significance with the new position of the commons under Elizabeth. Whatever the position may have been under Henry VIII (and it is very difficult to pronounce upon it) it is clear that under Elizabeth the

[76] D'Ewes, 410 *et seq*. The precise date of their release is unknown: see the article on Peter Wentworth in the *Dictionary of National Biography*, and Sir John Neale's articles, " Peter Wentworth," in the *English Historical Review*, xxxix, 36–54, 175–205.

[77] D'Ewes, 460; Prothero, 124–125. *Cf. infra*, p. 332.

[78] D'Ewes, 470; Tanner, 564–565.

[79] Townsend, *Historical Collections*, 60; D'Ewes, 479; D. Neal, *History of the Puritans*, i, 535 *et seq*; Tanner, 572–573. A few years later, in 1597, the queen set an example of what she conceived to be the proper procedure, by sending a formal message to the House inviting them to deal with certain ecclesiastical matters—D'Ewes, 557; Tanner, 573.

commons contained many men—possibly a majority—who were prepared to undertake the initiative in the work of government, and to that end eagerly urged a number of policies in church and state which embodied their ideas of how the country should be ruled. The partnership between crown and commons established by Henry VIII (for his own convenience) was undergoing some modification in the reign of his daughter. It was no longer merely a matter of the commons rejecting or amending government measures, as they had done under Henry, but of the commons themselves putting forth their own ideas. In the name of " freedom of speech " the commons were in effect claiming an equal right of initiative concurrent with the crown and its ministers. It seemed to them that if Mr. Cope's new prayer book received their approval, then they were entitled to pass Mr. Cope's bill, and (if the lords concurred) to present the queen with the choice of taking it or leaving it.

The queen felt instinctively that such a situation was impossible. In terms of practical politics she took her stand on the practice of her father. Her theoretical defence was the " prerogative." In modern language, her view might perhaps be expressed in the proposition that it is the duty of a government to place before parliament measures for dealing with the outstanding questions of the day; if that initiative on vital matters is allowed to pass into other hands, then the government has in effect ceased to govern. Under our present system all that is recognised and provided for by our political conventions. Governments change. But the only way of changing the government in the sixteenth century was to murder the queen, and a few desperate men were ready to do it. A few more in the seventeenth century added the refinement of a trial of the monarch and a public execution. In neither case was even the immediate problem necessarily solved, and still less was there any progress towards the general solution of all such situations which seems to us so simple—a peaceful change of government. The insoluble problem which caused the fall of the Stuarts was already well-nigh insoluble under Elizabeth. At best, all that she could devise was in the nature of a temporary expedient, as we shall see in the story of the monopoly debates.

The contemporary narratives of parliamentary proceedings do not conceal the fact that the commons were often afraid, but we must not misinterpret that fear. It was not physical fear; there was no reign of terror; no member of parliament suffered in life, limb or property. A few were lodged in the Tower for a few weeks but were certainly not treated rigorously. In the vast majority of cases a serious talk with the Privy Council was enough; and from time to time the speech from the throne explained in sonorous Tudor English the nature and difficulty of government as Elizabeth and her ministers felt it. The fear which beset the commons was rather a profound anxiety such as loyal and conscientious men must feel when they do not fully understand the crisis in which they live. The uncertainties of foreign affairs, the fear of a disputed succession which might well bring civil war and another religious revolution, and the appearance of strange and subversive doctrines were all grounds for great apprehension.[80]

The submissiveness with which the majority of the commons for so many years bowed to the haughty words and harsh acts of Elizabeth, was due in a great measure to a deep conviction of the perils and dangers which threatened the reformed church and the national independence, coupled with a firm reliance on the patriotic courage and wisdom of the queen. For these reasons, during the greater part of her reign, " the puritans in the House of Commons, though sometimes mutinous, felt no disposition to array themselves in systematic opposition to the government. But, when the defeat of the Armada, the successful resistance of the United Provinces to the Spanish power, the firm establishment of Henry IV on the throne of France, and the death of Philip II, had secured the state and the church against all danger from abroad, an obstinate struggle, destined to last through several generations, instantly began at home." [81]

Opposition to monopolies, 1601. "It was in the parliament of 1601 that the opposition which had, during forty years, been silently gathering and husbanding strength, fought its first great battle and won its first victory." [81a] The conflict arose concerning the enormous abuse of monopolies. Under cover of the loosely defined prerogative, possessed or assumed by the crown, of regulating all matters relating to commerce, the queen had taken upon herself to make to her courtiers lavish grants of patents to deal exclusively in a multitude of articles, mostly common necessaries of life. Coal, leather, salt, oil, vinegar, starch, iron, lead, yarn, glass and many other commodities were in consequence only to be obtained at ruinous prices. The grievance was first mooted in parliament in 1571 by Sir Robert Bell; but he was at once summoned before the council, and so hardly dealt with, that " it daunted all the House that for several days there was not one that durst deal in any matter of importance." [82] After the lapse of twenty-six years the commons ventured, in 1597, to present an address to the queen on the same subject, to which she replied, through the lord keeper, that she " hoped that her dutiful and loving subjects would not take away her prerogative, which is the choicest flower in her garden, and the principal and head pearl in her crown and diadem; but that they will rather leave that to her disposition," promising to examine all patents and " to abide the trial and true touchstone of the law." [83] In spite of these fair words, the abuse, far from being abated, rose to a still greater height. So numerous were

[80] For valuable discussions of Elizabeth's parliaments, see J. E. Neale, " Queen Elizabeth's quashing of bills," *English Historical Review*, xxxiv, 586; xxxvi, 480; " Parliament and the succession question," *ibid.*, xxxvi, 497; " Peter Wentworth," *ibid.*, xxxix, 36, 175; " Three Elizabethan Elections," *ibid.*, xlvi, 209. A valuable general survey will be found in Wallace Notestein, *The Winning of the Initiative by the House of Commons* (1924).
[81] Macaulay, *History of England*, i, 53.   [81a] *Ibid.*
[82] D'Ewes, *Journal*, 159. *Dictionary of National Biography*, ii, 172.
[83] D'Ewes, p. 547.

the articles subject to monopoly, that when the list of them was read over in the House in 1601, an indignant member exclaimed, " Is not bread there ? No, but if order be not taken for these, bread will be there before the next parliament." [84]   A bill " for the explanation of the common law in certain cases of letters-patent " was introduced by Laurence Hyde, and was debated with unprecedented warmth for four days. The ministers and courtiers, who endeavoured to support the prerogative, were overborne by a torrent of indignant and menacing eloquence. The populace openly cursed the monopolies, and declared that the prerogative should not be suffered to touch the old liberties of England. Seeing that resistance was no longer politic, or even possible, Elizabeth, with admirable tact, sent a message to the House, that " she understood that divers patents that she had granted were grievous to her subjects, . . . some should be presently repealed, some suspended, and none put in execution but such as should first have a trial according to the law, for the good of the people." Robert Cecil, the secretary, added the more direct assurance that all existing patents should be revoked, and no others granted for the future. Overjoyed at their victory, the commons waited upon the queen with an address of thanks, to which she replied in an affectionate and even apologetic tone. " Since I was a queen," she told them, " yet did I never put my pen unto any grant but that upon pretext and semblance made unto me it was both good and beneficial to the subject in general, though a private profit to some of my ancient servants who had deserved well. . . . Never thought was cherished in my heart that tended not to my people's good." [85]   By this adroit move, the queen induced the commons to drop their bill (which would have imposed statutory limitations upon the prerogative), while she abandoned the claim to base monopolies solely upon her prerogative. The question of validity was thrust upon the courts of law, where the patentees were left to fight their own battles. [86]   The great *Case of Monopolies* (1602) was a most interesting discussion, in which common law, political science and economic theory all contributed to the formation of the decision. [87]

PRIVILEGES OF PARLIAMENT

The reviving independence of the House of Commons under the Tudor sovereigns, especially during the reign of Elizabeth, is further evidenced in the care with which the peculiar privileges and immunities of parliament were from time to time vindicated. The case of Ferrers in 1543, in which the commons so signally maintained, by the mere warrant of their mace, the freedom of members from arrest, has been

[84] Townsend, *Journals*, 239; Prothero, 111 *et seq*; Tanner, 575.
[85] Townsend, 248, 264–265. *Cf.* Tanner, 572–575.
[86] Holdsworth, iv, 348–349.
[87] 11 Rep. 84*b*. See generally, Holdsworth, iv, 343–354; D. Seaborne Davies, " The Case of Monopolies," *Law Quarterly Review*, xlviii, 394, and " Acontius and the Patent System," *Economic History Review*, vii, 63.

already considered in treating of the three principal privileges of the commons.[88]

We have already seen the conflict which might arise between the privilege of the House and the interests of the public,[89] since the law regarded the body of an imprisoned debtor as a sort of pledge. The debtor's release therefore destroyed the creditor's security, or at least compelled the creditor to recover from the unlucky gaoler.

Smalley's Case, 1576. This situation contained possibilities for fraud. Thus, in 1576, Smalley, servant of Arthur Hall (a member of whom we shall have occasion to speak again), who had been arrested for debt, was set at liberty by the serjeant of the House; and on its being subsequently discovered that he had fraudulently procured this arrest, in order to get rid of the debt, was committed to prison for a month and ordered to pay the plaintiff £100.[90] There are several other instances under Elizabeth of privileged persons being liberated by the serjeant by warrant of the mace and not by writ.[91]

The privilege of freedom from arrest has always been limited to civil causes, and has never been allowed to interfere with the administration of the criminal law. But as regards one species of offence—contempt of a court of justice—which partakes of a criminal character, it was for some time doubtful how far privilege would avail as a protection for members.

Cromwell's Case, 1572. In 1572, Henry, Lord Cromwell, complained to the lords that his person had been attached by virtue of a writ out of chancery, for not obeying an injunction of that court. The situation was particularly obscure in the case of the chancery, for which the common lawyers felt some hostility, and whose position in the judicial system was as yet hardly settled. The lords agreed that the attachment did not appear to be warranted " by the common law or custom of the realm, or by any statute law, or by any precedent of the Court of Chancery," and ordered Lord Cromwell to be discharged. They added, however, that if at any future time it should be shown that by the queen's prerogative, or by common law or custom, or by any statute or precedents, the persons of lords of parliament are attachable, the order in this case should not affect their decision in judging according to the cause shown.[92] From this period down to 1757, the cases, as regards both lords and commons, were mainly in favour of privilege[93]; but in that year it was

---

[88] *Supra*, p. 249.   [89] *Supra*, pp. 197 *et seq.*

[90] Tanner, 580, 584–585; Prothero, 128; the first occasion of the release of a member's servant by mace. The lords used a similar procedure in 1584 by releasing James Digges, servant of the Archbishop of Canterbury, by sending the Gentleman Usher; D'Ewes, 314; Tanner, 585; Prothero, 128; see A. S. Turberville, " The protection of servants of members of parliament," *English Historical Review*, xlii, 590.

[91] See the case of Fitzherbert in 1593, Tanner, 588; Prothero, 127.

[92] D'Ewes, *Journal*, 203–204; Tanner, *Documents*, 578, 583; Prothero, 126. See also the cases of 1585 and 1597 holding that members were not liable to subpoena (the writ initiating chancery and Star Chamber proceedings) or to jury service.

[93] See the cases of Brereton in 1605 and of Lord Vaux in 1625—May, *Parliamentary Practice* (13th ed., 1924), pp. 124-125.

" ordered and declared by the lords that no peer or lord of parliament hath privilege of peerage, or of parliament, against being compelled by process of the courts of Westminster Hall to pay obedience to a writ of Habeas Corpus directed to him." [94]   In the case of Earl Ferrers, it was decided that an attachment may be granted, if a peer refuse obedience to the writ.[95]

In more recent times, members committed by courts of law for open contempt have failed in obtaining release by virtue of privilege.[96]   Not that either House of Parliament has waived its right to interfere when members are committed for contempt, but each case is considered upon its merits as it arises; and, although where the contempt has been flagrant protection has not been granted, " privilege might still be allowed against commitment under any civil process, or if the circumstances of the case appeared otherwise to justify it." [97]

County of Norfolk's Case, 1586.   The fifteenth-century cases [98] had left the decision of election disputes mainly in the hands of the council and the lords.   The matter was reopened in the case of the county of Norfolk, in 1586.   On account of some irregularity in the first return, the chancellor had issued a second writ for this county, and a different member had been elected.   The theory—plausible enough—seems to have been that since the Act of 1406 (7 Hen. 4, c. 15) made election writs returnable in chancery, it followed necessarily that the chancery must pass upon the sufficiency of the returns.   The circumstances having been noticed in the House of Commons, Queen Elizabeth directed the Speaker to express her displeasure that the House had been troubled with " a thing in truth impertinent for this House to deal withal, and only belonging to the charge and office of the lord chancellor," whom she had appointed to confer with the judges about the returns for the county of Norfolk, and to act therein according to justice and right.   The House, however, appointed a committee to investigate the circumstances, who reported in favour of the election under the first writ.   While intimating that they had reason to believe that the chancellor, and some of the judges, held the same opinion as themselves, the committee declared that they

---

[94] *Lords' Journal*, xxix, 181.

[95] Burrow, *Reports*, 631.

[96] See the cases of Long Wellesley in 1831, and of Lechmere Charlton in 1837, and the reports of the Committee of Privileges—*Commons' Journals*, lxxxvi, p. 701, vol. xxii, pp. 3 *et seq.* In 1873 Whalley and Guildford Onslow, members of parliament, were reprimanded and heavily fined by the Court of Queen's Bench for a contempt of court in connection with the celebrated Tichborne case: Chief Justice Cockburn remarking, that if he had seen fit to commit them, he would not have been restrained by privilege. And on January 23, 1874, parliament not being then in session, Whalley was committed by the same court for a contempt. He was discharged from custody before the 26th, on which day parliament was dissolved. On the meeting of a new parliament the Lord Chief Justice addressed a letter to the Speaker informing him of the facts, and a committee on privilege, to whom the letter was referred, reported that it did not demand the further attention of the House. Hansard, *Debates*, ccxviii, 52, 108; *Report of Parliamentary Committee*, 1874; May, *Parliamentary Practice*, p. 125.

[97] May, *Parliamentary Practice*, p. 127.

[98] *Supra*, pp. 199 *et seq.*

had not thought it proper to inquire of the chancellor what he had done, because " they thought it prejudicial to the privilege of the house to have the same determined by others than such as were members thereof. And though they thought very reverently of the said lord chancellor and judges, and thought them competent judges in their places; yet in this case they took them not for judges in parliament in this house: and thereupon required that, if it were so thought good, Mr. Farmer and Mr. Gresham (the members) might take their oaths and be allowed of by force of the first writ, as allowed by the censure of this house, and not as allowed of by the said lord chancellor and judges. Which was agreed unto by the whole house." [99]

The House and its members. But there was another species of privilege, relating to the internal discipline of the House—the power to punish offences against the established order committed by any of themselves —which, though apparently at all times an essential attribute of any assembly enjoying the right of free debate, first begins to attract attention during the Tudor period.

Story's Case, 1549. The journal of the commons records an early instance, under the date January 21, 1548, when John Story, one of the burgesses, was ordered to be committed to the custody of the serjeant of the House. On the next day but one, articles of accusation were read against him, and on the following day the commons, of their single authority, committed him to the Tower. The exact nature of his offence is not stated, but he is known to have been a zealous opponent of the reformation, and would appear to have used language disrespectful alike to the House and to the government of the protector Somerset. On March 2, Story sent a letter from the Tower with a full submission; whereupon the commons made an order " that the king's privy council in the nether House shall humbly declare unto the Lord Protector's grace that the resolution of the House is, that Mr. Story be enlarged and at liberty out of prison; and to require the king's Majesty to forgive him his offences in this case towards his Majesty and his council." Under Queen Mary, Story again fell under the censure of the House for disrespect to the Speaker; and in the same reign Thomas Copley, member for Gatton, was committed by the House to the custody of their serjeant for disrespectful words uttered of her Majesty. With less regard for their privileges, they directed the Speaker to declare this offence to the queen, and solicit her mercy for the offender.[1]

---

[99] D'Ewes, *Journal*, 393, 396–398; Tanner, 595–596; Prothero, 130; Hallam, *Constitutional History*, i, 275. The question was reopened in 1604 by James I; *infra*, pp. 331 *et seq.*

[1] Hallam, *Constitutional History*, i, 271–272. John Story, D.C.L., was the first Regius Professor of Civil Law at Oxford. Under Elizabeth he fled to the Netherlands, was there kidnapped by the queen's secret service, brought to England, tried and executed for treason in 1571. The government attempted to defend this in a number of pamphlets. He was beatified by the church in 1886. *Cf.* Maitland, " English Law and the Renaissance " in *Historical Essays* (ed. Cam), 139.

Hall's Case, 1581. The next case is more important, constituting as it does the leading precedent, so far as records show, for the power of the House to expel a member. Arthur Hall, a burgess for Grantham, was charged with having, on account of certain proceedings of the last session of parliament wherein he was privately interested, caused to be published a book, " not only greatly reproachful against some particular good members of this House, but also very much slanderous and derogatory to the general authority, power, and state of this House, and prejudicial to the validity of the proceedings of the same in making and establishing of laws, charging this House with drunkenness as accompanied in their councils with Bacchus. . . ." He had previously incurred the displeasure of the commons in 1572, when he was ordered to appear at the bar to answer " for sundry lewd speeches, used as well in this House as also abroad elsewhere." On another occasion he had been " charged with seven several articles," but, having " humbly submitted himself to the House and confessed his folly," was released " with a good exhortation from the Speaker." Regarded now as incorrigible, he was expelled the House, fined 500 marks, and sent to the Tower for six months, where he remained until the dissolution of parliament.[2] The power to impose a fine, and to imprison for a determinate length of time, are characteristics of a court of record, and such the House of Commons claimed to be until the middle of the next century, when the House finally abandoned the pretension to fine, or to imprison beyond the end of the session. The House of Lords retains both of these powers.

Dr. Parry's Case, 1585. The right of expulsion was again exercised by the commons in 1585 against William Parry, D.C.L., a burgess for Queenborough. He had denounced as cruel and bloody the bill to inflict the penalty of death on Jesuits and seminary priests and had voted against it, although without adducing his reasons—to the queen alone would he reveal them. The House seems to have regarded his speech as abusive instead of being argumentative, and forced him to apologise. A few months later, Parry lay in the Tower under a charge of treason which he confessed to be true. Thereupon the House expelled him and ordered a new writ.[3]

The House and strangers. So tenacious were they of their dignity, that they inflicted penalties upon strangers for words spoken by them outside the House. In 1585 they caused a currier named Bland, on account of contemptuous words uttered against the House, to be brought to their bar, whence he was discharged, since " he was a poor man and

[2] D'Ewes, 207, 212, 291; Tanner, 592–593; Prothero, 131; Hallam, *Constitutional History*, i, 273. In addition to the misconduct mentioned in the text, Hall was suspected of being privy to the fraud committed by his servant Smalley in 1576; see *supra*, p. 320. *Cf.* Herbert Wright, *Life and Works of Arthur Hall of Grantham* (1919).

[3] D'Ewes, 340–342, 352; Tanner, 593–594; Hallam, *Constitutional History*, i, 274. Parry was employed to spy on the catholics, but he became a convert, and formed a plan to assassinate the queen. Pollard, *Political History*, vi, 387–388.

had a great charge of children," on making submission and paying costs of twenty shillings.[4]

Long's Case, 1571. It is in the reign of Elizabeth also that the earliest precedent occurs for the punishment of bribery at elections. In 1571, the House inflicted a fine upon the borough of Westbury for receiving a bribe of four pounds from Thomas Long, the member returned, who is described as " a very simple man and of small capacity to serve in that place." The mayor was also ordered to refund the bribe; but Long, the briber, does not appear to have been expelled or otherwise punished.[5]

Money bills. In 1593 an attempt was made by the lords to encroach upon the commons' privilege of originating money bills. A message was sent from the Upper House referring to the queen's want of a supply, and requesting that a committee of conference might be appointed. This was acceded to; but it soon appeared that there was a difference of opinion between the upper and lower Houses. Sir Robert Cecil was instructed to report from the committee that the lords would not consent to grant anything less than three subsidies, while the commons wished to give only two. Hereupon Francis Bacon (afterwards the celebrated Chancellor) rose, and while disclaiming any wish to refuse a subsidy, " misliked that this House should join with the Upper House in the granting of it. For the custom and privilege of this House hath always been, first to make offer of the subsidies from hence, then to the Upper House; except it were that they present a bill unto this House, with desire of our assent thereto, and then to send it up again." The court party tried hard to bring about another conference with the lords, but their motion to that effect was lost on a division by 217 to 128.[6]

Views on the constitution. Notwithstanding the arbitrary practice of Elizabeth's government, and the submissive and adulatory strain in which she was always addressed by the commons, it is evident that the theory of the constitution, as a monarchy greatly limited by law, remained intact. The facts already cited might be regarded as sufficient proof of this assertion, but it is supported by still further evidence of much weight.

In the *Harborowe for Faithful and True Subjects*, published in 1559 by Aylmer, afterwards Bishop of London, in answer to John Knox's celebrated treatise against female monarchy entitled *The first blast of the trumpet against the monstrous regiment of women* (Geneva, 1558),[7] the author thus enumerates his reasons why " it is less danger to be governed in England by a woman than anywhere else ": " First, it is not she that

---

[4] D'Ewes, 366; Tanner, 594–595. In 1576, in *Williams' Case*, the House committed a stranger for abusive words and threatening a member with a dagger: *Commons' Journals*, i, 83; Prothero, 132.

[5] *Commons' Journals*, i, 88; Tanner 526–527; Prothero, 132.

[6] D'Ewes, 483, 486; Tanner, 610; Hallam, *Constitutional History*, i, 276.

[7] Knox's *Blast* was written in the time of Queen Mary and directed against her, but it was of course equally applicable to her sister Elizabeth.

ruleth, but the laws, the executors whereof be her judges appointed by her, her justices of peace, and such other officers. Secondly, she maketh no statutes or laws, but the honourable court of parliament; she breaketh none, but it must be she and they together, or else not. . . . If, on the other part, the regiment were such as all hanged upon the king's or queen's will and not upon the laws written; if she might decree and make laws alone without her senate; if she judged offences according to her wisdom and not by limitation of statutes and laws; if she might dispose alone of war and peace; if, to be short, she were a mere monarch, and not a mixed ruler, you might peradventure make me to fear the matter the more, and the less to defend the cause." [8]

Again, in 1566, Richard Onslow, then solicitor-general and Speaker of the commons, addressing Queen Elizabeth at the conclusion of the session, said: " By our common law, although there be for the prince provided many princely prerogatives and royalties, yet it is not such as the prince can take money or other things, or do as he will at his own pleasure without order; but quietly to suffer his subjects to enjoy their own without wrongful oppression; wherein other princes by their liberty do take as pleaseth them." [9]

William Harrison, in his *Description of England*, published with Holinshed's *Chronicles* in 1577, says of the parliament: " This House hath the most high and absolute power of the realm; for thereby kings and mighty princes have from time to time been deposed from their thrones; laws either enacted or abrogated; offenders of all sorts punished; and corrupted religion either disannulled or reformed. To be short, whatsoever the people of Rome did in their *centuriatis* or *tribunitiis comitiis*, the same is and may be done by authority of our Parliament House, which is the head and body of all the realm, and the place wherein every particular person is intended to be present, if not by himself, yet by his advocate or attorney. For this cause also, anything there enacted is not to be misliked, but obeyed by all men without contradiction or grudge." [10]

That the same theory of the constitution prevailed in the later period of Elizabeth's reign is evidenced by the words of the judicious Hooker in his *Ecclesiastical Polity*: " I cannot choose," he says, " but commend highly their wisdom, by whom the foundations of this commonwealth have been laid; wherein though no manner person or cause be unsubject to the king's power, yet so is the power of the king over all and in all limited, that unto all his proceedings the law itself is a rule. The axioms of our regal government are these: *Lex facit regem*—the king's grant of any favour made contrary to the law is void—*Rex nihil potest nisi quod jure potest* . . . what power the king hath, he hath it by law;

---

[8] *An Harborowe for faithful and trewe subiectes against the late blowne Blaste, concerning the Gouernement of Wemen*, Strassburg, 1559, pp. 52–55.
[9] D'Ewes, p. 115.
[10] Harrison, *Description of England* (ed. F. J. Furnivall), 173.

the bounds and limits of it are known, the entire community giveth general order by law how all things publicly are to be done; and the king as head thereof, the highest in authority over all, causeth, according to the same law, every particular to be framed, and ordered thereby. The whole body politic maketh laws which laws give power unto the king; and the king having bound himself to use according to law that power, it so falleth out that the execution of the one is accomplished by the other." [11] Similar views of the constitution—vaguely and somewhat timidly expressed it is true—are found in the *Commonwealth of England* of Sir Thomas Smith, one of Elizabeth's Secretaries of State.[12]

The theory of representation. In the reign of Elizabeth, in 1571, a bill was introduced in the commons to repeal, as to boroughs, the ancient statute of Henry V [13] and legalise the innovation which time had brought about. The bill appears to have been dropped, but it gave rise to an interesting debate which has been preserved in the pages of D'Ewes' *Journal*. The supporters of the bill argued the question on its merits, asserting that a man could not be presumed to be wiser for being a resident burgess, and that the whole body of the realm and the service of the same was rather to be respected than any private regard of place or person. "This," observes Hallam, "is a remarkable and perhaps the earliest assertion of an important constitutional principle that each member of the House of Commons is deputed to serve not only for his constituents but for the whole kingdom; a principle which marks the distinction between a modern English parliament and such deputations of the estates as were assembled in several continental kingdoms; a principle to which the House of Commons is indebted for its weight and dignity, as well as its beneficial efficiency, and which none but the servile worshippers of the populace are ever found to gainsay." Those who defended the existing law, and appeared anxious to restore it to vigour, urged that the inferior ranks using manual and mechanical arts ought, like the rest, to be regarded and consulted with on matters which concerned them (an argument which has been revived in the present day in favour of working-men candidates for parliament). But the chief mischief dwelt upon as resulting from non-resident borough members was the interference of noblemen in elections in favour of nominees. Some

[11] Richard Hooker, *Ecclesiastical Polity*, bk. viii, c. 11, 13. The first four books were published in 1594; the fifth in 1597; the remaining three not till forty-seven years after his death, which happened in the year 1600. The belief that the sixth book, though written by Hooker, did not belong to this work, and that the real sixth book has been lost, has been challenged by C. J. Sisson, *The Judicious Marriage of Mr. Hooker* (1940), who maintains the authenticity of the present books vi–viii. See Keble's edition and the essay on Hooker in A. Passerin d'Entrèves, *The Medieval Contribution to Political Thought* (Oxford, 1939).

[12] Smith's *Commonwealth*, Book ii, Chap. 3; extracts in Prothero, 176 *et seq*. This work was not published till 1583, six years after the author's death. The edition by L. Alston, under the title *De Republica Anglorum* (1906), has an introduction by Maitland.

[13] 1 Hen. 5, c. 1; above, p. 203.

members proposed to impose a fine of £40 on any borough making its election on a peer's nomination.[14]

On the other hand a novel theory—utterly unknown to the ancient English constitution—of an absolute and paramount power inherent in the very nature of the regal office, had already found not a few supporters among the lawyers and courtiers of Elizabeth's reign. It was only after long years of bitter conflict, after the decapitation of one monarch and the deposition of another, that this theory of government which the Stuart dynasty adopted, developed, and pushed to its extreme logical results, was at length finally vanquished by the ancient free principles of the constitution which it had attempted to supplant.

[14] D'Ewes, *Journal*, p. 168; and Hallam, *Constitutional History*, i, 266.

CHAPTER 12

THE REIGN OF JAMES I, 1603–1625

JAMES I came to the English throne at a critical period of our history. The movement towards despotism which was conquering most of the countries of Europe reached its climax in England under Henry VIII, and had since been slowly receding before the reviving spirit of freedom. During the later years of Elizabeth the puritan party had become organised and powerful. Whilst the old queen lived, they were, for the most part, content to postpone the active assertion of the rights of the people against the crown. They looked forward with hope to the advent of her successor, in the expectation of voluntary concessions; but were determined in any case to carry out further reforms in the ecclesiastical system, and to insist upon all the ancient privileges of parliament, and all the legal liberties of the subject. Violent changes were not, however, generally desired. Although there was a party bitterly hostile to the hierarchy, the bulk of the puritans had no very great desire to abolish episcopacy, and would possibly have been fully satisfied with a dispensation from certain ceremonies which too forcibly reminded them of the religion they had renounced—the relative strength of these parties is, of course, impossible to determine with much precision.

The king's character and upbringing. The presbyterian education of James had led some to anticipate a ready acquiescence in such a measure of reform. But the king's unhappy experience of the presbyterian clergy of Scotland had, in fact, been productive of prejudices the very opposite to what the English puritans had expected. According to the absurd caricature current a century ago, James had acquired more learning than he had understanding to digest, was puffed up with literary pride and self-sufficiency, imagined himself possessed of supereminent wisdom (although in reality lacking the judgment of a man of ordinary abilities), and, in the words of the Duc de Sully, was the " wisest fool in Europe." A human character is rarely as simple as that. In Scotland he had acted (as the occasion demanded) with almost Tudor vigour against rebellious nobles. In England he hoped for a period of settled peace, and in principle hoped for religious toleration—which in itself made him remarkable as a theologian. The country, on the other hand, was clamouring for war, and seething with sectarian passions. Between the two extremes there was no doubt a large mass of moderate peaceable men and it was the Stuart tragedy that so many of them were forced into the opposition camp.[1]

[1] See the estimates by S. R. Gardiner, *History of England*, i, 48–49, v. 315, and especially D. L. Keir, *Constitutional History of Modern Britain* (1938), 154–162.

The avowed antipathy of James to every kind of protestant non-conformity was based on political rather than on religious reasoning. "A Scottish presbytery," he said at the Hampton Court conference, "agreeth as well with a monarchy as God with the devil. Then Jack and Tom and Will and Dick shall meet, and at their pleasure censure me and my council."[2]   He was convinced that the hierarchy was the firmest support of the crown, and that where there was no bishop there would soon be no king. He determined, therefore, to allow not the slightest toleration to nonconformists, a resolution in which he was confirmed by the fulsome flattery of the prelates, some of whom, at the Hampton Court conference, did not hesitate to ascribe to him immediate inspiration from heaven.

The "Millenary Petition."   On his journey to London the puritan clergy presented to the king what is commonly called the "Millenary Petition," because it purported to proceed from 1,000 ministers, though the actual number of those who signified their assent to it is said not have exceeded 825.   It contained nothing inconsistent with the established hierarchy; but the petitioners prayed for a reformation in the church service, ministry, livings, and discipline which certainly "would have stirred up opposition from one end of the country to the other."[3]   In order to obtain further information on the points in dispute, James summoned the famous conference at Hampton Court between the Archbishop of Canterbury, eight bishops, five deans and two doctors, on the one side, and Dr. Reynolds and three other puritan divines on the other.   At the conference, which was held before the king on January 14, 15 and 16, 1604, James eagerly displayed his theological learning and sympathetically considered some of the suggestions.   One of them was carried out by the preparation of the new Authorised Version of the Bible (1611).   When Dr. Reynolds began to speak casually of "the bishop and his presbytery," however, deadlock was inevitable, and James was stung into the outburst we have already quoted.[4]   Transported with admiration, the primate exclaimed, "Undoubtedly your majesty speaks by the special assistance of God's spirit"; and the Bishop of London said his "heart melteth with joy, that Almighty God had given us such a king as, since Christ's time, the like hath not been."   Some slight alterations in the Book of Common Prayer were made after the conference; but ten of the men who had presented the Millenary Petition were committed to prison, "the judges having declared in the Star Chamber that

---

[2] William Barlow, *The Sum of the Conference*, p. 81.   Quoted by Tanner, *English Constitutional Conflicts*, p. 27.

[3] Gardiner, *History of England*, i, 149.   The petition is printed by Prothero, *Documents*, 413, and in Tanner, *James I*, 57–60.

[4] Gardiner, i, 156; extracts from the proceedings of the conference are printed in Tanner, *James I*, 60–69; a short minute by Bancroft (printed in Prothero, 416) shows the matters agreed upon.

it was an offence fineable at discretion, and very near to treason and
felony, as it tended to sedition and rebellion." [5]

While sternly repressing the nonconforming protestants, James at
the same time showed an inclination to grant some partial indulgence
to the Roman Catholics—a policy which excited disgust and jealousy
throughout the kingdom, and thus strengthened the hands of the puritan
faction. James soon found it necessary, in order to free himself from the
imputation of papistry, with which the puritans assailed him, to cause
the penal laws against the catholics to be put into execution. After the
discovery of the Gunpowder Plot, additional severity was added to the
statutes in force by two Acts of 1606 " containing more than seventy
articles inflicting penalties on the catholics in all their several capacities
of masters, servants, husbands, parents, children, heirs, executors,
patrons, barristers, and physicians." [6]

Theory of divine right. At a time when the growing spirit of freedom,
the general diffusion of knowledge and the revived study of Greek and
Roman authors [7] had caused a republican tendency to manifest itself
in parliament and among some of the people, the king was constantly
asserting, in the most offensive form, the novel theory of his divine
right—a doctrine already advanced by him some years before in Scotland,
in a treatise on the " True Law of Free Monarchies." [8] The circumstances
of his accession seemed to lend colour to the view. As an alien, the common law denied him inheritance [9]; the will whereby Henry VIII exercised
his statutory power of appointment also excluded him in favour of the
junior, Suffolk, line. His unopposed accession therefore seemed to
rest entirely upon a hereditary right which prevailed over common law
and statute. Parliament itself took this view in the Succession Act (1604)
which placed James's title on hereditary descent alone.[10]

In 1604, Convocation drew up a set of canons, 141 in number, which

[5] Hallam, *Constitutional History*, i, 298. (The allusion is possibly to the Act of Uniformity
(1559), s. 3).

[6] 3 & 4 James 1, c. 4, " For the better discovering and repressing of Popish recusants ";
and 3 & 4 James 1, c. 5, " To prevent and avoid dangers which grow by Popish recusants,"
Prothero, 256–268; Tanner, *James I*, 86–104. See also 7 James 1, c. 2, and c. 6.

[7] *Cf.* Hobbes, *Leviathan*, c. xxix, emphasises their anti-monarchical influence.

[8] *King James's Works*, ed. by James Montacute, Bishop of Winchester, 1616, p. 191 (ed.
C. H. McIlwain, 1918, pp. 53 *et seq*); extracts in Prothero, 400; Tanner, *James I*, 9 (*cf.*
14–22). The issues of political philosophy are too large for discussion here. See the
excellent introduction in G. P. Gooch, *Political Thought in England from Bacon to Halifax*
(Home University Library, 1914); J. N. Figgis, *Divine Right of Kings* (1896); G. P. Gooch,
English Democratic Ideas in the Seventeenth Century (1898; ed. H. J. Laski, 1927). Recent
studies of importance are J. W. Gough, *Fundamental Law in English Constitutional History*
(1955) and J. G. A. Pocock, *The Ancient Constitution and the Feudal Law* (1957).

[9] It seems that in 1705 parliament intended to prevent the recurrence of such a situation
by enacting that the lineal descendants of the Princess Sophia should be deemed to be
natural-born subjects; if they inherited the crown they could not in consequence be
represented as foreigners whose " divine right " over-rode the common law; 4 & 5 Anne,
i, 16. For the legal effect of that statute, see Att.-Gen. *v.* Prince Ernest Augustus of
Hanover [1957] A.C. 436, and the periodical literature on it mentioned in O. Hood
Phillips, *Constitutional Law* (2nd ed.), 197–198.

[10] Tanner, *James I*, 10–12; Prothero, 250; 1 Jac. 1, c. 1.

received the royal assent, but never having been sanctioned by parliament are not legally binding upon the laity. Besides declaring every man to be excommunicated who should question the complete accordance of the prayer book with the Word of God, they denounce as erroneous a number of tenets believed to be hostile to royal government, and inculcate the duty of passive obedience to the king in all cases without exception.[11]

Adopted by the hierarchy and the courtiers, the theory of divine right was later on elaborated into a system by Sir Robert Filmer,[12] and became the distinctive badge of the more violent high-churchmen and tories.

THE KING AND THE COMMONS

Such being the ideas of the king on regal government, it was inevitable that he should speedily come into conflict with the House of Commons. The very first acts of James's reign were ominous of the arbitrary manner in which he designed to rule his new kingdom. On his journey to London he ordered a thief, taken in the fact, to be executed without the formality of a trial,[13] and the proclamation summoning his first parliament was resented as an infringement upon the privileges and independence of the House of Commons. In it he took upon himself to specify the kind of men who were to be elected, and also directed that all returns should be sent to his Court of Chancery, and that such as should be there found contrary to the proclamation should be rejected as " unlawful and insufficient "— a procedure which had already produced a conflict between the commons and Queen Elizabeth in 1586.[14]

James's first parliament met on March 19, 1604. It was felt that a struggle with the crown was at hand. So large was the attendance of members in their places that additional seats had to be provided. The aggressive policy which produced James's proclamation naturally excited the commons into equally unwise pronouncements. In answer to the address from the throne, the Speaker, Sir Edward Phelips, was careful to remind the king of the limited nature of his regal powers. " New laws," said he, " could not be instituted, nor imperfect laws reformed nor inconvenient laws abrogated, by any other power than that of the High Court of Parliament, that is, by the agreement of the commons, the accord

[11] Extracts in Tanner, *James I*, 231–243.
[12] In his famous *Patriarcha*, written in the reign of Charles I, but not published till 1680; *cf.* Gooch, *Political Thought*, 161–164.
[13] "I hear our new king," said Sir John Harrington, "has hanged one man before he was tried; it is strangely done. Now, if the wind bloweth thus, why may not a man be tried before he has offended ?"—*Nugae Antiquae*.
[14] *Parliamentary History*, i, 969; *cf. supra*, p. 322. Gardiner, *History of England*, i, 163, shows from the *Egerton Papers*, 384, that of the " two sets of notes for the proclamation," it is that in Lord Chancellor Ellesmere's hand which " alone contains the direction for the reference of disputed elections to chancery, showing that this assumption originated with him." General admonitions (either separately, or in the preamble to the writs) to choose wise and moderate candidates had occasionally been issued under Richard II (Stubbs, ii, 479), Henry VII, Edward VI, and Elizabeth (*supra*, p. 244; Tanner, *Tudor Documents*, 523, 525—this last example as recent as 1597).

of the lords, and the assent of the sovereign; that to the king belonged
the right either negatively to frustrate, or affirmatively to ratify; but
that he could not institute: every bill must pass the two Houses before it
could be submitted to his pleasure." Only eleven years before, Elizabeth
had told the commons that " your privilege is *Ay* or *No*" [15]; the commons
now applied the same formula to the king. Their suggestion that a government cannot initiate measures, nor even consider them until they are
presented for the royal assent, but must abandon that function to a House
which regarded itself as normally an opposition,[16] is an indication of
how little understood were the essential lines of parliamentary government, and of how much remained to be learned in the expensive school
of experience before parliamentary government could work smoothly.

The first business of the commons was the vindication of their exclusive right to determine contested elections, against the attempt of James
to transfer the decision of such cases to his Court of Chancery.

Case of Goodwin and Fortescue, 1604. James I, in the proclamation
summoning his first parliament, attempted to exercise a wide control
over parliamentary elections, admonishing the sheriffs not to send precepts to rotten boroughs where there were insufficient residents, specifying
the kind of men who were to be elected, and specially forbidding the choice
of " bankrupts and outlaws." All returns were to be filed in chancery;
and any found contrary to this proclamation were to be rejected as unlawful and insufficient, and the constituencies fined. Any person elected
contrary to the proclamation was also to be fined and imprisoned.[17]
The question soon came to an issue. Sir Francis Goodwin was elected
for the county of Buckingham; but the clerk of the crown refused to
receive the return on the ground that Goodwin had been outlawed some
years before, and Sir John Fortescue, a member of the Privy Council,
was elected by virtue of a second writ. The commons, on the matter
being brought under their notice, voted that Goodwin was duly elected,
and ordered him to take his seat. The lords requested a conference
on the subject, which the commons at first refused, but afterwards
acceded to, on being informed that the request was made at the king's
special desire. They justified their decision as to Goodwin, by alleging
that owing to some technical informalities, he was not legally an outlaw,
and that even if he were, they could prove by precedents that outlaws
had sat in the House. The king, in his reply, going beyond the immediate
question, took the opportunity to enunciate a doctrine utterly subversive
of the free constitution of parliament. " He had no purpose," he said
" to impeach their privilege, but since they derived all matters of privilege
from him, and by his grant, he expected they should not be turned against

---

[15] *Supra*, p. 316.

[16] *Supra*, p. 317.

[17] Prothero, 280–281. Parliamentary returns went into chancery at least as early as the
statute of 1406 (*supra*, p. 202).

him." He then maintained that legally the House had no right to meddle with returns, which were made into the Court of Chancery, and were within its exclusive jurisdiction. He further denied their assertion that outlaws might legally sit, and requested them to confer with the judges. In face of the king's challenge of all the privileges of the House, involving as it did the vital question of its independence of, or subjection to, the royal will, it was impossible for the commons to give way on the main point of jurisdiction. But they acted with that combined firmness and reasonableness which in so many constitutional crises has characterised the political action of the English nation. They gave up the minor point, by bringing in a bill to disable outlaws in future from sitting in parliament, but they refused to confer with the judges, affirming that they themselves had always decided in cases of disputed elections. Two days later, after a further message from the king, in which he professed great regard for their privileges, declared himself distracted in judgment on the question in dispute, and desired and commanded as an absolute king that there should be a conference with the judges in the presence of his council, the commons gave way on the question of form. The conference with the judges, however, never came off. In an interview between the king himself and the committee who had drawn up the reply of the House, James admitted that the commons were the proper judges of the returns, but requested, as a personal favour, that the return of both Goodwin and Fortescue should be set aside and a new writ issued. To this the House assented, but to satisfy the scruples of certain members a letter was obtained from Goodwin expressing his concurrence in the arrangement—indeed, it was well known that Goodwin was elected against his own wish, as appears from the sheriff's interesting narrative of the election scene.[18] The apparent compromise was in effect a victory for the commons, whose right to decide upon the legality of returns, and the conduct of returning officers in making them, was thenceforth regularly claimed and exercised. It was fully recognised as their exclusive right by the court of Exchequer Chamber in 1674,[19] by the House of Lords in 1689,[20] and also by the courts of law in 1680[21] and 1702.[22] Their right was further recognised by the Act 7 & 8 William 3, c. 7, which declared that " the last determination in the House of Commons of the right of election " is to be pursued.

Shirley's Case, 1604: freedom from arrest. While the case of Goodwin and Fortescue was in progress there arose another case of great importance on another head of privilege, viz., freedom from arrest, which led

[18] *Commons' Journals*, i, 149–169; *Parliamentary History*, i, 993–1017; Tanner, *James I*, 202–217; Prothero, xci, 325–331; S. R. Gardiner, *History of England*, i, 167–170.

[19] *Barnardiston* v. *Soame* (1674) 6 St. Tr. 1092; Broom, *Constitutional Law* (ed. Denman), 800.

[20] *Barnardiston* v. *Soame* (1689) 6 St.Tr. 1119; Broom, *op. cit.*, 839.

[21] *Onslow's Case* (1680) 2 Ventris 37.

[22] *Prideaux* v. *Morris* (1702) 2 Salkeld 502.

to a more distinct recognition of the privilege by statute, and to an improvement in the law. Sir Thomas Shirley had been imprisoned in the Fleet, on an execution for debt, before the meeting of parliament. The commons sent their serjeant armed with a writ of privilege to demand his release. This being refused by the warden, he was committed to the Tower for contempt; but, still continuing obstinate through fear of becoming personally answerable for the debt, he was further committed to the prison called Little Ease in the Tower. Shortly afterwards, through the interposition of the king, which the commons had privately asked for, the warden delivered up the prisoner and was discharged after a reprimand. This proceeding directed attention to two legal hardships which for centuries had attended the release of members taken in execution: (1) the sheriff or warden was liable to an action for escape, and (2) the creditor lost his right to an execution. An Act was now passed by which it was for the first time declared : (1) that the officer should be discharged from all liability for delivering out of custody a person having a privilege of parliament, and (2) that the creditor, at the expiration of the time of privilege, might sue out a new writ of execution. The Act also distinctly recognised as existing law: (1) the privilege of freedom from arrest; (2) the right of either House of Parliament to set a privileged person at liberty; and (3) the right to punish those who make or procure arrests.[23]

The apology of the commons. During a long and stormy session the commons freely discussed their various grievances: the ancient abuse of purveyance, which, notwithstanding thirty-six restraining statutes, still flourished with scarcely diminished vigour; the hardships of feudal guardianship in chivalry; the monopolies of the great foreign trading companies, and several other matters of complaint. After granting the usual duties of tonnage and poundage for the king's life, they concluded by placing on record a remarkable protestation of their rights and liberties, drawn up by a committee of the House, and entitled a " form of apology and satisfaction to be delivered to his Majesty." In this important constitutional document the commons commence by expressing a desire to justify their recent conduct and to remove from the king's mind certain misinformations under which he appeared to be labouring, namely: First, that the privileges of the commons were not held " of right, but of grace only, renewed every parliament by way of donature, upon petition "; secondly, that they are " no court of record, nor yet a court that can command view of records, but that the attendance with the records is courtesy not duty "; and lastly, that the examination of the returns of writs for knights and burgesses is without their compass and belonging to the chancery—assertions against which, as " tending directly and apparently to the utter overthrow of the very fundamental privileges of our House,

---

[23] 1 Jac. 1, c. 13; Prothero, *Documents*, lxxxix, 254–255, 320–325; Tanner, *James I*, 302–317. The creditor's difficulties appeared early in the fifteenth century (*supra*, p. 198). In Shirley's case two private Acts were passed to protect the creditor and gaoler.

and therein of the rights and liberties of the whole commons of the realm
of England which they and their ancestors from time immemorial have
undoubtedly enjoyed," they protest, " in the name of the whole commons
of the realm of England, with uniform consent," for themselves and their
posterity.   In contradiction to these misinformations the commons
avouched: " (1) That our privileges and liberties are our right and due
inheritance no less than our very lands and goods [24]; (2) That they cannot
be withheld from us, denied, or impaired, but with apparent wrong to
the whole state of the realm; (3) That our making of request, in the
entrance of parliament, to enjoy our privilege, is an act only of manners,
and doth weaken our right no more than our sueing to the king for our
lands by petition, which form, though new and more decent than the old
by *praecipe*,[25] yet the subject's right is no less now than of old; (4) That
our House is a court of record and so ever esteemed; (5) That there is not
the highest standing court in this land that ought to enter into competency, either for dignity or authority, with this High Court of Parliament,
which, with your Majesty's royal assent, gives laws to other courts, but
from other courts receives neither laws nor orders; (6) And lastly, that
the House of Commons is the sole proper judge of return of all such writs
and of the election of all such members as belong unto it, without which
the freedom of election were not entire; and that the Chancery, though a
standing court under your Majesty, be to send out those writs and receive
the returns and to preserve them, yet the same is done only for the use of
the Parliament, over which neither the Chancery nor any other court,
ever had, or ought to have, any manner of jurisdiction." Further on they
inform the king that in regard to the late queen's " sex and age which we
had great cause to tender, and much more upon care to avoid all trouble,
which by wicked practice might have been drawn to impeach the quiet
of your Majesty's right in the succession [a gentle hint at the legal and
other difficulties which had stood in the way of James's claim to the
throne], those actions were then passed over which we hoped in succeeding
times . . . to redress restore and rectify; whereas, contrarywise in this
parliament, . . . not privileges, but the whole freedom of the parliament
and realm, hath from time to time, upon all occasions, been mainly
hewed at." They then enter into particulars of the various matters which
had arisen during the session—the business of Goodwin's election, of
Sir Thomas Shirley's arrest, and other causes of complaint. " For matter

[24] Inheritance was the most sacred right known to medieval law. The Conqueror's most
comforting promise to the Londoners was the continuance of inheritance; and much
use was made of the idea that the king " inherited " his prerogative, his parliament, his
taxes, etc., and that the subject " inherited " the common law (including constitutional
law). Cf. Plucknett, " The Lancastrian Constitution," *Tudor Studies presented to A. F.
Pollard*, 164.

[25] The allusion is to a famous legend: " in the middle of the fourteenth century the common
belief was that down to the time of Edward I the king could be sued like a private person,
and a judge said that he had seen a writ beginning *Praecipe Henrico Regi Angliae*. If
he had seen anything of the kind, it was some joke, some forgery. . . ." Pollock and
Maitland, *History of English Law*, i, 516; Holdsworth, ix, 11; and *cf.* the curious note in
Stubbs, *Constitutional History* (1875), ii, 238.

of religion," they assure his Majesty that he would be misinformed " if any man should deliver that the kings of England have any absolute power in themselves, either to alter religion (which God defend should be in the power of any mortal man whatsoever), or to make any laws concerning the same, otherwise than, as in temporal causes, by consent of parliament." Touching their own desires and proceedings therein, there had been not a little misconception and misinterpretation. " We have not come," they said, " in any puritan or Brownish [26] spirit to introduce their parity, or to work the subversion of the state ecclesiastical as now it standeth, things so far and so clearly from our meaning as that, with uniform consent, in the beginning of this parliament we committed to the Tower a man who out of that humour, in a petition exhibited to our House, had slandered the bishops; but according to the tenor of your Majesty's writ of summons directed to the counties from whence we came, and according to the ancient and long-continued use of parliaments, as by many records from time to time appeareth, we came with another spirit, even with the spirit of peace; we disputed not of matters of faith and doctrine, our desire was peace only, and our device of unity, how this lamentable and long-lasting dissension amongst the ministers (from which both atheism, sects, and all ill-life have received such encouragement and so dangerous increase) might at length, before help come too late, be extinguished. And for the ways of this peace we are not at all addicted to our own inventions, but ready to embrace any fit way that may be offered. Neither desire we so much that any man, in regard of weakness of conscience, may be exempted after parliament from obedience unto laws established, as that in this parliament such laws may be enacted as by relinquishment of some few ceremonies of small importance, or by any way better, a perpetual uniformity may be enjoyed and observed." They conclude by assuring the king that " Our care is, and must be, to confirm the love, and to tie the hearts of your subjects, the commons, most firmly to your Majesty. . . . Let no suspicion have access to their fearful thoughts that their privileges, which they think by your Majesty should be protected, should now by sinister information or counsel be violated or impaired, or that those which with dutiful respects to your Majesty speak freely for the right and good of their country shall be oppressed or disgraced. Let your Majesty be pleased to receive public information from your commons in parliament, as to the civil estate and government. For private informations pass often by practice. The voice of the people, in the things of their knowledge, is said to be as the voice of God. And if your Majesty shall vouchsafe, at your best pleasure and leisure, to enter into your gracious consideration of our petition for the ease of these burthens under which your whole people have of long time mourned,

---

[26] The " Brownists " took their name from Robert Browne (1550 ?-1633), a kinsman of Lord Burleigh, who is regarded as the founder of Congregationalism.

hoping for relief by your Majesty, then may you be assured to be possessed of their hearts, and if of their hearts, of all they can do and have." [27]

In this free and outspoken yet thoroughly conservative and monarchical address, the commons of England, at the commencement of their conflict for liberty with the House of Stuart, took up the position which they resolutely maintained during the eighty-four long and stormy years which ensued. "To understand this Apology," remarks S. R. Gardiner, "is to understand the causes of the success of the English Revolution. They did not ask for anything which was not in accordance with justice. They did not demand a single privilege which was not necessary for the good of the nation as well as for their own dignity." [28]

During the next two sessions of parliament (January 21 [29] to May 27, 1606; and November 18, 1606, to July 4, 1607) constant bickerings occurred between the king and the commons, but unmarked by any very decisive assertion of prerogative on the one hand or of privilege on the other.

The sessional rule. In the session of 1606, the rule that the same bill cannot be proposed twice in the same session was established, probably for the first time, by the action of the lords, who peremptorily rejected a bill respecting purveyance which the commons sent up to them very shortly after they had thrown out a previous bill to the same effect.

Jurisdiction over members. In the session of 1607 the commons, at the king's request, expelled and imprisoned one of their members, Sir Christopher Pigott (who had been chosen for Buckinghamshire on the resignation of Sir Francis Goodwin), for slanderous aspersions cast upon the national character of the Scots. But this was rather a confirmation of their jurisdiction over their own members than any surrender of their privileges. Three days after the speech had been uttered, the king sent them a message "how much he did mislike and tax the neglect of the House, in that the speech was not interrupted at the instant and the party committed before it became public, and to his Highness' ear." It was evident that the king had just cause to complain, and, after resolving that Pigott, being a member of the House, was not liable to be called in question elsewhere, the commons determined, in the exercise of their own discretion, to punish the intemperance of their own member. [30]

Union of the crowns: Calvin's Case (1608). During both sessions the principal subject of discussion was James's favourite, but premature, scheme for a perfect union between England and Scotland, so that all his subjects might enjoy the same rights and be amenable to the same laws. But the proposition was repugnant to both English and Scots, in whom

[27] *Parliamentary History*, i, 1030; and *State Papers Domestic*, viii, 70; Prothero, *Documents*, 286–293; more fully in Tanner, *James I*, 217–230.

[28] S. R. Gardiner, *History of England*, i, 186.

[29] By adjournment; the session began on November 5, the day of the Gunpowder Plot.

[30] *Commons' Journals*, i, 336.

the national prejudices and animosities of ages still warmly glowed, and the only result was the passing of an Act (4 Jac. 1, c. 1) by which all hostile laws between the two kingdoms, extending from the time of Henry V to the reign of Elizabeth, were repealed.

The king was anxious to have a declaratory Act pronouncing that the union of the crowns had effected a mutual naturalisation of the *post-nati* (*i.e.*, persons born after his accession to the throne of England), and also an enabling Act conferring the same right upon the *ante-nati*. The English House of Commons was averse to this proposal, and the king, knowing that the opinions of the judges were favourable to the *post-nati*, determined to get the point settled out of parliament by an English court of law. A piece of ground was accordingly bought in the name of Robert Calvin, an infant, born in Edinburgh in 1605, and an action was then brought in his name against two persons who, by collusion, were supposed to have deprived him of his land. This raised the question as to whether Calvin was an alien, as, in that case, he would be disabled from holding land in England. In the course of voluminous arguments examining the nature of monarchy, allegiance, conquest, settlement and many other points of public law, it was held by twelve judges out of fourteen, in the Exchequer Chamber, that the Scottish *post-natus* was a natural-born subject of the King of England.[31]

It may be added, to remind us of a fundamental principle of our constitutional law, that it was repeatedly laid down in this case that allegiance to the sovereign and protection by the sovereign are reciprocal.

Bate's Case (1606). Offended at the commons' bold assertion of their privileges and constant complaints of grievances, James allowed an interval of two years and a half to elapse without meeting his parliament (July 4, 1607, to February 9, 1610). In want of money, but unwilling to apply for a parliamentary grant, he had recourse to the expedient of increasing the duty on imports by his own sole authority. In 1606 the king had directed the collectors of customs to demand a duty of 5s. per cwt. on all currants imported, in addition to the 2s. 6d. granted by the statute of tonnage and poundage. John Bate, a merchant of the Levant Company, refused to pay the additional impost, alleging that it was illegal without the authority of parliament. An information was exhibited against him in the Court of Exchequer, and a unanimous decision of the four barons was soon given for the crown. But the language of Chief Baron Fleming and Baron Clarke (the only two whose judgments are reported) was even more subversive of liberty than the actual decision itself. On the basis of common law principles and the precedents, it is probable that the crown was entitled to succeed; but the court (as it frequently did in the period) found additional arguments in the nature of

---

[31] *Calvin's Case* (1608) 7 Co.Rep. 1; 2 St.Tr. 559. See also Broom, *Constitutional Law* (ed. Denman), pp. 4–26, and Tanner, *Constitutional Conflicts*, pp. 268–269. For a full discussion of this important case, see Holdsworth, *History of English Law*, ix, 72–86, xi, 234.

political theory, and that of a sort which very naturally produced great alarm. They maintained that the king's power is twofold, ordinary and absolute. His ordinary power is for the profit of particular subjects, for the execution of civil justice in the ordinary courts, and is called by civilians *jus privatum*, with us common law: it cannot be changed without parliament. The king's absolute power, on the contrary, is applied not for the benefit of particular persons, but for the general benefit of the people, and is *salus populi*. This power is not directed by the rules of common law, but is properly termed policy or government, varying according to the wisdom of the king for the common good. The matter in question is material matter of state, and ought to be governed according to the rules of policy by the king's extraordinary power. All customs (*i.e.*, duties), be they old or new, are the effects of foreign commerce: but commerce and all affairs with foreigners, war and peace, and all treaties whatsoever, are made by the absolute power of the king; he therefore who has power over the cause, has power also over the effect. No exportation or importation can be but at the king's ports. But the seaports are the king's gates which he may open or shut to whom he pleases. As to the statutes alleged on the part of the defendant, limiting the king's prerogative to impose duties, Baron Clark maintained the monstrous proposition that Edward III in giving his assent to the Act of the 45th of his reign, c. 4 (forbidding any new impositions to be laid on wool or leather), " did not bind his successors. "[32]

Impositions. Even while the case was pending the merchants hastened to appeal to the House of Commons; and in the Petition of Grievances presented by the House at the end of the session of 1606 a request was included that the impositions might cease to be levied, as no such duty could legally be demanded without the consent of parliament. When the commons reassembled in November, James informed them of the legal decision in his favour, and for a time the matter was allowed to drop. But the king soon determined to make a more extensive use of this power of taxation which the judges had declared to be vested in the crown. On July 29, 1608, a *Book of Rates* was published under the authority of the Great Seal, imposing heavy duties upon almost all mercantile commodities, " to be for ever hereafter paid to the king and his successors, on pain of his displeasure."

At length the financial difficulties of the king compelled him to recall parliament for a fourth session in February 1610.[33] The lawyers in the

---

[32] *Bate's Case* (the " Case of Impositions "), 2 St.Tr. 371; Broom, *Constitutional Law* (ed. Denman), pp. 245–302; Prothero, *Documents*, pp. 340–355; Tanner, *James I*, 338–345; Holdsworth, *History of English Law*, vi, 42–47; *The Antiquary*, vols. vi and vii G. D. G. Hall, " Impositions and the Courts, 1554–1606," *Law Quarterly Review*, lxix, 200, and " Bate's Case and Lane's Reports," *Bulletin of the John Ryland's Library*, xxxv, 405.

[33] Special precautions were taken to obtain a majority favourable to the crown. " During the long interval which had passed since the last session several vacancies had occurred. To four, at least, of the constituencies which had seats at their disposal, the treasurer,

Lower House had in the meantime been looking into the legal authorities, and were now prepared to dispute the decision of the judges on the question of impositions. Notwithstanding a message from the king forbidding them to discuss the question, the commons were not to be deterred. During a four days' debate [34] the illegality of impositions was argued from statutes and precedents, in the elaborate and luminous speeches of Hakewill, Yelverton and Whitelocke. The House was almost unanimous against the crown. They presented a strong remonstrance to the king on his attempt to prevent discussion, claiming as " an ancient, general, and undoubted right of parliament, to debate freely all matters which do properly concern the subject; which freedom of debate being once foreclosed, the essence of the liberty of parliament is withal dissolved." With regard to the impositions and judgment in the Exchequer, " the reasons may be extended much farther, even to the utter ruin of the ancient liberty of this kingdom, and of your subjects' right of propriety of their lands and goods." [35]   They remind the king, in a subsequent petition, that " the policy and constitution of this your kingdom appropriates unto the kings of this realm, with the assent of the parliament, as well the sovereign power of making laws as that of taxing or imposing upon the subjects' goods or merchandises wherein they have justly such a propriety as may not, without their consent, be altered or changed " : that whenever former kings, " occasioned either by their wars, or their over-great bounty, have without consent of parliament set impositions either within the land or upon commodities exported or imported by the merchants," the commons " have in open parliament complained of it, in that it was done without their consents, and thereupon never failed to obtain a speedy and full redress without any claim made by the kings of any powers or prerogative in that point " : that " these famous kings for the better contentment and assurance of their loving subjects agreed that this old fundamental right should be further declared and established by Act of Parliament, wherein it is provided that no such charges should ever be laid upon the people, without their common consent, as may appear by sundry records of former times." They proceed : " We, there-fore, your Majesty's most humble commons assembled in parliament, following the example of this worthy care of our ancestors, and out of a duty to those for whom we serve, finding that your Majesty, without advice or consent of parliament, hath lately, in time of peace, set both greater impositions, and far more in number than any your noble ancestors did in time of war, have with all humility presumed to present this most just and necessary petition unto your Majesty: That all impositions set

Salisbury, made applications in favour of nominees of his own. The answers which he received throw some light upon the manner in which elections were at that time con-ducted "—Gardiner, *History of England*, ii, 63 ; and see *State Papers, Domestic*, xlviii, 109, 116 ; xlix, 10.

[34] Copious extracts in Prothero, 342–353, and in Tanner, *James I*, 247–263. Hakewill's argument in full is in Broom, *Constitutional Law* (ed. Denman), 249–299.

[35] Prothero, 296–298 ; Tanner, *James I*, 245–247.

without the assent of parliament may be quite abolished and taken away; and that your Majesty, in imitation likewise of your noble progenitors, will be pleased that a law may be made during this session of parliament to declare that all impositions set, or to be set, upon your people, their goods or merchandises, save only by common assent in parliament, are and shall be void." [36] A bill was introduced and passed through the commons enacting that no imposition, other than those already in existence, should thereafter be laid without consent of parliament, but it was thrown out by the lords. The judgment in *Bate's Case* continued therefore to afford the shelter of a legal decision for the arbitrary exactions of the crown.

The use of proclamations. Besides the question of impositions, the commons brought forward a number of other grievances. They specially complained of the High Commission Court; of the abuse of proclamations, " by reason whereof," they said, " there is a general fear conceived and spread amongst your Majesty's people, that proclamations will by degrees grow up and increase to the strength and nature of laws; whereby not only that ancient happiness—freedom—will be much blemished (if not quite taken away), which their ancestors have so long enjoyed; but the same may also, in process of time, bring a new form of arbitrary government upon the realm, and this their fear is the more increased by occasion of certain books lately published, which ascribe a greater power to proclamations than heretofore had been conceived to belong unto them." [37] Dr. Cowell, regius professor of civil law at the University of Cambridge and eventually Master of Trinity Hall, had recently published, under the patronage of Archbishop Bancroft, a law dictionary called *The Interpreter*, containing most extravagant assertions in support of the king's absolute power. Under the title " King " was written: " He is above the law by his absolute power; and though for the better and equal course in making laws he do admit the three estates unto council, yet this in divers learned men's opinion is not of constraint, but of his own benignity or by reason of his promise made upon oath at the time of his coronation. And though at his coronation he take an oath not to alter the laws of the land, yet, this oath notwithstanding, he may alter or suspend any particular law that seemeth hurtful to the public estate. Thus much in short, because I have heard some to be of opinion that the laws are above the king." Of the parliament it is asserted: " Of these two, one must needs be true, that either the king is above the parliament, that is, the positive laws of his kingdom, or else that he is not an absolute king. . . . And, therefore, though it be a merciful policy, and also a politic mercy (not alterable without great peril) to make laws by the consent of the whole realm, because so no one part shall have cause to complain of a partiality, yet simply to bind a prince to or by those laws were repugnant to the nature and constitution of an absolute monarchy." Farther on he " holds it

---

[36] Petyt, *Jus Parliamentarium*, 322, 323; Prothero, 302.
[37] Prothero, 302–307; Tanner, *James I*, 148–156.

incontrollable [incontrovertible] that the king of England is an absolute king. "[38] The commons were so incensed at these opinions, more especially as the king was reported to have spoken in praise of the book, that they requested a conference on the subject with the lords. But before any further steps had been taken, James thought it expedient to express his displeasure at the imprudent language of this too zealous advocate of prerogative, and a proclamation was shortly afterwards issued prohibiting the purchase, uttering or reading of the book, and calling in all copies issued.[39]

The remonstrance of the commons on the subject of proclamations was not unproductive of good. Sir Edward Coke, Chief Justice of the King's Bench, was sent for to attend the council, and was asked by Salisbury (1) whether the king could by proclamation prohibit the building of new houses in London (with the object of checking what was regarded as the overgrowth of the capital), and (2) whether he could in the same way forbid the manufacture of starch from wheat (so as to preserve the latter

[38] Cowell's Interpreter, ed. 1607, articles " King," " Parliament," " Prerogative." See also extracts in Prothero, 409, and the paper by S. B. Chrimes, " Constitutional Ideas of Dr. John Cowell," English Historical Review, lxiv, 461 (1949).

[39] Lord Salisbury reported to the House of Lords that the king had acknowledged that, although he derived his title from his ancestors, " yet the law did set the crown upon his head," " and that he was a king by the common law of the land." He " had no power to make laws of himself, or to exact any subsidies de jure, without the consent of his three estates, and, therefore, he was so far from approving the opinion, that he did hate those who believed it "—Parliamentary Debates in 1610 (Camden Society, no. 81), p. 24, cited by Gardiner, History of England, ii, 67. In the proclamation suppressing the Interpreter, James took care to improve the occasion, by himself exalting the regal dignity to a level with the Deity: " This later age and times of the world wherein we are fallen," it begins, " is so much given to verbal profession, as well of religion as of all commendable moral virtues, but wanting the actions and deeds agreeable to so specious a profession, as it hath bred such an unsatiable curiosity in many men's spirits, and such an itching in the tongues and pens of most men, as nothing is left unsearched to the bottom both in talking and writing. For from the very highest mysteries in the Godhead and the most inscrutable counsels in the Trinity, to the very lowest pit of Hell, and the confused actions of the devils there, there is nothing now unsearched into by the curiosity of men's brains. Men not being contented with the knowledge of so much of the will of God as it hath pleased him to reveal, but they will needs sit with him in his most private closet and become privy of his most inscrutable counsels; and therefore it is no wonder that men in these our days do not spare to wade in all the deepest mysteries that belong to the persons or state of kings and princes, that are Gods upon earth: since we see (as we have already said) that they spare not God himself. And this licence that every talker or writer now assumeth to himself is come to this abuse, that many Phormios will give counsel to Hannibal, and many men that never went of the compass of cloysters or colleges will freely wade by their writings in the deepest mysteries of monarchy and politick government: whereupon it cannot otherwise fall out, but that when men go out of their element, and meddle with things about their capacity, themselves shall not only go astray and stumble in darkness, but will mislead also divers others with themselves into many mistakings and errors; the proof whereof we have lately had by a book written by Dr. Cowell called the Interpreter; for he being only a civilian by profession, and upon that large ground of a kind of dictionary (as it were) following the alphabet, having all kind of purposes belonging to government and monarchy in his way by meddling in matters above his reach, he hath fallen in many things to mistake and deceive himself: In some things disputing so nicely upon the mysteries of this our monarchy, that it may receive doubtful interpretations; yea, in some points very derogatory to the supreme power of this crown; in other cases mistaking the true state of the parliament of this kingdom and the fundamental constitutions and privileges thereof: and in some other points speaking unreverently of the common law of England and the works of some of the most famous and ancient judges therein; it being a thing utterly unlawful to any subject, to speak or write against that law under which he liveth, and which we are sworn and are resolved to maintain. Wherefore," etc. See the proclamation in Preface to the 1708 edition of the Interpreter.

for consumption of food only). Coke replied that it was a matter of great importance, on which he would confer with the other judges. To this the council reluctantly agreed, and Chief Justice Fleming, Chief Baron Tanfield, and Baron Altham were appointed to consider the matter in conjunction with him. Shortly afterwards the four judges delivered their opinion in the presence of the Privy Council. The king, they said, could not create any new offence by his proclamation; for then he might alter the law of the land in a high point; for if he may create an offence where none is, upon that ensues fine and imprisonment. But the king might admonish his subjects to keep the existing laws, on pain of punishment to be inflicted by the law. Further, the king could not by proclamation make an offence punishable in the Star Chamber, if it were not already by law under the jurisdiction of that court. They also formally declared that the king had no prerogative but what the law of the land allowed him. By their firmness on this occasion the judges rendered an important service to their country. A check was given to the exercise of arbitrary power in this direction, and for some time no proclamation imposing fine and imprisonment was issued.[40]

The " Great Contract." Another measure which occupied much of the attention of the king and parliament during this and the following session was what was termed the " Great Contract." The commons were desirous of getting rid of the irksome incidents of tenure in chivalry and the right of purveyance. After a great deal of negotiation between the parties, it was at length agreed that the king should receive the sum of £200,000 yearly as compensation for the abolition of both these feudal sources of revenue. The matter was adjourned to the next session of parliament; but in the meantime the commons had grown lukewarm. They were impressed with a sense of the insecurity of any contract made with the king in face of the doctrines maintained by himself and by the court lawyers, of a paramount royal prerogative uncontrollable by any statute. They were apprehensive that if the king's wants were fully supplied by a permanent grant, he might in future be tempted to govern without summoning parliaments; they were especially dissatisfied with his steady refusal to admit of any change, however slight, in the ceremonial of the national church, or of any reform in the system of the ecclesiastical courts, whose jurisdiction the bishops were persistently attempting to emancipate from all control by the courts of common law. James, too, on his part, appears to have become less eager to carry out the contract. It was represented to him that after all he would not gain much by the bargain; that by a little more care in managing the crown lands, by putting in force with the utmost rigour all the rights which he possessed against

[40] 12 Reports, 74; Tanner, *James I*, 187–188; Gardiner, *History of England*, ii, 85, 104. For a modern judicial authority that the purpose of a royal proclamation is to notify the existing law, and that it can neither make nor abrogate law, see *Ex parte Chavasse*; *Re Grazebrook* (1865) 4 De G.J. & S. at p. 662.

his subjects, he might obtain the required revenue without having recourse to parliament, and so retain his prerogative undiminished.[41] It became evident that the scheme must fall through; and Salisbury then pressed the commons for a supply for the king's immediate necessities. But the commons were in no humour to grant a subsidy unless the whole of their just grievances were redressed. If the king would not give way they were determined to fall back upon their right to refuse supplies. Some sharp things were said of the king's prodigality to his Scottish favourites; impatient and angry, he adjourned the House; and shortly afterwards the parliament was finally dissolved (December 6, 1610), after an existence of nearly seven years.

Rule without parliament, 1611–1614. For the next three years James endeavoured to rule without having recourse to parliament. His great difficulty was the financial one. His own extravagance, and the prodigality with which he rewarded the worthless favourites of his court, had involved him in a heavy debt and raised the ordinary expenditure far above the crown revenues. A vigorous effort was made to raise funds. Loans on privy seals were demanded, often unsuccessfully, from such as were supposed most capable of bearing the burden; the arrears of fines inflicted in the Star Chamber were rigorously exacted; the king of France was induced to pay up an old debt of £65,000; the Dutch were successfully pressed to liquidate their debt, contracted with Elizabeth, by annual instalments of £40,000; several peerages were sold at £10,000 apiece; and a new order of hereditary knights, called baronets, was created, each of whom paid £1,000 for his patent. In addition, large sums were raised by the sale of crown lands. But such resources were clearly temporary and inadequate. At the beginning of 1614 the king's liabilities amounted to £680,000 as contrasted with £300,000 at which they had stood at the opening of the session of 1610, whilst the actual expenditure exceeded the income by £200,000.

Sir Henry Nevill on parliament. For some time it had been evident that parliament must be summoned; a course which had always been consistently recommended to the king by Bacon and by Sir Henry Nevill, who, though an opposition member in the late parliament, had since been seeking the post of secretary of state. In a very statesmanlike memorial Nevill assured the king that it was a mistake to suppose that the opposition in the late parliament had arisen from factious motives. He had himself lived on familiar terms with the leaders of the opposition, and was able to affirm without fear of contradiction that they bore no ill-will towards the king. He was ready to undertake for the greater part of them that, if the king would act fairly by his people, he would find these men ready

---

[41] Gardiner, *History of England*, ii, 83, 106; Prothero, pp. lxx, 295, 298–300; Tanner, *James I*, 345–347. For the financial side, as seen by Sir Julius Caesar, Chancellor of the Exchequer, see Tanner, *op. cit.*, 348–354.

to exert themselves in support of the government. It would, of course, be necessary to grant certain things upon which those who would be called to pay the subsidies had set their hearts. Let the king consider what had been demanded, and what had been promised in the last session, granting the most reasonable of the commons' requests, in addition to performing all his own promises. Let him avoid any speech likely to excite irritation, and appear confident of the parliament's good affections, yielding what he meant to yield without waiting to be pressed. Let him communicate such proposals as he wished to lay before the commons, not through a member of the House of Lords, but either by his own mouth or by such of his ministers as were members of the Lower House, and let him request the commons to nominate a committee which might confer with him on all points on which any difference should arise between them. This last counsel shows Nevill's acute appreciation of the problem of parliamentary government. At his accession James not unnaturally honoured Elizabeth's old minister, Robert Cecil, by making him a baron, and later Earl of Salisbury. This deprived James of Cecil's great contribution to politics in explaining government policy to the House, answering objections, and generally maintaining liaison between king and commons. Time has shown the cardinal importance of that function, and the lack of men with the requisite gifts after Cecil's elevation had a serious effect. Difficulties which could have been overcome by a minister with the confidence of both king and commons were allowed to remain as sources of increasing friction. James's attempt to use selected peers as intermediaries was singularly unfortunate, since it touched upon the tender susceptibilities of the commons.[42]

Bacon also strongly advised the king to summon a parliament, and he too saw that the root of the problem was the king's relations with the commons, but his advice was much less straightforward and moral than that of Sir Henry Nevill. He submitted that there were many expedients for judiciously managing a House of Commons; that some of those who had been most forward in opposing were now won over, such as Nevill, Yelverton, Hyde, Crewe, Dudley Digges; that much might be done through intimidation or flattery towards filling the House with well-affected persons, winning or blinding the lawyers—the " *literae vocales* of the House "—and drawing the country gentlemen, the merchants, and the courtiers to act for the king's advantage.

The " Undertakers." Bacon's suggestion seems to resemble rather the " influence " and " management " which the eighteenth century politicians devised. The king might voluntarily tender such graces and modifications of his prerogative as might with smallest injury be conceded, in order to save the more important parts unimpaired.[43] Besides Nevill, who had offered to undertake, on behalf of the future House of Commons,

---

[42] See the memorial in Gardiner, *History of England*, ii, 202 *et seq.*, and *cf. ibid.*, i, 165.
[43] *Cf.* Gardiner, ii, 204 *et seq.*

that, if the king would concede the chief points in dispute, the House would not be niggardly in granting supplies, there were some others who appear to have engaged, not only to facilitate the king's dealings with the House, but to influence the elections. The project of these men, who, in the phraseology of the day, were termed the " Undertakers," soon leaked out, and excited much indignation throughout the country. The belief that a general attempt was being made to pack the parliament caused the government candidates to be rejected on all sides. Of the members returned to Westminster, three hundred, or nearly two-thirds of the whole assembly, were elected for the first time, the constituencies having evidently looked out for men who represented the determined spirit of the nation even more strongly than the members of the late parliament had done.[44]

James's second parliament met on April 5, 1614. In the king's speech certain concessions were offered, but of slight constitutional importance.

The Addled Parliament. The commons were not to be satisfied with these small instalments of justice. They went at once to the old grievance of impositions.[45] A unanimous vote was passed against the king's right of imposing taxes without the consent of parliament; and a conference on the subject was demanded of the lords. The lords requested the advice of the judges on the legal point; but this was adroitly refused by the mouth of Chief Justice Coke, on the ground that the question might come before them judicially. The lords, finally, declined the conference; but in the course of their debate an incident occurred which caused much excitement in the Lower House. Neile, Bishop of Lichfield, a sycophantic seeker after power and place, indulged in very abusive language towards the commons. The Lower House immediately demanded satisfaction from the lords. The bishop, when called upon to explain his words, protested " with many tears " that he had been misconstrued and never meant to speak any evil of the commons. The lords acquainted the Lower House with what had passed, but expressed an opinion that in future no member of their House ought to be called in question on the ground of common fame alone. The king now sent a message that unless the commons proceeded forthwith to treat of supply, he should dissolve parliament. But it was too late for intimidation. They declared that they would first proceed with the business of impositions before taking supply into consideration. A few days later, on June 7, James dissolved the parliament, which, from the circumstances of its not having passed a single bill, was nicknamed " the Addled Parliament." It had sat a little more than two months.

[44] " Amongst those who were thus elected were two men who were to set their mark upon the history of their country. Sir Thomas Wentworth, a young man of twenty-one, and heir to a princely estate in Yorkshire, represented the great county of the north; and John Eliot, a Devonshire country gentleman, nine years older than Wentworth, was sent to the House of Commons by the little borough of St. Germans "—*Ibid.*, ii, 230.

[45] Extracts in Tanner, *James I,* 267-268.

Members sent to the Tower. The sudden dissolution of parliament was not sufficient to appease the exasperation of James. Four members who had distinguished themselves by the warmth of their language, Wentworth, Hoskins, Christopher Nevill and Sir Walter Chute, were sent to the Tower. Sir Edwin Sandys and four other members were ordered, at the same time, not to leave London without permission, while Sir John Savile, Sir Roger Owen, Sir Edward Phelips and Nicholas Hyde were punished by dismissal from the Commission of the Peace.[46] This intemperate action of James committed him still more deeply to the conflict with the House of Commons.

A general benevolence (1614). During the next six years James pursued a career of arbitrary government unchecked by the existence of parliament. To supply the wants of his treasury, recourse was again had to the old expedients of forced loans, monopolies, heavy fines, and the rigorous exaction of the old feudal payments. At the time of the dissolution some of the bishops offered the king a contribution to help him out of his difficulties. In a few days their example was followed by the principal nobility and officers of the court; and a resolution was then taken to call upon all England for a general benevolence. Letters were written by the council to the sheriffs and magistrates in each county and borough, calling upon them to collect and send in contributions from all persons of ability. Although care was taken to represent these payments in the character of voluntary contributions, the council in their letters did not hesitate to give very strong hints that it would not be well with those who refused to pay. It was significant that the judges of assize were specially charged with the task of recommending payment, a mischievous resuscitation of the blended judicial and fiscal functions of the ancient justices itinerant. But despite all the exertions of the court only a very small sum was with much difficulty and pressure obtained. The bishops, courtiers, and the City of London had contributed £23,500 previously to the general appeal. From the general appeal itself, extending over nearly three years, the total sum obtained was no more than £42,600. In several counties the sheriffs and magistrates sent up united protests against the demand, appealing to the Act of 1 Richard 3, c. 2 against benevolences and expressing their unwillingness to injure their posterity by establishing a bad precedent.[47]

Prosecutions. *Mr. Oliver St. John,* on being applied to by the Mayor of Marlborough for a contribution, replied in a letter in which he maintained that all such contributions were contrary to Magna Carta and other statutes, including the well-known Act of Richard III, and that it was improper for private individuals to oppose their judgment to that of the

---

[46] Gardiner, *History of England,* ii, 249.
[47] *Ibid.,* ii, 265, 266.

commons in parliament who had refused to grant any supply. He concluded, somewhat intemperately, by charging the king with breaking the
coronation oath, and declaring his belief that all who paid the benevolence
were supporting their sovereign in perjury. This letter having come to the
knowledge of the council, St. John was sent for to London, committed to
the Tower, and sentenced by the Star Chamber to pay a fine of £5,000,
and to be imprisoned during the king's pleasure. The fine was afterwards
remitted, but he was not set at liberty for some time.

At this time the king and council were also engaged in investigating
another affair, which was probably clothed with an importance which it
did not possess in consequence of the excited feelings roused by the levy
of the benevolence. *Edmund Peacham*, rector of Hinton St. George,
Somersetshire (one of the counties which had taken the lead in remon-
strating against the benevolence), had recently been prosecuted in the
High Commission Court for a libel on his bishop and on the Consistory
Court, and was sentenced to be deprived of his orders. While the prosecution was pending, his house was searched, apparently for papers connected
with the alleged libel, and the officials happened to alight upon a manuscript treatise in the form of a sermon, together with some loose sheets,
containing in very offensive language such an attack upon the personal
conduct of the king and the actions of his ministers as would undoubtedly,
if published, have amounted to a seditious libel. These writings were
submitted to the council, who, there is little doubt (though there is no
direct evidence on the point), jumped to the conclusion that Peacham's
sermon, instead of being an isolated piece of puritanic intemperance,
had been prepared in connection with an organised conspiracy of the
Somersetshire gentry.[48] The government in fact felt sure that the phenomenon which we should now call an " opposition " was in fact a seditious
conspiracy, and it was on that ground that the four members were lodged
in the Tower in 1614. For a long while to come there was a very real
difficulty in drawing the line between a " conspiracy " and a " party."
Peacham was put to the rack and examined, as it is expressed by Secretary
Winwood, " before torture, in torture, between torture, and after torture,"
in the vain expectation that he would reveal a plot which had never existed.
No conspiracy or shadow of a conspiracy having been detected, the king
and his council determined to proceed directly against the prisoner,
not for a seditious libel, but for treason, under the statute of Edward III,
in compassing the king's death. The only semblance of evidence of an
overt act of treason was the manuscript sermon, never preached, nor
necessarily intended to be preached. James directed the attorney-general,
Bacon, to confer with the judges of the King's Bench separately, in order

---

[48] In consequence of the resistance to the benevolence shown by the county of Somerset,
three of its magistrates had recently been summoned before the council to receive a lecture on the impropriety of their conduct. Of these, one, Sir Maurice Berkeley, may have
been known to have been in communication with Peacham at the time of the last parliament,
and another, John Paulet, was his immediate neighbour, and had presented Peacham
with the living of Hinton—Gardiner, *History of England*, ii, 274.

to ascertain, and probably to influence, their opinion. Chief Justice Coke objected (so Bacon reported to the king) that " such particular and auricular taking of opinions is not according to the custom of this realm." [49] The three puisne judges made no difficulty in giving an opinion favourable to the crown; and Coke, finding himself unsupported by his brethren in his resistance to separate and private consultation of the judges, at length consented to give a written opinion, which proved, however, by no means satisfactory. Of the two grounds for questioning the treasonable nature of Peacham's writing, first, that it had never been published, secondly, that even if it had been published, it did not amount to treason, Coke appears to have passed over the first, but asserted boldly that no mere declaration of the king's unworthiness to govern, without words disabling his title, amounted to treason.[50] Peacham was brought to trial at the Taunton assizes, convicted, and sentenced to death. He was not, however, executed, but died in gaol about seven months afterwards.

The king and Chief Justice Coke. For some time there had been indications of an impending collision between the king and the Chief Justice of the King's Bench.[51] Now that James was at open war with the representatives of the nation, and was determined to govern as long as possible without the co-operation of a parliament, the only power in the state which he had to fear was the judicial power. It was impossible to prevent cases involving questions of the utmost constitutional importance from being submitted, as they arose from time to time, to the decision of the judges of the land. They were the authorised exponents of the existing law, and thus possessed the power, if so minded, effectually to check the encroachments of the royal prerogative.

Prior to Coke's accession to the bench, the judges had shown themselves, on the whole, sufficiently favourable to the prerogative. No reasons could be more satisfactory to the crown than those upon which the judges had founded their decisions in the celebrated cases of *Calvin* (or *post-nati*) and of *Bate* (or of the Impositions).[52] But Coke early developed upon the bench a sturdy personal independence, and a determination to appeal on

---

[49] Bacon's *Works* (ed. Spedding), v, 100; Tanner, *James I*, 188–192. Coke's objection was not to the consultation of the judges by the king, but to their being consulted separately and giving " opinion by fractions." At a later time he expressed himself against the propriety of the law-officers consulting the judges at all (3 Inst. 29), and quoted a conclusive precedent in his favour from the Year Books; but this point was never raised on the present occasion—Gardiner, *History of England*, ii, 277.

[50] " Innovations of Sir E. Coke," Bacon's *Works* (ed. Spedding), vi, 92. The report of the case (Cro.Car. 125) is too brief to be much use. Holdsworth, v, 313–315, suggests that it was Coke's view that an unpublished writing which did not impugn the king's title was not an overt act for the purposes of the Statute of Treasons. *Algernon Sidney's Case* (1683; *infra*, p. 515) seemingly overruled that view.

[51] There is an excellent account of Coke's public career in Holdsworth, *History of English Law*, v, 423–493. For a lively biography, see Hastings Lyon and Herman Block, *Edward Coke* (New York, 1929). The discussion of this period, with special reference to the history of public law, in Holdsworth, vi, 1–302, is of very great value and interest. For a short account of the common lawyers' position in the conflict, see Plucknett, *Concise History of the Common Law* (5th ed.), 191–198, 242–245.

[52] *Supra*, pp. 337, 338.

all occasions to the supremacy of the law, which frequently brought him into conflict with the king and the ecclesiastical and courtly supporters of the king's absolute power.[53] The claim, pertinaciously asserted by the king and his council, to interfere with the opinions of the judges in every case in which the rights of the crown were in the slightest degree involved was met by Coke with as pertinacious a denial.

The Case of Commendams (1616). Matters were brought to a crisis in 1616 by the proceedings in what is known as the " Case of Commendams." [54] During the time that Bishop Neile held the see of Lichfield, he had received from the king the grant of a living to be held " *in commendam*," that is, along with his bishopric. Two persons named Colt and Glover brought an action against the bishop on the ground that the presentation was theirs, and not the king's, and they further pleaded that, owing to certain legal objections, the king's grant was invalid in itself. On account of its great importance, the case was adjourned into the Exchequer Chamber before all the twelve judges. The king, hearing that his prerogative was likely to be called in question, deputed Bishop Bilson to sit in court, in his name, whilst the case was being argued, and to report on the language employed. Bilson reported that the counsel for the plaintiffs, besides arguing the special points of the case, had disputed the king's general prerogative to grant a commendam. Hereupon James directed the attorney-general Bacon to write to the chief justice, ordering him and the rest of the judges not to proceed to judgment until they had spoken with the king. Coke shortly replied that if it was wished that the other judges should receive the information just given to him, Bacon had better write to them himself. This was done; but the next day the judges, as if nothing had happened, proceeded with their arguments. On the day following they dispatched a letter to the king, signed by all the twelve, informing his Majesty that, as they were unanimously of opinion that the attorney-general's letter was contrary to law, they felt bound by their oaths to pay no attention to it, and had accordingly proceeded with the case on the appointed day.

The king, who was then at Newmarket, returned answer that the present case was one which concerned not merely the interests of private persons but in which he himself was to all intents and purposes a party; that delay was necessary in order that he might lay before them his own case, and that the oath not to delay justice was not meant to prejudice the king's prerogative; and concluded by commanding them, of his absolute power and authority royal, not to proceed further in the cause till they should

---

[53] The facts are concisely stated in Gardiner, *History of England*, iii, 7 *et seq*. See in particular the references there cited to the case of *Brownlow* v. *Mitchell*, and to Bacon's argument on the writ *De Rege Inconsulto*, and the case of *Glanville and Courtney*, which gave rise to Coke's quarrel with the Chancery.

[54] Reported as *Colt and Glover* v. *Bishop of Coventry*, Hobart 140. The right of granting a commendam was one of those papal prerogatives which passed to the crown at the Reformation. See generally, E. Gibson, *Codex Juris Ecclesiastici* (1761), ii, 912, 1528.

hear his pleasure from his own mouth. On his return to London, the twelve judges were summoned before the king and his council. James personally expatiated upon their misdemeanours both in substance and in the form of their letter, certifying him merely what they had done, instead of submitting to his judgment what they should do. He told them it was their duty to check those advocates who presumed to argue against his prerogative; that the popular lawyers were the men who, ever since his accession, had trodden on his prerogative in all parliaments; that his prerogative was double, the one ordinary, having relation to private interests, and which might be and was every day disputed in Westminster Hall; the other of a higher nature, referring to his supreme and imperial power and sovereignty, which ought not to be disputed or handled in vulgar argument; but that of late the courts of common law had grown so vast and transcendent as both to meddle with the king's prerogative and encroach upon all other courts of justice. As soon as he had concluded, all the judges fell upon their knees and asked pardon for their error. But Coke, though he joined in demanding pardon, entered on a justification of their conduct, reiterating his opinion that the postponement required by the king was in fact a real delay of justice, contrary to the law and their oaths. At the desire of James the lord chancellor Ellesmere and the attorney-general Bacon then delivered their opinions, which were directly opposed to that of the chief justice. The following question was then put to the judges, one by one: " Whether, if at any time in a case depending before the judges which his Majesty conceived to concern him either in power or profit, and thereupon required to consult with them, and that they should stay proceedings in the meantime, they ought not to stay accordingly ? " All, except Coke, fearful of offending the king, to whom they owed all their future prospects of professional advancement, promised to act in future according to the royal wishes. But from Coke no answer could be extracted than that, whenever such a case should come before him, he would do what was fitting for a judge to do. The noble conduct of the chief justice on this occasion has deservedly obtained for him the admiration of posterity. Rather than prostitute the independence of the judicial bench to the arbitrary interference of the king, he showed himself ready to sacrifice, for conscience' sake, the high position to which his own merits had raised him. Within a few weeks he was censured by the council and suspended from his office, and not long afterwards, in November 1616, received notice that he had ceased to be chief justice.[55]

" By the deprivation of Coke," observes Mr. Gardiner, " James obtained at a blow all that he had been seeking by more devious courses. The common law judges now held their offices practically, as well as theoretically, at the good pleasure of the sovereign. From henceforward

[55] Hallam, *Constitutional History*, i, 346–349; Gardiner, *History of England*, iii, 1 *et seq.*; Maitland, *Constitutional History*, 268–271. Some of the documents in the case are in Tanner, *James I*, 192–198.

the prerogative was safe from attack in the courts of law. From henceforth, however, it also stood on its own merits, and could no longer
expect to obtain that moral support which it had hitherto received from
the decisions pronounced from the bench by judges who were, comparatively at least with the men who held office subsequently to Coke's disgrace, independent of the favours and the anger of the crown." [56]

The king and the bar. This attack on the judiciary necessarily led the
king to assail the independence of the bar. In 1607, Nicholas Fuller,
a bencher of Gray's Inn (who had sat in James's first parliament, and
was returned for the City of London in 1614), was employed by two
Puritans, Ladd and Maunsell, committed by the High Commission
Court for refusing the oath *ex officio*, to move for their habeas
corpus. This he did on the ground that the commissioners had no
power to fine or imprison under the statute of Elizabeth I (1 Eliz. 1,
c. 1). Although this interpretation was not accepted by the judges at the
time, the language of the statute was such as to admit of argument. On
the ground that he had slandered the king's authority by questioning the
power of the commission, Fuller was himself summoned before the High
Commission Court, fined £200, and committed to prison. In 1613, James
Whitelocke, a barrister who had been brought into notice in James's
first parliament by his great speech on impositions, was summoned before
the Star Chamber on the charge of having given a private opinion to his
client that a commission issued by the king to inquire into the state of the
navy was illegal, on account of certain directions contained in it, as to
punishing offenders, which Whitelocke considered contrary to the well-
known clause of Magna Carta. He was committed to the Fleet, but, on
making humble submission, was set at liberty.[57]

Foreign policy of James. The foreign policy of James was scarcely,
if at all, less irritating to his people than his domestic misgovernment.
On coming to the throne he immediately declared for peace with Spain,
regardless of the wishes of the great body of Englishmen, who, looking
with twofold indignation on the Spanish power as the great supporter of
popery and tyranny, and feeling bound in honour not to desert their old
allies the Dutch in their gallant and now at length hopeful struggle for
independence, were eager to carry on the war. James, however, was not
only by nature averse from all war, but his notions of the divine right of
kings caused him to regard the Dutch war in particular as a contest of
rebels against their lawful sovereign, and therefore undeserving of any
assistance from him. There were indeed many circumstances in the
condition of England at the death of Elizabeth which rendered an honourable peace with Spain highly desirable; but not content with peace, James

---

[56] Gardiner, *History of England*, iii, 27.
[57] *Fuller's Case*, 12 Rep. 41; Whitelocke's *Liber Famelicus*, 33–40, 113–118; Gardiner,
History of England, ii, 36, 188.

must needs run counter to the whole current of national feeling and prejudice by setting his heart upon a marriage between his son and the Infanta. The execution of Sir Walter Raleigh (October 29, 1618), under a sentence of treason passed fifteen years previously, on evidence which was generally considered to be inconclusive, was regarded by the nation as a mean truckling to the revengeful demands of the court of Madrid; and the policy of alliance with Spain became still more odious after the outbreak of the war in Germany, in which the king's son-in-law, Frederick, Elector Palatine, was driven out of his hereditary dominions by the emperor. Despite his pacific temper, James was roused to attempt the restoration of his son-in-law, but while he was anxious to effect his object through the friendly mediation of Spain, the nation was clamouring to support the protestant interest in Germany by force of arms. In this state of affairs the ministers advised the king to take advantage of the war enthusiasm to summon a parliament, and James reluctantly gave his consent.

Third parliament, 1621. James's third parliament met on January 30, 1621, and was opened with a conciliatory speech from the throne. The commons made some complaints of the imprisonment of four of their members, at the close of the parliament of 1614, for words spoken in the House; but the matter was allowed to drop on certain explanations being given by Mr. Secretary Calvert, and an assurance from the king that he would faithfully maintain the privilege of freedom of speech demanded by the House. Two subsidies were then voted.

On the motion of the ex-chief justice, Sir Edward Coke, a committee of inquiry into grievances had been early appointed. The first abuse to which their attention was directed was that of monopolies, and this led to the revival of the ancient right of parliamentary impeachment—the solemn accusation of an individual by the commons at the bar of the lords— which had lain dormant since the impeachment of the Duke of Suffolk in 1450.[58]

Revival of impeachment. Under the Tudors impeachments had fallen into disuse, partly through the subservience of the commons, and partly through the preference of those sovereigns for bills of attainder, or of pains and penalties.[59] Moreover, the power wielded by the crown through the Star Chamber enabled it to inflict punishment for many state offences

[58] For the beginnings of impeachment, see *supra*, 164, 170–172, 193–194; *cf. infra*, pp. 529 *et seq.* For the reasons for its revival, Tanner, *James I*, 321–322.
[59] In 1534 the commons had complained to the lords of the conduct of Stokesley, Bishop of London, and called upon him to make answer. But the lords declared that it was unbecoming for any lord of parliament to make answer in that place; and the proceeding has not generally been regarded as a case of impeachment—*Lords' Journals*, i, 71; Hallam, *Constitutional History*, i, 357n. The proceedings against Wolsey in 1529 have sometimes been termed an "impeachment," but inaccurately. Articles against him were first presented to the Upper House and then sent down to the commons, who rejected them, chiefly through the eloquent defence of his patron made by Thomas Cromwell. *Cf.* Lingard, vi, 211.

without resorting to the assistance of parliament. With the revival of the spirit of liberty in the reign of James I, and the great outburst of historical research into the as yet unprinted records of the medieval parliaments, the practice of impeachment revived also, and was energetically used by the commons in the interest alike of public justice and of popular power; nor were they deterred by the obscurity of the precedents and the fact that even the main outlines of the procedure still remained to be settled. In the session of 1621, the commons impeached Sir Giles Mompesson and Sir Francis Mitchell, who, as patentees for the exclusive manufacture of gold and silver thread, for the licensing of ale-houses, and for the inspection of inns and hostelries, had been guilty of gross fraud, violence and oppression. The lords passed judgment on both, condemning them to be imprisoned, fined and degraded from the honour of knighthood.[60]

The impeachments of Mompesson and Mitchell were followed up by others against Sir John Bennett, judge of the Prerogative Court of Canterbury, for corruption in his office; and Field, Bishop of Llandaff, for brocage and judicial bribery.

Bacon (1621). As yet the commons had only attacked private persons; a much more important step was the impeachment of Lord Chancellor Bacon, which revived the right of impeaching the king's ministers. He was found guilty by the lords of receiving bribes from the suitors of his court, and condemned to pay a fine of £40,000, to be imprisoned in the Tower during the king's pleasure, to be for ever incapable of any office, place or employment, and never again to sit in parliament.[61] The constitutional right, revived by the proceedings against Bacon, was subsequently confirmed and completely re-established by the impeachment, in 1624, of *Lionel Cranfield, Earl of Middlesex,* Lord Treasurer of England, for bribery and other misdemeanours.[62] On his trial he maintained his innocence with much spirit, and bitterly complained of the law which denied to him the benefit of counsel's assistance. He was unanimously convicted, committed to prison, fined and disabled from holding office or sitting in parliament, but his remonstrance on the harshness of the law induced the lords to make an order that in future cases of impeachment the accused should be furnished with copies of the depositions for

[60] Mompesson had escaped beyond sea, but Mitchell suffered his punishment. The outlines of the procedure can be seen in the extracts in Tanner, *James I,* 322–324.

[61] Prothero, 334; more fully, Tanner, *James I,* 324–334. It is to the credit of James that, recognising the transcendent genius of the great philosopher, he mercifully released him from the Tower after a short confinement, remitting the fine and the other parts of the sentence, and conferred upon him a pension of £1,800. For the career and position of Bacon, see Holdsworth, *History of English Law,* v, 238–254. *Bacon's Case* and *Middlesex's Case* are the first examples of a particular person being disabled from sitting in parliament.

[62] See now, R. H. Tawney, *Business and Politics under James I; Lionel Cranfield as Merchant and Minister* (1958).

and against him, and that on demand he should be allowed the aid of counsel.[63]

Floyd's Case. Not content with reasserting their ancient right of impeachment, the commons, in the session of 1621, were hurried by their zeal against popery and their enthusiasm for the protestant Elector Palatine into an act which was at once an invasion of the judicial rights of the lords and a piece of gross and cruel injustice. It came to the knowledge of the House that Edward Floyd, a Roman Catholic barrister, then a prisoner in the Fleet, had expressed his satisfaction that " goodman Palsgrave and goodwife Palsgrave " (the Palatine and his consort) had been driven from the city of Prague. The commons, who suspected James of being very lukewarm in his son-in-law's cause, appear to have been lashed into a sudden paroxysm of rage by this flippant expression. Floyd was " impeached before the commons "—an unheard-of proceeding [64]—and condemned by the House to pay a fine of £1,000, to stand in the pillory in three different places for two hours each time, and to be carried from place to place on horseback, without a saddle, with his face to the horse's tail, and the tail in his hand. The jurisdiction of the commons in the matter rested on their assertion made earlier in the reign [65] that they were a " court of record." That assertion, in its turn, rested on the fact that the House had at various times imposed fine and imprisonment.[66] The lords, considering this proceeding to be an infringement of their privileges, and denying that the commons were entitled to that jurisdiction save over their own members, or over non-members who had infringed the privileges of the commons, requested a conference with the commons. As early as the first year of Henry IV, an entry on the rolls of parliament had declared that the judicial power of parliament did not belong to the commons,[67] and in this very session they had come to a vote, prior to impeaching Sir Francis Mitchell (whom they had at first condemned out of hand at their own bar), that they had no jurisdiction over cases which did not concern the privileges of their House. Without now formally confessing themselves in the wrong, they agreed that the prisoner should be arraigned before the lords, and entered a declaration in their journals that the proceedings in the Lower House

---

[63] *Lords' Journal*, iii, 307–383, 418. The proceedings against Middlesex were apparently promoted by Buckingham, who was at variance with him and determined on his ruin. See Montague, *Political History* (ed. Hunt and Poole), vol. vi, p. 118; Gardiner, *History of England*, v, 229–230.

[64] Impeachment was long a vague and ill-understood procedure; thus in 1626 Charles I (without the commons) proposed to " impeach " the Earl of Bristol: *infra*, p. 408.

[65] *Supra*, p. 335.

[66] It has been suggested that Coke was responsible for this seemingly oblique definition, and that political tactics dictated it: S. E. Thorne, " Courts of Record and Sir Edward Coke," *University of Toronto Law Journal*, ii, 24–49, and " Notes on Courts of Record," *West Virginia Law Quarterly*, xl, 347–359.

[67] *Supra*, pp. 193-194; *Rotuli Parliamentorum*, iii, 427.

should not be " drawn or used as a precedent to the enlarging or diminishing of the lawful rights or privileges of either House." [68]   The lords then
proceeded to impose an even more fantastic sentence. Their right to do
so was almost as dubious as that of the commons. Floyd had not attacked
the lords, nor was he a peer charged with felony. The later suggestion that
Floyd was impeached [69] by the commons before the lords is not warranted
by the journals of either House.

The parliament had now sat four months busily engaged in impeachments, inquiries into grievances and the preparation of bills of reform,
but without paying any attention to the king's request for a further supply
in addition to the two subsidies already granted. Impatient at the delay
and tired of listening to grievances, the king, much to the chagrin of the
commons, prorogued parliament till November.

When the commons reassembled in November they were in anything
but a complacent frame of mind. During the recess Sir Edwin Sandys,
a prominent parliamentary orator, had been arrested, together with the
eminent legal historian, John Selden, his legal adviser, examined before
the council on some secret charge, and kept in confinement for a month.
The commons took up the cause of their member with great warmth.
Sandys was absent through illness, but although Mr. Secretary Calvert
declared that his arrest had no connection with his speeches in the House,
two members were appointed to visit him and solicit a disclosure of the
truth. [70]

" **Mysteries of State.**"   While expressing themselves willing to grant
a moderate subsidy, the commons resolved first of all to enter upon the
question of grievances. On the proposition of Sir Edward Coke, a petition
was drawn up against the growth of popery. It asserted that both the
pope and the king of Spain were aspiring to universal dominion, the one
spiritual, the other temporal; that to these two powers the English papists
looked for support; and that their hopes had been recently raised by the
report of an intended marriage between the Prince of Wales and the Infanta
of Spain; the House therefore prayed that the king would marry his son
to a protestant princess, and would order an expedition to be sent against
that power (meaning Spain) which first maintained the war in the Palatinate. [71]   The king having furtively obtained a copy of this petition before
its presentation, wrote a peremptory letter to the Speaker, forbidding the

---

[68] Prothero, pp. 337-339. By the lords, Floyd was adjudged, in addition to the punishment
of the pillory, to pay a fine of £5,000, to be degraded from the estate of a gentleman and
held infamous, to be whipped at the cart's tail from the Fleet to Westminster Hall, and
to be imprisoned for life at Newgate. On the following day, the whipping was remitted
on a motion of Prince Charles—*Lords' Journal*, 148. At the end of the session the king
remitted the fine and gave Floyd his liberty. " Never," says Montague, *op. cit.*, p. 101,
" did he [the king] appear to more advantage in comparison with the houses than in his
mercy to Floyd."
[69] The conjecture of Lord Hale, *Jurisdiction of the Lords' House*, 101-102 (*cf.* Francis
Hargrave's cautious comment in his introduction, xix).
[70] *Commons' Journals*, i, 643, 644, 662; Gardiner, *History of England*, iv, 133, 233.
[71] Prothero, 307; Tanner, *James I*, 276-279.

House to meddle generally with mysteries of state, [71a] and in particular not to speak of his son's match with the daughter of Spain, or touch the honour of any prince his friend or ally. Sandys' commitment, he told them, was not for anything in his public conduct; adding, however: " We think ourself very free and able to punish any man's misdemeanours in parliament, as well during their sitting as after; which we mean not to spare hereafter, upon any occasion of any man's insolent behaviour there that shall be ministered unto us." [72]   Undismayed by the king's menacing language, the commons presented to him a strong but respectful justification of their conduct, in which, adverting to that part of the king's message which threatened them for freedom of speech, they claimed the privilege as their " ancient and undoubted right, and an inheritance received from their ancestors." [73]   In a long, laboured and sarcastic reply, James dwelt at length on their unfitness for meddling with matters of government far above their reach, commended to them the maxim *ne sutor ultra crepidam*, and concluded by remarking, " although we cannot allow of the style, calling it your ancient and undoubted right and inheritance, but could rather have wished that ye had said that your privileges were derived from the grace and permission of our ancestors and us (for most of them grow from precedents, which shows rather a toleration than inheritance), yet we are pleased to give you our royal assurance, that as long as you contain yourself within the limits of your duty, we will be as careful to maintain and preserve your lawful liberties and privileges as ever any of our predecessors were, nay, as to preserve our own royal prerogative; so as your house shall only have need to beware to trench upon the prerogative of the Crown, which would enforce us, or any just king, to retrench them of their privileges." [74]

Protestation of December 18, 1621. It was impossible for the commons to leave unanswered this explicit attack upon the essential privileges which they claimed as their birthright. On the eve of the Christmas recess they drew up and recorded in their journal their memorable protestation of December 18, 1621, in these words:

" The commons now assembled in parliament, being justly occasioned thereunto, concerning sundry liberties, franchises, and privileges of parliament, amongst others here mentioned, do make this protestation following:

" That the liberties, franchises, privileges, and jurisdictions of parliament, are the ancient and undoubted birthright and inheritance of the subjects of England:

" And that the arduous and urgent affairs concerning the king, state, and defence of the realm, and of the Church of England, and the maintenance and making of laws, and redress of mischiefs and grievances,

[71a] Ernst H. Kantorowicz, " Mysteries of State," *Harvard Theological Review*, xlviii, 65.
[72] Prothero, 310; Tanner, *James I*, 279.
[73] Prothero, 311; Tanner, *James I*, 280–283.
[74] Prothero, 312; Tanner, *James I*, 283–287.

which daily happen within this realm, are proper subjects and matter of counsel and debate in Parliament:

" And that in the handling and proceeding of those businesses, every member of the House of Parliament hath, and of right ought to have, freedom of speech to propound, treat, reason, and bring to conclusion, the same:

" And that the commons in parliament have like liberty and freedom to treat of these matters, in such order as in their judgments shall seem fittest:

" And that every member of the said House hath like freedom from all impeachment, imprisonment and molestation (other than by censure of the House itself), for or concerning any speaking, reasoning, or declaring of any matter or matters, touching the parliament, or parliament business:

" And that if any of the said members be complained of and questioned for anything done or said in parliament, the same is to be showed to the king by the advice and assent of all the commons assembled in parliament, before the king give credence to any private information." [74a]

Sending for the journals of the commons, James, in the presence of his council, tore up the obnoxious protestation with his own hand. He dissolved parliament by a lengthy proclamation setting forth his view of its proceedings [75]; and revenged himself on the " ill-tempered spirits " by committing Sir Edward Coke and Sir Robert Phelips to the Tower, and Selden, Pym and Mallory to other prisons: while Sir Dudley Digges, Sir Thomas Crewe, Sir Nathaniel Rich and Sir James Perrot were sent in a sort of honourable banishment to act as Royal Commissioners in Ireland. [76] " It is worthy of observation," remarks Hallam, " that in this session a portion of the Upper House had united in opposing the court. Their opposition must be reckoned an evident sign of the change that was at work in the spirit of the nation, and by which no rank could be wholly unaffected." This minority in the lords included Oxford, Southampton, Essex, Warwick, Saye and Spencer. The Earls of Oxford and Southampton were summoned before the council, and the former, on pretence of having spoken words against the king, was committed to the Tower. [77]

James's fourth and last parliament. From December 18, 1621, to February 19, 1624, James had again contrived to manage without a parliament. The bishops, judges, county and civic magistrates had been directed to collect a benevolence. [78] The abandonment of the projected marriage between the Prince of Wales and the Infanta of Spain, in which the king was reluctantly induced to acquiesce through the interested influence of the favourite Buckingham, rendered the commons unexpectedly complaisant. James on his part exhibited a condescension equally

---

[74a] *Commons' Journals*, i, 668; Rushworth, i, 53; Prothero, 313.
[75] Tanner, *James I*, 289–295; Prothero, 314–317.
[76] Rushworth, i, 55.
[77] Hallam, *Constitutional History*, i, 368.
[78] The documents are in Tanner, *James I*, 370–373; Prothero, 359–361.

unusual. He submitted for their consideration and advice the matrimonial negotiations with Spain, and the desirability of entering into a war for the recovery of the Palatinate, and even promised that if they would grant the money for the war, it should be paid into the hands of treasurers appointed by the commons, and that he would not treat of peace without previously taking their advice. The commons voted three subsidies and three-fifteenths (about £300,000); and eight citizens were appointed treasurers, and ten other selected persons a council of war, all of whom were to be accountable for their conduct to the commons in parliament.[79]

Act against monopolies. Besides confirming their right to impeach the ministers of the crown by their proceedings against the Earl of Middlesex, to which reference has been already made, the commons, in this session, procured the passing of several salutary statutes, of which the most important was a declaratory " Act concerning monopolies, and dispensations with penal laws and the forfeiture thereof." All monopolies; all licences to do, use, or exercise anything against the tenor or purport of any law or statute, or to agree or compound with others for any penalty or forfeiture limited by any statute; all grants or promises of the benefit of any forfeiture or penalty due on any statute, made before judgment thereupon had; and all proclamations, inhibitions, and other proceedings any way tending to the furthering or countenancing of the same or any of them— were declared to be contrary to the laws of the realm and utterly void.[80]

CONSTITUTIONAL RESULTS OF THE REIGN

On May 29, 1624, James parted with his last parliament,[81] in which, for the first time throughout his reign, hardly any difference had arisen between the crown and the commons. He died on March 27, 1625. The constitutional results of his reign are thus concisely summed up by Hallam: " The commons had now been engaged for more than twenty years in a struggle to restore and to fortify their own and their fellow subjects' liberties. They had obtained in this period but one legislative measure of importance, the late declaratory Act against monopolies. But they had rescued from disuse their ancient right of impeachment. They had placed on record a protestation of their claim to debate all matters of public concern. They had remonstrated against the usurped prerogatives of binding the subject by proclamation, and of levying customs at the out-ports. They had secured beyond controversy their

---

[79] 21 & 22 Jac. 1, cc. 33–43; Prothero, 278–280; Tanner, *James I*, 374–381.

[80] 21 & 22 Jac. 1, c. 3; Prothero, 275. It is under an exception contained in this Act that the crown has since exercised the right of granting letters-patent for new inventions, which would otherwise have been included in the general declaration against monopolies. It is provided that the Act " shall not extend to letters-patents and grants of privilege for the term of fourteen years or under, hereafter to be made, of the sole working or making of any manner of new manufactures within this realm to the true and first inventor or inventors of such manufactures, which others, at the time of making such letters-patents and grants, shall not use." See now, H. G. Fox, *Monopolies and Patents* (Toronto, 1947).

[81] He prorogued it, and his demise brought it to an end.

exclusive privilege of determining contested elections of their members. Of these advantages, some were evidently incomplete, and it would require the most vigorous exertions of future parliaments to realise them." [82]

The startling change in the temper of parliament is nowhere better seen than in the early proceedings of James's first parliament, when the commons denied to the crown all initiative and set themselves up as, in effect, the government. [83] Such a claim would have been impossible had not the king's own officers sadly defaulted in their duty—at the beginning of that same parliament, when members were expecting a statement from the privy councillors of the business to be brought before them on the king's behalf, there was complete silence from the official benches. [84] It is not surprising that after this awkward pause the house should proceed on its own account to the discussion of " grievances."

The crown and the commons. The crown evidently did not appreciate the need for skilful leadership by ministers and privy councillors in the House of Commons, in spite of the very able memorial by Sir Henry Nevill which has already been mentioned, [85] and its attempts to maintain contact with the House by other means produced irritation rather than loyal co-operation.   James himself sent frequent messages, attempting thereby to carry out what should have been the councillors' function of guiding the House; in fact, the result was to diminish the authority of the crown. Elizabeth's messages were rare but decisive; James's were extremely frequent, and were couched in extravagant terms which almost compelled the commons to put in controversial answers, the whole proceeding thus degenerating into an unseemly wrangle. [86] Another of James's expedients was equally ill-advised; this was his attempt to persuade the commons indirectly through conferences between the commons and the lords.   It is true that the lords selected for this purpose ministers and privy councillors from among their number; but in the nature of things, a conference occurred so late in the proceedings that success was unlikely when parties had already taken up positions from which they could not easily withdraw—to which must be added the unwillingness of the commons to accept guidance from the Upper House, and the fact that James had earned the ill-will of many of the peers.

Position of the Speaker. A third possibility was to use the Speaker, whose historical position gave him the opportunity of serving as a link between the crown and the House. The necessity of pleasing two masters made the Speaker's office very difficult; for the most part, he was a royal representative in the House, looking to the crown for the furtherance of a

---

[82] Hallam, *Constitutional History*, i, 373.
[83] *Supra*, p. 332.
[84] Wallace Notestein, *The Winning of the Initiative*, 56 n. 1.
[85] *Supra*, p. 344.
[86] Notestein, *op. cit.*, 41.

career in law or administration of which the speakership was the first considerable step. Nevertheless, at the express command of the House he might have to use language which differed widely from his own sentiments. In a moment of crisis he might have to choose between his masters, and on one momentous occasion of which we shall speak, he chose the House, even in the presence of the king himself [87]; on another, he had to be held in the chair while the House took action of which the Speaker's other master disapproved.[88] The result of so ambiguous a position was that neither the king nor the House could feel complete confidence in the Speaker.

The committee system. The distrust felt by the House is well illustrated by the rapid growth of the practice of the whole House going into committee; the result was that the Speaker left the chair, and quite possibly that circumstance contains the reason for the procedure.[89] At the same time, the influence of the privy councillors was less easily exerted in the larger body, while even on select committees the proportion of councillors declined.[90] James's growing reliance upon favourites such as Carr and Villiers also contributed to the decline of the councillors' prestige as it came to be realised that they were not completely admitted to the king's confidence.[91]

The lawyers. Left to rely upon its own resources, therefore, it is not surprising that the House should have sought in its lawyer-publicists that leadership which it had failed to find in the administrators and politicians of the council. The lawyers were a predominant element in the House, understood the growing complexities of parliamentary procedure, had a fairly clear idea of constitutional principles, and in several cases were good speakers and debaters. Moreover, they were thoroughly conscious of the need for intellectual foundations for the passions which so deeply moved them. To some of them the most promising course was to construct a suitable political theory,[92] and from this period date the beginnings of the common law's characteristic contributions to political science. To others the clue seemed to lie in legal history, where the study of the history of the monarchy, of parliament, and of feudalism led some investigators, at least, to blame the dark deeds of 1066 for our political, social and even economic woes.[93] Finally, the House and its proceedings aroused steadily increasing interest as the reign grew longer, and for the parliament of 1621 this is abundantly illustrated by the number and quality of the notes and diaries compiled by members for their own use.[94]

---

[87] *Infra*, pp. 410–411.   [88] *Infra*, p. 376.

[89] Notestein, *op. cit.*, pp. 41, 47.

[90] See now, D. H. Willson, *Privy Councillors in the House of Commons, 1604–1629* (Minneapolis, 1940).

[91] Notestein *Ibid.*, 46 n. 1.

[92] *Cf.* Holdsworth, *Some Lessons from our Legal History* (1928), and J. W. Gough, *Fundamental Law* (1955).

[93] *Cf.* J. G. A. Pocock, *The Ancient Constitution and the Feudal Law* (1957).

[94] Now printed as *Commons' Debates, 1621* (ed. W. Notestein, F. H. Relf and H. Simpson, 7 vols., 1935).

CHAPTER 13

CHARLES I FROM HIS ACCESSION TO THE MEETING OF THE LONG PARLIAMENT

CHARLES I succeeded to the throne on the death of his father, at the age of twenty-four. Nurtured from his infancy in the doctrine of the divine right and absolute power of kings, which James I had so industriously promulgated, and which the church, the court, and the judicial bench had openly espoused as the true principles of religion and policy, Charles " came a party man to the throne, and continued an invasion on the people's rights while he imagined himself only concerned in the defence of his own."[1] Distrust of his own judgment and too great a deference for the opinions of others, whose ill advice he followed, are the greatest faults admitted by his zealous partisan Lord Clarendon. Unhappy in the choice of his councillors—in Buckingham, Strafford, and Laud, more especially—he certainly was, but it was his own insincerity and innate propensity to intrigue which contributed more than anything else to embitter the struggle between him and his people, and which in the end effectually closed the door against reconciliation. " Faithlessness," observes Macaulay, " was the chief cause of his disasters, and is the chief stain on his memory. He was, in truth, impelled by an incurable propensity to dark and crooked ways. It may seem strange that his conscience, which, on occasions of little moment, was sufficiently sensitive, should never have reproached him with this great vice. But there is reason to believe that he was perfidious, not only from constitution and from habit, but also on principle. He seems to have learned from the theologians whom he most esteemed, that between him and his subjects there could be nothing of the nature of mutual contract; that he could not, even if he would, divest himself of his despotic authority; and that in every promise which he made, there was an implied reservation that such promise might be broken in case of necessity, and that of the necessity he was the sole judge."[2]

First parliament, 1625. The first fifteen months of Charles's reign saw two parliaments successively summoned and abruptly dissolved. Guided by the pernicious counsels of Buckingham, his heart was set upon a war with Spain, a war which, though approved by the last parliament of his father, had not yet been declared, and might easily have been avoided. Before commencing hostilities funds were absolutely necessary, and Charles expected from the commons a large and unconditional grant. But the members of the Lower House were much more

[1] Bolingbroke, *Works* (ed. Mallet, 1754), i, 516.
[2] Macaulay, *History of England*, i, 72.

impressed with the necessity of securing the redress of grievances and placing the enjoyment of civil liberty upon a secure basis, than eager for the prosecution of the war which their predecessors and the public had so loudly demanded. They accordingly doled out supplies very sparingly, granting in the first parliament but two subsidies (about £140,000). They further proposed to grant the customs duties of tonnage and poundage for one year only, instead of for the king's life as had for two centuries been the practice. The lords rejected this, with the result that Charles collected the tonnage and poundage without parliamentary authority.[3] They had no intention of refusing a further supply, but were resolved to avail themselves of their constitutional right to make it dependent upon redress of grievances—conspicuous among them being the fear of a Roman Catholic revival, augmented by the new tendencies in Anglicanism itself associated with Laud and the " Arminians." Professing themselves " ready in a convenient time, and in a parliamentary way, to afford all necessary supply to his Majesty upon his present and all other his just occasions," they were equally determined " freely and dutifully to do their utmost endeavours to discover and reform the abuses and grievances of the realm and state."[4] Indignant that they should thus dare to prescribe to him, the king hastily dissolved his first parliament, and endeavoured to raise money upon privy seals[5]; but within six months he again found it necessary to seek parliamentary aid.

Opposition to Buckingham. One of the chief causes of the late dissolution had been the desire of Charles to screen his favourite, the Duke of Buckingham, from anticipated impeachment by the commons. One of the most learned and moderate members, Sir Robert Cotton, in notes for a speech which was never actually delivered, alluded to " the young and simple counsel " by which the king was led. " We only," he said, " in loyal duty offer up our humble desires, that since his Majesty hath, with advised judgment, elected so wise, religious, and worthy servants to attend him in that high employment, he will be pleased to advise with them together a way of remedy for these disasters in state, brought on by long security and happy peace ; and not be led with young and simple counsel."[6]

Second parliament, 1626. Care had been taken to prevent several of the most popular orators of the last parliament from sitting in the new assembly by appointing them sheriffs[7] for the year; but this manoeuvre

---

[3] Hallam, i, 376; Gardiner, *History of England*, v, 364.

[4] Rushworth, i, 194; Gardiner, *Documents*, 2.

[5] Rushworth, i, 196; the parliament had adjourned to Oxford as the plague was raging in London.

[6] Forster, *Sir John Eliot*, i, 249; *cf.* Gardiner, *History of England*, v, 425 n.

[7] Among them were Sir Edward Coke, Sir Robert Phelips, Sir Thomas Wentworth (who had not yet gone over to the court party), and Sir Francis Seymour. Coke discovered the Act (*supra*, p. 167) in 1621; Holdsworth, v, 449; H. Hulme, "The Sheriff in the House of Commons from Elizabeth to Cromwell," *Journal of Modern History*, i, 361–377; Anson, i, 84.

failed in its effects. Irritated more than ever against the favourite, the new parliament determined to proceed to his impeachment. Whilst the commons were preparing materials for the charge, the king sent them word: " I would not have the house to question my servants, much less one that is so near me. And therefore I hope to find justice at your hands to punish such as shall offend in that kind." Buckingham, he assured them, had done nothing without his own special direction; " certain it is that I did command him to do what he hath done." At the same time he requested an immediate supply.[8]

The commons resolved that three subsidies and three fifteenths should be granted to the king: but with a proviso that the bill of supply should only be brought in after they had presented their grievances and received the king's answer. Addressing the king, they declared " that it hath been the ancient, constant and undoubted right and usage of parliaments to question and complain of all persons of what degree soever, found grievous to the commonwealth, in abusing the power and trust committed to them by their sovereign." And as to the supply, that " though it hath been the long custom of parliaments to handle the matter of supply with the last of their businesses; yet, at this time, out of extraordinary respect to your person and care of your affairs, we have taken the same into more speedy consideration," and have agreed to a resolution for a present supply.[9]

Buckingham impeached; members imprisoned. Buckingham was now formally impeached. Two of the managers on the part of the commons, Sir John Eliot and Sir Dudley Digges, were committed to the Tower by the king for alleged insolence of speech. The commons, incensed, declared that they would do no more business until their members were set at liberty. Sir Dudley Carleton, vice-chamberlain of the household, endeavoured to frighten the House into submission by insinuating that the king might very likely be tempted to govern without a parliament, like the princes on the Continent. But the commons compelled him to apologise, and a large number of peers having assured the king that Sir Dudley Digges had not spoken the words imputed to him, the two prisoners were shortly afterwards released.[10]

Privileges of the lords, 1626. Not contented with attacking the privileges of the commons, Charles was imprudent enough wantonly to provoke a quarrel with the House of Lords. For permitting his son, without the king's licence (as head of the house of Stuart), to marry Elizabeth Stuart, daughter of the Duke of Lennox, the Earl of Arundel (an enemy of Buckingham) was committed to the Tower during the session of parliament. The lords, resenting this attack upon their privileges, resolved,

[8] Gardiner, *Documents*,
[9] Rushworth, i, 249.
[10] Rushworth, i, 360–367.

" that no lord of parliament, the parliament sitting, or within the usual times of privileges of parliament, is to be imprisoned or restrained without sentence or decree of the House, unless it be for treason or felony, or refusing to give surety for the peace."[11] After a contest of three months between the king and the lords, Arundel was at length set at liberty.

The right to a summons. Another enemy whom Buckingham specially feared was the Earl of Bristol (John Digby), who having been ambassador to Spain at the time of Prince Charles's visit, had it in his power to make most damaging disclosures concerning the duke's conduct there. Charles refused him a writ of summons to parliament. Bristol complained to the peers of this violation of their common privilege; and the peers insisting, the king sent the writ, but with a letter forbidding the earl to avail himself of it on pain of the royal displeasure.[12] This letter he laid before the House of Lords, and the next day the attorney-general, by the king's order, charged him with high treason at the bar of the House in the hope that the Earl would be silenced in consequence. Bristol retaliated by accusing the Duke of Buckingham, who thus became the object of two concurrent prosecutions, respectively instituted by the House of Commons and by a former colleague in the late king's service.

To protect his favourite, and at the same time to thwart the pretension of parliament, involved in this attack upon Buckingham, to control the appointment of the ministers of the crown, Charles determined to dissolve parliament. The peers petitioned against this design, but the king angrily replied, " No, not a minute," and the dissolution was immediately declared.[13]

Expedients to raise money. By this hasty and ill-advised dissolution before the liberal subsidies conditionally promised had been granted, the king found himself without funds to carry on the war with Spain. He again had recourse to the old illegal methods of raising money.[14] Tonnage and poundage were arbitrarily exacted; commissions were issued to compound with recusants for dispensing with the penal laws; privy seals and benevolences were demanded from the rich; and the seaport towns were ordered to furnish vessels armed and equipped—the first attempt at ship-money. But that which excited the greatest indignation was the levying and exacting of a general loan from every subject, according to the rate at which he had been assessed to the last subsidy. The common people who refused to contribute were punished by impressment into the army or the navy; many of the gentry were committed to prison; several regiments of soldiers were sent into different counties and quartered upon

---

[11] *Ibid.*, i, 369; Gardiner, *Documents*, 44, 46.
[12] Gardiner, *Documents*, 44–45.
[13] For the impeachment of Buckingham, see Gardiner, *History of England*, vi, Chap. lviii, and *Documents*, pp. 3–45.
[14] See the materials in Gardiner, *Documents*, 46–57.

the inhabitants; and in some places martial law was enforced. Chief Justice Crewe, who refused to admit the legality of the loan, was punished by dismissal from his office.

Darnel's Case, 1627. Of the many persons imprisoned throughout England for refusing the loan, five only, Sir Thomas Darnel, Sir John Corbet, Sir Walter Earl, Sir John Heveningham and Sir Edmund Hampden (cousin of John Hampden, afterwards so celebrated), sued out their writs of habeas corpus in the King's Bench, to which the Warden of the Fleet returned that they were detained under a warrant from the Privy Council " by special command of the king." This gave rise to a most important discussion as to the sufficiency of such a return as a legal cause of detention, there being no charge made against the prisoners. Noy, Selden, and other eminent counsel for the prisoners, argued with much ability and learning in favour of the chartered immunity of English subjects from arbitrary detention, against the attorney-general, Sir Robert Heath, who upheld the absolute prerogative of the crown. The judges displayed great moderation and apparent impartiality while the question was being argued; but in the end Sir Nicholas Hyde, chief justice, gave the decision of the court in favour of the crown, and the prisoners were remanded to custody—a custody which, by this judgment, might be indefinitely prolonged, without any specific charge being brought against the prisoners, or any trial with its consequent condemnation or acquittal.[15] The judgment rested principally upon the " resolution in Anderson "[16] which was quoted by the attorney-general from a manuscript, and accepted by the court as decisive. The temporary triumph of the king was dearly bought at the price of the indignation which it spread among the people, who saw their right of personal liberty practically annihilated by this decision.

Undeterred by the difficulties which he had encountered in providing for the war with Spain, Charles rashly entered, at the instigation of Buckingham, upon a fresh war with France. After the disastrous and humiliating failure of the expedition of the favourite to the Isle of Ré (July 10–October 30, 1627), the absolute necessity of a large supply for carrying on the war forced the king to summon a third parliament.

Third parliament, first session, 1628. Previously to its assembling, it was deemed advisable to release the persons imprisoned for refusing the loan. Seventy-six were thus set at liberty; of whom twenty-seven (Sir Thomas Wentworth, afterwards Earl of Strafford, being of the number) were immediately returned to the new parliament. Charles opened the session (March 17, 1628) with a proud and threatening speech. " There is none here," he said, " but knows that common danger is the cause of this

[15] *Darnel's Case*, 3 St.Tr. 1; Gardiner, *Documents*, 57–64; *History of England*, vi, 213–217; Broom's *Constitutional Law* (ed. Denman), 158–204; Holdsworth, vi, 34–37.
[16] *Supra*, p. 309.

parliament, and that supply, at this time, is the chief end of it. . . . Every man now must do according to his conscience; wherefore, if you (which God forbid) should not do your duties in contributing what the state at this time needs, I must, in discharge of my conscience, use those other means, which God hath put into my hands, to save that which the follies of particular men may otherwise hazard to lose. Take not this as a threatening (for I scorn to threaten any but my equals), but an admonition from him that, both out of nature and duty, hath most care of your preservations and prosperities." The lord keeper added: " This way (of supply), as his Majesty hath told you, he hath chosen, not as the only way, but as the fittest; not as destitute of others, but as most agreeable to the goodness of his own most gracious disposition, and to the desire and weal of his people. If this be deferred, necessity and the sword of the enemy make way to the others. Remember his Majesty's admonition; I say remember it." [17] The commons were not at all disturbed by this menacing language. They had come together, said Wentworth, who was so soon to desert the popular cause, firmly determined on vindicating the " ancient vital liberties, by reinforcing the ancient laws made by our ancestors; by setting forth such a character of them as no licentious spirit shall dare to enter upon them." [18]

Committee of grievances. They at once resolved themselves into a committee of grievances to consider " the liberty of the subject in his person and in his goods." The principal matters discussed were: (1) illegal exactions under the name of loans; (2) the arbitrary commitment of those who refused compliance, and especially the recent decision of the King's Bench remanding Sir Thomas Darnel and others upon a habeas corpus; (3) the billeting of soldiers on private persons; and (4) the infliction of punishment by martial law. The commons passed resolutions " That no freeman ought to be detained or kept in prison or otherwise restrained by the command of the king or the Privy Council, or any other, unless some cause of his commitment, detainer or restraint be expressed for which by law he ought to be committed, detained or restrained "; and " that it is the ancient and undoubted right of every freeman that he hath a full and absolute property in his goods and estate; that no tax, tallage, loan, benevolence, or other like charge, ought to be commanded or levied by the king or any of his ministers, without common consent by act of parliament." Then for two months the attention of both Houses, either in conference or in separate debate, was almost exclusively devoted to the subject of a petition to the king for a declaratory confirmation of these liberties. The question was exhaustively argued by Selden, Coke, Littleton, Digges, Noy and other eminent lawyers on the part of the commons, and by the Attorney-General Heath, Serjeant Ashley, and others, as counsel for the crown. In the meantime the commons, anxious not to give the

[17] Rushworth, i, 480–484.
[18] *Ibid.*, i, 496.

king any just cause of offence, unanimously voted the unusually large amount of five subsidies (£350,000), but deferred the passing of a regular money bill until their grievances should be redressed. The king tried hard to satisfy the commons by offering his royal word not to arrest anyone without just cause, or a simple confirmation of the Great Charter and the other ancient statutes in favour of liberty. But Sir Edward Coke warned the House to proceed by bill. " Was it ever known," he said, " that general words were a sufficient satisfaction to particular grievances ? The king's answer is very gracious; but what is the law of the realm ? that is the question. I put no diffidence in his Majesty; the king must speak by a record, and in particulars, and not in general. Let us put up a Petition of Right; not that I distrust the king, but that we cannot take his trust but in a parliamentary way." [19]

The Petition of Right. The Petition of Right was then drawn up by the commons. The lords vainly proposed as an amendment : " We present this our humble petition to your Majesty with the care not only of preserving our own liberties, but with due regard to leave entire that sovereign power wherewith your Majesty is trusted for the protection, safety, and happiness of the people." [20] This insidious saving clause was firmly rejected by the commons. " Let us look into the records," said Alford, a member, " and see what they are: what is ' sovereign power '? Bodin saith that it is free from any condition. By this we shall acknowledge a regal as well as a legal power. Let us give that to the king that the law gives him, and no more." " I am not able," said Pym, " to speak to this question; I know not what it is. All our petition is for the laws of England; and this power seems to be another distinct power from the power of the law. I know how to add ' sovereign ' to his [the king's] person, but not to his power; also we cannot leave to him sovereign power; we never were possessed of it." Sir Edward Coke said : " This is *magnum in parvo*. This is propounded to be a conclusion of our petition. It is a matter of great weight; and, to speak plainly, it will overthrow all our petition; it trenches to all parts of it; it flies at loans, and at the oath, and at imprisonment, and billeting of soldiers; this turns all about again. Look into all the petitions of former times; they never petitioned wherein there was a saving of the king's sovereignty. I know that prerogative is part of the law, but sovereign power is no parliamentary word. In my opinion it weakens Magna Carta, and all our statutes; for they are absolute, without any saving of sovereign power; and shall we now add it, we shall weaken the foundation of law, and then the building must needs fall. Take we heed what we yield unto: Magna Carta is such a fellow that he will have no sovereign. I wonder this sovereign was not in Magna Carta, or in the

[19] Rushworth, i, 564. *Cf.* H. Hulme, " Opinion in the House of Commons on the proposal for a Petition of Right," *English Historical Review,* 1, 302; and for the procedural aspect, E. R. Adair, " The Petition of Right," *History,* v, 99.
[20] Rushworth, i, 567.

confirmations of it. If we grant this, by implication we give a sovereign power above all these laws. Power, in law is taken for a power with force; the sheriff shall take the power of the county; what it means here, God only knows. It is repugnant to our petition; that is, a Petition of *Right*, grounded on Acts of Parliament." [21]   In a further conference with the lords, Sir Henry Martyn dwelt with much force upon the moderation displayed by the commons as a reason for supporting the petition in its integrity. " This moderation will the better appear," he said, " if it be not forgotten how our ancestors and predecessors carried themselves in parliaments, when upon lighter provocations less would not serve their turns, but new severe commissions to hear and determine offences against their liberties, public ecclesiastical curses, or excommunications against the authors or actors of such violations, accusations, condemnations, executions, banishments. But what have we said all this parliament ? We only look forward, not backward; we desire amendment hereafter, no man's punishment for aught done heretofore; nothing written by us in blood, nay, not one word spoken against any man's person in displeasure. The conclusion of our petition is, that we may be better intreated in time to come: and doth not this moderate petition deserve your lordships' cheerful conjunction *ex congruo et condigno*? If a worm, being trodden upon, could speak, a worm would say, ' tread upon me no more I pray you '; higher we rise not, lower we cannot descend, and thus much we think in modesty may well be spoken in our own commendation, thence to move your lordships to vouchsafe us your noble company in this petition without surcharging it with this addition." [22]

At length the lords passed the petition without any material alteration, and it awaited only the royal assent to acquire the force of law. In the meantime Charles sent for the two chief justices, Hyde and Richardson, and submitted to them certain questions to be answered by themselves and the other judges. One was, " Whether, if the king grant the commons' petition, he doth not thereby exclude himself from committing or restraining a subject, for any time or cause whatsoever, without showing a cause ? " To this the judges replied, " Every law after it is made, hath its exposition, and so this petition and answer must have an exposition, as the case in the nature thereof shall require to stand with justice; which is to be left to the courts of justice to determine, which cannot particularly be discovered until such case shall happen. And although the petition be granted, there is no fear of conclusion as is intimated in the question." [23]   This indirect promise of compliance on the part of the judges was apparently unsatisfactory to the king, who had no intention of really parting with the prerogative of arbitrary commitment. On June 2, 1628, he attended in the House of Lords to give his answer to the bill, before the peers and commons in parliament. To the surprise of all men, instead of the usual

[21] Rushworth, i, 568.
[22] Rushworth, i, 590.
[23] Hargrave MSS. xxxii, 97, cited by Hallam, *Constitutional History*, i, 391.

concise and clear form of words by which a bill receives the royal assent, Charles returned a long and equivocal answer that " the king willeth that right be done according to the laws and customs of the realm, and that the statutes be put in due execution, that his subjects may have no cause to complain of any wrong or oppressions contrary to their just rights and liberties; to the preservation whereof he holds himself in conscience as well obliged, as of his prerogative." [24]   Highly incensed at this evasive reply, which was tantamount to a refusal to pass the bill, the commons gave vent to their ill humour by impeaching Dr. Mainwaring,[25] and were proceeding to censure the favourite Buckingham when on the joint application of the lords and commons the king at length signified the royal assent in the customary form—" Soit droit fait comme est désiré "— which was construed as giving to this second great fundamental compact between the crown and the nation the sanction of an Act of Parliament.[26]

THE PETITION OF RIGHT
3 Car. 1, c. 1.   (June 7, 1628.)

The Petition exhibited to his Majesty by the Lords Spiritual and Temporal and Commons, in this present Parliament assembled, concerning divers Rights and Liberties of the Subjects: with the King's Majesty's royal answer thereunto in full Parliament.

To the King's most Excellent Majesty.

I.   Humbly show unto our Sovereign Lord the King, the Lords Spiritual and Temporal and Commons in Parliament assembled, that whereas it is declared and enacted by a statute made in the time of the reign of King Edward the First, commonly called *Statutum de Tallagio non concedendo*,[27] that no tallage or aid shall be laid or levied by the king or his heirs in this realm, without the good will and assent of the archbishops, bishops, earls, barons, knights, burgesses, and other the freemen of the commonalty of this realm; and by authority of Parliament holden in the five-and-twentieth year of the reign of King Edward the Third,[28] it is declared and enacted, that from thenceforth no person shall be compelled to make any loans to the king against his will, because such loans were against reason and the franchise of the land; and by other laws of this realm, it is provided, that none should be charged by any charge or imposition called a benevolence, nor by such like charge,[29] by which the statutes before mentioned, and other the good laws and statutes of this realm, your subjects have inherited this freedom that they should not be compelled to contribute to any tax, tallage, aid, or other like charge, not set by common consent in Parliament.

II.   Yet nevertheless of late divers commissions directed to sundry commissioners in several counties, with instructions, have issued, by means whereof your people have been in divers places assembled, and required to lend certain

---

[24] Rushworth, i, 598.
[25] *Infra*, p. 530.
[26] F. H. Relf, *The Petition of Right* (1917) is an extended history of the document, the text of which here follows.
[27] *Supra*, p. 149.
[28] See *Rotuli Parliamentorum*, ii, 238.
[29] 1 Ric. 3, c. 2.

sums of money unto your Majesty, and many of them, upon their refusal so to do, have had an oath administered unto them not warrantable by the laws or statutes of this realm, and have been constrained to become bound to make appearance and give attendance before your Privy Council, and in other places, and others of them have been therefore imprisoned, confined, and sundry other ways molested and disquieted; and divers other charges have been laid and levied upon your people in several counties by lords lieutenants, deputy lieutenants, commissioners for musters, justices of peace and others, by command or direction from your Majesty, or your Privy Council, against the laws and free customs of this realm.

III. And where also by the statute called " The Great Charter of the Liberties of England," it is declared and enacted, that no freeman may be taken or imprisoned or be disseised of his freeholds or liberties, or his free customs, or be outlawed or exiled, or in any manner destroyed, but by the lawful judgment of his peers, or by the law of the land.[30]

IV. And in the eight-and-twentieth year of the reign of King Edward the Third, it was declared and enacted by authority of Parliament that no man, of what estate or condition that he be, should be put out of his lands or tenements, nor taken, nor imprisoned, nor disherited, nor put to death, without being brought to answer by due process of law.[31]

V. Nevertheless, against the tenor of the said statutes, and other the good laws and statutes of your realm to that end provided,[32] divers of your subjects have of late been imprisoned without any cause showed; and when for their deliverance they were brought before your justices by your Majesty's writs of *habeas corpus*, there to undergo and receive as the court should order, and their keepers commanded to certify the causes of their detainer, no cause was certified, but that they were detained by your Majesty's special command, signified by the lords of your Privy Council, and yet were returned back to several prisons, without being charged with anything to which they might make answer according to the law.

VI. And whereas of late great companies of soldiers and mariners have been dispersed into divers counties of the realm, and the inhabitants against their wills have been compelled to receive them into their houses, and there to suffer them to sojourn, against the laws and customs of this realm, and to the great grievance and vexation of the people.[33]

VII. And whereas also by authority of Parliament, in the five-and-twentieth year of the reign of King Edward the Third, it is declared and enacted, that no man shall be forejudged of life or limb against the form of the Great Charter and the law of the land; and by the said Great Charter and other the laws and statutes of this your realm, no man ought to be adjudged to death, but by the laws established in this your realm, either by the customs of the same realm or by Acts of Parliament; and whereas no offender, of what kind soever, is exempted from the proceedings to be used, and punishments to be inflicted by the laws and statutes of this your realm: nevertheless of late time divers commissions under your Majesty's Great Seal have issued forth, by which certain persons

---

[30] 9 Hen. 3, c. 29; *supra*, pp. 80–81.

[31] 28 Edw. 3, c. 3.

[32] See 37 Edw. 3, c. 18; 38 Edw. 3, stat. 1, c. 9; 42 Edw. 3, c. 3; 17 Ric. 2, c. 6.

[33] By stat. 31 Car. 2, c. 1, it is enacted that no officer, military or civil, or other persons, shall quarter or billet any soldier upon any inhabitant of this realm without his consent, and that every such inhabitant may refuse to quarter any soldier, notwithstanding any order whatsoever. The provisions of the Petition of Right and of this statute of Charles II against billeting are annually suspended by the Mutiny Act, which expressly gives permission to billet soldiers in inns and victualling houses.

have been assigned and appointed commissioners with power and authority to proceed within the land, according to the justice of martial law, against such soldiers and mariners, or other dissolute persons joining with them, as should commit any murder, robbery, felony, mutiny, or other outrage or misdemeanour whatsoever, and by such summary course and order as is agreeable to martial law, and as is used in armies in time of war, to proceed to the trial and condemnation of such offenders, and them to cause to be executed and put to death according to the law martial.

By pretext whereof some of your Majesty's subjects have been by some of the said commissioners put to death, when and where, if by the laws and statutes of the land they had deserved death, by the same laws and statutes also they might, and by no other ought to have been, adjudged and executed.

And also sundry grievous offenders, by colour thereof claiming an exemption, have escaped the punishments due to them by the laws and statutes of this your realm, by reason that divers of your officers and ministers of justice have unjustly refused or forborne to proceed against such offenders according to the same laws and statutes, upon pretence that the said offenders were punishable only by martial law, and by authority of such commissions as aforesaid; which commissions, and all other of like nature, are wholly and directly contrary to the said laws and statutes of this your realm.

VIII. They do therefore humbly pray your most excellent Majesty that no man hereafter be compelled to make or yield any gift, loan, benevolence, tax, or such like charge, without common consent by Act of Parliament; and that none be called to make answer or take such oath, or to give attendance, or be confined, or otherwise molested or disquieted concerning the same or for refusal thereof; and that no freeman, in any such manner as is before mentioned, be imprisoned or detained; and that your Majesty will be pleased to remove the said soldiers and mariners, and that your people may not be so burdened in time to come; and that the aforesaid commissions, for proceeding by martial law, may be revoked and annulled: and that hereafter no commissions of like nature may issue forth to any person or persons whatsoever to be executed as aforesaid, lest by colour of them any of your Majesty's subjects be destroyed or put to death contrary to the laws and franchise of the land.

All which they most humbly pray of your most excellent Majesty as their rights and liberties, according to the laws and statutes of this realm; and that your Majesty would also vouchsafe to declare, that the awards, doings and proceedings, to the prejudice of your people in any of the premises, shall not be drawn hereafter into consequence or example; and that your Majesty would be also graciously pleased, for the further comfort and safety of your people, to declare your royal will and pleasure, that in the things aforesaid all your officers and ministers shall serve you according to the laws and statutes of this realm, as they tender the honour of your Majesty and the prosperity of this kingdom.

Qua quidem petitione lecta et plenius intellecta per dictum dominum regem taliter est responsum in pleno parliamento, videlicet, Soit droit fait comme est désiré.[34]

The commons were triumphant, and grateful amidst their rejoicings. They immediately passed a bill granting the five subsidies already promised; and were preparing another giving the king tonnage and poundage for life, but delayed its passing in order to remonstrate against the continued illegal levying of those duties without the sanction of

[34] 3 Car. 1, c 1. *Statutes of the Realm*, v, 23, 24.

parliament,[35] and to pray for the removal from office of Buckingham, to whose evil influence they attributed all the misfortunes of the kingdom both at home and abroad. To prevent the delivery of this remonstrance the king suddenly (June 26) prorogued parliament.[36]

Third parliament, second session, 1629. On January 20, 1629, the two Houses reassembled. During the recess the assassination of Buckingham by Felton (August 23) had removed one great cause of contention between Charles and his people; but the king had continued to raise the customs duties as before, and several merchants, on refusal to pay, had been punished by distraint of their goods and imprisonment. On appealing to the courts of law, they were informed by the judges that the king's right was conclusively established by the decision in *Bate's Case*.[37]

The king's version of the Petition of Right. The natural irritation of the commons was increased on hearing that the speech in which Charles, at the close of the last session, had claimed tonnage and poundage as his due, had been entered on the parliament roll together with the Petition of Right, and that he had caused 1,500 copies of the great constitutional compact between the crown and the people to be circulated throughout the country with his first and repudiated answer annexed, in addition to the final answer, which alone formed part of the statute.[38] Selden at once complained to the House of the breach (as he alleged) of the Petition of Right in the case of the merchants whose goods had been seized, and also of the cutting off of a man's ears by an arbitrary judgment of the Star Chamber. " Next," he said, " they will take away our arms, and then our legs, and so our lives; let us all see we are sensible of this. Customs creep on us; let us make a just representation hereof unto his Majesty."

Question of privilege: Rolle's Case. The dispute as to tonnage and poundage was embittered and complicated by the fact that John Rolle, one of the merchants whose goods had been seized, was a member of the House. At this period, privilege of parliament was held to protect not only the persons but the goods of members from arrest[39]; and although, owing to the time (the middle of the parliamentary recess) when the seizure in *Rolle's Case* had been effected, it could only be brought technically within the privilege by means of a legal fiction, the

---

[35] Rushworth, i, 628; Gardiner, *Documents*, 70–72; they argued that the collection of these duties, however dubious before, was clearly illegal after the Petition of Right.

[36] In his speech (Gardiner, *Documents*, 73) he nevertheless replied to the argument in the undelivered remonstrance.

[37] The customs duties were not mentioned by name in the Petition of Right. Nevertheless, in the remonstrance which the commons were prevented from delivering by the prorogation, they had declared that the levying of tonnage and poundage without consent was illegal by the Petition of Right—Gardiner, *Documents*, 70; *History of England*, vi, 326 *et seq*.

[38] Gardiner, *History of England*, vii, 30.

[39] *Supra*, p. 197.

commons were disposed to resent the matter as an attack on their liberties; and while one member, Phelips, moved for a committee on the whole question of the levy of tonnage and poundage, another, Littleton, desired that " the parties be sent for that violated the liberties." [40] The king now thought it prudent to attempt to allay the rising storm. Sending for the two Houses to Whitehall, he explicitly renounced all claim to levy tonnage and poundage as of right. " It ever was, and still is my meaning," he told them, " by the gift of my people to enjoy it, and my intention in my speech at the end of the last session was not to challenge tonnage and poundage of right, but for expedience *de bene esse*, shewing you the necessity, not the right, by which I was to take it until you had granted it unto me; assuring myself, according to your general profession, that you wanted time and not good will to give it me." [41] This politic speech made a most favourable impression, and two days afterwards a proposal was made by Sir John Coke [42] to bring in a bill granting tonnage and poundage to the king; but there still remained a grievance which the commons had even more at heart than illegal taxation, and the latter question was postponed until the recent innovations in religion had been discussed.

Politics and religion. The position taken up by the commons alike in politics and religion was a conservative one. In politics they sought to preserve the free English constitution as it had existed prior to the despotic practices of the Tudors and the despotic theories, as well as practices, of the Stuarts. In religion they adhered to the strict calvinistic theology which had become increasingly prominent in the national church from the reformation to the beginning of the seventeenth century. This they regarded as the orthodox doctrine, and considered it to be supported by the Prayer Book, the Catechism, the Homilies, the writings of Bishop Jewel, the Lambeth Articles of 1595, the Resolutions of the Synod of Dort in 1618, the uniform consent of writers whose works had been published by authority, and by the submission enjoined by the two universities upon the opponents of the Lambeth Articles. They complained of the spread of popery and arminianism; the removal of communion tables to be set up as altars at the eastern end of churches; the placing of candlesticks on them; and the obeisance made towards them; the ordering that congregations should stand up at the singing of the *Gloria Patri*, and that women coming to be churched should wear veils; the setting up of pictures and lights and images in churches, praying towards the east, crossing and other devout but to them objectionable gestures.[43]

The king and Laud. In November 1628, at Laud's suggestion, the king had endeavoured to silence all religious controversy by issuing a

[40] Gardiner, *History of England*, vii, 32. For the sequel, see *infra*, p. 375.
[41] *Ibid.*, vii, 33.
[42] An industrious official, trained by Burleigh, who became Secretary of State in 1625, and the government's principal, though ineffective, spokesman in the commons.
[43] Gardiner, *Documents*, 77, and *History of England*, vii, 65. For a recent short survey of the religious situation at the moment, see Godfrey Davies, *The Early Stuarts*, 66–78.

new edition of the Articles of Religion, prefaced by a declaration (which is still printed in the Book of Common Prayer) directing that thereafter no man should either in writing or preaching put his own sense or comment as the meaning of the Articles, but should take them in their literal and grammatical sense.[44] He at the same time inferentially repudiated the right of parliament to deal with religious questions, by declaring that to the king, as supreme governor of the church, and to the Convocation, acting by his leave and with his approval, such matters exclusively belonged. But while professing to act impartially the king's sympathies were unmistakably shown not only by his close alliance with Laud, but his ostentatious bestowal of promotion upon those of the clergy who had rendered themselves notorious, and incurred the animosity of the House of Commons, by their simultaneous advocacy of anti-calvinistic doctrines in the church, and of the divine right of kings in the state. Dr. Montague, whose *Appello Caesarem* in 1625 had been condemned by the commons as containing matters contrary to the Thirty-nine Articles, and who in 1627 had been foremost in inculcating the duty of paying the forced loan, was promoted by the king to a bishopric shortly after the prorogation of parliament in 1628; and at the same time Dr. Mainwaring, who had but recently been impeached by the commons and condemned by the lords for his advocacy, in the pulpit and the press, of the right of the king to tax his subjects without the consent of parliament,[45] was rewarded with a rich living, and ultimately advanced to the bishopric of St. David's. The idea of toleration and religious liberty was as yet unthought of by either king or parliament, and the commons, having declared their interpretation of the Articles of Religion to be the only true one,[46] proceeded to summon the authors of the ceremonial innovations to answer at the bar of the House.

Tonnage and poundage. In the meantime the question of tonnage and poundage was again taken up, and, contrary to the advice of Pym, who wished the matter to be dealt with on the broad national basis of the illegality of taxation without consent, the commons resolved to give prominence to the breach of privilege in *Rolle's Case*,[47] and accordingly summoned the custom-house officers who had seized that member's goods to appear and answer for their contempt. The king refused to allow his officers to be questioned for obedience to his orders, and directed the House to adjourn for a few days until March 2.[48] During the short recess attempts were made to come to some private arrangement with the leaders of the commons, but these failing, the House, at its reassembling on March 2, was informed by the Speaker, Sir John Finch,

[44] Also printed in Gardiner, *Documents*, 75.
[45] *Infra*, p. 530.
[46] See the Resolution of the Commons of January 1629, Gardiner, *History of England*, vii, 41.
[47] *Supra*, p. 373.
[48] Gardiner, *History of England*, vii, 65, 66.

that the king again required them to adjourn, this time until the 10th. The right of the king to order an adjournment, which had always been admitted by the lords in reference to their own House, had never been acquiesced in by the commons, who, while complying with the king's wishes, had always been careful to make their adjournment their own formal act.

The Speaker held in the Chair. When the question of adjournment was now put by the Speaker a chorus of " Noes " resounded from every side. Sir John Eliot, who, anticipating the adjournment and speedy dissolution of parliament by the king, had prepared a protestation on the subjects of religion and taxation, which, if only passed by the House before its adjournment, would go forth to the country as an appeal against the king's arbitrary proceedings, rose to speak. He was interrupted by the Speaker, who, saying he had the absolute command of the king to leave the chair if any one should attempt to address the House, rose also, but was at once thrust back into his seat by Holles and Valentine. The whole House was now in an uproar. Some of the privy councillors present rushed to the assistance of the Speaker, who broke away for a moment, but only to be again seized and forced into the chair. " God's wounds," exclaimed Holles, " you shall sit till we please to rise." At the order of the House the door was locked by Sir Miles Hobart, who placed the key in his pocket. Eliot proposed that three resolutions, the substance of which he explained, should be formally put to the vote. Both the Speaker and the clerk refused. A confused and stormy debate ensued, and Eliot, despairing of getting the resolutions passed, had thrown them into the fire, when, just as the king's guard was approaching the House to effect a forcible entry, Holles who had hastily rewritten the resolutions from memory, read them to the House. They were carried by acclamation, and, the House having voted its own adjournment, the door was thrown open.[49]

The three resolutions declared: (1) that the introducers of innovation in religion, or of popery, or arminianism, or other opinions disagreeing from the true and orthodox church; and (2) all who should counsel or advise the taking and levying of the subsidies of tonnage and poundage, not being granted by parliament, or should be actors or instruments therein, should be reputed capital enemies to the kingdom and common-wealth; and (3) that all merchants or others who should voluntarily pay the said subsidies, should be reputed betrayers of the liberties of England, and enemies to the same. The commons thus made religion the primary issue, relating their other grievances to it. " Once the religious issue had been definitely raised, there was no longer any possibility of a com-promise. The commons were claiming the right to determine the religion of England."[50] The divergences which had caused anxiety in Elizabeth's

[49] Nicholas, *Notes of the Session of 1629*; State Papers, Domestic 1628–1629, p. 485, cxxxviii, 5, 6, 7; Gardiner, *History of England*, vii, 67–76.
[50] Godfrey Davies, *The Early Stuarts*, 42; the text of the resolutions is in Gardiner, *Documents*, 82–83.

later years, seemed now irreconcilable, and Charles became still more associated with the Laudian school of churchmen.

The House at its rising had adjourned until March 10. On that day the king dissolved parliament in person, subsequently stating his reasons in the course of a long and detailed criticism of the commons' behaviour,[51] while a little later in a proclamation he referred angrily to the " disobedient and seditious carriage of those ill-affected persons of the House of Commons," and a threat that " those vipers " amongst them " must look for their reward of punishment."

RULE WITHOUT PARLIAMENT, 1629–1640

On the dissolution of his third parliament, Charles I appears to have come to a settled determination to overthrow the old parliamentary constitution of England by governing, for the future, without the intervention of the national council. In an arrogant proclamation, referring to certain false rumours that he was about again to call a parliament, he announced " the late abuse having for the present driven us unwillingly out of that course, we shall account it presumption for any to prescribe any time unto us for parliaments, the calling, continuing, and dissolving of which is always in our own power. We shall be more inclinable to meet in parliament again when our people shall see more clearly into our intents and actions; when such as have bred this interruption shall have received their condign punishment." [52]

Imprisonment of members. Even before the actual dissolution, the king had hastened to take vengeance on the opposition " vipers." Sir John Eliot, Selden, Holles, Long, Valentine, Strode and three other members of the commons, were summoned before the council, interrogated as to their part in the scene of March 2 in the House, and committed to prison. Heath, the Attorney-General, who had the task of preparing a case against them in the Star Chamber, consulted all the judges, who reluctantly answered his inquiries. Legal difficulties still remained, and the king personally questioned all the judges some weeks later. Against Eliot, Holles and Valentine an information was finally filed in the King's Bench. The charges were that the prisoners, in the week preceding March 2, had formed a conspiracy to resist the king's lawful command that the House adjourn, to calumniate his ministers and to create discord between king and people, and further, had assaulted the Speaker. On being required to plead to the information, they demurred to the jurisdiction of the court on the ground that as their alleged offences had been committed in parliament, they were not punishable in any other place.[53] Very lengthy arguments ranging over a wide field of law and

[51] Gardiner, *Documents*, 83–99—" an able statement of the king's case against the House of Commons ": Gardiner, *History of England*, vii, 78.

[52] Rymer, xix, 62; Rushworth, ii, 3.

[53] 3 St.Tr. 294. As recently as 1621 (*Sandys' Case*) the commons had declared " that every member hath freedom from all impeachment, imprisonment or molestation (other than

political theory took place. Among other points, the prisoners referred to the Act 4 Hen. 8, c. 8, which terminated *Strode's Case* [54]; but the judges took the view that it was a private Act for the relief of Strode personally, and not a general recognition by statute of parliamentary free speech. This demurrer, which raised the great question of parliamentary privilege, was overruled; and as the defendants persisted in their refusal to plead further, judgment was given that they should be imprisoned during the king's pleasure, and not released until each had given surety for good behaviour and had made submission. In addition, Eliot, as the ring-leader, was fined £2,000, Holles 1,000 marks, and Valentine £500.[55] Other distinguished leaders of the opposition had been brought over to the king's side by the gift of office. Sir Dudley Digges was made Master of the Rolls; Noy, Attorney-General; and Littleton, Solicitor-General; Wentworth, created first a baron, then a viscount, and subsequently Earl of Strafford, was made president of the Council of the North, and afterwards lord deputy of Ireland.

Surrounded by these new counsellors, and guided chiefly by the advice of Laud and Wentworth, Charles now entered upon a career of despotism which he maintained for eleven years. This period of personal govern-ment, during which the king governed without parliament, was, constitu-tionally speaking, as much a revolutionary period as that during which, later on, parliament governed without the king. It should always be borne in mind that it was the aggression of Charles which provoked the counter-aggression of the parliament.

Financial Expedients. To raise a revenue, Charles had recourse to various exactions, many of which were clearly illegal, and nearly all odious and vexatious. " Obsolete laws," says Clarendon, " were revived and rigorously executed," and " projects of all kinds, many ridiculous,

by censure of the House itself) for or concerning any speaking, reasoning or declaring of any matter or matters touching the parliament or parliamentary business ": Prothero, *Documents*, 314. *Supra*, p. 358.

[54] *Supra*, pp. 248–249.

[55] Eliot died in prison some years afterwards (November 27, 1632); Holles gave security for good behaviour and was shortly afterwards released; Valentine remained in prison till the meeting of the Short Parliament in 1640. In 1641, the House of Commons declared all these proceedings in the King's Bench to be against the law and privilege of parliament; and in 1667, after the Restoration, they passed another resolution: " That the Act of Parliament in fourth Henry VIII commonly entitled ' an Act concerning Richard Strode ' is a general law, extending to indemnify all and every the members of both Houses of Parliament, in all Parliaments, for and touching any bills, speaking, reasoning, or declaring of any matter or matters in and concerning the Parliament to be communed and treated of; and is declaratory law of the ancient and necessary rights and privileges of Parliament." They subsequently resolved " that the judgment given, 5 Car. [1], against Sir John Eliot, Denzil Holles, and Benjamin Valentine, in the King's Bench, was an illegal judgment, and against the freedom and privilege of Parliament." On a conference, both these resolutions were agreed to by the lords; and finally, on a writ of error, the judgment of the court of King's Bench was reversed by the House of Lords, on April 15, 1668. (*Lords' Journal*, xii, 223; May, *Parliamentary Practice* (ed. 1924), 107). The privilege was confirmed, for the last time, by the Bill of Rights, the ninth article of which declared, " That the freedom of speech, and debates or proceedings in Parliament, ought not to be impeached or questioned in any court or place out of Parliament" (*supra*, p. 248; *infra*, p. 451 (sec. 9).

many scandalous, all very grievous, were set on foot." Tonnage and poundage and other duties were rigorously enforced by the royal authority alone. Monopolies, abolished by Act of Parliament in the last reign, were re-established and applied to almost every article of ordinary consumption, under cover of the remarkably ill-drawn section of the Act, which seemed to permit them in favour of corporations.[56] The ancient prerogative of compelling tenants in chivalry to receive the order of knighthood or pay a fine was revived, and extended to all men of full age seised of lands or rents (by whatever tenure) of the annual value of £40 or more. By this expedient " the king," says Clarendon, " received a vast sum of money from all persons of quality, or indeed of any reasonable condition, throughout the kingdom." [57] Commissioners were appointed to search out and compound for defects in titles to estates; and an attempt was even made to revive the ancient and odious forest laws. Under cover of the rule of law that no length of prescription could be pleaded in bar of the king's title, the boundaries of the royal forests were so extended that the forest of Rockingham alone was increased from six to sixty miles in circuit at the expense of the neighbouring landowners, who, at the same time, were mulcted in enormous fines for alleged encroachments, some of which were from three to four hundred years' standing,[58] " which burden," says Clarendon, " lighted most upon people of quality and honour, who thought themselves above ordinary oppression, and therefore like to remember it with more sharpness." [59]

Royal proclamations. In lieu of Acts of Parliament, royal proclamations, more numerous and oppressive than those which had excited so much opposition under James I, were issued from time to time and declared to have the force of laws. The common law judges, with a few honourable exceptions, upheld by their decisions the acts of the king; whilst the courts of Star Chamber and High Commission, by extending their authority and exercising a vigilant and severe coercive jurisdiction whenever the slightest opposition was manifested against the civil tyranny of the king or the ecclesiastical tyranny of Laud, maintained for some years what may not unfairly be designated as a reign of terror.

Punishments by the Star Chamber. Of the barbarous and tyrannical punishments inflicted by the court of Star Chamber it will be sufficient to refer to a few only of the more celebrated instances. (1) John Williams, Bishop of Lincoln, who, as a favourer of the Puritans, had excited the enmity of Laud, had received certain letters from Dr. Osbaldiston, the

---

[56] 21 & 22 Jac. 1, c. 3, s. 9; Tanner, *James I*, 271–272.

[57] *History of the Rebellion* (ed. Macray) i, 84, 85. *Supra*, pp. 97–98.

[58] On this ground Lord Salisbury was fined £20,000; Lord Westmorland, £19,000; Sir Christopher Hatton, £12,000; Sir Lewis Watson, £4,000; and many other persons in smaller amounts—Strafford's *Letters*, ii, 117. Cobbett's *Parliamentary History*, ii, 642. In fact, these fines were never paid, and the exchequer actually received only £23,000 from all the forests in England: Gardiner, *History of England*, viii, 282.

[59] Clarendon, *History*, i, 85.

master of Westminster School, wherein some contemptuous nickname was applied to the archbishop. For concealing (not publishing) this libellous letter, Williams was condemned, in 1637, to pay £5,000 to the king, and £3,000 to Laud, and to be imprisoned during pleasure. A few days afterwards he was suspended from his office by the High Commission Court. Osbaldiston was adjudged to pay a still heavier fine, to be deprived of his benefices, and to be imprisoned until he should make submission. In addition he was to stand in the pillory with his ears nailed to it, in front of his school in Dean's Yard.[60] (2) Alexander Leighton, a Scottish divine (whose son afterwards became Archbishop of Glasgow), was sentenced in 1630, for writing an able but scurrilous book entitled *An Appeal to Parliament, or Sion's Plea Against Prelacy*, to pay a fine of £10,000, to be degraded from his orders, to be whipped at Westminster and set in the pillory, to have one ear cut off, one side of his nose slit, and one cheek branded with S.S. (for " sower of sedition "), to have the whole of this repeated the next week at Cheapside, and to suffer imprisonment for life.[61] (3) In 1638, for refusing to swear to interrogatories while under a charge of distributing pamphlets against the bishops, John Lilburne, a London apprentice (who afterwards fought with great bravery in the parliamentary army, and attained the rank of lieutenant-colonel), was severely whipped from the Fleet to Westminster, set in the pillory, and kept in prison until released three years afterwards by the Long Parliament.[62] (4) But the case which excited the greatest popular indignation was that of Prynne, Burton, and Bastwick, who were together brought before the Star Chamber in 1637.

Cases of Prynne and others. *William Prynne*, a barrister of Lincoln's Inn, of great learning, but a bigoted Puritan, had already suffered, in 1633, for publishing a ponderous tome of 1,000 pages entitled *Histriomastix*, condemning stage-plays, may-games, and similar diversions. Unfortunately for Prynne, the queen, about ten weeks after the printing of this book had been completed, took part in a masque at court. A

[60] Rushworth, ii, 803–817. Osbaldiston managed to keep out of the way, but the bishop was imprisoned until released with other political prisoners, in 1640. There were other more serious charges against Williams: Gardiner, *History of England*, viii, 251–5.

[61] *State Trials*, iii, 383. *Sion's Plea* had been elaborated by Leighton out of a petition drawn up by him after the prorogation in 1628, for presentation to parliament at its next meeting, and to which he obtained five hundred signatures, including those of several members of the House of Commons. It assailed the bishops in unmeasured terms. They had promised the late king " absolute liberty to do what he list," if he would only support their authority. This was not so very far from the truth. But Leighton weakened his case against them as supporters of a regal autocracy by laying to their charge almost every evil which existed in the world; denouncing them as " men of blood," persecuting the saints, " knobs and wens of bunchy popish flesh," the " trumpery of Antichrist." The *Plea* was something more, however, than a mere attack upon the truth. It was an appeal to political presbyterianism, more especially as represented in parliament, to remove the evil counsellors of the king, and to resist a dissolution; " the invitation to Parliament to constitute itself into a permanent body was naturally regarded by the government as an invitation to revolution "—Gardiner, *History of England*, vii, 144.

[62] Gardiner, *History of England*, viii, 248–250.

passage reflecting in the strongest terms on female actors was now, unfairly as he contended, alleged to be an intentional insult to her Majesty [63]; and Prynne was condemned to stand twice in the pillory, to lose both ears, to pay a fine of £5,000, to be degraded from the bar and at his university (Oxford), and to be imprisoned until he should make entire submission. While in prison he managed to elude the prohibition of pen, ink, and paper, and published some fresh works in defence of his principles, one, a pamphlet entitled " News from Ipswich," containing charges of Romish innovations against Wren, Bishop of Norwich, which caused him to be now again brought before the Star Chamber. The offence of *Henry Burton*, a London rector, was the publication of two sermons, under the title " For God and the King," in which he implied that the innovations were the work of the bishops, and that their office should be abolished.

John Bastwick, a physician of Colchester, and formerly of Emmanuel College, Cambridge, was already, like Prynne, undergoing punishment for a former offence. Some years previously he had published a Latin work, called " Elenchus Papismi et Flagellum Episcoporum," in answer to a book written by one Short, a papist, in support of his religion. For this he was sentenced by the High Commission Court to a fine of £1,000, to be debarred his practice of physic, to be excommunicated, and imprisoned until he should make recantation. While in gaol he published a defence of himself and an acrimonious attack upon the church (" as full of ceremonies as a dog is full of fleas "), together with a Litany (" From bishops, priests and deacons, *Good Lord, deliver us* "); and for this publication he was summoned, at the same time as Prynne and Burton, before the Star Chamber. It was at first intended to proceed against the three for high treason, but the judges, on being consulted, had the courage to declare that their libels against the bishops did not amount to treason. The accused were all fined £5,000 each, condemned to the pillory, to lose their ears, to be branded on both cheeks, and to be imprisoned for life, without access to kindred or friends, and without books or writing materials. The sentence was executed in the most savage manner; the stumps of Prynne's ears, which had been mercifully spared by the hangman on the former occasion, being now pared off so closely as to endanger his life. So great was the sympathy expressed for them in London, and even in some country districts, that the council deemed it prudent to send Prynne to Jersey, Burton to Guernsey, and Bastwick to Scilly, where they remained in close confinement until released by order of the Long Parliament.[64]

[63] Prynne denied any reference to the queen, and argued that she could not have been aimed at in a publication the last proof-sheets of which had been corrected ten weeks before she acted in the court masque. But it appears by the newsletters of Salvetti, the Florentine agent, that the intention of the queen to act was known about the time Prynne was completing his proof, and the offending passage appears on the last page of the book then under revision. See Gardiner, *History of England*, vii, 329.

[64] Gardiner, *History of England*, viii, 226; Brodie, *History of the British Empire*, ii, 342. Several other instances of the merciless punishments inflicted by the Star Chamber are

Case of Ship-money. Shortly before these proceedings against Prynne, a decision had been pronounced by the Exchequer Chamber, in the famous case of ship-money. The idea of ship-money originated in the " venal diligence and prostituted learning " of Sir William Noy, the Attorney-General.[65] Alternatively, the commons' appeal to the medieval view of parliament tempted the king to appeal to the medieval view of the prerogative. The strictest technical legality was now the government's policy, under the guidance of Wentworth. Among the records in the Tower were found ancient writs compelling the seaports and even maritime counties to provide ships for the use of the king[66]; and upon these precedents Noy devised a plan by which a large fleet might be procured without any additional charge upon the revenue. In October, 1634, writs were issued to the magistrates of London and other ports ordering them to provide a certain number of ships of war of a specified tonnage and equippage, to be ready at Portsmouth on March 1, and empowering them to assess all the inhabitants, according to their substance, for the sum requisite for the fitting out and maintenance of the ships and their crews for the period of six months.[67]

Notwithstanding the remonstrances of London, and some other towns, obedience to these " new writs of an old edition " was enforced by the imprisonment of such persons as refused to pay their share of the assessment, and the experiment proved a great temporary success. " In this way," wrote the Venetian ambassador to his government, " did this most important affair begin and end. If it does not altogether violate the laws of the realm, as some think it does, it is certainly repugnant to usage and to the forms hitherto observed." [68] In effect, the levying of ship-money was regarded as the imposition of a " tax "; for the ships specified in the writs were of such a size as to render it impossible for any port in the kingdom (except London) to furnish them in kind as formerly, and the demand resolved itself into a demand for so much money. It was, therefore, in its essence, a distinct violation of the Petition of Right, notwithstanding the show of precedent in its favour. We now know that the fleet was being prepared in furtherance of a secret treaty which Charles had been negotiating, the ultimate object of which was the overthrow of the Dutch Republic and the division of its soil between Spain and England.[69] But there was also a real foundation for the pretext for arming with which the king endeavoured to hoodwink the nation, and

enumerated in the 4th chapter of Brodie's 2nd vol. It must be remembered that neither side had a monopoly of cruelty or illegality in that age of fierce political passions; *cf.* the sentences of the Commons and Lords in *Floyd's Case, supra,* pp. 355.

[65] Hallam, ii, 12.

[66] Ship-money had in fact been levied as recently as 1626—but at that moment the country was at war with Spain: Gardiner, *History of England,* vii, 356–357. Material on the history of the crown's right is collected by D. L. Keir, " The Case of Ship-Money," *Law Quarterly Review,* lii, 546 *et seq*; for the Anglo-Saxon ship-scot, see F. E. Harmer, *Anglo-Saxon Writs,* 269–270, and her notes at 266–268, 483.

[67] Rushworth, ii, 257; Gardiner, *Documents,* 105.

[68] Cited Gardiner, *History of England,* vii, 376.

[69] Clarendon, *State Papers,* i, 109, 112, 125; Gardiner, *History of England,* vii, 367–369.

even his own council, in the evident necessity at the time for a powerful fleet to repress as well the depredations of the Algerian pirates, who had become bold enough to infest the coasts both of England and Ireland, as the boldness of the Dutch, who had taken advantage of the naval weakness of England to dispute the ancient claim of the English crown to the dominion of the narrow seas.[70]

Noy died soon after suggesting the expedient of ship-money, but the Lord Keeper, Coventry, improved upon the original scheme by advising an extension of the writs from the seaports to the whole kingdom. Clarendon admits that this tax was intended not merely for the support of the navy, but " for a spring and magazine that should have no bottom, and for an everlasting supply of all occasions." [71] Writs were accordingly sent to the sheriff of every county in England and Wales ordering him to provide a ship of war of a prescribed tonnage, armed and equipped for the king's service; but as it was never intended that an actual ship should be provided, instructions were sent with each writ commanding the sheriff, instead of a ship, to levy upon his county a specified sum of money, and return the same to the treasurer of the navy for his Majesty's use, with directions to enforce payment by compulsory process. The collection of the money met with a good deal of resistance in the country. The chief constables of the hundred of Bloxham, Oxfordshire, replied to the warrant from the sheriff of the county directing the assessment, that they had " no authority to assess or tax any man," and that they did not conceive the warrant gave them any power to do so. Ultimately, the sheriff was obliged to make the assessment himself. Similar difficulties occurred also in Essex and Devonshire. In some places the incumbents, churchwardens and overseers utterly refused to produce their books. When cattle were distrained in default of payment no purchasers could be found, and the council found it necessary to direct them to be sent to London for sale by the king's officers.[72]

Richard Chambers, a London merchant, who had already suffered for his resistance to the imposition of tonnage and poundage, brought an action in the King's Bench against the Lord Mayor for imprisoning him on refusal to pay the assessment. The defendant pleaded the king's writ as a special justification, and the judges refused even to allow the question of right to be argued, Berkeley, one of their number, declaring that " there was a rule of law and a rule of government, and that many things which might not be done by the rule of law might be done by the rule of government." [73]

---

[70] It was to uphold these claims of the Dutch that Grotius wrote his celebrated *Mare Libeum* (1609), and his views were repeated in his more famous work on international law, *De Jure belli et pacis* (1625). These contentions were answered by Selden in the *Mare Clausum* (1635), proving that sovereignty over the narrow seas had been exercised by England from the earliest times. The controversy was ended by Bynkershoek, in his defence of the complete freedom of the seas, *De dominio maris* (1702), who, however, acknowledged, on the other hand, that the sovereignty of maritime states extended only to the so-called coast waters, the range of cannon-shot—*quousque tormenta exploduntur*; *terrae dominium finitur, ubi finitur armorum vis.*   [71] *History*, i, 85.

[72] Gardiner, *History of England*, viii, 93, 94, 102, 103.   [73] Rushworth, ii, 323.

The issuing of a third writ of ship-money, affecting, like its immediate predecessor, the whole of England, made it but too clear that ship-money was no longer a device to meet a sudden emergency in the national defence, and that it was the king's intention to retain this innovation as a permanent tax, to be levied at his pleasure, without the consent of the nation. The opposition to the writs, hitherto restricted to particular localities, now assumed a general aspect, and was taken up by men of the highest rank and of undoubted loyalty. The Earl of Danby (Henry Danvers), an old servant of the crown, wrote to the king, warning him of the universal discontent of his subjects. The new levies of money, he said, were repugnant to " the fundamental laws of England," [74] and to the privileges which their ancestors and they themselves had till the present time enjoyed. It was of the manner in which the money was raised, not of the amount, that they complained. The only way for the king to give satisfaction to his subjects was by summoning parliament.[75] The Earl of Warwick (Robert Rich) addressed him in much plainer language, and several peers drew up a protestation to the king, which, however, does not appear to have been actually presented.[76] But Charles had no intention either of calling a parliament or of desisting from the exaction of the obnoxious tax, which produced an annual revenue of over £200,000. The people murmured, but were obliged to yield to the overbearing power of the crown. Several attempts were made to raise the question of the legality of the levy in the courts of law, but the crown always found means to elude the discussion.

The government did not overlook the legal problem, however, and submitted to the judges the following questions : (1) " When the good and safety of the kingdom in general is concerned and the whole kingdom in danger; whether may not the king, by writ under the Great Seal of England, command all the subjects of our kingdom, at their charge, to provide and furnish such a number of ships, with men, victuals, and munition, and for such time as we shall think fit, for the defence and safe-guard of the kingdom from such danger and peril; and by law compel the doing thereof in case of refusal or refractoriness? (2) And whether, in such a case, is not the king the sole judge, both of the danger, and when and how the same is to be prevented and avoided ? " The judges (with the exception of Croke and Hutton, who, however, subscribed their names on the principle that the judgment of the majority was that of the whole body) answered both questions in favour of the prerogative, and this extra-judicial opinion was by the king's order publicly read in the

---

[74] This phrase came into popular use in 1635, and according to the conjecture of Gardiner, *History of England*, viii, 84–85, originated in the queen's household. James I had in fact used the phrase (McIlwain, *High Court of Parliament*, 79) as early as 1598. It was a technical term in French constitutional law in the sixteenth century, and it seems quite likely that we got it from France.

[75] Gardiner, *History of England*, viii, 201.

[76] *Ibid.*, 203.

Star Chamber, and enrolled in all the courts at Westminster, February 7, 1637.[77]

Charles's covering letter which accompanied the questions to the judges made the interesting suggestion that the publication of the judges' opinion would give immediate and authoritative guidance to the public, who would be spared the cost and delay of testing the validity of ship-money by means of private litigation. Such a view is certainly plausible under the régime of administrative and conciliar government which Charles had established; but there were others who clung to their common-law right of testing government action in court whenever they saw fit, and of themselves producing arguments which the law officers would be compelled to meet in public debate.

Hampden's Case. The contest could not be long avoided, and, in 1637, John Hampden, a gentleman of ancient family and good estate in Buckinghamshire, succeeded in obtaining a judicial decision upon the point of law. Having refused to pay the sum of 20s. assessed upon a portion of his estate,[78] proceedings were instituted against him in the Exchequer, to which he appeared and demurred to the writ as insufficient in law. Till this time " he was rather of reputation in his own country," says Clarendon, " than of public discourse or fame in the kingdom: but then he grew the argument of all tongues, every man inquiring who and what he was that durst, at his own charge, support the liberty and property of the kingdom." [79] The king awaited the decision of the judges with confidence.

During the twelve days the great case was argued in the Exchequer Chamber, by the celebrated Oliver St. John and Robert Holborne as counsel for Hampden, by the Attorney-General Bankes and the Solicitor-General Littleton on behalf of the crown. On the part of Hampden it was maintained:

[77] Rushworth, ii, 355; Gardiner, *Documents*, 108; *History of England*, viii, 206–209. On this opinion Strafford wrote: " The opinion delivered by the judges, declaring the lawfulness of the assignment for the shipping, is the greatest service that profession hath done the Crown in my time. But unless his Majesty hath the like power declared to raise a land army upon the same exigent of state, the Crown seems to me to stand but upon one leg at home, to be considerable but by halves to foreign princes abroad. Yet sure this methinks, convinces a power for the sovereign to raise payments for land forces, and consequently submits to his wisdom and ordinance the transporting of the money or men into foreign states, so to carry by way of prevention the fire from ourselves into the dwellings of our enemies . . . and if by degrees Scotland and Ireland be drawn to contribute their proportions to these levies for the public, *omne tulit punctum* "—*Letters and Despatches of the Earl of Strafford* (ed. Knowler, 1739), ii, 61. The judges had previously given similar answers to like questions in November 1635: Gardiner, *History of England*, viii, 94.

[78] The sum of 20s. was assessed on lands in Great Missenden, and another sum of 31s. 6d. on his lands in Great Kimble.

[79] *History*, iii, p. 62. Hampden, who was a cousin of Oliver Cromwell, had sat in Charles's first three parliaments. For refusing to contribute to the general loan in 1626, on the ground that " he feared to draw upon himself that curse in Magna Carta which should be read twice a year against those that do infringe it," he was committed to prison, but regained his freedom in time to be re-elected to the parliament of 1628. In the Long Parliament he sat for Buckinghamshire, and on the breaking out of the Civil War, took a colonel's commission in the parliamentary army. He died June 24, 1643, of wounds received in the skirmish at Chalgrove, near Oxford, six days previously.

(1) That the law and constitution of England had provided certain known and undoubted means for the defence of the realm whether by sea or land. (a) The military tenures of land bound a large part of the kingdom to a stipulated service at the charge of the holders. The Cinque Ports also, and some other towns held by an analogous tenure, were bound to furnish a quota of ships or men in return for the special privileges which they enjoyed. (b) In addition to these services in kind for defence by land and sea, things coming to the king by prerogative, as the profits arising from the feudal tenures, and various other emoluments received in right of the crown, were applicable so far as they could extend to the public use. (c) The king, moreover, had been specially provided with particular supplies of money for defence of the sea in time of danger, as the customs on wool and leather, tonnage and poundage. With regard to the legality of the modern impositions, far in excess of the ancient use, St. John said he did not intend to speak: " for in case his Majesty may impose upon merchandise what himself pleaseth, there will be less cause to tax the inland counties; and in case he cannot so do, it will be strongly presumed that he can much less tax them."

(2) When these ordinary revenues proved insufficient, the constitution had provided other sufficient and lawful means—*viz.*, aids and subsidies granted in parliament. To these the kings of England had at all times habitually had recourse. The fact that our kings also obtained supplies of money by loans on promise of repayment, or by benevolences which were in the nature of alms from their subjects, afforded additional proof that they possessed no prerogative of general taxation. It is rare in a subject, and more so in a prince, to ask and take that as a gift which he may and ought to have of right.

(3) But the most conclusive and irrefutable argument was founded on the long series of statutes, concluding with the recently granted Petition of Right, by which, in most emphatic language, it was provided that no tax should be levied on the subject without the consent of parliament.

(4) As to the precedents alleged on the crown side, it was answered that most or all of them applied to sea-towns and havens; and that it appeared that the inland counties had not so much as *de facto* been usually charged for ships. But even if precedents could be adduced, they could not be upheld in the teeth of so many statutes. The question was not what had been done *de facto*, for many things had been done which were never allowed, but what had been done, and might be done *de jure*. " Judicandum est legibus non exemplis." [80]

(5) Lastly, admitting that in a case of overruling necessity as of actual invasion, or its immediate prospect, not only the sovereign, but each man in respect of his neighbour, might do many things absolutely illegal at other seasons, yet in the present case there was no overwhelming danger; the nation was at peace with all the world; and it would be absurd to

---

[80] This maxim occurs both in Bracton and in the *Code*, vii, 45, 13.

reckon the piracies of a few Turkish corsairs among those instant perils for which a parliament would provide too late.

Judgment for the crown. The twelve judges took some time for deliberation, and delivered their judgments during the three next terms, four in each term. Seven pronounced in favour of the crown, and five in favour of Hampden; so that the majority against him was the least possible. Of the five who decided for Hampden, however, three based their judgments upon merely technical grounds peculiar to his particular case without dealing with the general question; but the other two, Croke and Hutton, boldly denied the right claimed by the crown, without the smallest qualification. The elaborate and learned judgment of Sir George Croke was grounded upon the following reasons: First, that the command by the king's writ to have ships at the charge of the inhabitants of the county was illegal and contrary to the common law, not being by authority of parliament. Secondly, that if at the common law it had been lawful, yet this writ was illegal, being expressly contrary to divers statutes prohibiting a general charge to be laid upon the commons without their consent in parliament. Thirdly, that it was not to be maintained by any prerogative, nor allegation of necessity or danger. Fourthly, admitting it were legal to lay such a charge upon maritime ports, yet to charge any inland county, as the county of Bucks, for making ships, and furnishing them with mariners, etc., was illegal and not warranted by any precedent. On the other hand, those who argued for the crown insisted that there was no question of taxation, but only of the fulfilment of a service due to the crown, and that if the writs demanded money, that was merely a convenient way of distributing the burden; several of the judges who pronounced for the crown, finding it almost impossible to elude the force of the numerous prohibitory statutes, rested their decision upon the intrinsic absolute authority of the king, and the inability of parliament to limit the high prerogative of the crown. As so often during the Stuart period, law abdicated in favour of the current political science. Thus Mr. Justice Crawley said: " This imposition without parliament appertains to the king originally, and to the successor *ipso facto*, if he be a sovereign in right of his sovereignty from the crown. You cannot have a king without these royal rights." Others fastened on the popular phrase " fundamental law " and neatly turned it against its authors by maintaining that the prerogative was " fundamental." " Where Mr. Holborne," said Mr. Justice Berkeley, " supposed a fundamental policy in the creation of the frame of this kingdom, that, in case the monarch of England should be inclined to exact from his subjects at his pleasure, he should be restrained, for that he could have nothing from them, but upon a common consent in parliament; he is utterly mistaken therein. . . . The law knows no such king-yoking policy. The law is of itself an old and trusty servant of the king's; it is his instrument or means which he useth to govern his people by: I never read nor heard that *lex* was *rex*; but it is

common and most true that *rex* is *lex*." " The king, *pro bono publico*,"
said Vernon, another judge, " may charge his subjects, for the safety and
defence of the kingdom, notwithstanding any act of parliament, and a
statute derogatory from the prerogative doth not bind the king; and the
king may dispense with any law in cases of necessity." Sir John Finch,
Chief Justice of the Common Pleas, followed in the same strain: " No
act of parliament," he said, " can bar a king of his regality, as that no
lands should hold of him, or bar him of the allegiance of his subjects
or the relative on his part, as trust and power to defend his people:
therefore acts of parliament to take away his royal power in the defence
of his kingdom are void; they are void acts of parliament to bind the
king not to command the subjects, their persons, and goods, and I say
their money too; for no acts of parliament make any difference." [81]

Effect of this judgment. Charles had little cause for rejoicing at the
legal decision in his favour. Its only effect was to make Hampden the
most popular man in England, and to strengthen and widely extend the
public indignation. " It is notoriously known," says Lord Clarendon,
" that pressure [ship-money] was borne with much more cheerfulness
before the judgment for the king than ever it was after; men before
pleasing themselves with doing somewhat for the king's service, as a
testimony of their affection, which they were not bound to do, many
really believing the necessity, and therefore thinking the burden reasonable; others observing that the access to the king was of importance,
when the damage to them was not considerable, and all assuring themselves
that when they should be weary or unwilling to continue the payment,
they might resort to the law for relief, and find it. But when they heard
this demanded in a court of law as a right, and found it, by sworn judges
of the law, adjudged so, upon such grounds and reasons as every stander-
by was able to swear was not law, and so had lost the pleasure and delight
of being kind and dutiful to the king, and instead of giving were required
to pay, and by a logic that left no man anything which he might call his
own; they no more looked upon it as the case of one man, but the case
of the kingdom, nor as an imposition laid upon them by the king, but
by the judges, which they thought themselves bound in conscience to
the public justice not to submit to. It was an observation long ago by
Thucydides, that ' men are more passionate for injustice than for violence,
because,' says he, ' the one coming as from an equal seems rapine, when
the other, proceeding from one stronger, is but the effect of necessity.'
So, when ship-money was transacted at the Council Board, they looked
upon it as a work of that power they were all obliged to trust, and an
effect of that foresight they were naturally to rely upon. Imminent

---

[81] 3 St.Tr., 825; Broom, *Constitutional Law* (ed. Denman), pp. 303–367; Hallam, *Constitutional History*, ii, 21, 22; Holdsworth, *History of English Law*, vi, 49 *et seq.*; selections
from the speeches of Oliver St. John and of Sir Robert Berkeley are given in Gardiner,
Documents, 109 *et seq.* A thorough examination of the legal arguments is given by
D. L. Keir, " The Case of Ship-Money," *Law Quarterly Review*, lii, 546–574.

necessity and public safety were convincing persuasions; and it might not seem of apparent ill-consequence to them, that upon an emergent occasion the regal power should fill up an hiatus, or supply an impotency in the law. But when they saw in a court of law (that law that gave them title and possession of all that they had) apophthegms of state urged as elements of law; judges as sharp-sighted as secretaries of state, and in the mysteries of state; judgment of law grounded upon matter of fact, of which there was neither inquiry nor proof, and no reason given for the payment of the thirty shillings in question, but what concluded the estates of all the standers-by; they had no reason to hope that that doctrine, or the preachers of it, would be contained within any bounds, and it was no wonder that they, who had so little reason to be pleased with their own condition, were not less solicitous for, or apprehensive of, the inconveniences that might attend any alteration.

" And here the damage and mischief cannot be expressed that the crown and state sustained, by the deserved reproach and infamy that attended the judges, by being made use of in this and the like acts of power; there being no possibility to preserve the dignity, reverence, and estimation of the laws themselves but by the integrity and innocency of the judges. And no question, as the exorbitancy of the House of Commons, this parliament, hath proceeded principally from their contempt of the laws, and that contempt from the scandal of that judgment; so the concurrence of the House of Peers in that fury, can be imputed to no one thing more than to the irreverence and scorn the judges were justly in, who had been always before looked upon there as the oracles of the law, and the best guides and directors of their opinions and actions. And they now thought themselves excused for swerving from the rules and customs of their predecessors (who, in altering and making of laws, in judging of things and persons, had always observed the advice and judgment of those sages), in not asking questions of those whom they knew nobody would believe: and thinking it a just reproach upon them (who, out of their gentilesses, had submitted the difficulties and mysteries of the law to be measured by the standard of general reason, and explained by the wisdom of state) to see those men make use of the licence they had taught, and determine that to be law which they thought reasonable, or found to be convenient. If these men had preserved the simplicity of their ancestors in severely and strictly defending the laws, other men had observed the modesty of theirs in humbly and dutifully obeying them." [82]

The Scottish rebellion. It was not long after the condemnation of Hampden that Charles entered upon his rash and unwise attempt to change the ecclesiastical position in Scotland, and to force upon the people of that kingdom a liturgy which the great body of them regarded with fanatical abhorrence. The Scots, having drawn up and signed their

[82] *History of the Rebellion,* i, 86.

celebrated Covenant (February 27, 1638),[83] at length took up arms in defence of their religious freedom. By the ignominious pacification of Berwick (June 18, 1639), the contest was only adjourned, and both sides almost immediately began to prepare for a renewal of the war. In this emergency, the real impotence of the king's arbitrary system of government became apparent. The illegal methods of supply so long practised proved utterly inadequate for the support of an army, and the king, after eleven years of despotic rule, most reluctantly yielded to the advice of his council, and issued writs for a parliament, which met on April 13, 1640.

Fourth (the Short) Parliament, 1640. It is remarkable that the House of Commons which met after so long a period of arbitrary misgovernment was admitted on all sides to be one of the most moderate and loyal assemblies which had been known for many years. " The House generally," says Clarendon, " was exceedingly disposed to please the king and do him service. It could never be hoped," he remarks elsewhere, " that more sober and dispassioned men would ever meet together in that place or fewer who brought ill purposes with them." [84]   Charles pressed for an ample and immediate supply, and pledged his word that if the commons would gratify him with the despatch of this matter, he would give them time enough afterwards to represent any grievances to him.

Redress before supply. But the commons, led by Pym and Hampden, and mindful how shamefully the royal word had been already violated, showed a thorough determination to have their accumulated grievances redressed before voting supplies. They declared that the conduct of the Speaker on the last day of the former parliament, in refusing, at the alleged command of the king, to put the question; and the prosecution and imprisonment of Eliot, Holles and Valentine, for their behaviour in parliament, were breaches of privilege. The proceedings against Hampden in the case of ship-money were inquired into by a committee and reported matter of grievance; and the various other illegal proceedings during the long discontinuance of parliament were discussed in detail. " Let us not stand too nicely upon circumstances," said Edmund Waller; " let us do what possibly may be done with reason and honesty on our part to comply with his Majesty's desires. Let us give new force to the old laws for the maintaining of our rights and privileges, and endeavour to restore this nation to the fundamental and vital liberties—to propriety of our goods, and the freedom of our persons. . . . The kings of this nation have always governed by parliament; . . . but his Majesty shall now hear the truth from us and we shall make appear the errors of divines who would persuade us that a monarch must be absolute, and that he

---

[83] Gardiner, *Documents*, 124. It was an amplification of previous covenants dating from 1581.
[84] *History*, i, 183.

may do all things *ad libitum*. . . . Since they are so ready to let loose the conscience of their kings, we are the more carefully to provide for our protection against this pulpit-law—by declaring and re-enforcing the municipal laws of this kingdom." [85]

Committee to confer with the lords. With this object, a committee was appointed to confer with the peers on a long list of grievances divided, by the advice of Pym, into the three heads of innovations in religion, invasions of private property, and breaches of the privileges of parliament. Impatient at the delay, Charles had recourse to the interposition of the lords. They voted that in their opinion " the supply should have precedency, and be resolved upon before any other matter whatsoever," and in a conference communicated this resolution to the commons. The latter at once voted this a high breach of their privileges, which the lords answered by a disclaimer of any intention to interfere with the undoubted right of the commons, admitting that " the bill of subsidies ought to have its inception in your House; and that when it comes up to their lordships, and is by them agreed to, it must be returned back to you, and be, by your Speaker, presented." [86]

In the meantime the king sent a message to the commons offering, if they would grant him twelve subsidies (about £850,000), payable in three years, to give up the prerogative of ship-money. But the commons were by no means inclined to purchase that which they justly claimed as their right. " Many observed ' that they were to purchase a release of an imposition very unjustly laid upon the kingdom, and by purchasing it, they should upon the matter confess it had been just; which no man in his heart acknowledged '; and therefore wished that the judgment might be first examined, and being once declared void, what they should present the king with would appear a gift and not a recompense." [87] The message was, however, taken into favourable consideration, and the commons were on the point of deciding that a supply should be granted to the king, leaving the amount and the manner for subsequent consideration, when Sir Henry Vane, Secretary of State, told them that if the supply were not voted in the amount and manner proposed in the king's message, it would not be accepted.

Parliament dissolved. This caused an adjournment of the debate, and the next day the king angrily dissolved parliament, which had sat only three weeks. " There could not a greater damp," says Clarendon, " have seized upon the spirits of the whole nation than this dissolution caused; and men had much of the misery in view which shortly after fell out. . . . Nor could any man imagine what offence they [the commons] had given, which put the king to that resolution. But it was observed

[85] Rushworth, ii, 1140–1142.
[86] Gardiner, *History of England*, ix, 110 *Lords' Journals*, iv, 76.
[87] Clarendon, *History*, i, 178.

that in the countenance of those who had most opposed all that was desired by his Majesty, there was a marvellous serenity; nor could they conceal the joy of their hearts: for they knew enough of what was to come, to conclude that the king would be shortly compelled to call another parliament, and they were as sure that so many grave and unbiased men would never be elected again." [88]

Autocracy again. Charles now returned to his old despotic courses. Several members of the late House of Commons were committed to prison. Forced loans were exacted; fresh monopolies were created. Ship-money was enforced with even greater rigour than before, and the Lord Mayor and sheriffs of London were summoned before the Council for neglecting to raise a loan demanded by the king. A new imposition was laid upon the counties, under the name of " coat and conduct money," for clothing and defraying the travelling expenses of the recruits whom the king had pressed into his services against the Scots.

In order to obtain a grant of six subsidies from the clergy, Convocation was unconstitutionally continued after the dissolution of parliament, under a fresh commission, authorising its sittings " during pleasure," and empowering it to alter and amend the laws of the church. It accordingly framed and promulgated a set of canons which greatly irritated both the political and religious feelings of a great part of the nation. In addition to inculcating the divine right of kings, and denouncing the damnable sin of resistance to authority, a new oath declaring approval of the established doctrine and government was appointed to be taken by all clergymen, and all graduates in the universities, and schoolmasters. [89]

In his military operations against the Scots, Charles failed utterly and ignominiously. After the defeat at the ford of Newburn-on-Tyne, the English army, disheartened, undisciplined, and disaffected, had retreated to York, leaving the counties of Northumberland and Durham to be possessed by the victors. " The game of tyranny," observes Macaulay, " was now up. Charles had risked and lost his last stake. . . . His army was mutinous, his treasury was empty; his people clamoured for a parliament; addresses and petitions against the government were presented. Strafford was for shooting the petitioners by martial law; but the king could not trust the soldiers."

A great council of peers. " A great council of peers was called at York, but the king could not trust even the peers. He struggled, evaded, hesitated, tried every shift, rather than again face the representatives of his injured people. At length no shift was left. He made a truce with the Scots and summoned a parliament." [90]

---

[88] Clarendon, *History*, i, 183.
[89] Rushworth, ii, 1186; Gardiner, *History of England*, ix, 146. The formula came to be known as the " et cetera oath " since the unskilful draftsman had used that lame compendium in enumerating the hierarchy which the subject swore to maintain. What he meant by et cetera has not been ascertained.   [90] Macaulay, " Essay on Hampden."

Chapter 14

FROM THE LONG PARLIAMENT TO THE RESTORATION

The Long Parliament

On November 3, 1640, met that renowned parliament " destined to every extreme of fortune, to empire and to servitude, to glory and to contempt; at one time the sovereign of its sovereign, at another time the servant of its servants "; but which, " in spite of many errors and disasters, is justly entitled to the reverence and gratitude of all who, in any part of the world, enjoy the blessings of constitutional government." [1] The elections had proceeded with the utmost excitement throughout England. The court candidates were rejected on all sides. The exertions of the leaders of the popular party—of Hampden in particular, who rode from shire to shire exhorting the electors to return worthy members—secured an overwhelming majority on the side of the opposition. "There was observed," says Clarendon, " a marvellous elated countenance in most of the members before they met together in the House; the same men who six months before were observed to be of very moderate tempers, and to wish that gentle remedies might be applied without opening the wound too wide and exposing it to the air, and rather to cure what was amiss than too strictly to make inquisition into the causes and origin of the malady, talked now in another dialect both of things and persons, . . . and said that they must now be of another temper than they were the last parliament; . . . that they had now an opportunity to make their country happy by removing all grievances and pulling up the causes of them by the roots, if all men would do their duties." [2]

The first day on which the House met for business, Pym delivered a long and eloquent speech on the miserable state and condition of the kingdom, denouncing the many arbitrary proceedings of the government as " done and contrived maliciously, and upon deliberation, to change the whole frame, and to deprive the nation of all the liberty and property which was their birthright by the laws of the land, which were now no more considered but subjected to the arbitrary power of the Privy Council, which governed the kingdom according to their will and pleasure." Of the persons who had contributed their joint endeavours to bring this misery upon the nation he named the Earl of Strafford, as "one more signal in that administration than the rest, being a man of

---

[1] Macaulay, "Hampden" (*Essays*, i, 566), and *History*, i, 87.

[2] Clarendon, *History*, i, 222; R. N. Kershaw, "The Elections for the Long Parliament, 1640," *English Historical Review*, xxxviii, 506, and "The Recruiting of the Long Parliament, 1645–1647," in *History*, viii, 169.

great parts and contrivance, and of great industry to bring what he designed to pass; a man who in the memory of many present, had sat in that House an earnest vindicator of the laws, and a most zealous asserter and champion for the liberties of the people; but that it was long since he turned apostate from those good affections, and, according to the custom and nature of apostates, was become the greatest enemy to the liberties of his country, and the greatest promoter of tyranny that any age had produced."

Impeachment of Strafford. Both sides were looking for support outside England. It had just been revealed that Strafford had at least contemplated the possibility of bringing over an army from Ireland. The parliamentarians were, on the other hand, in communication with the Scottish forces who were actually occupying the northern counties; Strafford was on the point of accusing Pym of treason [3] when parliament forestalled him. It was resolved, with " an universal approbation and consent from the whole House," to impeach Strafford of high treason. Pym immediately carried up the message to the bar of the lords, who, with very little debate, committed the earl to the custody of the Usher of the Black Rod, there to remain until the commons should bring in a particular charge against him.[4]

His attainder. That Strafford had been technically guilty of the crime of high treason was a matter of grave doubt, and his execution (May 12, 1641), under a bill of attainder, brought in after a lengthy trial had failed to secure the probability of a legal conviction, and passed, amidst popular tumults, by the small majority of seven in a House of Peers which could muster only forty-five votes, has procured for him that sympathy which violence invariably assures to its victims. But there can be no doubt that from the time when he devoted his consummate abilities to the establishment of that despotic system of government which he emphatically termed " Thorough," he became and continued a most formidable enemy to his country's freedom. However unsatisfactory in a purely legal point of view, the hesitating opinion of the judges may be taken as truly expressing at least his moral guilt, when they declared that he " deserved to undergo the pains and forfeitures of high treason by law." [5]

After a long and careful examination of the proceedings against Strafford, it was Gardiner's conclusion that " it is possible now to understand that in his own sense Strafford was speaking the truth when he declared his devotion to the parliamentary constitution, and that yet he was,

---

[3] " According to the letter of the law it was treason to bring in a foreign army against the king, whilst it was not treason to bring in a foreign army to support the king. Scotland, too, was a foreign country in a sense in which Ireland was not "—Gardiner, *History of England*, ix, 232. For a review of the scanty evidence on the affair of the Irish army, see *ibid.*, 318–321.

[4] Clarendon, *History*, i, 222 *et seq.*, 225 *et seq.*

[5] The text of the Act of Attainder is in Gardiner, *Documents*, 156. See *infra*, p. 530.

in the truest sense, the most dangerous enemy of parliaments. He attempted to maintain the Elizabethan constitution, long after it was possible to maintain it, and when the only choice lay between absolute government and parliamentary supremacy. In contending against the latter, he was, without knowing what he was doing, giving his whole strength to the establishment of the former. Yet, ruinous as his success would have been, in his devotion to the rule of intelligence he stands strangely near to one side of the modern spirit. Alone amongst his generation his voice was always raised for practical reforms. Pym and Hampden looked upon existing society as something admirable in itself, though needing to be quickened by a higher moral spirit, and to be relieved from the hindrances thrown in its way by a defective organisation. Strafford regarded that society as full of abuses, and sought in the organisation which was ready to his hand the lever by which those abuses might be removed. In happier times Pym and Strafford need never have clashed together, save in the bloodless contests of parliamentary debate." [6]

Impeachment of Laud, and others. The impeachment of Strafford was followed up by that of Archbishop Laud; of the Lord Keeper Finch; of Windebank, Secretary of State. The two latter, however, saved themselves by flight beyond the sea; thirteen bishops were impeached for having taken part in enacting canons, and six of the judges were impeached for their conduct in relation to ship-money; and the king agreed that for the future judges should be appointed for life *quamdiu se bene gesserint.*[6a]

The condemnation of Prynne, Burton, Bastwick, Leighton, and Lilburne, those victims of the tyranny of the Star Chamber, was declared illegal, and their liberation ordered. The return journey of the three former from their island prisons in Jersey, Guernsey, and Scilly, formed a triumphal procession, " great herds of people meeting them at their entrance into all towns, and waiting upon them out with wonderful acclamations of joy." Near London they were met by " above ten thousand persons, with boughs and flowers in their hands, the common people strewing flowers and herbs in the ways as they passed, making great noise and expressions of joy for their deliverance and return; and in those acclamations mingling loud and virulent exclamations against the bishops ' who had so cruelly prosecuted such godly men '." [7]

Assistance voted to the Scots. In the meantime, the presence of the Scottish army in the northern counties rendered the king powerless to resist the will of his parliament. Instead of aiding him " to chastising out of the rebels," as he had asked them to do in his opening speech,

---

[6] Gardiner, *History of England*, ix, 370–371; much the same problem is involved in the policy of the Earl of Clarendon after the Restoration.

[6a] Rushworth, ii, 1366. For the details of Laud's impeachment, see *infra*, p. 531.

[7] Clarendon, *History*, i, 269.

the commons agreed to grant the Scots " a brotherly assistance " afterwards fixed at £300,000.[8]

REFORMING LEGISLATION

Master of the situation, the parliament used its power with energy, tact, and moderation. During the first session of ten months a number of salutary Acts were passed, which, while sweeping away most of the accumulated abuses of recent times, left the ancient constitution intact, and the just prerogatives of the king undiminished.

Triennial Act, 1641. The first of these statutes regulated the intermission and duration of parliament. By the " Act for the preventing of inconveniences happening by the long intermission of parliaments," it was provided that if parliament was not duly summoned and assembled before the tenth day of September in the third year after the conclusion of the present (or any succeeding) parliament, it should, nevertheless, assemble on the second Monday in the ensuing November. For this purpose, the lord chancellor, or keeper of the great seal, should be sworn to issue the writs for a new parliament in due time, under pain of disability to hold his office, and further punishments; in case of his default, the peers were enabled and directed to meet at Westminster, and any twelve or more of them to issue the writs; failing the peers, the sheriffs, mayors, and bailiffs should cause elections to be made; and lastly, in their default, the electors themselves were to meet and proceed to choose their representatives, in the same manner as if writs had been regularly issued from the crown. No future parliament was to be dissolved, prorogued, or adjourned within fifty days after the time appointed for its meeting, except with its own consent.[9]

In the reign of Edward III, it had been provided by statute that parliament should be holden at least once in every year,[10] but as no provision was then made in case of the failure of the king to issue the necessary writs, the law had been disobeyed at pleasure. The known resolution of Charles to govern without a parliament made it absolutely necessary that the defect in the machinery of the constitution should be remedied. Carefully adhering to the old lines, the Triennial Act left untouched the king's prerogative of calling parliament, and even extended the legal period of intermission from one year to three. It was only in the event of the king failing to exercise his prerogative within the prescribed time that another mode was provided for ensuring the supremacy of the law.

Tonnage and poundage. An Act was passed (June 1641) putting an end to the long-contested prerogative of levying customs on merchandise.

---

[8] Montague, *Political History*, 232.
[9] 16 Car. 1, c. 1; Gardiner, *Documents*, 144; repealed in 1664, by 16 Car. 2, c. 1, which re-declared the principle, but made no provision of machinery to enforce it.
[10] *Supra*, p. 158.

By this Act (which granted to the king tonnage and poundage for less than two months), after reciting that these duties, not having been granted by parliament, had been collected against the laws of the realm, and that the farmers and collectors had deserved condign punishment, it was provided that in future any officer presuming to levy these customs, except during the time specified in the Act, should incur the penalties of praemunire, and be disabled during life to sue in any court. It was further, in general terms, " declared and enacted that it is, and hath been, the ancient right of the subjects of this realm, that no subsidy, custom, impost, or other charge whatsoever, ought or may be laid or imposed upon any merchandise exported or imported by subjects, denizens, or aliens, without common consent in parliament." [11]

Ship-money abolished, 1641. An " Act for the declaring unlawful and void the late proceedings touching ship-money, and for the vacating of all records and process concerning the same," was passed, declaring that charge illegal, and annulling the judgment in the Exchequer Chamber against Hampden as contrary to the laws and statutes of the realm, the right of property, the liberty of the subject, and the Petition of Right.[12] These two Acts closed the lengthy series of statutes which during the course of centuries had been passed in restraint of arbitrary taxation by the crown.

Star Chamber abolished. It had also been the care of parliament to sweep away all those conciliar tribunals which had become the principal instruments of despotic power. By an " Act for the regulating the Privy Council, and for taking away the court commonly called the Star Chamber," after reciting Magna Carta, and its train of statutes for protecting the liberty and property of the subject, the court of Star Chamber was abolished, and the old constitutional principle re-enunciated " that neither his Majesty nor his Privy Council hath, or ought to have, any jurisdiction, power, or authority, by any arbitrary way whatsoever, to examine or draw into question, determine, or dispose of the lands or goods of any subjects of this kingdom, but that the same ought to be tried and determined in the ordinary courts of justice, and by the ordinary course of the law." Under this statute, although the jurisdiction of the Privy Council, as well as of the Star Chamber, to try and determine any civil or criminal cause was abrogated, the Council still retained the power of examining and committing persons charged with offences.

Council's power of committal. But it was enacted that every person committed by the Council, or any member of it, or by the king's special

---

[11] 16 Car. 1, c. 8; Gardiner, *Documents*, 159. The grant was continued by six subsequent Acts (cc. 12, 22, 25, 29, 31, 36) for short periods down to July 2, 1642.

[12] 16 Car. 1, c. 14; Gardiner, *Documents*, 189. Five of the judges who had pronounced in favour of ship-money (Berkeley, Crawley, Davenport, Trevor, and Weston) were imprisoned for their judgment.

command, should, on application to the judges of the King's Bench or Common Pleas, have granted unto him, without delay on any pretence whatever, a writ of habeas corpus; that in the return to the writ the gaoler should certify the true cause of commitment, and that the court whence the writ had issued should, within three days, examine, and determine whether the cause were just and legal or not, and thereupon do what to justice should appertain, either by delivering, bailing, or remanding the prisoner.[13]   Another clause of this Act abolished the court of the President and Council of the North—which under Strafford's arbitrary administration had given so much offence—the court of the President and Council of the Welsh Marches (which extended its jurisdiction over the adjacent counties of Salop, Worcester, Hereford, and Gloucester), the court of the Duchy of Lancaster, and the Court of Exchequer of the County Palatine of Chester—all irregular tribunals which, " under various pretexts, had usurped so extensive a cognisance as to deprive one-third of England of the privileges of the common law." [14]

High Commission Court abolished, 1641.   With the court of Star Chamber and the provincial irregular tribunals fell also the court of High Commission.   By an Act intituled " A repeal of a branch of a statute *primo Elizabethae*, concerning commissioners, for causes ecclesiastical," after reciting that the commissioners, to the insufferable wrong and oppression of the king's subjects, had illegally assumed the right to fine and imprison for ecclesiastical offences, the clause of the statute under which the court had been erected was repealed, and the other ecclesiastical courts were deprived of all power to inflict fine, imprisonment, or corporal punishment.[15]

By other statutes the vexatious prerogative of purveyance was restrained, writs to compel the taking up of knighthood were abolished, and the boundaries of the royal forests were again reduced to their limits in the twentieth year of James I.[16]

Impressment declared illegal.   Among the beneficial Acts of the Long Parliament is also to be reckoned one which, while empowering the king

---

[13] 16 Car. 1, c. 10; Gardiner, *Documents*, 179.   This Act expressly overrode the Act *Pro Camera Stellata* (1487) and also 21 Hen. 8, c. 20.   The Petition of Right only dealt with committals " by special command of the King "; this Act deals with committals by the Council as a whole or by individual councillors, and required the cause (and not merely the fact) of committal to be returned on a habeas corpus.   Contrast the rule in Anderson, *supra*, p. 308.

[14] Hallam, *Constitutional History*, ii, 99.   By another Act (16 Car. 1, c. 15) certain abuses in the Stannary Courts of Cornwall and Devon were remedied.   *Cf. supra*, p. 248, n. Strafford, as president of the Council of the North, greatly extended the jurisdiction of that court, and excited much odium by his tyranny and arrogance.   The courts of the Council of the North and of the Marches of Wales were entirely abolished, but the jurisdiction of those of the Duchy of Lancaster and of the County Palatine of Chester was preserved as to matters touching the king's private estate.

[15] 16 Car. 1, c. 11; Gardiner, *Documents*, 186.   The latter part of the Act was repealed after the Restoration.

[16] 16 Car. 1, cc. 16, 19, 20; Gardiner, *Documents*, 192, 196.

to levy troops compulsorily for the suppression of the Irish rebellion, recites in the preamble that " by the laws of this realm none of his Majesty's subjects ought to be impressed or compelled to go out of his country to serve as a soldier in the wars, except in case of necessity of the sudden coming in of strange enemies into the kingdom, or except they be otherwise bound by tenure of their lands or possessions." [17]

Parliament indissoluble: Clerical Disabilities Act, 1642. Two other statutes of the Long Parliament are more open to animadversion. One provided that the parliament then sitting should not be prorogued or dissolved without its own consent, and the other (passed some months later than the others) deprived all clergy of temporal jurisdiction and especially the bishops of their suffrages among the peers. They were both grave departures from the old lines of the constitution; but the one, which was of a purely temporary nature, was rendered necessary by the deep and well-founded distrust which the character of Charles had inspired [18]; the other was the outcome of that abuse of their coercive jurisdiction and temporal power by which the bishops had rendered

---

[17] 16 Car. 1, c. 28; Gardiner, *Documents*, 242. Since this statute, impressment for the ARMY has never been exercised by virtue of the royal prerogative; but under the authority of parliament it has occasionally been resorted to, more especially during the American war, as, *e.g.*, in 1779, by statute 19 Geo. 3, c. 10. In later times, however, this odious violation of personal liberty—which has nothing in common with a national conscription applicable to all able-bodied citizens alike—has not been practised for strengthening the land forces, which have been recruited by enlistment, stimulated by bounties.

Impressment of sailors for the public service in the NAVY seems always to have stood on a somewhat different footing from military impressment. It is " a prerogative inherent in the crown," says Sir Michael Foster, " grounded upon common law and recognised by many Acts of Parliament." (2 Ric. 2, stat. 1, c. 4; 2 & 3 Phil. and Mary, c. 16; 7 & 8 Will. 3, c. 21; 2 & 3 Anne, c. 6; 4 & 5 Anne, c. 6; 5 & 6 Will. 4, c. 24.) Foster's view was affirmed by Lord Mansfield in *R. v. Tubbs* (1776) Cowp. 512; and by Lord Kenyon in *Ex parte Fox* (1793) 5 St.Tr. 276. Several early statutes against the impressment of soldiers (1 Edw. 3, c. 5; 25 Edw. 3, stat. 5, c. 8) are silent as to the impressment of sailors; a difference between the two services which was probably due in some measure to the fact that while the land service was provided for in ordinary cases by the military tenures and by the *jurati ad arma* or national militia, no competent provision was made by law for the ordinary sea-service (except in the case of the Cinque Ports and a few others, which were altogether inadequate for the public service). During the American war the hardships and cruelties of the system of naval impressment, carried out by armed press-gangs, were a disgrace to a free country; and since the conclusion of peace, ministers and parliament, alive to the dangerous principles on which recruiting for the navy had hitherto been conducted, have devised new expedients—higher wages, larger bounties, shorter periods of service, and a reserve volunteer force—more consistent with the liberty of the subject. The Commission on manning the navy, in 1859, reported that " the evidence of the witnesses, with scarcely an exception, shows that the system of naval impressment, as practised in former wars, could not now be successfully enforced."—See Foster, *Crown Law*, 158–179, and May, *Constitutional History*, iii, 20–24.

[18] The " Act to prevent inconveniences which may happen by the untimely adjourning, proroguing, or dissolving this present Parliament " (16 Car. 1, c. 7; Gardiner, *Documents*, 158), was ostensibly grounded on the necessity of speedily raising money for the relief of the army in the northern parts of the realm, and the impossibility of borrowing " on the authority of resolutions of parliament," unless some security was furnished to the creditors, that the assembly would not be dissolved before sufficient provision had been made for repayment of the moneys to be raised. But the chief motive was, undoubtedly, " a just apprehension of the king's intention to overthrow the parliament," and of personal danger to the popular leaders after a dissolution. It was known that the king had listened to and approved a proposal to bring up the English army from the north in order to overawe the parliament.—Hallam, *Constitutional History*, ii, 112, 113. On the army plot see Gardiner, *History of England*, ix, pp. 309–318.

themselves odious not merely to the puritans, but even to many of those who wished well to the cause of both church and king.[19]   After a session of ten months during which most of the series of Acts above enumerated were passed, the two Houses, in September 1641, adjourned for a short recess of six weeks.

Parliamentary party schism. It was about this time that a final schism in the parliamentary party developed itself. It was sharply divided on the matter of church government, and a large minority regarded the concessions already made by the king a sufficient surrender of the royal power. The leaders of the commons, however, were convinced that the king was bent upon recovering, by force or fraud, the arbitrary powers which he had been compelled to surrender; that unless further securities were taken, and a constant vigilance maintained, there was danger, not only of the loss of their newly vindicated liberties, but of the subversion of the existing free parliamentary constitution and the establishment in its stead of the personal government of the king. To them it seemed that as under Richard II, so now under Charles I the question between king and people was again practically narrowed to the simple issue of absolute monarchy versus parliamentary government. Pym and his co-workers in the parliament felt that the time had come to make an earnest appeal to the people, warning them, by a recital of the lessons of the past, that no faith could be reposed in the king.

In the meantime Charles had gone to Edinburgh, much against the wish of the commons, partly for the purpose of adjusting the points of difference which remained between him and his Scottish subjects, but mainly with the object of obtaining their assistance in his quarrel with his English subjects.[20]

The " Incident," 1641. At Edinburgh Charles set himself to winning over the parliament and church of Scotland, against the parliament of England, by granting all their demands, by assiduously attending the presbyterian worship, and by lavishing favours upon the chiefs of the covenanters. At the same time he was, it seems, secretly searching for proofs of the correspondence of the English political leaders with the Scots prior to the late invasion, with the object of bringing a charge of treason against the former, on his return.[21]   Acting on information, supplied by the Earl of Montrose in a letter to the king, that the Marquis of Hamilton and the Earl of Argyle had been implicated in the plans of the English malcontents, the Earl of Crawford formed a design for the

---

[19] In a very remarkable conversation with Hyde, Sir Edmund Verney, who was killed at the battle of Edgehill, declared his reluctance to fight for the bishops, whose quarrel he took it to be, though bound in gratitude not to desert the king.—Clarendon, *Life and Continuation* (ed. 1827), i, 160. The Act to disable persons in holy orders to exercise any temporal jurisdiction or authority (16 Car. 1, c. 27; Gardiner, *Documents*, 241), passed February 1642, was repealed after the Restoration by 13 Car. 2, stat. 1, c. 2.

[20] Gardiner, *History of England*, ix, 396.

[21] *Ibid.*, x, 28.

sudden arrest of the two noblemen and their removal to a safe place beyond the sea; if they resisted they were to be killed; but forewarned of the plot they frustrated it by publicly withdrawing from the Scottish parliament, and seeking refuge in Kinneil Castle, the residence of Hamilton's brother. The king, who was thought to have been an accomplice in the plot, complained of the suspicions of the lords as an insult to his honour. A committee of inquiry was ordered by the parliament, which elicited nothing decisive on either side, and Hamilton and Argyle were induced to return to parliament. But the leaders of the English House of Commons, which had sent a small committee to Scotland, with Hampden as its presiding member, to be near the king and watch proceedings, were kept well informed of what passed. And the news of the " Incident," as the affair of Hamilton and Argyle was termed, excited much agitation and alarm in London, lest this design against the two great leaders of the popular party in the northern kingdom should be followed by similar measures against the English malcontents.

Rebellion in Ireland. Parliament reassembled on October 20, 1641, and about the same time came tidings of the Irish rebellion, with its attendant massacre, which raised a fierce outcry against all papists, and was by many believed to have been secretly encouraged by the king. " The event," says Gardiner, " which precipitated the division of parties was the Ulster Rebellion. The first indication that the majority of the Commons felt that, with a war in Ireland in prospect, it was necessary that harmony should exist between the crown and parliament, is to be found in the instructions to the Commons' Committee in Scotland sent up to the Lords on November 8. The demand made in these instructions was for the appointment of councillors and ministers approved by parliament. To grant such a wish would practically annihilate the independent action of the crown, and the division of parties on ecclesiastical affairs now gave to the king a majority of the Lords and a large minority of the Commons upon whom he could rely. All those, in short, who wished to see considerable ecclesiastical changes made in the puritan direction supported the authority of the House of Commons, whilst those who wished the changes to be few or none supported the authority of the king." [22]

An examination into an alleged new army plot was instituted in the commons, and on November 17, Pym moved and carried a resolution " that upon examinations now read, there is sufficient evidence for this House to believe, that there was a second design to bring up the army against the parliament, and an intention to make the Scottish army stand as neutral." [23] Pym's object in producing this charge at this moment was an attempt to influence the voting on the Remonstrance.[24]

---

[22] Gardiner, *Documents*, p. xxxix. The Instructions referred to are printed, *ibid.*, p. 199.
[23] *Commons' Journal*, ii, 318.
[24] Gardiner, *History of England*, x, 74.

The Grand Remonstrance. On November 8, 1641, the draft of the Remonstrance, or " Declaration of the state of the kingdom," was laid upon the table of the House. Secretary Nicholas at once wrote to the king informing him of the fact, and urging his instant return to London. In reply the king wrote: " You must needs speak with such of my servants that you may best trust, in my name, that by all means possible this Declaration may be stopped." Under the leadership of Hyde, a band of members in the Lower House was now organised as what was truly to be called His Majesty's Opposition. With steady perseverance and tenacity the passage of the Remonstrance was disputed clause by clause during a seven days' debate, and only the most resolute determination on the part of the popular leaders availed to maintain any part of it unimpaired. At length the final debate was fixed for November 22. The king, eager at last to reach London before the final vote could be taken, was now hastening with all speed back from Edinburgh, and on the eventful 22nd was only distant two days' journey from the metropolis. For fourteen hours the debate was sustained with much warmth by Hyde, Falkland, Dering, Rudyard, Bagshaw, Culpepper, Pym, Orlando Bridgman, Waller, Hampden, Holles, Glyn, Coventry, Geoffrey Palmer and Maynard. Near midnight Secretary Nicholas retired, and wrote to the king that the commons had been in debate since twelve at noon and were at it still, it being then near twelve at midnight. " I stayed this dispatch," he continued, " in hopes to have sent your Majesty the result of that debate, but it is so late, as I dare not (after my sickness) adventure to watch any longer to see the issue of it: only I assure your Majesty there are divers in the Commons House that are resolved to stand very stiff for rejecting that Declaration, and if they prevail not then to protest against it."

At length, about two in the morning, the Remonstrance was carried by a majority of eleven only. So critical was the contest deemed, that Cromwell declared to Lord Falkland, as they were leaving the House together after the division, " that if the Remonstrance had been rejected, he would have sold all he had the next morning, and never have seen England more; and he knew there were many other honest men of the same resolution." [25]

The Remonstrance summarised. The preamble, consisting of twenty unnumbered clauses, and opening in the name of " The Commons in the present Parliament assembled," begins by declaring that for the past twelve months they had been carrying on a struggle of which the object was to restore and establish the ancient honour, greatness, and security of the nation and the crown—that the object of the Remonstrance was as well to answer the great aspersions cast upon what they had done, as to point out what remained for them to do, and the difficulties raised for

[25] Clarendon, *History*, i, 420.

their hindrance. In express terms they denounce the court conspiracy to subvert the fundamental laws and principles of government, to degrade the protestant religion, to discredit the claims and authority of parliament, and to introduce such opinions and ceremonies as would necessarily end in accommodation with popery.

The body of the Remonstrance is contained in 206 numbered clauses, and takes the form of practical proofs and illustrations of the statements advanced in the preamble.

After detailing, with vigorous and incisive rhetoric, all the invidious and tyrannical proceedings of the king during his first, second, and third parliaments, the government by prerogative from the third parliament to the pacification of Berwick, the Short Parliament and the Scottish invasion, the remedial Acts of the Long Parliament, and the practices of the court party, the Remonstrance proceeds to set forth the defence of the popular leaders.

" And now what hope," they said, " have we but in God, when as the only means of our subsistence and power of reformation is under Him, in the parliament? But what can we the commons, without the conjunction of the House of Lords, and what conjunction can we expect there, when the bishops and recusant lords are so numerous and prevalent that they are able to cross and interrupt our best endeavours for reformation, and by that means give advantage to this malignant party to traduce our proceedings?

" They infuse into the people that we mean to abolish all church government, and leave every man to his own fancy for the service and worship of God, absolving him of that obedience which he owes under God unto his Majesty, whom we know to be entrusted with the ecclesiastical law as well as with the temporal, to regulate all the members of the Church of England by such rules of order and discipline only as are established by parliament, which is his great council in all affairs, both in church and state.

" We confess our intention is, and our endeavours have been, to reduce within bounds that exorbitant power which the prelates have assumed unto themselves, so contrary both to the Word of God and to the laws of the land, to which end we passed the bill for the removing them from their temporal power and employments, that so the better they might with meekness apply themselves to the discharge of their functions, which bill themselves opposed, and were the principal instruments of crossing it.[26]

---

[26] Three bills were introduced by the commons for taking away the temporal power of the bishops. The first, " A Bill to restrain Bishops and others in Holy Orders from intermeddling in secular affairs," was sent up to the lords, May 1, 1641, where it was thrown out by a large majority. The second, popularly termed the " Root and Branch Bill," was intituled " For the utter abolishing and taking away all archbishops, bishops, their chancellors and commissaries, deans and chapters, archdeacons, prebendaries, chanters, canons, and all other their under-officers." It was introduced by Sir Edward Dering while the first bill was still pending, but after being long and vehemently debated,

" And we do here declare that it is far from our purpose or desire to let loose the golden reins of discipline and government in the church, to leave private persons or particular congregations to take up what form of divine service they please, for we hold it requisite that there should be throughout the whole realm a conformity to that order which the laws enjoin according to the Word of God.   And we desire to unburden the consciences of men of needless and superstitious ceremonies, suppress innovations, and take away the monuments of idolatry."

They then suggest a general synod of divines, the result of whose consultations should be represented to the parliament, there to be allowed of and confirmed, and to receive the stamp of authority.[27]

" They have maliciously charged us," they continue, " that we intend to destroy and discourage learning, whereas it is our chiefest care and desire to advance it, and to provide a competent maintenance for con-scionable and preaching ministers throughout the kingdom, which will be a great encouragement to scholars, and a certain means whereby the want, meanness and ignorance, to which a great part of the clergy is now subject, will be prevented.   And we intended likewise to reform and purge the fountains of learning, the two Universities, that the streams flowing from thence may be clear and pure, and an honour and comfort to the whole land.

" They have strained to blast our proceedings in parliament by wrest-ing the interpretations of our orders from their genuine intention.   They tell the people that our meddling with the power of episcopacy hath caused sectaries and conventicles, when idolatrous and popish ceremonies, introduced into the church by command of the bishops, have not only debarred the people from thence, but expelled them from the kingdom. Thus with Elijah, we are called by this malignant party the troublers of the state, and still, while we endeavour to reform their abuses, they make us the authors of those mischiefs we study to prevent."

Remedial measures demanded.   Finally, the Remonstrance specifies the remedial measures demanded :

(1) **Catholics.**   To keep papists in such condition, as that they might not be able to do any hurt ; and for avoiding such connivance and favour as had theretofore been shown to them, his Majesty was moved to grant a standing commission to some choice men named in parliament who might take notice of their increase, report upon their counsels and pro-ceedings, and use all due means, by execution of the laws, to prevent mischievous designs, from that quarter, against the peace and safety of

was allowed to drop on the king's departure for Scotland.   The third, which passed into a law in February 1642 (*supra*, p. 399), was the last concession made by Charles before finally quitting London with the intention of appealing to arms.

27 " The whole contention of the party of the Grand Remonstrance, the whole root of the baleful tree of the Civil War, lay in these words . . . ' No Popery ! ' was the cry on one side.   ' No sectarian meeting ! ' was the cry on the other.   ' No toleration ! ' was the cry on both "—Gardiner, *History of England*, x, 63.

the realm. And further, that some sufficient tests should be applied to discover the false conformity of papists to the English Church, by colour of which they had been admitted into places of highest authority and trust.

(2) **Judges.** That, for the better preservation of the liberties and laws, all illegal grievances and exactions should be presented and punished at the sessions and assizes; and that judges and justices should be sworn to the due execution of the Petition of Right and other laws.

(3) **Councillors.** A series of precautions were suggested to prevent the employment of evil councillors; and it was plainly stated that supplies for the support of the king's own estate could not be given, nor such assistance provided as the times required for the protestant party beyond the sea, unless only such councillors, ambassadors, and other ministers were in future employed as parliament could give its confidence to; and unless all councillors of state were sworn, as well to avoid receiving, in any form, reward or pension from any foreign prince, as to observe strictly those laws which concerned the subject at home in his liberty.[28]

It is evident that the Grand Remonstrance was produced in a fever of anxiety over popish intrigues at Court. It is now known that those intrigues were even more extensive than the commons suspected, but even so their actual political importance was very slight. The suggestion that the Anglican episcopate had entered into the plot was quite erroneous. It was natural, however, that the commons should make the most of this point in their appeal to the public—for that in substance is the true nature of the document. Of its specific proposals, two are of outstanding importance. First, it contemplated the House of Commons annexing the old royal supremacy over the church, and the enforcement throughout the country of a new ecclesiastical régime (whose nature still remained to be ascertained). Secondly, it proposed to transform the commons' old right of criticising ministers into a much more radical right of controlling their appointment in the first instance; in other words, the legislature claimed control over the executive.

Motion to print the Remonstrance. Immediately after the Remonstrance had been voted, there occurred an incident which plainly showed how exacerbated were the passions aroused by the debates which had occupied the last week or more. Peard, member for Barnstaple, moved that the Remonstrance should be forthwith printed. Hyde opposed the design as unlawful and mischievous, and in pursuance of the tactics already decided upon, said that if the motion were adopted, he should ask leave of the House to protest. Other voices cried out that they protested, and Geoffrey Palmer declared, " I protest for myself and all the rest." Protests, though in use with the lords, were utterly unknown to

---

[28] The Remonstrance is printed *in extenso* in Rushworth's *Collection*, part 3, i, 438 *et seq.*, and in Gardiner, *Documents*, 202 *et seq.*

the commons, and the presumption of Palmer, not merely in protesting at all without leave of the House, but also in the name of " all the rest," raised such a tumult that many members laid their hands upon their swords, and a violent conflict seemed imminent, " had not the sagacity and calmness of Mr. Hampden," says an eye-witness, " by a short speech prevented it." On a division it was decided by a majority of twenty-three that although the Remonstrance might be published, it should not be printed until the further order of the House.

The majority principle. The question whether the minority should be allowed to protest against a decision of the House of Commons was far too serious to admit of Palmer's offence being passed over unpunished. It was of vital importance to the authority and influence of the commons that, no matter what their internal divisions might be, their decisions should be kept before the people sole and intact. At the next sitting of the House, Palmer, after being heard in his defence, was committed to the Tower, but almost immediately afterwards released, on making a humble apology and retraction. This vain endeavour to preserve the appearance of unity in spite of a profound divergence could not long be maintained, and by the end of the century there was a growing practice of publishing votes and division lists; by this means the member was not only permitted, but was forced even against his will to reveal his position to the outside world. On December 15 (1641), the Remonstrance, having been previously presented to the king, was ordered to be printed by a majority of 135 votes to 83.

The Five Members. The next important, and indeed the critical, event in the relations between Charles I and his parliament was the impeachment and the attempted arrest of the Five Members. The king had no intention of submitting quietly to the adverse vote of the House of Commons. He, indeed, even with what he afterwards alleged to be the proofs of treason in his hands, attempted to make use of what Clarendon has termed " the strategem of winning men by places," by offering the chancellorship of the exchequer to Pym, the leader of the popular party.[29] But this attempt at conciliation failed, doubtless on account of the utter distrust and disbelief which the king in all his dealings had inspired. It is an interesting expedient, but at that date it could not be expected that statesmen would appreciate its possibilities, or realise that many political conflicts could be peacefully solved by calling upon a successful opposition to assume the responsibilities of office. Charles now seems to have resumed his original intention to crush his opponents. The leaders of the opposition to the Remonstrance were called to office. Hyde preferred for the present to serve the king as a private member of the House, but Falkland accepted the post of secretary of state, and Culpepper that

[29] Forster, *Arrest of the Five Members*, 55, 59; Gardiner, *History of England*, x, 127.

of chancellor of the exchequer. Balfour, the tried friend of the parliament, was removed from the governorship of the Tower—the " bridle " of the City—and Colonel Lunsford, a soldier of evil character and infamous name, was appointed in his place. But his appointment excited tumults in the City and at Westminster. The commons demanded his removal, and the king was persuaded to remove him within a week of his appointment and to put Sir John Byron in his place. Disturbed by secret reports, and the unusual concourse of armed men about the king at Whitehall, the commons sought the protection of a guard. On December 30, Pym (who seems to have already received intimation of the intended impeachment) moved " that there being a design to be executed this day upon the House of Commons, we might send instantly to the City of London . . . to come down with the train bands for our assistance." The next day the commons sent a verbal message to the king by Denzil Holles, expressing their earnest desire for a guard out of the City, under command of the Earl of Essex. The king required the message to be communicated to him in writing. This was immediately drawn up and presented, but no answer was returned for three days. At length, on January 3, 1642, the king's answer came. It was a refusal, but accompanied by a promise on " the word of a king, that the security of all and every one of you from violence, is and shall ever be as much our care as the preservation of us and our children." At that very time the Attorney-General was engaged in delivering a royal message to the House of Lords, impeaching for high treason Lord Kimbolton and five members of the commons, Pym, Hampden, Holles, Haslerigg and Strode,[30] and demanding that the House should secure the persons of the accused. The lords " somewhat appalled " (to quote Clarendon's expression) at this proceeding, appointed a committee to inquire into the legality of the accusation. In the meantime the king's officers had gone

---

[30] The Articles of Treason are printed in Gardiner, *Documents*, 236, from the *Journal of the House of Lords*, iv, 501 : " Articles of high treason and other high misdemeanours against the Lord Kimbolton, Mr. Denzil Holles, Sir Arthur Haslerigg, Mr. John Pym, Mr. John Hampden and Mr. William Strode.

1. That they have traitorously endeavoured to subvert the fundamental laws and government of the kingdom of England, to deprive the King of his regal power, and to place in subjects an arbitrary and tyrannical power over the lives, liberties, and estates of his Majesty's liege people.

2. That they have traitorously endeavoured by many foul aspersions upon his Majesty and his government, to alienate the affections of his people, and to make his Majesty odious unto them.

3. That they have endeavoured to draw his Majesty's late army to disobedience to his Majesty's commands, and to side with them in their traitorous designs.

4. That they have traitorously invited and encouraged a foreign power to invade his Majesty's kingdom of England.

5. That they have traitorously endeavoured to subvert the rights and very being of Parliaments.

6. That for the completing of their traitorous designs, they have endeavoured (as far as in them lay), by force and terror to compel the Parliament to join with them in their traitorous designs, and to that end have actually raised and countenanced tumults against the King and Parliament.

7. And that they have traitorously conspired to levy, and actually have levied, war against the King." (Referring to the armed guard which they had persisted in voting for the protection of the House.)

to the houses of the Five Members and were putting seals on their studies. The commons, having just heard of these proceedings, had voted them a breach of privilege when the king's serjeant appeared, and in the name of his master " required Mr. Speaker to place in his custody five gentlemen, members of this House (naming them), whom his Majesty had commanded him to arrest for high treason." The House appointed a committee, including two ministers of the crown, Lord Falkland and Sir John Culpepper, to attend on and inform the king that such an important message could only be answered after mature consideration, but that the accused would be ready to answer any legal charge made against them. The Five Members were ordered to attend daily in their places and the previous resolution for a military guard out of the City was turned into an Order of the House and sent by the hands of two of the members for the City to the Lord Mayor.

Was their impeachment illegal ?   Of this impeachment Macaulay has remarked in his essay on Hampden: " It is difficult to find in the whole history of England such an instance of tyranny, perfidy, and folly. The most precious and ancient rights of the subject were violated by this act. The only way in which Hampden and Pym could legally be tried for treason at the suit of the king was by a petty jury on a bill found by a grand jury. The Attorney-General had no right to impeach them. The House of Lords had no right to try them. . . . The tyrant resolved to follow up one outrage by another. In making the charge he had struck at the institution of juries. In executing the arrest, he struck at the privileges of parliament. He resolved to go to the House in person with an armed force, and there to seize the leaders of the opposition while engaged in the discharge of their parliamentary duties." These indignant remarks rest on the assumption that impeachment was a regular procedure with settled rules, and that Charles had broken the rules. In fact, impeachment was the creation of politicians, not of lawyers, and grievously lacked the logic and certitude which lawyers impart to the procedures under their control. Whether impeachment was at the suit of the crown, or the commons, or both, was an obscurity which Richard II noted long ago.[31]   In fact, there was the very recent case of the Earl of Bristol who had been impeached by the crown (without the commons) which was allowed to pass unchallenged.[32]   The committee, set up to show how all this infringed the privileges of the House (which had never extended to treason, felony and breach of the peace), had an impossible task and produced nothing which would bear examination.[33]   The truth is that events

---

[31] *Supra*, pp. 171–172.

[32] Gardiner, *History of England*, vi, 95; x, 143–144. For Floyd, who was " impeached before the commons," see *supra*, p. 355; *cf*. Mitchell, *supra*, p. 355–356.

[33] Gardiner, *History of England*, x, 144.   From time to time the lords, however, claimed that they were not bound to try commoners (as distinct from peers) save at the suit of the Lower House.   Such a rule, if it could be regarded as established, would have permitted the trial of Lord Bristol, although not the trial of the Five Members.

had reached the stage of crisis in which regard for law had disappeared, and its disappearance was all the more rapid since impeachment lacked the solid core of principle and procedure which alone could have checked its misuse.

Careful preparations were made to ensure the success of this *coup d'état*. Whitehall was fortified with a considerable accession of arms and ammunition, and the palace guards were ordered to hold themselves in readiness. Sir William Killigrew was sent round to each of the Inns of Court (collectively capable of furnishing a military guard of at least 500 men) with copies of the articles of treason, and with a request that they should be ready the next morning " at a moment's warning." Late in the night the king, after consultation with his secretary, Nicholas, sent instructions to the Lord Mayor of London not merely to refuse to the commons the guard which they had requested, but in its place to enrol such a guard for the royal service, with orders for its immediate employment in suppressing and dispersing all tumults and assemblages of the people in the streets of the City, and with express instructions, " by shooting with bullets, or otherwayes, to suppresse those tumults and destroy such of them as shall persist in the tumultuous wayes and disorders." [34]

The next morning, January 4, 1642, the accused members attended in their places and defended themselves from the charges which the king had brought against them. The commons sent up to the lords the articles of impeachment calling them " a scandalous paper," and requested them to institute inquiries as to who were its authors, to the end that they might receive condign punishment, and the commonwealth be secured against such persons.

The attempted arrest. Forewarned of the king's approach at the head of 300 or 400 armed men, the accused members, by the desire of the House, discreetly withdrew as the king was entering New Palace Yard.

At the entrance to Westminster Hall the king's armed band formed suddenly into a lane, ranging themselves on either side along the whole length of the Hall, and Charles, passing through this lane, ascended the stairs leading to the House of Commons. " The king's command had been, according to Sir Ralph Verney and Captain Slingsby, himself one of the company, that the great body should stay in the Hall; but, says D'Ewes, ' his Majesty coming into the lobby, a little room just without the House of Commons, divers officers of the late army in the north, and other desperate ruffians, pressed in after him to the number of about fourscore, besides some of his pensioners.' " Charles entered the House followed only by his nephew, the Elector Palatine, having commanded the rest of his followers " upon their lives not to come in "; but the door was not permitted to be closed behind him. " Visible now

---

[34] Forster, *Arrest of the Five Members*, 154–158. [Warrant dated January 3, 1642.]

at the threshold to all, were the officers and desperadoes above named, of whom D'Ewes proceeds, ' some had left their cloaks in the Hall, and most of them were armed with pistols and swords, and they forcibly kept the door of the House of Commons open, one Captain Hide standing next the door holding his sword upright in the scabbard '; a picture which Sir Ralph Verney, who was present that day in his place, completes by adding that ' so the doors were kept open, and the Earl of Roxborough stood within the door, leaning upon it.' As the king entered all the members rose and uncovered, and the king also removed his hat, and it would not have been easy, says Rushworth, to discern any of the Five Members had they been there, among so many bare faces standing up together. But there was one face among the five, which Charles knew too well not to have singled out even there; and hardly had he appeared within the chamber when it was observed that his glance and his step were turned in the direction of Pym's seat close by the bar. His intention, baffled by the absence of the popular leader, can only now be guessed at; but Rushworth adds, ' his Majesty not seeing Mr. Pym there, knowing him well, went up to the chair.' As he approached the chair, Lenthall stepped out to meet him; ' By your leave, Mr. Speaker,' he said, ' I must borrow your chair a little.' And then the king stepped up to his place and stood upon the step, but sat not down in the chair. And after he had looked a great while he spoke again. ' Gentlemen,' he said, ' I am sorry for this occasion of coming unto you. Yesterday I sent a serjeant-at-arms upon a very important occasion to apprehend some that by my command were accused of high treason; whereunto I did expect obedience, and not a message. And I must declare unto you here, that albeit no king that ever was in England shall be more careful of your privileges, to maintain them to the uttermost of his power than I shall be, yet you must know that in cases of treason no person hath a privilege. And therefore I am come to know if any of those persons that were accused are here.' Then he paused; and casting his eyes upon all the members of the House, said, ' I do not see any of them. I think I should know them.' ' For I must tell you, gentlemen,' he resumed, after another pause, ' that so long as those persons that I have accused (for no slight crime, but for treason) are here, I cannot expect that this House can be in the right that I do heartily wish it. Therefore I am come to tell you that I must have them wheresoever I find them.' Then again he hesitated, stopped, and called out, ' Is Mr. Pym here?' To which nobody gave answer. He then asked (continued D'Ewes) for Mr. Holles, whether he were present, and when nobody answered him, he pressed the Speaker to tell him." " Lenthall was not a great or heroic man, but he knew what his duty was. He now gave voice, in words of singular force and dexterity, to the common feeling that no individual expression of the intentions or opinions of the House was permissible. ' May it please your Majesty,' he said, falling on his knee before the king, ' I have neither eyes to see, nor tongue to speak, in this place but as this House is

pleased to direct me, whose servant I am here; and I humbly beg your
Majesty's pardon that I cannot give any other answer than this.' " [35]
Whereupon " the king answered ' Well, well; 'tis no matter. I think my
eyes are as as good as another's.' And then he looked round about the
House a pretty while to see if he could espie any of them." After that
long pause described by D'Ewes (" the dreadful silence," as one member
called it), Charles spoke again to the crowd of mute and sullen faces.
The complete failure of his scheme was now accomplished, and all its
possible consequences, all the suspicions and retaliations to which it had
laid him open, appear to have rushed upon his mind. " ' Well, since I
see all my birds are flown, I do expect from you that you shall send them
unto me as soon as they return hither. But, I assure you, on the word
of a king, I never did intend any force, but shall proceed against them in
a legal and fair way, for I never meant any other. And now, since I
see I cannot do what I came for, I think this is no unfit occasion to repeat
what I have said formerly, that whatsoever I have done in favour and to
the good of my subjects, I do mean to maintain it. I will trouble you no
more, but tell you I do expect, as soon as they come to the House, you
will send them to me; otherwise I must take my own course to find them.'
' After he had ended his speech,' continues D'Ewes, ' he went out of the
House in a more discontented and angry passion than he came in, going
out again between myself and the south end of the clerk's table, and the
Prince Elector after him.' Low mutterings of fierce discontent broke out
as he passed along, and ' many members cried out aloud, so as he might
hear them, *Privilege! Privilege!*' With those words, ominous of ill,
ringing in his ear, he repassed to his palace through the lane, again
formed, of his armed adherents, and amid audible shouts of as evil augury
from desperadoes disappointed of their prey. Eagerly in that lobby
had the word been awaited for, which must have been the prelude to a
terrible scene. ' For the design was,' pursues Sir Simonds D'Ewes,
writing at the close of his day's journal, ' to have taken out of our House
by force and violence the said Five Members, if we had refused to have
delivered them up peacefully and willingly; which, for the preservation
of the privileges of our House, we must have refused. And in the taking
of them away, they were to have set upon us all, if we had resisted, in a
hostile manner. It is very true that the plot was so contrived as that the
king should have withdrawn out of the House, and passed through the
lobby or little room next without it, before the massacre should have
begun, upon a watchword by him to have been given upon his passing
through them. But 'tis most likely that those ruffians, being about eighty
in number, who were gotten into the said lobby, being armed all of them
with swords, and some of them with pistols ready charged, were so
thirsty after innocent blood as they would scarcely have stayed the
watchword, if those members had been there; but would have begun

[35] Gardiner, *History of England*, x, 140.

their violence as soon as they had understood of our denial, to the hazard of the persons of the King and the Prince Elector, as well as of us. For, one of them understanding a little before the king came out that those five gentlemen were absent, " Zounds ! " said he, " they are gone ! and now we are never the better for our coming ! " ' " [36]

Its results. " The arrest of the Five Members," observes Mr. Forster, " was the final stage of the struggle against the Grand Remonstrance. It was a violent effort to reverse the eleven votes by which the victory was achieved, and to constitute the leaders of the minority to whom the highest offices in the state had meanwhile been given, masters of the House of Commons. When Charles and his armed attendants passed through the lobby of the House of Commons on January 4, the Civil War substantially had begun. Clarendon himself admits as much when he calls it ' the most visible introduction to all the misery that afterwards befel the king and kingdom.' " [37]

Question of the militia. The immediate question upon which the quarrel between king and parliament ultimately turned was the command of the militia. Ireland was in a state of rebellion, and a large army was absolutely necessary to reduce that kingdom to obedience. Justly persuaded of the utter insincerity of the king, and with the evidence before them of his intention to win back his authority at the sword's point, it would have been suicidal on the part of the commons to leave in the king's hands a military force which might, and probably would, have been used for their own overthrow. The bill for regulating the militia presented to the king in February 1642, by which persons to be nominated by the commons were to be entrusted with authority over the militia of the kingdom, was an undoubted encroachment upon the king's legal prerogative, unjustifiable perhaps as a permanent measure, but temporarily necessary in the crisis which the king himself had provoked. " When," says Clarendon, " it had been with much ado accepted, and first read, there were few men who imagined it would ever receive further countenance; but now there were very few who did not believe it to be a very necessary provision for the peace and safety of the kingdom, so great an impression had the late proceedings made upon them, that with little opposition it passed the commons, and was sent up to the lords." [38] The king's resolute refusal to pass the bill led by rapid steps to the Civil War.

The king did, however, make one last concession at this late hour, by assenting to the Clerical Disabilities Act on February 13, 1642.[39]

[36] Forster, *Arrest of the Five Members*, pp. 183 *et seq.*; Gardiner, *History of England*, x, 138 *et seq.*
[37] Forster, *Arrest of the Five Members*, p. 377. *Clarendon State Papers*, iii, p. lv. " The attempt to seize the Five Members was undoubtedly the real cause of the war "—Macaulay, " Essay on Hallam's *Constitutional History*," *Essays*, i, 188.
[38] Clarendon, *History*, i, 522; the Ordinance is printed in Gardiner, *Documents*, 245.
[39] *Supra*, p. 399.

This, and another accepted on the same day, is the last lawful statute until the Restoration. From 1642 to 1660 the traditional constitution ceased to work, and the considerable mass of ordinances [40] issued during the interval were necessarily treated as void at the Restoration. The constitutional period of the great contest between the king and the parliament may be said to have ended with the attempted arrest of the Five Members.

THE REVOLUTIONARY PERIOD, 1642–1660

The revolutionary period between 1642 and the restoration of Charles II in 1660—highly interesting and instructive to the student of political history, but complicated by numerous projects, counter-projects and fruitless negotiations—must necessarily be here passed over briefly. Within three years from the day (August 22, 1642) when Charles raised the royal standard at Nottingham, the Civil War was practically concluded. The crushing defeat of the king at Naseby (June 14, 1645) by the " New Model " army under Fairfax and Cromwell, followed by the rout of Montrose's forces at Philiphaugh (September 13, 1645), reduced Charles to the position of a fugitive in his own kingdom, and made a frank acceptance of the least onerous terms which, after a fair negotiation, he could obtain from the victorious parliament, the only means by which he could ever regain the exercise of his regal functions. In the political field, a long series of inconclusive negotiations showed what the king and parliament regarded as their respective war aims— the Nineteen Propositions of 1642, and the Propositions of Oxford (1643), Uxbridge (1645) and Newcastle (1646).[41] But the chance of a peaceful settlement was thrown away by the conduct of Charles himself, who, defeated in the field, betook himself to intrigue and double-dealing, in the hope that by fomenting discord between the Scots and the English, between the parliament and the army, and by dexterously playing off one against the other, he might ultimately regain the enjoyment of despotic power.

The religious difficulty. The great difficulty was the religious one. Laud and Charles had endeavoured to establish a rigid ceremonial uniformity; the parliament and the " Westminster Assembly " of divines (constituted June 12, 1643) had substituted an equally rigid uniformity of strict calvinistic dogma; the adoption of the " Solemn League and Covenant " [42] by the English parliament (September 25, 1643) had been exacted by the Scots as an indispensable preliminary to the aid which they rendered during the contest, and the maintenance of the presbyterian system in England was still with them an object of paramount importance. On the other hand, the victorious army of Fairfax and Cromwell, though

---

[40] Only in our own day have they been completely printed: C. H. Firth and R. S. Rait, *Acts and Ordinances of the Interregnum* (1911).

[41] All printed in Gardiner, *Documents*.

[42] Text in Gardiner, *Documents*, 267.

composed of men of widely differing views on religious matters, were agreed, as a body, in protesting against the refusal of toleration by both episcopalians and presbyterians alike, and in a determination to secure for themselves, and for all others, except the Roman Catholics, religious freedom of thought and of speech.

The Engagement, 1648. After nearly three years of intermittent negotiation, there seemed at last to be a possibility of an agreement with both army and parliament, on the basis of a presbyterian establishment for three years combined with a moderate measure of toleration. But the king, in the midst of the negotiations at Newport, entered into a secret treaty with the Scots, binding himself to maintain the presbyterian worship in England for three years and to suppress all other sects. In return, the Scots were to provide an army to replace him on the throne. This *renversement des alliances* had momentous consequences. The presbyterians grew accustomed to the idea that the *status quo* of 1641 was acceptable as a political settlement, and (coupled with the temporary imposition of their religious system) was preferable to the threatening supremacy of the army, whose religious " Independency " seemed to them little short of anarchy. In anticipation of the promised aid, the English royalists rose in various parts of the country, and on July 5, 1648, a Scottish royalist army entered England under the command of the Duke of Hamilton. The English army, under Cromwell and Fairfax, promptly took the field; and the total defeat of Hamilton's forces near Preston on August 17, followed by the surrender of Colchester, after a sharp siege, on the 27th of the same month, brought the second Civil War to a speedy close. Charles now returned to his old strategy of delusive negotiations with the parliament; but for the army, exasperated by the king's conduct and flushed with victory, the day of negotiation had passed.[43] To the fanatical belief of Charles in his divine right to govern the nation as to him seemed best, was at length opposed the equally fanatical belief of a bible-reading soldiery that it was their duty to see that " Charles Stuart, the capital and grand author of all the troubles and woes that the kingdom had endured, should be speedily brought to justice, for the treason, blood, and mischief of which he had been guilty."

Pride's Purge, December 6, 1648. By this time, the reins of government had passed alike from king, lords and commons, into the firm grasp of the leaders of the army. Royalist sympathisers had long ago left their

---

[43] It was Charles's ineradicable duplicity which caused all efforts at accommodation to fail. Even moderate men were oppressed with the feeling of utter distrust which his conduct inspired. In a curious pamphlet (preserved in the British Museum) entitled " Ten Necessary Quaeries touching the personall Treatie. Very useful and necessary to be considered. By James Taswell, a true lover of King, Parliament, Truth and Peace. London: Printed by R. I. for A. H. 1648," the working of this feeling is well brought out.

places in Parliament to serve in the king's army; the "Self-Denying Ordinance"[44] of 1645 placed an impassable barrier between the commons and the army; and after the "purging" of the House of Commons by Colonel Pride, the remnant, about fifty members in all, became a mere instrument for carrying out the will of the soldiery.

Trial and execution of the king. When the few peers who still continued to meet as the House of Lords refused to concur in bringing the king to trial, the truncated Lower House had assumed supreme authority by voting (January 4) that the people being, after God, the source of all legitimate power, the sovereign power in England resided in the commons who had been elected by and represented the people. Two days later, the commons, of their own sole authority, erected a High Court of Justice, which proceeded to arraign, try, convict and sentence the king.[45] The execution of the sentence took place on January 30, 1649.

Changes effected. Within a few weeks after the decapitation of the king, the House of Lords was voted "useless and dangerous," the kingship abolished as "unnecessary, burthensome, and dangerous," and the old constitutional form of government gave place to the Commonwealth of England.[46] In January 1649, the army officers had put forward a concrete proposal for a new constitution in a document called "The Agreement of the People."[47] This included a thorough redistribution of seats in the "Representative" (the new name for parliament), the compilation of voters' lists and biennial elections. The Representative was to appoint and control the Council of State, but certain matters were removed from its competence. There was naturally great reluctance to adopt a completely new and prefabricated constitution. At first, while the "Rump" House of Commons continued to exercise the functions of a parliament, the executive power was vested in a Council of State, consisting of forty-one persons, partly parliamentary, partly military. But the genius of Cromwell as a born "ruler of men," not less than the brilliant series of his military victories, culminating in the "crowning mercy" of Worcester (1651), soon caused the real executive power to be concentrated in his hands.

The Rump entertained a high esteem for itself, in spite of the derision with which the army treated it, and proposed to fill the hundreds of empty benches in the House by what amounted to co-opting new members. In exasperation, Cromwell ordered the removal of the Speaker from his chair, took away the mace ("that bauble"), and expelled the members (1653). The last link with legality had snapped—nearly, but not quite. John Bradshaw immediately reminded Cromwell of the Act of 16 Car. 1,

---

[44] Gardiner, *Documents*, 287.
[45] Gardiner, *Documents*, 357-358, 371-380.
[46] *Ibid.*, 384-388.
[47] *Ibid.*, 354-371. On this and several other documents of the same name, see J. W. Gough, "Agreements of the People," *History*, xv, 334.

c. 7, which provided that the Long Parliament should not be dissolved without its own consent.[48]   Those who had thought of the war as a war between traditional parliamentarism and a novel royal absolutism, took comfort in the thought, and years later the shadow of the ghost of the Long Parliament was yet to work constitutional wonders.[49]

Neither king, lords nor commons remained.   To fill the void, a caucus of officers and Congregational ministers selected a hundred and forty God-fearing men whose sessions acquired the nickname of " Barebones' Parliament."   After a day's debate they abolished chancery.   A committee was to reduce English law " to the bigness of a pocket-book, as it is . . . in New England."   Sectarian feuds soon frustrated its endeavours, until it was tricked into dissolving itself.

Instrument of Government.   By the close of the year 1653 a more permanent solution was tried in the " Instrument of Government," [50] which in effect restored the substance of a strictly limited monarchy under the style of " Protector," and an attenuated unicameral parliament for England, Scotland and Ireland limited by a powerful permanent Council, by a high property qualification for voters, and by the reservation in the Instrument of certain matters which parliament could not touch. Nor could ordinary revenue be withheld.   There can be no doubt that Cromwell aimed at establishing a form of government in which the nation would be ruled by the will of its elected representatives in parliament, and under which all men (with the considerable exception of Catholics and Anglicans) should possess the great boon of religious freedom.   But in practice he failed to carry out his ideal.   Toleration was only partially conceded; and " the government, though in form a republic, was in truth a despotism, moderated only by the wisdom, the sobriety, and the magnanimity of the despot." [51]   Justice between man and man seems to have been administered as fairly as, if not more fairly than, under the monarchy, but between the government and the subject arbitrary rule prevailed.   After the royalist rising at Salisbury (March 1655), when the judges on circuit were seized and even threatened with hanging, the country was mapped out into military districts, under the command

---

[48] *Supra*, p. 399.   On the expulsion of the Long Parliament, see the articles by C. H. Firth in the *English Historical Review*, viii, 526 and in *History*, ii, 129, 193.

[49] It must be remembered, however, that besides the Act to which Bradshaw referred, there was also the common-law rule that a parliament would be automatically dissolved by the demise of the crown.

[50] Gardiner, *Documents*, 405.   For the constitutional history of this period, see M. A. Thomson, *Constitutional History of England* (1938), iv, 32–49; C. H. Firth, *Oliver Cromwell*, c, xvi and his *House of Lords during the Civil War*, c, viii; A. F. Pollard, *Factors in Modern History*, c, ix; G. P. Gooch, *English Democratic Ideas in the Seventeenth Century*, and E. Jenks, *Constitutional Experiments of the Commonwealth.*   The political history is told at length by S. R. Gardiner, *Commonwealth and Protectorate*, continued by C. H. Firth, *Last Years of the Protectorate.*   Keith Feiling, *The Tory Party*, is valuable especially since its emphasis is on biographical and family history; to contemporaries the age seemed a series of personal problems, loosely linked up with national politics.

[51] Macaulay, *History*, i, 118.

of major-generals, by whom every insurrectionary movement was immediately suppressed and punished.

Cromwell's parliaments.   Ever since the Agreement of the People
(January 1649), the army leaders had been interested in electoral reform,
but experience soon taught them that they had nothing to hope for from
a freely elected parliament.   Two parliaments met under the Instrument
of Government; both were " purged," and both prepared new constitutions—which they had no right to do according to the Instrument.   The
device of constitutional limitations in a written document was one which
ran counter to everything which the public associated with the traditional
institution.   Cromwell had as much trouble with parliaments as had
Charles I—and treated them a good deal more roughly.   More adjustments were finally made by consent, and these showed unmistakably
a return to the essentials of the traditional constitution.   The Protectorate
was made more nearly like the old monarchy (although Cromwell refused
his consent to that clause in the " Humble Petition and Advice " [52]
which asked him to take the title of king), and a sort of House of Lords
was set up under the style of the " Other House."

All these institutions were merely shadows.   The Protector was not
a king, the Other House was not the heir of the ancient House of Lords
and the commons with their paper limitations and fancy franchise were
not the historic commons of England.   The death of Cromwell (September 3, 1658) removed the giant whose broad shoulders alone had sustained
the unstable edifice of the three kingdoms.

Steps towards the Restoration.   The army hoped for some good by
restoring the Rump, only to expel it again.   Then a Scottish army under
Monk made its contribution by restoring not merely the Rump but all
those who had been ejected by Pride's purge; the Long Parliament was
back again, with its presbyterian majority.   There were still a number of
projected constitutions under discussion (the actual authority at the
moment was a " Committee of Safety ").   The distant prospect of " Conservators " and even of a " Senate," however, could not distract the
nation from the solid fact that its feet were once more set in the ancient
ways now that a real parliament (or the remnants of one) had again
assembled.   Under General Monk's guidance, the Long Parliament
passed an Act recognising that the House of Lords was a part of parliament, recommending the election, according to the ancient methods, of
a convention for England (Scotland and Ireland being now left to their
own devices), and finally enacting its own dissolution.   This convention,
duly elected in all respects like a parliament save for the royal writ, accepted
the king's Declaration at Breda, and ordered the proclamation of Charles
II.[53]

[52] Gardiner, *Documents*, 447 *et seq.*   *Cf. supra*, p. 252.
[53] For an outline of the complicated process leading to the Restoration see D. Ogg, *Charles II*,
   i, 1–34.

Results of the Revolutionary Period

But although the legal constitution had been suspended during this period, and revived again at the accession of Charles II, the Great Rebellion could not fail to produce certain permanent political and constitutional results.[54] These may be summed up under the following heads:

(1) Although the cause of monarchy was gained, that of absolute monarchy was lost. There was indeed a vast amount of talk during the next thirty years ostentatiously supporting absolutist dogmas, and an attempt by James II to put them into practice, but when the crisis came, even non-resisters resisted, as they struck the final balance between the lessons of history and the abstractions of political science. Henceforth royalists and revolutionists alike regarded the close union and mutual interdependence of kings and parliaments as necessary for the good government of the country.

(2) The predominant influence of the House of Commons in the government of the nation was permanently established. The inability of the commons to restrain the army almost proved fatal, and a succession of pretentious and impotent assemblies, which quickly earned the contemptuous nicknames which still cling to them, might have done irreparable harm.[55] In the end it was realised that there was real significance in the fact that the army itself dared not face a regularly elected House. Monk's call for a " free parliament " was decisive—as was William of Orange's later. In that institution the country had found the sovereign test. This necessarily meant that the power and prestige of the House of Commons has ever since been growing more and more marked and decisive. The overthrow of the crown and the House of Lords had been so violent and complete, that even the unqualified restoration of their rights and dignity failed to reinstate them in their ancient ascendancy. The royalist House of Commons of Charles II, in its relations to the crown and the administration of the country, inherited, defended, and transmitted to its successors the conquests of the Long Parliament.

(3) The position of the national church after the restoration was no longer precisely the same as before the Rebellion. Down to the time of the Commonwealth the church had never ceased, in legal theory and to a great extent in actual fact, to be co-extensive with the nation, and the various changes in thought and practice which were advocated during the reign of Elizabeth I and onwards were regarded by their proponents as movements within the church. The developments of the interregnum

---

[54] " Of course, in seeming, Cromwell's work died with him; his dynasty was rejected, his republic cast aside; but the spirit which culminated in him never sank again, never ceased to be a potent, though often a latent and volcanic, force in the country. Charles II said that he would never go again on his travels, for anything or anybody; and he well knew that though the men whom he met at Worcester might be dead, still the spirit which warmed them was alive and young in others "—Bagehot, *English Constitution*, p. 282.

[55] John Milton, in a draft for a new constitution in 1660, proposed to have no parliament on the ground that it would save a lot of trouble.

showed that this theory was no longer tenable; toleration had been denied to " prelacy," and the sects denied the fundamentals of Anglicanism. The Restoration did not avail to cure this schism, and it was inevitable that the future should present the new problem of nonconformity. At the moment of its restoration by Charles II and his parliament it was patently the church not of the whole nation, but of a majority only. Thenceforward, as the other religious communities have gradually attained first to toleration and then to civil equality with the members of the national church, the ecclesiastical constitution, whilst still in theory national, has gradually come to be regarded not so much as the national church (which legally it still continues to be), but as the " Established " Church, using the word " established " in its modern signification, as denoting a religious body standing in a special relation to the state in contradistinction from all other religious bodies.

(4) Another important result of the revolutionary crisis through which the nation had passed was the development of an intense national antipathy to a standing army. This is all the more remarkable since the army's achievements had been so extraordinary, and (combined with the brilliant exploits of the navy), had raised England to an international position which all parties appreciated highly. On this occasion at least it is clear that conspicuous success in external affairs did not suffice to win public approval for the régime. Cromwell's army in fact possessed not only all the fundamental military virtues, but also the unusual qualities of genuine and ardent piety, which often took the form of extravagant sectarism. Impelled by a deep sense of its divine mission, and justified by its good intentions, the army tyrannised over the country for the country's good.

(5) It was indeed the psychological results of the nation's experience which were the most important. There was the dangerous heritage of fear, which (in the coming reign) magnified trivial incidents so much that parliament rushed into repressive legislation which bred two centuries of ill-feeling. The country's determination not to have another civil war was fortunately greatly helped by Charles' equal determination not to go on his travels again (it will be noted, however, that Clarendon and James II did " travel " again). Another heritage was the creation of incipient political parties. The close connection of political differences with the more fundamental religious differences brought the important consequence that a man's political attitude extended far beyond the matters of the moment, and, like his religion, became a general and permanent outlook upon affairs. Thus the ordinary man's political differences came to be systematised into political philosophies. It is, of course, true that it was only very slowly that political divisions became independent of religious divisions, and became organised independently of the corresponding religious bodies; nevertheless, there is no denying that the tragic divisions of the nation by the Civil War were perpetuated after the Restoration in the milder form of political parties. Furthermore,

the great achievement of 1660 had been to effect a compromise between two great parties of moderate opinion each of which rejected its extremists. The Civil War was a heavy price to pay for this first lesson in self-government, but the lesson was thoroughly learnt and faithfully applied in 1688. Politics steadily became less violent. For another fifty years or more statesmen were to be impeached, but Strafford was the last minister of the crown to suffer on the scaffold. And finally, the settlement reached constituted a clear answer to the political problem which had set the whole unhappy train of events in motion. In the issue between prerogative and law, it was law which won, and its victory was gained partly in battle against the Royalists, and partly in the minds of large numbers of ordinary citizens who resented the proceedings of the army and the sectaries. The discredit of extremists on both sides thus left the nation with the conviction, based upon experience, that political problems could best be dealt with within the framework of institutions and legal principles which history had made familiar. Upon that large measure of common ground the two political parties could compete without going to war, and in moments of supreme crisis could combine (as in 1660 and 1688) for the maintenance of the constitution.

CHAPTER 15

THE LATER STUART PERIOD
FROM THE RESTORATION TO THE REVOLUTION

THE Restoration was much more than the recall of a Stuart to the throne of his fathers; it was the restoration also of parliamentary government and of the Anglican ecclesiastical system. The whole operation was conducted through carefully devised forms which emphasised the legitimacy of these institutions and described their restoration as a return to paths of strict constitutional legality. The proclamation (May 8) issued by the Convention announced that the crown had descended immediately upon the death of Charles I to his son; consequently the year 1660 fell within the twelfth year of the reign of Charles II.

CHARLES II

A number of bills passed by the Convention Parliament received the royal assent. One of them dissolved the Long Parliament and declared that the Convention was a parliament and others dealt with the many technicalities of restoration. These naturally were numerous and knotty since it was necessary to regard as invalid all legislation which had not received the assent of king, lords and commons. At the same time, it was well understood that eighteen years of history could not be simply ignored. More difficult problems were the question of land-titles (and the settlement was surprisingly harsh upon royalists who had been ruined in the cause), and the punishment of the regicides. The most momentous of the Convention's acts was the abolition of tenure by knight's service.[1]

Abolition of Military Tenures. During the Commonwealth the vexatious emoluments derived from the military tenures had been suspended, and at the Restoration the feeling was unanimous in favour of abolishing those intolerable feudal burdens which had so long survived their original *raison d'être*. By the 12 Car. 2, c. 24, it was enacted that the Court of Wards and Liveries, and all wardships, liveries, primer seisins, and ousterlemains, values and forfeitures of marriages, by reason of any tenure of the king's majesty, or of any other, by knight's service, and all other gifts, grants, or charges incident or arising therefrom, be totally taken away, from February 24, [1646] (the date of the intermission of the Court of Wards by the Long Parliament); and that all fines for alienation, tenures by homage, knight's service, and escuage, and also aids for marrying the king's daughter, or knighting his son, and all tenures of the king *in capite*, be likewise taken

---

[1] *Supra*, pp. 37–38.

away; and that all sorts of tenures, held of the king or others, be turned into free and common socage, save only tenures in frankalmoign, copyholds, and the honorary services of grand serjeanty.[2] By the same statute the rights of purveyance and pre-emption were also finally abolished, with the result that the expenses of the royal household were considerably increased. The immediate and direct benefits conferred by this Act constituted a grateful boon to the landowners of the kingdom, and, so far as regards the abolition of purveyance, to the nation at large; indirectly, too, the whole nation gained by the simplification of tenure. In consideration of the surrender of these feudal privileges by the crown, the parliament resolved to make up the royal revenue to the annual sum of £1,200,000. As the landed gentry were the great gainers by the surrender, they ought, in justice, to have been subjected to some compensatory tax: and a proposal was made that a permanent tax should be laid on lands held in chivalry, which, as distinguished from those held in socage, had been alone liable to the feudal burdens.[3] But being powerful in parliament, the landowners succeeded, though only by the small majority of two, in substituting an hereditary excise on beer and some other liquors, thus transferring their own particular burden to the community at large.[4]

CAVALIER PARLIAMENT, 1661–1679

The Convention Parliament was dissolved in December, and writs issued for a new election. The new parliament—variously called the " Cavalier," the " Pensionary," or the " Long Parliament of the Restoration," which lasted from May 8, 1661, to January 24, 1679—was, during the first few years of its existence, " more zealous for royalty than the king, more zealous for episcopacy than the bishops." [5] As the terror from the late Civil War abated it gradually threw off its exuberant loyalty, and though its leaders were corrupt, they were too much alive to their own interests ever to sacrifice any of the powers of parliament. But the devoted attachment to the established church, and the hatred of sectaries, which distinguished its earlier sessions, continued unabated to the last.

Treason Act, 1661. The first act of the new parliament was to extend the scope of treason during the life-time of Charles II only, and to impose forfeiture upon any who should assert that the oft-dissolved Long Parliament was still in being—thus imposing a brusque and inelegant solution to an entertaining constitutional conundrum.[6] The disabilities of bishops

[2] The Act is printed in C. Grant Robertson's *Select Statutes, Cases and Documents of English Constitutional History*, 1660–1832, p. 11.

[3] On behalf of the landowners it could be urged that land bore the brunt of taxation and that finance and commerce largely escaped. Purveyance was unconnected with land-ownership.

[4] The excise was not a newly invented tax, having been originally imposed by the Long Parliament in 1643.

[5] Macaulay, *History*, i, 156.

[6] 13 Car. 2, st. 1, c. 1.

were next removed, and they forthwith resumed their seats in the House of Lords.[7]

Act Against Tumultuous Petitioning, 1661. By the 13 Car. 2, st. 1, c. 5, it was enacted that no petition to the king or either House of Parliament for alteration of matters established by law in church or state (unless the contents thereof had been previously approved in the country by three justices of the peace or the grand jury of the county, and in London by the lord mayor, aldermen and common council), should be signed by more than twenty, or delivered by more than ten, persons, under penalty in either case of £100 fine and three months' imprisonment.[8]

Corporation Act, 1661. By a series of Acts extending over several years, increasing restrictions were imposed on religious dissent. A number of incidents and plots, combined with the prevailing nervousness, was responsible for the fear of a rebellion by Cromwell's disbanded, but still formidable, soldiers. By the " Act for the well-governing and regulating of Corporations " (13 Car. 2, st. 2, c. 1) a religious test was combined with a political test. All corporate magistrates and office-bearers were obliged to take " the Sacrament of the Lord's Supper, according to the rites of the Church of England," to renounce the Solemn League and Covenant, and to swear that they believed it unlawful, on any pretence whatever, to take arms against the king, and that they abhorred the " traitorous position " of bearing arms by his authority against his person or his officers. " These provisions," remarks Hallam, "struck at the heart of the presbyterian party, whose strength lay in the little oligarchies of corporate towns, which directly or indirectly returned to parliament a very large proportion of its members." [9] But they equally affected all other nonconformists, and established an inequality of civil rights between churchmen and dissenters which continued down to recent times. The political test contained in the corporation oath of *non-resistance*, having been practically renounced at the Revolution, was abolished in 1718, shortly after the accession of the House of Hanover, by the " Act for quieting and establishing corporations" (5 Geo. 1, c. 6, s. 2). The religious test was not repealed till the reign of George IV.[10]

In the declaration issued by Charles II from Breda (April 14, 1660), he had stated the principle that no man should be called in question for differences of religious opinion not disturbing the peace of the kingdom.[11] But the great majority of the English people were not yet prepared to concede toleration; and by the Act of Uniformity all dissenters from the established church, protestant and Roman Catholic alike, were subjected to the bonds of a rigid conformity.

---

[7] 13 Car. 2, st. 1, c. 2, repealing 16 Car. 1, c. 27. The clergy lost their right of voting separate clerical taxes in 1664; *supra*, pp. 142–143.
[8] Robertson, *Documents*, 26; *infra*, p. 629.
[9] Hallam, *Constitutional History*, 330.
[10] 9 Geo. 4, c. 17 (1828); *infra*, p. 657.   [11] Gardiner, *Documents*, 466.

Act of Uniformity, 1662. The provisions of this celebrated statute (14 Car. 2, c. 4) may be divided into two classes: (1) Clauses which continue in force at the present day, *viz.*, those which legalise the Book of Common Prayer as then recently revised in convocation, with a direction for its use in every parish church and other places of public worship; and which require episcopal ordination of all persons holding ecclesiastical preferment, together with a declaration from all such persons of unfeigned assent and consent to the contents of the Book of Common Prayer. (2) Certain persecuting clauses directed against dissenters, which have since been repealed.[12]

The 14th section of the Act of Charles II declared " that no person . . . shall presume to consecrate and administer the holy sacrament of the Lord's Supper," until he should be ordained priest by episcopal ordination, under the penalty of £100 for such offence. This penalty was repealed in 1689 by the Toleration Act of William and Mary.[13]

By the 8th section not only all persons in holy orders, but all schoolmasters and persons instructing youth were required to subscribe a declaration of non-resistance, and that they would conform to the liturgy of the Church of England as by law established. Schoolmasters and private tutors were also subjected to the penalty of three months' imprisonment if they should present to exercise their calling without previous licence from the bishop of the diocese. That part of the declaration which related to non-resistance was abolished at the Revolution by statute 1 William & Mary, stat. 1, c. 8; but the licence of private tutors, though in later times practically obsolete, was not repealed till 1846 by the 9 & 10 Vict. c. 59.[14] The immediate result of the new Act of Uniformity was to eject from the established church about 2,000 ministers (for the most part non-episcopally ordained), who further recruited the ranks of protestant nonconformists.

Quakers' Act, 1662. An absurd adventure dignified by the name of Venner's Revolt frightened parliament into enacting a merciless statute, commonly called the Quakers' Act; it was enforced with rigour, large numbers of that body were imprisoned, and many died as a result of their harsh treatment.[15]

Conventicle Act, 1664. In 1663 a much more extensive plot in Yorkshire led to the mustering of 200 armed dissidents. The excitement over this affair produced the monstrous Conventicle Act (16 Car. 2, c. 4) whereby every person above sixteen years of age present at a conventicle (defined as any meeting for religious worship at which five persons were present besides the household) was subjected to the penalty of three months'

---

[12] 7 & 8 Vict. c. 102; 9 & 10 Vict. c. 59; 28 & 29 Vict. c. 122.
[13] 1 Will. & Mary, st. 1, c. 18. Robertson, 126. Tests in the older universities were not abolished until 1871.
[14] The Act of Uniformity is printed in Robertson's *Documents*, 37.
[15] 14 Car. 2, c. 1; Holdsworth, *History of English Law*, vi, 198; D. Ogg, *Charles II*, i, 208–210.

imprisonment for the first offence, of six for the second, and for the third to seven years' transportation. Two justices of the peace (or the chief magistrate if the offence is committed in a corporation where there are not two justices) were empowered to convict for the first and second offences, but transportation for the third offence could only be awarded on conviction by a jury. Return before the expiration of the term of banishment, or escape after conviction, was made felony punishable with death.[16]

Five-Mile Act, 1665. This enactment was followed in the next session by " An Act for restraining nonconformists from inhabiting in corporations " (17 Car. 2, c. 2). By this " Five-Mile Act," as it is usually termed, (1) a new test oath of non-resistance was imposed upon the clergy; (2) every nonconformist minister was prohibited, under the penalty of £40 for each offence, from coming within five miles of any corporate town; or of any parish, town, or place wherein he had been parson, vicar, curate, stipendiary, or lecturer, or had taken upon him to preach in unlawful assembly or conventicle; and (3) all nonconformists, whether lay or clerical, were restrained from teaching in any public or private school under the penalty of £40 fine and six months' imprisonment.

The provisions of these merciless statutes were not allowed to remain a dead letter. The religious persecution is said to have been far more severe than it had ever been at any period of the Commonwealth, and more widely extended than under Charles I.[17] No less than 8,000 Protestants are said to have been imprisoned during this reign, in addition to a large number of Roman Catholics. Of 1,500 Quakers who were confined, 350 died in prison.[18]

In 1660 by the first Declaration of Indulgence,[19] in 1661 at the Savoy Conference, in 1669 under the Cabal Ministry, and again in 1674, through the exertions of Tillotson and Stillingfleet, attempts were indeed made to bring about a reconciliation between the church and the protestant nonconformists; but the real difficulty of effecting a compromise and the unyielding temper of both parties, caused every effort at comprehension to fail.

The legislation so far considered was directed against nonconforming puritans. The second half of the reign shows parliament preoccupied with the catholic problem—once again, a religious question which was

[16] The Conventicle Act was limited in duration to three years, and expired in 1667. In 1670 it was renewed, with some mitigation of penalties, but with an extraordinary proviso, which reversed the established legal principle of construing penal acts: That all clauses in the Act " shall be construed most largely and beneficially for suppressing of conventicles, and for the justification and encouragement of all persons to be employed in the execution thereof "—22 Car. 2, c. 1; Robertson, 73.

[17] Hallam, *Constitutional History*, ii, 353.

[18] Neal, *History of the Puritans*, v, 17; Delaune, *Plea for Nonconformists*; Short's *History*, 559.

[19] In this document the king proposed an amalgamation of anglican and presbyterian institutions and a relaxation of divers statutory requirements, with an express renewal of his Declaration at Breda. In form, it was a statement of the king's intention to ask parliament for legislation to that effect.

inextricably connected with politics and the safety of the country in the minds of contemporaries.

Declaration of Indulgence, 1672. The famous Test Act of 1673 was provoked by a second " Declaration of Indulgence," recently issued by the king in virtue of his royal supremacy in ecclesiastical matters, suspending the laws against both recusants and nonconformists (1672). This declaration, though apparently a concession to the protestant dissenters, was really intended as a step towards the re-establishment of the Roman Catholic religion, in which the Duke of York was an avowed, Charles an unavowed, believer.

Secret Treaty of Dover, 1670. By this treaty the king, his brother, and Louis XIV of France, had entered into a royal conspiracy against the national church and civil liberties of England. The precise terms of this treaty were not then indeed authentically known, " but there can be no doubt," says Hallam, " that those who from this time displayed an insuperable jealousy of one brother, and a determined enmity to the other, had proofs enough for moral conviction of their deep conspiracy with France against religion and liberty. This suspicion is implied in all the conduct of that parliamentary opposition, and is the apology of much that seems violence and faction, especially in the business of the popish plot and the bill of exclusion." The secret Treaty of Dover " may be reckoned the first act of a drama which ended in the Revolution." [20] The course of the negotiations is a striking example of the absolute control still claimed by the crown in foreign affairs. Not only parliament, but the Privy Council also, was kept in ignorance. Indeed, of the king's five principal ministers (commonly referred to as the " Cabal ") only two had knowledge of the true nature of the engagement; a bogus treaty in different terms was put through for the benefit of the other three.

Suspending Power Attacked. The king's Declaration of Indulgence united in opposition to it not only the zealous churchmen, who were disgusted at the favour shown to both papists and dissenters, but also the dissenters themselves,[21] whose hatred of popery outweighed their gratification at their own toleration, as well as all lovers of liberty and law, who could not but regard the king's pretensions, in explicit terms, to suspend a body of statutes, and his command to magistrates not to put them in execution, as an assertion of despotic power capable of most dangerous extension. The House of Commons voted " that penal statutes in matters ecclesiastical cannot be suspended but by Act of Parliament," and addressed the king to recall his declaration. In his answer the king lamented that the

---

[20] Hallam, *Constitutional History*, ii, 386; the principal clauses are given by David Ogg, *Charles II*, i, 344 *et seq.*

[21] After a period of hesitation during which the ultimate object of the step was imperfectly understood. For the application of the Declaration, *cf.* David Ogg, *Charles II*, i, 355. For the suspending power, see *supra*, p. 190; *infra*, p. 442.

commons should question his ecclesiastical power, which had never, he said, been done before. To which they replied " we humbly conceive your Majesty hath been very much misinformed; since no such power was ever claimed or exercised by any your predecessors; and, if it should be admitted, might tend to the interrupting of the free course of the laws, and altering of the legislative power, which hath always been acknowledged to reside in your Majesty and your two Houses of Parliament." [22] At length the king was obliged to give way, and cancelled the declaration.

Test Act, 1673. But the commons, not satisfied with this concession, extorted his assent to the Test Act, 25 Car. 2, c. 2, as a measure of security against popish counsellors and officials. The Act, however, was so framed as to affect with equal disqualification nearly all classes of protestant dissenters as well as Roman Catholics. It provided that all persons holding any office or place of trust, civil or military, or admitted of the king's or the Duke of York's household, should publicly receive the Sacrament according to the rites of the Church of England, and also take the oath of supremacy, and subscribe a declaration against transubstantiation. The immediate effect of the Act was to compel Lord Clifford to resign his office of treasurer, and the Duke of York to quit the post of lord high admiral.

In return for the support given by the dissenters to the Test Act, a bill was passed, after some debate, by the House of Commons, giving a considerable amount of relief to protestant sectaries; but it was delayed in the Lords' House, who introduced several amendments, and a sudden prorogation caused it to be dropped.

Parliamentary Test Act, 1678. Five years later, in 1678, a parliamentary test was imposed which, for the first time, effectively excluded Roman Catholics from both Houses of Parliament. This was mainly due to the alarm excited in the nation by the discovery of the supposed popish plot.[23] By the " Act for the more effectual preserving the king's person and government, by disabling papists from sitting in either House of Parliament " (30 Car. 2, st. 2, c. 1), it was provided that no peer, or member of the House of Commons, should sit or vote without taking the oaths of allegiance and supremacy, and a declaration repudiating the doctrine of transubstantiation, the adoration of the Virgin, and the sacrifice of the mass.[24] Peers and members offending were to be deemed and judged popish recusants convict, and forfeit £500, besides suffering numerous disabilities. While the bill was in the Lords' House the Duke of York

---

[22] *Parliamentary History*, iv, 526, 551.

[23] As to this, see David Ogg, *Charles II*, ii, 559–584; Sir John Pollock, *The Popish Plot*.

[24] This declaration was later required of the king himself in consequence of the Bill of Rights: *infra*, p. 454.

moved that an exception might be admitted in his favour, and this was agreed to in the commons but only by a majority of two.[25]

Appropriation of Supplies. In the session of 1665 the commons took advantage of the necessity under which the king lay, of asking for extraordinarily large grants for the prosecution of the Dutch war, to establish the important principle of appropriating the supplies to specific purposes. Sir George Downing, one of the tellers of the exchequer, introduced into the Subsidy Bill granting the sum of £1,250,000 for the war with Holland a proviso that all moneys raised by virtue of that Act should be solely applicable to the service of the war, and should not be issued out of the exchequer except by order or warrant mentioning that they were payable for such service (17 Car. 2, c. 1). Despite the furious opposition of Clarendon, who stigmatised the proviso as derogatory to the honour of the crown, Charles himself insisted upon this restraint on the executive power, having been persuaded that the bankers would be more easily induced to advance the money, in anticipation of the revenue, upon this better security for speedy repayment. The principle of appropriating the supplies was by no means a novelty in the Constitution, but it had only been put into practice occasionally and at long intervals.[26] The complete authority exercised by the commons, during the late Civil War and the Commonwealth, over the whole receipts and expenditure of the national treasury had accustomed the House to regulate the disbursement of the sums which they granted; the advantage to the nation from their control of its finances was self-evident; and from the date of the Appropriation Act of Charles II it became " an undisputed principle, recognised by frequent and at length constant practice," that " supplies granted by parliament are only to be expended for particular objects specified by itself." [27] The principle of appropriation was not, however, carried into full effect till after the Revolution. But from the reign of William III it has been the invariable usage to insert a clause in the annual Appropriation Act prohibiting under severe penalties, as well the lords of the treasury from issuing, as the officers of the exchequer from obeying, any warrant for the expenditure of money in the national exchequer upon any other service than that to which it has been specifically appropriated. The permanent establishment of the principle and practice of appropriation " has given the House of Commons," remarks Hallam, " so effectual a control over the executive power, or, more truly speaking, has rendered it so much a participator in that power, that no administration

---

[25] Robertson, *Documents*, 86. From the time of Elizabeth the oath of supremacy had been exacted from members of the House of Commons, but not from the lords (*supra*, p. 294). Apparently it was felt to be insufficient. Roman Catholic lords were now for the first time excluded from their seats; and until the reign of George IV, 1829 (10 Geo. 4, c. 7), both Houses were effectually closed to the members of that religion.

[26] *Supra*, p. 169.

[27] Hallam, *Constitutional History*, ii, 357.

can possibly subsist without its concurrence, nor can the session of parliament be intermitted for an entire year, without leaving both the naval and military force of the kingdom unprovided for." [28]

Commission of Public Accounts. In the session of 1666, the demand for large additional supplies for the second Dutch war, coupled with the indifferent success which had attended the military operations, provoked suspicions of the dishonest appropriation of the money previously voted. The commons appointed a committee to inspect the accounts of the officers of the navy, ordnance, and stores, and subsequently sent up a bill appointing commissioners to inspect the public accounts, with full powers to inquire and report as to such persons as they should find to have broken their trust. While this measure was impending the king prorogued parliament, but promised to issue a royal commission for the examination of the accounts. In the following session, 1667 (Lord Clarendon having fallen in the interval, and the public being greatly perturbed by the appearance of a Dutch fleet in the Medway), the commons reintroduced their bill, which passed as " An Act for taking the accounts of the several sums therein mentioned." [29] Commissioners (who were to report from time to time to the king and both Houses of Parliament) were nominated in the Act and invested with most extensive powers, not only for auditing the public accounts, but for investigating frauds in the expenditure of money, and employment of stores. They were authorised to examine upon oath, to summon inquests, to commit to prison without bail all persons disobeying their orders, and to determine finally on the charge and discharge of all accounts; and upon a certificate of their judgment the barons of the exchequer were directed to issue process for recovering money to the king's use, as if there had been an immediate judgment of their own court.[30] The passing of this statute marked a further step in that transfer of the control of the executive administration from the crown to the House of Commons, which, throughout the long existence of the " Pensionary " Parliament of Charles II, was quietly but steadily proceeding.

The National Debt. The commencement of the National Debt dates from the reign of Charles II. During the Civil War large sums of money were deposited, for safe custody, with some of the most eminent London goldsmiths, who, after the Restoration, continued to act in their new capacity as bankers, and began to advance money to the national exchequer on the security of an assignment of some branch of the public revenue.

Stop of the Exchequer. Down to 1672 these loans were always punctually repaid; but in that year, at the outbreak of the third Dutch war, Charles II

[28] *Constitutional History*, iii, 117.
[29] 19 & 20 Car. 2, c. 1.
[30] Hallam, *Constitutional History*, ii, 360.

was persuaded by the Cabal administration to issue a proclamation deferring the payment of any money out of the exchequer due upon certain types of existing security, but promising, instead, to add the interest then due to the capital and to allow 6 per cent. interest on this new stock. By this proceeding the king acquired the disposal of about £1,300,000. Interest was paid down to the year 1683, when even this was stopped : and nothing was done for the public creditor until 1699, when an Act was passed (which was not to take effect till December 25, 1705) charging the excise with payment, from the latter date, of 3 per cent. interest on the principal sum of £1,328,526, redeemable on payment of a moiety, but no compensation was made for the loss of twenty-two years' arrears of interest.[31]

Bank of England Established, 1694. Five years previously, in 1694, the sum of £1,200,000 at 8 per cent. interest had been borrowed by the government from a body of merchants, who, in return, received the privilege of incorporation, by royal charter, as " The Governor and Company of the Bank of England." The charter was originally granted for only eleven years certain, parliament reserving the right to redeem the debt at any time after 1705, upon giving a year's notice : and with the redemption of the debt the charter was to expire. But far from paying off old debts, new loans were from time to time raised by the government in a similar manner, and the bank charter has been prolonged by several renewals.

Besides the economic and financial aspects of the crisis which the stop of the exchequer revealed, there were also important consequences in constitutional law, which were only fully settled some years later. Between 1690 and 1700 a long and tedious series of proceedings—the *Bankers' Case*—laid the foundations of the later doctrine that a subject has a remedy by petition of right for breach of contract by the crown.[32]

Original Civil Jurisdiction of the Lords. A singular proof of the influence of the commons under Charles II is furnished by the result of the famous controversy between the two Houses as to the original civil jurisdiction of the lords in the case of *Skinner* v. *The East India Company* (1666–1669). The lords entertained, upon reference by the crown, a petition of Skinner against the Company, overruled the defendant's plea to the jurisdiction, and condemned them to pay the plaintiff £5,000. In support of their jurisdiction the lords could show precedents from the Middle Ages (but not from the Tudor period) and from the reign of Charles I, together with learned arguments by such high authorities as Selden and Prynne. The Company, however, presented a complaint

---

[31] 12 & 13 Will. 3, c. 12, § xv. The principal was never repaid and was ultimately in 1716 incorporated in the general fund then established (3 Geo. 1, c. 7). For the financial crisis which caused the closing of the exchequer, see Shaw, " The Beginnings of the National Debt," in *Historical Essays of Owens College*, Manchester (1907); the effects of the " stop " have been greatly exaggerated. See R. D. Richards, " The Stop of the Exchequer," *Economic Journal* (Economic History Supplement), ii, 45.

[32] 14 St.Tr. 1; Denman's edition of Broom's *Constitutional Law*, 225; Holdsworth, *History of English Law*, ix, 32–39.

to the House of Commons. The commons resolved that the lords, in taking cognisance of an original complaint, and that relievable in the ordinary course of law, had acted illegally, and in a manner to deprive the subject of the benefit of the law. The lords, in return, voted, " That the House of Commons entertaining the scandalous petition of the East India Company against the Lords' House of Parliament, and their proceedings, examinations, and votes thereupon had and made, are a breach of the privileges of the House of Peers "; and that their own proceedings in *Skinner's Case* had been " agreeable to the laws of the land, and well warranted by the law and custom of parliament, and justified by many parliamentary precedents ancient and modern." After two conferences between the Houses had failed to produce an amicable settlement of the dispute, the commons voted Skinner into custody for a breach of privilege, and resolved that whoever should be aiding in execution of the order of the lords against the East India Company should " be deemed a betrayer of the rights and liberties of the commons of England and an infringer of the privileges of the House." The lords, in return, committed to prison Sir Samuel Barnardiston, deputy chairman of the Company, and imposed on him a fine of £300. By successive adjournments and prorogations the king managed to stop the course of the quarrel during fifteen months. But at the meeting of parliament in 1669, the commons renewed the dispute. Ultimately, the king recommended an erasure from the journals of all that had passed on the subject, and an entire cessation—an expedient which both Houses willingly embraced; and from that time the lords have tacitly abandoned all pretensions to an original jurisdiction in civil suits.[33]

Appellate Jurisdiction in Equity. In spite of a strong case, historically, the lords lost their jurisdiction as a result of *Skinner* v. *East India Co.* It is curious to note that in another case, where the position, historically, of the lords was weak, they actually extended their jurisdiction. This was a claim to hear appeals from the equity side of chancery in the celebrated case of *Shirley* against *Sir John Fagg*, in 1675. Since Fagg was a member of the House of Commons, there was great resentment at his being cited as respondent before the lords. The case gave rise to much intemperate behaviour on both sides, and the commons voted that no appeal lay to the judicature of the lords in parliament from courts of equity. The dispute was at length only terminated by the long prorogation from November 1675 to February 1677. The particular appeal of Shirley was never revived; but the lords continued to exercise their general jurisdiction over appeals from courts of equity.[34]

---

[33] The proceedings are printed in Robertson's *Documents*, 355. See also Hallam, *Constitutional History*, iii, 21; Anson, *Law and Custom*, 359; Pike, *House of Lords*, 281; Holdsworth, *History of English Law*, i, 367. Note that these proceedings did not touch the original criminal jurisdiction of the House (the trial of peers for treason or felony, impeachment, and breach of privilege).

[34] Robertson, *Documents*, 368; Hallam, *Constitutional History*, iii, 24; Holdsworth, i, 374.

The Lords and Money Bills. In 1671 the commons asserted, and in 1678 made good, their claim that money bills must originate in their house, and that the lords may reject, but cannot amend them. It was immediately perceived that both lords and king could be coerced by " tacking " financial clauses to a controversial measure. To this Charles II firmly replied that he would veto any bill which had been " tacked together " in this fashion.[35]

Royal Veto. The royal veto was still in use, although there were many occasions on which Charles felt it politically inexpedient to use it. Sometimes it was possible to secure the same result inconspicuously by contriving the disappearance of the engrossed bill at the critical moment.[36]

HABEAS CORPUS

Of all the statutes passed in the reign of Charles II, perhaps the most celebrated is the Habeas Corpus Amendment Act. But although this Act afforded to the subject a prompt and efficacious remedy in many cases of illegal imprisonment, it is a mistake to suppose that it introduced any new principle or conferred any new right.

Ancient Remedies for Illegal Detention. The right of personal liberty —the most precious of all rights—is as old as the constitution itself. It rests upon the common law, which was merely defined and declared by Magna Carta, and the stream of statutes which affirm that enactment.[37] The subject was, therefore, always legally free from detention except upon a criminal charge or conviction, or for a civil debt. Besides the ancient writs *De odio et atia* and *De homine replegiando* (which were available only in particular cases) any freeman imprisoned was entitled at common law to demand of the court of King's Bench a write of habeas corpus, or *corpus cum causa* as it was called, directed to the keeper of the prison, and commanding him to bring up the body of the prisoner, with the cause of the caption and detention, in order that the court might judge of its sufficiency, and either remand the prisoner, admit him to bail, or discharge him, according to the nature of the charge. In the fifteenth century it was used by the central courts to supervise commitments made by local and feudal courts; in the sixteenth it was used in the contest with the prerogative and admiralty courts, in the course of which it became apparent that the writ could be employed in the defence of the liberty of the person.

Inadequacy of the Ancient Remedies. This writ issued of right, and *ex debito justitiae*, and could not be denied. It possessed, however,

---

[35] Ogg, *Charles II*, ii, 472; *Commons' Journal*, ix, 239, 509; *Lords' Journal*, xiii, 223; *infra*, p. 549.

[36] C. E. Fryer, " The Royal Veto under Charles II," *English Historical Review*, xxxii, 103.

[37] See Holdsworth, ix, 104–125.

various defects. (1) The gaoler was not bound to make an immediate return to the writ, but might wait for a second writ called an " *alias,*" and a third, a "*pluries* "; and other expedients, such as shifting the prisoner about from prison to prison, were sometimes adopted in order to evade obedience. (2) It was doubtful whether the Court of Common Pleas could issue this writ; and the Court of Exchequer seems never to have done so. The Court of Chancery apparently did.[38] It was also doubtful whether a single judge of the Court of King's Bench could issue it during the vacation.

These defects caused much delay in obtaining the writ; but a more serious matter was the attempt made by the crown to defeat the right altogether, by maintaining that the "special command of the king " was *per se* a sufficient cause to justify the commitment and detention of a subject. This vitally important point was, as we have seen, elaborately argued in court and in parliament in the great *Case of the Five Knights* (*Darnel's Case*) in 1627, and was intended to have been settled by the Petition of Right, which declared against it.[39] The arbitrary arrest of Sir John Eliot, Selden, and other members, on the dissolution of parliament in 1629, and the attempt made to evade the words of the Petition of Right by setting forth in the warrant and in the return to the habeas corpus a colourable cause of commitment, " notable contempts of the king and government and stirring up sedition," led to the enactment of the remedial clauses concerning the writ of habeas corpus contained in the Act which abolished the Star Chamber.[40]

Abortive attempts at Reform. Under Charles II the arbitrary conduct of Lord Clarendon, in procuring political offenders to be illegally imprisoned in distant and unknown places, directed public attention to the necessity for a more speedy and effective process of enforcing the subject's right to personal liberty.[41] In April 1668 a bill to prevent the refusal of the writ of habeas corpus was introduced in the House of Commons, but did not pass through committee. In March 1670 another bill to the same effect was sent up to the lords, but fell through. In the session of 1673–1674, the commons passed two bills—one to prevent imprisonment in gaols beyond the seas, the other to give a more expeditious use of the writ of habeas corpus in criminal matters. These appear to have failed in the Upper House, as similar bills were sent up to the lords in 1675, and with a like result. In 1676 the delay and difficulty in procuring a habeas corpus were forcibly exemplified in the case of Francis Jenkes,[42] a citizen of London. He had delivered a speech at the Guildhall urging that a common council should speedily be held to petition the king, in

[38] *Cases in Exchequer Chamber* (Selden Society), ii, 76, 82 (c. 1474).
[39] *Supra,* pp. 356, 371.
[40] 16 Car. 1, c. 10. *Supra,* pp. 377, 398.
[41] *Infra,* p. 352.
[42] 6 St.Tr. 1190; 2 Swanst. 12, 83.

the name of the City, to call a new parliament. For this he was summoned before the Privy Council and committed to prison. Various attempts were unsuccessfully made to obtain his enlargement. The Court of Quarter Sessions for Westminster refused to admit him to bail, on the plea that he had been committed by a superior court; or to try him, because he was not entered in the calendar of prisoners. The lord chancellor, on being applied to for a habeas corpus, refused to issue it during the vacation; and the chief justice of the King's·Bench, to whom in the next place recourse was had, made so many difficulties that Jenkes lay in prison many weeks before he was eventually enlarged on bail.

The Act of 1679. At length, in 1679, three years after the proceedings in *Jenkes' Case*, the famous Habeas Corpus Act (31 Car. 2, c. 2) was passed. It is intituled " An Act for the better securing the liberty of the subject, and for prevention of imprisonments beyond the seas," and it is restricted to the case of persons imprisoned (before sentence) for " criminal or supposed criminal matters." It enacts: (1) That on complaint and request in writing by or on behalf of any person committed and charged with any crime (unless committed for treason or felony plainly expressed in the warrant; or as accessory or on suspicion of being accessory before the fact to any petty treason or felony; or upon suspicion of such petty treason plainly expressed in the warrant; or unless he is convicted or charged in execution by legal process) the lord chancellor or any of the judges of the superior courts in vacation or in term, upon viewing a copy of the warrant, or affidavit that a copy is denied, shall (unless the party has neglected for two whole terms after his imprisonment to apply to any court for his enlargement) award a habeas corpus for such prisoner, returnable immediately before himself or any other of the judges. And upon service thereof the officer in whose custody the prisoner is shall bring him before the said lord chancellor or other judge, with the return of such writ and the true cause of the commitment; and thereupon, within two days after the party shall be brought before them, the said lord chancellor or other judge shall discharge the prisoner, if bailable, upon giving security in any sum according to their discretion having regard to his quality and the nature of his offence, to appear and answer to the accusation in the proper course of judicature. (2) That such writs shall be endorsed as granted in pursuance of this Act, and signed by the person awarding the same. (3) That the writ shall be returned, and the prisoner brought up, within a limited time according to the distance, not exceeding in any case twenty days after service of the writ. (4) That officers and keepers neglecting or refusing to make due returns, or not delivering to the prisoner or his agent within six hours after demand a true copy of the warrant of commitment or shifting the custody of the prisoner from one to another, without sufficient reason or authority (specified in section 8 of the Act), shall for the first offence forfeit £100, and for the second offence £200 to the party grieved, and be disabled to hold his office. (5) That no person once delivered by habeas corpus shall be recommitted for the same offence, on penalty to the party of £500. (6) That every person committed for treason or felony, shall, if he requires it, the first week of the next term, or the first day of the next session of oyer and terminer, be indicted in that term or session, or else admitted to bail, unless it appear, upon oath made, that the king's witnesses cannot be produced at that time; and if acquitted, or not indicted and tried in the second term or session, he shall be discharged from his imprisonment for such imputed offence; but that no person, after the assizes shall be open for the county in which he is detained, shall be removed from the common gaol by habeas corpus till after the assizes are ended, but shall be left to the justice of the judges of assize. (7) That any such prisoner may move for and obtain his habeas corpus as well out of the chancery or exchequer as out of the King's Bench or Common Pleas; and the lord chancellor, or judges denying the same, on view of the copy of the warrant, or oath that such copy is refused, shall forfeit severally to the party grieved the sum of £500. (8) That this writ of habeas corpus shall run into the counties palatine, the cinque ports, and other privileged places, and the islands of Jersey and Guernsey. (9) That no inhabitant of England (except persons contracting, or convicts praying, to be transported, or having committed some capital offence in the place to which they are sent) shall be sent prisoner to Scotland, Ireland, Jersey, Guernsey, Tangier,[43] or any places beyond the seas within or without the king's dominions, on pain that the party committing, his advisers, aiders, and assistants, shall forfeit to the party aggrieved a sum not less than £500, to be recovered with treble costs; shall be disabled to bear any office of trust or profit; shall incur the penalties of praemunire; and shall be incapable of receiving the king's pardon for any of the said forfeitures, losses, or disabilities.[44]

Its Defects Remedied Later. Such is the substance of this great and important statute. It was subject, however, to three defects. (1) It fixed no limit on the amount of bail which might be demanded. (2) It only applied to commitments on criminal or supposed criminal charges; all other cases of unjust imprisonment being left to the habeas corpus at common law as it subsisted before this enactment. (3) It did not guard against falsehood in the return.

The first of these defects was remedied in 1689, by the Bill of Rights, which declared " that excessive bail ought not to be required." The other two (notwithstanding a serious attempt in 1757 to render the habeas corpus at common law more efficient) subsisted down to the year 1816, when they were at length removed by " an Act for more

---

[43] The fortress of Tangier in Africa (together with the island of Bombay) was acquired by Charles II, in 1661, as a portion with his wife Katherine of Braganza. It was abandoned in 1684.
[44] 31 Car. 2, c. 2; Robertson, 92. See also Holdsworth, *History of English Law,* ix, 117; Stephen, *Commentaries,* iv, 510.

effectually securing the liberty of the subject " (56 Geo. 3, c. 100). By this Act, in addition to various minor but important improvements, the statutory remedy was extended to cases of imprisonment on non-criminal charges, and the judges were empowered to examine and determine the truth of the facts set forth in the return, and in all cases of doubt to bail the prisoner.

The legislation in regard to the writ of habeas corpus terminates with the Act 25 & 26 Vict. c. 20 (passed in consequence of the decision of the Court of Queen's Bench in *Anderson's Case*,[45] where the writ was issued into Upper Canada), which provides: That " No writ of habeas corpus shall issue out of England by authority of any judge or court of justice therein into any colony or foreign dominion of the crown where her Majesty has a lawfully established court or courts of justice having authority to grant and issue the said writ and to ensure the due execution thereof throughout such colony or dominion."

Origin of the Whig and Tory Parties. It was in the year 1679, during the intense public agitation caused by the introduction of a bill to exclude the Duke of York from the throne, on the ground of his professed romanism, that the now familiar names of whig and tory were first applied to the two great political parties in the state. The king, having dissolved parliament on May 27, in order to quash the exclusion project, numerous petitions were sent up from all parts of the country praying for the speedy meeting of a new parliament. These were met by others from the adherents of the court party, expressing abhorrence at the attempt to coerce the king to summon parliament, as an encroachment on the royal prerogative. The rival parties were termed in consequence " petitioners " and " abhorrers," names which were soon afterwards changed for " whig " and " tory." [46]

But although the whigs and tories were first so designated at the time of the Exclusion bill, the germs of the two parties may be discerned in the opposition of the puritan members of the Lower House to the upholders of the royal prerogative under Elizabeth, and their continuous

---

[45] 3 El. & El. 487.

[46] *Infra*, p. 617. On the growth of parties, see Feiling, *History of the Tory Party*, 1640–1714 (1924). " It is a curious circumstance," observes Lord Macaulay, *History*, i, 244, " that one of these nicknames was of Scotch, and the other of Irish, origin. Both in Scotland and in Ireland misgovernment had called into existence bands of desperate men whose ferocity was heightened by religious enthusiasm. In Scotland, some of the persecuted Covenanters, driven mad by oppression, had lately murdered the primate, had taken arms against the government, had obtained some advantages against the king's forces, and had not been put down till Monmouth, at the head of some troops from England, had routed them at Bothwell Bridge. These zealots were most numerous among the rustics of the western lowlands, who were vulgarly called Whigs. Thus the appellation of Whig was fastened on the Presbyterian zealots of Scotland, and was transferred to those English politicians who showed a disposition to oppose the Court, and to treat Protestant Nonconformists with indulgence. The bogs of Ireland, at the same time, afforded a refuge to Popish outlaws, much resembling those who were afterwards known as Whiteboys. These men were then called Tories. The name of Tory was therefore given to Englishmen who refused to concur in excluding a Roman Catholic prince from the throne."

existence may be carried back at least to the schism in the constitutional party in the commons, which manifested itself during the debates on the Grand Remonstrance in 1641.[47]

Difference between the Two Parties. Both whigs and tories, it is to be observed, agreed in maintaining the system of government by king, lords, and commons, and all the ancient and fundamental institutions of the English constitution. But there was, nevertheless, a wide and irreconcilable difference of opinion between them. The tories looked towards the crown, and thought that the public good was best subserved by the exaltation of the royal prerogative; the whigs looked towards the people, whose welfare they regarded as the end and object of all governments. " They differed," says Hallam, " mainly in this; that to a tory the constitution, inasmuch as it was the constitution, was an ultimate point, beyond which he never looked, and from which he thought it altogether impossible to swerve; whereas a whig deemed all forms of government subordinate to the public good, and therefore liable to change when they should cease to promote that object. Within those bounds which he, as well as his antagonist, meant not to transgress, and rejecting all unnecessary innovation, the whig had a natural tendency to political improvement, the tory an aversion to it. The one loved to descant on liberty and the rights of mankind, the other on the mischiefs of sedition and the rights of kings. Though both, as I have said, admitted a common principle, the maintenance of the constitution, yet this made the privileges of the subject, the crown's prerogative, its peculiar care. Hence it seemed likely that, through passion and circumstance, the tory might aid in establishing despotism, or the whig in subverting monarchy. The former was generally hostile to the liberty of the press, and to freedom of inquiry, especially in religion; the latter their friend. The principle of the one, in short, was amelioration, of the other, conservation." [48]

Although both of these historic parties had been in existence for well over a generation, it was only very occasionally that they behaved like modern political parties. The Earl of Shaftesbury fought a general election with a remarkable degree of national organisation,[49] but it was an exceptional effort for a moment of extreme crisis. In normal times, the parties were apt to rely on local and family interests rather than upon political differences in rallying their forces, and this circumstance accounts for the existence of many groups which tended to impede both parties. It must also be remembered that as early as the reign of James I the natural differences of outlook between those in office and their critics played a certain part, and produced the terms " court " and " country " party. Thus Shaftesbury and his whig allies championed the " country " against

[47] *Supra*, pp. 402 *et seq.*, 420.
[48] Hallam, *Constitutional History*, iii, 200. *Cf.* B. Behrens, " The Whig Theory of the Constitution," in *Cambridge Historical Journal*, vii, 42, for a fuller treatment.
[49] E. Lipson, " Elections to the Exclusion Parliament," *English Historical Review*, xxviii, 59–85; C. S. Emden, *The People and the Constitution*.

the " court "; in the eighteenth century, however, it was the tories who described themselves as the " country," opposing the whigs who, being entrenched in office and favour, now constituted the " court " faction.

Charles Rules Without a Parliament, 1681–1685. The exposure of the Popish Plot, the failure of the Exclusion bill and the excesses of the Opposition were followed by a violent reaction in public opinion, which laid the whig party prostrate, and enabled Charles II to enjoy, during the last years of his reign, that despotic power for which he had long been languidly scheming. Having dissolved the Oxford parliament in April 1681, Charles ruled for the remainder of his reign without a parliament, in spite of the Triennial Act. Of the great whig leaders, Lord Russell and Algernon Sidney were executed, Shaftesbury was driven into exile in 1682 and died the next year, and municipalities, which were often strongholds of whiggery, had their charters revoked.

JAMES II, 1685–1688

James II ascended the throne in 1685, with a fixed design to make himself an absolute monarch, and to subvert the established church.

In many respects circumstances appeared peculiarly favourable to his despotic aims. The popular party were for the time completely crushed. The determination of Charles II's last parliament, in 1681, to accept of nothing but the Exclusion bill, had been punished by a sudden dissolution, after a session of only one week; and in violation of the plain letter of the Triennial Act, which required that no longer interval than three years should elapse between the dissolution of one parliament and the assembling of another, no writs had since been issued for an election. The high church and tory party were loud in their advocacy of hereditary monarchy as a divinely ordained institution, and the University of Oxford had but recently (July 1683) published a decree asserting the necessity of passive obedience, and condemning the works of Milton, Buchanan, and others, containing contrary propositions, to be publicly burnt. If it should be found necessary or expedient to summon a parliament, steps had been taken to render that assembly as subservient to the crown as its predecessors had been under Henry VIII.

Quo Warranto Against London. In 1683 an information *quo warranto* had been filed in the King's Bench against the Corporation of London, which, on the ground of some alleged irregularities, was adjudged to have forfeited its charters. The corporation was then remodelled in such a manner as to render it a mere tool of the court. The same policy was pursued during the next five years against several other obnoxious corporations; many others were intimidated into making quasi-voluntary surrenders, receiving in return new charters, framed on a far more oligarchical model, and reserving to the king the right of appointing the first members [50]; and the general result was to confine the power of returning a large proportion of the members of the House of Commons to nominees of the crown.

Customs: Parliament. James began his reign by an illegal proclamation ordering the continued payment of the customs duties, which had been granted only for the late king's life. With much misgiving, the king yielded to the advice of his ministers and summoned a parliament. " Those who look," says Hallam, " at the debates and votes of this assembly, their large grant of a permanent revenue to the annual amount of two millions, rendering a frugal prince, in time of peace, entirely out of all dependence on his people; their timid departure from a resolution taken to address the king, on the only matter for which they were really solicitous, the enforcement of the penal laws on a suggestion of his displeasure; their bill entitled, for the preservation of his majesty's person, full of dangerous innovations in the law of treason, especially one most unconstitutional clause, that any one moving in either House of Parliament to change the descent of the Crown should incur the penalties of that offence [51]; their supply of £700,000, after the suppression of Monmouth's rebellion, for the support of a standing army; will be inclined to believe that, had James been as zealous for the Church of England as his father, he would have succeeded in establishing a power so nearly despotic that neither the privileges of parliament, nor much less those of private men would have stood in his way. . . . Nothing less than a motive more universally operating than the interests of civil freedom would have stayed the compliant spirit of this unworthy Parliament, or rallied, for a time at least, the supporters of indefinite prerogative under a banner they abhorred." [52] This motive was supplied by the king himself, in the alarm for the reformed church inspired by his manifest determination gradually to fill all places of trust, civil and military, with professors of the Roman Catholic religion.

The opposition shown by the parliament to the king's avowed intention of keeping Romish officers in his service, contrary to the provisions of the Test Act, was punished by a hasty prorogation (November 20, 1685); and although parliament was continued in existence by further prorogations for about eighteen months before being dissolved, it was never again assembled during James's reign.

[50] Judge Jeffreys, on the northern circuit, in 1684, is said to have " made all the charters, like the walls of Jericho, fall down before him, and returned laden with surrenders, the spoils of towns."—North's *Examen*, 626, cited in Hallam, *Constitutional History*, ii, 455. A general attack upon corporate towns had been already advocated under the Protectorate by William Sheppard, author of the *Touchstone of Common Assurances* (1648) and of *England's Balme* (1657), a legal and economic adviser of Cromwell. See G. D. Ramsay, " Industrial *Laisser Faire* and the policy of Cromwell," *Economic History Review*, xvi, 93 at 97 (1946).

[51] This bill did not pass into law.

[52] Hallam, *Constitutional History*, iii, 50–52.

The Standing Army. Taking advantage of Monmouth's late insurrection, the king increased the number of regular troops in England from 6,000 to about 20,000; and as these were largely officered by Roman Catholics, he trusted that he had rendered himself independent of all forcible opposition. Throwing off all disguise, he soon made it apparent that " with a bench of judges to pronounce his commands, and an army to enforce them, he would not suffer the mockery of constitutional limitations to stand any longer in his way." [53]

The Dispensing Power. His first step was to procure a judicial decision in favour of his assumed prerogative of dispensing with the observance of the laws.[54] Having carefully eliminated from the bench such of the judges as would not promise to decide according to his wishes,[55] and having appointed others in their stead, a collusive action was brought against Sir Edward Hales, a recent convert to romanism, for the penalty of £500 incurred by accepting a military command without taking the oath and making the subscription required by the Test Act. The defendant having pleaded, in answer to the Act, a dispensation from the crown, eleven out of the twelve judges decided in favour of the prerogative. There were possibly sufficient technical grounds for their decision, but as so often happened in the seventeenth century, the judges preferred to rely on the political theory fashionable at the moment rather than upon legal principles; they therefore grounded their decision upon slavish maxims of absolute power which were capable of extension far beyond the immediate case.[56]

The dispensing power, which the courts of law had thus solemnly recognised, was now vigorously and systematically exercised. Four Roman Catholic peers, Powis, Belasyse, Arundell, and Jermyn of Dover, with Father Petre, a Jesuit, were sworn of the Privy Council. Several clergymen who had seceded to romanism were authorised to hold benefices without complying with the requirements of the Act of Uniformity; the vice-chancellor of the University of Cambridge was deprived of his office for declining to confer, at the king's request, an academical degree upon Alban Francis, a Benedictine monk; and the fellows of Magdalen

---

[53] *Ibid.*, p. 60.

[54] On the dispensing and suspending powers, see *supra*, pp. 190, 462.

[55] Jones, the Chief Justice of the Common Pleas, was plainly told that he must either give up his opinion or his place. " For my place," he answered, " I care but little. I am old and worn out in the service of the crown; but I am mortified to find that your Majesty thinks me capable of giving a judgment which none but an ignorant or a dishonest man could give." " I am determined," said the king, " to have twelve judges who will be all of my mind as to this matter." " Your Majesty," answered Jones, " may find twelve judges of your mind, but hardly twelve lawyers." He was dismissed, together with Montague, Chief Baron of the Exchequer, and two puisne judges, Neville and Charlton.— Macaulay, *History*, ii, 735. For a recent examination, see A. F. Havighurst, " The Judiciary and Politics in the Reign of Charles II," *Law Quarterly Review*, lxvi, 62, 229, and " James II and the Twelve Men in Scarlet," *ibid.*, lxix, 522.

[56] *Godden* v. *Hales* (1686) 2 Shower 475; 11 St.Tr. 1165; see also *Thomas* v. *Sorrell* (1674) Vaughan 330. *Cf.* Robertson, *Documents*, 384; Keir and Lawson, *Cases in Constitutional Law*, 55, and the discussion in Holdsworth, *History of English Law*, vi, 223–225.

College, Oxford, were expelled for refusing to elect as their president a Roman Catholic nominee of the crown.

New Commission for Ecclesiastical Causes. These last two acts of tyranny were accomplished under the summary and arbitrary jurisdiction of a new " Court of Commissioners for Ecclesiastical Causes," which the king had recently established by his royal supremacy in direct defiance of the Act of the Long Parliament (16 Car. 1, c. 11) abolishing the High Commission Court, and of the more recent statute, 13 Car. 2, c. 12, which, while reinstating the clergy in the ecclesiastical power, had expressly forbidden the creation by commission of any similar court. By this device, the king hoped to use the royal supremacy which parliament had conferred upon the crown in order to maintain the reformation settlement, as an instrument for undoing it. The whole government of the church was entrusted to seven commissioners (three clerics and four laymen), of whom the Chancellor Jeffreys was the chief. " The words in which the jurisdiction of these officers was described were loose, and might be stretched to almost any extent. All colleges and grammar schools, even those which had been founded by the liberality of private benefactors, were placed under the authority of the new board. All who depended for bread on situations in the church or in academical institutions, from the primate down to the youngest curate, from the vice-chancellors of Oxford and Cambridge down to the humblest pedagogue who taught Corderius, were subjected to this despotic tribunal. If any one of those many thousands was suspected of doing or saying anything distasteful to the government, the commissioners might cite him before them. In their mode of dealing with him they were fettered by no rule. They were themselves at once prosecutors and judges. The accused party was to be furnished with no copy of the charge. He was to be examined and cross-examined. If his answers did not give satisfaction, he was liable to be suspended from his office, to be ejected from it, to be pronounced incapable of holding any preferment in future. If he were contumacious, he might be excommunicated, or, in other words, be deprived of all civil rights and imprisoned for life. He might also, at the discretion of the court, be loaded with all the costs of the proceeding by which he had been reduced to beggary. No appeal was given. The commissioners were directed to execute their office notwithstanding any law which might be, or might seem to be, inconsistent with these regulations. Lastly, lest any person should doubt that it was intended to revive that terrible court from which the Long Parliament had freed the nation, the new visitors were directed to use a seal bearing exactly the same device and the same superscription with the seal of the old High Commission." [57]

[57] Macaulay, *History*, ii, 746.

Declaration of Indulgence: the Suspending Power. The dispensing power had been judicially recognised in *Godden* v. *Hales*, but the suspending power [58] had not yet been tested. This even more serious issue was raised in April 1687, when James published his famous Declaration for Liberty of Conscience, declaring it to be his " royal will and pleasure that from henceforth the execution of all and all manner of penal laws, in matters ecclesiastical, for not coming to church, or not receiving the sacrament, or for any other non-conformity to the religion established, or for or by reason of the exercise of religion in any manner whatsoever, be immediately suspended; and the further execution of the said penal laws, and every of them, is hereby suspended." [59]

The king's manifest object in issuing this Declaration was to obtain the support of the protestant nonconformists in his attempt to achieve despotic power; for the Roman Catholics had practically enjoyed religious toleration and freedom from civil disabilities from the date of James's accession to the throne. The nonconformists, however, for the most part, mistrusted the insidious advances of the king, and, against their own immediate interests, joined the church in resisting a measure which they well knew had for its ultimate object the restoration of romanism. It is to be observed that the Declaration went much further than the prerogative recognised in *Hales's Case* of dispensing with prohibitory statutes in the case of particular individuals, sweeping away, as it did in effect, a whole series of laws made for the security of the established church. It amounted, in the words of Mr. Justice Powell, " to an abrogation and utter repeal of all the laws; for I can see no difference, nor know of none, in law, between the king's power to dispense with laws ecclesiastical and his power to dispense with any other laws whatsoever. If this be once allowed of, there will need no parliament. All the legislature will be in the king, which is a thing worth considering." [60]

Second Declaration of Indulgence. After a year's interval, during which the king had made rapid and open advances towards the establishment of romanism, the Declaration of Indulgence was published a second time followed by an order in council directing it to be read in all churches, and for that purpose to be sent and distributed throughout their several dioceses by the bishops. A humble petition of the primate and six other prelates [61] against this order, presented to the king in his own closet,

---

[58] *Supra*, p. 190. Edward I's virtual suspension of the Statute of Carlisle seems to have been the nearest approach to a precedent, *supra*, p. 258. It would seem that Edward II had used such a power in 1315, *Rotuli Parliamentorum*, i, 292, no. 19. Under Charles II several Bills which proposed to confer a statutory suspending power upon the crown failed to pass, which indicated clearly that parliament did not consider that the power was part of the prerogative: Holdsworth, *History of English Law*, vi, 221–222.

[59] The whole document is printed by Robertson, 388.

[60] Judgment of Mr. Justice Powell in the *Seven Bishops' Case* (1688) 12 St.Tr. 427.

[61] Robertson, 391. Their names were Sancroft, Archbishop of Canterbury; Lloyd, Bishop of St. Asaph; Ken, of Bath and Wells; Trelawny, of Bristol; Lake, of Chichester; Turner, of Ely; and White, of Peterborough.

was pronounced a seditious libel; and the Seven Bishops were sent to the Tower, and soon afterwards brought to trial before the court of King's Bench.

The Seven Bishops. The extraordinary proceedings there revealed the extent to which the administration of justice had been debased by the king. His nominees on the bench were frightened and incompetent. Judges who had been dismissed from their posts had returned to practise at the bar and now appeared as counsel for the Seven Bishops. The principal legal issues were the alleged suspending power of the crown which was the basis of the Declaration of Indulgence, and the right of the subject to petition the crown, but the bench lost control of the proceedings and left everything, law and fact to, the jury. Amidst the enthusiastic rejoicings of the whole nation, the jury returned a verdict of acquittal (June 30, 1688). " The prosecution of the bishops," remarks Macaulay, " is an event which stands by itself in our history. It was the first and last occasion on which two feelings of tremendous potency—two feelings which have generally been opposed to each other, and either of which, when strongly excited, has sufficed to convulse the state—were united in perfect harmony. Those feelings were, love of the church and love of freedom. During many generations every violent outbreak of high church feeling, with one exception, has been unfavourable to civil liberty; every violent outbreak of zeal for liberty, with one exception, has been unfavourable to the authority and influence of the prelacy and the priesthood. In 1688 the cause of the hierarchy was for a moment that of the popular party. More than nine thousand clergymen, with the primate and his most respectable suffragans at their head, offered themselves to endure bonds and the spoiling of their goods for the great fundamental principle of our free constitution. The effect was a coalition which included the most zealous cavaliers, the most zealous republicans, and all the intermediate sections of the community. The spirit which had supported Hampden in the preceding generation, the spirit which, in the succeeding generation, supported Sacheverell,[62] combined to support the archbishop, who was Hampden and Sacheverell in one. . . . The names of whig and tory were for a moment forgotten. The old exclusionist took the old abhorrer by the hand. Episcopalians, presbyterians, independents, baptists, forgot their long feud, and remembered only their common protestantism and their common danger." [63]

Invitation to the Prince of Orange. On the day on which the verdict of " not guilty " was returned in the case of the Seven Bishops, the celebrated invitation, signed by the Earls of Danby, Devonshire, and Shrewsbury, Lord Lumley, Compton, Bishop of London, Admiral Edward Russell, and Henry Sydney, was despatched to William, Prince of

[62] *Infra*, p. 537.
[63] Macaulay, *History,* ii, 1035–1037.

Orange, and Stadtholder of the United Provinces. Danby and Compton were tories; Devonshire, Russell and Sydney were whigs; Shrewsbury and Lumley ex-catholics. Eminent leaders of both parties had thus joined in this momentous step. James now endeavoured to retrace his steps, but it was too late to regain the confidence of his people. Louis XIV bestirred himself to assist his royal brother. He gave notice to the States-General that he was strictly bound in friendship and alliance with his Britannic Majesty, and that any attack on England would be considered as a declaration of war against France. But James, who appeared bent on his own ruin, formally disowned the existence of any such alliance between France and England; and Louis, in disgust, withdrew his troops from the Netherlands and poured them into Germany, thus removing from before William one of his greatest obstacles.

On November 5, 1688, William landed at Torbay in Devonshire. It is unnecessary to enter at length into the details of a Revolution which the eloquent pages of Macaulay have rendered so generally familiar and which has since been still further illuminated by an eminent historian.[64]

After the second flight of James (December 23), the constitutional position was exceptionally difficult. Not only was there no king, but no parliament either, James's only parliament having been dissolved in November 1685. During the Civil War the survival of the Long Parliament had provided at least the semblance of continuity with legitimate authority, but the close of 1688 found the country in a constitutional void. Even the Great Seal, which in past centuries had usefully obscured the fact that the king was an infant, abroad, or sick, had been taken away by James, and thrown into the Thames. This emergency was met by an assembly composed of the lords spiritual and temporal then in London (about seventy in number) and of all persons who had been members of the House of Commons in the reign of Charles II, together with the lord mayor, aldermen, and fifty of the common council of London. This gathering requested the Prince of Orange to assume the provisional government of the country, and to summon all the constituent bodies of the kingdom to send up representatives to Westminster, to a Convention Parliament for the settlement of the affairs of the nation.

The Convention Parliament. The Convention Parliament met on January 22, 1689. The elections had been quiet, the candidates were chosen on the basis of their general reputation rather than as pledged to any particular solution. This freedom from commitments to the public was accompanied by a similar absence of pressure from patrons and official influence.[65] The nation was at this time divided into six parties, of which two—the blind enthusiasts for James II, who wished to

---

[64] G. M. Trevelyan, *The English Revolution* (Home University Library, 1938) is a study of fundamental importance.

[65] J. H. Plumb, "Elections to the Convention Parliament," *Cambridge Historical Journal*, v, 235–254.

recall him without stipulations, and the ultra-republicans, who wished to set up a Commonwealth—were too small and insignificant to exercise any appreciable influence. The bulk of the nation and of the Convention was divided among the remaining four parties, three being tories of varying shades, and the fourth and largest the whig party. Of the tories (1) Sherlock's party, which was especially strong among the clergy, wished that a negotiation should be opened with James for his restoration on such conditions as might fully secure the civil and ecclesiastical constitution of the realm. (2) Sancroft's party maintained that the king's stupidity, perverseness and superstition entitled the nation to treat him as though he were insane: they wished, therefore, to hand over the administration of the kingdom to a regent named by the estates of the realm, while continuing the title of James as nominal king. (3) Danby's party held that the king, by his flight, had abdicated his power and dignity; but that, as the throne of England could not be vacant for one moment, the crown had legally devolved on the next heir, who was the Princess of Orange. For as to James's infant son, his birth, they said, had been attended by such suspicious circumstances that it was impossible to admit his claim without inquiry [66]; and as those who called themselves his parents had removed him to France, together with all those French and Italian women of the bedchamber who, if there had been foul play must have been privy to it, inquiry had been rendered impossible. It only remained then, to proclaim the Princess of Orange, who was actually (under this theory) Queen-Regnant. (4) The whigs maintained that James, having by the gross abuse of his power broken the mutual contract between king and people—expressed on one side by the coronation oath and on the other by the oath of allegiance—had forfeited the crown; that the throne was therefore vacant; and that it was the right of the nation to elect a new king, and to impose upon him such conditions as might ensure the country against misgovernment.

In the Upper House the tories, who for the most part favoured the scheme of a regency, were in a majority; in the commons the whigs, though weaker than the combined tories, could predominate over any one section of them.

Resolutions of the Commons. On January 28, 1689, the commons passed their celebrated resolutions: (1) " That King James the Second having endeavoured to subvert the constitution of the kingdom by breaking the original contract between king and people, and by the advice of jesuits and other wicked persons, having violated the fundamental laws, and withdrawn himself out of the kingdom, hath abdicated the government, and that the throne is thereby vacant." (2) " That it hath

[66] The legitimacy of James II's son is now fully admitted by historians, but it was fiercely disputed at the time; " Anne for long honestly doubted whether the young James were her brother or not "—G. M. Trevelyan, *English Revolution*, 92.

been found by experience to be inconsistent with the safety and welfare of this protestant kingdom to be governed by a popish prince." [67]

To the second resolution, though obviously irreconcilable with the doctrine of indefeasible hereditary right, the lords at once gave their unanimous assent; but the first, which was debated clause by clause, encountered much opposition in the Upper House. The first division took place on the question whether or not there should be a regency; and a regency was negatived by fifty-one votes against forty-nine. The lords then voted, by fifty-three to forty-six, to accept the words which embodied the whig dogma that there was an original contract between the king and the people. They agreed, without a dissentient voice, to the commons' statement as to the misgovernment of James, but substituted the word " deserted " for " abdicated," and rejected the final and most important clause " that the throne was thereby vacant," by a majority of fifty-five to forty-one.

William Announces his Intentions. William had shown his wisdom and tact by leaving the nation to settle itself. But a crisis had now arrived when it became necessary for him to explain his views. Sending for Halifax, Danby, Shrewsbury and some other political leaders of note, he disclaimed any right or wish to dictate to the Convention, but gave them clearly to understand that he would not accept the position of regent, nor yet that of king consort with only such a share in the administration as his wife, as queen, might be pleased to allow him. If the estates offered him the crown for life, he would accept it; if not, he would return to his native country. It was only reasonable, he added, that the Lady Anne and her descendants should be preferred in the succession to any children whom he might have by any other wife than the Lady Mary.[68]

The Agreed Resolutions. After a conference between the two Houses, in which the questions between them were fully argued on both sides, the lords at length gave way. They resolved not to insist on their amendment to the original vote of the commons; they retained the word " abdicated " which the tory conscience found so helpful, and accepted the whiggish conclusion that the throne was vacant; and proposed and carried, without a division, that the Prince and Princess of Orange should be declared King and Queen of England.

New Oath of Allegiance. The adoption of this formula was a great advance towards a settlement, but many honest scruples still remained. The traditional form of the oath of allegiance which recognised the reigning monarch as " rightful " king might still have proved an insuperable barrier to many tories, had not the Earl of Nottingham made the suggestion that many could acknowledge William and Mary as king and queen

[67] *Commons' Journal*, x, 14, 15.
[68] Macaulay, *History*, iii, 1293.

de facto, who would be compelled to deny, or at least to doubt, their claim to be " rightful " sovereigns. The controversial adjective was therefore omitted and many honest men were able to think gratefully of Henry VII's famous statute about *de facto* kings.[69]

Proposed Constitutional Limitations. It was still to be decided upon what conditions William and Mary should be made king and queen. A committee of the commons appointed to consider what steps it might be advisable to take in order to secure law and liberty against the aggressions of future sovereigns, reported (1) that the great principles of the constitution which had been violated by James II should be solemnly asserted, and (2) that a long and varied list of new laws which they enumerated should be enacted in restraint of the prerogative and for the purer administration of justice. It was proposed that the militia should be remodelled; that the duration of parliaments should be limited, and the royal prerogative of prorogation and dissolution restricted; that the royal pardon should not be pleadable to a parliamentary impeachment; that toleration should be granted to protestant dissenters; that the crime of treason should be more precisely defined, and state trials be conducted in a manner more favourable to innocence; that the judges should hold their offices for life; that juries should be nominated in such a way as to exclude partiality and corruption; with many other salutary reforms, a remarkable omission, however, being the absence of any provision in favour of the liberty of the press. In a debate on the report it was urged that legislation on so many and important subjects would delay the settlement of the nation. The list of reforms was too long, if it referred only to what ought to be accomplished before the throne was filled; too short, if intended to include all reforms which the legislature would do well to make in proper season. It was finally decided to postpone all reforms until after the settlement of the government on its ancient constitutional basis had been accomplished, but to set forth in the instrument by which the Prince and Princess of Orange were called to the throne, and the order of succession settled, a distinct and solemn assertion of the fundamental principles of the constitution and of the ancient franchises of the English nation; so that the right of the king to his crown and of the people to their liberties might rest upon one and the same title-deed.

Declaration of Right. The Declaration of Right [70] was accordingly drawn up. It contains (1) a recital of all the illegal and arbitrary acts committed by James II; of his abdication, and of the consequent vacancy of the throne; (2) an emphatic assertion, nearly following the words of

---

[69] *Supra*, pp. 224-5. The vast and intricate subject of the oaths demanded of all sorts and conditions of men was greatly simplified by 1 Will. & Mary, sess. 1, c. 8 (1689) which notably abolished the oath of non-resistance imposed by 13 & 14 Charles 2, c. 3 (1662) on the Army, and by c. 4 (Act of Uniformity, 1662) on the clergy.
[70] The text of the Declaration is embodied in the preliminary portions of the Bill of Rights, printed, *infra*, pp. 449, *et seq.*

the previous recital, that all such enumerated acts are illegal; and (3) a resolution that the crown should be settled on William and Mary for their joint and separate lives, but with the administration of the government, during their joint lives, in William alone; and after the decease of the survivor, on the descendants of Mary, then on Anne and her issue, and lastly on the issue of William.

Tender and Acceptance of the Crown. On February 13, 1689, a tender of the crown, on the conditions set forth in the Declaration, was made by the Marquis of Halifax in the name of all the estates of the realm. " We thankfully accept," replied William, speaking for himself and his wife, " what you have offered us."

CHAPTER 16

THE REVOLUTION SETTLEMENT

THE reigns of William III and Mary II (1689–1694), of William III alone (December 28, 1694–March 8, 1702), and of Anne (1702–1714) were doubtless dominated in the minds of many contemporaries by the great series of wars which only concluded in 1713 with the Treaty of Utrecht; but in constitutional history these twenty-five years form a well-marked period of adjustment in which the implications of the Revolution were being discovered, discussed, and to some extent reduced to statutory form.

The Interregnum. We have seen in the last chapter that a most dangerous situation, which might easily have led to civil war, was resolved by the political technique of " finding a formula " which should seem to reconcile the divergent views of whigs and tories upon the nature of the English monarchy. Genuine concessions were made on both sides, but the substantial victory of the whig point of view is undeniable when the course of events is considered as a whole. A small but significant detail was the fact that the new joint reign was officially dated from February 13, 1689, when the new sovereigns accepted the formal offer of the crown. The constructive " abdication " of James II necessarily dated from his flight to France which began on December 11, 1688. The conclusion was inescapable: from December 12, 1688, to February 12, 1689, both days inclusive, there was no king. One very practical consequence of this, which all the world could see, was the fact that the courts of law did not sit during Hilary Term, 1689. This interregnum made an irreparable breach in the theory of divine hereditary right.

In the second session of the Convention Parliament, which reassembled on October 25, 1689, the Declaration of Right was recited at length and confirmed, with some slight but important amendments, in a regular Act of the legislature. The text of the Bill of Rights, the third great charter of English liberty and the coping-stone of the constitutional building, is as follows.[1]

BILL OF RIGHTS

1 Will. and Mary, sess. 2, c. 2 (1689)

An Act Declareing the Rights and Liberties of the Subject, and Setleing the Succession of the Crowne

I. Whereas the Lords Spirituall and Temporall and Commons, assembled at
    Westminster, lawfully, fully, and freely representing all the Estates of the

---

[1] *Statutes of the Realm*, vi, 142–145.

449

T.L.
15

people of this Realme, did, upon the thirteenth day of February, in the yeare of our Lord One thousand six hundred eighty-eight,[2] present unto their Majesties, then called and known by the names and stile of William and Mary, Prince and Princess of Orange, being present in their proper persons, a certaine Declaration in writeing, made by the said Lords and Commons, in the words following, *viz.* :

Whereas the late King James II by the assistance of diverse evill councellors, judges, and ministers imployed by him, did endeavour to subvert and extirpate the Protestant religion, and the lawes and liberties of this kingdome :

1. By assumeing and exerciseing a power of dispensing with and suspending of lawes and the execution of lawes without consent of Parlyament.

2. By committing and prosecuting diverse worthy prelates for humbly petitioning to be excused from concurring to the said assumed power.

3. By issueing and causeing to be executed a commission under the Great Seale for erecting a court called the Court of Commissioners for Ecclesiasticall Causes.

4. By levying money for and to the use of the Crowne, by pretence of prerogative, for other time, and in other manner than the same was granted by Parlyament.

5. By raising and keeping a standing army within this kingdome in time of peace without consent of Parlyament and quartering soldiers contrary to law.

6. By causing severall good subjects being Protestants to be disarmed at the same time when Papists were both armed and imployed contrary to law.

7. By violating the freedome of election of members to serve in Parlyament.

8. By prosecutions in the Court of King's Bench, for matters and causes cognizable onely in Parlyament and by diverse other arbitrary and illegal courses.

9. And whereas of late years, partiall, corrupt, and unqualifyed persons have been returned and served on juryes in tryalls and particularly diverse jurors in tryalls for high treason which were not freeholders.

10. And excessive baile hath beene required of persons committed in criminall cases to elude the benefitt of the lawes made for the liberty of the subjects.

11. And excessive fines have been imposed and illegall and cruell punishments inflicted.

12. And severall grants and promises made of fines and forfeitures before any conviction or judgement against the persons upon whome the same were to be levyed.

All which are utterly and directly contrary to the knowne lawes and statutes and freedome of this realme.

And whereas the said late King James the Second haveing abdicated the government and the throne being thereby vacant, his Highnesse the Prince of Orange (whome it hath pleased Almighty God to make the glorious instrument of delivering this kingdome from Popery and arbitrary power) did (by the advice of the Lords Spirituall and Temporall, and diverse principall persons of the Commons) cause letters to be written to the Lords Spirituall and Temporall being Protestants and other letters to the several countyes cityes universities burroughs and Cinque Ports for the choosing of such persons to represent them as were of right to be sent to Parlyament to meete and sitt at Westminster upon the two and twentyeth day of January in this yeare one thousand six hundred eighty and eight (1689) in order to such an establishment as that their religion

---

[2] That is, in modern reckoning, 1689; until 1752 the year was begun on March 25.

lawes and liberties might not againe be in danger of being subverted, upon which letters elections having beene accordingly made.

And thereupon the said Lords Spirituall and Temporall, and Commons pursuant to their respective letters and elections being now assembled in a full and free representative of this nation takeing into their most serious consideration the best meanes for attaining the ends aforesaid doe in the first place (as their auncesters in like case have usually done) for the vindicating and asserting their auntient rights and liberties, declare :

1. That the pretended power of suspending of laws or the execution of laws by regall authoritie without consent of Parlyament is illegall.[3]

2. That the pretended power of dispensing with laws or the execution of laws by regall authoritie as it hath beene assumed and exercised of late is illegall.[4]

3. That the commission for erecting the late Court of Commissioners for Ecclesiasticall Causes, and all other commissions and courts of like nature are illegall and pernicious.

4. That levying money for or to the use of the Crowne by pretence of prerogative without grant of Parlyament for longer time or in other manner than the same is or shall be granted is illegall.

5. That it is the right of the subject to petition the King and all commitments and prosecutions for such petitioning are illegall.[5]

6. That the raising or keeping a standing army within the kingdome in time of peace unlesse it be with consent of Parlyament is against law.

7. That the subjects which are Protestants may have arms for their defence suitable to their conditions and as allowed by law.[6]

8. That elections of members of Parlyament ought to be free.

9. That the freedome of speech, and debates or proceedings in Parlyament ought not to be impeached or questioned in any court or place out of Parlyament.

10. That excessive baile ought not to be required nor excessive fines imposed nor cruell and unusuall punishment inflicted.

11. That jurors ought to be duely impannelled and returned and jurors which passe upon men in trialls for high treason ought to be freeholders.

12. That all grants and promises of fines and forfeitures of particular persons before conviction are illegall and void.

13. And that for redresse of all grievances and for the amending strengthening and preserveing of the lawes Parlyaments ought to be held frequently.

---

[3] For the crown's assumption of suspending power in 1740 (on an address by the commons) and in 1766 (during a prorogation), and attempts by the House of Commons in 1783 to exercise a sort of suspending power by their mere resolution, see M. A. Thomson, *Constitutional History*, iv, 338–339.

[4] *Supra*, p. 190. In drawing up the Declaration of Right (which is here being recited) the lords were unwilling absolutely to condemn the dispensing power, and therefore inserted the qualifying words, " as it hath been assumed and exercised of late." By section XII of the Bill of Rights [*infra*, p. 454] the dispensing power was absolutely abolished, except in such cases as should be specially provided for by a bill to be passed during the then present session. No such bill was, however, passed.

[5] On the right of petitioning, see *infra*, pp. 669 *et seq.* The Act 13 Car. 2, c. 5, against *tumultuous* petitioning was not affected by this clause of the Bill of Rights.

[6] This declaration (says Blackstone) of the right of the subject to carry arms proper for his defence, " is a public allowance, under due restrictions, of the natural right of resistance and self-preservation, when the sanction of society and laws are found insufficient to restrain the violence of oppression." There is an ancient enactment, however (2 Edw. 3, c. 3), against going armed under such circumstances as may tend to terrify the people, or indicate an intention of disturbing the public peace ; and by a modern statute (60 Geo. 3, c. 1) the training of persons without lawful authority to the use of arms is prohibited ; and any justice of the peace is authorised to disperse such assemblies of persons as he may find engaged in that occupation, and to arrest any of the persons present.

And they doe claime demand and insist upon all and singular the premisses as their undoubted rights and liberties and that noe declarations judgments doeings or proceedings to the prejudice of the people in any of the said premisses ought in anywise to be drawne hereafter into consequence or example.

To which demand of their rights they are particularly encouraged by the declaration of his Highnesse the Prince of Orange as being the onely meanes for obtaining a full redresse and remedy therein.

Haveing therefore an intire confidence that his said Highnesse the Prince of Orange will perfect the deliverance soe farr advanced by him and will still preserve them from the violation of their rights which they have here asserted and from all other attempts upon their religion rights and liberties :

II. The said Lords Spirituall and Temporall and Commons assembled at Westminster doe resolve that William and Mary Prince and Princesse of Orange be and be declared King and Queene of England France and Ireland and the dominions thereunto belonging to hold the Crowne and royall dignity of the said kingdomes and dominions to them the said Prince and Princesse dureing their lives and the life of the survivor of them; and that the sole and full exercise of the regall power be onely in and executed by the said Prince of Orange in the names of the said Prince and Princesse dureing their joynt lives; and after their deceases the said Crowne and royall dignitie of the said kingdoms and dominions to be to the heires of the body of the said Princesse; and for default of such issue to the Princesse Anne of Denmarke and the heires of her body; and for default of such issue to the heires of the body of the said Prince of Orange. And the Lords Spirituall and Temporall and Commons do pray the said Prince and Princesse to accept the same accordingly.

III. And that the oathes hereafter mentioned be taken by all persons of whom the oathes of allegiance and supremacy might be required by law instead of them; and that the said oathes of allegiance and supremacy be abrogated.

I, A. B., doe sincerely promise and sweare, That I will be faithfull and beare true allegiance to their Majestyes King William and Queene Mary :
Soe helpe me God.

I, A. B., doe sweare That I doe from my heart abhorr, detest, and abjure as impious and hereticall this damnable doctrine and position that Princes excommunicated or deprived by the Pope or any authority of the see of Rome may be deposed or murdered by their subjects or any other whatsoever. And I doe declare That noe forreigne prince person prelate state or potentate hath or ought to have any jurisdiction power superiority pre-eminence or authoritie ecclesiasticall or spirituall, within this realme:
Soe helpe me God.

IV. Upon which their said Majestyes did accept the Crowne and royall dignitie of the kingdoms of England France and Ireland and the dominions thereunto belonging according to the resolution and desire of the said Lords and Commons contained in the said declaration.[7]

V. And thereupon their Majestyes were pleased that the said Lords Spirituall and Temporall and Commons being the two Houses of Parlyament [8] should continue to sitt, and with their Majesties royall concurrence make effectuall provision for the settlement of the religion lawes and liberties of this kingdome soe that the same for the future might not be in danger againe of being subverted; to which the said Lords Spirituall and Temporall and Commons did agree and proceede to act accordingly.

---

[7] At this point the recital of the Declaration of Right concludes.
[8] The royal assent to the convention's bill converting it into a parliament constitutes the statute 1 Will. & Mary, sess. 1, c. 1.

VI. Now in pursuance of the premisses, the said Lords Spirituall and Temporall and Commons in Parlyament assembled for the ratifying confirming and establishing the said declaration and the articles clauses matters and things therein contained by the force of a law made in due forme by authority of Parlyament doe pray that it may be declared and enacted That all and singular the rights and liberties asserted and claimed in the said declaration are the true auntient and indubitable rights and liberties of the people of this kingdome and soe shall be esteemed allowed adjudged deemed and taken to be and that all and every the particulars aforesaid shall be firmly and strictly holden and observed, as they are expressed in the said declaration; and all officers and ministers whatsoever shall serve their Majestyes and their successors according to the same in all times to come.

VII. And the said Lords Spirituall and Temporall and Commons seriously considering how it hath pleased Almighty God, in his marvellous providence, and mercifull goodness to this nation to provide and preserve their said Majestyes royall persons most happily to raigne over us upon the throne of their auncestors for which they render unto Him from the bottome of their hearts their humblest thanks and praises doe truly firmely assuredly and in the sincerity of their hearts thinke and doe hereby recognize acknowledge and declare that King James the Second haveing abdicated the government and their Majestyes haveing accepted the Crowne and royall dignity aforesaid their said Majestyes did become were are and of right ought to be by the lawes of this realme our soveraigne liege Lord and Lady King and Queene of England France and Ireland and the dominions thereunto belonging in and to whose princely persons the Royall State Crowne and dignity of the said realmes with all honours stiles titles regalities prerogatives powers jurisdictions and authorities to the same belonging and appertaining are most fully rightfully and intirely invested and incorporated united and annexed.

VIII. And for preventing all questions and divisions in this realme by reason of any pretended titles to the Crowne and for preserveing a certainty in the succession thereof in and upon which the unity peace tranquility and safety of this nation doth under God wholly consist and depend, the said Lords Spirituall and Temporall and Commons doe beseech their Majestyes that it may be enacted established and declared that the Crowne and regall government of the said kingdoms and dominions with all and singular the premisses thereunto belonging and appertaining, shall bee and continue to their said Majestyes and the survivour of them during their lives and the life of the survivour of them. And that the entire perfect and full exercise of the regall power and government be onely in and executed by his Majestie in the names of both their Majestyes dureing their joynt lives; and after their deceases the said Crowne and premisses shall be and remaine to the heires of the body of her Majestie and for default of such issue to her Royall Highnesse the Princesse Anne of Denmarke and the heires of her body and for default of such issue to the heires of the body of his said Majestie: and thereunto the said Lords Spirituall and Temporall and Commons doe in the names of all the people aforesaid most humbly and faithfully submitt themselves their heires and posterities for ever and doe faithfully promise. That they will stand to maintaine and defend their said Majestyes and alsoe the limitation and succession of the Crowne herein specified and contained to the utmost of their powers with their lives and estates against all persons whatsoever that shall attempt anything to the contrary.

IX. And whereas it hath beene found by experience that it is inconsistent with the safety and welfare of this Protestant kingdome to be governed by a Popish Prince or by any King or Queene marrying a Papist the said Lords Spirituall and Temporall and Commons doe further pray that it may be enacted, That all and every person and persons that is are or shall be reconciled to or shall hold communion with the See or Church of Rome or shall professe the Popish religion or shall marry a Papist [9] shall be excluded and be for ever uncapeable to inherit possesse or enjoy the Crowne and government of this realme and Ireland and the dominions thereunto belonging or any part of the same or to have use or exercise any regall power authoritie or jurisdiction within the same; and in all and every such case or cases the people of these realmes shall be and are hereby absolved of their allegiance, and the said Crowne and government shall from time to time descend to and be enjoyed by such person or persons being Protestants as should have inherited and enjoyed the same in case the said person or persons soe reconciled holding communion or professing or marrying as aforesaid were naturally dead.[10]

X. And that every King and Queene of this realme who at any time hereafter shall come to and succeede in the Imperiall Crowne of this kingdome shall on the first day of the meeting of the first Parlyament next after his or her comeing to the Crowne sitting in his or her throne in the House of Peeres in the presence of the Lords and Commons therein assembled or at his or her coronation before such person or persons who shall administer the coronation oath to him or her at the time of his or her takeing the said oath (which shall first happen) make subscribe and audibly repeate the declaration mentioned in the statute made in the thirtyeth yeare of the raigne of King Charles the Second entituled " An Act for the more effectuall preserveing the King's person and government, by disableing Papists from sitting in either House of Parlyament." But if it shall happen, that such King or Queene upon his or her succession to the Crowne of this realme shall be under the age of twelve yeares then every such King or Queene shall make subscribe and audibly repeate the said declaration at his or her coronation on the first day of the meeting of the first Parlyament as aforesaid which shall first happen after such King or Queene shall have attained the said age of twelve yeares.[11]

XI. All which their Majestyes are contented and pleased shall be declared enacted and established by authoritie of this present Parlyament and shall stand remaine and be the law of this realme for ever; and the same are by their said Majesties by and with the advice and consent of the Lords Spirituall and Temporall and Commons in Parlyament assembled and by the authoritie of the same declared enacted and established accordingly.

XII. And bee it further declared and enacted by the authoritie aforesaid, That from and after this present session of Parlyament noe dispensation by *non obstante* of or to any statute or any part thereof shall be allowed but that the same shall be held void and of noe effect except a dispensation be allowed of in such statute, and except in such cases as shall be specially provided for by one or more bill or bills to be passed dureing this present session of Parlyament.

---

[9] The marriage of George IV (while still Prince of Wales) to Mrs. Fitzherbert, a Roman Catholic, was void in English law as a consequence of not having complied with the Royal Marriage Act, 1772; the provisions of the Bill of Rights therefore could not apply.

[10] This provision, although not included in the Declaration of Right, was in accordance with the previous resolution of the Convention, that it was contrary to the interests of the kingdom to be governed by a papist.

[11] This clause supplements the preceding by enacting that every English sovereign shall, as a test of non-popery, repeat and subscribe, in full parliament or at the coronation, the declaration against transubstantiation, adoration of the Virgin, and the sacrifice of the mass, contained in the Parliamentary Test Act of the 30th Car. 2, st. 1, c. 1.—See *supra*, p.427. This declaration, which gave great umbrage to Roman Catholics, and was regarded as unnecessarily offensive by the majority of Anglicans and Free Churchmen alike, gave rise to much a crimonious discussion on the occasions of the successions of King Edward VII and King George V; and in August 1910, by Act 1 & 2 Geo. 5, c. 3, it was abolished in its entirety and replaced by a simple declaration of adhesion to the Protestant faith.

XIII. Provided that noe charter, or grant or pardon granted before the three-and-twentyeth day of October in the yeare of our Lord one thousand six hundred eighty nine shall be any wayes impeached or invalidated by this Act but that the same shall be and remaine of the same force and effect in law and noe other then as if this Act had never been made.

Many problems of fundamental importance and of extreme difficulty in view of the inevitably excited state of political feelings, were discussed in the new reign, and solutions found for them; the solutions were indeed very partial and insufficient, but they were first steps in the direction which subsequent events proved to be the right one, and therefore all the more creditable. Many of them will be described in our later pages and so it will suffice to recall them briefly at this point of the chronological narrative.

The Non-Jurors. The new oath, in spite of its conciliatory omission of the word " lawful," proved unacceptable to a small but distinguished group of ecclesiastics. Six bishops (five of whom had been among the famous seven of 1688) and a few others were in consequence deprived. These " Non-jurors " sacrificed themselves to their conscientious adherence to the doctrine of divine right. In their retirement they were not followed by any great number of the laity, since the oaths were not imposed upon the public at large. They were, however, a distinguished band whom the church could ill afford to lose—preachers, writers, and scholars, of whose works modern historians speak with respect.[12] The parochial clergy, even when they conformed and took the oaths, often did so with misgiving, and became sharply divided from the new latitudinarian bishops appointed after the Revolution. Of these one of the most prominent was Benjamin Hoadly, who, while Bishop of Bangor, defended the political revolution and at the same time denied the whole idea of the church as a " society " governed by a hierarchy.

Convocation Silenced. The fierce " Bangor Controversy " which ensued produced a deadlock in convocation where the lower clergy hotly maintained the thesis of episcopacy against the luke-warm bishops. In consequence, convocation was prorogued in 1717 and never transacted any important business again until the middle of the nineteenth century.[13]

---

[12] Among the non-juring bishops were Archbishop Sancroft and the hymn-writer Ken. Hickes was an eminent philologist, Carte and Hearne (later adherents to the sect) were distinguished historians; cf. D. C. Douglas, English Scholars (1939). At a later stage the non-jurors came to question the power of the state to deprive them of their dignities, and so there has been some recent disposition to treat them as the champions of the group against the state; but that, in any case, was not the original ground of their secession; cf. N. Sykes, Church and State (1934), 285 et seq., where the literature upon this question is examined.

[13] Convocations continued to be summoned at the same time as parliaments, and met; but were prorogued after presenting a formal address; F. Makower, Constitutional History of the Church of England, 371–372.

Dissenters and Catholics. The dissenters whose staunch resolution to refuse the tempting concessions of James II's Declarations of Indulgence had played so large a part in preparing for the Revolution, were rewarded with the Toleration Act of 1689, although its terms were by no means generous according to modern standards, and they still had to struggle to maintain the position thus acquired.[14] As for the catholics, it is noteworthy that William III came as the formal ally of Pope Innocent XI, and as the result of an understanding between them the penal laws against catholics were rarely enforced. They therefore enjoyed a *de facto* freedom of worship in private, although the civil disabilities which James II had tried to suspend or dispense with were maintained.[15]

The difficult question of the army was dealt with, temporarily at least,[16] the Press won its freedom almost by accident,[17] and the conduct of state trials and the law of treason finally received important legislative reforms in 1696 (7 & 8 Wil. 3, c. 3).[18]

The Revolution in the Colonies. James II had other dominions besides England, and in each of them the Revolution was accompanied by peculiarities derived from the state of local politics.

In the colonies [19] the seventeenth century brought great material development, but their politics were seriously confused by the repercussions of the civil war and the Revolution in the home country. Originally dependent upon the crown, the colonies were subjected to the rule of the English parliament after the outbreak of the civil war, and to this they at once raised theoretical objections. The Restoration brought back the crown to its traditional position in colonial government and a serious endeavour was made to govern the colonies through committees of the Privy Council. Charles II and James II continued the policy of the Navigation Act of Cromwell [20] and tried to plan the economic life of England and colonies alike as a whole. The colonial assemblies were the greatest obstacle to this project, for they embodied the local separatist sentiments which set one colony against another, and all (or nearly all) against England. James suppressed the assemblies of several colonies, organised vice-admiralty courts (he had been Lord High Admiral before his accession) to enforce the navigation acts, and attempted to unite several of the American colonies into a " Dominion of New England." These ambitious schemes were frustrated by the Revolution. The colonists resumed their old assemblies without waiting to hear William III's pleasure in the matter; the Privy Council through its committee continued to watch colonial affairs; the English parliament made still more sweeping

[14] *Infra*, p. 653.
[15] G. M. Trevelyan, *The English Revolution* (1938), 160.
[16] *Infra*, p. 673.
[17] *Infra*, p. 663.
[18] *Infra*, p. 519.
[19] On all this, see A. Berriedale Keith, *Constitutional History of the first British Empire* (1930).
[20] Enacted in 1651; text in S. R. Gardiner, *Constitutional Documents*, 468 *et seq.*

claims to legislative supremacy over the colonies; and the vice-admiralty courts did what they could to enforce navigation Acts. These last two circumstances were to be of decisive importance in the next century.

The Revolution in Ireland. To Ireland the Revolution merely added one more disaster. The agrarian settlement, dating from the attempt of Cromwell to use Irish land to pay for the English civil war, had resulted in a situation which only force could maintain. James II had indeed attempted to establish a catholic ascendancy in Ireland by means similar to those which he had employed in England. After his flight from England he was thus still in a position to fight in Ireland where he brought French troops to join the insurgent peasantry against William III, whose army consisted of protestant landlords, Ulstermen and Dutch. The relief of Londonderry, the Battle of the Boyne, and the fall of Limerick soon rendered his cause hopeless, and convinced English politicians that Ireland must be held at all costs lest it fall into the hands of France, and that religious persecution of the most ruthless kind was a necessary means to that end. Nor were the native catholic Irish the only victims. Ulster presbyterians were subjected to the anglican ascendancy by drastic laws, in spite of their great part in the defence of Londonderry. Moreover, the manufacturers of Ulster, like the great protestant landowners, were subjected to severe economic repression which the English parliament imposed in the supposed interests of English agriculture and industry. All this was possible since under Poynings' laws [21] the Irish parliament was completely controlled from England, while at the same time the English parliament legislated concurrently for Ireland.

The Revolution in Scotland. In Scotland the situation was very different. The only connection between her and England was the fact that both crowns had descended to the same monarch; neither English law nor the English parliament had any claim to interfere in Scottish affairs. There were important differences also in the general state of the two countries. The English Reformation had made the crown the head of a hierarchically organised church; in Scotland the Reformation had brought into being a democratically organised church which rejected the claims of the crown or any other authority to govern it. Charles I, by attempting to impose episcopacy, had made Scotland a party to the civil war. The Restoration had restored episcopacy, nominally at least, and it won the support of those who resented the high pretensions of the theocracy, but the Romanising policy of James II antagonised both whigs and tories. The Scottish revolution was an outcome of Scottish circumstances, and, although resembling the English movement, it was expressed in significantly different language, and accompanied by much

[21] *Supra*, p. 237.

more violence.[22] A significant difference in the two movements is the fact that the Scottish tories, possibly through lack of skilled leadership, did not take an important share in the conduct of the Revolution, but stood aside. In Scotland therefore the Revolution was the work of the whigs alone, and was embodied in documents which used the technical terminology of the whigs' political theory, while in England it was the result of a coalition and described in language which was a deliberate compromise between different views.

The English Declaration of Right, and the accompanying offer and acceptance of the crown of England, had taken place on February 13, 1689. The Scottish Convention of Estates [23] only met a month later, and not until April 11 did it pass resolutions framed, as far as possible, in conformity with those recently passed at Westminster. There was, however, one important deviation from the original. The English Convention, by voting a constructive abdication of the throne had, while actually deposing a bad king, endeavoured to evade the question whether subjects may lawfully perform such an act. The Scottish Convention did not shrink from using the bolder word " forfaulted " (forfeited). They resolved in their Claim of Right (the Scottish counterpart of the English Declaration of Right) " That James VII, being a professed papist, did assume the royal power and acted as king, without ever taking the oath required by law, and had, by the advice of evil and wicked counsellors, invaded the fundamental constitution of the kingdom, and altered it from a legal limited monarchy to an arbitrary despotic power, and hath exerted the same to the subversion of the protestant religion and the violation of the laws and liberties of the kingdom, whereby he hath forfaulted his right to the crown, and the throne has become vacant." They also voted papists incapable of wearing the crown, abolished episcopacy, made a Claim of Rights, asserted in dogmatic form their right to depose kings, and bestowed the crown on William and Mary, to descend afterwards in conformity with the limitations already marked out by the English Convention. William then took the accession oath—a formality which James VII had pointedly omitted—after assuring himself that the maintenance of Scottish religious institutions did not involve the persecution of non-presbyterians.

Consequences of the Revolution. Thus was accomplished the " glorious Revolution " of 1688, of all revolutions the least violent and the most beneficent. " It finally decided," says Macaulay, " the great question

---

[22] The course of the Revolution in Scotland has been described in Macaulay's *History of England*, c. xiii; P. Hume Brown, *History of Scotland*, ii 335 *et seq.*; G. M. Trevelyan, *The English Revolution*, 203 *et seq.*

[23] Besides a parliament (as to which see *infra*, p. 468) Scottish constitutional practice included a convention of estates whose composition was similar to that of the parliament, although less numerous. Conventions assumed practically all the powers of a parliament, but were more amenable to royal influence: A. V. Dicey and R. S. Rait, *Thoughts on the Union* (1920), 42 *et seq.* Cf. *infra*, pp. 491, 499.

whether the popular element which had, ever since the age of Fitzwalter and de Montfort, been found in the English polity should be destroyed by the monarchical element, or should be suffered to develop itself freely, and to become dominant. The strife between the two principles had been long, fierce and doubtful. It had lasted through four reigns. It had produced seditions, impeachments, rebellions, battles, sieges, proscriptions, judicial massacres. Sometimes liberty, sometimes royalty, had seemed to be on the point of perishing. During many years one half of the energy of England had been employed in counteracting the other half. The executive power and the legislative power had so effectually impeded each other that the state had been of no account in Europe. The king-at-arms who proclaimed William and Mary before Whitehall Gate, did in truth announce that this great struggle was over; that there was entire union between the throne and the parliament; and that England, long dependent and degraded, was again a power of the first rank; that the ancient laws by which the prerogative was bounded would henceforth be held as sacred as the prerogative itself, and would be followed out to all their consequences; that the executive administration would be conducted in conformity with the sense of the representatives of the nation; that that no reform, which the two Houses should, after mature deliberation, propose, would be obstinately withstood by the sovereign. The Declaration of Right, though it made nothing law which had not been law before, contained the germ . . . of every good law which has been passed during more than a century and a half, of every good law which may hereafter, in the course of ages, be found necessary to promote the public weal, and to satisfy the demands of public opinion." [24]

The Revolution of 1688 marks at once a resting-place and a fresh point of departure in the history of the English Constitution. The Bill of Rights was a summing-up, as it were, and final establishment of the legal bases of the constitution. With Magna Carta and the Petition of Right it forms the legal constitutional code to which no additions of equal importance (except the constitutional provisions of the Act of Settlement to be presently noticed) have since been made by legislative enactment. Political progress has indeed, from time to time, left its mark on the statute book, in laws the importance of which can hardly be exaggerated. But even the greatest of these enactments—as for instance the Reform Act of 1832—have been of the nature of amendments to the machinery of the constitution, supplying defects and correcting abuses, rather than alterations in the great constitutional principles finally established by the Revolution.

Customary Constitution. As might, however, be expected in a living organism, the constitution has not remained stationary during a period of more than two centuries. But its greatest changes have not been

---

[24] Macaulay, *History*, iii, 1310.

brought about by legislative enactments. Whilst the legal code has remained substantially unaltered, there has grown up by its side a purely unwritten and conventional code,[25] which, firmly established as a part of the constitution though still unknown to the law, has so completely modified the practical working of the legal code, as to form a present constitution which would be scarcely recognisable, except in its fundamental principles, by the authors of the Bill of Rights. The doctrines of divine hereditary right, of absolute royal power, of the passive obedience of the subject, were negatived once and for ever by the Revolution, and the rule of parliament was definitely established; but the mode of exercising that rule has since become something wholly different from what it then was and, in its present form of parliamentary government through a cabinet ministry, forms the main characteristic of our constitutional system.

Finally, it must be remarked that political freedom and national security were bought at the price of religious liberty. It is true that the Revolution was furthered by the designs of the saintly Innocent XI, who acquiesced in the expulsion of James II by William III; but the reason was the firm opposition of the Papacy to Louis XIV—and James was his tool. It is true that the opposition between king and popes resulted in a certain measure of toleration in England (but not in Ireland), yet it remains a fact that the prospect of foreign intervention served to maintain Anglican supremacy for nearly two hundred years after the Revolution.[26] The almost complete religious liberty of our own day has been achieved because it was now clear that religion could no longer hope for success from foreign arms.

Act of Settlement, 1701. As the reign advanced, it became clear that the succession clauses in the Bill of Rights were insufficient to deal with the future descent of the crown. Mary died at the close of the year 1694 without surviving issue; the last survivor of Princess Anne's issue died in her lifetime in 1700. William III had no issue, so that the question of the succession after the lifetimes of William and Anne was extremely obscure. By the Act of Settlement, therefore, new limitations of the crown were made to the Electress Sophia of Hanover and the heirs of her body; at the same time, some important constitutional restrictions were enacted which were to come into force when the new dynasty should come to the throne.

It will be convenient to set out the text of the Act of Settlement (12 & 13 Will. 3, c. 2), a statute important not only on account of the group of constitutional provisions embodied in it, which were to take effect from the accession of the House of Hanover, but also as the title-deed of the

[25] See Freeman, *Growth of the English Constitution,* p. 112.
[26] See p. 652, *infra.*

reigning dynasty, and a veritable original contract between the crown and the people.[27]

ACT OF SETTLEMENT

12 & 13 Will. 3, c. 2 (1701)

An Act for the further Limitation of the Crown and better securing the Rights and Liberties of the Subject [28]

Whereas in the first year of the reign of your Majesty and of our late most gracious Sovereign Lady Queen Mary (of blessed memory) an Act of Parliament was made intituled An Act for Declaring the Rights and Liberties of the Subject, and for settling the Succession of the Crown wherein it was (amongst other things) enacted established and declared that the Crown and Regall Government of the Kingdoms of England France and Ireland and the Dominions thereunto belonging should be and continue to your Majestie and the said late Queen during the joynt lives of your Majesty and the said Queen and to the survivor: And that after the decease of your Majesty and of the said Queen the said Crown and Regall Government should be and remain to the heirs of the body of the said late Queen: and for default of such issue to her Royall Highness the Princess Ann of Denmark and the heirs of her body: and for default of such issue to the heirs of the body of your Majesty. And it was thereby further enacted, That all and every person and persons that then were or afterwards should be reconciled to or shall hold communion with the See or Church of Rome or should professe the Popish Religion or marry a Papist should be excluded and are by that Act made for ever incapable to inherit possess or enjoy the Crown and Government of this Realme and Ireland and the Dominions thereunto belonging or any part of the same or to have use or exercise any regall power authority or jurisdiction within the same: And in all and every such case and cases the people of these Realms shall be and are thereby absolved of their allegiance: and that the said Crown and Government shall from time to time descend to and be enjoyed by such person or persons being Protestants as should have inherited and enjoyed the same in case the said person or persons so reconciled holding communion professing or marrying as aforesaid were naturally dead. After the making of which Statute and the Settlement therein contained your Majestie's good subjects who were restored to the full and free possession and enjoyment of their Religion Rights and Liberties by the providence of God giving success to your Majestie's just undertakings and unwearied endeavours for that purpose, had no greater temporall felicity to hope or wish for then [than] to see a Royall Progeny descending from your Majesty to whom (under God) they owe their tranquillity and whose ancestors have for many years been principall assertors of the reformed Religion and the liberties of Europe, and from our said most gracious Sovereign Lady whose memory will always be precious to the subjects of these Realms: And it having since pleased Almighty God to take away our said Sovereign Lady and also the most hopefull Prince William Duke of Gloucester (the only surviving issue of her Royall Highness the Princess Ann of Denmark) to the unspeakable grief and sorrow of your Majesty and your said good subjects, who under such

---

[27] The Act of Settlement is characterised by Hallam (*Constitutional History*, iii, 198) as " the seal of our constitutional laws, the complement of the Revolution itself and the Bill of Rights, the last great statute which restrains the power of the crown." The proposal to limit a further remainder to the Electress Sophia after the failure of the issue of Mary, Anne and William, had been first made in 1689, but after much controversy it was omitted from the Bill of Rights.

[28] *Statutes of the Realm*, vii, 636–638.

losses being sensibly put in mind that it standeth wholly in the pleasure of Almighty God to prolong the lives of your Majesty and of her Royall Highness, and to grant to your Majesty, or to her Royall Highness, such issue as may be inheritable to the Crown and Regall Government aforesaid by the respective limitations in the said recited Act contained doe constantly implore the Divine mercy for those blessings: And your Majestie's said subjects having daily experience of your royall care and concern for the present and future wellfare of these kingdoms and particularly recommending from your throne a further provision to be made for the Succession of the Crown in the Protestant line for the happiness of the Nation and the security of our Religion; and it being absolutely necessary for the safety peace and quiet of this Realm to obviate all doubts and contentions in the same by reason of any pretended titles to the Crown, and to maintain a certainty in the Succession thereof to which your subjects may safely have recourse for their protection in case the limitations in the said recited Act should determine: Therefore, for a further provision of the Succession of the Crown in the Protestant line we your Majestie's most dutifull and loyall subjects the Lords Spirituall and Temporall and Commons in this present Parliament assembled do beseech your Majesty that it may be enacted and declared and be it enacted and declared by the King's most excellent Majesty by and with the advice and consent of the Lords Spirituall and Temporall and Commons in this present Parliament assembled and by the authority of the same That the most excellent Princess Sophia Electress and Duchess Dowager of Hannover daughter of the most excellent Princess Elizabeth late Queen of Bohemia daughter of our late Sovereign Lord King James the First of happy memory be and is hereby declared to be the next in succession in the Protestant line to the Imperiall Crown and Dignity of the said Realms of England France and Ireland with the Dominions and territories thereunto belonging after his Majesty and the Princess Ann of Denmark and in default of issue of the said Princess Ann and of his Majesty respectively and that from and after the deceases of his said Majesty our now Sovereign Lord and of her Royall Highness the Princess Ann of Denmark and for default of issue of the said Princess Ann and of his Majesty respectively, the crown and Regall Government of the said Kingdoms of England France and Ireland and of the dominions thereunto belonging with the Royall State and Dignity of the said Realms and all honours stiles titles regalities prerogatives powers jurisdictions and authorities to the same belonging and appertaining shall be remain and continue to the said most excellent Princess Sophia and the heirs of her body being Protestants: And thereunto the said Lords Spirituall and Temporall and Commons shall and will in the name of all the people of this Realm most humbly and faithfully submit themselves their heirs and posterities and do faithfully promise that after the deceases of his Majesty and her Royall Highness and the failure of the heirs of their respective bodies to stand to maintain and defend the said Princess Sophia and the heirs of her body being Protestants according to the Limitation and Succession of the Crown in this Act specified and contained to the utmost of their powers with their lives and estates against all persons whatsoever that shall attempt anything to the contrary.

II. Provided always and it is hereby enacted that all and every person and persons who shall or may take or inherit the said Crown by vertue of the limitation of this present Act and is are or shall be reconciled to or shall hold communion with the See or Church of Rome or shall profess the Popish Religion or shall marry a Papist shall be subject to such incapacities as in such case or cases are by the said recited Act provided enacted and established: and that every King and Queen of this Realm who shall come to and succeed in the Imperiall Crown of this kingdom by vertue of this Act shall have the Coronation Oath administered to him her or them at their respective coronations according to the Act of Parliament made in the first year of the reign of his Majesty and the said late Queen Mary, intituled An Act for establishing the Coronation Oath, and shall make subscribe and repeat the Declaration in the Act first above recited mentioned or referred to in the manner and form thereby prescribed.

III. And whereas it is requisite and necessary that some further provision be made for securing our Religion Laws and Liberties from and after the death of his Majesty and the Princess Ann of Denmark and in default of issue of the body of the said Princess and of his Majesty respectively: Be it enacted by the King's most excellent Majesty by and with the advice and consent of the Lords Spirituall and Temporall and Commons in Parliament assembled and by the authority of the same:

1. That whosoever shall hereafter come to the possession of this Crown shall joyn in communion with the Church of England as by law established.

2. That in case the Crown and Imperiall Dignity of this realm shall hereafter come to any person not being a native of this kingdom of England this nation be not obliged to ingage in any warr for the defence of any dominions or territories which do not belong to the Crown of England without the consent of Parliament.

3. That no person who shall hereafter come to the possession of this Crown shall go out of the dominions of England Scotland or Ireland without consent of Parliament.[29]

4. That from and after the time that the further limitation by this Act shall take effect all matters and things relating to the well-governing of this kingdom which are properly cognisable in the Privy Councill by the laws and customs of this Realme shall be transacted there, and all resolutions taken thereupon shall be signed by such of the Privy Councill as shall advise and consent to the same.[30]

5. That after the said limitation shall take effect as aforesaid no person born out of the kingdoms of England Scotland or Ireland or the dominions thereunto belonging (although he be naturalised or made a denizen) except such as are born of English parents shall be capable to be of the Privy Councill or a member of either House of Parliament, or to enjoy any office or place of trust either civill or military or to have any grant of lands tenements or hereditaments from the Crown to himself or to any other or others in trust for him.[31]

6. That no person who has an office or place of profit under the king or receives a pension from the Crown shall be capable of serving as a member of the House of Commons.[32]

7. That after the said limitations shall take effect as aforesaid judges' commissions be made *quamdiu se bene gesserint* and their salaries ascertained and established but upon the address of both Houses of Parliament it may be lawfull to remove them.[33]

8. That no pardon under the Great Seal of England be pleadable to an impeachment by the Commons in Parliament.

IV. And whereas the Laws of England are the birthright of the people thereof and all the Kings and Queens who shall ascend the throne of this Realm ought to

---

[29] This clause was repealed by 1 Geo. 1, stat. 2, c. 51.

[30] Repealed by 4 & 5 Anne, c. 20, s. 27; *infra*, pp. 467, 624.

[31] As to the position of aliens, see *infra*, pp. 678 *et seq.*

[32] Modified by 4 & 5 Anne, c. 20; 6 Anne, c. 41; 1 Geo. 1, stat. 2, c. 56; *infra*, pp. 467, 565 *et seq.*

[33] This important provision, which established the independence of the judicial bench, as well as the provision in the 8th clause that the royal pardon should not be pleadable to an impeachment, had been omitted in the hasty and imperfect Bill of Rights. *Infra*, p. 465.

administer the government of the same according to the said laws and all their officers and ministers ought to serve them respectively according to the same; the said Lords Spirituall and Temporall and Commons do therefore further humbly pray That all the Laws and Statutes of this Realm for securing the established Religion and the Rights and Liberties of the people thereof and all other laws and statutes of the same now in force may be ratified and confirmed: And the same are by his Majesty by and with the advice and consent of the said Lords Spirituall and Temporall and Commons and by authority of the same ratified and confirmed accordingly.

Constitutional Clauses. The constitutional clauses in section III of the Act of Settlement are expressly stated to come into force only after the deaths of William III, and of Anne, and in default of their issue— in other words, whigs were able to represent these clauses as a new " compact " under which the House of Hanover was to rule. Several of these clauses are of great interest. The eighth was clearly a reminiscence of Danby's impeachment of 1679,[34] the second, third and fifth reflect the public attitude on William III's foreign policy and Dutch favourites. The sixth was the outcome of deep suspicion of place-men among the commons, but underestimated the ramifications of that difficult problem, as we shall see.[35] The fourth is the most conservative, with its insistence in almost medieval language that the formation of policy must take place in the Privy Council, and that resolutions must be signed by those who assent to them.[36] The last serious attempt to put such a scheme into practice was when Charles II gave his insincere support to Sir William Temple's scheme,[37] and that scheme had quickly yielded place to a succession of " cabinets," " juntos " and the like, which closely resembled the " cabal " which had preceded it, and which the scheme hoped to render impossible for the future. The immediate occasion for inserting this clause in the Act of Settlement was the great resentment felt at the secrecy which surrounded William III's conclusion of the Partition Treaties.

Tenure of the Judges. The seventh, unlike most of the rest, proved to be a permanent solution to a problem which had been acute throughout the Stuart age. Hitherto, judges had held office during pleasure, but had in practice enjoyed a considerable measure of independence. Edward I had indeed put some of his judges upon trial for oppression,[38] and Edward III had dismissed judges for reasons which seem largely independent of their strictly judicial functions.[39] Under Richard II the judges

---

[34] *Infra*, pp. 532-533.

[35] *Infra*, p. 565.

[36] *Supra*, pp. 213–215; the requirement that councillors should sign documents they approved is as old as 1424; *Rotuli Parliamentorum*, iv, 201, no. 17.

[37] *Infra*, p. 613.

[38] See the documents in T. F. Tout and H. Johnstone, *State Trials of Edward I*, 1289–1293; discussion in Sayles, *Cases in King's Bench* (Selden Society), i, intro., pp. lxvi–lxxi.

[39] J. H. Ramsay, *Genesis of Lancaster*, i, 284. The judges were soon restored. For other aspects of the crisis of 1340–1341, see *supra*, p. 163.

were forced by the king most unwillingly to take a side in the constitutional dispute; their subsequent banishment was the work of the lords appellants who actually executed only the Chief Justice of the King's Bench, Tresilian.[40] (One of his predecessors, Cavendish,[41] had been beheaded by the insurgent villeins.) In the fifteenth century the atmosphere was very different, and the judges (with the sole exception of Fortescue) kept resolutely apart even from the Wars of the Roses. Under the Tudors the judges were scarcely any more disturbed by political changes: the chief justices were dismissed at the accession of Mary,[42] whose accession they had tried to impede, and Elizabeth is suspected of dismissing a judge from political motives,[43] but beside these facts we must place others showing how the judges could take an independent stand against both queen and council.[44]

The Stuarts and the Judges. The situation first became serious with the advent of the Stuarts. The conflict of law and prerogative which runs all through Stuart history necessarily involved the judges of the common law courts, and dismissals—beginning with that of Coke in 1616—for political reasons occur under both James I and Charles I; at the same time, severe pressure was exerted by the crown by its habit of consulting the judges extra-judicially.[45] The Restoration brought no improvement. The new judges appointed immediately after 1660 though convinced royalists were excellent lawyers. Nevertheless, dismissals began again with Pemberton (in 1679 and again in 1683), and grossly political appointments such as Saunders, Scroggs and Jeffreys filled the gaps left by numerous political dismissals. The lowest point was reached under James II,[46] and we have already seen the result in the *Seven Bishops' Case.*[47]

These manipulations of the bench were possible because judges were ordinarily appointed *durante bene placito* and were thus removable at pleasure without assigning any professional default. After the Restoration on a few occasions a judge had been appointed *quamdiu se bene gesserit*, during good behaviour,[48] and this was not unusual with the barons of the exchequer[49]; removal could then be effected only by showing misconduct. The crown soon found the inconvenience of such a clause and so the crux of the problem was seen to consist in the wording

[40] *Supra*, pp. 192-194; *Year Book 11 Richard II* (Ames Foundation), ix, *et seq.*

[41] Cavendish had in fact been favourable to some of their demands; *Year Book 13 Richard II* (Ames Foundation), 123–124.

[42] Holdsworth, *History of English Law*, v. 349.

[43] *Ibid.*, p. 346.

[44] Holdsworth, *History of English Law*, v, p. 348; and *cf.* the incident related *supra*, pp. 308–310.

[45] *Ibid.*, v, 351.

[46] *Ibid.*, vi, 501–511.

[47] *Supra*, p. 443. In 1680 the whigs retaliated with an attempt to impeach some judges, and proposed legislation to make their tenure during good behaviour: B. Behrens " The Whig Theory of the Constitution," in *Cambridge Historical Journal*, vii, 62.

[48] Holdsworth, vi, 501.

[49] *Ibid.*, v, 351.

of the judges' patents. William III invariably made them during good behaviour, and the Act of Settlement now established that salutary rule as statute law. The first few years of the new reign had in fact shown that the judiciary, having been for so long at the storm-centre of affairs, could not immediately be freed from the entanglements of politics. Two of James II's judges, together with Jeffreys, only escaped a bill of pains and penalties by a timely death. Another, Holloway, was excepted from the Act of Grace [50] with which William III cut short the heated debates in which the whigs attempted to secure a long list of proscriptions. Such feelings had somewhat subsided by 1701, and this clause of the Act of Settlement was followed later in the century by Acts declaring that judges should no longer cease to sit by reason of the demise of the crown [51] —an old rule which enabled a sovereign upon his accession to appoint a new bench of judges (although the power was not used to its full extent), as well as hosts of other officers.[52] Events soon showed that the danger to the judiciary was to come in the future from parliament rather than from the crown. Thus the House of Lords once considered putting Lord Chief Justice Holt in the Tower because of his proceedings in *Knollys' Case*.[53] Even in the middle of the eighteenth century we find Lord Hardwicke and Lord Mansfield sitting in the cabinet as well as being chief justices of the king's bench; but such cases were rare, and excited much adverse comment.[54]

QUEEN ANNE

The reign of Queen Anne (1702–1714) contains many constitutional features which will be discussed elsewhere—great cases on parliamentary privilege, a marked advance towards cabinet government,[55] and the steady growth of party, especially symbolised in the impeachment of Dr. Sacheverell.[56] A slow decline in the practical power of the crown is typified by the fact that Anne was the last sovereign to exercise the royal veto [57]; on the other hand, her reign saw the first avowed attempt to pack the House of Lords.[58] For the purpose of this chapter her reign is chiefly interesting for two statutes which bear directly upon the Revolution settlement.

[50] 2 Will. & Mar., sess. 1, c. 10. " Between an Act of Grace originating with the sovereign and an Act of Indemnity originating with the estates of the realm there are some remarkable distinctions. An Act of Indemnity passes through all the stages through which other laws pass, and may, during its progress, be amended by either house. An Act of Grace is received with peculiar marks of respect, is read only once by the lords and once by the commons, and must be either rejected altogether or accepted as it stands " (Macaulay).
[51] Holdsworth, *History of English Law*, x, 415, n. 10.
[52] On the extent of the principle, *cf. ibid.*, 426.
[53] *R. v. Knollys* (1695) 1 Ld.Raym. 10; Holdsworth, vi, 270–271.
[54] *Cf.* Holdsworth, xii, 243–245 (Hardwicke), 473 (Mansfield).
[55] *Infra*, p. 625.
[56] *Infra*, p. 537.
[57] In 1708 she refused the royal assent to a Militia Bill relating to Scotland. Alternatively, it has been conjectured that the " veto " became unnecessary since the crown's influence was now sufficient to stop obnoxious bills at an earlier stage.
[58] In connection with the Treaty of Utrecht; *infra*, p. 541.

Regency Act, 1706. The first was the Regency Act, 1706.[59] The principal concern of the act was to remove the many practical and technical complications which might be anticipated if the queen died and the Hanoverian heir were at a great distance from England—as was certain to be the case. It declared that neither parliament nor Privy Council should henceforth be dissolved *ipso facto* by the demise of the crown [60]; parliament was to continue six months after that event, and so were many officers whose appointments were by commission; elaborate and curious machinery for a regency was set up until the next sovereign should reach the country. In the course of the lively debates upon this measure, other matters were raised and eventually incorporated in it. Accordingly, the clause about the Privy Council in the Act of Settlement [61] was repealed. The short and sweeping clause excluding place-men from the House of Commons, also contained in the Act of Settlement,[62] was likewise repealed and replaced by a clause excluding the holders of (1) any new office of profit which the crown may create in the future; and of (2) a list of offices set out in the clause. A proviso made it clear that naval and military officers were not excluded by this Act. The effect of these second thoughts upon the Revolution settlement was, broadly, to avoid a drastic change of political practice when the new dynasty should come to the throne. No attempt was to be made, after all, to enforce a medieval ideal upon the Privy Council, and in fact that body had already begun to lose its political importance. A symptom is the fact that Anne dropped the practice of regularly removing from the Privy Council ministers who were out of office or out of favour. As to the problem of place-men, zeal had outrun discretion in the Act of Settlement, which seemingly would have excluded even such place-holders as Secretaries of State or the Chancellor of the Exchequer. That rule would have given us a strict separation of executive and legislative organs such as still exists in the United States. Such a result was probably not intended, and the Regency Act was followed by other legislation which dealt with the problem in more practical ways.[63]

Union with Scotland. The second great constitutional statute of Anne's reign is the Act of Union, 1707.[64] The accomplishment by peaceful means of so great a design as the parliamentary union of England and Scotland, at a time when political passions ran high and many bitter memories were fresh in the minds of many people, is an event of exceptional interest. High credit belongs to the chief negotiators on either side, and

---

[59] 4 & 5 Anne, c. 20. For further changes made shortly after, see *infra*, p. 566.
[60] Early precedents are mentioned, *infra*, pp. 489–492. *Cf.* Holdsworth, *History of English Law*, x, 434; later legislation removed doubts (*e.g.*, as to the judges, *cf. supra*, p. 466) and extended the principle.
[61] *Supra*, p. 463.
[62] *Supra*, p. 463; *infra*, pp. 565-567.
[63] *Infra*, pp. 565-567 *et seq.*
[64] 5 & 6 Anne, c. 8; Grant Robertson, *Documents*, 162 *et seq.* (extracts); full text, documents and commentary in G. S. Pryde, *The Treaty of Union* (1950).

to those among the public who supported them—albeit with doubts and misgivings which it is easy to appreciate—and the whole episode deserves careful study.[65]

Ever since the two crowns had been united through the accession of James VI to the English kingdom as James I, there had been attempts to secure something more than this personal and accidental union. James himself desired it, and the judgment in *Calvin's Case* [66] was a first step in that direction. A parliamentary union was actually accomplished under the Instrument of Government [67] by force of arms, but the Rescissory Act of the Scottish parliament at the Restoration brought back the *status quo* of 1633. The English parliament authorised negotiations for a union in 1670 [68] and there was a Scottish overture in 1689; both parliaments appointed commissioners who negotiated during the winter of 1702–1703. None of these attempts succeeded, although there had been from time to time legislation in both countries removing some of the minor inconveniences of the situation.

The Scottish Parliament. The Scottish parliament had proceeded from origins presumably very similar to those which had produced the English parliament, but in the course of history several interesting divergences separated them.[69] In Scotland, bishops, lords and commons all sat in one chamber. It is difficult for us now to imagine several meetings going on simultaneously in one hall or room, but the Middle Ages seemed to be undismayed and it would probably be rash to assume that the Scottish parliament was necessarily " uni-cameral " in the modern sense of the word. The English law courts all sat in various corners of Westminster Hall (although they were separated by partitions of wainscoting in post-medieval times), and when the University of Paris held its " congregation " there might have to be seven discussions—the four nations each under its proctor, and the three superior faculties each under its dean—meeting in seven separate groups in the church of St. Julien le Pauvre, the nave of which measures 71 ft. 6 ins. by 53 ft. 6 ins. The English House of Commons had the great advantage of relatively commodious premises, separate from the lords, from the middle of the fourteenth century.[70] The representative part consisted of small tenants in chief or their representatives; in general, only " royal " boroughs

---

[65] See Hallam, c. xvii; A. V. Dicey and R. S. Rait, *Thoughts on the Union* (1920); P. Hume Brown, *History of Scotland*, iii, 35–122; Mark A. Thomson, *Constitutional History of England*, iv, 246–262.

[66] *Supra*, p. 337.

[67] *Supra*, p. 416.

[68] 22 Charles II, c. 9.

[69] See R. S. Rait *Parliaments of Scotland* (1925); C. S. Terry, *Scottish Parliament*, 1603–1707 (1912) which also contains an illuminating appendix of documents; Dicey and Rait, *op. cit.*

[70] Rashdall, *Universities of Europe* (ed. Powicke and Emden), i, 411; *cf.* A. G. Little in *English Historical Review*, lii, 309–310. See also " The Commons' Meeting-Places at Westminster " in J. G. Edwards, *The Commons in Medieval English Parliaments* (1958), pp. 25–27.

sent members; the franchise was extremely narrow; re-election was common and after 1661 was in a sort obligatory, with the result that general elections were rare.

Lords of the Articles. To all this must be added the practice of appointing " Lords of the Articles." An ingenious scheme, devised by the statecraft of James I and VI himself,[71] had converted their election into something akin to royal nomination. Their function was to prepare bills which the parliament subsequently accepted, generally without amendment or debate. These circumstances alone would have sufficed to reduce the Scottish parliament to impotence, but in addition there is the fact that the parliament had rivals. On the temporal side there were the Conventions of Estates, which were partly enlargements of the Privy Council, and partly diminutives of parliament, although possessing the crucial power of granting taxes. Still more serious was the fact that on the ecclesiastical side parliament had a powerful rival in the General Assembly of the Church of Scotland. This body, although strictly confined to presbyterians, was elected on a much broader basis than parliament, and its proceedings were followed with deep interest. Nor was it an exclusively clerical body, for a large minority of laymen were members of it. There can be no doubt that the assembly held a much higher place in the esteem of Scotsmen than parliament. To complete the picture, mention must be made of the Convention of the Royal Burghs which exercised considerable powers over trade and commerce, which in Scotland was still a legal monopoly, dating from the Middle Ages, of certain privileged boroughs.

Constitutional Results of the Scottish Revolution. The effect of the Revolution upon Scottish institutions was remarkable. The Convention of the Estates performed what it regarded as its traditional function in deposing James VII, but the legislation which accompanied this event effected a veritable revolution. The fifty years' struggle by the crown to impose episcopalianism was defeated by the abolition of episcopacy, and presbyterianism was finally established as the national church, and the General Assembly resumed its annual sessions after an eclipse of a generation. Still more remarkable is the radical change in the position of the Scottish parliament. This was due to its prompt imitation of English practice. When the Scots modelled their Claim of Right upon the English Declaration of Right, they were putting the Scottish parliament into the same position as the English one—a position which it had not, in fact,

---

[71] " The number of the prelates was small, and they were all the king's creatures. The peers, as he arranged it, were to choose the lords spiritual who should form part of the committee. Any bishop whom the peers chose would be, of necessity, not disagreeable to the king. The bishops were in turn to select the peers who should sit for the committee. They were certain to choose men as obsequious to the king as themselves. These chosen representatives of the bishops and the nobles were to select the most suitable members of parliament . . . to be Lords of the Articles "—Dicey and Rait, *op. cit.*, 36.

hitherto occupied, in spite of their daring assertion of the antiquity of their claims.[72] From 1690 to 1707, therefore, parliament for the first time became a focus of Scottish politics, and a serious rival of the assembly in popular esteem.

Scottish Commerce. The second half of the seventeenth century saw a remarkable increase of economic activity in Scotland. During the Cromwellian union Scotland was placed within the protective system of the Navigation Act, but that came to an end with the Restoration, which once again put Scottish merchants outside the pale. Soon after the Revolution the resurgent parliament established a company which embarked upon the famous and tragic Darien Scheme (1695). The constitutional and international complications of that venture—Darien was effectively a Spanish colony—made it clear that the dual monarchy of William III of England and William II of Scotland was unworkable, for one of those monarchies, Scotland, was actually at war with Spain which was the ally of the other, England. At the same time, the venture involved a serious collision between Scottish and English commercial interests.

The War Between the Parliaments. The Scottish parliament assumed the championship of the national cause, and embarked upon a spirited contest with Westminster, which had in fact already begun hostilities by protesting against the Act of 1695, and by encouraging William III to smother the Darien venture with the vast web of his European diplomacy. In exasperation the Scots drew the conclusion that the crowns would have to be separated; the English saw with dismay that the inevitable result of that would be the restoration of the Stuarts north of the Tweed. The last and greatest of the Scottish parliaments assembled in 1703. The Convention of 1689 (which later turned itself into a parliament) had been openly packed with whigs in order to carry out the Revolution; the parliament of 1703 was freely elected, and so all parties had their say in its momentous deliberations. So far, there had been no Scottish equivalent to the English Act of Settlement, and only a Scottish parliament could convey the Scottish crown to the Hanoverians after Anne's death. This they resolutely refused to do. Instead, the queen was compelled, by the parliament's refusal of supply on any other terms, to assent to two acts, (1) an Act Anent Peace and War (1703), making the Scottish parliament's consent necessary before a declaration of war or a treaty of peace or commerce could bind the Scottish people, and (2) an Act for the Security of the Kingdom (1704), providing that on the death of Anne the Scottish estates should choose as their new sovereign some person other than the one who succeeded to the English crown, unless there had been adequate safeguards against English control over Scottish politics and trade.[73]

[72] Dicey and Rait, pp. 63 *et seq.*
[73] These and the other statutes mentioned will be found in Sir C. Grant Robertson's *Select Statutes.*

The English parliament replied with the Alien Act,[74] which enacted that after Christmas Day, 1705, Scotsmen should be regarded in England as aliens born,[75] and that trade between England and Scotland should be suspended; both clauses, however, should cease to be effective as soon as the Scottish parliament should have adopted legislation entailing the crown in accordance with the English Act of Settlement, and if the Scottish parliament should authorise commissioners to treat for a union, then the queen was empowered to name commissioners on behalf of England to treat with them.

Drastic as all these proceedings were, it cannot be denied that each parliament was acting well within its jurisdiction; it is equally clear that they demonstrated, by a sort of *reductio ad absurdum*, as no doubt they were meant to do, that the existing constitutional position was intolerable and unworkable. Neither side regarded this legislation as a reckless exchange of threats, for both of them expressly provided for the contingency which all serious statesmen hoped for, namely, the opening of negotiations for a treaty.

Late in 1705 each country appointed commissioners; for three months in 1706 they conferred (or rather, exchanged memoranda, for it was not a round-table conference), and at last concluded their difficult and delicate task by producing a draft treaty of union. Amid fierce controversy, and even civil commotion, the Scottish parliament passed the treaty and made it (January 16, 1707) a statute of the Scottish parliament. On March 6, 1707, it also became an English statute, and the Union came into force on May, 1, 1707.

Terms of the Act of Union. The Act converted the dual monarchy of England and Scotland into the unitary realm of Great Britain, and confirmed the Hanoverian succession. The separate parliaments were replaced by a single parliament of Great Britain, each country retaining its electoral system. Complete commercial equality was conferred upon all British subjects, and detailed provisions for the transitional period prepared the way for a uniform system of taxation. To recompense Scotland for her share of liability for the national debt it was agreed to pay £398,085 10*s.* as an " Equivalent "—there was some anxiety about this, which was finally allayed by a long convoy of carts loaded with gold entering Edinburgh.[76] The Scottish law and judicial system were retained, and both countries adopted elaborate safeguards for their established churches. It was assumed that these churches were strictly territorial, and the Scots themselves deliberately refrained from asking for exemption from the sacrament test imposed upon the holders of certain offices and the members of certain professions in England by the Corporations

---

[74] 3 & 4 Anne, c. 7 (1705).
[75] Thus overruling the decision in *Calvin's Case* (supra, pp. 337-338).
[76] The Equivalent was used, in part, to meet the heavy losses incurred by investors in the Darien scheme.

Act (1661) and the first Test Act (1673). The Act of Union required Scottish members of the British parliament, like their English colleagues, to comply with the Parliamentary Test Act [77] which imposed a declaration (willingly taken by presbyterians) against certain Roman Catholic doctrines.

Scottish Appeals to the Lords. The details of Scottish representation in the British House of Lords and House of Commons will be considered later.[78] One important point upon the appellate jurisdiction of the British House of Lords was left open by the Act of Union, deliberately, it seems. It was a moot question whether before the Union the Scottish parliament had any right to review decisions of the Court of Session, and the silence of the Act of Union was significant. Shortly after the Union the British House of Lords entertained appeals from the Court of Session, and in *Greenshields' Case* (1711) the House reversed the Court of Session by holding that the use of the English Prayer Book by the episcopalians (who were, of course, a non-conforming minority in Scotland) was not a crime. There was less excitement than might have been expected over this, and the appellate jurisdiction has continued to this day to the great advantage of both legal systems.[79] The legislative and judicial union thus effected was accompanied by executive unity; this was achieved by the abolition of the Scottish Privy Council in 1708 (6 Anne, c. 40).

The Union enjoyed no popularity in either country, but slowly its solid benefits became apparent. Scotsmen took a large part in commercial, military and colonial adventure, and later became prominent in British politics,[80] while their representatives in both Houses, by constantly voting together in support of whatever government was in office, not only secured the tangible rewards of their policy, but contributed something amid the cross-currents of our early party system which made stable ministries possible.

Irish Union Refused. Unhappily the same story cannot be told of Ireland. The Irish parliament was completely under English control and was filled with men who had a property interest in the penal legislation which had contributed so largely to their landed fortunes. The

---

[77] 30 Charles 2, st. 2 (1678)—not 25 Charles 2, c. 2 (1673) as in Dicey and Rait, 247. Hence those authors are mistaken in concluding (pp. 202, 232, 247, 254–255) that Scottish members of the British Parliament were subjected to the sacrament test. The Corporations Act (1661) and the Test Act (1673) imposed a sacrament test on various persons, but not on members of parliament; the Parliamentary Test Act (1678) required a test of members of parliament, but it was a declaration, not the sacrament. I was only at the end of the eighteenth century that sufficient numbers of Scots had migrated to England, becoming candidates for English offices, to create a real problem under the Corporations Act and the first Test Act. See T. F. T. Plucknett, " The Union and the Tests," in *Studies presented to Sir Hilary Jenkinson* (1957), 320–325.

[78] *Infra*, pp. 529 (lords), 561 (commons).

[79] Holdsworth, *History of English Law*, xi, 14 *et seq.* By the end of the century, the house was overwhelmed by the number of Scottish appeals: Turberville, "The House of Lords as a Court of Law," *Law Quarterly Review*, lii, 205.

[80] Holdsworth, *loc. cit.*, has a detailed and illuminating discussion of these matters.

governing class, consequently, could expect no support from the mass of the Irish population in their resentment of English discriminatory legislation directed against their commerce (which was their principal grievance). The Irish House of Commons in 1707 congratulated Queen Anne upon the Scottish Union, and asked for a similar measure for Ireland, but without result. Ireland, clearly, had none of the bargaining power of the Scots.

Anne's Last Privy Council. From the English point of view, the Scottish Union was urgently needed in order to secure the Hanoverian succession. Even so, that succession was still precarious for the next forty years. During the last years of Anne, a Jacobite restoration seemed more likely than the Hanoverian accession, and many English ministers and politicians took the precaution of corresponding both with the Pretender and the Elector. Anne's last illness forestalled the Jacobites, whose plans were advanced, but not quite to the stage demanded by the sudden crisis. An obscure but dramatic scene in the Privy Council [81] showed how precarious the situation was. Many important posts were already in Jacobite hands, and Bolingbroke was trying to construct a Jacobite ministry, but the dying queen handed the staff of Lord Treasurer to Shrewsbury—" the baffling duke whose futility no one could understand, but who always knew his mind in an emergency." [82] He had signed the invitation to William III in 1688, and in 1714 he took equally decisive steps which secured the Hanoverian succession.

The Jacobites were thrown into confusion by this prompt action and by the defection of a group of " Hanoverian " tories (again 1688 was repeating itself). George I acceded peaceably, but there was so much violent Jacobite sentiment in England that the Riot Act [83] was passed to deal with it. Scotland rose in insurrection in 1715. Bad luck and bad management defeated it. Thirty years later the Young Pretender roused the Highlands and marched to Derby (1745). Once again the government survived in spite of its poor handling of the situation. It was clear that the Highlands were the real problem, and it was only by suppressing the feudal power of the chiefs (including their right to demand military service from their tenants) by the Heritable Jurisdictions Act [84] that at long last the Union and the Revolution settlement were placed beyond challenge.

---

[81] The contemporary rumour that the Dukes of Argyll and Somerset intruded upon the Privy Council unbidden, and turned the scale, seems to be without foundation: H. W. V. Temperley, in *English Historical Review*, xxvii, 686. It has been suggested that Shrewsbury arranged for their appearance: T. C. Nicholson and A. S. Turberville, *Charles Talbot, Duke of Shrewsbury* (1930), 211.

[82] G. N. Clark, *The Later Stuarts*, 237.

[83] 1 Geo. 1, stat. 2, c. 5 (1715); *infra*, p. 520. (*Cf.* the temporary riot Acts of 1 Mary, sess. 2, c. 12 and 1 Eliz. 1, c. 16).

[84] 20 Geo. 2, c. 43 (1747); *cf.* 21 Geo. 2, c. 34.

CHAPTER 17

SOME ASPECTS OF THE MONARCHY

SUCCESSION : REGENCIES : LAW OF TREASON

THE elective character of the old English kingship, but with the choice exclusively limited, under all ordinary circumstances, to the members of one royal house, has been already discussed in a previous chapter.[1]

This combination of the apparently incompatible principles of election and inheritance is very old, and evidently provided the necessary latitude of choice in times when the personality of the monarch was of paramount importance in national life. It may well be doubted whether monarchy would have been practicable as an institution if it had been either solely elective or solely hereditary. In other words, the rules (such as they were) frequently gave way to expediency and sometimes to the *fait accompli*. Any attempt to reduce them to a series of legal propositions (even with the admission of the necessary " exceptions ") will thus be extremely difficult, and in the end will produce an inaccurate impression. So intensely vital an institution as early monarchy would be gravely misrepresented by any attempt to ascribe to it a successoral law in terms suggestive of the placid devolution of a modern peerage. In all this, moreover, old English history is closely parallel to that of the kindred monarchies of the continent.[2]

Election. The Norman Conquest introduced a new dynasty, and a more comprehensive idea of royalty, combining both the national and feudal theories of sovereignty; but it effected no legal change in the nature of the succession to the crown. Election was still necessary to confer an inchoate right to become king—a right subsequently perfected by the ecclesiastical ceremony of unction and coronation. So strongly marked was the elective character of the kingly office that, even after the choice had been once made, the form of election was again gone through by the clergy and people assembled in the church at the coronation.[3] Needless to say, election does not imply a ballot or an electorate, but rather the acclamation of a leader by his followers; if there were a rival candidate, he, too, would be " elected " by his own partisans. There is thus a close connection between the " election " and the amount of political and military support a candidate was likely to receive.[4]

[1] *Supra*, p. 19.
[2] Continental material is discussed in Fritz Kern, *Kingship and Law in the Middle Ages* (ed. S. B. Chrimes, 1939), 12–27, and in P. Grierson, " Election and Inheritance in early Germanic Kingship," *Cambridge Historical Journal*, vii, 1.
[3] See Maskell, *Monumenta Ritualia Ecclesiae Anglicanae*, vol. ii; Freeman, *Norman Conquest*, iii, 42 *et seq.*, 626 *et seq.*
[4] The church, which had many elective offices (abbots, bishops, popes), played a large part in developing the theory and practice of elections. The universities (*e.g.* Paris) also had experience of the electoral process—and the majority rule.

Inheritance; Real Property Analogies. The inheritance of the crown has at all times been closely analogous to the contemporary idea of inheritance generally, and each has influenced the other. It is a matter of doubt how old is the concept of one person being the heir of another person; such an individualistic scheme may have replaced an earlier system where the main emphasis was on the headship of a family rather than the descent of the family lands from one individual to another.[5] The early evidence of the royal succession shows a bewildering confusion of practices, or even prejudices, rather than rules, and the rules for the descent of the crown could hardly be more precise than those governing the descent of a subject's land.[6] The introduction of a militant form of feudalism at the Conquest revolutionised thought upon the subject. It now became clear that a feudal fief was held not by a family but by a specific individual upon whom the king had placed responsibilities, and who in turn looked to his individual tenants for help in fulfilling them. It was so vitally important to the king that his tenant should be one man rather than another, since the relationship was personal, and demanded mutual trust, that there was little place at first for inheritance. When the inheritance of fiefs was finally admitted, it was naturally based upon primogeniture, although it was only slowly that even the elements of the system were formulated. Another result must be mentioned: feudalism looked not only to a particular man, but also to a particular area of land, for the performance of the services due. A reflection of this is seen in the fact that the " Duke of the Normans," the " Count of the Angevins " and the " King of the English " soon became " Duke of Normandy," " Count of Anjou " and " King of England." [7] Both of these tendencies, therefore, united in replacing the headship of a clan by the inheritance of a tract of land. The results of the change were important. The king lost his right of choosing a new tenant, and had to accept the heir of a deceased vassal; similarly, the nation (or the most considerable of its nobility) ceased in effect to choose the king, and accepted his predecessor's heir. The king, moreover, was associated with the land in a more intense degree than formerly, and thus there developed the idea of territorial sovereignty which has played so large a part in international relations.

Unction and Coronation. Finally, it remains to consider the nature and effect of coronation. In early times men were often more articulate in their ceremonial than in their treatises, and the history of the coronation rites contains valuable evidence upon the conception of monarchy current

[5] For inheritance, see Pollock and Maitland, *History of English Law*, ii, 240 *et seq.* *Cf.* Plucknett, *Concise History of the Common Law* (5th ed.), 522 *et seq.*, 712 *et seq.*

[6] For specimens of the various successoral notions to be found in the Anglo-Saxon period see P. E. Schramm, *History of the English Coronation* (1937), 145 *et seq.*; F. Kern, *Kingship and Law*, 12 *et seq.*; *supra*, p. 19.

[7] It was John who first made this change on his great seal: Stubbs, *Constitutional History*, i, 593.

in the various realms of medieval Europe.[8] The most ancient part of the ceremony was the unction—which was already established in several ecclesiastical rites, notably the consecration of bishops. It was first applied to a king in 751 when the French church used it to solemnise the abandonment of the Merovingian dynasty and the erection of a completely new royal house in the person of Pepin. The step was so revolutionary that every device that could be invented was employed in laying the foundation of the new monarchy. Unction first appears in England in 785; within a century we find the clergy investing the king with a golden helmet, which soon afterwards was replaced by a crown. Later still, the oath of allegiance (a Frankish institution) appears in England, in the time of King Edmund (940–946), and soon afterwards this serious exaction of an oath from the people is made more tolerable by the king undertaking a corresponding obligation in return. This was the *mandatum regis* whose three precepts we have already quoted. From precepts to promises was a short step, and the coronation oath later came to be supplemented in the coronation charter.[9]

The Effect of Unction. It was the unction which was the most significant part of the coronation rites, and its ecclesiastical effects were keenly debated on the continent as part of the great controversy between the *regnum* and the *sacerdotium*—did unction make the king an ecclesiastic, the equivalent of a bishop ? Did it authorise him to intervene in church matters ? Did it even make him superior to the clergy (as the eccentric *Anonymous* of York argued) ?[10] There was little attempt in England to draw practical consequences from speculations such as these, although it is worth remembering that a judge once said that "kings anointed with holy oil are capable of spiritual jurisdiction "[11] and that even a canonist could remark that " according to some, an anointed king is not a mere layman, but a *persona mixta* "—a sentiment in which a great common law judge concurred.[12] Such notions played an insignificant part, although

---

[8] For an exact description of the modern forms which were observed on the accession and coronation of King Edward VII, and which in their essential features were continued in those of George V, *cf.* Anson, *Law and Custom of the Constitution*, vol. ii, pt. 1, pp. 234 *et seq.*, and L. G. Wickham-Legg, *English Coronation Records*.

For more information on the details that follow, see the illuminating study of P. E. Schramm, *History of the English Coronation* (1937); P. L. Ward, " Coronation Ceremony in Medieval England," *Speculum*, xiv, 160 (1939); E. Kantorowicz, *The King's Two Bodies*, Chap. 3 ; a short account with special reference to medieval Germany and the peculiar position there will be found in Fritz Kern, *Kingship and Law*, 27 *et seq.*

[9] Schramm, *English Coronation*, 180 *et seq.* ; *supra*, p. 66.

[10] Extracts in R. W. and A. J. Carlyle, *Political Theory*, iv, 273 *et seq.*, and in C. H. McIlwain, *Political Thought*, 211 *et seq.* ; *cf.* Z. N. Brooke, *English Church and the Papacy*, 157 *et seq.* The latest edition is by G. H. Williams (Harvard Theological Studies); *cf.* Norman F. Cantor, *Church, Kingship and Lay Investiture*, 174 *et seq.* ; Walter Ullmann, *Papal Government*, 394 *et seq.*, and Ernst Kantorowicz, *The King's Two Bodies*, Chap. 3. See also Schulz, " Bracton on Kingship," *English Historical Review*, lx, 136.

[11] Fitzherbert, *Abridgement*, " Ayd de roy," 103, *per* Skipwith, in 1359 (from an unprinted Year Book). Skipwith became a judge in the course of the year.

[12] Lyndwood, *Provinciale* (Oxford, 1679), 126; compare the remark of Brian, C.J., in Y.B. 10 Hen. 7, Hil. no. 17 (1495) reprinted in Chrimes, *Constitutional Ideas in the Fifteenth Century*, 387.

it was realised that some people valued them; thus the change of dynasty in 1399 was helped a little by the story that Henry IV was anointed with a specially miraculous oil.[13]

The elaborate ceremonies contained much else besides. There was a perfunctory election duplicating the really effective election which preceded it; and there was the delivery of the ornaments of royalty—crown, sword, sceptre, rod, etc. That was clearly an investiture such as all landowners and beneficed clergy had often witnessed. It was natural that the king's reign should begin at the moment when he publicly received the insignia. There was therefore an interregnum between the death of one king and the complete institution of his successor, and that interregnum was unavoidable until the crown became strictly hereditary.

The Interregnum. Down to Henry III inclusive the reign of each king is dated from his coronation only. The interregnum between the death of the old and the coronation of the new king was always made as short as possible, in consequence of the serious inconvenience resulting from the doctrine that the king's peace was interrupted during a vacancy of the throne. But when the coronation was delayed, as happened in the cases of Henry II, Richard I, and John, who had each been absent in France at the death of his predecessor, the regal title was never assumed until the process of election and coronation had been gone through. Until then they were only entitled " Dux Normaniae," or, as Richard I was styled in the proclamation issued by his mother—and also in a charter granted by him before his coronation—" Dominus Angliae." [14] Edward I was the first king who reigned before his coronation. His father, Henry III, died on November 16, 1272, whilst Edward was absent in Palestine. Four days afterwards, when Henry was buried in Westminster Abbey, the Earl of Gloucester, with the prelates and barons, swore allegiance to Edward whom they " named " and " ordained " to be king.[15] His hereditary claim perfected by the fealty of the baronage—the old election in a feudal guise—appears to have been now regarded as conferring the name of king previous to coronation. But the idea of election and the necessity for consent to a king's accession were still preserved. During the four days which elapsed between the death of Henry and the recognition of Edward as king the throne was legally vacant. The new king's reign was dated not from the death of his father but from the day on which the oath of

---

[13] Schramm, *op. cit.*, 137; H. G. Wright, " Protestation of Richard II in the Tower," in *Bulletin of the John Rylands Library*, xxiii, 151, 159.

[14] Nicolas, *Chronology of History*, 272 *et seq.*; *Handbook of British Chronology* (ed. F. M. Powicke), 2; *Archaeologia*, xxviii, 110.

[15] *Annales Winton*, p. 112; " Magnates regni nominarunt Edwardum filium suum in regem," *Annales de Dunstaplia*, p. 254; " Recognoverunt paternique successorem honoris ordinaverunt," Rishanger, p. 75 (in all the Rolls series). "Nominare" and "ordinare' imply much more than impassive acquiescence in the succession of an heir. A somewhat similar emergency had arisen only two years earlier in France. Louis IX died, and Philip III succeeded him, in 1270 while both were on crusade. A coronation was impossible for many months, and so Philip was merely proclaimed and dated his regnal years from that date; Schramm, *History of the English Coronation*, 166.

fealty was taken [16]; and in the order for the proclamation of the king's
peace, issued in his name three days later by the royal council, Edward
is made to assert that the crown of England had devolved upon him
" successione haereditaria ac procerum regni voluntate et fidelitate nobis
praestita." [17] Shortly afterwards the oath of fealty was renewed in a great
assembly held at Westminster after the feast of St. Hilary, 1273, and
attended not only by all the prelates and other magnates of the kingdom,
but by four representatives from each county and each city.[18] Edward
did not get back to England until August 2, 1274, and was crowned on the
19th.

Edward II, who succeeded in 1307, was the first king whose reign was
dated from the day following the death of his predecessor. In him, then,
the principle of hereditary right appeared to have finally triumphed over
the old elective system.[19] But the true nature of the crown as an office of
trust, and the continuing right of the nation to regulate the succession to it,
were signally reasserted, not twenty years later, by the formal deposition
of the unfortunate king. This persistence of the national right to choose
the sovereign, the same in principle whether applied to the individual king
or to the selected dynasty, we shall now consider somewhat more in detail.

SUCCESSION TO THE CROWN

William the Conqueror, 1066. We have seen how William the Norman
found little difficulty, immediately after the battle of Hastings, in procuring
his election by the terrified witan. After taking the ancient oath of the
English kings, constituting a compact with the nation to govern with justice
and equity, he was duly crowned at Westminster by the Archbishop of
York.[20] On his death-bed the Conqueror bequeathed to his eldest
surviving son, Robert, the patrimonial Duchy of Normandy.

[16] Hardy, *Introduction to Close Rolls*, p. 136; Nicolas, *Chronology of History*, pp. 291–292;
Allen, *Royal Prerogative* (ed. 1849), 46 *et seq.*

[17] Rymer, i, 497. " For the first time," says Stubbs (*Constitutional History*, ii, 107) of
Edward I's accession, " the reign of the new king began, both in law and in fact, from
the death of his predecessor." With all deference, however, to so eminent a historian, it is
evident that although the hereditary claim of Edward was admitted without opposition,
yet in law, and in fact, there was actually no king for the space of four days. Indeed,
the author had just before told us that " his reign began on the day of his father's funeral."
The fact that the regnal years of Edward were dated only from the day of his recognition
as king by the baronage marks the persistence of the elective idea, and the difference still
recognised between the kingship and a private inheritance. It is important not to ante-
date the steps in the development of the hereditary doctrine. As Edward I was the first
king who reigned before coronation, so Edward II was the first whose reign is dated
from the day following the death of his predecessor. The theory embodied in the legal
maxim " the king never dies " is of still later growth. It may be said to have been practically accepted from the accession of the House of York; yet even Henry VIII's reign
commenced on the day after the death of his father (Nicolas, *Chronology of History*).
From the accession of Edward VI there has been no interregnum, however short, except
only where the line of succession has been broken.

[18] *Annales Winton*, p. 113; *Select Charters*, 421.

[19] Stubbs, *Constitutional History*, ii, 329–330. Edward V, Edward VI and all subsequent
monarchs date their accession from the day itself on which their predecessor died.

[20] *Supra*, p. 29. Stigand, Archbishop of Canterbury (and also Bishop of Winchester) was
regarded as a schismatic.

William Rufus, 1087. The Crown of England he would not attempt to bequeath, declaring that he held it not by hereditary right; he left the succession to the decision of God. He expressed, however, his ardent wish that his younger and favourite son William should succeed to the kingship of the English, in much the same way as formerly Edward the Confessor had recommended his brother-in-law Harold.[21] Furnished with a recommendatory letter from his father to Archbishop Lanfranc, William Rufus at once hastened to England. Here he was obliged to make a triple promise—to rule his future subjects with justice, equity, and mercy, to protect the rights and privileges of the church, and to conform to the primate's counsels in all things—before Lanfranc would declare in his favour. Having secured this powerful supporter, he was elected king at a meeting of the prelates and barons, in the third week after his father's death, and immediately crowned with the usual solemnities.[22]

Henry I, 1100. On the death of William Rufus in the New Forest, on August 2, 1100, his younger brother Henry, being close at hand, and having secured the royal treasure, was hastily elected king the following day at Winchester.[23] But although the election was the hurried act of a small number of the barons, it was something more than a mere form. The claims of Henry's absent elder brother, Robert the Crusader, were advanced and discussed. They rested not merely on priority of birth, but upon the wishes of the late king, expressed in the arrangement which he had made with Duke Robert, at Caen, in 1091, that each should be heir to the other in case of his dying childless. Ultimately the arguments of the Earl of Warwick gained a decision in Henry's favour. There were sound reasons of general policy for choosing Henry, who had been brought up in England, but it was felt necessary to adduce some general rule in his favour. This was successfully accomplished by stressing the fact that Robert was born before William I became king; Henry, born in 1068, was *porphyrogenite*, born in the purple, and therefore to be preferred. The argument served its purpose, and never appeared in England again.[24] Two days afterwards (August 5) he was crowned at Westminster by Maurice, Bishop of London,[25] and took the ancient coronation oath of the English kings. The exact words of the oath, agreeing with the ancient form used at the coronation of King Ethelred II, have been preserved:

[21] *Ordericus Vitalis*, vii, 15–16. The distinction between "conquest" and "heritage" and the possibility of their descent in different directions is common in medieval law: Pollock and Maitland, *History of English Law*, ii, 308.

[22] Eadmer, *Historiae Novorum*, lib. i, p. 25; *Select Charters*, p. 108. Some of the chroniclers state bluntly that Lanfranc "elected" Rufus, and Schramm, *op. cit.*, 153 (*cf.* 148–149) explains this by the theory, put forward by some clergy, that God was the effective elector and the people and clergy merely instruments; *cf. infra*, pp. 481, 491.

[23] *Anglo-Saxon Chronicle, s. a.* 1100.

[24] William of Malmesbury, *Gesta Regum*, v, 393; Schramm, 154.

[25] Anselm, Archbishop of Canterbury, was abroad, and the Archbishop of York seriously ill.

" In Christi nomine promitto haec tria populo Christiano mihi subdito. In primis me praecepturum et opem pro viribus impensurum ut ecclesia Dei et omnis populus Christianus veram pacem nostro arbitrio in omni tempore servet; aliud ut rapacitates et omnes iniquitates omnibus gradibus interdicam; tertium ut in omnibus judiciis aequitatem et misericordiam praecipiam, ut mihi et vobis indulgeat Suam misericordiam clemens et misericors Deus." [26] In the Charter of Liberties, which he issued at the same time, he announced to the nation his coronation " Dei misericordia et communi consilio baronum totius regni Angliae." [27]

The male line of the Conqueror became extinct on the death of Henry I.[28] The late king had endeavoured to secure the crown to his own offspring, first by inducing the baronage to do homage [29] and fealty to his son, William, and, after the untimely death of the Atheling, by exacting, on three separate occasions, an oath from the prelates and barons to acknowledge his daughter, the Empress Matilda, as his successor. The attempt to bind men's consciences more firmly by the triple repetition of the oath would seem to indicate his own mistrust; a recommendation to to the nation was all he could lawfully give, and it was a moot point whether even this recommendation had not been withdrawn on his deathbed.[30] Moreover, a woman was incapable of performing the martial duties which then appertained to royalty, and the acceptance of the Empress Matilda practically meant subjection to the rule of her husband, Geoffrey of Anjou —a man obnoxious to the Normans as an Angevin, to both English and Normans as a foreigner.[31] On the third occasion when fealty had been sworn to the Empress, her infant son, afterwards Henry II, was joined with her, and was nominated by his grandfather to be king after him. But, as the child was little more than two years old when the throne became vacant by Henry's death, he was clearly ineligible.

[26] Maskell, *Monumenta Ritualia,* ii, 6; *Select Charters,* 116. The ancient form of coronation oath, by which the king swore to maintain the laws and customs which the commonalty of the kingdom shall have chosen—*quas vulgus elegerit; les quels la communaute de vostre roiaume aura esleu*—has been at times altered to suit the various circumstances of accession to the throne. See Maitland, *Constitutional History,* p. 286; J. Wickham-Legg, *The Coronation Order of King James I,* xcvi, *et seq.*; L. G. Wickham-Legg, *The English Coronation Records,* Introduction, xxviii, *et seq.*; H. G. Richardson and G. O. Sayles, " Early Coronation Records," *Bulletin of the Institute of Historical Research,* xiii, 129, 139 *et seq.,* xiv, 1, 9 *et seq.*; Schramm, 179 *et seq.* The form of oath used at the Coronation of Edward VII, in its salient clause, runs: " Will you solemnly promise and swear to govern the people of this United Kingdom of Great Britain and Ireland, and the dominions thereto belonging, according to the statutes in Parliament agreed on, and the respective laws and customs of the same ?"—Anson, *Law and Custom,* ii, Part i, 236.

[27] *Select Charters,* 117.

[28] The Conqueror's eldest son, Robert, died without surviving issue a year earlier than Henry I.

[29] Similarly, subjects endeavoured to ensure the succession of their sons (generally the eldest) by persuading their feudal lord to accept, by anticipation, the son's homage; it was the frequency of these voluntary arrangements which soon hardened into the legal principle of primogeniture.

[30] Gervase of Canterbury, i, 94; Ralph de Diceto, i, 248; *cf.* also *Gesta Stephani* (*Chronicles of the Reigns of Stephen, Henry II and Richard I,* edited Howlett, Rolls Series), iii, 8–9.

[31] *Continuation of Florence of Worcester,* quoted by Stubbs, *Constitutional History,* i, 345 n. 3.

Stephen, 1135. Such being the position of affairs, the prompt action of Stephen of Blois, Count of Mortain and Boulogne,[32] his personal popularity with the men of London and Winchester, and the great influence of his brother Henry, Bishop of Winchester, ensured his election and coronation. To call him a usurper is an abuse of the term. His election, like that of his uncle, Henry I, was, indeed, somewhat irregular, few only of the magnates being present,[33] but the paucity of magnates was counterbalanced by the presence and support of the citizens of London, who might fairly claim to speak on behalf of the commonalty of the realm,[34] and the election was shortly afterwards confirmed by the adhesion of the great body of the baronage, clerical and lay. In the second of Stephen's charters his title to the throne is somewhat elaborately set forth: " Dei gratia assensu cleri et populi in regem Anglorum electus, et a Willelmo Cantuariensi archiepiscopo et sanctae Romanae ecclesiae legato consecratus, et ab Innocento sanctae Romanae sedis pontifice confirmatus." [35] Henry I, in a letter to Anselm, notifying his accession to the throne, had in like manner declared himself " nutu Dei a clero et a populo Anglia electus." [36] Both kings founded their title on the choice of the people. The confirmation by the pope was probably regarded, in Stephen's case, as a tacit condonation of the breach of their oaths by the king, prelates, and barons, who had all sworn to the late King Henry to support his daughter's claim.

Matilda. Matilda's claim was in fact put forward, and she was elected " Lady " of England by her supporters, presided over by Henry of Blois, Bishop of Winchester, who had for a short while deserted his brother, King Stephen, and now proposed that the clergy had the peculiar right of electing kings. The civil war ensued, but Matilda never secured coronation, and never used the title " Queen."

Feudal Influences. The kingship was now gradually passing out of the elective stage and becoming more feudal in character. Obtaining homage from all the feudatories was thought to give a secure title. The election became, as it were, feudalised in form, and to a great extent in spirit also. The action of Henry I, in exacting homage and fealty, first to his son William and then to his daughter and grandson, has already been noticed. In a similar manner Stephen, in 1152, endeavoured, unsuccessfully, to secure the recognition of his son Eustace as heir to the throne. On the death of Eustace, however, Stephen abandoned the struggle and made no

---

[32] Stephen was a younger son of Stephen, Count of Blois, by Adela, the only daughter of William the Conqueror who left surviving issue. His wife, Matilda, was the daughter and heiress of Eustace, Count of Boulogne, by Mary, younger sister of Matilda, wife of Henry I, and niece of Edgar Atheling.

[33] William of Malmesbury, *Historia Novella*, i, §§ 460–461; *Select Charters*, 136.

[34] *Gesta Stephani*, p. 5; *Select Charters*, 136. The claim of the Londoners to have the sole and special privilege of electing kings, is of course, baseless; Schramm, *ob. cit.*, 157. Cf. also *Anglo-Saxon Chronicle*, s. a. 1135.

[35] *Statutes of the Realm*—Charters of Liberties, p. 3; *Select Charters*, 143.

[36] Anselm's *Letters*, lib. iii, Ep. 41. *Select Charters*, 120. For divine election, *cf. supra*, p. 479 n. 22.

efforts on behalf of his second son. By treaty he recognised, not Matilda, but her son, Henry, as his successor and " heir "—language which some contemporaries construed as an adoption.

Henry II, 1154. At the time of Stephen's death, on October 25, 1154, Henry, Duke of Normandy, was absent from England. He returned on December 8, and after an interregnum of nearly two months, was elected and crowned king on the 19th of the same month.[37] He succeeded without opposition, not only by hereditary descent, but also by virtue of the recent compact of Winchester, ratified by the assent and homage of the baronage.[38] Henry II early procured the baronage to do homage, first to his young son William (who died at the age of three) and then to his son Henry. But he took a further and, as it turned out, most unfortunate step. Not satisfied with the homage of the baronage, which might be regarded as a prospective election, he borrowed from the practice of France and the Empires of the East and West,[39] the expedient of crowning and anointing the son during the lifetime of the father. The young Henry was twice solemnly crowned; on the first occasion by the Archbishop of York at Westminster in 1170, alone, and again, two years later, in company with his wife, daughter of Louis VII of France, the ceremony being now performed by the Archbishop of Rouen in Winchester Cathedral. Under the sinister guidance of his father-in-law he soon assumed the position of a rival and an enemy rather than of an heir-apparent, and died in arms against his father, in 1183.

Richard I, 1189. It was only a few days before his death, on July 6, 1189, that Henry II had recognised his eldest surviving son, Richard Cœur-de-Lion, as his successor. Richard remained absent from England about five weeks, engaged in receiving investiture of the Duchy of Normandy (July 20), and in concluding a treaty with Philip of France. In the meantime his mother, Queen Eleanor, issued a proclamation to the English, calling upon all freemen to take the oath of allegiance to her son Richard as " Lord of England." [40] No opposition of any kind was made by prelates, barons, or people, and on September 3, three weeks after he had landed in England, Richard took the usual coronation oaths, and was duly anointed and crowned, with extraordinary splendour and formality, in the presence of the assembled " archbishops, bishops, earls, barons, and a great multitude of knights."[41] In the Annals of Dunstable he is said to have been " elevated to the throne by hereditary right, after a solemn

---

[37] " Ab omnibus electus est "—Robert of Torigny, *Chronica, s. a.* 1145. *Cf.* William of Newburgh, ii, c. 1. *Select Charters*, 151.

[38] *Supra*, p. 55.

[39] It was also employed in Normandy, R. Foreville, *L'Eglise et la Royauté*, 282.

[40] Benedictus Abbas, ii, 74, 75.

[41] *Ibid.*, ii, 78. *Select Charters*, 244.

election by the clergy and people," [42] words which indicate that hereditary right was now beginning to prevail over the idea of election, the "election" being little more than a recognition of hereditary right.[43]

John, 1199. Richard I died without issue on April 6, 1199. After an interregnum of about six weeks, his younger brother John, to whom the barons, by Richard's death-bed orders, had already sworn fealty,[44] succeeded to the throne, with " a questionable title perfected by the election of the nation." [45] Even in private inheritances the doctrine of representation, by which the issue of a deceased elder brother would exclude the succession of the surviving younger brother, was as yet unsettled although it had in fact been making headway in private law until John's accession gave a check to it. The judges felt that they could not apply the principle without throwing doubt upon their master's title.[46] In the succession to the crown of England the doctrine had never hitherto obtained. Nearly two centuries had still to elapse before this stage in the growth of hereditary right was distinctly marked by the unopposed succession of Richard II as heir to his grandfather.[47] The claim of proximity of blood, which the uncle possessed, was much more obvious in early times than the subtle doctrine of representative primogeniture; and he was usually far better fitted by age, experience and personal authority to undertake the onerous duties of medieval royalty. In England there appears to have been an absence of any feeling in favour of the boy Arthur of Brittany, son of John's elder brother Geoffrey; while John's claim was supported by the death-bed recommendation of the late king, the influence of the queen-mother, and the adherence of a numerous and influential party among the barons. He was elected king without opposition, and crowned at Westminster on May 27.

At his election Archbishop Hubert, according to the account given by Matthew Paris, made a very remarkable speech, in which he declared the

---

[42] Annals of Dunstable, *s. a.* 1189 (*Annales Monastici*, iii, p. 24). The earlier portions of the Annals of Dunstable down to 1201 appear to be principally derived from the " Abbreviationes Chronicorum," and the " Imagines Historiarum " of Ralph de Diceto, the latter an original work of a contemporary. Hardy, *Catalogue of British History*, 1871, iii, 252.

[43] *Cf.* Schramm, 160–161. By the chroniclers Richard is termed " Earl " from his father's death till his investiture as Duke of Normandy on July 20, thenceforward " Duke Richard " till his coronation on September 3, 1189, when he became for the first time " Rex." His regnal years are reckoned only from this date. On his return from captivity he was crowned again at Winchester in 1194.

[44] Hoveden, *Chronica*, iv, 83.

[45] Stubbs, *Select Charters*, Introductory Sketch, 32; but see the rather different reading of events in Schramm, 161 *et seq.*

[46] Glanvill, lib. vii, c. 3. *Cf.* Plucknett, *History of the Common Law*, 5th ed., 716 *et seq.* The situation was commonly called the *casus regis*, and in Normandy the *mauvaise coutume*.

[47] " No opposition was made to the accession of Richard the Second, but there seems have been a strong notion in men's minds that John of Gaunt sought to displace his nephew. In earlier times, as the eldest and most eminent of the surviving sons of Edward the Third, John would probably have been elected without any thought of the claims of young Richard "—Freeman, *Growth of the English Constitution*, 213. Edward I, however, had already applied the principle of representation in adjudicating between Balliol and Bruce: Pollock and Maitland, *History of English Law*, ii, 298.

crown to be absolutely elective, giving even to the members of the royal stock no preference unless founded on their own personal merit.[48] The truth of this incident has been doubted by some; but from the mouth of a zealous partisan the speech is by no means improbable. Moreover, it is in accord with the church's views on fitness (as recognised by election) being preferable to mere inheritance. The archbishop, in fact, merely expressed, in very plain language indeed, what had been the theory of the constitution down to the time of Earl Harold, in whose person the theory was practically exemplified; and what, if we except the denial of any preference to members of the royal house, had actually been the ordinary practice both before and since the Conquest.[49] In the preamble of a charter issued by John shortly after his accession he was careful to unite both his titles: " Cum ad regimen regni Angliae, quod nobis jure competit haereditario, divina misericordia vocaverit, et mediante tam cleri quam populi unanimi consensu et favore." [50]

The Barons Choose an Anti-King. The struggle between John and the barons grew so bitter that they finally set up an anti-king in the now familar continental manner. As early as 1213, they had been negotiating with Louis (afterwards Louis VIII), the eldest son of Philip Augustus, King of France. The grant of Magna Carta produced only a short peace which John hastened to end by renewing the war. The barons then took the decisive step of again offering the crown to Louis, and again he accepted. The pope forbade this enterprise against a papal fief, but Louis built up his case on the facts that John had been condemned in England for his rebellion against Richard I and in France for the murder of Arthur; the surrender of England to the pope without consulting the barons entitled them to treat the throne as vacant; John's son Henry was born after these condemnations and so could not inherit [51]; and Louis was therefore entitled to prosecute his claim in right of his wife who was the daughter of the last of John's brothers and sisters to survive Richard I, and was therefore heir,[52] and, finally, that the election of John was invalid since it ignored this prior hereditary right.

Henry III, 1216. There was every probability that a justly incensed nation would have compelled the House of Anjou to yield the throne of

---

[48] Matthew Paris, ii, 454; *Select Charters*, 265–266.

[49] " Matthew Paris supposes that the archbishop, warned of John's utter faithlessness and foreseeing the troubles of his reign, wished to impress upon him and upon the people that as an elected king he must do his duty under pain of forfeiture. But the speech of Hubert was probably in itself nothing more than a declaration of John's fitness to be elected, the recollection of which would naturally recur to those who heard it when they found out how unfit he was to reign. The enunciation, however, of the elective character of the royal dignity is of very great importance "—Stubbs, *Constitutional History*, i, 554.

[50] Rymer, i, 75.

[51] On this curious point (which resembles the later notion of attainder) see Kern, *Kingship and Law*, 28 n. 10.

[52] Stubbs, *Constitutional History*, ii, 13 *et seq.*; Rymer, i, 140.

England to a new dynasty, when the death of John on October 19, 1216, removed the chief cause of offence, and gave his family one more chance before it was too late. The young Henry, who was barely nine years old, was knighted and hastily crowned at Gloucester on October 28 in the presence of the legate Gualo [53]; some years later, in 1220, when the country was more at peace, Archbishop Langton repeated the ceremony at Westminster. Arthur of Brittany had left a sister Eleanor, known as the " damsel of Brittany," who survived (although in strict confinement) till 1241, but she seems never to have been regarded as having a claim to the succession.

Edward I, 1272. The accession of Edward I, as we have already seen,[54] is notable because his reign began long before his coronation, leaving only a short interregnum of four days before the baronage gave their formal recognition. His son carried this development a stage further. Edward I's settlement of the line of succession and his treatment of the kingdom as if it were a private estate is worthy of note.[55]

Edward II, 1307. In the proclamation issued on the accession of Edward II he was declared to be already King of England by descent of heritage (" ja roi d'Engleterre par descente de heritage "), the words referring to the consent of the magnates of the realm being omitted.[56]

Hereditary Succession Established. From henceforth the old civil election dropped out, and hereditary succession became the established rule, subject, however, in cases of necessity, to the paramount power of parliament, not only to depose an individual sovereign, but also, for good reason, to set aside the direct line of descent and establish a new royal stock.[57] The ecclesiastical form of election by the clergy and people survived the civil form, and was maintained, in the coronation service down to the accession of Henry VIII [58]; since whose time a mere recognition by the people is all that takes place.[59]

[53] *Supra*, p. 88 n. 99. The Bishop of Winchester officiated, as neither archbishop was within reach; great care was taken to prevent any constitutional significance attaching to the legate's presence.

[54] *Supra*, pp. 477–478.

[55] On this, and the relevance of Chester and the Scottish throne, see Powicke, *Henry III and the Lord Edward*, ii, 732–733, 788.

[56] Rymer, ii, 1. Walsingham (i, 119) says: " Successit . . . non tam jure haereditario quam unanimi assensu procerum et magnatum."

[57] " Hereditary succession in monarchical states is nothing more than an expedient in government founded in wisdom, and tending to publick utility. And consequently whenever the safety of the whole requireth it, this expedient, like all rules of mere positive institution, must be subject to the controul of the supreme power in every state. . . . Title by descent was always esteemed by the legislature a wise expedient in government. But in cases of necessity, it was never thought to confer an indefeasible right, because that would have been *to defeat the end for the sake of the means* "—Sir Michael Foster, *Discourses on Crown Law*, p. 405.

[58] But see Schramm, 164, on the deliberate omission of the *collaudatio* at Edward II's coronation.

[59] The form for the coronation of Henry VIII, drawn up by that king himself, has been preserved. Hereditary right and elective right are set forth in equally strong terms. Prince Henry is described as " rightfull and undoubted enheritour by the lawes of God

Coronation Oath of Edward II. Although Edward II's reign began on July 8, 1307 (the day after his father's death), his coronation did not take place until February 25, 1308.[60] The coronation oath which he then took has aroused much discussion. On the one hand, it did not contain an engagement to maintain the rights of the crown such as Henry III and Edward I undertook, according to a recent conjecture [61]; on the other hand, it did contain a novel clause whose enigmatic wording has produced some centuries of controversy. The novel question and answer are as follows [62]:

> Sire, do you undertake to hold and keep the laws and the rightful customs which the commonalty of your realm shall have chosen, and will you defend and fortify them to the honour of God, to the best of your power ?
>
> I grant and promise them.

The Latin version (quas vulgus elegerit) agrees with the French (les quiels la communaute . . . aura esleu) in the uncertainty of the tense. Very eminent modern historians regard the " laws and customs " which the people " choose " as being legislation [63]; if this view is accepted, and if the tense is future, then the king swears to assent to future legislation not yet framed. In spite of the great weight of these authorities, it may be permissible to doubt whether the oath is concerned with legislation at all. The expression " laws and customs " is very common, but it does not occur with the meaning of " statutes." We need only examine the first folio of Bracton, *De Legibus et Consuetudinibus Angliae*, to see that these words meant the customary common law. To say that the people

and man," but also as " electe, chosen and required by all the thre estates of this lande, to take uppon hym the seid coroune and royall dignitie." The assent of the people is asked thus: " Woll ye serve at this tyme, and geve your wills and assents to the same consecration, enunction and coronacion ? Whereunto the people shall say with a grete voyce, Ye, Ye, Ye; So be it; Kyng Henry Kyng Henry "—Maskell, *Monumenta Ritualia*, ii, 75, n. 15; Freeman, *Norman Conquest*, iii, 627.

[60] There was a last minute delay which some chroniclers imply was caused by a political crisis; it has been suggested that Edward could not secure coronation until he had undertaken in advance to accept the demands which the barons were preparing to make: Wilkinson, " The Coronation oath of Edward II," in *Historical Essays in Honour of James Tait*, 405 *et seq.* For reasons *contra*, see Richardson, " The Coronation Oath," in *Transactions of the Royal Historical Society* (1941), at 142 *et seq.* Wilkinson returns to the subject in " The Coronation oath of Edward II and the Statute of York," *Speculum*, xix, 445–469.

[61] The evidence, all indirect, is presented by Richardson, *loc. cit.*, 131 *et seq.* (*Cf.* C. H. McIlwain, *Political Thought in the West*, 379.) That kings should have been sworn for centuries to maintain the rights of the people is quite natural; but at first sight it seems distinctly odd to require a king to swear to maintain his own rights—a thing that kings were generally only too eager to do. If it dates back to Henry III, then the reason for it may have been John's unauthorised surrender of the kingdom to the papacy. Edward I appealed to some such oath in resisting the papal provisors (an action which the barons appreciated); but when he also invoked it as invalidating concessions which he had been forced to accord, the barons may well have thought that the oath had outlived its usefulness. Hence the new oath administered to Edward II.

[62] Rymer, iii, 63 (Lodge and Thornton, *Documents*, 10–11).

[63] Stubbs, *Constitutional History*, ii, 331 ; Maitland, *Constitutional History*, 100 ; Richardson in *Transactions of the Royal Historical Society* (1941), 147. See, further, B. Wilkinson, " The Coronation Oath and the Statute of York," *Speculum*, xix, 445 ; Richardson, " The English Coronation Oath," *Speculum*, xxiv, 44, and for the oaths taken by Henry II's sons, R. Foreville, 313–314.

" choose " customs is quite in accord with medieval thought, which postulated an active rather than a passive assent by those who live under a custom. Bracton in fact uses words curiously appropriate to this clause in the coronation oath when he speaks of " customs approved by the consent of those who use them and confirmed by the oath of kings." [64] Thus interpreted,[65] the novel fourth clause might indeed seem a mere repetition of the traditional first clause. However, its presence might be accounted for by the excision of some clause to maintain the rights of the crown, the conjectural existence of which has just been mentioned. The new clause may therefore have been substituted for the old in order to protect not merely the prerogative but the whole fabric of common law, of which the prerogative was a part.[66]

Depositions. The right of the national assembly—whether acting as a technically constituted parliament, or as a convention of the estates of the realm—to regulate and vary the succession to the crown, has been constantly claimed and exercised whenever the safety and welfare of the kingdom have imperatively required it. The depositions by the witan of Sigebert in 755 and of Ethelred the Unready in 1017 have already been referred to in a previous chapter.[67] Since the Norman Conquest there had hitherto been no actual case of formal deposition; but we have seen the barons under King John renouncing their allegiance and electing Louis, son of the King of France, to be their king [68]; and the misgovernment of Henry III caused a change in the succession to be again mooted amongst the baronage.

Deposition of Edward II, 1327. There were no useful precedents at hand, therefore, when the queen, Mortimer and most of the barons, a number of bishops, and a violent mob of Londoners, all came to the conclusion that Edward II must be deposed. The participants realised that there was peril in the proceeding and took every care to spread the responsibility as widely as possible. The new parliament (which contained representatives from Wales) met in the king's absence on January 7, 1327, and all attempts to persuade him to come from Kenilworth to Westminster failed.[69] Much discussion in parliament, and noisy meetings in the City, occupied the ensuing week, in the course of which it was generally decided that the

---

[64] Bracton, f. 1b. *Cf.* R. S. Hoyt, " The Coronation Oath of 1308: the Background of the ' Leyes et les custumes,' " *Traditio*, xi, 235, and his " The Coronation Oath," *English Historical Review*, lxxi, 353.

[65] McIlwain, *op. cit.*, 196 and n. 2, seems in accord with this view.

[66] If so, the device nevertheless failed, for in 1322 Edward II was still able to say that the Ordinances (1311) were contrary to his coronation oath.

[67] *Supra*, p. 18.

[68] *Supra*, pp. 86, 484.

[69] The obscure course of events is discussed, and some new evidence is printed, in M. V. Clarke, *Representation and Consent*, 173 *et seq. Cf.* Lapsley in *English Historical Review*, xlix, 581, and Wilkinson, *ibid.*, liv, 223. There is no surviving official record of the proceedings, so we are dependent upon the chronicles. There may have been a " statute " (*supra*, p. 192), and, if so, Richard II may have destroyed it (M. V. Clarke, *op. cit.*, 177).

young Edward should replace his father on the throne.   On January 13 lords and commons assembled in Westminster Hall, and a bill of six articles, drawn up by Stratford, Bishop of Winchester, was exhibited against the king.   These articles set forth that he was devoid of the ability to govern, had suffered himself to be led in all things by evil counsellors, had neglected the business of the state, lost the crown of Scotland, broken his coronation oath, ruined his kingdom and people, and that there appeared no hope of his amendment.[70]   It was therefore resolved that the Lord Edward, the king's eldest son, should immediately take upon him the government of the kingdom and be crowned king.   Down to this point it would seem that nothing more than a political decision had been reached upon the desirability of a change of kings.   That decision had been reached both in parliament and in tumultuous meetings outside. There remained the much more difficult problem of clothing that policy with constitutional forms, so that the operation should seem reasonable and orderly when considered in the light of familiar procedures and accepted ideas of government.   It was therefore determined to procure a formal resignation from Edward II.   On January 20 a deputation of prelates, earls, barons, abbots and two judges waited upon the king, then a prisoner in Kenilworth Castle, and after notifying to him the resolution of parliament, obtained his consent to the election of his son. Then Sir William Trussel, in the name of the rest, and as " procurator of the prelates, earls, barons and others [and of the whole parliament]," renounced the homage and fealty which the members had severally made to the king, and declared that they should thereafter account him as a private person without any manner of royal dignity.   The ceremony ended by Sir Thomas Blount, the steward of the household, breaking his staff of office, as a sign that his master had ceased to reign as completely as if he were dead.[71]   In the proclamation of his peace [72] issued on January 24 the twofold title of Edward III, derived from the common counsel and consent of the estates of the realm and the voluntary resignation of his father, is carefully set forth; but there is no word of any deposition.   On January 25 his reign was held to begin (his father's having terminated it would seem, on the 20th, when for the last time documents went out in his name); on February 1 the young king, who was fourteen years of age, was crowned at Westminster.

[70] There seems no ground for treating these proceedings as a trial (as M. V. Clarke, *op. cit.*), still less as an impeachment (as Sir James Ramsay, *Genesis of Lancaster*, i, 162). The surviving narratives do not suggest that judicial forms were employed.

[71] Baker, *Chronicon* (ed. E. M. Thompson), 27; Knighton, i, 443; and see Stubbs, *Constitutional History*, ii, 380, and M. V. Clarke, *Representation and Consent*, 185–186. For Trussel, see *supra*, p. 208, n. 98. The form of words which he used is in Stubbs, *loc. cit.*; for another version (which omits the words in square brackets above), see *Rotuli Parliamentorum Inediti* (ed. H. G. Richardson and G. O. Sayles), 101.

[72] Rymer, ii, 683, 684; Lodge and Thornton, *Documents*, 20–21. The chancery soon found that " king Edward, son of king Edward, son of king Edward " was cumbrous, and adopted the form of " Edward, the third since the conquest." The unofficial dynastic numerals in the chronicles vary; one (in M. V. Clarke, *Representation and Consent*, 184, n. 3) refers to Edward II as " Edward V."

Much has been written of late concerning the part of parliament in all this. To the question: Did parliament depose the king? no short answer can be given. The official view was that Edward had abdicated, and that the ceremonies just mentioned were merely giving effect to his wish.[73] The session in Westminster Hall, in the course of which the lords and commons decided that Edward ought to reign no longer, might or might not have been a parliament according to later notions, and upon this point would partly depend the answer to our question. The really important feature, it may be suggested, is that contemporaries in 1327 seem unaware of this technical difficulty, and that they did not think it necessary to consider whether the lords and commons, summoned by the king as a parliament, might cease to be a parliament if they left a certain building, met without the king, or debated certain matters. For technicalities of this sort we must wait until 1399. Moreover, the parliament which met on January 7 in obedience to the writs of Edward II continued to sit after the revolution as the first parliament of Edward III—once again oblivious of technical objections which a later age was to find insuperable.[74]

Deposition of Richard II. The reign of Richard II presents many fascinating historical puzzles, and among them his deposition in 1399 has occupied the attention of several historians lately. A still more obscure incident, which seems now to be established as probable, is his earlier deposition during the last three days of the year 1387—a rash move which had to be hastily hushed up in view of disagreement among the conspirators as to who should be his successor.[75] The political decision was therefore rescinded before any steps had been taken to clothe it in constitutional form. The deposition in 1399 was preceded, as in Edward II's case, by a so-called voluntary resignation, and accompanied by Henry of Lancaster's very remarkable claim to the crown, in which an insinuated priority of descent from Henry III, a right of conquest, and the misgovernment of Richard, are artfully combined.

A parliament had been summoned to meet at Westminster on Tuesday, September 30, by writs issued in Richard's name at Chester on August 19. An official " record and process " of the deposition and a narrative of the events leading up to it was placed on the roll of parliament.[76] It is now known that that narrative is mendacious at a number of points, having been put together in the interests of Lancastrian propaganda.[77] It is, nevertheless, clear that Richard, while a prisoner in the Tower, executed a formal deed of resignation [78] on Monday, September 29, which was

---

[73] For an exact ecclesiastical parallel, see vol. clv of the Surtees Society, where a prior of Durham who resigned because of ill health was subsequently deposed.

[74] Some references are collected in Powicke, *Henry III*, ii, 594nn. *Cf. infra*, pp. 492, 528.

[75] M. V. Clarke, *Fourteenth Century Studies*, 91–95.

[76] *Rotuli Parliamentorum*, iii, 416 *et seq.* (extracts in Lodge and Thornton, *Documents*, 27 *et seq.*).

[77] Clarke, *op. cit.*, 67 *et seq.*; *cf.* A. Steel, *Richard II*, 260 *et seq.*

[78] Text in *Rotuli Parliamentorum*, iii, 416 no. 13.

presented to the magnates and commons, who had assembled for the first day of the parliament, on the following Tuesday, September 30. The " record and process " audaciously asserted that Richard II had performed this abdication ceremony with a cheerful countenance, and that he had already promised to abdicate while at Conway six weeks previously—statements which historians now agree are false. The record further alleges that Richard voluntarily intimated that he would like to have Henry of Lancaster as his successor, and gave his signet to Henry as a token thereof; this statement has also been received with suspicion.[79] However that may be, the assembled magnates accepted the abdication, and decided for greater surety to read some of a list of thirty-three articles [80] containing accusations against the king. The estates considered these articles notoriously true, and since the king had confessed his incompetence in the deed of resignation, they nominated commissioners who, sitting as a court (pro tribunali sedentes), out of still more abundant caution pronounced a decree of deposition: " Propter praemissa, et eorum praetextu, ab omni dignitate et honore regiis, si quid dignitatis et honoris hujusmodi in eo remanserit, merito deponendum pronunciamus, decernimus, et declaramus, et ipsum simili cautela deponimus." [81] The throne is then declared vacant: " ut constabat de praemissis, et oerum occasione, regnum Angliae, cum pertinentiis suis vacare." Finally Henry of Lancaster rose from his seat and claimed the throne as heir of Henry III—the most incredible of all the incredible things said on that strange day. The estates considered this " vindicatio " (for Romanistic language at this point succeeds the canonistic formulas of the deposition) and they " with all the people " agreed that Henry should reign over them: " ut Dux praefatus super eos regnaret unanimiter concesserunt." [82] Henry took his seat on the throne, the Archbishop of Canterbury preached, and the proceeding closed with a short speech of thanks from the newly recognised king. The next day (Wednesday, October 1), the sentence of deposition was published to Richard in the Tower by Chief Justice Thirning.[83]

One other fact needs mention. As soon as Henry IV had been recognised as king in the session of the lords and commons on September 30, he caused it to be announced [84] that a parliament would meet a week later (that is on Monday, October 6) in virtue of new writs, but that this exceptionally short notice was not to be a precedent. Upon that day,

---

[79] Clarke, op. cit., 78; B. Wilkinson, " The deposition of Richard II and the accession of Henry IV," in English Historical Review, liv, 215, at 219; A. Steel, Richard II, 278.

[80] Rotuli Parliamentorum, iii, 417–422 (extracts in Lodge and Thornton, 28–29).

[81] Ibid., 422 (Lodge and Thornton, 29–30).

[82] Ibid., 422–423 (Lodge and Thornton, 30–31). The " record and process " suppresses the fact that the Bishop of Carlisle had the temerity to make a speech protesting against the proceedings.

[83] Ibid., 424 (Lodge and Thornton, 31–32). In both texts the word " morne " is clearly a misreading for " morue," i.e., " morrow."

[84] Rotuli Parliamentorum, iii, 423, no. 57.

October 6, parliament was opened [85] by the new king, and Archbishop Arundel explained that the meeting of September 30 was not a parliament, since the writs had abated by reason of Richard II's abdication and deposition.[86]

Nature of the Proceedings. Such was the procedure, therefore, by which the Lancastrian dynasty came to the throne. The " record and process " is certainly an unreliable witness to the events before September 30 but we are bound to accept it as giving Henry's own view (true or false) of what happened when the estates met and accepted his claim. The document is, in fact, the considered statement of the Lancastrian case, and it remains to examine, however briefly, its constitutional implications.[87] The frequent references to the " abundant caution " with which the process was conducted are evidently truthful. Great care was taken; it has been asserted that a sort of commission of experts (upon which the chronicler Adam of Usk [88] claims to have sat) went into the legal position and drew comfort from canon law, and tried to find a plausible claim for Henry, and found none. Adam of Usk's commission reported that Richard could be deposed " by authority of the clergy and people called together for the purpose." The " clergy and people " have already been noticed in connection with coronations,[89] but a modern authority has suggested that Adam's words mean deposition by a parliament.[90] The further suggestion is made that Henry IV objected to taking the throne by a parliamentary title; that in consequence we have Arundel's ingenious doctrine that the assembly of September 30 was not technically a parliament; that the " record and process " strenuously maintains that view by speaking consistently of " estates," and by avoiding the word " parliament " [91]; and that, finally, by subtle manoeuvring Henry IV contrived to get the throne without the intervention of parliament. Subsidiary to this main thesis there is a controversy between modern scholars as to whether either, or both, or neither of the meetings on September 30 and October 6 were

---

[85] New elections were duly held, although many of the returns could not reach London until many days after October 6; meanwhile, those who were elected under Richard II's writs seem to have sat in anticipation of being re-elected—which they were, in due course.

[86] *Rotuli Parliamentorum*, iii, 415, no. 1.

[87] The controversial literature upon the course of events and their constitutional implications begins with the introduction by V. H. Galbraith and M. V. Clarke to the Dieulacres Chronicle, *Bulletin of the John Rylands Library*, xiv, 125–181 (reprinted in M. V. Clarke, *Fourteenth Century Studies*, 53–98; our citations are to that edition); G. Lapsley, " The Parliamentary Title of Henry IV," *English Historical Review*, xlix, 423–449, 577–606; S. B. Chrimes, *Constitutional Ideas in the Fifteenth Century*, esp. 106 *et seq.*; H. G. Richardson, " Richard II's Last Parliament," *English Historical Review*, lii, 39–47; G. Lapsley, " Richard II's 'Last Parliament,' " *ibid.*, liii, 53–78; B. Wilkinson, " Deposition of Richard II and the Accession of Henry IV," *ibid.*, liv, 216–239; H. G. Richardson, " Elections to the October Parliament of 1399, " *Bulletin of the Institute of Historical Research*, xiv, 137–143; Anthony Steel, *Richard II*, 260 *et seq.*

[88] Adam of Usk, *Chronicon* (ed. E. M. Thompson), 24.

[89] *Cf.*, *supra*, p. 481 n. 22.

[90] Lapsley, in *English Historical Review*, xlix, 586; *cf.* Chrimes, *op. cit.*, 106, and *contra*, Wilkinson in *English Historical Review*, liv, 230–231.

[91] *Cf.* the " estates " in Scottish history: *supra*, p. 458 n. 23.

in the eyes of contemporaries true parliaments. Instead of Bishop Stubbs'
view that Henry IV's title was purely parliamentary, Mr Lapsley would
urge that Henry deliberately rejected any such proposal and successfully
avoided owing his crown to parliament.

Was there a Parliamentary Title to the Crown? The principal difficulty
in both views is the conception of a " parliamentary title." As we saw at
the end of Chapter 8, *supra*, parliament was the king's court in the
same sense that a manorial court was the lord's; in the one case and
in the other, it is impossible to think of such a body as conferring
title upon its lord. The most it could do was to make a show of assent
and register the fact that it had a new master. It would be erroneous to
think of parliament as a college council electing to a scholarship, or as
the senate of the United States hearing the impeachment of a president.
Archbishop Arundel made it abundantly clear that parliament exists only
by virtue of the royal writ. It is difficult to find any contemporary trace
of the view that parliament could at this time confer a title to the crown;
on the other hand, it is undeniable that parliament's own title was derived
from the crown and ceased at the will of the crown. It is significant that
" technicalities " now begin to appear in Arundel's doctrine. There was
no precedent in favour of it, for as yet no king had died during the continuance of a parliament [92]; there was one precedent against it, for Edward
II's abdication had certainly not terminated his last parliament which, in
fact, continued to sit under his successor. Arundel's dogma that parliamentary writs become void upon the resignation of the king seems to be
derived by analogy from the fact that many other writs were abated by the
demise of the crown,[93] and may be a fruit of the deliberations by the
committee of experts upon which Adam of Usk served.[94] In adopting it as
the official view, Henry IV's advisers can hardly have been trying to avoid
a " parliamentary title " (for that conception, it is submitted, is an
anachronism). If they had a constitutional motive, it may perhaps be
found in the consideration that the new rule would emphasise the com-
pleteness with which Richard had ceased to be king, by equating the
situation caused by his resignation with the presumed results of a natural
demise of the crown, and in stating it Arundel made it clear that the
voidance of the writs took place " by reason of the acceptance of
the renunciation made by the said King Richard, and of the deposition of the
same King Richard, which was on Tuesday last." [95] The words are a

---

[92] It was the destiny of Henry himself to provide the first precedent of a parliament dissolved
by the demise of the crown, in 1413.

[93] The gradual legislative repeal of this rule has been noted, *supra*, p. 522; its early
history has not been collected. See 2 Edw. 3, c. 13; *Year Books of Edward II*, x, 265,
no. 70.

[94] A technicality which seems to have troubled no one is the statute of 1397 which made it
high treason to " compass or purpose . . . to depose the king ": 21 Ric. 2, c. 3. (*Cf.*
the judge's answer to question 9, *supra*, pp. 171. It was repealed by 1 Hen. 4, c. 10).

[95] *Rotuli Parliamentorum*, iii, 415, no. 1.

useful reminder that in 1327 and in 1399 the procedure consisted of (1) a " voluntary " abdication; (2) the acceptance of the abdication; and finally, (3) a formal deposition in which the legal bonds of king and subject are declared to be dissolved. No English king has been deposed until after he had abdicated; the " deposition," therefore, is not an aggressive act by subjects against monarch, but the final and formal ratification of the monarch's own resignation.

Henry IV's Claim to the Throne. The throne being thus vacant, it remains to consider the claim which Henry actually put forth before the lords and commons:

> In the name of Fadir, Son and Holy Ghost, I Henry of Lancastre chalenge yis Rewme of Yngland and the corone with all ye membres and ye appurtenances, als I yat am disendit be right lyne of the blode comyng fro the gude lorde Kyng Henry therde, and thorghe yat ryght yat God of his grace hath sent me, with helpe of my kyn, and of my frendes to recover it; the whiche Rewme was in poynt to be undone for defaut of governance and undoyng of the gode laws.[96]

Henry thus urged (1) his royal descent, (2) the fact that he had recovered the crown, and (3) the misdeeds of his predecessor. He subsequently explained that his " conquest " would not be used to the prejudice of his people.[97] The accession of Richard II (1377) had been, as we have seen, the first instance, in the succession to the crown of England, where the claim of representative primogeniture was preferred to that of proximity of blood. If the crown was to continue to descend according to the rules of real property, then the heir was the child Edmund Mortimer, Earl of March, the great-great-grandson of Edward III, through Philippa, daughter of Lionel, Duke of Clarence, third son, of that king (William, the second son having died in infancy). If England had adopted (or if Henry had established) the rule of descent called the " Salic Law " [98] then his claim would have been incontestable, for he was the son of the eldest of Edward III's sons to leave issue in the male line. But Henry did not take this course,[99] and relied upon his only other connection with the royal house, which was through his mother, Blanche of Lancaster, great-great-granddaughter of Henry III. Perhaps Henry thought it worth while to stress the long Lancastrian lineage with its growing legend of opposition to the crown; but all that was irrelevant as a basis for a claim to inherit, unless history could be falsified. Henry thought this desperate course worth trying. Henry III had two sons only who survived infancy, Edward I and Edmund " Crouchback," [1] first Earl of Lancaster. By means of a

---

[96] *Ibid.*, 422–423, no. 53. [97] *Ibid.*, 423, no. 56.

[98] At this moment the rule was becoming specially significant in France: J. M. Potter, " Development and Significance of the Salic Law," *English Historical Review*, lii, 235 *et seq.* One may wonder whether John of Gaunt had propounded the notion in 1376: *Chronicon Angliae* (Rolls Series, no. 64), 92.

[99] To have done so would have meant the abandonment of the English claim by Edward III, through his mother, to the French throne.

[1] So called because as a Crusader he wore a cross on his back. Later misunderstanding gave rise to the notion that he was deformed. The evidence is discussed by Lapsley in the *English Historical Review*, xlix, 593–595.

forged chronicle [2] it was alleged that Edmund was in fact the elder of the two. The implication was that the Lancaster line took priority over Edward I and all his descendants. Had the last four kings, then, reigned for a century and a quarter without lawful right? No one dared to draw this logical conclusion. The only claim by inheritance which Henry IV chose to make was thus demonstrably false. The only other matter in the claim which could entitle Henry IV was his military conquest—and he did at least apologise for that.[3]

The Crown Entailed. Under Henry IV the right of succession to the crown was settled, altered, and re-settled no less than four times. In his first parliament—the same which had been summoned by Richard II on September 30 and re-assembled under the new king's writs on October 6, 1399—the Lord Henry, Prince of Wales, was " created and ordained Heir Apparent " by the king with the assent of the lords spiritual and temporal and all the commons, " to have and enjoy the Realm in time to come when God it should will " ; and this was " entered of record on the rolls of this present parliament." [4] Four years afterwards, in the parliament which met at Westminster on January 14, 1404, the lords and commons " recognised " that the succession was entailed upon the Prince of Wales and the heirs of his body, and in default upon his brothers, the other sons of the king, and their issue in order of seniority.[5] In addition to his four sons, Henry (afterwards Henry V), Thomas (Duke of Clarence), John (Duke of Bedford), and Humphrey (Duke of Gloucester), Henry IV had two daughters who appear to have been intentionally ignored in this settlement; the daughters of his sons were, however, capable of inheriting under the entail. Two years later the lords and commons seem to have thought it desirable to exclude these also, probably with a view to negativing the right of succession through females, which was the basis of title of the young Earl of March, and asked the king and prince whether they agreed in the change. Accordingly, on June 7, 1406, the king resettled the crowns of England and France on himself, and the heirs male of his body by means of a remarkable charter, sealed with the great seal, and the seals of all the lords spiritual and temporal, and of the Speaker of the commons. This curious document, and the extraordinary form of its attestation, seem to indicate doubts whether the normal forms of parliamentary assent were adequate for so high a matter.[6] Very soon, however,

---

[2] Henry's father, John of Gaunt, has been accused of this, as part of an earlier scheme to place Henry in the line of succession during Richard II's reign.

[3] See *supra*, p. 493, n. 97.

[4] *Rotuli Parliamentorum*, iii, 434, no. 103. (Not on the statute roll.)

[5] *Ibid.*, 525, no. 17. (Not on the statute roll.) The distinction between the generic term " heirs," denoting all heirs, collateral as well as lineal, and the specific term " heirs of the body," which is restricted to lineal heirs alone, is sometimes overlooked.

[6] *Rotuli Parliamentorum*, iii, 575, 576. For the six months during which this *Hausgesetz* was in force, we therefore had a rule similar to the " Salic Law " ; if such a rule had been set up under Edward III, then Henry of Lancaster would have been the lawful successor of Richard II, and after the failure of the Lancastrian line, the line of York would have been entitled.

these limitations in tail male were perceived to involve certain inconvenient consequences, and so the last enactment was repealed on December 22 in that same year and by the same parliament, and the crown was finally settled upon King Henry and the heirs of his body, thus admitting into the line of succession his sons and their issue, female as well as male. Once again, a portentous charter with scores of seals was prepared, and a short statement of its effect was put on the statute roll—the first appearance of succession matters in the form of a statute.[7]

The Beauforts Legitimised. These vacillating dispositions, which resemble continental *Hausgesetze* rather than English statutes, are not the only products of Henry IV's dynastic anxieties. He had three half-brothers (John Beaufort, Earl of Somerset; Henry, Cardinal Beaufort; and Thomas Beaufort, Duke of Exeter) who were the illegitimate issue of his father John of Gaunt and Catherine Swynford. After a delay of some twenty-five years the parents were married, and the issue legitimised both by the Pope and by Richard II, who for this purpose assumed an imperial prerogative (come entier Emperour de son Roialme d'Engleterre) and asserted his royal plenary power (de plenitudine nostre regalis potestatis). This grant was confirmed by Henry IV in letters patent in which the significant words " excepta dignitate regali " appear to be mysteriously inserted.[8]

The Dynastic Situation. In the course of the fifteenth century the claim of the Mortimers (derived from Edward III's third son) had passed to Anne Mortimer, heiress of her house. Henry VI himself was heir of the fourth son, and the male line of Edward III's fifth son was represented by Richard, Earl of Cambridge. Anne Mortimer married Richard of Cambridge, and their son, Richard, Duke of York (1412–1460), was therefore heir general of Edward III, through his mother, and would become heir male of Edward III through his father, upon the death of Henry VI without issue. This conclusion can hardly be affected by the fact that there was a line of Beaufort Dukes of Somerset until 1471. As we have seen, their legitimation did not extend to the royal dignity; but even had they been born legitimate, they would possibly have been excluded by the common-law rule against the half-blood.[9] In any case, politically, the Beauforts were staunch supporters of the Lancastrian dynasty, and so there was a keen struggle for power between Richard, Duke of York, and the Duke of Somerset.

---

[7] 7 Hen. 4, c. 2. The reason for the change is given in the recited petition of the Lords and Commons. *Rotuli Parliamentorum*, iii, 581. It might be concluded from the beginning of the instrument that Henry's daughters would be entitled to take under it, but they are not included in that portion of the charter which sets out the remainders in detail.

[8] Richard II's patent of 1397 is in *Rotuli Parliamentorum*, iii, 343 no. 28. Henry IV's of 1407 was not put on the parliament roll. Both are edited with valuable textual and historical notes in A. F. Pollard, *Reign of Henry VII*, ii, 6–9.

[9] On half-blood, see Pollock and Maitland, *History of English Law*, ii, 303–305, and Plucknett, *Concise History* (5th ed.), 719–722. The point did not arise in the English royal succession, until Mary and Elizabeth succeeded Edward VI (but that was under an entail; no remainder had ever been created in favour of the Beauforts, and so they were at common law).

During two periods of the king's incapacity, York had been named Protector. He may have felt that his ultimate succession was assured as long as Henry VI remained childless; but in 1453 a Prince of Wales was born. Defeated at the battle of Bloreheath (1459), the Duke of York fled to Ireland, and was attainted in a parliament sitting at Coventry (1459). Assembling his friends, they invaded England, captured the king, and then, a new parliament having repealed the attainders passed at Coventry, York laid formal claim to the crown (1460).

The Yorkist Claim to the Throne. His first impulse was to march into parliament with a fanfare of trumpets (he already moved in royal state and had assumed the royal arms) and sit on the throne, but the stony silence of the astonished magnates showed that more ceremonious measures would be needed.[10] On October 16, 1460, therefore, he submitted to the lords spiritual and temporal in parliament (the commons were left out of the proceedings until the final treaty) a memorandum [11] consisting merely of his pedigree and the conclusion that as representing the line of the third of Edward III's sons he was entitled to the crown as against the descendants of the fourth son.

The king authorised the lords to draw up an answer. The lords called upon the judges to search out objections to York's claim, but they declined on the ground that they were judges and not advocates, and that the matter " touched the Kyng's high estate and regalie, which is above the lawe and passed ther lernyng "; they suggested that the royal family and the peers were alone competent to deal with it. The serjeants-at-law and king's attorney were next called, and their excuses cut short by the remark that this was the sort of work they were paid for; but no answer in support of the king's rights could be got from them, so the lords themselves prepared a defence of the Lancastrian title.[12]

The Lancastrian Defence. Sixty years after the revolution of 1399, therefore, the lords based the title of Henry VI upon (1) the " grete Othes " which they, and York himself, had sworn; (2) " the grete and notable Acts of Parlements . . . of dyvers of the Kyng's Progenitours, the which Acts be sufficient and resonable to be leyde ageyn the title of the seid Duc of York: the which Acts been of moche more auctorite than eny Cronycle, and also of auctorite to defete eny manere title made to eny persone "; (3) there were " dyvers entayles made to the heires males as for the Corone of Englond, as it may appere by dyvers Cronicles and Parlementes "; (4) the claimant has always borne the arms of York [Edward III's fifth son] and not those of Clarence [through whom he professed to claim]; and (5) Henry IV had entered as heir of Henry III.

[10] Stubbs, *Constitutional History*, iii, 184–185; J. H. Ramsay, *Lancaster and York*, ii, 231.
[11] *Rotuli Parliamentorum*, v, 375, no. 11.
[12] *Rotuli Parliamentorum*, v, 376, no. 13. There are brief extracts of some of the documents in Lodge and Thornton, 34–36.

This statement of Lancastrian doctrine deserves examination. The famous second point is significant for its weakness; the lords had no clear idea of the nature of these " acts of parliament," although they did esteem them more highly than mere chronicles. A judgment in parliament was admittedly conclusive as to private titles, but the lords did not venture to say that parliament could determine the succession to the crown, and had done so. Once again we must conclude that if the Lancastrians neither possessed, nor claimed to possess, a " parliamentary title," it was because that conception of the powers of parliament had not yet come into existence. Points (3) and (4) come to the root of the matter; the former alleges vaguely that there had been a number of entails in tail male—and, as we have already remarked, if there had been from the time of Edward III onwards a rule of male primogeniture, then Henry IV was the lawful successor of Richard II. The point about York's coat of arms similarly demonstrates that under a rule of tail male York was the heir of York and not of Clarence. The crown had in fact descended for centuries in what could be described as tail male, but there were two difficulties: first, some origin for the rule had to be found since it was not the common-law course of descent—hence the necessity to invoke, however vaguely, the " dyvers entayles made "; and secondly, there were the words of Henry IV himself claiming through his mother from Henry III—and the peers felt bound to stick by them.

The Yorkist Answer. Richard of York put in an answer point by point. The case of conscience in (1) he would submit to the church. To points (2) and (3) he replied, that only once had the crown been entailed,[13] and makes the point that if the title had been good there would have been no need for an Act "in a parlement by hym called." These disquieting although perfectly logical words suggested that Henry IV, being a king without title, could not call a truly lawful parliament; York therefore hastened to add that although the settling Acts were void against God's law and natural law, he regarded all other Lancastrian Acts of parliament as valid. As to (4) he bore the York arms out of policy only, and not as an indication that he or his ancestors had abandoned their claim,[14] adding that his proper arms were in truth neither York nor Clarence, but England. He treated (5) shortly, as a lie and a fraud.

The Compromise. The Lancastrian case, which might have been so strongly based in male inheritance consistently observed from the death of King John down to Henry VI had to be thrown away because of Henry IV's silly attempt to forge history; the alternative, a " parliamentary title,"

---

[13] Neither side had a detailed knowledge of the complicated dealings of Henry IV, recounted *supra*, p. 494, and York missed the point in his favour that only one of the settlements was in tail male, and that one was repealed six months later.

[14] Several rebels, at different times, had proposed the claim of the Clarence-March-York line.

was outside the range of contemporary thought.[15]   The argument that
Lancastrian parliaments were no more rightful than Lancastrian kings was
unanswerable and York's claim as heir general of Edward III had to be
admitted.   As so often happened in private litigation over land, the affair
ended with a final concord: York recognised Henry VI as king for life,
and the king recognised York as his successor after his death or resignation
—words which contain an unmistakable hint of what the Yorkists wanted
Henry to do.[16]

This accord did not even mention the young Prince of Wales, whose
appanage it transferred to York.   The civil war was renewed and at the end
of the year 1460 the Duke of York and his second son were slain at the
Battle of Wakefield; Edward, the eldest, inherited his father's claim to the
throne.   In spite of a Lancastrian victory in the second Battle of St.
Albans the new Duke of York got to London.

Accession of Edward IV, 1461.   The Chancellor addressed a mass
meeting of the citizens, and on March 4, 1461, Edward enthroned himself
in Westminster Hall, received the crown jewels at the Abbey, and proclaimed
himself Edward IV.   His reign was held to have begun on that day.   There
was no parliament in existence until eight months later when the official
account of the accession and its consequences was enrolled.[17]   The
proceedings are described with strict legal precision as the entry of the heir
at law upon his inheritance, which for sixty years had been held unlawfully
by usurpers.   The final concord had been broken at the Battle of Wakefield,
thus giving Edward a right of immediately entering.   Henry was " removed "; having never been king, there was no need to depose him.

During the brief Lancastrian restoration (October 1470–April 1471)
the crown was re-settled by parliament on Henry VI and his issue male
with remainder in default of such issue, to George, Duke of Clarence,
brother of Edward IV, and his heirs.[18]   Edward IV regained his throne,
and the Lancastrian line came to an end when Henry VI's only child,

---

[15] *Cf. supra*, p. 494.   Richard III caught the idea best: *infra*, pp. 499, 503.

[16] *Rotuli Parliamentorum*, v, 378 nos. 19 *et seq.*   The treaty received statutory ratification,
ibid., no. 27.

[17] *Rotuli Parliamentorum*, v, 463 *et seq.*; 1 Edw. 4, c. 1.

[18] " That if the said Henry, and Edward his first begotten son, died withoute Issue Male of
theire Body, that the seid Duke and his Heires shulde be Kynge of this Lande." *Rotuli
Parliamentorum*, vi, 191, no. 34, and *cf.* 194.   (Since Edward IV was attainted, his issue
was not capable of inheriting from or through him; the Yorkist claim therefore passed
to his brother.)   This Act is known only by the reference to it in the Act just cited (17 Edw.
4, 1477), by which it was repealed.   The petition of the commons on which the repealing
Act is founded is curious, and well brings out the Yorkist theory: "That where in your
moost dolorous absence oute of this your Reame, in the parties of Holond beyng, and
afore your moost victorious regresse into this same your Reame, in a pretensed Parlement,
unlaufully and by usurped auctorite summoned and called by your Rebell and Ennemye
Henry the VIth, late in dede, and not in right Kyng of Englond, holden here at your
Paloys of Westm', the xxvi day of November', the ixth yere of your moost noble reigne,
under the colored title of the said Henry from the begynnyng of this pretensed reigne,
and of the readeption of his usurped power and estate the first, dyvers and many maters
were treated, commoned and opened, to the anyntisyng and disheritaunce of You, Soveraigne Lord, and of your Roiall bloode," etc.   *Rotuli Parliamentorum*, vi, 191, no. 34.

Prince Edward, was murdered at Tewkesbury, and the unhappy king himself suffered the same fate a few weeks later in the Tower (1471).

Edward V, 1483. The accession of Edward V, elder of Edward IV's two young sons, was uneventful, but within two months it was plain that the late king's brother Richard, Duke of Gloucester, had designs upon the crown. The horror of the crime was matched by the ingenuity of the constitutional expedients employed.

Richard III, 1483. Most of the devices which we have already observed were pressed into service, and the proceedings summarised the results of almost two centuries of theory and practice. A sermon at St. Paul's explaining Richard's title, and a mass meeting at Guildhall, acknowledged the special position of London in these matters. Next, the lords spiritual and temporal and commons, who had come in obedience to writs summoning Edward V's first parliament, met on the appointed day (June 25), not at Westminster as a parliament, but at St. Paul's as the Three Estates of the Realm.[19] Thereupon " many and divers lords spiritual and temporal and other nobles and notable persons of the commons, in great multitude," professing to act " on the behalf and in the name of the three estates of this realm of England," presented to Richard a roll of parchment in which they recited his title to the throne,[20] and declared " we have chosen in all that that in us is, and by this writing choose you into our king and soveraigne lord, to whom we know for certain it appertaineth of inheritance so to be chosen." Richard accepted the proposal, and on the morrow he enthroned himself, as Edward IV had done, in Westminster Hall and took the coronation oath (an innovation), received the crown jewels at the Abbey, and proclaimed himself king. His reign dates from that day (June 26). His first and only parliament, after reciting the text of the roll of parchment, observed that the authors of it were not a parliament; but since " the court of parliament is of such authority and the people of this land of such nature and disposition, as experience teacheth, that manifestation and declaration of any truth or right made by the three estates of this realm assembled in parliament, and by authority of the same, maketh before all other things most faith and certainty," they proceeded to declare Richard " very and undoubted king of this realm of England, as well by

---

[19] It has been suggested that " the older royalist and legal idea of parliament as the king's court, summoned by the force of his writ, has seemingly had grafted on to it the extraneous political and social idea of the national sanction of the estates of the realm, acting— whether for themselves or through representatives—in their own name and with an authority of their own. It was, surely, this very idea, with the ultimate implications involved, which gradually worked that transformation in parliamentary theory which appeared during the three centuries from 1399 to 1688; and the fifteenth century, we may say, witnessed the completion of the grafting of this idea on to the older idea of parliament as a court ": S. B. Chrimes, *English Constitutional Ideas*, 125–126.

[20] Richard III (brother of Edward IV) founded his claim on (1) an alleged pre-contract of marriage of Edward IV, which rendered his issue by " dame Elizabeth Gray " illegitimate; (2) the attainder of the Duke of Clarence (Richard's elder brother), by which his children were debarred from the succession; and (3) the misgovernment of Edward IV. *Rotuli Parliamentorum*, vi, 240, 241.

right of consanguinity and inheritance as by lawful election, consecration and coronation "; and entailed the crown on the heirs of his body, particularly his son Edward, Prince of Wales, who was thereby declared heir-apparent.[21]   Richard III's plea rolls express the official view of the position: as occasion required they refer to " Henry VI, late king of England *de facto et non de jure*," [22] and to Edward V as " Edward V, the Bastard, formerly called Edward V king of England " [23]; Richard's own position is enrolled as " true and undoubted king of the realm of England, by divine and human right." [24]

Edward V and his still younger brother—the " Princes in the Tower "—were murdered; Richard III's only issue, the Prince of Wales, died shortly afterwards; Richard himself was slain at the Battle of Bosworth (1485). The House of York was therefore now represented in the first place by Edward IV's elder daughter Elizabeth (assuming her legitimacy); if Edward IV's marriage were invalid, then by the ten-year-old Earl of Warwick (unless he were barred by the attainder of his father, Clarence).

The Tudor Title. The victor of Bosworth, Henry VII, fulfilled his pledge to his followers by marrying Elizabeth, and took the precaution of putting Warwick in the Tower, where he remained until he was executed in 1499. He rejected the legitimist notion that he was king merely *jure uxoris*, but it is hardly possible to consider him as entitled through his mother, a Beaufort (moreover, she was still alive, and so whatever claim the Beaufort line might have was hers, and not yet Henry's); and still less through his father, Edmund Tudor, who had no English royal blood. In this case, therefore, since the title cannot be derived from any considerations of descent, an unusual degree of significance seems to attach to the Act of Parliament by which it was ordained and enacted with the assent of the lords and at the request of the commons " that the inheritance of the crowns of the realms of England and of France, with all the pre-eminence and dignity royal to the same pertaining, and all other seigneuries to the king belonging beyond the sea with the appurtenances thereto in any wise due or pertaining be, rest, remain, and abide in the most royal person of our own Sovereign Lord King Henry VIIth and in the heirs of his body lawfully coming perpetually with the Grace of God so to endure and in none other." [25] " Words," remarks Hallam, " studiously ambiguous, which while they avoid the assertion of an hereditary right that the public voice repelled, were meant to create a parliamentary title, before which the pretensions of lineal descent were to give way." [26] So it seemed, at least to later lawyers; but to a man in 1485 who remembered the history of the last twenty-five years,

[21] *Rotuli Parliamentorum*, vi, 240–242.
[22] M. Hemmant, *Exchequer Chamber* (Selden Society), ii, 77.
[23] *Ibid.*, 97.
[24] *Ibid.*, 65.
[25] 1 Hen. 7, c. 1.
[26] Hallam, *Constitutional History*, i, 8.

it would doubtless have been obvious that the victor, whoever he was, always got a parliamentary title—for what it was worth—and nevertheless might lose the crown afterwards. The question, raised in the case of Clarence, whether an attainder barred a claim to the throne, concerned Henry VII, for he himself was in that position. The judges advised that the attainder ceased as soon as he became king.[27]

Parliamentary Settlements under Henry VIII. In the reign of Henry VIII the succession to the crown was repeatedly altered by legislative enactment.

1. By the Royal Succession Act of 25 Hen. 8, c. 22 (1534), passed on the occasion of the king's marriage with Anne Boleyn, his previous marriage with Katherine of Aragon was annulled, and the crown was entailed on the king's issue male, " and for default of such sons of your body begotten, . . . that then the said imperial Crown . . . shall be to the issue female between your Majesty and your most dear and entirely beloved wife Queen Anne begotten, that is to say, first, to the eldest issue female, which is the Lady Elizabeth, now princess . . . and so from issue female to issue female, and to their heirs of their bodies, one after another, by course of inheritance, according to their ages, as the Crown of England hath been accustomed and ought to go, in cases when there be heirs females to the same." [28]

2. Subsequently to the king's marriage with Lady Jane Seymour, parliament passed an Act [29] by which (after declaring the king's marriage with Queen Katherine void, and his marriage with Anne Boleyn likewise void, and the issue of both marriages illegitimate) the crown was entailed on the sons of the king and Queen Jane successively and the heirs of their bodies, with remainder to the king's sons by any future wife in like manner, and on failure of such issue, to the daughters of the king and queen successively and their issue. And after reciting that if the king should die without lawful issue, no provision having been made in his lifetime touching the succession, the realm in that case would be destitute of a lawful governor, " or else percase encumbered with such a person that would covet to aspire to the same, whom the subjects of this realm shall not find in their hearts to love, dread, and obediently serve as their sovereign lord," [30] the Act proceeds to bestow upon the king the extraordinary power,

---

[27] Y. B. 1 Hen. 7, Mich., no. 5; and see Selden Society, *Publications*, vol. li, 185, for a reply to Bergenroth, who had held that the case was spurious. Other persons, however, were not rehabilitated (so as to sit in parliament, for example) until their attainders had been reversed in parliament.

[28] Tanner, *Tudor Constitutional Documents*, 382–388.

[29] 28 Hen. 8, c. 7 (1536); Tanner, *op. cit.*, 389–395.

[30] " This seemeth to be pointed at James V of Scotland, who was at this time the next in succession upon failure of the king's issue; not barely as being descended from the union of the two Roses, but under a parliamentary entail in favour of Henry VII and the heirs of his body made before that union took place. . . . Notwithstanding the near relation the House of Stuart stood in to the Crown of England, Scotland was, during all King Henry's reign, the same detested enemy it had been for ages past: and a national prejudice operated in both kingdoms as strongly as ever "—Foster, *Crown Law*, 407 n.

in default of lawful issue of his body, to limit the crown, by letters patent, or by his last will made in writing and signed with his hand, to such person or persons in possession and remainder, and according to such order or condition, as he should judge expedient. Not even a preference for persons of royal descent was reserved, but it was declared that the persons so to be appointed should enjoy the crown as if they " had been lawful heirs to the imperial Crown of this realm and as if the same crown of this realm had been given and limited to them plainly and particularly by special names and sufficient terms and words by the full and immediate authority of this your High Court of Parliament." [31] From the point of view of property law, the Act confers a "power of appointment" [32]; from the point of view of public law, it is an example of delegated legislation.

3. By a later Act, [33] after reciting the previous statute, Henry's two daughters, Mary and Elizabeth, were put into the entail next after the lawful issue male or female of the king and Prince Edward, but subject to such conditions as the king should, by letters patent or his last will, appoint. In the event of their failing to perform the conditions, or dying without issue, the king was again empowered to limit the succession as by the last Act.

The second Succession Act had declared Mary and Elizabeth to be illegitimate. The third, upon a supposition of their illegitimacy, now postponed them even to all the lawful issue female of the king; but yet in default of lawful issue of the king and of Prince Edward, it limited the crown to the illegitimate daughters of the king and their issue in preference to all the other descendants of Henry VII.[34]

Henry VIII Devises the Crown. In exercise of the power given to him by these Acts of Parliament, Henry VIII devised the crown, in remainder, on failure of issue of his three children, " to the heirs of the body of the Lady Frances our niece, eldest daughter to our late sister the French Queen " (i.e., his younger sister, Mary, dowager Queen of France and Duchess of Suffolk, who had died in 1533), thus postponing the descendants of his elder sister, Margaret, Queen of Scots.[35] It is worth remarking, however, that Henry made no mention in the will of the fact that he was using statutory powers in making it.

Edward VI,[36] Mary, and Elizabeth succeeded each other on the throne in strict accordance with, and by virtue of, the parliamentary entail. On

---

[31] These words mean that the royal appointment, in a subsequent document, will be as effective as if the name had been inserted in this present Act.

[32] Powers were beginning to come into common use at this very moment: Holdsworth, *History of English Law*, vii, 149 *et seq.*

[33] 35 Hen. 8, c. 1 (1544), strongly enforced by 1 Edw. 6, c. 12 (1544): Tanner, 398, 404.

[34] The legitimacy of each of the daughters of Henry VIII was liable to dispute, and it is impossible, on any theory, to support the legitimacy of both.

[35] On the validity of Henry VIII's will, see Pollard, *Political History*, 5–6. The Lady Frances lived in fact until 1559.

[36] Edward VI, under the influence of Northumberland, and without any parliamentary authority, had presumed to devise the crown to Lady Jane Grey (of the Suffolk line). She actually held the crown for a few days, but Mary counted them in her own regnal year. Jane was executed, 1554, in her sixteenth year.

the accession of Queen Mary an Act was passed (1 Mary, st. 2, c. 1) repealing, as far as concerned herself, all the Acts which stood in the way of her legitimacy, and declaring the marriage of her father and mother valid, the sentence of divorce a nullity, and that she was the legitimate issue of the king.

Queen Elizabeth's Title. On the first notice of Mary's death, Elizabeth was proclaimed, by order of the House of Lords then sitting, true and lawful heir to the crown according to the Act of Succession of the 35th year of Henry VIII. Whatever other title the queen might be presumed to have, her parliamentary title was clearly the one on which she relied. Discarding the precedent set by her sister, she suffered all altercation about the marriage of her father and mother, and the subsequent divorce, to sink into oblivion. The Act passed on her accession, though vaguely asserting in general terms her descent from the blood royal and that she was as fully entitled as her father or brother had been (which was perfectly true, since each reigned by a good parliamentary title), declared in guarded and limited terms that she was as fully entitled as her sister was at any time since the statute of the 35th year of King Henry VIII.[37]

So precariously established, even in the time of Elizabeth, was the power of parliament to alter the line of succession, that it was expressly enacted by statute that if any person should affirm or maintain that the laws and statutes did not bind the right of the crown and the descent, limitation, inheritance, and government thereof, his offence should be high treason. To affirm, by any book or work written or printed (before the same should be so established and affirmed by Act of Parliament), that any one particular person was or ought to be heir and successor to the queen, involved imprisonment for a year, and for the second offence, the penalties of praemunire.[38]

James I, 1603. On the death of Elizabeth, the Council [39] of the late queen proclaimed as her successor, James, King of Scots, the heir of Margaret, elder sister of Henry VIII. The claim of the House of Suffolk under the will of Henry VIII and the Acts of Parliament authorising him to dispose of the crown, had passed to Edward Seymour, called Lord

[37] 1 Eliz. 1, c. 3. Prothero, *Statutes and Constitutional Documents*, 21. " This declaration so guarded and limited seemeth strongly to imply, either that in the judgment of Parliament Queen Mary had no title antecedent to that Act (35 Hen. 8), or that Elizabeth, having no other, it was thought but decent to put the sisters upon an equal footing, as former Parliaments had done "—Foster, *Crown Law*, 409.

[38] 13 Eliz. 1, c. 1. Tanner, 413; Prothero, 57; *supra*, p. 298. The penalty for every person so affirming or maintaining after the decease of the queen, was forfeiture of goods and chattels only. This clause as to the power of parliament in the matter of the succession was, in substance and with almost identical words, revived and re-enacted by 4 & 5 Anne, c. 8, and 6 Anne, c. 7.

[39] The Earl of Northumberland protested that the death of the Queen had dissolved the council, and that the peers were the sole remaining authority until James should nominate a new one. Egerton, L. K., conceded the principle, which historically was sound; Gardiner, *History of England*, i, 85–86.

Beauchamp, but as his parents' marriage had been judicially declared invalid, he had to be considered illegitimate. Failing the Suffolk line, the crown had to go to the Stuarts, represented by James VI—an alien born— or his cousin Arabella who was English born. Enthusiasts for divine right gladly interpreted James's accession as the triumph of indefeasible royal right over both common law and statute. In fact, there was no alternative to James and parliament formally recognised his title and accession.[40] But even the ultra-royalist House of Commons under Charles II attempted to assert the right of parliament to alter the succession by twice passing, in 1679 and 1680, the bill for the exclusion of the Duke of York from the throne. At length in 1688 all doubts as to the power of parliament to regulate the succession as it should think fit, were finally set at rest by the "glorious revolution" which overturned the Stuart dynasty, and once more set an elective king upon the throne.

REGENCIES

There were numerous occasions when the king needed a substitute, either as a general assistant while he was within the realm, or as a deputy when he was out of the country; some similar arrangement might also become necessary in the event of a minority.[41] Under the Norman kings the justiciar was, as we have seen,[42] the king's general deputy and second in command, and usually carried on the government during the frequent absences [43] of the monarch. Sometimes a queen acted for her husband (as Matilda for Henry I, and Eleanor for Henry II; the latter was sometimes represented by his mother, the Empress). But these appointments scarcely fall within the stricter sense of the term "regency," which connotes the infancy or other natural incapacity of the reigning king. The common law makes no provision for the case of an infant king, who, in judgment of law, can never be a minor, and has therefore no legal guardian.[44] But with the gradual establishment of hereditary succession to the crown, the council (and, later, parliament), besides altering the course of succession as occasion required, began to exercise the power of vesting the royal authority, during the infancy or other incapacity of the reigning prince, in a protector, guardian, or council of regency. It is, however, remarkable that the practice only developed very slowly. When regents were appointed their title and powers varied. Other expedients than a regency were sometimes tried, as when the council (or, at times, a special council)

---

[40] 1 Jac. 1, c. 1. Prothero, 250. See *supra*, p. 330; 4 & 5 Anne, c. 14.

[41] A valuable discussion of continental examples will be found in Félix Olivier Martin, *Les Régences et Minorités des Rois*, 1060–1375 (Paris, 1931).

[42] *Supra*, pp. 45, 62–63, 94.

[43] The absences and regencies are listed in *Handbook of British Chronology* (ed. F. M. Powicke), 33–46.

[44] Co.Lit., 43. Coke reasons thus: "In judgment of law, the king, as king, cannot be said to be a minor: for when the royall bodie politique of the king doth meete with the naturall capacity in one person, the whole bodie shall have the qualitie of the royall politique, which is the greater and more worthy, and wherein is no minoritie." Lord Lyndhurst and Lord Eldon re-stated this doctrine in 1830.

conducted the government. Consequently, even in the later eighteenth century there were still important questions of principle unsettled. The following examples will illustrate the development.

Henry III, 1216. After the hasty coronation of Henry III, who at his father's death was only nine years old, a council of the prelates and barons who adhered to the young king was summoned to meet at Bristol a fortnight later. By common assent they committed the care of the king and kingdom to William, Earl of Pembroke, the earl marshal, with the title of *Rector Regis et Regni*. With the marshal was specially associated the legate Gualo, and the Bishop of Winchester (Peter des Roches) [45]; but his powers were practically limited by the advice of the baronage generally.

Edward I, 1272. In 1271, prior to Henry III's death, an arrangement had been made for the guardianship of the realm during his son's absence —there was, on this occasion, no question of a minority. In accordance with this, on the day after the king's decease, the Great Seal was delivered to Walter Giffard, Archbishop of York (the see of Canterbury being vacant), who, with the assistance of Roger de Mortimer, a baron, and Robert Burnell, one of the royal clerks, carried on the government until Edward's return in August 1274.[46] Their powers were confirmed in the national assembly which met at Westminster on January 14, 1273, and swore allegiance to the absent king.[47]

Edward III, 1327. After the deposition of Edward II and the election and coronation on February 1, 1327, of his eldest son Edward,[48] then of the age of fourteen, the parliament, which had been in session since January 7, proceeded to provide for the government of the kingdom. For this purpose they appointed a standing council, " a sort of parliamentary regency " as it has been termed, consisting of four bishops, four earls and six barons, with the king's cousin Henry, Earl of Lancaster, at their head, to advise the king in all matters of government.[49]

Richard II, 1377. Richard II was only eleven years old at the date of his accession. But however incapable naturally of exercising sovereign authority, he was regarded as in the legal enjoyment of it, and no regent was appointed. The Great Seal, according to the subtle reasoning of the lawyers of that age, was supposed to possess a sort of magical influence rendering any government legal. The day after his grandfather's death, Richard received the seal from the hands of its keepers, and delivered it to his uncle, John of Gaunt, Duke of Lancaster, for safe custody. Four days

---

[45] Walter of Coventry, ii, 233. Matthew Paris, *Chronica Majora* (Rolls Series), ii, 2.
[46] *Seventh Report of Deputy Keeper of the Public Records* (1846), App. ii, 259; *Royal and other Letters of Henry III*, Rolls Series, ii, 346; Stubbs, *Constitutional History*, ii, 108–109.
[47] *Annales Wintonie*, 113. See *supra*, pp. 136, 477.
[48] *Supra*, p. 487.
[49] *Rotuli Parliamentorum*, ii, 52; Knighton, i, 454.

afterwards it was handed over to the Bishop of St. David's who was thus enabled to legalise all acts of the government. But although no regent was appointed, the House of Lords nominated a council of twelve, composed of two bishops, two earls, two barons, two bannerets, and four knights, without whose concurrence no measure was to be carried into effect. This council was modified from time to time by parliament during the earlier years of Richard's reign.[50]

Henry VI's First Regency, 1422. At the accession of Henry VI (September 1, 1422) far more regularity and deliberation were shown in supplying the defect in the executive authority. Henry V on his deathbed had expressed a wish that his younger brother Humphrey, Duke of Gloucester, should act as regent in England, while his other brother John, Duke of Bedford, conducted the government in France.[51] But this disposition was disregarded by the parliament. On hearing of the late king's death, several of the lords, spiritual and temporal, chiefly members of the old council, met together and provided for the exigencies of government by issuing commissions to judges, sheriffs, and other officers, to continue in the exercise of their respective duties, and also writs for a new parliament. This was opened on November 9 by the Duke of Gloucester, as commissioner appointed in the king's name, with the consent of the council, under the Great Seal; and at once proceeded to ratify all the acts of the lords who had taken on themselves the administration and summoned the parliament. Some weeks later it is recorded in the rolls that the king, considering his tender age [which, in fact, was not quite twelve months] and his inability at present to direct in person the concerns of his realm, by the assent and advice of the lords spiritual and temporal, and of the commons, ordains and constitutes (after he shall have returned to England and so long as he shall remain in the kingdom, and it shall please the king) his uncle the Duke of Bedford, now in parts beyond sea, and during his absence the king's other uncle the Duke of Gloucester, now in England, to be protector and defender of the kingdom and English church, and the king's chief counsellor. Letters patent were afterwards passed to this effect, but the tenure of the office was expressly limited to the king's pleasure. Sixteen counsellors were afterwards appointed in parliament to assist the protector in the administration, with an almost unlimited power of veto on the removal and appointment of officers.[52]

The Protector's Powers Defined. The nature and extent of the powers committed to the protector may be learnt from the written answer of the lords to a request of the Duke of Gloucester, in the parliament of the sixth year of Henry's reign (1428), that he might be informed what authority he possessed as protector and defender of the realm and the king's chief

[50] *Rotuli Parliamentorum*, iii, 386; *cf.* Baldwin, *King's Council*, Chap, vi; *supra*, p. 168.
[51] See Ramsay, *Lancaster and York*, i, 303, and the authorities there cited.
[52] *Rotuli Parliamentorum*, iv, 169–176; *cf.* Baldwin, *King's Council*, 169 *et seq.*

counsellor. They reminded the duke that at first he had desired "to have had the governance of this land, affirming that it belonged unto you of right, as well by means of your birth as by the last will of the king that was, your brother, whom God assoile; alleging for you such grounds and motives as it was thought to your discretion made for your intent; whereupon the lords spiritual and temporal assembled there in parliament . . . had great and long deliberation and advice, searched precedents of the governail of the land in time and case semblable, when kings of this land have been tender of age, took also information of the laws of the land of such persons as be notably learned therein, and finally found your said desire not caused nor grounded in precedent nor in the law of the land; the which the king that dead is, in his life nor might by his last will nor otherwise alter, change, nor abrogate, without the assent of the three estates, nor commit or grant to any person governance or rule of this land longer than he lived." And that nevertheless "it is advised and appointed by authority of the king, assenting the three estates of this land, that ye, in absence of my lord your brother of Bedford, should be chief of the King's Council, and devised therefore unto you a name different from other counsellors, not the name of tutor lieutenant, governor, nor of regent, nor no name that should import authority of governance of the land, but the name of protector and defensor, the which importeth a personal duty of entendance to the actual defence of the land, as well against enemies outward, if case required, as against rebels inward, if any were, that God forbid; granting you therewith certain power, the which is specified and contained in an Act of the said parliament, it to endure as long as it liked the king." The lords then proceeded to exhort and require the duke, " to content you with the power above said and declared, of the which my lord your brother of Bedford, the king's eldest uncle, contented him; and that ye none larger power desire, will, nor use; giving you this that is above written for our answer to your foresaid demand, the which we will dwell and abide with withouten variance or changing." [53]

Principles Recognised, 1428. From these proceedings it appears to have been already recognised as constitutional law: (1) That the king does not possess the power of nominating a regent during the minority of his successor; and (2) that neither the heir presumptive, nor any other person, is entitled to exercise the royal prerogative during the king's infancy (or, by parity of reasoning, his infirmity); but that the sole right of determining the persons by whom, and the limitations under which, the executive government shall be conducted in the king's name and behalf, resides in the great council of parliament.[54] At least, that is how the barons interpreted the situation, obviously in harmony with their characteristic attitude upon the constitution. They tried hard to keep Richard II in a sort of life-long minority, and they had now no intention of allowing even the

---

[53] *Rotuli Parliamentorum*, iv, 326.
[54] Hallam, *Middle Ages*, iii, 189.

attenuated regality of a regent to diminish the large claims of the baronage, as an order, to control the government.[55]

Henry VI's Second Regency, 1454. In 1454 (32 Hen. 6), it having been reported to the House of Lords by a deputation of twelve peers who had waited upon the king, that his mental derangement was such that they " could get no answer nor sign " from him, the lords " elected and nominated Richard, Duke of York, to be protector and defender of the realm of England during the king's pleasure," with powers similar to those which had been formerly conferred upon the Duke of Gloucester. An Act of Parliament was subsequently passed, constituting the Duke of York protector of the church and kingdom and the king's chief counsellor during the royal pleasure, or until the Prince of Wales (then under two years old) should attain years of discretion, on whom the said dignity was immediately to devolve.[56] In less than a year the king became slightly better, and at once annulled the Duke of York's protectorate. Hitherto the lords had assumed the exclusive right of choosing the protector, the commons being merely assenting parties to the Act which ratified his election. But on the next occasion, the commons—who were for the most part strong partisans of the White Rose—took a much more active part, and would appear to have forced the lords unwillingly to reappoint the Duke of York.

Henry VI's Third Regency, 1455. The king being a prisoner in the hands of the Yorkists, after the first battle of St. Albans, was obliged to appoint the duke his lieutenant to open parliament in November 1455. The commons, doubtless inspired, as in the previous year, by the great personage whose interests they pressed, immediately proposed to the lords that whereas the king had deputed the Duke of York as his commissioner to proceed in this parliament, it was thought by the commons that, if the king hereafter could not attend to the protection and defence of the land, an able person should be appointed protector, to whom they might have recourse for redress of injuries. While the lords were considering the matter the commons, two days afterwards, repeated their request; and after they had left the chamber, the chancellor declared that " it is understood that they will not further proceed in matters of parliament to the time that they have answer to their desire and request." Having a third time pressed for an answer, the commons were at length informed that " the king our sovereign lord, by the advice and assent of the lords spiritual and temporal being in this present parliament, had named and desired the Duke of York to be protector and defensor of this land." In the act of ratification the duke was to hold his office not " during the king's pleasure," as formerly, but " until he should be discharged of it by the lords in

---

[55] *Cf. supra*, pp. 213–217.
[56] *Rotuli Parliamentorum*, v, 240–243.

parliament." [57] Before the end of February 1456 the king had once more recovered his reason, and resumed the personal exercise of the royal functions.[58]

Edward V, 1483. On the accession of Edward V at the age of thirteen, the queen-mother claimed and endeavoured to obtain the regency but the Duke of Gloucester (afterwards Richard III), having marched to London and secured the person of the king, was appointed by a Great Council of prelates, nobles, and chief citizens, " protector of the king and kingdom."

Regency Act, 1536. It is not to be expected that the Tudors would subscribe to the baronial dogma of which we have now seen the practical applications. Henry VIII (unlike his father) declined to leave the fate of an infant successor to be settled when the occasion arose, and in this, as in other respects, his will treats the crown as a prudent landowner of the time would treat his private fortune and family, as the commons themselves had suggested. By statute 28 Hen. 8, c. 7, it was provided that the successor to the throne, if a male and under eighteen, or if a female and under sixteen, should be until such age in the government of his or her natural mother (if approved by the king), and of such other counsellors as the king by his will should appoint; and the king accordingly appointed his sixteen executors to constitute the Privy Council, and exercise the authority of the crown, until his son Edward VI should attain the age of eighteen. By these executors the Earl of Hertford (afterwards Duke of Somerset), the king's maternal uncle, was appointed protector of the realm and guardian of the king's person. This arrangement, though contrary to the late king's will, was confirmed by the assent of the lords spiritual and temporal; and shortly afterwards the protector procured a grant of his office, with almost unlimited powers, by letters patent from the young king.[59]

Regency Act, 1751. No other instance of appointing a regent occurred till the year 1751, when, after the death of Frederick, Prince of Wales, an Act (24 Geo. 2, c. 24) was passed appointing the Princess Dowager of Wales to be guardian and regent, in case the crown should descend to any of the children of Frederick, Prince of Wales, under the age of eighteen years. A Council of Regency was also nominated by the Act; but the king was empowered to add four other members by instrument under his sign manual, to be opened after his death.

George III's First Regency Act, 1765. The proceedings during the reign of George III have a special importance as recent precedents. In 1765 an alarming illness led the king to consider the necessity of providing for a

[57] *Rotuli Parliamentorum*, v, 284–490; Hallam, *Middle Ages*, iii, 192.
[58] *Rotuli Parliamentorum*, v, 321.
[59] Burnet, ii, 4, 15.

regency in case of his death. At first he wished parliament to confer upon him the unconditional right of nominating any person as regent whom he might select. But by the Regency Act, as ultimately passed, the king was empowered to nominate, under his sign manual, either the queen, the Princess Dowager of Wales, or any descendant of George II residing in the kingdom, to be guardian of his successor (while under eighteen years of age) and " regent of the kingdom." A Council of Regency was appointed by the Act, which also defined its powers and those of the regent.[60]

On two occasions during the illness of George III, in 1788–1789, and again in 1810, the name and authority of the crown—through the means of letters patent under the Great Seal affixed by the authority of both Houses of Parliament—were used for the purpose of opening parliament when the king was personally incapable of exercising his constitutional functions. In 1788, in the discussions concerning the appointment of a regent, Fox " advanced the startling opinion that the Prince of Wales had as clear a right to exercise the power of sovereignty during the king's incapacity as if the king were actually dead; and that it was merely for the two Houses of Parliament to pronounce at what time he should commence the exercise of his right." [61] Pitt, however, firmly maintained the absolute right of parliament to make what provision it thought fit for carrying on the government, and the Duke of York, in the House of Lords, disclaimed the right on behalf of the prince, who " understood too well the sacred principles which seated the House of Brunswick on the throne, ever to assume or exercise any power, be his claim what it might, not derived from the will of the people, expressed by their representatives and their lordships in parliament assembled." [62] A Regency Bill was introduced in the commons and sent up to the lords, but the king's sudden recovery put a stop to all further proceedings. In 1810, when the king was seized with his last mental disorder, the proceedings of parliament were grounded generally upon the precedents of 1788.

Second Regency Act, 1811. An Act was ultimately passed—the royal assent being given by commission under the Great Seal authorised by a resolution of both Houses—by which the Prince of Wales was empowered to exercise the royal authority as regent, in the name and on behalf of the king but subject to many important limitations, particularly specified.[63]

Regency Act, 1830. By the statute 1 Will. 4, c. 2, the Duchess of Kent was appointed guardian and regent in the event of Queen Victoria coming to the throne before attaining the age of eighteen years; and, contrary to former precedents, no provision was made for a controlling council, but

---

[60] 5 Geo. 3, c. 27; May, *Constitutional History*, i, 168–175.

[61] May, *Constitutional History*, i, 177.

[62] *Parliamentary History*, xxvii, 678, 684.

[63] For a short but comprehensive summary of the important proceedings relative to the regency under George III, see May, *Constitutional History*, i, 175–215; Lecky, *History of England*, v, 387–447; Robertson, *Statutes and Documents*, 299–312.

the regent was left to carry on the government through the responsible ministers of the crown, and to act upon their advice alone.[64]

Victoria, First Regency Act, 1837. On the accession of Queen Victoria, the King of Hanover became presumptive heir to the throne, and an Act was passed providing that in the event of the queen's decease, while her successor was out of the realm, the government should be carried on in his name by lords justices until his arrival.[65]

Second Regency Act, 1840. The next occasion on which parliament exercised its powers of appointing a regent was on the queen's marriage, in 1840. An Act was passed by which, in the event of any of her children succeeding to the throne under the age of eighteen, Prince Albert, as the surviving parent, was appointed regent, without any Council of Regency, or any limitation upon the exercise of the royal prerogatives—except an incapacity to assent to any bill for altering the succession to the throne, or affecting the uniformity of worship in the Church of England, or the rights of the Church of Scotland.[66]

Royal absences. Royal absences have been dealt with in various ways. The earliest have already been mentioned.[67] It soon became clear that the problem was of much less moment, and could be treated on ceremonial lines. Thus Edward III left the kingdom in the care of the Duke of Cornwall as *Custos Regni* in 1338, and of the Duke of Clarence in 1345. The one was eight and the other seven years of age. Meanwhile the council conducted the government and kept in close touch with the king. Richard II and the Lancastrians appointed adult regents during absence, but Edward IV made the five-year-old Prince of Wales his regent during absence. Henry VIII twice appointed a queen and once a Duke of Norfolk, but no other royal absences occurred until William III. By statute [68] the office fell upon Mary, and after her death he inaugurated the practice of appointing a sort of commission with the title of "Lords Justices." This precedent was frequently followed, although occasionally a regency was conferred on a queen or Prince of Wales.

Regency Act, 1937. The Regency Act, 1937,[69] is a permanent measure designed to deal systematically with several different situations—the regency and guardianship of an infant sovereign; in the case of grave illness a regency, in the case of temporary incapacity or absence, a number of Counsellors of State.

---

[64] For the first time, it became necessary to contemplate the possibility that a presumptive heir might accede, and then have to yield the crown to the posthumous issue of the late monarch; this Act made provision for that contingency.

[65] 1 Vict. c. 72. The interval between the death of Anne and the arrival of George I had been similarly filled.

[66] 3 & 4 Vict. c. 52; May, *Constitutional History*, i, 223–224.

[67] *Supra*, p. 504.

[68] 2 Will. & Mary, sess. 1, c. 6.   [69] 1 Edw. 8 & 1 Geo. 6, c. 16.

LAW OF TREASON

Treason by the Common Law. The law of treason, with all its subtle distinctions and cruel constructions, is so interwoven with the thread of English constitutional history, that some notice of it is necessary. In the following brief sketch a few of the more important features gave been touched upon.[70] The crime of high treason as it existed at common law prior to the statute of Edward III was vague and indefinite. The fundamental principle upon which the law of treason was based was the allegiance, either natural or local, due from every man who lives under the king's protection. Every subject, from the age of fourteen, was bound to take the oath of allegiance if called upon to do so [71]; but allegiance was equally due whether the oath had been taken or not. The smallest breach of allegiance, was punished as treason; but the ruling of the judges as to what constituted a breach was at once arbitrary and unlimited, varying in different reigns according as the power of the king or of the barons happened to be in the ascendant. In the reign of Edward I, appealing to the French courts, in opposition to the king's, was adjudged high treason in the case of Nicholas Segrave. Under Edward II, the Despensers were accused of "accroaching," or exercising "royal power," by keeping the administration in their own hands, though without violence to the sovereign. A similar charge was brought against Roger Mortimer in Edward III's reign. Killing the king's uncle, father, brother, or even a messenger, was held to be treason, and a knight was indicted for the treason of "accroaching royal power "[72] by assaulting one of the king's subjects on the highway, and forcibly detaining him till he paid £90.

Statute of Treason, 1352. At length, after frequent complaints and petitions from the commons against arbitrary decisions of the courts the popular statute of 25 Edw. 3, st. 5, c. 2, was passed strictly defining the limits of treason.[73] The reason for the statute must be sought in the fact that a traitor's land, of whomsoever held, was forfeit to the crown, but a felon's land escheated to his immediate lord. Hence "kings wished to extend treason at the expense of felony; the magnates resisted. A lord whose tenant had, for example, slain a king's messenger was much concerned that this offence should be felony, not treason. In the one case he would get an escheat; in the other case far from getting an escheat, he would lose seignorial dues unless the king took pity on him, for the king would hold the traitor's land and no one can be the king's lord." [74]

[70] See, generally, J. F. Stephen, *History of Criminal Law*, ii, 241 *et seq.*; Pollock and Maitland, *History of English Law*, ii, 500 *et seq.*; Holdsworth, *History of English Law*, iii, 289 *et seq.*, iv, 492 *et seq.*, viii, 307 *et seq.* See further, Chrimes, "Richard II's Questions to the Judges," *Law Quarterly Review*, lxxii, 365; S. Rezneck, "History of the Parliamentary Declaration of Treason," *Law Quarterly Review*, xlvi, 80.

[71] Britton, lib. 1, c. 13.

[72] For this vague offence (which later could be used against over-mighty ministers), see M. V. Clarke, *Fourteenth Century Studies*, 126 *et seq.*, 247.

[73] *Supra*, p. 162, n. 46; Lodge and Thornton, *Documents*, 21–22.

[74] Pollock and Maitland, *History of English Law*, ii, 500.

Seven heads of treason were declared by this statute, which also provided that no other cases should be adjudged by the judges to be treason until the king and his parliament should declare whether they ought to be so judged. The treasons enumerated in the Statute of Edward are: (1) When a man doth compass or imagine the death of our lord the king, or of our lady his queen, or of their eldest son and heir; or (2) if a man do violate the king's "companion" (*i.e.*, the queen consort), or the king's eldest daughter unmarried, or the wife of the king's eldest son and heir; or (3) if a man do levy war against our lord the king in his realm; or (4) be adherent to the king's enemies in his realm, giving to them aid and comfort in the realm or elsewhere, and thereof be proveably attainted of open deed by people of their condition. (5) And if a man counterfeit the king's great or privy seal, or his money; (6) and if a man bring false money into this realm, counterfeit to the money of England; knowing the money to be false, to merchandise or make payment, in deceit of the king and his people; (7) and if a man slay the chancellor, treasurer, or the king's justices of the one bench or the other, justices in eyre, or justices of assize, and all other justices assigned to hear and determine, being in their places doing their offices.

The offence of counterfeiting the king's seals or his coins would now be regarded as a branch of the *crimen falsi*, or forgery, rather than a species of the *crimen laesae majestatis*, or treason; and by the modern statutes (24 & 25 Vict. cc. 98, 99) it is now punishable as felony only. Of the other species of treason enumerated it is unnecessary here to notice more than two, the 1st and 3rd.

(1) Compassing the King's Death. *Compassing or imagining the death of the king.* The word *compass* originally meant (as it still does) to achieve, to bring about. *Imagine* had the sense of planning or plotting, whether successfully or not. The two words are now taken to be synonymous, and to denote the purpose or design of the mind or will, even though the purpose or design take not effect; but the statute especially requires that the traitorous imagination be manifested by some *overt* or open act. Still, it is the mental act which, under this head of the statute, constitutes the crime of treason; and therefore in the trial of the Regicides, in 1660, it was held that not the decapitation of Charles I but the "compassing" his death constituted the treason, and that the killing was only an overt act proving the compassing. Meeting and consulting *how* to kill the king, although no scheme be finally adopted, is an overt act, and every person who assents to overtures for that purpose, or who encourages others, by advice, persuasion, or command, to commit the fact, shares in the guilt. Sir Everard Digby was convicted, in January 1606, of high treason for being privy to and not revealing the Gunpowder Plot, although it was not proved that he either said or did anything at the consultation. Not merely personal plots of assassination, but all wilful and deliberate attempts which may immediately, or consequently, endanger the life of the sovereign, have been held within the scope of the statute. Thus a conspiracy to depose or imprison the king has been constructively determined to be an overt act of compassing his death; "for experience hath shewn," observes Sir Michael Foster,[75] " that between the prisons and the graves of princes the distance is very small." Other offences still less personal, but having a remote tendency towards the same end, have been held to be overt acts under this head of treason. Entering into measures in concert with foreign powers to invade the kingdom would seem more properly to fall under the head of levying war or of adhering to the king's enemies. But unless the powers incited be actually at war it will not fall within any branch of the statute, except compassing the king's death. And even when the overt act would have properly fallen within the clause of adhering, it has been held an overt act of compassing, as in the case of Patrick Harding, who raised and sent men to France, then at open war with us, for the purpose of restoring James II.

Strained Constructions of the Statute. The Duke of Norfolk was convicted in 1572, contrary to all law and justice, of a treason resting on presumptions and inferences only. The overt act was his intended marriage with Mary Queen of Scots, and his correspondence with the Duke of Alva to raise an army to invade the kingdom. It was argued that as Mary had formerly laid claim to the crown, whoever married her would support her title, and consequently endeavour to depose Queen Elizabeth. The letters to Alva had no signatures, and were only proved to be the duke's by reading the confession of an agent, who vouched for their authenticity. A distinct act of treason, such as levying war, has been decided to be an overt act of compassing; thus the statute of 29 Hen. 6, c. 1 (1450), which attainted Jack Cade of rebellion, declared that gathering men together and inciting them to rise against the king was an overt act of imagining his death. Mere loose words spoken, not relating to any treasonable purpose, in agitation, are not an overt act; but words may expound an overt act, in itself indifferent, and words of advice and persuasion in contemplation or prosecution of a traitorous design, actually on foot, may be overt acts. Words written and published, either in letters or books, where the matter contained imports a compassing, have been held overt acts. It was held so in *Twyn's Case* (1663, 15 Car. 2), for publishing " A Treatise of the Execution of Justice," asserting that the supreme magistrate was accountable to the people, and that they might take up arms to put the king to death: and in *Williams's Case* (1619, 17 Jac. 1), for enclosing and sending in a box to James I a book declaring that the king would die in the year 1621, and that the kingdom would be destroyed.[76] Under the Stuarts, even unpublished writings were made use of to convict their authors of

---

[75] *Crown Law*, p. 196.
[76] Stephen, *History of Criminal Law*, ii, 306 n.; for a similar prophecy similarly punished four centuries earlier by King John, see Pollock and Maitland, ii, 507.

treason, as in *Peacham's Case* (1615), in whose study was found a manuscript sermon which had never been preached or published,[77] and in that of *Algernon Sidney*, at whose trial (in 1683) for participating in the Rye House Plot, the want of a second witness was supplied by the production of a discourse found in his closet, and evidently written many years before, in which it was maintained that kings were accountable to the people for their conduct.[78]

(2) **Levying War Against the King.** The third species of treason enumerated in the Statute of Edward III is that of levying war, which lies not in the intention or purpose, but in the act itself. It was only slowly that the common law took a serious view of armed rebellion. The numerous revolts of the twelfth and thirteenth centuries were dealt with most indulgently when contrasted with the fifteenth-century cases. The reason seems to be that while kings of England were at war with their overlord in France, it was impossible to hold that it was treason to levy war against a king in his realm. In 1340, however, Edward III claimed to be King of France; being himself no longer a " rebel," he felt free to deal severely with those who rebelled against him.[79] The levying must be against the king, which is either direct against his person or constructive against his government. Enlisting and marching have been held sufficient acts without coming to a battle or action. Attacking the king's forces in opposition to his authority, upon a march or in quarters, and holding a castle or fort against the king or his forces, if actual force be used in order to keep possession, have been held a sufficient levying of war. The true criterion as to what unlawful assemblies amount to a levying of war, is *Quo animo* did the parties assemble ? and in order to constitute the offence, the object of the assembly must be to effect by force something of a public and general concern. For if the assembly be upon account of some private quarrel, or to take revenge on particular persons, the statute of Edward itself has specially declared that it is no treason. " If any man," says the statute, " ride armed, open or secretly, with men of arms, against any other to slay or to rob him, or to take and keep him till he make fine or ransom for his deliverance,[80] it is not the mind of the king or his council that in such case it shall be judged treason; but it shall be judged felony or trespass according to the law of the land of old time used, and according as the case requireth." In accordance with this principle, and within the reason and equity of the statute, while on the one hand popular risings to maintain a private claim or to destroy particular enclosures, or to break prisons in order to release particular persons, and risings of men of a particular class against others of

---

[77] *Supra*, p. 348.

[78] These restoration cases, however, were governed by the Treason Act of 1661 (13 Charles 2, c. 1) under which written or spoken words were made substantive treasons, and not merely overt acts to compassing: Stephen, i, 411.

[79] Pollock and Maitland, ii, 505.

[80] These were the facts in *Gerberge's Case* (1347) which, with others, had provoked the statute of 1352: Stephen, ii, 246.

the same class—as of the weavers in and about London, who rose in 1675 to destroy all engine-looms because those machines enabled those of the trade who made use of them to undersell those who had them not [81]— have been held not to amount to levying war within the statute: on the other hand, with equal reason, every insurrection which in judgment of law is intended against the person of the king, either to dethrone or imprison him, or to oblige him to alter his measures of government, or to remove evil counsellors—although not conducted with military array—has been held to be a levying of war within the statute. Another class of popular risings, not levelled at the person of the king, but " against his Royal Majesty," that is, against the established law and government, have been brought within the clause of the statute against " levying war against the king," by constructions scarcely less strained than those upon compassing his death. Acting upon the logical distinction between general and particular purposes, but regardless of the fact that in the majority of cases there was an entire absence of any intention either to depose the sovereign or generally to subvert his government, the courts held trifling insurrections for the purpose of destroying all brothels,[82] or of throwing down all enclosures [83] or all dissenting meeting houses,[84] or to enhance the price of all labour,[85] or to open all prisons, or to expel all foreigners, or to redress real or imaginary national grievances in which the insurgents had no special interest—to be constructive " levyings " within the statute. The same doctrine was laid down by Lord Mansfield at the trial of Lord George Gordon for " levying war " by inciting a riot against the recent Act for the relief of Roman Catholics.[86]

Conspiracies to Levy War. It is to be noted that the Statute of Edward III entirely omitted, in its enumeration of the modes whereby treason could be committed, to include the act of conspiring or consulting to levy war. But by a strained construction it gradually became the established doctrine that a conspiracy to levy war against the king's person, though not in itself a distinct treason, might be received in evidence as an overt act of compassing his death.[87] Notwithstanding this construction, however, it was thought necessary under Elizabeth, Charles II and George III, to pass temporary Acts rendering a conspiracy to levy war treasonable (13 Eliz. 1, c. 1; 13 Car. 2, c. 1; 36 Geo. 3, c. 7). The disposition to extend a constructive interpretation to the Statute of Edward III continued to increase down to the end of George III's reign, during which it was carried to a great length, especially by Chief Justice Eyre in the trials of 1794.[88] These cases

---

81 1 Hale, *Pleas of the Crown*, 143.
82 *R.* v. *Messenger* (1668) Kelyng 75; 1 Hale, *Pleas of the Crown*, 134 (Hale dissenting).
83 *R.* v. *Bradshaw* (1597) 3 Inst. 9.
84 *Cf. Dammaree's Case* (1710) 15 St.Tr. 521; *Willis's Case* (1710) *ibid.* 613; *Purchase's Case* (1710) *ibid.* 651. (Cases arising out of Sacheverell's trial.)
85 *Temp.* Henry VIII; 3 Inst. 9; 1 Hale, *Pleas of the Crown*, 132.
86 *R.* v. *Gordon* (1781) 21 St.Tr. 485.
87 *R.* v. *Essex* (1600); *cf.* 3 Inst. 14 and Kelyng 20; Holdsworth, viii, 314.
88 *R.* v. *Hardy* (1794) 24 St.Tr. 199; *R.* v. *Horne Tooke* (1794) 25 St.Tr. 1.

arose out of the " Constitutional Society " and the " London Correspond-ing Society " which maintained a powerful agitation for universal suffrage and annual parliaments. Representatives of their local branches were to meet in a " Convention "—an alarming word in view of events in France. The prosecution failed to convince the jury that this meant an intention to depose the king, thus " compassing " his " death." The public properly resented these " constructive " treasons and the next year the law was clarified by the temporary Act, 36 Geo. 3, c. 7, the main object of which seems to have been to turn into substantive treasons certain things which had been judicially construed to be treasonable.[89] It was enacted: (1) That if any person shall, within the realm or without, compass, imagine, invent, devise or intend death, destruction, or any bodily harm tending to death or destruction, maiming or wounding, imprisonment or restraint of the person of the king, his heirs and successors; and shall express, utter, or declare such intention by publishing any printing or writing, or by any overt act or deed; being legally convicted thereof upon the oaths of two lawful and credible witnesses—he shall be adjudged a traitor and suffer as in cases of high treason. (2) It was also declared by the same Act that it should be treason to compass, imagine or intend (such intention being expressed by print, writing or overt act) to deprive or depose the king or his successors from the style, honour, or kingly name of the imperial crown, or to levy war within the realm in order by force to compel the sovereign to change his measures or counsels, or to overcome either House of Parlia-ment, or to stir any foreigner with force to invade this realm, or any of the king's dominions. Neither under this Act nor, as we have seen, under any of the judicial constructions was the speaking of words, not written or published, held to amount to an overt act of treason, unless the words were direct counsellings or persuasions in prosecution of a traitorous design actually on foot.

Treason-Felony Act, 1848. Thus the law continued down to the year 1848, when the 11 & 12 Vict. c. 12, " An Act for the better security of the Crown and Government of the United Kingdom," was passed. By this Act, commonly called the " Treason-Felony Act " the latter part of the statute of 1795 (as perpetuated by an Act of 1817), not relating to the king's person, was repealed, and the offences therein enumerated were made felonies,[90] but with the addition of the words " open and advised speaking " to the other modes of expressing the compassing.

Statutory Treasons. In addition to the species of treason already enumerated, the three following have been created by statutes at various times: (1) By 1 Anne, st. 2, c. 21, s. 3 (1702), the endeavouring to deprive or hinder any person being the next in succession, according to the

[89] Made perpetual in 1817 by 57 Geo. 3, c. 6.
[90] The Act of 1848 expressly saved the provisions of the Act of 1352; the effect thus was that the crown could choose between charging such conduct as treason or as felony.

limitations of the Act of Settlement, from succeeding to the crown, and maliciously and directly attempting the same by any overt act. (2) By 6 Anne, c. 41 (1707), any person who maliciously, advisedly and directly by writing or printing maintains and affirms that any other person has any right or title to the crown of this realm, otherwise than according to the Act of Settlement, or that the kings of this realm, with the authority of parliament, are not able to make laws and statutes to bind the crown and the descent thereof, shall be guilty of high treason. (3) By 3 & 4 Vict. c. 52 (1840), s. 4 (having reference to the contingency that any issue of the queen should happen to ascend the throne under the age of eighteen), it was enacted that any person aiding or abetting in bringing about a marriage to, as well as any person so marrying, such issue under the age of eighteen, without the consent in writing of the regent, and the assent of both Houses of Parliament previously obtained, should be guilty of treason.

Evidence: Statute of Edward VI. At common law, one positive witness was sufficient in the case of treason as in every other capital case. But by the salutary Act, 5 & 6 Edw. 6, c. 11 (1552), to which reference has been made above,[91] it was enacted " that no person or persons shall be indicted, arraigned, condemned, convicted or attainted, for any treasons that now be, or hereafter shall be, which shall hereafter be perpetrated, committed or done, unless the same offender or offenders be thereof accused by two lawful accusers; which said accusers, at the time of the arraignment of the party accused, if they be then living, shall be brought in person before the party so accused, and avow and maintain that that they have to say against the said party, to prove him guilty of the treasons or offences contained in the bill of indictment laid against the party arraigned." Yet for a century after the passing of this Act, little if any regard was paid to it in crown prosecutions, nor indeed had the common law as yet established any considerable body of rules of legal evidence; this very statute, it will be noticed, uses the curious word "accusers" in speaking of those whom later ages described as witnesses for the prosecution. It was even contended that a statute of 1 & 2 Phil. & Mary, c. 10, 1554 (which, as Sir Michael Foster has shown, was really meant to restore to the accused " the benefit of a trial by jury of the proper county, with all the advantages of defence peculiar to that method of trial, where former statutes had deprived him of it "), had repealed the statute of Edward VI by enacting that " all trials . . . for any treason shall be had and used according to the due order and course of the common law of this realm and not otherwise." At the trial of the Regicides, however, in 1660, and upon Lord Stafford's trial, in 1680, it was treated as a point beyond all doubt that the law required two witnesses; and from the date of the Restoration the wholesome distinction (subsequently established by the statute of William III) appears to have been taken, that although the two witnesses may depose

---

[91] *Supra*, p. 239.

to different overt acts, the acts must relate to the same species of treason; so that one witness to an alleged act of compassing the king's death cannot be conjoined with another deposing to an act of levying war, in order to make up the required number. In 1691, a bill for the regulation of trials upon charges of high treason passed the commons; but in consequence of the opposition of the court, and a dispute between the two Houses, it fell to the ground. Though more than once revived, the obstinacy of the commons in resisting a very just and reasonable amendment of the lords as to the trial of peers in the court of the High Steward, delayed the passing of the measure until 1696, when it became law as the Act 7 & 8 Will. 3, c. 3.

Statute of William III, 1696. Hitherto, persons accused of treason were under even more disadvantages than those accused of felony. As a result of this Act, treason trials now became remarkably more liberal, and set an example which was followed only haltingly and slowly in the conduct of the ordinary trial for felony. The Act provides that prisoners indicted for high treason shall have a copy of the indictment delivered to them five days at least before the trial, and a copy of the panel of the jurors two days before the trial; that they shall be allowed the assistance of counsel throughout the trial,[92] and be entitled to process of the court to compel the attendance of their witnesses, who must be examined on oath.[93] It removes any doubts as to the statute of Edward VI by requiring the oaths of two lawful witnesses either both to the same overt act, or one of them to one, and the other to another overt act of the same treason; unless the prisoner shall willingly, without violence, in open court, confess the charge. It is still more remarkable in that it limits prosecutions for treason to the term of three years from the commission of the offence, except in the case of attempted assassination of the king—a protection not enjoyed by murderers and thieves. The statute emanates from a period of great political uncertainty when many prominent persons, including ministers of the crown, felt that it was common prudence to maintain relations with the exiled Stuarts, just in case there should be a restoration, hence the singular indulgence of this provision. The contested provision as to the trial of peers (intended to remedy a serious defect in the constitution of the court of the High Steward, in which the peers-triers were a select number returned at the nomination of the High Steward) was included in the Act, which provided that all peers having a right to sit and vote in parliament shall be summoned on the trial of any peer for treason, and that every peer so summoned and appearing shall vote in the trial. By a later statute, 7 Anne, c. 21, the time for delivering a copy of the indictment to the prisoner was extended to ten days; and it was directed that a list of the witnesses intended

---

[92] The felon was not allowed counsel until 1837: 6 & 7 Will. 4, c. 114; although it had been permitted irregularly by indulgence of the court for some years.

[93] Sworn evidence for the defence (already possible in some special cases) was extended to all felonies in 1703: 1 Anne, st. 2, c. 9. But witnesses for the defence in felony cases were not yet compellable.

to be brought for proving the indictment, and of the jury, with their professions and places of abode, should be delivered to the prisoner at the same time with the copy of the indictment. But the operation of this clause was suspended until after the death of the Pretender. In our own day, it has been possible to simplify treason trials by applying to them the procedure of murder trials.[94]

The Riot Act. In recent times the tendency of the legislature has been to restrict rather than to enlarge the crime of treason. This has been made possible by creating statutory offences to replace those " constructive " treasons which the courts were compelled to create in their endeavours to provide a body of law to safeguard the state from sedition, treachery and serious disorder. The Statute of Treasons was never meant to be a systematic and exhaustive body of law on the safety of the state, and the attempt to use it for that purpose created many obscure problems which fell for consideration at the most inopportune time, namely, in moments of public excitement and danger. A good example of this type of reform is seen in the law of riot. Since the passing of the Riot Act, in 1715,[95] the government has possessed a great accession of strength in dealing with all tumultuous risings attended with violence, and can more advantageously treat the offence as felony under that Act than as treason. A large number of offences formerly punishable as treason have been removed into the class of " treason-felony " by the Act 11 & 12 Vict. c. 12 (1848), to which reference has already been made. By another Act, 5 & 6 Vict. c. 51 (1842), the offence of any person discharging, pointing, aiming, or presenting, at the person of the queen, any gun or other arms (whether containing explosive materials or not); or striking at or attempting to throw anything upon her person; or producing any firearms or other arms, or any explosive or dangerous matter near her Majesty's person—with intent to injure or alarm her, is declared to be a high misdemeanour and punishable by penal servitude for seven, and not less than three, years; or by imprisonment for not more than three years, and (if the court shall so direct) by a whipping not more than thrice during that period. A conviction under this statute may be supported by the like evidence as if the prisoner stood charged with murder, so that the rule requiring two witnesses is in this case dispensed with. By the 33 & 34 Vict. c. 23 (1870), forfeiture and attainder for treason or felony have been abolished.[96]

Recent Cases. In a case arising out of the South African War, 1899–1901, *Rex* v. *Lynch*,[97] the defendant was tried at bar for treason in adhering

---

[94] Treason Act, 1945 (8 & 9 Geo. 6, c. 44).

[95] 1 Geo. 1, st. 2, c. 5; *supra*, p. 473. It was based upon (expired) statutes of Mary and Elizabeth I.

[96] On the above subject see Foster, *Crown Law*; Hale, *Pleas of the Crown*; Kelyng, *Crown Cases* (1708); Hawkins, *Pleas of the Crown*. *Cf.* also Holdsworth, *English Law*, ii, 449; iii, 287; iv, 492; viii, 307; Stephen's *Commentaries* (19th ed.), iv, 121. For the Treason Acts under the Tudors, see Tanner, *Documents*, 375.

[97] [1903] 1 K.B. 444.

to and aiding the enemies of the queen in South Africa. This case established (a) that the Naturalisation Act (33 & 34 Vict. c. 14) does not permit naturalisation in a foreign state at war with Great Britain; that a British subject who renounces his allegiance and attempts to procure himself to be naturalised in an enemy's country in time of war is guilty of high treason; and (b) that the Statute of Treasons (25 Edw. 3, stat. 5, c. 2) applies to acts committed either within or without Great Britain; thus disposing of the contention that the words of the Act "adhering to the king's enemies in his realm" meant only that the accused must be at the time in the realm. In the case of Savarkar, a Hindu, in 1909, the offence was committed in India and sentence passed, in accordance with the provisions of the Indian Penal Code. The great notoriety the case attained was due to a point of international law, the prisoner having escaped at Marseilles and taken refuge on French territory. The Hague Tribunal for the adjustment of international differences rejected the claim of the French Government to asylum and extradited the prisoner to the British authorities. In *R.* v. *Ahlers*,[98] it was held that not only the bare acts, but also the purposes and intention of the accused must be taken into consideration. In *R.* v. *Casement*,[99] it was held after a most elaborate investigation of Edward III's statute, and the examination of numerous historical problems, that a British subject gives aid and comfort to the king's enemies, and is therefore guilty of treason, if he does an act which strengthens, or tends to strengthen, the enemies of the king in the event of a war against the king, or which weakens or tends to weaken, the power of the king and of the country to resist, or to attack, the enemies of the king and of the country; and the place of commission of the act of giving aid and comfort may be either at home, in the enemies' countries, or in a neutral State.

The raid made in 1896 by Dr. Jameson and his freebooters into the Transvaal Republic might presumably have been treated as being a treasonable act committed against Her British Majesty as suzerain of the Transvaal Republic. The prisoners were, however, tried under the Foreign Enlistment Act of 1870, s. 11, which provides that, "if any person within the limits of her Majesty's dominions, and without the licence of her Majesty, prepares or fits out any naval or military expedition to proceed against the dominions of any friendly State, he shall be liable to imprisonment not exceeding two years." In 1887 an offence was held to have been committed under this Act, when General Sandoval, Sir W. Call, and others were indicted for embarking on a naval expedition against the state of Venezuela.

The recent war produced the interesting case of *Joyce* v. *Director of Public Prosecutions*,[1] in which the House of Lords held that an alien who already owed local allegiance to the British crown by reason of his residence and who also obtained (though by false statements) a British passport, had

98 [1915] 1 K.B. 616, C.C.A.
99 [1917] 1 K.B. 98.
1 [1946] 1 All E.R. 186.

thereby voluntarily extended his obligation of allegiance so that it no longer ceased when he left the country, but continued while the crown assumed the duty of affording him protection (in the diplomatic sense).

British Colonies. As regard the British Colonies, the law in the main agrees with that of the mother country; but it is quite competent for a colony to deal with treason by its own legislation, which need not necessarily be in agreement with English law. The Indian Penal Code makes it punishable with transportation for life to wage war against the government of any Asiatic power in alliance or at peace with the Crown, or to attempt to excite feelings of disaffection to the government.

A striking feature of colonial legislation on this subject is the great number of Acts of indemnity passed after different rebellions. Instances of such Acts occur in the legislation of Canada, New Zealand, St. Vincent, and Jamaica. The most important in the history of law is the Jamaica Act (1866), which indemnified Governor Eyre for any acts done during the suppression of the rising in 1865. It was held by the Exchequer Chamber, in 1870, that this Act protected Governor Eyre from being successfully sued in England, on a cause of action arising out of his acts during the outbreak.[2]

It will have been obvious that the medieval law of treason is one of the sources from which has grown up a body of law for dealing with situations in which the state is imperilled. The other main source is the prerogative. Emergency legislation on these matters is rare in the Middle Ages. Under the Tudors the prerogative was freely used in emergency (*cf.* Elizabeth's measures for meeting the Spanish Armada, supplemented to some degree by martial law). The Stuart lawyers seized upon the indisputable need for such powers to make them the basis of a general doctrine of the prerogative, which they endeavoured to apply both in time of quiet and of emergency. Relics of Tudor practice and Stuart theory are still to be found in the eighteenth century when it was argued that the normal jurisdiction of a Secretary of State comprised some emergency powers. In the nineteenth century the growing complexity of society and the crises to which it is subject, compelled a growing recourse to legislation. The Napoleonic wars were the occasion of numerous statutes for the defence of the realm, some of them having the effect of suspending the operation of the Habeas Corpus Act as to some persons. The troubled years after the peace likewise produced legislation of the same sort—Lord Liverpool's " six Acts " are well-known examples.[3]

Defence of the Realm. In the twentieth century it has become the practice to deal with the subject as a whole rather than piecemeal, and to abandon the attempt to legislate directly upon it. The Defence of the Realm

---

[2] *Phillips* v. *Eyre* (1870) 6 Q.B.D. 1.
[3] *Infra*, p. 668 note.

Acts, 1914–15, conferred sweeping powers upon the government to legislate by orders, regulations and the like, and that is now the established procedure. Although those Acts died with the war, a similar scheme was set up by the Emergency Powers Act, 1920, as a permanent reserve of power for use upon emergency. For a third time the process was repeated when another war made necessary the Emergency Powers (Defence) Act, 1939.[4]

---

[4] The scope and mechanism of this Act can be seen from the summary in *Annual Survey of English Law* (1939) 34–49.

CHAPTER 18

PARLIAMENT

The Process of Modernisation. The Revolution which took place in the winter of 1688 and 1689 can be regarded as the first stage of the long, slow process in which the public institutions of the country were gradually transformed and modernised. From that date Englishmen ceased to feel at ease among the medieval monuments which surrounded them. The monarchy had been the first to feel the shock, and after that date, in spite of differences of detail, it is clear that the position of the crown was firmly placed in its modern setting rather than in that of Caroline or Elizabethan days.

This movement of cautious adaptation progressed at different paces in different departments. The law was feeling it, although to a less degree. Even so, the great medieval *corpus* of cases in the Year Books was printed for the last time in 1679; while, on the other hand, the great chancellorship of Lord Nottingham (1673–1682) laid the foundations of a system of equity which became a powerful means of modernising the country's legal system. By a curious coincidence that same year, 1679, saw the last edition of Lyndwood's *Provinciale*—the church, too, was abandoning its older constitutional history; Jeremy Taylor's *Ductor Dubitantium* (1660) was the last English essay in scholastic moral theology, and in 1664 the clergy lost the last remnant of self-government.[1]

Those political institutions which felt the new influences soonest were naturally those which were least tied to the past by elaborate procedures—for a rigid procedure was well known, all through the Middle Ages and for long afterwards, to be the surest bulwark against change, since nothing could destroy it save a solemn act of legislation. Thus the Privy Council, which had never had a rigid structure, responded rapidly to the changes of political life, and the Cabinet emerged during the eighteenth century as the result of practice alone. Several of the more recent government departments likewise developed so much that they were ripe for reorganisation by statute in 1784. Parliament and local government authorities, on the other hand, were too entangled with their own history to obtain release save by very drastic legislation. Although parliament was fettered—largely by the defects of municipal government—it was nevertheless a vigorous and living institution which all through the eighteenth century maintained a genuine political activity, of which no better proof can be found than the numerous occasions upon which it attempted to reform itself.

[1] *Supra*, p. 42; *cf. supra*, 455.

In this chapter we shall deal first with those matters which concerned parliament as a whole, and then with the affairs of each House separately.

The Duration of Parliament

The duration and intermission of parliament have been the subject of important legislative enactments in the period since the Revolution. By the ancient legal doctrine of the constitution, parliament can only be summoned by the king's writ; when summoned its duration was formerly limited by the king's pleasure alone; and on the death of the king who summoned it, it was held to be *ipso facto* dissolved. The parliament which deposed Richard II in 1399 was held, by a logical deduction of the constitutional lawyers of that day, to have ceased to exist when Richard ceased to be king.[2] Nearly three centuries later the Convention Parliament which restored Charles II was looked on as of doubtful validity because not summoned by the king's writ. The Convention acted indeed as a parliament, and even passed an Act declaring itself to be the two Houses of Parliament, " notwithstanding any want of the king's majesty's writ of summons," and " as if his majesty had been present in person at the assembling and commencement of the present Parliament "[3]: but it was deemed needful, or at all events prudent, that all its Acts should be confirmed by the succeeding parliaments summoned in due form. At the Revolution of 1688 legal subtleties, though still potent, were treated with greater boldness. The Convention Parliament which replaced James II by William and Mary, passed an Act indeed, like the Convention of 1660, declaring itself to be a legal parliament, notwithstanding any defect of form in its summons or other- wise [4]; but it was no longer thought necessary that its Acts should be confirmed by another parliament.

Triennial Acts. We have seen how the king's prerogative of calling parliament had been limited under Edward II and Edward III by statutes requiring annual parliaments,[5] and under Charles I by the Triennial Act, passed by the Long Parliament in 1641.[6] This Act was repealed, in 1664, by the " Pensionary Parliament " of Charles II (which lasted for nearly eighteen years), but it was at the same time provided by the re- pealing statute " that parliament should not be interrupted or discontinued above three years at the most "[7]; and the Bill of Rights declared in October, 1689, that " parliaments ought to be held frequently." [8] In 1692 a bill for establishing triennial parliaments was introduced in the

[2] *Supra*, p. 492; *infra*, p. 528.
[3] 12 Car. 2, c. 1; *supra*, p. 421.
[4] 1 Will. & Mary, sess. 1, c. 1.
[5] *Supra*, p. 158; these statutes were quite ineffective, as we have seen, *supra*, pp. 211, 228, 242.
[6] *Supra*, pp. 396 *et seq*.
[7] 16 Car. 2, c. 1.
[8] *Supra*, p. 451.

House of Lords and passed both Houses; but William refused his assent. It was reintroduced in 1693 but was rejected by the commons.

Triennial Act, 1694. A similar bill, however, was introduced in the following year and became the Triennial Act of William and Mary, in December, 1694. It provided that a new parliament should be called within three years after the dissolution of a former one, and introduced a new principle by enacting further that the utmost extent of time that any parliament should be allowed to sit should be limited to three years.[9] This continued to be the law for two-and-twenty years. But after the suppression of the Rebellion in 1715, the whig ministry of George I, still apprehensive of the machinations of the Jacobites, and fearful lest a general election should endanger the stability of the new dynasty, introduced and carried the Septennial Act of 1716, which extended the maximum period of parliamentary duration to seven years.[10]

Septennial Act, 1716. It is remarkable that the bill, although specially affecting the constitution of the Commons' House, was introduced in the House of Lords, its proposer being William, second Duke of Devonshire, whose father had been one of the chief promoters of the Triennial Act of 1694 (which also had begun in the lords). By passing the bill without a dissolution, parliament not only provided for the future, but extended the possible duration of the existing House of Commons (which indeed was its main object) for four years beyond the time for which it had been elected.[11] Such a proceeding, though perfectly legal—for to the authority of parliament there is no limit—had its best justification in the real and pressing danger which then menaced the reigning family, and with it, the whole of the Revolution settlement. The special emergency might indeed have been met by a temporary measure; but a permanent Act was deemed the safer and more constitutional course—at least, by the whigs. Moreover, there was much to be urged in favour of a change. "Ever since the Triennial Bill has been enacted," said Sir Richard Steele, who supported the septennial measure in the House of Commons, "the nation has been in a series of contentions; the first year of a triennial parliament has been spent in vindictive decisions and animosities about the late elections; the second session had entered into business; . . . the third session has languished in the pursuit of what little was intended to be done in the second; and the approach of an ensuing election has terrified the members into a servile management, according as their respective principals were disposed towards the question

---

[9] 6 Will. & Mary, c. 2; Robertson, *Documents*, 138.

[10] 1 Geo. 1, stat. 2, c. 38. It was introduced in the Lords on April 10, 1716, and received its third reading in the Commons, April 26, 1716; but the session began on March 17, 1715, which is, therefore, its official (but fictitious) date, and *The Statutes at Large*, using the old style, date it 1714.

[11] See Dicey, *Law of the Constitution*, pp. 42 *et seq.*: " The Septennial Act is at once the result and the standing proof " of parliamentary sovereignty (p. 46).

before them in the House." [12]   The bill was strongly opposed by the tories in both Houses who, having long inveighed against a standing army, asserted that it was now to be matched with a standing parliament, and denounced the bill as a breach of trust with the constituencies, declaring that parliamentary omnipotence could not thus be used to defeat a natural right [13]; nevertheless, it passed its third reading in the commons with a dissentient minority of only 122.

Among the most important effects of the extension of the natural duration of parliaments was a marked increase in the stability and power of the House of Commons, and a strengthening of the influence of the ministry.   Its political consequences were momentous, for it enabled the whigs to entrench themselves so deeply that they could not be shaken for almost half a century.   How demoralising the device was, can be seen from the unprincipled bargain suggested a few years later, whereby a further prolongation of the Septennial Act was to be passed in exchange for the Peerage Bill.[14]   Speaker Onslow declared that the Septennial Act formed " the era of the emancipation of the British House of Commons from its former dependence on the crown and the House of Lords," [15] but the lords were more frank, one remarking that an annuity for seven years was worth more than one for three, and another that " triennial parliaments destroy all family interest, and subject our excellent constitution to the caprice of the multitude."   It has been suggested that the difference between the position of the Lower House under the triennial and septennial systems is strongly brought out by the fact that in the reign of Anne party leaders, like Harley and St. John, joined the ranks of the peerage in the very midst of their political careers, while under the septennial system Sir Robert Walpole designedly confined himself to the House of Commons, and only accepted an earldom from George II when defeat had closed his long administration.   This is both true and significant; but it is not necessarily the result of the Septennial Act, and Walpole's long ministry was only made possible by the lavish use of that " influence " which became all the more permanent as a result of the Act. It is clear that the crown lost upon the transaction; as for the lords, those at least who were borough owners found their property enhanced in value.

Attempts to Repeal the Septennial Act.   From the reign of George II down to the reign of Victoria, attempts were made at different times to repeal the Septennial Act, and to shorten the duration of parliaments. In 1734 Walpole defended the Septennial Act in a speech which is a model

[12] Quoted by Lord Mahon, *History of England*, i, 305.

[13] K. G. Feiling, *The Second Tory Party*, 26.

[14] *Infra*, p. 542.   The incident is discussed in Basil Williams, *Stanhope*, 410 *et seq.*, 459 *et seq.*   The debates are summarised in A. S. Turberville, *House of Lords in the Eighteenth Century*, 164 *et seq.*

[15] Coxe's *Life of Sir Robert Walpole*, i, 75.

of whig political reasoning [16]; Chatham, in 1771, " with the most deliberate and solemn conviction, declared himself a convert to triennial parliaments " [17]; Burke, in 1780, argued that more frequent elections would favour the crown, which alone could bear the enormous expense [18]; but in 1849 Tennyson D'Eyncourt obtained leave to introduce a triennial bill by a majority of five. By that time the operation of an extended suffrage had brought the House of Commons into closer and more sympathetic relations with the mass of the people, and interest in this question sensibly declined.[19] There is no principle involved in either of the numbers 3 or 7. Any restriction on the duration of parliaments is but a means to an end—the maintenance of a House of Commons fairly representing the wishes of the nation, as those wishes periodically change amidst the vicissitudes of home and foreign politics. In practice it has been found that no parliament is continued longer than six years [20]; and indeed, whatever be the legal limit fixed, the practical limit will necessarily be somewhat less, in order that the government may retain its freedom of dissolving parliament untrammelled, and that the inconvenience of a forced dissolution at an untoward moment may be avoided. The Septennial Act remained in force till 1911, when by the seventh clause of the Parliament Act it was enacted that " Five years shall be substituted for seven years as the time fixed for the maximum duration of Parliament under the Septennial Act, 1715." During the First and Second World Wars it again became necessary to prolong a parliament beyond its statutory term, but this was done in the more seemly manner of annual renewal Acts.

Demise of the Crown. The rule that parliament was *ipso facto* dissolved by the death of the sovereign was abrogated in Queen Anne's reign by an enactment that the parliament in being at the time of a demise of the crown should continue for six months afterwards, unless specially prorogued or dissolved by the new sovereign.[21] A statute of George III

---

16 *Parliamentary History*, ix, 473; extracts in C. S. Emden, *Selected Speeches on the Constitution* (World's Classics), ii, 105.

17 *Parliamentary History*, xvii, 223.

18 *Parliamentary History*, xxi, 603; Emden, *Speeches*, ii, 113.

19 " It is a remarkable illustration of the changes that may pass over party warfare, that the republican Milton at one time advocated the appointment of members for life [in his ' Ready and Easy Way to Establish a Commonwealth ']; that the tory party under Walpole and Pelham advocated triennial, and even annual parliaments, which afterwards became the watchwords of the most extreme radicals; that the whigs, taking their stand upon the Septennial Act, contended against the tories for the greater duration of parliament; and that a reform which was demanded as of capital importance by the tories under George I and George II, and by the radicals in the succeeding reigns, has at present [1877] scarcely a champion in England "—Lecky, *History of England*, ii, 64.

20 Frequent dissolutions have reduced parliaments, at several periods, to an average duration of three or four years. Sir Samuel Romilly stated, in 1818, that out of eleven parliaments of George III eight had lasted six years. But from the accession of William IV in 1830 to the year 1860, there were no less than ten parliaments, showing an average duration of three years only. (May, *Constitutional History*, i, 444.) The parliament which met on May 31, 1859, was not dissolved till July 6, 1865, exceeding the six years' practical limit by 36 days.

21 7 & 8 Will. 3, c. 15; 6 Anne c. 41; *supra*, p. 467.

(1797) further provides that if the sovereign should die in the interval between the dissolution of one parliament and the day appointed by the writs of summons for the meeting of a new one, the last preceding parliament shall *ipso facto* revive and continue in being, unless again dissolved, for six months.[22] The six months' limit imposed by the Act of Anne was abolished by a clause in the Reform Act of 1867, so that now the continuance of a parliament in being at a demise of the crown is in no way affected by that event.[23]

IMPEACHMENT

Impeachment [24] was the last surviving occasion when lords and commons collaborated, save for purely ceremonial purposes. The procedure was cumbersome and in many points obscure, but it was nevertheless a formidable weapon in the seventeenth century. After the Revolution it became increasingly anachronistic as the criminal law gradually embraced a wider variety of financial misdeeds, and as the growth of ministerial responsibility provided a sufficient sanction against ministers whose political conduct gave offence. From the year 1621, when Sir Giles Mompesson and Lord Bacon were impeached, down to the Revolution in 1688, there were about forty cases of impeachment; under William III, Queen Anne, and George I, fifteen; and the reign of George II was marked by one only, that of Lord Lovat, impeached in 1746 for high treason.

The principal cases of constitutional importance since the impeachment of the Earl of Middlesex, in 1624, are the following:

George Villiers, Duke of Buckingham.[25]—Impeached by the commons before the lords on thirteen charges, of which the most important were that (1) he had neglected to guard the high seas; (2) had lent a squadron of English ships to be employed against the Huguenots; (3) had purchased for money and monopolised in his own person several of the highest offices of state. Sir Dudley Digges, Sir John Eliot, and six other members of the commons, managed the accusation before the lords. Buckingham delivered his answer, which was mostly concerned with the questions of fact, although he also invoked the king's general and special pardons; the commons were preparing to reply, when Charles I dissolved parliament. In 1628 the commons presented a remonstrance to the king, ascribing the evils which afflicted the kingdom to the excessive power exercised and abused by Buckingham, and prayed for his removal from

---

[22] 37 Geo. 3, c. 127. The intervening general election is therefore void. The Act contains several other inconvenient provisions; their original purpose was possibly to ensure that the new sovereign should not have to put up for seven years with a parliament elected shortly before his accession, but should have an early opportunity of exercising his " influence " in securing a satisfactory parliament.

[23] 30 & 31 Vict. c. 102, s. 51.

[24] For the earlier history, see *supra*, pp. 184, 190–193, 215–216.

[25] The documents relating to the impeachment of Buckingham are printed in Gardiner' *Documents*, pp. 3–44.

office and from about the king's person. Shortly afterwards Charles prorogued parliament, and during the recess Buckingham was assassinated by Felton.

Dr. Roger Mainwaring.—Impeached by the commons for three political sermons (two preached before the king), afterwards published under the title of " Religion and Allegiance." He maintained that " parliaments were not ordained to contribute any right to the king, but for the more equal imposing and easy exacting of that which unto kings doth appertain by natural and original law and justice, as their proper inheritance annexed to their imperial crowns from their birth " ; and that those who refused to pay taxes and loans imposed by the king's royal command, without consent of parliament, " did offend against the law of God and the king's supreme authority, and became guilty of impiety, disloyalty, and rebellion." He was condemned by the lords to imprisonment during the pleasure of the House, to pay a fine of £1,000, to be suspended for three years from the ministry, and to be incapable of holding any office, ecclesiastical or civil. Yet Charles almost immediately pardoned him, gave him an additional rectory, and some years afterwards made him Bishop of St. David's.[26]

Thomas Wentworth, Earl of Strafford.[27]—Impeached by the commons for high treason. Of the twenty-eight articles exhibited against him, having reference to his conduct as President of the Council of the North, as Lieutenant of Ireland, as a privy councillor, and as commander of the king's army in England, one only, the 15th, charging him with levying money by his own authority and quartering troops on the people of Ireland, in order to compel them to pay, could be fairly construed as a substantive treason—that of " levying war against the king "—within the statute of Edward III. The commons attempted to set up a principle of *cumulative* treason ; but even if the evidence as to all the charges had been legally sufficient, it appeared extremely doubtful whether the crime of treason could be established. The well-known provision of Edward III's statute was invoked in an endeavour to obtain a parliamentary declaration that his conduct constituted the crime of treason, but it was argued for the defence that this provision had been repealed by 1 Hen. 4, c. 10 (1399) and 1 Mary, sess. 1, c. 1 (1553). Firmly persuaded that Strafford was an enemy to his country, and, if not technically, yet to all intents and purposes, a traitor, some of the leaders of the commons resolved to avail themselves of one of the worst precedents of the Tudor times, and to proceed by bill of attainder.[28] The abandonment of the impeachment clearly shows how unsuitable was that procedure when the charges were political rather than criminal in nature. Pym and Hampden

---

[26] Gardiner, *History of England*, vi, 208–211, 312–313.

[27] See Gardiner, *Documents*, 156 ; Tanner, *Constitutional Conflicts*, App. v, p. 277.

[28] See Plucknett, " Impeachment and Attainder," *Transactions of the Royal Historical Society* (1953), 145.

opposed this course, but were outvoted; Falkland and Hyde, who shortly afterwards became the leaders of the royalist party, supported the attainder. Fifty-nine members of the commons voted against the bill when it was introduced in the Lower House, and were in consequence placarded in the streets as " Straffordians, who, to save a traitor, would betray their country." The lords requested the opinion of the judges whether some of the articles of accusation amounted to treason, and received a somewhat indecisively expressed answer, which, without distinctly stating that the prisoner was guilty of treason, declared that " they were of opinion, upon all which their lordships had voted to be proved, that the Earl of Strafford doth deserve to undergo the pains and forfeitures of high treason by law." Apprehension of popular tumult prevented more than forty-five peers from attending at the passing of the bill (May 7, 1641), and of these, nineteen voted against it. In the midst of violent anxiety and doubt, Charles I weakly and ungenerously gave the royal assent, thus sacrificing the man who had so faithfully served him, and whom he had promised that " not a hair of his head should be touched." " The execution of Strafford," as is remarked by Earl Russell,[29] " casts a stain upon all parties in the state. The House of Commons were instigated by passion; the House of Lords acted from fear; and Charles from some motive or other, which, at all events, was not the right one. The admission of the mob to overawe the deliberation of parliament was a sure sign that law was about to be subverted."

Archbishop Laud.—Impeached for high treason in December, 1640, and in March 1641, he was committed to the Tower, where he remained until his death. In October 1643, specific articles were exhibited against him, relating partly to religious matters and partly to the violent proceedings in the Star Chamber and High Commission Court, in which as a councillor he had borne a very prominent part. The charges may be summed up under the three heads of endeavouring (1) to subvert the fundamental laws of the realm and introduce arbitrary government; (2) to subvert true religion and introduce popery; and (3) to subvert the rights of parliament. After a long trial and the examination of more than 150 witnesses, there appeared so little likelihood of obtaining a judicial condemnation that the commons changed their impeachment into an ordinance (or bill) of attainder. The peers consulted the judges, who answered " that they could deliver no opinion in this case in point of law, because they could not deliver any opinion in point of treason but what was particularly expressed to be treason in the statute of 25 Edw. 3, and so referred it wholly to the judgment of this House."[30] This was tantamount to a declaration that the charges contained no legal treason; but the peers (twenty only were present) passed the bill; and the archbishop was beheaded on January 10, 1645.

[29] *English Government and Constitution*, p. 66.
[30] *Lords' Journal*, December 17, 1644 (vii, 103).

Edward Hyde, Earl of Clarendon, the lord chancellor and chief minister of Charles II from the Restoration till his own fall, impeached in 1667 on a " general " charge of high treason. Of the seventeen articles against him,[31] the most important were the first, the fourth, and the eleventh; *viz.* (1) " That the Earl of Clarendon hath designed a standing army to be raised, and to govern the kingdom thereby, advising the king to dissolve the present parliament, to lay aside all thoughts of parliaments for the future, to govern by military power, and to maintain the same by free quarters and contributions." (4) That he " advised and procured divers of his Majesty's subjects to be imprisoned against law, in remote islands, garrisons, and other places, thereby to prevent them from the benefit of the law and to introduce precedents for imprisoning of other of his Majesty's subjects in like manner." (11) That he had advised and effected the sale of Dunkirk (won by Oliver Cromwell from Spain), for a sum much below its value, to Louis XIV of France.

The lords, declining to follow the precedent of Strafford's case in favour of a " general charge " of treason (which the commons had endeavoured to set up by using the word " traitorously " in their impeachment), refused to commit Clarendon to the Tower. He fled from justice. In his absence an Act was passed (19 & 20 Car. 2, c. 2) commanding him to surrender for trial within a limited time, and in default of appearance banishing him for life, subjecting him to the penalties of high treason if he returned to England, and rendering him incapable of pardon, except by Act of Parliament. Illness prevented Clarendon from appearing within the prescribed time to take his trial, and he died in exile at Rouen in 1674.[31a]

Thomas Osborne, Earl of Danby.—Impeached for high treason and other high crimes and misdemeanours.[32] The resolve to impeach him was taken by the commons on December 20, 1678, and the principal charge against him was his having written a letter to Montagu, the English minister at the Court of Versailles, empowering him, only five days after an Act had been passed to raise supplies for carrying on the war with France, to make an offer of neutrality between France and Holland for the price of 6,000,000 livres. These negotiations were naturally very secret, and thus enabled the commons to allege that Danby had " accroached royal power " by dealing with them without consulting the council.

The impeachment of Danby brought forward several points of great constitutional importance:

(1) The letter to Montagu had been most unwillingly written by Danby at the express command of King Charles II, who, to satisfy the scruples of his minister, had even subjoined a postscript in his own handwriting—" This letter is writ by my order, C. R." As the king's authority

[31] The articles are printed in full by Robertson, *Documents*, p. 565.
[31a] Roberts in *Cambridge Historical Journal*, xiii, 1.
[32] See Robertson, *Documents*, 566–569.

for the letter was undeniable, " the commons," as Hallam has observed, " in impeaching Lord Danby, went a great way towards establishing the principle (recognised by the modern theory of the constitution) that no minister can shelter himself behind the throne by pleading obedience to the orders of his sovereign," but is answerable " for the justice, the honesty, the utility of all measures emanating from the crown, as well as for their legality "; thus rendering the executive administration " subordinate, in all great matters of policy, to the . . . virtual control of the two Houses of Parliament." [33] Indeed, the principle is already to be found as early as 1388.[34]

(2) As in the previous instance of Lord Clarendon, a difference arose in this case between the lords and commons as to committing the accused to the Tower. The charges against Danby, as specified in the articles of impeachment, could not be brought within any reasonable interpretation of the statutes relating to treason, and manifestly amounted to no more than a misdemeanour. After an adjourned debate, the lords refused to commit Danby to the Tower merely on the " general charge " contained in the word " traitorously," and in the absence of a specific allegation of some overt act of treason. The Cavalier parliament was shortly afterwards prorogued (December 30, 1678), and then dissolved; but the next House of Commons, which met on March 6, 1679, revived the impeachment, and passed a bill in similar terms to that which attempted to secure the appearance of Lord Clarendon; the lords then, of their own motion, ordered the Usher of the Black Rod to take the accused into custody. Although the lords thus receded from the position which they had originally taken up, their opposition in this case may be said to have checked the practice of " general " impeachments, whereby it had been dangerously maintained that any conduct could be construed as treason by the simple device of saying that the accused had acted " traitorously." [35]

3. Another point raised in this case was the right of pleading the king's pardon in bar of a parliamentary impeachment. On being called upon to give in his written answer to the charges of the commons, Danby pleaded a pardon, secretly obtained from the king, in discharge of all the offences of which he was accused. A committee of the commons found that there was " no precedent that ever any pardon was granted to any person impeached by the commons of high treason, or other high crimes, depending the impeachment "; and resolved " that the pardon pleaded by the Earl of Danby is illegal and void, and ought not to be allowed in bar of the impeachment of the commons of England." [36] The question was not

---

[33] *Constitutional History*, ii, 411.

[34] *Rotuli Parliamentorum*, iii, 240 b.

[35] The same question had arisen with the word "feloniously": see Y.B. 13 Hen. 4 Mich., no. 20, and Plucknett, " Commentary on the Indictments," in B. H. Putnam, *Proceedings before Justices of the Peace* (Ames Foundation), cxliv.

[36] *Commons' Journal*, April 28, and May 5, 1679 (ix, 606, 612). It is curious to note that an early case in 1348 shows the commons concerned over the same point: *Rotuli Parliamentorum*, ii, 201, no. 4.

settled on this occasion, as parliament was prorogued, and the impeachment was not afterwards revived. On both legal and political grounds the commons would seem to have been right in their contention. Although the king's prerogative to grant a pardon, even before trial, was undoubtedly in all ordinary criminal proceedings by indictment at the king's suit, it was equally undoubted that in any " appeal " or prosecution for felony, not at the suit of the king, but of the injured party or his next of blood, the king had no power to remit the capital sentence.[37] If the king could not deprive a private individual of his remedy at law, much less could he stop an impeachment at the suit of the whole commons of England. Whatever its original nature, it was now undoubted that impeachment was not at the suit of the crown. And on political grounds it was clear that if the plea of the accused were admitted, there would be an end to the pretended responsibility of the ministers of the crown, who by the intervention of prerogative might be screened from the inquiry and justice of parliament. The question was not finally decided till the Act of Settlement (12 & 13 Will. 3, c. 2) declared " that no pardon under the great seal of England be pleadable to an impeachment by the commons in parliament." The right of the crown to reprieve or pardon after sentence remains, however, unaffected. James I had remitted almost the whole sentence on Lord Chancellor Bacon; and after the impeachment and attainder of the six Scottish lords concerned in the rebellion of 1715, three of them received the king's pardon. Indirectly, the commons possess the power of pardoning by refusing to demand judgment after the lords have found the accused guilty; for no judgment can be pronounced by the lords till after it has been demanded by the commons.[38]

4. The right of the bishops to sit and vote on the trial of peers in capital cases was another question raised by the impeachment of Lord Danby. It was admitted that by ancient custom—originating in a claim of privilege by the church—the bishops never voted on judgment of life or limb. But the commons contended that as the final judgment often depends upon the preliminary proceedings—as in this case upon the validity of Danby's plea of a pardon in bar—the bishops ought not to vote on such preliminary proceedings. The lords, however, passed a resolution, which has ever since been adhered to, " that the lords spiritual have a right to stay and sit in court in capital cases till the court proceeds to the vote of guilty or not guilty." This is in conformity with the 11th chapter of the Constitutions of Clarendon (11 Hen. 2), which expressly required the bishops to be present on trials, but, in deference to the canon law, excused them from voting when it came to a question of life or limb (" episcopi . . . sicut barones ceteri, debent interesse judiciis curiae domini regis cum baronibus, usque perveniatur in judicio ad diminutionem membrorum vel mortem.")[39] The limited exclusion of the bishops applies only to

---

[37] Cf. supra, p. 78.
[38] See May, Parliamentary Practice (13th ed., 1924), p. 652.
[39] Supra, p. 60.

purely judicial proceedings. They are fully entitled to vote at every stage of a bill of attainder, which, though judicial in substance, is in form a legislative act—even though it affect the life of the person attainted. In the attainder of Sir John Fenwick, in 1696, the bishops voted in all the proceedings, including the final question for the passing of the bill.

5. Another point raised for the first time on the trial of Lord Danby was whether an impeachment abated on the prorogation or dissolution of parliament. A few years previously, in 1673, a committee of the lords appointed to inquire whether " appeals, either by writ of error or petition, from the proceedings of any other court, being depending and not determined in one session of parliament, continue *in statu quo* until the next next session," had reported in the affirmative, and their report had received the confirmation of the House. In March, 1679, a similar decision was come to by the lords with regard to the effect of a dissolution of parliament, as distinguished from a prorogation from session to session. It was also resolved (with special reference to *Lord Danby's Case*) " that the dissolution of the last parliament doth not alter the state of the impeachments brought up by the commons in that parliament." [40] This was logical, to the extent that it treated impeachments in the same manner as other judicial proceedings under the rule of 1673,[41] and continued to be the law of parliament until 1685, when, in order to secure the escape of the " popish lords " then under impeachment, the previous resolution was reversed and annulled.[42] The lingering impeachment of Lord Danby, which had been continued by the first decision, was put an end to by the last. He had suffered five years' imprisonment in the Tower, not being admitted to bail until 1684. He subsequently took an active part in public affairs under William III, by whom he was created Marquis of Carmarthen (1689), and, in 1694, Duke of Leeds. In 1695 he was again impeached by the commons on a charge of corruption; but the principal witness fled to the continent, and so no further proceedings were taken. He died in 1712. The question of abatement was not finally settled until 1791, when a dissolution having intervened during the impeachment of Warren Hastings, it became necessary for parliament to review the precedents of former impeachments and to pass its judgment on the contradictory decisions of the lords. After full discussion, it was voted in both Houses, by large majorities, that by the law and custom of parliament an impeachment pending in the House of Lords continued *in statu quo*, from one session and from one parliament to another, until a judgment shall have been given.[43]

[40] *Lords' Journal*, March 18, 19, 1679 (xiii, 466)
[41] But it made the discontinuance of legislative proceedings by a prorogation or dissolution look somewhat anomalous.
[42] *Lords' Journal*, May 22, 1685 (xiv, 11).
[43] Pike, *Constitutional History of the House of Lords*, p. 233, remarks, " It may perhaps, also be considered a general principle that neither prorogation nor dissolution of Parliament will put an end to impeachment by the commons before the lords." In the cases of Warren Hastings and Viscount Melville (*cf. infra*, p. 538), special Acts of Parliament were passed to remove all doubt on the matter, and " it is not improbable that these

Edward Fitzharris.—Impeached by the commons for high treason. Their real object was to elicit disclosures of a pretended " popish plot," and so aid the progress of the Exclusion Bill against the Duke of York. Fitzharris was (or had been) a secret agent and informer used by the court against the whigs. He doubtless knew a great deal—possibly too much, and it was thought that Charles II wanted him hanged. In order to prevent the commons from proceeding with the impeachment, Charles II instructed the attorney-general to proceed against Fitzharris in the King's Bench for a treasonable libel. At the same time, the lords raised an important point of constitutional law, namely, whether a commoner could be impeached for a capital offence, and in the interest of the court they voted that " Fitzharris should be proceeded with according to the course of common law, and not by way of impeachment." The grounds of their decision were not stated; but the fact of his being a commoner appears to have been mainly relied on. They were supported by a supposed authority in the case of Sir Simon de Bereford in the 4th Edward 3. Sir Simon, however, was not impeached by the commons, but charged before the lords, *at the suit of the crown*, of participation in the treason of Roger Mortimer. After giving judgment against him, the lords made a declaration (which, as being made " with the assent of the king, in full parliament," has been regarded by some as a statute), " that the aforesaid judgment be not drawn into example or consequence in time to come, whereby the said peers may be charged hereafter to judge other than their peers, contrary to the law of the land." [44] Even if this declaration amounted to a statute, which was doubtful, it clearly applied to cases similar to that of Bereford, and not to an impeachment at the suit of the commons. In subsequent cases the lords had violated their own declaration by trying commoners for capital offences at the suit of the crown. But an impeachment by the commons had come to be a proceeding of a totally distinct character. The reign of Richard II afforded several precedents of the impeachment of commoners; and the right had been exercised, without question, so recently as the time of Charles I.[45] The commons met the decision of the lords by voting it " a denial of justice, and a violation of the constitution of parliaments, and an obstruction to the further discovery of the popish plot," and " that for any inferior court to proceed against Edward Fitzharris, or any person, lying under an impeachment in parliament for the same crimes for which he or they stand impeached, is a high breach of the privileges of parliament." [46] The king shortly afterwards dissolved parliament, and the

---

precedents would be followed upon any future impeachment, as each of these Acts had reference only to the particular case under consideration at the time."—*Ibid.*, p. 234.

[44] *Rotuli Parliamentorum*, ii, 53, 54; *cf.* Hallam, *Constitutional History*, ii, 446. The principle used in the text to distinguish *Bereford's Case* could only be valid when impeachment came to be recognised as independent of the crown. It is not clear how early that view was; Richard II certainly cast doubt upon it (*supra*, p. 172), and so did Charles I (*supra.* p. 408).

[45] *Mainwaring's Case, supra*, p. 530.

[46] *Commons' Journal*, March 26, 1681.

prosecution of Fitzharris by indictment in the King's Bench was proceeded with. He pleaded in abatement that an impeachment was then pending against him for the same offence, but the plea was disallowed, and he was found guilty and executed.[47]

The unconstitutional theory of the lords put forward in the isolated case of Fitzharris has been superseded by a later decision. After the Revolution, in 1689, Sir Adam Blair and four other commoners were impeached of high treason in having published a proclamation of James II. A committee was appointed to search for precedents; and after full deliberation, and rejecting a motion requiring the opinion of the judges, the lords came to a resolution to proceed on the impeachments.[48]

William Bentinck, Earl of Portland; Edward Russell, Earl of Orford; Charles Montagu, Earl of Halifax; and *John, Lord Somers,* four whig peers impeached for high treason by a tory House of Commons for their share in promoting the Spanish partition treaties in 1700, and for other alleged illegal practices. The two Houses quarrelled as to the time and mode of the trial; and as the commons refused to appear on the day appointed to bring forward their evidence, the impeached ministers were acquitted.[49] There was probably some foundation for several of the minor charges, but few have pretended to justify the impeachments, which, as Hallam observes, " have generally been regarded as a disgraceful instance of party spirit."

Henry Sacheverell, rector of St. Saviour's, Southwark, impeached by the commons for two sermons preached, the one at Derby, the other at St. Paul's, in which he inculcated the doctrine of unlimited passive obedience. The prosecution was characterised by Hallam[50] as " of high importance in a constitutional light, and is not only the most authentic exposition but the most authoritative ratification of the principles upon which the Revolution is to be defended." " The managers appointed by the House of Commons," says Lockhart, an ardent Jacobite, " behaved with all the insolence imaginable. In their discourse they boldly asserted, even in her Majesty's presence, that, if the right to the crown was hereditary and indefeasible, the prince beyond seas (meaning the king), and not the queen, had the legal title to it, she having no claim thereto but what she owed to the people; and that by the Revolution principles, on which the constitution was founded, and to which the laws of the land agreed, the people might turn out or lay aside their sovereigns as they saw cause. Though, no doubt of it, there was a great deal of truth in these assertions, it is easy to be believed that the queen was not well pleased to hear them maintained, even in her own presence, and in so solemn a

---

[47] 8 St.Tr. 326. *Cf.* the account of this very mysterious affair in David Ogg, *Charles II,* ii, 617, 624 *et seq.*

[48] *Lords' Journal,* xiv, 260, 262–264; May, *Parliamentary Practice* (13th ed., 1924), 652.

[49] 14 St.Tr. 233.

[50] *Constitutional History,* iii, 204.

manner, before such a great concourse of her subjects. For, though princes do cherish these and the like doctrines whilst they serve as the means to advance themselves to a crown, yet, being once possessed thereof, they have as little satisfaction in them as those who succeed by an hereditary unquestionable title." [51] The lords found Sacheverell guilty by 69 votes to 52; but passed only a slight sentence, of suspension from preaching for three years and that his sermons should be burnt by the hands of the common hangman. Queen Anne afterwards rewarded him with the rich living of St. Andrew's, Holborn. He died in 1724. Politically, the whigs had made a tactical blunder of the first magnitude in prosecuting the Doctor, for the trial rallied a large body of tory opinion which broke up the ministry and returned a tory majority at the ensuing election.[52]

Robert Harley, Earl of Oxford; Henry St. John, Viscount Boling-broke; and *James Butler, Duke of Ormond.*—Tory ministers impeached by the commons for their share in negotiating the Peace of Utrecht, in 1713. Bolingbroke and Ormond fled to France, and were attainted in their absence. Oxford alleged in justification the immediate commands of the sovereign for what he had done, a defence which though it had failed to shelter Danby, and would not be tolerated now, found many supporters in the then unsettled state of the theory of ministerial responsibility. After two years' imprisonment in the Tower, Oxford was set at liberty, the commons, unable to agree with the lords as to the mode of procedure, having declined to continue the prosecution. The House of Lords, which contained so many ministers, ex-ministers and possible future ministers, fully realised that political life would be impossible if every new party victory were to be followed by the impeachment of the former ministry. The numerous obscurities of the procedure were therefore used to create delay while feeling died down.

This is the last instance of purely political impeachment. Constantly responsible to parliament, ministers have been restrained from the commission of the graver class of offences, and for minor errors of policy or conduct the loss of power has proved a sufficient punishment.

Warren Hastings; Lord Melville.—" The last hundred years," says May,[53] " present but two cases of impeachment—the one against Mr. Warren Hastings, on charges of misgovernment in India, the other against Lord Melville (in 1804), for alleged malversation in his office. The former was not a minister of the crown, and he was accused of offences committed beyond the reach of parliamentary control; and the offences charged against the latter had no relation to his political duties as a responsible minister."

[51] *Lockhart Papers*, i, 312.
[52] Keith Feiling, *Second Tory Party*, 411; A. S. Turberville, *House of Lords in the Eighteenth Century*, 96 *et seq.* ; Lecky, *History of England*, i, 63 *et seq.*
[53] May, *Constitutional History*, ii, 93.

THE HOUSE OF LORDS

Since the Revolution, the House of Peers—the lineal representative of the old *Curia Regis*—has undergone changes in its numbers, composition, and political weight and influence, greater even than the changes which, during the same period, have so materially affected the practical exercise of the authority of the crown in government and legislation.

Number of Peers. In the parliament of 1454, the last held before the outbreak of the Wars of the Roses, the number of lay peers who attended was fifty-six. In 1485, only twenty-eight received writs of summons to the first parliament of Henry VII. The greatest number summoned by Henry VIII was fifty-one, which was slightly increased during the reign of Elizabeth. In the meantime, by the suppression of the monasteries and the consequent removal from the Upper House of about thirty abbots and priors, the spiritual peerage (including five of the new sees created by Henry VIII) had been reduced to the number of twenty-six, at which it has ever since remained.[54] The four Stuart kings created 193 new peers, but as during their reigns ninety-nine peerages became extinct, the number of the peerage at the Revolution of 1688 actually stood at about 150, which was raised by William III and Queen Anne to 168.

Representative Peers. The House of Lords was further increased in 1707, on the passing of the Act of Union with Scotland, by the addition of sixteen representative peers from that kingdom, elected at the commencement of every Parliament. The lords were ill at ease with the introduction of so unfamiliar an element to their House. They soon found themselves in the odd position of having to sit on election petitions, as well as having to settle the difficult question of the relationship between Scottish, English and British peerages. The matters were dealt with in an atmosphere of some animosity, and the decisions were rendered the worse by their inconsistency, and under the influence of political considerations.[55] Thus what happened if a Scottish peer received a British peerage? In 1708 the Scottish Duke of Queensberry was created British Duke of Dover and took his seat as an hereditary peer; but in 1711, when the Scottish Duke of Hamilton was created Duke of Brandon, the House refused to allow him to sit, and maintained that attitude until it again reversed itself in 1782

---

[54] Attempts were made in 1834, 1836 and 1837, to exclude the episcopal element altogether from the House of Lords, but unsuccessfully. It was, however, determined by the legislature in 1847, when a new bishopric was created for Manchester, that no increase in the existing number of twenty-six bishops in the Upper House should take place (10 & 11 Vict. c. 108). The two archbishops, and the bishops of London, Durham and Winchester have always a right to sit in parliament, but the bishop last elected to any other see (except Sodor and Man, whose bishop is in no case a lord of parliament) cannot claim a seat until another vacancy has occurred. May, *Constitutional History*, i, 301; Pike, *Constitutional History of the House of Lords*, p. 369; Anson, *Law and Custom of the Constitution*, vol. i, 210.

[55] For the details of what follows, see May, *Constitutional History*, i, 192; Holdsworth, *History of English Law*, xi, 6; Turberville, *House of Lords in the Eighteenth Century*, Chap. v.

by permitting a later Duke of Hamilton to sit as Duke of Brandon. There was a feeling that the sixteen statutory representative peers was the maximum number of Scots which the House could tolerate in any capacity —even when furnished with British titles. Governments soon found a way round this rule by conferring British peerages upon the heirs apparent to Scottish titles; in such cases the House did not venture to unseat a British peer when he subsequently inherited a Scottish title.

In 1709 the lords heard their first election petition and reached the position that a Scottish peer who also held a British peerage was not entitled to vote for the Scottish representatives—which was logical under the rule of the Queensberry case, since a lord who sat in person had no need to be represented. But it created a grievance after the Hamilton case of 1711, for the position now was that a Scottish peer who also held a British peerage could neither sit nor elect, but was in " a worse condition than the meanest or most criminal of subjects." This disfranchising decision remained until it was reversed in 1793.

Problem of the Scottish Peer. Beneath all this lay a political and a social problem. Scotland was a much poorer country than England; even her dukes were much inferior to the English great families in material resources. It was the great pride of the House of Lords that there members were completely independent economically and politically of any outside power, whether it be the crown, the ministry, or an electorate. The House was an oligarchy, no doubt, but it was not unmindful of such merits as even an oligarchy might possess.[56] Into this scheme the Scots brought the anomaly of their election, and the defect of their economic weakness. We have just seen the vicissitudes of their struggle to obtain British (and therefore hereditary) seats; they were also mighty place-hunters. Inevitably they looked to the crown and the ministry of the day for the furtherance of their fortunes. They frequently voted as a solid block and could thereby hold the balance in many a division. Politically, they were an asset, or a menace, to any government. The machinery for the election of Scottish representative peers was immediately captured by the government and kept under government control. It must also be remembered that the Scottish lords could influence the elections of the forty-five Scottish members of the House of Commons to a very considerable extent, and so their support was desirable on that account also. The total result of all this was very curious: by holding the balance of power, and by selling their support to whatever ministry was in office, the Scots could exert a powerful influence upon English affairs; but when parliament came to deal with Scottish matters, the

---

[56] See the essay on the position of the aristocracy in Chap. II of Lecky's *History of England*, which admirably expresses eighteenth-century thought on the subject, although written about 1877.

Scottish representatives in both houses were easily voted down, as happened on a number of occasions.[57]

Party politics during the reign of Queen Anne were subject to violent changes and as party spirit came to be more and more a permanent factor in public affairs it necessarily followed that an hereditary chamber should respond imperfectly to sudden changes of the nation's mood, and that, even apart from moments of great crisis, the political complexion of the two chambers should not always match. Conflicts between the two Houses in the past had generally been on matters of privilege,[58] but there was now the possibility of conflict upon matters of general politics. Under these circumstances, ministers sometimes felt that they and their policies were insufficiently represented in the Upper House, and therefore asked the crown to exercise the prerogative of creating new peers to remedy the situation.

Partisan Creations of Peers. It was not a question of simply creating an arithmetical majority sufficient to pass a particular measure; neither party was sufficiently disciplined for accurate forecasts to be made, but ministries did feel that the proper presentation of their views in the lords was necessary, and they seem to have felt that generally that was sufficient. Such a situation arose in 1703 when a composite ministry dependent upon a tory majority in the commons, obtained the creation of four tory peers, although they had to yield to whig protests by also elevating a fifth, a whig, with them. The net gain was therefore three.[59]

More serious was the creation of the famous " tory dozen " in 1712. The government which took this decision [60] suffered from the weakness which often afflicted coalitions, and was further hampered by the personal feud between its two leaders, Harley (now Earl of Oxford) and St. John (soon to be Viscount Bolingbroke); its large tory majority in the commons was not unanimous (there was a vigorous October Club, and a still more vigorous March Club, while " highflyers " and " whimsicals " formed other groups); there was an alleged financial scandal, and an agitation against the Naturalisation Act resulting in its repeal [61]; Lord Nottingham, a staunch tory, but still more uncompromising churchman, deserted his party to enter into an unholy bargain with the whigs to pass his Occasional Conformity Bill [62]; the mysterious " Scottish plot " had set lords and commons at odds; and, above all, there was the great issue of peace or war, and the rapidly approaching problem of the succession. The

---

[57] The malt tax of 1713 (Turberville, 156) and the Act to amend the Scottish law of treason, 7 Anne, c. 21 (1709; *ibid.* 94) are examples.

[58] The proceedings in *Ashby* v. *White* (*infra*, p. 581) show that privilege was still a fruitful cause of dissension between the Houses.

[59] On this incident, see Turberville, *House of Lords in the Eighteenth Century*, 44.

[60] For the very complex political situation at the moment, see Turberville, *op. cit.*, 111–118, 155, and Keith Feiling, *The Tory Party*, 424–445. The principal issue was the Peace of Utrecht.

[61] *Infra*, p. 679.

[62] *Infra*, p. 654. The whigs in return abandoned the dissenters and their principle of toleration to get Nottingham's help against the peace.

House of Lords could, with an effort, produce a very slight whig majority against the government, but the cross-currents were so strong that a settled policy became exceptionally difficult. The sixteen Scottish peers added materially to the complexity of the situation.

The twelve new peers took their seats on January 2, 1712, and that very day voted for the court and turned the division. It was universally understood that their presence was intended to strengthen the peace party in the lords; but there was a secondary motive. " I asked Lord Oxford afterwards," wrote Lord Dartmouth, who as Privy Seal had the disagreeable duty of preparing the warrants, " what was the real inducement for taking so odious a course, when there were less shocking means to have acquired the same end. He said, the Scotch lords were grown so extravagant in their demands that it was high time to let them see they were not so much wanted as they imagined; for they were now come to expect a reward for every vote they gave." [63] These creations for partisan purposes were greatly resented, and furnished one of the articles of impeachment exhibited against Oxford in the next reign.

A few days later a royal message authorised the House to consider the possibility of substituting hereditary for elective Scottish peers,[64] for it was obvious that the two principles were then incompatible. There was no result, but in the next reign the matter was again raised in consequence of the political activities of the Prince of Wales who, at the head of a group of dissident whigs and tories which met at Leicester House, was in opposition to his father.

Stanhope's Peerage Bill, 1719. The fear that the Prince might, on coming to the throne, make use of his prerogative to overthrow the still subsisting whig majority in the Upper House by the creation of more tory peers induced the whig ministry of Sunderland and Stanhope in 1719 to put forward proposals for the limitation of the royal prerogative of creating peers. With the concurrence of George I, a Bill was introduced by the Duke of Somerset providing that, with an exception in favour of princes of the blood, the crown should be restrained from augmenting the then existing number of 178 peerages by more than six, although new peerages might be created in the place of any which should become extinct; and that twenty-five hereditary peers should be substituted for sixteen elective peers of Scotland. This unprecedented scheme aroused violent controversy in the Press and in the country, and even terminated the life-long friendship of Addison and Steele. In the lords great attention was directed to the question of the bearing of this Bill upon the Act of Union, whose provisions were generally felt to be in some way " fundamental." It was commonly realised that the change in the Scottish peerage was the crux of the whole scheme, and that the unlimited prerogative of creation was dangerous. The larger aspect of the probable effects of

[63] Burnet, vi, 95.
[64] *Ibid.* 99.

the Bill upon the balance of forces in the constitution gradually came to the fore, however, and the Bill was strongly opposed in the House of Commons by Sir Robert Walpole and others, and finally rejected by a large majority (269 to 177).[65] Had it passed into law it would have transformed the House of Lords into a close aristocratic body, independent alike of the crown and of the people. It would have eliminated from the complex mechanism of the constitution what has been termed its " safety-valve " [66]—that power of creating peers by which the sovereign, on the advice of his responsible ministers, is enabled, in cases of great emergency, to force the peers to bow to the will of the people, expressed by their representatives in the House of Commons, and thus to render possible the smooth and continuous working of our present system of parliamentary government.

Pitt and the Peerage. At the accession of George III the number of peerages amounted to only 174, but throughout his long reign new creations were multiplied with unprecedented profusion. In the earlier part of his reign the power of creating peers was mainly exercised by the king himself, as one means of carrying out his determination to break up the system of party government; but the younger William Pitt, on acceding to office, employed it for another and a far nobler purpose. The consolidation of his own authority as minister was naturally one of the objects which he had in view, but his great aim was to reform the House of Lords by changing it from a narrow and exclusive caste into a large representation of the intellect, the achievements, and more especially of the wealth of England. He wished, he said in effect, " to reward merit, to recruit the peerage from the great landowners and other opulent classes, and to render the crown independent of factious combinations among the existing peers." [67] This policy had in fact been the practice, to some extent, of his predecessors, and it is abundantly clear that among their creations there were many men whose merits were conspicuous.[68] With this object, while himself disdaining honours, Pitt dispensed them to others with the greatest profusion. In the first five years of his administration he created forty-eight new peers; at the end of eight years he had created between sixty and seventy; and later, in the two years 1796–1797, he created no less than thirty-five. In 1801, at the end of his seventeen years' administration, his creations had reached the total of 141.

The example set by Pitt was followed by succeeding ministers, and at the end of George III's long reign of sixty years the actual number of peerages conferred by that king (including some promotions of existing peers to a higher rank) amounted to the enormous number of 388.

---

[65] See E. R. Turner, " The Peerage Bill of 1719 " in *English Historical Review*, xxviii (1913), 243–259; Turberville, *The House of Lords in the Eighteenth Century* (1927), Chap. 6; C. S. Emden, *Speeches on the Constitution*, i, 105–111 for Walpole's speech.
[66] Bagehot, *English Constitution*, 229.
[67] Speech on January 16, 1789, quoted by May, *Constitutional History*, i, 278.
[68] See the instances cited in Turberville, *op. cit.*, 419.

Irish Peers, 1801. The House of Lords was further augmented on the union with Ireland in 1801, by the addition of twenty-eight Irish representative peers, elected, not for each parliament only like the Scottish representative peers, but for life—a variation evidently suggested by the experience of the older system. At the same time four Irish bishops were admitted to seats in the Upper House of the United Kingdom, sitting by rotation of sessions as representatives of the Irish episcopate. But on the disestablishment of the Church of Ireland in 1869, the Irish bishops lost their seats in parliament,[69] and no elections for the Irish representative peers have taken place since 1921.

The Later Peerage. The vast increase in the peerage under George III affected not merely the numbers but the whole character of the House of Lords. For the first time in our history, observes J. R. Green,[70] " it became the distinctly conservative element in our constitution. The full import of Pitt's changes has still to be revealed, but in some ways their results have been very different from the end at which he aimed. The larger numbers of the peerage, though due to the will of the crown, has practically freed the House from any influence which the crown can exert by the distribution of honours. This change, since the power of the crown has been practically wielded by the House of Commons, has rendered it far harder to reconcile the free action of the lords with the regular working of constitutional government. On the other hand, the larger number of its members has rendered the House more responsive to public opinion, when public opinion is strongly pronounced; and the political tact which is inherent in great aristocratic assemblies has hitherto prevented any collision with the Lower House from being pushed to an irreconcilable quarrel. Perhaps the most direct result of the change is seen in the undoubted popularity of the House of Lords with the mass of the people. The larger number of its members, and the constant additions to them from almost every class of the community, has secured it as yet from the suspicion and ill-will which in almost every other constitutional

---

[69] There were other differences in the mode of treating the Scottish and Irish peerages. From the date of the union with Scotland the crown has been debarred from creating any new Scottish peers, but the then existing peerage of Scotland was perpetuated in its integrity. On the union with Ireland, however, it was determined gradually to diminish the excessive numbers of the Irish nobility, and it was therefore provided by the Act of Union that only one Irish peerage should be created for every three which should become extinct, until the reduction of the number to 100, at which figure it should be maintained by the creation of one Irish peerage as often as a peerage became extinct, or as often as an Irish peer should become entitled, by descent or creation, to a peerage of the United Kingdom. At the same time the privilege was granted to all Irish peers (except the representative twenty-eight for the time being) of sitting in the House of Commons if elected by any constituency in Great Britain but not in Ireland. The peerage of both Scotland and Ireland has been undergoing a process of gradual absorption into the peerage of the United Kingdom. In order to adjust the inadequate representation of their peerage Scottish peers have, of recent years, been admitted in more considerable numbers to hereditary seats in the House of Lords of the United Kingdom. For the mode of election and the status of the Scottish and Irish peers, *cf.* L. O. Pike, *Constitutional History of the House of Lords*, pp. 358 *et seq.*; Anson, *Law and Custom*, i, 219–222.

[70] *Short History of the English People*, p. 792 (published in 1874).

country has hampered the effective working of a second legislative chamber."

The largely increased numbers of the House of Lords, and the more representative character which it had acquired through the changes in its composition here briefly sketched, had enabled it to preserve very much of its ancient authority and political influence. But it has nevertheless tended—especially since the Reform Act of 1832—to decline more and more from the position of a co-ordinate legislative power, and to become simply a revising and suspending House—altering and modifying bills sent up from the commons, rejecting them sometimes when the mind of the nation is not thoroughly made up in their favour, but yielding to the national will whenever unequivocally expressed.[71]

The Lords and the Reform Bills of 1831 and 1832. The constitutional position of the lords with regard to legislation of which they disapprove, but which is supported by the ministers of the crown, the House of Commons, and the people, may be said to have been definitely settled by the result of the memorable struggle with the Upper House in 1831 and 1832 on the passing of the Reform Bill. After sixteen peers had been created to assist the progress of the measure, the continued opposition of the House of Lords was at length overcome by the private persuasions of the king, and the knowledge that he had consented to his ministers' request for power to create a sufficient number of peers to ensure a majority.[72]

The threatened creation of peers was denounced at the time by the Duke of Wellington and the tory party generally as " an unconstitutional exercise of the prerogative "; but it was admirably answered by Earl Grey: " I ask what would be the consequences if we were to suppose that such a prerogative did not exist, or could not be constitutionally exercised ? The commons have a control over the power of the crown, by the privilege, in extreme cases, of refusing the supplies; and the crown has, by means

[71] The Earl of Derby, in speaking against the second reading of the Corn Importation Bill, in 1846: " My lords, if I know anything of the constitutional value of this House, it is to interpose a salutary obstacle to rash and inconsiderate legislation; it is to protect the people from the consequences of their own imprudence. It never has been the course of this House to resist a continued and deliberately formed public opinion. Your lordships always have bowed, and always will bow, to the expression of such an opinion; but it is yours to check hasty legislation leading to irreparable evils." (Hansard, *Debates*, lxxxvi, p. 1175.) Similarly, Lord Lyndhurst, speaking on the second reading of the Oaths Bill, in 1858, said in the House of Lords: " It is part of our duty to originate legislation; but it is also a most important part of our duty to check the inconsiderate, rash, hasty, and undigested legislation of the other House;—to give time for consideration; and for consulting and perhaps modifying the opinions of the constituencies; but I never understood, nor could such a principle be acted upon, that we were to make a firm, determined, and persevering stand against the opinion of the other House of Parliament, when that opinion is backed by the opinion of the people; and, least of all, on questions affecting, in a certain degree, the constitution of that House, and popular rights. If we do make such a stand, we ought to take care that we stand on a rock." (Hansard, *Debates*, cxlix, p. 1770.)

[72] " The king grants permission to Earl Grey, and to his chancellor, Lord Brougham, to create such a number of peers as will be sufficient to ensure the passing of the Reform Bill—first calling up peers' eldest sons. WILLIAM R., Windsor, May 17th, 1832." Roebuck, *History of the Whig Ministry*, ii, 331, 333, quoted by May, *Constitutional History*, i, 312.

of its power to dissolve the House of Commons, a control upon any violent and rash proceedings on the part of the commons; but if a majority of this House is to have the power, whenever they please, of opposing the declared and decided wishes both of the crown and the people, without any means of modifying that power—then this country is placed entirely under the influence of an uncontrollable oligarchy. I say that, if a majority in this House should have the power of acting adversely to the crown and the commons, and was determined to exercise that power, without being liable to check or control, the constitution is completely altered, and the government of this country is not a limited monarchy: it is no longer, my lords, the crown, the lords, and the commons, but a House of Lords —a separate oligarchy—governing absolutely the others." [73]

Less critical, but nevertheless serious, conflicts occurred on several occasions in the early nineteenth century. " The Lords," remarks May, " opposed themselves to concessions to the Roman Catholics, and to amendments of the criminal law, which had been approved by the commons. For several years neither the commons nor the people were sufficiently earnest to enforce the adoption of those measures; but when public opinion could no longer be resisted, the lords avoided a collision with the commons by acquiescing in measures of which they still disapproved. Since popular opinion has been more independently expressed by the commons, the hazard of such collisions has been greatly increased. The commons, deriving their authority direct from the people have increased in power; and the influences which formerly tended to bring them into harmony with the lords have been impaired." [74] In August, 1869, Mr. Gladstone obtained from the queen the creation of twelve liberal peers in order, not to create a majority, which was out of the question, but to present effectively before the lords his Irish Church Disestablishment Bill.[75] A collision between the two Houses was narrowly avoided in 1884, when the Representation of the People Bill was rejected by the House of Lords. The recurrence of such episodes made it appear as if the lords had the power of compelling a dissolution when they saw fit to do so. Gladstone firmly denied this proposition: " never will I be a party to dissolving in order to determine whether the lords or the commons were right upon the Franchise Bill," he wrote. " If I have anything to do with dissolution, it will be a dissolution upon organic change in the House of Lords." [76] A new departure at that crisis was taken by a correspondence carried on between the Marquis of Salisbury, as representing the opposition and the Conservative majority in the House of Lords, and the Right Hon. W. E. Gladstone, the then Prime Minister, through the medium of the sovereign. This was one of the rare instances in later English history of the sovereign stepping into the arena of party politics,

[73] Hansard, *Debates*, 3rd ser., xii, 1006 (May 17, 1832), quoted May, i, 314.
[74] May, *Constitutional History*, i, 307.
[75] E. Fitzmaurice, *Life of Lord Granville*, ii, 15–18 (cited in Turberville, *House of Lords in the Eighteenth Century*, 115 n. 3).
[76] Morley, *Life of Gladstone*, iii, 130.

in order to stay a political and, it might be, a constitutional crisis of threatening dimensions. That a collision between the two Houses was not precipitated at this juncture was primarily due to the good services of the sovereign in accepting the position of mediator between the two rival political forces, and, next, to the patriotic disposition shown by either statesman, who, while each asserting his own standpoint, finally made those mutual concessions which harmonised in the main with the prevailing popular opinion.

The Resolutions of 1907. The House of Lords continued to reject measures of capital importance, and it became abundantly clear that either the composition or the powers of the Upper House, or both, would have to be modified. This question of broad principle was advanced a stage by the debate in which the House of Commons adopted (June 26, 1907) a resolution proposed by Sir Henry Campbell-Bannerman that " in order to give effect to the will of the people as expressed by their elected representatives, it is necessary that the power of the other House to alter or reject bills passed by this House should be so restricted by law as to secure that within the limits of a single parliament the final decision of the commons should prevail." No legislation was proposed at the moment, but Campbell-Bannerman put forward the outlines of a scheme whereby a bill, passed by the commons and rejected by the lords, should become law if three successive private conferences between the two Houses failed to secure agreement, the bill having been passed by the commons afresh as a preliminary to the second and third conferences. The scheme did not touch the composition of the House of Lords, did not contemplate a general election intervening, and involved a delay which need not be much more than twelve months.[77]

Money-Bills in the Lords. The same political difficulties arose over financial measures as over general legislation, but the position of the House of Lords had for centuries been weaker in matters of taxation. Besides the exclusive right of initiating money-bills, a privilege which the House of Lords had readily admitted in the Short Parliament of 1640,[78] the commons also maintained that such bills should not be amended by the lords. In 1671, they successfully disputed the right of the lords to reduce the amount of an imposition; and since that year the lords have tacitly acquiesced in the contention of the commons. Whenever amendments have been made which the commons were desirous of adopting, they have invariably saved their privilege by throwing out the amended bill and sending up a fresh bill embodying the lords' amendments. But while abstaining from direct interference with grants of supply, the lords occasionally, without objection from the Lower House, rejected

---

[77] Campbell-Bannerman's speech (June 24) is in C. S. Emden, *Select Speeches on the Constitution* (World's Classics), i, 151–158.
[78] *Supra*, p. 391.

or postponed other bills incidentally affecting supply and taxation, such as bills for the regulation of trade and for imposing or repealing protective duties. When, however, in 1790, they amended a bill for regulating Warwick Gaol, by shifting the proposed rate from the owners to the occupiers of land, the commons vindicated their privilege by throwing out the bill. The right of the lords to reject a money-bill, " to pass all or reject all without diminution or alteration," was explicitly admitted by the Lower House in 1671 and 1689; but as the exercise of this right involved withholding supplies from the crown, the lords were loth to avail themselves of it, and, unable to exercise any control, ceased for the most part even to discuss financial measures. When, in 1763, they opposed the third reading of the Wines and Cider Duties Bill, it was observed that this was the first occasion on which they had been known to divide upon a money-bill.

Paper Duties Bill. At length, in 1860, the lords exercised their legal right of rejection, " in a novel and startling form," by rejecting a bill for the repeal of the paper-duty, after bills for the increase of the property tax and stamp duties, intended to supply the deficiency which would be caused by such repeal, had already received the royal assent. The legal right of the lords to reject any bill whatever was indisputable; and this particular bill (promoted by Gladstone in the interests of cheaper newspapers) had encountered stormy opposition in the Lower House, where it was only carried by a majority of nine. " Yet it was contended," observes Sir Erskine May, " with great force, that to undertake the office of revising the balances of supplies and ways and means—which had never been assumed by the lords during two hundred years—was a breach of constitutional usage, and a violation of the first principles upon which the privileges of the House are founded. If the letter of the law was with the lords, its spirit was clearly with the commons." After the lapse of six weeks, during which a committee of the commons had searched for precedents and reported to the House, Lord Palmerston, on the part of the Government, addressed the House, deprecating a collision with the lords, and expressing his opinion that, in rejecting the Paper Duties Bill, they had been actuated by motives of public policy merely, without any intention of entering upon a deliberate course of interference with the peculiar functions of the commons; adding, however, that should that appear to be their intention, the latter would know how to vindicate their privileges, if invaded, and would be supported by the people.

The Palmerston Resolutions, 1860. He concluded by proposing three resolutions, which were passed by the House (July 6, 1860): (1) " That the right of granting aids and supplies to the crown is in the commons alone "; (2) That although the lords had sometimes exercised the power of rejecting bills relating to taxation, yet the exercise of that power was " justly regarded by this House with peculiar jealousy, as affecting the right of the commons to grant supplies and to provide the ways and means for the service of the year "; and (3) That to secure to the commons their rightful control over taxation, " this House has in its own hands the power so to impose and remit taxes, and to frame bills of supply, that the right of the commons as to the matter, manner, measure, and time, may be maintained inviolate." In the following session the commons effectually prevented a second interference by the lords by including the repeal of the paper-duty in a general financial measure granting the property tax, the tea and sugar duties, and other ways and means for the service of the year, which the lords were constrained to accept.[79]

Tacking Money-Bills. For a short time the commons resorted to a somewhat dishonest device based upon this rule that the lords may not amend a money-bill. This consisted in including in a money-bill some other extraneous provisions which they had reason to believe would not be acceptable to the lords if presented as a separate measure. In this way the lords would be compelled to accept the whole, or reject the whole, since they could not amend what purported to be a money-bill. The device first appears in 1667, and in 1678 Charles II declared that he would veto any such bill. Tacking was successfully used in 1692 and 1698, but the most notable example occurred in 1701, when the commons " tacked " to the Land Tax Bill certain provisions dealing with the very delicate matter of William III's disposition of Irish forfeited estates. The lords were constrained to pass the whole, and the king himself to assent to the whole, since to reject a major financial measure would have crippled the government.[80] The practice was never adopted after the death of William III; under Queen Anne it was several times contemplated, but apparently never used.[81] The abandonment of the practice is due to the good sense of both Houses, and to the growing opinion that it was " unparliamentary "—in the wide sense of being a misuse of technicalities for the purpose of evading a recognised constitutional principle. Failing a solution by voluntary self-limitation, the problem was (as Maitland remarked in 1888) insoluble: " there is no impartial tribunal before which such questions can be brought, no tribunal which even pretends to be impartial." [82] As we shall see, some sort of tribunal may yet be devised to deal with such delicate problems.[83]

---

[79] May, *Constitutional History*, ii, 104–112. *Cf.* also May, *Parliamentary Practice*, 563–576, Some of the speeches, and a fuller text of the resolutions, will be found in C. S. Emden. *Select Speeches on the Constitution* (World's Classics), i, 137–154. " It would seem," writes Pike, *Constitutional History of the House of Lords*, p. 345, " that, should the commons always follow the same policy, the lords would lose even the power of throwing out a money-bill, or would be able to assert it only at the risk of interrupting all legislation affecting the public revenue and expenditure." This forecast of Mr. Pike was actually fulfilled.

[80] For these examples, see M. A. Thomson, *Constitutional History*, iv, 97–100, 204–205; David Ogg, *Charles II*, ii, 472.

[81] A. S. Turberville, *House of Lords in the Eighteenth Century*, 55, 57, 72.

[82] Maitland, *Constitutional History*, 399.

[83] See the Parliament Act, 1911, s. 1 (2), which defines a " money bill " and empowers the Speaker to apply that definition in certain circumstances.

The Crisis of 1910-11. The death of King Edward VII, in May 1910, found the country in the midst of a parliamentary crisis, from a constitutional point of view one of the most momentous in its whole political history. A finance bill giving effect to Mr. Lloyd George's budget, sent up by the House of Commons in 1909, having been rejected by the House of Lords on the ground of its not being purely a money-bill, an appeal was made by the government to the constituencies on the main question of the relations between the two Houses of Parliament; and a general election took place in January 1910.[84] The issue of this appeal to the electorate was decided in favour of the liberal party at the polls, and a liberal government was again returned to power. When the new parliament assembled on February 21 following, the speech from the throne formulated in distinct words the new situation, which cut at the very root of the hereditary principle in the House of Lords. " Recent experience," it said, " has disclosed serious difficulties, due to recurring differences of strong opinion, between the two branches of the legislature. Proposals will be laid before you, with all convenient speed, to define the relations between the Houses of Parliament so as to secure the undivided authority of the House of Commons over finance, and its predominance in legislation. These measures in the opinion of my advisers, should provide that that House should be so constituted and empowered as to exercise impartiality in regard to proposed legislation, the functions of initiation, revision, and, subject to proper safeguards, of delay."

The House of Lords, the conservative majority in which was represented by Lord Lansdowne, leader of the opposition, accepted the challenge, and immediately set to work to commence a reform of its existing constitution with a view to creating a strong and efficient Second Chamber, so as to combat the reactionary forces at work. On March 14 following, Lord Rosebery proposed resolutions stating the desirability of the reconstruction of the House and advancing the principle that " the possession of a peerage should no longer of itself give the right to sit and vote in the House of Lords." Accepting this resolution, though reluctantly and with protests from many sides, the House of Lords may be said to have itself signed its death-warrant as an hereditary chamber. Following on this resolution of the House manifold schemes were at once launched by publicists and others for its reconstitution. Foremost that of Lord Rosebery, who, on April 13 ensuing, gave notice of a resolution embodying a scheme of reform of that chamber: " (a) That, in future, the House of Lords shall consist of lords of parliament—(1) chosen by the whole body of hereditary peers from among themselves and by nomination by the crown, (2) sitting by virtue of offices and of qualifications held by them, (3) chosen from outside; (b) that the term of tenure of all lords of parliament shall be the same, except in the case of those who sit *ex officio*, who would sit so long as they hold the office for which they sit."

---

[84] Representative extracts from the debates during the crisis will be found in C. S. Emden, *Select Speeches*, i, 38–52, 165–199.

Parliament Bill Introduced. Meanwhile the House of Commons was not slow to act upon the mandate of the country. On April 11 the Parliament Bill was introduced by the prime minister (Mr. Asquith), who threw down the gauntlet to the lords with the words: " If the lords fail to accept our policy, or decline to consider it when it is formally presented to the House, we shall feel it our duty immediately to tender advice to the crown as to the steps which will have to be taken . . . if we do not find ourselves in a position to ensure that statutory effect will be given to this policy in this parliament, we shall then either resign our offices or recommend a dissolution of parliament." [85]

In the midst of this acrimonious political strife King Edward VII died, and his son, King George V, ascended the throne. Probably in order that the new reign should commence under calmer conditions the government and the unionist opposition called a truce, and endeavoured, in a private conference,[86] to find a *modus vivendi* touching the vexed question of the relations between the two Houses of Parliament. This conference, conducted with good feeling on both sides, failed after a final sitting in November 1910. A " state of war " ensued. In both Houses animated debates took place, and, Lord Rosebery having withdrawn his resolution as to a reconstitution of the Upper House, Lord Lansdowne moved the adjournment of the debate on the second reading of the Parliament Bill, attaching certain resolutions defining the attitude of the House of Lords, whenever sharp conflict of opinion should arise between the two Houses. These resolutions, while admitting the necessity of a reconstitution of the House of Lords on the lines already accepted under Lord Rosebery's motion, introduced two further proposals for the settlement of disputes, both alike alien to the spirit and tradition of the constitution. These were: submission of acute controversial differences to the electors for decision by referendum,[87] or (as to less serious matters) to a joint sitting of both Houses, with the Speaker of the House of Commons as chairman.[88] The lords were also prepared to relinquish their right to

[85] See Hansard, *Parliamentary Debates*, April 1910. The budget of 1909 was reintroduced, passed the commons, was accepted at last by the lords, and received the royal assent on April 29—a year after its original introduction.

[86] The members of the Conference were Mr. Asquith (Prime Minister), Mr. Lloyd George (Chancellor of the Exchequer), Mr. Birrell (Secretary for Ireland), and the Earl of Crewe (Colonial Secretary), on the part of the Government; Mr. Balfour, Mr. A. Chamberlain, Lord Lansdowne, and Lord Cawdor, on the part of the Opposition. The proceedings of the Conference were confidential and the cause of the breakdown (which was the application of its proposals to Irish Home Rule) not disclosed for many years. *Cf.* R. C. K. Ensor, *England, 1870–1914,* 422 *et seq.*

[87] A referendum, or plebiscite, is a popular vote on legal proposals which have been already considered by parliament. A like system was foreshadowed by Rousseau in *Le Contrat Social,* and, though attempted in France in 1793, was not put into practice in Europe until 1874—in Switzerland—where its working has been fairly successful. It has also been tried with no great results in the United States and in Belgium, and is embodied in the constitution of the Australian Commonwealth. *Cf.* Dicey, *Law of the Constitution* (8th ed., 1920), xci–c; Lowell, *Public Opinion and Popular Government,* pp. 152–195.

[88] A joint sitting of both Houses of the legislature is provided under the constitution in most of the self-governing British colonies, as also of the federated states of which they are composed, notably in the Cape parliament and various Australian colonies.

reject money-bills, provided that safeguards against " tacking " were adopted. The referendum had many advocates among the conservative party, as also among the advanced socialist wing of the radical party, but failed to find favour among the liberal party as a whole, where support of a popular vote might have been expected.

The parliament elected in January 1910 was dissolved in November of that year, and the liberals went to the country on the same issue on which they were returned to power eleven months previously—namely, the Parliament or " Veto Bill." The result of the election of December 1910 was to reinstate them in power, with the strength of the parties (or groups) in parliament practically unchanged.

The government at once indicated their line of action—the Parliament Bill was to be passed at all hazards. In the lords an interesting bill on the composition of the House of Lords had been introduced by Lord Lansdowne,[89] when the Parliament Bill, having once more passed through the House of Commons, was sent up to the lords in its substantial form. Around it raged one of the most memorable conflicts known to English political history. The lords' amendments were rejected, the most notable being one which endeavoured to list certain fundamental or constitutional matters (Home Rule among them) which were to be removed from the operation of the bill. At last, on July 21, the prime minister announced (what had long been surmised) that the government was prepared to advise the king to use the prerogative of creating sufficient peers to pass the bill, and that the king " has been pleased to signify that he will consider it his duty to accept and act on that advice." Some four hundred peerages would have been needed to " swamp the lords." The government did not make the creations, but took the risk of sending the bill back to the lords with their amendments negatived. Certain " die-hards " threatened resistance to the end, but calmer counsels prevailed, and the bill passed the House of Lords on August 10, 1911, owing to abstentions on the part of members rallying to Lord Lansdowne, who, in view of the momentous issues involved, and to save the sovereign from exercising his royal prerogative—a duty which was known to be distasteful to him—counselled this course as being the most loyal. There were some who supposed that only a few creations, just sufficient to deal with the existing situation and taking account of the many abstentions which had been promised, were in contemplation; but the announcement of Lord Morley, the leader of the government in the House of Lords, in the course of the final debate (August 10) made the situation clear: " If the Bill should be defeated tonight, His Majesty would assent to a creation of peers sufficient in number to guard against any possible combination of the different parties in opposition, by which the Parliament Bill might again be exposed

[89] *Cf.* Ensor, *op. cit.*, 428, and Francis Holland's continuation of May, *Constitutional History*, iii, 373 *et seq.*

a second time to defeat." [90]   A faction led by the Earl of Halsbury—
one containing among its members some of the most illustrious names in
contemporaneous history—insisted upon opposition to the bill, *i.e.*,
in their persistence in the lords' amendments.   By a majority of seventeen
the Parliament Bill passed,[91] without the exercise of the royal prerogative
being invoked.

PARLIAMENT ACT (1911)

(1 & 2 Geo. 5, c. 13)

An Act to make provision with respect to the powers of the House of Lords in
   relation to those of the House of Commons, and to limit the duration of
   Parliament.   [18th August, 1911]

Whereas it is expedient that provision should be made for regulating the
relations between the two Houses of Parliament:

And whereas it is intended to substitute for the House of Lords as it at
present exists a Second Chamber constituted on a popular instead of hereditary
basis, but such substitution cannot be immediately brought into operation:

And whereas provision will require hereafter to be made by Parliament in a
measure effecting such substitution for limiting and defining the powers of the
new Second Chamber, but it is expedient to make such provision as in this Act
appears for restricting the existing powers of the House of Lords:

Be it therefore enacted by the King's most Excellent Majesty, by and with
the advice and consent of the Lords Spiritual and Temporal, and Commons, in
this present Parliament assembled, and by the authority of the same, as follows: —

1.—(1) If a Money Bill, having been passed by the House of Commons, and
sent up to the House of Lords at least one month before the end of the session, is
not passed by the House of Lords without amendment within one month after
it is so sent up to that House, the Bill shall, unless the House of Commons direct
to the contrary, be presented to His Majesty, and become an Act of Parliament
on the Royal Assent being signified, notwithstanding that the House of Lords
have not consented to the Bill.

(2) A Money Bill means a Public Bill which in the opinion of the Speaker of
the House of Commons contains only provisions dealing with all or any of the
following subjects, namely, the imposition, repeal, remission, alteration, or
regulation of taxation; the imposition for the payment of debt or other financial
purposes of charges on the Consolidated Fund, or on money provided by
Parliament, or the variation or repeal of any such charges; supply; the appropriation, receipt, custody, issue or audit of accounts of public money; the raising
or guarantee of any loan or the repayment thereof; or subordinate matters incidental to those subjects or any of them.   In this subsection the expressions
" taxation," " public money," and " loan " respectively do not include any
taxation, money, or loan raised by local authorities or bodies for local purposes.

(3) There shall be endorsed on every Money Bill when it is sent up to the
House of Lords and when it is presented to His Majesty for assent the certificate
of the Speaker of the House of Commons signed by him that it is a Money Bill.

---

[90] *Parliamentary Debates*, House of Lords, August 10, col. 999.   There are extracts from the
speeches of Lord Curzon and Lord Haldane in Emden, *Select Speeches on the Constitution*,
i, 38–52.

[91] In the voting on non-insistence on the amendments to the Parliament Bill the numbers
were: For, 131; against 114; majority 17.   In the above text the words now enclosed in
square brackets have been amended by the Parliament Act, 1949, which substitutes for
them the words in italic.

Before giving his certificate, the Speaker shall consult, if practicable, two members to be appointed from the Chairmen's Panel at the beginning of each Session by the Committee of Selection.

2.—(1) If any Public Bill (other than a Money Bill or a Bill containing any provision to extend the maximum duration of Parliament beyond five years) is passed by the House of Commons in [three *two*] successive sessions (whether of the same Parliament or not), and, having been sent up to the House of Lords at least one month before the end of the session, is rejected by the House of Lords in each of those sessions, that Bill shall, on its rejection for the [third *second*] time by the House of Lords, unless the House of Commons direct to the contrary, be presented to His Majesty and become an Act of Parliament on the Royal Assent being signified thereto, notwithstanding that the House of Lords have not consented to the Bill: Provided that this provision shall not take effect unless [two years have *one year has*] elapsed between the date of the second reading in the first of those sessions of the Bill in the House of Commons and the date on which it passes the House of Commons in the [third *second*] of those sessions.

(2) When a Bill is presented to His Majesty for assent in pursuance of the provisions of this section, there shall be endorsed on the Bill the certificate of the Speaker of the House of Commons signed by him that the provisions of this section have been duly complied with.

(3) A Bill shall be deemed to be rejected by the House of Lords if it is not passed by the House of Lords either without amendment or with such amendments only as may be agreed to by both Houses.

(4) A Bill shall be deemed to be the same Bill as a former Bill sent up to the House of Lords in the preceding session if, when it is sent up to the House of Lords, it is identical with the former Bill or contains only such alterations as are certified by the Speaker of the House of Commons to be necessary owing to the time which has elapsed since the date of the former Bill, or to represent any amendments which have been made by the House of Lords in the former Bill in the preceding session, and any amendments which are certified by the Speaker to have been made by the House of Lords in the [third *second*] session and agreed to by the House of Commons shall be inserted in the Bill as presented for Royal Assent in pursuance of this section:

Provided that the House of Commons may, if they think fit, on the passage of such a Bill through the House in the second [or third *omit*] session, suggest any further amendments without inserting the amendments in the Bill, and any such suggested amendments shall be considered by the House of Lords, and, if agreed to by that House, shall be treated as amendments made by the House of Lords and agreed to by the House of Commons; but the exercise of this power by the House of Commons shall not affect the operation of this section in the event of the Bill being rejected by the House of Lords.

3. Any certificate of the Speaker of the House of Commons given under this Act shall be conclusive for all purposes, and shall not be questioned in any court of law.

4.—(1) In every Bill presented to His Majesty under the preceding provisions of this Act, the words of enactment shall be as follows, that is to say:

" Be it enacted by the King's most Excellent Majesty, by and with the advice and consent of the Commons in this present Parliament assembled, in accordance with the provisions of the Parliament Act, 1911, and by authority of the same, as follows."

(2) Any alteration of a Bill necessary to give effect to this section shall not be deemed to be an amendment of the Bill.

5. In this Act the expression " Public Bill " does not include any Bill for confirming a Provisional Order.

6. Nothing in this Act shall diminish or qualify the existing rights and privileges of the House of Commons.

7. Five years shall be substituted for seven years as the time fixed for the maximum duration of Parliament under the Septennial Act, 1715.

8. This Act may be cited as the Parliament Act, 1911.

The political crisis of 1947 resulted in the Parliament Act, 1949, which made the changes in the 1911 Act which are above indicated, and continues with a complicated proviso of temporary importance.[92]

Results. In effect the Parliament Act [93] has deprived the House of Lords of all legislative power in respect of money bills, while in respect of public bills other than money bills it has left it not a final but merely a suspensive veto. The general result is thus summarised by Professor Dicey [94]: "The simple truth is that the Parliament Act has given to the House of Commons, or, in plain language, to the majority thereof, the power of passing any Bill whatever provided always that the conditions of the Parliament Act, section 2, are complied with. But these provisions do leave to the House of Lords a suspensive veto which may prevent a Bill from becoming an Act of Parliament for a period of certainly more, and possibly a good deal more, than two years."

As the foregoing pages have shown, certain dramatic conflicts between lords and commons raised issues of the composition as well as the powers of the Upper House, and occasioned the production of a number of schemes for its reform. Other considerations pointed in the same direction. Comparative political science afforded interesting foreign analogies, while still more pressing was the need for lawyers of high eminence to assist the House in the exercise of its appellate duties.

Wensleydale Peerage, 1856. In 1856, with the object of improving the ancient appellate jurisdiction of the Upper House, an attempt was made to re-introduce life-peerages by means of the royal prerogative. Several cases of the creation of lay peerages—dukedoms and earldoms—for life only [95] occurred between the reigns of Richard II and Henry VI; but after that time, for more than four hundred years, no instance is recorded of any man [96] being admitted to a seat in the House of Lords as a peer for life. This departure was defeated, however, by the successful resistance of the House of Lords. Sir James Parke, late one of the barons of the Court of Exchequer, having been created Baron Wensleydale " for and during the time of his natural life," the lords referred the patent

---

[92] Parliament Act, 1949 (12, 13 & 14 Geo. 6, c. 99).

[93] For an examination of the constitutional effects of the Parliament Act, see Dicey, *Law of the Constitution*, 8th ed., Introduction, pp. xviii *et seq.*; 9th ed., Introduction, cxxix *et seq.*; W. I. Jennings, *Parliament*, 399 *et seq.*

[94] *Ibid.*, p. xxiii.

[95] *Cf.* Stubbs, *Constitutional History*, iii, 454 and n. 2.

[96] Certain German ladies received the titles of peerages, some in tail male, and some for life only; in neither case could the grantee sit, of course. A. S. Turberville, *House of Lords in the Eighteenth Century*, 417–418.

to a committee of privileges, and agreed, in accordance with its report, " that neither the letters patent, nor the letters patent with the usual writ of summons in pursuance thereof, can entitle the grantee to sit and vote in parliament." In consequence of this decision a new patent was issued creating Lord Wensleydale a hereditary peer of the realm. The resolution of the lords, remarks Sir Erskine May, " has since been generally accepted as a sound exposition of constitutional law. Where institutions are founded upon ancient usage, it is a safe and wholesome doctrine that they shall not be changed, unless by the supreme legislative authority of parliament." [97] The government brought in a bill to authorise the creation of two judicial life-peers; it passed the lords but was lost in the commons. Lord Russell's Bill (1869) to authorise the creation of twenty-eight eminent persons as life-peers failed to pass the lords.

After an interval of twenty years following the *Wensleydale Case* during which the appellate jurisdiction was at one time actually abolished prospectively as to England,[98] two lords of appeal in ordinary were at last constituted by the Appellate Jurisdiction Act, 1876 (39 & 40 Vict. c. 59), with the rank of baron for life and the right of sitting and voting during their tenure of office only.

Life Peers. These life peerages form such an important innovation from the standpoint of constitutional history as to deserve more than a passing notice. By this Act, power was also given to appoint a third lord of appeal in ordinary upon the demise or retirement of two paid judges of the Judicial Committee of the Privy Council, and a fourth when the two remaining paid judges retired or resigned. " An old principle was recognised and a new principle introduced. The principle that the holder of a barony for life only (as in the case of Lord Hay) enjoyed the rank of baron, and not the right of sitting and voting in parliament, was, as it were, reasserted. The introduction of lords with a right to be summoned, and to sit, and vote, not even for life, but only during the tenure of office, was quite new as applied to laymen, or was, at any rate, without precedent since the days of earlier chancellors." [99] The innovation thus made was still further extended by the Appellate Jurisdiction Act, 1887 (50 & 51 Vict. c. 70), which enables these life-peers to sit and vote as members of the House of Lords, even after retirement from office; and the vital clause (2) runs: " The sixth section of the Appellate Jurisdiction Act, 1876, shall be construed and take effect, as well in respect of any Lord of Appeal in Ordinary heretofore appointed under that Act, as of any such lord hereafter appointed, so as to entitle any person so appointed to sit and vote as a member of the House of Lords during his life as fully as if

[97] *Constitutional History*, i, 298. For a list of life peerages prior to the *Wensleydale Case*, see G. E. C., *Complete Peerage* (2nd ed.), viii, 751.
[98] By a provision of the Judicature Act, 1873, which was repealed before it came into force and replaced by the Judicature Act, 1875 (38 & 39 Vict. c. 77).
[99] Pike, *Constitutional History of the House of Lords*, p. 383. (Hay was one of James I's Scottish favourites, created a life-baron without a seat in the House of Lords in 1606.)

the words ' during the time that he continues in his office as a Lord of Appeal in Ordinary, and no longer,' had been omitted from the said section." The lords of appeal became now lords of parliament for life, but with no descendible dignity attached. By order of Queen Victoria, on the occasion of her Diamond Jubilee in 1897, precedence was given to the children of lords of appeal in ordinary immediately after the younger children of hereditary barons, though the warrant was not gazetted till August 1898.[1]

Further Projects of Reform. Following on the Appellate Jurisdiction Act of 1887, Lord Rosebery, in March 1888, brought forward a motion for the appointment of a selected committee to inquire into the constitution of the House of Lords. Although this motion was lost, it was followed, in the course of the same year, by schemes advanced by both the Earl of Dunraven and the Marquess of Salisbury for the reconstitution and reconstruction of the Upper Chamber. These proposals were withdrawn.[2]

Next, in the elation of victory at the polls, the radical party in the House of Commons agitated for a drastic reform of the Upper Chamber, through their spokesman, Labouchere (member for Northampton), who on March 13, 1894, moved an amendment to the address to the throne, which, in its wording, practically proposed the abolition of the House of Lords. The amendment was carried. On the same day, the address, thus amended, was negatived on the proposal of the government, and thus a serious constitutional crisis was averted: " the address to Her Majesty being recalled on the motion of those who originally proposed it," to use the words of Mr. Balfour, the leader of the opposition.

In the event, however, it was the powers of the House of Lords which were regulated by statute, not its composition, and the immediate occasion was the lords' rejection of the Finance Bill of 1909. That stormy episode concluded with the Parliament Act, 1911, which bears a preamble asserting the desirability of a Second Chamber " on a popular instead of hereditary basis."

Report of the Bryce Committee. The government did not abandon the opinion, which was everywhere gaining ground, that the reform of the constitution of the Upper House should be effected with as little delay as possible; but the outbreak of the First World War in August, 1914, postponed the consideration of the question; and it was not until August 25, 1917, that the prime minister appointed a committee (under the presidency of Lord Bryce) to inquire into the subject. The terms of reference were:

---

[1] For a further discussion on the various points, *cf.* Pike, *Constitutional History of the House of Lords*, pp. 383 *et seq*; Anson, *Law and Custom of the Constitution*, i, Chap. v.

[2] See Pike, *Constitutional History of the House of Lords*, pp. 384–387.

" To inquire and report—

(i) As to the nature and limitations of the legislative powers to be exercised by a reformed Second Chamber.

(ii) As to the best mode of adjusting differences between the two Houses of Parliament.

(iii) As to the changes which are desirable in order that the Second Chamber may in future be so constituted as to exercise fairly the functions appropriate to a Second Chamber."

The conference, which began on October 2, 1917, held forty-eight sittings, and extended over more than six months. Its report was issued in April 1918.[3]

As to the functions appropriate to a Second Chamber, the conference agreed on the following points:

" (1) The examination and revision of bills brought from the House of Commons, a function which has become more needed since, on many occasions, during the last thirty years, the House of Commons has been obliged to act under special rules limiting debate.

" (2) The initiation of bills dealing with subjects of a comparatively non-controversial character which may have an easier passage through the House of Commons if they have been fully discussed and put into a well-considered shape before being submitted to it.

" (3) The interposition of so much delay (and no more) in the passing of a bill into law as may be needed to enable the opinion of the nation to be adequately expressed upon it. This would be specially needed as regards bills which affect the fundamentals of the constitution or introduce new principles of legislation, or which raise issues whereon the opinion of the country may appear to be almost equally divided.

" (4) Full and free discussion of large and important questions, such as those of foreign policy, at moments when the House of Commons may happen to be so much occupied that it cannot find sufficient time for them. Such discussions may often be all the more useful if conducted in an assembly where debates and divisions do not involve the fate of the executive government." [4]

As to the elements that ought to find a place in the Second Chamber, it was agreed that persons of experience in various forms of public work, those who possess special knowledge of important departments of the national life and of imperial questions, and persons who are not extreme partisans, would be desirable members.[5]

Concerning the position which the Second Chamber ought to hold in our constitutional system, the following conclusions were submitted: " It was agreed that a Second Chamber ought not to have equal powers with the House of Commons, nor aim at becoming a rival of that assembly.

---

[3] *Parliamentary Papers* (1918), Cd. 9038: " Conference on the Reform of the Second Chamber."

[4] *Ibid.*, p. 4.

[5] *Ibid.*, pp. 4, 5.

In particular, it should not have the power of making or unmaking ministries, or enjoy equal rights in dealing with finance. . . . All precautions that could be taken ought to be taken to secure that in a reformed Second Chamber no one set of political opinions should be likely to have a marked and permanent predominance, and that the Chamber should be so composed as not to incur the charge of habitually acting under the influence of party motives.

" The Second Chamber should aim at ascertaining the mind and views of the nation as a whole, and should recognise its full responsibility to the people, not setting itself to oppose the people's will, but only to comprehend and give effect to that will when adequately expressed.

" It should possess that moral authority which an assembly derives not only from the fact that its members have been specially chosen to discharge important public duties but also from their personal eminence, from their acknowledged capacity to serve the nation, and from the confidence which their characters and careers are fitted to inspire. . . . So far as is possible a continuity should be preserved between the ancient House of Lords and the new Second Chamber, the best traditions of the former being handed on to the new body, so as to enhance its dignity, and make a seat in it an object of legitimate ambition. . . ." [6]

The above fundamental principles secured the unanimous agreement of the conference, as they will no doubt command general assent. But the question of the composition of the Second Chamber was found to be placed on more difficult and debatable ground. The desiderata dictated by the preliminary considerations were first that a certain portion of the new body should be taken from the existing peerage, and secondly that the large majority of the members should be so chosen as to enjoy popular authority. The idea of an election on the basis of a property qualification —either for electors or elected—was rejected; as also was the proposal to take persons chosen from certain prescribed categories. In order to make the popular element predominant, five alternative methods of composition were examined: (a) nomination, (b) direct election, (c) election by local authorities, (d) selection by a joint standing committee of both Houses, (e) election by the House of Commons.[7] The method recommended is that the Second Chamber should consist of two sections: (a) 246 persons elected by panels of members of the House of Commons distributed in certain territorial areas, the period of tenure to be twelve years (one-third to retire every four years); (b) eighty-one persons elected by a joint standing committee of both Houses, tenure and retirement as in the preceding section.[8] Further, the lord chancellor, ex-lord chancellors, and the law lords appointed under the Appellate Jurisdiction Acts should be members *ex officio* if the new Second Chamber is to discharge the judicial functions hitherto discharged by the House of Lords.[9]

[6] *Parliamentary Papers* (1918), Cd. 9038, p. 5.
[7] *Ibid.*, pp. 6–9.
[8] *Ibid.*, p. 11.
[9] *Ibid.*, p. 12.

The remainder of the report contains general recommendations relating to the first constitution of the new Chamber, and deals with the powers in respect of financial bills and the adjustment of differences between the two Houses.[10] The scheme never matured and no further definite steps have been taken towards the reconstruction of the Second Chamber.

One of the most ancient and historic privileges of peerage is " the trial of peers." This procedure was productive of much expense, and was abolished in 1948.[11]

As this revision was being prepared, the principle of life peerages and the admission of women into the House of Lords received legislative sanction.[12]

THE HOUSE OF COMMONS

Like the House of Lords, the House of Commons has also undergone very important changes in its numbers, its composition, and its political influence.

Number of Members. In the reign of Edward I the number of representatives of the commons varied considerably. A full parliament might contain 74 knights of the shire (2 from each of the 37 counties excluding the palatinates of Chester and Durham), and about 200 citizens and burgesses. Under Edward III and his three immediate successors the number of the burgesses was about 180, fluctuating in different parliaments according to the negligence or partiality of the sheriffs in omitting places which had formerly returned members. New boroughs, however, either on account of their growing importance or to increase the authority of the crown in the Lower House, were from time to time summoned to return representatives, and at the accession of Henry VIII we find 111 cities and boroughs (all of which retained the privilege down to the Reform Act of 1832) represented in parliament by 224 citizens and burgesses. In this reign the number of members was considerably increased by the addition of representatives for Wales,[13] and the Tudor sovereigns pursued the policy of creating insignificant boroughs [14] with the object of extending the influence of the crown in the House of Commons.[15] Between the reigns of Henry VIII and Charles II, no less than 180 members were added to the House by royal charter alone.[16] The borough of Newark,

---

[10] *Ibid.*, pp. 12 *et seq.*
[11] Criminal Justice Act, 1948.
[12] Life Peerages Act, 1958.
[13] *Supra*, pp. 235, 243.
[14] But among the towns which sent representatives for the first time during the Tudor period are Westminster, 1545, Peterborough, 1547, Maidstone, 1553, while Liverpool, which had not been represented since the reign of Edward I, was regularly represented from 1545 onwards. See the map, plate 23, in *Historical Atlas of Modern Europe* (ed. R. L. Poole).
[15] That object was not achieved: *supra*, p. 243, n. 77.
[16] May, *Constitutional History*, i, 329, citing Glanville's *Reports*, cii. In the reign of James I the commons, out of favour to popular rights, resolved that every town which had at any time returned members to parliament was entitled to a writ as a matter of course; and by virtue of this resolution fifteen boroughs regained the parliamentary franchise under

which received the parliamentary franchise by royal charter under Charles II, was the last instance of its kind. The House of Commons took the issue of writs into its own hands; and no new borough constituency was created in England or Wales until the Reform Act of 1832. At the date of the union with Scotland the number of members was 513. The Act of Union added forty-five representatives of that kingdom; and the Act of Union with Ireland in 1800 made a further addition to the House of 100 Irish members. The proportionate representation of the three kingdoms has since been a little varied, Scotland having seventy-two members, and Ireland 103.[17]

For some time after its establishment, the representative system, though never aiming at theoretical perfection, had been practically efficient. The knights of the shire and the burgesses who sat in the parliaments of the thirteenth and fourteenth centuries really did represent the wishes of the great majority of the free inhabitants of the counties and boroughs by whom they were elected.

Defects of the Representative System. But from the end of the fourteenth century to the passing of the Reform Act, in 1832, the House of Commons, as it gained in numbers lost more and more in real representative character. The inequalities in the representation which in course of time naturally grew up, through the simultaneous decay of ancient towns and rise into commercial importance of what had been once mere agricultural villages, were allowed to go on unheeded. Many new boroughs were, indeed, as we have seen, enfranchised by royal charter between the reign of Henry VIII and Charles II; but they were for the most part places of no special importance or size, and were, in many instances, endowed with the privilege of returning members to parliament for the express purpose of adding, as nomination boroughs, to the power of the crown in the House of Commons. In 1653, Cromwell made a statesmanlike effort to remedy the evil by disfranchising many small boroughs, giving members to Manchester, Leeds and Halifax, and increasing the numbers of county members; but his reforms, though characterised by Clarendon as a " warrantable alteration, and fit to be made in better times," were cancelled at the Restoration; and thenceforth, until the reign of George III, there was no further attempt to check the ever-growing abuses of the representative system.

James I and Charles I. In 1673 the County Palatine and City of Durham were for the first time admitted to the franchise by Act 25, Car. 2, c. 9. Hallam, *Constitutional History*, iii, 38.

[17] The Redistribution of Seats Act of 1885 made a new division of the United Kingdom into county and borough constituencies, and raised the number of members of parliament to 670, giving to England six and to Scotland twelve additional representatives. By the Representation of the People Act, 1918, the number of members was further increased to 707. The establishment of the Irish Free State removed the Irish members (except those from Northern Ireland) leaving the House of Commons at 615. It now stands at 640.

The Sale of Borough Seats. That system had become thoroughly venal and corrupt.[18] Most of the English boroughs—with a suffrage generally restricted to close corporations or to those bodies and their nominees, the freemen [19]—might be roughly divided into those which were sold by their " patrons," the great territorial proprietors, and those which sold themselves. Of the remainder, while many were under the influence of the crown, and obediently returned the crown's nominees, others were owned by patrons who exercised their powers of nomination honestly and conscientiously, and did a service to the country by introducing into the House of Commons young men of ability and promise, who, lacking money or connections, could not otherwise have found a seat. But the great majority of the boroughs were venal. The right to vote being attached to the ownership of certain tenements, it was simply a matter of buying sufficient properties in a borough to be able to control its election. Both the crown and the ministers of the day, either acting in unison, or, as was frequently the case under George III, in opposition to one another, bought seats alike of patrons and constituencies—titles, pensions, or hard cash satisfying the varying wants of all. The market for seats was further enlarged and their price enhanced by the competition of rich traders, more especially of the " nabobs," who had returned from the Indies with immense fortunes, and who anxiously sought entrance into the House of Commons as the avenue to social distinction or extended commercial advantage. The published correspondence and memoirs of men of the time attest the wholesale and unblushing bribery and barter of boroughs which prevailed. A few typical instances will serve as illustrations. In 1767, the borough of Ludgershall was sold by its proprietor, George Selwyn, for £9,000.[20] In 1807, £10,000 was offered for the two seats of Westbury, but was refused as inadequate by the trustees for the creditor of the late proprietor, Lord Abingdon.[21]

Corruption of Corporations. Sales by patrons were generally passed over without animadversion, but some of the attempts of corporations or constituencies to sell the seats at their disposal excited occasional indignation, and received a mild measure of punishment. In 1768, the corporation of Oxford took advantage of the general election to demand of the sitting members, Sir Thomas Stapleton and the Hon. Robert Lee, as the consideration for returning them again, the sum of £5,670, which was required to pay off the municipal debts. The request was not only refused, but reported to the House of Commons, who committed the mayor and ten of the aldermen to Newgate, whence they were soon

[18] See generally, Porritt, *Unreformed House of Commons*, and much detail of its working in Sir John Neale's *Elizabethan House of Commons*, where the system can be seen already well established.
[19] *Supra*, pp. 206 *et seq.*
[20] *Letters of Lord Chesterfield to his Son*, iv, 269.
[21] *Life of Sir Samuel Romilly*, ii, 200.

discharged after a reprimand from the Speaker. But with a sturdy determination to pay the corporation debts out of any other pockets rather than their own, the worthy mayor and aldermen, while still in Newgate, completed a sale of the two seats, already partly negotiated, to the Duke of Marlborough and the Earl of Abingdon; while the town clerk carried off the corporation books so as to prevent any evidence of the transaction from becoming public.[22] But perhaps the political morality of the times may be best exemplified by the borough of Sudbury which without any hesitation or attempt at decent disguise, shamelessly advertised itself for sale to the highest bidder.[23]

Corruption of Electors. In the larger boroughs and seaports the government not only had recourse to money bribes, but ensured the return of their candidates by the wholesale distribution of appointments in the customs and excise. In 1782, when Lord Rockingham carried a measure for the disfranchisement of revenue officers, no less that 11,500 were found to be electors, and seventy elections were said to depend mainly on their votes.[24]

The County Elections. The county constituencies of forty-shilling freeholders, although limited and unequal, were less corrupt and more independent than the voters in boroughs; but they were subject to the influence of the great nobles and local landowners. Their accessibility to none but the territorial aristocracy was further ensured by the enormous expense of a contest, which, in one instance, that of Yorkshire (a county of very exceptional size), amounted in 1807 to no less a sum than £200,000, as the joint expenses of two rival candidates, Lord Milton and Mr. Lascelles.[25]

Scottish Representation. The representation of the Scottish counties and boroughs was in even a worse condition than the English. In every borough in Scotland the franchise was vested in a self-elected corporation; while the county franchise belonged exclusively to the owners of feudal " superiorities," of the annual value of £400, who were not necessarily either landowners or residents in their counties. With a population of over 2,000,000, the total number of Scottish county electors in 1823 was

[22] *Parliamentary History*, xvi, 397–402; Horace Walpole, *Memoirs of The Reign of George III*, iii, 153; May, *Constitutional History*, i, 338.

[23] Horace Walpole, *Memoirs of the Reign of George III*, i, 42.

[24] *Parliamentary History*, xxiii, 101. Lord Rockingham said, in one borough having 500 voters, 120 had been appointed to places under government, through the influence of one of their number who happened to be a friend of the First Lord of the Treasury. *Ibid*. The electoral disabilities of revenue officers, no longer necessary in the large constituencies created by the Reform Act of 1867, were removed by 31 & 32 Vict. c. 73, and 37 & 38 Vict. c. 22.

[25] May, *Constitutional History*, i, 355, n. 2. For the whole subject see *ibid*., i, 327–354; Porritt, *The Unreformed House of Commons*, vol. i, *passim*; Sir Lewis Namier, *The Structure of Politics at the Accession of George III* (2 vols. 1929) is a valuable and illuminating study.

under 3,000; one county, Cromarty, having only nine. It was stated by the Lord Advocate, in 1831, that at an election, then within living memory, for the county of Bute, which had not more than twenty-one electors, of whom but one was resident, that resident, together with the sheriff and the returning officer, constituted the meeting; and having taken the chair, moved and seconded his own nomination, put the question to the vote, and elected himself.[26]

Irish Representation. In Ireland, most of the boroughs, from causes similar to those which affected the boroughs of England and Scotland, were equally subject to the patronage of noblemen and landowners. The counties possessed, indeed, a comparatively popular franchise; the electorate was composed of the forty-shilling freeholders, whose numbers had been multiplied alike by the action of the Irish land laws and of the protestant landowners who favoured sub-division with a view to extending their political influence. But though relatively far more numerous than the English county electors, the Irish peasant proprietors were also far less independent; so that the union with Great Britain in 1801 served only to add to the united parliament a further mass of nominee members.[27]

In 1793, when the members of the House of Commons numbered 558, a majority of 354 was nominally returned by " less than 15,000 electors," but in reality on the nomination or recommendation of the government and 197 private patrons.[28] The union with Ireland in 1801 added 100 members to the House, of whom seventy-one were nominated by fifty-six individuals. In 1816, Dr. Oldfield, in his *Representative History*, gave elaborate details showing that, of the 658 members, 487 were then returned by the nomination of the government or private patrons.[29] Well might the younger Pitt exclaim: " This House is not the representative of the people of Great Britain; it is the representative of nominal boroughs, of ruined and exterminated towns, of noble families, of wealthy individuals, of foreign potentates."

General Condition of Parliament. While all this is true, it is nevertheless likewise true that parliament was genuinely a political organ. The public took a keen interest in its proceedings, and contrived to make its feelings felt inside the House of Commons. Elections were costly, in part at least, because they were so hotly contested. Great landowners at immense expense contested the counties, but the contest was real and hard fought. The same vigorous campaigning took place in some at least of the boroughs, and since they were two-member constituencies an easy compromise

[26] Hansard, vii, 529; May, *Constitutional History*, i, 358.
[27] Wakefield, *Statistical and Political Account of Ireland*, ii, 299; Oldfield, *Representative History*, vi, 209 *et seq.*; May, *Constitutional History*, i, 359; see also Porritt, *The Unreformed House of Commons*, vol. ii, *passim*.
[28] *Annual Register for 1793*, App. to Chronicle, pp. 83–99.
[29] Oldfield's *Representative History*, vi, 285–300, cited by May, *Constitutional History*, i, 362.

was found by keeping one seat for the local patron, leaving the other for contest.[30] There was, in effect, a strong hereditary element even in the commons [31] which is not yet quite extinct. Not infrequently the electoral contest lay between two families who maintained an ancient historical feud. Only a small fraction of the constituencies actually went to the poll [32]; candidates frequently withdrew when they thought their chances unfavourable. But that again is more an indication of expense than of indifference. It is easy to over-emphasise the extent of patronage, " influence," and corruption, and care must be taken to retain the essential fact that through it all parliament was the centre of a vigorous and genuine political system, with the result that at the close of the eighteenth century parliament could still be sincerely defended—in other words, with all its defects and abuses, parliament was a sound institution, but one which needed, and was capable of, reform.

Exclusion of Placemen. The sixth clause of the Act of Settlement,[33] by which all placemen and pensioners were excluded from parliament, was directly aimed, not at the cabinet system, but at the dangerous influence which the crown had acquired through the profuse distribution of offices and pensions among the members of the legislature. This means of corrupting the representatives of the people had been extensively employed under the last two Stuarts; and William III, amidst the difficulties with which he found himself surrounded, adopted and even extended this baneful expedient for controlling his parliaments. To check this abuse the commons, in 1693, passed a bill to prohibit all members thereafter elected from accepting any office under the crown. Rejected by a small majority of the lords, the bill was reintroduced in the following year and passed both Houses; but William III refused the royal assent. A few years later, however, the principle of disqualification received a legislative sanction by the express exclusion from the House of Commons of the newly appointed commissioners of excise.[34] The total exclusion of all servants of the crown from the House of Commons enacted by the Act of Settlement was not only far too drastic a remedy for the special evil which it was intended to meet, but would also, if carried into practice, have brought the ministers of the crown into hopeless conflict with the House of Commons, and, by preventing the fusion of the legislative and

---

[30] Alternatively, two families might share the two seats: " at Yarmouth, between 1722 and 1784 one member was always a Townshend and the other a Walpole "—Sir Lewis Namier, *Structure of Politics*, i, 129. A Cavendish had always held one of the seats at Derby without a break from 1715 to 1835, but they never sought both, *ibid.*, 131. A Cavendish was a candidate in 1944.

[31] By no means all of them great families like the Cavendishes. See, for example, the Whitmores who have represented Bridgnorth with fair regularity from 1621 to 1870; the Foresters at Wenlock from 1678 to 1885; the Herberts and Clives at Ludlow from 1688 to 1923—in Namier, *op. cit.*, ii, 301 *et seq.*

[32] In 1761 at the general election 48 British constituencies went to the poll out of 315—Namier, i, 196.

[33] *Supra*, pp. 463, 467.

[34] 11 Will. 3, c. 2, s. 149 (Excise).

executive powers, have effectually stopped the development of the system of parliamentary or cabinet government which we now enjoy. The clause was, as we have seen, repealed before it could come into operation, in the fifth year of Queen Anne's reign (1706), but was re-enacted in a modified form [35]; and two years afterwards (1708), by the " Act for the security of her Majesty's person and Government, and of the succession to the Crown of Great Britain in the Protestant line," more reasonable provisions were enacted for the prevention of corrupt influence.[36] (1) Every person holding " any office or place of profit whatsoever under the crown " created since October 25, 1705, or in receipt of a pension during the pleasure of the crown, was incapacitated from sitting in the House of Commons; and (2) every member of that House accepting any of the previously existing offices under the crown (except a higher commission in the army) was obliged to vacate his seat, though still eligible for re-election. So long as the system of ministerial government, with responsibility to the House of Commons, was not fully established, and while the House of Commons itself remained liable to corrupt influences and, under a restricted franchise, failed to represent the people, such a provision as the latter, which compelled the acceptance of office by a representative to be submitted to the approval of his constituents, acted as a salutary check both upon the crown and the leading members of the commons. But now, with a reformed suffrage, and under a customary or unwritten constitution in which one of the principal functions of the members of the commons is, by an indirect process, to choose the ministers of the crown, the reasons for the enactment have ceased to exist. Although several attempts had been made to modify the principle, they were always unsuccessful, with the single exception contained in the Reform Act of 1867, dispensing with the requirement of re-election in the Act of 6 Anne, c. 41, in the case of the removal of a minister from one office under the crown to another.[37] In the twentieth century, however, these restrictions were found to be so obstructive in the rapid rearrangement of ministerial posts now in vogue, that they had to be removed. The Re-election of Ministers Act, 1919, relieved ministers who accepted office within nine months of the summoning of a new parliament from the requirement of re-election; by an Act of 1926 the requirement was completely abolished.

The exception from the Act of 6 Anne, c. 41, of all offices existing on October 25, 1705, enabled the crown still to exercise extensive corruption by means of places, and in 1741 no less than two hundred appointments

[35] *Supra*, p. 467; 4 & 5 Anne, c. 20, ss. 28–30. (*Statutes at Large*, 4 & 5 Anne, c. 8.)

[36] 6 Anne, c. 41, ss. 24–25. (*Statutes at Large*, 6 Anne, c. 7.) To check the increase of placemen, certain restrictions were also imposed on the multiplication of commissioners. (This act was a second Regency Act, necessitated by the fact that the Scottish union had supervened. As on the previous occasion, the commons seized the opportunity to tack hese place clauses to it.)

[37] 30 & 31 Vict. c. 102, s. 52. For the difficulties in which Gladstone was involved under this Act, see Morley, *Life of Gladstone*, ii, 465 *et seq.*

were held by members of the House of Commons.[38] In the following year, however, the Place Bill, which had been thrice rejected by the commons and twice by the lords, passed into an Act, excluding from the House a large number of officials, chiefly clerks and other subordinate officers of the public departments.[39] In 1782 several other offices which had been generally held by members of parliament were suppressed by Lord Rockingham's Civil List Act[40]; and the policy of official disfranchisement has been since almost invariably followed whenever new officers have been appointed by Acts of Parliament.[41]

Secret Pensions. The incapacity imposed by the Act 6 Anne, c. 41, upon pensioners of the crown during pleasure, though extended at the commencement of the next reign to pensioners for terms of years,[42] was eluded by the grant of secret pensions out of the large sum annually voted to the crown " as secret service money," and expended without any public account; but by Lord Rockingham's Act already referred to, the power of granting pensions out of the king's civil list was considerably limited, and secret pensions were abolished by a provision that in future all pensions should be paid at the public exchequer. In the same year a stop was put to another form of parliamentary corruption by an Act disqualifying contractors for the public service from sitting in the House.[43]

Exclusion of Judges. The common law judges had early been disqualified from sitting in the House of Commons; and this exclusion was extended to the Scottish judges under George II, and to the Irish judges under George IV. The same rule was applied in 1840 to the judge of the Court of Admiralty; and the holders of all newly created judicial posts have been disqualified by the Acts under which they were constituted. The Master of the Rolls—hitherto the sole judge who had retained the capacity of sitting in the commons—has been also at length disqualified by the clause of the Supreme Court of Judicature Act, 1873, which declares

---

[38] Lords' Protests, 1741, quoted May, *Constitutional History*, i, 272.

[39] 15 Geo. 2, c. 22.

[40] 22 Geo. 3, c. 82.

[41] The result of the large mass of legislation has been to create some obscurity, and Acts of Indemnity are occasionally necessary.

[42] 1 Geo, 1, c. 56.

[43] 22 Geo. 3, c. 45. The House of Commons (Disqualification) Act, 1931, was passed in consequence of the belated discovery that a member who was on the telephone was a contractor, and thus incurred penalties of £500 a day by sitting in the House. The Irish Parliament, in 1793, applied the principle of the English Act of Anne to its own members by disqualifying all holders of offices under the crown or lord lieutenant created after that time. This disqualification was extended, at the union, to the parliament of the United Kingdom; and at the same time several new disqualifications in respect of Irish offices were added (41 Geo. 3, c. 52).

In the first parliament of George I there were 271 members holding offices, pensions, and sinecures. In the first parliament of George II, 257; in the first parliament of George IV, but 89, exclusive of officers in the Army and Navy; and in 1833 there were only 60 members holding civil offices and pensions, and 83 holding naval and military commissions. On places and pensions in the House of Commons, see May, *Constitutional History*, i, pp. 369–375.

that no judge of the High Court of Justice or of the Court of Appeal shall be capable of being elected to or of sitting in that House.[44]

Bribery of Members. A House of Commons thus tainted at its source was peculiarly open to the attacks of political corruption. In his endeavour to break up the whig oligarchy which rested on the whole complex system, dominating parliament and reducing the crown to impotence, George III had to challenge the whigs on their own ground, and beat them at their own game. Like a Walpole or a Newcastle, he personally examined the voting list, and awarded honours, places, and pensions, or took means to signify his displeasure, in accordance with the votes of individual members. The great number of valuable appointments tenable by members of parliament operated like prizes in a lottery. " An interested man," said Lord Rockingham, " purchases a seat upon the same principle as a person buys a lottery-ticket." [45] But direct gifts of money to members were also resorted to by the ministers. Commenced under Charles II, and continued under William III, this method of "managing the House of Commons" was reduced to a system during the long tenure of office by Sir Robert Walpole. It continued to flourish during the remainder of George II's reign, and under George III was not only adopted and expanded by Lord Bute, but received a new and most pernicious development in the form of issuing public loans and lotteries privately to specially favoured persons on extravagantly easy terms, rewarding the supporters of the government by a distribution of the shares, which they were able to sell at once at a high premium as soon as they came on the public market.[46] In order to carry the preliminaries of the Peace of Paris in December, 1762, an office was publicly opened at the treasury for the bribery of members, and the sum of £25,000 was afterwards stated by the secretary of the treasury to have been expended in a single day in bribes, descending so low as a £200 bank-bill.[47]

---

[44] This large and tangled mass of legislation is now represented by the House of Commons Disqualification Act, 1957.

[45] Earl of Albemarle's *Rockingham Memoirs*, ii, 399.

[46] *Parliamentary History*, xv, 1305; Lord Mahon, *History of England*, v, 20; Lecky, *History of England*, i, 430.

[47] Horace Walpole, *Memoirs of George III*, i, 199. The following remarkable letter from Lord Saye and Sele to Mr. G. Grenville is often cited to show that even to members of the House of Lords money bribes were offered by ministers without any sense, on either side, of dishonour or insult: " London, November 26, 1763.

" HONOURED SIR,—I am very much obliged to you for that freedom of converse you this morning indulged me in, which I prize more than the lucrative advantage I then received. To show the sincerity of my words (pardon, Sir, the perhaps over niceness of my disposition) I return enclosed the bill for £300 you favoured me with, as good manners would not permit my refusal of it, when tendered by you. Your most obliged and most obedient servant,   " SAYE AND SELE

" P.S. As a free horse wants no spur, so I stand in need of no inducement or douceur to lend my small assistance to the king and his friends in the present Administration."
Grenville Correspondence, iii, 145–146, quoted Lecky, *History of England*, i, 431, n. Sir Lewis Namier, *Structure of Politics at the Accession of George III*, i, 221–222 shows that Saye and Sele was a parson's son who had inherited the title, but no fortune, from a collateral relative; the £300 was an instalment of the pension which the crown regularly offered at the time in such circumstances. For the financial history of the £25,000 mentioned in the text, see Namier, *op. cit.*, i, 226–229.

The System of Influence. It is easy to construct a lurid picture, so abundant and striking is the surviving evidence. But it is difficult to believe that the parliaments which contained such illustrious statesmen as Walpole, the Pitts, Carteret, the Stanhopes, Fox and so many others, worked in an atmosphere which was essentially that of jobbery and financial crookedness. The abundance of the surviving evidence in itself shows that no one hesitated to put his transactions into writing, or feared to keep his letters. The system was operated discreetly, perhaps, but not furtively. Sir Lewis Namier's *Structure of Politics at the Accession of George III* is an illuminating study of eighteenth-century " influence " in the light of contemporary constitutional ideas. " According to eighteenth-century theory," he writes,[48] " the executive, which had to carry on the business of the nation, consisted of the King and his Ministers, and the task of the legislature was to advise the King and to control his ' servants.' The proper attitude for right-minded members was one of considered support to the Government in the due performance of its task. What other grounds could there be for a systematic ' formed opposition ' than disloyalty to the established order (*e.g.*, Jacobitism) or a selfish, factious conspiracy of politicians to force their way into offices higher than they could obtain by loyal co-operation with their Sovereign and his Ministers ? But if it was proper for the well-affected member to co-operate with the Government so long as his conscience did not force him to give a contrary vote, attendance on the business of the nation was work worthy of its hire, and the unavoidable expenditure in securing a seat deserved sympathetic consideration. ' I have ever apprehended it to be reasonable,' wrote, in 1757, a Whig who after seventeen years in Parliament held neither place nor pension, ' that those who dedicate their time and fortune to the service of the Government should be entitled to a share of the rewards that are in its disposal. . . .' Nor did such a ' share ' necessarily deprive them of their independence—it is well known that about 1750 even Cabinet Ministers could speak and vote against Government measures; the one and only thing which place or office precluded was (what was anyhow considered reprehensible) a ' formed opposition.' . . . At the present day a member may accept from his party organisation payment of expenses incurred in his constituency; when faced by financial disaster some have applied, not unsuccessfully, to their Whips; but a member . . . must as a rule vote with his party. . . . The peculiarity of our own time is that the individual member can best pursue his interest by strictly adhering to his party, and that this is the only way in which he is entitled to pursue it. But about 1750 there were no parties in our sense of the term, certainly no party organisations, and His Majesty's government and the state as such were in theory the party which embraced all well-affected members. To adhere to them in spite of changes of Ministers did not necessarily mean changing sides,

[48] Namier, *op. cit.*, i, 262–265.

and to accept rewards from them was not necessarily synonymous with being bribed. Considering the matter from the other end, eighteenth-century administrations, not being able to control individual members through a party machine and a party-trained electorate, had to bind their following by posts of honour, places of profit, contracts and pensions."

How much worse than any other that system was, need not be debated here; that it was bad is obvious, and contemporaries made efforts to reform it.

Lord Chatham's Proposals. James I, as early as 1604, had admonished sheriffs to take no heed of rotten boroughs.[49] It was more than a century and a half later that the glaring defects of the representative system—the decayed and rotten boroughs, the private property of noblemen, the close corporations openly selling the seats at their disposal to members who in turn sold their own parliamentary votes, and the existence of great manufacturing cities distinguished by their wealth, industry, and intelligence, and yet possessing no right of sending representatives to parliament—led Lord Chatham as early as 1766 to advocate parliamentary reform. " Before the end of this century," he remarked to the Earl of Buchan, " either the parliament will reform itself from within, or be reformed with a vengeance from without." In the House he denounced the borough representation as " the rotten part of our constitution. It cannot continue a century; if it does not drop, it must be amputated." [50]

Wilkes' Proposals. Ten years later, in 1776, the notorious John Wilkes introduced a comprehensive scheme of reform in a bill proposing to give additional members to the metropolis and to Middlesex, Yorkshire and other large counties; to disfranchise the rotten boroughs and add the electors to the county constituency; and lastly, to enfranchise Manchester, Leeds, Sheffield, Birmingham and " other rich populous trading towns." " His scheme, indeed," remarks Sir Erskine May, " comprised all the leading principles of parliamentary reform which were advocated for the next fifty years without success, and have been sanctioned within our own time." [51] After some further abortive attempts at reform or protests against the system, such as Dunning's famous resolution of 1780 that " the influence of the crown has increased, is increasing, and ought to be diminished "[52]—of which the most noteworthy, on account of its extreme radicalism, was that of the Duke of Richmond, who in 1780 introduced a bill to establish annual parliaments, universal suffrage, and equal electoral districts—the subject was taken up by the younger Pitt in 1782 and 1783.

[49] *Supra*, p. 331.
[50] Debates on the Address, January 1766; *Parliamentary History*, xvi, 100; xvii, 223; May, *Constitutional History*, i, 394. In 1770 he raised the matter in the House of Lords: Emden, *Select Speeches*, ii, 111–112.
[51] *Constitutional History*, i, 394.
[52] May, *Constitutional History*, i, 36.

Pitt's Proposals. On May 7, 1782, when chancellor of the exchequer in Lord Rockingham's administration, Pitt moved for the appointment of a committee to inquire into the state of the representation. But the motion was rejected by 161 votes to 141. Exactly a year later, on May 7, 1783, being then in opposition to the coalition ministry, he submitted three resolutions affirming (1) the necessity of preventing bribery and expense at elections; (2) the expediency of disfranchising any borough whenever the majority of its voters should be convicted of corruption, and of transferring the unbribed minority to the county constituency; and (3) the desirability of increasing the number of county and metropolitan members. These resolutions were, however, negatived by 293 votes to 149.[53] Two years later, when prime minister Pitt again brought forward the question, this time by moving, on April 18, 1785, for leave to introduce a bill " to amend the representation of the people of England in parliament." He proposed the disfranchisement of thirty-six decayed boroughs and the transfer of their seventy-two members to the counties and the capital—the county constituencies being at the same time enlarged by the admission of copyholders. The seats of four other small boroughs were to be obtained by purchase and bestowed upon populous towns; while ten close corporations were to be similarly induced to surrender their exclusive rights for the benefit of their fellow townsmen. The bill was, however, purely permissive in character. No boroughs were to be disfranchised unless with the consent of the proprietors: and as compensation to them the sum of £1,000,000 was to be immediately set aside to accumulate at compound interest until it should become an irresistible bait.[54] This extraordinary proposal, which would have committed the state to the recognition of a saleable property in borough constituencies, was admitted by its author to be " a tender part," yet, in his opinion, " a necessary evil, if any reform was to take place." But the time was not yet ripe for parliamentary reform. The House of Commons being indifferent to it, the public generally apathetic, and George III distinctly adverse,[55] Pitt's Reform Bill was negatived by a majority of seventy-four. The matter was now allowed to drop, and the terror caused by the outbreak of the French Revolution some years later rendered all efforts at reform fruitless.

After the conclusion of the war in 1815 the question of reform was revived. Thenceforward it was again and again brought before parliament by Sir Francis Burdett, Lord John Russell, and others, until at length, under the whig ministry of Lord Grey (who had advocated the cause

---

[53] *Annual Register*, 1782, History, p. 181; 1783, History, p. 176.

[54] *Annual Register*, 1784–1785, p. 189, and Spencer Walpole, *History of England*, ii, 263; May, *Constitutional History*, i, 400.

[55] Pitt having written to the king insinuating a fear lest the personal influence of the crown should be employed to defeat the measure, George replied that " out of personal regard," he would " avoid giving any opinion to any one on the opening of the door to parliamentary reform, except to him "; but that he had " ever thought it unfortunate that he [Pitt] had early engaged himself in this measure." Tomline, *Life of Pitt* (4th ed.), ii, 40.

of reform for forty years), the Reform Bill, after defeats in both Houses of Parliament, a dissolution, the resignation and recall of the ministry, and the threatened creation of peers by the king,[56] was passed amidst the greatest popular excitement, and became an Act on June 7, 1832.[57]

The Reform Act, 1832. By this statute—"the Great Charter of 1832," as it has been deservedly called—fifty-six nomination or rotten boroughs with less than 2,000 inhabitants, and returning 111 members, were swept away. Thirty boroughs, having less than 4,000 inhabitants, each lost a member, and two more were taken from Weymouth and Melcombe Regis. In this way 143 seats were obtained for distribution among the towns and counties requiring additional representation. Forty-three new boroughs were created, twenty-two of which, including metropolitan districts, received the privilege of returning two members, and twenty-one one member each. The number of county members for England and Wales was increased from 94 to 159, the larger counties being divided, and a third member being assigned to other important county constituencies. All narrow rights of election were set aside in boroughs, and a £10 householder qualification (subject to conditions as to residence and payment of rates) was established instead, while the county franchise was extended by the addition to the old forty-shilling freeholders of copyholders and leaseholders for terms of years, and of tenants-at-will paying a rent of £50 a year.[58]

In the same session Reform Acts were passed for Scotland and Ireland. The number of Scottish representatives, fixed by the Act of Union at forty-five, was increased to fifty-three, of whom thirty were assigned to counties and twenty-three to cities and burghs. The county franchise was extended to all owners of "lands, houses, feu duties, or other heritable subjects," of the yearly value of £10, and to certain classes of leaseholders, and the burgh franchise to all £10 householders.[59]

In Ireland several rotten boroughs had been disfranchised at the time of the union: the right of election was now taken away from borough corporations, and vested in £10 householders. The qualification for the county franchise had been raised from 40s. to £10 freeholds by a measure [60] passed at the same time as the Roman Catholic Emancipation Act in 1829, and intended as a protection against the influence of the Roman Catholic priests and agitators, who had ousted the protestant landlords of their political influence over the poorer freeholders. By the present Act large additions were made to the county constituencies by the inclusion of certain classes of leaseholders and of £10 copyholders. The

---

[56] *Supra*, p. 545.
[57] There are several notable narratives of the movement: G. S. Veitch, *Genesis of Parliamentary Reform*; J. R. M. Butler, *The Passing of the Great Reform Bill*; G. M. Trevelyan, *Lord Grey of the Reform Bill*.
[58] 2 & 3 Will. 4, c. 45.
[59] 2 & 3 Will. 4, c. 65.
[60] 10 Geo. 4, c. 8.

number of Irish representatives, fixed by the Act of Union at 100, was increased to 105.[61]

Bribery Still Rampant. The Reform Act, great as were the efforts which put it on the statute book, and great as were its ultimate results, did not in fact provide a solution to the problems of representation; at most it showed the direction in which solutions were to be found. The pocket boroughs had gone, but there still remained many which were amenable to influence. The framers of the Act had also been unwilling to disfranchise persons who were voters under the old rules, however bizarre. Even the new electorate in a borough might be a small group which quickly learned the corrupt practices so long associated with borough electorates. Frequent legislation from 1841 onwards attempted to deal with the evil, and numbers of boroughs were disfranchised temporarily, and a few permanently.

Further Reform Proposed. At the same time the public became more and more engrossed in controversies then before parliament—the corn laws, factory legislation, the law of combinations as applied to trade unions—and it became clear that the demand for an extension of the franchise would soon have to be conceded. From 1833 onwards proposals were made for secret ballot instead of voters proclaiming their choice before a cheering or jeering multitude; but " to go sneaking to the ballot box " was thought to be " unworthy of the character of straightforward and honest Englishmen." [62] Reformers did succeed, however, in modifying (1838) and finally abolishing (1858) the property qualification for members.[63] Extension of the franchise and redistribution of seats was several times before parliament. Lord John Russell introduced bills in 1852 and 1854; Disraeli introduced a bill in 1859, Lord John Russell yet another in 1860, and finally it was a bill introduced by Disraeli which, after a curious adventure in the cabinet,[64] became the Reform Act of 1867.

The Reform Act, 1867. By the Reform Act of 1867, passed by Lord Derby's conservative ministry, a further extension of the electoral franchise in England and Wales was introduced scarcely less important than that conceded by the Reform Act of 1832.

The borough franchise was extended to all householders (subject to one year's residence and payment of poor rates) as well as to lodgers

---

[61] 2 & 3 Will. 4, c. 88. In 1850 the Irish borough franchise was extended to householders rated at £8, and the qualification required for the county franchise was also lowered, so as to include the owners of freeholds rated at £5 and occupiers rated at £12 (13 & 14 Vict. c. 69).

[62] Palmerston in 1852, cited in E. L. Woodward, *Age of Reform*, 162.

[63] *Supra*, pp. 204 *et seq.*

[64] For the famous " ten minutes " see Monypenny and Buckle, *Life of Disraeli* (1929), ii, 234.

occupying lodgings of the annual value of £10.[65] The county occupation franchise was reduced to £12. Eleven boroughs were disfranchised and thirty-five which had previously returned two members now returned only one. Twenty-five of the seats thus made available were transferred to English counties; eleven new boroughs were created and an additional seat was given to six large towns.[66]

In the following year Reform Acts were passed for Scotland and Ireland, similar to the English Act in principle, but differing from it in many of their details. In the Scottish counties the ownership franchise was reduced to " lands and heritages " of the yearly value of £5; and a £14 occupation franchise was established. The Scottish boroughs received a household and a lodger franchise. In Ireland no change was made in the county constituencies, but the borough franchise was further reduced to a £4 rating occupation (31 & 32 Vict. c. 48; 31 & 32 Vict. c. 49).

Representation of Minorities. By the Reform Act of 1867 a perfectly new principle, that of the representation of minorities, was introduced, in a tentative and partial manner, into the representative system. This principle had been embodied in Lord John Russell's abortive Reform Bill of 1854, which proposed to assign three members to certain counties, and other large places, the electors of which were to be entitled to vote for two only out of the three. The city of Manchester, and the boroughs of Liverpool, Birmingham and Leeds, were now each empowered to return three members to parliament; and it was declared (sections 8, 9) that at a contested election for any county or borough represented by three members, no person should vote for more than two candidates, nor in the city of London, which had four members, for more than three candidates.

The Ballot Act, 1872. It was left to Gladstone (who had succeeded Disraeli as prime minister in 1868) to carry a measure hardly less important than that of his great rival, namely, the Ballot Act, 1872.[67] The enlarged franchise could not be genuinely effective as long as workmen and tenants had to vote under the eye of their employers and landlords. The secret ballot was therefore necessary to implement the Reform Act. In Ireland it was a veritable deliverance.

Results. The two Acts—the Reform Act, and the Ballot Act— together have profoundly changed English political life. The older view was that the electorate consisted of selected persons who bore the main burden of taxation, and who exercised the trust of choosing members of parliament. It was thought to be but natural that that trust should be exercised publicly, and that it should result in a House which viewed its duties in very much the same light. The member, like the elector, was in

[65] *Supra*, pp. 206–207.
[66] 30 & 31 Vict. c. 102.
[67] 35 & 36 Vict. c. 33; *cf. supra*, p. 573.

a position of trust, exercising his discretion somewhat widely when called upon to decide whether he should support the king's ministers, or take the grave step of voting against them. The crown was the principal loser in 1832 since it could not support its ministers at the poll—witness the fall of Peel in 1835, when " for the first time in our political history a ministry was compelled to resign office as the direct result of a general election." [68] The result was that the decisive voice in forming a ministry passed from the crown to the House of Commons. The Acts of 1867 and 1872 brought into play a much larger electorate than had been enfranchised in 1832, and also a very different body of men. Their characteristic was, of course, inexperience and a certain instability due to their lack of strong political ties, as might be expected from the fact that they had been hitherto excluded from political activity. The subtle influences of locality, family and social connection which constituted the bond between the old historic parties and their loosely attached members, did not exist among the new electors. Their votes wavered disconcertingly: " the election of 1841 was the only occasion on which between 1832 and 1867 the electors returned a conservative majority; but from 1867 until 1910 every general election, except the abnormal one of 1900 held in the middle of the South African war, has resulted in a change of government." [69] The old concept of the vote as a trust, which the common law, in the case of *Ashby* v. *White*,[70] had treated as though it were property, and which resulted in members who used a wide discretion in the House, was equally foreign to the new electorate. Left to their own devices, they had evolved a different theory in which the right to vote was a right of man, and should therefore be universal; and the successful candidate was in their view a delegate. As soon as statesmen realised these changes, it was inevitable that the course of political practice should change. The fate of ministries was seen to depend on the electorate rather than on the House; ministers took the habit of addressing themselves to the electorate in public speeches during election campaigns—conduct which appeared undignified and unseemly to the more old-fashioned; party machinery was invented and perfected, and the party programme looking towards the future overshadowed the older type of party creed which looked towards the past for its origin and historical justification. The consequence was to alter profoundly the nature of the House of Commons. The broad discretion which governed the eighteenth-century member's vote gives place more and more to party discipline, and the more the House becomes representative of the electorate, the more evident it is that decisions lie with the electorate rather than with the House. This loss by the House was a gain to the cabinet. It was inevitable that ministers should look to the source from which they

[68] Francis Holland, continuation of May, *Constitutional History*, iii, 18.
[69] *Ibid*. iii, 22.
[70] *Infra*, p. 581.

drew their power; when they are clothed with that power it is hardly possible to discern any limits to what they can do.

The Reform Acts of 1884 and 1885. The Representation of the People Act of 1884 (48 & 49 Vict. c. 3), by assimilating the county to the borough franchise, gave the vote to rural labourers and to a large number of industrial workers, especially miners, who lived outside the limits of a parliamentary borough. The result was to increase the electorate by some two million voters, and a redistribution of seats was accordingly necessary. A measure to effect this was therefore introduced in the next year (the Redistribution of Seats Act, 1885, 48 & 49 Vict. c. 23). The old system of two-member constituencies was abandoned; only twenty-two towns and the Universities of Oxford and Cambridge continued to return two members. The short-lived experiment of three-member constituencies set up in 1867 was abandoned, and the other boroughs and the counties were divided into single-member constituencies. The smaller boroughs were left with a single member, the larger were divided into three or more separate constituencies. Similarly the counties were divided into single-member divisions.

Since the passing of the Reform Acts of 1884 and 1885 there have been increasing demands for further franchise and electoral reforms—the most important of these being the enfranchisement of women. In 1916 it was agreed to set up a conference, presided over by the Speaker, composed of thirty members of both Houses, representing the various shades of political opinion in parliament and in the country at large, to consider the question of parliamentary reform. The scheme proposed by this body was afterwards almost entirely accepted by the legislature and embodied in the Representation of the People Act, 1918 (7 & 8 Geo. 5, c. 64).

The New Reform Act, 1918. The changes introduced by this new Reform Act were conspicuous as much for their drastic character as for their significance. By the great Act of 1832 many seats were surrendered and redistributed, but the number of members remained unchanged at 658; franchise modifications were made whereby some 455,000 persons received the vote. The Act of 1867 made further changes, disfranchising a number of boroughs and redistributing the seats, but leaving the total number of members in the House of Commons the same as before, and by extending the franchise to artisans and labourers in the towns about 1,080,000 voters were added to the register. The Acts of 1884–1885 brought a further 2,000,000 electors (of whom the majority were agricultural labourers), and did much to establish equality in regard to electoral areas; the number of members was then increased from 658 to 670. The Act of 1918 added about 8,000,000 electors to the register, and extended the franchise to women, thus making the number of the electorate about 16,000,000.

The main subjects of this new enactment are the qualification of elec- tors, the registration of electors, the method and cost of elections, and the redistribution of seats. This Act itself was subjected to important changes by the Representation of the People (Equal Franchise) Act of 1928.

With regard to the franchise, instead of the seven alternative qualifica- tions, there are henceforth to be three, namely, in respect of (a) residence, (b) occupation of business premises, (c) the possession of a university degree (or, in the case of women, its equivalent). The ownership quali- fication is abolished, and plural voting along with it, save in a very limited form. In future no man may vote at a general election in more than two constituencies, one by reason of his residence, and a second either for the constituency in which he carries on his business or for his university. The qualifying period was fixed by the Act of 1918 at six months, but the law as it stands at present requires that a person must be living in the constituency on June 1, and must have resided there for at least thirty days at the time of registration. Further, he must have lived during the preceding three months either in the constituency itself, or in the same parliamentary county or borough, or in a county or borough adjacent to that in which the constituency is situated.

Women. As has been pointed out, the most remarkable innovation is the extension of the franchise to women; but under the Act of 1918 the basis of their qualification was different from that of men. A woman was entitled to vote if she had attained the age of thirty, and was not subject to any legal incapacity, and was qualified as a local government elector—that is, if she was a ratepayer or the occupant of unfurnished lodgings, or the wife of a man so qualified; also in respect of a university qualification. The Act of 1928, however, placed women on the same footing as men in respect of the franchise.[71]

The former disqualification on the ground of receipt of poor relief is removed. The old disqualifications through legal incapacity remain— that is, those applying to peers, infants, aliens, felons, convicts, idiots, lunatics, persons found guilty of corrupt and illegal practices, and persons disqualified for non-payment of rates.

The Act of 1918 made another innovation by requiring candidates to deposit £150, which should be forfeited if they failed to receive one- eighth of the votes cast; the object was to penalise frivolous candidatures.

A redistribution of seats was effected, chiefly on the ground of popula- tion, the unit being one seat for every 70,000 inhabitants, though in exceptional cases the commissioners were empowered to depart from this standard of division. Great Britain thus was allotted 602 members instead of 557, whilst the total number was increased from 670 to 707. The Universities of Oxford and Cambridge returned two members each,

[71] As a result women are now in a numerical superiority over men voters.

those of London and Wales one each, the Universities of Manchester, Liverpool, Leeds, Sheffield, Birmingham and Bristol two members elected jointly, and the combined Scottish Universities three members elected jointly.[72] In the case of Ireland, redistribution was effected by a separate Act,[73] the standard unit of population was taken as 43,000, and the number of members was increased from 103 to 105. But by the Irish Free State (Agreement) Act, 1922, it was enacted that "no writ shall be issued after the passing of this Act for the election of a member to serve in the Commons House of Parliament for a constituency in Ireland other than a constituency in Northern Ireland." Irish representation was therefore reduced to the thirteen representatives from Northern Ireland. The latest redistribution has left the membership of the House at 640.

Payment of Members. Both knights of the shire and burgesses were from the earliest time entitled to receive wages, or, more accurately payment for expenses from their constituents.[75] The amount was fixed under Edward II, by the writs *de levandis expensis*, at 4s. a day for a knight and 2s. for a burgess, for every day of the parliament and for the days spent on the journey. That rate was the maximum which the royal courts would help members to raise. It did not preclude private arrangements for less, or more expenses, and such bargains were frequent, especially with the boroughs. The members for London maintained considerable splendour and the city once had to borrow £10 from a fishmonger to meet their expenses. Other towns liked to see their members make a good impression—if only it could be done without charging the town. The county of Cambridge had a manor the revenues of which were devoted to the purpose.[76] These writs, which were issued, after the dissolution of parliament, at the request of the members who had served, may be traced to the end of Henry VIII's reign but by no means all the writs issued were enrolled, and the absence of a writ does not prove that the member got no wages, and still less does it prove that he never attended or that no election took place. The payment was unpopular in the counties and boroughs and was one of the reasons why representation in parliament was not eagerly sought for, but was regarded in the Middle Ages rather as a burden than a privilege. There were naturally attempts to escape liability, and they produced theories of the nature of representation which cannot be accepted without reserve. Ancient demesne and gavelkind

---

[72] The principle of proportional representation was applied to university elections when there were two or more candidates. Oxford and Cambridge were enfranchised by James I in 1603, London and the Scottish Universities in 1867. The University representation was abolished by the Representation of the People Act, 1948.

[73] The Redistribution of Seats (Ireland) Act, 1918 (7 & 8 Geo. 5, c. 65).

[75] M. McKisack, *Parliamentary Representation of Boroughs*, Chap. v; Pasquet (ed. Laffan), *Origin of the House of Commons*, 166 *et seq*; Latham, "Collection of Wages of Knights of the Shire," *English Historical Review*, xlviii, 455–464; Plucknett, "Parliament," in *English Government at Work* (ed. J. F. Willard and W. A. Morris), i, 127–128. Many writs are printed in W. Prynne, *Brief Register*, vol. iv.

[76] Prynne, *Brief Register*, iv, 540; Stubbs, *Constitutional History*, iii, 484.

claimed to be quit, and so did many franchises; there was also the suggestion that a lord who attended parliament was sufficiently representative of his tenants, and that they were not liable for the expenses of the knights of the shire.[77] In later times payments still continued to be made voluntarily by some boroughs to their representatives. Andrew Marvell, the witty member for Hull in the reign of Charles II, has been erroneously reputed the last recipient of a salary. But in 1681, three years after Marvell's death, Thomas King, who had been member for Harwich, obtained from the lord chancellor, after notice to the corporation of Harwich, a writ de expensis burgensium levandis. Lord Campbell, in his life of Lord Chancellor Nottingham, after citing the case of Thomas King, gave it as his opinion that the writ might still be claimed, and that no new law is required for those who desire to resume the ancient practice.[78]

The right of members to be paid not only grew obsolete; it was replaced, as we have seen,[79] by the contrary requirement of a property qualification. In 1830, a proposal to restore the practice of paying wages to members was included by Lord Blandford in a Reform Bill which he submitted to the House of Commons.[80] Resolutions were passed in the commons, in 1893 and 1895, in favour of payment of members of parliament, but failed to find acceptance by the House of Lords. At last this was successfully effected in 1911, in an expeditious manner and by the House of Commons alone. The matter had, in fact, become urgent in consequence of the decision of the courts that trade unions could not compulsorily raise funds from their members in order to provide salaries for members of parliament.[81] On August 10 (the very day on which the lords passed the Parliament Bill) the chancellor of the exchequer brought in a motion that provision should be made for paying a salary of £400 a year to every member of the House except ministers and officers of it or of the royal household. He pointed out that the principle had been frequently affirmed by the House, and had been adopted by the prime minister before the previous general election. It was not an innovation, but a reintroduction of an early practice, which had been originally applied by the constituencies, latterly in surreptitious and indirect ways, till 1780, when, however, the principle of " reasonable wages for all members " was affirmed by a sub-committee. There was now a much greater demand on members' time. The proposal met with a good deal of opposition; the principle of payment had been long debated, and it had been assumed that legislation would be necessary. There was some surprise, therefore, among the unlearned when it was proposed that members should vote themselves salaries by an obscure and little-known

[77] Rotuli Parliamentorum, ii, 258, no. 23; 287 no. 20.
[78] See Anson, Law and Custom of the Constitution, vol. i, p. 129, n.
[79] Supra, pp. 204 et seq.
[80] Hansard, Debates, 2nd ser. xxii, 678.
[81] Osborne v. Amalgamated Society of Railway Servants [1910] A.C. 87.

procedure; but at the further debate on August 14, the motion was carried by 241 to 128.[82]

PRIVILEGE

Freedom from Arrest. As we have seen in earlier chapters, privilege began as a means of assuring to the crown the unhampered attendance of its servants when engaged in public affairs, and privilege protected not only those called to parliament but also the staffs of various courts and offices, and persons within their jurisdiction, and members of the royal household. Its enforcement lay largely with the crown, until Henry VIII allowed the House of Commons to assume jurisdiction. Thenceforward, privilege served to enhance the prestige of the commons, and under the Stuarts it was more than once a weapon against the crown. In the eighteenth century it was the public which most suffered from the harsh and sometimes reckless assertion of parliamentary privilege. The extension of the privilege of peers and members from arrest, so as to protect, not only their own persons, but their property, their servants, and their servants' property, and even to protect their game from poaching, during the period of privilege, gave rise to very grave abuses, and the commons even took up the position that they and their servants were immune from civil proceedings of every kind—in spite of the fact that Sir Orlando Bridgeman (in *Benyon* v. *Evelyn*), and Lord Holt (in *Paty's Case*), had denied this pretension. This oppressive rule was partially restrained by several statutes,[83] and at length, in 1770, an Act was passed, by which the privilege was reduced to its ancient dimensions, protection from arrest for the persons of members only, leaving the course of justice as to their property and their servants entirely free.[84] By the effect of these various enactments the freedom of members from arrest has become not so much a parliamentary privilege as a legal right; and consequently " the arrest of a member in a civil cause is . . . irregular *ab initio*, and he may be discharged immediately, upon motion in the court from which the process issued." [85]

Election Disputes. The exclusive jurisdiction of the commons in matters of election, which, for the sake of their own independence, they had insisted

---

[82] The method had served in 1833 to provide the first grant of public money for elementary education. Parliamentary salaries were raised to £600 in 1937 and have been further increased subsequently.

[83] 12 & 13 Will. 3, c. 3; 2 & 3 Anne, c. 12; 11 Geo. 2, c. 24. For examples of the abuses mentioned, *cf.* Holdsworth, *History of English Law*, x, 545.

[84] 10 Geo. 3, c. 50.

[85] May, *Parliamentary Practice* (13th ed., 1924), p. 115, referring to *Colonel Pitt's Case* (1734) 2 Stra. 985; Anson, *Law and Custom of the Constitution*, vol. i, pp. 154–157. Freedom from arrest, though not taken away from the peers, lost much of its significance, when arrest on mesne process (before judgment given) was in all but certain special cases abolished in the year 1838 (1 & 2 Vict. c. 110, s. 1). See Pike, *Constitutional History of the House of Lords*, p. 259. On the more difficult matter of committals for contempt by the ordinary courts, see *supra*, p. 321, n. 96.

on and obtained,[86] became subsequently prostituted to the purposes of party, and this abuse reached its greatest height under George II and George III.[87] The evil was remedied as far as possible by the Grenville Act in 1770, which created a committee of the House into a statutory tribunal with the power (which the House by itself lacked) of administering an oath.[88] The mode of choosing the committee failed to eliminate party influences, and so also did the revised scheme enacted [89] at the instance of Sir Robert Peel in 1839; to the last the constitution and proceedings of election committees " too often exposed them to imputation of political bias." At length, in 1868, the trial of controverted elections was transferred to the judges of the superior courts of law,[90] thus recurring to the method adopted more than 450 years previously in the election statute of 11 Hen. 4.[91]

Ashby v. White, 1702–1704.

The claim by the commons of the exclusive right to determine, not merely the legality of elections, but the rights of the electors as well, gave rise, in 1702, to a memorable contest between the lords and commons. Ashby, a burgess of Aylesbury, having been refused permission to vote at an election, because the House had previously resolved that paupers in Aylesbury were disqualified, brought an action at common law against White and others, the returning officers of that borough. He obtained a verdict; but it was moved in the court of Queen's Bench in arrest of judgment, " that this action did not lie," and, contrary to the opinion of Lord Chief Justice Holt, judgment was entered for the defendant; a decision which was afterwards reversed, on a writ of error by the House of Lords, on the grounds upon which Chief Justice Holt had based his dissent in the court below. Upon this the commons, after lengthy debates passed resolutions affirming that: " It is the sole right of the commons of England in parliament assembled (except in cases otherwise provided for by act of parliament) to examine and determine all matters relating to the right of election of their own members," and that " neither the qualifications of any elector, or the right of any person elected, is cognisable or determinable elsewhere, than before the commons of England in parliament assembled, except in such cases as are specially provided for by act of parliament," and that " whoever shall presume to commence or prosecute any action, indictment, or information,

---

[86] *Supra*, pp. 321, 332 *et seq.* The Lords exercise a similar jurisdiction over the composition of their House by means of their Committee of Privileges. Chief Justice Holt successfully maintained in *R. v. Knollys* (1695) 1 Ld.Raym. 10, that the lords only had this jurisdiction when the matter came before them on a reference from the crown, and that their mere assertion that they had a privilege was not conclusive upon the courts. See Holdsworth, *History of English Law*, vi, 270–271.

[87] See May, *Constitutional History*, i, 362–369. " The struggle between Sir Robert Walpole and his enemies was determined in 1741—not upon any question of public policy— but by the defeat of the minister on the Chippenham Election Petition."—*Ibid.* p. 364.

[88] 10 Geo. 3, c. 16; made perpetual by 14 Geo. 3, c. 15.

[89] 2 & 3 Vict. c. 38 (there were several amending Acts).

[90] 31 & 32 Vict. c. 125.

[91] *Supra*, p. 200 n. 65.

which shall bring the right of electors, or persons elected to serve in parliament, to the determination of any other jurisdiction than that of the House of Commons, except in cases specially provided for by act of parliament, such person and persons, and all attornies, solicitors, counsellors, serjeants-at-law, soliciting, prosecuting or pleading in any such case, are guilty of a high breach of privilege of this House," [92] and they further resolved that Ashby was guilty of breach of privilege in bringing an action at common law. On the other side it was objected, as set forth in the judgment of the House of Lords, that " there is a great difference between the right of the electors and the right of the elected: the one is a temporary right to a place in parliament, *pro hac vice*; the other is a freehold or a franchise. Who has a right to sit in the House of Commons may be properly cognisable there; but who has a right to choose is a matter originally established, even before there is a parliament. A man has a right to his freehold by the common law, and the law having annexed the right of voting to his freehold, it is of the nature of his freehold, and must depend upon it. The same law that gives him his right must defend it for him, and any other power that will pretend to take away his right of voting may as well pretend to take away the freehold upon which it depends." [93]

Paty's Case. Shortly after the decision of the House of Lords, upholding the claim of Ashby against the returning officers, five other burgesses of Aylesbury, afterwards familiarly known as " the Aylesbury men," commenced similar actions against the constables in their borough. They were thereupon committed to Newgate by the House of Commons for a contempt of its jurisdiction. They endeavoured to obtain their discharge on writs of habeas corpus, but without effect, the majority of the judges holding that the commons were the sole judges of their own privileges. The commons further declared the counsel, agents, and solicitors of the plaintiffs guilty of a breach of privilege, and committed them also. The " Aylesbury men " then applied for a writ of error, in order to bring the decision of the judges refusing the habeas corpus before the House of Lords; but the commons resolved that no writ of error lay in this case, and petitioned the queen not to grant it. On the other hand, the lords addressed the queen, pointing out that writs of error are writs of right, *ex debito justitiae* (a contention which was upheld by ten out of the twelve judges, when appealed to by the queen for their advice), and prayed that the writ might be granted. At length the queen put an end to the unseemly contest by a prorogation of parliament, which at once set the

---

[92] *Commons' Journal*, xiv, 308; Robertson, *Documents*, 410–412.

[93] Report of Lords' Committee, March 27, 1704, upon the conferences in the case of *Ashby v. White*, 14 St.Tr. 792. The proceedings of the whole case are given *ibid.*, pp. 695–888. See also the Resolutions of the House of Lords, *Lords' Journals*, xvii, 534; Robertson, *Documents*, 412–413. There are copious extracts from Holt's judgment in Broom, *Constitutional Law* (ed. Denman), 846–868. For a commentary on the case, and its subsequent history, see Holdsworth, *History of English Law*, vi, 271 *et seq.*, x, 543 *et seq.*

" Aylesbury men " and their counsel at liberty. No longer impeded by the interposition of privilege, and supported by the judgment of the House of Lords, the plaintiffs proceeded with their actions, and obtained verdicts and execution against the returning officers.[94]

Conflict of Law and Privilege. These two cases brought to a head a controversy which had been smouldering for some few years on the relation of privilege to law, and of the House to the courts. The commons took the view that their privilege was above the law and not to be discussed in the courts; they further maintained that the content of privilege was not a closed list of matters but embraced anything which they declared by resolution to be matter of privilege, and that such a resolution was conclusive upon the courts. Just as the Stuarts had maintained that the prerogative was essentially elastic in its nature, and superior to the common law, so now the commons professed a similar mysticism of privilege. It is not surprising that they used the same inflated sort of language declaring that there were *arcana imperii* [95] which were not to be profaned— words which James I had used of the prerogative.

Such a claim imperilled the supremacy of the law, and upon that issue Chief Justice Holt withstood it, just as Coke had withstood the prerogative. In *Ashby* v. *White* he maintained that privilege is part of the law of the land, and that its existence in a particular circumstance will be decided, like any other point of law, by the court where the question is raised. From this it followed that a resolution of the house defining its privilege is ineffective—as indeed would be a resolution stating any other legal proposition. Holt first made this point in *Knollys' Case* [96] in 1695, when the lords claimed a privilege which Holt adjudged had no existence. The lords were angry, but finally dropped the matter. When *Ashby* v. *White* came up on a writ of error, the lords accepted Holt's doctrine, seeing in it a means whereby they could adjudicate upon the privileges of the commons. This latest aspect of the matter, which seemed to subordinate the commons to the lords, aroused intense feeling in the Lower House, which for over a century refused to acknowledge Holt's doctrine.

Expulsion of Members. From the reign of Elizabeth I onwards [97] the commons had occasionally expelled a member, and it continued to exercise the jurisdiction. Thus in 1714, Sir Richard *Steele* was expelled the House for writing " a seditious and scandalous libel " called *The Crisis*, a pamphlet reflecting on the tory ministry of Queen Anne as inimical to the Hanoverian succession. More serious was the expulsion

---

[94] *R.* v. *Paty* (one of the Aylesbury men) 2 Ld.Raym. 1109. *Cf.* Hargrave, *Juridical Arguments*.
[95] *Knollys' Case*, Skin. at p. 526 (quoted in Holdsworth, *History of English Law*, vi, 271 n. 2); Hale, *Jurisdiction of the Lords House*, ccxxvii–ccxxx; for James I, *cf. supra*, p. 342 n. 39.
[96] *Supra*, p. 581 n. 86.
[97] *Supra*, p. 323.

of Sir Robert *Walpole* [98] for corruption in December 1711. After some six months in the Tower, where the whigs regarded him as a political martyr, he was released in consequence of the prorogation. He was re-elected, and then the commons took the view that, having been expelled, he was therefore incapable of sitting in any session of that parliament; he was therefore excluded until the dissolution.[99]

The best known instance is in the proceedings against John *Wilkes* [1] in 1763, and the following years, when the commons first withdrew the shield of privilege in order to justify a judicial decision contrary to law and usage, and then, not content with expelling the obnoxious member, proceeded illegally to deprive the electors of Middlesex of their free choice of a representative. Wilkes had been arrested and imprisoned to await trial in consequence of the publication of the celebrated No. 45 of the *North Briton*, on a " general warrant "—*i.e.*, a warrant not specifying any person by name, but directed against " the authors, printers, and publishers generally "—signed by Lord Halifax, secretary of state.[2] He was released on a writ of habeas corpus, on the ground of his privilege as a member of the House of Commons (which, at the time, was in recess), and when it next met, the Lower House, eager to second the vengeance of the king, voted the publication, while still the subject of a prosecution in the King's Bench (which Wilkes declared himself ready to meet notwithstanding his privilege), " a false, scandalous, and seditious libel," tending to excite traitorous insurrections, and resolved " that privilege of parliament does not extend to the writing and publishing seditious libels." [3] The House thus eagerly surrendered an undoubted part of its privilege, in an angry attempt to attack one of its members. Wilkes, having been proved (to the satisfaction of the House) to be the author and publisher of the obnoxious No. 45, was expelled the House, and withdrew to France, an exile and an outlaw. In 1768 he came back to England, was elected M.P. for Middlesex, surrendered to his outlawry and served the sentence of two years, and in the meanwhile was again expelled [4]; and on his immediate re-election, the House not only expelled him a third time, but resolved that his expulsion rendered him " incapable of being elected a member to serve in this present parliament." Again re-elected by the county of Middlesex, the House declared his return to be null and void; and, on his being once more returned by the county, the House not only declared his election void but adjudged the seat to

---

[98] Stanhope, *History of England*, i, 398–400.

[99] The theory seems to have been that expulsion lasted as long as the parliament (although it has long been settled that a committal ended with the session).

[1] There is a lively account of Wilkes and his career in Stanhope, *History of England*, v, 25 *et seq.*

[2] On this aspect of the matter, see *infra*, p. 665.

[3] *Commons' Journal*, November 24, 1763.

[4] On April 24, 1768, we find George III writing to Lord North, then chancellor of the exchequer: " Though entirely confiding in your attachment to my person, as well as in your hatred of every lawless proceeding, yet I think it highly proper to apprize you that the expulsion of Mr. Wilkes appears to be very essential, and must be effected." *Correspondence of George III with Lord North* (ed. Donne) i, p. 2.

Colonel Luttrell, the second candidate, who had received only 296 votes, against 1,143 recorded for Wilkes. A profligate demagogue was thus turned into a popular hero and a champion of constitutional freedom. After a lapse of five years parliament was dissolved, and to the new parliament in 1774 Wilkes was again returned for Middlesex. The former intemperate proceedings respecting the Middlesex election, which Lord Camden said had " given the constitution a more dangerous wound than any which were given during the twelve years' absence of parliament in the reign of Charles I," were at length, in 1782, expunged from the journals of the commons, as being subversive of the rights of the whole body of electors in the kingdom.

The right of the commons to expel a member is undoubted; the further right of resolving that a specific person was ineligible had been exercised without a challenge at least once, in 1711, in Walpole's case. Assuming Wilkes' ineligibility, it followed (from a well-established principle of election law) that votes given for him were thrown away; the true result of the election was therefore the return of Colonel Luttrell. It will be seen that all this depends on the validity of the precedent of Walpole's ineligibility. The argument put forward on behalf of Wilkes was that the House in 1711 had done something which was beyond its powers, that it was attempting to establish a new privilege to the detriment of the electors, and that such an attempt was vain, in view of the principle contained in *Ashby* v. *White*.[5] For a long time the House was reluctant to accept that principle, but since the reversal in 1782 of the proceedings against Wilkes, it has been admitted that expulsion, though it vacates the seat of the expelled member, does not create any disability in him to serve again in parliament. In fact, " the commons have no control over the eligibility of candidates, except in the administration of the laws which define their qualification," for one House of Parliament cannot create a disability unknown to the law.[6]

Conviction of Treason or Felony. The question of the disability arising from conviction of treason or felony has been the subject of discussion in the commons on two or three occasions. By the common law a person attainted of treason or felony was incapable of being elected a member of parliament.[7] But a doubt was at one time entertained whether a person who was not attainted for treason or felony, but was merely convicted, was disqualified. In 1849, a resolution was brought before the House of Commons that Smith O'Brien, M.P., having been convicted of treason, was ineligible to sit in the House. It was proposed as an amendment that the resolution should run that he was attainted, but the amendment was rejected, and the resolution carried was, that having been adjudged guilty

---

[5] *Supra*, p. 583. For the arguments just mentioned, see Holdsworth, *History of English Law*, x, 540–544.
[6] May, *Parliamentary Practice* (13th ed., 1924), p. 66.
[7] Coke, 4th Inst., cap. 1, p. 47.

of treason, he was ineligible to sit in the House. The next case was that
of O'Donovan Rossa, in 1870, who was returned for Tipperary, while
undergoing sentence of penal servitude for treason-felony. As he had
been convicted and sentenced under the Treason-Felony Act, 11 & 12
Vict. c. 12,[8] it was contended that, not being attainted, there was no disqualification; but the House again rejected the contention, and resolved
that O'Donovan Rossa " having been adjudged guilty of felony, and
sentenced to penal servitude for life, and being now imprisoned under
such sentence, has become, and continues, incapable of being elected or
returned as a member of this House." In order, however, to obviate any
doubts as to the legality of this determination, a provision was inserted
in the Forfeiture Act, which abolished forfeiture and attainder for treason
or felony (33 & 34 Vict. c. 23, passed in the same year 1870), that any
person thereafter convicted of those offences should be incapable, while
undergoing punishment, of being elected a member of, or sitting or voting
in, parliament, or of exercising any parliamentary or municipal franchise.
The proceedings in O'Donovan Rossa's case also established that the
House, notwithstanding the Act of 1868 (31 & 32 Vict. c. 125),[9] reserved
in its own hands the power to decide on the eligibility of members. The
next leading case is that of John Mitchell. In 1848 he was tried for treason-
felony, found guilty, and sentenced to fourteen years' transportation.
After a comparatively short period he escaped from his imprisonment,
and after remaining abroad for many years returned to Ireland in 1874,
without having suffered his sentence or received a pardon. In February
1875, he was returned unopposed for Tipperary. On February 18, on
the motion of Disraeli, the prime minister, and notwithstanding the
expression of several doubts as to the legality of the course proposed to
be adopted, the House resolved " That John Mitchell, returned as a member for the county of Tipperary, having been adjudged guilty of felony
and sentenced to transportation for fourteen years, and not having
endured the punishment to which he was adjudged for such felony, or
received a pardon under the great seal, has become, and continues,
incapable of being elected or returned as a member of this House."
Mitchell was re-elected, but upon a petition lodged against his return it
was held that votes given to him were thrown away and that his opponent
was entitled to the seat.[10]

Privilege of Commitment. In the exercise of its powers of commitment
the House of Commons, on more than one occasion since the Revolution,
has been carried by passion beyond the reasonable and customary limits
of privilege. In 1721 a printer named Mist was committed to Newgate
by the House for printing a Jacobite newspaper which the commons
resolved to be " a false, malicious, scandalous, infamous, and traitorous

[8] *Supra*, p. 517.
[9] *Supra*, p. 581.
[10] Anson, *Law and Custom*, i, 87.

libel." As the offence of Mist could not possibly be interpreted as a contempt of the House, or a breach of its privileges, this proceeding of the commons was quite as unjustifiable, if not quite so violent, as their treatment of Floyd in the reign of James I.[11] The more recent practice of the House of Commons has been to avoid such excesses of jurisdiction by directing a prosecution by the Attorney-General for offences of a public nature which have been brought to their notice.

Case of Mr. Alex. Murray, 1751. The right of the commons to commit for breach of privilege was distinctly recognised by the judges in the two celebrated cases of the Hon. Alexander Murray (brother to Lord Elibank, a noted Scottish Jacobite), in 1751, and of Sir Francis Burdett in 1810. In the course of an inquiry before the House into a contested Westminster election, the high bailiff complained of Murray (who had been actively engaged in the election against the ministerial candidate) for obstructing and insulting him in the discharge of his duty. The commons decided to hear the parties by counsel, and after ordering Murray to give bail for his appearance from time to time, finally resolved that he should be committed to Newgate, and should receive his sentence on his knees. This humiliating command he steadily refused to obey. " Sir, I never kneel but to God," was his haughty reply to the Speaker [12]; and the commons were obliged to content themselves with ordering that he should be kept under the closest restrictions in Newgate, without pen, ink or paper, and that no person, not even his servant, should be admitted to him—a severity which, on account of his ill-health, was soon afterwards relaxed. On suing out his writ of habeas corpus in the King's Bench, the judges unanimously refused to discharge him, on the ground of their want of jurisdiction to judge of the privileges of the House of Commons or of contempts against them.[13] As the authority of the House to commit extends only to the duration of the session of parliament, Murray soon obtained his liberty, amidst the plaudits of the people, who regarded him as a martyr in the cause of popular freedom. On the first day of the following session, a motion was carried for his re-committal; but it was then found that he had withdrawn beyond sea, out of reach of the serjeant-at-arms.[14]

Sir Francis Burdett, 1810. In 1810 the commons committed to Newgate John Gale Jones, a prominent radical orator, for causing to be printed an offensive placard announcing for discussion in a debating

[11] *Supra*, pp. 355 *et seq.* See Hallam, *Constitutional History*, iii, 279, and Anson, *Law and Custom*, i, 360.
[12] Lord Orford, *Memoirs of last Ten Years of the Reign of George II*, i, 24. By a standing order of the commons, in 1772, the offensive custom of requiring prisoners to kneel at the Bar of the House was renounced. The lords, though silently discontinuing the practice, still affected to maintain it, in cases of privilege, by continuing the accustomed entries in their journals.—May, *Constitutional History*, ii, 75.
[13] *Cf.* Anson, *Law and Custom*, i, 187.
[14] Stanhope, *History of England*, iv, 28–30.

society, the conduct of two members of parliament. Sir Francis Burdett denied the authority of the commons, in his place in parliament, and enforced his denial by publishing his speech in Cobbett's *Political Register*. He was himself adjudged by the House guilty of contempt, and committed to the Tower by the warrant of the Speaker, but not until the aid of the military had been called in to overcome his forcible resistance. He then brought actions for redress against the Speaker and the serjeant-at-arms. The commons, instead of treating these actions as constituting an additional contempt of their authority, wisely directed the Speaker to plead and submit himself to the jurisdiction of the court. In the result the court of King's Bench, and, on appeal, the Exchequer Chamber and the House of Lords successively upheld the authority of the House.[15]

Publication of Debates. Of all the privileges of parliament, the one which has undergone the greatest modification, and of which the practical abandonment has produced the most momentous political results, is that which concerns the secrecy of its proceedings.

The original motive for secrecy of debate was the anxiety of the members to protect themselves against the action of the sovereign, but it was soon found equally convenient as a veil to hide their proceedings from the constituencies. " To print or publish the speeches of gentlemen in this House," said Mr. Pulteney in 1738, " looks very like making them accountable without doors for what they say within " [16]; and it was only after a prolonged struggle that the right of the electors, and of the public at large, to know what the representatives of the nation were doing in parliament was at length virtually conceded.

The Long Parliament, in 1641, had permitted the publication of its proceedings in the *Diurnal Occurrences in Parliament* (which continued until the Restoration), but prohibited the printing of speeches without leave of the House. For printing a collection of his own speeches, without such leave, Sir E. Dering was expelled the House and imprisoned in the Tower, and his book was ordered to be burned by the common hangman.[17] The prohibition was continued after the Restoration; but in 1680, to prevent inaccurate accounts of the business done, the commons directed their " votes and proceedings," without any reference to the debates, to be printed under the direction of the Speaker.[18] Thenceforward till the Revolution, we are almost entirely indebted for our knowledge of the parliamentary debates to the private memoranda and letters of members, which have since been published. Andrew Marvell, member for Hull, sent regular reports to his constituents during the eighteen

---

[15] *Burdett* v. *Abbott* (1811) 14 East 1; 4 Taunt. 401; *Annual Register for* 1810, pp. 67 *et seq.*; May, *Constitutional History*, ii, 76; Keir and Lawson, *Cases in Constitutional Law*, 94 *et seq.*

[16] *Parliamentary History*, x, 806; C. S. Emden, *Speeches on the Constitution*, i, 208 (*cf. ibid.*, 204, when in the same debate it was doubted whether the House could prevent such printing if it took place during recess).

[17] *Commons' Journal*, ii, 411 (February 2, 1641).

[18] *Ibid.*, ix, 74.

years from the Restoration to 1678. Anchitell Grey, who represented Derby for thirty years, took notes of the debates from 1667 to 1694, which were published, nearly a hundred years afterwards, in 1769. Locke, indeed, at the instigation of Shaftesbury, ventured in 1675 to write and publish a report of a debate in the House of Lords, under the title of " A Letter from a Person of Quality to a Friend in the Country "; but the Privy Council ordered it to be burnt by the hangman.

Debates were also frequently published anonymously in news-letters and pamphlets. After the Revolution frequent resolutions were passed by both Houses, from 1694 to 1698 to restrain " news-letter writers " from " intermeddling with their debates or other proceedings," or " giving any account or minute of the debates." But notwithstanding these resolutions, and the punishment of offenders, privilege was unable to prevail against the craving for political news natural to a free country; and from the accession of the House of Hanover imperfect reports of the more important discussions began to be published in Boyer's *Political State of Great Britain*, the *London Magazine*, and the *Gentleman's Magazine*, under the title of the " Senate of Great Lilliput," or the " Political Club," and with either simple initials, or feigned names for the speakers. The difficulties of reporting when notes had to be taken by stealth and the memory was mainly trusted to, naturally led to mis-representation. Dr. Johnson, who wrote the parliamentary reports in the *Gentleman's Magazine* from November 1740 to February 1743, is said to have confessed that " he took care that the Whig dogs should not have the best of it." [19]

In a debate on the subject in 1738, initiated by Speaker Onslow, Sir Robert Walpole humorously complained of the misrepresentation to which members were subjected. " I have read some debates of this House," he said, " in which I have been made to speak the very reverse of what I meant. I have read others, wherein all the wit, the learning and the argument has been thrown into one side, and on the other, nothing but what was low, mean, and ridiculous; and yet, when it comes to the question, the division has gone against the side which, upon the face of the debate, had reason and justice to support it." [20] Later reporters, moreover, too often indulged in offensive and scurrilous nicknames.

Contest with the Printers, 1771. In 1771 notes of speeches were pub-lished in several journals accompanied with the names of the speakers; and Col. George Onslow, member for Guildford, and a nephew of the late Speaker, who had been provoked by the approbrious terms applied to him by some of the reporters, precipitated a conflict between the House and the Press by making a formal complaint of several journals " as misrepresenting the speeches and reflecting on several of the members of this House." Certain printers were in consequence ordered to attend the

[19] See May, *Constitutional History*, ii, 34 *et seq.*
[20] *Parliamentary History*, x, 809.

bar of the House. Some appeared and were discharged, after receiving, on their knees, a reprimand from the Speaker. Others evaded compliance; and one of them, John Miller, who failed to appear, was arrested by its messenger, but instead of submitting, sent for a constable and gave the messenger into custody for an assault and false imprisonment. They were both taken before the Lord Mayor (Brass Crosby), and two aldermen, Oliver and the notorious John Wilkes. These civic magistrates, on the ground that the messenger was neither a peace officer nor a constable, and that his warrant was not backed by a city magistrate, discharged the printer from custody, and committed the messenger to prison for an unlawful arrest. Two other printers, for whose apprehension a reward had been offered by a government proclamation, were collusively apprehended by friends, and taken before Aldermen Wilkes and Oliver, who discharged the prisoners as " not being accused of having committed any crime." These proceedings at once brought the House into conflict with the Lord Mayor and Aldermen of London. The Lord Mayor and Alderman Oliver, who were both members of parliament, were ordered by the House to attend in their places, and were subsequently committed to the Tower. Their imprisonment, instead of being a punishment, was one long-continued popular ovation, and from the date of their release, at the prorogation of parliament shortly afterwards, the publication of debates has been pursued without any interference or restraint.[21]

Reporting as a Breach of Privilege. Though still in theory a breach of privilege, reporting is now encouraged by parliament as one of the main sources of its influence—its censure being reserved for wilful misrepresentation only. But reporters long continued beset with many difficulties. The taking of notes was prohibited, no places were reserved for reporters, and the power of a single member of either House to require the exclusion of strangers was frequently and capriciously employed. By the ancient usage of the House of Commons any one member by merely " spying " strangers present could compel the Speaker to order their withdrawal without putting the question. This power was exercised in 1849, and, after an interval of twenty-one years, in 1870. Its subsequent enforcement in 1872 and 1874 caused considerable inconvenience, and at length in 1875 the House was induced to adopt a modification of the rule. By a resolution passed in May of that year, while leaving the personal discretion of the Speaker unfettered, he was directed that whenever the presence of strangers should be brought to his notice by a member, he should, forthwith, without any debate or amendment, put the question of their withdrawal for the decision of all the members present. Although not made a standing order, this resolution, in the absence of further

[21] May, *Constitutional History*, ii, 43–49. *Cf.* C. S. Emden, *Speeches on the Constitution*, i, 211–223.

instructions from the House, has since been acted on by the Speaker in every case which has subsequently arisen.[22]

After the destruction of the Houses of Parliament by fire in 1834,[23] separate galleries were assigned for the accommodation of reporters, and in 1845 the presence of strangers in the galleries and other parts of the House not appropriated to members was for the first time officially recognised in the orders of the House of Commons. The daily publication of the division lists as part of the proceedings of the House—which alone was wanting to complete the publicity of its proceedings and the responsibility of members—was not adopted by the commons until 1836, an example which was only followed by the lords in 1857. Previously, it had been impossible to ascertain, in the great majority of cases, what members were present at a division and how they voted, the Houses themselves taking no cognisance of names, but only of numbers. On questions of great public interest, the exertions of individual members usually secured the publication of the names of the minority, and this practice—notwithstanding it was declared by the House of Commons in 1696 to be a breach of privilege " destructive of the freedom and liberties of parliament "—was persisted in, and latterly a list of the majority was also similarly published.

Parliamentary Reports and Papers. The official daily publication of the division lists was followed up by the adoption by the commons in 1839, and by the lords in 1852, of the practice of publishing the names of members addressing questions to witnesses before select committees, together with the minutes of evidence; and a few years previously, in 1835, the commons admitted the public into " community of knowledge as well as community of discussion " by directing all parliamentary reports and papers to be freely sold at a cheap rate.

" The entire people," it has been well observed, " are now present, as it were, and assist in the deliberations of parliament. An orator addresses not only the assembly of which he is a member but, through them, the civilised world. His influence and his responsibilities are alike extended. Publicity has become one of the most important instruments of parliamentary government. The people are taken into counsel by parliament, and concur in approving or condemning the laws, which are there proposed; and thus the doctrine of Hooker is verified to the very letter: ' Laws they are not, which public approbation hath not made so.' " [24]

Stockdale v. Hansard. The revolution which has taken place since the eighteenth century in the relations between the House of Commons and the people is forcibly brought out by the conflict which occurred

---

[22] Anson, *Law and Custom*, i, 162.
[23] Over a century before the fire, it had been proposed to replace the old Palace at Westminster by a more modern structure: Lord Ilchester, *Life of Henry Holland*, i, 70.
[24] May, *Constitutional History*, ii, 53.

in 1836 between the House and the courts of law consequent upon the publication of the parliamentary reports and proceedings. In 1771 we have seen the commons in conflict with the magistrates of London to uphold the privilege of the inviolable secrecy of the proceedings of the House; in 1836 the object of their contention with the courts of justice was the privilege of publishing all their own papers for the information of the nation. Certain reports of the inspectors of prisons, printed by Messrs. Hansard in obedience to the orders of the House of Commons, contained severe animadversions on a book written by a certain Stockdale, who thereupon brought an action for libel against the printers. It having been proved that the book was of an indecent character, a verdict was given for the defendants on a plea of justification; but Lord Chief Justice Denman, before whom the cause was tried, observed incidentally that " the fact of the House of Commons having directed Messrs. Hansard to publish all their parliamentary reports, is no justification for them, or for any bookseller who publishes a parliamentary report containing a libel against any man." This denial of parliamentary privilege was met by a declaration of the commons that the power of publishing their proceedings and reports was " an essential incident to the constitutional functions of parliament," and that any person instituting a suit as to, or any court deciding on, a matter of privilege contrary to the determination of either House, would be guilty of a breach of privilege. Stockdale at once proceeded to bring other actions, and on the issue whether the printers were justified by the privilege and order of the House, the court of Queen's Bench unanimously decided against them.[25] In a later action, however, Stockdale secured judgment by default. The sheriffs levied the amount of damages, and the House vindicated its privileges by committing Stockdale and his attorney Howard, and also the sheriffs.[26] While in prison, Stockdale repeated his offence by bringing other actions, for which his attorney's son and clerk were committed; and the deadlock was at length only removed by the passing of the Parliamentary Papers Act (1840) providing that all such actions should be stayed on the production of a certificate or affidavit that the paper complained of had been published by the order of either House of Parliament.[27] The publication by newspapers of the debates and proceedings in parliament was certainly tolerated, but it could not be said that it was " authorised," so as to be protected by the Act. It was determined in 1868 by the decision of the court of Queen's Bench in *Wason* v. *Walter*, that no action for libel would

---

[25] *Stockdale* v. *Hansard* (1839) 9 Ad. & E. 1 ; Broom, *Constitutional Law*, 870 *et seq.*; Keir and Lawson, *Cases in Constitutional Law*, 78 *et seq.*; May, *Constitutional History*, ii, 78 *et seq.*

[26] *Case of the Sheriff of Middlesex* (1840) 11 Ad. & E. 273; Broom, 960 *et seq.*; Keir and Lawson, 92 *et seq.*

[27] 3 & 4 Vict. c. 9. Subsequently Stockdale's attorney, Howard, brought two actions against the officers of the House, which, on the grounds of excess of authority and informality in the Speaker's warrant, were given in the plaintiff's favour. But on a writ of error the judgment in the second action was reversed by the Court of Exchequer Chamber. *Howard* v. *Gossett* (1842) 10 Q.B. 352; Broom, p. 969.

lie against the proprietor of *The Times* for printing a fair and faithful report.[28]

THE SPEAKER

As we have seen, the office of Speaker in the sixteenth century usually fell to a lawyer, and his subsequent career generally carried him to the judicial bench.[29] The same is true in the next century with few exceptions; Sir John Trevor (1685 and again in 1690–1695) and Henry Powle (1689, the Convention Parliament) both became master of the rolls, but none of their successors received judicial office in England.[30]

Speakers as Politicians. A new orientation of the speakership begins with the new century, when the chair was occupied by Robert Harley (1701–1705) whose future is well known—while still Speaker, he became secretary of state, and subsequently lord treasurer (1711), leader of the tory party, Earl of Oxford. From that moment the speakership was clearly a possible step in a political career. Both of his successors (John Smith, Richard Onslow) followed him to the exchequer, and the third Speaker after him became secretary of state (William Bromley). Sir Spencer Compton (Speaker, 1715–1727) left the chair[31] to become prime minister for a day or two in an endeavour by George II to oust Walpole. The venture was hopeless, and Compton had to wait until 1742 when Walpole's fall enabled him, now Lord Wilmington, to become prime minister again. He had been succeeded in the speakership by one of the most famous of all those who have held the office, Arthur Onslow, who sat continuously throughout the reign of George II (1727–1761). His abilities and long tenure enabled him to do much in settling the nature of the office and the traditions of the House. Unlike Spencer Compton and others, he divested himself of his sinecure office as soon as he was called to the chair.[32] Like other Speakers before and since, he took part in debates in committee, and maintained a close connection with politics as surviving papers show. Nevertheless, his frequent re-election shows that the House was inclined to separate the speakership from politics.

That separation was not easy, in spite of the fact that the House had secured unfettered control over elections to the office since 1679, when it refused to elect a person named to it by the king.[33] The younger Pitt, for example, secured the election of his cousin William Wyndham Grenville, who after a short term became home secretary and prime minister

---

[28] *Wason* v. *Walter* (1868) L.R. 4 Q.B. 73; Keir and Lawson, 105 *et seq.*

[29] *Supra*, pp. 207–211, 245–247. In 1566 Richard Onslow was both Solicitor-General and Speaker.

[30] One only, Sir John Mitford, left the chair (in 1802) to become chancellor of Ireland as Lord Redesdale. Sir Fletcher Norton had been Attorney-General before becoming Speaker, and claimed to have been promised a chief justiceship; he did not get it (1780): Lord Stanhope, *History of England*, vii, 15.

[31] He was concurrently Paymaster-General, a minor but very lucrative office.

[32] For a time he was concurrently treasurer of the Navy. The office of Speaker carried no salary, although certain fees were due, principally on Private Bills.

[33] A. I. Dasent, *Speakers of the House of Commons*, 226.

of "All the Talents." [34]   Grenville's successor, Henry Addington, was
also a member of Pitt's circle [35] and after several terms in the chair, he
left it in 1801 to become prime minister.

Mr. Speaker Manners Sutton. The speakership of Charles Manners
Sutton (1817–1834) is in many ways on the dividing line between the
old and the new conception of the Speaker's office—as it also spanned
the unreformed and the reformed House of Commons.   Like his predecessors, he took part in debates in committee, but in doing so he felt it
proper to offer an excuse.   In 1827 he was offered the Home Office, but
declined.   His conduct of the House's business was admirable, yet outside the House he was a partisan.   In 1831 the opponents of reform held
a meeting in his house; in 1832 there was talk of his becoming prime
minister.   In 1835, however, when Peel proposed him for re-election there
was strong opposition.   It was asserted that Manners Sutton had taken
part in the peculiar proceedings of Lord Melbourne's dismissal, and had
taken part in the negotiations for the formation of Peel's government.
Manners Sutton emphatically denied that he had indulged in cabinet-
making, or had taken any part in Melbourne's dismissal, or in advising
the late dissolution. [36]   His candidature was defeated by a strict party
vote—it was already known, of course, that Peel had not a majority.   His
practice, like his principles, was wavering between two conceptions of
the office; the vote of the House was similarly ambiguous, seeming to
condemn the alleged political activities of the late Speaker, and yet at the
same time electing a new Speaker of a different party from the old one,
the House having changed its political complexion.

The Speaker Becomes Neutral. These matters were rapidly clarified
in the years that followed, when the complete neutrality of the Speaker
was established.   Thus in 1841 a change in party was no longer the
occasion for opposing the re-election of Mr. Speaker Shaw Lefevre. [37]   It
became evident that members who had held important political office
were not suitable candidates under the new order—thus the proposal
to nominate Campbell-Bannerman (ex-secretary of state for war) was
not proceeded with, [38] although in 1871 an ex-whip became a most efficient
Speaker in the person of Mr. Brand.

The growth of complexity in parliamentary procedure is due to many
causes—vast increase of business, much of it of a peculiarly contentious
kind, and resort to obstruction.   To deal with this difficult situation the
House has constantly increased the discretionary powers of the Speaker,

---

[34] Owing to the king's illness he never received confirmation as Speaker.
[35] Son of the Pitt family doctor; went to Wimbledon to attend the duel between Pitt and
Tierney (1798); the first Speaker to have a salary in lieu of fees and sinecures (1790).
[36] Dasent, *Speakers*, 303–317.
[37] W. Ivor Jennings, *Parliament*, 57.
[38] *Ibid.*, 55.

making him in many matters a sort of judge of political warfare. The latest and most momentous step in the direction is to be found in the Parliament Act of 1911 which entrusts him with the duty of certifying those measures which are to enjoy the special procedure there prescribed for " money bills," it being expressly enacted that his decision is final, and not subject to review in any court.[39]

---

[39] *Supra*, p. 549. On the significance and working of the Speaker's power of certification under the Parliament Act, see *Jennings, op. cit.*, 61, 400–406.

CHAPTER 19

THE RISE OF THE MODERN POLITICAL SYSTEM

IN the preceding chapters we have discussed the Act of Settlement and have mentioned the various topics arising out of its provisions. Much more remains to be said on the progress of the constitution since the Revolution; and in the present chapter we shall examine briefly the delicate machinery which was evolved in the eighteenth century, with the cabinet as a subtle link between the crown and parliament, and the rise of parties as it affected the ministry and parliament.

KINGSHIP SINCE THE REVOLUTION

Prerogatives of the Crown. The legal prerogatives of the crown were only slightly affected by the Revolution settlement. It was still true that the king retained the supreme executive and a co-ordinate legislative power. He called parliament together, prorogued or dissolved it at pleasure, and might refuse the royal assent to any bills. He was the " fountain of justice," and as such dispensed royal justice through judges appointed to preside, in his name, over the various courts of judicature. As supreme magistrate and conservator of the peace he nominally prosecuted criminals, and might pardon them after conviction. As supreme military commander, he had the sole power of raising, regulating, and disbanding armies and fleets. As the " fountain of honour," he alone could create peers (a power of the highest constitutional importance) and confer titles, dignities, and offices of all kinds. He was the legal head and supreme governor of the national church, and in that capacity convened, prorogued, regulated, and dissolved all ecclesiastical synods or convocations. As the representative of the majesty of the state in its relations with foreign powers, he had the sole power of sending and receiving ambassadors, of contracting treaties and alliances, and of making war and peace.

Such, at least, is the analysis of the situation which Blackstone could still put forward some eighty years after the Revolution, and which his contemporaries (who were in a position to know) accepted as correct. As a statement of technical law it was of course subject to numerous qualifications, great and small, which are to be found in the law-books,[1] and the Revolution had made it indubitable that the whole discussion must take place under the paramount consideration that the prerogative is a part of the law, and neither outside it nor above it.

[1] Blackstone, *Commentaries*, bk. 1, c. 7; *cf.* Stephen, *Commentaries* (20th ed.), i, 302 *et seq.* For a detailed discussion, see Holdsworth, *History of English Law*, x, 340–425.

Rise of Constitutional Conventions. The most important qualification, however, was of a sort which is hardly amenable to the lawyer's characteristic mode of analysis, and which could hardly ever be brought to the lawyer's traditional touchstone—the decision of the courts. This qualification is the conventional mode of exercising the prerogative. It is the product of tradition, good sense, good manners, practical convenience and the pressure of circumstances. The eighteenth century had reduced social intercourse to something like a code of usages, which made contacts easy for those who had been early trained in its practice; in the same spirit it standardised its political conduct as a result of its experience of what facilitated the easy relationships of king, ministers and parliament. People acted on the assumption that others were acquainted with the conventions and would follow them, and so those conventions acquired an authority so great that the constitution cannot be correctly described in terms of law alone. Moreover, constitutional conventions, like their social counterparts, are subject to change as time goes on; those who are old-fashioned lament the intrusion of the new-fangled, and a later generation runs the risk of misunderstanding an earlier if it is unaware that the conventions have changed. That is particularly true of the reign of George III, which is peculiarly liable to misinterpretation if its contemporary conventions are not taken into account. It must also be remembered that in those days only the small group which worked the system was at all informed as to this sort of detail—unlike the present day, when every aspect of public affairs is scrutinised by authors and journalists.

Prerogative Exercised Through Ministers. In practice these vast prerogatives have now long been exercised not at the will of the sovereign, but of the responsible ministers of the crown, who represent the will of the majority in the House of Commons. " In outer seeming," it has been well observed, " the Revolution of 1688 had only transferred the sovereignty over England from James to William and Mary. In actual fact, it was transferring the sovereignty from the king to the House of Commons. From the moment when its sole right to tax the nation was established by the Bill of Rights, and when its own resolve settled the practice of granting none but annual supplies to the crown, the House of Commons became the supreme power in the state. It was impossible permanently to suspend its sittings, or, in the long run, to oppose its will, when either course must end in leaving the government penniless, in breaking up the Army and Navy, and in rendering the public service impossible." [2]

This result had been reached only after many centuries of slow development. The Middle Ages had already built up a vast mass of procedure which extended to administration as well as to law, and inevitably there

[2] J. R. Green, *Short History of the English People*, p. 680.

arose the view that the king should act through the recognised officers and with the usual formalities. At first, this was probably little more than prudent business management, but eventually its political implications became clearer, and much later it became possible to deduce that the king could only act through those channels, and not otherwise. Concurrently, the criminal responsibility of a minister for his official acts was asserted in a series of spectacular impeachments extending from Lord Latimer in 1376 down to Lord Somers in 1701 and Lord Oxford in 1715, while the further proposition was made clear (in *Danby's Case*) that the express command of the king was no defence.

Personal Influence of the Sovereign. The mode in which the executive power of the crown has gradually been transferred to what has been aptly termed "a board of control chosen by the legislature, out of persons whom it trusts and knows, to rule the nation " [3] will appear as we examine the growth of the cabinet. But though greatly weakened at the Revolution, the personal influence of the sovereign over the administration of affairs long continued to be openly exercised, and is still potent, to an extent which can be known only to the parties themselves, in the confidential intercourse of ministers with the head of the state.[4]

Several general causes tended to bring about a decline in the personal influence of the sovereign subsequent to the Revolution. Foremost amongst these may be placed the disputed succession to the crown. The Hanoverian succession was in very serious danger at the death of Queen Anne; and the continuing power of Jacobite intrigues was evidenced by the rebellions of 1715 and 1745. The divine right of kings, though permanently negatived at the Revolution, still continued for a time to be inculcated by the tory party, and by the great majority of the clergy, who taught the duty of passive obedience and the sinfulness of rebellion. But with the accession of the House of Hanover, the doctrine of divine right became attributable, in the minds of those who believed in it, not to the king *de facto* but to the heir of the Stuarts. Moreover, George I, from the necessity of the case, placed himself in the hands of the whig party, who claimed to have secured his accession to the throne; and the tories, influenced alike by party opposition and by personal objection to the new dynasty, found themselves in the somewhat unnatural position of opponents to the royal prerogative. And while on the one hand the

---

[3] Bagehot, *English Constitution*, p. 13.

[4] " There is not a doubt that the aggregate of direct influence normally exercised by the sovereign upon the counsels and proceedings of her ministers is considerable in amount, tends to permanence and solidity of action, and confers much benefit on the country, without in the smallest degree relieving the advisers of the crown from their undivided responsibility." . . . " It is a moral, not a coercive influence. It operates through the will and reason of the ministry, not over or against them. It would be an evil and a perilous day for the monarchy were any prospective possessor of the crown to assume or claim for himself, final, or preponderating, or even independent power, in any one department of the state "—Gladstone, *Gleanings of Past Years*, i, 42, 233. For more recent estimates see Frank Hardie, *Political Influence of Queen Victoria* (1935); A. Berriedale Keith, *The Constitution from Victoria to George VI* (2 vols., 1940), i, 132 *et seq.*

personal influence of the sovereign was opposed by the tories, both on account of his lack of hereditary right, and of his alliance with their political foes, that influence itself was rapidly diminished by the increased development of the system of party government working by means of the cabinet system.[5]

One very important factor in the declension of the sovereign's personal influence, was his abstention, since the death of Queen Anne, from presiding at cabinet councils. If the king was present, it followed that in the course of debate conflicting advice would be offered by individual councillors, and in practice the final decision would lie with the king; if he were absent, he would be presented with a recommendation in the name of the whole cabinet with no choice save of accepting or refusing it. William III, a man of consummate political ability, was, indeed, his own prime minister, his own foreign minister, and his own commander in-chief. Queen Anne not only regularly presided at cabinet councils, but occasionally attended debates in the House of Lords. It was only at the accession of George I that the king's ignorance of the English language and his indifference to English politics caused the introduction of the practice of cabinet councils being held without the presence of the sovereign. This practice—so essential to the free development of parliamentary government [6]—has ever since been maintained, and on the principle *optimus interpres usus* may now be regarded as having ripened into a fixed rule of the constitution. It is remarkable, however, that like some other important features of our political institution, such as the division of the legislative assembly into two instead of three Houses, the disappearance of the sovereign from the meetings of the cabinet should be due not to deliberate design but to a happy accident.

It is to the credit of George II that throughout his long reign of thirty-three years he discharged the duties of a constitutional king with honourable fidelity, loyally supporting the ministers to whom he had given his confidence, even at the expense of his own predilections. But it was not without an inward struggle that he did so. " Ministers are the king in this country," he once bitterly exclaimed [7]; and relying upon his legal right to choose his own ministers, he occasionally opposed the accession to office of persons whom he disliked. William Pitt, the " Great Commoner," was an especial object of his antipathy, having made himself personally offensive to the king by his somewhat intemperate attacks upon the sovereign's Hanoverian

[5] See Lecky, *History of England*, i, 271–281.
[6] " The presence of the king at the Cabinet either means personal government—that is to say, the reservation to him of all final decisions which he may think fit to appropriate— or else the forfeiture of dignity by his entering upon equal terms into the arena of general, searching, and sometimes warm discussion; nay, and even of voting too, and of being outvoted, for in Cabinets, and even in the Cabinets reputed best, important questions have sometimes been found to admit of no other form of decision "—Gladstone, *Gleanings of Past Years*, i, 85.
[7] Lord Mahon, *History of England*, iii, 280.

partialities.[8]   But when the king finally yielded, he honestly gave his new minister a hearty support.   " Sire," said Pitt, shortly after accepting office, " give me your confidence, and I will deserve it."   " Deserve my confidence," was the king's reply, " and you shall have it."   And the promise was faithfully kept.[9]

Revenues of the Crown.   The gradual development of what is now called the " civil list " is a long and complicated process.[10]   Some of the revenues of the crown were derived from crown lands, certain feudal rights (commuted into a hereditary excise by Charles II), such taxes as parliament had granted to the king for life at his accession, the post office and a large variety of sources producing comparatively insignificant sums.   To this must be added the duchies of Lancaster and Cornwall, and the equally complicated revenues drawn from Scotland and Ireland. From time to time these revenues were supplemented by parliamentary grants.   Under Charles II it was the theory that the king ought to run the country generally with these resources, calling upon parliament only in emergencies such as war.   Neither revenue nor expenditure was accurately known, and there was much guesswork in the arrangements.   At the accession of William and Mary, however, parliament fixed the annual revenue of the crown, in time of peace, at £1,200,000, of which about £700,000 (derived from the hereditary revenues of the crown, and from a part of the excise duties) was separately appropriated to what was afterwards called the king's " civil list," comprising not only the personal expenses of the king and the support of the royal household, but also the payment of civil officers and pensions, which according to modern notions would have been more fairly chargeable to the remaining portion of the crown revenue devoted to the strictly public expenditure of the state.

This arrangement was adhered to in succeeding reigns, and down to the accession of George II the civil list was maintained at £700,000.   Both Anne and George I, however, incurred debts, the former of £1,200,000, the latter of £1,000,000, which were discharged by parliament by loans charged upon the civil list itself.   The civil list of George II was fixed at a minimum of £800,000, parliament undertaking that if the hereditary revenues should produce less than that sum it would make up the deficiency—a liability which it discharged in 1746, by paying off a civil list

---

[8] In a debate, in December 1742, on a motion for defraying the cost of 16,000 Hanoverian troops, Pitt affirmed : " It is now too apparent that this great, this powerful, this formidable kingdom is considered only as a province to a despicable electorate, and that in consequence of a scheme formed long ago and invariably pursued, these troops are hired only to drain this unhappy nation of its money "—Lord Mahon, *History of England*, iii, 207.

[9] Lecky, *History of England*, ii, 380.

[10] The finances of Charles II are now known through the *Calendars of Treasury Books* (*cf.* David Ogg, *Charles II*, ii, 445 *et seq*).   For the later history, see May, *Constitutional History* (ed. Holland), i, 152 *et seq.*; Holdsworth, *History of English Law*, x, 482 *et seq.*; M. A. Thomson, *Constitutional History*, iv, 201, 341; Anson, *Law and Custom of the Constitution*, ii, pt. ii, 196–197; A. Berriedale Keith, *The Constitution from Victoria to George VI*, i, 40–45.

debt of £456,000. But the direct control of parliament over the personal expenses of the king was first acquired on the accession of George III, who surrendered to the nation his life interest in the hereditary revenues, and all claims to any surplus which might accrue from them, in return for a fixed civil list of £800,000 (increased in 1777 to £900,000) " for the support of his household, and the honour and dignity of the crown." In addition, however, to the fixed civil list, George III enjoyed a considerable further income, derived from the droits of the crown and admiralty and other sources, which was wholly independent of parliamentary control; and yet, notwithstanding the king's economical and even parsimonious mode of living, and the removal, from time to time, from the civil list of various charges which were unconnected with the personal comfort and dignity of the sovereign, his struggle to establish the ascendancy of the crown by systematic bribery of members of parliament with places, pensions, and direct gifts of money,[11] compelled him to make repeated applications to the nation for payment of debts upon the civil list. Altogether, the arrears paid off by parliament during his reign— exclusive of a debt of £300,000 charged on the civil list in 1782, when its expenditure was curtailed and split up into separate classes—amounted to a total of £3,398,000.

William IV, on his accession, surrendered not only the hereditary revenues, but all the other sources of revenue which had been enjoyed by his predecessors; receiving in return, a civil list of £510,000, which was at the same time relieved from most of the charges which more properly belonged to the civil government of the state. The civil list of Queen Victoria was settled, on the same principles, at the annual sum of £385,000; that of King Edward VII and Queen Alexandra at £470,000, and that of King George V and Queen Mary at a somewhat higher figure. The last three devolutions of the crown were each accompanied by Civil List Acts, in 1936, 1937 and 1952, whose terms follow what has now come to be the customary course. While the removal of civil charges has freed the crown from any suspicion of indirect influences, the improved administration and application of the finances available for the support of the dignity of the crown have, under the last six reigns, rendered it unnecessary to apply to parliament for the discharge of debts upon the civil list.[12]

Crown Lands. " The king," says Maitland, " is a great land-owner. Besides being the supreme lord of all land, he has many manors of his own; . . . some of them constitute, so to speak, the original endowment of the kingship, they are that ancient demesne of the crown which the Conqueror held when the great settlement of the Conquest was completed and was registered in Domesday Book." [13] This is the origin of the crown

---

[11] At least, so the Opposition professed to believe.
[12] For the whole subject see May, *Constitutional History*, i, Chap. iv; Anson, *Law and Custom*, ii, pt. ii, Chap. vii.
[13] Pollock and Maitland, *History of English Law*, i, 383.

lands. Continually augmented by feudal escheats and forfeitures the crown lands were as continually diminished by improvident grants to the royal favourites and followers. Attempts were made to check this abuse from time to time, by means of Acts of resumption, for example, but without effect, and Charles I still further diminished the royal patrimony by extensive sales and mortgages. His example was followed by the parliaments of the Commonwealth; and although at the Restoration these latter sales were declared void, Charles II soon squandered the estates which had been restored to the crown, and in three years reduced their annual income from £217,000 to £100,000. James II and William III were equally liberal and improvident, and, on the accession of Queen Anne, it was found by parliament that the crown lands had been so reduced that the net income from them scarcely exceeded the rent-roll of a squire.[14]   To preserve what still remained, an Act was passed (1 Anne, c. 1, s. 5) which, after sadly reciting "that the necessary expenses of supporting the crown, or the greater part of them, were formerly defrayed by a land revenue, which hath, from time to time, been impaired and diminished by the grants of former kings and queens of this realm, so that her Majesty's land revenue at present can afford very little towards the support of her government," prohibited absolute grants entirely, and prescribed stringent conditions as to the length of term and rentals of all future leases. Thus the small remnant of the crown lands was saved from utter dissipation. George III on his accession surrendered his interest in the crown lands, and received in return a fixed civil list.

Private Property of the Sovereign. This change has been accompanied by the restoration to the crown of a right which it had lost during its uncontrolled tenure of the hereditary estates. Before the Norman Conquest the king probably held no lands as king, but only as a private individual, and, equally with the subject, had enjoyed the right of inheriting, purchasing, devising, and otherwise disposing of his property. But when the kingship had become more strictly hereditary, the person and the office of the king were held to be so thoroughly identified that his private estates were merged in the royal demesne and made incapable of alienation by will. Accordingly when the crown lands were surrendered by George III the sovereign was again invested with the right of acquiring and disposing of private property in the same manner as any other member of the nation.[15]

[14] The crown lands received some augmentation from forfeitures after the rebellions of 1715 and 1745; but during the first 25 years of George III they produced a net average rental of little more than £6,000 a year. Improved administration and the rise in the value of land later rendered them much more productive. In 1798 they were valued at £201,250 a year; in 1812, at £283,160; in 1820 they actually yielded £314,852; in 1830 they produced £373,770; and in 1860 they returned an income of £416,530, exceeding the civil list granted to the queen. May, *Constitutional History*, i, 225. The net income from crown lands in 1958-1959 brought the Exchequer £1,530,000.

[15] See 39 & 40 Geo. 3, c. 88; 4 Geo. 4, c. 18; 25 & 26 Vict. c. 37.

THE KING'S MINISTERS

At all times it has been inevitable that a monarch who was burdened with the task of government should seek to share the load with others. The restless kings of the Norman and early Angevin line resorted to the justiciar, who advised them, and represented them while they roamed far and wide through their vast dominions. Routine could be carried out by administrative departments, and in time these were the nursery for a new race of professional civil servants. Kings thenceforward had the choice between (1) able men whom they had casually met, and whom they kept near for the sake of their counsel; (2) men who had shown ability and had attracted royal notice in the household; and (3) men who had worked their way up in the exchequer, chancery or other office, and showed conspicuous merit. All three types are amply represented in our medieval history.

The Medieval Chancellors. In the Middle Ages, the typical statesman was most generally chancellor,[16] and as a rule he came to the office through a career spent partly in politics and partly in the civil service; he was nearly always an ecclesiastic. This pre-eminence of the chancellor was natural, for the bulk of the work of government passed through his office. The finance offices with the treasurer at their head were so completely dominated by the accounting routine that they had little political importance; decisions, even on finance, were taken elsewhere. Wolsey was the last of the almost continuous line of great ecclesiastical chancellors; thenceforth there are only two great political chancellors, Bacon and Clarendon, and from Ellesmere's time [17] onwards the trend is for the great seal to go to a lawyer whose main duty will be to sit in the court of chancery. It must also be remembered that there might be a "favourite" who enjoyed great influence, without holding any high political office —Gaveston, the Despensers in the Middle Ages, and in the seventeenth century Buckingham, may be mentioned, among many. At the close of the century there was Lord Portland who alone shared the secrets of William III's foreign policy, although his only office was that of Groom of the Stole. In other words, the crown was not confined to officers of state for its advisers.

The Tudor Secretaries of State. Although Thomas Cromwell, Henry VIII's minister, was Lord Privy Seal from 1536 to 1540, it soon became evident that the still more intimate seal, the signet, was the real mainspring of the administrative machine. Its custodian was the king's secretary,

---

[16] The most recent lists of chancellors and other officers of state are in the *Handbook of British Chronology* (Royal Historical Society, 1939). The appendices of the *Oxford History of England* also contain lists of ministries. The last ecclesiastical chancellor was Bishop John Williams, 1621–1625. The last ecclesiastical lord treasurer was Bishop William Juxon, 1636–1641.

[17] Thomas Egerton became lord keeper in 1596, and Lord Ellesmere and chancellor in 1603, holding the great seal for twenty-one years until his death in 1617.

and his rise to prominence is marked by his ampler style of " secretary of state "—which is said to be of Spanish origin, just as our " masters of requests " got their title from France.[18]   But the mere names of the secretaries of state are enough to show the eminence of the office under the Tudors: William Cecil, Lord Burleigh, was secretary of state from 1550 to 1572 when he was raised to the dignity of lord treasurer, where he served from 1572 to 1599—in all, half a century of signal service in a momentous age.   Sir Francis Walsingham was secretary of state from 1573 to 1590, and Robert Cecil (Earl of Salisbury and second son of Lord Burleigh) followed his father's example by serving informally from 1590 onwards, and then with a formal appointment as secretary of state from 1596 to 1612, while he also became lord treasurer from 1608 to 1612 (holding both offices together).

Origins of the Secretary.   From insignificant beginnings [19] as the king's private secretary, the office grew slowly more important during the fifteenth century, especially since a warrant under the signet (normally in the secretary's custody) became of sufficient authority to " procure " the issue of the privy seal—and it had long been established that a warrant under the privy seal could procure the great seal.   The post was therefore responsible, but secretaries usually left it for a bishopric after a few years. In the sixteenth century the office rose rapidly in dignity; in 1509 it was held by Thomas Ruthall even after he became Bishop of Durham; Thomas Cromwell, early in his career, was the first layman to hold it; in 1539 the Statute of Precedence [20] gave the secretary a seat on the wool-sack; and in 1540 a royal warrant of Henry VIII gave to the office some of the characteristics which distinguish it to this day.

Royal Warrant of 1540.   By that warrant,[21] the king appointed two secretaries to one office.   Neither was senior to the other; each had a signet and so could act alone; they were not commissioners (such as were some-times appointed to hold the great seal); nor was there any apportionment of duties between them, with the result that either could do the whole work of the office.   That peculiar relationship still subsists and proves useful in practice.   Both of the two secretaries appointed in 1540 were

---

[18] Maitland, *English Law and the Renaissance* (1901) n. 17.   The French secretary Claude de l'Aubépine admits assuming the title while negotiating in 1559 with Spaniards who enjoyed it (Declareuil, *Histoire du droit Français*, 471 n. 98); we may have got it from France.   *Cf.* Basil Williams, " Secretaries of State in France and in England " (in *Studies in Anglo-French History*, ed. A. Coville and H. W. V. Temperley, 1935).

[19] The history of the office has attracted much attention.   N. H. Nicolas, *Observations on the office of Secretary of State* (1837) and in *Proceedings and Ordinances of the Privy Council*, vi, pp. xcvii–cxl; T. F. Tout, *Chapters in Administrative History*, vi, 397; L. B. Dibben, " Secretaries in the Thirteenth and Fourteenth Centuries," *English Historical Review*, xxv, 430; J. Otway-Ruthven, *The King's Secretary and Signet Office in the Fifteenth Century* (1939); F. M. G. Evans, *The principal Secretary of State, 1558–1680* (1923); Conyers Read, *Mr. Secretary Walsingham* (3 vols., 1925); M. A. Thomson, *Secretaries of State*, 1681–1782 (1932).

[20] 31 Hen. 8, c. 10 (partly in Tanner, *Tudor Constitutional Documents*, 204).

[21] *State Papers of Henry VIII*, ii, 623 (and in Tanner, *Tudor Constitutional Documents*, 206–207.)

members of the House of Commons, to which they had been elected in the ordinary way, but the royal warrant contained the remarkable provision that one of them should sit one week in the lords and the other in the commons, and during the next week they were to change places, although if business required, both might sit together in their places in the commons. For a time this curious scheme was put into effect. It shows how clearly Henry VIII realised the need for thoroughly competent and well-informed spokesmen to present the government's business in the two Houses of Parliament.

The Duties of the Secretary. A number of tracts and memoranda,[22] dating from around the year 1600, give us contemporary notes upon the duties of a secretary of state, and leave no doubt upon the enormous scope of his activities. He prepared the large number of judicial proceedings which came before the privy council, and generally sped them on their way to the chancery, star chamber or courts of law; he was in particular expected to be ready with information about anything likely to arise— he must understand the system of central and local government in England, Wales and Ireland—he must understand European diplomacy and know the exact state of negotiations in progress—he must understand commerce, and be ready in the descriptive economics of England—he should know the size and armaments of the Navy, the quantities of munitions available for the Army, its numbers, training and cost—he may be asked intricate questions upon the royal revenue, and the charges which have to be met out of it—and he must have a grasp of the English legal system, with civil and criminal procedure. Nicholas Faunt felt the need of having books on all these subjects, and conceived his office as a vast information bureau (his constant demand for statistics is remarkable) to which the king could turn, where vital facts were sought out and filed. And it is all very confidential; the first duty of a secretary is secrecy.

The Perils of Being Secretary. If Faunt called for figures, Robert Cecil was dazzled by the blaze of majesty, and intimidated by the perils of the office. He makes the point that the secretary's office is not known to the law and so has no customary bounds; no commission defines its authority; there is not even an oath of office [23] setting out the duties; and there is no administrative routine of warrants for his protection—the king merely

---

[22] A treatise by Robert Beale (1592) for the use of Sir Edward Wotton is printed in Conyers Read, *Mr. Secretary Walsingham*, i, 423–443; another of about the same date by Nicholas Faunt is edited by C. Hughes in *English Historical Review*, xx, 499–508 (large extracts in Tanner, *Constitutional Documents of James I*, 113–124); a brief memorandum ascribed to Dr. John Herbert, dated 1600, is printed in Prothero, *Statutes and Documents*, 166–168; and a short tract (*c.* 1605) by Robert Cecil is in the *Harleian Miscellany* (ed. T. Park), ii, 281 and in *Somers Tracts* (ed. Sir Walter Scott), v, 552 (extracts in Tanner, *op. cit.*, 124–126). At the trial of Davies for the execution of Mary Queen of Scots it was said " it was his duty to know the Queen's [Elizabeth's] mind ": E. S. M. Brooks, *Hatton*, 312 *Cf. English Historical Review*, xlvi, 632–636.

[23] A secretary's oath appears, *c.* 1613 (Tanner, *James I*, 127), but it is hardly distinguishable from that of a privy councillor.

speaks, the secretary acts. But what if there has been, shall we say, a mis-understanding? No document will protect him: "the place of Secretary is dreadful, if he serve not a constant Prince." Fifty years of experience of Tudor government from the inside prompted that remark. He deeply dis-trusted James I and felt he was entirely at the king's mercy, and might be disowned at any moment.[24] The impression left by the treatise is not so much that of a great officer of state as of an extremely confidential familiar, whose contact with the monarch was more constant and intimate than that of any other, not excluding the privy council. Great technical acquirements and great secrecy were needed, but it is assured that his duty is not to advise, but to prepare the materials for a decision, and to see that the decision is carried out. Such a situation might well exist under the Tudors, but it is evident that a capable secretary is in a position to influence, and even to form policy, if the monarch is not himself of exceptional ability and determination.

James I seems to have realised this and did not fill the place left vacant by the Earl of Salisbury [25]; instead, he tried to do all the work himself with an assistant secretary, and a favourite (Robert Carr, Earl of Somerset) as keeper of the signet. Pressure of business compelled the revival of the old system, but henceforth secretaries were industrious officials who were not admitted to the full confidence of the king.

Not until the Restoration did the secretaries begin to regain their former eminence, when the office was filled by such men as Henry Bennett, Lord Arlington (of the " cabal "), Sunderland, Godolphin, Nottingham, Oxford and Bolingbroke. With the accession of the Hanoverians the office became of great political importance. The Duke of Newcastle held it from 1724 to 1754, and among his partners in the dual office were Walpole and Carteret. Having become a political office held by nobles and great ministers, it was inevitable that routine work should be left to the growing staff of the signet office, and the senior clerk of the signet soon came to be described as the " under-secretary of state." [26]

Reforms of 1689 and 1782. Circumstances soon compelled some sort of allocation of duties between the two secretaries and this process went on through most of the seventeenth century, but not until 1689 was there the official division into the " Northern " and " Southern " departments,

---

[24] In his anxiety, Salisbury consulted the Attorney-General (who " is ever the rod and instrument to give the lash to those whom the King will cast down ") asking " how far shall that officer offend who hath no other commission but the King's word and command ?" Hobart's reply was vague and discouraging, and the privy councillors whom Salisbury canvassed would promise only to supplicate the king that he should be informed of his accusers and of the charge, and have a speedy trial—cold comfort indeed: G. Goodman, *Court of King James*, 42 (in Tanner, *James I*, 126–127). Salisbury's view of the secretary as mainly concerned, not with the signet, but with the king's oral command, recalls the parallel French development where the secretaries, who were originally notaries attesting the royal signature, came to be *secrétaires des commandements du roy*.

[25] Elizabeth had also left the office vacant for the period 1590–1596.

[26] It was also a well-established custom that when one of the secretaries was exceptionally prominent, his colleague should be an administrator rather than a politician.

which lasted until 1782. The division was worked out in foreign affairs, the northern department dealing with the northern powers, and the southern department with France, Spain, Portugal and other "southern" powers, together with Ireland, the colonies, and home affairs. The system was not too inconvenient in 1689, but changes in European diplomacy soon provided opportunities for the two secretaries, either accidentally or deliberately, to get at cross purposes. The great reform of 1782 was effected merely by word of mouth (and that, as we have seen, is quite in the tradition of the office). There is no order in council or royal warrant, and the nearest official evidence is a circular letter [27] to British representatives abroad directing them in the future to address their correspondence to Charles James Fox who has just been made secretary of state " with the sole direction of the department for foreign affairs "; the circular adds that Lord Shelburne holds " the department for domestic affairs."

Both before and after 1782 occasional experiments had been made with additional secretaries for special duties. There was a Secretary of State for Scotland from 1709 to 1746 and from 1926 onwards [28]; from 1768 to 1782 there was a secretary of state for the American colonies, but with the loss of America, the remaining colonies were dealt with by the Home Secretary. A third secretaryship was again created in 1794 with " War and the Colonies " as its province, and lasted until 1854 when each of those matters received a separate secretary.[29] Later, additional secretaries of state were set up for India (1858), for the Royal Air Force (1918—refounded as a Secretary of State for Air in 1919), for the Dominions (1924), and for Burma [30] (1935).

The Lord Treasurer. The treasurer was the head of the ancient office of the exchequer, and the earliest treasurer whose name is known to us for certain is none other than the famous Richard Fitz Neal, author of the *Dialogus de Scaccario*. The exchequer handled the most ancient types of revenue—crown lands, feudal dues and the like; more modern types, and emergency war taxation, for example, tended to be dealt with separately, often by *ad hoc* bodies, and sometimes by passing money through other institutions with a more expeditious accounting system, such as the court of wards or the chamber of the City of London. After the Restoration large numbers of special commissioners were erected to collect and account for this or that tax. The result was that the bulk of the nation's finance was removed from the

---

[27] Printed from a Foreign Office entry-book in Anson, ii, pt. i, 180.
[28] In 1885 the office of Secretary for Scotland was created by statute (48 & 49 Vict. c. 61) for the purpose of exercising various statutory powers transferred to it from other departments; it became a secretaryship of state by 16 & 17 Geo. 5, c. 18. *Cf.* A. Berriedale Keith, *British Cabinet System*, 216.
[29] The older office of Secretary at War dealt mainly with Army finance. For hints of its obscure history, see M. A. Thomson, *Constitutional History*, iv, 441 n.
[30] The separate offices for India and Burma while they lasted were held together.

exchequer, which became more and more a museum of constitutional antiquities.[31]

The medieval treasurer was a very eminent administrator, but only occasionally a political figure. In the later fifteenth century lords and even earls graced the office, while in the sixteenth it was held by two Dukes of Norfolk in succession from 1501 to 1547, by the Protector Somerset, and from 1550 to 1572 by William Paulet who rose from keeper of the king's widows and idiots to be Marquis of Winchester.[32] It seems clearly to have been honorific rather than politically or administratively important; we have seen that both the Cecils concluded their long careers with this dignity. Politically, the greatest of the later treasurers was Lord Danby (1673 to 1679), and the Duke of Shrewsbury was the last of all the treasurers (1714).

The Treasury as a Finance Ministry. In fact, the office had been considerably reorganised at the Restoration. The various boards and commissions dealing with particular taxes [33] were brought more effectively under the control of the treasurer,[34] and so for the first time there was one officer who could deal with large portions of the revenue, and take a broad view of national finance as a whole, and therefore frame some sort of financial policy. This concentration of financial machinery was for a long time only partial, however, for much annual expenditure did not come up for discussion in the annual budget— the civil list, for example, which contained a large part of the ordinary peacetime expenditure, was settled at the beginning of the reign only. In spite of such limitations there was still room for a real finance minister and it is well known that men such as Lord Godolphin, Sir Robert Walpole and Henry Pelham were alive to the possibilities.[35]

With the treasury, as with the chancery and the admiralty,[36] it was sometimes temporarily inexpedient to make an appointment, and instead a body of commissioners was set up to carry out the usual duties of the office. At first a temporary device, it became the permanent rule for the treasury in 1714, since which date the treasury has always been "in commission," the person first named in the commission being the "first

---

[31] Some of its very lucrative sinecures were used to supplement the salaries of less well-endowed offices, and others served as pensions to ex-ministers.

[32] His own comment on a life of ninety years spent in getting on under the Tudors was that he was sprung from the willow, not the oak.

[33] They are thus enumerated by M. A. Thomson, *Constitutional History*, iv, 436 n. 1 : Customs and Excise, wine licences, stamp duties, glass duties, hackney coaches; hawkers and pedlars, salt tax, land tax, hearth tax. Similarly special commissions were appointed for accounting, thus ignoring the ancient exchequer machinery: *op. cit.*, 208.

[34] D. M. Gill " The Treasury, 1660–1714," in *English Historical Review*, xlvi, 600; and " The Treasury and the Customs and Excise Commissioners," in *Cambridge Historical Journal*, iv. 94; *cf.* Sir T. L. Heath, *The Treasury*.

[35] For budgets of the mid-eighteenth century, and Pelham's policy, see Basil Williams, *The Whig Supremacy*, 315–318.

[36] The Admiralty has been in commission since 1708, save for a short period in 1827–1828 when the Duke of Clarence was Lord High Admiral.

lord of the treasury," and the others "junior lords." For a time the treasury board met regularly, but with the decline of that practice greater prominence fell to the chancellor of the exchequer.[37]

Chancellor of the Exchequer. An ancient office, the chancellorship of the exchequer had declined as the exchequer itself became more antiquated, and under the Tudors the office was generally combined (as it still is) with that of under-treasurer. From 1690 to 1827 the first lord of the treasury was also chancellor of the exchequer, if a commoner; but if the first lord was a peer, then a commoner was appointed as chancellor of the exchequer—in other words, it was already the rule that the chancellor of the exchequer must be a member of the House of Commons, although the first lord of the treasury could be (and often was) a peer. Such a rule seems to have naturally accompanied the growing preoccupation of the chancellor of the exchequer with financial matters, so far as that was possible under the old system, " but it would seem that the chancellorship did not begin to attain its present importance until after the death of Canning " [38]; in the meantime, the lords of the treasury became less active in finance and devoted themselves to the peculiar workings of the system of patronage or " influence " which came to be the effective basis of the great power exercised by the first lord of the treasury.[39]

The First Lord of the Treasury. A first lord of the treasury had numerous offices in his gift, partly as a result of the treasury's position as supervisor of the boards and commissions already mentioned, and many of these were disposed of at the instance of members among their supporters in the constituencies. A number of boroughs were so dominated by the department as to be called " treasury boroughs," [40] and in practice much of the crown's general patronage was administered through the same channels. Unification was indeed desirable; members liked to know " to whom they should address themselves "; the government needed to have one man who knew exactly the state of its affairs in this respect throughout the House of Commons. A first lord with these resources at his disposal, who also possessed the gift of " management," of maintaining the good will of members, and of " leading the house " generally, could therefore expect something like security of tenure.[41]

---

[37] Anson, ii, pt. i, 191 *et seq.*

[38] *Handbook of British Chronology* (ed. F. M. Powicke, 1939), 81.

[39] On this, see M. A. Thomson, *Constitutional History*, iv, 435–436. For the Treasury struggle to control the patronage of other departments, see Keir, 328, and Edward Hughes, *Studies in Administration and Finance*, 311.

[40] For the entertaining story of how the post office tried to gain control of the treasury borough of Harwich, see Sir Lewis Namier, *Structure of Politics*, ii, 441 *et seq.*

[41] M. A. Thompson, *op. cit.*, 365. *Cf.* the famous conversation in which Henry Fox refused to join the ministry of the Duke of Newcastle (1754) because the duke would not keep him informed as to the use of patronage: Lord Mahon, *History of England*, iv, 54–55. The Ministers of the Crown Act, 1937, assumes that in the future the prime minister will always be first lord of the treasury.

Some ministers achieved it; Walpole, from 1721 to 1742, Henry Pelham from 1743 to 1754, Lord North from 1770 to 1782, William Pitt from 1783 to 1801. These were the men, in fact, to whom the public applied, either derisively or resentfully, the name of " prime minister."

The Prime Minister. Like many another term of political abuse, the expression " prime minister " had some basis in fact, but not much. It originated in France, and at the moment when Walpole was rising to pre-eminence there were developments in France which English observers regarded as ominous warnings.[42] From time to time France had had a *premier ministre* or a *principal ministre* whose office was peculiarly powerful, and officially recognised; to him all other officers (especially the secretaries of state) were for the time being expressly subordinated. Such was the position, and style, of Cardinal Richelieu, and in England Lord Clarendon rejected the suggestion of some of his friends to give up the chancellorship and become prime minister.[43] The personal absolutism of Louis XIV could not tolerate so over-mighty a subject, but, soon after his death, the French premiership was restored by decree and conferred successively upon Cardinal Dubois (1722), after his death on the Duke of Orleans (1723), and eventually upon Cardinal Fleury (1726–1743) to whom, as before, the other ministers were directed to subordinate themselves.[44] When Walpole's enemies called him " prime minister " it was Fleury and his recent predecessors whom they had in mind. The comparison was very imperfect, at least on the formal side; at no time has an English prime minister been the official superior of the other ministers, nor has he ever been formally responsible for every department of government. On the other hand, there were incidents in Walpole's career which certainly were open to the construction that he was treating his colleagues much as if they were his subordinates, and that he monopolised the king's confidence. Again, Walpole did not nominate to the crown the complete list of his ministry. He succeeded in dismissing some and adding others, it is true, but these operations were effected by tortuous means and complicated intrigue; the theory was (and Walpole professed to adhere to it) that it was the duty of all who found themselves in the king's service to work together, in spite of mutual antipathies or differences. Very often they did; but there were times when human nature was too stubborn. In practice, Walpole made it very difficult for any colleague to work with him without becoming tacitly his subordinate. It seems probable that this result proceeded principally from Walpole's dominating personality, rather than from an overweening ambition as his enemies alleged. He doubtless realised

---

[42] For all this, see J. Declareuil, *Histoire générale du droit français*, 474–481. *Cf.* Léon Cahen, " The Prime Minister in France and England " (in *Studies in Anglo-French History*, ed. A. Coville and H. W. V. Temperley).

[43] M. A. Thomson, *op. cit.*, 109.

[44] Fleury did not, however, receive the title of principal minister, although he enjoyed the other attributes of the office.

that business was more easily conducted when ministers were agreed, but it would be hazardous to ascribe to him the desire to create a convention of ministerial solidarity. In official precedence he had no rank apart from that of his formal office—which (being generally that of first lord of the treasury) ranked below many of the other ministers. The office of prime minister was not known to the law until 1905, when by royal warrant of December 2, the holder of the office was given precedence next after the Archbishop of York, and his office was formally recognised as distinct from, although always held with, some other office. The only earlier official use of the designation was in the Treaty of Berlin, 1878, when Lord Beaconsfield was described as " prime minister." The position of prime minister has been combined on three occasions with the office of secretary for foreign affairs (*viz.*, by Lord Salisbury in his three administrations). This arrangement called forth some remonstrance from Mr. Gladstone, the leader of the opposition, solely on the ground that such an arrangement would not tend to the dispatch of public business. It was never hinted that it was unconstitutional; nor, indeed, considering the non-official nature of the cabinet, could a constitutional question arise on the point. Ramsay Macdonald combined the two offices in 1924. The Ministers of the Crown Act, 1937, which has tidied up many anomalies in the political hierarchy, seems to imply that in the future the prime minister will always be first lord of the treasury.

The first lord of the treasury and the secretaries of state have inevitably been the major offices of political influence. The nineteenth century promoted the chancellor of the exchequer to the front rank of ministers, and in our own day many new offices have been created whose holders become highly important, especially when the affairs of their department become a matter of urgency. At all times, moreover, it has been possible for the holder of a less important office to find opportunity for exerting considerable influence upon the general conduct of affairs when his abilities warranted it. In the eighteenth century, when the modern political system was beginning to take shape, there were many such offices, and in our own day they have multiplied. Some enjoyed high precedence and so were appropriate for peers whose position in the lords, and whose patronage in the constituencies, might be useful. Others were appointments at court, whose holders could create a friendly political atmosphere and exercise some influence. Others were recognised stepping-stones to higher things; thus a solicitor-general could hope to become attorney-general, and an attorney-general could aspire to a chief-justiceship or even to the woolsack. Meanwhile, as Murray did while attorney-general, he might even become an indispensable support of a weak ministry. Still other offices carried such considerable emoluments that they could be used to enable men to hold office who otherwise would be unable to do so —the paymaster-general was in this class. In short, the construction of a ministry was a work of social art such as the eighteenth century enjoyed, and did extremely well. It was rendered all the more difficult by the fact that a complete change of ministers was very rare: it happened in 1689, in 1714 and in 1782. With those signal exceptions, a slow but continuous series of partial changes was gradually transforming one ministry into its successor.

THE CABINET

The Privy Council. The privy council [45] continued to be the constitutional body of advisers of the king. There were those who held that he was bound by the laws and customs of the realm to consult it, but that was a political sentiment rather than a legal fact. At the Restoration the privy council was an active working body, transacting a large mass of business, great and small, political and administrative. But Charles II hated the delays and restraints imposed upon his designs by long debates in council, and having greatly augmented its numbers was able to allege with truth that "the great number of the council made it unfit for the secrecy and despatch which are necessary in great affairs." Availing himself of one of the peculiar characteristics of the council—its action through committees—Charles used as a confidential instrument its "committee for foreign affairs," with whom he concerted all measures of importance before submitting them, for a merely formal ratification, to the whole body of privy councillors. Unlike the other parallel bodies, this was not a true committee, since (1) it did not report back to the parent body, (2) it was selected by the king and not by the council, and (3) was not confined to matters referred to it by the council. As it dealt with momentous and secret matters of diplomacy, and consisted of a small number of important ministers, the king consulted it also on domestic matters of great importance—such as the Declaration of Indulgence; even in foreign affairs, however, some things might be hidden from it— such as the secret Treaty of Dover.

The Cabal Ministry, 1671. "Formerly," says Trenchard, writing towards the close of the seventeenth century, "all matters of state and discretion were debated and resolved in the privy council, where every man subscribed his opinion and was answerable for it. The late King Charles II was the first who broke this most excellent part of our constitution, by settling a cabal or cabinet council, where all matters of consequence were debated and resolved, and then brought to the privy council to be confirmed." [46] The word "cabal" with the meaning of "club" or "association of intriguers" had been popularly applied to the secret

---

[45] *Supra*, pp. 251–255. The best general account of privy council and cabinet is in M. A. Thomson, *Constitutional History*, iv, 102 *et seq.*, 211 *et seq.*, 349 *et seq.*, covering the seventeenth and eighteenth centuries. The four volumes by E. R. Turner on *The Privy Council and the Cabinet Council* are a massive collection of raw material. For the nineteenth century to the present day there is Sir Ivor Jennings, *Cabinet Government*, and A. Berriedale Keith, *The British Cabinet System*. W. Bagehot, *The English Constitution* (1867), contains a classical exposition.

[46] Trenchard, *Short History of Standing Armies* (1698), pp. vii, viii. "The very name of a cabinet council," says Hallam, "as distinguished from the larger body, may be found as far back as the reign of Charles I" (*Constitutional History*, iii, 184); but it occurs in the

councillors of the king even under James I, and the accidental coincidence that, in 1671, the cabinet consisted of five ministers, Clifford (Lord Treasurer), Arlington (Secretary of State), Buckingham (Master of the Horse), Ashley (for a short time Chancellor, later Earl of Shaftesbury), and Lauderdale (Secretary for Scotland), the initials of whose names made up the word "cabal," caused the latter designation to be used for some years as synonymous with cabinet. But, though convenient and even necessary for administrative purposes, cabinet government, in the form which it assumed at this period, was undoubtedly fraught with great evils. It deprived the privy council of whatever influence it might have had to check the actions of the king, especially since its non-official character was appreciated by the public, and vested the real government of the country in a body of ministers practically irresponsible to the nation. There were complaints in parliament that the privy council was not being regularly consulted, with the result that parliament did not know who was responsible for forming policy. Although the Test Act broke up the cabal, several of its members being Catholics, that was not enough to restore privy council government.

Temple's Scheme, 1679. Accordingly, in 1679, an attempt was made, on the advice (so it was said) of Sir William Temple, to restore the privy council to its former position. It was remodelled, and its numbers reduced from fifty to thirty, of whom fifteen were the chief officers of state, and the other fifteen were made up of ten lords and five commoners. The principle that political and economic power should go together was expressly recognised by the provision in the scheme that the joint income of the new council was not to fall below £300,000, a sum nearly equal to the estimated income of the whole House of Commons. Like similar experiments in the Middle Ages, it included all points of view, and seems actually to have contained a majority of persons associated with the opposition. It was hoped that a body thus constituted of great nobles and wealthy landed proprietors, too numerous for a cabal and yet not too numerous for secret deliberation, would form at once a check upon the crown and a counterbalance to the influence of parliament.[47] By the advice of this Council of Thirty, Charles II pledged himself to be guided in all affairs of state; but the pledge was quickly broken, and an interior or cabinet council was again formed.

The Revolution made little immediate change in the system. William III continued to give at least some of his confidence to a small group of principal ministers, although like Charles II he kept the most important steps in his foreign policy a secret from most of them—the exceptional

preceding reign in the writings of Lord Bacon, who, in treating of the "inconveniences of counsel," says: "for which inconveniences, the doctrine of Italy, and practice of France, in some kings' times, hath introduced *cabinet* counsels; a remedy worse than the disease." Bacon, *Works* (ed. Spedding, Ellis & Heath, 1858), vi, 424.

[47] See E. R. Turner, "The Privy Council of 1679," *English Historical Review*, xxx, 251. See also Anson, *Law and Custom*, ii, Pt. 1, pp. 76 *et seq.*

position in this respect of Lord Portland has already been mentioned.[48] Even so, the normal group was too large for the effective conduct of the war, and was deliberately reduced on the advice of Sunderland. For a time it was noticed that the closest circle of royal advisers was solidly Whig in composition and the abusive nickname of " the Junto " was popularly bestowed upon it in 1696. A similar situation persisted under the reign of Anne, although nomenclature continued to be unsettled.[49] Thus it seems that Anne regularly attended the " cabinet," but did not generally attend the " committee." The composition of the body, whatever its name, was becoming more settled, however, and came to be known in political circles. Nevertheless, there were moves in foreign diplomacy which were still kept secret from the cabinet.[50] That these developments had caused alarm can be seen from the clause in the Act of Settlement which would have imposed upon the House of Hanover the statutory duty of governing through the privy council instead of through a cabinet.[51] In fact the amateur politician was thereby making his almost last stand against the professional and official. The fact that under Anne that clause was repealed marks the advance made in the tolerance of the idea of a cabinet. As for the privy council, there was indeed the decisive meeting as Anne lay dying,[52] but it was the last example of spontaneous and independent action by the privy council.

The above summary of a very complicated situation is still sufficient to make a few important points evident. In the first place, the major factor in the formation of the cabinet as an institution was the crown. In its essentials a cabinet was a small and confidential group of advisers whom the sovereign consulted at its discretion. Whether the crown consulted the cabinet, or one or two ministers, or a few household officers, or nobody at all, was entirely a matter of discretion. There was no rule of law requiring the crown's acts to be fortified with advice or consent, save only in the case of legislation. Royal acts might in some cases need the application of a seal or similar formality which rendered the minister concerned responsible, but the crown could usually find a minister ready to take the risk. The very name suggests a small palace room where a very few can meet confidentially; later in the century we hear of a still more secret place than a cabinet, for very private talks took place in the " closet." It still remained a task for the future to determine the relation between the cabinet and the incipient party system, and the relation between the cabinet and parliament and the other ministers. The Junto of 1696 had indeed been mainly Whig, and had even made a practice of holding meetings of Whig members of parliament in a tavern [53]; but there

---

[48] *Supra,* p. 603.

[49] *Cf.* J. H. Plumb, " Organisation of the cabinet in the reign of Queen Anne," *Transactions of the Royal Historical Society* (1957), 137.

[50] M. A. Thomson, *Constitutional History,* iv, 214.

[51] *Supra,* pp. 463, sec. 4, 467.

[52] *Supra,* p. 473.

[53] Macaulay, *History of England,* Chap. xxii.

was no immediate development in permanent constitutional practice. The use of the word "committee" under Anne in contrast to "cabinet" possibly shows that for a time there was a secondary force at work, namely the need for ministers to consult among themselves. Indeed, the general public may well have thought that a cabinet was nothing more than a meeting of ministers, and that the privy council was substantially the same as both. Even the House of Lords was visibly puzzled: in 1711 the Earl of Scarsdale, in the House of Lords, having proposed a resolution in which the late advisers of the crown were referred to as the "cabinet council," afterwards substituted the word "ministers" as being "better known." This alteration gave rise to a discussion, in the course of which some peers maintained that "ministers" and "cabinet council" were synonymous, others that there might be a difference. The Duke of Argyle thought "all ministers were of the cabinet council, but that all the cabinet council were not ministers"; Lord Ferrers, that "the word ministry is more copious than cabinet council." Lord Cowper maintained that they were both terms of an uncertain signification, and "cabinet council" a word "unknown in our law"; while the Earl of Peterborough observed that "he had heard a distinction between the cabinet council and the privy council; that the privy councillors were such as were thought to know everything, and knew nothing, and those of the cabinet council thought nobody knew anything but themselves." [54] By that time there seems to be no resentment at the institution.

The Cabinet Under George I. The accession of the House of Hanover was a turning-point in the history of the cabinet, and of a very different nature from the plans which had been laid in the Act of Settlement. George I began his reign by appointing a cabinet of fifteen members, those most constantly attending being the secretaries of state, the first lord of the treasury, the chancellor, lord president of the council, lord privy seal and first lord of the admiralty. Others came irregularly or rarely, such as the Archbishop of Canterbury, the chief justice of the king's bench, the lord chamberlain and the lord steward. The household element, so prominent under William III, seems to have declined before the greater ministers. The debates seem to have been long and sometimes heated; George I evidently found them very trying, for he understood little of the English government system and of the personal and party issues which ran through it, and his knowledge of English was too slight to enable him to follow its discussions. After 1717 he rarely attended cabinet meetings. From these accidental circumstances flowed momentous results. The king no longer heard the conflicting views of different ministers, and no longer did he take part in their discussions; hence he was no longer constantly faced with the problem of himself reaching a decision

---

[54] *Parliamentary History*, vi, 971–974. "Ministry" is now used to include all those who hold political office, of whom only about twenty are in the "cabinet."

on the basis of the arguments put forward. Then again, having ceased to meet the cabinet as a group of contending politicians, he came to rely still more upon the incipient " prime minister " who necessarily derived much enhanced importance from the fact that he was the spokesman of the cabinet to the king, and of the king to the cabinet—the story is well known how Walpole and George I were reduced to conversing in Latin [55] as the one knew no German and the other no English. Then, too, there was the fact that when the king referred a matter to the cabinet, and the cabinet tendered its advice, the advice was more and more a single recommendation and not a choice of alternatives; in other words, the cabinet began to feel the need of speaking with one voice, of concealing its differences (if there were any), and of becoming a more compact and homogeneous body.

Cabinet Minutes. The advice was frequently conveyed in a formal minute drafted by a secretary of state. Of these documents a fair number have survived from the eighteenth century, together with casual notes made by members of the cabinet for their private use. Apart from this communication with the sovereign, the cabinet did not feel the need of records for its own use until comparatively recently, when the complexity of the issues made it necessary for ministers to have detailed directions approved by the cabinet for the guidance of their departments. There is now a considerable cabinet secretariat, distinct from that which is personal to the prime minister.[56]

The tendency towards closer cohesion and organisation may well have been strengthened by the fact that the absence of the king enabled the cabinet to develop its other function as a conference of the principal ministers upon problems common to them all (especially parliamentary management and party tactics), instead of being merely a collection of ministers whose principal duty was to the crown. How great these changes were can be seen when the policy of George III is examined.

Some expressions used by older writers, such as Lord Macaulay and Walter Bagehot, in describing the cabinet call for comment. In the first place, it is not helpful to describe the cabinet as a " committee," either of the Houses of Parliament or of the privy council. That word must mean a subordinate body, with terms of reference, reporting back to those who set it up. The cabinet is none of these things. Its functions

---

[55] Walpole's Latin was as good as that of most other well-educated people of his day, and the linguistic difficulties of Europe were then minimised by the common classical language. Thus Maria Theresa in 1741 addressed her Hungarian subjects in Latin, " a language which she had studied and spoke fluently, not from pedantry, as ladies elsewhere, but because it is to this day in common use with the Hungarian people, and still serves to convey the national deliberations ": Lord Mahon, *History of England* (1853), iii, 127; and when Dr. Johnson went to Paris he conversed with Voltaire in Latin, the only common language between them.

[56] It grew up in the course of the war of 1914–1918 and developed from the already existing secretariat of the Committee of Imperial Defence: Keith, *British Cabinet System*, 131 *et seq.* For the prime minister's cabinet letter to the king, *cf. ibid.*, 411.

are in no way ancillary, as are those of a true committee. It is also some-times remarked that the cabinet is " unknown to the law." This is true; the cabinet is indeed merely a conference of senior ministers, but the ministers are themselves very well known to the law, exercising powers which are now, in fact, very largely statutory. A decision of a modern cabinet (like a decision of the king in times past) can only be lawfully carried out if there is a minister or official with the authority in law to do it; the fact that the decision is one of the cabinet will not supply any defect in that authority. The cabinet is thus a means whereby the ministers exercise their powers, conduct their departments and advise the crown, in consultation with one another. The law is only concerned with what they do, and not with their preliminary consultations. The cabinet has, however, lately been mentioned in a statute. The Ministers of the Crown Act, 1937, has set up a salary scale for ministers high and low, and for some of those in the middle rank it provides an increase of salary if they are members of the cabinet, a fact which is to be ascertained from the *London Gazette*. It even goes further, by according a salary to the Leader of the Opposition.[57]

There still remains to consider the complex network of conventions which govern the selection, resignation or dismissal of cabinets and ministers, and their relation, individually and collectively, to parliament. Like the cabinet itself, they are the product of long years of practice; they have grown up, moreover, in an atmosphere increasingly charged with ideas based upon political parties. It is to the growth of parties, and the interplay between them and the cabinet, the ministry and parlia-ment, that we must therefore turn.

POLITICAL PARTIES AND MINISTRIES

The deep cleavage of opinion which is later associated with the names " whig " and " tory " has already been mentioned in connection with the religious dissensions under Elizabeth [58] and the formation of the " puri-tan" and "cavalier" groups whose conflict produced the Civil War.[59] The Restoration, as we have seen, was not due to any political or military triumph of royalists over republicans, but to a combination of groups in which the presbyterians occupied a crucial position. The old antagon-isms nevertheless survived, but in the form of party conflict. It would be misleading, however, to regard the whigs and tories of the seventeenth and eighteenth centuries as the exact counterparts of modern political parties. There was then no party organisation to enable the group to concert its activities and no attempt at party discipline. While there were certain ideas which were in the main characteristic of each of the parties, their expression was vague, and fell far short of a party " policy." In

---

[57] The expression " His Majesty's Opposition " occurs as early as 1820: *The Times Literary Supplement* (1948), 429.
[58] *Supra*, p. 318.
[59] *Supra*, pp. 328, 418.

consequence of this looseness of organisation, it followed that although each party had a nucleus of faithful adherents there was also a large proportion whose attachment to a party was somewhat slight, and whose action was difficult to predict. This did not necessarily mean that men changed party lightly; what usually happened was that groups formed within each party (and such small groups may well be more active and coherent than a large party); and so political tacticians had to deal, not with two parties, but with a larger number of groups. Thus Walpole led a group of whigs who allied with tories to oppose a whig ministry— his allies hailed him as almost a Jacobite [60]—but such temporary manoeuvres were common in the eighteenth century. Their significance is principally to remind us that it is an unwarrantable simplification to regard the politics of the eighteenth century as based upon a two-party system.

Opposition Discouraged. There were several factors which produced this state of affairs. We have already mentioned the view generally held that members should assist the government to carry on the king's business as far as they conscientiously could [61]; from this it is plain that the function of the opposition was not " to oppose " in the more modern sense in which that expression has been used. Hence the lack of that cohesion which a continuous conflict naturally produces in two forces habitually arrayed against one another.

Members and Mandates. Then, too, members of parliament strongly resented anything resembling a mandate, or " instructions " as they were generally called, from their electors. This represents to some extent a change in the conception of parliament. The medieval member came furnished, as we have seen, with express letters of attorney,[62] but their effect was to bind his constituents rather than himself. Nevertheless he was often the obvious spokesman of the locality when local interests were involved, and for centuries he was charged with such duties as securing local Acts. Mandates on public affairs, however, are hardly to be found before the reign of James I, and but rarely until after the Restoration. From then onwards, members were sometimes charged with mandates by their constituents in moments of political crisis such as the Exclusion Bill, the Peace of Utrecht, Walpole's Excise Bill, the Wilkes affair and the like. But these were exceptional cases. In 1745 a minister explained in parliament that a member was not the attorney of the locality

---

[60] Lord Mahon, *History of England*, i, 394–395.
[61] *Supra*, p. 569. The seating of members facing one another is a medieval plan. In the eighteenth-century opposition members already had the custom of sitting on one side (Dasent, *Speakers*, 262); but privy councillors sat together on what is now the Treasury bench—we have already mentioned the importance of those who, in Tudor times, sat near the Speaker. Thus Walpole and Pulteney sat side by side although Pulteney was leading the opposition to Walpole (Lord Mahon, *History of England*, iii, 102).
[62] *Supra*, p. 151. There are numerous examples in *York Civic Records*, v. 7, 31, 87, 93, etc., from about 1529 (Yorkshire Archaeological Society, Record Series, vol. cx).

which elected him, but "after a gentleman is chosen, he is the representative, or, if you please, the attorney of the people of England, and as such is at full freedom to act as he thinks best for the people of England in general. He may receive, he may ask, he may even follow the advice of his particular constituents; but he is not obliged, nor ought he to follow their advice if he thinks it inconsistent with the general interest of his country." [63] In 1797 Charles James Fox was somewhat less emphatic: "When gentlemen represent populous towns and cities, then it is a disputed point whether they ought to obey their voice, or follow the dictates of their own conscience," ironically adding "but if they represent a noble lord or a noble duke, then it becomes no longer a question of doubt; and he is not considered a man of honour who does not implicitly obey the orders of a single constituent." [64] The classical expression of the extreme view of parliamentary independence is Burke's *Letter to the Sheriffs of Bristol* (1777). With such a view prevailing in political circles it will be seen that a well-knit party was impossible. Just as it is commonly said that to-day an election is turned by the vagaries of a comparatively small number of unstable voters, so in the eighteenth century divisions in the House of Commons often depended upon a small but important group of members who acknowledged no permanent political ties.

Personal and Family Influences. The personal element was naturally stronger than the doctrinal element in the formation of parties. This followed partly from the patronage system already described, under which a few great families, Pelhams, Russells, Cavendishes, Spencers, Grenvilles (sometimes at variance, or competing among themselves) exercised much "influence" in the House and in the country. Closely related to one another, the great whig families were notoriously "all cousins," and commonly described themselves as "the connexion" rather than as a political party. But even so great a magnate as the Duke of Newcastle could not maintain anything approaching what would be called discipline in our own day. Such a system also implies that there will be disappointed men, and they will naturally tend to go into opposition. The ancient division between "court" (*i.e.*, the government) and "country" (those who for any reason are not with the government) is constantly reappearing, with the composition of the two groups varying according to temporary circumstances.

The Party Programme. A great point of difference between modern and older party systems is in the fact that today a party professes to have a broad and detailed programme, which is largely directed to the future. Any party can immediately state what it proposes to do if it gets the chance. The older system, however, had little need to make promises

---

[63] Sir William Yonge, *Parliamentary History*, xiii, 1076 *et seq.* (extracts in C. S. Emden, *Select Speeches on the Constitution*, ii, 108 *et seq.*).
[64] *Parliamentary History*, xxxiii, 709 *et seq.* (extracts in Emden, *op. cit.*, ii, 135).

to the electorate, and the electorate did not conceive itself as choosing between the several varieties of paradise offered by the candidates. Instead, their eyes were turned towards the past. The crucial question for an old whig or tory was not what he proposed to do in the future, but what he thought about the past—and the two great tests which were applied, long after the events, were the Revolution and the Peace of Utrecht. In 1792 Burke defended his orthodoxy by a detailed discussion of the year 1688 and of the arguments of *Dr. Sacheverell's Case* in 1711 (*Appeal from the New to the Old Whigs*), and even in the nineteenth century a detailed discussion of the events of 1688 might form part of a trial for seditious libel—the correct exposition of the Revolution was cardinal to whig orthodoxy.

Both parties had their scriptures. Whig doctrine was announced with singular force and lucidity in the treatises of John Locke, who set forth the reasonableness and moderation which were implicit in the contract-theory of government. The tories turned to one of the greatest monuments of English prose, Clarendon's *History of the Rebellion*, which produced a profound impression when it first appeared in 1702.[65] Beside it many placed the more brilliant and less solid essays of Lord Bolingbroke.

Party Condemned as Faction. For a long time party was deplored. It was commonly decried as " faction," and the concerted activity of partisans was roundly denounced as " conspiracy " and " combination." Not only Greek and Roman history but our own also could be used to provide warning examples: was not the Civil War itself the outstanding illustration of what faction might lead to ? The lesson was written at large in Clarendon's *History*, and Rochester's preface to it pointed the moral.[66] The tory sentiment was therefore in favour of unity within the nation, with men of all shades of opinion serving the crown side by side. That a group should force themselves upon the crown and compel it to forgo the services of members of a rival party seemed factious and presumptuous, derogatory to the monarch, and dangerous to the nation, which needs the service of its best men. The fact that the whigs had succeeded in carrying out this reprehensible manœuvre naturally confirmed the tories in their belief; the means whereby it had been effected—places and " influence "—made it more odious still.

Burke's Defence of Party. By slow degrees, opinion gradually came to tolerate parties. The charge of Jacobitism to which many tories were subject (more or less justifiably) enabled the whigs to maintain with some plausibility that the constitution and Protestantism were in peril, from

[65] *Cf.* K. G. Feiling, *History of the Tory Party*, 364, 372, 409.
[66] Feiling, *History of the Tory Party*, 364. One of the principal themes in Bolingbroke's works was an attack upon party, and at the Revolution, George Savile, Marquess of Halifax, had already set out in a famous tract *The Character of a Trimmer*.

which only whigs could save them. From 1714 the " whig supremacy " lasted until soon after the accession of George III in 1760. It was not a single party for long. It soon broke up into a number of groups which maintained a lively political warfare among themselves, and worked out the first principles of adjustment between party, parliament and cabinet. In short, party was coming to be tolerated. When George III and Lord Bute determined that the whig oligarchy must be broken, and office thrown open to tories as well as whigs, their attack was expressly directed to party as a principle; and it was on principle that Burke defended it in the closing pages of his *Thoughts upon the causes of the present Discontents* (1770). He skated lightly over the question of " influence," dismissed as mere cant the already venerable tag about " measures " rather than " men," and harked back to the remoter age of whig history, to " these wise men, for such I must call Lord Sunderland, Lord Godolphin, Lord Somers and Lord Marlborough . . . who were not afraid that they should be called an ambitious Junto; or that their resolution to stand or fall together should, by placemen, be interpreted into a scuffle for places. Party is a body of men united for promoting by their joint endeavours the national interest, upon some particular principle in which they are all agreed." [67] It remained for the nineteenth century to carry the process a stage further, and to accept the existence of party as one of the essential mechanisms of the political system.

THE SYSTEM AT WORK

All these factors which we have so far considered separately—the crown, the two houses, the ministers, the cabinet, the system of " influence," the political groups and parties—combined in actual practice to produce a remarkably subtle and delicate tissue of conventions and political habits, which, together with the underlying framework of the common law, made up the constitution.

The Fall of Clarendon. This era begins with the fall of Lord Clarendon in 1667. In his ideals and practices Clarendon was Tudor rather than Stuart. Queen Elizabeth and the practice of her day was often in his thoughts, and his belief in the privy council, in the role of the sovereign (a part which Charles II refused to play) and his dogma that parliament " was more, or less, or nothing, as the king chose to make it," and that parliament's sole function was to grant supply, were all much more Tudor than Stuart in character; indeed, the Stuart age was mainly concerned with demonstrating that these notions were already out of date. Clarendon's ministerial colleagues were not all of his way of thinking, and his fall was largely the work of cavaliers (like Lord Arlington) who had secured the sympathy of the king, while the king took to building

---

[67] Burke, *Select Works* (ed. E. J. Payne), i, 86. On " Measures and Men," see *ibid.*, 87 and the editor's notes, p. 279.

up a body of supporters in the commons which replaced the chancellor as the link between parliament and crown.[68]

The Cabal. With the fall of the *doctrinaire* Clarendon, English politics entered upon an experimental period under the guidance of men who were frankly opportunist in working out a new solution for a problem which was for the moment most obscure. The Cabal was a group of ministers whom the king consulted, owing duty to the king rather than to one another —indeed, their notorious divergence in religion and politics contrasts with later notions of ministerial behaviour. The results of such a system were the same whenever it was tried : the power of the crown was inevitably increased when the ministers no longer stood solidly together.

Lord Danby. The Test Act drove the Cabal from office, and into the breach stepped Sir Thomas Osborne, later Viscount Latimer, Earl of Danby, Marquis of Carmarthen and Duke of Leeds, who had steadily risen by his abilities through a long succession of financial offices, and enjoyed the patronage of Buckingham. Whereas Clarendon's system presupposed a king with a policy and vigour to carry it out, with parliament confined to voting supply, Danby's position was in some respects the reverse— " almost for the first time a minister who drew his entire resources from parliament presented the king with a clear and coherent programme of action." [69]   Soon raised to the peerage, Danby left the guidance of the commons in the hands of the Speaker, Sir Edward Seymour, but devoted himself to organising his own and the king's influence in the lower house, where he observed that even mediocrities could be extremely useful if their votes were organised—a portentous discovery.[70]

Danby for the first time organised a tory party, and carried out, as far as he could, the pro-Dutch and anti-French policy which the commons desired. But other questions supervened. The great Catholic problem was becoming acute, and the king pursued his own foreign policy, which was the opposite of his minister's. Thus although Danby effected the marriage of Princess Mary to William of Orange (1677), the king was still pro-French; indeed, so great was French influence that even whigs (including a Russell) were now on the pay-roll of Louis XIV, who was desperately anxious to get rid of Danby.

As it became clearer that Danby's policy would lead to the growth of royal independence of parliament, an opposition in the House of Commons took shape, with the Earl of Shaftesbury as its principal organiser. From that point the two parties were face to face, and the dramatic events which followed—the Popish Plot, the Exclusion Bill and the Revolution—have already been recounted,[71] and necessarily in terms of whig and tory politics.

---

[68] On the constitutional ideas of Clarendon, and the significance of his fall, see Keith Feiling, *History of the Tory Party*, 113–124; David Ogg, *Charles II*, i, 189, 451.

[69] Keith Feiling, *History of the Tory Party*, 154.

[70] David Ogg, *Charles II*, ii, 529.

[71] *Supra*, pp. 437 *et seq.*

With the accession of William III politics fell into quieter ways, and the long period of experiment in reconciling party politics with the traditional constitution began.

William III. The whigs, who claimed that they had secured the crown to William III, expected that he would choose his ministers solely from their ranks.[72] But the king was strongly opposed to government by party. He wished to retain the chief directing power himself, and to secure the support of a united parliament in carrying out his continental policy of opposition to Louis XIV of France. Accordingly, down to the year 1693, he distributed the chief offices in the government about equally between the two parties. Thus he gave office to professed tories such as Carmarthen and Nottingham, to professed whigs such as Russell, Pelham and Devonshire, as well as to the able but ambiguous Godolphin who was claimed (or disclaimed) by both parties.[73] But this policy, while it maintained the chief efficient power in the hands of the king, not only failed to secure unanimity among the various ministers of the crown, but even allowed of open hostility between them, as well in the discharge of their executive duties as in the discussions in parliament. The inconvenience of this state of things was so great that at length, between 1693 and 1696, acting on the advice of Robert Spencer, Earl of Sunderland, William abandoned the neutral position which he had hitherto maintained between the two parties, and entrusted all the chief administrative offices to the whigs, who commanded a majority in the House of Commons.

" The Junto," 1694–1698. The close union of the whig leaders, each promptly defending his colleagues against every attack, was so novel a spectacle that they became popularly known as " the Junto." The whigs monopolised office, ejected tories from the commissions of the peace, and used the recent plot to assassinate William as an excuse for rigorous measures against those whom they suspected of disaffection. But the ministerial system of government in its modern form was by no means as yet completely established. When, at the general election of 1698, a House of Commons was returned adverse to the Junto, and Montagu, who, as first lord of the treasury (and at the same time chancellor of the exchequer), had occupied the position and wielded the power of leader of the House, ceased to exercise any control over it, the ministry, instead of resigning office to their adversaries, as statesmen similarly situated would now do, kept their places. Nor did parliament address the king with a request to remove the ministers (as it had threatened to do earlier in the reign) since they had no charge of criminal misconduct to bring. Mere political disagreement was not yet sufficient cause by itself for demanding the resignation of a minister. Thus the old want of harmony between the

---

[72] *Cf.* Walcott, " English Party Politics, 1688–1714," in *Essays in Honor of W. C. Abbott.*
[73] See Feiling, *History of the Tory Party*, p. 275.

servants of the crown and the representatives of the people returned in full force, and continued, with some short intervals, until the general election of 1705 again sent up a whig majority to parliament.

Attempt to Revive Privy Council. It was during this interval of disunion between the cabinet and the majority in parliament, and while the possibility of still greater divergence, on the accession of a foreign dynasty, was present in men's minds, that an attempt was made at once to check the personal action of the king and to secure the responsibility of his ministers by the provisions of the 4th clause of the Act of Settlement. As a result of investigations into William III's diplomacy, the Lords presented an address complaining that the king had concluded the Partition Treaties without discussion in council. The matter was soon carried further by the Act of Settlement, which in its 4th clause provided, as we have seen, that after the accession of the House of Hanover, all matters relating to the government of the kingdom which were cognisable in the privy council, should be transacted there, and be authenticated by the signatures of such privy councillors as should advise and consent to the same. This and other clauses in the Act (on places, on judicial tenure, on foreign entanglements) finally enacted all those things which the opposition had been demanding since 1689, and are a notable example of what a ministry could be forced to accept by a hostile and determined House.[74] It was, however, soon perceived that this revival of the ancient authority of the privy council was an anachronism, and the clause was repealed, as already mentioned, early in Queen Anne's reign before it could come into operation.

Queen Anne's dislike of party. Queen Anne, equally with William III, displayed a strong and persistent preference for a mixed ministry, composed of the moderate men of each party. Her first ministry, throughout almost its whole existence, was of this character, consisting principally of Marlborough (whose only wish was adequate support for the war), Godolphin, Lord Treasurer (whom contemporaries were unable to classify), and Harley, Speaker (an ex-whig who was now the tory leader). A coalition of centre parties, it necessarily suffered attack by the extremer wings of both parties. The complete predominance of the whig element which finally ensued when Harley and St. John resigned in 1708 was very distasteful to the queen. In 1710 Harley and Shrewsbury formed a centre group to end the war, and by cautious stages extending over several months, the queen dismissed the leading members of the whig war party, notably Godolphin (Lord Treasurer) and Sunderland (Secretary of State)—in spite of the fact that whigs retained a solid parliamentary majority.[75] Both the queen and Harley were anxious to avoid a ministry

---

[74] On the political aspects see Keith Feiling, *History of the Tory Party*, 343 *et seq.* There is a real Clarendonian ring in the clause on the privy council.

[75] G. M. Trevelyan, *England under Queen Anne*, iii, 61 *et seq.*

entirely tory, and vainly endeavoured to induce the whig leaders to join in forming a coalition ministry, but with a preponderance of power in the hands of the tories.

The general election of that year, which was greatly influenced by the exertions of the clergy, who had been roused to opposition by the trial of Sacheverell, produced such a crushing defeat of the whigs, that the tory ministry under Harley, now made Earl of Oxford, retained undisputed sway until the close of the queen's reign (1714). It concluded the Peace of Utrecht against fierce opposition in the Lords [76] and came to an end in the extraordinary intrigue conducted in the Jacobite interest.

The Cabinet. It was, however, under the first two kings of the House of Hanover, the accession of whose dynasty was to have marked the extinction of the cabinet system, that parliamentary government by means of a ministry—nominally the king's servants, but really representing the will of the party majority for the time being in the House of Commons —was fully and finally established. This was due, in a great measure, to the personal character of George I and George II, who, aliens in blood, in language and in political sympathies, clung fondly to their beloved Hanover, and seemed to regard the kingship of Great Britain as an appendage, and rather an irksome appendage, to their small German Electorate.

" The troublesome energies of parliament," observes Sir Erskine May, " were an enigma to them; and they cheerfully acquiesced in the ascendancy of able ministers who had suppressed rebellions, and crushed pretenders to their crown—who had triumphed over parliamentary opposition, and had borne all the burden of the government. Left to the indulgence of their own personal tastes—occupied by frequent visits to the land of their birth, by a German court, favourites and mistresses —they were not anxious to engage more than was necessary in the turbulent contests of a constitutional government. Having lent their name and authority to competent ministers, they acted upon their advice, and aided them by all the means at the disposal of the court." [77] This indifference of the first two Georges to everything not affecting the interests of their continental dominions had most important and beneficial effects. It allowed the English constitution to develop freely under a kingship from which the element of personal royal power was for the time practically eliminated. George III strove hard throughout his reign to recover the ground lost under his two immediate predecessors; but the system of ministerial government with collective responsibility to the House of Commons was too firmly established to be overthrown, and is now regarded as a part of our polity almost as essential as the parliament itself.

[76] *Supra*, pp. 538, 541–542.
[77] May, *Constitutional History*, i, 7.

The desperate and unlucky intrigue of 1714 once again fastened the taint of Jacobitism on the tories, and the fact that many of them by their deeds belied their faith in legitimacy and non-resistance hindered rather than helped their prospects.[78] For half a century they were in the wilderness. Neither the '15 nor the '45 roused any hearty support, even among those who professed and called themselves Jacobites, but the entanglement was enough to keep the party impotent until the old cause was finally dead beyond recall. In the meantime there was a steady tory opposition all through the age of the whig supremacy which did useful work in criticism, and in denouncing certain elements which were indeed dangerous. " Standing armies, standing parliaments, and the moneyed interest " were their particular targets. Like their master Clarendon, they placed England's destiny in the hands of her navy instead of her army; frequently they denounced the Septennial Act; the Bank of England was in their eyes a whig contrivance, and they could point to the South Sea Bubble as a warning of the perils of financial speculation. The evils of party—another old tory tenet—were the more evident as the whigs dug in, and the tories strove hard (and sometimes with success) against " influence," " placemen " and parliamentary corruption in general. There was, therefore, a solid nucleus of opposition which could be augmented from time to time by dissident whigs so as to permit a genuine and lively political contest.[79]

The Stanhope Ministry of 1714–21. The new reign opened with an almost complete change of ministers—an occurrence of exceptional rarity, for the normal course was for changes to be made piecemeal, thus gradually altering the political complexion of government. For a precedent of so thorough a change we must go back to 1689, nor was the example followed so completely again until 1782 when Lord North was succeeded by Lord Rockingham. The principal figures were Lord Townshend as Secretary of State, replacing Bolingbroke,[80] and James Stanhope, his colleague, who spoke for the ministry in the Commons until he received a peerage in 1717. Montagu became first lord of the treasury and Earl of Halifax, and Lord Cowper received the great seal. Minor offices went to Townshend's brother-in-law, Robert Walpole, and to William Pulteney. The lord president of the council, the Earl of Nottingham, was by origin a tory, but had steadily co-operated with the whigs

---

[78] As Addison neatly put it, the tory creed was that " the Church of England will always be in danger till it has a Popish King for its defender ": Lord Mahon, *History of England*, i, 169n.

[79] " 162 tories voted against the Septennial Act in 1716 which clinched the whig power; in 1734, 154 voted for its repeal; 114 genuine tories (as opposed to courtiers) were returned to George III's first parliament." Keith Feiling, *Second Tory Party*, 2. Macaulay, in the opening of his essay on *Chatham*, roundly asserts that the parties had exchanged positions, " till at length the Tory rose up erect the zealot of freedom, and the Whig crawled and licked the dust at the feet of power." The controversy was continued by Lecky and Lord Mahon.

[80] In 1716 he was removed by the king and made Lord Lieutenant of Ireland.

to secure the Hanoverian accession; for practical purposes, therefore, the ministry was solidly of one party—another circumstance which made it remarkable.

Rise of Walpole. In the commons the skill in debate of Robert Walpole finally won him promotion, and before the end of the year 1715 he was first lord of the treasury. Meanwhile a new parliament had been elected (since Anne's would by statute expire six months after her demise), and a proclamation urged the electors to choose good Hanoverian Protestants—an impropriety which had frequently been condemned during the Middle Ages and later. As normally happened during the eighteenth century the elections agreed with the ministry. The new parliament's impeachment of Bolingbroke and Oxford for their part in the Peace of Utrecht was the last example of that procedure being used for merely political sanctions (as distinct from criminal) against a minister. At the same time, the Jacobite invasion of 1715 gave the excuse for the Septennial Act, and the whigs were now strongly entrenched. The ministry of Townshend and Stanhope soon began to fall apart, however, and Charles, Earl of Sunderland, led a secession, mainly on personal grounds. Many small causes of friction arose between the king and Townshend (and with him, Walpole) and in April 1717, Townshend was dismissed.[81] Walpole thereupon took the startling step of resigning in sympathy, and to contemporaries, and to the king, who had strongly urged him to desist, this seemed factious and intemperate behaviour. Pulteney and others likewise resigned in pursuance of their " criminal conspiracy " together.

There was worse to come. Walpole and his group entered upon the most factious opposition which had yet been witnessed; he fiercely denounced measures of which he had formerly approved, allied himself with the tories and even Jacobites, and showed what could be done by an opposition which regarded its only duty as being to oppose. Thus they defeated the Peerage Bill and other government measures; but, although troublesome, they did not shake the solid ministry of Lord Stanhope. In 1720 a pacification ensued between the king and the Prince of Wales (to whom Walpole had attached himself), accompanied by reconciliation among the ministers and ex-ministers; Walpole and Townshend accepted minor offices. The ministry fell with the South Sea Bubble. Lord Stanhope, who at least was innocent, died the day after an envenomed attack upon him in the lords; Craggs, secretary of state, died; his father, the postmaster-general, took poison; Aislabie resigned and was cast into the Tower, being succeeded [82] as chancellor of the exchequer by

---

[81] The very tangled story is told in Lord Mahon, *History of England*, i, Chaps. vii and viii. J. H. Plumb's *Life of Walpole* has begun to appear.

[82] After a brief interval during which Chief Justice Pratt was chancellor of the exchequer (*cf.* Lord Mansfield in 1757 and 1767, the object being to provide a titular head for the time being to the exchequer: Adolphus, *History of England*, i, 305). Walpole became chancellor of the exchequer (for the second time) on April 3, 1721 ; the next day he became first lord of the treasury, holding both offices until 1741.

Walpole, who had extricated himself from the market at the right moment with considerable profits. It was Walpole alone, in fact, who had sufficient technical skill to clear up the intricate relationships of the Treasury, the Bank and the South Sea Company. The success of his plan and the removal of so many rivals—Stanhope, Sunderland, Aislabie, Craggs— left Walpole the outstanding man of the day.

Walpole and his Colleagues. A new parliament maintained the whig majority, and vacant offices were filled, notably by Lord Carteret who as secretary of state stood for an active European foreign policy.[83] It was a severer strain than any cabinet could bear to have within it three such ambitious and imperious characters as Townshend, Walpole and Carteret. Carteret was the first to go, since the king was forced to choose between him and Townshend (1724). His successor was the Duke of Newcastle. The next year, through his own fault, Walpole lost a devoted friend in Pulteney, who had stood by him staunchly when he was in the Tower for corruption in 1711,[84] had resigned with him in 1717, and had long been an intimate companion. A brilliant parliamentarian, he was a potential rival, and Walpole refused his friend and ally a seat in his ministry until, after two years, he was admitted to the minor office of Cofferer of the Household. Pulteney finally learnt that there was nothing to be hoped for in working with Walpole and so went into opposition, joined Bolingbroke (now back from exile), and the two of them conducted the famous opposition paper *The Craftsman*. In 1725 Walpole procured the dismissal of the Duke of Roxburgh, Secretary of State for Scotland, on the express grounds that he consistently opposed the government's measures. Next appeared differences with Townshend over foreign policy; Walpole resented his brother-in-law's independent line, and in his own phrase, was determined that the firm should be " Walpole & Townshend," and not the reverse.

A crisis in Walpole's career came with the automatic termination of offices resulting from the death of George I. The new king's first act was an attempt to replace Walpole by Sir Spencer Compton (then Speaker of the House of Commons), but he abandoned it since the queen, for whose good judgment he had a well-founded respect, advised against it; indeed, two or three days were enough to show that Compton could neither form a ministry nor conduct the simplest business. To clinch matters, it was clear that Walpole could fulfil his promise to get a better civil list from parliament than Compton could. The old ministry was therefore renewed in office. The growing antipathy between Walpole and Townshend had almost culminated in a duel, when the latter retired from office

---

[83] See the valuable *Life of Stanhope*, and the study of *Carteret and Newcastle*, both by Basil Williams.

[84] Bills with Walpole's endorsements were put in evidence. Walpole seems to have regarded it as in his favour that he did not cash them, but negotiated them to certain political dependants.

and public life.[85] Henceforth Walpole was without a rival, supported by the House of Commons, and still more firm in his influence with the queen, and through her, with the king.

The Excise Bill. With Townshend and Carteret gone, a quiescent foreign policy ensued, and Walpole turned his attention to financial reform, and introduced his famous Excise Bill (1733). Unshakable at court, and supreme in his control of the commons, Walpole nevertheless failed to carry this reasonable and equitable measure. The opposition raised up a storm of protest throughout the country based on gross misrepresentation, and Walpole withdrew the measure, declaring that he would not collect any tax at the cost of bloodshed. It was his first defeat since the repeal of the patent for Wood's halfpence, which had united all Ireland against the ministry (1725). There had been some waverers in the ministry, alarmed at the menaces of the mob; with them Walpole dealt severely—vindictively, indeed, when it is remembered that ministerial solidarity was neither the theory nor the practice of the age: " surely, having yielded to the repugnance of the nation, Walpole might have forgiven the repugnance of his colleagues." [86] But two days after dropping the Bill, Lord Chesterfield and eight other peers were dismissed from Household offices, and the Duke of Bolton and Lord Cobham were deprived of their regiments. Such prompt and sweeping proscriptions were only possible through the complete ascendancy which Walpole exercised over the king; William III had refused to dismiss an officer for a parliamentary vote,[87] and the " Patriots " (as Bolingbroke and Pulteney had named their friends in opposition) vainly urged that senior officers should only be removed after a court martial. Walpole was unmoved; when in 1736 Cornet Pitt supported an address of congratulation on the marriage of the Prince of Wales, Walpole had him deprived of his commission. Contemporaries drew the conclusion that the minister meant to have no political dissent in any rank of the Army.[88] Equally unsuccessful was their motion to repeal the Septennial Act.

The Approach of War. The " Patriots " had hoped, but in vain, to draw some advantage from the death of Queen Caroline (November 1737) and fell back upon the stock topics of opposition, notably the " standing army " which a government spokesman in an unguarded

---

[85] That was in 1730. He devoted his leisure to the improvement of agriculture, and earned the nickname " Turnip Townshend " from his interest in that crop.

[86] Lord Mahon, *History of England*, ii, 255. (As a junior minister, Walpole had himself spoken against his chief's South Sea Bill.)

[87] Lord Mahon, *History of England*, ii, 263.

[88] Cornet is now replaced by second lieutenant; Pitt was already known as an ally of the Lord Cobham mentioned above. For some conjectures, see Lord Rosebery, *Chatham's Early Life and Connections*, 157 *et seq.* For the next seven years Pitt held an appointment in the prince's household.

moment declared to be necessary to the whig interest.[89]   In the classical manner of oppositions, the patriots demanded the reduction of the army and also the declaration of war against Spain.   On this issue Walpole was growing steadily weaker, and his neglect of the Press left him at a disadvantage in the pamphlet war which was—significantly—beginning to master the government.   His secretary of state, Newcastle, and his chancellor, Hardwicke, were against him; earlier in his career Walpole would have secured the summary dismissal of such dissident colleagues, but circumstances had changed, for the king was himself convinced that war was inevitable.   Walpole therefore had to tolerate as best he could these dissensions within the cabinet.   The public was equally incensed by the famous incident of " Jenkins' Ear."   The attack in the lords was led by Chesterfield and Carteret (ex-colleagues of Walpole); in the commons the government majority fell to 28.   Thereupon Pulteney and the opposition walked out in a dramatic gesture of secession.   This manoeuvre, as on the other occasions when it was attempted, failed to embarrass the government or excite the public.   Walpole yielded, but to the clamour for war which arose among the people and at court, rather than to the opposition.   War was declared in October, 1739.

Walpole as a War Minister.   Walpole was now a minister pursuing a policy which he believed to be wrong, and which he had tried hard to escape.   He stayed in office, nevertheless, partly no doubt because he was loth to leave it, partly perhaps because the old tradition still required the king's ministers to carry on his business, whether they liked it or not.   The war was far from successful, and the attacks upon Walpole for its failure grew more and more fierce as the operation of the Septennial Act brought a general election nearer.   In February 1741, it was moved by Samuel Sandys to address the king to remove Walpole from his presence and counsels for ever; he declared that all the nation's calamities were attributable to one person, Walpole, " because that one person has grasped in his own hands every branch of government; that one person has attained the sole direction of affairs, monopolised all the favours of the Crown, compassed the disposal of all places, pensions, titles, ribands, as well as all preferments, civil, military and ecclesiastical; that one person has made a blind submission to his will, both in elections and parliament, the only terms of present favour and future expectation." [90] Those words describe the nature of Walpole's government as his enemies saw it, and Walpole in his reply to the debate had to admit, at least for argument's sake, that he was " prime and sole minister in this country." Walpole defeated the motion by a large majority, partly because many opponents abstained from voting, and partly (it would seem) because, for the second time in his life, he had made an unholy pact with the

[89] Lord Mahon, *History of England*, ii, 397.
[90] *Ibid.*, iii, 104.

Jacobites.[91] However that may be, Walpole's triumph was apparent rather than real.

Walpole's Defeat. The general election of 1741 was tumultuous; the use of troops to keep order at the Westminster poll added point to the opposition's denunciation of the " standing army," and the Prince of Wales subscribed to their campaign fund. Walpole's majority fell in the new House to sixteen. Election petitions (which were then decided by the House in strict party votes) gave the ministry majorities of seven, and a defeat (on the Westminster petition) by four. Still Walpole hung on. When it seemed likely that the opposition could out-vote the government by one on the famous Chippenham election petition, Walpole allowed it to be known that he intended to resign, and the result was a majority of sixteen against him. He took leave of the king on February 1, 1742; the Chippenham division was on the 2nd; the Houses adjourned at the king's request on the 3rd for two weeks.

Walpole as Prime Minister. We are not here concerned with the charges hurled at Walpole, save those of a constitutional character. The passage just cited from Samuel Sandys' speech makes it clear that the opposition pressed its charge that he was a " prime minister." " According to our constitution," said Sandys, " we can have no sole and prime minister; we ought always to have several prime ministers [92] or officers of state; every such officer has his own proper department; and no officer ought to meddle in the affairs belonging to the department of another." The alternative to a prime minister is therefore the system which came to be called " government by departments." Walpole's defence may have been merely tactical, or it may have represented his genuine opinion upon the problem—it is difficult to say; in any case, Walpole did not deny Sandys' theory, but took his stand upon a denial of the fact, and maintained that he had not acquired the position ascribed to him. The fact that Walpole chose this very difficult ground for his defence seems to indicate that he felt it would be still more hazardous to attempt a defence of the principle of a prime minister. Forty years later Lord North was placed in the same quandary, and he, too, denied that he had been a " prime

---

[91] Jacobitism always revived in war time since there was more probability of foreign intervention in their favour (that was one of Walpole's principal reasons for avoiding war). At this moment, Walpole had secret communications with the Pretender, which were accepted with natural surprise and suspicion. This possibly accounts for the fact that the tories abstained from voting on the motion. Moreover, Walpole seems to have had in addition some secret hold over Shippen, the Jacobite leader in the House. See the letter in Lord Mahon, *History of England*, iii, app. l–li, who comments (iii, 34) that " no one will do Walpole the injustice to suspect him of sincerity." Lord Morley, *Walpole*, 231, unnecessarily would cast doubt upon Walpole's being implicated at all in the transaction. More recent discoveries make it clear that Walpole tricked the Jacobites. See I. S. Leadham, in *The Dictionary of National Biography*.

[92] This odd expression is matched by another mentioning " the queen and her prime ministers " Godolphin and Marlborough (G. M. Trevelyan in *The Times Literary Supplement*, xxix, 214).

minister "—although by now he permitted a doubt whether " government by departments " was altogether satisfactory, since it permitted so much power in the crown. By 1803 the younger Pitt at last ventured to maintain the constitutional propriety, and the practical necessity, of the office of prime minister. Walpole's twenty years of power, therefore, had not yet standardised the conception of the prime minister's constitutional position, nor even settled the question that such a position was desirable.

If we overrule Sir Robert's protests and persist in calling him " prime minister," we must do so on the grounds which Sandys adduced: Walpole had assumed the sole direction of affairs, had monopolised the ear of the king, and had made himself the sole source of favour. He had succeeded in this, however, as a result of his skill and personality; he was not using powers which were the normal attributes of an office. He had no predecessor, nor did he pass on this situation to a successor. Walpole's primacy was thus purely personal, and not official. It contrasted in other ways as well with that of a modern prime minister. Thus Walpole did not construct his ministry all at once. It was a slow process of modification, in which he could not simply call upon a colleague to resign, but had to persuade the king (or the colleague) that withdrawal was necessary. And just as Walpole's ministry was in fact a continuation of the one that preceded it, so on Walpole's fall his colleagues did not resign with him, many of them continuing in office after him.

Pulteney's Ministry. The political manoeuvres after Walpole's fall are good illustrations of how far removed the practice of the mid-eighteenth century was from that of the nineteenth. Walpole continued to be active behind the scenes, especially with a view to preventing his impeachment, for which there was a considerable clamour. The king asked the principal opposition leader, William Pulteney, to form an administration with as few changes as possible, and pledged not to impeach Walpole. This remarkable condition Pulteney refused,[93] but he finally accepted on the basis that he would not be vindictive; he added that " as the disposition of places is in my hands, I will accept none myself; I have so repeatedly declared my resolution on that point, that I will not now contradict myself." So Lord Wilmington became first lord of the treasury,[94] Samuel Sandys, chancellor of the exchequer, and Lord Carteret a secretary of state, the Duke of Newcastle remained the other secretary of state, his brother Henry Pelham remained as paymaster of the forces, and Lord Hardwicke remained as chancellor. For himself Pulteney asked for the earldom of Bath, and a seat in the cabinet. It will be seen that one of the principal attributes of a modern prime minister—that of selecting

[93] He was in doubt whether his followers would accept it: " for the heads of parties are like the heads of snakes, carried on by their tails." Lord Mahon, *History of England*, iii, 162 *et seq.*

[94] This was the Sir Spencer Compton who had tried to form a ministry in 1727; at this moment he was president of the council under Walpole.

his colleagues—was exercised by Pulteney, who himself held no office whatever; that he nevertheless sat in the cabinet; and that the office of first lord was given to a man whom everyone agreed was a moribund nonentity. Within a few hours Pulteney saw his blunder in leaving the House of Commons, where his influence was very great, and tried to stop the issue of his patent, but Walpole's influence was used against him inexorably: " the prostrate minister had from the dust worked Pulteney like a marionnette." [95] A great House of Commons man, Pulteney was ineffective in the lords, and realised too late that a seat in the cabinet without office carries very little power; the ministry was in effect Carteret's; and there was no one of his own weight to defend the ministry in the commons, save the solicitor-general, Sir William Murray, who was eager to leave the House for the bench. [96]

The Pelhams. On the death of Wilmington (1743), Henry Pelham became first lord (Walpole's influence again blocked Lord Bath, who had now changed his mind about taking office); then the two Pelhams forced Carteret out (again Walpole advised the king to submit). In 1745 the Pelhams made overtures to Pitt, who in all these changes had been left out. For years he had bitterly attacked the king, Carteret and Hanover. In 1745 he judged that the situation was different, and in 1746 he entered the ministry as paymaster. The opposition had thus lost its thunder, and some years of quiet followed. Pelham died in 1754 and the Duke of Newcastle became first lord. It was by now perfectly clear that no ministry could exist unless it made its peace with the perennial duke who specialised in patronage and held the great whig connection together. [97] No attempt was made by these ministries to maintain the strict Walpolean discipline. Thus Henry Fox, secretary-at-war, and Charles Townshend [98] of the Board of Trade fiercely attacked Lord Hardwicke's Marriage Act (1753), and in 1755 Fox and Pitt (paymaster) both began to attack Newcastle, although both retaining their offices. Newcastle dealt differently with his two rebels. Fox was tamed by admission to the cabinet [99]; Pitt was dismissed (1755).

The Seven Years War broke out in 1756, and the initial disasters created a grave situation. Admiral Byng was executed as a scapegoat

---

[95] Lord Rosebery, *Chatham: Early Life and Connections,* 177.

[96] Nevertheless, he faithfully served the Pelham administrations as Solicitor-General for twelve years, and two more as Attorney-General, before becoming Chief Justice of the King's Bench as Lord Mansfield.

[97] Thomas Pelham Holles (1693–1768), Lord Chamberlain, 1717–1724; Secretary of State, 1724–1754; First Lord of the Treasury, 1754–1756, 1757–1762; Privy Seal, 1765—a record of almost unbroken office exceeded only by Lord Burleigh. See Basil Williams, *Carteret and Newcastle.*

[98] Grandson of Walpole's rival.

[99] An earlier negotiation with Fox had broken down as the Duke refused to disclose the patronage position although he wanted Fox to lead the House: "If I am kept in ignorance of this," said Fox, " how shall I be able to talk to members, when some may have received gratifications, and others not ?" Lord Mahon, *History of England,* iv, 35. Very similar language was used by George Grenville when he attempted to lead the House, but without this indispensable information: Lecky, *History of England,* iii, 205.

for the ministers and in response to public clamour.[1] Newcastle (and Hardwicke with him) resigned. He realised that only able support in the commons could maintain a ministry, and that support was lacking, especially as Murray insisted upon becoming chief justice. The Duke of Devonshire consented to become first lord, and chose Pitt as secretary of state, on the ground that Pitt had much public support, to replace Fox, who had very little.

William Pitt's Ministry, 1756–1761. The rejected Duke of Newcastle taught Pitt a lesson. Some of the new ministers, Pitt among them, had the greatest difficulty in getting re-elected on their appointments; some were actually defeated. The king, too, could not forget the years of savage insults which Pitt had hurled at him while in opposition. In April 1757, the ministry was dismissed on the demand of the Duke of Cumberland, who refused to take up his command of the troops on the Continent as long as Pitt was in office. At last Pitt accepted the fact that Newcastle was indispensable to him, as Newcastle had already learned that his system by itself could not win a war. The ministry was reconstructed, with Newcastle as first lord. It would be idle to describe either Devonshire or Newcastle as " prime minister " in any reasonable sense of the word.[2] " I am sure," Pitt told the former, " that I can save this country, and that nobody else can." So Newcastle returned to his skilful jobbery, which kept the political machine running smoothly, while Pitt devoted himself to the most spectacular series of victories in our history.

Pitt's View of Politics. The political ideas which Pitt had long held were singularly well adapted to a war minister. In the first place, he eschewed political parties and connections. He soon broke with Lord Cobham [3] under whom he served his earliest years as one of " the Boys." He had powerful family connections with the Lytteltons through his mother, and the " cousinhood " of the Grenvilles through his wife (who was a sister of five Grenville brothers, the eldest of whom was Lord Temple). He quarrelled bitterly with both groups. By nature he was a free-lance, and he adopted that position as a principle. In October 1764 he wrote to the Duke of Newcastle: " As for my single self, I purpose to continue acting through life upon the best convictions I am able to form, and under the obligations of principles, not by the force of any particular bargains. . . . I have no disposition to quit the free condition of a man standing single, and daring to appeal to his country at large

---

[1] And *pour encourager les autres*, as Voltaire expressed it in *Candide*.

[2] A neat solution is to describe Devonshire as " for a while prime minister under Pitt ": Lord Rosebery, *Chatham*, 289.

[3] Sir Richard Temple, Lord Cobham (whose sister was mother of the Grenvilles and of Pitt's wife), took to politics when Walpole took away his regiment. On these connections, see Lord Rosebery, *Chatham: Early Life*, 130 *et seq.*

upon the soundness of his principles and the rectitude of his conduct." [4]
A little later it was reported " that he wished for the sake of his dear
country that all our factions might cease; that there might be a ministry
fixed such as the king should appoint and the public approve." [5] With
Pitt this was evidently an outcome of his own peculiar and difficult
character, but it brought him, in fact, to the same position as the tories
had reached generations ago, and the position to which George II latterly,
and George III soon, were to be led as they realised more and more keenly
how tight the hold of the whig magnates had become.

Pitt and the Party System. Party politics was, moreover, already
breaking down under its own complexity, and contemporaries had surprising difficulty in applying the terms " whig " and " tory " in the years
following 1750.[6] The timid Henry Pelham had robbed it of much of its
significance by drawing into his ministry all his outstanding opponents
or possible rivals—a striking reversal of Walpole's policy—and so produced the most uneventful epoch in English parliamentary annals.

Pitt and the House of Commons. Feeling as he did about party, and
party politics being in the chaotic state in which we find it in the middle
of the eighteenth century, it is not surprising that Pitt's attitude towards
the House of Commons, the great arena where the game was played,
was highly critical, and at times supercilious. He was occasionally
compelled, as we have seen, to take a hand in the business of politics as it
was conducted by Newcastle, Hardwicke, Fox, and his own embarrassing
train of Grenvilles; but it was only as a distasteful, if necessary, means
to an end. The House he frequently cowed with his famous glance,
crushing at least momentarily ministers, colleagues and opponents with
his overwhelming personality. He was the first to urge that there must
be a reform of the representative machinery, in 1766 and again in 1770.[7]

Pitt and the Public. As the passage already quoted has shown, Pitt
looked beyond the House of Commons to " his country at large," and
his political system consisted in the close union of king and country in
the person of the minister. So well was this understood, that it seemed
to George II incongruous when Pitt urged clemency for Admiral Byng
on the ground that the commons recommended it: " Sir," said the king,

[4] *Chatham Correspondence*, ii, 296–297; Lecky, *History of England*, iii, 283.

[5] *Bedford Correspondence*, iii, 333; Lecky, *loc. cit.*

[6] " ' Tory ' had become a label signifying independence or waywardness, yet perfectly
compatible with general support of ' Whig ' ministries. So Nugent had recommended
to Newcastle a Liverpool friend who ' though a dissenter and a good Whig, is a leading
man among the Tories.' Just as vague were the lists of members which were annotated
by Bute and his agents. Mr. Ongley of Bedford was ' Bedford ' but also ' Tory ' . . .
Armytage of York was Tory, though ' brought in by Lord Rockingham.' " Keith Feiling,
The Second Tory Party, 72.

[7] His thoughts were turned into this direction by the proposal to represent the American
colonies at Westminster.

" you have taught me to look for the sense of my people in other places than the House of Commons." His enemies roundly accused Pitt of cultivating the mob: at this juncture, however, Pitt and the mob took opposite views of the Byng question. They came together over the Wilkes issues, and separated again over the American question. It is true, however, that Pitt often received enthusiastic support from the towns and mercantile interests. For a large part of his career Pitt could indeed claim to have the nation behind him. Somehow he achieved this although none of the modern machinery for that purpose was yet available. He had little support from the pamphleteers; it was not yet the custom for ministers or politicians to organise and address large public meetings; his parliamentary speeches were very poorly reported, if at all; and his temperament did not make him easy of access. Such arts as lay within his reach, however, he employed to the full. All who knew him agree that he was intensely theatrical, and gave profound study to all the means of making a powerful impression; he " was perhaps the first of those statesmen who sedulously imbue the public with a knowledge of their merit." [8] All that is somewhat disquietingly modern; it was certainly very shocking to many of his contemporaries.

Pitt and the Cabinet. Neither Pitt's character nor his principles fitted with the contemporary idea of relationships among the ministers. His deliberate rejection of the party system would inevitably have led to " government by departments." On the other hand his imperious nature marked him out as a " prime or sole " minister. The famous incident which caused his resignation in 1761 summed up all these elements. The cabinet was solidly against Pitt on the question of declaring war against Spain, and he finally closed the proceedings with the famous words: " I was called by my sovereign and by the voice of the people to assist the state when others had abdicated the service of it. That being so, no one can be surprised that I will go on no longer since my advice is not taken. Being responsible I *will* direct; and will be responsible for nothing that I do not direct." Equally well known is the comment by Lord Granville (the Carteret of a previous generation): " when the gentleman talks of being responsible to the people, he talks the language of the House of Commons, and forgets that at this board he is responsible only to the king." [9]

George III; the "King's Friends." Pitt resigned on October 5, 1761. George III had succeeded his grandfather upon the throne on October 25, 1760. The young king's aims were, briefly, to break up the whig

[8] Lord Rosebery, *Chatham*, 258. Mr. Gladstone's preparations for an election campaign in 1874 seemed to Lord Shaftesbury " a new thing and a very serious thing ": F. Holland's continuation of May, *Constitutional History*, iii, 87.
[9] On the authenticity of this incident, see Basil Williams, *William Pitt, Earl of Chatham*, ii, 112–114 and *English Historical Review*, xxi, 119, 327.

hegemony which had reduced the crown to a humiliating position of insignificance in the last fifty years; to throw open to all who were worthy of it, irrespective of party connections, the service of the public in the ministry; and to end the war, which the country was beginning to feel a heavy drain.

In pursuance of his settled resolve to wrest all power from the hands of his ministers and to exercise it himself, George began his reign by calling to his aid a cabal of secret counsellors, with the Earl of Bute— a peer of Scotland, formerly his tutor, and at that time his groom of the stole—at their head. These were mainly composed of tories whose Jacobite tendencies had hitherto kept them apart from public affairs, but who now, having " abjured their ancient master, but retained their principles," [10] brought to the service of the new sovereign the reverential sentiments which had distinguished the adherents of the Stuarts. Tories alone, however, were much too weak, and in fact they were joined by several groups of dissident whigs, such as the Duke of Bedford's " Bloomsbury Gang," by Henry Fox himself (who was in the main Walpole tradition), and by George Grenville. Supported by these " king's friends " and their followers in the House of Commons, the king endeavoured to govern through ministers whose appointment was to a large extent dependent on the king's good will, and disposed at his own will the vast amount of ecclesiastical, military and civil patronage which, during the reigns of his two immediate predecessors, had been appropriated by the ministers of the hour, to supplement the already considerable political " influence " of the great whig houses.

The Bute and Grenville Ministries. On the second day after his accession (October 25, 1760), the king had caused Lord Bute to be sworn of the privy council, and admitted into the cabinet. The existing ministry, which had been formed in June, 1757, by a coalition of the Duke of Newcastle with the elder Pitt, were indeed retained in office, but Bute was the real adviser of the king, and held himself forth as the sole expounder of the royal will and opinions.[11] Within five months (March 25, 1761) he was gazetted a secretary of state; within thirteen—having in the meantime got rid of Newcastle and the other ministers who declined to retain responsibility without power—the favourite attained the object of his ambition in May, 1762, as prime minister. A few days afterwards he obtained the Order of the Garter. Such a rapid rise would have excited envy even in the case of a very able man; but Lord Bute was below mediocrity. In the minds of the populace, Bute's greatest fault was to be a Scot, and floods of lampoons inflamed this prejudice. He succeeded in putting an end to the Seven Years War, by the Peace of Paris (February 10, 1763). For the highly skilled, but very unsavoury, task of securing

---

[10] Walpole, *Memoirs*, i, 15, cited by May, *Constitutional History*, i, 13.
[11] Lord Mahon, *History of England*, iv, 322.

parliamentary approval, he employed Henry Fox—who had a number of personal scores to settle—and the traditional means of corruption, political bargaining, and the ruthless expulsion from office of opponents, were employed with a more than Walpolean severity. The affair earned for Fox much odium, and a peerage.[12] But Bute's intense unpopularity both within and without parliament soon rendered his position as minister untenable; and afraid, as he himself declared, " not only of falling himself, but of involving his royal master in his ruin," [13] he suddenly resigned on April 8, 1763. He retained, however, his influence at court and hoped to direct the measures of the new ministry which, under the leadership of George Grenville, the king had appointed, at his recommendation. But the new premier was by no means contented to be the mere agent of Lord Bute, and the king ultimately found himself bound to dismiss the favourite from court, and to promise that he should not be suffered to interfere in the royal councils " in any manner or shape whatever."

The Policy of Proscription. The " policy of proscription " carried out by Bute and Fox was primarily directed to carrying the Preliminaries of the Peace of Paris through parliament. The Duke of Devonshire— " the prince of the whigs," as the king's mother sarcastically termed him —having declined to attend the council summoned to decide upon the peace with France—a measure highly unpopular with the nation—was insulted by the king, forced to resign his office of lord chamberlain, and was struck out of the list of privy councillors by the king's own hand. For presuming, as peers of parliament, to express disapprobation of the peace, the Dukes of Newcastle and Grafton and the Marquis of Rockingham were dismissed from the lord-lieutenancies of their several counties, and the Duke of Devonshire, to avoid a similar affront, found it necessary to resign. Earl Temple was also dismissed from the lord-lieutenancy, and struck off the list of privy councillors on account of his friendship for John Wilkes, whose journal, the *North Briton*, had excited the anger of the court by denouncing the peace and the ministry with unexampled boldness and bitterness. For their votes in parliament, General Conway, a brave soldier and honourable politician, was dismissed from his civil and military commissions, Colonel Barré and Colonel à Court were deprived of their military commands, and Lord Shelbourne of his office of aide-de-camp to the king. Fitzherbert was removed from the Board of Trade, Calcraft from the office of deputy muster-master. All parliamentary placemen who failed to vote in accordance with the king's wishes were summarily dismissed, and even clerks in public offices and other small officials shared the fate of the patrons by whom they had been appointed.[14]

[12] See Lord Ilchester's biography of *Henry Fox, Lord Holland* (2 vols., 1920).
[13] Lord Mahon, *History of England*, v, 38. There has been much speculation why he resigned at this apparently triumphant moment.
[14] Lord Mahon, *History of England*, v, 33.

The " policy of proscription " was soon, however, destined for a time at least to very ignominious failure. Very shortly after Grenville's appointment to the premiership (April 16, 1763), differences sprang up between him and the king. It was the intention of Lord Bute and the king that he should be merely the agent for carrying out their wishes; but although as narrow-minded and imperious in his political views as the king himself, he was also equally confident in his own abilities, equally fond of power, and equally unbending in maintaining what he conceived to be his rights. Grenville and Bedford secured in 1765 a signal triumph in getting the king to promise to have no political dealings with Bute [15]; and George III scrupulously adhered to this undertaking,[16] although the gossips continued for some years to regard Bute as a secret influence, even while he was in Scotland or Italy. Twice during Grenville's ministry, and in spite of his objections, did the king open negotiations with Pitt for the formation of a new ministry, but on each occasion without success. Though willing to receive Pitt, he could not bring himself to admit those other " ministers of the late reign who had attempted to fetter and enslave him," whom Pitt demanded as colleagues, but whom the king had declared he would " never upon any account suffer to come into his service while he lived to hold the sceptre." [17]

The Rockingham Ministry, 1765. At length, in 1765, utterly wearied of the Grenville ministry, and determined at any cost to be rid of them, he found himself (July 13) reduced to the necessity of accepting as premier the whig Marquis of Rockingham, whom he had so recently removed from his lord-lieutenancy; while General Conway, who had been dismissed from an office in the king's household and from the command of his regiment, became secretary of state and ministerial leader of the House of Commons. Lord Rockingham's group of whigs consisted of younger men, it seems, who made some attempt to purge the old connection of those abuses which had brought it to disaster. To Macaulay " the Rockingham party was exactly what a party should be." [18] It had certainly the high merit of including Edmund Burke, who first entered public life as Rockingham's private secretary. But though forced by circumstances to place in office men whom he detested, George III was still determined to have his own way. He now adopted a different system of tactics. Having, in 1766, vainly resisted in council the proposal of his ministers to repeal the Stamp Act, which they deemed absolutely necessary for the conciliation of the American colonies, he opposed them in parliament by means of an organised opposition of the " king's friends," made up not only of independent members of the court party, but of office-holders under the crown, who were encouraged by the king to

---

[15] Lord Mahon, *History of England*, v, 159–160.
[16] *Ibid.*, v, 176.
[17] *Bedford Correspondence*, iii, 224.
[18] Macaulay, *Essay on Chatham*.

oppose his ministers, and were retained and protected in their offices while voting with the opposition.[19]

Ministry of Grafton and Chatham, 1766. After twelve months' tenure of office, Rockingham was dismissed by the king (July 1766); and Pitt, who was now raised to the Upper House as Earl of Chatham, was prevailed upon to form an administration on non-party lines, with the Duke of Grafton as first lord of the treasury, he himself taking the post of lord privy seal. The second ministry of Pitt was, however, anything but a success. The " Great Commoner " lost his popularity by the acceptance of a peerage, and the ministry was weakened by his absence from the commons. It is certain, however, that even in the Lower House Pitt could no longer have played his old part, for the mysterious and melancholy illness by which he was shortly prostrated soon prevented him from taking any active part in the administration, from which he retired in October 1768, leaving it to be carried on by the Duke of Grafton amidst ever-increasing difficulties.

At length, in 1770, the Grafton ministry resigned after an attack upon it in the lords by Chatham and Camden (at that very moment lord chancellor), and in the commons by another cabinet minister. The whig party being divided into two sections, composed of the respective followers of Rockingham and Chatham, the king adroitly seized the opportunity of their disunion to make Lord North—chancellor of the exchequer in the late administration—his prime minister, the seventh in ten years.

The King and Lord North's Ministry, 1770–1782. It was during Lord North's administration, which lasted for twelve years (1770 to 1782), that the personal influence of the king attained its highest pitch. " Not only," we are told, " did he direct the minister in all important matters of foreign and domestic policy, but he instructed him as to the management of debates in parliament, suggested what motions should be made or opposed, and how measures should be carried. He reserved to himself all the patronage; he arranged the entire cast of the administration; settled the relative places and pretensions of ministers of state, of law officers, and members of his household; nominated and promoted the English and Scottish judges; appointed and translated bishops, nominated deans, and dispensed other preferments in the church. He disposed of military governments, regiments, and commissions, and himself ordered the marching of troops. He gave and refused titles, honours, and pensions." [20] The king, in fact, exercised all those powers which the textbooks ascribed to the crown, but which had been captured by ministers during the whig

---

[19] The king's friends are principally known from Burke's fierce attack upon them in his *Thoughts upon the Present Discontents* (1770), echoed in Macaulay's *Essay on Chatham*. For an attempt to disentangle the facts from Burke's professedly partisan pamphlet, see Lord Mahon, *History of England*, v, 178 *et seq.*

[20] May, *Constitutional History*, i, 58; *Correspondence of George III with Lord North*, 1768–1783 (ed. Donne), *passim*.

ascendancy. He was, in fact, as declared by Mr. Fox in the House of Commons, " his own unadvised minister," Lord North submitting to be the mere mouthpiece of his royal master, and continuing to carry on the American war, although, as he informed the king in 1779, " he held in his heart, and had held for three years past," the opinion that its continuance " must end in ruin to his Majesty and the country."

Career and Character of North. Lord North's long ministry, coming after so many short and insecure administrations, calls for some examination. He entered politics under his kinsman the Duke of Newcastle, becoming a junior lord of the treasury in the great Pitt-Newcastle ministry in 1759, resigning on the accession of Rockingham in 1765. He was chancellor of the exchequer in 1767 in the Chatham-Grafton ministry, and continued so until his fall in 1782, adding the office of first lord of the treasury from 1770 to 1782 (the usual eighteenth-century practice unless the first lord was a peer, when the offices were separated).

Physically lazy, and temperamentally procrastinating and easy-going, North never sought office, and when he had it, was constantly trying to lay it down. Not being a careerist, he could afford to have principles and to vote as he thought fit, and justly claimed that he had never courted popularity. As chancellor of the exchequer during a very difficult period, and in his dealings with the East India Company, he showed his ability to deal with technical and complicated matters and to make them intelligible to the house. Above all, he was an admirable House of Commons man, humorous and unruffled under the heaviest fire of Burke, Fox, Dunning, and (at the end) the younger Pitt, and a most effective debater. In spite of these solid assets, Lord North was beset by a curious distrust of himself, and so too often allowed his better judgment to be deflected —especially by the king.[21]

North's Constitutional Practice. North, like the king, was jealous for the privileges and dignity of the House of Commons; it was on these grounds that they took their stand in the Wilkes affairs (mistakenly, perhaps, but sincerely), and it was in the name of parliament's (not the crown's) right to tax the colonies that they prosecuted the American war. Like many of his predecessors, North disliked being called a prime minister. Whereas Pitt had received a somewhat mysterious call from the voice of the people, North explained his position in terms which had long been familiar: " there are two grounds upon which a minister ought to stand; the first was that the king had an undoubted right of naming his own servants; the second, which formed the happiness of this country, that if the people by their representatives did really disapprove the

---

[21] *Cf.* Lord Mahon, *History of England*, v, 381 *et seq.*, the biography of *Lord North* by W. Baring Pemberton (1941), H. Butterfield, *George III, Lord North and the People*, 1779–1790, R. Pares, " George III and the Politicians," *Transactions of the Royal Historical Society* (1951), 127.

measures of any minister, to that degree that they would not go along with him, the king—however he might approve the minister—could not carry on business by him, and must part with him." [22]   North received ample parliamentary support, and he felt that as long as it lasted, and as long as the king also required his services, it was his duty to continue in office, although he often pleaded in vain for his release.

The constitutional issues raised by George III, however, concerned ministers and the cabinet rather than parliament.   On this matter North admitted that his practice was one of expedients rather than principle. He and most of his colleagues had been members of the previous admini-stration, which had been a typical Chatham construction of very mixed composition, and this lack of solidarity caused him trouble: " War can't be carried on in departments; there must be consultation, union and a friendly and hearty concurrence in all the several parts which set the springs at work, and give efficiency and energy to the movement, without which the machine must fail." [23]   Charles James Fox urged a strict cabinet discipline as a political principle, to which Lord North made the comment: " if you mean that there must not be a government by departments, I agree with you.   I think it a very bad system.   There should be one man or a cabinet to govern the whole, and direct every measure.   Government by departments was not brought in by me.   I found it so, and had not vigour and resolution to put an end to it." [24]

To enforce his system of personal government the king professed himself ready to adopt the most extreme measures.   In 1770, when Lord Chatham was about to move an address for dissolving parliament, the king, in a conversation with General Conway, said, laying his hand upon his sword: " I will have recourse to this sooner than yield to a dissolu-tion." [25]   He several times threatened to abdicate and retire to Hanover rather than accept ministers or measures of which he disapproved: a threat which was on one occasion met by the significant remark of Lord Thurlow: " Your Majesty may go; nothing is more easy; but you may not find it so easy to return when your Majesty becomes tired of staying there."

The Royal Veto.   Since the accession of the House of Hanover no sovereign of this country has exercised the prerogative of refusing the royal assent to a bill which has passed both Houses,[26] but it is not

---

[22] *Parliamentary History*, xviii, 994 (1775); W. B. Pemberton, *Lord North*, 256.

[23] Letter of Robinson (secretary to the treasury) to the first lord of the admiralty, who had not consulted the cabinet on various matters (1777); *Sandwich Papers* (Navy Records Society), i, 240.

[24] *Fox Correspondence*, ii, 38; C. S. Emden, *The People and the Constitution*, 151; North continued with the characteristic whig remark: " the king ought to be treated with all sort of respect and attention, but the appearance of power is all that a king of this country can have."

[25] Rockingham, *Memoirs*, ii, 179.

[26] The last occasions on which the prerogative of rejecting Bills was exerted were in 1692 and 1694, when William III refused the royal assent to the Bill for Triennial Parliaments and the Place Bill, and in 1707, when Queen Anne rejected a Scotch Militia Bill.

surprising to find that George III was prepared to do so. "I hope," he wrote to Lord North in 1774, " the crown will always be able in either House of Parliament to throw out a bill; but I never shall consent to use any expression that tends to establish that at no time the right of the crown to dissent is to be used." [27] This explanation of the disuse of the power is clearly correct. Royal influence (exercised either by the king, or by his ministers) could defeat a Bill in its earlier stages, and so the royal dissent was unnecessary.[28] Increasingly numerous attempts were made to deal with the problem of " influence," notably in a Bill for Economical Reform promoted by Burke, which would have abolished a number of rich sinecures. While the House was in committee upon various public petitions on the subject, in 1780 Dunning proposed and carried his celebrated resolution affirming " that it is now necessary to declare that the influence of the crown has increased, is increasing, and ought to be diminished " [29]; but it was not until the lapse of two more years, and after repeated motions of want of confidence in the government, that Lord North was compelled to resign office.

Rockingham's 2nd Ministry. The king was now once more forced to fall back upon the whigs, and Lord Rockingham again (March 1782) became prime minister. The circumstances of his new ministry are notable for the thoroughness with which offices were changed; practically an entirely new body of men took office, Lord Chancellor Thurlow being the only man of importance who had served under Lord North.

Reforms by Rockingham and Shelburne. The new ministry produced the Civil Establishment Act, 1782, the results of which were not very startling—at least as far as " influence " is concerned. Nevertheless, the Act did inaugurate an important movement. " The conclusion to be drawn," says a recent authority,[30] " would therefore seem to be that the true importance of economical reform cannot be found solely—or perhaps even mainly—in the history of parliament or of the whig legislation of 1782. The work of that year is important chiefly, it is suggested, in beginning a process of *administrative* reorganisation, to which the whigs were in the main indifferent and which was carried forward chiefly by tories. It did not attempt to eliminate influence, and was sometimes even charged with increasing it. It aimed only at more effectively organising the executive government. But in doing so, it profoundly changed the relation between the executive and the legislature. The former ceased to be the instrument of the crown, and began to become that of parliament." Rockingham died, however, in the July following, when

---

[27] June 26, 1774, in Lord Brougham's *Statesmen of the Time of George III*, i, p. 85.
[28] For a discussion of the views of Burke, Disraeli and Dicey on the later position of the veto, see Sir Ivor Jennings, *Cabinet Government*, 296–297.
[29] *Parliamentary History*, xxi, 347. The fact that some of North's followers voted with Dunning is explained by the fact that a general election was pending.
[30] D. L. Keir, " Economical Reform," *Law Quarterly Review*, 1, 368 at 373.

the king conferred the office of first lord of the treasury upon the Earl of Shelburne, the leader of the Chathamite section of the whig party—a choice which caused a large part of the ministry, including Charles James Fox, Burke and the Duke of Portland, who represented the Rockingham section, to resign and go into factious opposition. Some of them put forward the untenable doctrine that upon the death, in office, of a prime minister, it was the right of the cabinet, and not the king, to choose his successor.[31] Lord Shelburne continued in office long enough to conclude the Peace of Versailles (January 20, 1783), by which George III at length acknowledged, without reserve, the independence of the United States of America.

Coalition of Fox and North, 1783. But when the preliminary articles of peace were laid before parliament, the discontented whig faction led by Fox entered into an unnatural coalition with the followers of Lord North, and by their adverse majority in the House of Commons compelled Lord Shelburne to resign.

The king struggled hard against " his new tyrants," the successful leaders of the coalition. Twice he vainly solicited the younger Pitt [32] —who had recently held office for the first time as Lord Shelburne's chancellor of the exchequer—to form an administration; but at length (April 2, 1783), he found himself constrained to accept the coalition ministry, of which the Duke of Portland, Fox, and Lord North were the chiefs. Chafing at his renewed bondage, the king now thwarted his ministers to the utmost of his power, and revived the unconstitutional tactics of 1766, through an organised opposition in parliament by means of " the king's friends."

Fox's India Bill. In order to defeat in the lords the India Bill introduced by Fox, Secretary of State Lord Temple was authorised to protest against it in the king's name and to canvass the peers against this measure of his own ministers. " His Majesty," the king wrote on a card, as an authority for the proceeding, " allows Earl Temple to say that whoever voted for the India Bill was not only not his friend, but would be considered by him as an enemy ; and if these words were not strong enough, Earl Temple might use whatever words he might deem stronger, and more to the purpose." [33] Indignant at this conduct, the commons passed a resolution, on December 17, 1783, " that to report any opinion, or pretended opinion, of his Majesty, upon any Bill, or other proceeding, depending in either House of Parliament, with a view to influence the votes of the members, is a high crime and misdemeanour, derogatory to the honour of the crown, a breach of the fundamental privileges of parliament, and

---

[31] M. A. Thomson, *Constitutional History*, iv, 371, discusses the alleged precedent at the death of Pelham in 1754.

[32] Chatham had died May 11, 1778; William Pitt the younger was his second son.

[33] Duke of Buckingham's *Court and Cabinets of George III*, i, 285.

subversive of the constitution." [34]   On the very day that this resolution was passed, the House of Lords rejected the India Bill, and on the following day the king dismissed his ministers.[35]

Dismissal of the Coalition Ministry, 1783. This abrupt and contemptuous dismissal of a ministry who were supported by a vast majority in the House of Commons, although defeated on a major issue in the lords, brought the king into critical conflict with his parliament, from which he was only saved by the genius, perseverance, and tact of William Pitt, who now consented to undertake the formation of a government.   The fall of the coalition showed that a ministry supported by the commons might have to yield before the king and the lords.   The younger Pitt now demonstrated that a ministry supported by the king and lords might hold on long enough against a hostile House of Commons to acquire support in the nation, and win an election.   In spite of votes of want of confidence, and of attempts to prevent a dissolution by postponing the supplies, the youthful premier of twenty-five gained the enthusiastic support of the nation, and within four months the opposition majority, which had been two to one against the ministry, dwindled down to a bare majority of one.   Fox stoutly maintained that the whole course of events—the Temple incident, the dismissal of the coalition, and the continuance in office of Pitt after votes of censure had been passed against him—was unconstitutional.   Pitt replied that "the immediate appointment or removal of ministers does not rest with this house.   There is, therefore, nothing illegal in a minister's remaining in office after this house has declared against him."   He declared that the House had no right to ask the crown to remove ministers unless it brought criminal charges against them, and proved the charges.[36]   The lords joined in by censuring the commons for their unwarrantable attempt to dismiss a ministry.   Parliament was now dissolved; the old Pitt magic worked again; the great cities and the commercial interests rallied round him, and a general election gave to Pitt an overwhelming majority, which maintained him in power for seventeen years.   The triumph of the king and the minister was complete; the classical whig view that the crown was merely an ornament was gone [37]; the ascendancy of the crown was established, and continued, for nearly fifty years, to prevail over every other power in the state.   But the king's will was no longer supreme, as it had been during the administration of Lord North.   Although he continued his accustomed activity in public affairs, " he had now a minister who, with higher abilities and larger views of state policy, had a will even stronger than his own.   Throughout his reign it had been the tendency of the

[34] *Commons' Journals,* xxxix, 842.
[35] May, *Constitutional History,* i, 67–71; *infra,* p. 647 n. 44.
[36] C. S. Emden, *Speeches on the Constitution,* i, 59–61.   See generally, Lecky, *History of England,* v, 242–260.
[37] Horace Walpole observed that the crown devolved on the King of England upon the death of Lord Rockingham: Lecky, v, 164.

king's personal administration to favour men whose chief merit was their subservience to his own views, instead of leaving the country to be governed —as a free state should be governed—by its ablest and most popular statesmen. He had only had one other minister of the same lofty pretensions—Lord Chatham; and now, while trusting that statesman's son—sharing his councils, and approving his policy—he yielded to his superior intellect." [38] The wishes of the king, however, still exercised great influence on the ministers in the general policy of the government; and it was the king's persistent refusal to sanction the introduction of a measure for the relief of the Roman Catholics which at length caused Pitt in 1801 to resign. Out of personal regard for the king, he shortly afterwards promised never to revive the catholic question; and on his again taking office in 1804, he was prevented from strengthening his government by the admission of Mr. Fox to the cabinet, by the king's absolute refusal. George declared " that he had taken a positive determination not to admit Mr. Fox into his councils, even at the hazard of a civil war." [39]

Pitt's View of the Office of Prime Minister. Looking back over his long experience of office, the younger Pitt was able to describe the functions of a prime minister as not only a practical necessity, but as a generally recognised and settled part of the practice of English political life. The authority which many thought it was criminal for Walpole to use, and which Chatham had achieved only by sheer weight of personality, was now claimed by his son as the undoubted attribute of a position with which statesmen were by now perfectly familiar. He authorised Lord Melville to explain his attitude in a letter to Mr. Addington. Melville wrote (in 1803) that Pitt was emphatic " with regard to the absolute necessity there is in the conduct of the affairs of this country, that there should be an avowed and real minister, possessing the chief weight in the council, and the principal place in the confidence of the king. In that respect there can be no rivalry or division of power. That power must rest in the person generally called the prime minister, and that minister ought, he thinks, to be the person at the head of the finances. He knows, to his own comfortable experience, that notwithstanding the abstract truth of that general proposition, it is noways incompatible with the most cordial concert and mutual exchange of advice and intercourse amongst the different branches of executive departments; but still, if it should come unfortunately to such a radical difference of opinion that no spirit of conciliation or concession can reconcile, the sentiments of the minister must be allowed and understood to prevail, leaving the other members of administration to act as they may conceive themselves conscientiously called upon to act under the circumstances." [40]

[38] May, *Constitutional History*, i, 87.
[39] Rose's *Diaries and Correspondence*, ii, 156, 182: Horace Twiss, *Life of Eldon*, i, 446 *et seq.*
[40] The letter is in Lord Stanhope, *Life of Pitt*, iv, 24 (in ed. 1879, iii, 111–112).

During the successive ministries of Henry Addington (1801), Pitt (1804), Lord Grenville,[41] Charles James Fox and Addington, known as " All the Talents " (1806), the Duke of Portland (1807) and Spencer Perceval (1809), down to the year 1810, when the king's mental disease necessitated the appointment of a regency, the personal influence of the sovereign remained predominant. In 1807, George III even went so far as to require a written declaration from the Grenville ministry that they would never, under any circumstances, propose to him further concessions to the Roman Catholics, or even offer him any advice upon the subject.[42] This flagrantly unconstitutional pledge, which (so Sir Samuel Romilly maintained in parliament) would have rendered any ministers who gave it guilty of a high crime and misdemeanour,[43] was firmly but respectfully refused, and the refusal was immediately followed by their virtual dismissal. For the last time a sovereign dismissed a ministry.[44]

Since the reign of George III, but more especially since the Reform Act of 1832 made the House of Commons more like what it had ceased to be—a body really representing the opinions of the largest estate of the realm, the commons of England—the personal influence of the sovereign in the executive administration has steadily declined. It has, however, been asserted at intervals with effect. Under George IV, the influence of the crown remained paramount, and the two great parties in the state sought the royal favour first, as the avenue to parliamentary support. Yet it was in this reign that the remnant of independent kingship which had survived the Revolution, and even acquired renewed vigour and extension in the hands of George III, may be said to have expired on the day when that king's son and successor, after a prolonged struggle, finally gave his consent to the Bill for Roman Catholic emancipation in 1829.

Lord Melbourne's " Dismissal," 1834. It was believed by well-informed persons at the time, and long afterwards, that William IV, in November 1834, endeavoured to assert his personal wishes in the choice of a ministry, without reference to the will of parliament, by suddenly dismissing the whig ministry of Lord Melbourne, and entrusting to Sir Robert Peel the formation of a government from a party whose followers numbered less than a fourth of the House of Commons. It is now known that there was no question of dismissal; Melbourne had placed a number of possible courses before the king, leaving it expressly for him to choose between them or " any other course." The king, on the strength of this peculiar

---

[41] Youngest son of the prime minister of 1763–65.

[42] Letter of Lord Grenville to Marquis of Buckingham, March 17, 1807, in Buckingham's *Court and Cabinets of George III*, iv, 143. George II had exacted a pledge not to impeach Walpole: *supra*, p. 634.

[43] *Parliamentary Debates*, ix, 327.

[44] The last *formal* dismissal was in 1783. *Supra*, p. 645.

proceeding, chose the "other course" of inviting Peel to form a government.[45]

The new premier dissolved parliament; and the general election again returned a liberal majority, much smaller indeed than the former one, but sufficient, more compact, and better organised. After a gallant struggle —in which he rivalled the great qualities formerly displayed by Pitt, and defended himself by the same arguments [46]—against the hostile majority which his appeal to the country had evoked, Peel was compelled to resign, and in April 1835 the Melbourne ministry, with some alterations, was reinstated in office. The fact that Peel failed where Pitt had succeeded, is the measure of the great reform of 1832. In the eighteenth century the ministry in office could rely upon winning an election; but in 1834 the election was lost. While influence could turn an election, a dissolution was a powerful weapon for the crown, and language to that effect was used even after 1832 by both Peel and the queen [47]—the true significance of the new régime was not unmistakably clear until after 1867.

The Bedchamber Question, 1839. Growing unpopularity caused the Melbourne ministry to resign in 1839, and the summons of Sir Robert Peel to form an administration gave rise to what is known as the " Bed-chamber Question." Nearly all the ladies of the household were related to the members of the Melbourne cabinet, or to their political adherents; and Sir Robert Peel, convinced of the difficulties which would beset a minister who should leave about her Majesty's person the nearest relatives of his political opponents, informed the queen that he could not under-take the formation of a ministry unless he was permitted to make some changes in the higher offices of the court, including the ladies of her bed-chamber. The queen, by the advice of Lord Melbourne and his colleagues, refused " to adopt a course which she conceived to be contrary to usage, and which was repugnant to her feelings." Sir Robert Peel declined to accept office on those terms; and the Melbourne ministry conducted the government for two years longer. It again resigned in 1841, after an appeal to the country had failed to reverse the verdict of the House of Commons, pronounced by a majority of one, on a resolution of Sir Robert Peel, affirming that the ministers of the crown did not possess the confidence of the House of Commons, and " that their continuance in office under such circumstances was at variance with the spirit of the constitution." On assuming office, Peel met with no further difficulties on the bedchamber question; and the principle for which he

---

[45] Sir Ivor Jennings, *Cabinet Government*, 299–302. On the subtle question whether Peel was " responsible " (as he thought he was) for what was then believed to be the dismissal of Melbourne, see his speech in C. S. Emden, *Speeches on the Constitution*, i, 16; Sir Ivor Jennings, *op. cit.*, 338–340; A. Berriedale Keith, *The Constitution* (1940), i, 57–59.

[46] C. S. Emden, *Speeches on the Constitution*, i, 62–65, 66 *et seq.*

[47] Discussed in Jennings, *op. cit.*, 313 *et seq.*

contended has since been admitted, on all sides, to be constitutionally correct.[48]

The Queen's Memorandum, 1850. A more recent illustration of the personal share which the sovereign takes in public business is afforded by the memorandum communicated by the queen, in 1850, through Lord John Russell, her prime minister, to Lord Palmerston, the Secretary of State for Foreign Affairs. " The queen requires," it declared, " first, that Lord Palmerston will distinctly state what he proposes in a given case, in order that the queen may know as distinctly to what she has given her royal sanction. Secondly, having once given her sanction to a measure, that it be not arbitrarily altered or modified by the minister. Such an act she must consider as failure in sincerity towards the crown, and justly to be visited by the exercise of her constitutional right of dismissing that minister. She expects to be kept informed of what passes between him and the foreign ministers before important decisions are taken based upon that intercourse; to receive the foreign dispatches in good time; and to have the drafts for her approval sent to her in sufficient time to make herself acquainted with their contents before they must be sent off." But in controlling one minister the sovereign still acts upon the advice and responsibility of another—her first minister—to whom copies of dispatches and other information are also communicated in order to enable him to give such advice effectually.[49]

Constitutional Right of Dismissing a Minister. The constitutional right of dismissing a minister, asserted in the queen's memorandum, is now practically placed at the disposal of the premier and the cabinet, who are thus enabled as a whole, to exercise, through the crown, a check upon each individual member. This was exemplified, shortly after the French *coup d'état* of December 2, 1851, when Lord Palmerston was removed from the foreign secretaryship in Lord John Russell's administration on the ground that he had exceeded his authority in expressing to the French ambassador opinions favourable to the policy of the recent *coup d'état* and at variance with the non-intervention despatch agreed upon by the cabinet.[50]

Increased Power of the Executive. While the personal influence of the sovereign in the government of the country has steadily decreased since the reign of George III, the power of the crown, as wielded by its ministers, has continued to increase from the Revolution down to the present time.

---

[48] By the existing arrangement, which has now long prevailed, " the mistress of the robes, who is . . . only an attendant at court on great occasions, changes with the ministry; but the ladies in waiting, who enjoy much more personal contact with the sovereign, are appointed and continue in their appointments without regard to the political connections of their husbands "—Gladstone, *Gleanings*, i, 40.

[49] Martin, *Life of the Prince Consort*, ii, 305. Statement by Lord John Russell, Hansard, *Debates*, 3rd ser., cxix, 91; May, *Constitutional History*, i, 160; Sir Ivor Jennings, *Cabinet Government*, 276.

[50] May, i, 160–162.

The expansion of the empire, the great extension of public establishments, the vast increase of patronage—civil, military, and ecclesiastical—and the more profuse distribution of honours, have all largely added to the influence of the executive government, while its coercive power has been augmented by the establishment of the police, the recent concentration of the military forces, the abolition of purchase in the army, and the transfer of the command and jurisdiction over the auxiliary forces to the sovereign, to be exercised through the Secretary of State for War. During the reign of Queen Victoria the power and influence of the crown, always wisely and constitutionally exercised for the public benefit, on the advice of responsible ministers, provoked no attempts at restraint; and the personal power of the sovereign, as distinguished from the power of the regal office, having been restrained within due limits, the ancient jealousy of the crown, inherited from the struggles of our ancestors, may now almost be said to have died out.

Gladstone's Views. The delicate relations of the cabinet to the crown on the one hand, and to the Houses of Parliament and the people on the other, as well as the internal relations of its members to one another and to the premier, have not yet been touched upon. They are indeed topics upon which none but a cabinet minister is fully competent to speak. Fortunately, we now possess an account of them, at once graphic and authentic, from the pen of a most distinguished modern premier, which constitutes a classical statement of nineteenth-century practice. " The association," says Mr. Gladstone, " of the ministers with the parliament, and through the House of Commons with the people, is the counterpart of their association as ministers with the crown and the prerogative. The decisions that they take are taken under the competing pressure of a bias this way and a bias that way, and strictly represent what is termed in mechanics the composition of forces. Upon them, thus placed, it devolves to provide that the Houses of Parliament shall loyally counsel and serve the crown, and that the crown shall act strictly in accordance with its obligations to the nation. . . . In the face of the country the sovereign and the ministers are an absolute unity. The one may concede to the other; but the limit of concession by the sovereign is at the point where he becomes willing to try the experiment of changing his government; and the limit of concession by the ministers is at the point where they become unwilling to bear, what in all circumstances they must bear while they remain ministers, the undivided responsibility of all that is done in the crown's name. But it is not with the sovereign only that the ministry must be welded into identity. It has a relation to sustain to the House of Lords; which need not, however, be one of entire unity, for the House of Lords, though a great power in the state, and able to cause great embarrassment to an administration, is not able by a vote to doom it to capital punishment. Only for fifteen years out of the last fifty [1878] has the ministry of the day possessed the confidence of the House of

Lords. On the confidence of the House of Commons it is immediately and vitally dependent. This confidence it must always possess, either absolutely from identity of political colour, or relatively and conditionally."

Of the members of the cabinet, Mr. Gladstone proceeds: " Every one of them acts in no less than three capacities: as administrator of a department of state; as member of a legislative chamber; and as a confidential adviser of the crown. Two at least of them add to these three characters a fourth; for in each House of Parliament it is indispensable that one of the principal ministers should be what is termed its leader. This is an office the most indefinite of all, but not the least important. With very little of defined prerogative, the leader suggests, and in a great degree fixes, the course of all principal matters of business, supervises and keeps in harmony the action of his colleagues, takes the initiative in matters of ceremonial procedure, and advises the House in every difficulty as it arises.

Internal Relations of the Cabinet. " The nicest of all the adjustments involved in the working of the British government is that which determines, without formally defining, the internal relations of the cabinet. On the one hand, while each minister is an adviser of the crown, the cabinet is a unity, and none of its members can advise as an individual, without, or in opposition actual or presumed to, his colleagues. On the other hand, the business of the state is a hundredfold too great in volume to allow of the actual passing of the whole under the view of the collected ministry. It is therefore a prime office of discretion for each minister to settle what are the departmental acts in which he can presume the concurrence of his colleagues, and in what more delicate, or weighty, or peculiar cases, he must positively ascertain it. So much for the relation of each minister to the cabinet; but here we touch the point which involves another relation, perhaps the least known of all, his relation to its head.

" The head of the British government is not a grand vizier. He has no powers, properly so called, over his colleagues; on the rare occasions when a cabinet determines its course by the votes of its members, his vote counts only as one of theirs. But they are appointed and dismissed by the sovereign on his advice. In a perfectly organised administration, such for example as was that of Sir Robert Peel in 1841–1846, nothing of great importance is matured, or would even be projected, in any department without his personal cognisance; and any weighty business would commonly go to him before being submitted to the cabinet. He reports to the sovereign its proceedings, and he also has many audiences of the august occupant of the throne. He is bound, in these reports and audiences, not to counterwork the cabinet; not to divide it; not to undermine the position of any of his colleagues in the royal favour. . . . As the cabinet stands between the sovereign and the parliament, and is bound to be loyal to both, so he stands between his colleagues and the sovereign, and is bound to be loyal to both.

" As a rule, the resignation of the first minister, as if removing the bond of cohesion in the cabinet, has the effect of dissolving it. A conspicuous instance of this was furnished by Sir Robert Peel in 1846; when the dissolution of the administration, after it had carried the repeal of the Corn Laws, was understood to be due not so much to a united deliberation and decision as to his initiative. The resignation of any other minister only creates a vacancy. In certain circumstances, the balance of forces may be so delicate and susceptible that a single resignation will break up the government; but what is the rule in the one case is the rare exception in the other. The prime minister has no title to override any one of his colleagues in any one of the departments. So far as he governs them, unless it is done by trick, which is not to be supposed, he governs them by influence only. But upon the whole, nowhere in the wide world does so great a substance cast so small a shadow; nowhere is there a man who has so much power, with so little to show for it in the way of formal title or prerogative." [51]

Not the least of the many advantages which have accrued from the establishment of the cabinet form of parliamentary government has been the increase security of the crown and of its ministers. The old constitutional maxim that " the king can do no wrong " is now literally true, for his acts are really the acts of his ministers; and his ministers are responsible to the House of Commons not merely as of old, for any breach of the law, but for the general course of their policy, which must accord with the opinions of the majority of that House, or else, in conformity with a constitutional usage practically as binding as a legal enactment, the ministers are bound to resign office. Instead of a revolution or a parliamentary impeachment, a change of ministry suffices to preserve harmony between the crown and the people.

[51] " Kin beyond Sea," published in *North American Review*, September 1878, republished in *Gleanings of Past Years*, i, 225, 235, 241, 242–244. For a detailed examination of the working of the modern cabinet system see Sir Ivor Jennings, *Cabinet Government*, and A. Berriedale Keith, *The British Cabinet System* (both works survey the last hundred years of cabinet history).

CHAPTER 20

CIVIL LIBERTIES

GROWTH OF RELIGIOUS LIBERTY

PROTESTANT nonconformity, fostered instead of being crushed by the very efforts of the church to enforce unity, had gained considerably in numbers, organisation, and political weight, during the reigns of the last two Stuarts; and the important services of the dissenters, in combining with the church to bring about the revolution of 1688, were rewarded by the Toleration Act.[1]

Toleration Act, 1689. This famous statute was far indeed from granting religious freedom; it repealed none of the Acts by which conformity with the Church of England was exacted, and left the civil disabilities of nonconformists under the Corporation Act of 1661 and the Test Act of 1673 [2] intact; but it recognised, for the first time, the right of public worship beyond the pale of the state church, by exempting from the penalties of existing statutes against separate conventicles and absence from church, all persons who should take the oaths of allegiance and supremacy, and subscribe a declaration against transubstantiation. Dissenting ministers were relieved from the restrictions imposed by the Act of Uniformity and the Conventicle Act upon the administration of the Sacrament and preaching in meetings,[3] on condition that, in addition to taking the oaths, they signed the Thirty-nine Articles, with the exception of three and part of a fourth.[4] Quakers were allowed to make an affirmation in lieu of taking the oaths. All meeting-houses were required to be registered, but when registered their congregations were protected from molestation. For the purposes of this Act, "toleration" means that the criminal law ceased to compel all lay subjects to conform to the Church of England, and that it ceased to be a crime to profess certain non-Anglican forms of Christianity, or to assemble for the exercise of the religious rites of dissenters. Even in this restricted sense, toleration was not extended to Catholics: and the " civil disabilities " of dissenters, excluding them from office, etc., remained.

The principle of religious toleration was as yet, however, imperfectly established. Roman Catholics and unitarians were specially excepted

---

[1] 1 Will. & Mary, sess. 1, c. 18; Grant Robertson, *Documents*, 123.
[2] *Supra*, pp. 423 *et seq.*
[3] *Supra*, pp. 427 *et seq.*
[4] The articles excepted (as expressing the distinctive doctrines of the church) were arts. 34, 35, 36, and part of art. 20.

from the Act, and were soon afterwards subjected to additional penalties. Unitarians were disabled in 1698 from holding any office ecclesiastical, civil, or military [5] and Roman Catholics were placed under the most severe restrictions.[6]   In 1699 an Act was passed offering a reward of £100 for the discovery of any Roman Catholic priest exercising the functions of his office, and subjecting him to perpetual imprisonment. By the same Act every Roman Catholic was declared incapable of inheriting or purchasing land, unless he abjured his religion upon oath, and on his refusal his property was vested, during his life, in his next of kin, being a protestant.   He was also prohibited from sending his children abroad to be educated.[7]

During the tory ascendancy of the last four years of Queen Anne's reign, serious inroads were made upon the toleration formerly granted to protestant nonconformists, more especially by two statutes, the Occasional Conformity Act [8] and the Schism Act.[9]   The former, passed in 1711, was intended to prevent the evasion of the Test Act by occasional conformity on the part of those dissenters who, while adhering to their own form of worship, did not hesitate occasionally to receive the sacrament according to the rites of the established church.   The other Act, passed in 1713, " to prevent the growth of schism," was framed with the object of striking a blow at the political power of the whigs, who owed much to the support of the dissenters, and of securing to the Anglican church the control of education; it deprived dissenters of the means of educating their children in their own religious beliefs, by crushing all nonconformist schools, some of which had already attained a certain degree of eminence.

Indemnity Acts.   These reactionary statutes were, however, both repealed in 1718, under George I,[10] and from the beginning of the reign of George II civil offices were practically thrown open to protestant dissenters, by means of the Annual Indemnity Acts passed in favour of those who had failed to qualify themselves under the Corporation and Test Acts.[11]   The severe laws against the Roman Catholics, although enforced by a proclamation of Queen Anne in 1711, by a further Act of

[5] 9 Will. 3, c. 35.
[6] 1 Will. & Mary, sess. 1, c. 9 (1689).
[7] 11 Will. 3, c. 4; cf. 13 & 14 Will. 3, c. 6.
[8] 10 Anne, c. 6; Robertson, *Documents*, 187; *supra*, p. 541.
[9] 13 Anne, c. 7; Robertson, 190. See H. Mclachlan, *English Education under the Test Acts: Nonconformist Academies, 1662–1820* (Manchester, 1931).
[10] 5 Geo. 1, c. 4. In 1697, Sir Humphrey Edwin, Lord Mayor of London, and a presbyterian, gave great offence to churchmen by going in civic state to a dissenting meeting-house. To prevent any repetition of the scandal, the Act of 5 Geo. 1 (now repealed by the Statute Law Revision Act, 1871), while repealing the Occasional Conformity Act, enacted that no mayor, bailiff, or other magistrate should attend any public meeting for religious worship, other than that of the Church of England, in the gown or with the ensigns of his office, on pain of being disqualified to bear any public office whatsoever.
[11] The first Indemnity Act was passed in 1728 (1 Geo. 2, st. 2, c. 23). Since then, with a few exceptions, similar Acts were annually passed, until the repeal of the Test and Corporation Acts in 1828.

Parliament after the rebellion of 1715,[12] and by another royal proclamation after the rebellion of 1745, were also greatly mitigated in practice.

Lord Hardwicke's Marriage Act, 1753. In 1753, a fresh restriction was imposed upon dissenters by Lord Hardwicke's Marriage Act, the immediate object of which was to prevent clandestine marriages. While removing many serious scandals from English life, and putting the marriage law on a new and sounder basis, it added a new disability to nonconformists. Dissenters had previously been allowed to be married in their own places of worship; but by this Act all marriages, except those of Jews and Quakers, were required to be solemnised in a church, by ministers of the establishment and according to its ritual.[13]

Toleration under George III. It was not, indeed, till the reign of George III that the gradual relaxation of the religious penal code was commenced in earnest. Early in this reign the broad principles of toleration were judicially affirmed by the House of Lords, in the case of the City of London and the dissenters.[14] " It is now no crime," said Lord Mansfield in moving the judgment of the House, " for a man to say he is a dissenter; nor is it any crime for him not to take the sacrament according to the rites of the Church of England; nay, the crime is, if he does it contrary to the dictates of his conscience." " Persecution for a sincere, though erroneous, conscience, is not to be deduced from reason or the fitness of things; it can only stand upon positive law. The Toleration Act renders that which was illegal before, now legal; the dissenters' way of worship is permitted and allowed by this Act; it is not only exempted from punishment, but rendered innocent and lawful; it is established; it is put under the protection, and is not merely under the connivance, of the law." " There is nothing certainly," he added, " more unreasonable, more inconsistent with the rights of human nature, more contrary to the spirit and precepts of the Christian religion, more iniquitous and unjust, more impolitic, than persecution. It is against natural religion, revealed religion, and sound policy." [15]

The penal code, as regards both Roman Catholics and protestant dissenters, was gradually, though unsystematically, relaxed. By the Roman Catholic Relief Act of 1778, the precursor of the " No Popery " riots under Lord George Gordon in 1780, supplemented by another

---

[12] 1 Geo. 1, st. 2, c. 55.

[13] 26 Geo. 2, c. 33; Robertson, *Documents*, 223. For the evils of the old system which were removed by this Act see Lecky, *History of England*, ii, 115 *et seq*.

[14] *Chamberlain of London* v. *Allen Evans* (1767). The suit, originally instituted in the sheriff's court, was for a fine (under a by-law made in 1748) for refusing to serve as sheriff, on the ground of disability arising from not having taken the Sacrament, according to the rites of the Church of England, within a year before, as required by the Corporation Act of 13 Car. 2. (Judgment of the House for the defendant.)

[15] *Parliamentary History*, xvi, 313–327.

Act in 1791,[16] various penalties and disabilities were removed. Priests were no longer subjected to perpetual imprisonment for the performance of their sacred functions; Roman Catholic heirs educated abroad were relieved from forfeiture of their estates to the next protestant heir; the prohibition to purchase landed property was removed; a modified freedom of worship and education was permitted; and Roman Catholic peers, though still barred by the oath of supremacy from sitting in the House of Lords, were relieved from the banishment from the king's presence to which they had been subjected in 1678.[17]

In 1779, the Dissenting Ministers Act [18] relieved protestant dissenting preachers and schoolmasters from the limited subscription to the Thirty-nine Articles required by the Toleration Act, and a further measure in 1812 [19] relieved them from the remaining oaths and declaration required by the latter statute. The following year witnessed the removal of the disabilities under which unitarians had laboured by a statute,[20] repealing the exception of anti-trinitarians from the benefits of the Toleration Act, as well as the provisions against them in the Act of 9 Will. 3, c. 35 " for the suppression of blasphemy and profaneness."

The civil disabilities of dissenters under the Test and Corporation Acts still remained to be grappled with. These monuments of bygone bigotry were not only unjust to a large and worthy section of the community, but hurtful to the very cause of religion itself by turning the most sacred ordinance of Christianity into " an office-key, a pick-lock to a place." [21] As early as 1718 the first Lord Stanhope, anxious, as he declared, to place the dissenters on a footing of perfect equality with churchmen, had endeavoured to procure the repeal of the Test Act at the same time that the Occasional Conformity and Schism Acts were abrogated. But owing to the strong opposition, the repeal of the Test Act was deferred to a more favourable opportunity. In 1736, Plumer brought forward a motion for its repeal; but Walpole, who had for years obtained the support of the dissenters by holding out the hope of his assistance when an opportune moment should arrive, voted against the motion, which was defeated by a majority of 128.[22] Half a century passed before another attempt was made by Beaufoy, in 1787, but, though repeated in 1789, his motion was unsuccessful. Fox was the next to take up the subject, in 1790, yet even his advocacy was impotent to overcome the determined opposition to a repeal. After a lapse of nearly forty years, Lord John Russell, more fortunate than his predecessors, obtained in 1828 a success for which they had vainly striven. The civil disabilities of dissenters were at last swept away by the repeal of the Test and

[16] 18 Geo. 3, c. 60, and 3 Geo. 3, c. 32.
[17] 30 Car. 2, st. 2.
[18] 19 Geo. 3, c. 44.
[19] 52 Geo. 3, c. 155.
[20] 53 Geo. 3, c. 160.
[21] Cowper, *Works*, i, 80.
[22] Lord Mahon, *History of England*, i, 488; ii, 280.

Corporation Acts; the sacramental test previously required as a qualification for civil, military and corporate offices being replaced by a declaration, " upon the true faith of a Christian," against injuring or disturbing the established church.[23]

Roman Catholic Relief Act, 1829. The following year, 1829, witnessed the passing of the Roman Catholic Relief Act. From the date of the union with Ireland in 1801, the injustice of maintaining the political disabilities of the Roman Catholics in a United Kingdom of which they formed no inconsiderable portion of the population became more and more glaring. But George III declared that he " should reckon any man his personal enemy " who proposed any measure of relief; and during his life the liberal concessions which Pitt was anxious to make were compulsorily postponed. Under George IV the question, which was annually contested in parliament, assumed a graver aspect. The " Catholic Association," formed by Daniel O'Connell, kept up a constant appeal to the excited passions of the Irish people, and at length the tory ministry of the Duke of Wellington, finding it necessary to choose between concession and civil war, introduced and, with the aid of the whigs, carried through both Houses the Roman Catholic Relief Act of 1829. This measure, to which George IV was with difficulty induced to give a reluctant and hesitating assent, was tardy indeed, but complete. It admitted Roman Catholics, on taking the oath of allegiance with a repudiation of the doctrine that princes excommunicated by the pope might be deposed or murdered (instead of the oath of supremacy and declaration against transubstantiation and the adoration of the Virgin Mary), to both Houses of Parliament, to all corporate offices, to all judicial offices (except in the ecclesiastical courts), and to all civil and political offices, except those of regent, lord chancellor in England and Ireland,[24] and lord lieutenant of Ireland. Additional restraints were, however, imposed by the Act upon the interference of Roman Catholics in church patronage: Jesuits and monks were prohibited from coming into the realm without licence; and provisions were inserted for regulating the residence of such as were already within the kingdom.[25]

In 1832 an Act was passed providing that Roman Catholics in respect of their schools, places of worship, and charities, and of property held therewith, and of persons employed about them, should be subject to the same laws as were applicable to protestant dissenters.[26] A few years later the policy of according perfect religious liberty to the Roman Catholics was consummated by the repeal of many of the enactments

---

[23] 9 Geo, 4, c. 17; Robertson, *Documents*, 312.

[24] The Irish chancellorship was later thrown open to all creeds. The effect of later legislation upon the English chancellorship is obscure: see Lord Simon's reply to a debate in the House of Lords on May 11, 1943.

[25] 10 Geo. 4, c. 7; Robertson, *Documents*, 317.

[26] 2 & 3 Will. 4, c. 115.

against them which (though for the most part obsolete) still remained on the statute book.[27]   Still further repeals took place in 1926,[28] and the courts have made some notable decisions by upholding certain trusts which hitherto had failed as being " superstitious." [29]

A few supplementary measures were still required to complete the civil enfranchisement of dissenters.   In 1833, Joseph Pease, the first Quaker who had been elected to the House of Commons for 140 years, was allowed to take his seat on making an affirmation instead of an oath. In the same year Quakers, Moravians and separatists were enabled by statute to substitute an affirmation in all cases for an oath.[30]

Jewish Disabilities.   The Jews, banished from England under Edward I, had been suffered to return by Cromwell, but were not formally authorised to settle in England until after the Restoration.   An Act of James I passed in 1610, and directed against the Roman Catholics, had the collateral effect of debarring the Jews from the benefits of naturalisation, by making the reception of the sacrament a necessary preliminary to naturalisation in all cases.[31]   In the interest of trade and colonisation this requirement was partially relaxed by a subsequent statute, which dispensed with the sacramental test in favour of all Jews and protestant foreigners who had resided seven years continuously in the American plantations.[32]   Notwithstanding the political disabilities attaching to them in England, the number of foreign Jewish settlers continued to increase with the expansion of English commerce; and at length, in 1753, an attempt was made to extend to all Jews applying for parliamentary naturalisation the exemption from the sacramental test, already conceded to those who had resided in the colonies, or been engaged in the manufacture of hemp or flax.   But the celebrated " Jew Bill," by which this very moderate measure of toleration was effected, proved to be in advance of the opinion of the age.   " No Jews ! No Jews ! No wooden shoes ! " became the popular cry; and although the Bill, after a fierce opposition in the House of Commons, obtained a fleeting place upon the statute book, it raised such a storm of opposition throughout the country as to necessitate its repeal in the following session.[33]   Jews were occasionally admitted to municipal offices, together with protestant nonconformists, under cover of the annual Indemnity Acts; but the declaration " on the true faith of a Christian," imposed by the Act 9 Geo. 4, c. 17, while relieving dissenters from the requirements of the Test and Corporation Acts, had forged new fetters for the Jew.   These were removed, so far as

27 7 & 8 Vict. c. 102 (1844); 9 & 10 Vict. c. 59 (1846).
28 Roman Catholic Relief Act, 1926; 16 & 17 Geo. 5, c. 55.
29 *Bourne* v. *Keane* [1919] A.C. 815; *Re Caus* [1934] Ch. 162.
30 3 & 4 Will, 4, cc. 49, 82; and see 1 & 2 Vict. c. 77.
31 *Infra*, p. 680.
32 1739, 13 Geo. 2, c. 7; *Parliamentary History*, xiv, 1373; Lecky, *History of England*, i, 262.
33 Lord Mahon, *History of England*, iv, 35–37.   *Cf. Infra*, p. 680.

regards corporations, in 1845 [34]; and, after a lengthened struggle, the only legal obstacle to the admission of Jews to parliament was also removed, in 1858, by an Act which empowered either House of Parliament, by resolution, to omit (in certain cases) the words " upon the true faith of a Christian " from the oath of abjuration.[35] These Acts did not benefit persons who professed to have no religious belief, as the case of Mr. Bradlaugh showed.[36]

Civil Marriage: University Tests. In 1836 a civil registration of births, marriages, and deaths was established; and by another Act, dissenters were permitted to solemnise marriages in their own chapels, registered for that purpose.[37] Lastly, in 1871, one of the few remaining disabilities of dissenters was redressed by the Universities Tests Act, which opened all lay academical degrees and all lay academical and collegiate offices in the universities of Oxford, Cambridge and Durham to persons of any religious belief.[38]

Disestablishment in Ireland and Wales. Presbyterianism remained the established religion in Scotland after the Union of 1707; but the Anglican Church was the established religion in Ireland and Wales, in spite of the fact that the inhabitants of the former were predominantly Roman Catholic and of the latter predominantly nonconformist. To remedy this obvious injustice the church was disestablished in Ireland in 1869, and in Wales in 1914. Owing, however, to the outbreak of war in that year, the Act for the disestablishment of the church in Wales was suspended and only became operative in 1920.

Convocation. The alliance between the crown and the Church of England which resulted from the Reformation, produced on the one hand all those disabilities upon non-Anglicans which we have just described; but it also produced, on the other hand, an almost total extinction of the church's autonomy. The revolution imposed upon the church a bench of latitudinarian bishops in the whig interest, who were unable to work with the tory and high church clergy in the Lower House of Convocation. On the early history of Convocation and its relation to the king and parliament something has been said.[39] From the passing of the Act for the Submission of the Clergy, 25 Hen. 8, c. 19,[40] Convocation has ceased to possess any independent legislative power, church and

[34] 8 & 9 Vict. c. 52.
[35] 21 & 22 Vict. c. 49; 23 & 24 Vict. c. 63. By the 29 & 30 Vict. c. 19, all distinctions between Jewish and other members were removed by the enactment of a new form of oath from which the words " on the true faith of a Christian " were omitted.
[36] Anson, *Law of the Constitution*, i, 95 *et seq.*; Oaths Act, 1888, 51 & 52 Vict. c. 46.
[37] 6 & 7 Will. 4, cc. 85, 86.
[38] 34 & 35 Vict. c. 26. Nonconformists were admitted to Degrees in Divinity at Oxford in 1920.
[39] *Supra*, pp. 142 *et seq.*, and notes.
[40] *Supra*, p. 277, and note.

state being alike subjected to the supreme power of parliament. Under
Elizabeth it was occasionally consulted on questions affecting religion,
and it confirmed, in 1563, the Thirty-nine Articles.[41] By the king's
licence Convocation established certain canons in 1604 (which, however,
not having been confirmed by parliament, are not binding on the laity);
and attempted to make further regulations in 1640 [42]; but from the year
1664, when the practice of ecclesiastical taxation was discontinued, even
discussions in Convocation practically ceased. About the time of the
revolution attempts were made to resuscitate the action of Convocation,
more especially by Atterbury (afterwards Bishop of Rochester and banished
for his Jacobite intrigues), who published a book entitled *The Rights and
Privileges of an English Convocation*. In 1717, the religious ferment
excited by the controversy arising out of the denunciation by the Lower
House of Convocation of a sermon in favour of religious liberty preached
by Hoadly, Bishop of Bangor, induced the ministers of George I suddenly to prorogue the Convocation.[43] From this time Convocation,
though regularly summoned, was for more than a century regularly
prorogued immediately after it had assembled. In 1850 it was again
allowed to resume the discussion of church matters, and in 1861 was
empowered by royal licence to alter the 29th canon of 1604, which prohibited parents from acting as sponsors to their children; but it was
specially provided in the licence that no alteration should be of any validity
until confirmed by letters patent under the great seal. In 1872, letters of
business were issued by the crown empowering Convocation to frame
resolutions on the subject of public worship, and these were afterwards
incorporated in an Act of Parliament (Act of Uniformity Amendment
Act, 35 & 36 Vict. c. 35).[44]

The Enabling Act, 1919. The co-operation of the lay element in the
deliberations of both Houses of Convocation had long been felt desirable,
and in 1919 this was achieved by the Church of England Assembly
(Powers) Act, commonly known as the " Enabling Act," which gave
statutory authority for the setting up of the National Assembly of the
Church of England.[45] It consists of three houses—the House of Bishops,
the House of Clergy, and the House of Laity. The first two are formed
of the Upper and Lower Houses of the two Convocations of Canterbury
and York; the third, the representatives of the laity, are elected by the
lay members of the Diocesan Conference, who in turn are elected at
parochial church meetings. The Church Assembly may discuss any

[41] *Supra*, pp. 291–292.
[42] *Supra*, p. 392.
[43] On the intermission of Convocation, and the effect of the "Bangor Controversy," see
Norman Sykes, *Church and State in the Eighteenth Century*, 287–314. Atterbury was
controverted by William Wake, whose *State of the Church* (folio, 1703) assembles the
original sources for the history of Convocation, and is still the standard work.
[44] See Hallam, *Constitutional History*, iii, 242–247 ; Anson, *Law and Custom of the Constitution*,
vol. ii, Pt. ii, pp. 263 *et seq.*
[45] 9 & 10 Geo. 5, c. 76.

matter relating to the Church of England and may propose measures which, if they receive the assent of the two Houses of Parliament and of the king, have the effect of an Act of Parliament.[46]

LIBERTY OF THE PRESS

Of the political privileges of the people acquired or enlarged since the revolution, we have still to consider the liberty of the Press.

Censorship. We have seen how freedom of opinion in religious matters was early restrained by the action of the church against the Lollard teachers and writers [47]; and soon after the invention of printing in the fifteenth century the Press was placed under a rigorous censorship, not only in England but throughout Europe. After the Reformation in England, the censorship of the Press in matters of dogma passed with the ecclesiastical supremacy to the crown. Many of the Treason Acts passed in the Tudor period deal with the printing of treasonable matter. It became a part of the royal prerogative to appoint a licenser, without whose *imprimatur* no writings could be lawfully published; and the printing of unlicensed works was visited with the severest punishments in the prerogative courts. Printing was further restrained by patents and monopolies which, together with the practice of the Stationers' Company, laid the foundation of the law of copyright.[48] The privilege was confined, in the first instance, under regulation established by the Star Chamber in Queen Mary's reign, to members of the Stationers' Company, and the number of presses, and of men to be employed on them, was strictly limited. Under Elizabeth I, the censorship was enforced by more rigorous penalties. All printing was interdicted elsewhere than in London, Oxford and Cambridge; and nothing whatever was allowed to be published until it had first been " seen, perused and allowed " by the Archbishop of Canterbury or the Bishop of London, except only publications by the queen's printers, to be appointed for some special service, or by law-printers, for whom the licence of the chief justices was sufficient.[49] Mutilation or death was the penalty of those who dared to print anything which the judges might choose to construe as seditious or slanderous of the government in church or state.[50]

Early Stuarts: Commonwealth. Under James I and Charles I, political and religious discussion was repressed by the Star Chamber with the greatest severity.[51] By an ordinance of the Star Chamber, issued in

---

[46] Stephen, *Commentaries* (20th ed.), i, 522; A. Berriedale Keith, *The Constitution* (1940) ii, 429 *et seq.*

[47] *Supra*, pp. 265 *et seq.*

[48] See Holdsworth, *History of English Law*, vi, 360 *et seq.*, for the regulatory aspect; and iv, 496, 511–512 for the criminal aspect; v, 205 for the beginning of the law of libel.

[49] Ordinances of the Star Chamber for the regulation of the Press in 1586, *supra*, p. 310.

[50] St. 23 Eliz. 1, c. 2. See the cases of Stubbe, Udal, Barrow, Greenwood and Penry, *supra*, pp. 301 and 305.

[51] *Supra*, pp. 379 *et seq.*

July 1637, the number of master printers was limited to twenty, who were to give sureties for good behaviour, and were to have not more than two presses and two apprentices each (unless they were present or past masters of the Stationers' Company, when they were allowed three presses and three apprentices): and the number of letter-founders was limited to four. The penalty for practising the arts of printing, bookbinding, letter-founding or making any part of a press, or other printing materials, by persons disqualified, or not apprenticed thereto, was whipping, the pillory and imprisonment. Even books which had been once examined and allowed were not to be reprinted without a fresh licence; and books brought from abroad were to be landed in London only, and carefully examined by licensers appointed by the Archbishop of Canterbury and the Bishop of London, who were empowered to seize and destroy all such as were " seditious, schismatical or offensive." Periodical searches, both of booksellers' shops and private houses, were also enjoined and authorised. Yet it was during this inauspicious period that the first newspaper, the *Weekly Newes*, made its appearance, late in the reign of James I [52]; and during the contest between crown and parliament tracts and newspapers issued forth in shoals.[53] The Long Parliament, however, while abolishing the Star Chamber, continued the censorship of the Press; and endeavoured to silence all royalist and prelatical writers by most tyrannical ordinances, " to repress disorders in printing," by which the messengers of the government were empowered to break open doors and locks, by day or by night, in order to discover unlicensed printing presses, and to apprehend authors, printers and others.[54] These proceedings called forth the *Areopagitica* of Milton, in which he branded the suppression of truth by the licenser as the slaying of " an immortality rather than a life," maintained that " she needs no policies, no stratagems, no licensings, to make her victorious," and nobly, but ineffectually, pleaded for " the liberty to know, to utter, and to argue freely according to conscience, above all [other] liberties." [55] Milton agreed, however, that it was necessary to censor news, and himself was appointed a licenser.[56]

Licensing Act, 1662. After the Restoration, the entire control of printing was placed in the hands of the government by the Licensing Act of 1662, which, though originally passed only for three years, was continued by subsequent renewals until 1679. Printing was strictly confined

---

[52] The *Weekly Newes*, May 23, 1623, printed for Nicholas Bourne and Thomas Archer—May, *Constitutional History*, ii, 240.

[53] More than 30,000 political pamphlets and newspapers were issued from the Press during the twenty years from 1640 to the Restoration. They may be seen in the *Thomason Collection* at the British Museum bound up in 2,000 volumes. (Catalogue (1908) by G. K. Fortescue.)

[54] On this period, see W. M. Clyde, *The Struggle for Freedom of the Press from Caxton to Cromwell* (1934).

[55] Milton, *Areopagitica: a Speech for Liberty of Unlicensed Printing*, in *Works*, ed. 1863, iv, 400, 442.

[56] Clyde, *op. cit.*, 79-80.

to London, York and the two.universities; the number of master printers was limited, as in the ordinances of the Star Chamber, in 1637, to twenty; and no private person was to publish any book or pamphlet unless it were first licensed—law books by the lord chancellor, or one of the chiefs of the common law courts, historical or political books by the Secretary of State, books of heraldry by the earl marshal, and all other books by the Archbishop of Canterbury, or the Bishop of London, or by the chancellor or vice-chancellor of one of the universities.[57] Authors and printers of obnoxious works were to be hanged, quartered, mutilated, exposed in the pillory, flogged, or simply fined and imprisoned, according to the nature of the offence; and the works themselves were burned by the common hangman.[58] After the Licensing Act had been temporarily suffered to expire in 1679, the twelve judges, with Chief Justice Scroggs at their head, declared it to be criminal at common law to publish anything concerning the government, whether true or false, of praise or censure, without the royal licence.[59] All newspapers were in consequence stopped; and the people were reduced for political intelligence and instruction to two government publications, the official *London Gazette*, which furnished a scanty supply of news without comment, and the *Observator*, which consisted of comment without news. In the absence of newspapers, the coffee-houses became the chief organs through which the public opinion of the capital vented itself, while the inhabitants of provincial towns, and the great body of the gentry and country clergy, depended almost exclusively on newsletters from London for their knowledge of political events.[60]

Licensing Act Expired, 1695. At the accession of James II, in 1685, the Licensing Act was revived for seven years, and was thus in force at the revolution. It was once more renewed in 1692, for one year and until the end of the following session of parliament; but a further attempt to renew it in 1695 was negatived by the commons,[61] and thenceforth the censorship of the Press has ceased to form part of the law of England.

The Press was now theoretically free; but in practice it was still subject to several methods of restraint. The principle laid down by Chief Justice Scroggs in 1679 was affirmed by the more respectable authority of Lord Holt in 1704.[62] The way in which the summary jurisdiction of Parliament was employed to check the publication of debates has already been

---

[57] 14 Car. 2, c. 33; Robertson, *Documents*, 60.

[58] See the cases of John Twyn, St.Tr. vi, 659; of Keach, *ibid.*, 710; of Harris, Smith, Curtis, Carr and Cellier, *ibid.*, vii, 926–1043, 1111, 1183; and *cf.* May, *Constitutional History*, ii, 242.

[59] Cases of Harris and Carr, 1680, 7 St.Tr. 929, 1127. *Cf.* David Ogg, *Charles II*, ii, 515 *et seq.* This monstrous opinion was not judicially condemned until 1765, by Lord Camden, Chief Justice of the Common Pleas, in the case of *Entick* v. *Carrington*, 19 St.Tr. 1030; Broom, *Constitutional Law*, pp. 558–623.

[60] See Macaulay, *History of England*, i, Chap. iii, 360, 380.

[61] For the curious reasons given, see Holdsworth, vi, 375–376.

[62] *R.* v. *Tutchin*, 14 St.Tr. 1095 at 1128.

referred to, with reference to the privileges of the House of Commons[63]; and the government also made use of two other means of controlling the Press: (1) the stamp duty on newspapers, and (2) the law of libel. Newspapers, however, quickly multiplied when freed from the censorship, and in the reign of Queen Anne assumed their present form, combining intelligence with political discussion.[64] At the same time the intellectual character of the periodical literature was raised, and its influence widely extended, by the talents of writers like Addison, Steele, Swift and Bolingbroke.

But the Press soon became the favourite instrument of party warfare, and by its scurrilous language excited a strong feeling of opposition to it among the governing classes. Each party, when in power, endeavoured to crush its opponents by prosecuting as seditious libels all publications which supported the opposition.

Stamp Duty on Newspapers. The revival of the Licensing Act was even suggested, but dismissed as impracticable; and a stamp duty on newspapers and advertisements was adopted instead, avowedly for the purpose of restraining the Press generally and of crushing the smaller papers. The first Stamp Act was passed in the tenth year of Queen Anne,[65] and being found efficient both as a check on the circulation of cheap periodicals and as a source of revenue, the stamp was gradually raised to fourpence. At the end of George III's reign it was extended, by one of the series of statutes known as the Six Acts,[66] to tracts and other unstamped periodicals which, while professing not to be newspapers, had obtained a wide circulation among the poor as disseminators of political news and dissertations. Evasions of the stamp duty were frequent, and the state and the contraband Press continued at war until after the Reform Act of 1832. In 1833 the advertisement duty, which had been increased under George III, was reduced in amount, and in 1853 was relinquished altogether. In 1836 the stamp on newspapers was lowered to 1d., and in 1855 abandoned.[67] The duty on paper, which had latterly proved a serious stumbling-block in the way of popular education, was swept away in 1861.[68]

Law of Libel. A far more powerful instrument for the suppression of freedom of discussion than the Stamp Act was the law of criminal libel. This was rigorously enforced by the government under William III and Anne; but during the reigns of the first two Georges the Press generally enjoyed more toleration, Sir Robert Walpole being indifferent

---

[63] *Supra*, pp. 585 *et seq.*
[64] The first daily paper, the *Daily Courant*, was issued in 1709.
[65] 10 Anne, c. 18 (1711).
[66] In 1819; see *infra*, p. 668, n. 83.
[67] *History of The Times*, ii, 194, 200, has facsimiles of stamps.
[68] *Supra*, p. 548.

to its attacks, and openly avowing his contempt for political writers of all parties. Shortly after the accession of George III, the nation, taking a keen interest in political affairs, and finding itself unrepresented in a corrupt House of Commons, sought utterance for its opinions in the columns of the Press, which from this time rapidly rose into a formidable political power.

No. 45 of the " North Briton." A renewed conflict with the government was the natural result. Lord Bute, the premier, was driven from power (April 8, 1763) mainly by the criticism of Wilkes in the *North Briton*, and a fortnight afterwards (April 23) the celebrated No. 45 of that journal appeared, commenting in severe and offensive terms on the king's speech at the prorogation of parliament and upon the unpopular Peace of Paris recently (February 10, 1763) concluded. By a strained exercise of prerogative a general warrant was issued for the discovery and apprehension of the authors and printers (not named) of the obnoxious No. 45. Forty-nine persons, including Wilkes, were arrested on suspicion under the general warrant: and it having been ascertained that Wilkes was the author, an information for libel was filed against him in the King's Bench on which a verdict was obtained.[69] Released from prison on the ground of privilege as a Member of Parliament,[70] Wilkes brought an action against Mr. Wood, the Under-Secretary of State, and obtained a verdict of £1,000 damages, the court holding that the general warrant was invalid [71]; and four days afterwards Dryden Leach, one of the printers arrested on suspicion, gained another verdict with £400 damages against the messengers. On a bill of exceptions, which was argued before the court of King's Bench in 1765, Lord Mansfield and the other three judges pronounced the general warrant illegal, declaring that " no degree of antiquity could give sanction to an usage bad in itself." [72]

General Warrants. In the same year, 1765, an action brought by John Entick, the suspected author of the *Monitor, or British Freeholder*, against the messengers who had seized all his books and papers under a general search warrant from the secretary of state was decided against the government. Lord Camden, Chief Justice of the Commons Pleas, determined that such warrants, which had originated in the practice of the Star Chamber, and had been unjustifiably continued since the expiration of the Licensing Act of Charles II, were absolutely illegal.[73] The

---

[69] *R.* v. *Wilkes*, 4 Burr. 2527, 2574.

[70] *Supra*, pp. 584 *et seq.*

[71] *Wilkes* v. *Wood* (1765) 19 St.Tr. 1153. Broom, *Constitutional Law*, pp. 548 *et seq*; Holdsworth, *History of English Law*, x, 659.

[72] *Leach* v. *Money* (1765) 3 Burr. 1692, 1742; 19 St.Tr. 1001. Broom's *Constitutional Law*, pp. 524 *et seq.*

[73] *Entick* v. *Carrington* (1765) 19 St.Tr. 1030. Broom, *Constitutional Law*, pp. 558–623; Keir and Lawson, *Cases in Constitutional Law*, 145. Holdsworth, *History of English Law*, x, 661 *et seq.* The issue of search warrants was later regulated by the Larceny Act, 1861 (24 & 25 Vict. c. 96), s. 103, and a large number of other statutes for specified purposes.

court refused to accept the arguments for the government (1) that the use of these powers of search was justifiable on grounds of public necessity, or (2) that they belonged to the office of secretary of state, or of privy councillor, under the " rules in Anderson," [74] or (3) that they could be justified by long user. It was held that long use and practice in a court can become law—the common law itself arose in this way; but the practice of an office which is not judicial cannot become legal merely because of long user.

Junius' " Letter," 1769. The excitement caused by the proceedings against Wilkes and the printers had scarcely subsided when the prosecutions which followed upon the publication of Junius' celebrated " Letter to the King " in the *Morning Advertiser* of December 19, 1769, forcibly directed the attention of the public to the severe and extended interpretation of the law of libel adopted by the judges since the revolution. Already, in 1731, on the trial of one Richard Franklin for publishing a libel in the *Craftsman*, it had been held that falsehood, though always alleged in the indictment, was not essential to constitute the libel, and Lord Raymond positively refused to admit of any evidence to prove the truth of the statements complained of.[75] On the trial of John Almon,[76] a bookseller, for selling a reprint of Junius' letter, two other doctrines were maintained by the courts. (1) It was held that the publisher of a libel was criminally liable for the acts of his servants, unless proved to be neither privy nor assenting thereto; and afterwards the judges decided that exculpatory evidence was inadmissible, and that publication of a libel by the servant was conclusive proof of the criminality of the master. (2) Lord Mansfield laid it down that it was the province of the judge alone to determine the criminality of a libel, leaving to the jury to determine merely the fact of publication, and whether the libel meant what it was alleged in the indictment to mean. On the trial of Woodfall,[77] the original publisher of the " Letter to the King," the jury, in order to defeat this interpretation of the law, found the defendant " guilty of printing and publishing only "—a verdict which the court held to be uncertain, necessitating a new trial. Miller [78] and other printers who were subsequently tried for printing the same letter were boldly declared by the jury to be " not guilty."

Rights of Juries in Libel Cases. The doctrine held by the judges in these trials, though clearly right as a statement of the law, was entirely at variance with contemporary thought upon the nature of government

---

[74] *Supra*, p. 308.

[75] *R.* v. *Franklin* (1731) 17 St.Tr. 626. Holdsworth, viii, 344; J. F. Stephen, *History of Criminal Law*, ii, 324. The *Craftsman* was the paper conducted by Pulteney and Bolingbroke in opposition to Walpole.

[76] *R.* v. *Almon* (1770) 20 St.Tr. 803; Holdsworth, x, 675; Stephen, ii, 324.

[77] *R.* v. *Woodfall* (1770) 20 St.Tr. 870.

[78] *R.* v. *Miller* (1770) 20 St.Tr. 895.

and the extent of the subject's liberties, and was strongly animadverted upon in both Houses of Parliament; and the rights of juries in cases of libel were nobly and eloquently maintained by the advocacy of Erskine in the cases of the *Dean of St. Asaph* [79] in 1783 and of *Stockdale*, 1789, the latter being a prosecution for publishing what was charged as " a scandalous and seditious libel " concerning the conduct of the House of Commons in its impeachment of Warren Hastings.[80] At length, in 1792, the ruling of the judges as to the province of juries was in effect reversed by Fox's Libel Act, which declared their right, on any trial or information for libel, to give a general verdict of guilty or not guilty on the whole matter.[81]

Effect of Fox's Libel Act, 1792. In so far as there was (and still is) any legal definition of a seditious libel, it is extremely wide. Nor did Fox's Act attempt any curtailment, or indeed any definition at all. Its effect was in terms procedural; but in transferring from the judge to the jury the power of saying whether any particular publication was a seditious libel, it placed the decision in the hands of twelve men whose views were more likely to be representative of general opinion than would be judges and lawyers who perforce had studied the sweeping assertions of the older law cases—which were often relics of Stuart and Star Chamber days. The Act did not reduce the number of convictions for libel, and as events were to show, juries a century ago were far from sympathetic to authors of Jacobin tendencies. The jury's acquittal is indeed conclusive; but the jury's conviction is still subjected by the Act to the defendant's right (by means of a motion in arrest of judgment) to convince the judge, if he can, that under the law the publication is not libellous. " It is, broadly speaking, true to say that a man can publish anything he pleases provided that, if proceedings against him are taken, he can induce either a jury, or the court, to say that the matter published is not a libel." [82]

Reactionary Period, 1792–1832. The law of seditious libel is not the only peril which besets the political writer, and soon the signal advance made by liberty of opinion during the first thirty years of George III's reign was to receive a decided check. The proceedings of the French revolutionists created a widespread terror of democracy among the great body of the English people, which was aggravated by the extravagance of a small but turbulent body of social and political reformers in England itself. With the publication by the government, in 1792, of a proclamation warning the people against wicked and seditious writings industriously dispersed among them, and commanding magistrates to discover the

---

[79] *R. v. Shipley* (1783) 21 St.Tr. 847; Holdsworth, x, 677–688; Stephen, ii, 330–343, has a full narrative and discussion.
[80] *R. v. Stockdale* (1789) 22 St.Tr. 237.
[81] 32 Geo. 3, c. 60; Grant Robertson, *Documents*, 272; Holdsworth, x, 688–696.
[82] Holdsworth, x, 692.

authors, printers and promulgators of such writings, began a reactionary period in the growth of liberty of opinion which cannot be said to have entirely passed away until after the passing of the Reform Act of 1832. During this period, prosecutions of the Press abounded; seditious speaking was severely restrained [83]; and the regulation of newspapers frequently occupied the attention of the legislature.

Freedom of the Press from 1832. But from the year 1832, at latest, the freedom of the Press has been completely established. The utmost latitude of criticism and invective has been allowed it in discussing the actions of the government and of all public men and measures. By Lord Campbell's Libel Act, passed in 1843, the defendant on an indictment or information for a defamatory libel is allowed to plead its truth, and that its publication was for the public benefit; and the harsh extension of the ruling in *Almon's* case,[84] as to the criminal liability of the publisher for the unauthorised acts of his servants, has been altered by allowing the defendant in all cases to prove that such publication was made without his authority, consent, or knowledge, and that it did not arise from want of due care or caution on his part.[85] State prosecution for libel is now as much a thing of the past as the censorship itself. The policy of repression has been finally discarded; and rulers have at length recognised in practice the truth and wisdom of Lord Bacon's maxim that the " punishing of wits enhances their authority; and a forbidden writing is thought to be a certain spark of truth, that flies up in the faces of them that seek to tread it out." [86]

Nevertheless, it must not be thought that the problem of the freedom of the Press has been solved. It is insoluble, save by a compromise, and a compromise necessarily varies with circumstances. In our own day the discussion turns upon recent legislation, such as the Official Secrets

---

[83] The Six Acts (60 Geo. 3 & 1 Geo. 4, cc. 1, 2, 4, 6, 8, 9) were a batch of repressive measures passed at the instance of the government, in 1819, in consequence of the disturbed state of the country. By the first (c. 1) the training of persons to the use of arms was prohibited; by the second (c. 2) the magistrates in the disturbed counties were authorised to search for and seize arms; by the third (c. 4) defendants in cases of misdemeanour in the King's Bench were deprived of the right of imparling; by the fourth (c. 6), called the Seditious Meetings Act, extraordinary powers were conferred on the executive, and all meetings of more than fifty persons for the discussion of public grievances were prohibited, except under very stringent conditions; by the fifth (c. 8) the courts of law were enabled, on the conviction of a publisher of a seditious or blasphemous libel, to order the seizure of all copies of the libel in his possession or that of any other person specified, and on a second conviction to punish him with fine, imprisonment, or banishment. The sixth (c. 9) extended the newspaper stamp duty to cheap political pamphlets and periodicals, as mentioned in the text. All these Acts were permanent except the Seditious Meetings Act, which was limited to five years, and the Seizure of Arms Act, which expired on March 25, 1822. The punishment of banishment inflicted by the Seditious Libels Act was repealed in 1830 by 11 Geo. 4 & 1 Will. 4, c. 73. See, especially, W. H. Wickwar, *The Struggle for the Freedom of the Press 1819–1832* (1928).

[84] *Supra*, p. 666.

[85] 6 & 7 Vict. c. 96.

[86] On liberty of the Press, see Hunt, *Fourth Estate*; Andrews, *History of British Journalism*; Hallam, *Constitutional History*, iii, 2–6, 166–168; May, *Constitutional History*, ii, 238–383.

Acts, 1911 and 1920, and the Incitement to Disaffection Act, 1934, rather than upon the law of seditious libel.

THE RIGHT TO PETITION

The right of petitioning the crown and parliament was one of the most valuable possessed by the subject, and seems to have been exercised from the earliest times. But for many centuries it was practically restricted to petitions for redress of private and local grievances, and the remedies prayed for were such as have since been provided by courts of equity and by private Acts of Parliament. The practice of petitioning on political subjects came into vogue during the period of the Great Rebellion, many petitions, signed by large bodies of people, being presented both to Charles I and the Long Parliament; and it was probably the recollection of the intimidation exercised by numerous bodies of petitioners in the early days of the Long Parliament which prompted the restraining Act of 13 Car. 2, st. 1, c. 5, passed in 1661.[87] In December 1679, in consequence of the dissatisfaction of the nation at the repeated prorogations, great exertions were made to get up numerously signed petitions to the king for the assembling of parliament. A royal proclamation was thereupon issued, forbidding all persons to sign such petitions under pain of punishment. This, though it checked, did not entirely prevent the presentation of these petitions. Counter-addresses were therefore sent up to the throne from grand juries, magistrates, and many corporations, expressing their *abhorrence* of the petitions for the assembling of parliament; whence the two principal parties in the country, subsequently distinguished as whigs and tories, obtained for the time the names of petitioners and abhorrers.

By the Bill of Rights the right of the subject to petition the king was expressly sanctioned, in view of the attempt by the late king to deny it in the *Seven Bishops' Case*; but the House of Commons for a long time showed itself intolerant of such expressions of opinion, and extremely jealous of any semblance of interference with its functions.

Petitions to the Commons. In 1701 the commons imprisoned five of the Kentish petitioners until the end of the session, for praying the House to attend to the voice of the people and " turn its loyal addresses into bills of supply." Any petition expressing opinions of which the majority of the House did not approve was, of course, liable to summary rejection.

The right to petition is not a right to a favourable reply. In 1772 a most temperate petition, signed by about 250 of the clergy and by several members of the professions of law and physic, praying for relief from subscription to the Thirty-nine Articles, was rejected by a large majority of the commons. Seven years later, however, in 1779, a widely organised attempt to procure parliamentary and economical reform gave rise to a

[87] *Supra*, p. 423.

general system of petitioning, in which the freeholders of Yorkshire led the way, and were soon followed by many other important counties and by the principal cities. " This," observes Sir Erskine May, " may be regarded as the origin of the modern system of petitioning, by which public measures, and matters of general policy, have been pressed upon the attention of parliament. Corresponding committees being established in various parts of the country were associated for the purpose of effecting a common object by means of petitions, to be followed by concerted motions made in parliament. An organisation which has since been so often used with success was now first introduced into our political system." [88]

The great movement for the abolition of the slave trade, which began with a petition from the Quakers in 1782, affords the most remarkable example of direct influence of petitions upon the deliberations of parliament. But it was not until the latter part of the reign of George IV that petitioning obtained the development which has since distinguished it in all the great political movements. Not only is the right to petition now fully recognised, but " the act of petitioning is free to all, and parliament will receive any petition respectfully worded, and complying with the forms of the House, whilst the statute of 13 Car. 2 has nearly become a dead letter, and under ordinary circumstances no one dreams of enforcing that Act (intended to prevent violent and tumultuous petitioning), or of inquiring, when a petition is presented, whether its conditions have been complied with." [89]

For a time, petitions to the House of Commons served a useful purpose in calling its attention to matters which were agitating the public, or some section of it, and a full debate might be initiated in this way. By their frequency they later came to be a nuisance, disorganising the work of the House; it was therefore resolved in 1839 that for the future petitions should not be debated.

The decline of the procedure was no great loss, as alternative methods are now available for raising matters in parliament. Temporary matters are ventilated in the Press, and in the House by question and answer. Sectional interests, which formerly made great use of petitions, now have other techniques at hand,[90] and general questions upon which there is public interest will often be adopted by one or another of the political parties.

THE ARMED FORCES AND THE POLICE

The opinion gradually formed that there was a close connection between the extent of the civil liberties of the subject and the amount of

[88] May, *Constitutional History*, ii, 63 *et seq.*
[89] Broom, *Constitutional Law*, p. 511. It was, however, expressly decided by Lord Mansfield, on the trial of Lord George Gordon for his share in the " No Popery " riots of 1780, that the Act of Charles II had not been repealed; and it was cited in 1848, when it was found necessary to prohibit the large body of Chartist petitioners from carrying out their declared intention of marching to the House to present their petition. On the subject of public petitions see also Anson, *Law and Custom*, i, 371 *et seq.*
[90] Learnedly and entertainingly divulged by Sir Ivor Jennings, *Parliament*, Chap. vii.

armed forces at the disposal of the crown. This was amply confirmed when Englishmen saw the erection on the Continent of absolute monarchies whose existence was seemingly rendered possible only by well organised and comparatively numerous military forces. In the seventeenth and eighteenth centuries, therefore, the size of the standing army was closely examined and debated at endless length year after year in parliament. The mode of recruitment—whether by voluntary enlistment, or by compulsory impressment—was a much less serious matter, since the persons normally picked up by the press gangs had as yet no means of exerting any political influence.

It must also be remembered that the machinery for raising armed forces, and the forces so raised, served at the same time two distinct purposes. There was first the necessity of maintaining order at home; this took the form of putting down brigandage, riots and insurrections as they occurred, rather than of steady and continuous preventive watch (and similarly there was the need to protect shipping in time of peace from pirates). And, secondly, there was the more serious business of war. This generally involved an invasion of Scotland or the Continent, and consequently service outside of the realm—although it was often necessary to put the maritime counties in a state of defence against invasion or, more frequently, forays against the coastal districts by foreign powers, or even pirates.

How Forces were Raised. The crown had two modes of raising military forces.

(1) To call upon those who owed military service to the crown as a result of the tenure by which they held their land, or as a result of their status as subjects of the king. Such forces therefore consisted of (a) the feudal tenants, bound by the tenure of their lands to serve the king both at home and abroad (summoned for the last time to render personal service in the expedition of Charles I against the Scots in 1640, and extinguished by the Act 12 Car. 2, c. 24, abolishing the military tenures), and (b) the national militia, bound exclusively to service at home, and already sufficiently described.[91] In either case, service was obligatory, although it was in various ways limited.

(2) To engage at a wage such men as could be persuaded to enlist voluntarily, upon a contractual basis. These forces were also of two kinds: (a) those of a more or less permanent character, such as the small bodyguard of the sovereign and the garrisons, insignificant in number, maintained in a few fortified places—the Tower of London, Portsmouth, Dover, Tilbury and, before the union of the crowns, Berwick and some other places on the Scottish border; (b) those raised for special emergencies, comprising stipendiary troops, which even in feudal times were regularly employed by English kings for the purposes of foreign warfare.

[91] *Supra*, pp. 32–33, 120–125.

Of military service due by tenure, and of the legal limitations upon it, we have already spoken [92]; but Edward I and Edward II on several occasions had recourse to the compulsory conscription of others than those obliged to serve by tenure. But here also there were doubts as to the nature and extent of the service; and accordingly the first parliament of Edward III passed a statute (1 Edw. 3, st. 2, c. 5), " That no man from henceforth shall be charged to arm himself otherwise than he was wont in the time of the king's progenitors; and that no man be compelled to go out of his shire but when necessity requireth and sudden coming of strange enemies into the realm; and then it shall be done as hath been used in times past for the defence of the realm." Edward also endeavoured to call, not on individuals, but on the counties and chief towns to furnish him with troops. The object was possibly to mobilise only part of the men liable, the others being called upon to pay instead of to serve, thus financing the forces actually in the field. This operation was denounced as an unparliamentary tax, and parliament met the new demand by a statute (25 Edw. 3, stat. 5, c. 8) providing " that no man shall be constrained to find men-at-arms, hobblers, nor archers, other than those who hold by such service, if it be not by common consent and grant made in parliament." Both these statutes were confirmed in the fourth year of Henry IV (c. 13). For some time compulsory levies carried out by commissioners of array for foreign warfare were discontinued, and a system of contracting by indenture with men of rank and influence to raise troops at a high rate of pay was adopted. But as the great cost of stipendiary troops caused our kings to disband them as soon as the particular necessity for which they were engaged had ceased, the country escaped the danger of a standing army.

Compulsion by the Tudors. Under the despotic sway of the Tudors the prerogative of pressing men for military service out of the kingdom was to some extent revived, and Elizabeth used the army and its peculiar martial law as a means of preserving public order.[93] Its exercise by Charles I called forth, as we have seen, the declaratory statute against impressment of the sixteenth year of his reign.[94] The great object of Charles and of Strafford was to obtain a standing army; but the popular party in parliament, aware that the free states of the Continent had been turned into despotisms through this very means, offered a determined opposition.

The Civil War. The outbreak of the Civil War ultimately turned upon the question who should command the military forces; and it was in the Civil War that the system of standing armies in this country

---

[92] *Supra*, pp. 32–33, 144 *et seq.* In the fifty years of his reign, Edward III only once (in 1327) called up the feudal forces: A. E. Prince, " The Army and the Navy," in *English Government at Work, 1327–1336* (ed. J. F. Willard and W. A. Morris), i, 344, where much detailed information is given.

[93] *Supra*, pp. 307 *et seq.*

[94] *Supra*, pp. 399 *et seq.*

originated. By the " Instrument of Government," in 1653, which invested Cromwell with the title of " the Lord Protector," provision was made for the support of a regular army of 30,000 men; and the military subjection in which Cromwell held the country excited amongst all parties a deep-rooted antipathy to a standing army. At the Restoration the people clamoured for the disbandment of the army of the Commonwealth, to which Charles II somewhat reluctantly assented. General Monk's foot regiment (the Coldstream) and one other of horse were, however, retained in the king's service; another was formed out of troops brought from Dunkirk; and these, amounting in 1662 to 5,000 men, formed, under the name of guards, the nucleus of the present regular army.[95]

Standing Army at the Revolution. Towards the end of Charles II's reign, in 1684, the garrison of Tangier (consisting of one regiment of horse and two of foot) was recalled to England, and this raised the numbers of the regular force to about 7,000 foot and 1,700 cavalry and dragoons. James II endeavoured to make himself absolute by means of a great standing army. Taking advantage of Monmouth's insurrection, he made large additions to the military force left by his brother, and brought up their numbers to about 30,000 men. He formed a vast camp at Hounslow for the purpose of overawing London, and induced the judges to pronounce sentence of death on deserters, contrary to both the letter and spirit of the law. But under both Charles II and James II the parliament took every opportunity of opposing the permanent retention of the troops which were necessarily raised from time to time for special purposes. When, in 1667, 12,000 fresh troops were hastily levied for the Dutch war, the commons at once came to a unanimous resolution to request the king to disband them immediately on the conclusion of peace. Similarly, in 1673, after fresh levies had been raised for the second Dutch war, the commons resolved " that the continuing of any standing forces in this nation, other than the militia, is a great grievance and vexation to the people "; and when, in 1678, Charles II suddenly levied 20,000 men, on the pretext of a war with France, the Commons only consented to vote supplies on condition that these troops should be disbanded. One of the principal articles of Clarendon's impeachment was that he had " designed a standing army to be raised and to govern the kingdom thereby."

The Mutiny Act. The illegality of raising or keeping a standing army within the kingdom in time of peace, except with consent of parliament, is expressly declared by the Bill of Rights. This declaration has been regularly repeated in the Mutiny Act (passed for the first time in 1689, for one year only, and annually [96] renewed ever since), together with the

[95] See Fortescue, *History of the British Army*, i, 289 *et seq.*
[96] With rare exceptions: Holdsworth, vi, 241, n. 2, and x, 378, n. 10.

further declaration that " no man may be forejudged of life and limb, or subjected in time of peace to any kind of punishment within this realm by martial law, or in any other manner than by the judgment of his peers and according to the known and established laws of this realm." Then follow provisions for embodying an army for the safety of the kingdom and its dependencies, and authorising the sovereign to make articles of war for the government of the troops by martial law.[97]

The Army after the Revolution. Although the maintenance of a military force has been absolutely dependent, since the Revolution, upon the will of parliament, so strong was the national prejudice under William III against a standing army, that in 1697, after the Peace of Ryswick, the commons insisted upon the dismissal of the king's Dutch guards, and on the reduction of the number of troops to 7,000 (afterwards increased to 10,000) for the defence of England and 12,000 for Ireland. The great victories of Marlborough reconciled the nation somewhat to the idea of a standing army; and it was, moreover, necessary during the life of the Pretender, in order to prevent the Scottish and other adherents of the exiled Stuarts from rising in rebellion; yet, under George I and down to the close of the eighteenth century, the ordinary peace establishment, exclusive of the troops in Ireland, but including the garrisons of Minorca and Gibraltar, only slightly exceeded 17,000 men. The question of billeting troops upon innkeepers and the public caused much trouble, but parliament was extremely unwilling to authorise the construction of barracks, fearing that they would become engines of tyranny. In 1735, parliament manifested its jealousy of the military power by passing an Act (8 Geo. 2, c. 30) forbidding any troops to come within two miles of any place, except the capital or a garrison town, during an election. In the same spirit, the commons resolved, in 1741, consequent upon the military having been called in to quell some riotous proceedings at a Westminster election, " that the presence of a regular body of armed soldiers at an election of members to serve in parliament is a high infringement of the liberties of the subject, a manifest violation of the freedom of elections, and an open defiance of the laws and constitution of this kingdom "; and the persons concerned in the matter were ordered to attend the House, and received on their knees a severe reprimand from the Speaker.

It was also objected with reason that the articles of war provided only an obscure, unsystematic and harsh body of military law. This was at long last remedied by reframing the Mutiny Act and replacing it by the Army Act, 1879 (renewed annually), in which the articles of war were embodied as a code of military law. It is now replaced by the Army and Air Force (Annual) Act.

The French Revolution and the Peninsular War not only finally reconciled the nation to a standing army, but excited a desire in

---

[97] 1 Will. & Mary, c. 5; Robertson, *Documents*, 108; *cf.* Holdsworth, x, 379.

many—the country gentlemen especially—for a very large permanent force. The vast scale upon which warfare has been conducted in recent years has, of course, rendered it necessary that the " nucleus," even for purely defensive purposes, should be much larger than formerly.[98]

Reforms. Since 1890, successive governments, through their ministers of war, have been busy with schemes (some of which were short-lived) for the reorganisation of the British military forces, so as to adapt them more or less to the altered conditions and exigencies of modern warfare. Great Britain alone of all the Great Powers of Europe has, partly owing to reliance on its maritime ascendancy, and partly to a supposed unwillingness (though this had never been ascertained) on the part of the people to submit to the burden of universal military service (conscription), been slow to welcome any departure from her ancient and obsolete military régime. Able-bodied unemployed could be put into the army under a series of Acts of Queen Anne,[99] and men convicted or charged with crime might settle with the crown by offering to serve with the army. But the first attempts to make the army a more or less national institution was that inaugurated by a commission appointed in 1890 by both Houses of Parliament to advise on the question of army reform.

The Hartington Commission. This commission, presided over by Lord Hartington, issued a report, the result of which was a rearrangement of the military command upon a new basis.[1] The primary object of the scheme was to co-ordinate the work of the army and the navy; this was done, and, to effect it, many reforms in the organisation of both services were brought about. The proposals embodied in the report were carried into effect in 1895, and a Committee of Imperial Defence, with a cabinet minister as its president, superseded the office of commander-in-chief, and, in its place, an Army Council was appointed to deal with essentially executive matters. The change was one of far-reaching importance. The commander-in-chief hitherto represented the sovereign as the supreme general of the forces; and the delegation to the Imperial Defence Committee of the cabinet of the control and inspection of the military forces of the realm carried with it a recognition of the standing army as a national institution. The office of commander-in-chief was now no longer a representative office; it became an executive post, the occupier of which was amenable and responsible to the committee for his conduct of the affairs entrusted to him, and through the committee to parliament, whilst he was himself a member of the committee. The Imperial Defence Committee was then formed into a government department. This system was

---

[98] Anson, *Law and Custom*, ii, Pt. ii, Chap. 8; Hallam, *Constitutional History*, iii, 105–106, 259–263; Maitland, *Constitutional History*, pp. 447–459.
[99] 2 & 3 Anne, c. 13; 3 & 4 Anne, c. 10; and others. An Act of 1708 gave £3 to the overseers of the poor for every pauper who " enlisted ": Max Beloff, *Public Order* (1938), 118.
[1] Anson, *loc. cit.*, p. 203.

framed on a German model, the Landesverteidigungskommission, which corresponds more or less to our Committee of National Defence, as does the German office of chief of the general staff to that of the commander-in-chief. With the retirement of the Duke of Cambridge in 1895, the old office of commander-in-chief came to an end, and the new order commenced. With this change, a new era in the history of our national defences began; the standing army became the national army, and the auxiliary forces, including the old militia, were practically merged into it. Under this new army organisation scheme, Arnold-Forster, the then Secretary for War, proposed to divide the regular army into two parts: (1) the general service army, and (2) the home service army. The former, being designed for foreign service, to consist of men joining the colours for a period of long service—six months at a depôt, eight and a half years on active service, and three years with the reserve; the home service army to be territorialised and be made up of troops raised by enlistment, together with certain numbers of militia battalions.

The Haldane Reforms. This scheme had not yet been put into operation, when the unionist government went out of power. The succeeding Minister of War, Lord Haldane, at once introduced new ideas, which, incorporated in a Bill, speedily became law. The Territorial and Reserve Forces Act, 1907 (7 Edw. 7, c. 9), presents the following main features. It provided for: (a) An active field force of 168,000 officers and men, composed of regulars, regular reserves and a special reserve; (b) a special contingent of 80,000 men, recruited from the old militia, which, like the active field force, is also liable to service abroad; and (c) a territorial army, composed of volunteers and yeomanry, the numbers of which (though they have never reached that figure) were fixed at 315,000. The men in this force enlist for four years, but are not liable to foreign service. The duty of raising and administering the territorial force is vested in county associations, which are composed (1) of officers from the territorial army in the county in question; (2) of representatives of the county and borough councils, nominated by the Army Council; (3) a president, vice-president and chairman, nominated by the Army Council; and (4) a secretary and treasurer. The necessary drill halls, rifle butts and other material and equipment, as part and parcel of the organisation, are provided by the county association. The regular army suffered in numbers in consequence of these innovations, many units having to be disbanded in order to make the arrangements complete. The old historical militia does not constitute a portion of the territorial force. As above seen, it is associated, as a " special reserve," to the battalions of the regular troops, to which it locally belongs. This Act (7 Edw. 7, c. 9) finally submerged this old historic force, which has now ceased to exist, although the name " militia " was conferred by statute in 1921 on certain classes of reservists. It was scarcely possible to believe that the present régime would be lasting.

During the First World War, conscription was introduced into Great Britain and several of the colonies.[2]

Compulsory National Service. The approach of the Second World War brought a remarkable extension of the principle of conscription. The Military Training Act, 1939 (May 25) for the first time made military service compulsory in time of peace. The National Service (Armed Forces) Act, 1939, replaced it (September 3) with a more comprehensive scheme and, as the war proceeded, further legislation introduced compulsory "national service" as the industrial counterpart of military conscription, and eventually these provisions were extended to women as well as to men.

The Police Forces. The ancient power of the county—*posse comitatus* —was both military and civil in its function. For ordinary purposes, the maintenance of order rested on the compulsory, unpaid office of constable (and from Elizabethan times to the eighteenth century there were women constables).[3] The towns relied on watch and ward as set up by the Statute of Winchester,[4] but their watchmen were apt to be aged and infirm.[5] The larger towns obtained local Acts empowering them to levy rates to maintain a salaried system of watch.[6] In London the multiplicity of local units and the special problems of a large metropolis created a dangerous situation, which was met by Peel's Metropolitan Police Act, 1829.[7] There was much misgiving at the exercise by the Secretary of State of this jurisdiction, but it was the only solution possible which permitted the whole of London to be treated as a police unit. The name "police" was of foreign origin and irresistibly reminded people of the reactionary Continental powers, whose strength was largely now in their "police" rather than in their armies. The scheme was effective; so much so that the criminal gangs migrated to provincial towns. With the reform of the municipal corporations and the erection of active watch committees, a fresh migration thence took place to the suburbs and more rural areas. Here the justices of the peace were unable to cope with the problem. County constabularies existed in some counties and not in others. A national system was not created out of these fragments until 1856 when the Home Office received powers of

---

[2] *Cf.* Military Service Act, 1916 (5 & 6 Geo. 5, c. 104); Military Service Act, 1916 (Session 2) (6 & 7 Geo. 5, c. 15); Military Service (No. 2) Act, 1918 (8 & 9 Geo. 5, c. 5); and the regulations made thereunder (S.R. & O., 1916, Nos. 53, 54, 210, 342, 343).

[3] Holdsworth, x, 153; *cf.* S. A. H. Burne, *Staffordshire Quarter Session Rolls*, iv, 186 (1600).

[4] *Supra*, p. 124.

[5] The evils of "trading justices" of the peace, and incompetent watchmen, were tackled with great spirit and skill by Sir John Fielding (the blind half-brother of the novelist): see the biography by R. Leslie-Melville (1934), and B. M. Jones, *Henry Fielding, Novelist and Magistrate* (1933).

[6] L. Radzinowicz, *History of Criminal Law* (1950, three vols., in progress) contains an extended history of the police in the eighteenth and nineteenth centuries.

[7] 10 Geo. 4, c. 44.

inspection by the County and Borough Police Act [8]—again amid forebodings of ministerial espionage. The fears were doubtless exaggerated, but not entirely groundless.

The Navy. Although it is true that the Tudors created the Royal Navy, yet it is worthy of note than even Edward II and Edward III had a few ships which they owned, and a few permanent officers whom they paid.[9] In time of emergency these resources were supplemented by calling upon the Cinque Ports to do their duty in providing ships and men, and by impressing mariners—who by the mere fact of being mariners, were liable to compulsory naval service. It was the technical progress of shipbuilding which finally evolved specialised craft for war purposes superior to the ordinary merchantmen, and thus rendered necessary a standing navy. A deep-rooted tradition held that all this was the affair of the ports and coasts, and Charles I's attempt, by the writs of ship money, to distribute the burden of naval defence upon the country at large has already been mentioned.[10] Apart from this, and the use of impressment which the courts fully recognised,[11] the navy presented no constitutional problem, and was not distrusted by the public as was the army.

ALIENS AND NATURALISATION

By way of conclusion we may consider the position of the alien, who strictly had no civil liberties. There were many reasons for this. He was often a merchant intent on the dangerous operation of taking money out of the realm; he was sometimes a usurer; he might be a cleric with obnoxious bulls and provisions from Rome; he might be an enemy; after the Reformation his theology as well as his trading might arouse antipathy.

Common Law Disabilities. English kings at war with France had seized the lands of Frenchmen (or rather Normans) in England; at first a temporary defence measure, this grew into the rule that an alien cannot hold land [12]; he cannot inherit; a claim to inherit cannot be made through him; obviously, then, he can bring no real action, and, according to Littleton, he can bring no personal action—debt, for example; he can hold no public office; and although subject to the criminal law, he did not enjoy its full protection.[13] It was, therefore, a most dangerous situation, and was only rendered tolerable by special dispensations. These were

---

[8] 19 & 20 Vict. c. 69.

[9] A. E. Prince, " The Army and Navy," in *English Government at Work* (ed. J. F. Willard and W. A. Morris), i, 377.

[10] *Supra*, pp. 382 *et seq.*

[11] Holdsworth, x, 381; *Broadfoot's Case* (1743) Foster 154; *Barrow's Case* (1811) 14 East 346. *Supra*, pp. 398-399 n. 7

[12] The curious story is in Pollock and Maitland, *History of English Law*, i, 461–463.

[13] Holdsworth, ix, 93–94.

of various sorts. Magna Carta, as we have seen,[14] contains a few general protective clauses; by the close of the Middle Ages the matter was often covered by treaty with friendly powers; and individual aliens often obtained letters of safe conduct.[15] The close monopolies of trade enjoyed in England by guilds and municipal corporations seriously hampered alien merchants, and in some cases they organised themselves as guilds with privileges from the crown, the Hansa being the most famous example, but all aliens dwelling in England long remained subject to higher taxation and to many vexatious restrictions, more particularly as to retail trade. By statute 32 Hen. 8, c. 16, they were further prohibited from taking any shop or dwelling-house on lease, and they were at all times liable to be ordered by the crown to quit the realm. The last occasion on which this right of expulsion was exercised occurred in 1575 under Elizabeth I.

Denization and Naturalisation. An alien might become, to a certain extent, an English subject, either by *denization* under the king's letters patent, or by *naturalisation* by a personal Act of Parliament, the latter mode not merely enabling him to hold land, but to inherit it from others and to transmit it by inheritance to his children, whether born before or after his naturalisation. By statute 7 Jac. 1, c. 2 (1610), it was, however, enacted that no person should be naturalised unless he should first take the oaths of allegiance and supremacy in the presence of the parliament, and also take the Sacrament.

The fifth clause of the constitutional provisions of the Act of Settlement [16] imposing various disabilities on aliens was founded, like the second and third, on a very reasonable jealousy of a foreign king and foreign favourites, in consequence of the conduct of William III in appointing foreigners who accompanied him from Holland to high positions in the English state, but the feeling had always existed more or less. The clause expressly affects all aliens, even those naturalised or made denizens. It was confirmed in 1715 by statute 1 Geo. 1, st. 2, c. 4, which, " for the better preserving the said clause in the said Act entire and inviolate," provided that no bill for the naturalisation of any person should be received without a clause disqualifying him from sitting in parliament or enjoying the prohibited offices or places of trust. But as it was impossible to limit the action of future parliaments, these provisions, as well as those of 7 Jac. 1, c. 2, were occasionally dispensed with by special Acts of Parliament passed previously to the introduction of the private bills for the naturalisation of particular individuals. In 1708 one general Act was passed (7 Anne, c. 5) for the naturalisation of all foreign protestants, but this was repealed three years afterwards

---

[14] *Supra*, p. 83; *cf.* the *Carta Mercatoria* (1303).
[15] Specimens and a general discussion will be found in A. Beardwood, *Alien Merchants in England* (1931).
[16] *Supra*, p. 464.

(10 Anne, c. 5). In 1753, the famous " Jew Bill " was passed (26 Geo. 2, c. 26) enabling foreign Jews to be naturalised without taking the Sacrament as required by the 7 Jac. 1, c. 2; but the popular dislike excited by this measure was so great that it was repealed in the following session of parliament.[17] At length, in 1825, by 6 Geo. 4, c. 67, the preliminary sacramental test imposed by the 7 Jac. 1, c. 2, was abolished in all cases; and in 1844 the provision of 1 Geo. 1, st. 2, c. 4, as to naturalisation bills was also repealed by 7 & 8 Vict. c. 66, s. 2.

The Control of Aliens. While in the interest, or supposed interest, of the English people, aliens were subjected to certain disabilities, and even to liability to expulsion when the safety of the state should require it, their right of asylum against foreign governments was ever maintained inviolate. But in 1793 the suspicion that some of the political refugees who came over in great numbers at the time of the French Revolution were in league with democratic associations in England in conspiracies against the government, led to the passing of an Alien Act (33 Geo. 3, c. 4) placing all foreigners under strict surveillance, and empowering the secretary of state to remove any who were suspected out of the realm. The Alien Act, which was passed for one year only, was renewed from time to time, but its more stringent provisions were relaxed as soon as peace was temporarily restored in 1802. In that year the arrogant demand of Napoleon that we should " remove out of the British dominions all the French princes and their adherents, together with the bishops and other individuals whose political principles and conduct must necessarily occasion great jealousy to the French Government," was firmly refused, except in the single instance of M. Georges, who, having been concerned in circulating papers hostile to the government in France, was removed from our European dominions. On the resumption of war the Alien Act was again renewed in its integrity; after the peace of 1814, its provisions were again relaxed; and from 1816 its re-enactment, even in a modified form, was strongly opposed in parliament, until its final abandonment in 1826.

The registration of aliens was still, however, insisted on, and fresh provisions for this purpose were enacted in 1836 by the 6 & 7 Will. 4, c. 11; but their execution gradually fell into disuse. During the political disturbances of 1848 the English executive were empowered by parliament (11 & 12 Vict. c. 20), for the space of one year, to remove from the kingdom any foreigners who should be considered dangerous to its peace, but this power was never exercised.

Naturalisation Act, 1844. In the meantime, in 1844, the naturalisation of aliens had been greatly facilitated by Hutt's Act, 7 & 8 Vict. c. 66, which enabled them, on obtaining a certificate from the home secretary

[17] *Supra*, pp. 658.

and taking the oath of allegiance, to acquire all the rights and capacities of natural-born British subjects, except the capacity of becoming a member of either House of Parliament, or of the privy council, or any other rights and capacities specially excepted in the certificate. This Act has since been repealed by the Naturalisation Act of 1870 (33 & 34 Vict. c. 14, amended by 35 & 36 Vict. c. 39), which has completely altered the status of aliens and naturalised subjects, upsetting the ancient maxim, " nemo patriam in qua natus est exuere, aut ligeantiae debitum ejurare potest," and rendering much of the learning as to allegiance and aliens contained in the famous *Calvin's Case* [18] and in subsequent cases now only historically interesting. Under the existing law an alien may take, acquire, hold, and dispose of real and personal property in the United Kingdom, of every description (except British ships) in the same manner in all respects as a natural-born British subject, but without the right to any office or franchise, municipal, parliamentary, or other; and on obtaining a certificate of naturalisation from one of her Majesty's principal secretaries of state, he becomes entitled, in the United Kingdom, to all political and other rights and privileges, and subject to all the obligations, of a natural-born subject. It is also provided that a natural-born subject may become a " statutory alien " by being voluntarily naturalised in a foreign state, and may again acquire British nationality by permission of a secretary of state. The Act of 1870 is repealed by the British Nationality and Status of Aliens Act, 1914, and the law is contained in the British Nationality and Status of Aliens Acts, 1914 to 1943.[19]

[18] *Supra*, p. 337.
[19] 4 & 5 Geo. 5, c. 17; 8 & 9 Geo. 5, c. 38; 12 & 13 Geo. 5, c. 44; 23 & 24 Geo. 5, c. 49; 6 & 7 Geo. 6, c. 14.

Chapter 21

LOCAL GOVERNMENT AND SOCIAL SERVICES

From what has already been said [1] it will be apparent that local government in England is at least as old as the royal central government. Its history is not only long but obscure in the earlier periods and complicated as we approach modern times. Much of the complication is due to the reluctance (until the nineteenth century) of parliament to abolish rules and institutions. There were experiments and reforms, but they took the shape of additional machinery and new institutions which were set to work amid all the wreckage of the centuries. Hence there are successive layers of institutions as one age after another took in hand the problems of local government.

The oldest scheme of local government consisted of the ancient communities of the county, the hundred, the township and the borough. Their powers and duties were entirely traditional and were not derived from the crown, parliament or any other central body, but formed a part of the great mass of traditional principles and practices known as the common law. Some of these institutions became modified by feudalism, and some features of feudal geography still remain (the Isle of Ely, for example, which was once a feudal franchise, survives with a modern county council of its own). Like all our oldest institutions they recognised no specialisation of functions, and exercised judicial, legislative and administrative powers. There was always the possibility that localities with peculiar characteristics should develop, purely as a matter of custom, a governmental system more suitable to their needs—the law of the marsh in Essex and in Kent, the stannaries of Cornwall and other mining jurisdictions elsewhere and the group of the Cinque Ports are well-known examples.

The next stage occurs when the central government undertakes to confer additional powers (or to impose additional duties) upon local authorities. This might be by charter, as when a borough received new powers, or a locality was created a borough; or it might be by statute, as when the Statute of Winchester of 1285 dealt with the policing of towns generally. After the Middle Ages a long line of statutes conferred powers upon the parish.

A more drastic method was for the central authority to undertake some function of local government and carry out the work through its agents, appointed centrally but working locally. The sheriff is the oldest

---

[1] *Supra*, pp. 20–22, 120–124, 126, 134, 206–207. The fundamental work on the subject is Sidney and Beatrice Webb, *English Local Government from the Revolution to the Municipal Corporations Act*, 9 vols., 1906–1929. The legal and constitutional (as distinct from political and social) aspects can be found in Holdsworth, x, 126–339.

example of this, but soon we find very numerous bodies of commissioners appointed by the crown to do work locally and independent to a large extent of the older institutions. Commissions of sewers, justices of labourers and especially the justices of the peace fall into this category, and although their authority originally came from the prerogative, they later received very wide statutory powers.

A variety of influences either warped or moulded this structure. As seats in parliament became desirable, much harm was done by the fact that the borough government was often the parliamentary constituency, with the result that the borough constitution was completely atrophied for all purposes save that of returning members to the House of Commons. Thus the boroughs which became " rotten " in the parliamentary sense, were equally rotten as organs of local government. Consequently those townsmen who desired an active local government were forced to seek it in some other quarter than the mayor and town council—recourse was generally had to special bodies erected by local Acts of parliament. To a lesser extent the same is true of the county. On the other hand, an enormous stimulus to experiment and development in local government came from the ever-growing need of organising a system of poor law, which was the parent (or at least the pattern) of many features of the present local government system.

Finally, there are a number of functions which were originally performed by voluntary bodies but which later were absorbed by the organs of central or local government. Medieval guilds and fraternities provided a certain amount of social relief for their members, and charitable foundations and hospitals of various sorts abounded. The guilds also managed a system of controls over trade and industry which has now passed to the central government. A very remarkable example is education which, at first largely initiated by voluntary bodies, is now shared by the local and central authorities.

The Borough. The history of boroughs in the Middle Ages is largely a matter of local variations, each town pursuing its own destiny. There were, however, some features which became fairly general. Many towns had as their head an officer with the French title of mayor, and frequently during the thirteenth century we find a sort of council of twelve, twenty-four or some other number of burgesses. Whether these were the old hundred court in a new guise (as Maitland thought), or whether they were imported, if only in outline, with the mayor from the French commune (as Tait suggests) is a difficult question.[2] In any case it is now agreed that the borough government was distinctly oligarchic by about 1300, and in the course of the fourteenth century many towns witnessed a popular movement directed against the local magnates.

[2] Pollock and Maitland, *History of English Law*, i, 657; J. Tait, *The Medieval English Borough*, 286.

The Common Council. The first-fruits of the movement were the establishment of the " common council " in London in 1376, an example which was followed by other towns in the course of the fifteenth and sixteenth centuries. The object of these common councils was to give the lesser townsfolk some share in the government. It was an attempt to place political power in the hands of some, while others retained economic power. After a momentary success, a reaction set in, although by no means all the gains were lost, and many boroughs became permanently endowed with two councils, the more popular being twice the size of the more ancient.[3] The outline still survives in the two degrees of " alderman " and " councillor " which were retained in the Municipal Corporations Act of 1835—thanks to an amendment inserted by the House of Lords.

The powers of the medieval borough are difficult to define. Those which they prized most and recorded most carefully in early times [4] became unimportant in later centuries; some of them defeated themselves, as when the borough control of trade and industry forced economic activity to take refuge outside the borough in the suburbs or in the countryside, thus producing stagnation within the walls. This vagueness was an actual advantage, however, when an active borough wanted to do things, for it was difficult to show a legal reason why they should not. So we find in the sixteenth century boroughs which had street-cleaning and lighting, fire brigades, piped water supplies, salaried doctors to look after the poor, relief for the unemployed and municipal stocks of coal and candles for use when these commodities became seasonally rare and costly.[5]

The seventeenth century submerged the borough in the tumult of national politics. The Test and Corporation Acts excluded some of its most energetic members from office, the Stuarts attacked the borough charters in the *quo warranto* cases, and the fatal gift of the parliamentary franchise reduced many to the position of rotten boroughs. Meanwhile, a seeming change in legal theory led to the view that the simplest activity could only be carried on by means of a local act of parliament—a slow and costly procedure which earlier ages had not found necessary. To some extent the somnolence of the borough was compensated by the greater activity of other institutions; thus the justices of the peace (where there was a borough commission) became the effective judiciary, while the parishes now had statutory powers of various sorts. Where a considerable body of inhabitants wanted to get effective action, their best course was to get themselves constituted " improvement commissioners " with statutory powers of levying a rate.

Municipal Corporations Act, 1835. The modern age of borough history begins with the repeal of the Test and Corporation Acts in 1828

---

[3] Tait, *op. cit.*, 302 *et seq.*

[4] *i.e.*, the farm of the borough, freedom from toll, return of writs, peculiarities of tenure and succession law, preference for compurgation instead of jury trial, etc.

[5] These examples are from J. H. Thomas, *Town Government in the Sixteenth Century* (1933).

and the passing of the Reform Act of 1832, which separated completely
the functions of parliamentary representation and local government.
The way was then clear for the Municipal Corporations Act, 1835.[6]
By this Act (developed by the Municipal Corporations Act of 1882)
the municipal oligarchies were swept away and the government vested in
the mayor, aldermen and councillors. The mayor holds office for one
year and is elected by the council; the aldermen, in number one-third of
the number of the councillors, are elected by the council for a period of
six years. The councillors are elected for three years by the burgesses.
This body manages the property of the corporation, maintains the police
force, and administers the affairs of the town generally. It has the power
to make by-laws for the good governing of the borough and for the prevention of nuisances, and can inflict fines not exceeding £5 for breach of
them. Specially significant points are that the municipal franchise was
based upon rateable occupation and not limited (as was the parliamentary
franchise) by a minimum figure; the requirement that accounts be audited
and published; the extinction of ancient trading rights; and the publicity
of the council's proceedings. On the other hand, the Act made no great
extension in the borough's general powers. The various *ad hoc* bodies
which actually did the work of local government were empowered by the
Act to transfer their powers to the corporation if they chose; they were
in fact reluctant to do so, until the Board of Health in later years pressed
them.[7] Finally, the legislature made boroughs the statutory health
authority, and a mass of detailed legislation was consolidated and codified
by the Municipal Corporations Act, 1882.[8]

The County. The ancient machinery of the county had suffered much
the same fate as the boroughs in the course of centuries. The county
had once upon a time been a court of wide jurisdiction. Those days had
long since passed, and even as a court of small civil claims it had in many
cases become almost useless. The county of Middlesex in 1750 obtained
an Act [9] empowering it to act as a small debts court, and a similar scheme
was applied to all counties by the County Courts Act of 1846.[10] This
Act only touched the county judiciary, and left the local government of
the county unaffected. Just as the old municipalities had allowed their
powers of local government to fall into the hands of special commissioners,
vestries and the like, so also the government of the county had passed
out of the hands of its historic institutions of county court, sheriff and
lord lieutenant. The principal organ in fact had come to be the justices
of the peace. Their early history has already been mentioned [11]; as time

---

[6] 5 & 6 Will. 4, c. 76.
[7] J. Redlich and F. W. Hirst, *Local Government in England*, i, 132.
[8] 45 & 46 Vict. c. 50.
[9] 23 Geo. 2, c. 33; Holdsworth, i, 191; for similar courts elsewhere, see Winder, " Courts
    of Requests," *Law Quarterly Review*, lii, 369.
[10] 9 & 10 Vict. c. 95.
[11] *Supra*, p. 126.

went on their duties were immensely increased by statute, not only in the sphere of criminal administration but also in that of poor law and general local government. A vast and confused mass of legislation which defies analysis conferred wide and very miscellaneous powers. In the sixteenth and seventeenth centuries the central government succeeded in making the justices of the peace its agents in a real sense, by maintaining constant and close contact between the Privy Council and the justices. In the eighteenth century the Privy Council silently withdrew from the business of local government and left the justices to a large extent to their own devices. They took up the burden manfully, worked long and hard, and tackled some of the most difficult problems of government without guidance or expert help from Westminster—indeed, parliament regarded the justices as themselves being experts to whom proposed bills would be sent for their opinion before proceeding to second reading.[12] The principal other contact between the justices and the central government was provided by the ordinary courts of law which through the forms of litigation exerted a control which was necessarily fitful.[13]

In addition to their extensive criminal jurisdiction, the justices had important supervisory powers by statute over the poor law administration, highways, the licensing of ale-houses, the maintenance of public order generally, and even (for a time) the inspection of cotton mills.

The reform of municipal government in 1835 naturally raised the question of the reform of county government. The two cases were very different, however. Anything in the nature of a county council analogous to the borough council was dependent upon the existence of really good roads and cheap railways. Then, too, the county justices, in spite of inevitable shortcomings, had a record of service which could, and did, survive keen examination, and so their case was far removed from that of the undeniably corrupt or impotent municipal corporations.[14] There was also a traditional fear of either increasing the power of the government, or of setting up little local tyrants such as were believed to exist on the Continent. Some of the justices' powers were transferred to other bodies, the Home Office, for example; but in the main the system was kept on until 1888.[15] This is all the more remarkable since the wide powers of levying rates, which the justices exercised under many statutes, constituted a system of taxation unaccompanied by any form of representation.

---

[12] Webb, *Local Government*, i, 555; hence the opinion of the knights of the shire often decided the fate of bills which dealt with local government.

[13] The fact that a justice was personally liable for any misuse of his powers was a serious (although capricious) check, which bore heavily on them, in spite of over a hundred statutes, from James I onwards, which give them some relief. These statutes were later consolidated and revised in the Public Authorities Protection Act, 1893 (56 & 57 Vict. c. 61), in part repealed and replaced by the Limitation Act, 1939 (2 & 3 Geo. 6, c. 21), s. 21. See generally, Holdsworth, x, 155–158.

[14] Webb, *Local Government*, i, 605–607.

[15] *Infra*, pp. 693–694.

History of the Poor Law. So far, we have considered ancient institutions which had either inherent or acquired powers of local government. A different type of development must now be examined which consists of a continuous problem which pressed so heavily upon the nation that a new series of institutions and administrative arrangements had to be devised. The oldest and most important example is the history of the poor law, and somewhat similar methods were later applied to such matters as public health and elementary education. The result in each case was a set of institutions which were not concerned with local government generally, but only with their own special function.

In pre-Norman times the state did not directly relieve poverty, but by enforcing by legal sanctions the payment of tithes to the church, it may be said to have indirectly provided for the relief of the poor. In their inception tithes were voluntary offerings of the people, made under the belief—carefully inculcated by the clergy—of the religious duty of every Christian to bestow on God's service a tenth part of his goods. " But it was not possible or desirable," observes Stubbs,[16] " to enforce " this duty " by spiritual penalties: nor was the actual expenditure determined except by custom, or by the will of the bishop, who usually divided it between the church, the clergy and the poor. . . . The recognition of the legal obligation of tithes dates from the eighth century, both on the Continent and in England. In A.D. 779 Charles the Great ordained that everyone should pay tithe, and that the proceeds should be disposed of by the bishop; and in A.D. 787 it was made imperative by the legatine councils held in England, which being attended and confirmed by the kings and ealdormen had the authority of witenagemots. From that time it was enforced by not unfrequent legislation . . . the cathedral church being, it would seem, the normal recipient, and the bishop the distributor." By a law of Ethelred II the tithes were directed to be applied, in accordance with the ancient usage, one-third to church fabrics, one-third to the clergy, and the remaining third to the poor.[17] It was not until the council held in 1200 that the principle of the prior claim of the parochial clergy on tithes was summarily stated.[18] In the *Mirror of Justices*, it is boldly asserted to be the right of the poor to be " sustained by parsons, rectors of churches, and by the parishioners, so that none should die for default of sustenance,"[19] but the duty was one of imperfect obligation, there being no compulsory method of enforcing it. The clergy, however, more especially the monastic bodies, who, as impropriators of many parochial benefices, had managed to secure a large portion of the tithes, by no means neglected this duty; but unfortunately "the blind eleemosynary spirit " which led them to practise and inculcate indiscriminate alms-

---

[16] *Constitutional History*, i, 248.
[17] VIII Ethelred, c. 6.
[18] Stubbs, *Constitutional History*, i, 250.
[19] Ed. Whittaker (Selden Society), lib. i, c. 3. See the suggestive study by J. de Laplanche, *La Soutenance*. (It should be remembered that the *Mirror* only expresses the extremely individual views of the author; his attitude to ecclesiastical questions is peculiar.)

giving had a direct tendency to foster " that vagabond mendicity which unceasing and very severe statutes were enacted to repress." By Edward III's Statute of Labourers, it was forbidden to give alms, under colour of charity, to the able-bodied poor; every man having no means of his own was to accept service under pain of imprisonment. By 12 Ric. 2, cc. 3–9, begging was permitted, subject to regulations—certificates might be given to poor men and women authorising them to beg within specified local limits.

Henry VIII's Poor Laws. Under Henry VIII the same policy with regard to the poor was maintained, but with a great increase of severity. By 22 Hen. 8, c. 12, all beggars and vagrants—as well aged and impotent as able-bodied—were ordered to repair to the place of their birth. Justices of the peace were authorised to give licences to " aged and impotent persons " to beg within certain prescribed districts, but licensed beggars transgressing their limits, and all unlicensed beggars, were to be whipped or else set in the stocks three days and three nights with bread and water only. By 27 Hen. 8, c. 25, all cities, counties, towns and parishes were directed to maintain their aged and impotent poor by voluntary alms, and to set the able-bodied to work; but valiant beggars or sturdy vagabonds refusing to work were to be punished by whipping for the first offence, loss of an ear for the second, and hanging for the third. By the same Act indiscriminate almsgiving was forbidden on pain of forfeiting ten times the value of the gift; but a collection was to be made in every parish church on Sundays, to which the clergy were to exhort the people to contribute.

Suppression of the Monasteries. By the suppression of the monasteries the chief support of vagrant mendicity was withdrawn; and under Edward VI and Elizabeth I numerous statutes were passed enforcing with greater stringency and severity the provisions already in existence for the relief of the aged and impotent, and the punishment of the " valiant and sturdy " poor.

The Act of 1601. At length in 1601, the Act of 43 Eliz. I, c. 2 [20] introduced regular local taxation for the relief of the poor and thus furnished the foundation of modern Poor Law. Every parish was to be responsible for the maintenance of its own poor out of a rate to be levied on the landed property of the parish by " overseers of the poor," consisting of the churchwardens, and from two to four substantial householders nominated yearly by two justices of the neighbourhood. The rate was to be applied by the overseers (1) in providing work for all able-bodied persons who had no means to maintain themselves, and (2) in relieving the lame, impotent, old, blind, and such other persons as were poor and not able to work, and who had no parents, grandparents, or children competent to maintain them.

[20] Text in A. E. Bland, P. A. Brown and R. H. Tawney, *Select Documents*, 380.

The Act of 43 Eliz. 1 involved two principles : (1) the relief of the impotent and aged, and the providing work for the able-bodied poor; (2) that this should be done parochially, each parish providing for its own poor. It had already been directed by certain earlier statutes that paupers unable or unwilling to work should be compellable to remain in the particular parishes where they were settled (*i.e.*, where they were born, or had resided for a certain period, varying from one to three years). But there was nothing to prevent able-bodied and industrious paupers from resorting to any parish that they pleased for employment; and the irregular and imperfect manner in which the Act of Elizabeth was for many years carried out in many parishes caused a migration of poor into those which were better regulated. To relieve the latter from this unfair burthen, an Act was passed in 1662 (14 Car. 2, c. 12) providing that within forty days after the coming of any person to settle in any parish, he might, on complaint of the churchwardens or overseers that his circumstances were such that he was likely to become a charge upon the parish, be removed, by the warrant of two justices, back to the parish in which he was born, or had been last settled for at least forty days. Thus originated the law of settlement, which has been the subject of a vast amount of subsequent legislation (and litigation) and still retains a close connection with the relief of the poor.

The relief of the poor in all its various details continued for more than a century under the uncontrolled management of the overseers, who, in too many instances, proved quite unequal to the duty of effectively working the Act.

Eighteenth-Century Acts. In 1722, by 9 Geo. 1, c. 7, churchwardens and overseers of parishes were empowered, with the consent of the vestry, to purchase or hire houses, or to contract with any person, for the lodging and employment of the poor; three small parishes were permitted to unite in establishing a single workhouse; and it was declared that such persons as declined to submit to the lodging provided for them should not be entitled to any relief. In 1782, Mr. Davies Gilbert's Act (22 Geo. 3, c. 83) authorised parishes in which the adoption of the Act should be agreed upon by two-thirds in number and value of the owners and occupiers, to appoint guardians to act in place of overseers of the poor; and also to enter into voluntary unions with each other for the accommodation, employment, and maintenance of their paupers. In 1819 the Act 59 Geo. 3, c. 12, empowered the vestry of any parish to commit the management of its poor to a committee of substantial householders, termed a select vestry, to whose directions the overseers should be bound to conform.

Select Vestries. These were onerous duties, requiring constant work. The churchwardens were, indeed, an ancient institution, but the overseers were the product of the poor-law statutes, and most of the duties of the parish meeting in the vestry were also statutory. It was inevitable that the nature of the vestry should undergo changes as a result of these stresses, and the law felt bound to recognise the growth of the " select vestry." As Sir Erskine May observed [21]: " Every parish is the image and reflection of the state. The land, the church, and the commonalty share in its government; the aristocratic and democratic elements are combined in its society. The common law, in its grand simplicity, recognised the right of all the rated parishioners to assemble in vestry and administer parochial affairs. But in many parishes this popular principle gradually fell into disuse; and a few inhabitants—self-elected and irresponsible—claimed the right of imposing taxes, administering the parochial funds, and exercising all local authority. This usurpation, long acquiesced in, grew into a custom, which the courts recognised as a legal exception from the common law. The people had forfeited their rights, and select vestries ruled in their behalf." A partial remedy for this abuse of parochial government was applied by Sturges Bourne's Act in 1818 (58 Geo. 3, c. 69), and by Sir John Hobhouse's Vestry Act (1 & 2 Will. 4, c. 60) in 1831.

Both the Gilbert Act and the Select Vestry Act being permissive only and not compulsory, the relief of the poor in the great majority of parishes continued to be administered by the overseers. Under their unskilful administration the wise and simple provisions of the law for the relief of the poor gradually assumed the proportions of a gigantic national evil. " The industrial population of the whole country," observes Sir Erskine May,[22] " was being rapidly reduced to pauperism, while property was threatened with no distant ruin. The system which was working this mischief assumed to be founded upon benevolence; but no evil genius could have designed a scheme of greater malignity for the corruption of the human race. The fund intended for the relief of want and sickness— of age and impotence—was recklessly distributed to all who begged a share. Everyone was taught to look to the parish, and not to his own honest industry, for support."

Poor Law Amendment Act, 1834. At length, in 1834, on the recommendation of a Royal Commission appointed at the request of parliament in the preceding year, to inquire into the state and administration of the laws relating to the poor, was passed the important Poor Law Amendment Act, 4 & 5 Will. 4, c. 76. Not the least significant feature of this memorable Commission was the fact that one of its most active members was Edwin Chadwick, the enthusiastic disciple of Bentham. He was an ardent advocate of the control of local activity by a central authority, which by means of the technique of public administration should enable the central expert to guide the work of the local staffs.

[21] May, *Constitutional History*, iii, 276. Select vestries are discussed at length in Webb, *Local Government*, i, cc. i–vii.
[22] *Constitutional History*, iii, 405.

The Workhouse Test. As for the new Act which he inspired, "the principle was that of the Act of Elizabeth, to confine relief to destitution; and its object to distinguish between want and imposture. This test was to be found in the workhouse.   Hitherto pauperism had been generally relieved at home, the parish workhouse being the refuge for the aged, for orphans and others, whom it suited better than out-door relief.   Now out-door relief was to be withdrawn altogether from the able-bodied, whose wants were to be tested by their willingness to enter the workhouse. This experiment had already been successfully tried in a few well-ordered parishes, and was now generally adopted.   But instead of continuing ill-regulated parish workhouses, several parishes were united, and union workhouses established common to them all.   The local administration of the poor was placed under elected boards of guardians; and its general superintendence under a central Board of Commissioners in London."[23]

The Commissioners were a new departure in English government, and had wide powers of making orders and regulations, could dismiss local officers without consulting the local board of guardians which appointed them, and exerted detailed control by a system of inspection and audit.   In this Act Benthamism secured its most conspicuous triumph. The Poor Law Commissioners were appointed for five years, with Chadwick as their secretary, but the duration of the Commission was afterwards extended from time to time till 1847, when, by statute 10 & 11 Vict. c. 109, it was superseded by a new Commission, afterwards known as the Poor Law Board, consisting of the lord president of the council, lord privy seal, home secretary, and chancellor of the exchequer for the time being, and of such other persons as the crown might appoint.   Under this Act the President of the Board became for the first time a minister with a seat in parliament.

Within three years from the passing of the Act of 1834 its beneficial effects were manifested in a reduction, to the extent of three millions, in the annual expenditure for the relief of the poor.   Some of the provisions of the Act have since been partially relaxed; and the strict and universal application of the workhouse test could hardly then be hoped for until supplemented by an efficient organisation of private charity, working in independent but harmonious correlation with the public system, for the relief of industrious and deserving persons in temporary difficulties, who, by timely aid, may be kept from falling into the ranks of paupers.

In short, the history of the Poor Law down to 1834 is one of strict localism, every parish supporting its own poor, and particularly in the case of the agricultural areas, every bench of justices devising its own economic and social policy, until it became necessary to impose at the head a new national authority to regulate and control the whole administration.

---

[23] May, *Constitutional History*, iii, 407.   For an excellent analysis of the Act, see Redlich and Hirst, *Local Government*, i, 105 *et seq.*

Public Assistance. The enormous body of statutory provisions for the relief of the poor was consolidated by the Poor Law Act, 1927 (17 & 18 Geo. 5, c. 14), which wholly repealed some sixty Acts and partly repealed thirty-nine others. This Act retained the boards of guardians as the authority administering the Poor Law in the Poor Law unions, but the boards of guardians were abolished in 1930 and their powers were transferred to the county and county borough councils by the Local Government Act, 1929 (19 & 20 Geo. 5, c. 17). This was followed by the Poor Law Act, 1930 (20 & 21 Geo. 5, c. 17), which replaced the Act of 1927 with the amendments made necessary by the transfer.[24] Poor Law relief is now termed Public Assistance and is administered under the Public Assistance Order, 1930, as amended from to time. Counties are divided into districts, each equipped with an advisory committee of not more than thirty-six persons. These committees include county councillors, town and district councillors and " persons experienced in the relief of distress," mainly ex-guardians, and to them is delegated most of the business of outdoor relief. In London there are no advisory committees, but the London County Council may establish some similar bodies in the boroughs, and may allow metropolitan borough councils to control maternity and child welfare services.

Public Health Act, 1848. The various activities which have long been classed as " public health " show a somewhat similar course of development, again under the strenuous leadership of Edwin Chadwick. The principal difference was that the existing public health organisation was much more recent in most cases than that of the Poor Law, and also that it was non-existent in the places where it was needed most—those new " populous places " springing up as a result of the industrial revolution in places where there was no tradition of local government and no existing institutions. The health problem was therefore not so much one of controlling old institutions as of creating them where none existed. The need was urgent. Epidemics of cholera caused grave anxiety. The Poor Law Commission urged that public health and poverty were related problems, and the new system of registration (also a creation of Chadwick) enabled for the first time a statistical approach to be made.[25] The result was a still more complete embodiment of Chadwickian bureaucracy in the Public Health Act, 1848 (11 & 12 Vict. c. 63), after the failure of bills in 1845 and 1847.

The Act set up a General Board of Health as the central authority. The local administration was in the hands of Local Boards of Health; these were new institutions brought into existence under the Act either

---

[24] See also the Poor Law Act, 1934 (24 & 25 Geo. 5, c. 59) and the Poor Law (Amendment) Act, 1938 (1 & 2 Geo. 6, c. 23).

[25] 6 & 7 Will. 4, c. 86, Births and Deaths Registration Act, 1836. The Registrar-General compiled statistics from data collected locally by officials connected with the boards of guardians. The "bills of mortality," dating from Tudor times, were kept by the company of parish clerks down to the nineteenth century, but were very imperfect statistically.

at the request of the inhabitants of a place, or imposed upon them by the Central Board if the death rate in the area exceeded twenty-three per thousand annually. If a borough adopted the Act, it became the sanitary authority. As with the Poor Law Act of 1834, the local authority (not being a borough council) was elected by a system giving additional votes (up to a maximum of six) to the larger ratepayers. The principal spheres of action were sewerage, paving, lighting, street regulation, water supply, burial grounds and offensive trades. Local by-laws needed the confirmation of a Secretary of State. There was a paid staff centrally and locally, with powers to inspect public nuisances and to levy rates.

The opposition was strong and the bill was much limited before it was allowed to pass. The public awoke with a shock to discover that a new force was at work, and soon the opposition to " centralisation " was organised. A curious constitutional romanticism [26] sought ammunition in Anglo-Saxon history where (it was contended with truth) local institutions were autonomous. Just as Coke used the common law against James I, so Toulmin Smith used the Anglo-Saxon laws against the Poor Law Commissioners and the General Board of Health. This Gothic revival in local government gathered such force that the General Board of Health was dissolved in 1854. Various expedients culminated in the Local Government Act of 1858 [27] which reduced the powers of the central authorities (now distributed between the Privy Council and the Local Government Department of the Home Office) and increased the powers of the local boards.

Surveying all this generally, it will appear that by the middle of the century local government had been broken up into fragments in an attempt to make it functional. Locally there was a vast tangle of boards of health, guardians, improvement commissions, highway districts, petty sessional divisions, boroughs, parishes, counties, all with varying franchise systems levying separate rates, maintaining separate staffs and operating in geographical areas of the utmost complexity. Some of their activities were permissive, others compulsory. Central control came from the Poor Law Board, the Home Office, the Privy Council, the Medical Office or the Board of Trade.

Local Government Board, 1871. The next stage was the reconstruction of local government by fitting together these fragments into a new system which should be simpler and more effective. A Royal Sanitary Commission reported weightily in 1871 in favour of a reconstruction of the system, and the first result was the creation of the Local Government Board in 1871,[28] receiving powers transferred from the Poor Law Board (which this Act abolished) and several other central departments. This unified

---

[26] The phrase is from Redlich and Hirst, i, 145, who describe the movement. It influenced scholarship, especially in Germany, through Rudolf von Gneist.
[27] 21 & 22 Vict. c. 98.
[28] 34 & 35 Vict. c. 70.

central authority was given a coherent body of law by the codification and revision of a large number of statutes by the Public Health Act, 1875.[29] That Act attempted a corresponding degree of unification in local authorities. As far as the boroughs were concerned it succeeded, for it made the town council the local authority for health; outside the boroughs it was more difficult, and so the Act transferred public health powers generally to the guardians, they being as yet the nearest approach to a unit of general local government.

The problem of county government was brought to the fore as a result of the Reform Act of 1884 which enfranchised so many rural inhabitants, and fifty years of endeavour [30] finally produced the Local Government Act of 1888.

Local Government Act, 1888: County Councils. The Local Government Act of 1888 (51 & 52 Vict. c. 41) practically established the system of local authority in the counties, as it now obtains in England and Wales, by depriving the justices of the right to administer the affairs of the counties, and vesting it in elective county councils. This Act took within its view of local administration three areas; the largest, the county; next, the sanitary district, whether urban or rural, which also comprehended municipal boroughs, themselves urban districts; lastly, the parish. The county council is composed of a chairman, county aldermen, and county councillors; the latter are elected for three years by the county electors, the chairman and aldermen are elected by the council. The whole administrative business, with the powers which formerly resided in the justices, were, by the Act, practically transferred to this new representative body, the county council. An exception was the police, which was only transferred in part, the control being thenceforth vested in a standing joint committee of quarter sessions and county council. The Act of 1888 has been largely replaced by the Local Government Act, 1933 (23 & 24 Geo. 5, c. 51).

The local government franchise is now regulated by section 3 of the Representation of the People Act, 1918, and sections 1 and 2 of the Representation of the People Act, 1945 (8 & 9 Geo. 6, c. 5). A person is entitled to be registered as a local government elector for a local government electoral area if he or she is of full age and not subject to any legal incapacity, and (a) is on the last day of the qualifying period occupying as owner or tenant, any land or premises in that area, and (b) has during the whole qualifying period, *i.e.*, three months, so occupied any land or premises in that area, or if that area is not an administrative county or county borough, in any administrative county or county borough in which the area is wholly or partly situated. A lodger who occupies rooms let

---

29 38 & 39 Vict. c. 55.
30 As early as 1836 Joseph Hume had introduced a Bill for transferring the administrative functions of justices of the peace to " county boards." The attempt was renewed in 1849, 1850, 1851, 1852, 1860 and 1868: Redlich and Hirst, i, 164–168.

to him unfurnished is regarded as a tenant. In addition, any person who has, or but from an incapacity arising from his status as a peer would have, a qualification as a parliamentary elector for a local government area is qualified as a local government elector. The Act of 1918 imposed a minimum age of thirty years upon women voters; that was removed by the Representation of the People (Equal Franchise) Act of 1928 (18 & 19 Geo. 5, c. 12). The Act also conferred a qualification upon the spouse of an elector which has been abolished by section 2 of the Act of 1945.

The main object of the Local Government Act, 1888, was, so far as possible, to give to counties the form of government which had previously pertained only to English boroughs. The county council was made a corporation with perpetual succession and a common seal with power to hold land without licence in mortmain. Thus were transferred to the county council the administrative functions formerly exercised by quarter sessions, but the poor law was left with the boards of guardians and elementary education with the school boards.[31]

Urban and Rural District Councils. By the Local Government Act of 1894 (56 & 57 Vict. c. 73) (now largely replaced by the Local Government Act, 1933 (23 & 24 Geo. 5, c. 51)), each administrative county was subdivided into urban or rural districts, with their own councils elected by the county electors within the district. The most important duty imposed on the district councils is the care of the public health of their areas—sanitation, isolation of disease, sewage, etc. They are also responsible for the maintenance of highways other than main roads, housing, etc. By the same Act, in every rural parish which is not included in an urban district a parish meeting was set up, consisting of persons in the parish whose names are enrolled as electors on the parliamentary or local government registers. The powers and duties of the parish council consist mainly: in the appointment of overseers, the custody of the parish books and registers, management of parish property, other than that vested in the ecclesiastical commissioners, lighting, watching, the establishment of baths and wash-houses and the provision of burial grounds. The primary purpose of this measure was to reorganise the old vestries on a democratic basis.

London County Council. By the London Government Act of 1899 (now replaced by the London Government Act, 1939), the administrative County of London (which came into existence, with the London County Council, in 1888) has been divided into twenty-eight metropolitan boroughs, and the town councils, constituted for these boroughs by Order in Council under the Act, have taken over the powers and duties of the district boards, together with some of the duties of the county council.

---

[31] As to poor law, see *infra*, p. 699; as to education, see *infra*, pp. 696–698.

Education. We have so far considered the interplay between the traditional organs of local government and the needs created by two of the oldest " social services "—poor relief, and public health regulation. Many other services have their own history, often with interesting constitutional implications. Only one more can be considered here, and that is public education.

The beneficence of private founders spread over many centuries had provided schools in many places large and small down to the middle of the eighteenth century. At the same time, the system of apprenticeship afforded some sort of technical training, and " parish children " could be apprenticed by the parish.[32] The industrial revolution had seriously dislocated this system; population had shifted to places where schools did not exist, and even in corporate towns all was not well, for the corruption of the corporation had brought much neglect, mismanagement and even embezzlement of educational endowments. Most serious of all was the plight of poor-law children compulsorily apprenticed in mills, which the exigencies of water-power had caused to spring up in hitherto remote places.

Sir Robert Peel, himself a large mill-owner, made a beginning with the first of the Factory Acts, the Health and Morals of Apprentices Act, 1802,[33] which required that apprentices in mills should receive a modicum of instruction. The Act was ineffective, but it turned attention to the problem. In 1811 members of the Church of England by their subscriptions formed the National Society, and in 1814 an undenominational British and Foreign School Society was formed; both of them tackled the initial difficulty of the capital outlay needed to provide a building. In 1833 parliament voted a small sum equally to both societies, and from 1839 onwards the Education Committee of the privy council administered the grants and inspected the schools. By 1856 the vice-president of the committee was a minister in parliament, and in 1860 its regulations were codified. The situation was curious: the central authority had a large measure of control, but it did not own any schools, while an institution so necessarily bound to its locality as a school was not subject to any local control.

There had been unsuccessful attempts in parliament since the beginning of the nineteenth century to provide parochial schools with support from the rates, but this decisive step was not taken until the Education Act of 1870.[34] Elected and rate-levying local school boards were set up, and they established a system of schools parallel with the voluntary schools (but the latter did not participate in the local rate). Education first became a concern of the county councils when they were given powers

---

[32] The institution is old (see an indenture dated 1309 in Selden Society, *Year Book Series*, xxii, 126–128), and was regulated by the great Statute of Artificers, 1563 (5 Eliz. 1, c. 4). Apprenticeship of paupers was provided for in the Poor Law Act of 1601 (43 Eliz. 1, c. 2).

[33] 42 Geo. 3, c. 73.

[34] 33 & 34 Vict. c. 75.

by the Technical Instruction Act, 1889,[35] and those powers came to be used for secondary education. Meanwhile the school boards had also been entering the field of secondary education by maintaining " higher grade schools " and evening schools. This they had no legal authority to do, as the *Cockerton* case [36] was to show.

A measure of unification at the centre was clearly desirable, since elementary schools were governed by the education committee of the privy council, while technical schools were controlled by a different body the " Science and Art Department." The course adopted by an Act of 1899 (62 & 63 Vict. c. 33) was to erect a Board of Education as the central authority for both types.

Education Act, 1902. The whole situation was ripe for review, however, and momentous reforms were effected by the Education Act of 1902 (2 Edw. 7, c. 42) which abolished school boards and transferred their powers to councils of counties, boroughs, and larger urban districts, which became local education authorities. Secondary education was encouraged, and voluntary schools were henceforth to be supported by the local educational authorities from the rates.

A local education authority was made responsible for the efficiency of all public elementary schools, and over those schools which it provided itself, its powers were made absolute. But a sharp distinction was made between those which it provided itself—the successors of the board schools —and those which it maintained but did not provide, that is, the voluntary schools. In the non-provided schools, the appointment of a majority of the managers was carefully kept in the hands of the religious bodies and thus the denominational character of the voluntary schools was preserved, and the control of the local education authority strictly limited to the secular side of the education. The greater part of the burden, however, hitherto borne by private subscribers was now transferred to the ratepayers, but these subscribers had now to pay the local school rate. This led to the enforced support by the ratepayers of denominational schools under private management which was bitterly opposed by nonconformists.

The system of education established by the Act of 1902 continued until 1944. Meanwhile the compulsory school attendance age was raised to fourteen by the Education Act, 1918 (8 & 9 Geo. 5, c. 39), which required provision to be made for practical or advanced instruction in elementary schools; and the Education Acts were consolidated by the Education Act, 1921 (11 & 12 Geo. 5, c. 51).

Education Act, 1944. Under the Education Act, 1944 (7 & 8 Geo. 6, c. 31), the statutory system of education was organised in three progressive stages known as primary education (for children up to twelve), secondary

---

[35] 52 & 53 Vict. c. 76.
[36] [1901] K.B. 322, 726.

education (for children up to between fifteen and nineteen) and further education (for children over the compulsory school age). The central authority is the Ministry of Education, and the Minister has the duty of promoting education and of securing the effective execution of the national policy of providing a varied and comprehensive educational service in every area. He is assisted by a Central Advisory Committee for England and one for Wales. The county council or county borough councils are the local education authorities responsible for all education in their areas. The compulsory school age is raised to fifteen and will be raised to sixteen when practicable. No fees are to be charged for admission to any school maintained by a local education authority. Religious education is to be given in all schools maintained by a local education authority. The school day in all schools maintained by a local education authority is to begin with a single act of collective worship unless the school premises render this impracticable. The distinction between provided non-denominational (now county) schools and non-provided denominational (now voluntary) schools remains, but assistance from public funds may be given to the managers of voluntary schools to enable the school buildings to be brought up to the standard of the county schools. Medical treatment at the schools is to be free and assistance may be given in providing clothing and footwear. A system of compulsory free part-time education in county colleges is to be set up for young persons under eighteen. Independent schools are required to be registered and are subject to inspection and control if unsatisfactory.

Highways. It was the common law liability of the parish (or the customary liability of some subdivision thereof) to repair the highways lying within it. Under the Highway Act, 1835 (5 & 6 Will. 4, c. 50), this duty was performed by the surveyor of highways of the parish (district surveyor in groups of parishes and highway board in certain populous parishes). The office of surveyor in respect of ordinary highways is now vested in borough councils and urban district councils, and, in respect of highways in rural districts, the county councils.

The principal roads constituting the national system of routes for through traffic (other than in London or a county borough) have become trunk roads and are the responsibility of the Minister of Transport (Trunk Roads Act, 1936 (1 Edw. 8 & 1 Geo. 6, c. 5)). Other main roads are the responsibility of the county and county borough councils (Local Government Act, 1929 (19 Geo. 5, c. 17), ss. 29–39).

The Rating System. To obtain the funds required for the relief of the poor the Poor Relief Act, 1603 (43 Eliz. 1, c. 2), as amended by later statutes, established a system whereby the overseers of the poor in every parish were given power to raise money by the taxation of every occupier of lands, houses, tithes impropriate, propriations of tithes, coal mines and mines of every other kind, woodlands and sporting rights. In course of time the bulk of the funds required for local government purposes was raised by means of the poor rate.

The duties of the overseers of the poor in relation to the rates were transferred by the Rating and Valuation Act, 1925 (15 & 16 Geo. 5, c. 90), to the councils of boroughs (including county boroughs) and of urban and rural districts, and a consolidated general rate was substituted for the poor rate and all other rates which the rating authority had power to make. In rural areas the rating authority has also power to make a special rate in any part of its area which is liable to be separately rated in respect of lighting and watching and other special expenses.

In London the duties of overseers have been performed by the metropolitan borough councils since the London Government Act, 1899 (62 & 63 Vict. c. 14), and levy the poor rate and the general rate together, as one rate called the general rate.

Derating. The severe economic depression in 1929 accentuated certain defects which had appeared in the rating system. So long as distress was principally agricultural distress it was reasonable to assume that it would be much the same all over the country, and it was a fair distribution of the burden to expect each rating area to maintain its own poor. The economic geography of the country is now very different, and a " depressed area " which would attempt to maintain its poor would have to levy such prohibitive rates that the last relics of prosperity would be banished. In other words, distress is no longer a local problem, but a national one. Moreover, the old rating system assumed that the amount of land occupied was a rough indication of taxability. That was true in a mainly agricultural country, but has long ceased to be equitable, and a series of Agricultural Rates Relief Acts began in 1896 to deal with the problem.

Under the Local Government Act of 1929 (19 & 20 Geo. 5, c. 17) farmers are relieved of the whole of their rates except on their private houses and cottages, which are to be rated as houses used for the particular purpose of farming and not as ordinary dwelling-houses. Productive industries and freight and transport hereditaments will pay a quarter rate. But the money saved in rates by railway companies is to be passed on to· the producer in the shape of reduced freight charges on certain selected traffics. In preparation for this relief, special lists were prepared under the Rating and Valuation (Apportionment) Act. The loss of revenue is to be made up by a readjustment of the burden among local authorities, by extra assistance from the state, from changes in local government and by the revision of the system of grants in aid.

The Labour Exchanges Act, 1909 (9 Edw. 7, c. 7), enabled the Board of Trade to furnish information as to employers desiring workpeople and vice versa. Labour exchanges are now called employment exchanges.

The problem of the areas suffering from industrial depression was tackled by the Special Areas (Development and Improvement) Act, 1934 (25 & 26 Geo. 5, c. 1), providing for the initiation, organisation, prosecution and assistance of measures designed to facilitate the economic and social improvement of such areas.

The poor law has always been unpopular, and during the nineteenth century workers made a gallant effort to help themselves without recourse to it. Various organisations for thrift, and especially building societies, were created; the accidents of sickness and unemployment prompted the creation of friendly societies and thereby introduced the idea that these were insurable risks to be met by foresight rather than by poor law methods. Much legislation was passed to secure the sound management of these concerns.[37] Finally, the government accepted the principle of contributory schemes involving the worker, the employer and the exchequer.

Unemployment Insurance. Compulsory insurance against unemployment was first introduced by Part II of the National Insurance Act, 1911 (1 & 2 Geo. 5, c. 55). The classes of persons within the scheme were greatly extended by the Unemployment Insurance Act, 1920 (10 & 11 Geo. 5, c. 30). The law was consolidated by the Unemployment Insurance Act, 1935 (25 & 26 Geo. 5, c. 8), and agricultural workers were brought within the scheme by the Unemployment Insurance (Agriculture) Act, 1936 (26 Geo. 5 & 1 Edw. 8, c. 13). Some classes of domestic servants have been brought within the scheme by orders made under the Unemployment Insurance Act, 1938 (1 & 2 Geo. 6, c. 8).

Social Security. Provision for assisting unemployed persons otherwise than under the poor law or unemployment insurance was rendered necessary by the acute unemployment in the years following the 1914–1918 War. The relief of unemployed persons was ruining the unemployment insurance scheme and the finances of local authorities in depressed areas. Unemployment assistance was introduced by the Unemployment Assistance Act, 1934, which constitutes Part II of the Unemployment Act, 1934 (24 & 25 Geo. 5, c. 29), which set up an Unemployment Assistance Board for the assistance, retraining and rehabilitation of unemployed persons.

Compulsory health insurance was introduced by Part I of the National Insurance Act, 1911 (1 & 2 Geo. 5, c. 55). The law is now contained in the social legislation of 1946.

The New Approach to Social Services. The Local Government Act of 1929 is in fact only one aspect of a complete change of view in the last generation upon the functions of government and the methods of dealing

[37] *Cf.* H. E. Raynes, *Social Security in England: a History* (1957).

with social problems; it had been preceded by changes at the centre which had produced new ministries.

The necessary implication of these measures was that there should be vast bureaucracies in the central government; without such machinery these projects could not exist. Other problems besides poverty have likewise ceased to be local and have become national—the road system, for example. Consequently, the end of the First World War brought with it a number of new ministries embodying the new attitude, and developing the new technique. The old Local Government Board was refounded as the Ministry of Health in 1919. The Ministry of Labour grew out of the Ministry of National Service (1917), and in 1919 there was also created the Ministry of Transport which later was to bring into being two very interesting bodies, the Central Electricity Board (1927) (now broken into autonomous regions) and the London Passenger Transport Board (1933) (now the London Transport Executive).

The Second World War has seen the Minister of Labour become the Minister of Labour and National Service and the creation of two ministries of great importance, the Ministry of Town and Country Planning (1943) (now Ministry of Housing and Local Government) and the Ministry of National Insurance (1944) (now Ministry of Pensions and National Insurance). The Board of Education has become the Ministry of Education (1944).

To all this must now be added the " nationalisation " of some of the major industries and their government by " Authorities," " Commissions," " Boards " and the like. Their relationship to parliament is one of the outstanding problems of contemporary constitutional law.

INDEX

The following abbreviations have been used:

abp.	= archbishop.		d.	= duke, duchess.
A.-G.	= attorney-general.		e.	= earl.
b.	= baron.		J.	= justice.
B.	= baron of the exchequer.		K.B.	= king's bench.
bp.	= bishop.		l.	= lord.
card.	= cardinal.		L.K.	= lord keeper.
C.	= chancellor.		m.	= marquess.
C.B.	= chief baron of the exchequer.		P.M.	= prime minister.
			Sec. St.	= secretary of state.
C.J.	= chief justice.		S.G.	= solicitor-general.
C.P.	= common pleas.		v.	= viscount.

Courtesy titles are indicated by italic. Different persons of the same name or title are arranged in chronological order. The sub-headings within the longer subject-titles are generally arranged chronologically or systematically instead of alphabetically.